Fodor's 08

FRANCE

**Where to Stay and Eat
for All Budgets**

**Must-See Sights
and Local Secrets**

Ratings You Can Trust

Fodor's Travel Publications   New York, Toronto, London, Sydney, Auckland
www.fodors.com

FODOR'S FRANCE 2008

Editors: Robert I. C. Fisher, *lead editor;* Rachel Klein

Editorial Production: Tom Holton

Editorial Contributors: Nancy Coons, Jennifer Ditsler-Ladonne, John Fanning, Sarah Fraser, Simon Hewitt, Rosa Jackson, Christopher Mooney, Lisa Pasold, George Semler, Heather Stimmler-Hall

Maps & Illustrations: David Lindroth, *cartographer;* William Wu; additional cartography provided by Henry Colomb, Mark Stroud, Moon Street Cartography; Bob Blake and Rebecca Baer, *map editors*

Design: Fabrizio LaRocca, *creative director;* Guido Caroti, Siobhan O'Hare, *art directors;* Tina Malaney, Chie Ushio, Ann McBride, *designers;* Melanie Marin, *senior picture editor*

Cover Photo: Château de Chenonceau, Loire Valley: David Barnes/age fotostock

Production/Manufacturing: Angela L. McLean

ISBN 978-1-4000-1804-8

ISSN 0532-5692

SPECIAL SALES

This book is available at special discounts for bulk purchases for sales promotions or premiums. Special editions, including personalized covers, excerpts of existing books, and corporate imprints, can be created in large quantities for special needs. For more information, write to Special Markets/Premium Sales, 1745 Broadway, MD 6-2, New York, New York 10019, or e-mail specialmarkets@randomhouse.com.

AN IMPORTANT TIP & AN INVITATION

Although all prices, opening times, and other details in this book are based on information supplied to us at press time, changes occur all the time in the travel world, and Fodor's cannot accept responsibility for facts that become outdated or for inadvertent errors or omissions. So **always confirm information when it matters**, especially if you're making a detour to visit a specific place. Your experiences—positive and negative—matter to us. If we have missed or misstated something, **please write to us**. We follow up on all suggestions. Contact the France editor at editors@fodors.com or c/o Fodor's at 1745 Broadway, New York, NY 10019.

Be a Fodor's Correspondent

Your opinion matters. It matters to us. It matters to your fellow Fodor's travelers, too. And we'd like to hear it. In fact, we need to hear it.

When you share your experiences and opinions, you become an active member of the Fodor's community. That means we'll not only use your feedback to make our books better, but we'll publish your names and comments whenever possible. Throughout our guides, look for "Word of Mouth," excerpts of your unvarnished feedback.

Here's how you can help improve Fodor's for all of us.

Tell us when we're right. We rely on local writers to give you an insider's perspective. But our writers and staff editors—who are the best in the business—depend on you. Your positive feedback is a vote to renew our recommendations for the next edition.

Tell us when we're wrong. We're proud that we update most of our guides every year. But we're not perfect. Things change. Hotels cut services. Museums change hours. Charming cafés lose charm. If our writer didn't quite capture the essence of a place, tell us how you'd do it differently. If any of our descriptions are inaccurate or inadequate, we'll incorporate your changes in the next edition and will correct factual errors at fodors.com immediately.

Tell us what to include. You probably have had fantastic travel experiences that aren't yet in Fodor's. Why not share them with a community of like-minded travelers? Maybe you chanced upon a beach or bistro or B&B that you don't want to keep to yourself. Tell us why we should include it. And share your discoveries and experiences with everyone directly at fodors.com. Your input may lead us to add a new listing or highlight a place we cover with a "Highly Recommended" star or with our highest rating, "Fodor's Choice."

Give us your opinion instantly at our feedback center at www.fodors.com/feedback. You may also e-mail editors@fodors.com with the subject line "France Editor." Or send your nominations, comments, and complaints by mail to France Editor, Fodor's, 1745 Broadway, New York, NY 10019.

You and travelers like you are the heart of the Fodor's community. Make our community richer by sharing your experiences. Be a Fodor's correspondent.

Bon voyage!

Tim Jarrell, Publisher

CONTENTS

CLOSEUPS

FRANCE IN FOCUS

CONTENTS

ABOUT THIS BOOK

Sometimes you find terrific travel experiences and sometimes they just find you. But usually the burden is on you to select the right combination of experiences. That's where our ratings come in.

As travelers we've all discovered a place so wonderful that its worthiness is obvious. And sometimes that place is so experiential that superlatives don't do it justice: you just have to be there to know. These sights, properties, and experiences get our highest rating, **Fodor's Choice,** indicated by orange stars throughout this book.

Black stars highlight sights and properties we deem **Highly Recommended,** places that our writers, editors, and readers praise again and again for consistency and excellence.

By default, there's another category: any place we include in this book is by definition worth your time, unless we say otherwise. And we will.

Disagree with any of our choices? Care to nominate a place or suggest that we rate one more highly? Visit our feedback center at www.fodors.com/feedback.

Hotel and restaurant price categories from ¢ to $$$$ are defined in the opening pages of each chapter. For attractions, we always give standard adult admission fees; reductions are usually available for children, students, and senior citizens. Want to pay with plastic? **AE, D, DC, MC, V** following restaurant and hotel listings indicate whether American Express, Discover, Diners Club, MasterCard, and Visa are accepted.

Unless we state otherwise, restaurants are open for lunch and dinner daily. We mention dress only when there's a specific requirement and reservations only when they're essential or not accepted—it's always best to book ahead.

Hotels have private bath, phone, TV, and air-conditioning and operate on the European Plan (aka EP, meaning without meals), unless we specify that they use the Continental Plan (CP, with a Continental breakfast), Breakfast Plan (BP, with a full breakfast), or Modified American Plan (MAP, with breakfast and dinner) or are all-inclusive (AI, including all meals and most activities). We always list facilities but not whether you'll

be charged an extra fee to use them, so when pricing accommodations, find out what's included.

Many Listings

★ Fodor's Choice
★ Highly recommended
⊠ Physical address
✛ Directions
🕮 Mailing address
☎ Telephone
🖷 Fax
⊕ On the Web
✇ E-mail
🎫 Admission fee
☉ Open/closed times
Ⓜ Metro stations
▭ Credit cards

Hotels & Restaurants

🏨 Hotel
🛏 Number of rooms
🖒 Facilities
🍽 Meal plans
✕ Restaurant
🖎 Reservations
🚭 Smoking
🍺 BYOB
✕🏨 Hotel with restaurant that warrants a visit

Outdoors

⛳ Golf
🏕 Camping

Other

☾ Family-friendly
⇨ See also
⊠ Branch address
☞ Take note

WHAT'S WHERE: NORTHERN FRANCE

1 Paris. A quay-side vista that takes in the Seine, a passing boat, Notre Dame, the Eiffel Tower, and mansard roofs all in one generous sweep is enough to convince you that Paris is indeed the most beautiful city on earth.

2 Ile-de-France. Appearing like all France in miniature, the Ile-de-France region is the nation's heartland. Here Louis XIV built vainglorious Versailles, Chartres brings the faithful to their knees, and Monet's Giverny enchants all.

3 Loire Valley. Chenonceaux, Chambord, and Saumur—the parade of royal and near-royal châteaux magnificently captures France's golden age of monarchy in an idyllic region threaded by the Loire river.

4 Normandy. Sculpted with cliff-lined coasts, Normandy has been home to saints and sculptors, with a dramatic past marked by Mont-St-Michel's majestic abbey, Rouen's towering cathedral, and the D-Day beaches.

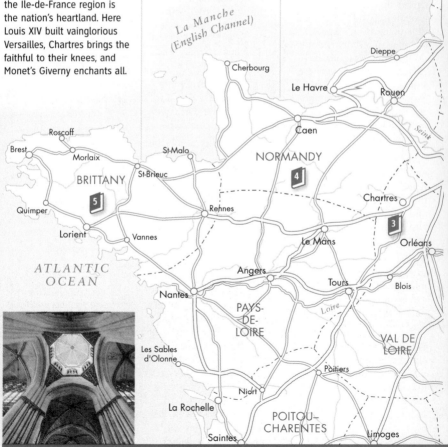

La Manche (English Channel)

Dieppe

Cherbourg

Le Havre

Rouen

Seine

Caen

Roscoff

Brest

Morlaix

St-Malo

NORMANDY

St-Brieuc

BRITTANY

Quimper

Lorient

Vannes

Rennes

Chartres

ATLANTIC OCEAN

Nantes

Angers

Le Mans

Tours

Orléans

Blois

Loire

PAYS-DE-LOIRE

VAL DE LOIRE

Les Sables d'Olonne

Poitiers

Niort

La Rochelle

POITOU-CHARENTES

Saintes

Limoges

5 **Brittany.** A long arm of rocky land stretching into the Atlantic, Brittany is a place unto itself, with its own language and time-defying towns such as Gauguin's Pont-Aven and the pirate haven of St-Malo.

6 **Champagne Country.** "Brother, come quickly, I'm drinking stars," exclaimed Dom Pérignon upon first sipping the sublime beverage he invented. The capital of bubbly is Reims, set near four great Gothic cathedrals.

7 **Alsace-Lorraine.** Although this region bordered by the Rhine often looks German and sounds German, its main sights—18th-century Nancy, medieval Strasbourg, and the lovely Route du Vin—remain proudly French.

8 **Burgundy.** Hallowed ground for wine lovers, Burgundy hardly needs to be beautiful—but it is. Around the gastronomic hub of Dijon, the region is famed for its verdant vineyards and Romanesque churches.

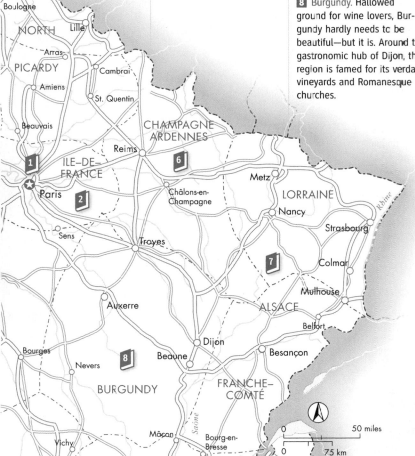

Calais

Boulogne

NORTH   Lille

Arras

PICARDY   Cambrai

Amiens

St. Quentin

Beauvais

CHAMPAGNE
ARDENNES

Reims

1   ILE–DE–
FRANCE   **6**

Paris   **2**   Metz

Châlons-en-
Champagne   LORRAINE

Nancy

Sens

Strasbourg

Troyes

7   Colmar

Mulhouse

Auxerre   ALSACE

Belfort

Bourges   Dijon   Besançon

Nevers   **8**   Beaune

BURGUNDY   FRANCHE–
COMTÉ

Saône

Rhine

0   50 miles

Mâcon
Vichy   Bourg-en-
Bresse   0   75 km

WHAT'S WHERE: SOUTHERN FRANCE

9 Lyon & the Alps.
Local chefs rival their Parisian counterparts in treasure-filled Lyon, heart of a diverse region where you ski down Mont Blanc or take a heady trip along the Beaujolais Wine Road.

10 Provence. Famed for its Lavender Route, the honey-gold hill towns of the Luberon, and vibrant cities like Aix and Marseilles, this region was dazzlingly abstracted into geometric daubs of paint by Van Gogh and Cézanne.

11 French Riviera.
From glamorous St-Tropez through beauteous Antibes to sophisticated Nice, this sprawl of pebble beaches and zillion-dollar houses has always captivated sun lovers and socialites.

12 Midi-Pyrénées & Languedoc-Roussillon.
Rose-hued Toulouse, once-upon-a-timefied Carcassone, and Matisse's beloved Vermillon Coast are among France's southwest's most colorful sights.

13 Basque Country, Gascony & the Hautes-Pyrénées. Whether you head for Bay of Biscay resorts like Biarritz, coastal villages such as St-Jean-de-Luz, or the Pyrénéan peaks, this region will cast a spell.

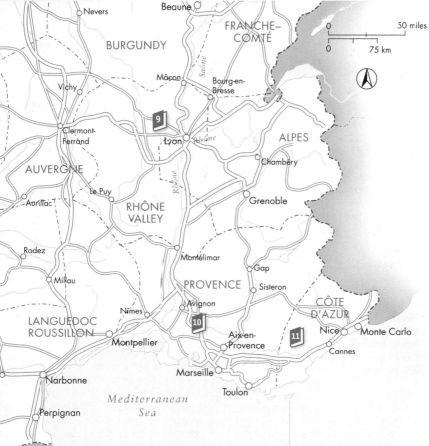

Nevers

Beaune

FRANCHE–
COMTÉ

BURGUNDY

Mâcon

Saône

Bourg-en-
Bresse

Vichy

9

Clermont-
Ferrand

Lyon   Rhône

ALPES

Chambéry

AUVERGNE

Le Puy

Aurillac

RHÔNE
VALLEY

Rhône

Grenoble

Rodez

Montélimar

Gap

Millau

PROVENCE   Sisteron

Nîmes

Avignon

CÔTE
D'AZUR

LANGUEDOC
ROUSSILLON

10

Nice   Monte Carlo

Montpellier

Aix-en-
Provence

11

Cannes

Narbonne

Marseille

Toulon

*Mediterranean
Sea*

Perpignan

0 ____ 50 miles
0 ____ 75 km

**14 Bordeaux & the Wine
Country.** The wines of Bordeaux tower as a standard
against which others are
measured, and they made
the city of Bordeaux rich and
owners of its vineyards—like
Château Mouton-Rothschild—
even richer.

15 The Dordogne. One of
the hottest destinations in
France, the Dordogne is a
stone-cottage pastorale studded with fairy-tale castles,
storybook villages, and
France's top prehistoric sights.

QUINTESSENTIAL FRANCE

Café Society

Along with air, water, and wine, the café remains one of the basic necessities of life in France. You may prefer a posh perch at a renowned Paris spot such as the Deux Magots on boulevard St-Germain or opt for a tiny *café du coin* (corner café) in Lyon or Marseilles, where you can have a quick cup of coffee at the counter. Those on Paris's major boulevards (such as Boulevard St-Michel and the Champs-Élysées) will almost always be the most expensive and the least interesting. In effect, the more modest establishments (look for nonchalant locals) are the places to really get a feeling for French café culture. And we do mean culture—not only the practical rituals of the experience (perusing the posted menu, choosing a table, unwrapping your sugar cube) but an intellectual spur as well. You'll see businessmen, students, and pensive types pulling out notebooks for intent scribblings. In fact,

some Paris landmarks like the Café de Flore host readings, while several years ago a trend for *cafés philos* (philosophy cafés) took off. And there's always the frisson of history available at places like La Closerie des Lilas, where an expensive drink allows you to rest your derrière on the spots once favored by Baudelaire and Apollinaire. Finally, there's people-watching, which goes hand in glove with the café lifestyle—what better excuse to linger over your *café crème* or Lillet? So get ready to settle in, sip your *pastis,* and pretend your travel notebook is a Hemingway story in the making.

Street Markets

Browsing through the street markets and *marchés couverts* (covered markets) of France is enough to make you regret all the tempting restaurants around. But even though their seafood, free-range poultry, olives, and produce cry out to be

If you want to get a sense of contemporary French culture, and indulge in some of its pleasures, start by familiarizing yourself with the rituals of daily life. These are a few highlights—things you can take part in with relative ease.

gathered in a basket and cooked in their purest form, you can also enjoy them as a simple visual feast. Over at flea and *brocante* (collectibles) markets, food plays second fiddle. With any luck, you'll find a little 18th-century engraving that makes your heart go *trottinant*.

Bistros & Brasseries

The choice of restaurants in France is a feast in itself. Of course, at least once during your trip you'll want to indulge in a luxurious meal at a great haute cuisine restaurant—but there's no need to get knee-deep in white truffles at Paris's Alain Ducasse to savor the France the French eat. For you can discover the most delicious *French-Women-Don't-Get-Fat* food with a quick visit to a city neighborhood bistro. History tells us that bistros served the world's first fast food—after the fall of Napoléon, the Russian soldiers who occupied Paris were known to cry *bistro* ("quickly" in Russian) when ordering. Here, at zinc-topped tables, you'll find the great delights of *cuisine traditionelle* like *grand-mère's* lamb with white beans. Today, the bistro boom has meant that many are designer-decorated and packed with trendoise. If you're lucky, the food will be as witty and colorful as the clientele. Brasseries, with few exceptions, remain unchanged—great bustling place with white-aproned waiters and hearty, mainly Alsatian, food, such as pork-based dishes, *choucroute* (sauerkraut), and beer ("brasserie" also means brewery). *Bon appétit!*

IF YOU LIKE

Great Food

Forget the Louvre or the Château de Che-nonceau—the real reason for a visit to France is to dine at its famous temples of gastronomy. Once you dive into Taillev-ent's lobster soufflé, you'll quickly real-ize that food in France is far more than fuel. The French regard gastronomy as essential to the art of living, so don't feel guilty if your meal at Paris's Le Grand Véfour takes as long as your visit to the Musée d'Orsay: two hours for a three-course menu is par, and you may, after relaxing into the routine, feel pressured at less than three. Gastronomads—those who travel to eat—won't want to miss a pilgrimage out to Megève to witness the culinary acrobatics of superchef Marc Veyrat, half mad scientist, half inspired artist. These days, la haute cuisine in the States and England is nearly as rare as Tibetan food, so plan on treating din-ing as religiously as the French do—at least once.

- **La Maison de Marc Veyrat, Annecy.** Bil-lionaires and foodies fight for seats at Marc Veyrat's Alpine aerie, France's newest culinary shrine.

- **Le Grand Véfour, Paris.** Guy Martin's Savoyard creations are extraordinaire, but the 18th-century decor is almost more delicious.

- **L'Auberge de L'Ill, near Ribeauville.** Mas-ter chef Paul Haeberlin marries grand and Alsatian cuisine, with the empha-sis on proper marriage, not passion-ate love.

- **Le Louis XV, Monaco.** If you're going to feast like a king, this Alain Ducasse outpost is the place to do it.

La Vie de Châteaux

From the humblest feudal ruin to the most delicate Loire Valley spires to the grand-est of Sun King spreads, the châteaux of France evoke the history of Europe as no museum can. Standing on their castel-lated ramparts, it is easy to slip into the role of a feudal lord scrambling to protect his patchwork of holdings from kings and dukes. The lovely landscape takes on a strategic air and you find yourself role-playing thus, whether swanning aristo-cratically over Chenonceau's bridgelike *galerie de bal* spanning the River Cher or curling a revolutionary lip at the splendid excesses of Versailles. These are, after all, the castles that inspired Charles Perrault's "Sleeping Beauty" and "Beauty and the Beast," and their fairy-tale magic—rich with history and Disney-free—still holds true. Better yet, enjoy a "queen-for-a-stay" night at one of France's many châteaux-hotels. Many are surprisingly affordable—even though some bathrooms look like they should be on a postcard.

- **Château de la Bourdaisière, Loire Valley.** Not one but *two* princes de Broglie welcome you to this idyllic and ele-gant neo-Renaissance hotel.

- **Vaux-le-Vicomte, Ile-de-France.** Louis XIV was so jealous when he saw this 17th-century xanadu, he commis-sioned Versailles.

- **Chambord, Loire Valley.** This French Renaissance extravaganza—all 440 rooms and 365 chimneys—will take your breath away. Be sure to go up the down staircase designed by Da Vinci.

- **Château d'Ussé, Loire Valley.** Step into a fairy tale at "Sleeping Beauty"'s leg-endary home.

Beautiful Villages

Nearly everyone has a mind's-eye view of the perfect French village. Oozing half-timber houses and roses, these once-upon-a-time-ified villages have a sense of tranquillity not even tour buses can ruin. The Loire Valley's prettiest village, Saché is so small it seems your own personal property—an eyebrow of cottages, a Romanesque church, a 17th-century auberge inn, and a modest château. Little wonder Honoré de Balzac came here to write some of his greatest novels. Auvers-sur-Oise, the pretty riverside village in the Ile-de-France, inspired some of Van Gogh's finest landscapes. In the Dordogne region, hamlets have a Walt Disney–like quality, right down to Rapunzel windows, flocks of geese, and storks'-nest towers. Along the Côte d'Azur you'll find the sky-kissing, hilltop *villages perchés*, like Èze. All in all, France has an *embarras de richesses* of nestled-away treasures—so just throw away the map. After all, no penciled itinerary is half as fun as stumbling upon some half-hidden Brigadoon.

- **Riquewihr, Alsace.** Full of storybook buildings, cul-de-sac courtyards, and stone gargoyles, this is the showpiece of the Alsatian Wine Route.

- **Haut-de-Cagnes, French Riviera.** This perfect example of the eagle's nest village near the coast is nearly boutique-free, was once adored by Renoir, and remains ancient in atmosphere.

- **La Roque-Gageac, Dordogne.** Lorded over by its immense rock cliff, this centuries-old, riverside village is the perfect backdrop for a beautiful pique-nique.

Monet, Manet & Matisse

It is through the eyes of its artists that many first get to know France. No wonder people from across the globe come to search for Gauguin's bobbing boats at Pont-Aven, Monet's bridge at Giverny, and the gaslit Moulin Rouge of Toulouse-Lautrec—not hung in a museum but alive in all their three-dimensional glory. In Arles you can stand on the spot where van Gogh painted and compare his perspective to a placard with his finished work; in Paris you can climb into the garret-atelier where Delacroix created his epic canvases, or wander the redolent streets of Montmartre, once haunted by Renoir, Utrillo, and Modigliani. Of course, an actual trip to France is not necessary to savor this country: a short visit to any major museum will probably just as effectively transport the viewer—by way of the paintings of Pisarro, Millet, Poussin, Sisley, and Matisse—to its legendary landscapes. But go beyond museums and discover the actual towns that once harbored these famed artists.

- **St-Paul-de-Vence, Côte d'Azur.** Pose oh-so-casually under the Picassos at the famed Colombe d'Or inn, once favored by Signac, Modigliani, and Bonnard.

- **Céret, Languedoc-Roussillon.** Pack your crayons for a trip to Matisse Country, for this is where the artist fell in love with the fauve ("savage") hues found only in Mother Nature.

- **Giverny, Ile-de-France.** Replacing paint and water with earth and water, Monet transformed his 5-acre garden into a veritable live-in Impressionist painting.

IF YOU LIKE

Le Shopping

Although it's somewhat disconcerting to see Gap stores gracing almost every major street corner in Paris and other urban areas in France, if you take the time to peruse smaller specialty shops, you can find rare original gifts—be it an antique brooch from the 1930s or a modern vase crafted from Parisian rooftop-tile zinc. It's true that the traditional gifts of silk scarves, perfume, and wine can often be purchased for less in the shopping mall back home, but you can make an interesting twist by purchasing a vintage Hermés scarf, or a unique perfume from an artisan perfumer. Bargaining is traditional in outdoor and flea markets, antiques stores, small jewelry shops, and craft galleries, for example. If you're thinking of buying several items, or if you're simply in love with something a little bit too expensive, you've nothing to lose by cheerfully suggesting to the proprietor, "Vous me faites un prix?" ("How about a discount?"). The small-business man will immediately size you up, and you'll have some good-natured fun.

- **Colette, Paris.** Wiggle into the ultimate little black dress at this fashionista shrine.

- **L'Isle-sur-la-Sorgue, Provence.** This canal-laced town becomes a Marrakech of marketeers on Sunday, when dazzling antiques and brocante dealers set up shop.

- **Grain de Vanille, Cancale.** These sublime tastes of Brittany—salted butter caramels, rare honeys, and malouine cookies—make great gifts, *non*?

Gothic Churches & Cathedrals

Their extraordinary permanence, their everlasting relevance even in a secular world, and their transcending beauty make the Gothic churches and cathedrals of France a lightning rod if you are in search of the essence of French culture. The product of a peculiarly Gallic mix of mysticism, exquisite taste, and high technology, France's 13th- and 14th-century "heavenly mansions" provide a thorough grounding in the history of architecture (some say there was nothing new in the art of building between France's Gothic arch and Frank Lloyd Wright's cantilevered slab). Each cathedral imparts its own monumental experience—knee-weakening grandeur, a mighty resonance that touches a chord of awe, and humility in the unbeliever. Even cynics will find satisfaction in these edifices' social history—the anonymity of the architects, the solidarity of the artisans, and the astonishing bravery of experiments in suspended stone.

- **Notre-Dame, Paris.** Make a face back at the gargoyles high atop Quasimodo's home.

- **Reims, Champagne.** Tally up the 34 V.I.P.s crowned at this magnificent edifice, age-old setting for the coronations of French kings.

- **Chartres, the Ile-de-France.** Get enlightened with France's most beautiful stained-glass windows.

- **Mont-St-Michel, Normandy.** From its silhouette against the horizon to the abbey and gardens at the peak of the rock, you'll never forget this awe-inspiring sight.

L'Esprit Sportif

Though the physically inclined would consider walking across Scotland or bicycling across Holland, they often misconstrue France as a sedentary country where one plods from museum to château to restaurant. But it's possible to take a more active approach: imagine pedaling past barges on the Saône River or along slender poplars on a route départementale (provincial road); hiking through the dramatic gorges in the Massif Central or over Alpine meadows in the Savoie; or sailing the historic ports of Honfleur or Cap d'Antibes. Experiencing this side of France will take you off the beaten path and into the countryside. As you bike along French country roads or along the extensive network of Grands Randonnées (Lengthy Trails) crisscrossing the country, you will have time to tune into the landscape—to study crumbling garden walls, smell the honeysuckle, and chat with a farmer in his potager vegetable garden.

- **The VBT Loire Biking Tour.** Stunning châteaux-hotels, Pissarro-worthy riverside trails, and 20 new best friends make this a fantastique way to go "around the whirl."

- **Sentier des Cascades, Haute-Pyrénéees.** Near Cauterets is the GR10 walk, which features stunning views of the famous waterfalls and abundant *marmottes* (Pyrenean groundhogs).

- **Tracking the Camargue Reserve, Provence.** Take an unforgettable *promenade équestre* (horseback tour) of this amazing nature park, home to bulls and birds—50,000 flamingos, that is.

Clos Encounters

Bordeaux or Burgundy, Sauternes or Sancerre, Romanée-Conti or Côte du Rhône—wherever you turn in France, you'll find famous Gallic wine regions and vineyards, born of the country's curvaceous landscape. Speckled unevenly with hills, canals, forests, vineyards, châteaux, and the occasional cow clinging to 30-degree inclines, the great wine regions of France attract hordes of travelers more interested in shoving their noses deep into wine glasses than staring high into the stratosphere of French cathedral naves. Fact is, you can buy the bottles of the fabled regions—the Côte d'Or, the Rhône Valley, or that oenophile's nirvana, Bordeaux—anywhere, so why not taste the lesser-known local crus from, say, the lovely vineyards in the Loire Valley. Explore the various *clos* (enclosures) and *côtes* (hillsides) that grow golden by October, study the *vendangeur* grape-pickers, then drive along the wine routes looking for those "Dégustation" signs, promising free sips from the local vintner. Pretty soon you'll be expert on judging any wine's aroma, body, and backwash.

- **Mouton-Rothschild, Route de Médoc.** Baron Philippe perfected one of the great five premiers crus here—and there's a great visitor's center.

- **Clos de Vougeot, Burgundy.** A historic wine-making barn, 13th-century grape presses, and its verdant vineyard make this a must-do.

- **The Alsace Route de Vin.** Between Mulhouse and Strasbourg, many picture-book villages entice with top vintners.

GREAT ITINERARIES

THE GOOD LIFE
7 to 9 Days
Great châteaux, fine porcelain, superb wine, brandy, truffles, and foie gras sum up France for many. Beginning in château country, head south and west, through Cognac country into wine country around Bordeaux. Then lose yourself in the Dordogne, a landscape of rolling hills peppered with medieval villages, fortresses, and prehistoric caves.

Loire Valley Châteaux
3 or 4 days. Base yourself at the crossroads of Blois, starting with its multi-era château. Then head for the huge château in Chambord. Amboise's château echoes with history, and the neighboring manor, Clos Lucé, was Leonardo da Vinci's final home—or instead of this "town" château, head west to the tiny village of Rigny-Ussé for the "Sleeping Beauty" castle of Ussé. Heading southeast, finish up at Chenonceau—the most magical one of all—then return to the transportation hub city of Tours. ⇨ *The Loire Valley in Chapter 3*

Bordeaux Wine Country
2 days. Pay homage to the great names of Médoc, north of the city of Bordeaux, though the hallowed villages of Margaux, St-Julien, Pauillac, and St-Estèphe aren't much to look at. East of Bordeaux, via the prettier Pomerol vineyards, the village of St-Émilion is everything you'd want a wine town to be, with ramparts and medieval streets. ⇨ *Bordeaux in Chapter 14*

Dordogne & Périgord
2 or 3 days. Follow the famous Dordogne River east to the half-timber market town of Bergerac. Wind through the green, wooded countryside into the region where humans' earliest ancestors left their mark, in the caves in Les Eyzies-de-Tayac and the famous Grotte de Lascaux. Be sure to sample the region's culinary specialties: truffles, foie gras, and preserved duck. Then travel south to the stunning and sky-high village of Rocamadour. ⇨ *Dordogne in Chapter 15*

By Public Transportation
It's easy to get to Blois and Chenonceaux by rail, but you'll need to take a bus to visit other Loire châteaux. Forays farther into Bordeaux country and the Dordogne are difficult by train, involving complex and frequent changes (Limoges is a big railway hub). Further exploration requires a rental car or sometimes sketchy bus routes.

FRANCE FROM NORTH TO SOUTH
6 to 9 Days.
So, you want to taste France, gaze at its beauty, and inhale its special joie de vivre—all in a one-week to 10-day trip. Let's assume at least that you've seen Paris, and you're ready to venture into the countryside. Here are some itineraries to help you plan your trip. Or create your own route using the suggested itineraries in each chapter. First, zoom from Paris to the heart of historic Burgundy, its rolling green hills traced with hedgerows and etched with vineyards. From here, plunge into the arid beauty of Provence and toward the spectacular coastline of the Côte d'Azur.

Burgundy Wine Country
2 to 3 days. Base yourself in the market town of Beaune and visit its famous Hospices and surrounding vineyards. Make a day trip to the ancient hill town of Vézelay, with its incomparable basilica, stop-

ping in Autun to explore Roman ruins and its celebrated Romanesque cathedral. For more vineyards, follow the Côte d'Or from Beaune to Dijon. Or make a bee-line to Dijon, with its charming Vieille Ville and fine museums. From here it's a two-hour drive to Lyon, where you can feast on this city's famous earthy cuisine. Another three hours' push takes you deep into the heart of Provence. ⇨ *Northwest Burgundy and Wine Country in Chapter 8 and Lyon in Chapter 9*

Arles & Provence
2 to 3 days. Arles is the atmospheric, sun-drenched southern town that inspired Van Gogh and Gauguin. Make a day trip into grand old Avignon, home to the 14th-century rebel popes, to view their imposing palace. And make a pilgrimage to the Pont du Gard, the famous triple-tiered Roman aqueduct west of Avignon. From here two hours' drive will bring you to the glittering Côte d'Azur. ⇨ *Arles, Avignon, and Pont du Gard in Chapter 10*

Antibes & the Côte d'Azur
2 to 3 days. This historic and atmospheric port town is well positioned for day trips. First head west to glamorous Cannes. The

next day head east into Nice, with its exotic Vieille Ville and its bounty of modern art. There are ports to explore in Villefranche and St-Jean-Cap-Ferrat, east of Nice. Allow time for a walk out onto the tropical paradise peninsula of Cap d'Antibes, or for an hour or two lolling on the coast's famous pebble beaches. ⇨ *Cannes, Nice, Villefranche-sur-Mer, St-Jean-Cap-Ferrat, and Cap d'Antibes in Chapter 11*

By Public Transportation
The high-speed TGV travels from Paris through Burgundy and Lyon, then zips through the south to Marseille. Train connections to Beaune from the TGV are easy; getting to Autun from Beaune takes up to two hours, with a change at Chagny. Vézelay can be reached by bus excursion from Dijon or Beaune. Rail connections are easy between Arles and Avignon; you'll need a bus to get to the Pont du Gard from Avignon. Antibes, Cannes, and Nice are easily reached by the scenic rail line, as are most of the resorts and ports along the coast. To squeeze the most daytime out of your trip, take a night train or a plane from Nice back to Paris.

GREAT ITINERARIES

A CHILD'S-EYE VIEW
9 Days.
Lead your children (and yourself) wide-eyed through the wonders of Europe, instilling some sense of France's cultural legacy. Make your way through Normandy and Brittany, with enough wonders and evocative topics, from William the Conqueror to D-Day, to inspire any child to put down his computer game and gawk. Short daily drives forestall mutiny, and you'll be in crêperie country, satisfying for casual meals.

Paris
2 days. Paris's major museums, like the Louvre, can be as engaging as they are educational—as long as you keep your visits short. Start out your Paris stay by giving your kids an idea of how the city was planned by climbing to the top of the Arc de Triomphe. From here work your way down the Champs-Élysées toward Place de la Concorde. Stop for a puppet show at the Marionettes des Champs-Élysées, at Avenues Matignon and Gabriel, halfway down the Champs. Continue walking down the Champs, to the Jardin des Tuileries, where kids can sail boats on a small pond. Then taxi or hike over to the Louvre for an afternoon visit. Your reward? Stop in at Angélina (on Rue de Rivoli, across the street), a tearoom famous for its thick hot chocolate. If you want to see the puppet show, do this on a Wednesday, Saturday, or Sunday. The next morning, head to the Eiffel Tower for a bird's-eye view of the city. After you descend, ride on one of the Bateaux Mouches at Place de l'Alma, nearby. Then take the métro to the hunchback's hang-out, Notre-Dame Cathedral. Finish up your Paris visit by walking several blocks over, through the center of the Ile de la Cité, to Paris's most storybook sight—the Sainte-Chapelle, a fairy-tale, stained-glass chapel that looks like a stage-set for Walt Disney's *Sleeping Beauty.* ⇨ *Exploring Paris in Chapter 1*

Versailles
1 day. Here's an opportunity for a history lesson: with its amazing Baroque extravagance, no other monument so succinctly illustrates what inspired the rage of the French Revolution. Louis XIV's eye-popping château of Versailles pleases the secret monarch in most of us. ⇨ *Southwest from Versailles to Chartres in Chapter 2*

Honfleur
1 day. From this picture-book seaport lined with skinny half-timber row houses and salt-dampened cobblestones, the first French explorers set sail for Canada in the 15th century. ⇨ *Upper Normandy in Chapter 4*

Bayeux
2 days. William the Conqueror's extraordinary invasion of England in 1066 was launched from the shores of Normandy. The famous Bayeux tapestry, showcased in a state-of-the-art museum, spins the tale of the Battle of Hastings. From this home base you can introduce the family to the modern saga of 1944's Allied landings with a visit to the Museum of the Battle of Normandy, then make a pilgrimage to Omaha Beach. ⇨ *Lower Normandy in Chapter 4*

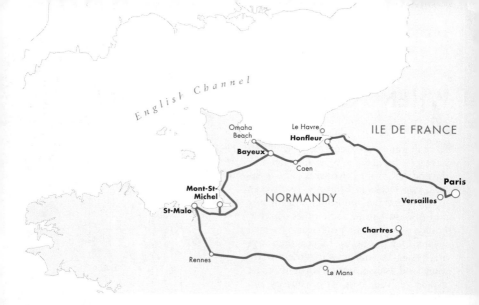

Mont-St-Michel

1 day. Rising majestically in a shroud of sea mist over vacillating tidal flats, this mystical peninsula is Gothic in every sense of the word. Though its tiny, steep streets are crammed with visitors and tourist traps, no other sight gives you a stronger sense of the worldly power of medieval monasticism than Mont-St-Michel. ⇨ *Lower Normandy in Chapter 4*

St-Malo

1 day. Even in winter you'll want to brave the Channel winds to beachcomb the shores of this onetime pirate base. In summer, of course, it's mobbed with sun seekers who stroll the old streets, restored to quaintness after World War II. ⇨ *Northeast Brittany and the Channel Coast in Chapter 5*

Chartres

1 day. Making a beeline on the autoroute back to Paris, stop in Chartres to view the loveliest of all of France's cathedrals. ⇨ *Southwest from Versailles to Chartres in Chapter 2*

By Public Transportation

Coordinating a sightseeing tour like this with a limited local train schedule isn't easy, and connections to Mont-St-Michel are especially complicated. Versailles, Chartres, and St-Malo are easy to reach, and Bayeux and Honfleur are doable, if inconvenient. But you'll spend a lot of vacation time waiting along train tracks.

WHEN TO GO

Keep in mind that French schoolchildren have *five* holidays a year: one week at the end of October, two weeks at Christmas, two weeks in February, two weeks in April, and the two full months of July and August. During these times travel in France is truly at its peak season, which means that prices are higher, highways are busier, the queues for museums are long, and transportation is at its most expensive. Your best bet for quality and calm is to travel off-season. June and September are the best months to be in France, as both are free of the midsummer crowds. Try to avoid the second half of July and all of August, when almost everyone in France goes on vacation. July and August in southern France can be stifling. Paris can be stuffy and uncomfortable in August. Many restaurants, theaters, and small shops close, but enough stay open these days to make a low-key, unhurried visit a pleasure. Anytime between March and November will offer you a good chance to soak up the sun on the Côte d'Azur. If Paris and the Loire are among your priorities, remember that the weather is unappealing before Easter. If you're dreaming of Paris in the springtime, May is your best bet, not rainy April. But the capital remains a joy during midwinter, with plenty of things to see and do.

Climate

At left are average daily maximum and minimum temperatures for Paris and Nice.

FORECASTS

Weather Channel Connection (⊕*www. weather.com*).

Nice

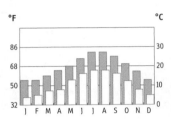

Paris

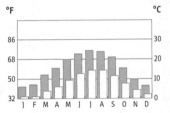

Paris

Champs Elysées

WORD OF MOUTH

"Go to the Impressionist floor at the Museé d'Orsay. View the Renoirs on one side, the Monets on the other, and the Eiffel Tower straight through the window. Think how lucky you are to be in Paris!"

—IdsantTK

"Take one of the sunset cruises that leave from the Iles. Then return to the restaurant you chose earlier. Lastly, a late walk back to your hotel past Paris's softly lit monuments and bridges. Sigh.'

—JeanneB

WELCOME TO PARIS

TOP REASONS TO GO

★ **Masterpieces Theater:** There will always be something new to see at the Louvre—after all, the Mona Lisa is just one of its 800,000 treasures.

★ **Feasting at Le Grand Véfour:** Back when Napoléon dined here, this was the most beautiful restaurant in Paris. Guess what? It is still is.

★ **Quasimodo's Notre Dame:** Get to know the stone gargoyles high atop this erstwhile playground of Victor Hugo's hunchback, then savor the splendor inside this great Gothic cathedral.

★ **Café Society:** Whether you prefer a posh perch at Les Deux Magots or just the corner café *du coin,* be sure to Hemingway an afternoon away over two café *filtrés.*

★ **A Walk along the Seine:** Pretend you're Cary Grant and Audrey Hepburn in *Charade* with a jaunt along the Rive Gauche or a romance aboard the Bateaux Mouches.

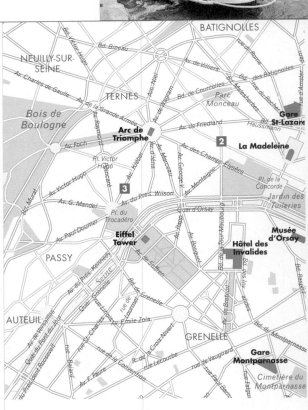

1 **From Notre-Dame to the Place de la Concorde.** Spend time wandering around the lovely Ile de la Cité, home of Notre-Dame, and relaxing in the Tuileries before and after tackling the Louvre.

2 **The Faubourg St-Honoré.** Chic spots in cities come and go, but the Faubourg's always had it and probably always will, with its well-established shops and cafés.

3 **From the Tour Eiffel to the Arc de Triomphe.** You won't be able to cover this whole area in one day, but plan lots of time for what could be called "monumental" Paris. In addition to the Eiffel Tower, the Champs-Élysées, and the Arc de Triomphe, there are several excellent museums worth planning your days around.

4 **The Grands Boulevards.** Use the Opéra Garnier as your orientation landmark and set out to do some power shopping. There are some intriguing small museums in the neighborhood, too, if you want a dose of culture.

GETTING ORIENTED

Proudly displaying its illustrious 2,000-year history, and serving today as home to some 2 million people, Paris could take you multiple lifetimes to explore from top to bottom—and that's not counting the Louvre. Happily, the métro system is extremely efficient and will aid you in see-and-flee sightseeing. But to truly savor Paris's heady parfum, opt for the bus, or even better, your feet. In no time at all, you'll be strolling like a true Parisian from the arty Rive Gauche (Left Bank) to the regal Rive Droite (Right Bank).

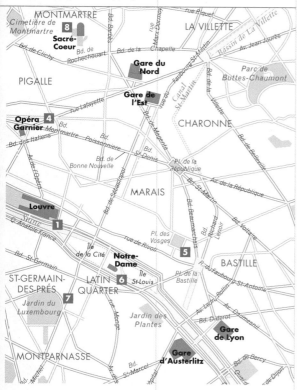

5 **The Marais & the Bastille.** The Marais is Paris's most popular Sunday-afternoon-lazing neighborhood, where you can while away the afternoon at the Place des Vosges or shop to your heart's content. And if it's new and happening in Paris, the Bastille is where you'll find it.

6 **Ile St-Louis & the Quartier Latin.** Ile St-Louis is one of the most romantic spots in Paris. Leave time to wander the Latin Quarter, a 'hood known for its vibrant student life.

7 **From Orsay to St-Germain-des-Prés.** Great cafés and two of the city's most fabulous museums are found here. Also, don't miss the Jardins du Luxembourg.

8 **Montmartre.** Like a small village inside a big city, Montmartre feels distinctly separate from the rest of Paris—but it's prime tourist territory with Sacré-Coeur as its main attraction (pictured below).

PARIS PLANNER

Getting Around

Paris is without question best explored on foot and, thanks to Baron Haussmann's mid-19th-century redesign, the City of Light is a compact wonder of wide boulevards, gracious parks, and leafy squares. When you want a lift, though, public transportation is easy and inexpensive. The métro (subway) goes just about everywhere you're going for €1.40 a ride (a carnet, or "pack" of 10 tickets is €10.90); tickets are good for the vast bus network, too.

Paris is divided into 20 *arrondissements* (or neighborhoods) spiraling out from the center of the city. The numbers reveal the neighborhood's location, and its age: the 1st arrondissement at the city's heart being the oldest. The *arrondissements* in central Paris—the 1st to 8th—are the most-visited.

It's worth picking up a copy of Paris Pratique, the essential map guide, available at bookstores, and souvenir shops.

Hours

Paris is by no means a 24/7 city so planning your days beforehand can save you aggravation. Museums are closed one day a week, usually Tuesday, and most stay open late at least one night each week, which is also the least crowded time to visit. Store hours are generally 10 AM to 7:30 PM, though smaller shops may not open until 11 AM, only to close for several hours during the afternoon. Some retailers are still barred by law from doing business on Sunday, but exceptions include the shops along the Champs-Elysées, the Carrousel du Louvre, and around the Marais, where most boutiques open at 2 PM.

When to Go

The City of Light is magical all year round, but it's particularly gorgeous in June when the long days (the sun doesn't set until 10 PM) stretch sightseeing hours and make it ideal to linger in the cafés practicing the city's favorite pastime—people-watching.

Winter can be dark and chilly, but it's also the best time to find cheap airfares and hotel deals.

April in Paris, despite what the song says, is often rainy.

Summer is the most popular (and expensive) season, and at the height of it, in July, Paris can feel like a city under siege, bursting at the seams as crowds descend en masse. Keep in mind that, like some other European cities, Paris somewhat shuts down in August—some restaurants are closed for the entire month, for example—though there are still plenty of fun things to do, namely free open-air movies and concerts, and the popular Paris Plage, the "beach" on the right bank of the Seine.

September is gorgeous, with temperate weather, saner airfares, and cultural events timed for the rentrée (or return), signifying the end of summer vacation.

Saving Time & Money

Paris is one of the world's most visited cities—with crowds to prove it, so it pays to be prepared. Buy tickets online when you can: most cultural centers and museums offer advance ticket sales and the small service fee you'll pay is worth the time saved waiting in line. Investigate alternate entrances at popular sites (there are three at the Louvre, for example) and check when rates are reduced, often during once-a-week late openings. Also, most major museums—including the Louvre and the Musée d'Orsay—are free the first Sunday of each month.

A Paris Museum Pass can save you money if you're planning serious sightseeing, but it might be even more valuable for the fact that it allows you to bypass the lines. It's sold at the destinations it covers and at airports, major métro stations, and the tourism office in the Carrousel du Louvre (two-, four- or six-day passes are €30, €45, and €60 respectively; for more information visit www.paris-museumpass.com).

Stick to the omnipresent ATMs for the best exchange rates; exchanging cash at your hotel or in a store is never going to be to your advantage.

Eating Out

Restaurants follow French mealtimes, serving lunch from noon to 2:30 PM and dinner from 7:30 or 8 PM on. Some cafés serve food all day long. Always reserve a table for dinner, as top restaurants book up months in advance. When it comes to the check, you must ask for it. (It's considered rude to bring it unbidden.) In cafés you'll get a register receipt with your order. Gratuities (*servis*) are almost always included in the bill but it's good form to leave some small change on the table: a few centimes for drinks, or €2–€3 at dinner.

What to Wear

When it comes to dress, the French reserve athletic-type clothing for sports. Sneakers are fine as long as they're not "gym shoes" (think urban hip). You'll feel comfortable wearing jeans just about anywhere as long as they're neat, although before you head out for the evening make sure to check if they're acceptable.

Paris Etiquette

The Parisian reputation for rudeness is undeserved. In fact, Parisians are sticklers for "politesse" and exchanging formal greetings is the rule. Informal American-style manners are considered impolite. Beginning an exchange with a simple "Do you speak English?" will get you off on the right foot. Learning a few key French words will take you far. Offer a hearty *bonjour* (bohn-zhoor) when walking into a shop or café and an *au revoir* (o ruh-vwahr) when leaving, even if nobody seems to be listening (a chorus may reply). When speaking to a woman over age 16, use *madame* (ma-dam), literally "my lady." For a young woman or girl, use *mademoiselle* (mad-mwa-zel). A man of any age goes by *monsieur* (muh-syuh). Always say please, *s'il vous plaît* (seel-voo-play), and thank you, *merci* (mair-see).

Introduction by
Nancy Coons

Updated by
Elizabeth
Bard, Jennifer
Ditsler-
Ladonne,
Rosa Jackson,
Lisa Pasold,
and Heather
Stimmler-Hall

IF THERE'S A PROBLEM WITH a trip to Paris, it's the embarrassment of riches that faces you. No matter which aspect of Paris you choose— touristy, historic, fashion-conscious, pretentious-bourgeois, thrifty, or the legendary bohemian arty Paris of undying attraction—one thing is certain: you will carve out your own Paris, one that is vivid, exciting, ultimately unforgettable. Wherever you head, your itinerary will prove to be a voyage of discovery. But choosing the Paris of your dreams is a bit like choosing a perfume or cologne. Do you want something young and dashing, or elegant and worldly? How about sporty, or perhaps strictly glamorous? No matter: they are all here—be it perfumes, famous museums, legendary churches, or romantic cafés. Whether you spend three days or three months in this city, it will always have something new to offer you, which may explain why the most assiduous explorers of Paris are the Parisians themselves.

Veterans know that Paris is a city of vast, noble perspectives and intimate, ramshackle streets, of formal *espaces vertes* (green open spaces) and quiet squares. This combination of the pompous and the private is one of the secrets of its perennial pull. Another is its size: Paris is relatively small as capitals go, with distances between many of its major sights and museums invariably walkable.

For the first-timer there will always be several must-dos at the top of the list, but getting to know Paris will never be quite as simple as a quick look at Notre-Dame, the Louvre, and the Eiffel Tower. You'll discover that around every corner, down every *ruelle* (little street) lies a resonance-in-waiting. You can stand on the Rue du Faubourg St-Honoré at the very spot where Edmond Rostand set Ragueneau's pastry shop in *Cyrano de Bergerac.* You can read the letters of Madame de Sévigné in her actual *hôtel particulier,* or private mansion, now the Musée Carnavalet. You can hear the words of Racine resound in the ringing, hair-raising diction of the Comédie Française. You can breathe in the fumes of hubris before the extravagant onyx tomb Napoléon designed for himself. You can gaze through the gates at the school where Voltaire honed his wit, and you can lay a garland on Oscar Wilde's poignant grave at Père-Lachaise Cemetery.

If this is your first trip, you may want to take a guided tour of the city— a good introduction that will help you get your bearings and provide you with a general impression before you return to explore the sights that particularly interest you. To help track those down, this chapter's exploration of Paris is divided into eight neighborhood walks. Each *quartier,* or neighborhood, has its own personality, which is best discovered by foot power. Ultimately, your route will be marked by your preferences, your curiosity, and your state of fatigue. You can wander for hours without getting bored—though not, perhaps, without getting lost. By the time you have seen only a few neighborhoods, drinking in the rich variety they have to offer, you should not only be culturally replete but downright exhausted—and hungry, too. Again, take your cue from Parisians and think out your next move in a sidewalk café. So you've heard stories of a friend who paid $8 for a coffee at a café. So what? What you're paying for is time, and the opportunity to watch the intricate drama of Parisian street life unfold. Hemingway knew the rules; after all, he would have remained just another unknown sports-writer if the waiters in the cafés had hovered around him impatiently.

EXPLORING PARIS

Updated by
Lisa Pasold

As world capitals go, Paris is surprisingly compact. The city is divided in two by the River Seine, with two islands (Ile de la Cité and Ile St-Louis) in the middle. Each bank of the Seine has its own personality; the Rive Droite (Right Bank), with its spacious boulevards and formal buildings, generally has a more genteel feel than the carefree Rive Gauche (Left Bank), to the south. The east–west axis from Châtelet to the Arc de Triomphe, via the Rue de Rivoli and the Champs-Élysées, is the Right Bank's principal thoroughfare for sightseeing and shopping.

Numbers in the text correspond to numbers in the margin and on the Exploring Paris, from the Tour Eiffel to the Arc de Triomphe, and Montmartre maps.

FROM NOTRE-DAME TO THE PLACE DE LA CONCORDE: THE HISTORIC HEART

In the center of Paris nestled in the River Seine are the two celebrated islands, the Ile de la Cité and the Ile St-Louis. Of the two, it's the Ile de la Cité that forms the historic ground zero of Paris. It was here that the earliest inhabitants of Paris, the Gaulish tribe of the Parisii, settled in about 250 BC, calling their home Lutetia, meaning "settlement surrounded by water." Today it's famed for the great, brooding cathedral of Notre-Dame, the haunted Conciergerie, and the dazzling Sainte-Chapelle. If Notre-Dame represents Church, another major attraction of this walk—the Louvre—symbolizes State. A succession of French rulers was responsible for filling this immense structure with the world's greatest paintings and works of art. It's the largest museum in the world, as well as one of the easiest to get lost in. Beyond the Louvre lie the graceful Tuileries Gardens, the grand Place de la Concorde—the very hub of the city—and the Belle Epoque splendor of the Grand Palais and the Pont Alexandre III. All in all, this area comprises some of the most historic and beautiful sights to see in Paris.

WHAT TO SEE

2 **Ancien Cloître Quartier.** Hidden in the shadows of Notre-Dame, this

Fodor'sChoice
★

adorable and often overlooked nook of Paris was thankfully spared when Baron Georges Eugène Haussmann knocked down much of the Ile de la Cité in the 19th century. Enter the quarter—originally the area where seminary students boarded with the church canons—by heading north toward the Seine to reach Rue Chanoinesse, once the seminary's cloister walk. Here, at No. 10, is the house (sadly renovated) that was once paradise to those fabled lovers of the Middle Ages, Héloïse and Abélard. Although defaced by a modern police station and garage, this tiny warren of six streets still casts a spell, particularly at the intersection of Rue des Ursins and Rue des Chantres, where a lovely medieval

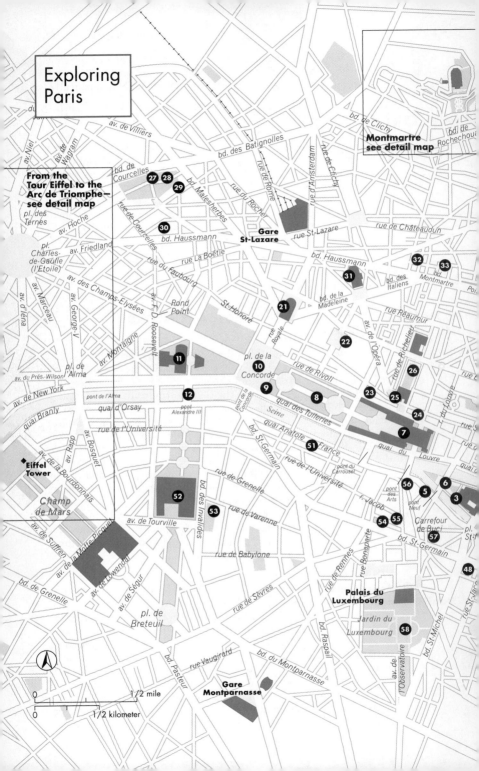

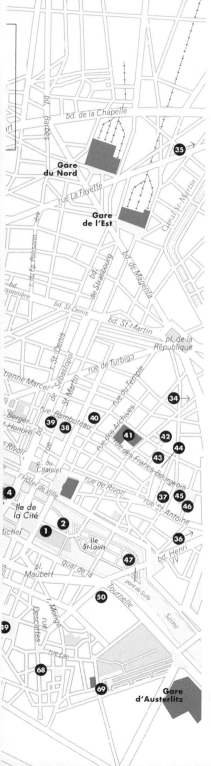

palace, tiny flower garden, and quayside steps form a cul-de-sac where time seems to be holding its breath. ⊠ *Rue du Cloître-Notre-Dame north to Quai des Fleurs, Ile de la Cité* Ⓜ *Cité.*

❹ **Conciergerie.** Bringing a tear to the eyes of *ancien régime* devotees, this is the famous prison in which dukes and duchesses, lords and ladies, and, most famously, Queen Marie-Antoinette were imprisoned during the Revolution before being carted off to the guillotine. Originally part of a royal palace, the turreted medieval building still holds Marie-Antoinette's cell; a chapel, embellished with the initials M. A., which was commissioned after the queen's death by her daughter, occupies the true site of her confinement. Out of one of these windows, the queen saw a notorious scene of the Revolution: her best friend, the Comtesse de Lamballe—lover of the arts and daughter of the richest duke in France—torn to pieces by a wild mob, her dismembered limbs then displayed on pikes. Elsewhere are the courtyard and fountain where victims of the Terror spent their final days. ⊠ *1 quai de l'Horloge, Louvre/Tuileries* ☎ *01–53–40–60–93* ⊕ *www.monum.fr* ☎ *€7.50, joint ticket with Sainte-Chapelle €10.40* ⊙ *Daily 9:30–6* Ⓜ *Cité.*

⓫ **Grand Palais** *(Grand Palace).* With its curved glass roof, the Grand Palais is unmistakable when approached from either the Seine or the Champs-Élysées, and forms a turn-of-the-20th-century Beaux Arts showpiece with the **Petit Palais** on the other side of Avenue Winston-Churchill. Today, the Grand Palais plays host to major exhibitions (some of blockbuster status, so book tickets in advance). Its smaller counterpart, the Petit Palais, set just off the Champs-Élysées, presents a permanent collection of French painting and furniture, with splendid canvases by Courbet and Bouguereau. Along with temporary exhibitions and antiques fairs, the building itself is a real draw, a 1902 cream puff of marble and gilt, with huge windows overlooking the Seine. ⊠ *Av. Winston-Churchill, Champs-Élysées* ☎ *01–44–13–17–30 Grand Palais, 01–42–65–12–73 Petit Palais* ⊕ *www.paris.fr/musees/* ☎ *Grand Palais: €11.10. Petit Palais: free, temporary exhibit entry fees vary* ⊙ *Grand Palais: hrs vary; Petit Palais: Tues.–Sun. 10–6* Ⓜ *Champs-Élysées–Clemenceau.*

Ⓒ ❽ **Jardin des Tuileries** *(Tuileries Gardens).* Monet and Renoir captured this gracious garden (really more of a long park) with paint and brush, Left Bank songstresses warble about its beauty, and all Parisians know it as a charming place to stroll and survey the surrounding cityscape. A palace once stood here on the site of a clay pit that supplied material for many of the city's tile roofs. (Hence the name *tuileries,* or tile works.) During the Revolution, Louis XVI and his family were kept in the Tuileries under house arrest. Now the Tuileries is a typically French garden: formal and neatly patterned, with statues, rows of trees, fountains with gaping fish, and gravel paths. No wonder the Impressionists liked it here—note how the gray, austere light of Paris makes green trees look even greener. ⊠ *Bordered by Quai des Tuileries, Pl. de la Concorde, Rue de Rivoli, and the Louvre, Louvre/Tuileries* Ⓜ *Tuileries.*

Continued on page 37

NOTRE-DAME

Notre-Dame is the symbolic heart of Paris and, for many, of France itself. Napoléon was crowned here, and kings and queens exchanged marriage vows before its altar. There are a few things worth seeing inside the Gothic cathedral, but the real highlights are the exterior architectural details and the unforgettable view of Paris, framed by stone gargoyles, from the top of the south tower.

OUTSIDE NOTRE-DAME

Begun in 1163, completed in 1345, badly damaged during the Revolution, and restored by the architect Eugène Viollet-le-Duc in the 19th century, Notre-Dame may not be France's oldest or largest cathedral, but in beauty and architectural harmony it has few peers. The front entranceways seem like hands joined in prayer, the sculpted kings on the facade form a noble procession, and the west (front) rose window gleams with what seems like divine light.

The most dramatic approach to Notre-Dame is from the Rive Gauche, crossing at the Pont au Double from quai de Montebello, at the St-Michel métro or RER stop. This bridge will take you to the open square, place du Parvis, in front of the cathedral. (The more direct metro stop is Cité.)

THE WEST (FRONT) FACADE
The three front entrances are, left to right: the Portal of the Virgin, the Portal of the Last Judgment (*above*), and the Portal of St. Anne, the oldest of the three.

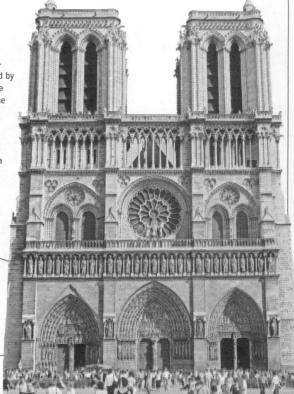

THE STONE GARGOYLES
Notre-Dame's gargoyles were designed by Eugène Viollet-le-Duc, the architect who oversaw the cathedral's 19th-century renovations. Technically they're chimeras, not gargoyles, as they're purely ornamental; a true "gargoyle" is a carved sculpture that functions as a waterspout.

THE GALLERY OF KINGS
Above the three front entrances are the 28 restored statues of the kings of Israel, the Galerie des Rois.

INSIDE THE CATHEDRAL

❶ **The Pietà,** behind the choir, represents the Virgin Mary mourning over the dead body of Christ.

❷ **The biblical scenes** on the north and south screens of the choir represent the life of Christ and the apparitions of Christ after the Resurrection.

❸ **The north rose window** is one of the cathedral's original stained-glass panels; at the center is an image of Mary holding a young Jesus.

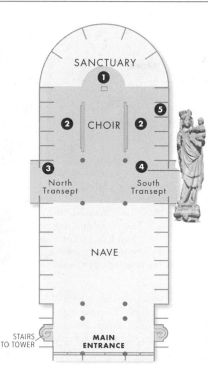

SANCTUARY

❶

❷ CHOIR ❷

❺

❸

❹

North Transept

South Transept

NAVE

STAIRS TO TOWER

MAIN ENTRANCE

❹ At the south (right) entrance to the choir, you'll glimpse the haunting 12th-century statue of **Notre-Dame de Paris,** "Our Lady of Paris," the Virgin, for whom the cathedral is named.

❺ **The treasury,** on the south side of the choir, holds a small collection of religious garments, reliquaries, and silver- and gold-plate.

■**TIP**➔ The best time to visit Notre-Dame is early in the morning, when the cathedral is at its brightest and least crowded.

MAKING THE CLIMB

A separate entrance, to the left of the front facade if you're facing it, leads to the 387 stone steps of the south tower. These steps take you to the bell of Notre-Dame (as tolled by the fictional Quasimodo). Looking out from the tower, you can see how Paris—like the trunk of a tree developing new rings—has grown outward from the Ile de la Cité. To the north is Montmartre; to the west is the Arc de Triomphe, at the top of the Champs-Elysées; and to the south are the towers of St-Sulpice and the Panthéon. ■**TIP**➔**Lines to climb the tower are shortest in the morning, Tuesday to Friday.**

SOMETHING TO PONDER

Do Notre-Dame's hunchback and its gargoyles have anything in common other than bad posture? Quasimodo was created by Victor Hugo in the novel *Notre-Dame de Paris,* published in 1831. The incredible popularity of the book made Parisians finally take notice of the cathedral's state of disrepair and spurred Viollet-le-Duc's renovations. These included the addition of the gargoyles, among other things, and resulted in the structure we see today.

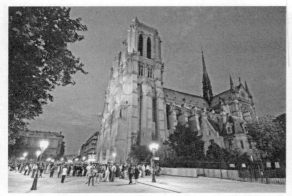

Place du Parvis

Flying buttresses

Notre-Dame was one of the first Gothic cathedrals in Europe. It was also one of the first buildings to make use of **flying buttresses**—exterior supports that spread out the weight of the building and its roof. At first people thought they looked like scaffolding that the builders forgot to remove. ■**TIP**➔ **The most tranquil place to appreciate the architecture of Notre-Dame is from the lovely garden behind the cathedral, Square Jean-XXIII.**

Place du Parvis is *kilomètre zéro*, the spot from which all distances to and from the city are officially measured. A polished brass circle set in the ground, about 20 yards from the cathedral's main entrance, marks the exact spot.

The Archaeological Crypt (entrance down the stairs in front of the cathedral) is a quick visit but very interesting, especially for kids and archaeology buffs. It gives an "under the city" view of the area, with remains from previous churches that were built on this site, scale models charting the district's development, and artifacts dating from the Parisii, who lived here 2,000 years ago. The **Musée de Notre-Dame**, on the other hand, has little to interest the average visitor.

☎ 01–53–10–07–00
✕ www.monum.fr
▨ Cathedral free. Towers: €7. Crypt €3.30. Treasury €2.50. Museum €2.50.
☺ Cathedral daily 8–7. Towers Apr.–June and Sept., daily 9:30–7:30; July and Aug., weekdays 9–7:30, weekends 9 AM–11 PM; Oct.–Mar., daily 10–5:30. Note: towers close early when overcrowded. Treasury Mon.–Sat. 9:30–11:30 and 1–5:30. Crypt Tues.–Sun. 10–6. Museum Wed. and weekends 2:30–6.

TIMELINE

1160	Notre-Dame is conceived by Bishop Maurice de Sully, the bishop of Paris.	**c. 1200–1245**	The western facade and towers are completed.	**1345**	Construction of the original cathedral is completed.
1163	Construction begins.	**1208**	The Nave is completed.	**1699–1723**	The original Gothic choir is replaced with a Baroque one.
1182	Choir is completed; the main altar is consecrated.	**1235–1250**	A series of chapels are added to the nave.		
1196	Bishop de Sully dies.	**1250–1270**	The High Gothic–style north and south Rose windows are installed.	**c 1790**	The church is plundered during the Revolution.
		1296–1330	A series of chapels are added to the apse.	**1845**	Viollet-le-Duc's restoration begins, lasting 23 years.

NEED A BREAK? Stop for a snack or lunch at Dame Tartine (📞 *01-47-03-94-84*), one of the two designer brasseries erected in the Tuileries in the late 1990s (it's on the left as you arrive from the Place de la Concorde). With its glass-paneled walls and roof and light wood and aluminum accents, the restaurant is sober and airy. The cuisine is inventive and offers good value—try the lamb flan with tomato puree and a carafe of red Ventoux from the Rhône. You can also eat outdoors in the leafy shade.

❼ Louvre. Leonardo da Vinci's *Mona Lisa* and *Virgin and St. Anne,* Veronese's *Marriage at Cana,* Giorgione's *Concert Champêtre,* Delacroix's *Liberty Guiding the People,* Whistler's *Mother (Arrangement in Black and White)* … you get the picture. After two decades of renovations, the Louvre is a coherent, unified structure, and search parties no longer need to be sent in to bring you out. Begun by Philippe-Auguste in the 13th century as a fortress, it was not until the reign of pleasure-loving François I, 300 years later, that the Louvre of today gradually began to take shape. Through the years Henri IV (1589–1610), Louis XIII (1610–43), Louis XIV (1643–1715), Napoléon I (1804–14), and Napoléon III (1852–70) all contributed to its construction.

Fodor'sChoice
★

The number one attraction is the "Most Famous Painting in the World": Leonardo da Vinci's enigmatic *Mona Lisa* (*La Joconde,* to the French), painted in 1503–06 and now cynosure of all eyes in the museum's Salle des États, where it was ensconced in its own special alcove in 2005. The story behind her face—one that is still emerging—is fascinating. The portrait of the wife of one Francesco del Giocondo, a 15th-century Florentine millionaire, Leonardo's masterpiece is now believed to have been painted for her husband as a memorial after the lady's death. Some historians now maintain that her black garb is in honor of her baby who died in 1502. If so, however, this may be at odds with the famous smile, which critics point to as another example of Leonardo's famous wit: the family name Giocondo is derived from the Latin word for "jocundity," or humor. More great High Renaissance masterpieces line nearby walls, including Leonardo's *Virgin and St. Anne* and Raphael's *La Belle Jardinière.* The Salle des États also contains one of the largest pictures in the Louvre: the *Feast at Cana,* by Pablo Veronese (1528–88), a sumptuous painting reminiscent of the Venetian painter's *Christ in the House of Levi* (which is in Venice). These paintings, filled with partygoers, prompted a formal summons from the pope, asking Veronese to explain in person why he had scandalously included the chaos of drunken revelers, dwarves, and animals in what was purportedly a holy scene.

The Louvre is packed with legendary collections, which are divided into eight curatorial departments: Near Eastern Antiquities; Egyptian Antiquities; Greek, Etruscan, and Roman Antiquities; Islamic Art; Sculptures; Decorative Arts; Paintings; and Prints and Drawings. Don't try to see it all at once; try, instead, to make repeat visits. Some other highlights of the painting collection are Jan van Eyck's magnificent *The Madonna and Chancellor Rolin,* painted in the early 15th century; *The Lacemaker,* by Jan Vermeer (1632–75); *The Embarkation for*

Cythera, by Antoine Watteau (1684–1721); *The Oath of the Horatii*, by Jacques-Louis David (1748–1825); *The Raft of the Medusa*, by Théodore Géricault (1791–1824); and *La Grande Odalisque*, by Jean-Auguste-Dominique Ingres (1780–1867).

The French crown jewels (in the Gallerie d'Apollon—a newly renovated 17th-century extravaganza) include the mind-boggling 186-carat Regent diamond. Atop the marble Escalier Daru is the Nike, or *Winged Victory of Samothrace*, which seems poised for flight over the stairs. Among other much-loved pieces of sculpture are Michelangelo's two *Slaves*, intended for the tomb of Pope Julius II. These can be admired in the Denon Wing, where a medieval and Renaissance sculpture section is housed partly in the former imperial stables. The Richelieu Wing is the new home of the famous *Venus de Milo*. If you're a fan of the Napoléon III style—the apotheosis of 19th-century, red-and-gilt opulence—be sure to see the galleries that once housed the Ministry of Finance.

To get into the Louvre, you may have to wait in two long lines: one outside the Pyramide entrance portal and another downstairs at the ticket booths. You can avoid the first by entering through the Carrousel du Louvre, but you can't avoid the second. Your ticket (be sure to hold on to it) will get you into any and all of the wings as many times as you like during one day—and once you have your ticket you can skip the entry line. Once inside, you should stop by the information desk to pick up a free color-coded map and check which rooms are closed for the day. (Closures rotate through the week, so you can come back if something is temporarily unavailable.) Beyond this, you'll have all you need—shops, a post office, and places to eat. Café Marly may have an enviable location facing into the Cour Napoléon, but its food is decidedly lackluster. For a more soigné lunch, keep your appetite in check until you get to the museum's stylish Café Richelieu, or head outside the palace walls. There's also a full calendar of lectures, films, concerts, and special exhibits; some are part of the excellent lunch-hour series called Les Midis du Louvre. Most are not included in the basic ticket price—pick up a three-month schedule at the information desk or check online for information. Remember that the Louvre is closed Tuesday. ⊠*Palais du Louvre, Louvre/Tuileries* 🕾*01–40–20–53–17 information* ⊕*www. louvre.fr* 🖾*€8.50, €6 after 6* PM *Wed. and Fri. Free 1st Sun. of month; €8.50 for Napoléon Hall exhibitions* ⊙*Mon., Thurs., and weekends 9–6, Wed. and Fri. 9* AM–*10* PM Ⓜ*Palais-Royal.*

★ ❾ **Musée de l'Orangerie.** The most beautiful Claude Monet paintings in the world—eight vast mural-size *Nymphéas* (Water Lilies)—can be found at this newly removed museum, which also includes a collection of early-20th-century paintings, with works by Renoir, Paul Cézanne, Henri Matisse, and Marie Laurencin, among other masters. The museum's name, by the way, isn't misleading; the building was originally used to store the Tuileries' citrus trees over the winter. ⊠*Pl. de la Concorde, Louvre/Tuileries* 🕾*No phone* ⊕*www.musee-orangerie.fr/* 🖾*€7* ⊙*Wed.–Mon. 12:30–6* Ⓜ*Concorde.*

❶ Notre-Dame.

See highlighted listing in this chapter.

❿ Place de la Concorde. This majestic square at the foot of the Champs-Élysées was laid out in the 1770s, but there was nothing in the way of peace or concord about its early years. Between 1793 and 1795 more than a thousand victims, including Louis XVI and Marie-Antoinette, were sent into oblivion at the guillotine, prompting Madame Roland's famous cry, "Liberty, what crimes are committed in thy name." The top of the 107-foot **Obelisk**—a present from the viceroy of Egypt in 1833—was regilded in 1998. The Place continues to have politically symbolic weight. Demonstrations center here, since the Assemblée Nationale is right across the river and the Palais de l'Élysée (the French presidential palace) and the U.S. Embassy are just around the corner. Among the handsome, symmetrical 18th-century buildings facing the square is the Hôtel Crillon, originally built by Gabriel—architect of the Petit Trianon—as an 18th-century home for three of France's wealthiest families. At the near end of high-walled Rue Royale is the legendary Maxim's restaurant, but unless you choose to eat here, you won't be able to see the riot of crimson velvets and florid Art Nouveau furniture inside. ⊠ *Champs-Élysées* Ⓜ *Concorde.*

❺ Place Dauphine. The Surrealists loved Place Dauphine, which they called "*le sexe de Paris*" because of its location—at the far-western end of the Ile de la Cité—and suggestive V-shape. Its origins were much more proper: built by Henri IV, it was named in homage to his successor, the dauphin, who grew up to become Louis XIII. The triangular square is lined with some charming 17th-century houses that the writer André Maurois felt represented the very quintessence of Paris and France. Take a seat on a park bench, enjoy a picnic, and see if you agree. ⊠ *Ile de la Cité* Ⓜ *Cité.*

⑫ Pont Alexandre-III *(Alexander III Bridge).* No other bridge over the Seine epitomizes the fin de siècle frivolity of the Belle Epoque (or Paris itself) like the exuberant, bronze-lamp–lined Pont Alexandre-III. An urban masterstroke that seems as much created of cake frosting and sugar sculptures as stone and iron, it was built, like the Grand and Petit Palais nearby, for the 1900 world's fair. It was inaugurated by the ill-fated czar Nicholas II, and ingratiatingly named in honor of his father. ⊠ *Invalides* Ⓜ *Invalides.*

❻ Pont Neuf *(New Bridge).* Crossing the Ile de la Cité, just behind Square du Vert-Galant, is the oldest bridge in Paris, confusingly called the New Bridge—the name was given when it was completed in 1607, and it stuck. It was the first bridge in the city to be built without houses lining either side, allegedly because Henri IV wanted a clear view of Notre-Dame from his windows at the Louvre. ⊠ *Ile de la Cité* Ⓜ *Pont-Neuf.*

❸ Sainte-Chapelle *(Holy Chapel).* Not to be missed and one of the most
magical sights in European medieval art, this Gothic chapel was built by Louis IX (1226–70; later canonized as St. Louis) in the 1240s to house

what he believed to be Christ's Crown of Thorns, purchased from Emperor Baldwin of Constantinople. A dark lower chapel is a gloomy prelude to the shimmering upper one. Here the famous beauty of Sainte-Chapelle comes alive: instead of walls, all you see are 6,458 square feet of stained glass, delicately supported by painted stonework that seems to

GO CLASSICAL

Catching a classical music concert at the jewel-box Sainte-Chapelle can be a highlight of your trip to Paris—log on to ⊕ *www.ampconcerts.com* for the recital schedule there and at other historic churches in Paris.

disappear in the colorful light streaming through the windows. The lowest section of the windows was restored in the mid-1800s, but otherwise this chapel presents intact incredibly rare stained glass. Deep reds and blues dominate the background glass here, noticeably different from later, lighter medieval styles such as those in Notre-Dame's rose windows. The Sainte-Chapelle is essentially an enormous magic lantern illuminating the 1,130 figures from the Bible, to create—as one writer poetically put it—"the most marvelous colored and moving air ever held within four walls." Originally, the king's holy relics were displayed in the raised apse and shown to the faithful on Good Friday. Today the magic of the chapel comes alive during the regular concerts held here; call to check the schedule. ⊠ *4 bd. du Palais, Ile de la Cité* ☎ *01–53–73–78–51* ⊕ *www.monum.fr* ✉ *€6.10, joint ticket with Conciergerie €10.40* ◷ *Daily 9:30–6, entry closes at 5:30, or 4:30 Nov.–Feb.* Ⓜ *Cité.*

FROM THE EIFFEL TOWER TO THE ARC DE TRIOMPHE: MONUMENTS & MARVELS

The Eiffel Tower (or *Tour Eiffel,* to use the French) lords over southwest Paris, and from nearly wherever you are on this walk you can see its jutting needle. For years many Parisians felt it was an iron eyesore and called it the Giant Asparagus, a vegetable that weighed 15 million pounds and grew 1,000 feet high. But gradually the tower became part of the Parisian landscape, entering the hearts and souls of Parisians and visitors alike. Thanks to its stunning nighttime illumination, topped by four 6,000-watt projectors creating a lighthouse beacon visible for 80 km (50 mi) around, it continues to make Paris live up to its moniker *La Ville Lumière*—the City of Light. Water is the second highlight here: fountains playing beneath Place du Trocadéro and boat tours along the Seine on a Bateau Mouche. Museums are the third; the area around Trocadéro is full of them. Style is the fourth, and not just because the buildings here are overwhelmingly elegant—but because this is also the center of haute couture, with the top names in fashion all congregated around Avenue Montaigne, only a brief walk from the Champs-Élysées, to the north.

The 2-km (1-mi) Champs-Élysées was originally laid out in the 1660s by landscape gardener André Le Nôtre as parkland sweeping away from the Tuileries. In an attempt to reestablish this thoroughfare as

1

one of the world's most beautiful avenues, the city has planted extra trees, broadened sidewalks, refurbished Art Nouveau newsstands, and clamped down on garish storefronts. One legacy of this much-advertised renovation are some excellent megastores, including Virgin (music and video) and Sephora (makeup and perfume), along with a few chic restaurants, plus an opulent branch of the pâtissier Ladurée. Site of most French national celebrations, the Champs-Élysées is the last leg of the Tour de France bicycle race, on the third or fourth Sunday in July, and the site of vast ceremonies on Bastille Day (July 14) and Armistice Day (November 11).

WHAT TO SEE

★ ⓴ **Arc de Triomphe.** Set on Place Charles-de-Gaulle—known to Parisians as L'Étoile, or the Star (a reference to the streets that fan out from it)—the colossal, 164-foot Arc de Triomphe arch was planned by Napoléon but not finished until 1836, 20 years after the end of his rule. It's decorated with some magnificent sculptures by François Rude, such as the *Departure of the Volunteers,* better known as *La Marseillaise,* to the right of the arch when viewed from the Champs-Élysées. A small museum halfway up the arch is devoted to its history. France's Unknown Soldier is buried beneath the archway; the flame is rekindled every evening at 6:30. ✉ *Pl. Charles-de-Gaulle, Champs-Élysées* ☎ 01–55–37–73–77 ⊕ *www.monum.fr* ✆ €8 ⊘ *Apr.–Sept., daily 10* AM*–11* PM*; Oct.–Mar., daily 10* AM*–10:30* PM Ⓜ *Métro or RER: Étoile.*

⓳ **Fondation Pierre Bergé–Yves Saint Laurent.** With his business partner, Pierre Bergé (who had the Napoléon-size ego to include his name in this museum's name), iconic fashion designer Yves Saint Laurent reopened his former atelier in 2004—this time as a gallery and archive of his work. Temporary exhibits, some fashion-related, rotate roughly every six months. The first, a show of Saint Laurent's art-inspired clothing, including his Mondrian dress, was a knockout; a more recent exhibit was devoted to theater artist Robert Wilson. ✉ *5 av. Marceau, Trocadéro/ Tour Eiffel* ☎ 01–44–31–64–00 ⊕ *www.fondation-pb-ysl.net* ✆ €5 ⊘ *Tues.–Sun. 11–6* Ⓜ *Alma-Marceau.*

★ ⓱ **Maison de Baccarat.** Famed modernist designer Philippe Starck brought an irreverent, Alice-in-Wonderland approach to the HQ of the venerable Baccarat crystal firm. Opened in 2003, the Baccarat museum plays on its building's Surrealist legacy: Cocteau, Dalí, Buñuel, and Man Ray were all frequent guests of the mansion's onetime owner, Countess Marie-Laure de Noailles. At the entrance, talking heads are projected onto giant crystal urns, and a lighted chandelier is submerged in an aquarium. Other fairy-tale touches include a 46-foot-long crystal-legged dinner table and an 8-foot-high chair, perfect for seating a giant princess. Not all the marvels come from Starck though; Baccarat has created exquisite crystal pieces since Louis XV conferred his seal on the glassworks in 1764. Many of the company's masterworks are on display, from the soaring candlesticks made for Czar Nicholas II to the perfume flacon Dalí designed for Schiaparelli. The museum's Cristal Room café–restaurant attracts an appropriately glittering crowd, so book well in advance for lunch or dinner. ✉ *11 pl. des Etats-Unis,*

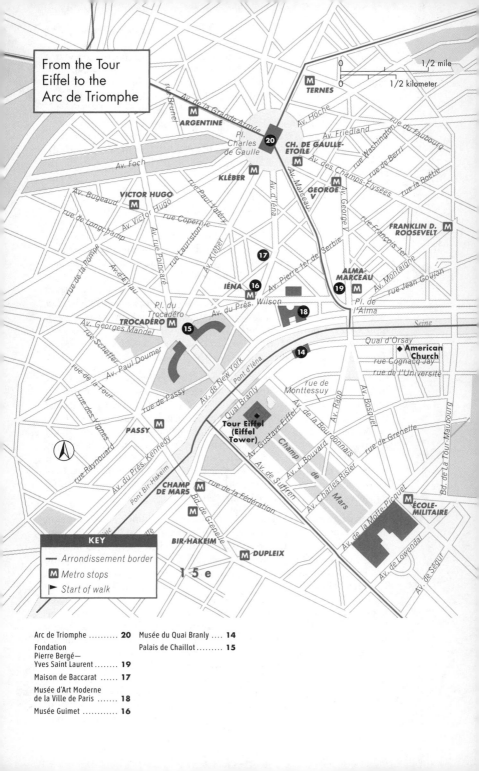

From the Tour Eiffel to the Arc de Triomphe

Trocadéro/Tour Eiffel ☎01–40–22–11–00 ⊕*www.baccarat.fr* ☒€7 ⊗*Mon.–Sat. 10–7* Ⓜ*Trocadéro.*

⓲ Musée d'Art Moderne de la Ville de Paris *(City Museum of Modern Art).* Although the city's modern-art museum hasn't attracted a buzz comparable to that of its main Paris competitor, the Centre Georges Pompidou, it can give a more pleasant museum-going experience. Like the Pompidou, it shows temporary exhibits of painting, sculpture, installation and video art, plus a permanent collection of top-tier 20th-century works from around the world—but it happily escapes the Pompidou's overcrowding. The building reopened in February 2006 and its vast, white-walled galleries are an ideal backdrop for the bold statements of 20th-century art. The collection takes over, chronologically speaking, where the Musée d'Orsay leaves off; among the earliest works are Fauvist paintings by Vlaminck and Derain, followed by Picasso's early experiments in Cubism. Just next door, the **Palais de Tokyo** (☒*13 av. du Président-Wilson* ☎01–47–23–38–86 ⊕*www.palaisdetokyo. com* ☒€6 ⊗*Tues.–Sun. noon–midnight*), the Art Nouveau twin of the Musée d'Art Moderne, reemerged in 2002 as a trendy stripped-down space for contemporary arts. There's no permanent collection, just dynamic temporary exhibits, along with a bookstore and the hippest museum restaurant in town, Tokyo Eat. ☒*11 av. du Président-Wilson, Trocadéro/Tour Eiffel* ☎01–53–67–40–00 ⊕*www.paris.org* ☒*Permanent collection free, temporary exhibitions €7* ⊗*Tues.–Fri. 10–5:30, weekends 10–6:45* Ⓜ*Iéna.*

⓰ Musée Guimet. Prized by connoisseurs the world over, this museum was founded by Lyonnais industrialist Émile Guimet, who traveled around the world in the late 19th century amassing Indo-Chinese and Far Eastern objets d'art, plus a fabled collection of Cambodian art. Be sure to peer into the delicate round library (where you'd swear Guimet has just stepped out for tea) and toil up to the top floor's 18th-century ivory replica of a Chinese pavilion. ☒*6 pl. d'Iéna, Trocadéro/Tour Eiffel* ☎01–56–52–53–00 ⊕*www.museeguimet.fr* ☒€6 ⊗*Wed.–Sun. 10–6* Ⓜ*Iéna or Boissiére.*

⓮ Musée du Quai Branly. Picasso was inspired by African and Oceanic art to create his revolutionary *Demoiselles d'Avignon* and if he were around today he would make a beeline for this brand new museum (opened in 2006). Set alongside the Seine, this controversial museum, also known as the Musée des Arts Premiers, displays state-held troves of African, Asian, and Oceanic art, including anthropological collections previously shown in the Louvre. Make sure to get the telephone-style audio guide, as printed information is limited. Architect Jean Nouvel meant the long, low outline of the museum to suggest the Tour Eiffel's shadow—you can see the Tour towering above the classy museum restaurant and the less-expensive main-floor café. ☒*Quai Branly, Trocadéro/Tour Eiffel* ☎01–53–57–41–20 ⊕*www.quaibranly. fr* Ⓜ*Alma-Marceau.*

⓯ Palais de Chaillot *(Chaillot Palace).* This honey-color, Art Deco culture center facing the Seine, perched atop tumbling gardens with sculpture and fountains, was built in the 1930s and houses three museums: the **Musée de l'Homme** (Museum of Mankind); the **Musée de la Marine** (Maritime Museum), with a collection of model ships, marine paintings, and naval paraphernalia salty enough to delight all fans of Patrick O'Brien's novels (and anyone who has ever thought of running away to sea); and the new **Cité de l'Architecture et du Patrimoine.** The latter two are worth visiting but the only reason to visit the first is for its café (see the Need A Break entry for this chapter). The garden leading to the Seine has sculptures and dramatic fountains and is the focus for fireworks demonstrations on Bastille Day. The palace terrace, flanked by gilded statuettes (and often invaded by roller skaters and skateboarders), offers a wonderful picture-postcard view of the Tour Eiffel and is a favorite spot for fashion photographers. ⊠ *Pl. du Trocadéro, Trocadéro/ Tour Eiffel* ☎ *01–44–05–72–72 Museum of Mankind, 01–53–65– 69–69 Maritime Museum* ⊕ *www.mnhn.fr* ⊠ *Museum of Mankind €7, Maritime Museum €6.50* ⊗ *Museum of Mankind: Wed.–Fri. and Mon. 9:45–5:15, weekends 10–6:30; Maritime Museum: Wed.–Mon. 10–6* Ⓜ *Trocadéro.*

NEED A BREAK? You'll get a tremendous view of the Eiffel Tower and the Invalides dome with your ice cream, cocktail, or lunch at Le Totem (⊠ *Pl. du Trocadéro, Troca-déro/Tour Eiffel* ☎ *01–47–27–28–29*), an elegant bar and restaurant in the south wing of the Palais de Chaillot.

☾ ★ **Tour Eiffel** *(Eiffel Tower).*

See highlighted listing in this chapter.

THE FAUBOURG ST-HONORÉ: LE STYLE, C'EST PARIS

Fashions change, but the Faubourg St-Honoré, just north of the Champs-Élysées and the Tuileries, has been unfailingly chic since the early 1700s. The streets of this walk include some of the oldest in Paris. As you stroll from the President's Palace through arcaded streets and 19th-century passageways to the much-renovated market zone of Les Halles, you'll see all that is elegant in Paris, from architecture to fashion to food, all presented with typical Parisian insouciance. The centerpiece of the area is the stately Place Vendôme; on this ritzy square, famous boutiques sit side by side with famous banks—but then elegance and finance have never been an unusual combination. It's not surprising to learn that one of the main arteries of the area, Rue de Castiglione, was named after one of its former residents—the glamorous fashion-plate Countess de Castiglione, sent to plead the cause of Italian unity with Napoléon III. The emperor was persuaded (he was easily susceptible to feminine charms), and the area became a Kingdom of Woman: famous dressmakers, renowned jewelers, exclusive perfume shops, and the most chic hotel in Paris, the Ritz, made this *faubourg* (district) a symbol of luxury throughout the world. Long a neighborhood for ambitious beauties, it's no surprise to learn that Coco Chanel established her fashion house here on Rue Cambon. Today the tradition continues, with leading names in fashion found farther east on Place des Victoires, close to what was, for centuries, the gastronomic heart of Paris: Les Halles (pronounced "lay-*ahl*"), once the city's main market. These giant glass-and-iron market halls were demolished in 1969 and replaced by a park and the Forum des Halles, a dismal underground "shopping mall" now scheduled for a big makeover by a big-name architect. The surrounding streets underwent a transformation and are now filled with shops, cafés, restaurants, and chic apartment buildings.

WHAT TO SEE

★ ㉓ **Les Arts Décoratifs** *(Decorative Arts Center).* A must for lovers of fashion and the decorative arts, this northwestern wing of the Louvre building houses three high-style museums in one: the newly renovated **Musée des Arts Décoratifs,** with furniture, tapestries, glassware, paintings, and other necessities of life from the Middle Ages through Napoléon's time and beyond—a highlight here are the sumptuous period-style rooms; **Musée de la Mode,** devoted to costumes and accessories dating from the 16th century to today; and the **Musée de la Publicité,** with temporary exhibits of advertisements and posters. ⊠ *107 rue de Rivoli, Louvre/Tuileries* ☎ *01–44–55–57–50* ⊕ *www.ucad.fr* ☒ *€6* ⊙ *Tues.–Sun. 11–6* Ⓜ *Palais-Royal.*

㉕ **Comédie Française.** Famous for its classical French drama, this theater company was founded in 1680 by Louis XIV, a king more interested in controlling theater than promoting it. This building opened in 1799 but burned almost to the ground a hundred years later; what you're looking at dates from 1900. The *comédienne* Sarah Bernhardt, who famously performed from palaces in St. Petersburg to tents in Texas, began her career here. Today, mannered productions of Molière, Racine, and Corneille appear regularly on the bill—enjoyable if you understand French and don't mind declamatory formal acting. ⊠ *Pl. Colette, Louvre/Tuileries* ☎ *01–44–58–15–15* Ⓜ *Palais-Royal.*

㉑ **Église de La Madeleine** *(Church of La Madeleine).* With its rows of uncompromising columns, this sturdy Neoclassical edifice—designed in 1814 but not consecrated until 1842—looks more like a Greek temple than a Christian church. In fact, La Madeleine, as it's known, was nearly selected as Paris's first train station (the site of the Gare St-Lazare, just up the road, was chosen instead). Inside, the walls are richly and harmoniously decorated; gold glints through the murk. The portico's majestic Corinthian colonnade supports a gigantic pediment with a frieze of the Last Judgment. ⊠ *Pl. de la Madeleine, Opéra/Grands Boulevards* ⊕ *www.eglise-lamadeleine.com* ⊙ *Mon.–Sat. 7:30–7, Sun. 8–7* Ⓜ *Madeleine.*

㉔ **Louvre des Antiquaires.** This "shopping mall" of superelegant antiques dealers, off Place du Palais-Royal opposite the Louvre, is a minimuseum in itself. Its stylish glass-walled corridors—lined with Louis XVI *boiseries* (antique wood paneling), Charles Dix bureaus, and the pretty sort of bibelots that would have gladdened the heart of Marie-Antoinette—deserve a browse whether you intend to buy or not. Don't wear your flip-flops in here. ⊠ *Main entrance: Pl. du Palais-Royal,*

Continued on page 48

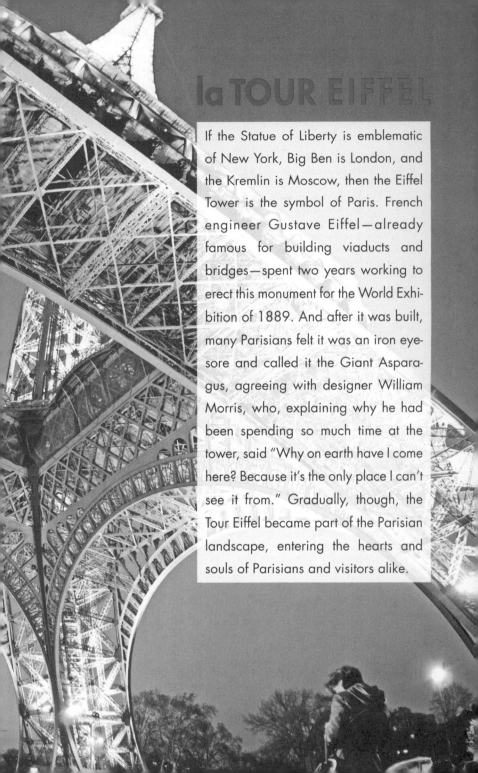

la TOUR EIFFEL

If the Statue of Liberty is emblematic of New York, Big Ben is London, and the Kremlin is Moscow, then the Eiffel Tower is the symbol of Paris. French engineer Gustave Eiffel—already famous for building viaducts and bridges—spent two years working to erect this monument for the World Exhibition of 1889. And after it was built, many Parisians felt it was an iron eyesore and called it the Giant Asparagus, agreeing with designer William Morris, who, explaining why he had been spending so much time at the tower, said "Why on earth have I come here? Because it's the only place I can't see it from." Gradually, though, the Tour Eiffel became part of the Parisian landscape, entering the hearts and souls of Parisians and visitors alike.

Total height: 1,063 feet ↑

■ The 200 millionth visitor went to the top of the Eiffel Tower in 2002.

■ You can take the stairs as far as the third level (check out the fantastic ironwork), but if you want to go to the very top you'll have to take the elevator.

■ To get to the first viewing platform, Gustave Eiffel originally used avant-garde hydraulic cable elevators designed by American Elisha Otis for two of the curved base legs of the tower. French elevators with a chain-drive system were used in the other two legs. During the 1989 renovation, all the elevators were rebuilt by the Otis company.

■ Every 7 years the tower is repainted. The job takes 15 months and uses 60 tons of "Tour Eiffel Brown" paint in three shades—lightest on top, darkest at the bottom.

Jules Verne

← The Eiffel Tower contains 12,000 pieces of metal and 2,500,000 rivets.

■ An expensive way to beat the queue is to dine at the **Jules Verne** restaurant on the second level. You ascend on a private elevator to the dining room. It's run by chef Alain Ducasse and open for lunch and dinner (☎ 01–45–55–61–44 for reservations). **Attitude 95** on level one is slightly less pricey.

■ The tower almost became scrap iron in 1909, when its concession expired, but its use as a radio antenna saved the day.

■ The tower is most breathtaking at night, when every girder is illuminated. The light show, conceived to celebrate the turn of the millennium, was so popular that the 20,000 lights were reinstalled for permanent use in 2003. It does its electric shimmy for 10 minutes every hour on the hour until 1 AM in winter and 2 AM in summer.

The base formed by the tower's feet is 410 by 410 feet. ↑

☎ 01–44–11–23–23

⊕ www.tour-eiffel.fr

▨ By elevator: 2nd fl., €4.20, 3rd fl. €7.70, 4th fl. €11. Climbing: 2nd and 3rd fl. only, €3.80

☉ June–late Aug., daily 9 AM–midnight; late Aug.–May, daily 9 AM–11 PM, stairs close at dusk in winter

Ⓜ Bir-Hakeim, Trocadéro, Ecole Militaire; RER Champ de Mars

■TIP➔ A **Museums and Monuments Pass** will let you skip long lines but might not be worth the investment.

DINING ON A BUDGET

Looking for an inexpensive option near the tower? Head to nearby **Café du Marché** (✉ 38 rue Cler, Trocadéro/Tour Eiffel, ☎ 01–47–05–51–27), a relaxed restaurant where drinks are cheap, the salads gigantic, and the daily specials truly special.

CLOSE UP

Hemingway's Paris

There is a saying: "Everyone has two countries, his or her own—and France." For the Lost Generation after World War I, these words rang particularly true. Lured by favorable exchange rates, free-flowing alcohol, and a booming artistic scene, many American writers, composers, and painters moved to Paris in the 1920s and 1930s, Ernest Hemingway among them. He arrived in Paris with his first wife, Hadley, in December 1921 and made for the Rive Gauche—the Hôtel Jacob et d'Angleterre, to be exact (still operating at 44 rue Jacob). To celebrate their arrival the couple went to the Café de la Paix for a meal they nearly couldn't afford.

Hemingway worked as a journalist and quickly made friends with other expat writers such as Gertrude Stein and Ezra Pound. In 1922 the Hemingways moved to 74 rue du Cardinal Lemoine, a bare-bones apartment with no running water (his writing studio was around the corner, on the top floor of 39 rue Descartes). Then in early 1924 the couple and their baby son settled at 113 rue Notre-Dame des Champs. Much of *The Sun Also Rises,* Hemingway's first serious novel, was written at nearby café La Closerie des Lilas. These were the years in which he forged his writing style, paring his sentences down to the pith. As he noted in *A Moveable Feast,* "hunger was good discipline." There were some particularly hungry months when Hemingway gave up journalism and tried to publish short stories, and the family was "very poor and very happy."

They weren't happy for long. In 1926, just when *The Sun Also Rises* made him famous, Hemingway left Hadley and the next year wedded his mistress, Pauline Pfeiffer, across town at St Honoré-d'Eylau, then moved to 6 rue Férou, near the Musée du Luxembourg, whose collection of Cézanne landscapes (now in the Musée d'Orsay) he revered.

For gossip and books, and to pick up his mail, Papa would visit Shakespeare & Co., at 12 rue de l'Odéon, owned by Sylvia Beach, who became a trusted friend. For cash and cocktails Hemingway usually headed to the upscale Rive Droite. He collected the former at the Guaranty Trust Company, at 1 rue des Italiens. He found the latter, when he was flush, at the bar of the Hôtel Crillon, or, when poor, at the Caves Mura, at 19 rue d'Antin, or Harry's Bar, still in brisk business at 5 rue Daunou. Hemingway's legendary association with the Hôtel Ritz was sealed during the Liberation in 1944, when he strode in at the head of his platoon and "liberated" the joint by ordering martinis all around. Here Hemingway asked Mary Welsh to become his fourth wife, and here also, the story goes, a trunk full of notes on his first years in Paris turned up in the 1950s, giving him the raw material to write *A Moveable Feast.*

Louvre/Tuileries ⊕ *www.louvre-antiquaires.com* ☉ *Tues.–Sun. 11–7* Ⓜ *Palais-Royal.*

Once patronized by Proust and Gertrude Stein (who loved the chocolate cake here) Angélina (✉ *226 rue de Rivoli, Louvre/Tuileries* ☎ *01-42-60-82-00*), founded in 1903, is an elegant *salon de thé* (tearoom), famous for its *chocolat africain,* a jug of incredibly thick hot chocolate served with whipped cream (irresistible even in summer). Although it's still among the city's best chocolate hits, finicky Proust would probably sniff at the slightly shopworn air of the place today and reserve his affections for the ever-elegant teas served at historic Ladurée, a short walk to the east at 16 rue Royale.

㉖ **Palais-Royal** *(Royal Palace).* One
Fodor'sChoice of the most Parisian sights in all
★ of Paris, the Palais-Royal is especially loved for its gardens, where children play, lovers whisper, and senior citizens crumble bread for the sparrows, seemingly oblivious to the ghosts of history that haunt this place. The buildings of this former palace—royal only

> **ROOM WITH A VIEW**
>
> Visit the arcades of the Palais-Royal to see why the French writer Colette called the view from her window "a little corner of the country" in the heart of the city.

in that all-powerful Cardinal Richelieu (1585–1642) magnanimously bequeathed them to Louis XIII—date from the 1630s. In front of one of its shop fronts Camille Desmoulins gave the first speech calling for the French Revolution in 1789. Today the Palais-Royal is occupied by the French Ministry of Culture and private apartments (Colette and Cocteau were two lucky former owners), and its buildings are not open to the public. You can, however, visit its colonnaded courtyard—the setting where Audrey Hepburn had to choose between Cary Grant and Walter Matthau at the climax of Stanley Donen's *Charade*—and classical gardens, a tranquil oasis prized by Parisians. Around the exterior of the complex are famous arcades—notably the Galerie Valois—whose elegant shops have been attracting customers since the days when Thomas Jefferson used to come here for some retail therapy. ✉ *Pl. du Palais-Royal, Louvre/Tuileries* Ⓜ *Palais-Royal.*

㉒ **Place Vendôme.** Snobbish and self-important, this famous square is also gorgeous; property laws have kept away cafés and other such banal establishments, leaving the plaza stately and refined, the perfect home for the rich and famous (Chopin lived and died at No. 12; today's celebs camp out at the **Hôtel Ritz,** while a lucky few, including the family of the Sultan of Brunei, actually own houses here). Mansart's rhythmic, perfectly proportioned example of 17th-century urban architecture still shines in all its golden-stone splendor. Napóleon had the square's central column made from the melted bronze of 1,200 cannons captured at the Battle of Austerlitz in 1805. There he is, perched vigilantly at the top. If you're feeling properly soigné, repair to Hemingway's Bar at the Hôtel Ritz and raise a glass to "Papa" (see the Close-Up box, "Hemingway's Paris"). Ⓜ *Opéra.*

THE GRANDS BOULEVARDS: URBAN KALEIDOSCOPE

The French have a word for it: *flâner*—to stroll, promenade, dawdle. Back in the 19th century, the Parisians made this a newly fashionable activity, thanks to the magisterial boulevards Baron Haussmann—the regional prefect who oversaw the reconstruction of the city in the 1850s and 1860s—had designed and laid out. The focal point of this walk is the uninterrupted avenue that runs in almost a straight line from St-Augustin, the city's grandest Second Empire church, to Place de la République, whose very name symbolizes the ultimate downfall of the imperial regime. The avenue's name changes six times along the way, which is why Parisians refer to it as the *Grands Boulevards* (plural). The makeup of the neighborhoods along the Grand Boulevards changes steadily as you head east from the posh 8e arrondissement toward working-class east Paris. The *grands magasins* (department stores) at the start of the walk epitomize upscale Paris shopping and stand on Boulevard Haussmann. The opulent Opéra Garnier, just past the grands magasins, is the architectural showpiece of the period (often termed Second Empire and corresponding to the rule of Napoléon III). Though big banks moved into the area between the World Wars, the Olympia concert hall has survived on the Boulevard des Capucines, helping to keep alive *l'esprit boulevardier*. And recently, trendy cafés have sprouted up, attracting a fresh crop of fashionable wanderers to this perennially interesting strip.

WHAT TO SEE

㉞ Cimetière du Père-Lachaise *(Père-Lachaise Cemetery).* Cemeteries may not be your idea of the ultimate attraction, but this is the largest and most interesting in Paris. It forms a veritable necropolis, with cobbled avenues and tombs competing in pomposity and originality. Named after the Jesuit father—Louis XIV's confessor—who led the reconstruction of the Jesuit Rest House in 1682, the cemetery houses the tombs of the famed medieval lovers Héloïse and Abélard; composer Chopin; artists Ingres and Georges Seurat; playwright Molière; writers Balzac, Proust, Colette, Wilde (usually covered in lipstick kisses), and (buried in the same grave) Gertrude Stein and Alice B. Toklas; popular French actress Simone Signoret and her husband, singer–actor Yves Montand; singer Edith Piaf; and rock-star Jim Morrison of the Doors. Make sure to get a map at the entrance (it's easy to get lost!) and track them down. ⊠*Entrances on Rue des Rondeaux, Bd. de Ménilmontant, Rue de la Réunion, Père Lachaise* ⊕*www.pere-lachaise.com* ⊙*Apr.–Sept., daily 8–6; Oct.–Mar., daily 8–5* Ⓜ*Gambetta, Philippe-Auguste, Père-Lachaise.*

㉜ Hôtel Drouot. Paris's central auction house has everything from stamps and toy soldiers to Renoirs and 18th-century commodes. The 16 salesrooms make for fascinating browsing, and there's no obligation to bid. Although much of the auction action has moved to the glamorous Parisian venues of Sotheby's and Christie's, Drouot is still as lively as ever. ⊠*9 rue Drouot, Opéra/Grands Boulevards* ☎*01–48–00–20–00* ⊕*www.gazette-drouot.com* ⊙*Mid-Sept.–mid-July, viewings Mon.–Sat. 11–noon and 2–6, with auctions starting at 2* Ⓜ*Richelieu-Drouot.*

28 Musée Cernuschi. Newly renovated, this connoisseur's favorite includes Chinese art from Neolithic pottery (3rd millennium BC) to funeral statuary, painted 8th-century silks, and contemporary paintings, as well as ancient Persian bronze objects. ⊠ *7 av. Velasquez, Parc Monceau* ☎ *01–53–96–21–50* ⊕ *www.paris.fr/musees* 🖾 *Free* ☉ *Tues.–Sun. 10–5:40* Ⓜ *Monceau.*

★ **30 Musée Jacquemart-André.** Often compared to New York City's Frick Collection, this was one of the grandest private residences of 19th-century Paris. Built between 1869 and 1875, it found Hollywood fame when used as Gaston Lachaille's mansion in the 1958 musical *Gigi*, as a great stand-in for the floridly opulent home of a sugar millionaire played by Louis Jourdan. Edouard André and his painter-wife, Nélie Jacquemart, the house's actual owners, were rich and cultured, so art from the Italian Renaissance and 18th-century France compete for attention here. Note the freshly restored Tiepolo frescoes in the staircase and on the dining-room ceiling, while salons done in the fashionable "Louis XVI–Empress" style (favored by Empress Eugénie) are hung with great paintings, including Uccello's *Saint George Slaying the Dragon*, Rembrandt's *Pilgrims of Emmaus*, Jean-Marc Nattier's *Mathilde de Canisy*, and Jacques-Louis David's *Comte Antoine-Français de Nantes*. You can tour the house with the free English audio guide. The Tiepolo salon now contains a café, so why not lunch here and enjoy the Fragonard, Mantegna, and Chardin salads, named after great painters. ⊠ *158 bd. Haussmann, Parc Monceau* ☎ *01–45–62– 11–59* ⊕ *www.musee-jacquemart-andre.com/jandre* 🖾 *€8.50* ☉ *Daily 10–6* Ⓜ *St-Philippe-du-Roule or Miromesnil.*

NEED A BREAK?

Opened by superchef Alain Ducasse and renowned baker Eric Kayser, Be (⊠ *73 bd. de Courcelles, Parc Monceau* ☎ *01–46–22–20–20*), a *boulangerie-épicerie*, is a hybrid bakery and corner store stocked with gastronomic grocery items like candied tomatoes and walnut oil from the Dordogne. Pick up a superlative sandwich to eat in the nearby Parc Monceau or, if the weather's not cooperating, grab a seat in the back and order soup.

29 Musée Nissim de Camondo. Molière made fun of the *bourgeois gentilhomme*, the middle-class man who aspired to the class of his royal betters, but the playwright would have been in awe of Comte Moïse de Camondo, whose sense of style, grace, and refinement could have taught the courtiers at Versailles a thing or two. This immensely rich businessman built his grand hôtel particulier in the style of the Petit Trianon and proceeded to furnish it with some of the most exquisite furniture, *boiseries* (carved wood panels), and bibelots of the mid- to late 18th century. His wife and children (the museum is named after his son, who died in combat during World War I) then moved in and lent the house enormous warmth and charm. From ancien régime splendor, however, the family descended to the worst horrors of World War II: after the death of Count Moïse in 1935, the estate left the family's house and treasures to the government, while shortly thereafter family descendants were packed off to Auschwitz by the Nazis, where several of them were murdered. Today, the wealthy matrons of Paris have

Fodor's Choice ★

made this museum their own, and it shines anew with the beauty of the 18th century. No other house in Paris gives you such a sense of high French elegance as this one. ✉ *63 rue de Monceau, Parc Monceau* ☎ *01–53–89–06–50* ⊕ *www.ucad.fr* 🎫 *€6* ⊙ *Wed.–Sun. 10–5* Ⓜ *Villiers.*

㉛
Fodor's Choice
★

Opéra Garnier. Haunt of the *Phantom of the Opera*, setting for Degas's famous ballet paintings, and still the most opulent theater in the world, the Paris Opéra was begun in 1862 by Charles Garnier at the behest of Napoléon III. But it was not completed until 1875, five years after the emperor's abdication. Awash with Algerian colored marbles and gilt putti, it's said to typify Second Empire architecture: a pompous hodgepodge of styles with about as much subtlety as a Wagnerian cymbal crash. The composer Debussy famously compared it to a Turkish bathhouse, but lovers of pomp and splendor will adore it. If you're one of those who decide to opt for one of the cheaper *sans-visibilité* (without a view of the stage) seats, at least you'll have images from Chagall's favorite operas and ballets to stare at on the ceiling. To see the theater and lobby, you don't actually have to attend a performance: after paying an entry fee, you can stroll around at leisure and view the auditorium and the Grand Foyer, whose grandeur reminds everyone that this was a theater for bejeweled Parisians who wanted to watch a little bit of opera and a lot of each other. The **Musée de l'Opéra,** containing a few artworks (including a Degas sketch of Wagner) and theatrical mementos, is unremarkable. Technically the official home of the Paris Ballet, this auditorium usually mounts one or two full-scale operas a season, although most operas are presented at the drearily modern Opéra de la Bastille. ✉ *Pl. de l'Opéra, Opéra/Grands Boulevards* ☎ *01–40–01–22–63* ⊕ *www.opera-de-paris.fr* 🎫 *€6* ⊙ *Daily 10–5* Ⓜ *Opéra.*

OF OPERATIC PROPORTIONS

Over-the-top with gilt and multicolor marble both inside and out, it's no wonder the Phantom haunted the Palais Garnier. Unable to settle on any one style, Charles Garnier, the designer, chose them all: a Renaissance-inspired detail here, a Rococo frill there, Greek shields put up at random. To best appreciate the luxury of the Second Empire style, walk around the outside of the Opéra, then pause on the steps to watch the world rush by. The building is magically illuminated on performance nights—it's worth dropping by to admire the spectacle even if you're not heading inside.

㉗
Parc Monceau. The most picturesque gardens on the Right Bank were laid out as a private park in 1778 and retain some of the fanciful elements then in vogue, including mock ruins and a faux pyramid. Captured in all its verdant glory in Vincente Minelli's *Gigi*, it remains today the green heart of one of Paris's most fashionable neighborhoods. The rotunda—known as the Chartres Pavilion—is surely the city's grandest public restroom; it started life as a tollhouse. ✉ *Entrances on Bd. de Courcelles, Av. Velasquez, Av. Ruysdaël, and Av. van Dyck, Parc Monceau* Ⓜ *Monceau.*

🐦 **㉟** **Parc de La Villette.** Usually known simply as La Villette, this ambitiously landscaped, futuristic park (designed by noted modernist Bernard Tschumi) has several attractions, including the **Cité de la Musique,** designed by geometry-obsessed Christian de Portzamparc. This giant Postmodern musical academy also houses the **Musée de la Musique** (Museum of Musical Instruments). At the **Géode** cinema, which looks like a huge silver golf ball, films are shown on an enormous 180-degree curved screen. The science museum, the **Cité des Sciences et de l'Industrie,** contains dozens of interactive exhibits (though most displays are in French only). *Science Museum* ✉ *30 av. Corentin-Cariou, Parc de la Villette* ☎ *01–40–05–80–00* ⊕ *www.cite-musique.fr* ✉ *Museum of Musical Instruments €7.50, Science Museum €7.50, Planetarium, €3* ⊙ *Museum of Musical Instruments Tues.–Sat. noon–6, Sun. 10–6; Science Museum Tues.–Sun. 10–6* Ⓜ *Porte de La Villette, Porte de Pantin.*

㉝ **Passage Jouffroy.** Built in 1846, as its giant clock will tell you, this shop-filled passage was one of the favorite haunts of 19th-century dandies and flaneurs like the author Gérard de Nerval, who often strolled here in top hat and tails, with a large lobster on a pink-ribbon leash. ✉ *Entrances on Bd. Montmartre, Rue de la Grange-Batelière, Opéra/Grands Boulevards* Ⓜ *Richelieu Drouot.*

THE MARAIS & THE BASTILLE: C'EST *SUPER*COOL

The Marais is one of the city's most historic and sought-after residential districts. Except for the architecturally whimsical Pompidou Center, the tone here is set by the gracious architecture of the 17th and 18th centuries (the Marais was spared the attentions of Haussmann, the man who rebuilt so much of Paris in the mid-19th century). Today most of the Marais's spectacular hôtels particuliers—loosely translated as "mansions,"—the onetime residences of aristocratic families—have been restored; many are now museums, including the noted Musée Picasso and Musée Carnavalet. There are hyper-trendy boutiques and cafés among the kosher shops in what used to be a predominantly Jewish neighborhood around Rue des Rosiers.

The Marais, which means "marsh" or "swamp" (so don't be surprised by the sulfurous smell after heavy rainfall, even today), first became a fashionable address back when King Charles V moved his court here from the Ile de la Cité in the 14th century. However, it wasn't until Henri IV laid out Place Royale, today the gorgeous Place des Vosges, in the early 17th century, that the Marais became *the* place to live. All that came to an end on July 14, 1789, when the Bastille prison—once located on the eastern edge of the Marais—was stormed. Largely in commemoration of the bicentennial of the French Revolution, the Bastille area was renovated and became one of the trendiest sections of Paris. Galleries, shops, theaters, cafés, restaurants, and bars now fill formerly decrepit buildings and alleys. Strolling through the bustling Marais streets today, it's easy to appreciate the fabulous gold-hue facades of these buildings. Also keep your eyes peeled for open passages (*portes cochères*), leading to elegant courtyards that speak of times gone by. You may flee into one of them on weekends when massive crowds descend on the Marais. In the end, however, the squeak-through streets, noisy traffic jams, and half-pint sidewalks are part of the game.

WHAT TO SEE

㊶ Archives Nationales *(National Archives)*. If you're a serious history buff, you'll be fascinated by the thousands of intricate historical documents, dating from the Merovingian period to the 20th century, at the National Archives. Louis XVI's diary is here, containing his sadly ignorant entry for July 14, 1789, the day the Bastille was stormed and when, for all intents and purposes, the French Revolution began: "*Rien*" ("Nothing"). But even if you're not into history, the buildings themselves are worth seeing, as the Archives are housed in the **Hôtel de Soubise,** one of the grandest of all 18th-century Parisian mansions, whose salons were among the first to show the Rococo, light-filled curving style that followed the heavier Baroque opulence of Louis XIV. ✉*60 rue des Francs-Bourgeois, Le Marais* ☎*01–40–27–62–18* ⊕*www.archivesnationales.culture.gouv.fr* ⊠*€3* ⊙*Mon. and Wed.–Fri. 10–5:45, weekends 1:45–5:45* Ⓜ*Rambuteau.*

㊴ Atelier Brancusi *(Brancusi Studio)*. Romanian-born sculptor Constantin Brancusi settled in Paris in 1898 at age 22. This small, airy museum in front of the Pompidou Center contains four glass-front rooms that re-create Brancusi's studio, crammed with smooth, stylized works from all periods of his career. ✉*Pl. Georges-Pompidou, Beaubourg/Les Halles* ☎*01–44–78–12–33* ⊠*€7, €10 including Centre Pompidou* ⊙*Wed.–Mon. 2–6* Ⓜ*Rambuteau.*

★ **㊳ Centre Georges Pompidou.** Known as Beaubourg (for the neighborhood), this modern art museum and performance center is named for French president Georges Pompidou (1911–74), although the project was actually initiated by his art-loving wife. Designed by then-unknowns Renzo Piano and Richard Rogers, the Centre was unveiled in 1977, three years after Pompidou's death. Its radical purpose-coded colors and spaceship appearance scandalized Parisians, but they've learned to love the futuristic apparition. You approach the center across **Place Georges-Pompidou,** a sloping piazza, where you can find (if you look carefully enough) the **Atelier Brancusi.** The **Musée National d'Art Moderne** (Modern Art Museum, entrance on Level 4) has doubled in size to occupy most of the center's top two stories: one devoted to modern art—including major works by Matisse, the Surrealists, Modi-

---

MUSEUM KNOW-HOW

If you choose to spend an hour or two in any of the museums along the way, allow a full day. Be prepared to wait in line at the Picasso Museum. Note that some of the museums don't open until the afternoon. If you're interested in Judaica, don't plan this tour for a Saturday, when almost all Jewish-owned and -related stores, museums, and restaurants are closed. The place to lunch? No question: a café table under the arcades lining the magnificent Place des Vosges.

gliani, Duchamp, and Picasso—the other to contemporary art from the 1960s onward, including video installations. Also look for blockbuster temporary exhibitions on such subjects as Dada and Pop Art. In addition, there are a public reference library, a language laboratory, an industrial design center, two cinemas, and a snazzy and sophisticated rooftop restaurant, Georges, which is noted for its great view of the skyline and Eiffel Tower. ⊠*Pl. Georges-Pompidou, Beaubourg/Les Halles* ☎*01–44–78–12–33* ⊕*www.cnac-gp.fr* ☎*€10, including Atelier Brancusi; €7 for permanent collection only; €7–€9 for temporary exhibits; free 1st Sun. of month* ✪*Wed.–Mon. 11–9* Ⓜ*Rambuteau.*

OBERKAMPF
Take the métro to République, the district north of the Bastille, where you can check out the hopping nightlife Oberkampf district: walk along Rue du Faubourg-du-Temple until you hit Rue St-Maur, turn right and head to the action on Rue Jean-Pierre-Timbaud and Rue Oberkampf.

NEED A BREAK? Cross the plaza in front of the Pompidou and grab a table at Café Beaubourg (⊠*100 rue St-Martin, Beaubourg/Les Halles* ☎*01-48-87-63-96*), an early brainchild of French architecture star Christian de Portzamparc. Flawed service is redeemed by great people-watching and the large no-smoking section on the ground floor, not to mention the well-designed bathrooms in the basement.

37 Hôtel de Sully. The best surviving example of early Baroque in Paris, this mansion was built in 1624 with Flemish-inspired carving and a stately secret garden. Like much of the area, the hotel fell into ruin until the 1950s, when it was rescued by the administration of French historic monuments, **Caisse Nationale des Monuments Historiques.** This is now the administration's head office, complete with an excellent bookshop featuring innumerable publications in French and English about Paris (be sure to look up at the shop's original Louis XIII ceiling). Guided visits to Paris sites and buildings begin here, though all are conducted in French. There are also photography exhibitions here, organized by the **Patrimoine Photographique,** an outpost of the Jeu de Paume museum. ⊠*62 rue St-Antoine, Le Marais* ☎*01–44–61–20–00* ⊕*www.monum.fr* ✪*Tues.–Sun. 10–6:30* Ⓜ*St-Paul.*

46 Maison de Victor Hugo. Set on beautiful 17th-century Place des Vosges, this house was the residence of the workaholic French author famed for *Les Misérables* and the *Hunchback of Notre-Dame.* He lived here between 1832 and 1848 and memorabilia on view include several of his atmospheric, Gothic-horror-movie-like ink sketches, tribute to Hugo's unsuspected talent as an artist, along with illustrations for his writings by other artists, including Bayard's rendition of Cosette (which has graced countless *Les Miz* T-shirts). Upstairs, in Hugo's original apartment, you can see the tall desk where he stood to write, along with furniture from several of his homes—including the Chinese-theme panels and woodwork he commissioned for his mistress. ⊠*6 pl. des Vosges, Le Marais* ☎*01–42–72–10–16* ☎*Free* ✪*Tues.–Sun. 10–5:45* Ⓜ*St-Paul.*

40 **Musée d'Art et d'Histoire du Judaïsme** *(Museum of Jewish Art and History)*. With its clifflike courtyard ringed by giant pilasters, Pierre Le Muet's Hôtel St-Aignan—completed in 1650—is one of the most awesome sights in the Marais. It opened as a museum in 1998 after a 20-year, $35 million restoration. The interior has been remodeled to the point of blandness, but the displays, including 13th-century tombstones excavated in Paris; wooden models of destroyed East European synagogues; a roomful of early Chagalls; and Christian Boltanski's stark, two-part tribute to Shoah (Holocaust) victims, are carefully presented. Nearby, at 17 rue Geoffroy-l'Asnier, is the extremely moving Mémorial du Martyr Juif Inconnu, adjacent to the Centre de Documentation Juive Contemporaine. France's Jewish population sank from 300,000 to 180,000 during World War II but has since grown to around 700,000, the largest in Europe. ⊠ *71 rue du Temple, Le Marais* ☎ *01–53–01–86–60* ⊕ *www.mahj.org* ✉ *€6.80* ☉ *Sun.–Fri. 11–6* Ⓜ *Rambuteau.*

★ **44** **Musée Carnavalet.** If it has to do with Paris, it's here. This collection is a fascinating hodgepodge of Parisian artifacts, from the prehistoric canoes used by Parisii tribes to the furniture of the bedroom where Marcel Proust wrote his evocative, legendarily long novel *In Search of Lost Time.* Material dating from the city's origins until 1789 is housed in Hôtel Carnavalet, the setting for the most brilliant 17th-century salon in Paris, presided over by Madame de Sévigné, best known for the hundreds of letters she wrote to her daughter; they've become one of the most enduring chronicles of French high society in the 17th century. The section on the Revolution includes riveting models of guillotines and objects associated with the royal family's final days, including the king's razor and the chess set used by the royal prisoners at the approach of their own endgame. Lovers of the decorative arts will enjoy the period rooms here, especially those devoted to that most French of French styles, the 18th-century Rococo. Be sure to see the evocative re-creations of Proust's cork-lined bedroom, the late-19th-century Fouquet jewelry shop, and a room from the Art Nouveau monument the Café de Paris. ⊠ *23 rue de Sévigné, Le Marais* ☎ *01–44–59–58–58* ⊕ *www.paris.fr/musees/musee_carnavalet* ✉ *Free* ☉ *Tues.–Sun. 10–5:30* Ⓜ *St-Paul.*

43 **Musée Cognacq-Jay.** Another rare opportunity to see how cultured and rich Parisians once lived, this 16th-century mansion contains an outstanding collection of 18th-century artwork in its wood-panel, boiseried rooms. Ernest Cognacq, founder of the department store La Samaritaine, and his wife, Louise Jay, amassed furniture, porcelain, and paintings—notably by Fragonard, Watteau, Boucher, and Tiepolo—to create one of the world's finest private collections of this period. ⊠ *8 rue Elzévir, Le Marais* ☎ *01–40–27–07–21* ⊕ *www.paris.fr/musees/cognacq_jay* ✉ *Free; temporary exhibits €4.60* ☉ *Tues.–Sun. 10–5:40* Ⓜ *St-Paul.*

★ **42** **Musée Picasso.** Housed in the 17th-century Hôtel Salé, this museum has the largest collection of Picassos in the world—and these are "Picasso's Picassos," not necessarily his most famous works but rather the paintings and sculptures the artist valued most. Arranged chronologically, the museum gives you a great snapshot (with English info panels) of the painter's life. There are also works by Cézanne, Miró, Renoir, Braque, Degas, and Matisse. The building is showing some of the wear and tear that goes with being one of the city's most popular museums; on peak summer afternoons this place is more congested than the Gare du

Lyon. ✉ *5 rue de Thorigny, Le Marais* ☎ *01–42–71–25–21* ⊕ *www. musee-picasso.fr* ☎ *€5.50; €6.70 including temporary exhibits; Sun. €4; free 1st Sun. of month* ☉ *Wed.–Mon. 9:30–5:30* Ⓜ *St-Sébastien.*

NEED A BREAK?

"The dormouse in the teapot," Le Loir dans la Théière (✉ *3 rue des Rosiers, Le Marais* ☎ *01–42–72–90–61*) is aptly named for the dormouse who fell asleep at Alice in Wonderland's tea party. This is the perfect place to recover from museum overload—cozy into a leather chair, order a silver pot of tea, and choose a homemade cake.

㊱ **Place de la Bastille.** An excellent place to visit if you're planning to overthrow a monarchy, the Place de la Bastille is also a great jumping-off point for lunch (especially with the Richard Lenoir market on Thursday and Sunday mornings). Nothing remains of the infamous Bastille prison destroyed at the beginning of the French Revolution. In the midst of the large traffic circle is the **Colonne de Juillet** (July Column), commemorating the overthrow of Charles X in July 1830. As part of the countrywide celebrations for July 1989, the bicentennial of the French Revolution, the **Opéra de la Bastille** was erected, inspiring substantial redevelopment on the surrounding streets, especially along Rue de Lappe and Rue de la Roquette. What was formerly a humdrum neighborhood rapidly gained art galleries, clubs, and bars. Ⓜ *Bastille.*

㊺ **Place des Vosges.** The oldest monumental square in Paris—and probably

Fodor'sChoice
★

still its most nobly proportioned—the Place des Vosges was laid out by Henri IV at the start of the 17th century. Originally known as Place Royale, it has kept its Renaissance beauty nearly intact, although its buildings have been softened by time, their pale pink brick crumbling slightly in the harsh Parisian air and the darker stone facings pitted with age. It was always a highly desirable address, reaching a peak of glamour in the early years of Louis XIV's reign, when the nobility were falling over themselves for the privilege of living here. The two larger buildings on either side of the square were originally the king's and queen's pavilions. The statue in the center is of Louis XIII. It's not the original; that was melted down in the Revolution, the same period when the square's name was changed in honor of the French département of the Vosges, the first in the country to pay the new revolutionary taxes. With its arcades, symmetrical pink-brick town houses, and trim green garden, bisected in the center by gravel paths and edged with plane trees, the square achieves harmony and balance: it's a pleasant place to tarry on a sultry summer afternoon. Better yet, grab an arcade table at one of the many cafés lining the square—even a simple cheese crepe becomes a feast in this setting. To get inside one of the imposing town houses, visit the **Maison de Victor Hugo,** at No. 6 *(see above)*, on the southeast corner of the square. Ⓜ *Chemin Vert or St-Paul.*

THE ILE ST-LOUIS & THE LATIN QUARTER: ACROSS THE SEINE

Set behind the Ile de la Cité is one of the most romantic spots in Paris, tiny Ile St-Louis. Of the two islands in the Seine—the Ile de la Cité is just to the west—the St-Louis best retains the romance and loveliness of *le Paris traditionnel.* It has remained in the heart of Parisians as it has remained in the heart of every tourist who came upon it by accident, and without warning—a tiny universe unto itself, shaded by trees, bordered by Seine-side quais, and overhung with ancient stone houses. Up until the 1800s it was reputed that some island residents never crossed the bridges to get to Paris proper—and once you discover the island's quiet charm, you may understand why. South of the Ile St-Louis on the Left Bank of the Seine is the bohemian Quartier Latin (Latin Quarter), with its warren of steep, sloping streets, populated largely by Sorbonne students and academics.

The name Latin Quarter comes from the old university tradition of studying and speaking in Latin, a tradition that disappeared during the Revolution. The university began as a theology school in the Middle Ages and later became the headquarters of the University of Paris; in 1968 the student revolution here had an explosive effect on French politics, resulting in major reforms in the education system. The aging *soixante-huitards* continue to influence French politics, as shown by the election of openly gay, Green Party member Bertrand Delanoë to the mayoralty of Paris. Most of the district's appeal is less emphatic: Roman ruins, tumbling street markets, the two oldest trees in Paris, and chance glimpses of Notre-Dame all await your discovery.

TIMING   You can spend a day leisurely exploring this area—given that several sites, notably the Musée National du Moyen-Age, deserve a lengthy visit.

WHAT TO SEE

Ⓒ ⑥⑨ **Grande Galerie de l'Evolution** *(Great Hall of Evolution).* Visitors young and old will be charmed by the parade of taxidermied animals at this flagship of the Paris natural history museums, in the Jardin des Plantes. With displays ranging from the tiniest dung beetle to the tallest giraffe, this museum is an excellent break for kids who have been trudging, sour-pussed, around the Louvre. The original 1889 building was recently redone and updates include a ceiling that changes color to suggest storms, twilight, or the hot savanna sun. Don't miss the gigantic skeleton of a blue whale, and the stuffed royal rhino—he came from the menagerie at Versailles, where he was a pet to Louis XV. There are some English-language information boards available, but not many. ✉ *36 rue Geoffroy-St-Hilaire, Quartier Latin* ☎ *01–*

40–79–30–00 ⊕*www.mnhn.fr* ✉€8 ⊙*Wed.–Mon. 10–6* Ⓜ*Place Monge or Jussieu.*

❹❼ **Ile St-Louis.** One of the more fabled addresses in Paris, this tiny island has
Fodor'sChoice long harbored the rich and famous, including Chopin, Daumier, Hel-
★ ena Rubinstein, Chagall, and the Rothschild family, who still occupy
the island's grandest house. In fact, the entire island displays striking
architectural unity, stemming from the efforts of a group of early-17th-
century property speculators led by Christophe Marie. The group commissioned leading Baroque architect Louis Le Vau (1612–70) to erect a
series of imposing town houses. Other than some elegant facades and
the island's highly picturesque quays along the Seine, there are no major
sights here—just follow your nose and soak in the atmosphere. Study
the plaques on the facades of houses describing who lived where when.
An especially somber reminder adorns 19 quai de Bourbon: "Here lived
Camille Claudel, sculptor, from 1899 to 1913. Then ended her brave
career as an artist and began her long night of internment." Rodin's
muse, she was committed to an insane asylum by her family where she
was forbidden to practice her art. In your tour of the St-Louis, don't
miss the views of Notre-Dame from the Quai d'Orleans, the historic
Hôtel Lauzun museum, or, *bien sûr,* the Grand-Marnier ice cream or
Pamplemousse Rose sorbet at Berthillon, found on the center street of
the island. Ⓜ*Pont-Marie.*

NEED A BREAK? Cafés all over town sell Berthillon, the haute couture of ice cream, but the
Berthillon (✉*31 rue St-Louis-en-l'Ile, Ile St-Louis* ☎*01–43–54–31–61*) shop
itself is the place to go. More than 30 flavors are served; expect to wait in
line. The shop is open Wednesday–Sunday but closes in August.

❺⓿ **Institut du Monde Arabe** *(Institute of the Arab World).* Jean Nouvel's
striking 1988 glass-and-steel edifice adroitly fuses Arabic and European styles. Note the 240 shutterlike apertures that open and close
to regulate light exposure. Inside, the institute tries to do for Arab
culture what the Pompidou Center does for modern art, with the help
of a sound-and-image center, a vast library and documentation center,
and an art museum. The top-floor café provides a good view of Paris.
✉*1 rue des Fossés-St-Bernard, Quartier Latin* ☎*01–40–51–38–38*
⊕*www.imarabe.org* ✉*Exhibitions €7, museum €3* ⊙*Tues.–Sun. 10–
6* Ⓜ*Cardinal Lemoine.*

★ ❹❽ **Musée National du Moyen-Age** *(National Museum of the Middle Ages).*
Rivaling New York City's Cloisters as the greatest museum of medieval
art in the world, the Musée Cluny—a name that is more popularly
used—is housed in the 15th-century Hôtel de Cluny, erstwhile residence
of the abbots of Cluny (the famous—but now largely destroyed—abbey
in Burgundy). A stunning selection of tapestries, including the exquisite
Dame à la Licorne (*Lady and the Unicorn*) series, headlines its exhibition of medieval decorative arts. Alongside the mansion are the city's
Roman baths and the *Boatmen's Pillar,* Paris's oldest sculpture. ✉*6
pl. Paul-Painlevé, Quartier Latin* ☎*01–53–73–78–00* ⊕*www.musee-
moyenage.fr* ✉*€5.50, free 1st Sun. of month, otherwise €4 on Sun.*
⊙*Wed.–Mon. 9:15–5:45* Ⓜ*Cluny–La Sorbonne.*

⑭ Panthéon. Originally commissioned as a church by Louis XV as a mark of gratitude for his recovery from a grave illness in 1744, the Panthéon is now a monument to France's most glorious historical figures, including dozens of French statesmen, military heroes, Voltaire, Zola, Rousseau, and other thinkers. Germain Soufflot's building was not begun until 1764, and was not completed until 1790, during the French Revolution, whereupon its windows were blocked and it was transformed into the national shrine it is today. Its newest resident is Alexandre Dumas, whose remains were interred there in November of 2002. ✉ *Pl. du Panthéon, Quartier Latin* ☎ *01–44–32–18–00* ⊕ *www.monum.fr* ✇ *€7* ⊙ *Apr.–Sept., daily 10–6:30; Oct.–Mar., daily 10–6* Ⓜ *Cardinal Lemoine; RER: Luxembourg.*

㊿ Rue Mouffetard. The narrow windy cobblestone street is one of Paris's
Fodor'sChoice   oldest—it was once a Roman road leading south from Lutecia (Roman
★   Paris) to Italy. The lower half of the hilly street has a lively street market, open every morning from 8 AM to 1 PM. Chocoholics will love Nicholson (No. 112), and those with a nose for strong cheese will be in heaven at Androuët (No. 134). It's worth the detour to the nearby Boulanger de Monge (No. 123 rue Monge) for one of the best baguettes in Paris. The shops along the street are closed Monday. The restaurants on the upper half of the street get pretty touristy at night, so you'll probably enjoy this more during the day.

FROM ORSAY TO ST-GERMAIN-DES-PRÉS: TOUJOURS LA POLITESSE

This walk covers the Left Bank, from the Musée d'Orsay in the stately 7e arrondissement to the chic and colorful area around St-Germain-des-Prés in the 6e. The Musée d'Orsay, in a daringly converted Belle Epoque rail station on the Seine, houses one of the world's most spectacular arrays of Impressionist paintings. Farther along the river, the 18th-century Palais Bourbon—now home to the National Assembly—sets the tone for the 7e arrondissement. This is Edith Wharton territory—select, discreet *vieille France,* where all the aristocrats live in gorgeous, sprawling, old-fashioned apartments or *maisons particulières* (*very* private town houses). Embassies—and the Hôtel Matignon, residence of the French prime minister—line the surrounding streets, their majestic scale in total keeping with the Hôtel des Invalides, whose gold-leaf dome climbs heavenward above the regal tomb of Napoléon. The Rodin Museum—set in a gorgeous 18th-century mansion—is only a short walk away. This remains a district where manners maketh the man.

To the east, away from the splendor of the 7e, the Boulevard St-Michel slices the Left Bank in two: on one side, the Latin Quarter; on the other, the Faubourg St-Germain, named for St-Germain-des-Prés, the oldest church in Paris. Ask Parisians and tourists alike and many venture that this is their favorite district in Paris, stuffed as it is with friendly cafés, soigné boutiques, and adorably quaint streets. The venerable church tower has long acted as a beacon for intellectuals, most famously

Continued on page 67

THE SEINE

No matter how you approach Paris—historically, geographically, or emotionally—the Seine flows through its heart, dividing the City of Light into two banks, the generally upscale *Rive Droite* (Right Bank) and the more bohemian *Rive Gauche* (Left Bank).

The Seine has long been used as a means for transportation and commerce and although there are no longer any factories along its banks, all manner of boats still ply the water. You'll see tugboats, fire and police boats, the occasional bobbing houseboat, and many kinds of tour boats; it might sound hokey, but there's really no better introduction to the City of Light than a boat cruise, and there are several options, depending on whether you want commentary on the sights or not. Many of the city's most famous attractions can be seen from the river, and are especially spectacular at dusk, as those celebrated lights of Paris glint against the sky.

FROM ILE DES CYGNES TO THE LOUVRE

Musée d'Orsay clock

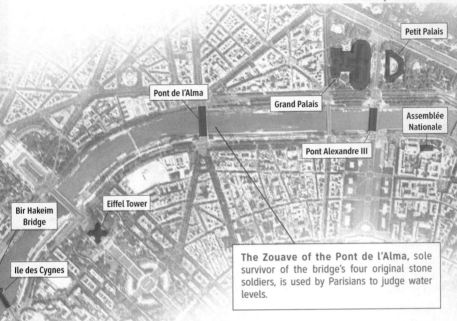

Petit Palais

Grand Palais

Assemblée Nationale

Pont de l'Alma

Pont Alexandre III

Eiffel Tower

Bir Hakeim Bridge

Ile des Cygnes

The Zouave of the Pont de l'Alma, sole survivor of the bridge's four original stone soldiers, is used by Parisians to judge water levels.

Whether you hop on a boat cruise or stroll the quays at your own pace, the Seine comes alive when you get off the busy streets of Paris. At the western edge of the city on the **Ile des Cygnes** (literally the Isle of Swans), a small version of the Statue of Liberty stands guard. Auguste Bartholdi designed the original statue, given as a gift from France to America in 1886, and in 1889 a group of Americans living in Paris installed this ¼ scale bronze replica—it's 37 feet, 8 inches tall.

You can get to the Ile des Cygnes via the **Bir Hakeim** bridge—named for the 1942 Free French battle in Libya—whose lacy architecture horizontally echoes the nearby **Eiffel Tower**. You might recognize the view of the bridge from the movie *Last Tango in Paris*.

As you make your way downstream you can drool in envy at the houseboats docked near the bronze lamp-lined **Pont Alexandre III.** No other bridge over the Seine epitomizes the fin-de-siècle frivolity of the Belle Epoque: It seems as much created of cake frosting and sugar sculptures as of stone and iron, and makes quite the backdrop for fashion shoots and weddings. The elaborate decorations include Art Nouveau lamps, cherubs, nymphs, and winged horses at either end. The bridge was built, like the Grand Palais and Petit Palais nearby, for the 1900 World's Fair.

Strollers by the water   Along the banks of the Seine

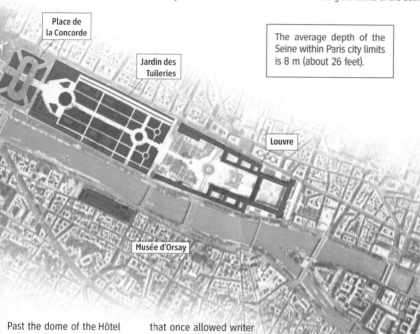

Place de la Concorde

Jardin des Tuileries

The average depth of the Seine within Paris city limits is 8 m (about 26 feet).

Louvre

Musée d'Orsay

Past the dome of the Hôtel des Invalides, is the 18th-century neoclassical façade of the **Assemblée Nationale**, the palace that houses the French Parliament. Across the river stands the **Place de la Concorde**. Also look for the great railway station clocks of the Musée d'Orsay that once allowed writer Anaïs Nin to coordinate her lovers' visits to her houseboat, moored below the Tuileries. The palatial **Louvre** museum, on the Right Bank, seems to go on and on as you continue up the Seine.

PERFECT PICNIC PLACES

Paris abounds with romantic spots to pause for a picnic or a bottle of wine, but the Seine has some of the best.

Try scouting out a place on the point of Ile St-Louis; at sunset you can watch the sun slip beneath receding arches of stone bridges.

The long, low quays of the Left Bank, with its public sculpture work, are perfect for an al-fresco lunch.

FROM PONT DES ARTS TO JARDIN DES PLANTES

At the water's edge.

Pont des Arts

Pont Neuf

Châtelet Theatres

Hotel de Ville

Institut de France

Ile de la Cité

Conciergerie

Notre-Dame

The Institut de France

Parisians love to linger on the elegant **Pont des Arts** footbridge that streches between the palatial Louvre museum and the Institut de France. Napoléon commissioned the original cast-iron bridge with nine arches; it was rebuilt in 1984 with seven arches.

Five carved stone arches of the **Pont Neuf**—the name means "new bridge" but it actually dates from 1605 and is the oldest bridge in Paris—connect the Left Bank to the Ile de la Cité. Another seven arches connect the Ile and the Right Bank. The pale gray curving balus-

trades include a row of stone heads; some say they're caricatures of King Henry IV's ministers, glaring down at the river.

On the Right Bank at the end of the Ile de la Cité is the **Hôtel de Ville (City Hall)**—this area was once the main port of Paris, crowded with boats delivering everything from wood and produce to visitors and slaves.

Medieval turrets rise up from **Ile de la Cité,** part of the original royal palace; the section facing the Right Bank includes the **Conciergerie**, where Marie Antoinette was imprisoned in 1793 before her execution.

PARIS PLAGE

Paris Plage, literally Paris Beach, is Mayor Bertrand Delanoë's summer gift to Parisians and visitors. In August the roads along the Seine are closed, tons of sand are brought in and decorated with palm trees, and a slew of activities are organized, from free early morning yoga classes to evening samba and swimming (not in the Seine, but in the fabulous Josephine Baker swimming pool). Going topless is discouraged but hammocks, kids' playgrounds, rock-climbing, and cafés keep everyone entertained.

Pont des Arts

Paris Plage

Notre-Dame

As you pass the end of the island, you'll notice a small grated window: this is the evocative memorial to the dead of World War II.

Next to the Ile de la Cite is the lovely residential **Ile St-Louis**; keep an eye out for the "proper" depth measuring stick on Ile St-Louis, near the Tour d'Argent restaurant.

Also on the Ile de la Cité is the cathedral of **Notre-Dame,** a stunning sight from the water. From the side it looks almost like a great boat sailing down the Seine.

Sightseeing boats turn near the public sculpture garden at the **Jardin des Plantes**, where you'll get a view of the huge national library, **Bibliothèque François Mitterrand**—the four towers look like opened books. Moored in the Seine near the bibliothèque is the Josephine Baker swimming pool with its retractable roof. Paris used to have several floating pools, including the elaborate Piscine Deligny, which was used in the Paris Olympics in 1924; it inexplicably sank in 1993.

Ile St-Louis

Jardin des Plantes

Bibliothéque Francois Mitterand

PLANNING A BOAT TOUR ON THE SEINE

■ Most boat tours last about an hour; in the winter, even the interior of the boats can be cool, so take an extra scarf or sweater.

■ It never hurts to book ahead since schedules vary with the season and the (unpredictable) height and mood of the Seine.

■ As you float along, consider that Parisians used similar boats as a form of public transportation until the 1930s. Not really like Venice; more like the Staten Island ferry.

■ For optimal Seine enjoyment, combine a boat tour with a stroll—walk around Ile St-Louis, stroll along the Left Bank quays near the Pont Neuf, or start at the quay below the Louvre and walk to the Eiffel Tower, past the fabulous private houseboats.

WHICH BOAT IS FOR YOU?

If you want... lots of information	☎ 01–40–76–99–99 ⊕ www.bateaux-mouches.fr 💳 €8 Ⓜ Alma-Marceau	
	The massive, double-decker **Bateaux Mouches**, literally "fly boats," offer prerecorded commentary in seven languages.	Departs from the Pont de l'Alma (Right Bank) daily April to September: every half hour from 10 AM to 11 PM; daily: October through March approximately every three hours from 11 AM to 9 PM.
If you want... to do your own thing	☎ 08–25–05–01–01 ⊕ www.batobus.com 💳 €11, €13 for 2 consecutive days	
	The commentary-free **Batobus** boat-bus service allows you to hop on and off the river. (Note: there's no service early January through early February.)	Departs from 8 locations: Eiffel Tower, Champs Elysées, Musée d'Orsay, Louvre, St. Germain-des-Pres, Notre-Dame, Hotel de Ville, and Jardin des Plantes.
If you want... to impress a date or client	☎ 01–44–54–14–70 ⊕ www.yachtsdeparis.fr 💳 €165 for dinner cruise Ⓜ Bastille	
	The **Yachts de Paris** specialize in gorgeous boats—expensive, yes, but glamorous as all get-out, with surprisingly good meals.	Departs from Quai de Javel (west of the Eiffel Tower); dinner cruises leave from Port Henri IV (near Bastille).
If you want... the Seine, with music	☎ 01–43–54–50–04 ⊕ www.lecalife.com 💳 €40 and up for dinner cruise Ⓜ Louvre-Rivoli	
	Le Calife is the Aladdin's lamp of the Seine, moored across from the Louvre. Jazz, piano music, and evenings devoted to French song makes this a quirky and charming choice.	Departs from the Quai Malaquais, opposite the Louvre and just west of the Pont des Arts footbridge.

during the 1950s when Albert Camus, Jean-Paul Sartre, and Simone de Beauvoir ate and drank existentialism in the neighborhood cafés. Today most of the philosophizing is done by tourists, yet a wealth of bookshops, art stores, and antiques galleries ensures that St-Germain, as the area is commonly known, retains its highbrow and very posh appeal. In the southern part of this district is the city's most colorful park, the Jardin du Luxembourg.

TIMING   Aim for an early start—that way you can hit the Musée d'Orsay early, when crowds are smaller, then get to the Rue de Buci street market when it's in full swing, in the late afternoon (the stalls are generally closed for lunch until 3 PM). Note that the Hôtel des Invalides is open daily, but Orsay is closed Monday.

You might consider returning to one or more museums on another day or night—the Orsay is open late Thursday evening, along with its stylish restaurant.

WHAT TO SEE

57   **Cour du Commerce St-André.** Like an 18th-century engraving come to

Fodor's Choice   life, this exquisite, cobblestone-street arcade is one of Paris's loveliest

★   sights. Although it's been tatted up with some faux cafés, its shop signs, awnings, and outdoor tables make it a most festive tableau, where Napoléon himself still wouldn't look too out of place taking his coffee (as he did back when). One of the restaurants on the Cour is actually Paris's oldest café, Le Procope (☎01–40–46–79–00), opened in 1686 by an Italian named Francesco Procopio. Many of Paris's most famous literary sons and daughters imbibed here through the centuries, including Voltaire, Balzac, George Sand, Victor Hugo, and even Benjamin Franklin, who popped in whenever business brought him to Paris. The café started out as the Sardi's of its day, because the Comédie-Française was nearby. Racine and Molière were regulars. The place is still going strong, so you, too, can enjoy its period (though now gussied-up) trimmings and traditional menu. Just opposite Procope is that hidden 18th-century treasure, the Cour de Rohan, a series of three cloistered courtyards. ⊠ *Linking Bd. St-Germain and Rue St-André-des-Arts, St-Germain-des-Prés* Ⓜ *Odéon.*

NEED A   If you are in search of the mysterious glamour of the Rive Gauche, you can
BREAK?   do no better than to station yourself at one of the sidewalk tables—or at a window table on a wintry day—to watch the passing parade outside and in Les Deux Magots (⊠ 6 pl. St-Germain-des-Prés, St-Germain-des-Prés ☎ 01–45–48–55–25), the immortal old-fashioned St-Germain café named after the two Chinese figurines, or *magots.* Today, tourists crowd the tables, but in its yesteryear this was the place where Oscar Wilde drank his evening absinthe at a sidewalk table, Hemingway raised glasses with James Joyce, and those 1950s coffee enthusiasts Jean-Paul Sartre and Richard Wright often talked late into the night.

56   **Institut de France** *(French Institute).* Built to the designs of Louis Le Vau from 1662 to 1674, the institute's curved, dome-top facade is one of the Left Bank's most impressive waterside sights. It also houses one of France's most revered cultural institutions, the Académie Française, created by Cardinal Richelieu in 1635. Unfortunately, the interior is closed to the general public. ⊠*Pl. de l'Institut, St-Germain-des-Prés* Ⓜ*Pont-Neuf.*

★ ❺❷ **Les Invalides.** Famed as the final resting place of Napoléon, the Hôtel des Invalides, to use its official name, is an outstanding monumental Baroque ensemble, designed by Libéral Bruand in the 1670s at the behest of Louis XIV to house wounded, or invalid, soldiers. Although no more than a handful of old-timers live at the Invalides these days, the army link remains in the form of the **Musée de l'Armée,** a military museum. The **Musée des Plans-Reliefs,** also housed here, contains a fascinating collection of old scale models of French towns. The 17th-century **Église St-Louis des Invalides** is the Invalides's original church. More impressive is Jules Hardouin-Mansart's **Église du Dôme,** built onto the end of the church of St-Louis but blocked off from it in 1793. The showpiece here is that grandiose monument to glory and hubris, **Napoléon's Tomb.** ⊠*Pl. des Invalides, Trocadéro/Tour Eiffel* ☎*01–44–42–37–72 Army and Model museums* ⊕*www.invalides.org* ✍*€7* ⊗*Église du Dôme and museums Apr.–Sept., daily 10–6; Oct.–Mar., daily 10–5. Closed 1st Mon. of every month* Ⓜ*La Tour-Maubourg.*

☺ ❺❽ **Jardin du Luxembourg** *(Luxembourg Gardens).* Immortalized in countless paintings, the Luxembourg Gardens possess all that is unique and befuddling about Parisian parks: swarms of pigeons, cookie-cutter trees, ironed-and-pressed dirt walkways, and immaculate lawns meant for admiring, not touching. The tree- and bench-lined paths offer a reprieve from the incessant bustle of the Quartier Latin, as well as an opportunity to discover the dotty old women and smooching university students who once found their way into Doisneau photographs. The park's northern boundary is dominated by the Palais du Luxembourg, surrounded by a handful of well-armed guards; they're protecting the senators who have been deliberating in the palace since 1958. Although the garden may seem purely French, the original 17th-century planning took its inspiration from Italy. When Maria de' Medici, widow of Henri IV, acquired the estate of the deceased Duke of Luxembourg in 1612 she decided to turn his mansion into a version of the Florentine Medici home, the Palazzo Pitti. Today, an adjacent wing of her former palace houses the **Musée de Luxembourg,** open only for special temporary major exhibitions. ⊠*Bordered by Bd. St-Michel and Rues de Vaugirard, de Médicis, Guynemer, and*

THE WORLD ON STRINGS

One of the great attractions of the park is the Théâtre des Marionnettes, where on weekends at 11 and 3:15 and on Wednesday at 3:15 you can catch one of the classic *guignols* (marionette shows) for a small admission charge. The wide-mouthed kids are the real attraction; their expressions of utter surprise, despair, or glee have fascinated the likes of Henri Cartier-Bresson and François Truffaut.

1

Auguste-Comte, St-Germain-des-Prés ⊕*www.museeduluxembourg.fr*
Ⓜ*Odéon; RER: Luxembourg.*

❺❺ **Musée Delacroix.** Set on **Place Furstenberg**—one of the tiniest, posh-
Fodor's Choice est, and most romantic squares in Paris—the studio of artist Eugène
★ Delacroix (1798–1863) contains only a small collection of his sketches
and drawings but is redolent of the spirit of France's foremost Romantic painter. The hidden surprise here is that just beyond the museum
salons lies the loveliest backyard garden in Paris—an enchanting retreat
that is sure to bring out the artist in you. ✉*6 rue Furstenberg, St-
Germain-des-Prés* ☎*01–44–41–86–50* 🖅*€5* ⊘*Wed.–Mon. 9:30–5*
Ⓜ*St-Germain-des-Prés.*

★ ❺❶ **Musée d'Orsay.** In a spectacularly converted Belle Epoque train station, the Orsay Museum—devoted to the arts (mainly French) spanning the period 1848–1914—is one of the city's most popular, thanks
to the presence of the world's greatest collection of Impressionist and
Postimpressionist paintings. Here you can find Manet's *Déjeuner sur
l'Herbe* (*Lunch on the Grass*), the painting that scandalized Paris in
1863 when it was shown at the Salon des Refusés, an exhibit organized
by artists refused permission to show their work at the Academy's official annual salon, as well as the artist's provocative nude, *Olympia.*
There's a dazzling rainbow of masterpieces by Renoir (including his
beloved *Le Moulin de la Galette*), Sisley, Pissarro, and Monet. The
Postimpressionists—Cézanne, van Gogh, Gauguin, and Toulouse-
Lautrec—are on the top floor. On the ground floor you can find the
work of Manet, the powerful realism of Courbet, and the delicate
nuances of Degas. If you prefer more academic paintings, look for
Puvis de Chavannes's larger-than-life classical canvases. And if you're
excited by more modern developments, look for the early-20th-century
Fauves (meaning "wild beasts," the name given them by an outraged
critic in 1905)—particularly Matisse, Derain, and Vlaminck.

The museum is arranged on three floors. Once past the ticket booths
(get your tickets in advance through the Web site to avoid the lines),
you can pick up an English-language audio guide along with a free
color-coded map of the museum. Then step down the stairs into the
sculpture hall. Here the vastness of the space complements a ravishing
collection of French sculpture from 1840 to 1875. ✉*1 rue de la Légion
d'Honneur, St-Germain-des-Prés* ☎*01–40–49–48–14* ⊕*www.musee-
orsay.fr* 🖅*€7.50, €5.50 on Sun.* ⊘*Tues., Wed., Fri., and Sat. 10–6,
Thurs. 10–9:45, Sun. 9–6* Ⓜ*Solférino; RER: Musée d'Orsay.*

**NEED A
BREAK?** If those *Déjeuner sur l'Herbe* paintings make you think about lunch, stop at
the middle floor's Musée d'Orsay Restaurant (☎*01–45–49–47–03*) in the
former train station's sumptuous dining room. Train food, however, this is
not: an elegant lunch is available 11:30 to 2:30, high tea from 3:30 to 5:40
(except on Thursday, when dinner is served instead, from 7 to 9:30 PM). For a
simpler snack anytime, visit the top-floor Café des Hauteurs and drink in its
panoramic view across the Seine toward Montmartre.

★ ⑤ **Musée Rodin.** The exquisitely palatial 18th-century Hôtel Biron makes a gracious stage for the sculpture of Auguste Rodin (1840–1917). You'll doubtless recognize the seated *Le Penseur* (*The Thinker*), with his elbow resting on his knee, and the passionate *Le Baiser* (*The Kiss*). From the upper rooms, which contain some fine if murky paintings by Rodin's friend Eugène Carrière (1849–1906), there are some fine views of the lovely gardens. Elsewhere are fine sculptures by Rodin's mistress, Camille Claudel (1864–1943), a remarkable artist in her own right. Her torturous relationship with Rodin drove her out of his studio— and out of her mind. In 1913 she was packed off to an asylum, where she remained, barred from any artistic activities, until her death. For much more soothing scenarios, repair to the mansion garden: it's exceptional not only for its rosebushes and sculpture, but also its view of the Invalides dome with the Eiffel Tower behind and its superb cafeteria. ⊠ *77 rue de Varenne, Invalides/Eiffel Tower* ☎ *01–44–18–61–10* ⊠ *€5, Sun. €3, gardens only €1* ⊙ *Easter–Oct., Tues.–Sun. 9:30–5:45; Nov.–Easter, Tues.–Sun. 9:30–4:45* Ⓜ *Varenne.*

⑤ **St-Germain-des-Prés.** Paris's oldest church was first built to shelter a relic of the true cross brought from Spain in AD 542. The chancel was enlarged and the church then consecrated by Pope Alexander III in 1163; the tall, sturdy tower—a Left Bank landmark—dates from this period. The church stages superb organ concerts and recitals. ⊠ *Pl. St-Germain, St-Germain-des-Prés* ⊙ *Weekdays 8–7:30, weekends 8* AM*–9* PM Ⓜ *St-Germain-des-Prés.*

MONTMARTRE: THE CITADEL OF PARIS

On a dramatic rise above the city is Montmartre, site of the Sacré-Coeur Basilica and home to a once-thriving artist community. This was the quartier that Toulouse-Lautrec and Renoir immortalized with a flash of their brush and a tube of their paint. Although the great painters have long departed, and the fabled nightlife of Old Montmartre has fizzled down to some glitzy nightclubs and skin shows, Montmartre still exudes history and Gallic charm. Windmills once dotted Montmartre (often referred to by Parisians as *La Butte*, meaning "mound"). They were set up here not just because the hill was a good place to catch the wind—at more than 300 feet it's the highest point in the city—but because Montmartre was covered with wheat fields and quarries right up to the end of the 19th century. Today only 2 of the original 20 windmills remain. Visiting Montmartre means negotiating a lot of steep streets and flights of steps. The crown atop this urban peak, the Sacré-Coeur Basilica, is something of an architectural oddity, with a silhouette that looks more like that of a mosque than a cathedral. No matter: when viewed from afar at dusk or sunrise, it looks like Paris's "sculpted cloud."

SOAK UP THE SCENE

Carré Roland Dorgelès, the tiny square just across from the Lapin Agile, has benches perfect for gazing at Montmartre's historic vineyard or pausing for a picnic.

Long a draw because of its bohemian–artistic history, Montmartre became even more popular after its starring role in the 2001 smash-hit films *Amélie* and *Moulin Rouge* (the latter entirely re-created on a film set, though). Now you not only have to contend with art lovers seeking out Picasso's studio and Toulouse-Lautrec's favorite brothel, but movie fans looking for Amélie's café and *épicerie*. Yet you can still give the hordes on the Place du Tertre the slip and discover some of Paris's most romantic and picturesque corners.

WHAT TO SEE

67 **Au Lapin Agile.** One of the most picturesque spots in Paris, this leg-
Fodor'sChoice endary bar-cabaret (sorry—open nights only) is a miraculous sur-
★ vivor from the 19th century. It got its curious name—the Nimble Rabbit—when the owner, André Gill, hung up a sign (now in the Musée du Vieux Montmartre) of a laughing rabbit jumping out of a saucepan clutching a bottle of wine. Founded in 1860, this ador-able maison-cottage was a favorite subject of painter Maurice Utrillo. Once owned by Aristide Bruant (immortalized in many Toulouse-Lautrec posters), it became the home-away-from-home for Braque, Modigliani, Apollinaire, and Vlaminck. The most famous habitué, however, was Picasso, who once paid for a meal with one of his paintings, then promptly went out and painted another, which he named after this place (it now hangs in New York's Metropolitan Museum, which purchased it for $50 million). ⊠ *22 rue des Saules, Montmartre* ☎ *01–46–06–85–87* ⊕ *www.au-lapin-agile.com* ✆ €24 ⊗ *Tues.–Sun. 9 PM–2 AM* Ⓜ *Lamarck-Caulaincourt.*

63 **Bateau-Lavoir** *(Boat Wash House).* Montmartre poet Max Jacob coined the name for the original building on this site (which burned down in 1970), saying it resembled a boat and that the warren of artists' studios within was perpetually paint-splattered and in need of a good hosing down. Wishful thinking, since the building only had one water tap. It was here that Pablo Picasso and Georges Braque made their first bold stabs at the concept of Cubism. The replacement building also contains art studios, but is the epitome of poured-concrete drabness. ⊠ *13 pl. Émile-Goudeau, Montmartre* Ⓜ *Abbesses.*

61 **Moulin de la Galette** *(Wafer Windmill).* This is one of two remaining windmills in Montmartre. It was once the focal point of an open-air cabaret (made famous in the painting by Renoir that hangs in the Musée d'Orsay). Rumor has it that in 1814 the miller Debray, who had struggled in vain to defend the windmill from invading Cossacks, was then strung up on its sails and spun to death by the invaders. Unfortunately, it's privately owned and can only be admired from the street below. ⊠ *Rue Tholozé, Montmartre* Ⓜ *Abbesses.*

59 **Moulin Rouge** *(Red Windmill).* This world-famous cabaret was built in 1885 as a windmill, then transformed into a dance hall in 1900. Those wild, early days were immortalized by Toulouse-Lautrec in his posters and paintings. It still trades shamelessly on the notion of Paris as a city of sin: if you fancy a gaudy Vegas-style night out—sorry, admirers of the Baz Luhrmann film won't find any of its charm here—this is the place to go. The cancan, by the way—still a regular sight here—was considerably raunchier when Toulouse-Lautrec was around. ✉*82 bd. de Clichy, Montmartre* ☎*01–53–09–82–82* ⊕*www.moulin-rouge. com* ✉*€80–€125* ⊘*Shows nightly at 9 and 11* Ⓜ*Blanche.*

⓺ **Musée de Montmartre** *(Montmartre Museum).* In its turn-of-the-20th-century heyday, Montmartre's historical museum was home to an illustrious group of painters, writers, and assorted cabaret artists. Foremost among them were Renoir and Maurice Utrillo. The museum also provides a view of the tiny **vineyard**—the only one in Paris—on neighboring Rue des Saules. A token 125 gallons of wine are still produced here every year. ✉*12 rue Cortot, Montmartre* ☎*01–46–06–61–11* ✉*€5.50* ⊘*Tues.–Sun. 10–6* Ⓜ*Lamarck-Caulaincourt.*

★ ⓿ **Musée de la Vie Romantique.** Lovers of all things "romantique" will enjoy visiting this tranquil, 19th-century countrified town house, set in a little park at the foot of Montmartre (head down Rue Blanche from Place Blanche; the third left is Rue Chaptal). For years the site of Friday-evening salons hosted by the Dutch-born painter Ary Scheffer, the house often welcomed such guests as Ingres, Delacroix, Turgenev, Chopin, and Sand. The memory of author George Sand (1804–76)—real name Aurore Dudevant—haunts the museum. Portraits, furniture, and household possessions, right down to her cigarette box, have been moved here from her house in Nohant in the Loire Valley. There's also a selection of Scheffer's competent artistic output on the first floor. Take a moment to enjoy a cup of tea in the garden café. ✉*16 rue Chaptal, Montmartre* ☎*01–55–31–95–67* ⊕*www.paris.fr/musees* ✉*Free for permanent collection, exhibitions €4.50* ⊘*Tues.–Sun. 10–5:40* Ⓜ*St-Georges.*

⓺ **Place des Abbesses.** The triangular square is typical of the picturesque, slightly countrified style that has made Montmartre famous. Now the hub of the local arts and fashion scene, the Place is surrounded by trendy shops, sidewalk cafés, and shabby-chic restaurants, a prime habitat for the young, neo-bohemian crowd and a sprinkling of expats. The entrance to the Abbesses métro station, a curving, sensuous mass of delicate iron, is one of only two original Art Nouveau entrance canopies left in Paris. ✉*Montmartre* Ⓜ*Abbesses.*

⓺ **Place du Tertre.** This tumbling square (*tertre* means "hillock") regains its village atmosphere only in winter, when the branches of the plane trees sketch traceries against the sky. At any other time of year you can be confronted by crowds of tourists and a swarm of third-rate artists clamoring to do your portrait (if one of them whips up an unsolicited portrait, you are not obliged to buy it). **La Mère Catherine,** on one corner of the square, was a favorite with the Russian Cossacks who occupied Paris in 1814. They couldn't have suspected that by banging on the table and yelling "*bistro*" (Russian for "quickly"), they were inventing a new breed of French restaurant. ✉*Montmartre* Ⓜ*Abbesses.*

NEED A BREAK? There are few attractive food options around Place du Tertre; locals know to slip away to La Divette du Moulin (✉*98 rue Lepic at Rue Orchampt, Mont-*

A GOOD WALK

Begin at Place Blanche, landmarked by the Moulin Rouge **59** ►, the windmill-turned–dance hall immortalized by Toulouse-Lautrec. Prior to the raucous time of the cancan was the dreamy age of Romanticism; to discover its exquisite 19th-century charm, you need only visit the lovely Musée de la Vie Romantique **60**, set three blocks south of Place Blanche. Heading down Rue Blanche until the third left onto Rue Chaptal, this country-house-in-the-city was the former haunt of such greats as Georges Sand, Chopin, Ingres, and Delacroix.

After savoring its delicate salons, backtrack up to Place Blanche and then walk up lively Rue Lepic. Few people notice the tiny Lux Bar at No. 12, with its original Art Nouveau woodwork and tiled murals from 1910—most are too busy looking across the street at the Café des Deux Moulins, where Amélie Poulain served coffee and brewed up schemes for helping strangers in the noted 2001 movie. Up Rue Lepic you'll find the Moulin de la Galette **61**, atop its leafy hillock opposite Rue Tholozé, once a path over the hill. Turn right down Rue Tholozé, past Studio 28, the first cinema built expressly for experimental films.

Continue down Rue Tholozé to Rue des Abbesses and turn left toward the triangular Place des Abbesses **62**. Follow Rue Ravignan as it climbs north, via Place Émile-Goudeau, an enchanting little cobbled square, to the "cradle of Cubism," the Bateau-Lavoir **63**, or Boat Wash House, at its northern edge. Unfortunately the building burned in 1970 and is now rebuilt

rather blandly. Painters Picasso and Braque had studios in the original building; this drab concrete edifice was built in its place (check out the historic photographs in the window of No. 11 bis for an idea of how it used to look). Continue up the hill via Rue de la Mire to Place Jean-Baptiste Clément, where Amedeo Modigliani had a studio.

The upper reaches of Rue Lepic lead to Rue Norvins, formerly Rue des Moulins. At the end of the street to the left is stylish Avenue Junot. Back on Avenue Junot, continue right past the bars and tourist shops until you reach Place du Tertre **64**, the heart of Montmartre. Fight your way through to the southern end of the square for a breathtaking view of the city.

Around the corner on Rue Poulbot, the Espace Salvador-Dalí houses works by Salvador Dalí, who once had a studio in the area. Return to Place du Tertre. Looming behind is the scaly white dome of the Basilique du Sacré-Coeur **65** The cavernous interior is worth visiting for its golden mosaics; climb to the top of the dome for the view of Paris. Walk back toward Place du Tertre. Turn right onto Rue du Mont-Cenis and left onto Rue Cortot, site of the Musée de Montmartre **66**, which, like the Bateau-Lavoir, once sheltered an illustrious group of painters, writers, and assorted cabaret artists. Another famous Montmartre landmark is at No. 22: the bar-cabaret Au Lapin Agile **67**, former haunt of Picasso.

1

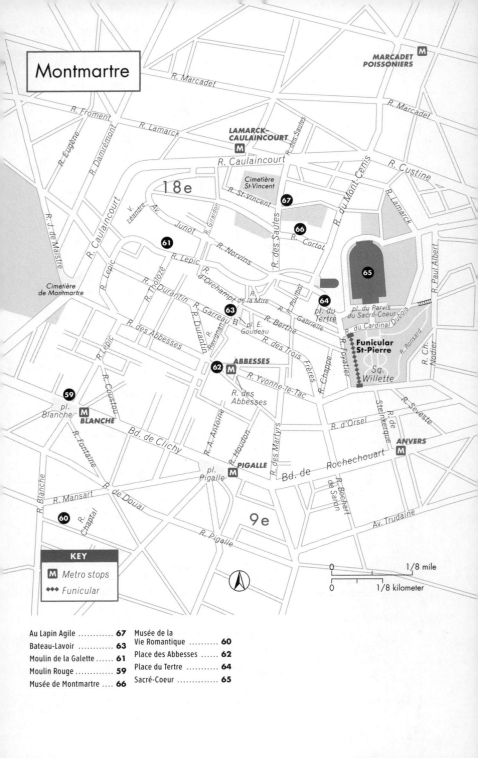

Montmartre

martre ☏ *01–46–06–34–84*) to regain a sense of camaraderie and rest their weary feet—there's tasty food or simply a decent cup of coffee, every day of the week.

★ ⑥⑤ **Sacré-Coeur.** Often compared to a "sculpted cloud" atop Montmartre, the Sacred Heart Basilica was erected as a sort of national guilt offering in expiation for the blood shed during the Paris Commune and Franco-Prussian War in 1870–71, and was largely financed by French Catholics fearful of an anticlerical backlash under the new republican regime. The basilica was not consecrated until 1919. Stylistically, the Sacré-Coeur borrows elements from Romanesque and Byzantine models. The gloomy, cavernous interior is worth visiting for its golden mosaics; climb to the top of the dome for the view of Paris. Try to visit at sunrise or long after sunset, as otherwise this area is crammed with bus groups, young lovers, postcard sellers, guitar-wielding Christians, and sticky-finger types; be extra cautious with your valuables. ✉ *Pl. du Parvis-du-Sacré-Coeur, Montmartre* ☏ *01–53–41–89–00* 🔲 *Free, dome €4.50* ⊙ *Basilica daily 6:45 AM–11 PM; dome and crypt Oct.–Mar., daily 9–6; Apr.–Sept., daily 10–5* Ⓜ *Anvers.*

WHERE TO EAT

Updated by
Rosa Jackson

Whether you get knee-deep in white truffles at Les Ambassadeurs or merely discover pistachio sausage (the poor man's foie gras) at a classic corner bistro, you can discover that food in Paris is an obsession, an art, a subject of endless debate. From the edible genius of haute cuisine wizards Eric Frechon and Alain Ducasse to the sublime creations of Pierre Gagnaire (whose marriage of heated foie gras, pressed caviar, and Japanese seaweeds will make you purr), dining in Paris can easily leave you in a pleasurable stupor. And when it all seems a bit overwhelming, you can slip away to a casual little place for an earthy, bubbling cassoulet, have a midnight feast of the world's silkiest oysters, or even opt out of Gaul altogether for superb pasta, couscous, or an herb-bright Vietnamese stir-fry. Once you know where to go, Paris is a city where perfection awaits at all levels of the food chain.

Generally, restaurants are open from noon to about 2:30 and from 7:30 or 8 to 10 or 10:30. It's best to make reservations, particularly in summer, although the reviews only state when reservations are absolutely essential. If you want no-smoking seating, make this clear; the mandatory no-smoking area is sometimes limited to a very few tables. Brasseries have longer hours and often serve all day and late into the evening; some are open 24 hours. Assume a restaurant is open every day, unless otherwise indicated. Surprisingly, many prestigious restaurants close Saturday as well as Sunday and sometimes Monday. July and August are the most common months for annual closings, although Paris in August is no longer the wasteland it once was. For help with the vocabulary of French cooking, see the Menu Guide at the end of this book. Places where a jacket and tie are de rigueur are noted. Otherwise, use common sense—jeans and T-shirts are not suitable in Paris restaurants, nor are shorts or running clothes, except in the most casual bistros and cafés.

PRICES & RESERVATIONS

By French law, prices must include tax and tip (*service compris* or *prix nets*), but pocket change left on the table in basic places, or an additional 5% in better restaurants, is always appreciated. Beware of bills stamped "Service Not Included" in English or restaurants slyly using American-style credit-card slips, hoping that you'll be confused and add the habitual 15% tip. In neither case should you tip beyond the guidelines suggested above.

Here are a few key sentences for booking, if needed: "*Bonjour madame/ monsieur* (ma'am, sir; say *bonsoir* after 6 PM). *Je voudrais faire une reservation pour X (1, un/une; 2, deux; 4, quatre; 6, six) personnes pour le diner* (dinner)/*le déjeuner* (lunch) *aujourd'hui à X heures* (today at X o'clock)/*demain à X heures* (tomorrow at X o'clock)/*lundi* (Monday), *mardi* (Tuesday), *mercredi* (Wednesday), *jeudi* (Thursday), *vendredi* (Friday), *samedi* (Saturday), *dimanche* (Sunday) *à X heures* (at X o'clock). *Le nom est* (your own name). *Merci bien.*" Many of these restaurants have their own Web sites and you can e-mail them for reservations instead of making a telephone call—readers report that they get fast and courteous replies. Note that reservations are unnecessary for brasserie and café meals at odd hours.

WHAT IT COSTS				
¢	$	$$	$$$	$$$$
AT DINNER under €11	€11–€16	€17–€22	€23–€30	over €30

Restaurant prices are for a main course only at dinner, including tax (19.6%) and service; note that if a restaurant offers only prix-fixe (set-price) meals, it is given a price category that reflects the full prix-fixe price.

1ER ARRONDISSEMENT (LOUVRE/LES HALLES)

CONTEMPORARY

$$-$$$ ✗ **Pinxo.** The word *pinxo* means "to pinch" in Basque, and this is how the food in this fashionable hotel restaurant is designed to be eaten—often with your fingers, and off your dining companion's plate. (Each dish is served in three portions to allow for sharing.) Alain Dutournier, who also runs the more formal Carré des Feuillants nearby and Trou Gascon in the 12th arrondissement, drew on his southwestern roots to create this welcoming modern spot. Freed from the tyranny of the *entrée-plat-dessert* cycle, you can nibble your way through such minidishes as marinated herring with Granny Smith apple and horseradish, and squid cooked *à la plancha* (on a griddle) with ginger and chili peppers. Some dishes work better than others, but it's hard not to love a place that serves deep-fried Camembert as a cheese course. ✉*Hôtel Plaza Paris Vendôme, 4 rue du Mont Thabor, Louvre/*

> ### WORD OF MOUTH
>
> "Romantic Dining in Paris? Hey, Le Grand Véfour is supposedly where Napoléon courted Josephine."
> –cheyne

Tuileries ☎*01–40–20–72–00* ⊕*www.pinxo.fr* ▬*AE, DC, MC, V*
⊘*Closed 1 wk at Christmas* Ⓜ*Tuileries.*

FRENCH

$$$$ ✗ **Le Grand Véfour.** Victor Hugo could stride in and still recognize this

Fodor'sChoice place—in his day, as now, a contender for the prize of most beautiful

★ restaurant in Paris. Originally built in 1784, set in the arcades of the Palais-Royal, it has welcomed everyone from Napoléon to Colette to Jean Cocteau—many seats bear a plaque commemorating a famous patron. The mirrored ceiling and Restoration-era glass paintings of goddesses beguile the foodies as well as the fashionable who gather here to enjoy chef Guy Martin's delights. He hails from Savoie, so you can find lake fish and mountain cheeses on the menu alongside such luxurious dishes as foie gras–stuffed ravioli. If you can't spring for the extravagant à la carte menu or the 10-course, €250 *menu plaisir,* try the lunchtime prix-fixe for €75. ⊠*17 rue Beaujolais, Louvre/Tuileries* ☎*01–42–96–56–27* ⌕*Reservations essential*Jacket and tie ▬*AE, DC, MC, V* ⊘*Closed weekends, July, 1 wk at Easter, 1 wk at Christmas. No dinner Fri.* Ⓜ*Palais-Royal.*

★ **$$–$$$$** ✗ **Restaurant du Palais-Royal.** Tucked away in the northeast corner of the magnificent Palais-Royal garden, this stylish modern bistro decorated in jewel tones serves food to match its stunning location under the palace arcades. Sole, scallops, and risotto—including a dramatic squid-ink and lobster version—are beautifully prepared, but juicy steak with *pommes Pont Neuf* is also a favorite of the expense-account lunchers who love this rather pricey place. Finish up with an airy *mille-feuille* pastry that changes with the seasons—berries in summer, chestnuts in winter. Be sure to book in advance, especially in summer, when the terrace tables are hotly sought after. ⊠*Jardins du Palais-Royal, 110 Galerie Valois, Louvre/Tuileries* ☎*01–40–20–00–27* ▬*AE, DC, MC, V* ⊘*Closed Dec. and Jan., weekends Oct.–Apr., Sun. in summer* Ⓜ*Palais-Royal.*

★ **$$** ✗ **L'Ardoise.** This minuscule storefront painted white and decorated with enlargements of old sepia postcards of Paris is the very model of the contemporary bistros making waves in Paris. Chef Pierre Jay's first-rate three-course menu for €31 tempts with such original dishes as mushroom and foie gras ravioli, scallops panfried with oyster mushrooms, and a langoustine risotto (you can also order à la carte, but it's less of a bargain). Just as enticing are the desserts, such as a superb *feuillantine au citron*—caramelized pastry leaves filled with lemon cream and lemon slices—and a boozy baba au rhum. With friendly waiters, service all weekend, and a small but well-chosen wine list, L'Ardoise would be perfect if it weren't often crowded and noisy. ⊠*28 rue du Mont Thabor, Beaubourg/Les Halles* ☎*01–42–96–28–18* ▬*MC, V* ⊘*Closed Mon. in Aug. No lunch Sun.* Ⓜ*Concorde.*

$–$$ ✗ **Willi's Wine Bar.** Don't be fooled by the name—this British-owned spot is no modest watering hole but rather a stylish haunt for Parisian and visiting gourmands, who might stop in for a glass of wine at the polished oak bar or settle into the beamed dining room. The selection of reinvented classic dishes changes daily to reflect the market's offerings, and might include roast cod with artichokes and asparagus in

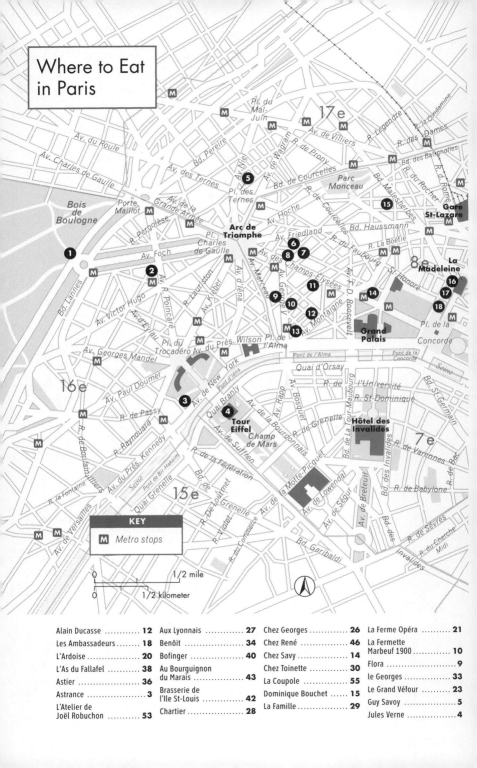

Where to Eat in Paris

KEY

Ⓜ *Metro stops*

Paris Now: The New Dining Trends

What are the latest fashions on the Paris dining scene? Not everyone wants a three-course blowout every time they go to a restaurant. While meals have long followed a predictable *entrée-plat-dessert* pattern, this is changing thanks to pioneering chefs such as Joël Robuchon. In his Atelier and his Table, the man once voted "chef of the 20th century" encourages dining in small or larger portions, according to your appetite. His opening hours even suggest that it's OK to graze outside traditional mealtimes—*une révolution*. Taking a similar approach is Alain Dutournier of Pinxo, who has actually persuaded Parisians to eat with their fingers and steal food off their companions' plates. Chefs are also developing a freer hand with spices, thanks to their experiences abroad. One of the first to incorporate spices into French cuisine without falling into fusion follies was Pascal Barbot at L'Astrance. During a stint in Australia, Barbot learned to juggle Asian flavors, then honed his French technique at L'Arpège. Most recently, chef Michel Troisgros of the famed Roanne restaurant has created an innovative new menu for the bijou Hôtel Lancaster, introducing such bold dishes as frogs' legs with tamarind. Even as their palates grow more adventurous, however, the French are reembracing *terroir*. Nothing illustrates this better than the purchase of the turn-of-the-20th-century bistro Aux Lyonnais by superchef Alain Ducasse. Never one to miss a trend, Ducasse knows that Parisians will always love earthy regional food when it's prepared with care and served in a gorgeous setting.

spring, venison in wine sauce with roast pears and celery-root chips in fall, and mango candied with orange and served with vanilla cream in winter. The extensive list of about 250 wines reflects co-owner Mark Williamson's passion for the Rhône Valley and Spanish sherries. ⊠*13 rue des Petits-Champs, Louvre/Tuileries* ☎*01–42–61–05–09* ⊕*www. williswinebar.com* ⊟*MC, V* ☉*Closed Sun.* Ⓜ*Bourse.*

¢–$ ✕ **Rouge Tomate.** The name of this *épicerie-restaurant* is misleading, since not all the tomatoes served here are red—the shop specializes in little-known varieties sourced mostly in France, with green, yellow, and striped varieties on display in summer. Off-season, rather than rely on pallid imports, the cook uses homemade preserves (jars of tomato sauces and jams are sold in the shop). The airy space feels like a coffee shop and adjoins a quiet terrace. Enjoy such reasonably priced dishes as goat-cheese-and-tomato terrine with tomato confit, tagliatelle with yellow-tomato sauce, chicken and cumin, and chocolate fondant with tomato-orange confit. ⊠*34 pl. du Marché St-Honoré, Louvre/Tuileries* ☎*01–42–61–16–09* ⊕*www.rouge-saint-honore.com* ⊟*AE, MC, V* ☉*Closed 1 wk at Christmas* Ⓜ*Tuileries, Pyramides.*

2ᴱ ARRONDISSEMENT (LA BOURSE/OPÉRA)

FRENCH

$$$ ✕ **Chez Georges.** If you were to ask Parisian bankers, aristocrats, or antiques dealers to name their favorite bistro for a three-hour weekday lunch, many would choose Georges. The traditional fare, written

in authentically hard-to-decipher handwriting, is good—chicken liver terrine, curly endive salad with bacon and a poached egg, steak with béarnaise—and the atmosphere is better, compensating for the rather steep prices. In the dining room a white-clothed stretch of tables lines the mirrored walls; attentive waiters sweep efficiently up and down its length. Order one of the wines indicated in colored ink on the menu and you can drink as much or as little of it as you want (and be charged accordingly); there's also a separate wine list that has grander bottles. ⊠ *1 rue du Mail, Louvre/Tuileries* ☎ *01–42–60–07–11* ▭ *AE, MC, V* ⊘ *Closed weekends and Aug.* Ⓜ *Sentier.*

$$–$$$ ✕ **Aux Lyonnais.** For Alain Ducasse it's not enough to run three of
Fodor'sChoice   the world's most expensive restaurants (in Paris, Monte Carlo, and
★   New York) and an ever-expanding string of Spoon, Food & Wine fusion bistros. He also has a passion for the old-fashioned bistro, so he has resurrected this 1890s gem by appointing a terrific young chef to oversee the short, frequently changing, and reliably delicious menu of Lyonnais specialties (if you're watching your pennies, opt for the limited-choice €28 set menu). Dandelion salad with crisp potatoes, bacon, and silky poached egg, watercress soup poured over parsleyed frogs' legs, and a sophisticated rendition of coq au vin show he is no bistro dilettante. The decor hews to tradition, too; there's a zinc bar, an antique coffee machine, and original turn-of-the-20th-century woodwork. ⊠ *32 rue St-Marc, Opéra/Grands Boulevards* ☎ *01–42–96–65–04* ▭ *AE, MC, V* ⊘ *Closed Sun. and Mon., Aug., 1 wk at Christmas. No lunch Sat.* Ⓜ *Bourse.*

$–$$ ✕ **Le Vaudeville.** This Art Deco brasserie is filled with journalists, bankers, and locals *d'un certain âge* who come for its good-value assortment of prix-fixe menus and highly professional service. Shellfish, house-smoked salmon, and desserts such as profiteroles are particularly enticing. Enjoy the graceful 1920s decor—almost the entire interior of this intimate dining room is done in real or faux marble—and lively dining until 1 AM daily. ⊠ *29 rue Vivienne, Opéra/Grands Boulevards* ☎ *01–40–20–04–62* ▭ *AE, DC, MC, V* Ⓜ *Bourse.*

¢   ✕ **La Ferme Opéra.** If your arm is aching from trying to flag down café waiters, take a break in this bright, super-friendly self-service restaurant not far from the Louvre, specializing in produce from the Ile de France region (around Paris). Inventive salads and sandwiches, quiches such as the three-cheese with pecan, hot dishes like chicken with dates and prunes served with polenta, and fruit crumbles, tarts, and cheesecakes are all impeccably fresh. ⊠ *55–57 rue St-Roch, Opéra/Grands Boulevards* ☎ *01–40–20–12–12* ▭ *AE, MC, V* Ⓜ *Pyramides.*

3ᴱ ARRONDISSEMENT (BEAUBOURG/MARAIS)
CONTEMPORARY

$$$–$$$$ ✕ **Le Murano.** If you love Baccarat's Cristal Room, you'll simply adore the restaurant of the swank, new Murano Urban Resort in the achingly chic northern Marais. There's nothing subtle about the ostentation in this hip hotel's dining room, whose ceiling drips with white tubes of various lengths. Dress to the nines and arrive with plenty of attitude (or brace yourself with three test tubes of alcohol at the bar). The light, modern, Mediterranean-inspired food neither distracts nor offends—

smoked salmon with too-pink *tarama* (cod roe), sautéed squid, waffle-style potato chips. If you can survive the sneering once-over at the door, surprisingly good-humored dining room staff add to the experience. ⊠*13 bd. du Temple, Le Marais* ☎*01–42–71–20–00* ⚸*Reservations essential* ▤*AE, DC, MC, V* Ⓜ*Filles du Calvaire.*

★ $$$ ✕ **Le Petit Pamphlet.** Around the same time that his popular bistro Le Pamphlet closed for renovations (it reopened in early 2007), chef Alain Carrère launched this casual annex two streets north of Place des Vosges. Run by the same professional team that made Le Pamphlet such a success, this bistro couldn't be more welcome in a part of the Marais where good value can prove elusive. In a rather impersonal setting brightened by Jacquard, table runners, and framed sketches, happy diners tuck into dishes such as a snail brochette with semolina gnocchi and sorrel sauce, Parmesan risotto topped with griddled shrimp, steak with potato gratin, and a crumble made with Mirabelle plums. The friendly staff are eager to please. ⊠*15 rue Saint-Gilles, Le Marais* ☎*01–42–71–22–21* ⚸*Reservations essential* ▤*MC, V* ⊙*Closed Sun., 1 wk in Jan., and 2 wks in Aug. No lunch Mon. or Sat.* Ⓜ*Chemin Vert.*

4ᴱ ARRONDISSEMENT (BEAUBOURG/MARAIS/ ILE ST-LOUIS)

CONTEMPORARY

$$$–$$$$ ✕ **Le Georges.** One of those rooftop showstopping venues so popular in Paris, Le Georges preens atop the Centre Georges Pompidou. The staff is as streamlined and angular as the furniture, and at night the terrace has distinct snob appeal: come snappily dressed or suffer the consequences (you may be relegated to something resembling a dentist's waiting room). Part of the Costes brothers' empire, the establishment trots out predictable fare such as penne with morel mushrooms and raw tuna with a sesame crust. It's all considerably less dazzling than the view, except for the suitably decadent desserts (try the Cracker's cheesecake with fromage blanc). ⊠*Centre Pompidou, 6th fl., Rue Rambuteau, Beaubourg/Les Halles* ☎*01–44–78–47–99* ▤*AE, DC, MC, V* ⊙*Closed Tues.* Ⓜ*Rambuteau.*

FRENCH

$$$ ✕ **Benoît.** If you loved Benoît (founded 1912) before it became the recent property of überchef Alain Ducasse and Thierry de la Brosse—the pair that revived Aux Lyonnais—chances are you'll adore it now. Without changing the vintage setting, which needed nothing more than a minor dusting, the illustrious new owners have subtly improved the menu with dishes such as marinated salmon, frogs' legs in a morel mushroom cream sauce, and an outstanding cassoulet, served in a cast-iron pot. Hardworking young chef David Rathgeber, formerly of Aux Lyonnais, keeps the kitchen running smoothly and the waiters are charm incarnate. It's a splurge to be here, so go all the way and top off your meal with tarte tatin that's caramelized to the core or a rum-doused baba. ⊠*20 rue St-Martin, Le Marais* ☎*01–42–72–25–76* ▤*AE, MC, V* Ⓜ*Châtelet.*

🕒 $–$$$ ✕ **Bofinger.** One of the oldest, loveliest, and most popular brasseries in Paris has generally improved in recent years. Stake out one of the tables dressed in crisp white linen under the glowing Art Nouveau glass cupola—this part of the dining room is no-smoking—and enjoy classic brasserie fare such as oysters, seafood-topped choucroute, lamb fillet, and orange-spiked chocolate mousse (stick to simple fare as some of the more ambitious dishes can be simply odd). The prix-fixe includes a decent half bottle of red or white wine, and there's an especially generous children's menu. ⊠ *5–7 rue de la Bastille, Bastille/ Nation* ☎ *01–42–72–87–82* ⊕ *www.bofingerparis.com* ⊟ *AE, DC, MC, V* Ⓜ *Bastille.*

$–$$$ ✕ **Au Bourguignon du Marais.** The handsome, contemporary look of this Marais bistro and wine bar is the perfect backdrop for the good traditional fare and excellent Burgundies served by the glass and bottle. Always on the menu are Burgundian classics such as *jambon persillé* (ham in parsleyed aspic jelly), escargots, and *oeufs en meurette* (eggs poached in a red-wine sauce); more up-to-date picks include a cèpe mushroom velouté with poached oysters (though the fancier dishes are generally less successful). In summer, the terrace is the place to be. ⊠ *19 rue de Jouy, Beaubourg/Les Halles* ☎ *01–48–87–15–40* ⊟ *AE, DC, MC, V* ☺ *Closed weekends* Ⓜ *St-Paul.*

$–$$$ ✕ **Brasserie de l'Ile St-Louis.** Set on picturesque Ile St-Louis and opened in 1870—when Germany took over Alsace-Lorraine and its chefs decamped to the capital—this outpost of Alsatian cuisine remains a cozy cocoon filled with stuffed animal heads, antique fixtures fashioned from barrels, and folk-art paintings. The food is gemütlich, too: *coq-au-Riesling*, omelets with Muenster cheese, onion tarts, and *choucroutes garni* (sauerkraut studded with ham, bacon, and pork loin—one variant is made with smoked haddock). In warm weather, the crowds move out to the terrace overlooking the Seine and Notre-Dame. With the famed *glacier* Berthillon so close by, it's best not to bother with the pricey desserts here. ⊠ *55 quai de Bourbon, Ile St-Louis* ☎ *01–43–54–02–59* ⊟ *DC, MC, V* ☺ *Closed Wed. and Aug. No lunch Thurs.* Ⓜ *Pont Marie.*

$–$$ ✕ **Mon Vieil Ami.** "Modern Alsatian" might sound like an oxymoron,
Fodor's Choice   but once you've tasted the cooking at this bistro run by the celebrated
★   Strasbourg chef Antoine Westermann you'll understand. The updated medieval dining room—stone walls, wooden beams, dark-wood tables, and small glass panes—provides a stylish milieu for his inventive cooking, which showcases perfect produce. Pâté *en croûte* (wrapped in pastry) with a knob of foie gras is hard to resist among the starters. Long-cooked, wine-marinated venison comes with succulent accompaniments of quince, prune, celery root, and chestnuts. Panfried skate paired with sautéed potatoes and lemon confit also earns kudos. Call during opening hours (11:30–2:30 and 7–11) to book, since they don't answer the phone the rest of the time. ⊠ *69 rue St-Louis-en-l'Isle, Ile St-Louis* ☎ *01–40–46–01–35* ⊟ *AE, DC, MC, V* ☺ *Closed Mon. and Tues.* Ⓜ *Pont Marie.*

MIDDLE EASTERN

⟳ ¢–$ ✕ **L'As du Fallafel.** Look no farther than the fantastic falafel stands on Rue de Rosiers for some of the cheapest and tastiest meals in Paris: L'As (the Ace) is widely considered the best of the bunch. A falafel costs €5, but shell out a little extra money for the *spécial* with grilled eggplant, cabbage, hummus, tahini, and hot sauce. The chawarma, made with chicken or lamb, is also one of the finest in town. Though takeout is popular, it can be more fun (and not as messy) to eat off a plastic plate in one of the two frenetic but fascinating fast-food-style dining rooms. The fresh lemonade is the falafel's best match. ⊠ *34 rue des Rosiers, Le Marais* ☎*01–48–87–63–60* ✺*MC, V* ⊘*Closed dusk Fri.–dusk Sat. and Jewish holidays* Ⓜ*St-Paul.*

5ᴱ ARRONDISSEMENT (LATIN QUARTER)

CONTEMPORARY

★ $–$$$ ✕ **Le Pré Verre.** Chef Philippe Delacourcelle knows his cassia bark from his cinnamon, thanks to a long stint in Asia. He opened this sharp bistro (with purple-gray walls and photos of jazz musicians) to showcase his unique culinary style, rejuvenating archetypal French dishes with Asian and Mediterranean spices. His bargain prix-fixe menu (€12.50 at lunch, €25.50 at dinner) changes constantly, but his trademark crisp salt cod with cassia bark and supersmooth smoked potato purée is a winner, as is his rhubarb compote with gingered white chocolate mousse. Ask for advice in selecting one of the wines from small producers. The main floor is no-smoking, with smokers relegated to the cellarlike downstairs space. ⊠ *8 rue Thénard, Quartier Latin* ☎*01–43–54–59–47* ✺*MC, V* ⊘*Closed Sun., Mon., and 2 wks in Aug.* Ⓜ*Maubert-Mutualité.*

FRENCH

★ $$$$ ✕ **La Tour d'Argent.** La Tour d'Argent had a difficult year in 2006 with the loss of a Michelin star, the death of owner Claude Terrail, and a change of chefs. It remains to be seen whether this landmark restaurant will rise to the challenge a more youthful approach, but there's no denying the splendor of its setting overlooking the Seine. If you don't want to splash out on dinner at around €200 a head, treat yourself to the set-price lunch menu for a relatively accessible €70. This entitles you to succulent slices of one of the restaurant's numbered ducks (the great duck slaughter began in 1919 and is now well past the millionth mallard, as your numbered certificate will attest). The most celebrated dish, *canard au sang* (duck in a blood-based sauce), is available à la carte or for a €22 supplement. Don't get too daunted by the wine list—more of a Bible, really—with the help of one of the sommeliers you can splurge a little (about €80) and perhaps taste a rare vintage Burgundy from the extraordinary cellars, which survived World War II. ⊠ *15 quai de la Tournelle, Quartier Latin* ☎*01–43–54–23–31* ⊕*www.latourdargent.com* ⌕*Reservations essential*Jacket and tie ✺*AE, DC, MC, V* ⊘*Closed Mon. and Aug. No lunch Tues.* Ⓜ*Cardinal Lemoine.*

★ $–$$$ ✕ **Chez René.** Think there's nowhere left in Paris that serves *boeuf bourguignon,* coq au vin, and frogs' legs in a timeworn bistro setting—crisp white tablecloths, burgundy woodwork, waiters in black aprons? Then you haven't been to Chez René, whose specialty—aside from robust Burgundian classics—is reassuring continuity, as illustrated by the photos of the staff taken every decade that adorn the walls. ⊠*14 bd. St-Germain, Quartier Latin* ☎*01–43–54–30–23* ⊟*MC, V* ⊘*Closed Sun., Mon., Christmas wk, and Aug. No lunch Sat.* Ⓜ*Maubert-Mutualité.*

★ **$-$$** ✕ **Le Reminet.** Chandeliers and mirrors add an unexpected grace note to this mellow bistro set in a narrow salon with stone walls (there's a second room upstairs) and run by a friendly couple. The menu changes regularly and showcases the young chef's talent with dishes like shrimp ravioli with coconut milk and grilled lamb with a cumin-and-red pepper crust. Desserts are equally inventive: don't even try to resist the mini baba au rhum with panfried winter fruits. You can score a deal with the weekday €13 prix-fixe lunch or the €17 dinner menu on Monday and Thursday. ⊠*3 rue des Grands-Degrés, Quartier Latin* ☎*01–44–07–04–24* ⊟*MC, V* ⊘*Closed Tues., Wed., and last 3 wks in Aug.* Ⓜ*Maubert-Mutualité.*

¢–$ ✕ **Les Pipos.** The tourist traps along romantic Rue de la Montagne Ste-Genevieve are enough to make you despair—and then you stumble across this bistro, bursting with chatter and laughter. Slang for students of the famous École Polytechnique nearby, Les Pipos is everything you could ask of a Quartier Latin bistro: the space is cramped, the food (such as Charolais steak and duck confit) is substantial (the cheese comes from the Lyon market, though the Poilâne bread could be fresher), and conversation flows as freely as the wine. It gets crowded, so arrive early to snag a table. You can also stop in for a glass of wine and a plate of *saucisson* in the late afternoon and watch the sun go down behind the Panthéon. ⊠*2 rue de L'École Polytechnique, Quartier Latin* ☎*01–43–54–11–40* ⊟*No credit cards* ⊘*Closed Sun. and 2 wks in Aug.* Ⓜ *Maubert-Mutualité.*

6ᴱ ARRONDISSEMENT (ST-GERMAIN-DES-PRÉS/ LATIN QUARTER)

CONTEMPORARY

$-$$ ✕ **Ze Kitchen Galerie.** William Ledeuil made his name at popular Les Bouquinistes (a Guy Savoy baby bistro) before opening this pareddown contemporary bistro in a loftlike space nearby. If the name isn't exactly inspired, the cooking shows unbridled creativity and a sense of fun: from a deliberately deconstructed menu featuring raw fish, soups, pastas, and *à la plancha* (grilled) plates, consider chicken wing, broccoli, and artichoke soup with lemongrass, or pork ribs with curry jus and white beans. Worldly eaters might find the flavors rather subtle, but the food here is adventurous for Paris. The menu changes monthly, and art exhibits rotate every three months; Ledeuil also gives cooking classes. The only thing missing is a no-smoking section. ⊠*4 rue des Grands-Augustins, Quartier Latin* ☎*01–44–32–00–32* ⊕*www.zekitchengalerie.fr* ⊟*AE, DC, MC, V* ⊘*Closed Sun. No lunch Sat.* Ⓜ*St-Michel.*

FRENCH

★ **$$$–$$$$** ✕ **Lapérouse.** Émile Zola, George Sand, and Victor Hugo were regulars, and the restaurant's mirrors still bear diamond scratches from the days when mistresses didn't take jewels at face value. It's hard not to fall in love with this 17th-century Seine-side town house whose warren of intimate, boiserie-graced salons breathes history. The latest chef, Alain Hacquard, has found the right track with a daring (for Paris) spice-infused menu: his lobster, Dublin Bay prawn, and crayfish bisque is flavored with Szechuan pepper and lemon. Game is prominent in fall, with a selection of southwestern wines to accompany dishes like Scottish grouse. For a truly intimate meal, reserve one of the legendary private salons where anything can happen (and probably has). ⊠ *51 quai des Grands Augustins, Quartier Latin* ☎ *01–43–26–68–04* ⚖ *Reservations essential* ▭ *AE, DC, MC, V* ⊘ *Closed Sun. No lunch Sat.* Ⓜ *St-Michel.*

★ $–$$ ✗ **Le Timbre.** Working in a tiny open kitchen, Manchester native Chris Wright could teach many a French chef a thing or two about *la cuisine française.* He works with only the finest suppliers to produce a constantly changing seasonal menu that keeps the locals coming back. A spring meal might begin with lightly cooked vegetables atop tapenade on toast, and fat, halved asparagus spears dabbed with an anise-spiked sauce, balsamic vinegar, and Parmesan. The mille-feuille is spectacular, but try not to miss *le vrai et le faux fromage,* a two-year-old British cheddar juxtaposed with a farmer's goat cheese from the Ardèche. Black-and-white photos of Paris add real charm to the narrow dining room. ⊠ *3 rue Ste-Beuve, Montparnasse* ☎ *01–45–49–10–40* ▭ *MC, V* ⊘ *Closed Sun., 3 wks in Aug., and 1 wk at Christmas.* Ⓜ *Vavin.*

$ ✗ **Le Comptoir du Relais Saint-Germain.** Run by legendary bistro chef Yves
Fodor's Choice   Camdeborde, this tiny, Art Deco hotel restaurant is booked up several
★   months in advance for the single dinner sitting (a five-course, €40 set menu of haute-cuisine-quality food). So it's probably best to try your luck at lunch (noon–6 PM) or on weekends (noon–11 PM), when no bookings are taken and brasserie-style food is served. Start with charcuterie or pâté, then choose from open-faced sandwiches, salads, and a handful of hot dishes such as braised beef cheek, roast tuna, and Yves's famed deboned and breaded pig's trotter. Sidewalk tables make for prime people watching in summer and Le Comptoir recently opened a down-to-earth snack shop next door serving crepes and sandwiches. ⊠ *9 carrefour de l'Odéon, St-Germain-des-Prés* ☎ *01–44–27–07–50* ▭ *AE, MC, V* Ⓜ *Odéon.*

SPANISH

★ $–$$ ✗ **Fogòn St-Julien.** The most ambitious Spanish restaurant in Paris has shed its tiny yellow dining room near St-Julien-le-Pauvre church for an airy Seine-side space—and chef Alberto Herraiz seems in his element. The seasonal all-tapas menu is tempting at €40 per person, but that would mean missing out on what must be the city's finest paella: saffron with seafood, inky squid, or Valencia-style with rabbit, chicken, and vegetables. Finish up with the custardy Crème Catalan accompanied by a glass of muscatel. ⊠ *45 quai des Grands-Augustins, Quartier Latin* ☎ *01–43–54–82–62* ⚖ *Reservations essential* ▭ *MC, V* ⊘ *Closed Mon.* Ⓜ *St-Michel.*

7ᴱ ARRONDISSEMENT (INVALIDES/EIFFEL TOWER)

FRENCH

$$$$ ✗ **Jules Verne.** A table at this all-black restaurant on the second level of the Tour Eiffel, 400 feet removed from the gritty reality of Parisian life, is one of the hardest to snag in Paris. At its best, Alain Reix's cooking justifies a wait of two months or more for dinner (lunch is more accessible), but lately his food has been a deflating experience. The wisest approach, then, is to go for the €53 lunch menu (weekdays only) and expect good but not exquisite food, such as pigeon fricassee or squid with duck liver, an intriguing meeting of land and sea. There's always the exceptional view—the highlight of any meal here has to be the ride up the restaurant's private elevator. Arrive early for a window seat. ⊠ *Tour Eiffel, Trocadéro/Tour Eiffel* ☎ *01–45–55–61–44* ⌖ *Reservations essential*]acket and tie ▤ *AE, DC, MC, V* Ⓜ *Bir-Hakeim.*

★ $$$–$$$$ ✗ **L'Atelier de Joël Robuchon.** Chef Frédéric Simonin lends northern and southern French touches to Robuchon's style in veal rib chops with olives, fava beans, and tiny artichokes or, for dessert, the "total *rhubarbe*," which raises this humble cold-weather stalk to sublime heights. As at Robuchon's L'Atelier, you can find a selection of small plates alongside more substantial dishes, but the seating arrangement is more conventional (no bar, just tables and chairs) and La Table accepts reservations—in fact, you should book weeks in advance for a seat in this small dining room somewhat disconcertingly decorated in gold leaf. ⊠ *5 rue Montalembert, St-Germain-des-Prés* ☎ *01–42–22–56–56* ⌖ *Reservations essential* ▤ *MC, V* Ⓜ *Rue du Bac.*

★ $ ✗ **Le Café Constant.** Parisian thirty- and fortysomethings are a nostalgic bunch, which explains the popularity of this down-to-earth venue from esteemed chef Christian Constant. This is a relatively humble bistro with cream-color walls, red banquettes, and wooden tables. You can sometimes spot Constant relaxing in the dining room after the lunch rush; the chef seems to feel most at home here. The menu reads like a French cookbook from the 1970s—who cooks veal *cordon bleu* these days?—and, with Constant overseeing the kitchen, the dishes taste even better than you remember. There's a delicious creamy lentil soup with morsels of foie gras, and the artichoke salad comes with fresh—not bottled or frozen—hearts. A towering *vacherin* (meringue layered with ice cream) might bring this delightfully retro meal to a close. ⊠ *139 rue St-Dominique, Invalides* ☎ *01–47–53–73–34* ⌖ *Reservations not accepted* ▤ *MC, V* ⊗ *Closed Sun. and Mon.* Ⓜ *Métro Ecole Militaire, Pont de l'Alma; RER: Pont de l'Alma.*

8ᴱ ARRONDISSEMENT (CHAMPS-ÉLYSÉES/LOUVRE)

CONTEMPORARY

$$$$ ✗ **Maison Blanche.** The celebrated Pourcel twin brothers preside over this edgy "White House," which basks in its show-off view across Paris from the top floor of the Théâtre du Champs-Élysées. Typical of the globe-trotting, southern French–inspired (and not always successful) fare are the vegetable pot-au-feu with white Alba truffle (a section of the menu is dedicated to vegetarian dishes), crisp-crusted scallop tart with crab and baby leeks, and French beef with an herb crust,

mushrooms, and shallots slow-cooked in Fitou wine. A side order of mashed potatoes, green beans, or salad will set you back a sobering €10—this is a place for the fat of wallet and trim of figure. Desserts are divided into chocolate and fruit sections, the fruit options being the most playful. In keeping with the snow-white setting, staff can be rather frosty. ⊠*15 av. Montaigne, Champs-Élysées* ☎*01–47–23–55–99* ⊕*www.maison-blanche.fr* ▭*AE, MC, V* ⊘*No lunch weekends* Ⓜ*Franklin-D.-Roosevelt.*

★ $$$$ ✕ **La Table du Lancaster.** Operated by one of the most enduring families in French gastronomy—the Troisgros clan has run a world-famous restaurant in Roanne for three generations—this stylish boutique-hotel restaurant is the perfect setting for tasting the stellar cosmopolitan cuisine. Try to sit in the stunning Asian-inspired courtyard with its red walls and bamboo trees. Often drawing on humble ingredients, such as eel or even pigs' ears, the food reveals fascinating flavor and texture contrasts, as in silky sardines on crunchy melba toast, or tangy frogs' legs in tamarind. A classic borrowed from the menu in Roanne is cod in a seaweed bouillon over short-grain white rice, a subtle and sensual dish. Don't miss the desserts, such as not one but two slices of sugar tart with grapefruit slices for contrast. ⊠*Hotel Lancaster, 7 rue de Berri, Champs-Élysées* ☎*01–40–76–40–18* ⊕*www.hotel-lancaster.fr* ⌂*Reservations essential* ▭*AE, DC, MC, V* ⊘*Closed Aug. No lunch Sat. and Sun.* Ⓜ*George V.*

$$$–$$$$ ✕ **Spoon, Food & Wine.** Decorator Jean-François Auboiron has revamped Alain Ducasse's original fusion bistro with a silver screen lighted with sculptures by Patricia Zurini and a long central table where strangers share a unique dining experience. The mix 'n' match menu hasn't changed significantly since the restaurant first opened, but you can now order a three-course lunch served in 40 minutes for €38 or try the featured Travel Spoon dish at dinner, which comes from one of the Spoon branches around the world. Fashion folk love this place for its many vegetable and pasta dishes and its irresistible desserts, particularly the TobleSpoon, a takeoff on Toblerone. If you've sampled the Spoon concept elsewhere in the world, don't expect the same here; each branch is tailored to a particular city's tastes, and what looks exotic in Paris (bagels and bubble-gum ice cream) might seem humdrum in New York. ⊠*14 rue de Marignan, Champs-Elysées* ☎*01–40–76–34–44* ⊕*www.alain-ducasse.com or www.spoon.tm.fr* ⌂*Reservations essential* ▭*AE, MC, V* ⊘*Closed weekends, Aug., and 1 wk at Christmas* Ⓜ*Franklin-D.-Roosevelt.*

FRENCH

$$$$ ✕ **Alain Ducasse au Plaza Athénée.** This previously sober dining room glimmers with 10,000 crystals following a whirlwind revamp by decorator Patrick Jouin. Clementine-color tablecloths and space-age cream-and-orange chairs with pull-out plastic trays (a bit airplane-like) provide a more cheerful setting for the cooking of young chef Christophe Moret, who still seems to be finding his footing in a dining room heavy with gastronomic expectations. Some dishes taste too subtle, while in others strong flavors overwhelm more delicate ingredients. Even so, a meal here is delightfully luxe, starting with a heavenly

amuse-bouche of Dublin Bay shrimp with caviar and a tangy lemon cream. You can continue with a full truffle-and-caviar fest, or opt for slightly more down-to-earth dishes such as lobster in spiced wine with quince or saddle of lamb with small sautéed artichokes. If you find yourself hesitating over dessert, opt for the baba au rhum, which comes with a trolley of fine rums. ✉*Hôtel Plaza Athenée, 27 av. Montaigne, Champs-Élysées* ☎*01–53–67–66–65* ⊕*www.plaza-athenee-paris.com* ⌨*Reservations essential*Jacket required ▤*AE, DC, MC, V* ⊘*Closed weekends, 2 wks in late Dec., and mid-July–mid-Aug. No lunch Mon.– Wed.* Ⓜ*Alma-Marceau.*

★ $$$$ ✗ **Les Ambassadeurs.** A former star—more of a comet, really—in the Alain Ducasse galaxy, Jean-Francois Piége is now establishing his own identity in Le Crillon's hallowed 18th-century dining room, recently updated in muted tones that offset the glistening marble and dripping chandeliers. Born in 1970, he is young enough to play with food— deconstructing and reconstructing an egg to look like a square marsh-mallow, its yolk studded with white truffle—and grown-up enough to serve unabashedly rich classics of French cooking, such as deboned squab stuffed with foie gras. An expert at pairing langoustines and caviar, he has come up with a new version for the Crillon, this time wrapping the ingredients in a delicate crepe. À la carte, it's easily one of the city's priciest restaurants, but there is a relatively democratic €70 lunch menu. Happily, the waiters will make you feel at home no matter what your budget. ✉*Hôtel de Crillon, 10 pl. de la Concorde, Louvre/ Tuileries* ☎*01–44–71–16–17* ⌨*Reservations essential* Ⓜ*Concorde.*

$$$$ ✗ **Maxim's.** Count Danilo sang "I'm going to Maxim's" in Lehar's *The Merry Widow,* Leslie Caron was klieg-lighted here by Cecil Beaton for *Gigi,* and Audrey Hepburn adorned a banquette with Peter O'Toole in *How to Steal a Million.* In reality, Maxim's has lost some of its luster— the restaurant had its heyday 100 years ago during the Belle Epoque, when *le tout Paris* swarmed here—but this exuberant Art Nouveau sanctuary still offers a taste of the good life under its breathtaking painted ceiling. It's just a shame that Maxim's is so jaw-droppingly expensive for food—like the Billy-bi mussel consommé with cream or braised sole in vermouth—that would feel at home in a brasserie. A set menu would attract a bigger crowd and make the room feel more fes-tive. Still, there's no place like Maxim's—especially on the last Friday of every month when they present a 1900 cabaret evening, replete with gypsy violins. ✉*3 rue Royale, Louvre/Tuileries* ☎*01–42–65–27– 94* ⊕*www.maxims-de-paris.com* ⌨*Reservations essential* ▤*AE, DC, MC, V* ⊘*Closed Sun. and Mon. No lunch Sat.* Ⓜ*Concorde.*

$$$$ ✗ **Pierre Gagnaire.** If you want to venture to the frontier of luxe cooking today—and if money is truly no object—a dinner here is a must. Chef Pierre Gagnaire's work is at once intellectual and poetic,

---

LA VIE EST BELLE

To see Maxim's in all its eye-knocking Belle Epoque splendor, just log on to their Web site at ⊕ *www.maxims-de-paris.com* and check out those photos (wait for the text to disappear) under its "Evening of Cabaret" section—dig those ostrich feathers, gypsy vio-lins, and joie-de-vivre.

often blending three or four unexpected tastes and textures in a single dish. Just taking in the menu requires concentration, so complex are descriptions such as "suckling lamb from Aveyron: sweetbreads, saddle, and rack; green papaya and turnip velouté thickened with Tarbais beans." The Grand Dessert, a seven-dessert marathon, will leave you breathless. The businesslike gray-and-wood dining room feels

refreshingly informal, especially at lunch, but it also lacks the grandeur expected at this level. The uninspiring prix-fixe lunch, uneven service, and occasional ill-judged dishes linger as drawbacks, and prices keep shooting skywards, making Pierre Gagnaire an experience only for the financial elite. ⊠6 rue de Balzac, Champs-Élysées ☎01–58–36–12–50 ⊕www.pierre-gagnaire.com ⚠Reservations essential ☰AE, DC, MC, V ☉Closed Sat. and 2 wks in July. No lunch Sun. and Aug. Ⓜ Charles-de-Gaulle–Étoile.

$$$$
Fodor'sChoice
★

✕ **Taillevent.** Perhaps the most traditional—for many diners this is only high praise—of all Paris luxury restaurants, this grande dame basks in newfound freshness under brilliant chef Alain Solivérès and a subtly modernized dining room, with particular attention paid to the lighting. Look for southern French–inspired dishes such as a splendid spelt risotto with truffles and frogs' legs or panfried duck liver with caramelized fruits and vegetables. One of the 19th-century paneled salons has been turned into a winter garden, and contemporary paintings adorn the walls. The service is flawless and the exceptional wine list is well priced. All in all, a meal here comes as close to the classic haute-cuisine experience as you can find in Paris—and it's not the priciest, especially if you ask for the little-advertised €70 lunch menu and choose one of the many reasonably priced wines. Not surprisingly, you must reserve your table for dinner a month in advance. ⊠15 rue Lamennais, Champs-Élysées ☎01–44–95–15–01 ⊕www.taillevent.com ⚠Reservations essentialJacket and tie ☰AE, DC, MC, V ☉Closed weekends and Aug. Ⓜ Charles-de-Gaulle–Étoile.

★ $$$–$$$$

✕ **Flora.** Alain Passard–trained Flora Mikula made her name at Les Olivades, a Provençal bistro in the 7e, before joining a gaggle of ambitious restaurateurs in this platinum-card area. Moving away from the bistro register, she's turning out refined food with southern twists in a dressed-up setting with plaster moldings and mirrors of various sizes that feels much like a bourgeois apartment, with a distinctive feminine touch that comes from the many pink details. Standout dishes on the frequently changing seasonal menu are a scallop *tarte fine* with truffle vinaigrette, roast sea bass with a potato-olive puree, roasted-apple mille-feuille with salted-caramel ice cream, and a spectacular Grand Marnier soufflé. Order from the pricier *carte* if you want to take advantage of the superb cheese trolley from fromager Laurent Dubois (a cheese plate is available on the €36 menu for a €2 supplement). Service, like the food, is generally impeccable, with the occasional minor slip-up. ⊠*36 av. George V, Champs-Elysées* ☎*01–40–70–10–49* ⊕*www.les-saveursdeflora.com* ☰*AE, MC, V* ⊘*Closed Sun. and Aug. No lunch Sat.* Ⓜ*Franklin-D.-Roosevelt.*

$$$–$$$$ ✕ **Senderens.** Iconic chef Alain Senderens waited until he reached retirement age to make a rebellious statement against the all-powerful Michelin inspectors, "giving back" the three stars he had held for 28 years and juxtaposing modern furniture against the former Lucas Carton's splendid Art Nouveau interior before renaming the restaurant after himself. The

WORD OF MOUTH

"At Senderens (once known as Lucas Carton), just the ballet of the waitstaff in their tails, the sterling silver cheese wagon with more than 150 different varieties, the wine suggestions geared to each menu option, and the real niceness of the people who work there, despite—or perhaps because—it is highly choreographed, make for an experience you'll never forget."

–Former NY resident

new curvy white furnishings and craterlike ceiling lights would look at home in an airport lounge, as would the slightly bewildered staff. Gone are the dishes that made Lucas Carton great—most notably the chef's signature duck à l'Apicius—in favor of a fusion menu that spans the globe. Sometimes his new dishes work, as in warm semi-smoked salmon with Thai spices and iced cucumber, and sometimes they fall flat, as in a too-rich starter of roast foie gras with fig salad and licorice powder. Senderens has also taken his passion for food-and-drink matches to extremes, suggesting a glass of wine, whiskey, sherry, or even punch to accompany each dish. What will he do next—dye his hair pink? ⊠*9 pl. de la Madeleine, Opéra/Grands Boulevards* ☎*01–42–65–22–90* ☰*AE, DC, MC, V* Ⓜ*Madeleine.*

$$$ ✕ **Dominique Bouchet.** To taste the cooking of one of the city's great chefs, you no longer need to pay for the sumptuous backdrop once provided by the Hôtel Crillon. Dominique Bouchet has left that world behind for an elegant bistro where contemporary art brightens cream-painted walls, and he seems all the happier for it. The kitchen sends out the perfect combination of refined French technique and country-style cooking, as in an iced velouté of green peas with almonds and summer truffles, duck breast with confit turnips, or poached pear with chocolate sauce and caramel ice cream. Everything sparkles except the service, which occasionally has trouble keeping up. ⊠*11 rue Treilhard, Champs-Élysées* ☎*01–45–61–09–46* ⊕*www.dominique-bouchet.com* ☰*AE, DC, MC, V* ⊘*Closed weekends and Aug.* Ⓜ*Miromesnil.*

$$–$$$ ✕ **La Fermette Marbeuf 1900.** Graced with one of the most mesmerizing Belle Epoque rooms in town—accidentally rediscovered during renovations in the 1970s—this is a favorite haunt of French celebrities, who adore the sunflowers, peacocks, and dragonflies of the Art Nouveau mosaic and stained-glass mise-en-scène. The menu rolls out a solid, updated classic cuisine. Try the snails in puff pastry, saddle of lamb with *choron* (a tomato-spiked béarnaise sauce), and bitter-chocolate fondant—but ignore the rather depressing €30 prix-fixe unless you're on a budget. Popular with tourists and businesspeople at lunch, La Fermette becomes truly animated around 9 PM. ✉ *5 rue Marbeuf, Champs-Élysées* ☎ *01–53–23–08–00* ⊕ *www.fermettemarbeuf.com* ▤ *AE, DC, MC, V* Ⓜ *Franklin-D.-Roosevelt.*

$–$$$ ✕ **Chez Savy.** Just off the glitzy avenue Montaigne, Chez Savy exists in its own circa-1930s dimension, oblivious to the area's galloping fashionization. The Art Deco cream-and-burgundy interior looks blissfully intact (avoid the back room unless you're in a large group), and the waiters show not a trace of attitude. Fill up on rib-sticking specialties from the Auvergne in central France—lentil salad with bacon, foie gras (prepared on the premises), perfectly charred lamb with featherlight shoestring frites—order a celebratory bottle of Mercurey and feel smug that you've found this place. ✉ *23 rue Bayard, Champs-Élysées* ☎ *01–47–23–46–98* ▤ *MC, V* ⊙ *Closed weekends and Aug.* Ⓜ *Franklin-D.-Roosevelt.*

9ᴱ ARRONDISSEMENT (OPÉRA/PIGALLE-CLICHY)

FRENCH

¢–$ ✕ **Les Vivres.** The brainchild of Jean-Luc André, chef at the elegant Pétrelle next door, Les Vivres translates as "survival supplies," and many devotees now feel they couldn't live without it. Down the hill from Montmartre on a quiet residential street, this stylish dining room—like the French country home you wish you had—serves lunch nonstop from 11 to 7 and dinner on Friday nights. You can always find seasonal vegetables, which are grilled, marinated, or slow-roasted; a savory tart; and such hearty dishes as farmer's rabbit with Nyons olives, *hachis parmentier* (shepherd's pie), and squid fricassee. Jars of jams and preserves are available to take home for future emergencies. ✉ *28 rue Pétrelle, Montmartre* ☎ *01–42–80–26–10* ▤ *MC, V* ⊙ *Closed Sun., Mon., and Aug.* Ⓜ *Anvers.*

¢ ⊙ ✕ **Chartier.** People come here more for the bonhomie and the stunning 1896 interior than the cooking, which could be politely described as unambitious. This cavernous restaurant—the only original turn-of-the-century *bouillon* to remain true to its mission of serving cheap, sustaining food to the masses—enjoys a huge following. You may find yourself sharing a table with strangers as you study the long, old-fashioned menu of such standards as hard-boiled eggs with mayonnaise, pot-au-feu, and *blanquette de veau* (veal stew in a white sauce). ✉ *7 rue du Faubourg-Montmartre, Opéra/Grands Boulevards* ☎ *01–47–70–86–29* ⚠ *Reservations not accepted* ▤ *MC, V* Ⓜ *Montmartre.*

11ᴱ ARRONDISSEMENT (BASTILLE/RÉPUBLIQUE)

FRENCH

★ $$$ ✕ **Astier.** The prix-fixe menu (there's no à la carte) at this tried-and-true restaurant must be one of the best values in town, with a lunch menu for €23.50 and a second lunch menu and dinner menu for €28. Among the deftly prepared seasonal dishes are tomato-and-goat-cheese tart on curly endive, rabbit in mustard sauce with fresh tagliatelle, an old-fashioned blanquette de veau, and *marquise au chocolat* (chocolate mousse cake). This is a great place to come if you're feeling cheesy, since it's locally famous for having one of the best *plateaux de fromages* (cheese plates) in Paris—a giant wicker tray lands on the table and you help yourself. The lengthy, well-priced wine list is a connoisseur's dream. ✉*44 rue Jean-Pierre Timbaud, République* ☎*01–43–57–16–35* ⊕*www.restaurant-astier.com* ⚐*Reservations essential* ☰*MC, V* ☉*Closed weekends, Aug., Christmas wk, and Easter wk* Ⓜ*Parmentier.*

$$–$$$ ✗ **Le Repaire de Cartouche.** In this split-level, dark-wood bistro between Bastille and République, chef Rodolphe Paquin applies a disciplined creativity to earthy French regional dishes. The menu changes regularly, but typical are a salad of *haricots verts* (string beans) topped with tender slices of squid, scallops on a bed of diced pumpkin, juicy lamb with white beans, and old-fashioned desserts like custard with tiny madeleine cakes. The wine list is very good, too, with bargains like a Cheverny from the Loire Valley for €17. ✉*99 rue Amelot, Bastille/Nation* ☎*01–47–00–25–86* ⚐*Reservations essential* ☰*MC, V* ☉*Closed Sun., Mon., and Aug.* Ⓜ*Filles du Calvaire.*

12ᴱ ARRONDISSEMENT (BASTILLE/NATION)

FRENCH

★ **$$–$$$** ✗ **Le Square Trousseau.** This beautiful Belle Epoque bistro is a favorite of the fashion set. Even models can't resist the peppered country pâté, slow-cooked lamb, or tender baby chicken with mustard and bread-crumb crust. Wines might seem a little pricey but are lovingly selected from small producers—you can also buy them, along with superb Spanish ham, at the restaurant's small boutique–wine bar next door. If you're on a budget, try the lunch menu at €20 or €25. ✉*1 rue Antoine Vollon, Bastille/Nation* ☎*01–43–43–06–00* ☰*AE, MC, V* ☉*Closed Sun. and Mon.* Ⓜ*Ledru-Rollin.*

14ᴱ ARRONDISSEMENT (MONTPARNASSE)

FRENCH

$–$$$ ✗ **La Coupole.** This world-renowned cavernous spot with Art Deco murals practically defines the term *brasserie*. La Coupole might have lost its intellectual aura since the Flo group's restoration, but it has been popular from the days when Jean-Paul Sartre and Simone de Beauvoir were regulars and is still great fun. Today it attracts a mix of bourgeois families, tourists, and elderly lone diners treating themselves to a dozen oysters. Expect the usual brasserie menu—including perhaps the largest shellfish platter in Paris—choucroute, a very un-Indian but tasty lamb curry, and some great over-the-top desserts. They don't take reservations after 8:30 PM Monday–Thursday and after 8 PM Friday–Sunday, so be prepared for a wait at the bar. ✉*102 bd. du Montparnasse, Montparnasse* ☎*01–43–20–14–20* ⊕*www.flobrasseries.com* ☰*AE, DC, MC, V* Ⓜ*Vavin.*

16ᴱ ARRONDISSEMENT (TROCADÉRO/BOIS DE BOULOGNE)

CONTEMPORARY

$$$$ ✗ **Astrance.** Pascal Barbot may have risen to fame thanks to his restau-
Fodor'sChoice rant's amazing-value food and casual atmosphere, but a few years later
★ Astrance has become resolutely haute with prices to match. Most diners put their faith in the chef by ordering his €150 tasting menu, which unfolds over two to three hours in a series of surprisingly light courses.

Even à la carte meals here—available only at lunch—cost at least €120, but Barbot's cooking has such an ethereal quality that it's worth even the monthlong wait for a table at dinner. His dishes often draw on Asian ingredients, as in grilled lamb with miso-laquered eggplant and a palate-cleansing white sorbet spiked with chili pepper and lemongrass. Wines by the glass offer great value but don't always match the quality of the food. If you're looking for an affordable lunch menu, you sadly must look elsewhere. ⊠ *4 rue Beethoven, Trocadéro/Tour Eiffel* ☎*01–40–50–84–40* ✄*Reservations essential* ▭*AE, DC, MC, V* ⊘*Closed Sat.–Mon., Aug., and 1 wk in Feb.* Ⓜ*Passy.*

$$–$$$$

Fodor'sChoice

★

✕ **La Table de Joël Robuchon.** Frédéric Simonin, who formerly worked with Ghislaine Arabian, lends northern and southern French touches to Joël Robuchon's fabled style in such dishes as veal rib chops with olives, fava beans, and tiny artichokes or, for dessert, the "total rhubarbe," which raises this humble cold-weather stalk to sublime heights. As at Robuchon's L'Atelier you'll find a selection of small plates alongside more substantial dishes, but the seating arrangement is more conventional (no bar, just tables and chairs) and La Table accepts reservations—in fact, you should book weeks in advance. ⊠*16 av. Bugeaud, Trocadéro/Tour Eiffel* ☎*01–56–28–16–16* ✄*Reservations essential* ▭*MC, V* ⊘*Closed Sun. and 2 wks in Aug. No lunch Mon. and Sat.* Ⓜ*Victor-Hugo.*

FRENCH

$$$$

✕ **Le Pré Catelan.** Live a Belle Epoque fantasy by dining beneath the chestnut trees on the terrace of this fanciful landmark *pavillon* in the Bois de Boulogne. Among the winning dishes that have appeared on chef Frédéric Anton's menu are spit-roasted squab in a caramelized sauce, sweetbreads with morels and asparagus tips, and roasted pear on a caramelized waffle with bergamot ice cream. For a taste of the good life at a (relatively) gentle price, order the €55 lunch menu and soak up the opulent surroundings along with service that's as polished as the silverware. ⊠*Rte. de Surèsnes, Bois de Boulogne* ☎*01–44–14–41–14* ✄*Reservations essential* Jacket and tie ▭*AE, DC, MC, V* ⊘*Closed Sun., Mon., mid-Feb., and 1 wk in Nov.* Ⓜ*Porte Dauphine.*

17ᴱ ARRONDISSEMENT (MONCEAU/CHAMPS-ÉLYSÉES)

FRENCH

★ $$$$

✕ **Guy Savoy.** Revamped with dark African wood, rich leather, and cream-color marble, Guy Savoy's luxury restaurant has stepped gracefully into the 21st century. Come here for a perfectly measured contemporary haute-cuisine experience, since Savoy's several bistros have not lured him away from his kitchen. The artichoke soup with black truffles, sea bass with spices, and veal kidneys in mustard-spiked jus reveal the magnitude of his talent, and his mille-feuille is an instant classic. Half portions allow you to graze your way through the menu—unless you choose a blowout feast for €210 or €285—and reasonably priced wines are available (though beware the cost of wines by the glass). Best of all, the atmosphere is joyful—Savoy senses that having fun is just as important as eating well. ⊠*18 rue Troyon, Champs-Élysées* ☎*01–43–80–40–61* ⊕*www.guysavoy.com* ✄*Reservations essential* Jacket and tie ⊟*AE, MC, V* ⊗*Closed Sun., Mon., and mid-July–mid-Aug. No lunch Sat.* Ⓜ*Charles-de-Gaulle-Étoile.*

18ᴱ ARRONDISSEMENT (MONTMARTRE)

FRENCH

$–$$ ✕ **Chez Toinette.** Between the red lights of Pigalle and the Butte Montmartre, this cozy bistro with red walls and candlelight hits the romance nail on the head. In autumn and winter game comes into play in long-simmered French dishes—choose from *marcassin* (young wild boar), venison, and pheasant. Regulars can't resist the crème brûlée and the raspberry tart. Prices have crept up and a new owner took over in 2005, but quality has remained high and Chez Toinette is still a rare find for this neighborhood. ⊠*20 rue Germaine Pilon, Montmartre* ☏*01–42–54–44–36* ⊟*MC, V* ⊗*Closed Sun., Mon., Aug., and 2 wks at Christmas. No lunch* Ⓜ*Pigalle.*

$–$$ ✕ **La Famille.** Inaki Aizpitarte, originally from the Basque region, opened this hip restaurant on a street known for its role in the film *Amélie.* Happily, La Famille is worth visiting for what it brings to the plate, not the screen. The spare space attracts the *bobo* (bohemian bourgeois) neighbors who are bringing a new energy to Montmatre. Aizpitarte's globetrotting menu might include panfried foie gras with miso sauce or chocolate custard with fiery Basque peppers. On the last Sunday of every month a tasting menu is served (the restaurant is otherwise closed Sunday). ⊠*41 rue des Trois-Frères, Montmartre* ☏*01–42–52–11–12* ⊟*MC, V* ⊗*Closed Sun., Mon., and 3 wks in Aug. No lunch* Ⓜ*Abbesses.*

CAFÉS & SALONS DE THÉ

Along with air, water, and wine (Parisians eat fewer and fewer three-course meals), the café remains one of the basic necessities of life in Paris; following is a small selection of cafés and *salons de thé* (tearooms) to whet your appetite. **Au Père Tranquille** (⊠*16 rue Pierre Lescot, Beaubourg/Les Halles, 1ᵉʳ* ☏*01–45–08–00–34* Ⓜ*Les Halles*) is one of the best places in Paris for people-watching. **Brasserie Lipp** (⊠*151 bd. St-Germain, St-Germain-des-Prés, 6ᵉ* ☏*01–45–48–53–91* Ⓜ*St-Germain-des-Prés*), with its turn-of-the-20th-century decor, was a favorite spot of Hemingway's; today television celebrities, journalists, and politicians come here for coffee on the small glassed-in terrace off the main restaurant. **Café Beaubourg** (⊠*43 rue St-Merri, Beaubourg/Les Halles, 4ᵉ* ☏*01–48–87–63–96* Ⓜ*Hôtel-de-Ville*), near the Pompidou Center and designed by architect Christian de Portzamparc, is one of the trendiest rendezvous spots for fashion and art types. **Café Marly** (⊠*Cour Napoléon du Louvre, 93 rue de Rivoli, Louvre/Tuileries, 1ᵉʳ* ☏*01–49–26–06–60* Ⓜ*Palais-Royal*), overlooking the main courtyard of the Louvre, is perfect for an afternoon break or a nightcap, though the food could be better. Note that ordinary café service shuts down during meal hours, when overpriced, mediocre food is served.

★ **La Charlotte en l'Île** (⊠*24 rue St-Louis-en-l'Ile, Ile St-Louis, 4ᵉ* ☏*01–43–54–25–83* Ⓜ*Pont-Marie*) would be fancied by the witch who baked gingerbread children in *Hansel and Gretel*—set with fairy lights, carnival masques, and decoupaged detritus, it's a tiny, storybook spot that offers more than 30 varieties of tea along with a sinfully good hot chocolate. **La Crémaillère** (⊠ *15 pl. du Tertre, Montmartre, 18ᵉ* ☎ *01–46–06–58–59* Ⓜ *Anvers*) is a veritable monument to fin de siècle art in Montmartre. **Les Editeurs** (⊠ *4 carrefour de l'Odéon, St-Germain-des-Prés, 6ᵉ* ☎ *01–43–26–67–76* Ⓜ *St-Germain-des-Prés*), strategically placed near prestigious Rive Gauche publishing houses, attracts passersby with red velour seats and glossy books on

display. The terrace just off the Boulevard St-Germain is great for people-watching, but not ideal for catching a waiter's eye. **Le Flore en l'Ile** (⊠ *42 quai d'Orléans, Ile St-Louis, 4ᵉ* ☎ *01–43–29–88–27* Ⓜ *Pont-Marie*) is on the Ile St-Louis and has a magnificent view of the Seine. **Ladurée** (⊠ *16 rue Royale, Opéra/Grands Boulevards, 8ᵉ* ☎ *01–42–60–21–79* ⊕ *www.laduree.fr* Ⓜ *Madeleine* ⊠ *75 av. des Champs-Élysées, Champs-Élysées, 8ᵉ* ☎ *01–40–75–08–75* Ⓜ *Georges V*) is pretty enough to bring a tear to Proust's eye—these salons de thé have barely changed since 1862 (there's another outpost on the Left Bank at 21 rue Bonaparte). For sheer Traviata opulence, the one on the Champs-Élysées can't be beat: wait until you see the pâtisserie counter or the super-sumptuous Salon Paéva. You can dote on the signature lemon-and-caramel macaroons, or try them in a dazzling array of other flavors including hazelnut praline, rose petal, pistachio, blackcurrant violet, or salted butter caramel. Oooooh! **Ma Bourgogne** (⊠ *19 pl. des Vosges, Le Marais, 4ᵉ* ☎ *01–42–78–44–64* Ⓜ *St-Paul*), on magical Place des Vosges, is a calm oasis for a coffee or a light lunch away from the noisy streets. **Mariage Frères** (⊠ *30 rue du Bourg-Tibourg, Le Marais, 4ᵉ* ☎ *01–42–72–28–11* Ⓜ *Hôtel-de-Ville*) is an outstanding tea shop serving 500 kinds of tea, along with delicious tarts.

WHERE TO STAY

Updated
by Heather
Stimmler-Hall

Winding staircases, flower-filled window boxes, concierges who seem to have stepped out of a 19th-century novel—all of these can still be found in Paris hotels, and despite the scales being tipped in favor of the well-heeled, overall there's good news for travelers of all budgets. Increased competition means the bar for service and amenities has been raised everywhere. Many good-value establishments in the lower-to-middle price ranges have updated their funky '70s wallpaper and "Why should I care, Madame?" attitudes, while still keeping their prices in check. Virtually every hotel is now equipped with cable TV to meet the needs of international guests. Now it's not uncommon for mid-range hotels to have a no-smoking floor, for inexpensive hotels to offer air-conditioning and buffet breakfast service, and even for budget places to have wireless Internet or an Internet terminal in their little lobbies. So, whatever price you're looking for, compared to most other cities Paris is a paradise for the weary traveler tired of dreary, out-of-date, or cookie-cutter rooms. The best hotels still emanate an unmistakable Paris vibe: weathered beamed ceilings, vaulted stone breakfast crypts, tall windows overlooking zinc rooftops, and leafy courtyards where you can sit and linger over your daily croissant and café.

Despite the huge choice of hotels, you should always reserve well in advance, especially if you're determined to stay in a specific place. You can do this by telephoning, faxing, or e-mailing ahead, then asking for confirmation of your reservation, detailing the duration of your stay, the price, the location and type of your room (single or double, twin beds or double), and the bathroom (shower—*douche*—or bath—*baignoire*—private or shared). Assume that hotel rooms have air-conditioning, TV, telephones, and private bath, unless otherwise noted. Remember that the *very* top Paris hotels retain their ranks among the world's priciest. Room rates at these legendary places can range from €400 to €700—and upward—for a night. These rates can artificially skew our price chart figures for, in truth, a $$$ hotel listed below can be as reasonable as €160.

PRICES

Almost all Paris hotels charge extra for breakfast, with prices ranging from €5 to more than €40 per person in luxury establishments. For anything more than the standard Continental breakfast of café au lait and croissants, the price will be higher. You may be better off finding the nearest café. Occasionally breakfast is included in the hotel rate—this is denoted below with a BP (Breakfast Plan) in the review. If not, presume all hotels reviewed operate on the EP (European Plan), with no breakfast included in the basic room rate. A nominal *séjour* (lodging) tax of €1.07 per person per night is charged to pay for promotion of tourism in Paris.

	WHAT IT COSTS				
	¢	$	$$	$$$	$$$$
FOR TWO PEOPLE	under €75	€75–€100	€101–€150	€151–€225	over €225

Prices are for two people in a standard double room in high season, including tax (19.6%) and service charge.

1ER ARRONDISSEMENT (LOUVRE/LES HALLES)

$$$$ **Hôtel Costes.** The place that put Jacques Garcia on the map as France's ritziest designer, Jean-Louis and Gilbert Costes's eponymous hotel is the darling of decorating magazines and a magnet for the sunglasses-at-night set. Nearly every room is swathed in enough pomegranate-red, $400-a-yard fabrics, swagging, and braided trim to choke a runway of supermodels. A seductive bar with its labyrinth of secluded nooks is *the* place in Paris to be seen trying not to be seen. For taste, many consider this the top Paris hotel, but better wear thick skin: unless you're an off-duty celeb, the army of perfectly coiffed hosts and hostesses has a knack for making you feel underdressed and unimportant. ✉239 *rue St-Honoré, Louvre/Tuileries, 75001* 🕾*01–42–44–50–50* 🖵*01–42–44–50–01* ⊕*www.hotelcostes.com* 🗫*77 rooms, 5 suites* ⟳*In-room: safe, VCR, Wi-Fi. In-hotel: restaurant, room service, bar, pool, parking (fee), some pets allowed* ⊟*AE, DC, MC, V.*

★ $$$$ 🎬 **Hôtel Meurice.** With millions lavished on this famous hotel in recent years by its owner, the Sultan of Brunei, the Meurice sparkles as never before—and that's saying something, since it has welcomed royalty and celebrity since 1835. The restaurant—a fabled extravaganza of cream boiseries and glittering chandeliers—and the elaborately gilded 18th-century Rococo salons cast a spell as they have always done, and who can resist afternoon tea under the Winter Garden's stunning stained-glass ceiling and palm trees. Guest rooms are aswim in Persian carpets, marble mantelpieces, and ormolu clocks and are in either a gilded Louis XVI or Napoleonic-Empire style. Most have a Tuileries/Louvre or Sacré-Coeur view, but the massive Royal Suite takes in a 360-degree panorama (reportedly Paris's only). Baths are marble, with two sinks and deep, spacious tubs. The health club includes grape seed–based Caudalíe treatments, such as "cabernet sauvignon" massages, while children are pampered with their own Meurice teddy bear and tot-size slippers and bathrobe. Every room has complimentary broadband Internet. ✉*228 rue de Rivoli, Louvre/Tuileries, 75001* 🕾*01–44–58–10–10* 🖵*01–44–58–10–15* ⊕*www.meuricehotel.com* 🗫*160 rooms, 36 suites* ⟳*In-room: safe, dial-up. In-hotel: 2 restaurants, room service, bar, gym, concierge, public Internet, no-smoking rooms, some pets allowed* ⊟*AE, DC, MC, V* Ⓜ*Tuileries, Concorde.*

$$$$ 🎬 **Hôtel Ritz.** Festooned with Napoleonic gilt, sparkling crystal chandeliers, and *qualité de Louvre* antiques, this majestic and legendary hotel was founded back in 1896 by Cesar Ritz. Yes, the glamour quotient declines precipitously in the back wing, but even if you get one of the humbler chambers, you could easily spend days without venturing past the main gates, thanks to the hotel's dazzling shops, bars, clubs, and restaurants. There's the luxe Espadon restaurant, which overlooks the prettiest dining courtyard in Paris; the famed Ritz Escoffier cooking school where you can learn the finer points of *gâteaux*; the Cambon Champagne Bar and the famous Hemingway Bar; not to mention the basement health club—a veritable Louis XIV temple of sweat. Kids get a special welcome gift, their own bathrobe and slippers, and can participate in swimming or cooking lessons with bilingual babysitters. ✉*15 pl. Vendôme, Louvre/Tuileries, 75001* 🕾*01–43–16–30–30* 🖵*01–43–16–36–68* ⊕*www.ritzparis.com* 🗫*106 rooms, 56 suites* ⟳*In-room: safe, ethernet, dial-up. In-hotel: 3 restaurants, room service, bars, pool, gym, spa, children's programs (ages 6–12), parking (fee)* ⊟*AE, DC, MC, V* Ⓜ*Opéra.*

$$$$ 🎬 **Hôtel de Vendôme.** With a discreet entrance on the posh Place Vendôme and tiny jewel box of a lobby with inlaid marble and carved mahogany paneling, this hotel has all the comfort and luxury of its

neighboring palace hotels without the ostentatious size. Rooms are handsomely done in French period styles from Louis XIV to Art Deco, with marble baths, antique furnishings, and hand-carved wood detailing throughout. Technical touches include wireless Internet access, flat-screen TVs, and a bedside console that controls the lights, curtains, music, and an electronic DO-NOT-DISTURB sign. The British-style restaurant and bar, decorated with leather chesterfields and wood paneling, hosts a live pianist Thursday through Saturday and presents contemporary French-fusion fare. ☒*1 pl. Vendôme, Louvre/Tuileries, 75001* ☎*01–55–04–55–00* 🖷*01–49–27–97–89* ⊕*www.hoteldevendome. com* 📲*18 rooms, 11 suites* &*In-room: safe, DVD (some), Wi-Fi. In-hotel: restaurant, room service, bar, parking (fee), some pets allowed (fee)* ═*AE, DC, MC, V* Ⓜ*Concorde, Opéra.*

$$$ 🖭 **Hôtel Brighton.** Many of Paris's most prestigious palace hotels face the Tuileries or Place de la Concorde. The Brighton breathes the same rarified air under the arcades for a fraction of the price. Smaller rooms with showers look onto a courtyard; street-facing chambers have balconies and a royal view onto the gardens and the Rive Gauche in the distance. Extensive renovations updated all of the rooms between 2001 and 2004, with the newest ones featuring flat-screen TVs and heated towel racks. The least expensive rooms have windows under the arches along Rue de Rivoli, while the first floor rooms have high ceilings. ☒*218 rue de Rivoli, Louvre/Tuileries, 75001* ☎*01–47–03–61–61* 🖷*01–42–60–41–78* ⊕*www.esprit-de-france.com* 📲*61 rooms* &*In-room: Wi-Fi, safe. In-hotel: laundry service, some pets allowed* ═*AE, DC, MC, V* Ⓜ*Tuileries.*

$$ 🖭 **Hôtel Londres St-Honoré.** An appealing combination of character and comfort distinguishes this small, inexpensive hotel, which is a five-minute walk from the Louvre. Exposed oak beams, statues in niches, and rustic stone walls give this place an old-fashioned air. Though rooms have floral bedspreads and standard hotel furniture, they are pleasant, and the price is right. Note that the elevator only starts on the second floor. ☒*13 rue St-Roch, Louvre/Tuileries, 75001* ☎*01–42–60–15–62* 🖷*01–42–60–16–00* ⊕*www.123france.com* 📲*21 rooms, 4 suites* &*In-room: no a/c (some). In-hotel: public Internet, no-smoking rooms, some pets allowed* ═*AE, DC, MC, V* Ⓜ*Pyramides.*

¢ 🖭 **Hôtel Henri IV.** Princes once made the regal Ile de la Cité their home but even paupers can call it home, thanks to one of Paris's most beloved (and popular) rock-bottom sleeps. Set in a 400-year-old building that once housed Henri IV's printing presses, it has a drab lobby and narrow staircase (five flights, no elevator) but guest rooms wear their age with pride. Nothing beats the top location, set on gorgeous Place Dauphine and just a short stroll to the Louvre and Notre-Dame. Bathrooms are in the hallway; pay a little extra and get a room with a private shower, or reserve room No. 16, the only one with a tub. ☒*25 pl. Dauphine, Ile de la Cité, 75001* ☎*01–43–54–44–53* 📲*20 rooms, 7 with shower/bath* &*In-room: no a/c, no phone, no TV* ═*MC, V* Ⓜ*Cité, St-Michel, Pont Neuf.*

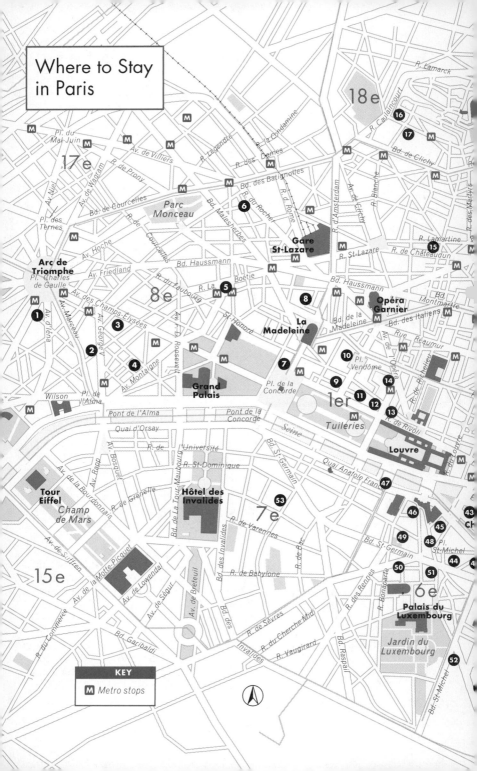

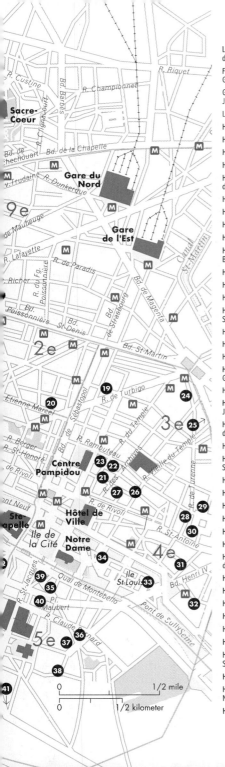

2ᴱ ARRONDISSEMENT (BOURSE/LES HALLES)

¢ 🖼 **Hôtel Tiquetonne.** Just off the Montorgueil market and a short hoof from Les Halles (and the slightly seedy Rue St-Denis), this is one of the least expensive hotels in the city center. The so-old-fashioned-they're-re-vintage rooms aren't much to look at, nor do they offer amenities, but they're always clean and some are downright spacious. Book one of the top two floors facing the quiet, pedestrian Rue Tiquetonne, not the loud, car-strangled Rue Turbigo. ⊠*6 rue Tiquetonne, Beaubourg/Les Halles, 75002* 🏠*01–42–36–94–58* 🖶*01–42–36–02–94* ☎*45 rooms, 33 with bath* ⚷*In-room: no a/c, no TV. In-hotel: some pets allowed* ▭*AE, MC, V* ☉*Closed Aug. and last wk in Dec.* Ⓜ*Étienne Marcel.*

3ᴱ ARRONDISSEMENT (BEAUBOURG/MARAIS)

★ $$$$ 🖼 **Murano Urban Resort.** As the epicenter of Parisian cool migrates east-ward, it's no surprise that a design-conscious hotel has followed. On the trendy northern edge of the Marais, this cheeky hotel that dares to call itself a resort combines Austin Powers playfulness with serious 007-inspired gadgetry. A psychedelic elevator zooms guests to ultraviolet-light hallways, where they enter pristine white rooms via fingerprint sensor locks. White shag carpeting, black-slate bathrooms, pop-art fur-niture, and bedside control panels that change the color of the lighting to keep guests amused until it's time for aperitifs. Two suites have private terraces with heated, countercurrent pools. Stylish Parisians pack the hotel's vodka bar and sleek restaurant, where a live DJ holds court in the elevated booth. ⊠*13 bd. du Temple, République, 75003* 🏠*01–42–71–20–00* 🖶*01–42–71–21–01* ⊕*www.muranoresort.com* ☎*43 rooms, 9 suites* ⚷*In-room: safe, DVD, Wi-Fi. In-hotel: restaurant, room service, bar, pool, gym, spa, concierge, laundry service, parking (fee), some pets allowed* ▭*AE, DC, MC, V* Ⓜ*Filles du Calvaire.*

★ $$$$ 🖼 **Pavillon de la Reine.** The former hangout of the Marais elite—Madame de Sévigné, Racine, La Fontaine, and Molière—this gorgeous Place des Vosges mansion dating from 1612 competes with Ritz-level luxury but on a more intimate scale. *Entrez* through a spectacular courtyard-driveway into a luscious lobby that recalls a royal hunting lodge: massive beams overhead, tapestries, and a salon with the original 300-year-old fireplace. The hotel has large doubles, duplexes, and gen-uine suites decorated in either contemporary or 18th-century-style wall fabrics—modern or historic, make your request known when book-ing. Many rooms look out on the entry court or an interior Japanese-inspired garden. A spiral-posted wooden canopy bed is the centerpiece of Suite 58. There's wireless Internet throughout, and a computer station in the lobby. ⊠*28 pl. des Vosges, Le Marais, 75003* 🏠*01–40–29–19–19, 800/447–7462 in U.S.* 🖶*01–40–29–19–20* ⊕*www.pavillon-de-la-reine.com* ☎*30 rooms, 26 suites* ⚷*In-room: safe, Wi-Fi. In-hotel: room service, bar, parking (no fee), some pets allowed* ▭*AE, DC, MC, V* Ⓜ*Bastille, St-Paul.*

¢ 🖼 **Hôtel Bellevue et du Chariot d'Or.** Here you have a Belle Epoque time traveler, proud to keep its dingy chandeliers and faded gold trimming as is. Budget groups from France and the Netherlands come for the clean but sans-frills rooms; some rooms sleep four. Halls are lined with stamped felt that helps muffle sound trickling up from the spacious marble-floor lobby and bar. There may be some quirks, like the hefty old-fashioned room keys and the bathtub–showers without curtains, but you're just a few blocks from hipper addresses in the heart of the Marais. ⊠*39 rue de Turbigo, Beaubourg/Les Halles, 75003* ☎*01–48–87–45–60* 🖶*01–48–87–95–04* ⊕*www.hotelbellevue75.com* ➟*59 rooms* ⅍*In-room: no a/c. In-hotel: bar* ⊟*AE, DC, MC, V* ⦿*BP* Ⓜ*Réaumur-Sébastopol, Arts et Métiers.*

4ᴱ ARRONDISSEMENT (MARAIS/ILE ST-LOUIS)

$$$$ 🏨 **Hôtel du Jeu de Paume.** Set off the street by heavy doors and a small courtyard, this unique hotel on Ile St-Louis has been built within the stone walls and wooden beams of a 17th-century court where French aristocrats once played *jeu de paume,* an early version of tennis. The lounge bar and breakfast room, decorated with both contemporary and antique artworks, allow the best views of this amazing architecture. The rooms themselves are modern, with wood or tile floors, basic furnishings, small closets, and tiled bathrooms. Some bilevel rooms have narrow spiral staircases. Bonuses include Annick Goutal toiletries and, on the upper floors, ceiling fans. Superior rooms and suites open onto a sunny garden patio. ⊠*54 rue St-Louis-en-l'Ile, Ile St-Louis, 75004* ☎*01–43–26–14–18* 🖶*01–40–46–02–76* ⊕*www.jeudepaumehotel. com* ➟*23 rooms, 5 suites* ⅍*In-room: no a/c, safe. In-hotel: bar, public Internet, some pets allowed* ⊟*AE, DC, MC, V* Ⓜ*Pont Marie.*

★ **$$$–$$$$** 🏨 **Hôtel Bourg Tibourg.** Scented candles and subdued lighting announce the designer-du-jour Jacques Garcia's theatrical mix of haremlike romance and Gothic contemplation. Royal blue paint and red velvet line the claustrophobic halls. The rooms are barely bigger than the beds, and every inch has been upholstered, tasseled, and draped in a cacophony of stripes, florals, and medieval motifs; Byzantine alcoves hold mosaic-tiled tubs. A pocket-size garden has room for three tables, leafy plants, and a swath of stars above. ⊠*19 rue Bourg Tibourg, Le Marais, 75004* ☎*01–42–78–47–39* 🖶*01–40–29–07–00* ⊕*www. hotelbourgtibourg.com* ➟*29 rooms, 1 suite* ⅍*In-room: safe, refrigerator, Wi-Fi* ⊟*AE, DC, MC, V* Ⓜ*Hôtel de Ville.*

$$$ 🏨 **Hôtel Saint Merry.** Due south of the Pompidou Center is this small
Fodor'sChoice and stunning Gothic hideaway, once the presbytery of the adjacent
★ Saint Merry church. In its 17th-century stone interior you can gaze through stained glass, relax on a church pew, or lean back on a headboard recycled from an old Catholic confessional. With a massive hardwood table, fireplace, and high ceiling, the suite is fit for a royal council. Room 9 is bisected by stone buttresses still supporting the church. The Saint Merry's lack of an elevator and 21st-century temptations like TV is also in keeping with its ascetic past (and keeps the place monkishly quiet). ⊠*78 rue de la Verrerie, Beaubourg/Les Halles, 75004* ☎*01–42–78–14–15* 🖶*01–40–29–06–82* ⊕*www.hotelmarais. com* ➟*11 rooms, 1 suite* ⅍*In-room: no a/c, safe, no TV (some). In-hotel: room service, some pets allowed* ⊟*MC, V* Ⓜ*Châtelet.*

★ **$$–$$$** 🏨 **Hôtel Caron de Beaumarchais.** The theme of this intimate hotel is the work of former next-door neighbor Pierre-Augustin Caron de Beaumarchais, supplier of military aid to American revolutionaries and author of *The Marriage of Figaro.* First-edition copies of his books adorn the public spaces, and the salons faithfully reflect the taste of 18th-century French nobility, right down to the wallpaper and 1792 pianoforte. Richly decorated with floral fabrics and white wooden period furnishings, the rooms have original wooden beams, hand-painted bathroom tiles, and gilded mirrors. All rooms have flat-screen TVs and wireless Internet access. ⊠*12 rue Vieille-du-Temple, Le Marais, 75004* ☎*01–42–72–34–12* 🖷*01–42–72–34–63* ⊕*www. carondebeaumarchais.com* ↩*19 rooms* ₳*In-room: safe, refrigerator, dial-up, Wi-Fi* ⊟*AE, DC, MC, V* Ⓜ*Hôtel de Ville.*

$$–$$$ 🖳 **Hôtel Saint Louis.** Louis XIII–style furniture, oil paintings, exposed beams, bare stone, and various antiques invite speculation about which duke may have owned this 17th-century building on the coveted Ile St-Louis. Minibalconies on the upper levels also have Seine views. Number 51 has a tear-shape tub and a peek at the Panthéon. Breakfast is served in the vaulted stone cellar. ⊠*75 rue St-Louis-en-l'Ile, Ile St-Louis, 75004* ☎*01–46–34–04–80* 🖷*01–46–34–02–13* ⊕*www. hotelsaintlouis.com* ↩*19 rooms* ₳*In-room: safe. In-hotel: some pets allowed* ⊟*MC, V* Ⓜ*Pont Marie.*

$$–$$$ 🖳 **Hôtel Saint-Louis Marais.** Once an annex to a local convent, this 18th-century hotel has retained its stone walls and beams while adding red-clay tile floors and antiques. A wooden-banistered stair leads to the small but proper rooms, decorated with basic red carpet and green bed-spreads. (Those with heavy luggage, beware: no elevator.) One room is equipped with a kitchenette. The hotel's in Village St-Paul, a little tangle of medieval lanes just south of the well-traveled Marais that has an excellent English-language bookstore and is not yet overrun by tourists. ⊠*1 rue Charles V, Le Marais, 75004* ☎*01–48–87–87–04* 🖷*01–48–87–33–26* ⊕*www.saintlouismarais.com* ↩*20 rooms* ₳*In-room: no a/c, safe, dial-up, Wi-Fi. In-hotel: public Internet, some pets allowed* ⊟*DC, MC, V* Ⓜ*Sully Morland, Bastille.*

$$ 🖳 **Hôtel de la Bretonnerie.** This small hotel is in a 17th-century *hôtel particulier* (town house) on a tiny street in the Marais, a few minutes' walk from the Centre Pompidou and the bars and cafés of Rue Vieille du Temple. Rooms are classified as either *chambres classiques* or *chambres de charme*, the latter being more spacious, and naturally pricier, but with more elaborate furnishings, like Louis XIII–style four-poster canopy beds and marble-clad bathtubs. Overall, the establishment is spotless, and the staff is welcoming. A computer station in the lobby is available for Internet access. ⊠*22 rue Ste-Croix-de-la-Bretonnerie, Le Marais, 75004* ☎*01–48–87–77–63* 🖷*01–42–77–26–78* ⊕*www. bretonnerie.com* ↩*22 rooms, 7 suites* ₳*In-room: no a/c, safe, refrigerator. In-hotel: public Internet* ⊟*MC, V* Ⓜ*Hôtel de Ville.*

$$ 🖳 **Hôtel de la Place des Vosges.** Despite a lack of some expected comforts and an elevator that doesn't serve all floors, a loyal clientele swears by this small, historic hotel on a street leading directly into Place des Vosges. The Louis XIII–style reception area and rooms with oak-beam ceilings, rough-hewn stone, and a mix of rustic finds from second-hand shops evoke the Old Marais. The lone top-floor room, the hotel's largest, has a Jacuzzi and a view over Rive Droite rooftops. Other, considerably smaller rooms are cheaper. All rooms have duvet com-

forters, and some are equipped with flat-screen TVs or invigorating multijet showers. Fans are provided in summer. ⊠ *12 rue de Birague, Le Marais, 75004* 🕾*01–42–72–60–46* 🖷*01–42–72–02–64* ⊕*www. hotelplacedesvosges.com* ⤣*16 rooms* ♿*In-room: no a/c, safe, Wi-Fi* ⊟*AE, DC, MC, V* Ⓜ*Bastille.*

$$ 🏨 **Hôtel du Vieux Marais.** A great value for the money in one of the most popular neighborhoods in Paris, this pleasingly minimalist hotel with a turn-of-the-20th-century facade is on a quiet street in the heart of the Marais. Rooms are bright and impeccably clean, with contemporary oak furnishings, burgundy-leather seating, and velour curtains. Bathrooms are immaculately tiled in Italian marble, with walk-in showers or combination shower/bathtub. The staff is exceptionally friendly, and the lobby has Wi-Fi access. ⊠ *8 rue du Plâtre, Le Marais, 75004* 🕾*01–42–78–47–22* 🖷*01–42–78–34–32* ⊕*www.vieuxmarais.com* ⤣*30 rooms* ♿*In-room: safe, Wi-Fi* ⊟*MC, V* Ⓜ*Hôtel de Ville.*

★ $ 🏨 **Grand Hôtel Jeanne-d'Arc.** You can get your money's worth at this hotel in an unbeatable location off the tranquil Place du Marché Ste-Catherine, one of the city's lesser-known pedestrian squares. The 17th-century building has been a hotel for more than a century, and although rooms are on the spartan side they're well maintained, with spotless tiled bathrooms and cheery, if somewhat mismatched, colors (back rooms are dimmer). The welcoming staff is informal and happy to recount the history of this former market quartier. ⊠ *3 rue de Jarente, Le Marais, 75004* 🕾*01–48–87–62–11* 🖷*01–48–87–37–31* ⊕*www. hoteljeannedarc.com* ⤣*36 rooms* ♿*In-room: no a/c. In-hotel: some pets allowed* ⊟*MC, V* Ⓜ*St-Paul.*

5ᴱ ARRONDISSEMENT (LATIN QUARTER)

★ $$–$$$ 🏨 **Les Degrés de Notre Dame.** On a quiet street a few yards from the Seine, this cozy budget hotel is lovingly decorated with the owner's flea-market finds. The most expensive room, 501, occupies the entire top floor, with views of Notre Dame and room for four. There's no elevator, but colorful murals of Parisian scenes decorate the winding stairwell. The restaurant–bar, frequented by local Parisians, serves French and North-African specialties and has a large sidewalk terrace. ⊠ *10 rue des Grands Degrés, Quartier Latin, 75005* 🕾*01–55–24–88–88* 🖷*01–40–46–95–34* ⊕*www.lesdegreshotel.com* ⤣*10 rooms* ♿*In-room: no a/c, safe. In-hotel: restaurant, bar, no kids under 12* ⊟*MC, V* �Ⓞⅼ*BP* Ⓜ*Maubert-Mutualité.*

$$ 🏨 **Hôtel Grandes Écoles.** Guests enter Madame Lefloch's country-style domain through two massive wooden doors. Distributed among a trio of three-story buildings, rooms have a distinct grandmotherly vibe with their flowery wallpaper and lace bedspreads, but are downright spacious for this part of Paris. And the Grandes Écoles is legendary for its stunning interior cobbled courtyard and garden, which becomes the second living room and a perfect breakfast spot when *il fait beau*. Rooms in the "garden" wing are coolest in summer. ⊠ *75 rue du Cardinal Lemoine, Quartier Latin, 75005* 🕾*01–43–26–79–23* 🖷*01–43–25–28–15* ⊕*www.hotel-grandes-ecoles.com* ⤣*51 rooms* ♿*In-room: no a/c, no TV. In-hotel: room service, parking (fee), some pets allowed* ⊟*MC, V* Ⓜ*Cardinal Lemoine.*

★ $$ ⊞ **Hôtel des Jardins du Luxembourg.** Blessed with a personable staff and a smart, stylish look, this hotel, on an unbelievably calm cul-de-sac just a block from the Luxembourg Gardens, is an oasis for contemplation—even Freud stayed here for six weeks during the winter of 1885–86. A cheery hardwood-floor lobby with fireplace leads to smallish rooms furnished with wrought-iron beds, puffy duvets, contemporary bathrooms, and equally contemporary Provençal fabrics. Ask for one with a balcony, or request one of the larger ground-floor rooms with private entrance directly onto the street. A hot buffet is served in the cheerful breakfast room. It's also an easy commute to either airport or the Eurostar via the RER train that stops at the end of the street. ⊠*5 impasse Royer-Collard, Quartier Latin, 75005* ☏*01–40–46–08–88* 🖶*01–40–46–02–28* ⊕*www.les-jardins-du-luxembourg.com* ⇦*26 rooms* ♿*In-room: safe, refrigerator, Wi-Fi* ▭*AE, DC, MC, V* Ⓜ*RER: Luxembourg.*

$–$$ ⊞ **Hôtel Familia.** Owners Eric and Sylvie continue to update and improve their popular budget hotel without raising the prices. They've added custom-carved wooden furniture from Brittany, new carpeting, and antique tapestries and prints on the walls. The second and fifth floors have balconies (some with views of Notre-Dame) and all of the rooms are perfectly soundproof from traffic below. Their slightly more expensive sister hotel next door, the Minerve, offers the added luxury of air-conditioning. ⊠*11 rue des Ecoles, Quartier Latin, 75005* ☏*01–43–54–55–27* 🖶*01–43–29–61–77* ⊕*www.hotel-paris-familia.com* ⇦*30 rooms* ♿*In-room: no a/c. In-hotel: laundry service, concierge, public WiFi, parking (fee)* ▭*AE, DC, MC, V* Ⓜ*Cardinal-Lemoine.*

★ $–$$ ⊞ **Hôtel Minerve.** Fans of the Gaucheron family will be delighted to learn that the Minerve is now part of the Familia fold. Just next door to the Familia, and twice as big, the hotel has been completely refurbished in the inimitable Gaucheron style: flowers and breakfast tables on the balconies, frescoes in the spacious lobby, tapestries on the walls, and cherrywood furniture in the rooms. It's less intimate than the Familia—but just as charming. ⊠*13 rue des Écoles, Quartier Latin, 75005* ☏*01–43–26–26–04* 🖶*01–44–07–01–96* ⊕*www.hotel-paris-minerve.com* ⇦*54 rooms* ♿*In-room: no a/c, dial-up* ▭*AE, MC, V* ⍐*BP* Ⓜ*Cardinal Lemoine.*

★ $–$$ ⊞ **Hôtel Saint-Jacques.** Nearly every wall in this bargain hotel is bedecked with faux-marble and trompe-l'oeil murals. As in many old and independent Paris hotels, each room is unique, but a general 19th-century theme of Empire furnishings and paintings dominates, with a Montmartre cabaret theme in the new breakfast room that includes a player piano. Wireless Internet is available in the lounge bar. About half the rooms have tiny step-out balconies that give a glimpse of Notre-Dame and the Panthéon. Room 25 has a round-the-corner balcony; Room 16 is popular for its historic ceiling fresco and moldings. Repeat guests get souvenir knickknacks or T-shirts. ⊠*35 rue des Écoles, Quartier Latin, 75005* ☏*01–44–07–45–45* 🖶*01–43–25–65–50* ⊕*www.hotel-saintjacques.com* ⇦*38 rooms* ♿*In-room: no a/c, safe. In-hotel: Wi-Fi* ▭*AE, DC, MC, V* Ⓜ*Maubert Mutualité.*

$ **Hôtel Esméralda.** A Parisian flea market meets the Renaissance at this legendary shabby-chic hotel with superior views of Notre-Dame if you're lucky enough to get a front room. A vertiginous, ancient spiral staircase (no elevator) leads to a rabbit warren of low corridors, mismatched doors, and even funkier decor. Some rooms surprise with their marble fireplaces and chandeliers; others could be cleaner. The Esméralda's foyer may be its highlight: wood-beamed, strewn with art and tapestries, with classical music playing, it's right out of Flaubert's *Madame Bovary.* You'll decide whether it's "Paris charm" or "low-cost chaos." ⊠4 *rue St-Julien-le-Pauvre, Quartier Latin, 75005* ☎*01–43–54–19–20* 🖷*01–40–51–00–68* ⇖*19 rooms, 15 with bath* ♿*In-room: no a/c, no TV. In-hotel: some pets allowed* ⊟*No credit cards* Ⓜ*St-Michel.*

☾ ¢–$ **Hôtel Marignan.** Paul Keniger, the energetic third-generation owner, has cultivated a convivial atmosphere here for independent international travelers. The Marignan lies squarely between no-star and youth hostel (no TVs or elevator) and offers lots of communal conveniences—a fully stocked and accessible kitchen, free laundry machines, and copious tourist information. Rooms are modest (some sleeping four or five) but have firm mattresses and clean bathrooms. The least expensive rooms share toilets and/or showers with one other room on the same floor. Room phones only take incoming calls. ⊠*13 rue du Sommerard, Quartier Latin, 75005* ☎*01–43–54–63–81* 🖷*01–43–25–16–69* ⊕*www.hotel-marignan.com* ⇖*30 rooms, 12 with bath* ♿*In-room: no a/c, kitchen, no TV. In-hotel: laundry facilities* ⊟*MC, V* Ⓜ*Maubert Mutualité.*

★ ¢   **Port-Royal Hôtel.** The spotless rooms and extra-helpful staff at the Port-Royal are well above average for this price range. Just below the Rue Mouffetard market at the edge of the 13e arrondissement, it may be somewhat removed from the action, but the snug antiques-furnished lounge areas, garden courtyard, and rooms with wrought-iron beds, mirrors, and armoires make it worth the trip. Rooms at the lower end of the price range are equipped only with sinks (an immaculate shared shower room is in the hallway). ⊠*8 bd. de Port-Royal, Les Gobelins, 75005* ☎*01–43–31–70–06* 🖷*01–43–31–33–67* ⇖*46 rooms, 20 with bath/shower* ♿*In-room: no a/c, no TV* ⊟*No credit cards* Ⓜ*Les Gobelins.*

6^E ARRONDISSEMENT (ST-GERMAIN)

$$$$ **L'Hôtel.** Rock stars love this eccentric and opulent boutique hotel, and

Fodor's Choice   we can see why. Though sophisticated in every way, there's something

★   just a bit naughty in the air. Is it its history as an 18th-century *pavillion d'amour* (inn for trysts)? Is it that Oscar Wilde permanently checked out in Room 16, back in 1900? Or is it Jacques Garcia's makeover—rooms done in yards of thick, rich fabrics in colors like deep red and emerald green? All of the above. And the intimate bar and restaurant allow guests to mingle with the Parisian *beau-monde.* The only complaint? Snug rooms. A skylight tops a circular atrium; a grotto holds a countercurrent pool and a steam room. ⊠*13 rue des Beaux-Arts, St-Germain-des-Prés, 75006* ☎*01–44–41–99–00* 🖷*01–43–25–64–81* ⊕*www.l-hotel.com* ⇖*16 rooms, 4 suites* ♿*In-room: safe, Wi-Fi. In-*

hotel: restaurant, room service, bar, pool, laundry service, some pets allowed ☐*AE, DC, MC, V* Ⓜ*St-Germain-des-Prés.*

$$$$ ⚟ **Hôtel d'Aubusson.** Dapper in their pinstripe suits, the staff greets you
Fodor'sChoice warmly at this 17th-century town house and former literary salon. The
★ showpiece is the stunning salon spanned by massive beams and headed
by a gigantic fireplace. Decked out in rich burgundies, greens, or blues,
the bedrooms are filled with Louis XV– and Regency-style antiques
and have Hermès toiletries; even the smallest rooms are a good size by
Paris standards. Behind the paved courtyard (where in warmer weather
you can have your breakfast or predinner drink) there's a second structure with three apartments handy for families. The Café Laurent café–
piano bar hosts jazz three time per week. All returning guests (and new
guests who book at least four days) get special V.I.P. treatment such as
champagne and flowers on arrival. ☒*33 rue Dauphine, St-Germain-
des-Prés, 75006* ☎*01–43–29–43–43* ☐*01–43–29–12–62* ⊕*www.
hoteldaubusson.com* ⚟*49 rooms* ☾*In-room: safe, DVD (some), dial-
up, Wi-Fi. In-hotel: room service, bar, public Internet, parking (fee),
no-smoking rooms, some pets allowed, public Internet* ☐*AE, DC,
MC, V* Ⓜ*Odéon.*

★ **$$$$** ⚟ **Le Relais Christine.** This exquisite property was once a 13th-century
abbey, but don't expect monkish quarters. You enter from the impressive stone courtyard into a lobby and fireside honor bar done up in rich
fabrics, stone, wood paneling, and antiques. The cavernous breakfast
room and adjacent fitness center flaunt their vaulted medieval stonework. The spacious, high-ceilinged rooms (many spanned by massive
beams) offer a variety of classical and contemporary styles: Asian-theme
wall fabrics or plain stripes, rich aubergine paints or regal scarlet-and-
gold. Split-level lofts house up to five people, and several ground-level
rooms open onto a lush garden with private patios and heaters. ☒*3 rue
Christine, St-Germain-des-Prés, 75006* ☎*01–40–51–60–80, 800/525–
4800 in U.S.* ☐*01–40–51–60–81* ⊕*www.relais-christine.com* ⚟*33
rooms, 18 suites* ☾*In-room: safe, DVD (some), dial-up. In-hotel: room
service, parking (no fee), no-smoking rooms, some pets allowed* ☐*AE,
DC, MC, V* Ⓜ*Odéon.*

$$$ ⚟ **Hôtel de Fleurie.** On a quiet side street near Place de l'Odéon, a series
of statues set into the facade invite you into this spiffy, super-pretty,
family-run hotel. Antiques, Oriental rugs, and rich upholsteries fill the
18th-century building. The warm-color rooms, mostly done in yellows
with wood paneling and checked drapes, include amenities such as
heated towel racks in the bathroom. The location is ideal: equidistant
from the Seine and the Jardin du Luxembourg. ☒*32–34 rue Grégoire-
de-Tours, St-Germain-des-Prés, 75006* ☎*01–53–73–70–00* ☐*01–
53–73–70–20* ⊕*www.hotel-de-fleurie.tm.fr* ⚟*29 rooms* ☾*In-room:
dial-up. In-hotel: bar, public Internet* ☐*AE, DC, MC, V* Ⓜ*Odéon.*

$$$ ⚟ **Hôtel Millésime.** Step through the doors of this St-Germain-des-Prés
hotel and you can find yourself transported to the sunny south of
France. Rooms are decorated in warm reds, yellows, and royal blues
with rich fabrics, padded headboards, and sparkling tiled bathrooms.
The centerpiece is the gorgeous Provençal-style courtyard with ocher
walls and wrought-iron balconies (Room 15 has direct access). Friendly

service and a bountiful buffet breakfast make this a fine find. ✉ *15 Rue Jacob, St-Germain-des-Prés, 75006* ☎ *01–44–07–97–97* 🖷 *01–46–34–55–97* ⊕ *www.millesimehotel.com* ⚑ *22 rooms* ⚷ *In-room: safe, Wi-Fi. In-hotel: room service, bar, public Internet, some pets allowed* ▤ *AE, MC, V* Ⓜ *St-Germain-des-Prés.*

\$\$–\$\$\$ 🖾 **Hôtel Bonaparte.** The congeniality of the staff only makes a stay in this intimate place more of a treat. Old-fashioned upholsteries, 19th-century furnishings, and paintings make the relatively spacious rooms feel comfortable and unpretentious. Rooms have empty refrigerators; you're invited to stock them with drinks and snacks. Facilities may be basic, but the location in the heart of St-Germain about 30 steps from Place St-Sulpice is nothing short of fabulous. Light sleepers should request rooms overlooking the courtyard. ✉ *61 rue Bonaparte, St-Germain-des-Prés, 75006* ☎ *01–43–26–97–37* 🖷 *01–46–33–57–67* ⚑ *29 rooms* ⚷ *In-room: safe, refrigerator* ▤ *MC, V* ❍❘*BP* Ⓜ *St-Sulpice.*

\$\$ 🖾 **Hôtel du Lys.** To jump into an inexpensive Parisian fantasy, just climb the convoluted stairway to your room (there's no elevator) in this former 17th-century royal residence. Well maintained by Madame Steffen, the oddly shaped guest rooms have tiny nooks, weathered antiques, and exposed beams throughout. Breakfast is served in the lobby or in your room. It may be modest, but it's extremely atmospheric. ✉ *23 rue Serpente, Quartier Latin, 75006* ☎ *01–43–26–97–57* 🖷 *01–44–07–34–90* ⊕ *www.hoteldulys.com* ⚑ *22 rooms* ⚷ *In-room: no a/c, safe. In-hotel: some pets allowed* ▤ *MC, V* ❍❘*BP* Ⓜ *St-Michel, Odéon.*

★ \$ 🖾 **Hôtel de Nesle.** This one-of-a-kind budget hotel is like a quirky and enchanting dollhouse. The facilities are bare-bones—no elevator, phones, or breakfast—but the payoff is in the petite rooms cleverly decorated by theme. Sleep in Notre-Dame de Paris, lounge in an Asian-style boudoir, spend the night with writer Molière, or steam it up in Le Hammam. Decorations include colorful murals, canopy beds, custom lamps, and clay tiles. Most rooms overlook an interior garden, and the dead-end street location keeps the hotel relatively quiet. If you book one of the rooms without a shower, you'll have to share the one on the second floor. ✉ *7 rue de Nesle, St-Germain-des-Prés, 75006* ☎ *01–43–54–62–41* 🖷 *01–43–54–31–88* ⊕ *www.hoteldenesleparis.com* ⚑ *20 rooms, 9 with bath* ⚷ *In-room: no a/c, no phone, no TV. In-hotel: no-smoking rooms, some pets allowed* ▤ *MC, V* Ⓜ *Odéon.*

7ᴱ ARRONDISSEMENT (TOUR EIFFEL/INVALIDES)

★ \$\$\$\$ 🖾 **Hôtel Duc de Saint-Simon.** If it's good enough for the notoriously choosy Lauren Bacall, you'll probably fall for the Duc's charms, too. Its hidden location between Boulevard St-Germain and Rue du Bac is one plus; another is the shady courtyard entry. Rooms in shades of yellow, green, pink, and blue teem with antiques and countrified floral and striped fabrics. Four rooms have spacious terraces overlooking the courtyard and the drooping wisteria. The 16th-century basement lounge is a warren of stone alcoves with a zinc bar and plush seating. To keep the peace, parents are discouraged from bringing children along. ✉ *14 rue St-Simon, St-Germain-des-Prés, 75007* ☎ *01–44–39–20–20* 🖷 *01–45–48–68–25* ⊕ *www.hotelducdesaintsimon.com* ⚑ *29 rooms,*

5 suites ♨ *In-room: no a/c (some), safe, ethernet, dial-up. In-hotel: bar, parking (fee), no kids* ⊟ *AE, DC, MC, V* Ⓜ *Rue du Bac.*

$$ 🛏 **Hôtel Verneuil.** Set near the Seine, the Verneuil is just across the street from the former home of famed French songster Serge Gainsbourg. Guest rooms may be more petite than you'd hoped for, but each is painstakingly decorated. The white-cotton quilts on the beds, framed pressed flowers on the walls, and faux-marble trompe-l'oeil trim work and stained-glass windows in the hall make you feel you've arrived at *chez grandmère.* ⊠ *8 rue de Verneuil, St-Germain-des-Prés, 75007* ☏ *01–42–60–83–14* 🖷 *01–42–61–40–38* ⊕ *www.hotelverneuil.com* ➳ *26 rooms* ♨ *In-room: no a/c (some), safe, Wi-Fi. In-hotel: bar, public Internet, some pets allowed (fee)* Ⓜ *RER: Musée d'Orsay.*

8ᴱ ARRONDISSEMENT (CHAMPS-ÉLYSÉES)

$$$$ 🛏 **Four Seasons Hôtel George V Paris.** The George V is as poised and pol-
Fodor'sChoice   ished as the day it opened in 1928: the original Art Deco detailing and
★   17th-century tapestries have been restored, the bas-reliefs regilded, the marble-floor mosaics rebuilt tile by tile. Rooms are decked in fabrics and Louis XVI trimmings but have homey touches like selections of CDs and French books. Le Cinq restaurant is one of Paris's hottest tables, and a newly opened business center has six fully equipped working stations with computers and printers. The low-lighted spa and fitness center pampers guests with 11 treatment rooms, walls covered in *toile de Jouy* fabrics, and an indoor swimming pool evoking Marie-Antoinette's Versailles. A relaxation room is available for guests who arrive before their rooms are ready. Even children get the four-star treatment with personalized T-shirts and portable DVD players to distract them at dinnertime. ⊠ *31 av. George V, Champs-Elysées, 75008* ☏ *01–49–52–70–00, 800/332–3442 in U.S.* 🖷 *01–49–52–70–10* ⊕ *www.fourseasons.com/paris* ➳ *184 rooms, 61 suites* ♨ *In-room: safe, kitchen (some), DVD, ethernet. In-hotel: 2 restaurants, room service, bar, pool, gym, spa, concierge, children's programs (ages 1–12), laundry service, airport shuttle, some pets allowed* ⊟ *AE, DC, MC, V* Ⓜ *George V.*

$$$$ 🛏 **Hôtel de Crillon.** Home away from home for movie stars and off-duty celebrities, the Crillon has long been one of Paris's greatest hotels. It began life as a regal palace designed for Louis XV in 1758 by Jacques-Ange Gabriel to preside over the north side of the fabled Place de la Concorde. In 1909 it became a hostelry and since then has played host to generations of diplomats and refined travelers. Most rooms are lavishly decorated with Rococo and Directoire antiques, crystal-and-gilt wall sconces, and gilt fittings. The sheer quantity of marble downstairs—especially in the highly praised Les Ambassadeurs restaurant—is staggering. ⊠ *10 pl. de la Concorde, Champs-Élysées, 75008* ☏ *01–44–71–15–00, 800/888–4747 in U.S.* 🖷 *01–44–71–15–02* ⊕ *www.crillon.com* ➳ *90 rooms, 57 suites* ♨ *In-room: safe, dial-up. In-hotel: 2 restaurants, room service, bars, gym, spa, children's programs (ages 6–12), no-smoking rooms, public Internet* ⊟ *AE, DC, MC, V* Ⓜ *Concorde.*

★ **$$$$**   🛏 **Hôtel Plaza-Athenée.** Prime-time stardom as Carrie Bradshaw's Parisian pied-à-terre in the final episodes of *Sex & the City* may have boosted the street cred of this 1911 palace hotel, but its revival as the city's last word in luxury owes more to the meticulous attention of the renowned chef Alain Ducasse, who overlooks everything from the hotel's flagship restaurant and restored 1930s Relais Plaza brasserie to the quality of the croissants served at breakfast. You can choose your preferred guest-room look; each accommodation has been redone in either Regency, Louis XVI, or Deco style, with remote control air-conditioning, mini-hi-fi/CD players, and even a pillow menu. May to September, all guests repair to the gorgeously red-parasoled Cour Jardin since this courtyard restaurant has long been one of the prettiest sights in Paris. Interact with the unflagging energy of the 460 staff members and you can see why the Athenée continues to be the choice of the Jagger-Paltrow set. ⊠25 av. Montaigne, Champs-Élysées, 75008 ☎01–53–67–66–65, 866/732–1106 in U.S. ⎕01–53–67–66–66 ⊕www.plaza-athenee-paris.com ↩145 rooms, 43 suites ⬩In-room: safe, DVD, dial-up. In-hotel: 3 restaurants, room service, bar, no-smoking rooms, some pets allowed ⊟AE, DC, MC, V Ⓜ Alma-Marceau.

$$$$ 🏨 **Hôtel Relais Monceau.** The Royal Monceau entered 2005 remodeled and restyled by in-demand hotel designer Jacques Garcia. The grand lobby feels intimate with pale turquoise walls and deep, gold-and-green velour sofas and chairs. The hotel's Sicilian Carpaccio Restaurant captures the sexy feel of an Italian palazzo. Mirrored tiles and burgundy velour dominate the maharaja-style Royal's Bar. Rooms have been enlarged and outfitted with taffeta, velour, and silk in gold, royal blue, copper, or deep purple. Cabinets containing CD/DVD players and fax/printer/scanners are disguised behind discreet screens. The indoor swimming pool is as divine, and new massage treatments have an Asian influence. ⊠37 av. Hoche, Champs-Élysées, 75008 ☎01–42–99–88–00 ⎕01–42–99–89–90 ⊕www.royalmonceau.com ↩124 rooms, 56 suites ⬩In-room: safe, DVD, Wi-Fi. In-hotel: 2 restaurants, room service, bar, pool, gym, concierge, laundry service, parking (fee) ⊟AE, DC, MC, V Ⓜ Charles-de-Gaulle-Etoile/Ternes.

$$$$ 🏨 **Pershing Hall.** Formerly an American Legion hall, this circa-2001 boutique hotel designed by Andrée Putman champions masculine minimalism, with muted surfaces of wood and stone and even cooler attitudes to match. Rooms have stark-white linens, triptych dressing mirrors, slender tubelike lamps, and tubs perched on round marble bases. The only trace of lightheartedness is the free minibars. All deluxe rooms and suites face the courtyard dining room whose west wall is a six-story hanging garden with 300 varieties of plants. The lounge bar serves drinks, dinner, and DJ-driven music until 2 AM. ⊠49 rue Pierre Charron, Champs-Élysées, 75008 ☎01–58–36–58–00 ⎕01–58–36–58–01 ⊕www.pershinghall.com ↩20 rooms, 6 suites ⬩In-room: safe, DVD, ethernet, dial-up, Wi-Fi. In-hotel: restaurant, room service, bar, some pets allowed ⊟AE, DC, MC, V Ⓜ George-V, Franklin-D.-Roosevelt.

$$$ 🏨 **Hôtel Queen Mary.** A warm welcome (and a gentle price tag) awaits you at this cheerfully elegant hotel, set just two blocks from the Place de la Madeleine and Paris's famous department stores. Sunny yellow walls, fabrics in burgundy, gold, and royal blue, and plush carpeting throughout soften the historic architectural detailing and high ceilings. Rooms are nicely appointed with large beds, and thoughtful extras like

trouser presses, Roger & Gallet toiletries, and complimentary decanters of sherry. Guests mingle in the bar during happy hour, and breakfast can be served in the enchantingly trellised garden courtyard in summer. ✉*9 rue Greffulhe, Opéra/Grands Boulevards, 75008* ☎*01–42–66–40–50* 🖷*01–42–66–94–92* ⊕*www.hotelqueenmary.com* ↩*35 rooms, 1 suite* ♿*In-room: safe, dial-up, Wi-Fi. In-hotel: room service, bar, some pets allowed* ▭*MC, V* Ⓜ*Madeleine.*

$$ 🖼 **Hôtel d'Albion.** The modestly stylish Albion reveals an eclectic taste in art. The halls are hung with children's-book illustrations, while African art decorates guest-room doors. The cheerful lobby meanders around to a small breakfast area and even smaller outdoor garden terrace. Apricot and beige predominate in the snug and simply furnished rooms, whose details hint at particular themes: music (with framed sheet-music collages) or theater (comedy–tragedy mask motifs). The staff may be lackadaisical, but this is a rare cheap sleep with character in an otherwise budget-busting neighborhood. ✉*15 rue de Penthièvre, Champs-Élysées, 75008* ☎*01–42–65–84–15* 🖷*01–49–24–03–47* ⊕*www.hotelalbion.net* ↩*22 rooms, 4 suites* ♿*In-room: no a/c, safe, dial-up. In-hotel: restaurant, room service, laundry service* ▭*AE, DC, MC, V* Ⓜ*Miromesnil.*

9ᴱ ARRONDISSEMENT (OPÉRA)

$$
Fodor'sChoice
★

🖼 **Hôtel Langlois.** After starring in *The Truth About Charlie* (a remake of *Charade*), this darling hotel gained a reputation as one of the most atmospheric budget sleeps in the city. Rates have crept up, but the former circa-1870 bank retains its beautiful wood-paneled reception area and wrought-iron elevator. The individually decorated and spacious rooms are decked out with original glazed-tile fireplaces and period art. Some rooms, such as Nos. 15, 21, and 41, have enormous retro bathrooms. Street-facing rooms can be noisy, but the top-floor views over the rooftops make up for it. ✉*63 rue St-Lazare, Opéra/Grands Boulevards, 75009* ☎*01–48–74–78–24* 🖷*01–49–95–04–43* ⊕*www.hotel-langlois.com* ↩*24 rooms, 3 suites* ♿*In-hotel: public Internet, some pets allowed* ▭*AE, MC, V* Ⓜ*Trinité.*

$ 🖼 **Hôtel Chopin.** At the end of the passage Jouffroy—one of the many glass-roof shopping arcades built in Paris in the early 19th century—the Chopin recalls its 1846 birth date with a creaky-floored lobby and aged woodwork. The basic but comfortable rooms overlook the arcade's quaint boutiques or the rooftops of Paris. The decor leans heavily toward salmon walls and green carpets, but rooms on the first and second floors have blue toile de Jouy prints. The best rooms end in 7 (No. 407 overlooks the Grevin waxwork museum's ateliers), while the cheapest are the smaller rooms ending with a 2. ✉*10 bd. Montmartre, 46 passage Jouffroy, Opéra/Grands Boulevards, 75009* ☎*01–47–70–58–10* 🖷*01–42–47–00–70* ↩*36 rooms* ♿*In-room: no a/c, safe* ▭*AE, MC, V* Ⓜ*Grands Boulevards.*

11ᴱ ARRONDISSEMENT (BASTILLE)

$$ 🖼 **Hôtel Beaumarchais.** This bold hotel straddles the fashionable Marais district in the 3ᵉ and the hip student and artist neighborhood of Oberkampf in the 11ᵉ. Brightly colored vinyl armchairs, an industrial

1

metal staircase, and glass tables mark the lobby, which hosts monthly art exhibitions. Out back, a small courtyard is decked in hardwood, a look you'll rarely see in Paris. The rooms hum with primary reds and yellows, some with Keith Haring prints. Kaleidoscopes of ceramic fragments tile the bathrooms. ⊠*3 rue Oberkampf, République, 75011* ☎*01–53–36–86–86* ⏚*01–43–38–32–86* ⊕*www.hotelbeaumarchais. com* ⟿*31 rooms* ⅃*In-room: safe, Wi-Fi. In-hotel: some pets allowed* ⊟*AE, MC, V* Ⓜ*Filles du Calvaire, Oberkampf.*

12ᴱ ARRONDISSEMENT (BASTILLE/GARE DE LYON)

$$ ⛿ **Le Pavillon Bastille.** The transformation of this 19th-century hôtel particulier (across from the Opéra Bastille) into a mod, colorful, high-design hotel garnered both architectural awards and a fiercely loyal, hip clientele. Some clients take to the hotel's blue-and-gold color scheme, but others find it brash. ⊠*65 rue de Lyon, Bastille/Nation, 75012* ☎*01–43–43–65–65, 800/233–2552 in U.S.* ⏚*01–43–43–96– 52* ⟿*24 rooms, 1 suite* ⅃*In-room: safe, VCR (some), Wi-Fi. In-hotel: room service, bar, no-smoking rooms, some pets allowed* ⊟*AE, DC, MC, V* Ⓜ*Bastille.*

16ᴱ ARRONDISSEMENT (ARC DE TRIOMPHE/LE BOIS)

★ $$$$ ⛿ **Hôtel Raphael.** This discreet palace hotel was built in 1925 to cater to travelers spending a season in Paris, so every space is generously sized for such long, lavish stays—the closets, for instance, have room for ball gowns and plumed hats. Guest rooms, most with king-size beds, are turned out in 18th- and early-19th-century antiques and have 6-foot windows, Oriental rugs, silk damask wallpaper, chandeliers, and ornately carved wood paneling. Bathrooms are remarkably large; most have claw-foot bathtubs and separate massage-jet showers. The roof terrace, topped with a summer restaurant, has a panoramic view of the city, with the Arc de Triomphe looming in the foreground. Parents will find a friend in the concierge, who can arrange for bilingual babysitters and priority access to amusement parks, and offers recommendations on kid-friendly restaurants and entertainment. ⊠*17 av. Kléber, Trocadéro/ Tour Eiffel, 75116* ☎*01–53–64–32–00* ⏚*01–53–64–32–01* ⊕*www. raphael-hotel.com* ⟿*52 rooms, 38 suites* ⅃*In-room: safe, DVD (some), VCR (some), dial-up, Wi-Fi. In-hotel: 2 restaurants, room service, bar, gym, no-smoking rooms, some pets allowed (fee)* ⊟*AE, DC, MC, V* Ⓜ*Kléber.*

18ᴱ ARRONDISSEMENT (MONTMARTRE)

★ $$ ⛿ **Hôtel Prima Lepic.** An impressive value, the Prima Lepic stands out among dozens of mediocre hotels in this perennial tourist zone. Elements from the original 19th-century building remain, such as vintage tiling in the entry and heavy-duty white iron furniture in the breakfast area. The bright rooms are full of spring colors and florals; the so-called Baldaquin rooms have reproduction canopy beds. Extra comforts include in-room teapots and bathrobes, and—in some cases— flat-screen TVs. Larger rooms are suitable for families but have little natural light. ⊠*29 rue Lepic, Montmartre, 75018* ☎*01–46–06–44–64*

🏠*01–46–06–66–11* ⊕*www.hotel-paris-lepic.com* 🛏*38 rooms* ♿*In-room: no a/c, safe, dial-up, Wi-Fi* 💳*AE, DC, MC, V* Ⓜ*Blanche.*

$ 🏨 **Hôtel des Arts.** The location in the heart of Montmartre's winding streets would be reason enough to stay at this budget-priced hotel, but the scattering of antiques in the lounge, bookcases in the lobby, and vintage cabaret scenes painted onto each elevator door give it a welcoming feel usually lacking in this price range. Rooms have red or green carpeting, modern wooden furnishings, and floral or plaid linens. No. 42 is a larger double with a balcony overlooking Paris, but the best views are from the sixth floor (these cost an additional €20). ✉*5 rue Tholozé, Montmartre, 75018* ☎*01–46–06–30–52* 🏠*01–46–06–10–83* ⊕*www.arts-hotel-paris.com* 🛏*50 rooms* ♿*In-room: no a/c, safe, Wi-Fi. In-hotel: room service* 💳*AE, DC, MC, V* Ⓜ*Abbesses.*

NIGHTLIFE & THE ARTS

With a heritage that includes the cancan, the Folies-Bergère, the Moulin Rouge, Mistinguett, and Josephine Baker, Paris is one city where no one has ever had to ask, "Is there any place exciting to go to tonight?" Today the city's nightlife and arts scenes are still filled with pleasures. Hear a chansonnier belt out Piaf, take in a *Victor/Victoria* show, or catch a Molière play at the Comédie Française. Detailed entertainment listings can be found in the weekly magazines *Pariscope* (⊕*www.pariscope.fr) and L'Officiel des Spectacles.* Also look for *Aden* and *Figaroscope,* and the free *Paris Voice* (⊕*www.parisvoice.com*), Wednesday supplements to the newspapers *Le Monde* and *Le Figaro,* respectively. The 24-hour hotline and the Web site of the **Paris Tourist Office** (☎*08–92–68–30–00 in English [€0.34 per min]* ⊕*www.parisinfo.com*) are other good sources of information about activities in the city.

The best place to buy tickets is at the venue itself; try to purchase in advance, as many of the more popular performances sell out. Also try your hotel or a ticket agency, such as www.theatreonline.com or **Opéra Théâtre** (✉*7 rue de Clichy, Montmartre, 9ᵉ* ☎*01–42–81–98–85* Ⓜ*Trinité*). Tickets for most concerts can be bought at **FNAC** (✉*1–5 rue Pierre Lescot, Forum des Halles, 3rd level down, Beaubourg/Les Halles, 1ᵉʳ* ☎*08–92–68–36–22* Ⓜ*Châtelet–Les Halles*). The **Virgin Megastore** (✉*52 av. des Champs-Élysées, Champs-Élysées, 8ᵉ* ☎*01–49–53–50–00* Ⓜ*Franklin-D.-Roosevelt*) also sells theater and concert tickets. Half-price tickets for many same-day theater performances are available at some venues and at the **Kiosques Théâtre** (✉*Across from 15 pl. de la Madeleine, Opéra/Grands Boulevards* Ⓜ*Madeleine* ✉*Outside Gare Montparnasse on Pl. Raoul Dautry, Montparnasse, 15ᵉ* Ⓜ*Montparnasse-Bienvenüe*); open Tuesday–Saturday 12:30 PM–8 PM and Sunday 12:30 PM–4 PM. Expect to pay a €3 commission per ticket and to wait in line.

THE ARTS

DANCE

The biggest news on the French dance scene is the spanking new **Centre National de la Danse** (⊠*1 rue Victor Hugo, Pantin* ☎*01–41–83–27–27* ⊕*www.cnd.fr* Ⓜ*Hoche or RER: Pantin*), which opened in 2004 in a former jailhouse on the canal of the Pantin suburb of Paris. Dedicated to teaching dance, it also has a regular program of performances

★ open to the public. The super-spectacular 19th-century **Opéra Garnier** (⊠*Pl. de l'Opéra, Opéra/Grands Boulevards, 9ᵉ* ☎*08–92–89–90–90* ⊕*www.opera-de-paris.fr* Ⓜ*Opéra*) is home to the reputable Ballet de l'Opéra National de Paris and hosts other troupes like Merce Cunningham. Seat prices range €6–€57; note that many of the cheaper seats have obstructed views, more of an obstacle in dance than in opera performances. The **Opéra de la Bastille** (⊠*Pl. de la Bastille, Bastille/ Nation, 12ᵉ* ☎*08–92–69–78–68* ⊕*www.opera-de-paris.fr* Ⓜ*Bastille*) occasionally hosts major dance troupes, often modern and avant-garde in tenor. The **Théâtre de la Bastille** (⊠*76 rue de la Roquette, Bastille/ Nation, 11ᵉ* ☎*01–43–57–42–14* Ⓜ*Bastille*) is where innovative modern-dance companies perform. At its two houses, the **Théâtre de la Ville** (⊠*2 pl. du Châtelet, Beaubourg/Les Halles, 4ᵉ* ☎*01–42–74–22–77 for both* Ⓜ*Châtelet* ⊠*31 rue des Abbesses, Montmartre, 18ᵉ* Ⓜ*Abbesses*) is *the* place for contemporary dance. Troupes like La La La Human Steps and Anne-Teresa de Keersmaeker's Rosas company are presented here and sell out quickly.

EARLY & CLASSICAL MUSIC

Classical- and world-music concerts are held at the **Cité de la Musique** (⊠*221 av. Jean-Jaurès, Parc de la Villette, 19ᵉ* ☎*01–44–84–44–84* Ⓜ*Porte de Pantin*). The **Théâtre des Champs-Élysées** (⊠*15 av. Montaigne, Champs-Élysées, 8ᵉ* ☎*01–49–52–50–50* ⊕*www.theatrechampselysees. fr* Ⓜ*Alma-Marceau*), an Art Deco temple and famed site of the premiere of Stravinsky's 1913 *Le Sacre du Printemps*, hosts concerts and ballet. Many **churches** hold classical concerts (often free). For musical events at **Notre-Dame** (⊠*Pl. du Parvis Notre-Dame, Ile de la Cité, 4ᵉ* Ⓜ*Cité*) tickets are through **Musique Sacrée à Notre-Dame** (☎*01–44–41–49–99*).

★ **Sainte-Chapelle** (⊠*4 bd. du Palais, Ile de la Cité, 1ᵉʳ* ☎*01–42–77– 65–65* Ⓜ*Cité*), a Gothic tour-de-force of shimmering stained glass, holds memorable candlelighted concerts March through November; make reservations well in advance. The **Musée du Moyen Age** (⊠*6 pl. Paul Painlevé, Quartier Latin, 5ᵉ* ☎*01–53–73–78–16* Ⓜ*Cluny–La Sorbonne*) stages medieval music concerts between October and July, including the free *l'Heure Musicale* every Friday at 12:30 and Saturday at 4.

FILM

Many movie theaters, especially in principal tourist areas such as the Champs-Élysées, St-Germain-des-Prés, Les Halles, and the Boulevard des Italiens near the Opéra, show first-run films in English. Check the weekly guides for a movie of your choice. Look for the initials *v.o.*, which mean *version originale*, that is, not dubbed. Cinema admission runs from €6 to €10. Most theaters will post two showtimes: the first is the *séance*, when commercials, previews, and sometimes short films start, and the second is the actual feature presentation time, which is usually 10–20 minutes later. Paris has many small cinemas showing classic and independent films, especially in the Latin Quarter. For the *cinéphile* (movie lover) brought up on Fellini, Bergman, and Resnais, the main mecca is the famed **Cinémathèque Française** (✉ *51 rue de Bercy, Bercy, 12ᵉ* ☎ *01–56–26–01–01* Ⓜ *Bercy*), which pioneered the preservation

> **THE SEVENTH ART**
>
> The French call movies the *septième art* (seventh art) and discuss the latest releases with the same intensity as they do gallery openings or theatrical debuts. That's not to say they don't like popcorn flicks, but you're as likely to see people standing in line for a Hitchcock retrospective or a hard-hitting documentary as for a Hollywood cream puff.

of early films (note: most films here are shown in French). Its dramatic new home, designed by Frank Gehry, opened in fall 2005 and includes a museum and video library, as well as four theaters.

★ **La Pagode** (✉ *57 bis, rue de Babylone, Trocadéro/Tour Eiffel, 7ᵉ* ☎ *08–92–89–28–92* Ⓜ *St-François Xavier*)—where else but in Paris would you find movies screened in an antique pagoda? A Far East fantasy, this structure was built in 1896 for the wife of the owner of the Le Bon Marché department store. Who can resist seeing a flick in the silk-and-gilt Salle Japonaise? Come early to have tea in the bamboo-fringed garden. In the heart of the Left Bank, **St-André-des-Arts** (✉ *30 rue St-André-des-Arts, Quartier Latin, 6ᵉ* ☎ *01–43–26–48–18* Ⓜ *St-Michel*) is one of the best art cinemas in Paris.

OPERA

Paris offers some of the best opera in the world—and thousands know it. Consequently, getting tickets to a performance of the **Opéra National de Paris** at its two main venues, the Opéra de la Bastille and the Opéra Garnier, can be difficult on short notice; it's a good idea to plan ahead. There's even been renewed interest since the 2004–05 season under the new direction of Gérard Mortier, famous for his turnaround of the Salzburg Festival. Review a list of performances by checking the Web site ⊕ *www.opera-de-paris.com*, getting a copy of the Paris Tourist Office's *Saison de Paris* booklet, or by writing to the Opéra de la Bastille (✉ *120 rue de Lyon, Bastille/Nation, 75576 cedex 12*) well in advance. Make your selection and send back the booking form, giving several choices of nights and performances. If the response is affirmative, just pick up and pay for your tickets before the performance (you can also pay for them by credit card in advance). For performances at either the Opéra de la Bastille or the Palais Garnier *(for complete info on this theater, see Dance, above),* seats go on sale at the box office two weeks before any given show or a month ahead by phone or online; you must go in person to buy the cheapest tickets. Last-minute discount tickets, if available, are offered 15 minutes before a performance for seniors and anyone under 28. The box office is open 11 to 6:30 PM daily. Prices for tickets start at €5 for standing places (at the Opéra Bastille, only) and go up to €160.

The **Opéra de la Bastille** (⊠ *Pl. de la Bastille, Bastille/Nation, 12ᵉ* ☎ *08– 92–89–90–90* ⊕ *www.opera-de-paris.fr* Ⓜ *Bastille*), a modern auditorium, has taken over the role of Paris's main opera house from the Opéra Garnier. The grandest opera productions are usually mounted here, while the Garnier now presents smaller-scale operas such as Mozart's *La Clemenza di Tito* and *Così Fan Tutte.* Gorgeous though the Garnier is, its tiara-shape theater means that many seats have limited sight lines, so it's best to ask specifically what the sight lines are when booking (partial view in French is *visibilité partielle*). Needless to say, the cheaper seats are often those with partial views—of course, views of Garnier's house could easily wind up being much more spectacular than any sets on stage, so it's not really a loss. The opera season usually runs September through July.

The **Opéra Comique** (⊠ *5 rue Favart, Opéra/Grands Boulevards, 2ᵉ* ☎ *08–25–00–00–58* ⊕ *www.opera-comique.com* Ⓜ *Richelieu-Drouot*) is a lofty old hall where comic operas are often performed. **Théâtre Musical de Paris** (⊠ *Pl. du Châtelet, Beaubourg/Les Halles, 1ᵉʳ* ☎ *01–40– 28–28–40* ⊕ *www.chatelet-theatre.com* Ⓜ *Châtelet*), better known as the Théâtre du Châtelet, puts on some of the finest opera productions in the city and regularly attracts international divas like Cecilia Bartoli and Anne-Sofie von Otter. It also plays host to classical concerts, dance performances, and the occasional play.

THEATER

A number of theaters line the Grands Boulevards between Opéra and République, but there's no Paris equivalent of Broadway or the West End. Shows are mostly in French. Information about performances can be obtained on a Web site (⊕ *www.theatreonline.fr*), which lists 170 different theaters, offers critiques, and provides an online reservation service. **Bouffes du Nord** (⊠ *37 bis, bd. de la Chapelle, Stalingrad/La Chapelle, 10ᵉ* ☎ *01–46–07–34–50* Ⓜ *La Chapelle*) is the wonderfully atmospheric theater that is home to English director Peter Brook. The **Comédie-Française** (⊠ *Pl. Colette, Louvre/Tuileries, 1ᵉʳ* ☎ *01–44–58– 15–15* ⊕ *www.comedie-francaise.fr* Ⓜ *Palais-Royal*) is a distinguished venue that stages classical French drama in the very regal surroundings of the 18th-century Palais-Royal. The legendary 19th-century **Odéon Théâtre de l'Europe** (⊠ *Pl. de l'Odéon, St-Germain-des-Prés, 6ᵉ* ☎ *01– 44–41–36–36* Ⓜ *Odéon*), once home to the Comédie Française, has today made pan-European theater its primary focus. **Théâtre National de Chaillot** (⊠ *1 pl. du Trocadéro, Trocadéro/Tour Eiffel, 16ᵉ* ☎ *01– 53–65–30–00* Ⓜ *Trocadéro*) has two theaters dedicated to drama and dance. Since 2003, it has hosted the groundbreaking duo of Deborah Warner (director) and Fiona Shaw (actress) for several excellent English-language productions. **Théâtre du Palais-Royal** (⊠ *38 rue Montpensier, Louvre/Tuileries, 1ᵉʳ* ☎ *01–42–97–59–81* Ⓜ *Palais-Royal*) is a sparkling 750-seat Italian theater bedecked in gold and purple. For children, one "theatrical" experience can be a delight—the **Marionnettes du Jardin du Luxembourg** (⊠ *St-Germain-des-Prés* ☎ *01–43–26–46–47*

Ⓜ *Vavin*) stages the most traditional performances, including *Pinocchio* and *The Three Little Pigs*.

NIGHTLIFE

The City of Light truly lights up after dark. So, if you want to paint the town *rouge* after dutifully pounding the parquet in museums all day, there's a dazzling array of options to discover. In the early 1990s the Bastille was the hottest nightlife area in town. Though the scene has migrated north toward the Belleville and Oberkampf districts, the Bastille remains popular. Fun and flashy, the block-long Rue de Lappe has the most bars per foot in Paris; nearby Rue de la Roquette and Rue de Charonne also have many en vogue options. Up north, Rue Oberkampf and surrounding streets abound with laid-back theme bars—many playing live music—while the yuppie-bohemian types head up to the latest lounges around métro Belleville and the Canal St-Martin. The Left Bank is definitely a lot less happening. The Champs-Élysées is making a comeback, though the clientele remains predominantly foreign. Take note: the last métro runs between 12:30 AM and 1 AM and 2 AM on Saturday (you can take a taxi, but they can be hard to find, especially on weekend nights). For information about dates for the dazzling one-night-only soirees, keep an eye out for the free listings mag *Lylo* or flyers in bars.

BARS & CLUBS

American Bar at La Closerie des Lilas (✉ *171 bd. du Montparnasse, Montparnasse, 6ᵉ* ☎*01–40–51–34–50* Ⓜ *Montparnasse*) lets you drink in the swirling action of the adjacent restaurant and do it at a bar hallowed by plaques honoring such former habitués as Man Ray, Jean-Paul Sartre, and Samuel Beckett. Happily, many Parisians still call this watering hole their home away from home. A cherished relic from the days of Picasso and Modigliani, **Au Lapin Agile** (✉ *22 rue des Saules, Montmartre, 18ᵉ* ☎*01–46–06–85–87* Ⓜ *Lamarck-Caulaincourt*), the fabled artists' hangout in Montmartre, is a miraculous survivor from the early 20th century. This is an authentic French cabaret of songs, poetry, and humor in a publike setting where the audience comes and goes throughout the evening show (Tuesday–Sunday 9 PM–2 AM). **Barramundi** (✉ *3 rue Taitbout, Opéra/Grands Boulevards, 9ᵉ* ☎*01–47–70–21–21* Ⓜ *Richelieu Drouot*) is one of Paris's hubs of nouveau-riche chic. The lighting is dim, the copper bar is long, and the walls are artfully textured. **Le Bilboquet** (✉ *13 rue St-Benoît, St-Germain-des-Prés, 6ᵉ* ☎*01–45–48–81–84* Ⓜ *St-Germain-des-Prés*) is the place to sip cocktails in a ritzy Belle Epoque salon while a jazz combo sets the mood. The namesake of **Buddha Bar** (✉ *8 rue Boissy d'Anglas, Champs-Élysées, 8ᵉ* ☎*01–53–05–90–00* Ⓜ *Concorde*), a towering gold-painted Buddha, contemplates enough Dragon Empress screens and colorful chinoiserie for five MGM movies. Although quite past its prime as a Parisian hot spot, it manages to remain packed in the evenings with an eclectic crowd.

1

Le Cab (✉ *2 pl. du Palais Royal, Louvre/Tuileries, 1ᵉʳ* ☎*01–58–62–56–25* Ⓜ*Palais-Royal*) heats up during Fashion Week with models, photographers, and stylists bypassing the lesser beings at the velvet rope. **Café Charbon** (✉*109 rue Oberkampf, Oberkampf, 11ᵉ* ☎*01–43–57–55–13* Ⓜ*St-Maur, Parmentier*) is a beautifully restored 19th-century café with a trendsetting crowd that has made this place one of the mainstays of trendy Okerkampf.

★ **De la Ville Café** (✉*34 bd. Bonne Nouvelle, Opéra/Grands Boulevards, 10ᵉ* ☎*01–48–24–48–09* Ⓜ*Bonne Nouvelle, Grands Boulevards*) is a funky, industrial-baroque place, with its huge, heated sidewalk terrace, mosaic-tile bar, and swish lounge. As the anchor of the slowly reawakening Grands Boulevards scene, it requires that you arrive early on weekends for a seat.

Le Gibus (✉*18 rue du Faubourg du Temple, République, 11ᵉ* ☎*01–47–00–78–88* Ⓜ*République*) is one of Paris's most famous music venues and has hosted everyone from the Police to Billy Idol). Today the Gibus's cellars are *the* place for trance, techno, hip-hop, hard-core, and jungle music. **Harry's New York Bar** (✉*5 rue Daunou, Opéra/Grands Boulevards, 2ᵉ* ☎*01–42–61–71–14* Ⓜ*Opéra*), a cozy, wood-paneled hangout decorated with dusty college pennants and popular with expatriates, is haunted by the ghosts of Ernest Hemingway and F. Scott Fitzgerald. This place claims to have invented the Bloody Mary, and one way or another, the bartenders here do mix a mean one. Don't miss the piano bar downstairs where Gershwin composed "An American in Paris." The ravishing Asian–Art Deco **Man Ray** (✉*34 rue Marbeuf, Champs-Élysées, 8ᵉ* ☎*01–56–88–36–36* Ⓜ*Franklin-D.-Roosevelt*) keeps its profile high, not surprising given that it is owned by Johnny Depp, Sean Penn, and Simply Red's Mick Hucknall. The clientele come to flash their bling and don't bat an eye at the pricey drinks (starting at €10 for a Coke). **Wagg** (✉*62 rue Mazarine, St-Germain-des-Prés, 6ᵉ* ☎*01–55–42–22–00* Ⓜ*Odéon*), in a vaulted stone cellar that was Jim Morrison's hangout back when it was the Whiskey-a-Go-Go, has been turned into a small, sleek club run by the übertrendy London club Fabric, with large helpings of house techno music. It's beneath the popular Alcazar restaurant.

FLOOR SHOWS & CABARET

Paris's cabarets are household names, though mostly just tourists go to them these days. Prices range from €40 (simple admission plus one drink) to more than €125 (dinner plus show). **Crazy Horse** (✉*12 av. George-V, Champs-Élysées, 8ᵉ* ☎*01–47–23–85–56* ⊕*www.lecrazyhorseparis.com* Ⓜ*Alma-Marceau*) is one of the best-known cabarets, with pretty dancers and a new risqué routine called "teasing" that involves top hats, fishnets, dark pink lipstick, and little else. **Lido** (✉*116 bis, av. des Champs-Élysées, Champs-Élysées, 8ᵉ* ☎*01–40–76–56–10* ⊕*www.lido.fr* Ⓜ*George-V*) stars the famous Bluebell Girls; the owners claim that no show in Las Vegas can rival it for special effects. **Michou** (✉*80 rue des Martyrs, Montmartre, 18ᵉ* ☎*01–46–06–16–04* ⊕*www.michou.fr* Ⓜ*Pigalle*) is owned by the always blue-clad Michou, famous in Paris circles. The men on stage wear extravagant drag—high camp and parody are the order of the day. That old favorite at the foot of Montmartre, **Moulin Rouge** (✉ *82 bd. de Clichy, Montmartre, 18ᵉ* ☎ *01–53–09–82–82* Ⓜ *Blanche*), mingles the Doriss Girls, the cancan, and a horse in an extravagant (and expensive) spectacle.

HOTEL BARS

Some of Paris's best hotel bars mix historic pedigrees with hushed elegance—and others go for a modern, edgy luxe. Following are some **Fodor's Choice** perennial favorites. The super-chic bar at **L'Hôtel** (✉ *10 rue des Beaux-★ Arts, St-Germain-des-Prés, 6ᵉ* ☎ *01–44–41–99–00* Ⓜ *St-Germain-des-Prés*) had stylemeister Jacques Garcia revamp its gorgeously historic decor. **Hôtel Le Bristol** (✉ *112 rue du Faubourg–St-Honoré, Champs-Élysées, 8ᵉ* ☎ *01–53–43–43–42* Ⓜ *Miromesnil*) attracts the rich and powerful. **Hôtel Costes** (✉ *239 rue Saint-Honoré, Louvre/Tuileries, 1ᵉʳ* ☎ *01–42–44–50–25* Ⓜ *Tuileries*) draws many big names in the fashion world during Collections weeks to its red-velvet interior. **Hôtel Plaza Athénée** (✉ *25 av. Montaigne, Champs-Élysées, 8ᵉ* ☎ *01–53–67–66–00* Ⓜ *Alma Marceau*) is Paris's perfect chill-out spot; the bar was designed by Starck protegé Patrick Jouin.

★ **Murano Urban Resort** (✉ *13 bd. du Temple, République, 3ᵉ* ☎ *01–42–71–20–00* ⊕ *www.muranoresort.com* Ⓜ *République*) is by far the hippest hotel bar *du jour,* with its never-ending black stone bar, candy-color fabric wall panels, and packed nightly with beautiful art and fashion types.

Hot–cool **Pershing Hall** (✉ *49 rue Pierre Charron, Champs-Élysées, 8ᵉ* ☎ *01–58–36–58–00* Ⓜ *George V*) has a stylish lounge bar with muted colors and an enormous "wall garden" in the courtyard. Colin Field, the best barman in Paris, presides

★ at the **Ritz's Hemingway Bar** (✉ *15 pl. Vendôme, Louvre/Tuileries, 1ᵉʳ* ☎ *01–43–16–33–65* Ⓜ *Opéra*), but with a dress code and cognac aux truffes on the menu, Hemingway might raise an eyebrow. Across the hallway is the hotel's Cambon Bar, a soigné setting where Cole Porter composed "Begin the Beguine."

JAZZ CLUBS

For nightly schedules consult the specialty magazines *Jazz Hot, Jazzman,* or *Jazz Magazine.* Nothing gets going until 10 PM or 11 PM; entry prices vary widely from about €10 to more than €25. **Caveau de la Huchette** (✉ *5 rue de la Huchette, Quartier Latin, 5ᵉ* ☎ *01–43–26–65–05* Ⓜ *St-Michel*), one of the few surviving cellar clubs from the 1940s, is a

> ### COOL PLACES IN A HOT SPOT
>
> Once it was the Bastille area, then gritty Oberkampf; today the trendy nightlife zone is the Canal St-Martin, a working-class neighborhood just east of Gare de l'Est and clustered around the canal built by Napoléon I. While you're likely to spot celebrity photographer Mario Testino, the neighborhood feels refreshingly relaxed. A top hangout is the Hôtel du Nord (✉ 102 quai de Jemmapes ☎ 01–40–40–78–78), once famous as the setting for Marcel Carné's 1938 film, now transformed into a restaurant where you might see Christian Lacroix. Also chic is nearby Chez Prune (71 quai de Valmy).

Paris classic, big with swing dancers and Dixieland musicians. **Le Petit Journal** (⊠*71 bd. St-Michel, Quartier Latin, 5e* ☎*01–43–26–28–59* Ⓜ*Luxembourg* ⊠*13 rue du Commandant-Mouchotte, Montparnasse, 14^e* ☎*01–43–21–56–70* Ⓜ*Montparnasse Bienvenüe*), with two locations, has long attracted the greatest names in French and international jazz. It now specializes in big band (Montparnasse) and Dixieland (St-Michel) jazz and also serves dinner 8:30–midnight.

ROCK, POP & WORLD-MUSIC VENUES

Upcoming concerts are posted on boards in FNAC and Virgin Megastores. **L'Olympia** (⊠*28 bd. des Capucines, Opéra/Grands Boulevards, 9e* ☎*08–92–68–33–68* ⊕*www.olympiahall.com* Ⓜ*Madeleine*), a legendary venue once favored by Jacques Brel and Edith Piaf, still plays host to leading French vocalists. **Palais Omnisports de Paris-Bercy** (⊠*8 bd. de Bercy, Bercy/Tolbiac, 12e* ☎*08–92–69–23–00* Ⓜ*Bercy*) is the largest venue in Paris; English and American pop stars shake their spangles here (we see you, Mademoiselle Spears). **Zénith** (⊠*Parc de la Villette, 19e* ☎*01–42–08–60–00* Ⓜ*Porte-de-Pantin*)—here's your chance to see White Stripes or Limp Bizkit while surrounded by screaming Parisians.

SHOPPING

Updated by
Jennifer Ditsler-
Ladonne

In the most beautiful city in the world, it's no surprise to discover that the local greengrocer displays his tomatoes as artistically as Cartier does its rubies. The capital of style, Paris has an endless panoply of delights to tempt shop-'til-you-droppers, from grand couturiers like Dior to the funkiest flea markets. Today every neighborhood seems to reflect a unique attitude and style: designer extravagance and haute couture characterize Avenue Montaigne and Rue Faubourg St-Honoré; classic sophistication pervades St-Germain; avant-garde style dresses up the Marais; while a hip feel suffuses the area around Les Halles. With the euro trouncing the dollar, here are some words to remember: *soldes,* sale; *fripes,* secondhand clothing; *dépôt vente,* secondhand shop; and *dégriffé,* designer labels, often from last year's collection, for sale at a deep discount. And if you do decide to indulge that special bauble, what better place to make that once-in-a-blue-moon splurge than Paris?

Most stores—excepting department stores and flea markets—stay open until 6 or 7 PM, but many take a lunch break sometime between noon and 2 PM. Many shops traditionally close Sunday. If you're from outside the European Union, age 15 and over, and stay in France and/or the European Union for less than six months, you can benefit from Value Added Tax (V.A.T.) reimbursements, known in France as TVA; the sum remitted to non-EU folk is known as the *détaxe* (détaxe forms must be shown and stamped by a customs official before leaving the country). To qualify, non-EU residents must spend at least €175 in a single store on a single day. Refunds vary from 13% to 19.6% and are mailed to you by check or credited to your charge card.

SHOPPING BY NEIGHBORHOOD

AVENUE MONTAIGNE
Shopping doesn't come much more chic than on Avenue Montaigne, with its graceful town mansions housing some of the top names in international fashion: **Chanel, Dior, Céline, Valentino, Krizia, Ungaro, Prada, Dolce & Gabbana,** and many more. Neighboring Rue François 1er and Avenue George-V are also lined with many designer boutiques: **Versace, Fendi, Givenchy,** and **Balenciaga.**

CHAMPS-ÉLYSÉES
Cafés and movie theaters keep the once-chic Champs-Élysées active 24 hours a day, but the invasion of exchange banks, car showrooms, and fast-food chains has lowered the tone. Four glitzy 20th-century arcade malls—**Galerie du Lido, Le Rond-Point, Le Claridge,** and **Élysées 26**—capture most of the retail action, not to mention the **Gap** and the **Disney Store.** Some of the big luxe chain stores—also found in cities around the globe—are here: **Sephora** has reintroduced a touch of elegance and the cool factor soared skyward when the mothership **Louis Vuitton** (on the Champs-Élysées proper) reopened in spring 2005 after a year of renovations.

THE FAUBOURG ST-HONORÉ
This chic shopping and residential area is also quite a political hub. It's home to the Élysée Palace as well as the official residences of the American and British ambassadors. The Paris branches of **Sotheby's** and **Christie's** and renowned antiques galleries such as **Didier Aaron** add artistic flavor. Boutiques include **Hermès, Lanvin, Gucci, Chloé,** and **Christian Lacroix.**

LEFT BANK
For an array of bedazzling boutiques with hyper-picturesque goods—antique toy theaters, books on gardening—and the most fascinating antiques stores in town, be sure to head to the area around Rue Jacob, nearly lined with *antiquaires,* and the streets around super-posh Place Furstenberg. After decades of clustering on the Right Bank's venerable shopping avenues, the high-fashion houses have stormed the Rive Gauche. The first to arrive were **Sonia Rykiel** and **Yves St-Laurent** in the late '60s. Some of the more recent arrivals include **Christian Dior, Giorgio Armani,** and **Louis Vuitton.** Rue des St-Pères and Rue de Grenelle are lined with designer names.

LOUVRE–PALAIS ROYAL
The elegant and eclectic shops clustered in the 18th-century arcades of the Palais-Royal sell such items as antiques, toy soldiers, cosmetics, jewelry, and vintage designer dresses. There are even handmade gardening tools sold by a prince at **Le Prince Jardinier.**

LE MARAIS
The Marais is a mixture of many moods and many influences; its lovely, impossibly narrow cobblestone streets are filled with some of the most original, small-name, nonglobal goods to be had—a true haven for the original gift—including the outposts of **Jamin Puech,** the **Red Wheel-**

barrow, and **Sentou Galerie.** Avant-garde designers **Azzedine Alaïa** and **Tsumori Chistato** have boutiques within a few blocks of stately Place des Vosges and the Picasso and Carnavalet museums. The Marais is also one of the few neighborhoods that has a lively Sunday afternoon (usually from 2 PM) shopping scene.

OPÉRA TO LA MADELEINE

Two major department stores—**Printemps** and **Galeries Lafayette**—dominate Boulevard Haussmann, behind Paris's ornate 19th-century Opéra Garnier. Place de la Madeleine tempts many with its two luxurious food stores, **Fauchon** and **Hédiard.**

PLACE VENDÔME & RUE DE LA PAIX

The magnificent 17th-century Place Vendôme, home of the Ritz Hotel, and Rue de la Paix, leading north from Vendôme, are where you can find the world's most elegant jewelers: **Cartier, Boucheron, Bulgari,** and **Van Cleef and Arpels.** The most exclusive, however, is the discreet **Jar's.**

PLACE DES VICTOIRES & RUE ÉTIENNE MARCEL

The graceful, circular Place des Victoires, near the Palais-Royal, is the playground of fashion icons such as **Kenzo,** while **Comme des Garçons** and Yohji Yamamoto line Rue Étienne Marcel. In the nearby oh-so-charming Galerie Vivienne shopping arcade, **Jean-Paul Gaultier** has a shop that has been renovated by Philippe Starck, and is definitely worth a stop.

RUE ST-HONORÉ

A fashionable set makes its way to Rue St-Honoré to shop at Paris's trendiest boutique, **Colette.** The street is lined with numerous designer names, while on nearby Rue Cambon you can find the wonderfully elegant **Maria Luisa** and the main **Chanel** boutique.

DEPARTMENT STORES

For an overview of Paris *mode,* visit *les grands magasins.* Paris's monolithic department stores. Most are open Monday through Saturday from about 9:30 AM to 7 PM, and some are open until 10 PM one weekday evening.

★ **Le Bon Marché** (✉ *24 rue de Sèvres, St-Germain-des-Prés, 7ᵉ* ☎ *01–44–39–80–00* Ⓜ *Sèvres-Babylone*) has undergone a complete face-lift and is now Paris's chicest department store, with an impressive array of designers represented for both men and women. **La Grande Épicerie** is one of the largest groceries in Paris and a gourmand's home away from home. **Bazar de l'Hôtel de Ville** (✉ *52–64 rue de Rivoli, Beaubourg/Les Halles, 4ᵉ* ☎ *01–42–74–90–00* Ⓜ *Hôtel de Ville*), better known as BHV, has minimal fashion offerings but is noteworthy for its enormous basement hardware store. **Printemps** (✉ *64 bd. Haussmann, Opéra/Grands Boulevards, 9ᵉ* ☎ *01–42–82–50–00* Ⓜ *Havre-Caumartin, Opéra, or Auber*) has everything plus a whopping six floors dedicated to men's fashion. **Galeries Lafayette** (✉ *40 bd. Haussmann, Opéra/Grands Boulevards, 9ᵉ* ☎ *01–42–82–34–56* Ⓜ *Chaussée d'Antin, Opéra, or Havre-*

Caumartin) is dangerous—the granddaddy of them all—everything you never even dreamt of and then some.

BUDGET

Monoprix (✉ *21 av. de l'Opéra, Opéra/Grands Boulevards, 1er* ☎ *01– 42–61–78–08* Ⓜ *Opéra* ✉ *6 av. de la Plaine, Nation, 20e* ☎ *01–43– 73–17–59* Ⓜ *Nation* ✉ *50 rue de Rennes, St-Germain-des-Prés, 6e* ☎ *01–45–48–18–08* Ⓜ *St-Germain-des-Prés*) is the French dime store par excellence—with scores of branches throughout the city—and stocks inexpensive everyday items like toothpaste, groceries, toys, and paper. It also carries inexpensive children's clothes and makeup of surprisingly good quality.

MARKETS

The lively atmosphere that reigns in most of Paris's open-air food markets makes them a sight worth seeing even if you don't want or need to buy anything. Every neighborhood has one, though many are open only a few days each week. Sunday morning until 1 PM is usually a good time to go. Many of the better-known markets are in areas you'd visit for sightseeing; here's a list of the top bets. **Boulevard Raspail** (✉ *Between Rue de Rennes and Rue du Cherche-Midi, Quartier Latin, 6e* Ⓜ *Rennes*) has a great organic market on Tuesday and Friday. **Rue de Buci** (✉ *St-Germain-des-Prés, 6e* Ⓜ *Odéon*), in the chic and lively St-Germain-des-Prés quarter, is closed Sunday evening and Monday. **Rue Mouffetard** (✉ *Quartier Latin, 5e* Ⓜ *Place Monge*), near the Jardin des Plantes, is best on weekends. **Rue Montorgueuil** (✉ *Beaubourg/ Les Halles, 1er* Ⓜ *Châtelet Les Halles*) is closed Sunday afternoon and Monday. **Rue Lepic** (✉ *Montmartre, 18e* Ⓜ *Blanche or Abbesses*) is best on weekends. The **Marché d'Aligre** (✉ *Rue d'Aligre, Bastille/Nation, 12e* Ⓜ *Ledru-Rollin*), open until 1 PM every day except Monday, is a bit farther out but is the cheapest and probably most locally authentic market in Paris.

On Paris's northern boundary, the **Marché aux Puces** (Ⓜ *Porte de Clignancourt*), which takes place Saturday through Monday, is a centuryold labyrinth of alleyways spreading for more than a square mile packed with antiques dealers' booths, junk stalls—and world-class pickpockets; arrive early. On the southern and eastern sides of the city—at **Porte de Vanves** (Ⓜ *Porte de Vanves*) and **Porte de Montreuil**—are other, smaller flea markets. Vanves is a hit with the fashion set and specializes in smaller objects—mirrors, textiles, handbags, clothing, and glass. Arrive early if you want to find a bargain; the good stuff goes fast and stalls are liable to be packed up before noon.

SHOPPING ARCADES

Paris's 19th-century commercial arcades, called *passages* or *galeries*, are the forerunners of the modern mall. Glass roofs, decorative pillars, and mosaic floors give the passages character. The major arcades are on the Right Bank in central Paris. **Galerie Vivienne** (✉ *4 rue des Petits-*

Champs, Opéra/Grands Boulevards, 2ᵉ Ⓜ *Bourse*) is home to a range of interesting shops, including **Jean-Paul Gaultier's** Philippe Starck–designed fantasy, an excellent tearoom, and a quality wineshop.

★ **Passage du Grand-Cerf** (⊠*Entrances on Rue Dussoubs, Rue St-Denis, Beaubourg/Les Halles, 4ᵉ* Ⓜ *Étienne-Marcel*) is a pretty, glass-roofed gallery filled with crafts shops offering an innovative selection of jewelry, paintings, and ceramics. **Passage Jouffroy** (⊠*12 bd. Montmartre, Opéra/Grands Boulevards, 2ᵉ* Ⓜ *Montmartre*) is full of shops selling toys, postcards, antique canes, and perfumes. **Passage des Panoramas** (⊠*11 bd. Montmartre, Opéra/Grands Boulevards, 2ᵉ* Ⓜ *Montmartre*),

★ built in 1800, is the oldest of them all. The elegant **Galerie Véro-Dodat** (⊠*19 rue Jean-Jacques Rousseau, Louvre/Tuileries, 1ᵉʳ* Ⓜ *Louvre*) has shops selling old-fashioned toys, contemporary art, and stringed instruments. It's best known, however, for its antiques stores.

SPECIALTY STORES

ACCESSORIES, COSMETICS & PERFUMES

By Terry (⊠*36 Galerie Véro-Dodat, Louvre/Tuileries, 1ᵉʳ* ☎*01–44–76–00–76* Ⓜ *Louvre, Palais-Royal*) is the brainchild of Yves Saint Laurent's former director of makeup, Terry de Gunzberg; it offers her own brand of "ready-to-wear" cosmetics as well as a personalized cosmetics service.

Fodor's Choice **Chantal Thomass** (⊠*211 rue St-Honoré, Louvre/Tuileries, 1ᵉʳ* ☎*01–*
★ *42–60–40–56* Ⓜ *Tuileries*), a legendary lingerie diva, is back with this *Pillow Talk*–meets–Louis XV–inspired boutique. This is French naughtiness at its best, striking just the right balance between playfulness and straight-on seduction. Upstairs are lingerie-inspired swimsuits and beaded crop tops with Thomass's own sweetly subversive messages. **Christian Louboutin** (⊠*19 rue Jean-Jacques Rousseau, Louvre/Tuileries, 1ᵉʳ* ☎*01–42–36–05–31* Ⓜ *Palais-Royal* ⊠*38–40 rue de Grenelle, St-Germain-des-Prés, 7ᵉ* ☎*01–42–22–33–07* Ⓜ *Sèvres Babylone*) is famous for his wacky but elegant shoes, trademark blood-red soles, and impressive client list (Caroline of Monaco, Catherine Deneuve, Elizabeth Taylor). **E. Goyard** (⊠*233 rue St-Honoré, Louvre/Tuileries, 1ᵉʳ* ☎*01–42–60–57–04* Ⓜ *Tuileries*) has been making the finest luggage since 1853.

★ **Hermès** (⊠*24 rue du Faubourg St-Honoré, Louvre/Tuileries, 8ᵉ* ☎*01–40–17–47–17* Ⓜ *Concorde* ⊠*42 av.*

UNCOMMON-SCENTS

Guerlain (⊠68 av. des Champs-Élysées ☎01–45–62–52–57 Ⓜ Franklin-D.-Roosevelt) has reopened its historic address after a spectacular renovation befitting the world-class perfumer. Still the only Paris outlet for legendary perfumes like Shalimar and L'Heure Bleue, they've added several new signature scents (Rose Barbare, Cuir Beluga), and the perfume "fountain" allows for personalized bottles to be filled on demand. Or, for a mere 30,000 euros, a customized scent can be blended just for you. Also here are makeup, scented candles, and a spa.

Georges V, 8ᵉ, Champs-Élysées 🕾*01–47–20–48–51* Ⓜ*George V*) created the eternally chic Kelly (named for Grace Kelly) and Birkin (named for Jane Birkin) handbags, but is keeping ahead of the luxury game with new designs by superstar Jean-Paul Gaultier. Some accessories may not have waiting lists but are extremely covetable: enamel bracelets, intricately patterned silk twill ties, small leather goods.

★ **Jamin Puech** (⊠*43 rue Madame, St-Germain-des-Prés, 6ᵉ* 🕾*01–45–48–14–85* Ⓜ*St-Sulpice* ⊠*68 rue Vieille-du-Temple, Le Marais, 3ᵉ* 🕾*01–48–87–84–87* Ⓜ*St-Paul*) thinks of its bags as jewelry, not just a necessity. Nothing's plain-Jane here—everything is whimsical, unusual, and fun.

Fodor'sChoice
★ **Loulou de la Falaise** (⊠*7 rue de Bourgogne, Trocadéro/Tour Eiffel, 7ᵉ* 🕾*01–45–51–42–22* Ⓜ*Invalides*) was the original muse of Yves Saint Laurent; she was at his side for more than 30 years of collections and designed his accessories line. Now this paragon of the fashion aristocracy has her own two-floor boutique filled with the best style around. **Sabbia Rosa** (⊠*73 rue des Sts-Pères, St-Germain-des-Prés, 6ᵉ* 🕾*01–45–48–88–37* Ⓜ*St-Germain-des-Prés*) sells French lingerie favored by celebrities like Catherine Deneuve and Claudia Schiffer.

BOOKSTORES

The scenic open-air bookstalls along the Seine sell secondhand books (mostly in French), prints, and souvenirs. Numerous French-language bookstores—specializing in a wide range of topics, including art, film, literature, and philosophy—are found in the Latin Quarter and around St-Germain-des-Prés. **Brentano's** (⊠*37 av. de l'Opéra, Opéra/Grands Boulevards, 2ᵉ* 🕾*01–42–61–52–50* Ⓜ*Opéra*) is well known for its selection of English-language books. **Comptoir de l'Image** (⊠*44 rue de Sévigné, Le Marais, 3ᵉ* 🕾*01–42–72–03–92* Ⓜ*St-Paul*) is where designers John Galliano, Marc Jacobs, and Emanuel Ungaro stock up on old copies of *Vogue, Harper's Bazaar,* and *The Face.* **Galignani** (⊠*224 rue de Rivoli, Louvre/Tuileries, 1ᵉʳ* 🕾*01–42–60–76–07* Ⓜ*Tuileries*) is especially known for its extensive collection of art and coffee-table books.

★ **La Hune** (⊠*170 bd. St-Germain, St-Germain-des-Prés, 6ᵉ* 🕾*01–45–48–35–85* Ⓜ*St-Germain-des-Prés*), sandwiched between the Café de Flore and Les Deux Magots, is a landmark for intellectuals. French literature is downstairs, but the main attraction is the comprehensive collection of international books on art and architecture upstairs. Stay here until midnight with all the other genius-insomniacs. he **Red Wheelbarrow** (⊠*22 rue St-Paul, Le Marais, 4ᵉ* 🕾*01–42–77–42–17* Ⓜ*St-Paul* ⊠*13 rue St-Charles, Le Marais, 4ᵉ* 🕾*01–40–26–76–20* Ⓜ*St-Paul*) is *the* anglophone bookstore—if it was written in English, they can get it. It also has a complete academic section and every literary review you can think of. **Shakespeare and Company** (⊠*37 rue de la Bûcherie, Quartier Latin, 5ᵉ* 🕾*01–43–26–96–50* Ⓜ*St-Michel*), the sentimental Left Bank favorite, is named after the publishing house that first edited James Joyce's *Ulysses.* Nowadays, it specializes in expatriate literature. You can count on a couple of eccentric characters somewhere in the stacks, a sometimes-spacey staff, the latest titles from British presses, and hidden secondhand treasures in the odd corners and crannies. Poets give readings upstairs on Monday at 8 PM; there are also tea-party talks on Sunday at 4 PM.

CLOTHING

MEN'S WEAR

Berluti (✉26 rue Marbeuf, Champs-Élysées, 8ᵉ ☎01–53–93–97–97 Ⓜ Franklin-D.-Roosevelt) has been making the most exclusive men's shoes for more than a century. **Charvet** (✉28 pl. Vendôme, Opéra/ Grands Boulevards, 1ᵉʳ ☎01–42–60–30–70 Ⓜ Opéra) is the Parisian equivalent of a Savile Row tailor. **Madélios** (✉23 bd. de la Madeleine, Opéra/Grands Boulevards, 1ᵉʳ ☎01–53–45–00–00 Ⓜ Madeleine) gathers up all kinds of menswear labels from classy (Dior, Kenzo) to quirky (Paul Smith) to casual (Diesel, Levi's).

WOMEN'S WEAR

It doesn't matter, say the French, that fewer and fewer of their top couture houses are still headed by compatriots. It's the chic elegance, the classic ambience, the je ne sais quoi, that remains undeniably Gallic. Here are some meccas for Paris chic. **Antik Batik** (✉4 rue Cambon, Louvre/Tuileries, 1ᵉʳ ☎01–40–15–01–45 Ⓜ Concorde) has a wonderful line of ethnically inspired clothes. There are row upon row of beaded and sequined dresses, Chinese silk tunics, short fur jackets, flowing organza separates, and some of Paris's most popular handbags. **Azzedine Alaïa** (✉7 rue de Moussy, Le Marais, 4ᵉ ☎01–42–72–19–19 Ⓜ Hôtel-de-Ville) is the undisputed "king of cling" and a supermodel favorite.

★ **Chanel** (✉42 av. Montaigne, Champs-Élysées, 8ᵉ ☎01–47–23–74–12 Ⓜ Franklin-D.-Roosevelt ✉31 rue Cambon, Louvre/Tuileries, 1ᵉʳ ☎01–42–86–26–00 Ⓜ Tuileries) is helmed by svelte Karl Lagerfeld who whips together nouvelle takes on all of Coco's favorites: the perfectly tailored tweed suit; a lean, soigné black dress; a quilted bag with a gold chain; a camellia brooch. **Chloé** (✉54–56 rue du Faubourg St-Honoré, Louvre/Tuileries, 8ᵉ ☎01–44–94–33–00 Ⓜ Concorde) is enjoying a renaissance with Phoebe Philo at the helm; her flowing layered dresses brought the label instant cachet. This season's above-the-knee A-line skirts, cropped jackets in '60s silhouettes, and lots of sheer organza made news with fashionistas.

Christian Dior (✉30 av. Montaigne, Champs-Élysées, 8ᵉ ☎01–40–73–54–44 Ⓜ Franklin-D.-Roosevelt ✉16 rue de l'Abbé, St-Germain-des-Prés, 6ᵉ ☎01–40–73–54–44 Ⓜ St-Germain-des-Prés) features the flamboyant John Galliano … so what if he pairs full-length body-skimming evening dresses with high-tops and a Davy Crockett raccoon hat? It's just fashion, darling.

Fodor'sChoice
★ **Christian Lacroix** (✉73 rue du Faubourg St-Honoré, Louvre/Tuileries, 8ᵉ ☎01–42–68–79–00 Ⓜ Concorde ✉2 pl. St-Sulpice, St-Germain-des-Prés, 6ᵉ ☎01–46–33–48–95 Ⓜ St-Sulpice) masters color and texture to such an ultra-Parisian extent that his runway shows leave fans literally weeping with pleasure—and not just Eddy from Absolutely Fabulous.

The Rue du Faubourg St-Honoré location is the Lacroix epicenter; on the ground floor you'll find the ready-to-wear line "Bazar"; haute couture is through the courtyard.

★ **Colette** (⊠ *213 rue St-Honoré, Louvre/Tuileries, 1ᵉʳ* ☎ *01–55–35–33–90* Ⓜ *Tuileries*) is the most fashionable, most hip, and most hyped store in Paris (and possibly the world). The ground floor, which stocks design objects, gadgets, and makeup, is generally packed with fashion victims and the simply curious. Upstairs are handpicked fashions, accessories, magazines, and books, all of which ooze trendiness.

> ### GRAND COUTURE REDUX
>
> Didier Ludot (⊠ Jardins du Palais-Royal, 24 Galerie Montpensier ☎ 01–42–96–06–56 Ⓜ Palais-Royal) is one of the world's most famous vintage-clothing dealers and an incredibly charming man to boot. Check out the wonderful vintage Chanel suits, Balenciaga dresses, and Hermès scarves, and bring lots of money. (A tip: be nice to the dogs.)

★ **Jean-Paul Gaultier** (⊠ *44 av. George V, Champs-Élysées, 8ᵉ* ☎ *01–44–43–00–44* Ⓜ *George V* ⊠ *6 Galerie Vivienne, Opéra/Grands Boulevards, 2ᵉ* ☎ *01–42–86–05–05* Ⓜ *Bourse*) first made headlines with his celebrated corset with the ironic i-conic breasts for Madonna, but now sends fashion editors into ecstasy with his sumptuous haute couture creations. Designer Philippe Starck spun an *Alice in Wonderland* fantasy for the boutiques, with quilted cream walls and Murano mirrors. **Shine** (⊠ *15 rue de Poitou, Le Marais, 3ᵉ* ☎ *01–48–05–80–10* Ⓜ *Filles du Calvaire*) outshines even the old Bastille boutique in its new digs in the Marais's greener pastures. Retro and übermodern all at once, here you can find only the cutting-edge of chic (with a clientele to match): Marc by Marc Jacobs, See by Chloë, jeans by Stitch, and True Religion. **Sonia Rykiel** (⊠ *175 bd. St-Germain, St-Germain-des-Prés, 6ᵉ* ☎ *01–49–54–60–60* Ⓜ *St-Germain-des-Prés* ⊠ *70 rue du Faubourg St-Honoré, Louvre/Tuileries, 8ᵉ* ☎ *01–42–65–20–81* Ⓜ *Concorde*) is the queen of French fashion. Since the '60s she's been designing stylish knit separates and has made black her color of preference.

GIFTS FOR THE HOME

★ **Maison de Baccarat** (⊠ *11 pl. des Etats-Unis, Trocadéro/Tour Eiffel, 16ᵉ* ☎ *01–40–22–11–00* Ⓜ *Trocadéro*) was once the home of Marie-Laure de Noailles, known as the Countess of Bizarre; now it's a museum and crystal store of the famed manufacturer. Philippe Starck revamped the space with his signature cleverness—yes, that's a chandelier floating in an aquarium and, yes, that crystal arm sprouting from the wall alludes to Jean Cocteau (a friend of Noailles).

★ **Muji** (⊠ *47 rue des Francs Bourgeois, Le Marais, 4ᵉ* ☎ *01–49–96–41–41* Ⓜ *St-Paul* ⊠ *27 and 30 rue St-Sulpice, St-Germain-des-Prés, 6ᵉ* ☎ *01–46–34–01–10* Ⓜ *Odéon*) runs on the concept of *kanketsu*, or simplicity. The resultant streamlined designs for sportswear, housewares, and other supplies are all the rage in Europe. Must-haves include a collection of mini-necessities—travel essentials, wee office gizmos, purse-size accoutrements—so useful and adorable you'll want them all. **Résonances** (✉ *Carrousel du Louvre, 99 rue de Rivoli, Louvre/Tuileries, 1er* ☎01–42–97–06–00 Ⓜ *Louvre/Palais-Royal*) specializes in nostalgic French lifestyle items: 1950s-style soap holders that attach to the wall, everything you need to cook the perfect egg, a neat porcelain figurine called Pierrot le Gourmand that holds lollipops.

GOURMET GOODIES

À la Mère de Famille (✉*35 rue du Faubourg-Montmartre, Opéra/Grands Boulevards, 9e* ☎01–47–70–83–69 Ⓜ *Cadet*) is an enchanting shop well versed in French regional specialties and old-fashioned bonbons, sugar candy, and more. **Fauchon** (✉*26 pl. de la Madeleine, Opéra/Grands Boulevards, 8e* ☎01–70–39–38–00 Ⓜ *Madeleine*) is the most famous and iconic of all Parisian food stores.

PARIS ESSENTIALS

To research prices, get advice from other travelers, and book travel arrangements, visit www.fodors.com.

TRANSPORTATION

AIR TRAVEL TO & FROM PARIS

CARRIERS

Major carriers fly daily from the United States; Air France, British Airways, British Midland, and EasyJet fly regularly from London.

AIRPORTS & TRANSFERS

Paris is served by two international airports:

Charles de Gaulle/Roissy (☎*01–48–62–22–80 in English* ⊕*www.adp. fr*), 26 km (16 mi) northeast, and

Orly (☎*01–49–75–15–15* ⊕*www.adp.fr*), 16 km (10 mi) south. Orly has two terminals: Orly Ouest (domestic flights) and Orly Sud (international, regular, and charter flights). Charles de Gaulle has three terminals: Aérogare 1 (foreign flights), Aérogare 2 (Air France flights), and Aérogare T-3 (discount airlines and charter flights). Terminal information should be noted on your ticket. Terminals within each airport are connected with a free shuttle service, called the *navette*.

From Charles de Gaulle, the RER-B, the suburban commuter train, beneath Terminal 2, has trains to central Paris (Les Halles, St-Michel, Luxembourg) every 20 minutes; the fare is €8.10, and the journey takes 30 minutes. Note that you have to carry your luggage up from and down to the platform and that trains can be crowded during rush hour. **Remember you must retain the train ticket sold to you at Charles de Gaulle Airport because you will need it at the end of the ride to exit the métro system** once you are in the city center. Without a ticket stub, you will not be able to get the métro turnstiles to open to exit the subway system in Paris and you could wind up paying a fine or being trapped in the station until a passerby can aid you *(also see the note about métro mugging in the Métro Travel section, below)*.

Buses operated by Air France (you need not have flown with the airline) run every 15 minutes between Charles de Gaulle and western Paris (Porte Maillot and the Arc de Triomphe). The fare is €13 or €14, and the trip takes about 40 minutes, though rush-hour traffic may make it longer. Additionally, the Roissybus, operated by the RATP, runs directly between Charles de Gaulle and Rue Scribe by the Opéra every 15 minutes and costs €8.50. Taxis are readily available; the fare will be around €50–€60, depending on traffic, but traffic jams can make this a frustrating venture. Aeroports Limousine Service can meet you on arrival in a private car and drive you to your destination; reservations should be made two or three days in advance; MasterCard and Visa are accepted—readers report inordinate delays, however. The following minibus services—with fixed prices—can also meet you on arrival.

The RER-C line is one way to get to Paris from Orly Airport; there's a free shuttle bus from the terminal building to the train station, and trains leave every 15 minutes. The fare is €5.70 (métro included), and the train journey takes about 35 minutes. The Orlyval service is a shuttle train that runs direct from each Orly terminal to the Antony RER-B station every seven minutes; a one-way ticket for the entire trip into Paris is €9.05. Buses operated by Air France (you need not have flown with the airline) run every 12 minutes between Orly Airport, Montparnasse station, and Les Invalides. On the Left Bank, the fare is €8, and the trip can take from 30 minutes to an hour, depending on traffic. RATP also runs the Orlybus between the Denfert-Rochereau métro station and Orly every 15 minutes, and the trip costs €5.80. You can economize using **RATP Bus 285,** which shuttles you from the airport to Line 7, métro Villejuif Louis Arragan station for the price of a city bus ticket. It operates daily from 6:45 AM (from 5:15 AM weekdays) to 12:45 AM at the Orly Sud terminal. A 20-minute taxi ride costs about €20–€30.

Taxis & Shuttles Air France Bus (▦ *08–92–35–08–20 recorded information in English €0.35 per min* ⊕ *www.cars-airfrance.com).* **Airport Connection** (▦ *01–43–65–55–55* 🖥 *01–43–65–55–57* ⊕ *www.airport-connection.com).* **Paris Airports Services** (▦ *01–55–98–10–80* 🖥 *01–55–98–10–89* ⊕ *www.parisairportservice. com).* **RATP (Paris Transit Authority: including Roissybus, Orlybus, Orlyval)** (▦ *08–92–68–77–14 €0.35 per min* ⊕ *www.ratp.com).*

BUS TRAVEL TO & FROM PARIS

Long-distance bus journeys within France are uncommon, which may be why Paris has no central bus depot. *See By Bus in France Essentials for information on traveling to and from Paris by bus.*

BUS TRAVEL WITHIN PARIS

The Paris bus system is user-friendly and a great way to see the city. Buses are marked with the route number and destination in front and with major stopping places along the sides. The brown bus shelters contain timetables and route maps. Maps are also found on each bus. To get off, press one of the red buttons mounted on the silver poles that run the length of the bus and the *arrêt demandé* (stop requested) light directly above the driver will light up. Use the rear door to exit (some require you to push a silver button to open the door).

TICKETS & SCHEDULES

You can use your métro ticket on buses; if you have individual tickets (as opposed to weekly or monthly tickets), be prepared to punch your ticket in the gray machines on board the bus. Your best bet is to buy a *carnet* of 10 tickets for €10.90 at any métro station, or you can buy a single ticket onboard (exact change appreciated) for €1.40. You need to show (but not punch) weekly, monthly, and Paris-Visite/Mobilis tickets to the driver. Tickets can be bought on buses, in the métro, or in any bar–tabac store displaying the lime-green métro symbol above its street sign. Most routes operate from 6 AM to 8:30 PM; some continue until midnight. During weekday rush hours there are usually buses every 5 minutes, with waits up to 15 minutes on weekends or evenings. Some bus shelters have digital signs indicating the wait time. The newly improved night bus service, called the *Noctilien,* has 35 routes that operate within Paris every 15–30 minutes (12:30 AM–5:30 AM) between Châtelet, four of the city's five train stations, and various nearby suburbs.

Bus Information RATP (✉ *54 quai de la Rapée, 75012* ☎ *08–92–68–77–14 €0.35 per min* ⊕ *www.ratp.com*).

CAR TRAVEL

The aggressive and bewildering style of Parisian drivers is usually enough to deter visitors from getting behind the wheel. Traffic moves at a snail's pace, and parking is a nightmare. Meters and ticket machines (pay and display) are common and in Paris work only with parking cards (*cartes de stationnement*). They work like credit cards in the parking meters and come in three denominations: €10, €20, and €30. Since parking in Paris runs a whopping €2 per hour, you should invest in the €30 option if you can. Parking cards are available at any café posting the red TABAC sign. Insert your card into the nearest meter, choose the approximate amount of time you expect to stay, and you'll receive a green receipt, which must be clearly visible to the meter patrol; place it on the dashboard on the inside of the front window on the passenger side. There's no shortage of underground parking garages, with the most expensive ones in the center of town, designated by a white "P" on a blue square. The only time parking is free is on Sunday and in certain streets in August, designated with a yellow circle sticker on the parking meter. Although the speed limits are rarely enforced in France, parking fines are handed out regularly, and any cars illegally parked will be towed.

Gasoline stations are usually well hidden on small streets within the city and charge absurdly high prices; the ones in hypermarket parking lots around the city's *périphérique,* or ring road, are a better deal and open 24 hours.

The major ring road encircling Paris is called the *périphérique,* with the *périphérique intérieur* going counterclockwise around the city, and the *périphérique extérieur,* or the outside ring, going clockwise. Up to five lanes wide, the périphérique is a major highway from which *portes* (gates) connect Paris to the major highways of France. The names of these highways function on the same principle as the métro, with the final destination as the determining point in the direction you must take. For instance, heading north, look for Porte de la Chapelle (direction Lille and Charles de Gaulle Airport); east, for Porte de Bagnolet (direction Metz and Nancy); south, for Porte d'Orléans (direction Lyon and Bordeaux); and west, for Porte d'Auteuil (direction Rouen and Chartres) or Porte de St-Cloud. Other portes include Porte de la Villette; Porte de Pantin; Porte de Bercy (A4 to Reims); Porte d'Italie; and Porte de Maillot (A14 to Rouen).

MÉTRO TRAVEL

The métro is by far the quickest and most efficient way to get around. Trains run from 5:30 AM until 1 AM and 2 AM on Saturday (and be forewarned—this means the famous "last métro" can pass your station anytime after 12:30 AM on weekdays). Stations are signaled either by a large yellow M within a circle or by their distinctive curly green Art Nouveau railings and archway entrances bearing the subway's full title (Métropolitain). It's essential to **know the name of the last station on the line you take,** as this name appears on all signs. A connection (you can make as many as you like on one ticket) is called a *correspondance.* At junction stations illuminated orange signs bearing the name of the line terminal appear over the correct corridors for correspondances. Illuminated blue signs marked SORTIE indicate the station exit. In general, the métro is safe, although try to avoid the larger, mazelike stations at Les Halles and République if you're alone late at night, and try and ride in the first car behind the conductor. Access to métro platforms is through an automatic ticket barrier. Slide your ticket in and pick it up and retrieve it as it pops up. **Keep your ticket during your journey; you will need it to leave the RER system,** and you'll be glad you have it in case you run into any green-clad inspectors when you're leaving—they can be very unpleasant and will impose a big fine on the spot if you do not have a ticket.

Speaking of unpleasant, many readers have written to us about being mugged in the métro system. A favorite mode is for muggers to "sandwich" you as you attempt to exit the rather tricky turnstiles; others make their attack on the lengthy escalators at the métro exits. Pickpockets are close enough and nimble-fingered enough (think Oliver Twist) to rob you in a split second. These pickpockets work in groups, never alone—one will divert your attention (think the Artful Dodger) while the other whisks away your wallet or your passport (which should not be in your back pocket or shoulder purse). Prevention of petty crime is the same all over the world. Just use discretion and caution while maintaining your physical comfort zone in crowded places. Happily, as large cities go, Paris remains—for the most part—a safe place.

FARES & SCHEDULES

All métro tickets and passes are valid not only for the métro but also for all RER, tram, and bus travel within Paris. Métro tickets cost €1.40 each; a *carnet* (10 tickets for €10.90) is a better value. The best deal for long visits is the new, unlimited usage *Carte Navigo*, an electronic ticket sold according to zone. Zones 1 and 2 cover the entire métro network; tickets cost €52.50 a month. For these monthly tickets, you need a pass (available from rail and major métro stations) and a passport-size photograph (many stations have photo booths). ■**TIP→Because they're meant to be for residents and not visitors, you may have to ask at more than one window before a ticket agent will let you get a Carte Navigo.** The Carte Navigo replaces the weekly Carte Orange, but the latter is still available, for an undetermined amount of time. The Carte Orange is only valid for weekly travel, Monday morning to Sunday night. It's €16, for travel within Paris.

Visitors are usually directed to purchase the one-day (Mobilis) and two- to five-day (Paris-Visite) tickets for unlimited travel on the entire RATP (Paris transit authority) network: métro, RER, bus, tram, funicular (Montmartre), and Noctilien (night bus). The Mobilis and Paris-Visite passes are valid starting any day of the week. Paris-Visite also gives you discounts on a few museums and attractions. Mobilis tickets cost €5.50. Paris-Visite is €8.50 (one day), €13.95 (two days), €18.60 (three days), and €27.20 (five days) for Paris only. Children ages 4–11 receive approximately 50% off.

Métro Information RATP (☎ 08–92–68–41–14 ⊕ www.ratp.fr).

TAXIS

On weekend nights after 11 PM it's nearly impossible to find a taxi—you're best off asking hotel or restaurant staff to call you one, but, be forewarned: you'll have to pay for them to come get you and, depending on where they are, the fare can quickly add up. If you want to hail a cab on your own, look for the taxis with their signs lighted up (their signs will be glowing white as opposed to the taxis that are already taken whose signs will be a dull orange). There are taxi stands on almost every major street corner but again, expect a wait if it's a busy weekend night. Taxi stands are marked by a square dark blue sign with a white T in the middle. Daytime rates, denoted A (7 AM–7 PM), within Paris are €0.82 per km (½ mi), and nighttime rates, B, are €1.10 per km. Suburban zones and airports, C, are €1.33 per km. There's a basic hire charge of €2.10 for all rides, a €1 supplement per bag after the second piece, and a €0.75 supplement if you're picked up at an SNCF station. Waiting time is charged at €26.28–€29.90 per hour.

Taxi Companies **Alpha Taxis** (☎ *01–45–85–85–85*) operate 24 hours throughout the Ile-de-France region. **Taxi G7** (☎ *01–47–39–47–39*) have cars that can accommodate wheelchairs.

Taxis Bleus (☎ *08–91–70–10–10, 08–25–16–66–66 for airport service*) is one of the largest taxi companies in Paris.

TRAIN TRAVEL

Paris has five international train stations run by the SNCF: Gare du Nord (northern France, northern Europe, and England via Calais or the Channel Tunnel); Gare St-Lazare (Normandy and England via Dieppe); Gare de l'Est (Strasbourg, Luxembourg, Basel, and central Europe); Gare de Lyon (Lyon, TGV to Aix-en-Provence, Marseille, the Riviera, Geneva, Italy); and Gare d'Austerlitz (Loire Valley, southwest France, Spain). The Gare Montparnasse is used by the TGV *Atlantique* bound for Nantes or Bordeaux. Call 08–92–35–35–35 for information. Trains heading outside of Ile-de-France are usually referred to as *Grandes Lignes,* while regional train service is referred to as *trains de banlieue,* or *Le Transilien.*

RER trains travel between Paris and the suburbs and are operated by the RATP. When they go through Paris, they act as a sort of supersonic métro—they connect with the métro network at several points—and can be great time-savers. Access to RER platforms is through the same type of automatic ticket barrier (if you've started your journey on the métro, you can use the same ticket), but you'll need to have the same ticket handy to put through another barrier when you leave the system.

Train Information RER/RATP (☎ *08–92–68–77–14* ⊕ *www.ratp.fr*). **SNCF Nationale** (☎ *36–35 [€0.34 per min]* ⊕ *www.voyages-sncf.com*). **TGV** (⊕ *www.tgv.com*). **SNCF/Transilien** (☎ *08–91–36–20–20* ⊕ *www.sncf.fr*).

CONTACTS & RESOURCES

CAR RENTAL

Cars can be rented at both airports, as well as at locations throughout the city, including the ones listed below.

Local Agencies Avis (✉ *60 rue de Ponthieu, Champs-Élysées, 8e* ☎ *01–43–59–03–83* Ⓜ *St-Philippe du Roule*). **Europcar** (✉ *60 bd. Diderot, Bastille/Nation, 12e* ☎ *08–25–82–54–63* Ⓜ *Gare de Lyon*). **Hertz** (✉ *193 rue de Bercy, Bercy/Tolbiac, 12e* ☎ *01–43–44–06–00* Ⓜ *Gare de Lyon*). **National/Citer** (✉ *18 rue de Dunkerque, Gare du Nord, 10^e* ☎ *01–53–20–06–52* Ⓜ *Gare du Nord*).

EMERGENCIES

A 24-hour emergency service is available at American Hospital. Hertford British Hospital also has all-night emergency service. This guidebook does not list the major Paris hospitals, as the French government prefers an emergency operator to make the judgment call and assign you the best option. Note that if you're able to walk into a hospital emergency room by yourself, you are often considered "low priority." So if time is of the essence, the best thing to do is to call the fire department (🕮18); a fully trained team of paramedics will usually arrive within five minutes. You may also dial for a Samu ambulance (🕮15); there's usually an English-speaking physician available. In a less urgent situation, SOS Medecin (doctor) or SOS Dentiste services send a certified, experienced doctor or dentist to your door, a very helpful 24-hour service to use for common symptoms of high fever, toothache, or upset stomach (the visit usually costs €75). It's important to check with your insurance company before you leave for your trip to make sure that you are covered internationally.

Doctors & Dentists SOS Dentiste (🕿01-43-37-51-00). **SOS Medecin** (🕿01-43-07-77-77).

Emergency Services Ambulance (🕿15 or 01-45-67-50-50). **Fire Department** (🕿18). **Police** (🕿17).

Hospitals American Hospital (✉63 bd. Victor-Hugo, Neuilly 🕿01-46-41-25-25). **Hertford British Hospital** (✉3 rue Barbès, Levallois-Perret 🕿01-46-39-22-22).

Late-Night & 24-Hour Pharmacies Dhéry (✉Galerie des Champs, 84 av. des Champs-Élysées, Champs-Élysées, 8e 🕿01-45-62-02-41) is open 24 hours. **Pharmacie Internationale** (✉5 pl. Pigalle, Pigalle-Clichy, 9e 🕿01-48-78-38-12) is open 24 hours some days. **Pharmacie Matignon** (✉2 rue Jean-Mermoz, at the Rond-Point de Champs-Élysées, Champs-Élysées, 8e) is open daily until 2 AM.

INTERNET & MAIL

Almost all hotels in Paris, save for the resolutely old-fashioned, have a tiny Internet kiosk that guests can use for free or for a fee. There are also several Internet cafés that can provide more services and offer competitive rates. **XS Arena Internet** (✉43 bd. Sebastopol, Châtelet, 75001 🕿01-40-13-06-51 ✉17 rue Soufflot, Quartier Latin, 75005 🕿01-43-54-55-55), usually full of young gamers, is open daily, 24 hours. **La Baguenaude** (✉30 rue Grande Truanderie, Châtelet, 75001 🕿01-40-26-27-74 ⊕www.baguenaude-cafe.com) is smaller and has shorter opening hours, but more specialized equipment, including scanners, CD burners, and color printers. **Cyber Cube** (✉12 rue Daval, Bastille, 75011 🕿01-49-29-67-67 ⊕www.cybercube.fr) is open daily 10–10, with rates by the minute.

If you bring your laptop with you, be sure to be prepared with adaptors and foreign access numbers for your home ISP . Wireless Internet access is more and more common in Paris, particularly in hotels and cafés, although not always for free.

Post offices, or PTT, are found in every neighborhood and are recognizable by a yellow and blue LA POSTE sign. They're usually open weekdays 8 AM–7 PM, Saturday 8 AM–noon, but the **main Paris post office** (✉52 rue du Louvre, 1er) is open 24 hours, seven days a week. For a memorable souvenir, get your postcards stamped at the post office inside the Louvre Museum or the Eiffel Tower (on the first level).

TOUR OPTIONS
BY BOAT

Hour-long boat trips on the Seine can be fun if you're in Paris for the first time; the cost is €9–€15. A few lines serve lunch and dinner (for an additional cost); make reservations in advance. The massive, double-decker Bateaux Mouches (with commentary in seven languages) depart from the Pont de l'Alma (Right Bank) every half hour from April to September from 10 AM to 11 PM and approximately every three hours during the gray winter months from 11 AM to 9 PM. Bateaux Parisiens boats depart every half hour in summer and every hour in winter, starting at 10 AM; the last boat departs at 10 PM (11 PM in summer). Canauxrama organizes half- and full-day barge tours along the canals of east Paris. Vedettes du Pont-Neuf offer one-hour trips with live commentary in French and English; boats depart daily from Square du Vert Galant every 30 to 60 minutes 10 AM to 10:30 PM (with a 90-minute lunch break from noon) March through October, and from 10:30 AM to 10 PM with a two-hour lunch break November through February. Yachts de Paris organizes romantic 2½-hour "gourmand cruises" (for about €149) year-round.

Fees & Schedules Bateaux Mouches (⊠ *Pont de l'Alma, Trocadéro/Tour Eiffel, 8ᵉ* ☎ *01–42–25–96–10* ⊕ *www.bateauxmouches.com* Ⓜ *Alma-Marceau*). **Bateaux Parisiens** (⊠ *Port de la Bourdonnais, at foot of Eiffel Tower, Trocadéro/Tour Eiffel, 7ᵉ* ☎ *08–25–01–01–01* ⊕ *www.bateauxparisiens.com* Ⓜ *Trocadéro*). **Canauxrama** (⊠ *13 quai de la Loire, Gare de l'Est, 19ᵉ* ☎ *01–42–39–15–00* ⊕ *www.canauxrama. com* Ⓜ *Jaurès* ⊠ *For information: Bassin de l'Arsenal, opposite 50 bd. de la Bastille, Bastille/Nation, 12ᵉ* ☎ *01–42–39–15–00* Ⓜ *Bastille*). **Vedettes du Pont-Neuf** (⊠ *Below Sq. du Vert-Galant, Ile de la Cité, 1ᵉʳ* ☎ *01–46–33–98–38* ⊕ *www.vedettesdupontneuf.com* Ⓜ *Pont Neuf*). **Yachts de Paris** (⊠ *Port de Javel* ☎ *01–44–54–14–70* ⊕ *www.yachtsdeparis.com*).

BY BUS

For a two-hour orientation tour by bus, the standard price is about €25. The two largest bus-tour operators are Cityrama and Paris Vision; for a more intimate tour of the city, Cityrama also runs several minibus excursions per day with a private multilingual tour operator for €74. Paris Vision runs nonstop two-hour tours with multilingual commentary available via individual headphones with more than 10 languages for €19. Paris L'Open Tour gives tours in a double-decker bus with an open top; commentary is available in French and English on individual headphones. Get on or off at one of the 50 pickup points indicated by the lime-green sign posts; tickets may be purchased on board and cost €25 for one day, €28 for unlimited use for two days. Les Cars Rouges offer double-decker London-style buses with nine stops—a ticket for two consecutive days is available for €22. RATP (Paris Transit Authority) also offers economical, commentary-free excursions; the Montmartrobus departs from métro Anvers and zips through the winding cobbled streets of Montmartre to the top of the hill for those of you who don't want to brave the walk; the trip is the price of one métro ticket (€1.40). The RATP Balabus Bb line goes from Gare du Lyon to the Grande Arche at La Défense passing by all major tourist attractions on the way for the price of one to three métro tickets. The Balabus Bb line runs Sunday and holidays from mid-April to September.

Information Cityrama (✉ 4 pl. des Pyramides, 1er ☎ 01–44–55–61–00 ⊕ www. ecityrama.com). **Les Cars Rouges** (☎ 01–53–95–39–53 ⊕ www.carsrouges. com). **Paris L'Open Tour** (✉ 13 rue Auber, 9e ☎ 01–42–66–56–56 ⊕ www. paris-opentour.com). **Paris Vision** (✉ 214 rue de Rivoli, 1er ☎ 01–42–60–30–01 ⊕ www.parisvision.com.

BY FOOT

The team at Paris Walking Tours offers a wide selection of tours, from neighborhood visits to museum tours and theme tours such as "Hemingway's Paris," "The Marais," "Montmartre," and "The Latin Quarter." A two-hour tour costs about €10. Context Paris offers more intimate tours (small groups only) of the city, including orientation cruises and specialized art and history tours led by qualified academics. Three-hour tours average €200 per group. A list of walking tours is also available from the Caisse Nationale des Monuments Historiques, in the weekly magazines available at any kiosk in the city, *Pariscope* and *L'Officiel des Spectacles,* which list walking tours under the heading "*Conférences*" (most are in French, unless otherwise noted).

Fees & Schedules Caisse Nationale des Monuments Historiques (✉ Bureau des Visites: Hôtel de Sully, 62 rue St-Antoine, Bastille/Nation, 4e ☎ 01–44–61–21–70 Ⓜ St-Paul). **Context Paris** (☎ 06–13–09–67–11 ⊕ www.contextparis.com).

Paris Walking Tours (☎ 01–48–09–21–40 ⊕ www.paris-walks.com).

VISITOR INFORMATION

There are more than five branches of the Paris tourist office located at key points in the capital. Don't call with a question though—you'll get a host of generic recorded information that will cost you €0.34 per minute.

Information Espace du Tourisme d'Ile-de-France (✉ Carrousel du Louvre, 99 rue de Rivoli, 75001 ☎ 08–92–68–30–00 ⊕ www.pidf.com Ⓜ Palais-Royal Musée du Louvre). **Office du Tourisme de la Ville de Paris Pyramides** (✉ 25 rue des Pyramides, 75001 ☎ 08–92–68–30–00 €0.34 per min Ⓜ Pyramides). **Office du Tourisme de la Ville de Paris Gare du Lyon** (✉ Arrivals, 20 bd. Diderot, 75012 Ⓜ Gare du Lyon). **Office du Tourisme de la Ville de Paris Gare du Nord** (✉ 18 rue de Dunkerque, 75010 Ⓜ Gare du Nord). **Office du Tourisme de la Ville de Paris Opéra–Grands Magasins** (✉ 11 rue Scribe, 75009 Ⓜ Opéra). **Office du Tourisme de la Ville de Paris Tour Eiffel** (✉ Between east and north legs of Eiffel Tower Ⓜ Champs de Mars/Tour Eiffel).

BY FOOT

The team at Paris Walking Tours offers a wide selection of tours, from neighborhood visits to museum tours and theme tours such as "Hemingway's Paris," "The Marais," "Montmartre," and "The Latin Quarter." A two-hour tour costs about €10. Context Paris offers more intimate tours (small groups only) of the city, including orientation cruises and specialized art and history tours led by qualified academics.

VISITOR INFORMATION

There are more than five branches of the Paris tourist office located at key points in the capital. Don't call with a question though—you'll get a host of generic recorded information that will cost you €0.34 per minute.

Information **Espace du Tourisme d'Ile-de-France** (⊠ *Carrousel du Louvre, 99 rue de Rivoli, 75001* ☎ *08–92–68–30–00* ⊕ *www.pidf.com* Ⓜ *Palais-Royal Musée du Louvre*). **Office du Tourisme de la Ville de Paris Pyramides** (⊠ *25 rue des Pyramides, 75001* ☎ *08–92–68–30–00* *€0.34 per min* Ⓜ *Pyramides*). **Office du Tourisme de la Ville de Paris Gare du Lyon** (⊠ *Arrivals, 20 bd. Diderot, 75012* Ⓜ *Gare du Lyon*). **Office du Tourisme de la Ville de Paris Gare du Nord** (⊠ *18 rue de Dunkerque, 75010* Ⓜ *Gare du Nord*). **Office du Tourisme de la Ville de Paris Opéra–Grands Magasins** (⊠ *11 rue Scribe, 75009* Ⓜ *Opéra*). **Office du Tourisme de la Ville de Paris Tour Eiffel** (⊠ *Between east and north legs of Eiffel Tower* Ⓜ *Champs de Mars/Tour Eiffel*).

Ile-de-France

WORD OF MOUTH

"Last summer at Versailles, the regular State Rooms were crowded with a river of people. So we took the tour of the Private Apartments and, wow, was it great! We got to see how Louis XV really lived his life…the dog room, the library, his famous desk, and also the theater he had build for his sons—even his commode. The group was very small and the person (who spoke in English) was so informative. As for the State Rooms, opt for the helpful audioguides."

— Hypatia2A

WELCOME TO ILE-DE-FRANCE

TOP REASONS TO GO

★ **Louis XIV's Versailles:**
Famed as glorious testimony to the Sun King's megalomania, this is the world's most luxe palace and nature-tamed park.

★ **Creamy Chantilly:**
Stately château, stellar art collection, pretty park, boaty lakes, fabulous forest, regal racecourse, palatial stables…all within the same square mile.

★ **Van Gogh in Auvers:**
The great painter spent his last, manically productive three months here—you can see where he painted, where he got drunk, where he shot himself, and where he remains.

★ **Chartres Cathedral:**
A pinnacle of Gothic achievement, this 13th-century masterpiece has peerless stained glass and a hilltop silhouette visible for miles around.

★ **Monet's Waterlilies:**
Come to Giverny to see his lily pond—a half-acre "Monet"—then peek around his charming home and stroll the time-warped streets to the ultrastylish American Art Museum.

Château de Chantilly

1 The Western Ile-de-France: Versailles to Malmaison. The Ile-de-France's richest frontier for you, if you want to dig into the past, is the western half of the 60-km (35mi) circle that orbits Paris. These sylvan woods are literally full of châteaux of all descriptions, the towns are charming, and no one should miss the world's grandest palace. Haunt of Louis XIV, Madame de Pompadour, and Marie-Antoinette, **Versailles** is a monument to splendidly wretched excess and once home to 20,000 courtiers and servants. Nearby *la vie de châteaux* continues to dazzle at **Dampierre, Rambouillet, Maintenon, Thoiry, St-Germain,** and Napoléon's **Malmaison.** More spiritual concerns are embodied in **Chartres Cathedral,** the soaring pinnacle of Gothic architecture. Thirty miles north are landscapes of lasting impressions: **Giverny** and **Auvers,** immortalized by Monet and Van Gogh, respectively.

2

GETTING ORIENTED

Appearing like all France in miniature, the Ile-de-France region is the heartland of the nation. The "island of France" is the poetic name for the area surrounding Paris and taking in the valleys of three rivers, the Seine, the Marne, and the Oise. Ever since the days of Julius Caesar, this has been the economic, political, and religious hub of France and, consequently, no other region boasts such a wealth of great buildings, from Chartres to Fontainebleau and Versailles. Though small, this region is so rich in treasures that a whole day of fascinating exploration may take you no more than 60 km (35 mi) from the capital.

2 The Eastern Ile-de-France: Chantilly to Fontainebleau. By traveling an eastward arc through the remainder of the Ile you can savor the icing on the cake. Begin with **Chantilly,** one of the most opulent châteaux in France, noted for its royal stables, art treasures, and gardens by André Le Nôtre. Northward lies medieval **Senlis,**

the storybook castle of **Pierrefonds,** and **Compiégne's** palace, where Napoléon III had his court. Heading south, **Disneyland Paris** is where the Mickey-smitten rejoice. Continuing south, three magnificent châteaux—**Vaux-le-Vicomte, Courances,** and **Fontainebleau**—were built for some of France's most pampered monarchs and merchants.

Versailles

ILE-DE-FRANCE PLANNER

Getting Around

A comprehensive rail network ensures that most towns in Ile-de-France can make comfortable day trips from Paris, but make sure you know the right station to head out from (Gare de Lyon for Fontainebleau, Gare St-Lazare for Vernon, Gare du Nord for Compiègne, or Gare Montparnasse for Chartres). RER (commuter train) tunnels through central Paris en route to Versailles, St-Germain-en-Laye, and Disneyland.

A handful of venues need other means of access. To reach Giverny, rail it to Vernon, then use the taxi or local bus (or bike). To reach Vaux-le-Vicomte, head first for Melun, then take a taxi or local bus (in summer a shuttle service). Senlis can be reached by bus from Chantilly. And note that Fontainebleau station is in neighboring Avon, and getting to the château means a 10-minute bus ride.

The best way to crisscross the region without returning to the capital is by car. There's no shortage of expressways or fast highways. Expressways fan out from Paris in all directions: A13 northwest to Versailles and Giverny; A1 north to Senlis and Compiegne; A4 east to Disneyland.; A6 southeast to Fontainebleau; and A10 southwest to Chartres.

The Impressionist Ile

Paris's Musée d'Orsay may have some of the most fabled Monet and Van Gogh paintings in the world, but the Ile-de-France has something (almost) better—the actual landscapes that were rendered into masterpieces by the brushes of many great Impressionist and Postimpressionist artists.

At Giverny, Claude Monet's house and garden is a moving visual link to his finest daubs—its famous lily-pond garden, designed by the artist himself, gave rise to his legendary water-lilies series (some historians feel it was the other way around). Elsewhere, villages like Vétheuil—where the master liked to set up his easel—still look like three-dimensional "Monets."

In Auvers-sur-Oise, Vincent van Gogh had a final burst of creativity before ending his life; the famous wheat field where he was attacked by crows and painted his last painting is just outside town. Back then, they called him Fou-Roux (mad redhead) and derided his art. But now, more than a century after his passionate rendering of life and landscape, the townspeople here love to pay tribute to the "Van Go Go"—as Japanese tourists like to call him—who helped make their village famous.

André Derain lived in Chambourcy, Camille Pissarro in Pontoise, Alfred Sisley in Moret-sur-Loing—all were inspired by the silvery sunlight that tumbles over these hills and towns. Earlier, Rousseau, Millet, and Corot paved the way for Impressionism with their penchant for outdoor landscape painting in the village of Barbizon, still surrounded by its romantic, quietly dramatic forest. A trip to any of these towns will provide lasting impressions.

Finding a Place to Stay

In summer, hotel rooms are at a premium, and making reservations is essential; almost all accommodations in the swankier towns—Versailles, Rambouillet, and Fontainebleau—are on the costly side. Take nothing for granted; picturesque Senlis, for instance, does not have a single hotel in its historic downtown area.

Making the Most of Your Time

With so many legendary sights in the Ile-de-France—many of which are gratifying human experiences rather than just guidebook necessities—you could spend weeks visiting the region. For a stimulating mix of pomp, nature, and spirituality, we suggest your three priorities should be Versailles, Giverny, and Chartres. You definitely need a day for Versailles. the world's grandest palace. For that sublime treat of medieval art and architecture, the cathedral of Chartres, you need at least half a day. Ditto for Monet's ravishing home and garden at Giverny.

If you have time, combine Versailles with nearby St-Germain-en-Laye, and Chartres with Maintenon and Rambouillet. There are two other zones to concentrate on. To the north, Chantilly acts as a hub, between the painters' village of Auvers-sur-Oise and historic Senlis. To the southeast, Fontainebleau is the anchor. Nearby lurk the romantic forest village of Barbizon, and the splendiferous château and gardens of Vaux-le-Vicomte.

WHAT IT COSTS

	¢	$	$$	$$$	$$$$
Restaurants	Under €11	€11–€17	€17–€23	€23–€30	Over €30
Hotels	Under €50	€50–€80	€80–€120	€120–€190	Over €190

Restaurant prices are per person for a main course at dinner, including tax (19.6%) and service; note that if a restaurant offers only prix-fixe (set-price) meals, it has been given the price category that reflects the full prix-fixe price. Hotel prices are for a standard double room in high season, including tax (19.6%) and service charge. Hotels operate on the European Plan (EP, with no meal provided) unless we note that they use the Breakfast Plan (BP), or also offer such options as Modified American Plan (MAP, with breakfast and dinner daily, known as demi-pension), or Full American Plan (FAP, or pension complète, with three meals a day). Inquire when booking if these all-inclusive meal plans (which always entail higher rates) are mandatory or optional.

How's the Weather?

With its extensive forests, Ile-de-France is especially beautiful in fall, particularly October. May and June are good months, too, while July through August can be sultry and crowded.

On a Saturday night in summer, however, you can see a son-et-lumière show in Moret-sur-Loing and make a candlelight visit to Vaux-le-Vicomte.

Be aware when making your travel plans that some places are closed one or two days a week.

The château of Versailles is closed Monday; and the châteaux of Chantilly and Fontainebleau are closed Tuesday.

In fact, as a rule, well-touristed towns make their fermeture hebdomadaire (weekly closing) on Monday or Tuesday, when museums, shops, and markets may be closed—call ahead if in doubt.

Disneyland Paris gets really crowded on summer weekends.

So does Giverny (Monet's garden), which is at its best May through June and, like Vaux-le-Vicomte, is closed November to March.

During the winter months, it is always best to check and phone ahead to make sure your sightseeing stops are still open.

Introduction by
Nancy Coons

Updated by
Simon Hewitt

TO SOME OBSERVERS THE ILE-DE-FRANCE is the most heartwarming of all the French provinces. First, there's the pleasure of imagination fulfilled: there's something comfortingly familiar about the lanes bordered with silvery poplar trees, the golden haze in the air, the gray stone of a village steeple. And no wonder, for scores of painters have immortalized these very features. Corot began with the forest of Fontainebleau and the village of Barbizon. Camille Pissarro worked at Pontoise. Alfred Sisley's famous riverside canvases were painted at Moret-sur-Loing, near Fontainebleau. Claude Monet painted the Epte River. And Vincent van Gogh thrived (creatively, at least) and died in Auvers.

But aside from these things, just what is it that makes the Ile-de-France so attractive? Is it its proximity to the great city of Paris—or perhaps that it's so far removed? Had there not been this world-class cultural hub right nearby, would Monet have retreated to his Japanese gardens at Giverny? Or Paul Cézanne and Van Gogh to bucolic Auvers? Kings and courtiers to the game-rich forests of Fontainebleau, Rambouillet, and Dampierre? Would medieval castles and palaces have sprouted in the town of St-Germain-en-Laye? Would abbeys and cathedrals have sprung skyward in Chartres and Senlis?

If you asked Louis XIV, he wouldn't have minced his words: the city of Paris—yawn—was simply *démodé*—out of fashion. In the 17th century, the new power base was going to be Versailles, once a tiny village in the heart of the Ile-de-France, now the site of a gigantic château from which the Sun King's rays (Louis XIV was known as *le roi soleil*) could radiate, unfettered by rebellious rabble and European arrivistes. Of course, later heirs kept the lines open and restored the grandiose palace as the governmental hub it was meant to be—and commuted to Paris, well before the high-speed RER.

That, indeed, is the dream of most Parisians today: to have a foot in both worlds. Paris may be small as capital cities go, with just under 2 million inhabitants, but Ile-de-France, the region around Paris, contains more than 10 million people—a sixth of France's entire population. That's why on closer inspection the once rustic villages of Ile-de-France reveal cosseted gardens, stylishly gentrified cottages, and extraordinary country restaurants no peasant farmer could afford to frequent. And that's why Ile-de-France retains a sophisticated air, along with a glowing patina of history, not found in any of France's other patches of verdure.

The Ile-de-France is the ancient heartland of France, the core from which the French kings gradually extended their power over the rest of a rebellious, individualistic nation. Since the time when it was first wrested from savage Gauls by Julius Caesar, in 52 bc, the region has played a leading role in French history; its towns and villages intimately entwined with the course of national fact and legend. Charlemagne confirmed his power in France after generations had fought against the Romans near Soissons. There is Versailles, from which the three Louis gloriously reigned until the forces of Revolution dealt the French monarchy a deathblow. And Napoléon, after ruling for a time from Malmaison, abdicated his rule in the courtyard at Fontainebleau.

The Ile-de-France is not really an *île* (island), of course. This green-forested buffer zone that enfolds Paris is only vaguely surrounded by the three rivers that meander through its periphery. But France's capital city seems to crown this genteel sprawl of an atoll, peppered with pretty villages, anchored by grandiose châteaux. The spokes of railway and freeway that radiate every which way from the Paris ring road all merge gently into this verdant countryside. Ile-de-France strikes a mellow balance, offering a rich and varied cross section of Gallic culture...a minisampling of everything you expect from France, and all within easy day trips from Paris. With cathedrals, châteaux, and places immortalized by great painters, what more could you wish for? Well, how about Goofy on parade along Main Street USA? Pirates of the Caribbean? And Disney's own answer to Versailles, the bubble-gum-pink turrets of Sleeping Beauty's Castle? Yes, Disneyland Paris has taken root, drawing sellout crowds of Europeans wanting a taste of the American Dream—and crowds of American families stealing a day from their Louvre schedule. It's just another epic vision realized against the green backdrop of Ile-de-France.

EXPLORING ILE-DE-FRANCE

Though small, the Ile-de-France is so rich in treasures that a whole day of fascinating exploration may take you no more than 60 km (35 mi) from the capital. Thus, a great advantage to exploring this region is that all its major monuments are within a half-day's drive from Paris, or less, if you take the trains that run to many of the towns in this chapter. The catch is that most of those rail lines connect the towns of the Ile with Paris, not, in general, with neighboring towns of the region. Thus, it may be easier to plan on "touring" the Ile in a series of side trips from Paris, rather than expecting to travel through the Ile in clockwise fashion (which, of course, can be handily done if you have a car). This chapter is broken up into two halves. Threading the western half of the Ile, the first tour heads southwest from Paris to Versailles and Chartres, turns northwest along the Seine to Monet's Giverny, and returns to Paris via St-Germain-en-Laye and Malmaison after visiting Vincent van Gogh's Auvers. Exploring the eastern half of the Ile, the second tour picks up east of the Oise Valley in glamorous Chantilly, then detours north to Compiène and Pierrefonds, and finishes up southward by heading to Disneyland Paris, Vaux-le-Vicomte, and Fontainebleau.

THE WESTERN ILE-DE-FRANCE: VERSAILLES TO MALMAISON

Not only is majestic Versailles one of the most unforgettable sights in Ile-de-France, it's also within easy reach of Paris, less than 30 minutes by either train or car (A13 expressway from Porte d'Auteuil). It's also

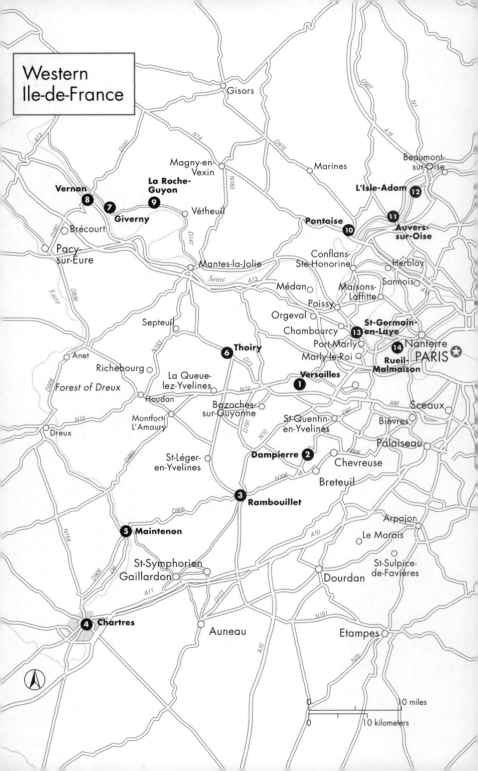

Western Ile-de-France

Gisors

Magny-en-Vexin

Marines

Beaumont-sur-Oise

Vernon ⑧

La Roche-Guyon ⑨

Vétheuil

L'Isle-Adam ⑫

⑦ **Giverny**

Brécourt

Pontoise ⑩

⑪ **Auvers-sur-Oise**

Pacy-sur-Eure

Mantes-la-Jolie

Conflans-Ste-Honorine

Herblay

Seine

Médan

Maisons-Laffitte

Sannois

Poissy

Septeuil

Orgeval

Chambourcy

St-Germain-en-Laye ⑬

⑥ **Thoiry**

Port-Marly

Anet

Richebourg

La Queue-lez-Yvelines

Marly-le-Roi

⑭ **Rueil-Malmaison**

Nanterre

PARIS ★

Forest of Dreux

Houdan

Bazoches-sur-Guyonne

Versailles ①

Sceaux

Montfort-L'Amaury

St-Quentin-en-Yvelines

Bièvres

Palaiseau

Dreux

St-Léger-en-Yvelines

Dampierre ②

Chevreuse

Breteuil

③ **Rambouillet**

Arpajon

⑤ **Maintenon**

Le Marais

St-Symphorien Gaillardon

Dourdan

St-Sulpice-de-Favières

④ **Chartres**

Auneau

Etampes

0   10 miles

0   10 kilometers

the starting point for a visit to the western half of the Ile-de-France, which is studded with a number of spectacular châteaux—including Maintenon and St-Germain-en-Laye—and is anchored by holy Chartres to the south and Vincent van Gogh's Auvers-sur-Oise to the north.

VERSAILLES

❶ *16 km (10 mi) west of Paris via A13.*

GETTING HERE

Versailles has three train stations, all reached from different stations in Paris (journey-time 25–40 mins). The handiest is Versailles Rive Gauche, reached by the RER-C5 line (main stations at Paris's Austerlitz, St-Michel, Invalides, and Champ-de-Mars). The round-trip fare is €6. There are also regional SNCF trains from Gare Montparnasse to Versailles Chantiers, and from Gare St-Lazare to Versailles Rive Droite. Versailles Chantiers (about a 20-min walk from Versailles's front gates, although a municipal bus runs between the two) connects Versailles with several other towns in the Ile-de-France, notably Chartres (with about three trains every two hours for the 50-min trip). The other two stations in Versailles are about a 10-minute walk to the château, although the municipal Bus B or a summertime shuttle service (use métro ticket or pay small fee in coins) can also deposit you at the front gates.

EXPLORING

FodorsChoice It's hard to tell which is larger at **Château de Versailles**—the world-
★ famous château that housed Louis XIV and 20,000 of his courtiers, or the mass of tour buses and visitors standing in front of it. The grandest palace in France remains one of the marvels of the world and its full story is covered in the special photo feature on the château in this chapter, "Gilt Trip: A Tour of Versailles." But this edifice was not just home to the Sun King, it was to be the new headquarters of the French government capital (from 1682 to 1789 and again from 1871 to 1879). To accompany the palace, a new city—in fact, a new capital—had to be built from scratch. Tough-thinking town planners took no prisoners, dreaming up vast mansions and avenues broader than the Champs-Élysées. If you have any energy left after exploring Louis XIV's palace and park, a tour of Versailles—a textbook 18th-century town—offers a telling contrast between the majestic and the domestic.

From the front gate of the palace turn left onto the Rue de l'Independence Américaine and walk over to Rue Carnot past the stately Écuries de la Reine, once the queen's stables, now the regional law courts, to octagonal Place Hoche. Down Rue Hoche to the left is the powerful Baroque facade of **Notre-Dame,** built from 1684 to 1686 by Jules Hardouin-Mansart as the parish church for Louis XIV's new town.

Around the back of Notre-Dame, on Boulevard de la Reine (note the regimented lines of trees), are the elegant Hôtel de Neyret and the **Musée Lambinet,** a sumptuous mansion from 1751, furnished with paintings, weapons, fans, and porcelain. ⊠*54 bd. de la Reine* 🕿*01–39–50– 30–32* 🖻*€5.30* ⊘*Tues.–Sun. 2–6.*

Take a right onto Rue Le Nôtre, then go left and right again into Passage de la Geôle, a cobbled alley, lined with quaint antiques shops, which climbs up to **Place du Marché-Notre-Dame,** whose open-air morning market on Tuesday, Friday, and Sunday is famed throughout the region (note the four 19th-century timber-roof halls).

Cross Avenue de St-Cloud and head to **Avenue de Paris**; its breadth of 120 yards makes it wider than the Champs-Élysées, and its buildings are just as grand and even more historic. Cross the avenue and return toward the château. Avenue de Paris leads down to Place d'Armes, a vast sloping plaza usually filled with tourist buses. Facing the château are the Trojan-size royal stables.

The **Grandes Écuries** *(Grand Stables)*, to the right, house the **Musée des Carrosses** (Carriage Museum), open April through October weekends only (€2), and the **Manège,** where you can see 28 white horses and their riders, trained by the great equine choreographer Bartabas, practicing every morning. Fodor's Talk Forum readers rave about the show. ⊠*1 av. de Paris* 🕿*01–39–02–07–14* 🖻*€8* ⊘*Tues.–Fri. 9–noon, weekends 11–2.*

Turn left from the Grandes Écuries, cross Avenue de Sceaux and Avenue de Paris, pass the imposing chancellery on the corner, and take Rue de Satory—a cute pedestrian shopping street—to the domed **Cathédrale St-Louis,** with its twin-towered facade, built from 1743 to 1754 and enriched with a fine organ and paintings.

Rue d'Anjou leads down to the 6-acre **Potager du Roi,** the lovingly restored, split-level royal fruit-and-vegetable garden created in 1683 by Jean-Baptiste de La Quintinye. ⊠*Entrance at 4 rue Hardy* 🕿*01– 39–24–62–62* ⊕*www.potager-du-roi.fr* 🖻*€6.50* ⊘*Apr.–Oct., daily 10–6; Nov.–Mar., weekdays 2–5.*

WHERE TO STAY & EAT

★ $$$$ ✕ **Les Trois Marches.** In the Trianon Palace hotel, celebrated chef Gérard Vié's take on *cuisine bourgeoise* is one of the most luxe around—you'll find it hard to wait for your meal after perusing the menu, studded with delights like turbot *galette* (cake) with onions and *pommes Anna,* cassoulet with Codiza sausages, and a sublime duck simmered with turnips and truffles. In pleasant weather, you can opt to dine on the long, attractive terrace. ⊠*1 bd. de Reine* 🕿*01–30–84–52–00* ⚒*Reservations essential*Jacket and tie ⊟*AE, DC, MC, V* ⊘*Closed Sun., Mon., and Aug.*

$$–$$$ ✕ **Au Chapeau Gris.** This bustling wood-beamed restaurant just off Avenue de St-Cloud, overlooking elegant Place Hoche, offers a sturdy choice of meat and fish dishes, ranging from boeuf rossini with wild mushrooms to salmon and scallops marinated in lime and the top-price lobster fricasseed in Sancerre. The wine list roams around the vineyards of Bordeaux and Burgundy, while desserts include crème brûlée with lemon zest, and apricot and caramel tart. The €28 prix-fixe

menu makes a filling lunchtime option. ⊠7 *rue Hoche* ☎*01–39–50–10–81* ⊕*www.auchapeau.gris.com* ▤*MC, V* ⊘*Closed Wed. No dinner Tues.*

★ $$$$ ✕⊡ **Trianon Palace.** A modern-day Versailles, this deluxe hotel is in a turn-of-the-20th-century, creamy white creation of imposing size, filled with soaring rooms (including the historic Salle Clemenceau, site of the 1919 Versailles Peace Conference), palatial columns, and with a huge garden close to the château park. Once faded, the hotel is now aglitter with a health club (the pool idles beneath a glass pyramid) and Les Trois Marches restaurant, one of France's best. Try to avoid the newer annex, the Pavillon Trianon, and insist on the full treatment in the main building (ask for one of the even-numbered rooms, which look out over the woods near the Trianons; odd-numbered rooms overlook the modern annex). ⊠*1 bd. de la Reine, 78000* ☎*01–30–84–51–20* ☎*01–30–84–50–01* ⊕*www.trianonpalace.fr* ⇨*165 rooms, 27 suites* ⟡*In-room: refrigerator, Wi-Fi. In-hotel: 2 restaurants, bar, pool, gym* ▤*AE, DC, MC, V* ⟐*BP.*

WORD OF MOUTH

"You could try the Café Trianon in the splendiferous Trianon Palace. It's a little annex to the incredibly posh and expensive Les Trois Marches restaurant. The food is reasonably priced and the setting is magnificent. I don't usually pay that much for lunch but at Versailles it somehow seems appropriate." –StCirq

$–$$ ⊡ **Le Cheval Rouge.** This unpretentious old hotel, built in 1676, is in a corner of the town market square, close to the château and strongly recommended if you plan to explore the town on foot. Some rooms around the old stable courtyard have their original wood beams. ⊠*18 rue André-Chénier, 78000* ☎*01–39–50–03–03* ☎*01–39–50–61–27* ⊕*www.chevalrouge.fr.st* ⇨*38 rooms* ⟡*In-room: no a/c. In-hotel: bar, some pets allowed (fee)* ▤*AE, MC, V.*

$ ⊡ **Home St-Louis.** This family-run, three-story stone-and-brick hotel is a good, cheap, quiet bet—close to the cathedral and not too far from the château. ⊠*28 rue St-Louis, 78000* ☎*01–39–50–23–55* ☎*01–39–21–62–45* ⇨*25 rooms* ⟡*In-room: no a/c. In-hotel: some pets allowed* ▤*AE, MC, V.*

NIGHTLIFE & THE ARTS
Directed by Bartabas, the **Académie du Spectacle Equestre** (☎*01–39–02–07–14* ⊕*www.acadequestre.com*) stages hour-long shows on weekend afternoons of horses performing to music—sometimes with riders, sometimes without—in the converted 17th-century Manège (riding school) at the Grandes Écuries opposite the palace. The **Centre de Musique Baroque** (⊕*www.cmbv.com*) often presents concerts of Baroque music in the château opera and chapel. The **Mois Molière** (☎*01–30–97–84–48*) in June heralds a program of concerts, drama, and exhibits inspired by the famous playwright. The **Théâtre Montansier** (☎*01–39–20–16–00*) has a full program of plays.

Continued on page 159

GILT TRIP
A TOUR OF VERSAILLES

Louis XIV's Hall of Mirrors

A two-century spree of indulgence in the finest bling-bling of the age by the consecutive reigns of three French kings produced two of the world's most historic artifacts: gloriously, the Palace of Versailles and, momentously, the French Revolution.

Less a monument than an entire world unto itself, Versailles is the king of palaces. The end result of 380 million francs, 36,000 laborers, and enough paintings, if laid end to end, to equal 7 miles of canvas, it was conceived as the ne plus ultra expression of monarchy by Louis XIV. As a child, the king had developed a hatred for Paris (where he had been imprisoned by a group of nobles known as the Frondeurs), so, when barely out of his teens, he cast his cantankerous royal eye in search of a new power base. Marshy, inhospitable Versailles was the stuff of his dreams. Down came dad's modest royal hunting lodge and up, up, and along went the minion-crushing, Baroque palace we see today.

Between 1661 and 1710, architects Louis Le Vau and Jules Hardouin Mansart designed everything his royal acquisitiveness could want, including a throne room devoted to Apollo, god of the sun (Louis was known as *le roi soleil*). Convinced that his might depended upon dominating French nobility, Louis XIV summoned thousands of grandees from their own far-flung châteaux to reside at his new seat of government. In doing so, however, he unwittingly triggered the downfall of the monarchy. Like an 18th-century Disneyland, Versailles kept its courtiers so richly entertained they all but forgot the murmurs of discontent brewing back home.

As Louis XV chillingly fortold, "After me, the deluge." The royal commune was therefore shocked—shocked!—by the appearance, on October 5, 1789, of a revolutionary mob from Paris ready to sack Versailles and imprison Louis XVI. So as you walk through this awesome monument to splendor and excess, give a thought to its historic companion: the French Revolution. A tour of Versailles's grand salons inextricably mixes pathos with glory.

CROWNING GLORIES: TOP SIGHTS OF VERSAILLES

Seducing their court with their self-assured approach to 17th- and 18th-century art and decoration, a trinity of French kings made Versailles into the most vainglorious of châteaux.

Versailles from the outside

Galerie des Glaces (Hall of Mirrors). Of all the rooms at Versailles, none matches the magnificence of the Galerie des Glaces (Hall of Mirrors). Begun by Mansart in 1678, this represents the acme of the Louis Quatorze (Louis-XIV) style. Measuring 240 feet long, 33 feet wide, and 40 feet high, it is ornamented with gilded candlesticks, crystal chandeliers, and a coved ceiling painted with Charles Le Brun's homage to Louis XIV's reign.

Detail of the ceiling

In Louis's day, the Galerie was laid with priceless carpets and filled with orange trees in silver pots. Nighttime galas were illuminated by 3,000 candles, their blaze doubled in the 17 gigantic mirrors that precisely echo the banner of windows along the west front. Lavish balls were once held here, as was a later event with much greater world impact: the signing of the Treaty of Versailles, which put an end to World War I on June 28, 1919.

Hall of Mirrors

The Grands Appartements (State Apartments). Virtual stages for ceremonies of court ritual and etiquette, Louis XIV's first-floor state salons were designed in the Baroque style on a biceps-flexing scale meant to one-up the lavish Vaux-le-Vicomte château recently built for Nicolas Fouquet, the king's finance minister.

Inside the Apollo Chamber

Flanking the Hall of Mirrors and retaining most of their bombastic Italianate Baroque decoration, the Salon de la Guerre (Salon of War) and the Salon de la Paix (Salon of Peace) are ornately decorated with gilt stucco, painted ceilings, and marble sculpture. Perhaps the most extravagant is the Salon d'Apollon (Apollo Chamber), the former throne room.

Hall of Battles

Appartements du Roi (King's Apartments). Completed in 1701 in the Louis-XIV style, the king's state and private chambers comprise a suite of 15 rooms set in a "U" around the east facade's Marble Court. Dead center across the sprawling cobbled forecourt is Louis XIV's bedchamber—he would awake and rise (just as the sun did, from the east) attended by members of his court and the public. Holding the king's chemise when he dressed soon became a more definitive reflection of status than the possession of an entire province. Nearby is Louis XV's magnificent Cabinet Intérieur (Office of the King), shining with gold and white boiseries; in the center is the most famous piece of furniture at Versailles, Louis XV's roll-top desk, crafted by Oeben and Riesener in 1769.

Louis XIV

King's Apartments

Chambre de la Reine (Queen's Bed Chamber). Probably the most opulent bedroom in the world, this was initially created for Marie Thérèse, first wife of Louis XIV, to be part of the Queen's Apartments. For Marie Antoinette, however, the entire room was glammed up with silk wall-hangings covered with Rococo motifs that reflect her love of flowers. Legend has it that the gardens directly beyond these windows were replanted daily so that the queen could enjoy a fresh assortment of blossoms each morning. The bed, decked out with white ostrich plumes *en panache*, was also redone for Louis XVI's queen. Nineteen royal children were born in this room.

VINTAGE BOURBON

Versailles was built by three great kings of the Bourbon dynasty. Louis XIV (1638—1715) began its construction in 1661. After ruling for 72 years, Louis Quatorze was succeeded by his great grandson, Louis XV (1710—74), who added the Royal Opera and the Petit Trianon to the palace. Louis XVI (1754—93) came to the throne in 1774 and was forced out of Versailles in 1789, along with Marie Antoinette, both guillotined three years later.

Queen's Bed Chamber

2

GILT TRIP: A TOUR OF VERSAILLES

Petits Appartements (Small Apartments). As styles of decor changed, Louis XIV's successors felt out of sync with their architectural inheritance. Louis XV exchanged the heavy red-and-gilt of Italianate Baroque for lighter, pastel-hued Rococo. On the top floor of the palace, on the right side of the central portion, are the apartments Louis XV commissioned to escape the wearisome pomp of the first-floor rooms. Here, Madame de Pompadour, mistress of Louis XV and famous patroness of the Rococo style, introduced grace notes of intimacy and refinement. In so doing, she transformed the daunting royal apartments into places to live rather than pose.

Parc de Versailles. Even Bourbon kings needed respite from Versailles's endless confines, hence the creation of one of Europe's largest parks, designed to surround the palace. The 250-acre grounds (☎ 01–30–83–77–88 for guided tour) are the masterpiece of André Le Nôtre, presiding genius of 17th-century classical French landscaping. Le Nôtre was famous for his "green geometries": ordered fantasies of clipped yew trees, multicolored flower beds (called parterres), and perspectival allées cleverly punctuated with statuary, laid out between 1661 and 1668. The architectonic effect is best admired from inside the palace, views about which Le Nôtre said, "Flowers can only be walked on by the eyes."

Ultimately, at the royal command, rivers were diverted—to flow into more than 600 fountains—and entire forests were imported to ornament the park, which is centered around the mile-long Grand Canal. As for the great fountains, their operation costs a fortune in these democratic days, and so they perform only on Saturday and Sunday afternoons (☉ 3:30–5:30) from mid-April through mid-October; admission during this time is €6. The park is open daily 7 AM–8 PM or dusk.

LIGHTING UP THE SKY

The largest fountain in Versailles' château park, the Bassin de Neptune, becomes a spectacle of rare grandeur during the Fêtes de Nuit (☎ 01–30–83–78–88 for details), a light-and-fireworks show held on ten nights (usually Saturday) between late July and early September. Starting at 10:30 PM, with upwards of 200-plus actors costumed in knee-breeches and curled wigs, the 90-minute show is well worth the ticket admission of €16 to €48.

Dauphin's Apartments

Bassin de Neptune

Chapel and Opéra Royal: In the north wing of the château are three showpieces of the palace. The solemn white-and-gold Chapelle was completed in 1710—the king and queen attended daily mass here seated in gilt boxes. The Opéra Royal (Opera House), entirely constructed of wood painted to look like marble, was designed by Jacques-Ange Gabriel for Louis XV in 1770. Connecting the two, the 17th-century Galeries have exhibits retracing the château's history.

Opéra Royal

2

GILT TRIP: A TOUR OF VERSAILLES

VERSAILLES: FIRST FLOOR, GARDENS & ADJACENT PARK

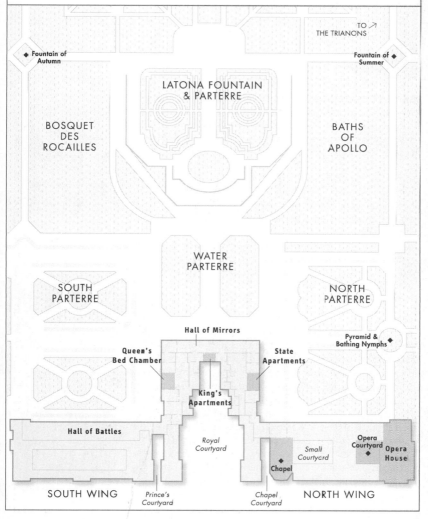

TO ↗
THE TRIANONS

◆ Fountain of
Autumn

Fountain of ◆
Summer

LATONA FOUNTAIN
& PARTERRE

BOSQUET
DES
ROCAILLES

BATHS
OF
APOLLO

WATER
PARTERRE

SOUTH
PARTERRE

NORTH
PARTERRE

Hall of Mirrors

Pyramid &
Bathing Nymphs ◆

Queen's
Bed Chamber

State
Apartments

King's
Apartments

Hall of Battles

Royal
Courtyard

Opera
Courtyard

Small
Courtyard

Opera
House

◆
Chapel

SOUTH WING

Prince's
Courtyard

Chapel
Courtyard

NORTH WING

LET THEM EAT CRÊPE: MARIE ANTOINETTE'S ROYAL LAIR

Was Marie Antoinette a luxury-mad butterfly flitting from ball to costume ball? Or was she a misunderstood queen who suffered a loveless marriage and became a prisoner of court etiquette at Versailles? Historians now believe the answer was the latter and point to her private retreats at Versailles as proof.

R.F.D. VERSAILLES?

Here, in the northwest part of the royal park, Marie Antoinette (1755–93) created a tiny universe of her own: her comparatively dainty mansion called Petit Trianon and its adjacent "farm," the relentlessly picturesque Hameau ("hamlet"). In a life that took her from royal cradle to throne of France to guillotine, her happiest days were spent at Trianon. For here she could live a life in the "simplest" possible way; here the queen could enter a salon and the game of cards would not stop; here women could wear simple gowns of muslin without a single jewel. Toinette only wanted to be queen of Trianon, not queen of France. And considering the horrible, chamber-pot-pungent, gossip-infested corridors of Versailles, you can almost understand why.

TEEN QUEEN

From the first, Maria-Antonia (her actual name) was ostracized as an outsider, "l'Autrichienne"—the Austrian. Upon arriving in France in 1770—at a mere 15 years of age—she was married to the Dauphin, the future King Louis XVI. But shamed by her initial failure to deliver a royal heir, she grew to hate overcrowded Versailles and soon escaped to the Petit Trianon. Built between 1763 and 1768 by Jacques-Ange Gabriel for Madame de Pompadour, this bijou palace was a radical statement: a royal residence designed to be casual and unassuming. Toinette refashioned the Trianon's interior in the sober Neoclassical style.

Hameau

Queen's House

Temple of Love

Petit Trianon

"THE SIMPLE LIFE"

Just beyond Petit Trianon lay the storybook Hameau, a mock-Norman village inspired by the peasant-luxe, simple-life daydreams caught by Boucher on canvas and by Rousseau in literature. With its water mill, thatched-roof houses, pigeon loft, and vegetable plots, this make-believe farm village was run by Monsieur Valy-Busard, a farmer, and his wife, who often helped the queen—outfitted as a Dresden shepherdess with a Sèvres porcelain crook—tend her flock of perfumed sheep.

Marie Antoinette

As if to destroy any last link with reality, the queen built nearby a jewel-box theater (open by appointment). Here she acted in little plays, sometimes essaying the role of a servant girl. Only the immediate royal family, about seven or so friends, and her personal servants were permitted entry; disastrously, the entire official-dom of Versailles society was shut out—a move that only served to infuriate courtiers. This is how fate and destiny close the circle. For it was here at Trianon that a page sent by Monsieur de Saint-Priest found Marie-Antoinette on October 5, 1789, to tell her that Paris was marching on an already half-deserted Versailles.

Was Marie Antoinette a political traitor to France whose execution was well merited? Or was she the ultimate fashion victim? For those who feel that this tragic queen spent—and shopped—her way into a revolution, a visit to her relatively modest Petit Trianon and Hameau should prove a revelation.

FACTS & FANCIES

Sharing a joint ticket—€9—with the Petit Trianon is the Grand Trianon, also found in the northwest sector of Versailles's park. Created by Hardouin Mansart in 1687, it was used as a retreat for Louis XIV but restored in the early 19th century, with Empire-style salons. Both Trianons are open Tuesday—Sunday noon–5:30. As for the Hameau, the grounds are open to the public, but its rooms are now undergoing a 10-year renovation.

TAKING ON VERSAILLES (WITHOUT LOSING YOUR HEAD)

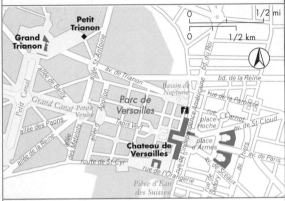

Statue of King Louis XIV

TOURING THE PALACE

The army of 20,000 noblemen, servants, and sycophants who moved into Louis XIV's huge Château de Versailles is matched today by the battalion of 3 million visitors a year. You may be able to avoid the crowds (and lines for tours) if you arrive here at 9 AM. The main entrance is near the top of the courtyard to the right; there are different lines depending on tour, physical ability, and group status. Frequent guided tours in English visit the private royal apartments. More detailed hour-long tours explore the opera house or Marie Antoinette's private parlors. You can go through the grandest rooms—including the Hall of Mirrors and Marie Antoinette's stunningly opulent bed chamber—without a group tour. To figure out the system, pick up a brochure at the information office or ticket counter.

TOURING THE PARK

If the grandeur of the palace begins to overwhelm, the Parc de Versailles is the best place to come back down to earth. The distances of the park are vast—the Trianons themselves are more than a mile from the château—so you might want to climb aboard a horse-drawn carriage (€7, ⊕ www.calechesversailles.com), take the electric train (🎫 5.80 round-trip, ⊕ www.train-versailles.com), or rent a bike from Petite-Venise (🎫 €5.20 per hr or €26 for 6 hrs, ☎ 01–39–66–97–66), the building at the top of the Grand Canal, where you can also hire a rowboat (🎫 €8.50 per hr). You can also drive to the Trianons and canal through the Grille de la Reine (🎫 €5.50 per car).

PICNIC IN THE PARK

If you don't opt for a luncheon at La Flotille restaurant (by the Grand Canal), take a cue from the locals, picnicking in grand fashion, as only the French know how. The brochures request that you don't picnic on the lawns, but they don't mention the groves scattered throughout the woods.

✉ Place d'Armes, Versailles

⊕ www.chateauversailles.fr

☎ 01–30–83–78–00

🎫 €13.50; Petit and Grand Trianons (joint ticket) €9; Parc de Versailles free; Sunday fountain show €6; Fêtes de Nuit €16–€48.

🚪 Main palace Apr.–Oct., Tues.–Sun. 9–6:30; Nov.–Mar., Tues.–Sun, 9–5:30. Trianons Tues.—Sun. noon–6. Park daily dawn—dusk.

Ⓜ RER Line C from Paris to Versailles Rive Gauche station or SNCF trains from Paris's Gare St-Lazare and Gare Montparnasse.

SHOPPING

Aux Colonnes (⊠ *14 rue Hoche*) is a highly rated *confiserie* (candy shop) with a cornucopia of chocolates and candies; it's closed Monday. **Les Délices du Palais** (⊠ *4 rue du Maréchal-Foch*) has all the makings for an impromptu picnic (cold cuts, cheese, salads); it's also closed Monday. **Legall** (⊠ *Place du Marché*) has a huge choice of cheeses—including one of France's widest selections of goat cheeses; it's closed Sunday afternoon and Monday. **Passage de la Geôle,** which is open Friday–Sunday 9–7 and is close to the town's stupendous market, houses several good antiques shops.

DAMPIERRE

② *21 km (13 mi) southwest of Versailles via D91.*

The unspoiled village of Dampierre is adorned with one of the most elegant family seats in Ile-de-France. The stone-and-brick **Château de Dampierre,** surrounded by a moat and set well back from the road, was rebuilt in the 1670s by Hardouin-Mansart for the Duc de Luynes. Much of the interior retains its 17th-century decoration—portraits, wood paneling, furniture, and works of art. But the main staircase, with its trompe-l'oeil murals, and the richly gilded **Salle des Fêtes** (ballroom) date from the 19th century. This second-floor chamber contains a huge wall painting by the celebrated artist Jean-Auguste-Dominique Ingres (1780–1867), an idealized evocation of the mythical Age d'Or (Golden Age)—fitting, perhaps, since this aristocratic family did many good deeds and was even beloved by locals and farmers during the French Revolution. The large park, fronted by gigantic gates, was planned by Versailles landscape architect André Le Nôtre. ⊠ *2 Grande-Rue* ☏ *01–30–52–52–83* ⊕ *www.chateau-de-dampierre.fr* ☏ *€9.50, grounds only €6* ⊙ *Apr.–mid-Oct., Mon.–Sat. 11–6:30, Sun. 11–noon and 2–6:30.*

RAMBOUILLET

③ *16 km (10 mi) southwest of Dampierre via D91 and D906, 32 km (20 mi) southwest of Versailles, 42 km (26 mi) southwest of Paris.*

Haughty Rambouillet, once favored by kings and dukes, is now home to affluent gentry and, occasionally, the French president. The **Château de Rambouillet** is surrounded by a magnificent 30,000-acre forest that remains a great place for biking and walking. Most of the château dates from the early 18th century, but the brawny **Tour François-Ier** (François I Tower), named for the king who died here in 1547, was part of the fortified castle that stood on this site in the 14th cen-

MOVE THAT BARGE, LIFT THAT SAIL

The park's exotic, storybook beauty once inspired Jean-Honoré Fragonard to paint his 18th-century *Fête at Rambouillet* (now in the Gulbenkian Museum in Lisbon), which tellingly depicts a gilded, courtier-filled barge about to enter a stretch of a river torn by raging rapids. "Apres moi, le deluge," indeed.

THE ILE-DE-FRANCE THROUGH THE AGES

In 987 Hugues Capet was crowned the first King of France in...Senlis, not Paris. You could say Ile-de-France has been something of an Anti-Paris ever since. In medieval times, long before the name Ile-de-France was first coined (in 1380), the region witnessed the birth of Gothic architecture—not in Paris—but in Morienval and St-Denis, and was subsequently peppered with glorious churches and cathedrals, such as Chartres, whose majesty rivaled that of hunchback-ridden Notre-Dame.

Napoléon I preferred La Malmaison and Fontainebleau (where he abdicated in 1814) to Paris, while Napoléon III spent all fall hunting and partying in Compiègne. Louis XIV quit Paris for good, to Versailles, his brand-new, purpose-built capital (which is what it remained until 1789, and was again from 1871 to 1879, as its imposing buildings—many once foreign embassies—testify to this day). Everyone's heard of the Treaty of Versailles after World War I, but an earlier Versailles Treaty, in 1783, put paid to the American War of Independence, and Bismarck had the new German Empire proclaimed in Versailles after the Franco-Prussian War in 1871. Versailles remains the largest town in Ile-de-France but, with 85,000 inhabitants, it's no city—you have to go outside Ile-de-France, to Rouen in Normandy (137 km [85 mi] from Paris), to find one of those.

Like Versailles, Ile-de-France has changed little down the ages—all the region's modernity seems channelled into the five villes nouvelles (new towns) decreed in the 1960s. The rural charm and sleepy pace help explain why so many creators have preferred Ile-de-France to the bustle of Paris—be they composers like Debussy (St-Germain) or Ravel (Montfort); writers like Zola (Medan) or Dumas (Port Marly); or, above all, painters like Monet (Giverny), Van Gogh (Auvers), Millet (Barbizon), or Pissarro (Pontoise), to name but a few....

tury. Highlights include the wood-paneled apartments, especially the **Boudoir de la Comtesse** (Countess's Dressing Room); the marble-wall **Salle de Marbre** (Marble Hall), dating from the Renaissance; and the **Salle de Bains de Napoléon** (Napoléon's Bathroom), adorned with Pompeii-style frescoes. Compared to the muscular forecourt, the château's lakeside facade is a sight of unsuspected serenity and, as flowers spill from its balconies, cheerful informality. ☎01–34–83–00–25 ⊕*www. monum.fr* ✆€6.10 ⊗*Daily 10–11:30 and 2–5:30.*

An extensive **park,** with a lake with small islands, stretches behind the château, site of the extraordinary **Laiterie de la Reine** (Queen's Dairy), built for Marie-Antoinette, who, inspired by the writings of Jean-Jacques Rousseau, came here to escape from the pressures of court life, pretending to be a simple milkmaid. It has a small marble temple and grotto and, nearby, the shell-lined Chaumière des Coquillages (Shell Pavilion). The **Bergerie Nationale** (National Sheepfold) is the site of a more serious agricultural venture: the merinos raised here, prized for the quality and yield of their wool, are descendants of sheep imported from Spain by Louis XVI in 1786. A museum alongside tells the tale and evokes shepherd life. ⊠*Dairy and Shell Pavilion* €3, *Sheepfold* €4 ⊙*Dairy Apr.–Sept., Wed.–Mon. 10–noon and 2–6; Oct.–Mar., Wed.–Mon. 10–noon and 2–4:30; Sheepfold mid-Jan.– mid-Dec., Wed.–Sun. 2–5.*

Some 4,000 models, some dating back to 1885, and more than 1,300 feet of track make the **Musée Rambolitrain** a serious model-train museum. It has historic steam engines, old-time stations, and a realistic points and signaling system. ⊠*4 pl. Jeanne-d'Arc* ☎*01–34–83–15–93* ⊠*€3.50* ⊙*Wed.–Sun. 10–noon and 2–5:30.*

WHERE TO EAT

$-$$ ✕ **La Poste.** You can bank on traditional, unpretentious cooking at this lively former coaching inn in the center of town, close to the château park. Service is good, as is the selection of prix-fixe menus (€21–€36). Chicken fricassee with crayfish is a specialty, along with game in season. ⊠*101 rue du Général-de-Gaulle* ☎*01–34–83–03–01* ▭*AE, MC, V* ⊙*Closed Mon. No dinner Sun. or Thurs.*

CHARTRES

4 *39 km (24 mi) southwest of Rambouillet via N10 and A11, 88 km (55 mi) southwest of Paris.*

GETTING HERE

Both regional and main-line (Le Mans–bound) trains leave Paris's Gare Montparnasse for Chartres (50–70 mins); ticket price is around €24 round-trip. Chartres's train station on Place Pierre-Sémard puts you within walking distance of the cathedral.

EXPLORING

If Versailles is the climax of French secular architecture, perhaps Chartres is its religious apogee. All the descriptive prose and poetry that have been lavished on this supreme cathedral can only begin to suggest the glory of its 12th- and 13th-century statuary and stained glass, somehow suffused with burning mysticism and a strange sense of the numinous. Chartres is more than a church—it's a nondenominational spiritual experience. If you arrive in summer from Maintenon across the edge of the Beauce, the richest agrarian plain in France, you can see Chartres's spires rising up from oceans of wheat. The whole town— with its old houses and picturesque streets—is worth a leisurely exploration. From Rue du Pont-St-Hilaire there's an intriguing view of the rooftops below the cathedral. Ancient streets tumble down from the cathedral to the river, lined most weekends with bouquinistes selling old books and prints. Each year on August 15 pilgrims and tourists flock here for the Procession du Voeu de Louis XIII, a religious procession through the streets commemorating the French monarchy's vow to serve the Virgin Mary.

Fodor'sChoice Worship on the site of the **Cathédrale Notre-Dame,** better known as Chartres Cathedral, goes back to before the Gallo-Roman period; the crypt contains a well that was the focus of druid ceremonies. In the late 9th century Charles II (known as the Bald) presented Chartres with what was believed to be the tunic of the Virgin Mary, a precious relic that went on to attract hordes of pilgrims. The current cathedral, the sixth church on the spot, dates mainly from the 12th and 13th centuries and was erected after the previous building, dating from the 11th century, burned down in 1194. A well-chronicled outburst of religious fervor followed the discovery that the Virgin Mary's relic had miraculously survived unsinged. Princes and paupers, barons and bourgeois gave their money and their labor to build the new cathedral. Ladies of the manor came to help monks and peasants on the scaffolding in a tremendous resurgence of religious faith that followed the Second Crusade. Just 25 years were needed for Chartres Cathedral to rise again, and it has remained substantially unchanged since.

The lower half of the facade survives from the earlier Romanesque church: this can be seen most clearly in the use of round arches rather than the pointed Gothic type. The **Royal Portal** is richly sculpted with scenes from the life of Christ—these sculpted figures are among the greatest created during the Middle Ages. The taller of the two spires (380 feet versus 350 feet) was built at the start of the 16th century, after its predecessor was destroyed by fire; its fanciful Flamboyant intricacy contrasts sharply with the stumpy solemnity of its Romanesque counterpart (access €3, open daily 9:30–noon and 2–4:30). The **rose window** above the main portal dates from the 13th century, and the three windows below it contain some of the finest examples of 12th-century stained-glass artistry in France.

As spiritual as Chartres is, the cathedral also had its more earthbound uses. Look closely and you can see that the main nave floor has a subtle slant. This was built to provide drainage as this part of the church was often used as a "hostel" by thousands of overnighting pilgrims in medieval times.

Your eyes will need time to adjust to the somber interior. The reward is seeing the gemlike richness of the stained glass, with the famous deep Chartres blue predominating. The oldest window is arguably the most beautiful: **Notre-Dame de la Belle Verrière** (Our Lady of the Lovely Window), in the south choir. The cathedral's windows are being gradually cleaned—a lengthy, painstaking process—and the contrast with those still covered in the grime of centuries is staggering. It's worth taking a pair of binoculars along with you to pick out the details. If you wish to know more about stained-glass techniques and the motifs used, visit the small exhibit in the gallery opposite the north porch. For even more detail, try to arrange a tour (in English) with local institution Malcolm Miller, whose knowledge of the cathedral's history is formidable. (He leads tours twice a day Monday through Saturday; the cost is €10. You can reach him at the telephone number below.) The vast black-and-white labyrinth on the floor of the nave is one of the few to have survived from the Middle Ages; the faithful were expected to travel along its entire length (some 300 yards) on their knees. Guided tours of the **Crypte** start from the Maison de la Crypte opposite the south porch. You can also see a 4th-century Gallo-Roman wall and some 12th-century wall paintings. ⊠16 cloître Notre-Dame

☎02–37–21–75–02 ⊕*www.char-tres-tourisme.com* ▭*Crypt €3* ⊙*Cathedral 8:30–7:30, guided tours of crypt Easter–Oct., daily at 11, 2:15, 3:30, and 4:30; Nov.–Easter, daily at 11 and 4:15.*

The **Musée des Beaux-Arts** *(Fine Arts Museum)* is in a handsome 18th-century building just behind the cathedral that used to serve as the bishop's palace. Its varied collection includes Renaissance enamels, a portrait of Erasmus by Holbein, tapestries, armor, and some fine (mainly French) paintings from the 17th, 18th, and 19th centuries. There's also a room devoted to the forceful 20th-century landscapes of Maurice de Vlaminck, who lived in the region. ▭*29 cloître Notre-Dame* ☎*02–37–90–45–80* ▭*€2.30* ⊙*Wed.–Sat. and Mon. 10–noon and 2–5, Sun. 2–5.*

The Gothic church of **St-Pierre** (▭*Rue St-Pierre*), near the Eure River, has magnificent medieval windows from a period (circa 1300) not represented at the cathedral. The oldest stained glass here, portraying Old Testament worthies, is to the right of the choir and dates from the late 13th century.

Exquisite 17th-century stained glass can be admired at the church of **St-Aignan** (▭*Rue des Grenets*), around the corner from St-Pierre.

WHERE TO STAY & EAT

$$$–$$$$
Fodor's Choice
★

✕ **Moulin de Ponceau.** Ask for a table with a view of the River Eure, with the cathedral looming behind, at this 16th-century converted water mill. On sunny days you can eat outside, by the water's edge—an idyllic setting. Choose from a regularly changing menu of French stalwarts such as rabbit terrine, trout with almonds, and tarte tatin. ▭*21 rue de la Tannerie* ☎*02–37–35–30–05* ⊕*www.lemoulindeponceau.fr* ▭*AE, MC, V* ⊙*Closed 2 wks in Feb. No lunch Sat., no dinner Sun.*

$$$–$$$$

✕ **La Vieille Maison.** Just 100 yards from the cathedral, in a pretty 14th-century building with a flower-decked patio, this restaurant is a fine choice for either lunch or dinner. Chef Bruno Letartre changes his menu regularly, often including such regional specialties as asparagus, rich duck pâté, and superb homemade foie gras. Prices, though justified, can be steep, but the €20 lunch menu served on summer weekdays is a good bet. ▭*5 rue au Lait* ☎*02–37–34–10–67* ⊕*www.lavieillemaison.fr.st* ▭*AE, MC, V* ⊙*Closed Mon. No dinner Sun.*

$$$–$$$$
Fodor's Choice
★

✕▭ **Château d'Esclimont.** On the way south from Rambouillet to Chartres is the town of St-Symphorien, famed for one of France's most spectacular château-hotels. Adorned with pointed turrets, *pièces d'eau* (moated pools), and a checkerboard facade, the 19th-century Esclimont domaine—built by the de La Rochefoucaulds—is well worth seeking out if you wish to eat and sleep like an aristocrat. This member of the

Relais & Châteaux group is replete with luxuriously furnished guest rooms (many are loftily dimensioned, others snug in corner turrets) adorned with reproduction 18th-century French pieces. Carved stone garlands, cordovan leathers, brocades, and period antiques grace the public salons; the superbly manicured grounds cradle a heated pool. The cuisine is sophisticated: quail, duck, lobster, and mushroom and chestnut fricassee top the menu at the restaurant, La Rochefoucauld (dinner reservations are essential, and a jacket and tie are required, as is a very fat wallet). ⊠ *2 rue du Château-d'Esclimont (24 km [15 mi] northeast of Chartres via N10/D18, 28700 St-Symphorien-le-Château* ☎ *02–37–31–15–15* 🖷 *02–37–31–57–91* ⊕ *www.esclimont.com* ⤳ *46 rooms, 6 suites* ♿ *In-room: no a/c, refrigerator, ethernet. In-hotel: restaurant, tennis courts, pool* ▭ *AE, DC, MC, V* ❙◎❙ *MAP.*

★ $$-$$$ ✕▣ **Le Grand Monarque.** Set on Chartres's main town square not far from the cathedral, this is a delightful option with decor that remains seductively and warmly redolent of the 19th century. Built originally as a coaching inn (and today part of the Best Western chain), the hotel has numerous rooms, many attractively set with brick walls, wood antiques, lush drapes, and modern bathrooms; the best are in a separate turn-of-the-20th-century building overlooking a garden, while the most atmospheric are tucked away in the attic. Downstairs, the stylishly decorated Georges restaurant has prix-fixe menus starting at €29. There's a winning hand in the kitchen, as such delicacies as pheasant pie and scallops with lentils attest. It's closed Monday and there's no dinner Sunday, but the hotel's Madrigal brasserie is open daily. ⊠ *22 pl. des Épars, 28000* ☎ *02–37–18–15–15* 🖷 *02–37–36–34–18* ⊕ *www.bwgrand-monarque.com* ⤳ *55 rooms* ♿ *In-room: no a/c (some), refrigerator, dial-up. In-hotel: restaurant, bar, some pets allowed (fee)* ▭ *AE, DC, MC, V* ❙◎❙ *BP.*

MAINTENON

⑤ *17 km (10 mi) northwest of Chartres via D6 and D906, 65 km (41 mi) southwest of Paris.*

Several trains daily, on the Paris-Rambouillet-Chartres line, stop in Maintenon, site of the famed **Château de Maintenon**. This regal structure once belonged to Louis XIV's second wife, Françoise Scarron—better known as Madame de Maintenon—whom he married morganatically in 1684 (as social inferiors, neither she nor her children could claim a royal title). She had acquired the château as a young widow 10 years earlier, and her private apartments are the focus of an interior visit. A round brick tower (16th century) and square 12th-century keep give the ensemble a muscular dignity. Mirrored in a canal that contains the waters of the Eure, this is one of the most picturesque châteaux in France. Inside, lush salons are done up in the Louis XIII style (or rather, in the Second Empire, 19th-century version of it), a homage to royal roots created by the Ducs de Noailles, one of France's most aristocratic families, which has maintained Maintenon as one of its family homes for centuries. ⊠ *2 pl. Aristide-Briand* ☎ *02–37–23–00–09* 🎫 *€6.20* ⊗ *Apr.–Oct., Wed.–Mon. 2–6:30; Nov.–Mar., weekends 2–5:30.*

2

Looming at the back of the château garden and extending through the village almost from the train station to highway D6 are the unlikely ivy-covered arches of a ruined **aqueduct**, one of the Sun King's most outrageous projects. The original scheme aimed to provide the ornamental lakes in the gardens of Versailles (some 50 km [31 mi] away) with water from the River Eure. In 1684, 30,000 men were signed up to construct a three-tier, 5-km (3-mi) aqueduct as part of the project. Many died in the process, and construction was called off in 1689.

WHERE TO EAT

★ ¢–$ ✕ **Bistrot d'Adeline.** This small, rustic bistro on the main street close to the château in Maintenon offers a cheerful welcome and home cooking with stews and *tête de veau* (calf's head) among the specialties. There's a good-value three-course set menu at lunchtime for €11. ⊠ *3 rue Collin-d'Harleville* ☎ *02–37–23–06–67* ⚎ *Reservations essential* ▭ *No credit cards* ⊘ *Closed Sun., Mon., and part of Aug.*

THOIRY

❻ *47 km (27 mi) north of Maintenon via D983 and N12, 44 km (28 mi) west of Paris.*

Thoiry is most famous for its 16th-century château with beautiful gardens, a wild-animal preserve, and a gastronomy museum. The village makes an excellent day trip from Paris, especially if you're traveling with children. The showpiece remains the **Château de Thoiry,** built by Philibert de l'Orme in 1564. Its handsome Renaissance facade is set off by gardens landscaped in the disciplined French fashion by Le Nôtre, in this case with unexpected justification: the château is positioned directly in line with the sun as it sets in the west at the winter solstice (December 21) and as it rises in the east at the summer solstice (June 21). Heightening the effect, the central part of the château appears to be a transparent arch of light because of its huge glass doors and windows. Owners Vicomte Paul de La Panouse and his American wife Annabelle have restored the château and park, opening both to the public. The distinguished history of the La Panouse family—a Comte César even fought in the American Revolution—is retraced in the **Musée des Archives** (Archives Museum), where papal bulls and Napoleonic letters mingle with notes from Thomas Jefferson and Benjamin Franklin. You're allowed to wander at leisure, although it's best not to stray too far from the official footpath through the **Parc Zoologique** (animal preserve). Note that the parts of the reserve that contain the wilder beasts—zebras, camels, hippos, bears, elephants—can be visited only by car. Tigers can be seen from the safety of a raised footbridge, and lions from inside a glass-walled tunnel. Nearby is a children's play area with a burrow to wriggle through and a huge netted cobweb to bounce around in. There's also a maze formed by impenetrable yew hedges. ☎ *01–34–87–52–25* ⊕ *www.thoiry.tm.fr* ⊡ *Château €6, park and game reserve €22* ⊘ *June–Sept., daily 10–6; Oct.–May, daily 10–5.*

WHERE TO STAY & EAT

$ ✕⊞ **L'Auberge de Thoiry.** Conveniently situated on Thoiry's village street, 300 yards from the château, this sturdy hotel has small but cozy rooms; Nos. 3 and 4 can be joined together as a family suite (€128). Snails, gizzard salad, spareribs, and pizza are staples on the unadventurous menu in the spacious restaurant (closed Monday). ⊠*38 rue de la Porte-St-Martin, 78770* ☎*01–34–87–40–21* 🖹*01–34–87–49–57* ⊕*www.aubergedethoiry.fr* ⤸*12 rooms* ♿*In-room: no a/c. In-hotel: restaurant, some pets allowed (fee), no elevator* ▭*MC, V* ⦿*MAP.*

**EN
ROUTE**   As you begin to enter the region of the Ile-de-France the Impressionists made their own, cross the Seine at Vernouillet and follow D190 to **Mantes-la-Jolie.** Arriving from Limay, look out for the old, now ruined bridge over the Seine once painted by Jean-Baptiste-Camille Corot. Another painter, the Postimpressionist Maximilien Luce, is the hero of the fine town museum alongside the 12th-century Église Notre-Dame, whose twin-towered silhouette was another favorite Corot motif. The small, circular windows ringing the east end of the church are an unusual local architectural characteristic—you can also see them 11 km (7 mi) north, at the church in **Vétheuil**—a town immortalized in many a magnificent Monet canvas—where the road regains the riverbank beneath impressive chalk cliffs.

GIVERNY

❼ *8 km (5 mi) west of La Roche-Guyon on D5, 45 km (27 mi) northwest of Thoiry via D11 and D147, 70 km (44 mi) northwest of Paris.*

GETTING HERE
Take a main-line train (departures every couple of hours) from Paris's Gare St-Lazare to Vernon (50 mins) on the Rouen–Le Havre line, then a taxi, bus, or bike (which you can hire at the café opposite Vernon station) to Giverny, 6 mi away. Buses, which run April through October only, meet the trains daily and whisk you away to Giverny for €4 more.

EXPLORING
The small village of Giverny (pronounced jee-vair-knee), just beyond the Epte River, which marks the boundary of Ile-de-France, has become a place of pilgrimage for art lovers. It was here that Claude Monet lived for 43 years, until his death at the age of 86 in 1926. Although his house is now prized by connoisseurs of 19th-century interior decoration, it's his garden, with its Japanese-inspired water-lily pond and its bridge, that remains the high point for many—a 5-acre, three-dimensional Impressionist painting you can stroll around at leisure. It's easy to get to Giverny from Paris—trains leave every couple of hours from Gare St-Lazare for the 50-minute ride to Vernon; buses and taxis meet the trains and whisk you to Giverny, or you can rent a bike from the café opposite the station (head down to the river and take the cycle path once you've crossed the Seine). Most make this a day trip, although Giverny has some jewel bed-and-breakfasts, so you should consider an

overnight or two. Vernon itself *(see below)* is a well-preserved old town with a magisterial Gothic church.

FodorsChoice The **Maison et Jardin Claude-Monet** *(Monet's House and Garden)* has
★ been lovingly restored. Monet was brought up in Normandy and, like many of the Impressionists, was captivated by the soft light of the Seine Valley. After several years in Argenteuil, just north of Paris, he moved downriver to Giverny in 1883 along with his two sons, his mistress, Alice Hoschedé (whom he later married), and her six children. By 1890 a prospering Monet was able to buy the house outright. With its pretty pink walls and green shutters, the house has a warm feeling that may come as a welcome change after the stateliness of the French châteaux. Rooms have been restored to Monet's original designs: the kitchen with its blue tiles, the buttercup-yellow dining room, and Monet's bedroom on the second floor. The house was fully and glamorously restored only in the 1970s, thanks to the millions contributed by fans and patrons (who were often Americans). Reproductions of his works, and some of the Japanese prints he avidly collected, crowd its walls. During this era, French culture had come under the spell of Orientalism and these framed prints were often gifts from visiting Japanese diplomats, whom Monet had befriended in Paris.

Three years after buying his house and cultivating its garden—which the family called the "Clos Normand"—the prospering Monet purchased another plot of land across the lane to continue his gardening experiments, even diverting the Epte to make a pond. The resulting garden *"à la japonaise"* (reached through a tunnel from the "Clos"), with flowers spilling out across the paths, contains the famous "tea-garden" bridge and water-lily pond, flanked by a mighty willow and rhododendrons. Images of the bridge and the water lilies—in French, *nymphéas*—in various seasons appear in much of Monet's later work. Looking across the pond, it's easy to conjure up the grizzled, bearded brushsmith dabbing at his canvases—capturing changes in light and pioneering a breakdown in form that was to have a major influence on 20th-century art.

The garden is a place of wonder, filled with butterflies, roosters, nearly 100,000 plants bedded every year, and more than 100,000 perennials. No matter that nearly 500,000 visitors troop through it each year; they fade into the background thanks to all the beautiful roses, purple carnations, lady's slipper, aubrieta, tulips, beaded irises, hollyhocks, poppies, daises, lambs' ears, larkspur, and azaleas, to mention just a few of the blooms (note that the water lilies flower during the latter part of July and the first two weeks of August). Even so, during the height of spring, when the gardens are particularly popular, try to visit during midweek. If you want to pay your respects, Monet is buried in the family vault in Giverny's village church. ⊠ *84 rue Claude-Monet* ☎ *02–32–51–28–21* ⊕ *www. fondation-monet.com* ⊠ *Gardens and home €5.50, gardens only €4* ⊙ *Apr.–Oct., Tues.–Sun. 10–6.*

After touring the painterly grounds of Monet's house, you may wish to see some real paintings at the airy **Musée Américain** *(American Museum)*, farther along the road. Endowed by the late Chicago art patrons Daniel and Judith Terra, it displays works by American Impressionists who were influenced by Claude Monet. After the master made Giverny his home, other artists, including Willard Metcalf, Louis Ritter, Theodore Wendel, and John Leslie Breck, "discovered" Giverny, too (truth be known, Monet soon tired of being a cult figure). On-site are a restaurant and *salon de thé* (tearoom), as well as a garden "quoting" some of Monet's plant compositions. Head down the road to visit Giverny's landmark Hôtel Baudy *(see below)*, now a restaurant and once the stomping grounds and watering hole of many of these 19th-century artists. ⊠ *99 rue Claude-Monet* ☎ *02-32-51-94-65* ⊕ *www.maag.org* ⊠ *€5.50* ☉ *Apr.–Nov., Tues.–Sun. 10–6.*

> ### IF YOU COULD SEE WHAT HE SAW
>
> Monet also immortalized the countryside surrounding Giverny—notably, its haystacks and poplar trees—in oils, but these motifs have often been altered beyond recognition. The haystacks are no more (wheat is now rolled up), while Monet's famous rows of poplar trees along the River Epte, near Limetz, about 3 km (2 mi) south of Giverny, are completely overgrown. But to enjoy these hills and dales, hike or bike the 20 trails that link Giverny and Vernon; to find the best of them, pick up the hiking guide from Vernon's tourist office (bike rental places are nearby).

WHERE TO STAY & EAT

$–$$ ✕ **Les Jardins de Giverny.** This tile-floor 1912 restaurant, overlooking a rose garden, is a few minutes' walk from Monet's house. Enjoy the two-course €21 menu or choose from a repertoire of inventive dishes such as foie gras spiked with calvados, duck with honey, or lamb with thyme. ⊠ *1 rue du Milieu* ☎ *02-32-21-60-80* ▤ *AE, MC, V* ☉ *Closed Mon. and Dec.–Feb. No dinner Wed. or Sun.*

$ ✕ **Hôtel Baudy.** Back in Monet's day, this pretty-in-pink villa, originally an *épicerie-buvette* (café-cum-grocer's store), was the hotel of the American painters' colony. Today, the rustic dining room and flowery patio, overlooked by a rose garden and the hut Cézanne once used as a studio, retain more historic charm than the simple cuisine (mainly warm and cold salads) or the busloads of tour groups (luckily channeled upstairs). ⊠ *81 rue Claude-Monet* ☎ *02-32-21-10-03* ▤ *MC, V* ☉ *Closed Mon. and Nov.–Mar. No dinner Sun.*

$ ✕▦ **La Musardière.** Just a short stroll from chez Monet, this 1880 manor house (the name means "Place to Idle") has a cozy lobby, guest rooms with views overlooking a leafy garden, and its own restaurant–crêperie (closed November–March, no lunch Monday). ⊠ *123 rue Claude-Monet, 27620* ☎ *02-32-21-03-18* ▤ *02-32-21-60-00* ⇴ *10 rooms, 1 suite* ⚲ *In-room: no a/c. In-hotel: restaurant, tennis court, pool, no elevator* ▤ *AE, DC, MC, V* ⑩ *MAP.*

★ $–$$$ ▦ **Giverny B&Bs.** Giverny's dire shortage of hotels is made up for by several enticing, stylish, and affordable B&Bs set up in village homes. Particularly notable are **Le Clos Fleuri** (⊠ *5 rue de la Dîme* ▦▱ *02–32–21–36–51*), a Norman manor house set in a lovely garden and run by the Fouché family; **La Réserve** (⊠ *Rue Blanche-Hoschedé* ☎ *02–32–21–99–09*), about a mile outside town, an expansive residence surrounded by orchards and with gorgeous, antiques-adorned and wood-beamed guest apartments, some of which have fireplaces and canopy beds; and the residence of **Marie-Claire Boscher** (⊠ *1 rue du Colombier* ▦▱ *02–32–51–39–70*), which used to be a hotel-restaurant that Monet frequented. Log onto the Web site www.giverny.org/hotels for all the details.

2

VERNON

❽   *5 km (3 mi) northwest of Giverny on D5, 73 km (46 mi) northwest of Paris.*

The Vieille Ville (Od Town) of Vernon, on the Seine, has a medieval church, which Monet painted from across the Seine, and several fine timber-frame houses (the most impressive, on Rue Carnot, houses the tourist office).

The church of **Notre-Dame** (⊠ *Rue Carnot*), across from the tourist office, has an arresting rose-window facade that, like the high nave, dates from the 15th century. Rounded Romanesque arches in the choir, however, attest to the building's 12th-century origins.

A few minor Monet canvases, along with other late-19th-century paintings, can be admired in the town museum, the **Musée Poulain.** This rambling old mansion is seldom crowded, and the helpful curators are happy to explain local history. ⊠ *12 rue du Pont* ☎ *02–32–21–28–09* ▱ *€2.60* ◷ *Apr.–Sept., Tues.–Fri. 10–12:30 and 2–6; weekends 2–6; Oct.–Mar., Tues.–Sun. 2–5:30.*

WHERE TO STAY & EAT

$$–$$$ ✕ **Les Fleurs.** This small, white-walled restaurant in the center of Vernon looks unremarkable inside and out, but the food on your plate has far more personality—as you can see with one bite of the roast salmon with herbs, or the snails in a Roquefort cheese sauce. Fresh flowers on the tablecloths add a colorful touch. Service is slick and friendly, while fixed-prices run €24–€47. ⊠ *71 rue Sadi-Carnot* ☎ *02–32–51–16–80* ⊕ *www.restaurantlesfleurs.com* ▤ *AE, MC, V* ◷ *Closed Aug. and Mon. No dinner Sun.*

★ $$–$$$ ✕▦ **Château de Brécourt.** This 17th-century stone-and-brick château close to the expressway outside Vernon has high-pitched roofs, an imposing forecourt, and extensive grounds. Guest rooms follow the same exuberant turn-of-the-19th-century lines. Even if you're not staying here, you can dine on the inventive food in the august restaurant, Le Grand Siècle. A sumptuous, €42 four-course menu, and dishes such as lobster mousse and veal with truffles make it a popular spot—and it's relatively easy to get to from Giverny, a few miles across the Seine from Vernon. As such châteaux-hotels go, a stay here is a relatively good value. ⊠ *Rte. de Brécourt, 8 km (5 mi) southwest of Vernon on*

D181–D75, 27120 Douains ☏*02–32–52–40–50* 🖶*02–32–52–69–65*
⊕*www.chateaudebrecourt.com* ⊷*25 rooms, 4 suites* ♿*In-room: no
a/c, refrigerator. In-hotel: restaurant, tennis court, pool, some pets
allowed (fee)* ▤*AE, MC, V* ⦿*MAP.*

LA ROCHE-GUYON

➒ *8 km (5 mi) east of Giverny via D147, 7 km (4 mi) northwest of
Vétheuil on D913, 69 km (43 mi) northwest of Paris.*

Ruins of a medieval cliff-top castle look down on the River Seine and
the quaint village of La Roche-Guyon. A steep-climbing stairway, hewn
through the rock, links the castle to the classical **château** below, constructed mainly in the 18th century. The château has impressive iron
gates incorporating the arms of the owners, the Rochefoucauld family; its main building is one story higher than ground level, behind an
arcaded terrace that towers above the stables and grassy forecourt.
An interior highlight is the *Story of Esther* tapestry series. ✉*1 rue
de l'Audience* ☏*01–34–79–74–42* ⊕*www.chateaudelarocheguyon.
fr* 🎟*€7.50* ⦿*Mar.–Oct., Tues.–Sun. 10–5; Nov.–mid-Dec. and mid-
Jan.–Feb., weekends 10–5.*

WHERE TO EAT

$$ ✕ **Le Moulin de Fourges.** Nestled in verdant countryside by the River
Epte, 5 km (3 mi) north of La Roche-Guyon, this converted 18th-cen-
tury water mill has a mouthwatering setting. Succulent dishes range
from braised lamb with apple and celery, to duck with polenta and
coffee grains. The €38 four-course menu is a good bet. ✉*38 rue du
Moulin, Fourges* ☏*02–32–52–12–12* ⊕*www.moulin-de-fourges.com*
♿*Reservations essential* ▤*MC, V* ⦿*Closed Mon. Apr. –Sept. and
weekdays Oct. –Mar.*

PONTOISE

➓ *47 km (28 mi) east of La Roche-Guyon via D147, N183, and N14, 29
km (19 mi) northwest of Paris via A15.*

A pleasant old town on the banks of the Oise, Pontoise is famous for
its link with the Impressionists.

The small **Musée Pissarro,** high up in the Vieille Ville, pays tribute to
one of Pontoise's most illustrious past residents, Impressionist painter
Camille Pissarro (1830–1903). The collection of prints and drawings is
of interest mainly to specialists, but the view across the valley from the
museum gardens will appeal to all. ✉*17 rue du Château* ☏*01–30–38–
02–40* ⊕*www.ville-pontoise.fr* 🎟*Free* ⦿*Wed.–Sun. 2–6.*

The **Musée Tavet-Delacour,** housed in a turreted mansion in the center of
Pontoise, stages good exhibitions and has a permanent collection that
ranges from street scenes and landscapes by Norbert Goenutte and
other local painters to contemporary art and the intriguing abstractions
of Otto Freundlich. ✉*4 rue Lemercier* ☏*01–30–38–02–40* ⊕*www.
ville-pontoise.fr* 🎟*€4* ⦿*Wed.–Sun. 10–12:30 and 1:30–6.*

AUVERS-SUR-OISE

Fodor'sChoice
★

7 km (4 mi) east of Pontoise via D4, 33 km (21 mi) northwest of Paris via N328.

GETTING HERE

Getting to Auvers from Paris (Gare du Nord) invariably requires a change of train, either in Valmondois (suburban trains) or St-Ouen l'Aumone (RER-C). Journey time is 45–55 minutes. There is no connecting public transportation from the area around Vernon.

EXPLORING

The tranquil Oise River valley, which runs northeast from Pontoise, retains much of the charm that attracted Camille Pissarro, Paul Cézanne, Camille Corot, Charles-François Daubigny, and Berthe Morisot to Auvers-sur-Oise in the second half of the 19th century. But despite this lofty company, it's the spirit of Vincent van Gogh that haunts every nook and cranny of this pretty riverside village. Van Gogh moved to Auvers from Arles in May 1890 to be nearer his brother. Little has changed here since that summer of 1890, during the last 10 weeks of Van Gogh's life, when he painted no fewer than 70 pictures. You can find out about his haunts and other Impressionist sites in Auvers by stopping in at the tourist office at Les Colombières, a 14th-century manor house, set on the Rue de la Sansonne (closed from 12:30 to 2 pmevery day). Short hikes outside the town center—sometimes marked with yellow trail signs—will lead you to rural landscapes once beloved by Pissarro and Cézanne, including the site of one of Van Gogh's last paintings, *Wheat Fields with Crows.* On July 27, 1890, the great painter laid his easel against a haystack, walked behind the Château d'Auvers, shot himself, then stumbled to the Auberge Ravoux, where the owner sent to Paris for the artist's brother, Theo. Van Gogh died on July 29. The next day, using a hearse from neighboring Méry (because the priest of Auvers refused to provide his for a suicide victim), Van Gogh's body was borne up the hill to the village cemetery. His heartbroken brother died the following year and, in 1914, was reburied alongside Vincent in his simple ivy-covered grave.

Set opposite the village town hall, the Auberge Ravoux, the inn where Van Gogh stayed, is now the **Maison de van Gogh** *(Van Gogh House).* The inn opened in 1876 and owes its name to Arthur Ravoux, the landlord from 1889 to 1891. He had seven lodgers in all, including the minor Dutch painter Anton Hirsching; they paid 3.50 francs board and lodging, cheaper than the other inns in Auvers, where 6 francs was the going rate. A dingy staircase leads up to the tiny, spartan wood-floor attic where Van Gogh stored some of modern art's most famous pictures under his bed. A short film retraces Van Gogh's time at Auvers, and there's a well-stocked souvenir shop. Stop for a drink or for lunch in the ground-floor restaurant. ⊠*8 rue de la Sansonne* ☎*01–30–36–60–60* 💷*€5* ⊘*Mar.–Nov., Wed.–Sun. 10–6.*

A major town landmark opened to the public for the first time in 2004: the house and garden of Van Gogh's closest friend in Auvers, Dr. Paul Gachet. Documents and souvenirs at the **Maison du Dr Gachet** evoke Van Gogh's stay in Auvers and Gachet's passion for the avant-garde art of his era. The good doctor was himself the subject of one of the artist's most famous portraits (and the world's second-most expensive painting when it sold for $82 million in the late 1980s), the actual painting of which was reenacted in the 1956 Kirk Douglas biopic, *Lust for Life*. Friend and patron to many of the artists who settled in and visited Auvers in the 1880s, among them Cézanne (who immortalized the doctor's house in

> ## IN SEARCH OF VINCENT
>
> Auvers-sur-Oise is peppered with plaques marking the spots that inspired his art. The plaques bear reproductions of his paintings, enabling you to compare his final works with the scenes as they are today. His last abode—the Auberge Ravoux—has been turned into a shrine. You can also visit the medieval village church, subject of one of Van Gogh's most famous paintings, *L'Église d'Auvers*, admire Osip Zadkine's powerful statue of Van Gogh in the village park, and visit the restored house of Dr. Gachet, Vincent's best friend.

a famous landscape), Gachet also taught them about engraving processes. The ivy covering Van Gogh's grave in the cemetery across town was provided by Gachet from this house's garden. ⊠ *78 rue du Dr-Gachet* 🕾 *01–30–36–60–60* 🎫 *€4* ⊙ *Apr.–Oct., Tues.–Sun. 10–6.*

☙ The elegant 17th-century village château—also depicted by Van Gogh—set above split-level gardens, now houses the **Voyage au Temps des Impressionnistes** *(Journey Through the Impressionist Era)*. You'll receive a set of headphones (English available), with commentary that guides you past various tableaux illustrating life during the Impressionist years. Although there are no Impressionist originals—500 reproductions pop up on screens interspersed between the tableaux—this is one of France's most imaginative, enjoyable, and innovative museums. Some of the special effects—talking mirrors, computerized cabaret dancing girls, and a simulated train ride past Impressionist landscapes—are worthy of Disney. The museum restaurant, Les Canotiers—named after Renoir's famous painting of boaters—offers dishes favored by such artists as Morisot, Degas, and Manet, while more casual fare is offered at a re-creation of a 19th-century *guinguette* (riverbank café). ⊠ *Rue de Léry* 🕾 *01–34–48–48–40* ⊕ *www.chateau-auvers.fr* 🎫 *€10.50* ⊙ *Apr.–Sept., Tues.–Sun. 10–6; Oct.–mid-Dec. and mid-Jan.–Mar., Tues.–Sun. 10:30–4:30.*

The landscape artist Charles-François Daubigny, a precursor of the Impressionists, lived in Auvers from 1861 until his death in 1878. You can visit his studio, the **Maison-Atelier de Daubigny,** and admire the mural and roof paintings by Daubigny and fellow artists Camille Corot and Honoré Daumier. ⊠ *61 rue Daubigny* 🕾 *01–34–48–03–03* 🎫 *€5* ⊙ *Easter–Oct., Thurs.–Sun. 2–6.*

2

You may also want to visit the modest **Musée Daubigny** to admire the drawings, lithographs, and occasional oils by local 19th-century artists, some of which were collected by Daubigny himself. The museum is opposite the Maison de Van Gogh, above the tourist office, which shows a free 15-minute film (in English on request) about life in Auvers, "From Daubigny to Van Gogh." ⊠*Manoir des Colombières, Rue de la Sansonne* ☎*01–30–36–80–20* ⊠*€4* ⊙*Apr.–Oct., daily 2–6; Nov.– mid-Dec. and mid-Jan.–Mar., Wed.–Sun. 2–5.*

WHERE TO STAY & EAT

★ $$–$$$ ✕ **Auberge Ravoux.** For total Van Gogh immersion, have lunch in the restaurant he patronized regularly more than 100 years ago, in the building where he finally expired. The €35, three-course menu changes regularly, but it's the genius loci that makes eating here special, with glasswork, lace curtains, and wall blandishments carefully modeled on the original designs. A magnificently illustrated book, *Van Gogh's Table* (published by Artisan), by culinary historian Alexandra Leaf and art historian Fred Leeman, recalls Vincent's stay at the Auberge and describes in loving detail the dishes served there at the time. ⊠*52 rue Général-de-Gaulle* ☎*01–30–36–60–63* ⊛*Reservations essential* ▤*AE, DC, MC, V* ⊙*Closed Nov.–Feb. No dinner Sun. or Mon.*

$$–$$$ ✕▣ **Hostellerie du Nord.** This sturdy white mansion began life as a coach house in the 17th century, and is conveniently and attractively situated close to the Oise River and rail station, a short walk from Van Gogh's former house. Rubicund owner Joël Boilleaut is a noted chef and expects his diners to linger over the cheeseless three-course €43 lunch menu (coffee and a half bottle of wine thrown in) or the €55 four-course dinner banquet, when tuna carpaccio with fennel and spinach, and guinea fowl with licorice and apple, raise gastronomic eyebrows. The restaurant is closed Monday, Saturday lunch, and Sunday dinner, but no worries: a scaled-down bistro service provides a more than adequate alternative, with scallops and jugged hare among a healthy choice. Joël's wife Corinne oversees the prim hotel, whose small, white-walled bedrooms, adorned with gilt-framed pictures, are named after artists, including Cézanne, who stayed here in 1872, and Van Gogh, whose junior suite provides your wood-beamed quaintest, if priciest, slumbertime option. ⊠*6 rue du Gal-de-Gaulle, 95430* ☎*01–30–36– 70–74* 🖷*01–30–36–72–75* ⊕*www.hostelleriedunord.fr* 🛏*10 rooms* ⌂*In-room: dial-up. In-hotel: restaurant, no elevator* ▤*AE, MC, V* ⊙*Closed part of Feb.* ⏻*MAP.*

L'ISLE-ADAM

⑫ *6 km (4 mi) northeast of Auvers-sur-Oise via D4, 40 km (25 mi) north of Paris via N1.*

Residentially exclusive L'Isle-Adam is one of the most picturesque towns in Ile-de-France. Paris lies just 40 km (25 mi) south, but it could be 161 km (100 mi) and as many years away. The town has a sandy beach along one stretch of the River Oise (via rue de Beaumont); a curious pagodalike folly, the Pavillon Chinois de Cassan; and an unassuming local museum.

The **Musée Louis-Senlecq,** on the main street behind the tall-towered town church, features the ceramic figures produced in L'Isle-Adam a century ago, and contains numerous attractive works by Jules Dupré and other local landscapists. ⊠ *46 Grande-Rue* ☎ *01–34–69–45–44* ⊕ *www.ville-isle-adam. fr* ☎ *€3.20* ⊙ *Wed.–Mon. 2–6.*

WHERE TO STAY & EAT

$–$$$ ✕▣ **Le Cabouillet.** The riverside Cabouillet aptly reflects the quiet charm of L'Isle-Adam, thanks to its pretty views over the Oise. You

> ## AN EXUBERANCE OF FORM
>
> You may find that the Château de Monte-Cristo's fanciful exterior, where pilasters, cupolas, and stone carvings compete for attention, crosses the line from opulence to tastelessness, but—as in such swashbuckling novels as *The Count of Monte Cristo*—swagger, not subtlety, is what counts.

can savor these from each of its cozy rooms or from the chic restaurant, where the cooking can be inspired—try the sea bass with cockles and fennel, or the chicken with morels and asparagus. ⊠ *5 quai de l'Oise, 95290* ☎ *01–34–69–00–90* ☎ *01–34–69–33–88* ⊕ *www.le-cabouillet. com* ⊠ *5 rooms* ⅙ *In-room: no a/c. In-hotel: restaurant, no elevator* ▭ *AE, DC, MC, V* ⊙ *Closed Mon. and late Dec.–early Feb. No dinner Sun.* ❙◎❙ *MAP.*

ST-GERMAIN-EN-LAYE

⓭   *29 km (18 mi) southwest of L'Isle-Adam via D64/N184, 17 km (11 mi) west of Paris.*

The elegant town of St-Germain-en-Laye, encircled by forest and perched behind Le Nôtre's Grande Terrace overlooking the Seine, has lost little of its original cachet, despite the invasion of wealthy former Parisians who commute to work on the RER (the station is in the center of town and has frequent trains to and from Paris).

If you're fond of the swashbuckling novels of Alexandre Dumas (who, incidentally, enjoyed the rare honor of reburial in the Paris Panthéon in 2002), then you can enjoy the **Château de Monte-Cristo** *(Monte Cristo Castle)* at Port-Marly on the southern fringe of St-Germain (signposted to your left as you arrive from Marly-le-Roi). Dumas built the château after his books' surging popularity made him rich in the 1840s. Construction costs and lavish partying meant he went broke just as quickly, and he skedaddled to a Belgian exile in 1849. The château contains pictures, Dumas mementos, and the luxurious Moorish Chamber, with spellbinding, interlacing plasterwork executed by Arab craftsmen (lent by the Bey of Tunis) and restored thanks to a donation from the late Moroccan king Hassan II. ⊠ *Av. du Président-Kennedy* ☎ *01–39–16–49–49* ☎ *€5* ⊙ *Apr.–Oct., Tues.–Fri. 10–12:30 and 2–6, weekends 10–6; Nov.–Mar., Sun. 2–5.*

Next to the St-Germain RER train station is the stone-and-brick **Château de St-Germain,** with its dry moat, intimidating circular towers, and La

Grande Terrasse, one of the most spectacular of all French garden set-pieces; the château itself dates from the 16th and 17th centuries. A royal palace has existed here since the early 12th century, when Louis VI—known as Le Gros (the Plump)—exploited St-Germain's defensive potential in his bid to pacify Ile-de-France. A hundred years later Louis IX (St. Louis) added the elegant **Sainte-Chapelle**, the château's oldest remaining section; note the square-topped, not pointed, side windows and the filled-in rose window on the back wall. Charles V (1364–80) built a powerful defensive keep in the mid-14th century, but from the 1540s François I and his successors transformed St-Germain into a palace with more of a domestic than a warlike vocation. Louis XIV was born here, and it was here that his father, Louis XIII, died. Until 1682—when the court moved to Versailles—it remained the country's foremost royal residence outside Paris; several Molière plays were premiered in the main hall. Since 1867 the château has housed the impressive **Musée des Antiquités Nationales** (Museum of National Antiquities), holding a trove of artifacts, figurines, brooches, and weapons, from the Stone Age to the 8th century. Behind the château is André Le Nôtre's **Grande Terrasse**, a terraced promenade lined by century-old lime trees. Directly overlooking the Seine, it was completed in 1673 and has rarely been outdone for grandeur or length. ⊠*Pl. Charles-de-Gaulle* ☎*01–39–10–13–00* ⊕*www.musee-antiquitesnationales.fr* ☞*€4* ⊙ *Wed.–Mon. 9–5:15.*

The quaint **Musée du Prieuré** *(Priory Museum)* is devoted to the work of the artist Maurice Denis (1870–1943) and his fellow Symbolists and to Nabis—painters opposed to the naturalism of their 19th-century Impressionist contemporaries. Denis found the calm of the former Jesuit priory, set above tiered gardens with statues and rose-bushes, ideally suited to his spiritual themes, which he expressed in stained glass, ceramics, and frescoes as well as oils. ⊠*2 bis, rue Maurice-Denis* ☎*01–39–73–77–87* ☞*€5.30* ⊙ *Tues.–Fri. 10–5:30, weekends 10–6:30.*

WHERE TO STAY & EAT

$$ ✗ **La Feuillantine.** An imaginative, good-value prix-fixe €35 menu has made this wood-beamed restaurant an often crowded success. Scallops with fennel, salmon with endive, and herbed chicken fricassee with morels are among chef Francis Porier's specialties. Try for a table near the window; those near the back of the restaurant can be a bit gloomy. ⊠*10 rue des Louviers* ☎*01–34–51–04–24* ⊕*www.lafeuillantine.com* ▭*AE, MC, V.*

$$$$
Fodor'sChoice
★ ✗▦ **La Forestière.** A quintessentially beautiful Ile-de-France country retreat surrounded by forest, this hotel, run by Philippe Cazaudehore, is St-Germain's most stylish. The rambling house itself is a solid, shuttered-window affair with 18th-century–style furniture. The fine restaurant, the Cazaudehore (closed Monday, no dinner on Sunday from November to February), sees chef Grégory Balland major in sole with mushroom risotto, steamed turbot and beef tartare with oysters, and hare stuffed with olives and foie gras. Dining on the garden veranda on such delights as Balland's melt-in-the-mouth foie gras with gingerbread

can prove a most seductive experience. ⊠*1 av. du Président-Kennedy, 78100* ☎*01–30–61–64–64* 🖷*01–39–73–73–88* ⊕*www.cazaudehore. fr* ⇆*25 rooms, 5 suites* ⚫*In-room: no a/c, refrigerator. In-hotel: restaurant, bar, some pets allowed (fee)* ▱*AE, DC, MC, V* ⦿❘*BP.*

NIGHTLIFE & THE ARTS
The **Fête des Loges** *(Loges Festival)* is a giant fair and carnival held in the Forest of St-Germain from July to mid-August. Hordes of fans of cotton candy, roller coasters, and Ferris wheels turn up every year.

RUEIL-MALMAISON

⓮ *8 km (5 mi) southeast of St-Germain-en-Laye via N13, 8 km (5 mi) west of Paris on N13 via La Défense.*

Rueil-Malmaison is a slightly dreary western suburb of Paris, but the memory of the legendary pair Napoléon and Joséphine still haunts its château. Built in 1622, **La Malmaison** was bought by the future empress Joséphine in 1799 as a love nest for Napoléon and herself (they had married three years earlier). Theirs is one of Europe's most dramatic love stories, replete with affairs, hatred (the emperor's family often disparaged Joséphine—a name bestowed on her by Napoléon: her real name was Rose—as "the Creole"), and scandal. After the childless Joséphine was divorced by the heir-hungry emperor in 1809, she retired to La Malmaison and died here on May 29, 1814.

The château has 24 rooms furnished with exquisite tables, chairs, and sofas of the Napoleonic period; of special note are the library, game room, and dining room. The walls are adorned with works by artists of the day, such as Jacques-Louis David, Pierre-Paul Prud'hon, and Baron Gérard. Take time to admire the clothes and hats that belonged to Napoléon and Joséphine, particularly the empress's gowns. Their carriage can be seen in one of the garden pavilions, and another pavilion contains a unique collection of snuffboxes donated by Prince George of Greece. The gardens themselves are delightful, especially the regimented rows of tulips in spring. The Bois Préau, Josephine's house after her divorce from the emperor, is located nearby but is now undergoing a multi-year renovation. ⊠*15 av. du Château* ☎*01–41–29–05–57* ⊕*www.chateau-malmaison.fr* ▱*€4.50* ☉ *Wed.–Mon. 10–12:30 and 1:30–5:15.*

> **WORD OF MOUTH**
>
> "Going via public transport, I took the RER to Rueil-Malmaison (the métro doesn't go there) on the line A. Incorrect is the info to take Bus 258 from there to the château; instead, take Bus 2A or 2B from the RER station to the main road near the château (I think the stop is called Château). They only run about once every half hour or even once an hour during some periods." –Christina

THE EASTERN ILE-DE-FRANCE: CHANTILLY TO FONTAINEBLEAU

This area covers a broad arc, beginning northeast of Paris in Chantilly, one of the most popular day trips from the French capital. From the frozen-in-time medieval town of Senlis, we detour north to visit Compiègne—hyperopulent outpost of the Napoleonic dynasty—and neighboring Pierrefonds, a fairy-tale 19th-century castle that may even outdo the one at Disneyland Paris, the very next stop on this tour heading south. The grand finale comprises three of the most spectacular châteaux in France: Vaux-le-Vicomte, Courances, and Fontainebleau.

CHANTILLY

⑮ *37 km (23 mi) north of Paris via N16, 23 km (14 mi) east of L'Isle-Adam via D4.*

GETTING HERE

Chantilly can be reached on both suburban (Transilien) and main-line (to Creil and beyond) trains from Paris's Gare du Nord; the trip takes 25–40 minutes and costs €8.

EXPLORING

Celebrated for lace, cream, and the most beautiful medieval manuscript in the world—*Les Très Riches Heures du Duc de Berry*—romantic Chantilly has a host of other attractions: a faux Renaissance château with an eye-popping art collection, splendid Baroque stables, a classy racecourse, and a 16,000-acre forest.

Fodor's Choice ★ Although its lavish exterior may be 19th-century Renaissance pastiche, the **Château de Chantilly,** sitting snugly behind an artificial lake, houses the outstanding **Musée Condé,** with illuminated medieval manuscripts, tapestries, furniture, and paintings. The most famous room, the **Santuario** (sanctuary), contains two celebrated works by Italian painter Raphael (1483–1520)—the *Three Graces* and the *Orleans Virgin*—plus an exquisite ensemble of 15th-century miniatures by the most illustrious French painter of his time, Jean Fouquet (1420–81). Farther on, in the **Cabinet des Livres** (library), is the world-famous Book of Hours whose title translates as *The Very Rich Hours of the Duc de Berry,* which was illuminated by the Brothers Limbourg with magical pictures of early-15th-century life as lived by one of Burgundy's richest lords (unfortunately, due to their fragility, painted facsimiles of the celebrated calendar illuminations are on display, not the actual pages of the book). Other highlights of this unusual museum are the **Galerie de Psyché** (Psyche Gallery), with 16th-century stained glass and portrait drawings by Flemish artist Jean Clouet II; the **Chapelle,** with sculptures by Jean Goujon and Jacques Sarrazin; and the extensive collection of paintings by 19th-century French artists, headed by Jean-Auguste-Dominique Ingres. In addition, there are grand and smaller salons, all stuffed with palace furniture, family portraits, and Sèvres porcelains, making this a must for lovers of the decorative and applied arts.

☎03–44–62–62–62 ⊕*www.cha-
teaudechantilly.com* ⊠€9, *including park* ⊘*Apr.–Oct., daily 10–6;
Nov.–Mar., daily 10:30–5.*

Le Nôtre's **park** is based on that
familiar French royal combination of formality (neatly planned
parterres and a mighty, straight-
banked canal) and romantic
eccentricity (the waterfall and the
Hameau, a mock-Norman village
that inspired Marie-Antoinette's
version at Versailles). You can
explore on foot or on an electric train, and take a **hydrophile**
(electric-powered boat) for a glide
down the Grand Canal. ☎*03–44–
57–35–35* ⊠*Park only €4, with
boat €9, with train and boat €14;
€16 joint ticket including château* ⊘*Apr.–Oct., daily 10–8; Nov.–Mar.,
daily 10:30–6.*

> ## A DAY AT THE RACES
>
> Since 1834 Chantilly's fabled race-
> track, the Hippodrome des Princes
> de Condé (⊠Rte. de la Plaine-
> des-Aigles ☎03–44–62–44–00
> ⊕www.france-galop.com/hip-
> pos/h60500.htm) has come into
> its own each June with two of
> Europe's most prestigious events:
> the **Prix du Jockey-Club** (French
> Derby) on the first Sunday of the
> month, and the **Prix de Diane** for
> three-year-old fillies the Sunday
> after. On main race days, a free
> shuttle bus runs between Chantil-
> ly's train station and the racetrack.

The palatial 18th-century **Grandes Écuries** *(Grand Stables)* by the race-
track, built by Jean Aubert in 1719 to accommodate 240 horses and
500 hounds for stag and boar hunts in the forests nearby, are the grandest stables in France. They're still in use as the home of the **Musée
Vivant du Cheval** (Living Horse Museum), with 30 breeds of horses
and ponies housed in straw-lined comfort—in between dressage performances in the courtyard or beneath the majestic central dome. The
31-room museum has a comprehensive collection of equine paraphernalia: everything from saddles, bridles, and stirrups to rocking horses,
anatomy displays, and old postcards. There are explanations in English throughout. ⊠*7 rue du Connétable* ☎*03–44–57–40–40* ⊕*www.
museevivantducheval.fr* ⊠*€8.50* ⊘*Apr.–Oct., Wed.–Mon. 10:30–
5:30; Nov.–Mar., Wed.–Fri. and Mon. 2–6, weekends 10:30–6:30.*

WHERE TO STAY & EAT

★ $$-$$$ ✕ **La Capitainerie.** Housed in the stone-vaulted kitchens of the Châ-
teau de Chantilly's legendary 17th-century chef Vorace Vatel, with an
open-hearth fireplace big enough for whole lambs or oxen to sizzle
on the spit, this quaint restaurant is no ordinary museum cafeteria.
Reflect at leisure on your cultural peregrinations over mouthfuls of
grilled turbot or roast quail, and don't forget to add a good dollop
of homemade crème de Chantilly to your dessert. ⊠*In Château de
Chantilly* ☎*03–44–57–15–89* ⊟*MC, V* ⊘*Closed Tues. No dinner
Wed.–Mon.*

$-$$$ ✕ **La Ferme de Condé.** At the far end of the racetrack, in a building that
began life as an Anglican chapel, lost its tower, then served as a private
gym, is one of the classier restaurants in Chantilly. Dishes include roast
suckling pig, duck with honey and spices, and lobster terrine. An €18
menu makes it a suitable lunch spot. There's a good wine list and choice

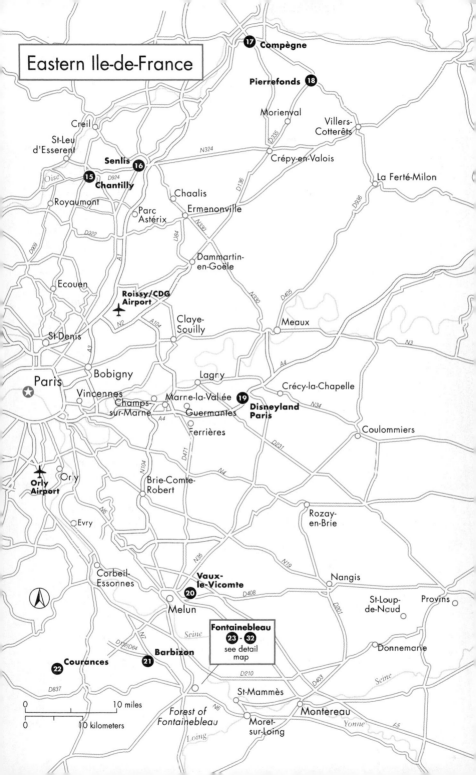

of wine by the jug. ✉*42 av. du Maréchal-Joffre* ☎*03–44–57–32–31* ⊕*bbnours.free.fr* ♤*Reservations essential* 🍴*AE, DC, MC, V.*

$$$$ 🏨 **Dolce Chantilly.** Surrounded by forest and its own 18-hole golf course, this luxe, highly restored, and meetings-friendly hotel is set 1½ km (1 mi) northeast of the château. The marble-floor reception hall creates a glitzy impression not quite matched by the guest rooms, which are functional, modern, and a bit small. The Le Swing brasserie, in the golf clubhouse, serves lunch for €16, and the deluxe Carmontelle has formal dining under top-ranked chef Alain Montigny. ✉*Rte. d'Apremont, Vineuil–St-Firmin 60500* ☎*03–44–58–47–77* 🖨*03–44–58–50–11* ⊕*chantilly.dolce.com* 🛏*200 rooms, 4 suites* ♤*In-room: refrigerator, Wi-Fi. In-hotel: 3 restaurants, golf course, tennis court, pool, gym* 🍴*AE, DC, MC, V* 🍽*FAP.*

$ 🏨 **Campanile.** This functional, modern motel is in quiet Les Huit Curés, on the northern outskirts of Chantilly on the banks of the Nonette River (which compensates for the lack of interior charm). There's a grill room for straightforward meals, with a buffet for appetizers, cheese, and desserts. You can dine outside on the terrace in summer. ✉*Rte. de Creil, on N16 toward Creil, Les Huit Curés 60500* ☎*03–44–57–39–24* 🖨*03–44–58–10–05* 🛏*45 rooms* ♤*In-room: no a/c. In-hotel: restaurant, bar, some pets allowed* 🍴*AE, DC, MC, V.*

SENLIS

⑯ *10 km (6 mi) east of Chantilly via D924, 45 km (28 mi) north of Paris via A1.*

Senlis is an exceptionally well-preserved medieval town with crooked, mazelike streets dominated by the svelte, soaring spire of its Gothic cathedral. Be sure to also inspect the moss-tile church of St-Pierre, with its stumpy crocketed spire. You can enjoy a 40-minute tour of the Vieille Ville by horse and carriage, departing from in front of the cathedral, daily April–December (€35 for up to three people).

★ The **Cathédrale Notre-Dame** (✉*Pl. du Parvis*), one of France's oldest and narrowest cathedrals, dates from the second half of the 12th century. The superb spire—arguably the most elegant in France—was added around 1240, and the majestic transept, with its ornate rose windows, in the 16th century.

The town's excellent **Musée d'Art** *(Art Museum)*, built atop an ancient Gallo-Roman residence, displays archaeological finds ranging from Gallo-Roman votive objects unearthed in the neighboring Halatte Forest to the building's own excavated foundations (uncovered in the basement), including some macabre stone heads bathed in half light. Paintings upstairs include works by Manet's teacher Thomas Couture (who lived in Senlis) and a whimsical fried-egg still life by 19th-century realist Théodule Ribot. ✉*Palais Épiscopal, Pl. du Parvis-Notre-Dame* ☎*03–44–32–00–83* 💶*€4* ⊙*Mon., Thurs., and Fri. 10–noon and 2–6; weekends 11–1 and 2–6; Wed. 2–6.*

**OFF THE
BEATEN
PATH**

Parc Astérix. A great alternative to Disneyland, and a wonderful day out for young and old, this Gallic theme park, 10 km (6 mi) south of Senlis via A1, opened in 1989 and takes its cue from a French comic-book figure whose adventures are set during the Roman invasion of France 2,000 years ago. Among the 30 rides and six shows that attract thundering herds of families each year are a mock Gallo-Roman village, costumed druids, performing dolphins, splash-happy waterslides, and a giant roller coaster. ☎03–44–62–34–04 ⊕*www.parcasterix.com* ☎€35 ⊙*Apr.–Aug., daily 10–6; Sept.–mid-Oct., Wed. and weekends 10–6.*

WHERE TO STAY & EAT

$$$ ✕ **Le Bourgeois Gentilhomme.** This pink-and-cream restaurant in old Senlis, named for dapper chef Philippe Bourgeois, serves such interesting dishes as pigeon with cabbage and bacon, fricassee of burbot with mushrooms, and crab lasagna with cress, to name but three. ⊠*3 pl. de la Halle* ☎03–44–53–13–22 ⊕*www.bourgeois-gentilhomme.com* ▤*AE, DC, MC, V* ⊙*Closed Mon. and 2 wks in Aug. No lunch Sat., no dinner Sun.*

$–$$ ▦ **L'Hostellerie de la Porte-Bellon.** This old stone house with garden, just a five-minute walk from the cathedral and close to the bus station, is the closest you can get to spending a night in the historic center of Senlis. The restaurant (no dinner Sunday) has menus at €21 and €27. ⊠*51 rue Bellon, 60300* ☎03–44–53–03–05 ⊟03–44–53–29–94 ⟲*17 rooms* △*In-room: no a/c. In-hotel: restaurant, some pets allowed (fee), no elevator* ▤*AE, MC, V* ⊙*Closed mid-Dec.–mid-Jan.* ⦿*MAP.*

COMPIÈGNE

⑰ *32 km (20 mi) northeast of Senlis via D932a.*

Compiègne, a bustling town of some 40,000 people—frequent trains connect with Paris's Gare du Nord (the trips takes 45 minutes and costs €28 round-trip)—is at the northern limit of the Forêt de Compiègne. Set on the edge of the misty plains of Picardy, this is prime hunting country, so you can be sure there's a former royal hunting lodge in the vicinity. The one here enjoyed its heyday in the mid-19th century under upstart emperor Napoléon III. But the town's history stretches further back—to Joan of Arc, who was captured in battle and held prisoner here, and to its 15th-century Hôtel de Ville (Town Hall), with its jubilant Flamboyant Gothic facade; and further forward—to the World War I armistice, signed in Compiègne Forest on November 11, 1918.

Fodor's Choice
★
☾

The 18th-century **Château de Compiègne,** where the future Louis XVI first met Marie-Antoinette in 1770, was restored by Napoléon I and favored for wild weekends by his nephew Napoléon III. The first Napoléon's legacy is more keenly felt: his state apartments have been refurbished using the original designs for hangings and upholstery, and bright silks and damasks adorn every room. Much of the mahogany furniture gleams with ormolu, and the chairs sparkle with gold leaf. Napoléon III's furniture looks ponderous by comparison. Behind the palace is a gently rising 4-km (2½-mi) vista, inspired by the park at Schönbrunn, in Vienna, where Napoléon I's second wife, Empress Marie-Louise, grew up. Also here is the **Musée du Second Empire**, a collection of Napoléon III–era decorative arts. The showstopper here is Franz-Xaver Winterhalter's *Empress Eugénie Surrounded by Her Ladies in Waiting*, a famed homage to the over-the-top hedonism of the Napoléon Trois era. Make time for the **Musée de la Voiture** and its display of carriages, coaches, and old cars, including the *Jamais Contente* (*Never Satisfied*), the first car to reach 100 kph (62 mph). ⊠ *Pl. du Général-de-Gaulle* ☎ *03–44–38–47–02* ⊕ *www.musee-chateau-compiegne.fr* ☛ *€5* ⊙ *Mar.–Oct., Wed.–Mon. 10–6; Nov.–Feb., Wed.–Mon. 10–4.*

☺ A collection of 85,000 miniature soldiers—fashioned of lead, cardboard, and other materials—depicting military uniforms through the ages is found in the **Musée de la Figurine Historique** *(Toy Soldier Museum).* ⊠ *28 pl. de l'Hôtel-de-Ville* ☎ *03–44–40–72–55* ☛ *€2* ⊙ *Mar.–Oct., Tues.–Sat. 9–noon and 2–6, Sun. 2–6; Nov.–Feb., Tues.–Sat. 9–noon and 2–5, Sun. 2–5.*

Some 7 km (4 mi) east of Compiègne via N31 and D546, off the road to Rethondes, is the **Wagon de l'Armistice** *(Armistice Railcar),* a replica of the one in which the World War I armistice was signed in 1918. In 1940 the Nazis turned the tables and made the French sign their own surrender in the same place—accompanied by Hitler's infamous jig for joy—then tugged the original car off to Germany, where it was later destroyed. The replicated car is part of a small museum in a leafy clearing. ⊠ *Clairière de l'Armistice* ☎ *03–44–85–14–18* ☛ *€3* ⊙ *Apr.–Oct., Wed.–Mon. 9–noon and 2–6:30; Nov.–Mar., Wed.–Mon. 10–noon and 2–5.*

WHERE TO STAY & EAT

$–$$ ✕ **Rôtisserie du Chat qui Tourne.** This nice spot (no lunch Monday, no dinner Sunday), with its brass lights, plush curtains, and waiters in black tie, tries valiantly to be upper crust, while its adjacent brasserie serves a lighter, more casual fare. ⊠ *17 rue Eugène-Floquet* ☎ *03–44–40–02–74* ▭ *AE, MC, V.*

$ ⊞ **Harlay.** A family-run hotel in a foursquare stone building, the Harlay is conveniently sited by the bridge linking the rail station and downtown. Rooms are soberly decorated; the best overlook the River Oise and are soundproofed with double-glazing. ⊠ *3 rue de Harlay, 60200* ☎ *03–44–23–01–50* 🖶 *03–44–20–19–46* ⊕ *www.hotel-compiegne.net* ⇖ *20 rooms* ▭ *AE, DC, MC, V.*

PIERREFONDS

18 *14 km (9 mi) southeast of Compiègne via D973.*

Dominating the attractive lakeside village of Pierrefonds, a former spa resort, is its immense ersatz medieval castle. Built on a huge mound in the 15th century, the **Château de Pierrefonds** was dismantled in 1620 then comprehensively restored and re-created in the 1860s to imagined former glory at the behest of Emperor Napoléon III, seeking to cash in on the craze for the Middle Ages. Architect Viollet-le-Duc left a crenelated fortress with a fairy-tale silhouette, although, like the fortified town of Carcassonne, which he also restored, Pierrefonds is more a construct of what Viollet-le-Duc thought it should have looked like than what it really was. A visit takes in the chapel, barracks, and the majestic keep holding the lord's bedchamber and reception hall, which is bordered by a spiral staircase whose lower and upper sections reveal clearly what is ancient and modern in this former fortress. Don't miss the plaster casts of tomb sculptures from all over France in the cellars, and the **Collection Monduit**—industrially produced, larger-than-life lead decorations made by the 19th-century firm that brought the Statue of Liberty to life. Buses from Compiègne runs three times daily (fewer on Sunday) from the train station. Taxis are pricey but bikes are another option—this is great bicycling countryside. ⊠*Rue Viollet-le-Duc* ☎*03–44–42–72–72* 🖃*€6.10* ☉*Tues.–Sun. 9:30–12:30 and 2–5:30.*

WHERE TO STAY & EAT

$ ╳🏠 **Le Relais Brunehaut.** Five km (3 mi) north of Pierrefonds, in the hamlet of Chelles, is this quaint hotel–restaurant with a view of the abbey church next door. It's made up of a tiny ensemble of stucco buildings bordered by several acres of pleasant park and a small duck-populated river. An old wooden waterwheel in the dining room and the good, simple seasonal fare make eating here a pleasure. The dining room is closed Monday and Tuesday for lunch year-round. ⊠*3 rue de l'Église, 5 km (3 mi) east of Pierrefonds on D85, 60350 Chelles* ☎*03–44–42–85–05* 🖶*03–44–42–83–30* 🛏*11 rooms* 🛆*In-room: no a/c. In-hotel: restaurant, no elevator* ▭*DC, MC, V* ☉*Closed mid-Jan.–mid-Feb.* ❏*MAP.*

DISNEYLAND PARIS

☾ **19** *68 km (40 mi) southwest of Pierrefonds via D335, D136, N330, and*
Fodor'sChoice *A4, 38 km (24 mi) east of Paris via A4.*
★

GETTING HERE

Take the RER from central Paris (stations at Étoile, Auber, Les Halles, Gare de Lyon, and Nation) to Marne-la-Vallée–Chessy, 100 yards from the Disneyland entrance. Journey time is around 40 minutes, and trains operate every 10–30 minutes, depending on the time of day. Note that a TGV (Train à Grande Vitesse) station links Disneyland to Lille, Lyon, Brussels, and London (via Lille and the Channel Tunnel). Disneyland's hotel complex offers a shuttle bus service to Orly and Charles de Gaulle airports for €20.

EXPLORING

Disneyland Paris (originally called Euro Disney) is probably not what you've traveled to France to experience. But if you have a child in tow, the promise of a day here may get you through an afternoon at Versailles or Fontainebleau. If you're a dyed-in-the-wool Disney fan, you'll want to make a beeline for the park to see how it has been molded to appeal to the tastes of Europeans (Disney's "Imagineers" call it their most lovingly detailed park). And if you've never experienced this particular form of Disney showmanship, you may want to put in an appearance if only to see what all the fuss is about. When it opened, few turned up to do so; today the place is jammed with crowds, and Disneyland Paris is here to stay—and grow, with **Walt Disney Studios** opened alongside it in 2002.

Disneyland Park, as the orginal theme park is styled, consists of five "lands": Main Street U.S.A., Frontierland, Adventureland, Fantasyland, and Discoveryland. The central theme of each land is relentlessly echoed in every detail, from attractions to restaurant menus to souvenirs. The park is circled by a railroad, which stops three times along the perimeter. **Main Street U.S.A.** goes under the railroad and past shops and restaurants toward the main plaza; Disney parades are held here every afternoon and, during holiday periods, every evening.

Top attractions at **Frontierland** are the chilling Phantom Manor, haunted by holographic spooks, and the thrilling runaway mine train of Big Thunder Mountain, a roller coaster that plunges wildly through floods and avalanches in a setting meant to evoke Utah's Monument Valley. Whiffs of Arabia, Africa, and the West Indies give **Adventureland** its exotic cachet; the spicy meals and snacks served here rank among the best food in the park. Don't miss the Pirates of the Caribbean, an exciting mise-en-scène populated by eerily humanlike, computer-driven figures, or Indiana Jones and the Temple of Doom, a breathtaking ride that re-creates some of this luckless hero's most exciting moments.

Fantasyland charms the youngest parkgoers with familiar cartoon characters from such classic Disney films as *Snow White, Pinocchio, Dumbo,* and *Peter Pan.* The focal point of Fantasyland, and indeed Disneyland Paris, is Le Château de la Belle au Bois Dormant (Sleeping Beauty's Castle), a 140-foot, bubblegum-pink structure topped with 16 blue- and gold-tipped turrets. Its design was allegedly inspired by illustrations from a medieval *Book of Hours*—if so, it was by way of Beverly Hills. The castle's dungeon conceals a 2-ton scaly green dragon that rumbles in its sleep and occasionally rouses to roar—an impressive feat of engineering, producing an answering chorus of shrieks from younger children. **Discoveryland** is a futuristic eye-knocker for high-tech Disney entertainment. Robots on roller skates welcome you on your way to Star Tours, a pitching, plunging, sense-confounding ride based on the *Star Wars* films. In Le Visionarium, a simulated space journey is presented by 9-Eye, a staggeringly realistic robot. One of the park's newest attractions, the Jules Verne–inspired **Space Mountain Mission 2,** pretends to catapult *exploronauts* on a rocket-boosted, comet-battered journey through the Milky Way.

2

Walt Disney Studios opened next to the Disneyland Park in 2002. The theme park is divided into four "production zones." Beneath imposing entrance gates and a 100-foot water tower inspired by the one erected in 1939 at Disney Studios in Burbank, California, **Front Lot** contains shops, a restaurant, and a studio re-creating the atmosphere of Sunset Boulevard. In **Animation Courtyard,** Disney artists demonstrate the various phases of character animation; Animagique brings to life scenes from *Pinocchio* and *The Lion King*; while the Genie from *Aladdin* pilots Flying Carpets over Agrabah. **Production Courtyard** hosts the Walt Disney Television Studios; Cinémagique, a special-

---

PUTTING THE PARIS IN DISNEYLAND PARIS

The following are quirks unique to Mickey's European pied-à-terre. Wine is served in the park (they changed their no-alcohol policy in the 1990s). Tombstone inscriptions at Phantom Manor read: "Jasper Jones, loyal manservant, kept the master happy; Anna Jones, faithful chambermaid, kept the master happier." No Mickey walking around—he was too mobbed by kiddies, so he stays in one spot, and you have to line up to see him.

---

effects tribute to U.S. and European cinema; and a behind-the-scenes Studio Tram tour of location sites, movie props, studio decor, and costuming, ending with a visit to Catastrophe Canyon in the heart of a film shoot. **Back Lot** majors in stunts. At Armageddon Special Effects you can confront a flaming meteor shower aboard the Mir space station, then complete your visit at the giant outdoor arena with a Stunt Show Spectacular involving cars, motorbikes, and Jet Skis. ☎01–60–30–60–30 ⊕*www.disneylandparis.com* ✉*€43, €115 for 3-day Passport; includes admission to all individual attractions within Disneyland or Walt Disney Studios, but not meals; tickets for Walt Disney Studios are also valid for admission to Disneyland during last 3 opening hrs of same day* ⊘*Disneyland mid-June–mid-Sept., daily 9 am–10 pm; mid-Sept.–mid-June, weekdays 10–8, weekends 9–8; Dec. 20–Jan. 4, daily 9–8; Walt Disney Studios daily 10–6* ⊟*AE, DC, MC, V.*

WHERE TO STAY & EAT

¢–$$$ ✕ **Disneyland Restaurants.** Disneyland Paris is peppered with places to eat, ranging from snack bars and fast-food joints to five full-service restaurants—all with a distinguishing theme. In addition, Walt Disney Studios, Disney Village, and Disney Hotels have restaurants open to the public. But since these are outside the park, it's not recommended that you waste time traveling to them for lunch. Disneyland Paris has relaxed its no-alcohol policy and now serves wine and beer in the park's sit-down restaurants, as well as in the hotels and restaurants outside the park. ☎01–60–45–65–40 ⊟*AE, DC, MC, V.*

$$$–$$$$ ☷ **Disneyland Hotels.** The resort has 5,000 rooms in six hotels, all a short distance from the park, ranging from the luxurious Disneyland Hotel to the not-so-rustic Camp Davy Crockett. Free transportation to the park is available at every hotel. Packages including Disneyland lodging, entertainment, and admission are available through travel agents

in Europe. *⏍Centre de Réserva-
tions, B.P. 100, cedex 4, 77777
Marne-la-Vallée* ☎*01–60–30–60–
30, 407/934–7639 in U.S.* 🖷*01–
49–30–71–00* ⌕*All hotels have
at least 1 restaurant, café, indoor
pool, health club, sauna, bar, Wi-Fi*
🗖*AE, DC, MC, V* ⍢*FAP.*

NIGHTLIFE & THE ARTS
Nocturnal entertainment outside
the park centers on **Disney Village,**
a vast pleasure mall designed by
American architect Frank Gehry.
Featured are American-style restaurants (crab shack, diner, deli,
steak house), including **Billybob's
Country Western Saloon** (☎*01–60–
45–70–81*). Also in Disney Village is **Buffalo Bill's Wild West Show**

WORD OF MOUTH

"The most surprising thing to me
was that we had trouble getting
decent food. We wanted to eat
dinner about 7 before the light
parade, but most of the restaurants closed before that. When
we finally landed a reservation,
it was simply mediocre—worse
than food at WDW in Orlando or
in Anaheim. I was very surprised.
But the light parade was really
special—lots of blacklight effects,
and each float stopped while the
people performed, then moved
on." –WoodyVQ

(☎*01–60–45–71–00 for reservations*), a two-hour dinner extravaganza with a menu of sausages, spare ribs, and chili; performances
by a talented troupe of stunt riders, bronco busters, tribal dancers,
and musicians; plus some 50 horses, a dozen buffalo, a bull, and an
Annie Oakley–style sharpshooter, with a golden-maned "Buffalo Bill"
as emcee. A re-creation of a show that dazzled Parisians 100 years ago,
it's corny but great fun. There are two shows nightly, at 6:30 and 9:30;
the cost is €60 for adults, €40 for children under 12.

VAUX-LE-VICOMTE

 *48 km (30 mi) south of Disneyland Paris via N36, 5 km (3 mi) north-
east of Melun via N36 and D215, 56 km (35 mi) southeast of Paris via
A6, N104, A5, and N36.*

GETTING HERE
Get to Vaux by taking the train on a 45-minute trip to Melun, then taxi
(for about €30 each way) the 7 km (4 mi) to the château. However,
from mid-March to mid-November, Vaux runs a special Châteaubus
shuttle, which you can get at the Melun train station and costs €7
round-trip.

EXPLORING
A manifesto for French 17th-century splendor, the **Château de Vaux-le-
Vicomte** was built between 1656 and 1661 by finance minister Nicolas
Fouquet. The construction program was monstrous: entire villages were
razed, 18,000 workmen called in, and architect Louis Le Vau, painter
Charles Le Brun, and landscape architect André Le Nôtre recruited at
vast expense to prove that Fouquet's taste was as refined as his busi-
ness acumen. The housewarming party was so lavish it had star guest
Louis XIV, tetchy at the best of times, spitting jealous curses. He hurled

Fouquet in the slammer and set about building Versailles to prove just who was top banana.

The high-roofed château, partially surrounded by a moat, is set well back from the road behind iron railings topped with sculpted heads. A cobbled avenue stretches up to the entrance, and stone steps lead to the vestibule, which seems small given the noble scale of the exterior. Charles Le Brun's captivating decoration includes the ceiling of the **Chambre du Roi** (Royal Bedchamber), depicting *Time Bearing Truth Heavenward,* framed by stuccowork by sculptors François Girardon and André Legendre. Along the frieze you can make out small squirrels, the Fouquet family's emblem—squirrels are known as *fouquets* in local dialect. But Le Brun's masterwork is the ceiling in the **Salon des Muses** (Hall of Muses), a brilliant allegorical composition painted in glowing, sensuous colors that some feel even surpasses his work at Versailles. On the ground floor the impressive **Grand Salon** (Great Hall), with its unusual oval form and 16 caryatid pillars symbolizing the months and seasons, has harmony and style even though the ceiling decoration was never finished. The state salons are redolent of *le style louisquartorze,* thanks to the grand state beds, Mazarin desks, and Baroque marble busts—gathered together by the current owners of the château, the Comte et Comtesse de Vogüé—that replace the original pieces, which Louis XIV trundled off as booty to Versailles. In the basement, whose cool, dim rooms were used to store food and wine and house the château's kitchens, you can find rotating exhibits about the château's past and life-size wax figures illustrating its history, including the notorious 19th-century murder-suicide of two erstwhile owners, the Duc et Duchess de Choiseul-Praslin. The house has been featured in many Hollywood films, including *The Man in the Iron Mask, Dangerous Liaisons,* and *Moonraker*.

Le Nôtre's carefully restored **gardens** are at their best when the fountains are turned on (the second and final Saturday of each month from April through October, 3 pm –6 pm). Also visit the **Musée des Équipages** (Carriage Museum) in the stables, and inspect a host of carriages and coaches in wonderful condition. ☎01–64–14–41–90 ⊕*www. vaux-le-vicomte.com* ✉*€12.50, candlelight château visits €15.50; gardens only €7.50.*

> ### DES SOIRÉES À CHANDELLES?
>
> Perhaps the most beautiful time to visit the château and gardens is when they are illuminated by thousands of candles during the Candlelight Evenings, held every Saturday night, from 8 to midnight, from May through mid-October (also Friday in July and August). Readers complain, however, that at night the vast and grand gardens are nearly invisible and the low candlepower doesn't really do justice to the splendor of the salons.

WHERE TO EAT

¢–$ ✕ **L'Écureuil.** An imposing barn to the right of the château entrance has been transformed into this self-service cafeteria, where you can enjoy fine steaks (insist yours is cooked enough), salads, pastries, coffee, or a snack beneath the ancient rafters of a wood-beam roof. The restaurant is open daily for lunch and tea, and for dinner during candlelight visits. ⊠*Château de Vaux-le-Vicomte* ☎*01–60–66–95–66* ▭*MC, V.*

BARBIZON

㉑ *17 km (11 mi) southwest of Vaux-le-Vicomte via Melun and D132/ D64, 52 km (33 mi) southeast of Paris.*

On the western edge of the 62,000-acre Forest of Fontainebleau, the village of Barbizon retains its time-stained allure despite the intrusion of art galleries, souvenir shops, and busloads of tourists. The group of landscape painters known as the Barbizon School—Camille Corot, Jean-François Millet, Narcisse Diaz de la Peña, and Théodore Rousseau, among others—lived here from the 1830s on. They paved the way for the Impressionists by their willingness to accept nature on its own terms rather than using it as an idealized base for carefully structured compositions. Sealed to one of the famous sandstone rocks in the forest—which starts, literally, at the far end of the main street—is a bronze medallion by sculptor Henri Chapu, paying homage to Millet and Rousseau.

Corot and company would often repair to the Auberge Ganne after painting to brush up on their social life; the inn is now the **Musée de l'École de Barbizon** *(Barbizon School Museum).* Here you can find documents of the village as it was in the 19th century, as well as a few original works. The Barbizon artists painted on every available surface, and even now you can see some originals on the upstairs walls. Two of the ground-floor rooms have been reconstituted as they were in Ganne's time—note the trompe-l'oeil paintings on the buffet doors. There's also a video on the Barbizon School. ⊠*92 Grande-Rue* ☎*01–60–66– 22–27* ✑*€6, joint admission with Musée-Atelier Théodore-Rousseau* ⊗ *Wed.–Mon. 10–12:30 and 2–5:30.*

Though there are no actual Millet works, the **Atelier Jean-François Millet** *(Millet's Studio)* is cluttered with photographs and mementos evoking his career. It was here that Millet painted some of his most renowned pieces, including *The Gleaners.* ⊠*27 Grande-Rue* ☎*01–60–66–21–55* ✑*Free* ⊗ *Wed.–Mon. 9:30–12:30 and 2–5:30.*

By the church, beyond the extraordinary village war memorial featuring a mustached ancient Gaul in a winged helmet, is the **Musée Théodore-Rousseau** *(Rousseau's House-cum-Studio),* in a converted barn. It's crammed with personal and artistic souvenirs and also has an exhibition space for temporary shows. ⊠*55 Grande-Rue* ☎*01–60–66–22–38* ✑*€6, joint admission with Barbizon School Museum* ⊗ *Wed.–Mon. 10–12:30 and 2–5:30.*

2

WHERE TO STAY & EAT

$–$$ ✕ **Le Relais de Barbizon.** French country specialties are served at this rustic restaurant with a big open fire and a large terrace shaded by lime and chestnut trees. The four-course weekday menu is a good value, but wine here is expensive and cannot be ordered by the *pichet* (pitcher). Reservations are essential on weekends. ✉2 av. Général-de-Gaulle ☎01–60–66–40–28 ▭MC, V ⊘ *Closed part of Aug., part of Feb., and Wed. No dinner Tues.*

> ### SHARE THE FANTASY
>
> The most spectacular element of Courances's gardens is *Le Miroir*— "The Mirror." This perfect sheet of water, surrounded by parterre hedges, was immortalized in the famous "Share the Fantasy" television ads of Chanel.

★ $ ✕▣ **Les Alouettes.** This delightful, family-run 19th-century inn is set in 2 acres of leafy parkland, which the better rooms overlook. The interior is '30s style, and many rooms have oak beams. Lionel Ménard's rustic restaurant (reservations essential; no dinner Sunday), with its large open terrace, serves traditional French cuisine such as hare with mushrooms and lamb with eggplant. ✉4 *rue Antoine-Barye, 77630* ☎01–60–66–41–98 🖷01–60–66–20–69 ⊕*www.barbizon.net/lesalouettes* ⇝*20 rooms, 2 suites* ⌂*In-room: no a/c. In-hotel: restaurant, bar, some pets allowed (fee), public Internet, no elevator* ▭AE, DC, MC, V †⊙†MAP.

COURANCES

22

Fodor'sChoice

★

11 km (7 mi) west of Barbizon via the A6, Exit 13, a few miles from Milly-la-Fôret.

Set within one of the most lavish water gardens in Europe, the **Château de Courances** is a byword for beauty and style among connoisseurs. Framed by majestic avenues of centuries-old plane trees, the house's style is Louis Treize, although its finishing touch—a horseshoe staircase (mirroring the one at nearby Fontainebleau)—was an opulent 19th-century statement made by Baron Samuel de Haber, a banker who bought the estate and whose daughter then married into the regal family of the de Behagués. Their descendants, the Marquises de Ganay, have made the house uniquely and famously "chez soi," letting charming personal taste trump conventional "bon goût," thanks to a delightful mixture of 19th-century knickknacks and grand antiques. Outside, the vast French Renaissance water gardens create stunning vistas of stonework, grand canals, and rushing cascades. The house can only be seen on a 40-minute tour. By public transport, take the train from Paris's Gare de Lyon to Fontainebleau-Avon, then use La Patache shuttle bus to Courances. ☎01–40–62–07–71 ⊕*www.courances.net* ✍€8.50, park only €6.50 ⊙*Apr.–Oct., weekends 2–6.*

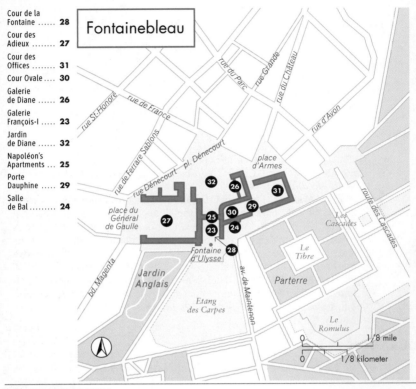

FONTAINEBLEAU

9 km (6 mi) southeast of Barbizon via N7, 61 km (38 mi) southeast of Paris via A6 and N7.

GETTING HERE

Fontainebleau—or, rather, neighboring Avon, 2 km (1½ mi) away (there's frequent shuttle bus service to the château for €3 round-trip)—is a 45-minute rail ride from Paris's Gare de Lyon; tickets are €1.75 one-way.

EXPLORING

Like Chambord, in the Loire Valley, or Compiègne, to the north, Fontainebleau was a favorite spot for royal hunting parties long before the construction of one of France's grandest residences. Although not as celebrated as Versailles, this palace is almost as spectacular.

★ ❷❸ – ❸❷   The **Château de Fontainebleau** you see today dates from the 16th century, although additions were made by various royal incumbents through the next 300 years. The palace was begun under the flamboyant Renaissance king François I, the French contemporary of England's Henry VIII. The king hired Italian artists Il Rosso (a pupil of Michelangelo) and Primaticcio to embellish his château. In fact, they did much more: by introducing the pagan allegories and elegant lines of Mannerism to France, they revolutionized French decorative art. Their virtuoso frescoes and stuccowork can be admired in the **Galerie François-Ier** (Francis I Gallery) and in the jewel of the interior, the 100-foot-long **Salle de Bal** (ballroom), with its luxuriant wood paneling, completed under Henri II, François's successor, and its gleaming parquet floor that reflects the patterns on the ceiling. Like the château as a whole, the room exudes a sense of elegance and style—but on a more intimate, human scale than at Versailles: this is Renaissance, not Baroque. **Napoléon's apartments** occupied the first floor. You can see a lock of his hair, his Légion d'Honneur medal, his imperial uniform, the hat he wore on his return from Elba in 1815, and one bed in which he definitely did spend a night (almost every town in France boasts a bed in which the emperor supposedly snoozed). Joséphine's **Salon Jaune** (Yellow Room) is one of the best examples of the Empire style—the austere Neoclassical style promoted by the emperor. There's also a throne room—Napoléon spurned the one at Versailles, a palace he disliked, establishing his imperial seat in the former King's Bedchamber here—and the Queen's Boudoir, also known as the Room of the Six Maries (occupants included ill-fated Marie-Antoinette and Napoléon's second wife, Marie-Louise). The sweeping **Galerie de Diane,** built during the reign of Henri IV (1589–1610), was converted into a library in the 1860s. Other salons have 17th-century tapestries and paintings, and frescoes by members of the Fontainebleau School.

Although Louis XIV's architectural fancy was concentrated on Versailles, he commissioned Mansart to design new pavilions and had André Le Nôtre replant the gardens at Fontainebleau, where he and his court returned faithfully in fall for the hunting season. But it was Napoléon who spent lavishly to make a Versailles, as it were, out of Fontainebleau. He held Pope Pius VII here as a captive guest in 1812, signed the second church-state concordat here in 1813, and, in the cobbled **Cour des Adieux** (Farewell Courtyard), said good-bye to his Old Guard on April 20, 1814, as he began his brief exile on the Mediterranean island of Elba. The famous **Horseshoe Staircase** that dominates the Cour des Adieux, once the Cour du Cheval Blanc (White Horse Courtyard), was built by Androuet du Cerceau for Louis XIII (1610–43); it was down this staircase that Napoléon made his way slowly to take a final salute from his Vieille Garde. Another courtyard—the **Cour de la Fontaine** (Fountain Courtyard)—was commissioned by Napoléon in 1812 and adjoins the Étang des Carpes (Carp Pond). Across from the pond is the formal Parterre (flower garden) and, on the other side, the leafy Jardin Anglais (English Garden).

The **Porte Dauphine** is the most beautiful of the various gateways that connect the complex of buildings; its name commemorates the christening of the dauphin—the heir to the throne, later Louis XIII—

LIAISONS DANGEREUSES

Henri II added the decorative interlaced initials found throughout the palace. You might expect to see the royal *H* woven with a *C* (for Catherine de' Medici, his wife). Instead you'll find a *D*—indicating his mistress, Diane de Poitiers.

under its archway in 1606. The gateway fronts the **Cour Ovale** (Oval Court), shaped like a flattened egg. Opposite the courtyard is the **Cour des Offices** (Kitchen Court), a large, severe square built at the same time as Place des Vosges in Paris (1609). Around the corner is the informal **Jardin de Diane** (Diana's Garden), with peacocks and a statue of the hunting goddess surrounded by mournful hounds. ⊠ *Pl. du Général-de-Gaulle* ☎ *01–60–71–50–70* ⊕ *www.musee-chateau-fontainebleau. fr* ⊠ *€5.50, Napoléon's Apartments €3 extra; gardens free* ☉ *Palace: Oct.–May, Wed.–Mon. 9:30–5, June–Sept., Wed.–Mon. 9:30–6; gardens May–Sept., daily 9–7; Oct. and Apr., daily 9–6; Nov.–Mar., daily 9–5.*

WHERE TO STAY & EAT

$–$$$ ✕ **Arrighi.** This cozy, pink-walled, Art Deco restaurant near the château pulls in local gourmets with its three-course €18 menu that sometimes includes salmon or boeuf bourguignon. Jugged hare, pavé de biche (venison), and scallops with ginger and *roquette* salad are among seasonal specialties à la carte. ⊠ *53 rue de France* ☎ *01–64–22–29–43* ⊟ *MC, V* ☉ *Closed Mon. No dinner Sun.*

$$$ ✕ 🖵 **Napoléon.** This former post office close to the palace counts as one of the best local hotels. Pastel-color rooms have modern furniture and marble baths and look out onto terraces or the indoor patio. The plush restaurant, La Table des Maréchaux, with its golden wallpaper and crimson velvet seating, is the smartest in town and serves satisfying, deftly prepared classics, and the €40 Menu Napoléon, featuring rabbit with apricots and pike-perch with celery puree in Sancerre sauce, is a succulent deal. ⊠ *9 rue Grande, 77300* ☎ *01–60–39–50–50* 🖷 *01–64–22–20–87* ⊕ *www.hotelnapoleon-fontainebleau.com* 🛏 *58 rooms* ⚅ *In-room: no a/c, refrigerator, ethernet. In-hotel: restaurant, some pets allowed (fee)* ⊟ *AE, DC, MC, V* ⦿ *MAP.*

★ $$$ 🖵 **L'Aigle Noir.** This may be Fontainebleau's costliest hotel, but you can't go wrong if you request one of the rooms overlooking either the garden or the palace. They have late-18th- or early-19th-century reproduction furniture, creating a Napoleonic vibe. Sadly the excellent restaurant, Le Beauharnais, no longer exists. ⊠ *27 pl. Napoléon-Bonaparte, 77300* ☎ *01–60–74–60–00* 🖷 *01–60–74–60–01* ⊕ *www. hotelaiglenoir.com* 🛏 *18 rooms* ⚅ *In-room: refrigerator. In-hotel: pool, gym, some pets allowed (fee)* ⊟ *AE, DC, MC, V* ⦿ *BP.*

$$–$$$ 🖵 **Londres.** Established in 1850, the Londres is a small, family-style hotel with Louis XV accents. Six rooms have balconies overlooking Fontainebleau's palace entrance and the Cour des Adieux, where Napoléon bade his troops an emotional farewell; the best views are from Rooms 8, 10 and 11 on the top floor. The hotel's prim 19th-century facade is a registered landmark. ⊠ *1 pl. du Général-de-Gaulle, 77300* ☎ *01–64–22–20–21* 🖷 *01–60–72–39–16* ⊕ *www.hoteldelondres.com* 🛏 *12 rooms* ⚅ *In-room: no a/c, dial-up. In-hotel: restaurant, bar, no elevator* ⊟ *AE, DC, MC, V* ☉ *Closed 1 wk Aug. and mid-Dec.–early Jan.* ⦿ *BP.*

SPORTS & THE OUTDOORS

The Forest of Fontainebleau is laced with hiking trails; for more information ask for the *Guide des Sentiers* (trail guide) at the tourist office. Bikes can be rented at the Fontainebleau-Avon train station. The forest is also famed for its quirky rock formations, where many a novice alpinist first caught the climbing bug; for more information contact the **Club Alpin Français** (⊠ *24 av. Laumière, 75019 Paris* ☎ *01–53–72–87–00* ⊕ *www.ffcam.fr*).

ILE-DE-FRANCE ESSENTIALS

TRANSPORTATION

If traveling extensively by public transportation, be sure to load up on information (schedules, the best taxi-for-call companies, etc.) upon arriving at the ticket counter or help desk of the bigger train and bus stations in the area, such as Versailles, Chantilly, and Fontainebleau. Note that many of this chapter's destinations are easily reached as day trips from Paris.

BY AIR

Major airports in the Ile-de-France area are Charles de Gaulle, commonly known as Roissy, 25 km (16 mi) northeast of Paris, and Orly, 16 km (10 mi) south. Shuttle buses link Disneyland to the airports at Roissy, 56 km (35 mi) away, and Orly, 50 km (31 mi) distant; buses take 45 minutes and run every 45 minutes from Roissy, every 60 minutes from Orly (less frequently in low season), and cost €15.

Airport Information Charles de Gaulle (☎ *01–48–62–22–80* ⊕ *www.adp.fr*). **Orly** (☎ *01–49–75–15–15* ⊕ *www.adp.fr*).

BY BUS

Although many of the major sights in this chapter have train lines connecting them on direct routes with Paris, the lesser towns and destinations pose more of a problem. You often need to take a local bus or taxi after arriving at a train station (for instance, to get to Senlis from Chantilly Gare SNCF, or Fontainebleau and Barbizon from Avon Gare SNCF, or Vaux-le-Vicomte from Melun Gare SNCF, or Giverny from Vernon Gare SNCF). Other buses travel outward from Paris's suburbs—the No. 158A bus, for instance, which goes from La Défense to St-Germain-en-Laye and Rueil-Malmaison.

Bus Information SNCF (☎ *36–35, €0.34 per min* ⊕ *www.transilien.com*).

BY CAR

A13 links Paris (from the Porte d'Auteuil) to Versailles. You can get to Chartres on A10 from Paris (Porte d'Orléans). For Fontainebleau take A6 from Paris (Porte d'Orléans), or for a more attractive, although slower route through the Forest of Sénart and the northern part of the Forest of Fontainebleau, take N6 from Paris (Porte de Charenton) via Melun. A4 runs from Paris (Porte de Bercy) to Disneyland. Although a comprehensive rail network ensures that most towns in Ile-de-France can make comfortable day trips from Paris, the only way to crisscross the region without returning to the capital is by car. There's no shortage of expressways or fast highways, but be prepared for delays close to Paris and during the morning and evening rush hours.

BY TRAIN

Many sights can be reached by train from Paris. Both regional and main-line (Le Mans–bound) trains leave Gare Montparnasse for Chartres (50–70 mins); the former also stop at Versailles, Rambouillet, and Maintenon. Gare Montparnasse is also the terminal for the suburban trains that stop at Montfort-L'Amaury, the nearest station to Thoiry (35 mins).

Some main-line trains from Gare St-Lazare stop at Mantes-la-Jolie (30 mins) and Vernon (50 mins) on their way to Rouen and Le Havre. Suburban trains leave the Gare du Nord for L'Isle-Adam (50 mins). Chantilly is on the main northbound line from Gare du Nord (the trip takes 25–40 mins), and Senlis can be reached by bus from Chantilly. Fontainebleau—or, rather, neighboring Avon, 2 km (1½ mi) away (there is frequent bus service)—is 45 minutes from Gare de Lyon. To reach Vaux-le-Vicomte, head first for Melun, then take a taxi or local bus (in summer a shuttle service); to reach Giverny, rail it to Vernon, then use the taxi or local bus.

St-Germain-en-Laye is a terminal of the RER-A (commuter train) that tunnels through Paris (main stations at Étoile, Auber, Les Halles, and Gare de Lyon). The RER-A also accesses Maisons-Laffitte and, at the other end, the station for Disneyland Paris (called Marne-la-Vallée–Chessy), within 100 yards of the entrance to both the theme park and Disney Village. Journey time is around 40 minutes, and trains operate every 10–30 minutes, depending on the time of day. The handiest of Versailles's three train stations is the one reached by the RER-C line (main stations at Austerlitz, St-Michel, Invalides, and Champ-de-Mars); the trip takes 30–40 minutes. Special *forfait* tickets, combining travel and admission, are available for several regional tourist destinations (including Versailles, Fontainebleau, and Auvers-sur-Oise). A main-line TGV (Trains à Grande Vitesse) station links Disneyland to Lille, Lyon, Brussels, and London (via Lille and the Channel Tunnel).

Train Information Gare SNCF Fontainbleau (⊠ *1 pl. François-Mitterrand* ☎ *03–80–43–16–34*). **Gare SNCF Versailles** (⊠ *Cour de la Gare* ☎ *03–80–43–16–34*). **SNCF** (☎ *08–91–36–20–20 €0.23 per min* ⊕ *www.transilien.com*). **TGV** (⊕ *www.tgv.com*).

CONTACTS & RESOURCES

CAR RENTAL

Cars can be rented from agencies in Paris or at Orly or Charles de Gaulle airports.

2

EMERGENCIES

The American Hospital and the British Hospital are closer to Paris, and other regional hospitals are listed by town below.

Contacts Ambulance (☎*15*). **American Hospital** (✉*63 bd. Victor-Hugo* ☎*01-46-41-25-25*) in Neuilly. **Franco-British Hospital** (✉*3 rue Barbès* ☎*01-46-39-22-22*) in Levallois-Perret. **Chartres** (✉*34 rue du Dr-Maunoury* ☎*02-37-30-30-30*). **Melun** (✉*2 rue Fréteau-de-Pény* ☎*01-64-71-60-00*). **Versailles** (✉*177 rue de Versailles, Le Chesnay* ☎*01-39-63-91-33*).

INTERNET & MAIL

In smaller towns, ask your hotel concierge if there are any Internet cafés nearby.

Internet & Mail Information Aux Petits Buffons (✉*68 rue d'Anjou, behind cathedral, Versailles* ☎*01-30-21-80-80*). **Cybercafé** (✉*10 rue Ducastel, near château, St-Germain-en-Laye* ☎*01-39-21-90-27*). **Fontainebleau main post office** (✉*2 rue de la Chancellerie* ☎*01-60-74-51-40*). **Versailles main post office** (✉*3 av. de Paris* ☎*01-39-49-65-20*).

MEDIA

With Paris so close, regional newspapers do not exist as they do elsewhere in France. But *Le Parisien* (published in Paris) has regional news sections, and *Paris-Normandie* has an Yvelines edition.

TOUR OPTIONS

Cityrama organizes guided excursions to Giverny, Chartres, and Fontainebleau/Barbizon (€55–€63) from April through October. Cityrama and Paris Vision run half- and full-day trips to Versailles (€39–€85).

Contacts Cityrama (✉*2 rue des Pyramides, 75001 Paris* ☎*01-44-55-60-00* ⊕ *www.cityrama.fr*). **Paris Vision** (✉*214 rue de Rivoli, 75001 Paris* ☎*01-42-60-30-01* ⊕ *www.parisvision.com*).

PRIVATE GUIDES

Alliance Autos has bilingual guides who can take you on a private tour around the Paris area in a luxury car or minibus for a minimum of four hours for about €80 an hour (call to check details and prices). Euroscope runs minibus excursions to Versailles (€75) and Giverny (€80).

Contacts Alliance Autos (✉*149 rue de Charonne, 75011 Paris* ☎*01-55-25-23-23*). **Euroscope** (✉*27 rue Taitbout, 75009 Paris* ☎*01-56-03-56-81* ⊕ *www.euroscope.fr*).

VISITOR INFORMATION

Contact the Espace du Tourisme d'Ile-de-France (⊕*www.pidf.com* ☉Wed.–Mon. 10–7), under the inverted pyramid in the Carrousel du Louvre, for general information on the area. Information on Disneyland is available from the Disneyland Paris reservations office. Local tourist offices are listed below by town.

Tourist Information Espace du Tourisme d'Ile-de-France (✉*Pl. de la Pyramide-Renversée, 99 rue de Rivoli, 75001 Paris* ☎*08-03-81-80-00*). **Disneyland Paris reservations office** (✉*B.P. 100, cedex 4, 77777 Marne-la-Vallée* ☎*01-60-30-60-30, 407/824-4321 in U.S.*). **Auvers-sur-Oise** (✉*Rue de la Sansonne*

☎ *01–30–36–10–06* ⊕ *www.auvers-sur-oise.com*). **Barbizon** (✉ *41 Grande-Rue* ☎ *01–60–66–41–87* ⊕ *www.barbizon-france.com*). **Chantilly** (✉ *60 av. du Maréchal-Joffre* ☎ *03–44–57–08–58* ⊕ *www.ville-chantilly.fr*). **Chartres** (✉ *Pl. de la Cathédrale* ☎ *02–37–18–26–26* ⊕ *www.chartres-tourisme.com*). **Compiègne** (✉ *28 pl. de l'Hôtel-de-Ville* ☎ *03–44–40–01–00* ⊕ *www.compiegne-tourisme. fr*). **Fontainebleau** (✉ *4 rue Royale* ☎ *01–60–74–99–99* ⊕ *www.fontainebleau-tourisme.com*). **Rambouillet** (✉ *1 pl. de la Libération* ☎ *01–34–83–21–21* ⊕ *www.ot-rambouillet.fr*). **St-Germain-en-Laye** (✉ *38 rue au Pain* ☎ *01–34–51–05–12* ⊕ *www.ville-st-germain-en-laye.fr*). **Senlis** (✉ *Pl. du Parvis Notre-Dame* ☎ *03–44–53–06–40* ⊕ *www.ville-senlis.fr*). **Versailles** (✉ *2 bis, av. de Paris* ☎ *01–39–24–88–88* ⊕ *www.versailles-tourisme.com*).

The Loire Valley

Chambord Castle

WORD OF MOUTH

"Chenonceau is the most famous Loire château and certainly one of the most beautiful, built straddling the lazy Cher River. During World War II, folks escaped from Nazi France by going through the castle to cross the Cher to the Vichy-controlled part of France. Happily, the Chenonceaux rail station was recently relocated to now let you off right in front of the château, thus a day trip by rail from Paris is possible!"

— PalQ

WELCOME TO THE LOIRE VALLEY

Place Plumereau, Tours

TOP REASONS TO GO

★ **Sleeping Beauty's Castle:** Play once-upon-a-time at Ussé—gleaming white against an emerald forest backcloth, it's so beautiful it inspired Perrault's immortal tale.

★ **Kingly Chambord:** The world's wackiest rooftop, with a forest of chimneys to match the game-rich woodlands extending in all directions, marks the Loire's grandest château.

★ **Splendor in the Grass:** The Renaissance re-blooms at Villandry, whose geometric gardens have been lovingly restored to floricultural magnificence.

★ **Romantic Chenonceau:** Half bridge, half pleasure palace, this epitome of picturesque France extends across the Cher River, so why not row a boat under its arches?

★ **Medieval Magic:** Fontevraud is the majestic medieval abbey that is the resting-place of English kings...and you can sleep on the spot.

1 From Tours to Orleans. East from **Tours**, strung like precious gems along the peaceful Loire, the royal and near-royal châteaux are among the most fabled sights in France. From magical **Chenonceau**—improbably suspended above the River Cher—to mighty **Chambord**, with its 440 rooms, to **Amboise** (where Leonardo da Vinci breathed his last), this architectural conveyor belt

moves up along the southern bank to deposit you at **Orléans**, newly burnished to old-world splendor with its pedestrianized *centre ville historique* (it was here that Joan of Arc had her most rousing successes against the English). Heading back to Tours on the northern bank, you'll discover the immense palace at **Blois** and some of the best hotels in the region.

Orléans

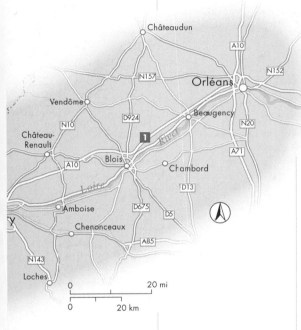

GETTING ORIENTED

The Loire Valley, which pretty much splits France in two, has been much traversed down the ages, once by Santiago pilgrims, now by Bordeaux-bound TGV trains. It retains a backwater feel that mirrors the river's sluggish, meandering waters, although trade along the river resulted in major towns sprouting along its banks: Angers, Saumur, Blois, Orléans. But Tours remains the gateway to the region, not only for its central position but because the TGV links it with Paris in little more than an hour. From Angers you can drive northeast to explore the winding, intimate Loir Valley. Continue along the Loire as far as Nantes, the southern gateway to Brittany.

2 From Villandry to Langeais. Step into a fairy tale by castle-hopping among the most beautiful châteaux in France, from **Villandry's** fabled gardens to **Ussé**, which seems to levitate over the unicorn-haunted Forest of Chinon. From the Renaissance jewel of **Azay-le-Rideau**, continue west to **Chinon** for a dip in the Middle Ages along its Rue Haute St-Maurice—a pop-up illuminated manuscript. Continue time-traveling at the 12th-century royal abbey of **Fontevraud**, resting place of Richard the Lion-Hearted and Eleanor of Aquitaine. Then fast-forward to the 15th century at the storybook castle at **Saumur**—looming over the Loire's chicest town—**Angers's** brooding fortress, and the Camelot-worthy château at **Langeais**.

Langeais

LOIRE VALLEY PLANNER

Making the Most of Your Time

More than a region in the usual sense, the Loire Valley is just that: a valley, and although most of the sites are close to the meandering river, it's a long way—140 mi—between Orléans, on the eastern edge, and Angers away to the west.

If you have 10 days or so you can visit the majority of the sites we cover.

Otherwise we suggest you divide the Valley into three segments and choose the base(s) as your time and tastes dictate.

To cover the eastern Loire (Chambord, Cheverny, Chaumont), base yourself in or near Blois.

For the central Loire (Amboise, Chenonceau, Villandry, Azay-le-Rideau), base yourself in or around Tours. For the western Loire (Ussé, Chinon, Fontevraud, Angers), opt for pretty Saumur.

Of course if you can base yourself at one of the region's beautiful château-hotels (sometimes on country roads), do so.

Finding a Place to Stay

Even before the age of the railway, the Loire Valley drew vacationers from far afield, so there are hundreds of hotels of all types. At the higher end are sumptuously, stylishly converted châteaux, but even these are not as pricey as you might think. Note that most of these are in small villages, and that upscale hotels are in short supply in the major towns. At the lower end are a wide choice of gîtes, bed-and-breakfasts, and small, traditional inns in towns, usually offering terrific value for the money. The Loire Valley is a popular destination, so make reservations well in advance—in July and August, this is essential (and we're talking weeks, not days). Beware that from November through Easter, many properties are closed. Assume that all hotel rooms have air-conditioning, telephones, TV, and private bath, unless otherwise noted.

WHAT IT COSTS

	¢	$	$$	$$$	$$$$
Restaurants	Under €11	€11–€17	€17–€23	€23–€30	Over €30
Hotels	Under €50	€50–€80	€80–€120	€120–€190	Over €190

Restaurant prices are per person for a main course at dinner, including tax (19.6%) and service; note that if a restaurant offers only prix-fixe (set-price) meals, it has been given the price category that reflects the full prix-fixe price. Hotel prices are for a standard double room in high season, including tax (19.6%) and service charge. Hotels operate on the European Plan (EP, with no meal provided) unless we note that they use the Breakfast Plan (BP), or also offer such options as Modified American Plan (MAP, with breakfast and dinner daily, known as demi-pension), or Full American Plan (FAP, or pension complète, with three meals a day). Inquire when booking if these all-inclusive meal plans (which always entail higher rates) are mandatory or optional.

Wheel Estate: Biking the Loire Valley

A fairy-tale realm par excellence, the Loire Valley is studded with storybook castles, forests primeval, time-burnished towns, and—*bien sûr*—the famous châteaux de la Loire, which are strung like a strand of pearls across a countryside so serene it could win the Nobel peace prize. With magic at every curve in the road, Cinderella's glass coach might be the optimum way to get around, but the next best thing is to tour the Val de Loire by bike. There's nothing like seeing Chenonceaux with your head pumped full of endorphins, surrounded by 20 new best friends, and knowing you'll be spending the night in a pointed turret bedroom that savors of sleeping princesses. If you want to experience this region at its most blissful—but not blisterful!—take the VBT (Vermont Biking Tours) Loire Valley Tour. Many participants found it to be the most wonderful, truly oooooooooo-lala travel experience they ever had in France.

Every morning, for six days, you sally forth not to kill dragons, but to cycle down village roads that look like Corot paintings, visit feudally luxurious châteaux, and explore medieval towns like Chinon at 180 heartbeats a mile. Each day sees from two to four hours of biking (about 34 to 56 km [19 to 35 mi]), with an option of either calling it quits at lunch and returning to your hotel or continuing on with the rack pack for the afternoon. The tour guide likes to joke that "real men don't ask for directions—at least not in English," but since the instructions direct you along the route virtually pebble-to-pebble, this faux pas never arose. The itinerary reads like the pages of a Perrault fairy tale, studded as it is with such legendary abodes as Azay-le-Rideau, Chenonceau, Villandry, and Ussé. It's a good morning's work to see two châteaux, *non*?

You can have an even better evening of it, thanks to VBT's splendid choice of châteaux-hotels. At the 16th-century La Bourdaisière, retreat of King François I, you'll feel a wand has been waved over you as you repair to the candlelighted Richelieu-red dining room to enjoy a supper-lative *filet de carpe au Bourgueil*. Audrey Hepburn's favorite, the Domaine de la Tortinière, fulfills anyone's "Queen-for-a-Stay" fantasies. Your final hotel, the Château de Rochecotte, was the 19th-century Xanadu of Prince de Talleyrand-Périgord. It's little wonder that most of the 20 bikers in the group were in a state of dumb intoxication after six days with VBT (✉614 Monkton Rd., Bristol, VT 05443 ☎800/245–3868 ⊕www.vbt.com). And we're not talking about all the wine tastings.

Getting Around

The regional rail line along the riverbank will get you to the main towns (Angers, Saumur, Tours, Blois, Orleans, along with 10 other towns), while some other châteaux are served by branch lines (Chenonceau, Azay, Langeais, Chinon, along with 20 or so other towns) or SNCF bus.

Occasionally, you can arrive at the rail station and need to invest in a taxi ride to get to the châteaux buried deep in the countryside.

The station staff can recommend the best regional taxi services, many of whom have advertisements at the stations.

The downside of train travel is having to fit your visits within the constraints of a railroad timetable.

For some, that makes a hired car a particularly practical option (although minimal signage in this rural area can turn a half-hour trip into a two-hour ordeal).

The N152, hugging the riverbank, is the region's four-wheeled backbone.

Given the region's flattish terrain, hiring a bike may well appeal. There are also local bus services and coach excursions, notably from Tours.

If you're driving down from Paris, take the A10 to Orléans/Tours, or the A11 to Angers/Saumur.

Introduction by
Nancy Coons

Updated by
Simon Hewitt

A DIAPHANOUS AURA OF SUBTLY shifting light plays over the luxuriant countryside of the Loire Valley, a region blessedly mild of climate,
richly populated with game, and habitually fertile. Although it had
always been viewed as prime real estate, the victorious Valois dynasty
began to see new possibilities in the territory once the dust from the
Hundred Years' War began to settle and the bastions of the Plantagenet
kings lost some of their utility. This, they mused, was an ideal spot for a
holiday home. Sketching, no doubt, on a tavern napkin at Blois, Louis
XII dreamed of a tasteful blend of symmetry and fantasy, of turrets and
gargoyles, while Anne of Brittany breathed down his neck for more
closet space. In no time at all, the neighboring Joneses had followed
suit, and by the 16th century the area was a showplace of fabulous
châteaux *d'agrément,* or pleasure castles—palaces for royalty, yes, but
also love nests for mistresses and status statements for arrivistes (Chenonceau was built by a tax collector). There were boxwood gardens
endlessly receding toward vanishing points, moats graced with swans,
parades of delicate cone-topped towers, frescoes, and fancywork ceilings. The glories of the Italian Renaissance, observed by the Valois
while making war on their neighbor, were brought to bear on these
mega-monuments with all the elegance and proportions characteristic
of antiquity.

By the time François I took charge, extravagance knew no bounds: on
a 13,000-acre forest estate, hunting parties at Chambord drew A-list
crowds from the far reaches of Europe—and the availability of 430
rooms made weekend entertaining a snap. Queen Claudia hired only
the most recherché Italian artisans: Chambord's famous double-helix
staircase may, in fact, have been Leonardo da Vinci's design (he was
a frequent houseguest there when not in residence in a manor on the
Amboise grounds). From massive kennels teeming with hunting hounds
at Cheverny to luxurious stables at Chaumont-sur-Loire, from endless
allées of pollarded lime trees at Villandry to the fairy-tale towers of
Ussé—worthy of Sleeping Beauty herself—the Loire Valley became the
power base and social center for the New France, allowing the monarchy to go all out in strutting its stuff.

All for good reason. In 1519 Charles V of Spain, at the age of 19, inherited the Holy Roman Empire, leaving François and his New France—
as well as England's Henry VIII—out in the cold. It was perhaps no
coincidence that in 1519 François, in a grand stab at face-saving one-
upmanship, commenced construction on his ultimate declaration of
dominion, the gigantic château of Chambord. After a few skirmishes
(the Low Countries, Italy), and no doubt a few power breakfasts, François was confident enough to entertain the emperor on his lavish Loire
estates, and by 1539 he had married Charles V's sister.

Location is everything, as you realize when you think of Hyannisport,
Kennebunkport, and Balmoral: homesteads redolent of dynasty, where
natural beauty, idyllic views, an invigorating hunt with the boys, and
a barefoot stroll in the great outdoors liberate the mind to think great

thoughts and make history's decisions. Perhaps this is why French Revolution have-nots sacked so many of the châteaux of the Loire Valley; today most of the châteaux have been restored, and are maintained as museums in the public domain. Although these châteaux are testimony to France's most fabled age of kings, their pleasures, once restricted to royalty and members of the nobility, are now shared by the populace. Yet the Revolution and the efforts of latter-day socialists have not totally erased a lingering gentility in the people of the region, characterized by an air of refined assurance far removed from the shoulder-shrugging, chest-tapping French stereotypes. Here life proceeds at a pleasingly genteel pace, and you can find a winning concentration of gracious country inns and discerning chefs, a cornucopia of local produce and game, and the famous, flinty wines of Vouvray and Chinon—all regional blessings still truly fit for a king, but now available to his subjects as well.

EXPLORING THE LOIRE VALLEY

Pick up the Loire River halfway along its course from central France to the Atlantic Ocean. Châteaux and vineyards will accompany you throughout a 225-km (140-mi) westbound course from the cathedral city of Orléans to the bustling city of Angers. Towns punctuate the route at almost equal distances—Orléans, Blois, Tours, Saumur—and are useful bases if you're relying on public transportation. But don't let the lack of a car prevent you from visiting and overnighting in the lovely villages of the region because a surprising number can be accessed via train, bus, or taxi. Although you may be rushing around to see as many famous châteaux as possible, make time to walk through the poppy-covered hills, picnic along the riverbanks, and sample the famous local wines.

Tours, the capital city of the province of Touraine, is the gateway to the entire region, not only for its central position but because the TGV high-speed train can deposit you there from Paris in little more than an hour. This chapter is divided into two tours, and the first explores a string of fine châteaux east of Tours; Blois, Chaumont, and Amboise lead the way, but two of the area's most stunning monuments lie south of the Loire—romantic Chenonceau, with its arches half-straddling the River Cher, and colossal Chambord, its forest of chimneys and turrets visible above the treetops. By heading westward from Tours, our second tour allows you to enter a storyland par excellence, address to such fairy-tale châteaux as Ussé and Azay-le-Rideau and the more muscular castles of Chinon and Saumur. From Angers you can drive northeast to explore the winding, intimate Loir Valley all the way to Châteaudun, just south of Chartres and the Ile-de-France; or continue along the Loire as far as Nantes, the southern gateway to Brittany.

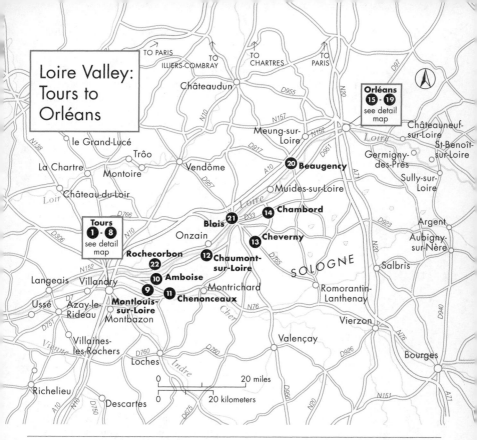

Loire Valley:
Tours to
Orléans

SO NEAR & YET SO LOIRE:
FROM TOURS TO ORLÉANS

At Orléans, halfway along the route of the Loire—the longest river in France—the river takes a wide, westward bend, gliding languidly through low, rich country known as the Val de Loire—or Loire Valley. In this temperate region—a 225-km (140-mi) stretch between Orléans and Angers—scores of châteaux built of local *tufa* (white limestone) rise from the rocky banks of the Loire and its tributaries: the rivers Cher, Indre, Vienne, and Loir (with no *e*).

The Loire is liquid history. For centuries the river was the area's principal means of transportation and an effective barrier against invading armies. Towns arose at strategic bridgeheads, and fortresses—the earliest châteaux—appeared on towering slopes. The Loire Valley was hotly disputed by France and England during the Middle Ages; it belonged to England (under the Anjou Plantagenet family) between 1154 and 1216 and again during the Hundred Years' War (1337–1453). It was the example of Joan of Arc, the Maid of Orléans (so called after the site of one of her most stirring victories), that crystallized French efforts to expel the English.

The Loire Valley's golden age came under François I (ruled 1515–47)—flamboyant contemporary of England's Henry VIII—whose salamander emblem can be seen in many châteaux, including Chambord, the mightiest of them. Although the nation's power base shifted to Paris around 1600, aristocrats continued to erect luxurious palaces along the Loire until the end of the 18th century.

TOURS

3

240 km (150 mi) southwest of Paris.

GETTING HERE

The handful of direct TGV trains from Paris (Gare Montparnasse) to Tours each day cover the 150 mi in 70 minutes; fare is €39–€51 depending on time of day. A more frequent service, but involving a change in suburban St-Pierre-des-Corps, takes 65 minutes and costs €53. A cheaper, slower alternative is the twice-daily traditional (non-TGV service) from Gare d'Austerlitz that takes 2 hours, 30 minutes but costs only €28. Tours is the Loire Valley rail hub. Trains leave every couple of hours or so for Chinon (50 mins, €8); Langeais (15 mins, €5); Azay-le-Rideau (30 mins, €5); Amboise (20 mins, €5); Saumur (40 mins, €10); and Blois (30–40 mins, €10), in addition to other towns. To reach Chenonceaux from Tours (€6), there are buses in the morning (45 mins), then trains in the afternoon (30 mins).

EXPLORING

Little remains of Tours's own château—one of France's finest cathedrals more than compensates—but the city serves as the transportation hub for the Loire Valley. Trains from Tours (and from its adjacent terminal at St-Pierre-de-Corps) run along the river in both directions, and regular bus services radiate from here; in addition, the city is the starting point for organized bus excursions (many with English-speaking guides). The town has mushroomed into a city of a quarter of a million inhabitants, with an ugly modern sprawl of factories, high-rise blocks, and overhead expressway junctions cluttering up the outskirts. But the timber-frame houses in **Le Vieux Tours** (Old Tours) and the attractive medieval center around place Plumereau were smartly restored after extensive damage in World War II.

Only two sturdy towers—the Tour Charlemagne and the Tour de l'Horloge (Clock Tower)—remain of the great medieval abbey built over the tomb of St. Martin, the city's 4th-century bishop and patron saint. Most of the abbey, which once dominated the heart of Tours, was razed during the French Revolution. Today's bombastic neo-Byzantine church, the **Basilique St-Martin,** was completed in 1924. There's a shrine to St. Martin in the crypt. ⊠ *Rue Descartes.*

Old mosaics and Romanesque sculptures from the former abbey

LUSCIOUS LOIRE

If the natives of Tours are known for one thing, it's their elegant French. Paris may be the capital, but for the Tourangeaux, Parisians are the ones with the accent.

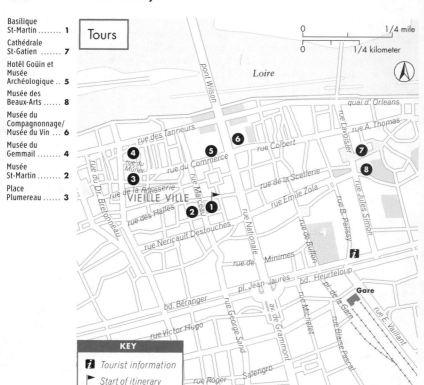

are on display in the **Musée St-Martin,** a small museum housed in a restored 13th-century chapel that adjoined the abbey cloisters. The museum retraces the life of St. Martin and the abbey's history. ⊠*3 rue Rapin* ☎*02–47–64–48–87* ⊠*Free* ⊙*Mid-Mar.–mid-Nov., Wed.–Sun. 9:30–12:30 and 2–5:30.*

North from the Basilique St-Martin to the river is **Le Vieux Tours,** the lovely medieval quarter. A warren of quaint streets, wood-beam houses, and grand mansions once home to 15th-century merchants, it has been gentrified with chic apartments and pedestrianized streets— Tours's college students and tourists alike love to sit at the cafés lining

Place Plumereau, once the town's *carroi aux chapeaux* (hat market).

Fodor's Choice Lining the square, Nos. 1 through 7 form a magnificent series of half-
★ timber houses; note the wood carvings of royal moneylenders on Nos. 11 and 12. At the top of the square a vaulted passageway leads on to a cute medieval **Place St-Pierre-le-Puellier.** Running off the Place Plumereau are other streets adorned with historic houses, notably Rue Briçonnet—No. 16 is the **Maison de Tristan** with a noted medieval staircase. ⊠*Bordered by Rues du Commerce, Briçonnet, de la Monnaie, and du Grand-Marché.*

🐚 ❹ The **Musée du Gemmail,** in the imposing 19th-century Hôtel Raimbault, contains an unusual collection of three-dimensional colored-glass window panels. Depicting patterns, figures, and portraits, the panels are beautiful and intriguing—most of the gemlike fragments of glass came from broken bottles. Incidentally, Jean Cocteau coined the word *gemmail* by combining *gemme* (gem) with *émail* (enamel). ✉*7 rue du Mûrier* ☎*02–47–61–01–19* ⊕*www.gemmail.com* 🎫*€5.40* ⊙*Apr.– mid-Oct., Tues.–Sun. 2–6:30.*

❺ The **Hôtel Gouin** *(archaeology museum)* is set in Tours's most extravagant example of early Renaissance domestic architecture (too bad its immediate vicinity was among the hardest hit by German bombs), its facade covered with carvings that seemed to have grown like Topsy. Inside are assorted oddities ranging from ancient Roman finds to the scientific collection of Dupin de Chenonceau (owner of the great château in the 18th century). The museum is closed in December. ✉*25 rue du Commerce* ☎*02–47–66–22–32* ⊕*www.monuments-touraine. fr* 🎫*€4.50* ⊙*Wed.–Mon. 10–1 and 2–6.*

❻ The **Musée du Compagnonnage** *(Guild Museum)* and the **Musée du Vin** (Wine Museum) are both in the cloisters of the 13th-century church of St-Julien. *Compagnonnage* is a sort of apprenticeship–cum–trade union system, and here you see the masterpieces of the candidates for guild membership: virtuoso craft work, some of it eccentric (an Eiffel Tower made of slate, for instance, or a château constructed of varnished noodles). ✉*8 rue Nationale* ☎*02–47–21–62–20* 🎫*Musée du Compagnonnage €4.90, Musée du Vin €2; joint ticket €5.50* ⊙*Wed.–Mon. 9–noon and 2–6.*

★ ❼ The **Cathédrale St-Gatien,** built between 1239 and 1484, reveals a mixture of architectural styles. The richly sculpted stonework of its majestic, soaring, two-tower facade betrays the Renaissance influence on local château-trained craftsmen. The stained glass dates from the 13th century (if you have binoculars, bring them). Also take a look at the little tomb with kneeling angels built in memory of Charles VIII and Anne of Brittany's two children; and the **Cloître de La Psalette** (cloister), on the south side of the cathedral. ✉*Rue Lavoisier* ☎*02–47–47–05–19* ⊙*Daily 8–noon and 2–6.*

❽ The **Musée des Beaux-Arts** *(Fine Arts Museum),* in what was once the archbishop's palace, has an eclectic selection of furniture, sculpture, wrought-iron work, and pieces by Rubens, Rembrandt, Boucher, Degas, and Calder. It even displays Fritz the Elephant, stuffed in 1902. ✉*18 pl. François-Sicard* ☎*02–47–05–68–73* 🎫*€4* ⊙*Wed.–Mon. 9–12:45 and 2–6.*

WHERE TO STAY & EAT

$–$$ ✗ **Les Tuffeaux.** This friendly restaurant, between the cathedral and the Loire, is the city's best value. Chef Gildas Marsollier wins customers with delicious fennel-perfumed salmon, oysters in an egg sauce seasoned with Roquefort, and remarkable desserts. Wine is served by the glass, a great way to try some of the local *appellations*. Gentle lighting and the 17th-century wood beams and stone walls provide a soothing

EATING WELL IN THE LOIRE VALLEY

The Loire Valley is known as the Garden of France and is home to several of the country's top restaurants. Lush pastures, a temperate climate, and rich soil make this a food-producing paradise. Seasonal delights among a year-round cornucopia of fruit and vegetables include asparagus in spring, and mushrooms (and game) in fall.

There's also wonderful goat-cheese and freshwater fish, notably salmon, pike, and carp. To wash it all down,

the Loire offers a greater variety of wine than any region in France: from dry whites (Savennières, Sancerre, Cheverny) to full-bodied reds (Bourgueil, Chinon, and Saumur-Champigny), via sweet whites (Coteâux du Layon and Montlouis) to rosé (Cabernet d'Anjou, often sweet), not forgetting versatile Vouvray, a white that comes sweet, dry...and with a sparkle!

background. ✉19 *rue Lavoisier* ☎02–47–47–19–89 ▤AE, MC, V ⊘Closed Sun. and part of July. No lunch Mon. or Wed.

★ $$$–$$$$ ✕▣ **Domaine de la Tortinière.** South of Tours atop a vast, sloping lawn, this storybook, toy-size, neo-Gothic château comes complete with two fairy-tale towers and a heated, terraced pool. Built in 1861, La Tortinière is now nearing perfection in all things bright and beautiful. Guest rooms in the main building convey quiet, rustic luxury; the conversation pieces are those in the two turrets, while others delight with beamed ceilings. Most beds are so comfy it's hard to wake up. In recent years the owners have smartly done up the former stables, warehouses, and servants' quarters (all just a path away from the main building). Replete with Louis XVI chairs, taffeta curtains, chiffonière tables, plate-glass windows, and air-conditioning, these are almost more alluring than the rooms in the main château. The stylish rotunda restaurant looks out over the lawn and showcases David Chartier's cuisine, including *beuchelle tourangelle,* sautéed veal sweetbreads with morels in white wine (no dinner Sunday, November through March). The main lawn overlooks the Indre River, bordered by a line of towering oak trees that have been trimmed back to make a "frame." The sweet life, indeed. ✉10 *rte. de Ballan-Miré, 12 km (7 mi) south of Tours, 37250 Veigné* ☎02–47–34–35–00 ≖02–47–65–95–70 ⊕www.tortiniere. com ⇨24 rooms, 6 suites ♿In-room: no a/c (some) refrigerator, WiFi (some). In-hotel: restaurant, tennis court, pool, no elevator ▤MC, V ⊘Closed mid-Dec.–late Feb. ❑MAP.

★ $$$–$$$$ ✕▣ **Jean Bardet.** King of Tourangeau chefs, Jean Bardet has a propensity for quoting philosophers, is as happy as a rabbit in a garden (his is packed with heirloom blooms and plants), and is celebrated for showcasing exotic fruits and vegetables in his signature creations. Specials served up in his plush yellow dining salon on his eight-course, €135 *menu dégustation* (tasting menu) and the mighty à la carte menu might include pigeon with foie gras in cabbage-leaf papillote, baby eel in red wine, oysters poached in Muscadet on a puree of watercress, or roast lobster with duck gizzards. Reservations are essential (April to October, there's no lunch Saturday, Monday, and Tuesday; November to March, there's no lunch Saturday and Tuesday, no dinner Sunday, and it's closed Monday). If you want to enjoy what some might deem the ultimate luxury—a breakfast masterminded by Bardet—book one of the guest rooms upstairs at this stately Directoire-style mansion; all luxuriously mix-and-match antiques and modern touches in the distinctive Relais & Châteaux manner. ☒*Château Belmont, 57 rue Groison, 37100* ☎*02–47–41–41–11* 🖷*02–47–51–68–72* ⊕*www.jean-bardet.com* 🛏*16 rooms, 5 suites* ♿*In-room: refrigerator. In-hotel: restaurant, pool, some pets allowed (fee)* ▭*AE, DC, MC, V* ⏐⊙⏐*MAP.*

> ### QUEEN FOR A STAY
>
> Distinguished by its elegance and *bon ton*, the Château de la Tortinière was reputedly Audrey Hepburn's favorite when she checked in for a visit. If you want to keep the fairy-tale vibe going, head just down the road to Monts to visit the newly restored Château de Candé, open to visitors in summer, and scene of the notorious wedding of the Duke and Duchess of Windsor on June 3, 1937.

$-$$ ⏐⊡⏐ **Central.** A delightfully friendly city-center oasis, this Best Western hotel near the Musée du Compagnonnage is set back from the street behind a gravel court and terraced garden. Inside, the welcome is vivacious, the lobby daguerreotype charming, and the clientele a pleasant mix of foreign students and happy travelers. The guest rooms are comfortable; the best look onto the garden, but cost 40% more. A walk of about eight blocks east takes you to the historic center of Tours. ☒*21 rue Berthelot, 37000* ☎*02–47–05–46–44* 🖷*02–47–66–10–26* ⊕*www.bestwesterncentralhoteltours.com/* 🛏*38 rooms* ♿*In-room: refrigerator, no a/c (some). In-hotel: bar, parking (no fee), some pets allowed* ▭*AE, MC, V* ⏐⊙⏐*BP.*

¢–$ ⏐⊡⏐ **Mondial.** Tucked away in the city center on a small leafy square 300 yards from the Loire, this is the closest hotel to historic half-timber Place Plumereau, a five-minute walk away. The white-walled, postwar building has some rooms with floral-patterned quilts and curtains, others in pastel shades. All are on the small side but spotlessly clean and offer good value, and service is friendly. There's no restaurant but the brasserie Bure is right next door. ☒*3 pl. de la Résistance, 37000* ☎*02–47–05–62–68* 🖷*02–47–61–85–31* ⊕*www.hotelmondialtours.com* 🛏*19 rooms* ▭*AE, MC, V.*

MONTLOUIS-SUR-LOIRE

❾ *11 km (7 mi) east of Tours on south bank of the Loire.*

Like Vouvray—its sister town on the north side of the Loire—Montlouis is noted for its white wines. On Place Courtemanche the **Cave Touristique** will help you learn all about the fine vintages produced by the wine growers of Montlouis. On the eastern side of town is one of the most alluring châteaux of the region, **La Bourdaisière.** Although open to day-trippers for guided tours, this once-royal retreat

Continued on page 215

ONCE UPON A CHATEAU

Loire and château are almost synonymous. There may be châteaux in every region of France, but nowhere are they so thickly clustered as they are in the Loire Valley. There are several reasons for this. By the early Middle Ages, prosperous towns had already evolved due to being strategically sited on the Loire, and defensive fortresses—the first châteaux—were built by warlords to control certain key points along the route. And with good reason: the riches of this wildly fertile region drew many feuding lords; in the 12th century, the medieval Plantagenet kings of France and England had installed themselves here (at Chinon and Fontevraud, to be exact).

During this time, dukes and counts began to build châteaux, from which they could watch over the king's lands and also defend themselves from each others' invasions. Spare, cold, and uninviting (that being the point), their châteaux were compartmented to house whole courts which settled in with their own furniture, pantry, and wall-sized tapestries (for insulation against the drafts). The notion of defense extended to the décor: massive high-back chairs protected the sitter from being stabbed in the back dur-

The châteaux of the Loire Valley range in style from medieval fortresses to Renaissance country homes, and they don't skip a beat in between. Today, travelers hop their way from the fairy-tale splendor of Ussé to the imposing dungeons at Angers to the graceful spans of Chenonceau. But to truly appreciate these spectacular structures, it helps to review their evolution from warlike stronghold to Sleeping Beauty's home.

ing dinner, and the *crédence* (credenza) was a table used by a noble's official taster to test for poison in the food.

These fortifications continued to come in handy during the Hundred Years' War, during which France and England quibbled over the French crown, for 116 years. When that war came to an end, in 1453, King François I went to Italy, looking for someone else to beat up on, and came back with the Renaissance (he literally brought home Leonardo da Vinci). The king promptly built a 440-room Xanadu, Chambord, in the Italianate style.

By the 15th century, under the later medieval Valois kings, the Loire was effectively functioning as the country's capital, with new châteaux springing up apace, advertising their owners' power and riches. Many were built using a chalky local stone called *tuffeau* (tufa), whose softness and whiteness made it ideal for the sculpted details which were the pride of the new architectural style. The resulting Renaissance pleasure palaces were sumptuous both inside and out—Charles Perrault found the Château de Ussé to be so peaceful and alluring it inspired him to write "Sleeping Beauty" in 1697. A few years before, Louis XIV had started building his new seat of government. It wasn't long before it was goodbye Loire Valley, hello Versailles.

Above: Château de Chambord

FROM DEFENSE TO DECORATION

13ᵀᴴ CENTURY

Angers

The parade of châteaux began with the medieval fortress at Angers, a brooding, muscular fort built by St. Louis to defend the gateway to the Loire against pesky English invaders. Military architecture gave birth to this château, a perfect specimen of great, massive defensiveness. Such castles were meant to look grim, advertising horrid problems for attackers—defenders shot cross-bow arrows from the slit windows—and unpleasant conditions for prisoners in the dungeons. The most important features of these fortress-châteaux were the *châtelets* (twin turrets that frame the drawbridge), the *chemin de ronde* (the machicolated passageways between towers), and the *donjon* (fortress keep).

14ᵀᴴ CENTURY

Saumur

When the battle cries faded and periods of peace once more beguiled the land, the château changed its appearance and the picture palaces of the Loire came into being. Elegance arrived early at Saumur, built in 1360 by Louis I of Anjou. His heir, the luxury-loving Duc de Berri, dressed up the sturdy fort with high, pointed roofs, gilded steeples, iron weather vanes, and soaring pinnacles, creating a Gothic-style castle that Walt Disney would have been proud of. Former cross-bow apertures were replaced with good-size windows, from which love-sick princesses would gaze down on chivalric tournaments, now featuring fancy cloth-of-gold trappings, and festive banquets with blaring trumpet backup became the norm.

| 1214 | French king **Philippe Auguste** defeats English and German armies in Anjou. | 1270 | **Death of Louis IX** (St. Louis) in Tunis during the 8th Crusade. | | 1337 | **Hundred Years' War** between France and England. begins. | 1360 | Louis I of Anjou tranforms **Saumur** into his elegant residence. |

1300

1400

| 1228 | 1238 Constructuion of **Angers Castle.** | | | 1348 | The **Black Death** kills one third of the French population. |

3

Azay-le-Rideau

16TH CENTURY

By the Renaissance—brought to France from Italy by Charles VIII at the end of the 15th century—balance, harmony, and grace were brought to the fore. Rich officials wowed the womenfolk with châteaux that were homages to the bygone days of chivalry, such as Azay-le-Rideau.
■ The château may look Gothic from a distance, but its moat is actually the River Indre, and its purpose is to provide a pleasing reflection, thereby emphasizing the Italianate symmetry of this architectural bijou. Funded by the royal financier Berthelot but designed by his wife, Philippe, this was a fairy-tale castle. The turrets and machicolations were just for fun, and a grand staircase was added to showcase the ladies' sweeping skirts.

Chenonceau

16TH CENTURY

Its architecture is civilized, peaceful, and feminine, aptly so since it was constructed by three ladies. Catherine Briçonnet, a tax collector's wife, built the Gothic-style château; Diane de Poitiers, the mistress of Henri II, extended it by adding a bridge across the river (for easy access to her hunting grounds), before
■ being kicked out by Henri's wife, Catherine de Medici, who tacked galleries onto the bridge in homage to the Ponte Vecchio in Florence, her home town. Although its broad facade offers a curtsey to the virtues of Baroque style, Chenonceau is actually only two rooms deep— the château had become an exquisite stage curtain and little more.

1518 | **Azay-le-Rideau** is rebuilt with Italian influences.

1431 | After rallying the French to victory in Orléans, **Joan of Arc** is burned at the stake by the English.

1525 | **François I** builds **Chambord.**

1547 | King Henri II gives **Chenonceau** to his mistress Diane de Poitiers.

1500

1600

1485 | **Charles VIII** invades Italy, importing home the Renaissance.

LA VIE DE CHATEAUX

To truly savor the châteaux of the "Valley of the Kings," you can do more than just tour them: You can sleep in them, party in them, and helicopter-ride over them.

Château de la Bordaisière, Montlouis-sur-Loire.

QUEEN FOR A STAY

Here are the crème de la crème of the Loire Valley's magical château-hotels:

Château de la Bordaisière, Montlouis-sur-Loire. Not far from Chenonceau, this enchanting neo-Renaissance castle is run by princes Louis-Albert and Philippe-Maurice de Broglie. Royal red salons, chic bedrooms, a famous tomato potager, a vast pool, and heirloom gardens are just a few of the goodies here.

Château de Colliers, Muides-sur-Loire. Close to Chambord, this *très charmant* jewel has ravishing Rococo salons and the most beautiful hotel river terrace along the Loire.

Château de Reaux, Bourgueil. With its red-and-white chessboard facade, swans in the moat, and the Comtesse Florence de Bouillé in residence, this 17th-century castle is right out of a storybook.

AN EYE ON HIGH

Thanks to helicopter excursions, you can get a new perspective on the grand châteaux by taking to the air—appropriately so, since Leonardo da Vinci invented the contraption while residing in Amboise. Jet Systems (☎ 02–47–30–20–21, ⊕ www.jet-systems.fr) makes helicopter trips over the Loire Valley on Tuesday, Thursday, and weekends from the aerodrome at Dierre, just south of Amboise; costs range from €57 (10 minutes, flying over Chenonceau) to €229 (50 minutes, covering six châteaux) per person. For a more leisurely airborne visit, contact France Montgolfière (☎ 02–54–32–20–48, ⊕ www.franceballoons.com) for details of their balloon trips over the Loire; prices run €180–€225.

LET THERE BE A LIGHT SHOW

In summer, several châteaux offer celebrated *son-et-lumière* (sound-and-light) extravaganzas after dark. Some are historical pageants—with huge casts of people dressed in period costume, all floodlit (the flicker of flames helps dramatize the French Revolution), and accompanied by music and commentary, sometimes in English; Amboise and Loches are the top examples. Other châteaux—including Chenonceau, Chambord, and Azay-le-Rideau—offer recorded commentary and magical effects created by slide projections (pictured), smoke-machines, and color spotlights.

and birthplace of noted 17th-century courtesan Gabrielle d'Estrées is today the enchanted hotel–domain of the Princes de Broglie.

WHERE TO STAY

$$$–$$$$
Fodor'sChoice
★

 Château de la Bourdaisière. Few other hotels so magically distill all the grace, warmth, and elan of *la vie de château* as does this 15th-century, 100-carat jewel. Once the favored retreat of two kings, François I and Henri IV, today its presiding spirits are only slightly less royal: brother-Princes Philippe-Maurice and Louis-Albert de Broglie, scions of one of France's top families (two prime ministers and one Nobel Prize winner, at last count). Louis-Albert is one of Paris's most famed gardeners, who here cultivates 400 types of tomatoes in the château's *potager* (vegetable garden). It's not surprising, then, to find the three main public salons suavely done up in shades of tomato red, sumptuously offsetting such accents as an immense marble fireplace and large bouquets designed by the prince. You can start your gawking, however, at the park entrance—motorists often stop to drink in the view of the neo-Renaissance castle perched atop its picture-perfect hill. Guest rooms range from the grand—*François-Premier* is a timber-roof cottage blown up to ballroom dimensions—to more standard-issue, yet always stylish salons (garden-view rooms away from the gravel driveway are best). Cheaper rooms are found in the adjoining 17th-century "stables" fitted out with a gardening shop and a tiny eatery that serves up dazzling salads and confections (lunch only, June–September). What more can you ask? What about an enormous secluded pool—a gift from heaven during hot summer days. Life-changingly gracious, La Bourdaisière makes a truly princely base for exploring the Loire. ✉*25 rue de la Bourdaisière, 37270* ☎*02–47–45–16–31* 🖷*02–47–45–09–11* ⊕*www.chateaulabourdaisiere.com* 📞*17 rooms, 3 suites* ♿*In-room: no a/c, dial-up. In-hotel: restaurant, tennis court, pool* ▬*MC, V* ☺*Closed Nov. 15–Mar. 15* ⦿*BP.*

AMBOISE

❿ *13 km (8 mi) east of Montlouis via D751, 24 km (15 mi) east of Tours.*

GETTING HERE

Amboise has frequent train connections with Tours (20 mins, €5), Blois (24 mins, €6), and many other towns that lie along the main train route which follows the banks of the river; about 10 trains a day make the Tours–Blois transit. From Amboise's station, the town is across the Loire (the island in the middle of the river is the less-than-exciting Ile d'Or); follow the signs across two bridges to the centre ville and Place Richelieu.

EXPLORING

The Da Vinci trail ends here in one of the more popular towns along the river. Site of Leonardo's final home, crowned with a royal château, and jammed with bustling markets and plenty of hotels and restaurants, Amboise is one of the major hubs of the Loire. On hot summer days, however, the plethora of tour buses turn the Renaissance town into a carbon monoxide nightmare. So why come? The main château is soaked in history (and blood), while Leonardo's Clos-Lucé is a must-do on any Val de Loire itinerary.

The **Château d'Amboise** became a royal palace in the 15th and 16th centuries. Charles VII stayed here, as did the unfortunate Charles VIII, best remembered for banging his head on a low doorway lintel (you will be shown it) and dying as a result. The gigantic **Tour des Minimes** drops down the side of the cliff, enclosing a massive circular ramp designed to lead horses and carriages up the steep hillside. François I, whose long nose appears in so many château paintings, based his court here, inviting Leonardo da Vinci as his guest. The castle was also the stage for the Amboise Conspiracy, an ill-fated Protestant plot against François II; you are shown where the corpses of 1,200 conspirators dangled from the castle walls. This is one reason why the château feels haunted and forlorn—another is the fact that most of its interior furnishings have been lost. But don't miss the lovely grounds, adorned with a Flamboyant Gothic gem, the little chapel of St-Hubert with its carvings of the Virgin and Child, Charles VIII, and Anne of Brittany, and once graced by the tomb of Leonardo. ☎02–47–57–00–98 ⊕*www.chateau-amboise.com* ✉*€8.50* ⊗*Nov.–Mar., daily 9–noon and 2–4:45; Apr.–June, Sept., and Oct., daily 9–6; July and Aug., daily 9–7.*

☾ ★ If you want to see where "the 20th century was born"—as the curators here like to proclaim—head to the legendary **Clos Lucé**, about 600 yards up Rue Victor-Hugo from the château. Here, in this handsome Renaissance manor, Leonardo da Vinci (1452–1519) spent the last four years of his life, tinkering away at inventions, amusing his patron, King François I, and gazing out over a garden that was planted in the most fashionable Italian manner (and which now contains a dozen full-size renderings of machines designed by Leonardo, which you can activate as you stroll round). The **Halle Interactive** contains working models, built by IBM engineers using the detailed sketches in the artist's notebooks, of some of Leonardo's extraordinary inventions; by this time, Leonardo had put away his paint box because of arthritis. Mechanisms on display include three-speed gearboxes, a military tank, a clockwork car, and a flying machine complete with designs for parachutes. Cloux, the house's original name, was given to Anne of Brittany by Charles VIII, who built a chapel for her that is still here. Some of the house's furnishings are authentically 16th century—indeed, thanks to the artist's presence, this house was one of the first places where the Italian Renaissance made inroads in France: Leonardo's *Mona Lisa* and *Virgin of the Rocks*, both of which graced the walls here, were bought by the king, who then moved them to the Louvre. ✉*2 rue du Clos-Lucé* ☎*02–47–57–00–73* ⊕*www.vinci-closluce.com* ✉*€12* ⊗*Sept.–Dec. and Feb.–June, daily 9–6; July and Aug., daily 9–8; Jan., daily 10–5.*

Just 3 km (2 mi) south of Amboise on the road to Chenonceaux, the **Pagode de Chanteloup** is a remarkable sight—a 140-foot, seven-story Chinese-style lakeside pagoda built for the Duke of Choiseul in 1775.

Children will adore puffing their way to the top for the vertigo-inducing views, but some adults will find the climb—and the 400-yard walk from the parking lot—a little arduous. Sadly, the adjoining lake and park have become the worse for wear. ⊠*Rte. de Bléré* ☏*02–47–57–20–97* ⊕*www.pagode-chanteloup.com* 🖃€*6.90* ⊙*May, June, and Sept., daily 10–6:30; Mar. and Apr., daily 10–noon and 2–6; July and Aug., daily 9:30–7.30; Oct.–mid-Nov., weekends 10—5.*

WHERE TO STAY & EAT

★ $$$–$$$$ ✕▥ **Château de Noizay.** Filled with the mystery of the past—this was once the fabled redoubt of the Protestant plotters in the 1559 Amboise Conspiracy—this château is fitted out with Renaissance chimneys and salons, a parterre garden, and, best of all, one of the finest chefs around. Guest rooms are so regal you may feel like bowing or curtsying to the staff; if so, opt for the adjacent 19th-century "Clock House"—a gracious pastel-hue haven with lush air-conditioning. Noizay itself is a tiny, off-the-beaten-path treasure—don't miss the idyllic countryside hike down Rue François-Poulenc, past the famous composer's pretty 18th-century house, a troglodyte hamlet, and endless poppy fields right out of a Monet painting. ⊠*Rte. de Chançay, 8 km (5 mi) west of Tours, 37210 Noizay* ☏*02–47–52–11–01* 🖷*02–47–52–04–64* ⊕*www.chateaudenoizay.com* ⇆*14 rooms* ♿*In-room: no a/c (some). In-hotel: restaurant, tennis court, pool* ▭*AE, MC, V* ⊙*Closed mid-Jan.–mid-Mar.* ¶⊙*FAP.*

$$$ ✕▥ **Château de Pray.** Fifty years ago Loire Valley guidebooks praised
Fodor'sChoice   this domain and, delightfully, things have only gotten better. Like a
★   Rolls-Royce Silver Cloud, this hotel keeps purring along, offering many delights: a romantic, twin-towered château, Loire River vista, tranquil guest rooms (four of the less expensive are in a charming "Pavillon Renaissance"), and excellent restaurant. The latter is set in two salons, one in Charles-Dix golds, the other lighted with chandeliers and stained-glass windows, lined with tapestries, and spectacularly centered around a neo-Gothic, sculpted-wood fireplace. Chef Ludovic Laurenty loves his independence: he has his own vegetable garden in the grounds, and cooks his own bread. You can sample his skill for €30 with the lunchtime menu, or by enrolling for a cooking class. Just outside is the elegant lawn terrace, where tipsy guests assemble to toast their friends with magnums of Veuve Clicquot. ⊠*Rte. de Chargé, 4 km (2 mi) east of Amboise, 37400* ☏*02–47–57–23–67* 🖷*02–47–57–32–50* ⊕*praycastel.online.fr* ⇆*17 rooms, 2 suites* ♿*In-room: no a/c. In-hotel: restaurant, pool, no elevator, public Wi-Fi* ▭*MC, V* ⊙*Closed Jan.* ¶⊙*MAP.*

¢–$ ✕▥ **Le Blason.** Two blocks behind Château d'Amboise and a five-minute walk from the town center, this small, old hotel has enthusiastic owners and rooms of different shapes and sizes: No. 229, for example, has exposed beams and a cathedral ceiling; No. 109 is comfortably spacious with a good view of the square. The on-site restaurant, L'Alliance (under different management; no lunch Tuesday or Wednesday), offers menus starting €18 and scrumptious roast lamb with garlic, tuna with sesame seeds, and salmon carpaccio with mustard dressing. But beware: you must arrive by 8:45 for dinner. ⊠*11 pl. Richelieu,*

3

37400 ☎02–47–23–22–41 🖷02–47–57–56–18 ⊕www.leblason.fr
🗬25 rooms 🐾In-hotel: restaurant, some pets allowed (fee), no elevator ☰AE, DC, MC, V ⊘Closed mid-Jan.–early Feb. ¶○¶MAP.

$$$ ⊡ **Le Vieux Manoir.** An ultimate welcome mat for anyone visiting the
Fodor'sChoice Loire Valley, this lovely hotel is the creation of Gloria Belknap—a
★ Californian whose immense style Edith Wharton would have cot-
toned to immediately. You'll have a hard time tearing yourself away
from your guest room, as Gloria has turned loose some decorators
extraordinaires on her inn: toile de Jouy screens, gilt-framed paintings,
comfy Napoléon III covered-in-jute armchairs, timeworn armoires,
and tables adorned with Shaker baskets make this place *House &*
Garden–worthy. Each chamber—named after a great French lady,
such as George Sand, Madame du Barry, or Colette—is a delight:
a bleached redbrick chimney and red-and-white calico accent one,
while ceiling beams and a French Provincial four-poster bed warm
another. But you'll probably spend more time in the book-filled
library or in the main salon—soaking up the wit and wisdom of Glo-
ria and husband Bob—or by the fountain in the leafy garden. ⊠13
rue Rabelais, 37400 ☎☎02–47–30–41–27 ⊕www.le-vieux-manoir.
com 🗬6 rooms, 1 cottage 🐾In-room: no TV (some). In-hotel: no
elevator ☰MC, V ¶○¶BP.

★ $$–$$$ ⊡ **Le Manoir Les Minimes.** Picture-perfect and soigné as can be, this gor-
geously stylish hotel is lucky enough to preside over a Loire riverbank
under the shadow of Amboise's great cliff-side château. Set within its
own compound, this quaintly shuttered late-18th-century manoir looks
like it's on sabbatical from a Fragonard landscape. Inside, the grand
staircase, dining room, and main salon are all a-dazzle in daffodil yel-
low silks and gilt-framed mirrors, with ruby accents of Louis Seize
sofas and bergères. The standard guest rooms are pleasant enough but
try to spring for the showpieces, such as the Suite Prestige (in a stunning
blue toile de Jouy). Eric Deforges and Patrice Longet have made this
hotel very *chez soi*, with all sorts of loving details—at night, you can
even find the weather forecast for the following day on your pillow. At
dusk, cap it all off by stepping beyond the French doors to the man-
oir's exquisite gravel terrace to enjoy a Kir Royale. ⊠34 quai Charles-
Guinot, 37400 ☎02–47–30–40–40 🖷02–47–30–40–77 ⊕www.man-
oirlesminimes.com 🗬10 rooms, 8 suites 🐾In-room: refrigerator, no
TV, dial-up. In-hotel: no elevator ☰MC, V.

CHENONCEAUX

⓫ 12 km (8 mi) southeast of Amboise via D81, 32 km (20 mi) east of
Tours.

GETTING HERE

Three to fivetrains run daily between Tours and Chenonceaux (30
mins, €6), one of the main destinations on one of the extensive branch
lines of the Loire rail system. The station is especially convenient, just
a minute's walk from the front gates of the château; across the tracks
is the one-road town.

EXPLORING

Achingly beautiful, the **Château de Chenonceau** has long been considered the "most romantic" of all the Loire châteaux, thanks in part to its showpiece—a breathtaking *galerie de bal* that spans the River Cher like a bridge. The gallery was used as an escape point for French Resistance fighters during World War II, since all other crossings had been bombed. Set in the village of Chenonceaux (spelled with an *x*) on the River Cher, this was the fabled retreat for the *dames de Chenonceau*, Diane de Poitiers, Catherine de' Medici, and Mary Queen of Scots. Happily spending at least half a day wandering through the château and grounds, you can see that this monument has an undeniable feminine touch. During the peak summer season the only drawback is the château's popularity: if you want to avoid a roomful of schoolchildren, take a stroll on the grounds and come back to the house at lunchtime.

> ### HAVE THAT NIKON READY
>
> Be sure to walk to the most distant point of Chenonceau's largest parterre garden, le Jardin de Diane de Poitiers—there you can find a tiny bridge leading to a river lookout point where you can find the most beautiful view of France's most glorious château. Sorry, no picnics allowed.

More pleasure palace than fortress, the château was built in 1520 by Thomas Bohier, a wealthy tax collector, for his wife, Catherine Briçonnet. When he went bankrupt, it passed to François I. Later, Henri II gave it to his mistress, Diane de Poitiers. After his death, Henri's not-so-understanding widow, Catherine de' Medici, expelled Diane to nearby Chaumont and took back the château. Before this time, Diane's five-arched bridge over the River Cher was simply meant as a grand ceremonial entryway leading to a gigantic château, a building never constructed. It was to Catherine, and her architect, Philibert de l'Orme, that historians owe the audacious plan to transform the bridge itself into the most unusual château in France. Two stories were constructed over the river, including an enormous gallery that runs from one end of the château to the other. This design might seem the height of originality but, in fact, was inspired by Florence's covered Ponte Vecchio bridge, commissioned by a Medici queen homesick for her native town.

July and August are the peak months at Chenonceau: only then can you escape the maddening crowds by exiting at the far end of the gallery to walk along the opposite bank (weekends only), rent a rowboat to spend an hour just drifting in the river (where Diane used to enjoy her morning dips), and enjoy the **Promenade Nocturne,** an evocative son et lumière performed in the illuminated château gardens.

Before you go inside, pick up an English-language leaflet at the gate. Then walk around to the right of the main building to see the harmonious, delicate architecture beyond the formal garden—the southern part belonged to Diane de Poitiers, the northern was Catherine's—with the river gliding under the arches (providing superb "air-conditioning" to the rooms above). Inside the château are splendid ceilings, colossal fireplaces, scattered furnishings, and paintings by Rubens, del Sarto, and Correggio. The curatorial staff have delightfully dispensed with velvet ropes and adorned some of the rooms with bouquets designed in 17th-century style. As you tour the salons, be sure to pay your respects to former owner Madame Dupin, tellingly captured in Nattier's charming portrait: thanks to the affection she inspired among her proletarian neighbors, the château and its treasures survived the Revolution intact (her grave is enshrined near the northern embankment). The château's history is illustrated with wax figures in the **Musée des Cires** (Waxwork Museum) in one of the château's outbuildings. A cafeteria, tearoom, and the ambitious Orangerie restaurant handle the crowds' varied appetites. 🕿 *02–47–23–90–07* ⊕*www.chenonceau. com* 🖅*Château €9.50; including Musée des Cires, €11; night visit of gardens €5* ⊙*Mid-Mar.–mid-Sept., daily 9–7; mid-Feb.–mid-Mar. and mid-Sept.–mid-Oct., daily 9–6; mid-Oct.–mid-Feb., daily 9–5.*

WHERE TO STAY & EAT

$$–$$$
Fodor$Choice
★

✕🖾 **Le Bon Laboureur.** In 1882 this ivy-covered inn won Henry James's praise and the famed author might be even more impressed today. Thanks to four generations of the Jeudi family, this remains one of the Loire's most stylish auberges. Charm is in abundance—many guest rooms are enchantingly accented in toile de Jouy fabrics, rustic wainscotting, tiny lamps, and Redouté pink-and-blue pastels. Those in the main house are comfortably sized (a few overlook the main street—avoid these if you are a light sleeper), those in the former stables are larger (some overlook a pert vegetable garden) and more renovated, but our favorites are the quaint rooms in the separate patio house near the terrace. Don't lose any time bagging a table in the "old" dining room (book this room, not the more modern ones), whose wood-beamed ceiling, glazed terra-cotta walls, and Louis XVI chairs are almost as elegant as chef Jean-Marie Burnet's turbot with red pepper and fennel. And that is saying something: meals here are marvels. ✉*6 rue du Dr-Bretonneau, 37150* 🕿*02–47–23–90–02* 🖷*02–47–23–82–01* ⊕*www.amboise.com/laboureur* 🖙*24 rooms* ⌂*In-room: refrigerator, no a/c (some), dial-up. In-hotel: restaurant, bar, pool, bicycles, some pets allowed (fee), no elevator* ▤*AE, DC, MC, V* ⊙*Closed Jan.–mid-Feb. and mid-Nov.–mid-Dec.* ¶⊙*MAP.*

★ $–$$

✕🖾 **La Roseraie.** The Bon Laboureur may be Chenonceaux's most famous hostelry, but this runs close for charm, thanks in part to the joyful welcome of its English-speaking hosts, Laurent and Sophie Fiorito. But let's not forget the guest rooms, many of which are designed with florals, checks, and lace, or the copious meals served in the wood-beamed dining room (where foie gras, duck with fruit and honey, and apple tart are among the specialties), or the pretty pool. Try to get a garden-side room, even if too many pink tablecloths and white chairs make the patio less than restful. If car traffic bothers you, be sure to avoid the rooms overlooking the main street. ✉*7 rue du Dr-Bretonneau, 37150* 🕿*02–47–23–90–09* 🖷*02–47–23–91–59* ⊕*www.charmingroseraie.com* 🖙*17 rooms* ⌂*In-room: no a/c. In-hotel: restaurant, bar, pool, no elevator* ▤*AE, DC, MC, V* ⊙*Closed mid-Nov.–mid-Feb.* ¶⊙*BP.*

CHAUMONT-SUR-LOIRE

12 *26 km (16 mi) northeast of Chenonceaux via D176/D62, 21 km (13 mi) southwest of Blois.*

★ Although a favorite of Loire connoisseurs, the 16th-century **Château de Chaumont** is often overlooked by visitors who are content to ride the conveyor belt of big châteaux like Chambord and Chenonceau, and it's their loss. Set on a dramatic bluff that towers over the river, Chaumont has always cast a spell—perhaps literally so. One of its fabled owners, Catherine de' Medici, occasionally came here with her court "astrologer," the notorious Ruggieri. In one of Chaumont's bell-tower rooms, the queen reputedly practiced sorcery. Whether or not Ruggieri still haunts the place (or Nostradamus, another on Catherine's guest list), there seem to be few castles as spirit-warm as this one.

Centerpiece of a gigantic park (a stiff walk up a long path from the little village of Chaumont-sur-Loire; cars and taxis can also drop you off at the top of the hill) and built by Charles II d'Amboise between 1465 and 1510, the château greets visitors with glorious, twin-tower *châtelets*—twin turrets that frame a double drawbridge. The castle became the residence of Henri II. After his death his widow Catherine de' Medici took revenge on his mistress, the fabled beauty Diane de Poitiers, and forced her to exchange Chenonceau for Chaumont. Another "refugee" was the late-18th-century writer Madame de Staël. Exiled from Paris by Napoléon, she wrote *De l'Allemagne* (*On Germany*) here, a book that helped kick-start the Romantic movement in France. In the 19th century her descendants, the Prince and Princess de Broglie, set up regal shop, as you can still see from the stone-and-brick stables, where pure-bred horses (and one elephant) lived like royalty in velvet-lined stalls. The couple also renovated many rooms in the glamorous neo-Gothic style of the 1870s. Today, their sense of fantasy is retained in the castle's **Festival International des Jardins** (⊕www.chaumont-jardin.com €9), held May to October in the extensive park and featuring the latest in horticultural invention. Chaumont is one of the more difficult locations to reach via public transportation, with a long cab ride needed from the nearest train station across the river at Onzain. ☎02–54–51–26–26 €6.50 ⊙Apr.–Sept., daily 9:30–6:30; Oct.–Mar., daily 10–5.

WHERE TO STAY & EAT

★ $$$–$$$$ ╳ ▣ **Domaine des Hauts-de-Loire.** Long a landmark of Loire luxe, this aristocratic outpost is across the river from Chaumont (which has a handy bridge) and some 4 km (2 mi) inland. This is no château but an 18th-century, turreted, vine-covered hunting lodge, replete with a grand salon furnished with 18th-century antiques, a lovely pool, an adorable swan lake, a helipad, 180 acres of forest for hikes, and the most blissful air-conditioning in all Touraine. Guest rooms are beige, suave, and tranquil; those in the adjacent coach house are more modern but can be considerably more spectacular—the best have exposed brick walls, couture fabrics, and timbered cathedral ceilings. The restaurant (closed Monday and Tuesday) is famous for its style and quality—an evening here glows with mellow lights, sumptuous white bouquets, and dazzling dishes like goose Rossini with mushroom risotto, showcased in the €75 and €95 prix-fixe menus. Later, purring patrons often repair to the salon for champagne to swap stories and toast their good luck at being here—and *here.* ⊠*Rte. de Herbault, across Loire from Chaumont, 41150 Onzain* ☎*02–54–20–72–57* 🖷*02–54–20–77–32* ⊕*www. domainehautsloire.com* ⌨*25 rooms, 10 suites* ♿*In-room: refrigerator, ethernet. In-hotel: restaurant, tennis court, pool, no elevator* ▤*AE, DC, MC, V* ⊗*Closed Dec.–Feb.* ⦿*MAP.*

$ ✕🏨 **Hostellerie du Château.** Set on a bank of the Loire and directly opposite the road leading up to Chaumont's château, this quaint edifice was—rather uniquely for these parts—built in the early 20th century as a hotel pure and simple. Four stories tall, fitted out with half-timber eaves, the hotel conjures up the grace of earlier days. Today, happily, it's purring along as a reasonably priced option. The entry hall soars, the restaurant is cozy and friendly, and the staff is Chaumont-courteous. Who cares if the rooms are on the simple side and a bit the worse for wear? The hotel does however front the main road zipping through Chaumont (with loads of traffic), so be sure to bag a room away from the street, preferably on the side facing the Loire. ⊠*2 rue du Mal-de-Lattre-de-Tassigny, 41150* ☎*02–54–20–98–04* 🖷*02–54–20–97–98* ⊕*www.hostellerie-du-chateau.com* ⌨*15 rooms* ♿*In-room: no phone. In-hotel: restaurant, pool* ▤*MC, V* ⊗*Closed Feb.*

CHEVERNY

⑬ *24 km (15 mi) east of Chaumont, 14 km (9 mi) southeast of Blois.*

Perhaps best remembered as Capitaine Haddock's mansion in the Tintin comic books, the **Château de Cheverny** is also iconic for its restrained 17th-century elegance. One of the last in the area to be built, it was finished in 1634, at a time when the rich and famous had mostly stopped building in the Loire Valley. By then, the taste for quaintly shaped châteaux had given way to disciplined Classicism; so here a white, elegantly proportioned, horizontally coursed, single-block facade greets you across manicured lawns. To emphasize the strict symmetry of the plan, a ruler-straight drive leads to the front entrance. The Louis XIII interior with its stridently painted and gilded rooms, splendid furniture, and rich tapestries depicting the Labors of Hercules is one of the few still intact in the Loire region. Despite the priceless Delft vases and Persian embroideries, it feels lived in. That's because it's one of the rare Loire Valley houses still occupied by a noble family. You can visit a small Tintin exhibition called *Le Secret de Moulinsart* (admission extra) and are free to contemplate the antlers of 2,000 stags in the Trophy Room: hunting, called "venery" in the leaflets, continues vigorously here, with red coats, bugles, and all. In the château's kennels, hordes of hungry hounds lounge around dreaming of their next kill. Feeding times—*la soupe aux chiens*—are posted on a notice board, and you are welcome to watch the "ceremony" (delicate sensibilities beware: the dogs line up like statues and are called, one by one, to wolf down their meal from the trainer). ☎*02–54–79–96–29* ⊕*www. chateau-cheverny.fr* ✉€*6.80,* €*11.80 with Tintin exhibition,* €*16.50 including. boat-and-buggy rides* ⊘*Apr.–Sept., daily 9:15–6:15; Oct.– Mar., daily 9:45–5.*

CHAMBORD

⓮ *13 km (21 mi) northeast of Chaumont-sur-Loire via D33, 19 km (12*
Fodor'sChoice *mi) east of Blois, 45 km (28 mi) southwest of Orléans.*
★

GETTING HERE

There is surprisingly little public transportation to Chambord. There are no trains, but Transports du Loir et Cher (⊕*tlcinfo.net*) offers a bus route from Blois (departures 9 AM and 1 PM) only from June 15 to September 15.

EXPLORING

The "Versailles" of the 16th century and the largest of the Loire châteaux, the **Château de Chambord** is the kind of place William Randolph Hearst might have built if he'd had the money. Variously dubbed "megalomaniacal" and "an enormous film-set extravaganza," this is one of the most extraordinary structures in Europe, set in the middle of a royal game forest, with just a cluster of buildings—barely a village—across the road. With a facade that is 420 feet long, 440 rooms and 365 chimneys, a wall 32 km (20 mi) long to enclose a 13,000-acre forest (you can wander through 3,000 acres of it; the rest is reserved for wild boar and other game), this is one of the greatest buildings in France. Under François I, building began in 1519, a job that took 12 years and required 1,800 workers. His original grandiose idea was to divert the Loire to form a moat, but someone (perhaps his adviser, Leonardo da Vinci, who some feel may have provided the inspiration behind the entire complex) persuaded him to make do with the River Cosson. François I used the château only for short stays; yet when he came, 12,000 horses were required to transport his luggage, servants, and entourage. Later kings also used Chambord as an occasional retreat, and Louis XIV, the Sun King, had Molière perform here. In the 18th century Louis XV gave the château to the Maréchal de Saxe as a reward for his victory over the English and Dutch at Fontenoy (southern Belgium) in 1745. When not indulging himself with wine, women, and song, the marshal planted himself on the roof to oversee the exercises of his personal regiment of 1,000 cavalry. Now, after long neglect—all the original furnishings vanished during the French Revolution—Chambord belongs to the state.

There's plenty to see inside. You can wander freely through the vast rooms, filled with exhibits (including a hunting museum)—not all concerned with Chambord, but interesting nonetheless—and lots of Ancien

Régime furnishings. The enormous double-helix staircase (probably envisioned by Leonardo, who had a thing about spirals) looks like a single staircase, but an entire regiment could march up one spiral while a second came down the other, and never the twain would meet. But the high point here in more ways than one is the spectacular chimneyscape—the roof terrace whose forest of Italianate towers, turrets, cupolas, gables, and chimneys have been compared to everything from the minarets of

> **PLANET CHAMBORD**
>
> As you travel the gigantic, tree-shaded roadways that converge on Chambord, you first spot the château's incredible towers—19th-century novelist Henry James said they were "more like the spires of a city than the salient points of a single building"—rising above the forest. When the entire palace breaks into view, it is an unforgettable sight.

Constantinople to a bizarre chessboard. The most eye-popping time to see this roof is at night, when the château is spectacularly illuminated with slide projections; the presentation, called "Les Claires de Lune," is free and held nightly during July and August from 10 PM to midnight. During the year there's a packed calendar of activities on tap, from 90-minute tours of the park in a 4x4 vehicle (€15) to guided tours on bike or horseback. A soaring three-story-tall hall has been fitted out to offer lunches and dinners. ☎02–54–50–40–00 ⊕www.chambord.org ☞€8.50, €9.50 in July and Aug. ☉Apr.–Sept., daily 9–6:15; Oct.–Mar., daily 9–5:15.

WHERE TO STAY & EAT

★ **$$$$** ✕ **Relais de Bracieux.** Masterminded by chef Bernard Robin, this is one of the Loire's top restaurants. Out of the gleaming kitchens comes sumptuous nouvelle cuisine: lobster with dried tomatoes and shepherd's pie with oxtail and truffles. Connoisseurs also savor Robin's simpler fare: carp, game in season, and salmon with beef marrow. Others delight in his opulent details—accompanying your dessert you may find a fairy-tale forest of mushrooms and elves spun in sugar. The four-course menu costs €60, and there's a three-course menu weekdays at €39. The dining room is traditional-modern, with cane-back chairs, and the best tables are by the large windows overlooking the garden. ✉1 av. de Chambord, 8 km (5 mi) south of Chambord, 9 km (6 mi) northeast of Cour-Cheverny on road to Chambord, Bracieux ☎02–54–46–41–22 ⊕www.relaisdebracieux.com ♠Reservations essentialJacket and tie ▤AE, DC, MC, V ☉Closed mid-Dec.–end Jan. and Tues. and Wed.

★ **$–$$** ✕▦ **Grand St-Michel.** The village of Chambord is as tiny as its château is massive. Its leading landmark is this historic hotel, a revamped hunting lodge set across the lawn from the château. Guest rooms once boasted fabled views of the palace but towering oak trees now block the view from all but two. No matter—this is a most enjoyable hotel, with a cozy lobby, solidly bourgeois guest rooms, and a 19th-century-flavored restaurant. Adorned with mounted deer heads, majolica serving platters, and thick curtains, this room is straight out of a Flaubert novel. The fare is local, hearty (including deer pâté, pumpkin soup, and game

Parisian magic: *l'heure bleue* (twilight) arrives in the Latin Quarter.

Masterpieces Theater: Paris is a pageant of magnificent art, whether you visit the modern Centre Beaubourg (top left), medieval Notre Dame (top right), or the *Mona Lisa* at the Louvre (bottom).

Make time stand still at Sleeping Beauty's Château de Ussé (top) or at Louis XIV's Versailles (bottom).

Tipple your way through Beaune (top), the heart of Burgundy's wine country, then paint yourself into Monet's favorite corner at his lily-pond garden in Giverny (bottom).

Lift your spirits at Mont-St-Michel (top) or indulge more earthly pleasures at one of Lyon's famous *bouchon* taverns (bottom).

The red roofs and cliffs of Roussillon (top) evoke the sun of France's south while greener pastures beckon along Alsace's famous Wine Road (bottom).

Step into the pages of a storybook in golden-stoned Sarlat-la-Caneda, the hub of the Dordogne region, one of France's hottest destinations.

Escape the madding crowds along Provence's Lavender Route (top), then go celeb-spotting at a harbor café in sizzling St-Tropez (bottom) for a change of pace.

in fall), attractively priced (especially the €21 menu), and there's a delightfully leafy terrace café facing the château. ⊠*Pl. St-Louis, 41250* ☎*02–54–20–31–31* 🖷*02–54–20–36–40* ⊕*www.saintmichel-chambord.com* ⏍*40 rooms* ♿*In-room: no a/c. In-hotel: restaurant, tennis court, some pets allowed (fee), no elevator* ☐*MC, V* ⊘*Closed mid-Nov.–mid-Dec.* ⭗|*BP.*

> **SWEET DREAMS**
>
> The Château de Colliers has a vast river terrace over a magnificently stretch of the Loire—there's nothing like drifting off to sleep with the burbling sound of the water as your lullaby.

$$
Fodor'sChoice
★
⚃ **Château de Colliers.** Keep Chenonceau. You can have Chambord. For a few lucky travelers, the most unforgettable château in the Loire proves to be this tiny, overlooked treasure. Other château-hotels may have pomp but this has something more precious—*authenticité*. The home of Christian and Marie-France de Gélis (both of whom are charming and speak English), it was sold to their family in 1779 by the Marquis de Vaudreuil, first French governor of Louisiana. At the end of a long allée, this "pavillon Mansart" embraces you in a semicircular layout (the *collier*, or necklace). Ten family descendants study you from gilded Charles-Dix frames in the main salon, a confectionery vision of white Rococo moldings, glittering chandelier, and furniture that Madame Bovary would have loved. The breakfast room is covered with quaint 16th-century Italian frescoes and each guest room is a bouquet of antiques and comfy furniture. Unfortunately, Monsieur and Madame de Gélis don't hold down the fort year-round any longer. While their housekeepers are friendly, they don't provide that distinctive family feeling. ⊠*Rue Nationale, Muides-sur-Loire, 8 km (4 mi) northwest of Chambord; 17 km (10 mi) southwest of Blois, 41500* ☎*02–54–87–50–75* 🖷*02–54–87–03–64* ⏎*chcolliers@aol.com* ⏍*4 rooms, 1 suite* ♿*In-room: no a/c, no TV. In-hotel: pool, no elevator* ☐*MC, V* ⭗|*BP.*

THE OUTDOORS
Rent a horse from the former stables, **Les Écuries du Maréchal de Saxe** (⊠*On grounds of Château de Chambord* ☎*02–54–20–31–01*), and ride through the vast national park surrounding the château. From April through October you can hire a rowboat or join a boat tour to explore the château moat and the **Grand Canal** (☎*02–54–33–37–54 for details*) linking it to the River Cosson.

ORLÉANS

115 km (23 mi) northeast of Chambord, 112 km (70 mi) northeast of Tours, 125 km (78 mi) south of Paris.

GETTING HERE
Trains from Paris (Gare d'Austerlitz) leave for Orléans every hour or so; the 85-mi trip (€17) takes between 1 hour, 5 minutes and 1 hour, 25 minutes with a change in suburban Les Aubrais sometimes necessary. Trains run every couple of hours from Orléans to Tours (50 mins,

€15) via Blois (30 mins, €9.50). Three trains daily continue to Angers (1 hr, 50 mins, €27).

EXPLORING

Orléans once had the biggest inferiority complex this side of Newark, New Jersey. The city paled pitifully in comparison with other cities of central France, so the townsfolk clung to the city's finest moment—the coming of *la pucelle d'Orléans* (the Maid of Orleans), Joan of Arc, in 1429 to liberate the city from the English during the Hundred Years' War. There's little left from Joan's time, but the city is festooned with everything from her equestrian monument to a Jeanne d'Arc Dry Cleaners. Today, however, Orléans is a thriving commercial city and wonderfully sensitive urban renewal has added enormous charm, especially to the medieval streets between the Loire and the cathedral.

The story of the Hundred Years' War, Joan of Arc, and the Siege of Orléans is widely known. In 1429 France had hit rock bottom. The English and their Burgundian allies were carving up the kingdom. Besieged by the English, Orléans was one of the last towns about to yield, when a young Lorraine peasant girl, Joan of Arc, arrived to rally the troops and save the kingdom. During the Wars of Religion (1562–98), much of the cathedral was destroyed. A century ago ham-fisted town planners razed many of the city's fine old buildings. Both German and Allied bombs helped finish the job during World War II.

⓯ The **Cathédrale Ste-Croix** is a riot of pinnacles and gargoyles, both Gothic and pseudo-Gothic, embellished with 18th-century wedding-cake towers. After most of the cathedral was destroyed in the 16th century during the Wars of Religion, Henry IV and his successors rebuilt it. Novelist Marcel Proust (1871–1922) called it France's ugliest church, but most find it impressive. Inside are vast quantities of stained glass and 18th-century wood carvings, plus the modern **Chapelle de Jeanne d'Arc** (Joan of Arc Chapel), with plaques in memory of British and American war dead. ⊠*Pl. Ste-Croix* ☉*Daily 9–noon and 2–6.*

⓰ Just across the square from the cathedral is the **Hôtel Groslot,** a
Fodor'sChoice Renaissance-era extravaganza (1549–55) bristling with caryatids, strap
★ work, and Flemish columns. Inside are regal salons redolent of the city's history (this used to be the Town Hall), all done in the most sumptuous 19th-century Gothic Troubadour style and perhaps haunted by King François II (who died here in 1560 by the side of his bride, Mary Queen of Scots). ⊠*Pl. de l'Etape* ☎*02–38–24–05–05* ☞*€4* ☉*Daily 9–6.*

⓱ The modern **Musée des Beaux-Arts** *(Fine Arts Museum)* is across from the cathedral. Take the elevator to the top of the five-story building; then make your way down to see works by such artists as Tintoretto, Velázquez, Watteau, Boucher, Rodin, and Gauguin. The museum's richest collection is its 17th-century French paintings. ⊠*1 rue Fernand-Rabier* ☎*02–38–79–21–55* ☞*€3, joint ticket with History Museum* ☉*Tues.–Sat. 9:30–12:15 and 1:30–5:45, Sun. 2–6:30.*

⓲ The **Musée Historique** *(History Museum)* is housed in the **Hôtel Cabu,** a Renaissance mansion restored after World War II. It contains works of

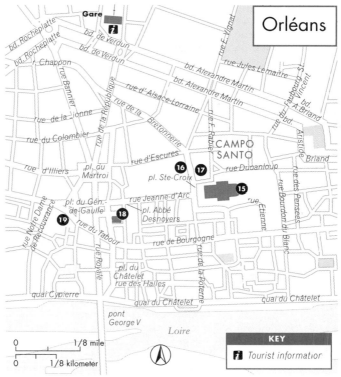

both "fine" and "popular" art connected with the town's past, including a remarkable collection of pagan bronzes of animals and dancers. These bronzes were hidden from zealous Christian missionaries in the 4th century and discovered in a sandpit near St-Benoît in 1861. ⊠*Sq. de l'Abbé-Desnoyers* ☎*02–38–79–25–60* ⊠*€3, joint ticket with Arts Museum* ⊙*July and Aug., Tues.–Sun. 9:30–12:15 and 1:30–5:45; May, June, and Sept. Tues.–Sat. 1:30–5:45 and Sun. 2–6:30; Oct.–Apr., Wed. 1:30–5:45 and Sun. 2–6:30.*

❶⑨ During the 10-day Siege of Orléans in 1429, 17-year-old Joan of Arc stayed on the site of the **Maison de Jeanne d'Arc** *(Joan of Arc House).* This faithful reconstruction of the house she knew contains exhibits about her life and costumes and weapons of her time. Several dioramas modeled by Lucien Harmey recount the main episodes in her life, from the audience at Chinon to the coronation at Reims, her capture at Compiègne, and her burning at the stake at Rouen. ⊠*3 pl. du Général-de-Gaulle* ☎*02–38–52–99–89* ⊕*www.jeannedarc.com. fr* ⊠*€2* ⊙*May–Oct., Tues.–Sun. 10–noon and 1:30–6; Nov.–Apr., Tues.–Sun. 1:30–6.*

WHERE TO STAY & EAT

★ $$–$$$$ ✗ **Les Antiquaires.** The flamboyant opulence of this cozy, wood-beamed restaurant close to the river, with its red walls, cane-backed chairs, and brass chandeliers, is a perfect setting for Philippe Bardau's colorfully presented dishes. Some have a Mediterranean flavor, like his mullet with eggplant or sea bass with artichokes and fennel. Richer fare includes pigeon with truffle risotto, fillet of beef with truffled gnocchi, and foie gras with artichoke mousseline. For dessert, try the red berries with blackberry milk shake. ✉ *2–4 rue au Lin* ☎ *02–38–53–63–48* ⊕ *www.restaurantlesantiquaires.com* ▭ *AE, MC, V* ✆ *Closed Mon. No dinner Sun.*

★ $$$–$$$$ ✗⌨ **Château de La Verrerie.** While set outside Aubigny-sur-Nère—some 90 km (55 mi) south of Orléans—this fabled hotel is well worth the detour. Set in the Forêt d'Ivoy next to its own mirror-lake, the turreted fairy-tale landmark dates from the 15th century and was once owned by royal Stuarts; it is now a famously elegant retreat run by Comte Béraud and Comtesse Florence de Vogüé, whose ancestors acquired the place in 1842. Guest rooms are spacious (six have twin beds, six are doubles) with high ceilings, family heirlooms, and sweeping views of the estate. A half-timber 17th-century cottage on the estate has been transformed into the Maison d'Hélène restaurant, an excellent spot for light lunches and sumptuous dinners (closed Tuesday and Wednesday). Don't forget to visit the château's delightful Renaissance chapel, with frescoes dating from 1525—nor, for that matter, the historic Franco-Scottish sites of Aubigny itself. ✉ *11 km (7 mi) southeast of Aubigny, 18700 Oizon* ☎ *02–48–81–51–60 château, 02–48–58–24–27 restaurant* ☎ *02–48–58–21–25* ⊕ *www.chateaux-france.com/verrerie* ⇨ *11 rooms, 1 suite* ⚿ *In-room: no a/c, no TV. In-hotel: restaurant, tennis court, some pets allowed (fee)* ▭ *MC, V* ✆ *Closed mid-Dec.–late Jan.* ⍓ *BP.*

$$ ✗⌨ **Le Rivage.** This small, white-walled hotel makes a pleasant base, though can be a little hard to find—take the N20 south from Orléans to Olivet, then turn right into Avenue de Verdn and continue parallel to the River Loiret for a mile or so. Each of the compact rooms has a little balcony with a view of the tree-lined Loiret River; the bathrooms are tiny. But this place is best known for its excellent restaurant (no lunch Saturday; no dinner Sunday, November–April), which has a wonderful terrace with lovely views of the Loiret River. The stylish menu changes with the season—if you're lucky, chef François Tassin's memorable lobster salad with mango or glazed green-apple soufflé with apple marmalade will be on tap. ✉ *635 rue de la Reine-Blanche, 5 km (3 mi) south of Orléans, 45160 Olivet* ☎ *02–38–66–02–93* ☎ *02–38–56–31–11* ⇨ *17 rooms* ⚿ *In-hotel: restaurant, bar, tennis court, some pets allowed (fee), no elevator* ▭ *AE, DC, MC, V* ✆ *Closed late Dec.–mid-Jan.* ⍓ *MAP.*

NIGHTLIFE & THE ARTS

The two-day **Fêtes de Jeanne d'Arc** *(Joan of Arc Festival)*, on May 7 and 8, celebrates the heroic Maid of Orléans with a parade and religious procession.

BEAUGENCY

20 *32 km (17 mi) west of Orléans via N152, 24 km (15 mi) northeast of Chambord via D112 and D951.*

A clutch of historic towers and buildings around a 14th-century bridge over the Loire lends Beaugency its charm. The buildings in this town on the north bank of the river include the massive 11th-century **donjon** (keep), the Romanesque church of **Notre-Dame**, and the **Tour du Diable** (Devil's Tower), overlooking the river.

The **Château Dunois** contains a regional museum with traditional costumes and peasant furniture. ✉ *2 pl. Dunois* ☎ *02–38–44–55–23* ⊕ *www.beaugency.fr* ☉ *Closed for renovation at this writing.*

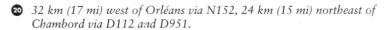

3

BLOIS

21 *27 km (17 mi) southwest of Beaugency via N152, 54 km (34 mi) southwest of Orléans, 58 km (36 mi) northeast of Tours.*

GETTING HERE

Trains from Paris (Gare d'Austerlitz) leave for Blois every 1 or 2 hours; the 115-mi trip (€23) takes between 1 hour, 35 minutes and 1 hour, 55 minutes, according to service. There are trains every 2 hours or so from Blois to Tours (30–40 mins, €10) and Orléans (30–50 mins, €9.50).

EXPLORING

Perched on a steep hillside overlooking the Loire, site of one of France's most historic châteaux, and birthplace of those delicious Poulain chocolates and gâteaux (check out the bakeries along Rue Denis-Papin and tour the nearby Poulain factory), the bustling big town of Blois is a convenient base, well served by train and highway. A signposted route leads you on a walking tour of the **Vieille Ville** (Old Town)—a romantic honeycomb of twisting alleys, cobblestone streets, and half-timber houses—but it's best explored with the help of a map available from the tourist office. The historic highlight is Place St-Louis, where you can find the Maison des Acrobats (note the timbers carved with *jongleurs,* or jugglers), Cathédrale St-Louis, and Hôtel de Villebresme, but unexpected Renaissance-era galleries and staircases also lurk in tucked-away courtyards, such as the one in the Hôtel d'Alluye, built by Florimond Robertet, finance minister to three kings and the last patron to commission a painting from Leonardo da Vinci. The best view of the town, with its château and numerous church spires rising sharply above the river, can be had from across the Loire.

The massive **Château de Blois** spans several architectural periods and is among the valley's finest. Your ticket entitles you to a guided tour—given in English when there are enough visitors who don't understand French—but you're more than welcome to roam around without a guide if you visit between mid-March and August. Before you enter, stand in the courtyard to admire examples of four centuries of architecture. On one side stand the 13th-century hall and tower, the latter offering a stunning view of the town and countryside. The Renaissance begins to flower in the Louis XII wing (built between 1498 and 1503), through which you enter, and comes to full bloom in the François I wing (1515–24). The masterpiece here is the openwork spiral staircase, painstakingly restored. The fourth side consists of the Classical Gaston d'Orléans wing (1635–38). Upstairs in the François I wing is a series of enormous rooms with tremendous fireplaces decorated with the gilded porcupine, emblem of Louis XII, the ermine of Anne of Brittany, and, of course, François I's salamander, breathing fire and surrounded by flickering flames. Many rooms have intricate ceilings and carved, gilt paneling; there's even a sad little picture of Mary, Queen of Scots. In the council room the Duke of Guise was murdered by order of Henri III in 1588. In the **Musée des Beaux-Arts** (Fine Arts Museum), in the Louis XII wing, you can find royal portraits, including Rubens's puffy portrayal of Maria de' Medici as France Personified. Every evening mid-April through mid-September, **son-et-lumière** shows are staged (in English on Wednesday). Call 02–54–90–33–33 for details; tickets cost €7. ☎02–54–90–33–33 ⊠€7 ⊙Apr.–Sept., daily 9–6:30; Oct.–Mar., daily 9–12:30 and 1:30–5:30.

WHERE TO STAY & EAT

★ $$$–$$$$ ✕ **Au Rendez-Vous des Pêcheurs.** This friendly restaurant in an old grocery near the Loire has simple decor but offers excellent value for its creative cooking. Chef Christophe Cosme studied under Burgundy's late Bernard Loiseau and his inventive dishes range from fish and seafood specialties (try the crayfish-and-parsley flan) to succulent baby pigeon on a bed of cabbage. ⊠27 rue du Foix ☎02–54–74–67–48 ⊕www.rendezvousdespecheurs.com ⊰Reservations essential ⊟AE, MC, V ⊙Closed Sun., Aug., and 2 wks Jan. No lunch Mon.

$$–$$$ ✕ **L'Espérance.** In a bucolic setting overlooking the Loire, chef Raphaël Guillot serves up inventive cuisine, like fried mangoes with lavender and five different kinds of scallop dishes. ⊠189 quai Ulysse-Besnard ☎02–54–78–09–01 ⊟AE, MC, V ⊙Closed Mon. and part of Aug. No dinner Sun.

$$ ✕▣ **Le Médicis.** Rooms at this smart little hotel 1 km (½ mi) from the château de Blois are comfortable, air-conditioned, and soundproof; all share a joyous color scheme but are individually decorated. The restaurant alone—done Renaissance-style with a coffered ceiling—makes a stay here worthwhile. Chef-owner Damien Garanger turns his innovative classic dishes into a presentation—coquilles St-Jacques (scallops) with bitter roquette lettuce, roast pigeon, and thin slices of roast hare with a black-currant sauce. For dessert, try the raspberry sorbet with brioche and chocolate sauce. The staff is cheerful and there are 250 wines to choose from (the restaurant does not serve dinner Sunday October–March). ⊠2 allée François-Ier, 41000 ☎02–54–43–94–04 ⊠02–54–42–04–05 ⊕www.le-medicis.com ⇥12 rooms ⌖In-room: refrigerator. In-hotel: restaurant, no elevator ⊟AE, DC, MC, V ⊙Closed Jan. ⫶⧉MAP.

ROCHECORBON

㉒ *5 km (3 mi) east of Tours on north bank of the Loire.*

One of the poshest villages in the Loire, this is a favored forgetaway for Parisians and vacationers. Spread out along the Loire-bank N152 road, with a tiny center set with a church and fine restaurants, Rochecorbon is overshadowed by its immense cliff studded with curious troglodyte dwellings—caves-cum-cottages sculpted out of tufa, that milky-white porous stone which lines the Loire Valley (and was used to build so many great châteaux). Unfortunately, the town's Manoir des Basses-Rivières—an exquisite, 18th-century rock-face manor—is in the throes of a lengthy renovation.

★ Rochecorbon is the only place from which you can actually take a boat-ride excursion out on the Loire. The hour-long **Bateau-Promenade** glides you along a magnificently tranquil stretch of the river to Vouvray and back. Although the commentary on the boat is in French, the sights alone—riverside caves, deserted towers, distant châteaux (like Moncontour, made famous by Balzac)—make for a most enjoyable outing. ⊠*56 quai de la Loire* ☎*02–47–52–68–88* ☜*€9* ⊙*July and Aug., daily 3 and 5* PM*; Apr.–June, Sept., and Oct., daily by reservation.*

Find the little town center midway along the Quai de la Loire embankment by taking the road leading into the highlands of "upper" Rochecorbon. Past the elegant L'Oubliette restaurant and an attractive church (elsewhere in town is the Chapelle St-Georges, with Romanesque frescoes), the road gently mounts the tufa cliff to arrive at a vast plateau studded with Vouvray vineyards. The one attraction hereabouts is found two-thirds up along the route—the **Caves Rupestres,** an abandoned 600-year-old quarry now carved, in a folkloric-modern manner, with 34 wall bas-reliefs detailing the legends of wine in the region, which you can admire with a glass of the grape in your hand. ⊠*Rue Vaufoynard* ☜*€5.50* ⊙*Apr., weekends 2–6; May, June, Sept., and Oct., daily 2–6; July and Aug., daily 10:30–7.*

WHERE TO STAY & EAT

★ $$$–$$$$ ✕⌂ **Les Hautes Roches.** *Extraordinaire* is the word for some of the dozen luxe-troglodyte rooms at this famous hotel, which stud a towering cliff-face with their elegant sash windows, gas-lantern lamps, and finished marble steps. Don't expect furnishings à la Fred Flintstone: half the guest-room walls are Ice Age, but stylish fabrics, Louis Treize seating, and carved fireplaces are the main allurements. Some prefer rooms in the regular house—no cave-dwelling drama, but exquisitely comfortable and air-conditioned. The restaurant (closed Monday, no lunch Wednesday, no dinner Sunday) has an extremely staid decor, so most everyone repairs to the enchanting terrace to feast on a panoply of foie gras, fish and duck dishes, and architectonic desserts—one of the best kitchens in the Loire (don't forget to order a selection from the gigantic cheese tray). To top it all off, a sapphire pool tempts all during the Loire's *grandes chaleurs (heat spells).* ⊠*86 quai de la Loire, 37210 Rochecorbon* ☎*02–47–52–88–88* 🖷*02–47–52–81–30* ⊕*www.leshautesroches. com* ➭*15 rooms* &*In-room: refrigerator, no a/c (some). In-hotel: res-*

taurant, pool, some pets allowed (fee) ⊟AE, DC, MC, V ⊘Closed mid-Jan.–mid-Mar. ⦿*MAP.*

THE STORYBOOK LOIRE: VILLANDRY TO LANGEAIS

To the west of Tours, breathtaking châteaux dot the Indre Valley between the regional capital and the historic town of Chinon on the River Vienne. This is the most glamorous part of the Val de Loire and the beauty pageant begins with the fabled gardens of the Château de Villandry. Your journey then continues on to the fairytale châteaux of Azay-le-Rideaux, Ussé, and Montreuil-Bellay. Farther on, no one will want to miss the towns of Chinon, Saumur, Angers, Fontevraud, and Langeais, which contain sights that remain the quintessence of romantic medievalism. Along the way, you can savor such storybook delights as Saché—perhaps the Loire's prettiest town—and the Château de Réaux, with its picture-perfect pepper-pot towers, moat, and swans.

VILLANDRY

❷❸ *18 km (11 mi) west of Tours via D7, 48 km (30 mi) northwest of Loches.*

FodorśChoice ★ Green-thumbers get weak in the knees at the mere mention of the **Château de Villandry,** a grand estate near the Cher River, thanks to its painstakingly relaid 16th-century **gardens,** now the finest example of Renaissance garden design in France. These were originally planted in 1906 by Dr. Joachim Carvallo and Anne Coleman, his American wife, whose passion resulted in two terraces planted in styles that combine the French monastic garden with Italianate models depicted in historic Du Cerceau etchings. Seen from Villandry's cliff-side walkway, the garden terraces look like flowered chessboards blown up to the nth power—a breathtaking sight.

Beyond the water garden and an ornamental garden depicting symbols of chivalric love is the famous *potager,* or vegetable garden, which stretches on for bed after bed—the pumpkins here are *les pièces de résistance.* Flower lovers will rejoice in the main *jardin à la française* (French-style garden): framed by a canal, it's a vast carpet of rare and colorful blooms planted *en broderie* ("like embroidery"), set into patterns by box hedges and paths. The aromatic and medicinal garden, its plots neatly labeled in three languages, is especially appealing. Below an avenue of 1,500 precisely pruned lime trees lies an ornamental lake that is home to two swans: not a ripple is out of place. The château interior was restored in the mid-19th century; of particular note are the painted and gilt Moorish ceiling from Toledo and the collection of Spanish pictures. Note that the quietest time to visit is usually during the two-hour French lunch break, while the most photogenic is during the **Nuits des Mille Feux** (Nights of a Thousand Lights, usually held in early July), when paths and pergolas are illuminated with myriad lanterns and a dance troupe offers a tableau vivant. There are also a Baroque music festival in late August and a gardening weekend held in early September. There is no train station at Villandry, so train to nearby Savonnières and taxi the 4-km (2½-mi) distance. ☎02–47–50–02–09 ⊕*www.chateauvillandry.com* ✉*Château and gardens €8, gardens only €5.50* ⊙*Château Apr.–Oct., daily 9–6; mid-Feb., Mar., and 1st half Nov., daily 9–5. Gardens Apr.–Sept., daily 9–7; Oct.–mid-Nov., daily 9–5.*

WHERE TO STAY & EAT

¢–$ ✕🏨 **Le Cheval Rouge.** A half-minute walk from the great château of Villandry, this is a fine, comfortable, and casual hotel-restaurant. Since it's set on a major traffic route, book one of the quieter rooms at the back. The restaurant is popular with locals, who come for the surprisingly good and classic food and wine; menus start at €18. Best bets are the terrine of foie gras, the calf sweetbreads, and the wood-fired-grill fare. ✉*9 rue Principale, 37510* ☎*02–47–50–02–07* 🖷*02–47–50–08–77* ⊕*www.lecheval-rouge.com* ⇆*41 rooms* ♿*In-room: no TV. In-hotel: restaurant, some pets allowed (fee), no elevator* ▭*MC, V* ⊙*Closed Jan.* ⦿❘*BP.*

AZAY-LE-RIDEAU

🔵 *11 km (7 mi) south of Villandry via D39, 27 km (17 mi) southwest of Tours.*

A largish town surrounding a sylvan dell on the banks of the River Indre, pleasant Azay-le-Rideau (located on the main train line between Tours and Chinon) is famed for its white-walled Renaissance pleasure palace, called "a faceted diamond set in the Indre Valley" by Honoré de Balzac.

★ The 16th-century **Château d'Azay-le-Rideau** was created as a literal fairy-tale castle. When it was constructed in the Renaissance era, the nouveau-riche treasurer Gilles Berthelot decided he wanted to add tall corner turrets, moat, and machicolations to conjure up the distant seigneurial past when knighthood was in flower and two families, the Azays and the Ridels, ruled this terrain. It was never a serious fortress—it certainly offered no protection to its builder when a financial scandal forced him to flee France shortly after the château's completion in 1529. For centuries the château passed from one private owner to another until it was finally bought by the State in 1905. Though the interior contains an interesting blend of furniture and artwork (one room is an homage to the Marquis de Biencourt who, in the early 20th century, led the way in renovating château interiors in sumptuous fashion—sadly, many of

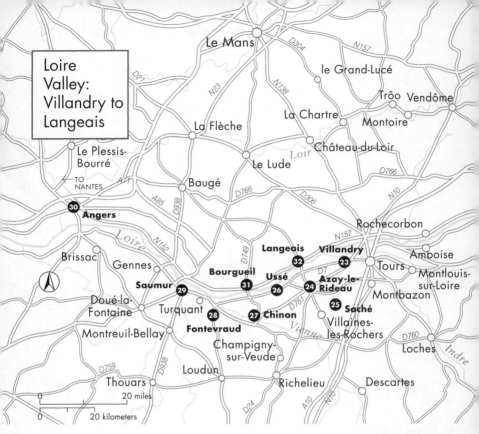

Loire
Valley:
Villandry to
Langeais

Le Mans

le Grand-Lucé

Trôo   Vendôme

Montoire

La Chartre

La Flèche

Château-du-Loir

Le Plessis-
Bourré

TO
NANTES

Baugé

Le Lude

Loir

Angers

Rochecorbon

Brissac   Gennes

Langeais   Villandry

Amboise

Bourgueil

Tours   Montlouis-
sur-Loire

Saumur

Ussé   Azay-le-
Rideau

Montbazon

Doué-la-
Fontaine

Turquant

Chinon   Saché

Montreuil-Bellay

Fontevraud

Villaines-
les-Rochers

Loches

Champigny-
sur-Veude

Loudun

Richelieu

Descartes

Thouars

0   20 miles

0   20 kilometers

his elegant furnishings were later sold), you may wish to spend most of your time exploring the enchanting gardens, complete with a moatlike lake. Innovative **son-et-lumière** shows are held on the grounds from 10:30 PM, May through September. ☎02–47–45–42–04 ⊕*www.cha-teaux-france.com/azaylerideau* ≣€7.50 ♘*Apr.–Sept., daily 9:30–6; Oct.–Mar., daily 10–12:30 and 2–5:30.*

WHERE TO STAY & EAT

$-$$$ ✕⌂ **Le Grand Monarque.** Grand and elegant, this famous town landmark is about a three-minute walk from Azay's château. Some complain that its fame brings a captive audience, which can result in offhand service. However, rooms, which vary in size and style, have character; most are simple, with an antique or two, and many have exposed beams. Public salons are luxe and alluring, while the restaurant (which, from mid-October to December and mid-February to late March, is closed Monday, and does not serve dinner Sunday) serves high-style food and boasts one of the region's most extensive wine lists, with more than 700 choices. There's also a bistro for a quicker, cheaper lunch, with a menu at €15. Weekend stays must include dinner. ⊠*3 pl. de la République, 37190* ☎*02–47–45–40–08* 🖷*02–47–45–46–25* ⊕*www.legrandmonarque. com* ⇆*24 rooms* ⌂*In-room: no a/c, dial-up. In-hotel: restaurant, bar,* some pets allowed (fee), no elevator $=$AE, MC, V ⊘Closed Dec.–mid-Feb. ᵀ⊙⎮MAP.

★ ¢–$ 🏠 **Biencourt.** Charmingly set on the pedestrian street that leads to Azay's château gates, this red-shuttered town house hides an authentic, 19th-century schoolhouse within a delightful courtyard-garden, now fitted out with cozily traditional guest rooms (and the stray blackboard and school desk). No matter if you can't land one of the conversation pieces in "La Classe"—the other chambers are fine enough, decorated in pastels as warm as the delightfully helpful owners, the Mariotons. The village has quite a few restaurant selections—if you just don't want to stroll around and pick, ask Cédric and Emmanuelle about the best. ⊠7 rue Balzac, 37190 🕾02–47–45–20–75 🖷02–47–45–91–73 ⊕www.hotelbiencourt.com ⋐17 rooms, 12 with bath ♿In-room: no a/c (some), no TV. In-hotel: no elevator $=$MC, V ⊘Closed mid-Nov.–late Feb.

A GARDEN NAMED L'ÉLÉGANCE

Set 4 km (2½ mi) north of Azay-le-Rideau and tended by Madame Béatrice de Andia—one of the grandes dames of the Loire—and her staff are the Jardins de la Chatonnière, a 15-acre rose and lily garden that will make most emerald-green with envy. Framing the private, turreted Renaissance château are six spectacular visions, with each garden devoted to a theme, including L'Élégance and L'Abondance, in the extraordinary shape of a gigantic leaf. (⊠Rte. D57, direction Lignières-Langeais 🕾02–47–45–40–29 ⊕www.lachatonniere.com ⊠€6 ⊘Mid-Mar.–mid-Nov., daily 10–7.)

THE OUTDOORS

Rent bikes from **Leprovost** (⊠13 rue Carnot 🕾02–47–45–40–94) to ride along the Indre; the area around Azay-le-Rideau is among the most tranquil and scenic in Touraine.

SACHÉ

㉕
Fodor'sChoice
★

7 km (4½ mi) east of Azay-le-Rideau via D17.

A crook in the road, a Gothic church, the centuries-old Auberge du XIIᵉ Siècle, an Alexander Calder stabile (the great American sculptor created a modern atelier nearby), and the country retreat of novelist Honoré de Balzac (1799–1850)—these few but choice elements all add up to Saché, one of the prettiest (and most undiscovered) nooks in the Val de Loire. If you're heading in to the town from the east, you're first welcomed by the **Pont-de-Ruan**—a dream-sequence of a flower-bedecked bridge, water mill, and lake that is so picturesque it will practically click your camera for you.

Two kilometers (1 mi) farther, you hit the center of Saché and the **Château de Saché**, which contains the **Musée Balzac**. If you've never read any of Balzac's "Comédie Humaine," you might find little of interest here; but if you have, and do, you can return to such novels as *Cousin Bette* and *Eugénie Grandet* with fresh enthusiasm and understanding.

Much of the landscape around here, and some of the people back then, found immortality by being fictionalized in many a Balzac novel. The present château, built between the 16th and the 18th century, is more of a comfortable country house than a fortress. Born in nearby Tours, Balzac came here—to stay with his friends, the Margonnes—during the 1830s, both to write such works as *Le Père Goriot* and to escape his creditors. The château houses substantial exhibits, ranging from photographs to original manuscripts to the coffeepot Balzac used to brew the caffeine that helped to keep him writing up to 16 hours a day. A few period rooms are here and impress with 19th-century charm, including a lavish emerald-green salon and the author's writing room. Be sure to study some of the corrected author proofs on display. Balzac had to pay for corrections and additions beyond a certain limit. Painfully in debt, he made emendations filling all the margins of his proofs, causing dismay to his printers. Their legitimate bills for extra payment meant that some of his books, best-sellers for nearly two centuries, failed to bring him a centime. ☎*02–47–26–86–50* ⊕*www.musee-balzac.fr* ✉*€4.50* ⊘*Apr.–Sept., daily 10–6; Oct.–Mar., Wed.–Mon. 10–12:30 and 2–5.*

WHERE TO EAT

★ **$$$**   ✗ **Auberge du XIIe Siècle.** You half expect Balzac himself to come strolling in the door of this half-timber, delightfully historic auberge, so little has it changed since the 19th century. Still sporting a time-stained painted sign and its original exterior staircase, and nearly opposite the great author's country retreat, this inn retains its centuries-old dining room, now warmed by a fireplace, bouquets, and rich wood tables. Beyond this room is a modern extension—all airy glass and white walls but not exactly what you're looking for in such historic surrounds. Balzac's ample girth attested to his great love of food, and he would no doubt enjoy the nouvelle spins on his classic *géline* chicken favorites served here today, or the *aiguillettes de canard rosées en réduction de Chinon* (slices of duck flavored in Chinon wine). Dessert is excellent, and so is the coffee, a refreshment Balzac drank incessantly (little wonder he created more than 2,000 characters). ✉*1 rue du Château* ☎*02–47–26–88–77* ▤*MC, V* ⊘*Closed 3 wks in Jan., 1 wk in June, 1 wk in Sept., 1 wk in Nov., and Mon. No dinner Sun., no lunch Tues.*

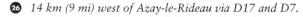

USSÉ

㉖ *14 km (9 mi) west of Azay-le-Rideau via D17 and D7.*

Fodor's Choice   The most beautiful castle in France is first glimpsed as you approach
★   the **Château d'Ussé** and an astonishing array of blue-slate roofs, dormer
♻   windows, delicate towers, and Gothic turrets greets you against the flank of the Forest of Chinon. Literature describes this château, overlooking the banks of the river Indre, as the original *Sleeping Beauty* castle; Charles Perrault—author of this beloved 17th-century tale—spent time here as a guest of the Count of Saumur and legend has it that Ussé inspired him to write the famous story. Though parts of the

THE LOIRE VALLEY THROUGH THE AGES

Marauding Huns laid siege to Orléans in AD 451 , just 44 years after the death of St. Martin, fabled Bishop of Tours. The next invaders were the Vikings, who pillaged their way down to Angers in the 9th century. Then came the English: in 1154—two years after wedding Eleanor of Aquitaine—Henry Plantagenet became King of England and sovereign of almost all western France, the Loire included. In 1189 he died (as Henry II) in Chinon. In 1199 his son, Richard the Lion-Hearted, died there, too; both are buried (alongside Eleanor) in Fontevraud Abbey, founded a century earlier.

But the French were having none of this foreign hegemony. Beefy castles (Langeais, Chinon) sprouted up along the valley. In 1429 Joan of Arc kicked the English out of Orléans.

Her triumph was short-lived but soon the Loire was back in French hands, and a period of peace and prosperity ensued that saw the region become the center of French culture and politics. The Renaissance arrived in the 1490s, when Charles VII hired Italian craftsmen to update his château at Amboise; then Renaissance prince François I lured Leonardo da Vinci to Amboise, where he died in 1519—the year François began building the world's most fanciful château, Chambord.

The next hundred years were the Loire's pleasure-palace golden age. The decline set in with Louis XIV and his obsession with Versailles. Tours served briefly as French capital in 1870 during the Franco-Prussian War, and the region enjoyed an unwelcome spotlight in 1940, when Petain met Hitler in Montoire-sur-Loir. When France freed itself from the Nazi yoke four years later, the Loire was briefly in the frontline, as bombarded Tours and Orléans recall. But, elsewhere, its rural tranquillity emerged untouched. You'll mostly have the impression that time has stopped still.

castle are from the 1400s, most of it was completed two centuries later. By the 17th century, the region was so secure one fortified wing of the castle was demolished to allow for grand vistas over the valley and the castle gardens, newly designed in the style Le Nôtre had made so fashionable at Versailles. Only Disney could have outdone this white-tufa marvel: the château is a flamboyant mix of Gothic and Renaissance styles—romantic and built for fun, not for fighting. Its history supports this playful image: it endured no bloodbaths—no political conquests or conflicts—while a tablet in the chapel indicates that even the French Revolution passed it by. Inside, a tour leads you through several sumptuous period salons, a 19th-century French fashion exhibit, and the Salle de Roi bedchamber built for a visit by King Louis XV (who never arrived—his loss, as the red-silk, canopied four-poster bed here is the stuff of dreams). At the end of the house tour, you can go up the fun spiral staircases to the *chemin de ronde* of the lofty towers; there are pleasant views of the Indre River from the battlements, and you can also find rooms filled with waxwork effigies detailing the fable of Sleeping Beauty herself. Kids will love this.

Before you leave, visit the exquisite Gothic-becomes-Renaissance chapel in the garden, built for Charles d'Espinay and his wife in 1523–35. Note the door decorated with pleasingly sinister skull-and-crossbones carvings. Just a few steps from the chapel are two towering cedars of Lebanon—a gift from the genius-poet of Romanticism, Viscount René de Chateaubriand, to the lady of the house, the Duchess of Duras. When her famous amour died in 1848, she stopped all the clocks in the house—à la Sleeping Beauty—"so as never to

> ### SWEEPING BEAUTY
>
> When the inventor of the fairy tale, Charles Perrault, happened on the Château de Ussé one stormy night, he asked for permission to stay over (back then, châteaux were often used as "hotels" by travelers). He was so swept away by the castle's grandeur—it sprawls along a lengthy river embankment—he was inspired to write *Sleeping Beauty* and *Puss in Boots*.

hear struck the hours you will not come again." The castle then was inherited by her relations, the Comte and Comtesse de la Rochejacquelin, one of the most dashing couples of the 19th century. Today, Ussé belongs to their descendant, the Duc de Blacas, who is as soigné as his castle. If you do meet him, proffer thanks, as every night his family floodlights the entire château, a vision that is one of the Loire Valley's dreamiest sights. Regarded as a symbol of *la vieille France*, Ussé can't be topped for fairy-tale splendor, so make this a must-do. ⊠*Rigny-Ussé* 🕾*02–47–95–54–05* 🎫*€12* ⊘*Mid-Feb.–mid-Nov., daily 10–6.*

WHERE TO STAY & EAT

★ ¢–$ ✕🏠 **Le Clos d'Ussé.** Thank heavens for this delightful inn. The best time to see the great Château d'Ussé is in early morning light or illuminated at night, and the easiest way to do that is to overnight in the village of Rigny-Ussé here at the home of the *famille* Duchemin. Eric runs the place, Muriel is in charge of the extremely cozy restaurant, while *grand-mère* offers a warm smile. Not surprisingly, families will adore this place, especially as three of the rooms are custom-built for them (and rather stylish, to boot). Best of all, a one-minute walk from the front door takes you to the castle gates. ⊠*7 rue Principale, 37420 Rigny-Ussé* 🕾🖷*02–47–95–55–47* ➛*8 rooms, 4 with bath* ⚐*In-room: no a/c, no phone. In-hotel: restaurant, bar, some pets allowed (fee), no elevator* ⊟*MC, V* ⊘*Closed Nov.–mid-Feb.*

CHINON

㉗ 13 km (8 mi) southwest of Rigny-Ussé via D7 and D16, 44 km (28 mi)
Fodor's Choice southwest of Tours.
★

GETTING HERE

SNCF trains (50 mins, €8) leave for Chinon from Tours' train station at least three times a day.

EXPLORING

The historic town of Chinon—birthplace of author François Rabelais (1494–1553)—is dominated by the towering ruins of its medieval castle, perched high above the River Vienne. The medieval heart of the town is a storybook warren of narrow, cobbled streets (some are pedestrian-only) lined with half-timber houses; its fairy-tale allure was effectively used to frame Josette Day when she appeared as Beauty in Jean Cocteau's 1949 film *La Belle et la Bête*. The main road of the historic quarter, Rue Haute St-Maurice (a continuation of Rue Voltaire, which begins at the central Place du Général-de-Gaulle) is a virtual open-air museum; other towns may have one or two or three blocks lined with medieval and Renaissance houses, but this street runs, spectacularly, for more than 15 blocks. Although there are some museums in town—the **Musée d'Art et d'Histoire** (Art and History Museum) in a medieval town house on Rue Haute St-Maurice, the **Maison de la Rivière**, devoted to Chinon's maritime trade and set along the embankment, and the **Musée du Vin** (Wine Museum) on Rue Voltaire—the medieval quarter remains the must-do, as a walk here catapults you back to the days of Rabelais. Because both the village and the château are on steep, cobbled slopes, it's a good idea to wear comfortable walking shoes.

The vast **Château de Chinon,** currently undergoing restoration and only partly visitable at this writing, a veritable fortress with walls 400 yards long, dates from the time of Henry II of England, who died here in 1189 and was buried at Fontevraud. Two centuries later the castle witnessed an important historic moment: Joan of Arc's recognition of the disguised Dauphin, later Charles VII; the castle was also one of the domiciles of Henri II and his warring wife, Eleanor of Aquitaine. At Chinon everything is open to the elements, except the **Logis Royal** (Royal Chambers). Here there's a small museum containing a model of the castle when it was intact, various old tapestries, and precious stones. For a fine view of the region, climb the **Tour Coudray** (Coudray Tower), where in 1307 leading members of the crusading Knights Templar were imprisoned before being taken to Paris, tried, and burned at the stake. The **Tour de l'Horloge** (Clock Tower), whose bell has sounded the hours since 1399, contains the **Musée Jeanne d'Arc** (Joan of Arc Museum). There are sensational views from the ramparts over Chinon, the Vienne Valley, and, toward the back of the castle, the famous vineyard called Le Clos de l'Echo. ☎02–47–93–13–45 ✆€3 ☉Apr.–Sept., daily 9–7; Oct.–Mar., daily 9:30–5.

"DRINK ALWAYS AND NEVER DIE"

Participants in Chinon's medieval festival, the Marché à l'Ancienne (⊕ *www.chinon.com*), are fond of quoting the presiding muse of the city, Renaissance writer François Rabelais. Held on the third Saturday of August, this free wine-tasting extravaganza has stalls, displays, and costumed locals recalling rural life of a hundred years ago. For details, contact the tourist office.

WHERE TO STAY & EAT

$$$–$$$$ ✕ **Au Plaisir Gourmand.** Jean-Claude Rigollet's tufa-stone 18th-century restaurant by the Vienne River is the finest in Chinon. Specialties served in the Renaissance-style dining room include crayfish salad, snails in garlic, jellied rabbit, *sandre* (pike-perch) with butter sauce, and braised oxtail in red wine. ⊠*2 rue Parmentier* ☎*02–47–93–20–48* ▭*AE, MC, V* ⊘*Closed Mon. and mid-Feb.–mid-Mar. No dinner Sun., no lunch Tues.*

$$ ✕▦ **France.** Right on Chinon's most charming square—a picture post-card come to life with splashing fountain and a bevy of cafés—this sweetly agreeable Best Western hotel, two blocks from the medieval quarter, has been an hotel since 1577. Many regional notables lived here before the Revolution, when it became the Hôtel Lion d'Or, the first hostelry in the region. The wood-beamed guest rooms are comfortable and cozy; some overlook two tiny, flowerpot-bedecked court-yards, while others take in views that include Chinon's castle ruins. The restaurant, Au Chapeau Rouge (closed Monday and no dinner Sunday), serves regional cuisine, and there's also a brasserie for cheaper snacks. ⊠*47 pl. du Général-de-Gaulle, 37500* ☎*02–47–93–33–91* 🖷*02–47–98–37–03* ⊕*www.hotel-france-chinon.federal-hotel.com* ⟿*30 rooms* ⚹*In-room: no a/c (some). In-hotel: restaurant* ▭*AE, DC, MC, V* ⊘*Closed Nov. and mid-Feb.–mid-Mar.* ⦿|*MAP.*

FONTEVRAUD-L'ABBAYE

㉘ *20 km (12 mi) northwest of Chinon via D751.*

A refreshing break from the worldly grandeur of châteaux, the small vil-lage of Fontevraud is crowned with the largest abbey in France, a mag-nificent complex of Romanesque and Renaissance buildings that were of central importance in the history of both England and France.

Fodor'sChoice ★ Founded in 1101, the **Abbaye Royale de Fontevraud** had separate churches and living quarters for nuns, monks, lepers, "repentant" female sinners, and the sick. Between 1115 and the French Revolution in 1789, a suc-cession of 39 abbesses—among them a granddaughter of William the Conqueror—directed operations. The great 12th-century **Église Abba-tiale** (Abbey Church) contains the tombs of Henry II of England, his wife Eleanor of Aquitaine, and their son, Richard Coeur de Lion (the Lion-Hearted). Though their bones were scattered during the Revolu-tion, their effigies still lie *en couchant* in the middle of the echoey nave. Napoléon turned the abbey church into a prison, and so it remained until 1963, when historical restoration work—still under way—began. The **Salle Capitulaire** (Chapter House), adjacent to the church, with its collection of 16th-century religious wall paintings (prominent abbesses served as models), is unmistakably Renaissance; the paving stones bear the salamander emblem of François I. Next to the long refectory is the famously octagonal **Cuisine** (kitchen), topped by 20 scaly stone chim-neys led by the **Tour d'Evrault**. ⊠*Pl. des Plantagenêts* ☎*02–41–51–71–41* ⊕*www.abbaye-fontevraud.com* ▦*€6.50* ⊘*June–Sept., daily 9–6:30; Oct.–May, daily 10–6.*

After touring the Abbaye Royale, head outside the gates of the complex a block to the north to discover one of the Loire Valley's most time-machine streets, the **Allée Sainte-Catherine.** Bordered by the Fontevraud park, headed by a charming medieval church, and lined with a few scattered houses (which now contain the town tourist office, a gallery that sells medieval illuminated manuscript pages, and the delightful Licorne restaurant), this street still looks like the 14th century aborning.

> ### FAITH, HOPE & CLARITY
>
> With its clean-cut lines, Fontevraud's Abbey Church is a gigantic monument of the French Romanesque, the solid style of simple geometric forms eschewing ornamentation. Home to the tombs of Eleanor of Aquitaine and Richard the Lion-Hearted, the soaring nave was intended to elevate the soul.

WHERE TO STAY & EAT

★ $$$–$$$$ ✕ **La Licorne.** A hanging shop sign adorned with a painted unicorn beckons you to this pretty-as-a-picture town-house restaurant just off Fontevraud's idyllic Allée Sainte-Catherine. Past a flowery garden and table-adorned terrace, tiny salons glow with happy folks feasting on some of the best food in the region: Loire salmon, guinea fowl in Layon wine, and lobster with fava beans should make most diners purr with contentment. ✉*31 rue Robert-d'Arbrissel* ☎*02–41–51–72–49* ✍*Reservations essential* ▭*AE, DC, MC, V* ☉*Closed late Dec.–mid-Jan. and Mon. mid-Sept.–Mar. No dinner Sun. and Wed.*

★ $–$$ ✕▥ **Hostellerie de l'Abbaye Royale.** One of the more unusual hotels in the Loire Valley and set right within the medieval splendor of Fontevraud, this series of outbuildings was once the abbey's lepers' hospice. The entrance gives onto the vast *salle capitulaire* conference room and the cloisters now house a restaurant, Le Cloître (reservations essential), where Eroc Bichon's delicacies, such as swordfish simmered in Saumur-Champigny wine, entice. In a muscular side wing the erstwhile monks' cells have been transformed into small but alluring guest rooms, chic and bright in modern checks and fine wood accents. Staying here lets you explore the abbey grounds when its gates are closed to the public—an exceptional experience. ✉*Abbaye Royale, 49590* ☎*02–41–51–73–16* ▤*02–41–51–75–50* ⊕*www.hotelfp-fontevraud.com* ⬅*52 rooms* ⌂*In-room: no a/c, refrigerator, dial-up. In-hotel: restaurant, no elevator* ▭*AE, MC, V* ☉*Closed mid-Nov.–Mar.* ▯*MAP.*

SAUMUR

★ ㉙ *15 km (9 mi) northwest of Fontevraud via D947, 68 km (43 mi) west of Tours.*

GETTING HERE

To reach Saumur by train from Paris (Gare Montparnasse) requires a change in either Angers (2 hrs, 20 mins, €63) or Tours (3 hrs, €58). Regional trains link Saumur to Tours (40 mins, €10) and Angers (20–30 mins, €7.50) every 2 hours or so.

EXPLORING

You'll find putting up with the famous *snobisme* of the Saumurois well worth it once you get a gander at Saumur's magnificent historic center. Studded with elegant 19th-century town houses and the charming Place St-Pierre, lorded over by the vast 14th-century church of St-Pierre and centerpiece of a warren of streets, cafés, and ice-cream parlors, this *centre historique* is sheer delight. Looming over it all—icon of the town and a vision right out of a fairy tale—is Saumur's mighty turreted castle high above the river. But Saumur is not content to rest on former glories: today, it is one of the larger towns along the Loire and a key transportation hub for Anjou, the province just to the

> **THE VERY RICH HOURS**
>
> Presided over by its magnificent cliff-top castle—which has a starring role in *Les Très Riches Heures du Duc de Berry*, France's most famous illuminated book—Saumur is known as one of the ritziest towns in France. Regional government offices, wealthy wine producers, and hordes of *bon chic, bon genre* shoppers means you can probably enjoy a blast of old-time French attitude (the waiters are even snobbier than the matrons). Little seems to have changed over the centuries: Honoré de Balzac famously wrote up the surly side of the Saumurois in *Eugénie Grandet.*

west of Touraine. Saumur is also known for its riding school and flourishing mushroom industry, which produces 100,000 tons per year. The same cool tunnels in which the mushrooms grow provide an ideal storage place for the local *mousseux* (sparkling wines); many vineyards hereabouts are open to the public for tours.

If you arrive in the evening, the sight of the elegant, floodlighted, white 14th-century **Château de Saumur** takes your breath away. Look familiar? Probably because you've seen it in reproductions from the famous *Très Riches Heures* (Book of Hours) painted for the Duc de Berry in 1416 (now in the Musée Condé at Chantilly). Inside it's bright and cheerful, with a fairy-tale gateway and plentiful potted flowers. Owing to renovation of the castle walls, the two museums based here, the **Musée des Arts Décoratifs** (Decorative Arts Museum) and the **Musée du Cheval** (Equestrian Museum), were still closed for restoration at this writing. Until the museums reopen (hopefully in 2008), visitors will only have access to the garden and terrace. However, for July and August, guided tours of some castle interiors can be arranged, 10:15–4:45. From the cliff-side promenade beyond the carpark there's a thrilling vista of the castle on its bluff against the river backdrop. ⊠ *Esplanade du Château* ☎ *02–41–40–24–40* ⊕ *www.saumur-tourisme.net/chateausaumur.html* ⊡€2 ⊗ *Apr.–Sept., Wed.–Mon. 10–1 and 2–5:30.*

♻ The **Cadre Noir de Saumur** *(Riding School)* is unique in Europe, with its 400 horses, extensive stables, five Olympic-size riding schools, and miles of specially laid tracks. Try for a morning tour, which includes a chance to admire the horses in training. During the **Carrousel de Saumur,** on the last two weekends in July, the horses put on a full gala display for enthusiastic crowds. ⊠ *Rue de l'Abbaye* ☎ *02–41–53–50–60* ⊕ *www.*

cadrenoir.fr ☒*€7.50* ⊙*Guided tours only, Apr.–mid-Oct., Tues.–Fri. 9–6, Sat. 9–12:30, Mon. 2–6.*

Saumur is the heart of one of the finest wine regions in France. To pay a call on some of the vineyards around the city, first stop into the **Maison du Vin** *(House of Wine)*, for the full scoop on hours and directions; also consult the Web site for Loire wines, www.vinsdeloire.com. ✉*Quai Lucien-Gautier* ☎*02–41–38–45–83* ⊙*Easter–mid-Nov., daily 10–5.*

Here are some of the top vineyards of the Saumur region. Note that Loire wine is not a practical buy—except for instant consumption—but if wine-tasting tours of vineyards inspire you, enterprising winemakers will arrange shipments.

For sparkling Saumur wine try **Ackerman** (✉*13 rue Léopold-Palustre, St-Hilaire* ☎*02–41–03–30–20*).

Veuve Amiot (✉*21 rue Jean-Ackerman, St-Hilaire* ☎*02–41–83–14–14*) is a long-established producer of Saumur wines.

You can visit the cavernous premises of **Gratien-Meyer** (✉*Rte. de Montsoreau* ☎*02–41–83–13–32* ☒*€3* ⊙*Daily, 9–noon and 2–6*) on the east side of Saumur, April through September.

Just southeast of Saumur, in Dampierre-sur-Loire, stop in at the **Château de Chaintres** (✉*54 rue de la Croix-de-Chaintre* ☎*02–41–52–90–54*), where Krishna Lester, a husky English eccentric, produces the region's finest red and enjoys expounding on the unexpected links between frogs in the throat, toads in the hole, and malolactic fermentation.

WHERE TO STAY & EAT

$$–$$$ ✕🏨 **Anne d'Anjou.** The spectacular setting at the foot of Saumur castle may appeal to you most about this elegant 18th-century hotel—or maybe the flower-strewn courtyard, or perhaps the views of the Loire from some of the guest rooms (although not the traffic rushing by). The finest retain their original, late-18th- and early-19th-century decoration, and one is even furbished to the designs of Percier and Fontaine, Napoléon's favorite architects. A real plus is the restaurant Les Ménestrels (closed Sunday), found in a lovingly restored 16th-century house up against the castle cliff. The menu here changes regularly under the eye of virtuoso chef Christophe Hosselet, who has a penchant for perch with spring-onion fondue, partridge with walnuts, and wild mushrooms with ham and foie gras. ✉*32 quai Mayaud, 49400* ☎*02–41–67–30–30* 📠*02–41–67–51–00* 🌐*www.hotel-anneanjou.com* *45 rooms* *In-room: refrigerator. In-hotel: public Internet, some pets allowed (fee)* ▭*AE, DC, MC, V* *MAP.*

$–$$$ Fodor's Choice ★ 🏨 **Saint-Pierre.** At the very epicenter of historic Saumur, this gorgeous little jewel is hidden beneath the medieval walls of the church of Saint-Pierre—look for the hotel's storybook entrance on one of the pedestrian *passages* that circle the vast nave. Once inside the 15th- to 17th-century house, you can find a sweet reception area and suave staff to welcome you. Up the Renaissance corkscrew staircase (or modern mini-elevator) you can find the astonishingly refined guest rooms. Designer fabrics, antique *pont* cabinets (forming a "bridge" over bed headboards), elegant wainscoting, Persian rugs, tuffeau fireplaces, and bathrooms replete with Paloma Picasso designs make this a favored home-away-from-home for Saumur's most savvy visitors. The smaller rooms face the church but they also are quieter than those overlooking the road leading up to the castle. There's no restaurant, but steps away is lovely Place St-Pierre, lined with outdoor cafés. ⊠*Rue Haute-Saint-Pierre, 49400* 🕾*02–41–50–33–00* 🖷*02–41–50–38–68* ⊕*www.saintpierre-saumur.com* ⇨*15 rooms* ⅍*In-room: refrigerator, ethernet. In-hotel: some pets allowed (fee)* ▤*AE, DC, MC, V.*

$-$$ 🎟 **Loire.** This hotel wins no prizes for charm or friendly service, but it is clean, spacious, and functional. It's also inconveniently located across the river from the main part of town, though this makes parking easier and affords a stunning view of the château from its restaurant, Les Mariniers (closed Saturday and November through March, no dinner Friday). ⊠*Rue de Vieux-Pont, 49400* 🕾*02–41–67–22–42* 🖷*02–41–67–88–80* ⊕*www.loire-hotel.fr* ⇨*44 rooms* ⅍*In-hotel: restaurant* ▤*AE, DC, MC, V.*

ANGERS

③⓪ *45 km (28 mi) northwest of Saumur, 88 km (55 mi) northeast of Nantes.*

GETTING HERE

TGV trains from Paris (Gare Montparnasse) leave for Angers every hour or so; the 180-mi trip takes 90 minutes (€59). Trains run every two hours or so to Saumur (20–30 mins, €7.50) and Tours (1 hr, €15). Three regional trains daily continue to Blois (1 hr, 20 mins, €21) and Orléans (1 hr, 50 mins, €27).

EXPLORING

The bustling city of Angers, on the banks of the Maine River, just north of the Loire, is famous for its towering castle filled with the extraordinary Apocalypse Tapestry. But it also has a fine Gothic cathedral, a selection of art galleries, and a network of pleasant, traffic-free streets around Place Ste-Croix, with its half-timber houses. The town's principal sights lie within a compact square formed by the three main boulevards and the Maine.

★   The banded black-and-white **Château d'Angers,** built by St. Louis (1228–38), glowers over the town from behind turreted moats, now laid out as gardens and overrun with flowers and deer. As you explore the grounds, note the startling contrast between the thick defensive walls, defended by a drawbridge and 17 massive round towers in a distinctive pattern, and the formal garden, with its delicate white-tufa chapel, erected in the 16th century. For a sweeping view of the city and surrounding countryside, climb one of the castle towers. A well-integrated modern gallery on the castle grounds contains the great **Tenture de l'Apocalypse** (Apocalypse Tapestry), woven in Paris in the 1380s for the Duke of Anjou. Measuring 16 feet high and 120 yards long, its many panels show a series of 70 horrifying and humorous scenes from the Book of Revelation. In one, mountains of fire fall from heaven while boats capsize and men struggle in the water. Another has the Beast with Seven Heads. ✉ *2 promenade du Bout-du-Monde* ☎ *02–41–86–48–77* 🌐 *www.monuments-nationaux.fr* 🎟 *€7* ⏲ *May–Aug., daily 9:30–6:30; Sept.–Apr., daily 10–5:30.*

The **Cathédrale St-Maurice** (✉ *Pl. Monseigneur-Chappoulie*) is a 12th- and 13th-century Gothic cathedral noted for its curious Romanesque facade and original stained-glass windows; bring binoculars to appreciate both fully.

To learn about the heartwarming liqueur made in Angers since 1849, head to **Cointreau** on the east of the city. It has a museum and offers a guided visit of the distillery, which starts with an introductory film, moves past cointreauversial advertising posters, through the bottling plant and alembic room, with its gleaming copper-pot stills, and ends with a tasting. English tours are staged at 3 PM . ✉ *2 bd. des Bretonnières, St-Barthélémy d'Anjou* ☎ *02–41–31–50–00* 🌐 *www.cointreau.com* 🎟 *€5.50* ⏲ *Tours daily July and Aug., 10:30, 2:30, 3:30, and 4:30; May, June, Sept., and Oct., 10:30 and 3, also Sun. 4:30; Nov.–Apr., 3, also Sun. 4:30.*

WHERE TO STAY & EAT

$ ✕ **La Treille.** For traditional, simple fare at affordable prices, try this small two-story mom-and-pop restaurant off Place Ste-Croix and across from Maison d'Adam, Angers's finest timber-frame house. The prix-fixe menu may start with a *salade au chèvre chaud* (warm goat-cheese salad), followed by confit of duck and an apple tart. The upstairs dining room draws a lively crowd; downstairs is quieter. ✉ *12 rue Montault* ☎ *02–41–88–45–51* 💳 *MC, V* ⏲ *Closed Sun.*

$$–$$$ ✕🏨 **Anjou.** In business since 1846, the Anjou, now part of the Best Western chain, has a vaguely 18th-century style, and stained-glass windows in the lobby. The spacious rooms have high ceilings, double doors, and modern bathrooms where terry robes await you. There's a fine restaurant, La Salamandre (closed Sunday), where Danie Louboutin's meticulously prepared classic cuisine ranges from lamb and duck with cranberries to calamari with crab sauce. Opt for one of the reasonably priced prix-fixe menus. ✉ *1 bd. du Maréchal-Foch, 49100* ☎ *02–41–21–12–11, 800/528–1324 in U.S.* 📠 *02–41–87–22–21* 🌐 *www.hoteldanjou.fr* 🛏 *53 rooms* 👍 *In-room: refrigerator. In-hotel: restaurant, some pets allowed (fee)* 💳 *AE, DC, MC, V* 🍽 *BP.*

$ 🏨 **Mail.** A stately lime tree stands sentinel behind wrought-iron, wisteria-framed gates outside this 17th-century mansion on a calm street between the Hôtel de Ville and the river. The smallish rooms are individually decorated in pastel shades. ✉ *8 rue des Ursules, 49100* ☎ *02–41–25–05–25* 📠 *02–41–86–91–20* 🌐 *www.hotel-du-mail.com* 🛏 *26 rooms* 👍 *In-room: no a/c. In-hotel: some pets allowed (fee), no elevator* 💳 *AE, DC, MC, V.*

NIGHTLIFE & THE ARTS

July and August see the **Angers L'Eté** *(Angers Summer)* festival (☎ *02–41–23–50–00*), with concerts at the Cloître Toussaint.

LANGEAIS

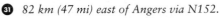 *82 km (47 mi) east of Angers via N152.*

Sometimes unjustly overlooked, the **Château de Langeais**—a castle in the true sense of the word—will particularly delight those who dream of lions rampant, knights in shining armor, and the chivalric days of yore. Built in the 1460s, bearing a massive portcullis and gate, and never altered, it has an interior noted for its superb collection of medieval and Renaissance furnishings—fireplaces, tapestries, chests, and beds—which would make Guinevere and Lancelot feel right at home. Outside, gardens nestle behind sturdy walls and battlements. The town itself has other sites, including a Renaissance church tower, but chances are you won't want to move from the delightful outdoor cafés that face the castle entrance. Do follow the road a bit to the right (when looking at the entrance) to discover the charming historic houses grouped around a waterfall and canal. ☎02–47–96–72–60 ⊕*www.chateau-de-langeais. com* ☜€7.80 ☉*Apr.–mid-Nov., daily 9:30–6:30; mid-Nov.–Mar., daily 10–5.*

LOIRE VALLEY ESSENTIALS

TRANSPORTATION

If traveling extensively by public transportation, be sure to load up on information (*Guide Régional des Transports* schedules, the best taxi-for-call companies, etc.) upon arriving at the ticket counter or help desk of the bigger train and bus stations in the area, such as Tours, Orléans, and Angers.

BY AIR

The closest international airports are Paris's Charles de Gaulle and Orly, although Ryanair flies to Tours from London Stansted.

BY BIKE

With its nearly flat terrain, the Loire Valley is custom-built for traveling by bike; however, a single-day expedition visiting three or more châteaux would be difficult, except for professional bicyclists, considering the distances involved. *Vélos tout-terrain* (mountain bikes) are the sturdiest models. When renting, inquire about bike-repair kits. As Tours is the heart of the region, it's the best base.

Bike Rentals Détours de Loire (✉*5 rue du Rempart, Tours* ☎*02–47–61–22–23* ⊕ *www.loire-a-velo.fr*) has more than a dozen outlets along the Loire, where you can rent bikes from €14 a day or €57 a week.

BY BUS

Local bus services are extensive and reliable, providing a link between train stations and scenic areas off the river; it's possible to reach many villages and châteaux by bus (although many routes are in place to service schoolchildren, meaning service is less frequent in summer and sometimes all but nonexistent on Sunday)—most of the big towns and châteaux are more handily reached by train, however. Inquire at tourist offices for information about routes and timetables, available in very handy form. The leading companies are Les Rapides du Val de Loire, based in Orléans; TLC, serving Chambord and Cheverny from Blois; Touraine Fil Vert and Fil Bleu, both of which serve the Touraine region, including out-of-the-way Loches; and Anjou Bus (Anjou region). The hardest place to reach is the magical Château d'Ussé but there's one municipal bus line to Rigny-Ussé that connects with Chinon—when in doubt, taxi. For Fontevraud, catch buses from Saumur.

Bus Information Anjou Bus (⊠ *Pl. Michel-Debré, Angers* ☎ *02–41–81–49–72* ⊕ *www.cg49.fr/services/voyager/anjou-bus*). **Fil Bleu** (⊠ *Pl. Jean-Jaurès, Tours* ☎ *02–47–66–70–70*). **Les Rapides du Val de Loire** (⊠ *27-B bd. Marie-Stuart, Orléans* ☎ *02–38–61–90–00* ⊕ *www.rvl-info.com*). **TLC (Transports du Loir-et-Cher)** (⊠ *9 rue Alexandre-Vézin, Blois* ☎ *02–54–58–55–44* ⊕ *tlcinfo.net*).

Touraine Fil Vert (⊠ *10 rue Alexander-Fleming, Tours* ☎ *02–47–47–17–18* ⊕ *www.touraine-filvert.com*).

BY CAR

The Loire Valley is an easy drive from Paris. A10 runs from Paris to Orléans—a distance of around 125 km (80 mi)—and on to Tours, with exits at Meung, Blois, and Amboise. After Tours, A10 veers south toward Poitiers and Bordeaux. A11 links Paris to Angers and Saumur via Le Mans. Slower but more scenic routes run from the Channel ports down through Normandy into the Loire region.

The "easiest" way to visit the Loire châteaux is by car; N152 hugs the riverbank and is excellent for sightseeing. But note that signage can be few and far between once you get off the main road and many a traveler has horror stories about a 15-minute trip lasting two hours ("Next time, by bus and train …"). You can rent a car in all the large towns in the region, or at train stations in Orléans, Blois, Tours, or Angers, or in Paris.

BY TRAIN

The great writer Henry James used the train system to tour Touraine back in the late 19th century and found it a most convenient way to get around. Things have only gotten better since then. Thanks to superbly organized timetables, you can whisk around from château to château with little worry or stress. True, you may sometimes need to avail yourself of a quick taxi ride from the station to the château door, but compared to renting a car, this adds up to little bother and expense. As gateways to the region, Tours (70 mins, €38.40) and Angers (95 mins, €58.50) are both served by the superfast TGV (Trains à Grande Vitesse) from Paris (Gare Montparnasse); note that the main-line station in Tours is in suburban St-Pierre-des-Corps. There are also TGV trains from Charles-de-Gaulle Airport direct to the Loire Valley to Angers (2 hrs, 30 mins, €50.60), and St-Pierre-des-Corps (for Tours, 1 hr, 45 mins, €43.50). Express trains run every two hours from Paris (Gare d'Austerlitz) to Orléans (1 hr, 5 mins, €17, usually you must change at nearby Les Aubrais) and Blois (1 hr, 40 mins, €23).

The main train line follows the Loire from Orléans to Angers (1 hr, 50 mins, €26.70); there are trains every two hours or so, stopping in Blois, Tours, and Saumur; trains stop less frequently in Onzain (for Chaumont), Amboise, and Langeais. There are branch lines with trains from Tours to Chenonceaux (30 mins, €5.60), Azay-le-Rideau (30 mins, €5), and Chinon (50 mins, €8). You can reach Loches from Tours with an SNCF bus (50 mins, €7.70). Ask the SNCF for the brochure *Les Châteaux de la Loire en Train* for more detailed information. Helpful train-schedule brochures are available at most stations.

Train Information Gare SNCF Tours (✉ *Cour de la Gare* ☎ *03–80–43–16–34*). **Gare SNCF Orléans** (✉ *1 pl. François Mitterand* ☎ *03–80–43–16–34*). **SNCF** (☎ *36–35,€0.34 per min* ⊕ *www.voyages-sncf.com*). **TGV** (⊕ *www.tgv.com*).

CONTACTS & RESOURCES

CAR RENTAL
Local Agencies Avis (✉ *58 rue de Vendôme, Blois* ☎ *02–54–45–10–61* ✉ *Gare SNCF, Orléans* ☎ *02–38–62–27–04* ✉ *Gare SNCF, Tours* ☎ *02–47–20–53–27*). **Europcar** (✉ *76 rue Bernard-Palissy, Tours* ☎ *02–47–64–47–76*). **Hertz** (✉ *Pl. de la Gare, Angers* ☎ *02–41–88–15–16* ✉ *57 rue Marcel-Tribut, Tours* ☎ *02–47–75–50–00*).

EMERGENCIES
Contacts General Ambulance (☎ *15*). **General Fire Department** (☎ *18*). **General Police** (☎ *17*). **Regional hospitals** (✉ *4 rue Larrey, Angers* ☎ *02–41–35–36–37* ✉ *14 av. de l'Hôpital, Orléans* ☎ *02–38–51–44–44* ✉ *2 bd. Tonnellé, Tours* ☎ *02–47–47–47–47*).

INTERNET & MAIL
In smaller towns, ask your hotel concierge if there are any Internet cafés nearby.

Internet & Mail Information Cyberspace (✉ *27 rue Lavoisier, near cathedral, Tours* ☎ *02–47–20–89–69*). **Ambiance Multimedia** (✉ *10 rue Bodinier, off Rue de la Roë, north of cathedral, Angers* ☎ *02–41–18–26–24*). **La Poste (main post office)** (✉ *75b rue Marceau, Tours* ☎ *02–47–31–11–41*). **La Poste (main post office)** (✉ *Pl. de la Gare, Angers* ☎ *02–41–88–19–92*).

MEDIA
La Nouvelle République covers the whole of the region while the *Courrier de l'Ouest* concentrates on the western Loire, as do the local editions of *Ouest France*.

TOUR OPTIONS
CHÂTEAU TOURS
Many châteaux insist that you follow one of their tours; try to get a booklet in English before joining, as most are in French. Bus tours of the main châteaux leave daily in summer from Tours, Blois, Angers, Orléans, and Saumur: ask at the relevant tourist office for latest times and prices. If you want to do the top châteaux with the convenience of a van tour, readers rave about Acco-Dispo—usually three are included

on the tour (for example, Chambord, Cheverny, and Chaumont). The half-day trips cost around €32 a person and leave from Tours.

Contacts **Acco-Dispo Tours** (⊠ *18 rue des Vallées, Amboise* ☎ *06–82–00–64–51* ⊕ *www.accodispo-tours.com*).

HELICOPTERS & BALLOONS

Jet Systems makes breathtaking helicopter trips over the Loire Valley on Tuesday, Thursday, and weekends from the aerodrome at Dierre, just south of Amboise; cost ranges from €60 (10 mins, flying over Chenonceau) to €230 (35 mins, covering six châteaux) per person.

For a more leisurely airborne visit, contact France Montgolfière for details of their balloon trips over the Loire; prices run €180–€225.

Fees & Schedules **France Montgolfières** (☎ *02–54–32–20–48* ⊕ *www.franceballoons.com*). **Jet Systems** (☎ *02–47–30–20–21* ⊕ *www.jet-systems.fr*).

PRIVATE GUIDES

The tourist offices in Tours and Angers arrange city and regional excursions with personal guides.

WALKING TOURS

Two-hour walking tours of Tours set out from the tourist office every morning at 10 AM or 2:30 PM in July and August, weekends only April–June, September , and October (€5.50). English-speaking guides show you around Blois on a tour that starts from the château at 4 (€5).

VISITOR INFORMATION

The Loire region has two area tourist offices, both of which are for written inquiries only. For Chinon and points east, contact the Comité Régional du Tourisme Centre-Val de Loire. For Fontevraud and points west, contact the Comité Départemental du Tourisme de l'Anjou.

Tourist Information **Comité Régional du Tourisme Centre-Val de Loire** (⊠ *37 av. de Paris, 45000 Orléans* ⊕ *www.loirevalleytourism.com*). **Comité Départemental du Tourisme de l'Anjou** (⊠ *Pl. Kennedy, 45000 Angers* ☎ *02–41–23–51–51* ⊕ *www.anjou-tourisme.com*).

Amboise (⊠ *Quai du Général-de-Gaulle* ☎ *02–47–57–09–28* ⊕ *www.amboise-valdeloire.com*). **Angers** (⊠ *7 pl. Kennedy* ☎ *02–41–23–51–11* ⊕ *www.angers-tourisme.com*). **Blois** (⊠ *3 av. du Dr-Jean-Laigret* ☎ *02–54–90–41–41* ⊕ *www.loiredeschateaux.com*). **Fontevraud-L'Abbaye** (⊠ *Pl. St-Michel* ☎ *02–41–51–79–45* ⊕ *www.cote-saumuroise.com*). **Montlouis-sur-Loire** (⊠ *Pl. François-Mitterrand* ☎ *02–47–45–00–16* ⊕ *www.ville-montlouis-loire.fr*). **Orléans** (⊠ *6 rue Albert-Ier* ☎ *02–38–24–05–05* ⊕ *www.tourisme-orleans.com*). **Rochecorbon** (⊠ *Pl. de la Lanterne* ☎ *02–47–52–80–22*). **Saumur** (⊠ *Pl. de la Bilange* ☎ *02–41–40–20–60* ⊕ *www.ot-saumur.fr*). **Tours** (⊠ *78 rue Bernard-Palissy* ☎ *02–47–70–37–37* ⊕ *www.ligeris.com*).

Normandy

Le Touquet

WORD OF MOUTH

"I believe you make a mistake if you do not spend a night at Mont-St-Michel. The Mont is completely different after the day-trippers leave in the late afternoon. In the early evening you can see the tide come rushing back in to make the Mont an island again—this alone makes staying into the evening worthwhile. The soft gold glow of the lights throughout the village at night is very beautiful."

—LarryJ

WELCOME TO NORMANDY

TOP REASONS TO GO

★ **Mont-St-Michel:** The spire-topped silhouette of this mighty offshore mound, dubbed the Marvel of the Occident, is one of the greatest sights in Europe. Get there at high tide, when the water races across the endless sands.

★ **Bayeux:** Come not just for the splendor of the tapestry telling how William conquered England, but for untouched medieval buildings and the beefy, bonnet-topped cathedral.

★ **Honfleur:** From France's prettiest harbor, lined with beam-fronted houses, you can head to the ravishing wooden church of Ste-Catherine.

★ **Rouen:** Sanctified by the memory of Jeanne d'Arc, hallowed by its towering Gothic cathedral (immortalized by Monet), and lined with medieval half-timber houses, Rouen makes a great gateway city to Normandy.

★ **D-Day Beaches:** From rocky Omaha to pancake-flat Utah, muse on the stirring deeds of World War II.

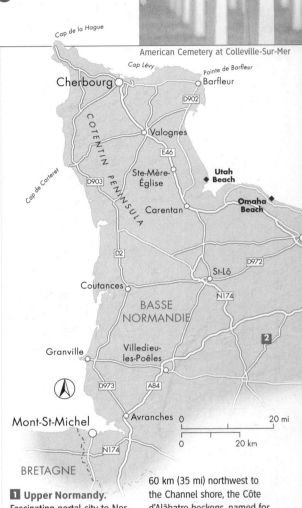

American Cemetery at Colleville-Sur-Mer

1 Upper Normandy. Fascinating portal city to Normandy, **Rouen** still contains—despite World War II's battering—such an overwhelming number of lovely churches, chapels, towers, fountains, and old cross-beamed houses that many take two full days to enjoy this commercial and cultural hub. Heading some

60 km (35 mi) northwest to the Channel shore, the Côte d'Alâbatre beckons, named for the white cliffs that stretch south, including the spectacular rock formations often painted by Monet at **Etretat**. Nearby seaside **Fécamp** regals with its noted Benedictine palace and distillery, while **Le Havre** remains a busy commercial port.

Harbor of Honfleur

4

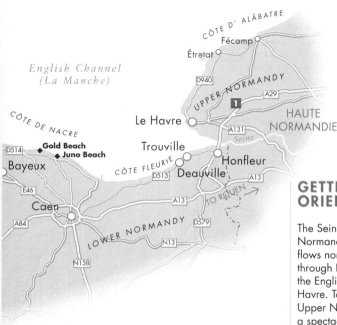

English Channel
(La Manche)

CÔTE D' ALÂBATRE
Fécamp
Étretat
CÔTE DE NACRE
Gold Beach
Juno Beach
Bayeux
D514
Le Havre
Trouville
CÔTE FLEURIE
Deauville
D513
Caen
E46
A84
LOWER NORMANDY
N13
N158
D579
UPPER NORMANDY
D940
A29
HAUTE
NORMANDIE
A131
Seine
Honfleur
A13
A13
TO ROUEN

GETTING ORIENTED

The Seine Valley divides Normandy in two as it flows northwest from Paris through Rouen and into the English Channel at Le Havre. To the north lies Upper Normandy and a spectacular coastline lined with towering chalk cliffs called the Côte d'Alabâtre, or Alabaster Coast. West of the Seine lies Lower Normandy, full of lush meadows and lined with the sandy beaches of the Côte Fleurie, or Flower Coast. (These are some of the same beaches where the allies landed on D-Day.) Far to the west, at the foot of the sparsely populated Cotentin Peninsula, the offshore Mont-St-Michel patrols one of the continent's biggest bays.

2 **Honfleur to Mont-St-Michel.** Basse (or Lower) Normandie begins with the sandy Côte Fleurie (Flower Coast), announced by seaside **Honfleur**, full of half-timber houses that were favored by the Impressionists. Just south, Rothschilds by the Rolls arrive in season at the Belle Epoque seaside resorts of **Trouville** and **Deauville**—both beautiful if hard-on-the pocket. Modern and student-filled **Caen** is famed for its two gigantic abbey churches,

one begun by William the Conqueror, who is immortalized in nearby **Bayeux's** legendary tapestry. This town makes a great base to explore the somber D-Day sites along Utah and Omaha beaches; bus tours and moving memorials make a fitting prelude for a drive across Normandy's Cotentin Peninsula to **Mont-St-Michel**, whose tiny island is crowned by one of the most beautiful Gothic abbeys in France.

NORMANDY PLANNER

Eating Well

Apples and cows are at the base of Normandy's rich cuisine. This is no place for the faint-stomached. The favored main course is veal or beef in a cream sauce, followed by a chunk of regional cheese like Camembert, Livarot, or Pont-L'Eveque. An apple tart with cream usually wraps things up. Other local specialties include foie gras, duck cooked in blood, and *andouille de Vire* (cold smoked sausage served in thin slices). Sound a bit heavy? If you're near the sea, you'll be fine. Shrimp and oysters abound, herring and scallops warrant coastal festivals each fall, and cod and sole are served swimming in cider and cream; *sole à la dieppoise* comes with a sauce made of white wine, cream, mussels, and mushrooms. There are no vineyards hereabouts but you won't go thirsty: take cider during your meal, calvados (apple brandy) afterward, and pommeau if you fancy a sweet, tangy, apple-tinged aperitif.

Making the Most of Your Time

Normandy is a big region with lots to see. If you have 10 days or so you can do it justice. If not, you'll need to prioritize. Is search of natural beauty? Head to the coastline north of Le Havre. Prefer sea and sand? Beat it to the beaches west of Trouville. Like city life? You're likely to love pretty Rouen. Are you a history buff? Base yourself in Caen to tour the D-Day beaches. Can't get enough of churches and cathedrals? You can go pretty much anywhere, but don't miss Bayeux, Rouen, or Mont-St-Michel. (The last is a bit isolated, so you might want to get there directly from Paris, or at the start or end of a tour of Brittany.)

Getting Around

Although this is one of the few areas of France with no high-speed rail service—perhaps because it's so close to Paris, or because it's not on a lucrative route to a neighboring country—Normandy's regional rail network is surprisingly good, meaning that most towns can be reached by train. Rouen is the hub for Upper Normandy, Caen for Lower Normandy. Unless you're driving, you'll need a bus to reach the coastal resorts like Étretat, Honfleur, and Houlgate. For Mont-St-Michel, a combination of train and bus is required. To visit the D-Day beaches, a guided minibus tour, leaving from Caen or Bayeux, is your best bet. The A13 expressway is the gateway from Paris, running northwest to Rouen and then to Caen. From there the A84 takes you almost all the way to Mont St-Michel, and the N13 brings you to Bayeux. If you're arriving from England or northern Europe, the A28 via to Rouen is a scenic (and near-empty) delight.

Touring the D-Day Beaches

One of the great events of modern history, the D-Day invasion of June 1944, was enacted on the beaches of Normandy. Omaha Beach (site of an eye-opening museum), Utah Beach, as well as many sites on the Cotentin Peninsula, and the memorials to Allied dead, all bear witness to the furious fighting that once raged in this now-peaceful corner of France. Today, as seagulls sweep over the cliffs where American rangers scrambled desperately up ropes to silence murderous German batteries, visitors now wander through the blockhouses and peer into the bomb craters, the carnage of *Saving Private Ryan* thankfully now a distant, if still horrifying, memory. Unless you have a car, the D-Day beaches are best visited on a bus tour from Bayeux. Public buses are rare, although Bus No. 75 heads to Arromanches and Bus No. 70 goes to Omaha Beach and the American cemetery (during summer only). However, Bus Verts du Calvados (www.busverts.fr/_hiver/dday/caen_omaha.asp), offers a "Circuit Caen-Omaha Beach" route that connects many of the D-Day sights. As for guided tours, Normandy Tours (02–31–92–10–70; www.normandy-tours-hotel.com), which carries up to eight in its minivan, leaves from Bayeux's Hotel de la Gare. The guides are walking encyclopedias of local war lore and may be flexible about visiting beaches or cemeteries of interest to you. The half-day tours (€50) are available all year in English. In addition, other Bayeux-based tour outfitters include D-Day Tours (02–31–51–70–52; www.d-daybeaches.com), with half-day tours (€50) and full-day tours (€75). Battlebus (02–31–22–28–82; www.battlebus.fr) has a full-day extravaganza (€75).

Finding a Place to Stay

Accommodations to suit every taste can be found throughout Normandy, from basic bed-and-breakfasts to the most luxurious hotel. Even in the ultraswank resorts of Deauville and Trouville, it is possible to find delightful and inexpensive little vacation spots. Prices are ratcheted up in summer along the coast, so be sure to book ahead, especially on weekends when half of Paris heads to the seaside. Many hotels are closed in winter. In the beach resorts the season runs from the end of April to October.

The region's two largest cities, Rouen and Caen, are not among France's best-endowed when it comes to high-end hotels.

To stay the night on Mont-St-Michel is a memorable experience, but be sure to reserve your room weeks in advance.

WHAT IT COSTS

	¢	$	$$	$$$	$$$$
Restaurants	Under €11	€11– €17	€17– €23	€23– €30	Over €30
Hotels	Under €50	€50– €80	€80– €120	€120– €190	Over €190

Restaurant prices are per person for a main course at dinner, including tax (19.6%) and service; note that if a restaurant offers only prix-fixe (set-price) meals, it has been given the price category that reflects the full prix-fixe price. Hotel prices are for a standard double room in high season, including tax (19.6%) and service charge. Hotels operate on the European Plan (EP, with no meal provided) unless we note that they use the Breakfast Plan (BP), or also offer such options as Modified American Plan (MAP, with breakfast and dinner daily, known as demi-pension), or Full American Plan (FAP, or pension complète, with three meals a day). Inquire when booking if these all-inclusive meal plans (which always entail higher rates) are mandatory or optional.

Introduction by
Nancy Coons

Updated by
Simon Hewitt

SAY THE NAME "NORMANDY," AND which Channel-side scenario comes to mind? Could it be long ships bristling with oars scudding into the darkness toward Hastings? Such ships were immortalized in the Bayeux Tapestry, which traces step-by-step the epic tale of William the Conqueror, who in 1066 sailed across the Channel to claim his right to England's throne. Or do you think of iron-gray convoys massing silently along the shore at dawn, lowering tailgates to pour troops of young Allied infantrymen into the line of German machine-gun fire? At Omaha Beach you may marvel at the odds faced by the handful of soldiers who in June 1944 were able to rise above the waterfront carnage to capture the cliff-top battery, paving the way for the Allies' reconquest of Europe.

Perhaps you think of Joan of Arc—imprisoned by the English yet burned at the Rouen stake by the Church she believed in? In a modern church you may light a candle on the very spot where, in 1431, the Maiden Warrior sizzled into history at the hands of panicky politicians and time-serving clerics: a dark deed that marked a turning point in the Hundred Years' War. Or are you reminded of the dramatic silhouette of Mont-St-Michel looming above the tidal flats, its cobbles echoing with the footfalls of medieval scholars? You may make a latter-day pilgrimage to the famous island-abbey, one of the most evocative monuments in Europe behind its crow's-nest ramparts.

The destinies of England and Normandie (as the French spell it) have been intertwined ever since William, duke of Normandy, insisted that King Edward the Confessor had promised him the succession to the English crown. When a royal council instead anointed the Anglo-Saxon Harold Godwinsson, the irate William stormed across the Channel with 7,000 well-equipped archers, well-mounted knights, and well-paid Frankish mercenaries. They landed at Pevensey Bay on September 28, 1066, and two weeks later, at Hastings, saw off a ragtag mix of battle-weary English troops hastily reinforced with peasant conscripts swinging stones tied to sticks. Harold met his maker, an arrow through his eye. William progressed to London and was crowned King of England on Christmas Day.

There followed nearly 400 years of Norman sovereignty in England. For generations England and Normandy vacillated and blurred, merged, and diverged. Today you can still feel the strong flow of English culture over the Channel, from the Deauville horse races frequented by high-born ladies in gloves, to silver spoons mounded high with teatime cream; from the bowfront, slope-roof shops along the harbor at Honfleur to the black-and-white row houses of Rouen, which would seem just as much at home in the setting of *David Copperfield* as they would in *Madame Bovary*.

And just as in the British Isles, no matter how you concentrate on history and culture, sooner or later you'll find yourself beguiled by the countryside, by Normandy's rolling green hills dotted with dairy cows and half-timber farmhouses. Like the locals, you'll be tempted by seafood fresh off the boat, by sauces rich with crème fraîche, by cheeses redolent of farm and pasture. And perhaps with cheeks pink from the apple-scented country air, you'll eventually succumb to the local antidote to northern damp and chill: a mug of tangy hard cider sipped by a crackling fire, and the bracing tonic of Normandy's famous apple brandy, calvados.

EXPLORING NORMANDY

You won't want to miss medieval Rouen, seaside Honfleur, or magnificent Mont-St-Michel. But if you get away from these popular spots you can lose yourself along the cliff-lined coast and in the green spaces inland, where the closest thing to a crowd is a farmer with his herd of brown-and-white cows. From Rouen to the coast—the area known as Upper Normandy—medieval castles and abbeys stand guard above rolling countryside, while resort and fishing towns line the white cliffs of the Côte d'Alabâtre. Popular seaside resorts and the D-Day landing sites occupy the sandy beaches along the Côte Fleurie; apple orchards and dairy farms sprinkle the countryside of the area known as Lower Normandy. The Cotentin Peninsula to the west juts out into the English Channel. Central Normandy encompasses the peaceful, hilly region of La Suisse Normande, along the scenic Orne River.

UPPER NORMANDY

The French divide Normandy into two: Haute-Normandie and Basse-Normandie. Upper (Haute) Normandy is delineated by the Seine as it meanders northwest from Ile-de-France between chalky cliffs and verdant hills to Rouen—the region's cultural and commercial capital—and on to the port of Le Havre. Pebbly beaches and even more impressive chalk cliffs line the Côte d'Alabâtre (Alabaster Coast) from Le Havre to Dieppe. In the 19th century, the dramatic scenery and bathing resorts along the coast attracted and inspired writers and artists like Maupassant, Monet, and Braque. Lower (Basse) Normandy encompasses the sandy Côte Fleurie (Flower Coast), stretching from the resort towns of Trouville and Deauville to the D-Day landing beaches and the Cotentin Peninsula, jutting out into the English Channel. Inland, lush green meadows and apple orchards form the heart of calvados country west of the pilgrim town of Lisieux. After the World War II D-Day landings, some of the fiercest fighting took place around Caen and Bayeux, as many monuments and memorials testify. To the south, in the prosperous Pays d'Auge, dairy farms produce the region's famous cheeses. The hilly Suisse Normande provides the region's most rugged scenery. Rising to the west is the fabled Mont-St-Michel. Our tour starts in Rouen, then heads north to the Channel Coast, which we follow all the way from Dieppe to Mont-St-Michel.

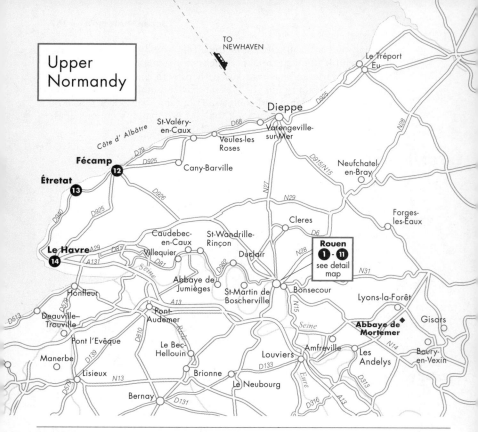

TO NEWHAVEN

Le Tréport
Eu

Dieppe

St-Valéry-
en-Caux

Côte d' Albâtre

Veules-les
Roses

Varengeville-
sur-Mer

Neufchatel-
en-Bray

Fécamp
12

Cany-Barville

Étretat
13

Cleres

Forges-
les-Eaux

Caudebec-
en-Caux

St-Wandrille-
Rinçon

Le Havre
14

Villequier

Duclair

Rouen
1 - **11**
see detail
map

Abbaye de
Jumièges

St-Martin de
Boscherville

Bonsecour

Lyons-la-Forêt

Honfleur

Pont-
Audemer

Abbaye de
Mortemer

Gisors

Deauville-
Trouville

Le Bec-
Hellouin

Amfreville

Les
Andelys

Boury-
en-Vexin

Pont l'Evêque

Manerbe

Louviers

Lisieux

Brionne

Bernay

Le Neubourg

Seine

Eure

ROUEN

32 km (20 mi) north of Louviers, 130 km (80 mi) northwest of Paris, 86 km (53 mi) east of Le Havre.

GETTING HERE

Trains from Paris (Gare St-Lazare) leave for Rouen every two hours or so (€22); the 85-mi trip takes 70 minutes. Change in Rouen for Dieppe (2 hrs from Paris, €25). Several trains daily link Rouen to Caen (90 mins, €21.50) and Fecamp (90 mins, €12), sometimes requiring a change to a bus at Bréauté-Beuzeville.

EXPLORING

"O Rouen, art thou then to be my final abode!" was the agonized cry of Joan of Arc as the English dragged her out to be burned alive on May 30, 1431. The exact spot of the pyre is marked by a concrete-and-metal cross in front of the Église Jeanne-d'Arc, an eye-catching modern church on Place du Vieux-Marché, just one of the many landmarks that make Rouen a fascinating destination. Although much of the city was destroyed during World War II, a wealth of medieval half-timber houses still lines the cobblestone streets, many of which are pedestrian-only—most famously Rue du Gros-Horloge between Place du Vieux-Marché and the cathedral, suitably embellished halfway along with a giant Renaissance clock. Rouen is also a busy port—the fifth largest in France.

Rouen is known as the City of a Hundred Spires, because many of its important edifices are churches. Lording it over them all is the highest spire in France, erected in 1876, a cast-iron tour-de-force rising 490 feet above the crossing of the **Cathédrale Notre-Dame.** The original 12th-century construction was replaced after a devastating fire in 1200; only the left-hand spire, the **Tour St-Romain** (St. Romanus Tower), survived the flames. Construction on the imposing 250-foot steeple on the right, known as the **Tour de Beurre** (Butter Tower), was begun in the 15th century and completed in the 17th, when a group of wealthy citizens donated large sums of money for the privilege of continuing to eat butter during Lent. Interior highlights include the 13th-century choir, with its pointed arcades; vibrant stained glass depicting the crucified Christ (restored after heavy damage during World War II); and massive stone columns topped by some intriguing carved faces. The first flight of the famous **Escalier de la Librairie** (Library Stairway), attributed to Guillaume Pontifs (also responsible for most of the 15th-century work seen in the cathedral), rises from a tiny balcony just to the left of the transept. ⊠*Pl. de la Cathédrale, St-Maclou* ☎*02–32–08–32–40* ☉*Daily 8–6.*

❷ The late-Gothic church of **St-Maclou,** across Rue de la République behind the cathedral, bears testimony to the wild excesses of Flamboyant architecture. Take time to examine the central and left-hand portals of the main facade, covered with little bronze lion heads and pagan engravings. Inside, note the 16th-century organ, with its Renaissance wood carving, and the fine marble columns. ⊠*Pl. St-Maclou, St-Maclou* ☎*02–35–71–71–72* ☉*Mon.–Sat. 10–noon and 2–6, Sun. 3–5:30.*

❸ A former ossuary (a charnel house used for the bodies of plague victims), the **Aître St-Maclou** is a reminder of the plague that devastated Europe during the Middle Ages; these days it holds Rouen's Fine Art Academy. French composer Camille Saint-Saëns (1835–1921) is said to have been inspired by the ossuary when he was working on his *Danse Macabre.* The half-timber courtyard, where you can wander at leisure and maybe visit a picture exhibition, contains graphic carvings of skulls, bones, and grave diggers' tools. ⊠*186 rue Martainville, St-Maclou.*

❹ A stupendous example of high Gothic architecture is the **Abbaye St-Ouen** next to the imposing Neo-classical City Hall. The abbey's stained-glass windows, dating from the 14th to the 16th century, are the most spectacular grace notes of the spare interior, along with the 19th-century pipe organ, among the finest in France. ⊠*Pl. du Général-de-Gaulle, Hôtel de Ville*

MONET IN 3-D

If you're familiar with the works of Impressionist artist Claude Monet, you'll immediately recognize Rouen cathedral's immense west front, rendered in an increasingly hazy fashion in his series Cathédrales de Rouen—you can enjoy a ringside view and a coffee at the Brasserie Paul, just opposite. The facade is illuminated by a free light show, based on Monet's canvases, for an hour every evening from June through mid-September.

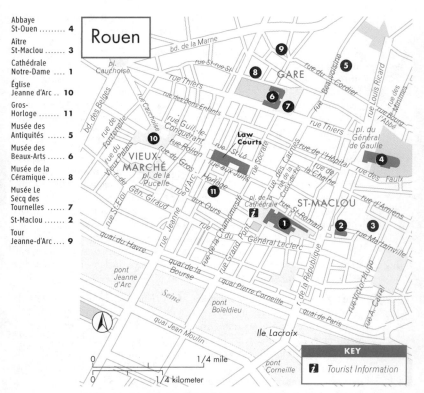

☎02–32–08–13–90 ⊙Mid-Mar.–Oct., Wed.–Mon. 8–12:30 and 2–6; Nov.–mid-Dec. and mid-Jan.–mid-Mar., Wed. and weekends 10–12:30 and 2–4:30.

⑤ Gallo-Roman glassware and mosaics, medieval tapestries and enamels, and Moorish ceramics vie for attention at the **Musée des Antiquités,** an extensive antiquities museum housed in a former monastery dating from the 17th century. A new display devoted to natural history, which includes some skeletons dating back to prehistoric times, opened in February 2007. ✉198 rue Beauvoisine, Gare ☎02–35–98–55–10 ✇€3 ⊙Mon.–Sat. 10–12:15 and 1:30–5:30, Sun. 2–6.

⑥ One of Rouen's cultural mainstays is the **Musée des Beaux-Arts** (Fine Arts Museum), which has a scintillating collection of paintings and sculptures from the 16th to the 20th century, including works by native son Géricault as well as by David, Rubens, Caravaggio, Velasquez, Poussin, Delacroix, Chassériau, Degas, and Modigliani, not to mention the impressive Impressionist gallery, with Monet, Renoir, and Sisley, and the Postimpressionist School of Rouen headed by Albert Lebourg and Gustave Loiseau. ✉Square Verdrel, Gare ☎02–35–71–28–40 ⊕www. rouen-musees.com ✇€3, €5.35 includes Musée Le Secq des Tournelles and Musée de la Céramique ⊙Wed.–Mon. 10–6.

❼ The **Musée Le Secq des Tournelles** (*Wrought-Iron Museum*), near the Musée des Beaux-Arts, claims to have the world's finest collection of wrought iron, with exhibits spanning from the 4th through the 19th century. The displays, imaginatively housed in a converted medieval church, include the professional instruments of surgeons, barbers, carpenters, clockmakers, and gardeners. ⊠*2 rue Jacques-Villon, Gare* 🕾*02–35–88–42–92* 🖅*€2.30, €5.35 includes Musée des Beaux-Arts and Musée de la Céramique* ⊘ *Wed.–Mon. 10–1 and 2–6.*

❽ A superb array of local pottery and European porcelain can be admired at the **Musée de la Céramique** (*Ceramics Museum*), in an elegant mansion near the Musée des Beaux-Arts. ⊠*1 rue Faucon, Gare* 🕾*02–35–07–31–74* 🖅*€2.30, €5.35 includes Musée Le Secq des Tournelles and Musée des Beaux-Arts* ⊘ *Wed.–Mon. 10–1 and 2–6.*

❾ Sole remnant of the early-13th-century castle built by French king Philippe-Auguste, the beefy **Tour Jeanne-d'Arc,** a pointed-top circular tower, houses a small exhibit of documents and models charting the history of the castle where Joan of Arc was tried and held prisoner in 1430. ⊠*Rue Bouvreuil, Gare* 🕾*02–35–98–55–10* 🖅*€1.50* ⊘ *Mon. and Wed.–Sat. 10–12:30 and 2–6, Sun. 2–6:30.*

❿ Dedicated to Joan of Arc, the **Église Jeanne d'Arc** (*Joan of Arc Church*) was built in the 1970s on the spot where she was burned to death in 1431. The aesthetic merit of its odd cement-and-wood design is debatable—the shape of the roof is *supposed* to evoke the flames of Joan's fire. Not all is new, however: the church showcases some remarkable 16th-century stained-glass windows taken from the former Église St-Vincent, bombed out in 1944. The adjacent **Musée Jeanne-d'Arc** evokes Joan's history with waxworks and documents. ⊠*33 pl. du Vieux-Marché, Vieux-Marché* 🕾*02–35–88–02–70* ⊕*www.jeanne-darc.com* 🖅*€4* ⊘*Museum: mid-Apr.–mid-Sept., daily 9:30–1 and 1:30–7; mid-Sept.–mid-Apr., daily 10–noon and 2–6:30.*

■ NEED A BREAK? The friendly Maison Hardy (⊠*Pl. du Vieux-Marché, Vieux-Marché* 🕾*02-35-71-81-55)* offers zestful service and a splendid view of the picturesque market-square, scene of the burning of Joan of Arc, whose story is retraced in colorful frescoes on the café wall.

⓫ The name of the pedestrian Rue du Gros-Horloge, Rouen's most popular street, comes from the **Gros-Horloge** itself, a giant Renaissance clock. In 1527 the Rouennais had a splendid arch built especially for it, and today its golden face looks out over the street. You can see the clock's inner workings from the 15th-century belfry. Though the street is crammed with stores, a few old houses, dating from the 16th century, remain. Wander through the surrounding **Vieux Rouen** (Old Rouen), a warren of tiny streets lined with more than 700 half-tim-

THE MESSENGER

Before Joan of Arc was torched on Rouen's Place du Vieux-Marché, she asked a friar to hold a crucifix high in the air and to shout out assurances of her salvation so that she could hear him above the roar of the fire.

ber houses, many artfully transformed into fashionable shops. ⊠*Rue du Gros-Horloge, Vieux-Marché* ☎*€6* ☉*Apr.–Oct., Tues.–Sun. 10–6; Jan.–Mar., Tues.–Sun. 2–5.*

WHERE TO STAY & EAT

$$$$ ✕ **La Couronne.** If P. T. Barnum, Florenz Ziegfeld, and Cecil B. DeMille
Fodor'sChoice had put together a spot distilling all the charm and glamour of Nor
★ mandy, this would be it. Behind a half-timber facade gushing geraniums, the "oldest inn in France," dating from 1345, is a sometimes-ersatz extravaganza crammed with stained leaded glass, sculpted wood beams, marble Norman chimneys, leather-upholstered chairs, and damasked curtains. The Salon Jeanne d'Arc is the largest room and has a wonderful wall-wide sash window and quaint paintings, but the only place to sit is the adorably cozy, wood-lined Salon des Rôtisseurs, an antiquarian's delight. The star attractions on the €29 menu—lobster soufflé, sheeps' feet, duck in blood sauce—make few modern concessions. Dine at La Couronne and you'll be adding your name to a list that includes Sophia Loren, John Wayne, Jean-Paul Sartre, Salvador Dalí, and Princess Grace of Monaco. ⊠*31 pl. du Vieux-Marché, Vieux-Marché* ☎*02–35–71– 40–90* ⊕*www.lacouronne.com.fr* ⊟*AE, DC, MC, V.*

★ **$$–$$$** ✕ **Dufour.** Opened in 1906 on an old street near the cathedral, this woodbeamed, stone-walled restaurant is a local institution. Character is here aplenty—model ships sway overhead, a variety of quirky brass lamps bedeck the walls, the city's steepest, narrowest staircase leads up to the restrooms, and overdressed bourgeois arrive early to claim the best tables (in the corner beneath the large, pastel-paned windows). But it's the cuisine that keeps them coming back. Fish is a specialty—try the grilled sole or brill in cider nicely lubricated by some startlingly tasty Quincy (a white wine from south of the Loire). Among the welter of fixed-price menus, the choice extends from plump green asparagus, in lightly whisked butter sauce, to a sagging platter of Normandy cheeses, followed by a copious helping of homemade apple tart or chocolate profiteroles. ⊠*67 bis, rue St-Nicolas, St-Maclou* ☎*02–35–71–90–62* ⊕*www.restaurant-dufour. com* ⊟*AE, MC, V* ☉*Closed Mon. No dinner Sun.*

$–$$ ✕ **La Toque d'Or.** Overlooking the Église Jeanne d'Arc, this large, bustling restaurant has been renowned since time immemorial for Jean-Jacques Baton's Normandy classics such as veal with Camembert flamed in calvados, breast of duck glazed in cider, or spicy braised turbot. Try the excellent house-smoked salmon (they'll give you a tour of the smokehouse if you wish) and the Norman apple *tarte soufflée.* Cheaper meals are available in the *grill* upstairs. ⊠*11 pl. du Vieux-Marché, Vieux-Marché* ☎*02–35–71–46–29* ⊟*AE, DC, V.*

$$ ✕▦ **Dieppe.** Established in 1880, the Dieppe remains up-to-date thanks to resolute management by five generations of the Guéret family. Staff members also are helpful, and they speak English. The compact rooms are cheerful and modern; street noise can be a problem, however, despite double-glazed windows. The restaurant, Les Quatre Saisons (no lunch Saturday), serves seasonal dishes with an emphasis on fish, such as the sole Michèle (poached in a light wine sauce), but is best known for its pressed duckling. ⊠*Pl. Bernard-Tissot, Gare, 76000* ☎*02–35–71–96– 00, 800/334–7234 for U.S. reservations* ☎*02–35–89–65–21* ⊕*www.*

hotel-dieppe.fr ↻*41 rooms* ♿*In-room: no a/c. In-hotel: restaurant, bar, some pets allowed* ⊟*AE, DC, MC, V* ⧆*MAP.*

$ ✕⊞ **Vieux Carré.** In the heart of Old Rouen, this cute hotel has small, practical, and comfortable rooms furnished with a taste for the exotic: lamps from Egypt, tables from Morocco, and 1940s English armoires. Ask for one of the rooms on the third floor for a view of the cathedral. Breakfast and lunch are served in the leafy courtyard, weather permitting, or in the cozy little bistro (closed Monday) off the reception area. Lunches are light and simple. Brunch is served both Saturday and Sunday until 2 PM. ⊠*34 rue Ganterie, Gare, 76000* ☎*02–35–71–67–70* ⊟*02–35–71–19–17* ↻*14 rooms* ♿*In-room: no a/c, dial-up. In-hotel: restaurant, no elevator, some pets allowed* ⊟*AE, DC, MC, V.*

$$$ ⊞ **Mercure Centre.** In the jumble of streets near the cathedral—a navigational challenge if you arrive by car—this modern chain hotel has small, comfortable rooms done in breezy pastels. The hotel is handy for exploring the old streets of the city center. ⊠*7 rue de la Croix-de-Fer, St-Maclou, 76000* ☎*02–35–52–69–52* ⊟*02–35–89–41–46* ⊕*www. mercure.com* ↻*125 rooms* ♿*In-room: ethernet. In-hotel: bar, parking (fee)* ⊟*AE, DC, MC, V* ⧆*BP.*

★ $–$$ ⊞ **Cathédrale.** This hotel, in a 17th-century building built around a flower-laden patio, sits on a narrow pedestrian street behind the cathedral. (You can sleep soundly, though: the cathedral bells do not boom out the hour at night.) Rooms are petite, but neat and comfortable. Breakfast is served in the beamed tearoom. ⊠*12 rue St-Romain, St-Maclou, 76000* ☎*02–35–71–57–95* ⊟*02–35–70–15–54* ⊕*www.hotel-de-la-cathedrale.fr* ↻*25 rooms* ♿*In-room: no a/c, ethernet. In-hotel: bar, no elevator, parking (fee), some pets allowed (fee)* ⊟*MC, V.*

NIGHTLIFE & THE ARTS

The **Fête Jeanne d'Arc** *(Joan of Arc Festival)* takes place on the Sunday nearest to May 30, with parades, street plays, concerts, exhibitions, and a medieval market. Operas, plays, and concerts are staged at the **Théâtre des Arts** (⊠*7 rue du Dr-Rambert, Vieux-Marché* ☎*02–35–71–41–36* ⊕*www.operaderouen.com*). Visit the popular local haunt **Bar de la Crosse** (⊠*53 rue de l'Hôpital, St-Maclou* ☎*02–35–70–16–68*) for an aperitif and a good chat with some friendly Rouennais.

FÉCAMP

★ ⑫ *42 km (26 mi) northeast of Le Havre.*

The ancient cod-fishing port of Fécamp was once a major pilgrimage site. The magnificent abbey church, **Abbaye de La Trinité** (⊠*Rue Leroux*), bears witness to Fécamp's religious past. The Benedictine abbey was founded by the Duke of Normandy in the 11th century and became the home of the monastic order of the Précieux Sang de la Trinité (Precious Blood of the Trinity—referring to Christ's blood, which supposedly arrived here in the 7th century in a reliquary from the Holy Land).

Fécamp is also the home of Benedictine liqueur. The **Palais de la Bénédictine** *(Benedictine Palace)*, across from the tourist office, is a florid building dating from 1892 that mixes neo-Gothic and Renaissance styles. Watery pastiche or taste-tingling architectural cocktail? Whether you're shaken or stirred, this remains one of Normandy's most popular attractions. The interior is just as exhausting as the facade. Paintings, sculptures, ivories, advertising posters, and fake bottles of Benedictine compete for attention with a display of the ingredients used for the liqueur, and a chance to sample it. There's also a shop selling Benedictine products and souvenirs. ⊠110 rue Alexandre-le-Grand ☏02–35–10–26–10 ⊕www.benedictine.fr ⌕€6 ⊗July and Aug., daily 10–7; Sept.–Dec. and Feb.–June, daily 10–12:45 and 2–6.

> **THE ALABASTER COAST**
>
> Named for the white cliffs that stretch between Dieppe and Le Havre, the scenic Côte d'Albâtre attracted writers and artists like Maupassant, Proust, and Monet in the 19th century. Perhaps they were inspired by the area's châteaux and rock formations, but they probably didn't spend time sunbathing in their Speedos; the coast is known for its galets—large pebbles that cover the beaches.

WHERE TO STAY & EAT

$ ✗ **L'Escalier.** This delightfully simple little restaurant overlooking the harbor serves traditional Norman cuisine, such as mussels in calvados and homemade fish soup. ⊠101 quai Bérigny ☏02–35–28–26–79 ⌕Reservations essential ▭DC, MC, V ⊗Closed 2 wks in Nov.

★ $$–$$$ ✗▥ **Les Hêtres.** Top chef Bertrand Warin runs this restaurant in Ingouville, east of Fécamp. Reservations are essential—as are jacket and tie—for the elegant 17th-century dining room (except in midsummer, it's closed Monday and Tuesday, with no lunch Wednesday). Half-timber walls and Louis XIII chairs contrast with sleek, modern furnishings. The five pretty guest rooms, each with old wooden furniture and engravings, are for diners only; the largest has a terrace overlooking the garden. ⊠24 rue des Fleurs, 28 km (17 mi) east of Fécamp, 76460 Ingouville ☏02–35–57–09–30 ☐02–35–57–09–31 ⊕www.leshetres.com ⌕5 rooms ⌂In-room: no a/c, ethernet. In-hotel: restaurant, no elevator, some pets allowed (fee) ▭MC, V ⊗Closed Jan.–mid-Feb. ⊠MAP.

$ ✗▥ **Auberge de la Rouge.** The Enderlins welcome you to this little inn just south of Fécamp. Rooms overlook the garden and are actually good-size lofts that sleep four. The restaurant (closed Monday; no dinner Sunday) showcases modern classics by chef Paul Durel, such as scallops with ham and leek shoots, and local specialties like roast turbot, veal and mushrooms in wine, or beef with toasted thyme. Top it off, if you can, with a local favorite, soufflé à la Bénédictine. ⊠1 rue du Bois-de-Boclion, 1 km (½ mi) south of Fécamp, 76400 St-Léonard ☏02–35–28–07–59 ☐02–35–28–70–55 ⊕www.auberge-rouge.com ⌕8 rooms ⌂In-room: no a/c. In-hotel: restaurant, no elevator ▭AE, DC, MC, V ⊠BP.

$ ✗▥ **La Ferme de la Chapelle.** The charm of this former priory lies neither in the simple, comfortable rooms around the courtyard, nor in the restaurant with its no-frills menu, but rather in its outstanding location high atop the cliffs overlooking Fécamp. There's a breathtaking, dramatic view over the entire coastline—explore it on an invigorating hike along the nearby coastal footpath. The €110 split-level family room can accommodate up to five people. ⊠*Côte de la Vierge, 76400* ☏*02–35–10–12–12* 🖷*02–35–10–12–13* ⊕*www.fermedelachapelle.fr* ⇆*17 rooms, 5 studios* ⚐*In-room: no a/c. In-hotel: restaurant, pool, no elevator, some pets allowed (fee)* ❗⃝*MAP.*

ÉTRETAT

⓭ *17 km (11 mi) southwest of Fécamp via D940, 88 km (55 mi) north-west of Rouen.*

GETTING HERE

There are no trains to Étretat. Your best bet is to take the bus from either from Fécamp (30 mins) or Le Havre (60 mins). Occasional trains from Paris (Gare St-Lazare) are met at Bréauté-Beuzeville station, between Rouen and Le Havre, by a bus that reaches Étretat in 30 minutes. All buses are operated by **Autos-Cars Gris** (02–35–27–04–25).

EXPLORING

Fodor'sChoice ★ This large village, with its promenade running the length of the pebble beach, is renowned for the magnificent tall rock formations that extend out into the sea. The **Falaises d'Étretat** are white cliffs that are as famous in France as Dover's are in England—and have been painted by many artists, Claude Monet chief among them. At low tide it's possible to walk through the huge archways formed by the rocks to neighboring beaches. The biggest arch is at the **Falaise d'Aval,** to the south. For a breathtaking view of the whole bay, take the path up to the top of the Falaise d'Aval. From here you can hike for miles across the Manneporte Hills...or play a round of golf on one of Europe's windiest and most scenic courses, overlooking **L'Aiguille** (The Needle), a 300-foot spike of rock jutting out of the sea just off the coast. To the north towers the **Falaise d'Amont,** topped by the chapel of Notre-Dame de la Garde.

WHERE TO STAY & EAT

$ ✕ **Les Roches Blanches.** The exterior of this family-owned restaurant off the beach is a post–World War II concrete eyesore. But take a table by the window with a view of the cliffs, order Georges Trézeux's superb fresh seafood (try the sea bass roasted in calvados), and you'll be glad you came. Reservations are essential for Sunday lunch. ⊠*Rue de l'Abbé-Cochet* ☏*02–35–27–07–34* ☰*MC, V* ⊙*Closed Tues. and Wed. and mid-Nov.–mid-Jan.*

★ $$$–$$$$ ✕▥ **Donjon.** This charming ivy-covered château, built in 1862 in a park overlooking the town, has lovely sea views. Rooms are individually furnished, spacious, comfortable, and quiet. For a spectacular view, request the Oriental Suite, the Horizon Room, or the Marjorie Room. Wilfrid Chaplain's flamboyant cuisine, ranging from warm hare terrine to scallops and salmon in cider, is dished up in a cozy, romantic restaurant. Rooms are reserved on a half-board basis on weekends. ⊠*Chemin de St-Clair, 76790* ☏*02–35–27–08–23* 🖷*02–35–29–92–24* ⊕*www.ledonjon-etretat.fr* ⇆*21 rooms* ⚐*In-room: no a/c, ethernet. In-hotel: restaurant, bar, pool, some pets allowed (fee)* ☰*AE, DC, MC, V* ❗⃝*MAP.*

$–$$$ ✕⊞ **Dormy House.** This unpretentious hotel is ideally located halfway up the Étretat cliffs. The rooms are simple and comfortable, but the real beauty is right out your bedroom window, thanks to views of *la mer,* so wonderful they would have Debussy humming in no time. The restaurant specializes in fresh fish and seafood platters, ranging from simple delights such as the sole stew to the full-scale *symphonie* of fish. Request a table near the window for a panoramic view of the coast. ⊠*Rte. du Havre, 76790* ☎*02–35–27–07–88* 🖷*02–35–29–86–19* ⊕*www. dormy-house.com* ⇨*62 rooms, 1 suite* ♿*In-room: no a/c, dial-up. In-hotel: restaurant* ☰*AE, MC, V* ❙◎❙*MAP.*

¢–$$ ✕⊞ **Résidence.** The cheapest rooms in this gorgeous 16th-century house in the heart of Étretat are pretty basic—both the bathroom and the shower are in the hallway—but the more expensive have in-room bathrooms, and one even has a hot tub. The service is friendly; the staff is young and energetic. The brasserie-type restaurant on the ground floor, Le Salamandre, is rather cutting-edge for the region; all products are certified organic, farm-raised, and homemade, from the vegetable terrine to the nougat ice cream. In winter a fire crackles in the hearth. ⊠*4 bd. du Président-René-Coty, 76790* ☎*02–35–27–02–87* 🖷*02–35–27–17–07* ⇨*15 rooms* ♿*In-room: no a/c, no TV (some). In-hotel: restaurant, no elevator* ☰*AE, MC, V* ❙◎❙*BP.*

SPORTS

Don't miss the chance to play at **Golf d'Étretat** (⊠*Rte. du Havre* ☎*02– 35–27–04–89*), where the breathtaking 6,580-yard, par-72 course drapes across the cliff tops of the Falaise d'Aval; it's closed Tuesday.

LE HAVRE

❶ *28 km (18 mi) southwest of Étretat via D940, 88 km (55 mi) west of Rouen, 200 km (125 mi) northwest of Paris.*

Le Havre, France's second-largest port (after Marseille), was bombarded 146 times during World War II. You may find the rebuilt city, with its uncompromising recourse to reinforced concrete and open spaces, bleak and uninviting; on the other hand, you may admire Auguste Perret's rational planning and audacious modern architecture, which earned the city UNESCO World Heritage status. The hilly suburb of **Ste-Adresse**, just west of town, is resplendent with Belle Epoque villas and an old fortress. It's also worth a visit for its beach, often painted by Raoul Dufy, and for its fine views of the sea and port, immortalized in a famous Monet masterpiece.

The **Musée André-Malraux,** the city art museum, is an innovative 1960s glass-and-metal structure surrounded by a moat, and includes an attractive sea-view café. Two local artists who gorgeously immortalized the Normandy coast are showcased here—Raoul Dufy (1877–1953), through a remarkable collection of his brightly colored oils, watercolors, and sketches; and Eugène Boudin (1824–98), a forerunner of Impressionism, whose compelling beach scenes and landscapes tellingly evoke the Normandy sea and skyline. ⊠*2 bd. Clemenceau* ☎*02–35– 19–62–62* 🖾*€5* ⊗ *Wed.–Mon. 11–6.*

Normandy on Canvas

Long before Claude Monet created his Giverny lily pond by diverting the Epte River that marks the boundary with Ile-de-France, artists had been scudding into Normandy. For two watery reasons: the Seine and the sea. Just downstream from Vernon, where the Epte joins the Seine, Richard the Lion-Hearted's ruined castle at Les Andelys, immortalized by Paul Signac and Félix Vallotton, heralds the soft-lighted, cliff-lined Seine Valley, impressionistically evoked by Albert Lebourg and Gustave Loiseau in the Arts Museum in Rouen—where Camille Corot once studied, and whose mighty cathedral Monet painted until he was pink, purple, and blue in the face.

The Seine joins the sea at Le Havre, where Monet grew up, a protégé of Eugène Boudin, often termed the precursor of Impressionism. Boudin would boat across the estuary from Honfleur, where he hobnobbed with

Gustave Courbet, Charles Daubigny, and Alfred Sisley at the Ferme St-Siméon. Le Havre in the 1860s was base camp for Monet and his pals Frédéric Bazille and Johan Barthold Jongkind to explore the rugged coast up to Dieppe, with easels opened en route beneath the cliffs of Étretat.

The railroad from Gare St-Lazare (smokily evoked by Monet) put Dieppe within easy reach of Paris. Eugène Delacroix daubed seascapes here in 1852. Auguste Renoir visited Dieppe from 1878 to 1885; Paul Gauguin and Edgar Degas clinked glasses here in 1885; Camille Pissarro painted his way from Gisors to Dieppe in the 1890s. As the nearest port to Paris, Dieppe wowed the English, too. Walter Sickert moved in from 1898 to 1905, and artists from the Camden Town Group he founded back in London often painted in Dieppe before World War I.

★ The other outstanding building in Le Havre, and one of the most impressive 20th-century churches in France, is the **Église St-Joseph,** built to the plans of Auguste Perret in the 1950s. The 350-foot tower powers into the sky like a fat rocket. The interior is just as thrilling. No frills here: the 270-foot octagonal lantern soars above the crossing, filled almost to the top with abstract stained glass that hurls colored light over the bare concrete walls. ⊠ *Bd. François-Ier* ☎*02–35–42–20–03.*

WHERE TO STAY & EAT

$$–$$$ ✗ **L'Odyssée.** With the port and fish market within netting distance, seafood is guaranteed to be fresh here. It's a no-frills place—the visual appeal is on your plate, in the pinks and greens of the smoked salmon and avocado sauce that accompany the chef's homemade fish terrine. Although it specializes in fresh fish, notably sea bass and turbot, the Odyssée has its share of meat dishes—the breast of duck with three-pepper sauce is usually a winner. ⊠ *41 rue du Général-Faidherbe* ☎*02–35–21–32–42* ▤*AE, MC, V* ⊘*Closed Mon. and mid-Aug.–early Sept. No dinner Sun., no lunch Sat.*

$$ ▦ **Art Hotel.** This hotel, in a Perret building, is handily located by the Bassin de Commerce. The light, airy rooms have modern furniture; the best have views of the port. As at all hotels in Le Havre, the prices are high for the size of the rooms. ⊠ *147 rue Louis-Brindeau, 76600*

🖼02–35–22–69–44 🖨02–35–42–09–27 ⊕*www.bestwestern.fr* ₪*30 rooms* ⚒ *In-room: no a/c, refrigerator. In-hotel: bar, public Wi-Fi, parking (fee)* ▤*AE, DC, MC, V.*

HONFLEUR TO MONT-ST-MICHEL

Basse Normandy (Lower Normandy) begins to the west of the Seine Estuary, near the Belle Epoque resort towns of Trouville and Deauville, extending out to the sandy Côte Fleurie (Flower Coast), stretching northwest from the D-Day landing sites past Omaha Beach and on to Utah Beach and the Cotentin Peninsula, which juts out into the English Channel. After the World War II D-Day landings, some of the fiercest fighting took place around Caen and Bayeux, as many monuments and memorials testify. Heading south, in the prosperous Pays d'Auge, dairy farms produce the region's famous cheeses. Rising to the west is the fabled Mont-St-Michel. Inland, heading back toward central France, lush green meadows and apple orchards cover the countryside starting west of the market town of Lisieux—the heart of calvados country.

HONFLEUR

⑮   24 *km (15 mi) southeast of Le Havre via A131 and the Pont de Nor-*
Fodor'sChoice *mandie, 27 km (17 mi) northwest of Pont-Audemer, 80 km (50 mi)*
★   *west of Rouen.*

GETTING HERE
To Whom It May Concern: get to Honfleur, take the bus from Deauville (30 mins, €3); from Caen (1 hr, 45 mins, €13); or from Le Havre (30 mins, €6.50). Buses run every two hours or so and are operated by **Bus Verts du Calvados** (🖼08–10–21–42–14 ⊕www.busverts.fr).

EXPLORING
The colorful port town of Honfleur has become increasingly crowded since the opening of the elegant Pont de Normandie, providing a direct link with Le Havre and Upper Normandy. (The world's largest cable-stayed bridge, it's supported by two concrete pylons taller than the Eiffel Tower and is designed to resist winds of 160 mph.) Honfleur, full of half-timber houses and cobbled streets, was once an important departure point for maritime expeditions, including the first voyages to Canada in the 15th and 16th centuries. The 17th-century harbor is fronted on one side by two-story stone houses with low, sloping roofs and on the other by tall, narrow houses whose wooden facades are topped by slate roofs. Note that parking can be a problem. Your best bet is the parking lot just beyond the Vieux-Bassin (old harbor) on the left as you approach from the land side.

★   Soak up the seafaring atmosphere by strolling around the old harbor and paying a visit to the ravishing wooden church of **Ste-Catherine,** which dominates a tumbling square. The church and the ramshackle belfry across the way were built by townspeople to show their gratitude for

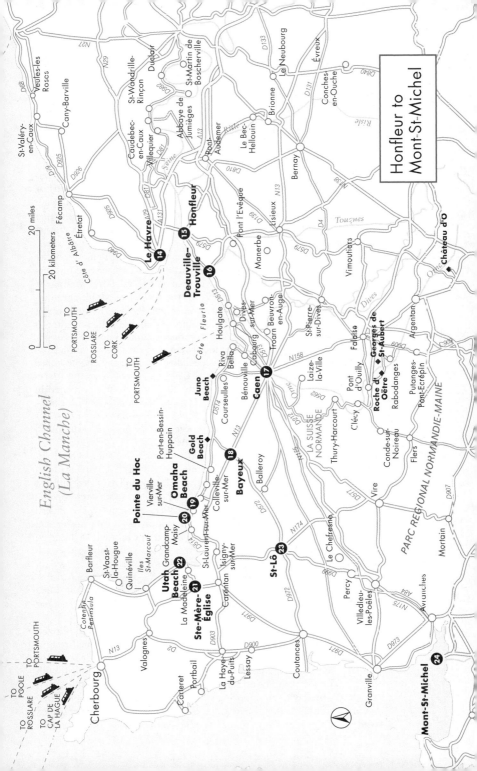

the departure of the English at the end of the Hundred Years' War, in 1453. ⊠*Rue des Logettes* ☎*02–31–89–11–83.*

WHERE TO STAY & EAT

$$$ ✕ **La Terrasse de L'Assiette.** Gérard Bonnefoy, one of Honfleur's top chefs, offers seasonal delights such as succulent scallops with hazelnut risotto and roast lamb from the salt marshes. ⊠*8 pl. Ste-Catherine* ☎*02–31–89–31–33* ▤*AE, DC, MC, V* ⊗*Closed Mon. No dinner Sun. except July and Aug.*

$ ✕ **L'Ancrage.** Massive seafood platters top the bill at this bustling restaurant in a two-story 17th-century building overlooking the harbor. The cuisine is authentically Norman—simple but good. If you want a change, try the succulent calf sweetbreads. ⊠*16 rue Montpensier* ☎*02–31–89–00–70* ▤*MC, V* ⊗*Closed Wed. and last 2 wks in Mar. No dinner Tues. except July and Aug.*

★ **$$$–$$$$** ✕▦ **Ferme St-Siméon.** The story goes that this 19th-century manor house was the birthplace of Impressionism, and that its park inspired Monet and Sisley. Rooms are opulent, with pastel colors, floral wallpaper, antiques, and period accents. Those in the converted stables are quieter but have less character. Be aware, however, that the high prices have more to do with the hotel's reputation than with the amenities it offers (although spa treatments are among them). Under chef Patrick Ogheard, the sophisticated restaurant (closed February to mid-March and Monday; no lunch Tuesday) specializes in fish; the cheese board does justice to the region, as does the €125 gastronomic menu. A second, (slightly) more modest restaurant, La Table Toutain, opened in 2007. ⊠*Rue Adolphe-Marais on D513 to Trouville, 14600* ☎*02–31–81–78–00* ▤*02–31–89–48–48* ⊕*www.fermesaintsimeon.fr* ⤴*31 rooms, 3 suites* ⌂*In-room: no a/c, refrigerator. In-hotel: 2 restaurants, tennis court, pool* ▤*AE, MC, V* ⎮◎⎮*MAP.*

$$$–$$$$ ✕▦ **Le Manoir de Butin.** An archetypal fin de siècle "villa," this half-timber, dormer-roofed manor welcomes you with a pretty facade in the Anglo-Norman style. Perched on top of a small wooded hill just 650 feet meters from the sea, the hotel offers guest rooms with appetizing views, all traditionally and tastefully furnished, and with modern marble bathrooms. The room on the first floor has a four-poster bed and its own balcony. The atmospheric restaurant (closed Wednesday; no lunch Thursday or Friday) specializes in seasonal fish dishes such as a light lobster consommé and braised freshwater cod. ⊠*Phare du Butin, 14600* ☎*02–31–81–63–00* ▤*02–31–89–59–23* ⊕*www.hotel-lemanoir.fr* ⤴*10 rooms* ⌂*In-room: no a/c. In-hotel: restaurant, some pets allowed (fee), public Internet* ▤*AE, MC, V* ⊗*Closed Nov. and mid-Dec.–Jan.* ⎮◎⎮*MAP.*

★ **$$–$$$** ✕▦ **L'Absinthe.** A 16th-century presbytery with stone walls and beamed ceilings houses a small and charming hotel and the acclaimed restaurant of the same name. Rooms are comfortable but small, except for the attic suite, which has a private living room. All are equipped with large modern bathrooms and hot tubs. The elegant and cozy reception area is adorned with an imposing stone fireplace. Chef Antoine Ceffrey is famous for his seasonal seafood and fish dishes such as turbot grilled with leeks. On sunny days request a table on the terrace; the restaurant is closed for dinner Monday. The Grenouille brasserie serves simpler fare. ☒*10 quai de la Quarantaine* ☏*02–31–89–23–23* 🖷*02–31–89–53–60* ⊕*www.absinthe.fr* 🛏*6 rooms, 1 suite* ⚘*In-room: no a/c. In-hotel: restaurant, no elevator, some pets allowed (fee)* ▤*DC, MC, V* ☽*Closed mid-Nov.–mid-Dec.* ⊖|*MAP.*

$$–$$$ ☖ **Cheval Blanc.** Most guest rooms at this cozy quayside hotel have fine views of the port. No. 34 is larger and is furnished with a couch, queen-size bed, and has gabled ceilings and a Jacuzzi. There are also two spacious suites at €425 with hammam (steam room) and balcony. ☒*2 quai des Passagers, 14600* ☏*02–31–81–65–00* 🖷*02–31–89–52–80* ⊕*www.hotel-honfleur.com* 🛏*33 rooms* ⚘*In-room: no a/c* ▤*MC, V* ☽*Closed Jan.*

NIGHTLIFE & THE ARTS

The two-day **Fête des Marins** *(Marine Festival)* is held on Pentecost Sunday and Monday. On Sunday all the boats in the harbor are decked out in flags and paper roses, and a priest bestows his blessing at high tide. The next day, model boats and local children head a musical procession. There's also a five-day **Fête du Jazz** *(Jazz Festival)* in August.

DEAUVILLE-TROUVILLE

❶⑥   *16 km (10 mi) southwest of Honfleur via D513, 92 km (57 mi) west*
Fodor's Choice *of Rouen.*
★

GETTING HERE

Trains to Deauville-Trouville (the station is between the two towns) from Gare St-Lazare in Paris (2 hrs, €26) often require a change at Lisieux. There also buses to Deauville from Le Havre (1 hr, €9); Honfleur (30 mins, €3); and Caen (75 mins, €9). Buses run every two hours or so and are operated by **Bus Verts du Calvados** (☏08–10–21–42–14 ⊕www.busverts.fr).

EXPLORING

Twin towns on the beach, divided only by the River Touques, Deauville and Trouville compete for the title of Most Extravagant Norman Town. The two towns have distinctly different atmospheres, but it's easy (and common) to shuttle between them. Trouville—whose beaches were immortalized in the 19th-century paintings of Eugène Boudin (and Vincente Minelli's 1958 Oscar-winner, *Gigi*)—is the oldest seaside resort in France. In the days of Louis-Philippe, it was discovered by artists and the upper crust; by the end of the Second Empire it was the beach à la mode. Then the Duc de Mornay, half brother of Napoléon III, and other aristocrats who were looking for something more exclusive, built their villas along the deserted beach across the Touques (more than a few of these were built simply as love-shacks for their mistresses).

Thus was launched Deauville, a vigorous grande dame who started kicking up her heels during the Second Empire, kept swinging through the Belle Epoque, and is still frequented by a fair share of Rothschilds, princes, and movie stars. Few of them ever actually get in the water here, since other attractions—casino, theater, music hall, polo, galas, racecourses (some of the world's most fabled horse farms are here), marina and regattas, palaces and gardens, and extravagant shops along the Rue Eugène-Colas—compete for their attention. Fashionable avenues like Rue des Villas and Place Morny also entice. But perhaps Deauville is known best for its **Promenade des Planches**—the boardwalk extending along the seafront and lined with deck chairs, bars, striped cabanas, and an array of lovely half-timber Norman villas—*the* place for celebrity-spotting. With its high-price hotels,

> ## HOOFBEATS YOU CAN BET ON
>
> If you can't catch up with a Rothschild bidding on a new colt at Deauville's famous August yearling sales, aim for the Grand Prix de Deauville race held on the last Sunday in August. Throughout the summer, Deauville's Toques and Clairefontaine hippodromes hold horse races (or polo matches) nearly every afternoon.

designer boutiques, and one of the smartest gilt-edge casinos in Europe, Deauville is often jokingly called Paris's 21st arrondissement.

Trouville—a short drive or five-minute boat trip across the Touques River from its more prestigious neighbor—remains more of a family resort, harboring few pretensions. If you'd like to see a typical French holiday spot rather than look for glamour, stay in Trouville. It, too, has a casino and boardwalk, an aquarium and bustling fishing port, a lively Sunday morning market, plus a native population that makes it a livelier spot out of season than Deauville.

WHERE TO STAY & EAT

$$$$
Fodor's Choice
★

✕🖼 **Normandy-Barrière.** With a facade that is a riot of pastel-green timbering, checkerboard walls, and Anglo-Norman balconies, the Normandy has been one of the town's most beautiful landmarks since it opened in 1912. From the beginning it attracted well-heeled Parisians (many of whom appreciated the underground passage to the casino), but it has kept them coming as its grand salons have been transformed by Jacques Garcia—France's chicest and most aristo decorator—and now overflow with needlepointed sofas, fin de siècle chandeliers, and opulent silks. The lobby is a Belle Epoque blowout, with soaring oak walls, a forest of columns, and islands of comfy, 19th-century-style armchairs. The courtyard is its outdoor version, with a grassy patio surrounded by a spectacular panoply of turrets and balconies. Request a room with a sea view, and don't forget to ask about the special thalassotherapy rates with full or half days of mud baths, salt massages, and soothing heated-seawater swims. Breakfast is served around the indoor pool. Creamy sauces are much in evidence in the mouthwatering Norman dishes served up in the L'Etrier restaurant, set in a grand hall which glitters like the salons of Versailles. ✉ *38 rue Jean-Mermoz, 14800 Deauville* ☎ *02–31–98–66–22, 800/223–5652 for U.S. reservations* 🖷 *02–31–98–66–23* ⊕ *www.normandy-barriere.com* ➷ *290 rooms, 31 suites* ♿ *In-room: no a/c, refrigerators. In-hotel: 2 restaurants, bar, pool, public Wi-Fi, some pets allowed (fee)* ⊟ *AE, DC, MC, V* ⍾⦿*BP.*

$–$$$ ✕▥ **Le Clos Deauville-St-Gatien.** Starting out as an old Norman half-timber farmhouse, this hotel now sprawls with more than 50 rooms and a rather lush and glossy swimming pool terrace. Set just outside Honfleur, near the Forest of St-Gatien, it remains a fine base for horseback riding (on-site facilities) or a round of golf at the nearby 18-hole course. Rooms in the main house are rustic, with exposed beams and traditional furniture; those in the annex lack character but have terraces that open out to the swimming pool. The restaurant, Le Michel's, serves succulent Norman fare, such as blood sausage with roast apples, or grilled lamb with eggplant caviar. Reservations are essential. ⊠*4 chemin des Bricoleurs, 14130* ☎*02–31–65–16–08* 🖷*02–31–65–10–27* ⊕*www.clos-st-gatien.fr* 🖙*58 rooms* ⚒*In-room: dial-up. In-hotel: restaurant, tennis courts, pool, gym, no elevator* ▤*AE, MC, V.*

$–$$ ▥ **Continental.** One of Deauville's oldest buildings is now this provincial hotel, close to the train station yet within easy walking distance of the town center. Rooms are small but simple, pristine, and reasonably priced for Deauville. ⊠*1 rue Désiré-Le-Hoc, 14800Deauville* ☎*02–31–88–21–06* 🖷*02–31–98–93–67* ⊕*www.hotel-continental-deauville. com* 🖙*42 rooms* ⚒*In-room: no a/c, dial-up. In-hotel: bar* ▤*AE, DC, MC, V* ⊘*Closed mid-Nov.–mid-Dec.*

¢–$ ▥ **Carmen.** This straightforward, unpretentious little hotel is around the corner from the casino and a block from the sea. Rooms range from plain and inexpensive to comfortable and moderately priced. The owners, the Bude family, are on hand to give advice. Breakfast runs €5.75. ⊠*24 rue Carnot, 14360 Trouville* ☎*02–31–88–35–43* 🖷*02–31–88–08–03* 🖙*18 rooms* ⚒*In-room: no a/c. In-hotel: restaurant, public Internet* ▤*AE, DC, MC, V* ⊘*Closed Jan.–mid-Feb.*

NIGHTLIFE & THE ARTS

One of the biggest cultural events on the Norman calendar is the weeklong **American Film Festival,** held in Deauville in early September. Formal attire is required at the **Casino de Deauville** (⊠*2 rue Edmond-Blanc* ☎*02–31–14–31–14*). Trouville's **Casino de Trouville** (⊠*Pl. du Maréchal-Foch* ☎*02–31–87–75–00*) is slightly less highbrow than Deauville's. Night owls enjoy the smoky **Amazone** (⊠*13 rue Albert-Fracasse, Deauville*); it's open until 5 AM. The **Y Club** (⊠*14 bis, rue Désiré-le-Hoc, Deauville*) is the place to go out dancing.

SPORTS & THE OUTDOORS

Deauville becomes Europe's horse capital in August, when breeders jet in from around the world for its yearling auctions and the races at its two attractive *hippodromes* (racetracks). Afternoon horse races are held in the heart of Deauville at the **Hippodrome de Deauville—La Toques** (⊠*Blvd. Mauger* ☎*02–31–14–20–00*). Horse and polo races can be seen most summer afternoons at the **Hippodrome de Deauville Clairefontaine** (⊠*Rte. de Clairefontaine* ☎*02–31–14–69–00*). Head for the **Poney Club** (⊠*Rue Reynoldo-Hahn* ☎*02–31–98–56–24*) for a wonderful horseback ride on the beach. (The sunsets can be spectacular.) It's open weekends and holidays, but be sure to call early to reserve a horse, or a pony for your little one. Sailing boats large and small can be rented from the **Club Nautique de Trouville** (⊠*Digue des Roches Noires* ☎*02–31–88–13–59*).

CAEN

🔞 *28 km (17 mi) southeast of Bayeux, 120 km (75 mi) west of Rouen.*

Fodor's Choice
★

GETTING HERE

Trains from Paris (Gare St-Lazare) leave for Caen every two hours or so (€19); the 150-mi trip takes less than two hours. Some trains continue to Bayeux (2 hrs, €31). Several trains daily link Caen to Rouen (90 mins, €21.50) and St-Lô (45 mins, €11). Bus Verts du Calvados (☎08-10–21–42–14 ⊕www.busverts.fr) operate buses every two hours or so from Caen train station to Le Havre (2 hrs, 15 mins, €18) via Deauville (75 mins, €9) and Honfleur (1 hr, 45 mins, €11.50).

EXPLORING

With its abbeys and castle, Caen, a busy administrative city and the capital of Lower Normandy, is very different from the coastal resorts. William of Normandy ruled from Caen in the 11th century before he conquered England. Nine hundred years later, during the two-month Battle of Caen in 1944, a fire raged for 11 days, devastating much of the town. Today, the city is basically modern and commercial, with a vibrant student scene. The Caen Memorial, an impressive museum devoted to World War II, is considered a must-do by travelers interested in 20th-century history (many avail themselves of the excellent bus tours the museum sponsors to the D-Day beaches). But Caen's former grandeur can be seen in its extant historic monuments and along scenically restored Rue Ecuyère and Place St-Sauveur.

A good place to begin exploring Caen is the **Hôtel d'Escoville,** a stately mansion in the city center built by wealthy merchant Nicolas Le Valois d'Escoville in the 1530s. The building was badly damaged during the war but has since been restored; the austere facade conceals an elaborate inner courtyard, reflecting the Italian influence on early Renaissance Norman architecture. The on-site city **tourist office** is an excellent resource. ✉*Pl. St-Pierre* ☎*02–31–27–14–14* ⊕*www.ville-caen.fr.*

Across the square, beneath a 240-foot spire, is the late-Gothic church of **St-Pierre,** a riot of ornamental stonework.

Looming on a mound ahead of the church is the **château**—the ruins of William the Conqueror's fortress, built in 1060 and sensitively restored after the war. The castle gardens are a perfect spot for strolling, and the ramparts afford good views of the city. The citadel also contains two museums and the medieval church of **St-Georges,** used for exhibitions.

The **Musée des Beaux-Arts,** within the castle's walls, is a heavyweight among France's provincial fine-arts museums. Its old masters collection includes works by Poussin, Perugino, Rembrandt, Titian, Tintoretto, van der Weyden, and Paolo Veronese; there's also a wide range of 20th-century art. ✉*Entrance by castle gateway* ☎*02–31–30–47–70* ⊕*www.ville-caen.fr/mba* 🎫*Free* ⊙ *Wed.–Mon. 9:30–6.*

The **Musée de Normandie** *(Normandy Museum),* in the mansion built for the castle governor, is dedicated to regional arts, such as ceramics and sculpture, plus some local archaeological finds. ✉*Entrance by* *castle gateway* 🕿*02–31–30–47–60* ⊕*www.ville-caen.fr/mdn* ✉*Free* ⊘*June–Sept., daily 9:30–6; Oct.–May, Wed.–Mon. 9:30–6.*

Fodor'sChoice Caen's finest church, of cathedral proportions, is part of the **Abbaye**
★   **aux Hommes** *(Men's Abbey)*, built by William the Conqueror from local
Caen stone (also used for Canterbury Cathedral, Westminster Abbey,
and the Tower of London). The abbey was begun in Romanesque style
in 1066 and expanded in the 18th century; its elegant buildings are now
part of City Hall and some rooms are brightened by the city's fine collection of paintings. Note the magnificent yet spare facade of the abbey
church of **St-Étienne**, enhanced by two 11th-century towers topped by
octagonal spires. Inside, what had been William the Conqueror's tomb
was destroyed by 16th-century Huguenots during the Wars of Religion.
However, the choir still stands; it was the first to be built in Norman
Gothic style, and many subsequent choirs were modeled after it. ✉*Pl.
Louis-Guillouard* 🕿*02–31–30–42–81* ✉*Tours €2.20* ⊘*Tours daily
at 9:30, 11, 2:30, and 4.*

The **Abbaye aux Dames** *(Ladies' Abbey)* was founded by William the
Conqueror's wife, Matilda, in 1063. Once a hospital, the abbey—rebuilt
in the 18th century—was restored in the 1980s by the Regional Council, which then promptly requisitioned it for office space; however, its
elegant arcaded courtyard and ground-floor reception rooms can be
admired during a free guided tour. You can also visit the squat **Église
de la Trinité** (Trinity Church), a fine example of 11th-century Romanesque architecture, though its original spires were replaced by timid
balustrades in the early 18th century. Note the intricate carvings on
columns and arches in the chapel; the 11th-century crypt; and, in the
choir, the marble slab commemorating Queen Matilda, buried here in
1083. ✉*Pl. de la Reine-Mathilde* 🕿*02–31–06–98–98* ✉*Free* ⊘*Tours
daily at 2:30 and 4.*

★ The **Mémorial,** an imaginative museum erected in 1988 in the north side
of the city, is a must-see if you're interested in World War II history. The
stark, flat facade, with a narrow
doorway symbolizing the Allies'
breach in the Nazi's supposedly
impregnable Atlantic Wall, opens
onto an immense foyer containing
a café, brasserie, shop, and British
Typhoon aircraft suspended overhead. The museum itself is down
a spiral ramp, lined with photos
and documents charting the Nazi's
rise to power in the 1930s. The
idea—hardly subtle but visually
effective—is to suggest a descent
into the hell of war. The extensive
displays range from wartime plastic jewelry to scale models of bat-
tleships, with scholarly sections on
how the Nazis tracked down radios

FROM WAR TO PEACE

Normandy war museums are
legion, but the Mémorial, its
one and only peace museum,
is special. Even better, readers
rave about the museum's four-
hour minibus tours of the D-Day
beaches, run daily April to September. You can even make a day
trip from Paris for this by catching
the 8:40 AM train out of Gare St-
Lazare to Caen and returning on
the 7:55 PM train. Besides the tour,
this €100 trip includes pickup at
the station and lunch.

used by the French Resistance and on the development of the atomic bomb. A room commemorating the Holocaust, with flickering candles and twinkling overhead lights, sounds a jarring, somewhat tacky note. The D-Day landings are evoked by a tabletop Allied map of the theater of war and by a spectacular split-screen presentation of the D-Day invasion from both the Allied and Nazi standpoints. Softening the effect of the modern 1988 museum structure are tranquil gardens; the newest is the British Garden, inaugurated by Prince Charles in 2004. The museum itself is fittingly set 10 minutes away from the Pegasus Bridge and 15 minutes from the D-Day beaches. ⊠*Esplanade Dwight-D.-Eisenhower* ☎*02–31–06–06–44* ⊕*www.memorial.fr* ✍*€17* ⊙*Mid-Feb.–Oct., daily 9–7; Nov., Dec., and late Jan.–mid-Feb., daily 9–6.*

WHERE TO STAY & EAT

$–$$$ ✕ **Le P'tit B.** On one of Caen's oldest pedestrian streets near the castle, this typically Norman, half-timber 17th-century dining room—stone walls, beamed ceilings, and large fireplace—showcases the good-value regional cuisine of Cédric Mesnard. ⊠*15 rue de Vaugueux* ☎*02–31–93–50–76* ⚱*Reservations essential* ▭*MC, V.*

$$–$$$ ✕⌨ **Dauphin.** Despite being in the heart of the city, this hotel, in a former 12th-century priory, is surprisingly quiet. Some of the smallish rooms have exposed beams; those overlooking the street are soundproof; the ones in back look out on the courtyard. Service is friendly and efficient in the hotel and in the excellent though expensive restaurant (no lunch in summer). ⊠*29 rue Gémare, 14000* ☎*02–31–86–22–26* ☎*02–31–86–35–14* ⊕*www.le-dauphin-normandie.com* ⤴*32 rooms, 5 suites* ⚴*In-room: no a/c, refrigerator. In-hotel: restaurant, bar* ▭*AE, DC, MC, V* ⊙*Closed 2 wks Nov. and part of Feb.* ⦿*MAP.*

SHOPPING

A *marché aux puces (flea market)* is held on Friday morning on Place St-Saveur and on Sunday morning on Place Courtonne. In June, collectors and dealers flock to Caen's bric-a-brac and **antiques fair.**

THE OUTDOORS

Take a barge trip along the canal that leads from Caen to the sea on the *Hastings* (⊠*Quai Vendeuvre* ☎*02–31–34–00–00*); there are four daily departures: 9 AM, noon, 3 PM, and 7 PM.

EN ROUTE Early on June 6, 1944, the British 6th Airborne Division landed by glider and captured **Pegasus Bridge** (named for the division's emblem, showing Bellerophon astride his winged horse, Pegasus). This proved the first step toward the liberation of France from Nazi occupation. To see this symbol of the Allied invasion, from Caen take D514 north and turn right at Bénouville. The original bridge—erected in 1935—has been replaced by a similar but slightly wider bridge; but the actual original can still be seen at the adjacent **Mémorial Pegasus** visitor center (⊙Feb.–Nov. daily ✍ €6). Café Gondrée by the bridge—the first building recaptured on French soil—is still standing, still serving coffee, and houses a small museum. A 40-minute son-et-lumière show lights up the bridge and the café at nightfall between June and September.

Five kilometers (3 mi) north of here, just beyond Ouistreham and its **Grand Bunker** museum recalling Hitler's Atlantic Wall, lie the easternmost D-Day landing beaches: **Sword Beach** extends to Luc-sur-Mer; **Juno Beach** to Courseulles; and **Gold Beach** to Arromanches. These flat, sandy beaches, stormed by British (Gold and Sword) and Canadian (Juno) troops, extend beneath pretty resort towns like Lion-sur-Mer, Langrune, and St-Aubin. Inland, slender church spires patrol the vast, flat horizon.

WHERE TO STAY & EAT

$ ✕▣ **Le Mulberry.** This small hotel, one block back from the seafront, is run by a cheerful young couple, Aline and Damien Debaudre. Rooms are small and basic, but a good value, and the restaurant (closed Tuesday and Wednesday) serves up Aline's homemade tuna pâté and ham in cider on the €14.50 set menu. ⊠ *6 rue Maurice-Lithare* ☎ *02–31–22–36–05* 🖷 *02–31–21–59–66* ⊕ *www.lemulberry.fr* ▭ *MC, V* ⊗ *Closed Jan.*

BAYEUX

⑱ *28 km (17 mi) northwest of Caen.*

Bayeux, the first town to be liberated during the Battle of Normandy, was already steeped in history—as home to a Norman Gothic cathedral and the world's most celebrated piece of needlework: the Bayeux Tapestry. Bayeux's medieval backcloth makes it a popular base, especially among British travelers, for day trips to other towns in Normandy. Since Bayeux had nothing strategically useful like factories or military bases, it was never bombed on either side, leaving its beautiful cathedral and old town intact. The old-world mood is at its most boisterous during the Fêtes Médiévales, a market-cum-carnival held in the streets around the cathedral on the first weekend of July. A more traditional market is held every Saturday morning. The town is a good starting-point for visits to the World War II sites; there are many custom-tour guides, but Taxis du Bessin (☎ 02–31–92–92–40) is one of the best.

Fodor's Choice Really a 225-foot-long embroidered scroll stitched in 1067, the **Bay-** ★ **eux Tapestry** *(Tapestry Museum)*, known in French as the *Tapisserie de la Reine Mathilde* (Queen Matilda's Tapestry), depicts, in 58 comic strip–type scenes, the epic story of William of Normandy's conquest of England in 1066, narrating Will's trials and victory over his cousin Harold, culminating in the Battle of Hastings on October 14, 1066. The tapestry was probably commissioned from Saxon embroiderers by the count of Kent—who was also the bishop of Bayeux—to be displayed in his newly built cathedral, the Cathédrale Notre-Dame. Despite its age, the tapestry is in remarkably good condition; the extremely detailed, often homey scenes provide an unequaled record of the clothes, weapons, ships, and lifestyles of the day. It's showcased in the **Musée de la Tapisserie;** free headphones let you to listen to an English commentary about the tapestry. ⊠ *Centre Guillaume-le-Conquérant, 13 bis, rue de Nesmond* ☎ *02–31–51–25–50* ▣ *€7.70, includes Musée Baron-Gérard* ⊗ *May–Aug., daily 9–7; Sept.–Apr., daily 9:30–12:30 and 2–6.*

Housed in the Bishop's Palace beneath the cathedral, and fronted by a majestic plane tree planted in March 1797 and known as the Tree of Liberty, the **Musée Baron-Gérard** contains a fine collection of Bayeux porcelain and lace, ceramics from Rouen, a marvelous collection of pharmaceutical jars from the 17th and 18th centuries, and 16th- to 19th-century furniture and paintings by local artists. ⊠*1 pl. de la Liberté* ☎*02–31–92–14–21* ☑*€3.50, €7.70 includes Tapestry Museum* ⊘*Daily 10–12:30 and 2–6.*

Bayeux's mightiest edifice, the **Cathédrale Notre-Dame,** is a harmonious mixture of Norman and Gothic architecture. Note the portal on the south side of the transept that depicts the assassination of English archbishop Thomas à Becket in Canterbury Cathedral in 1170, following his courageous opposition to King Henry II's attempts to control the church. ⊠*Rue du Bienvenu* ☎*02–31–92–01–85* ⊘*Daily 8:30–6.*

Handmade lace is a specialty of Bayeux. The best place to learn about it and to buy some is the **Conservatoire de la Dentelle** near the cathedral, which has a good display. ⊠*6 rue du Bienvenu* ☎*02–31–92–73–80* ☑*Free* ⊘*Mon.–Sat. 10–12:30 and 2:30–6.*

At the **Musée de la Bataille de Normandie** *(Battle of Normandy Museum)* exhibits trace the story of the struggle from June 7 to August 22, 1944. This modern museum near the moving British War Cemetery, sunk partly beneath the level of its surrounding lawns, contains some impressive war paraphernalia. ⊠*Bd. du Général-Fabian-Ware* ☎*02–31–51–46–90* ⊕*www.normandiememoire.com* ☑*€6.50* ⊘*May–Sept., daily 9:30–6:30; Oct.–Apr., daily 10–12:30 and 2–6.*

Fodor's Choice   About 16 km (10 mi) southwest of Bayeux stands the **Château de Balleroy.**
★   A connoisseur's favorite, it was begun by architect François Mansart in 1626 and took a decade to complete. The *cour d'honneur* is marked by two stylish side pavilions—an architectural grace note adapted from Italian Renaissance models—which beautifully frame the small, but very seignorial, central mass of the house. Inside, the *salon d'honneur* is the very picture of Louis XIV decoration, while other rooms were recast in chic 19th-century style by Malcolm Forbes, who bought the château in 1970. A gallery houses the fascinating **Musée des Ballons** (Balloon Museum). The companion village to the château was designed by Mansart in one of the first examples of town planning in France. Note that the château itself is closed mid-October to mid-March, but the museum remains open. ⊠*Balleroy* ☎*02–31–21–60–61* ⊕*www. chateau-balleroy.com* ☑*€7* ⊘ *Château and museum:Mid-Mar.–mid-Oct., Wed.–Mon. 10–6; museum also open mid-Oct.–mid-Mar., weekdays 10–noon and 1:30–5.*

WHERE TO STAY & EAT

$$–$$$ ✕ **L'Amaryllis.** Pascal Marie's small restaurant has three prix-fixe menus, running €12 to €29. The three-course dinner, with six selections per course, may include a half dozen oysters, fillet of sole with a cider-based sauce, and pastries or chocolate gâteau for dessert. Lobster and skate with shallots lurk *à la carte.* ⊠*32 rue St-Patrice* ☎*02–31–22–47–94* ⊟*MC, V* ⊘*Closed Mon. and Jan. No dinner Sun. Nov.–Mar.*

> **HOW WILL GOT HERE**
>
> Kind of like the world's longest cartoon, the Bayeux Tapestry features 58 gloriously hand-embroidered scenes, some amusing but also including gory battles and the hand of God reaching down from the sky to meddle in human activities and help Will out. If you know nothing of the conqueror, read the history blurb in the museum before seeing the tapestry—you'll enjoy it more that way.

★ $$$–$$$$ ✕🏨 **Château d'Audrieu.** This family-owned château with an elegant 18th-century facade fulfills a Hollywood notion of a palatial property: princely opulence, overstuffed chairs, wall sconces, and antiques. Rooms 50 and 51 have peaked ceilings with exposed-wood beams. The restaurant (closed Monday except for guests; no lunch weekdays) has an extensive wine list. Chef Cyril Haberland explores an exotic repertoire of dishes, like scallops with chestnuts and cranberry juice. ✉ *13 km (8 mi) southeast of Bayeux off N13, 14250 Audrieu* ☎ *02–31–80–21–52* 📠 *02–31–80–24–73* 🌐 *www.chateaudaudrieu.com* *29 rooms* *In-room: no a/c, refrigerator. In-hotel: restaurant, bar, pool, no elevator* ▭ *AE, MC, V* ⏲ *Closed Dec.–mid-Feb.* 🍴 *MAP.*

$–$$ ✕🏨 **Grand Hôtel du Luxembourg.** The Luxembourg has small but adequate rooms; all but two face a courtyard garden. It has one of the town's best restaurants, Les Quatre Saisons (closed January), with a seasonal menu. Depending on the time of year, choose the honey-roasted ham with melted apples, or braised turbot with sage. ✉ *25 rue des Bouchers, 14400* ☎ *02–31–92–00–04, 800/528–1234 for U.S. reservations* 📠 *02–31–92–54–26* 🌐 *www.adeauville.com/henri/hotelbayeux* *24 rooms, 3 suites* *In-room: dial-up. In-hotel: restaurant, bar, some pets allowed (fee)* ▭ *AE, DC, MC, V* 🍴 *MAP.*

★ $$ 🏨 **Manoir du Carel.** The narrow slits serving as windows on the tower recall the origins of the 17th-century Manoir du Carel, set nicely halfway between Bayeux and the sea, and built as a fortified manor during the Hundred Years' War. Owner Jacques Aumond enjoys welcoming guests to his comfortable rooms with modern furnishings. The cottage on the grounds, ideal for families, has a kitchen plus a fireplace that masks a brick oven where villagers once had their bread baked. Pets are not allowed. ✉ *5 km (3 mi) northwest of Bayeux, 14400 Maisons* ☎ *02–31–22–37–00* 📠 *02–31–21–57–00* 🌐 *www.bienvenue-au-chateau.com* *2 rooms, 1 cottage* *In-room: no a/c. In-hotel: tennis court, no elevator* ▭ *DC, MC, V* 🍴 *BP.*

THE D-DAY BEACHES

History focused its sights along the coasts of Normandy at 6:30 AM on June 6, 1944, as the 135,000 men and 20,000 vehicles of the Allied troops made land in their first incursion in Europe in World War II. The entire operation on this "Longest Day" was called Operation Overlord—the code name for the invasion of Normandy. Five beachheads (dubbed Utah, Omaha, Gold, Juno, and Sword) were established along the coast to either side of Arromanches. Preparations started in mid-

1943, and British shipyards worked furiously through the following winter and spring building two artificial harbors (called "mulberries"), boats, and landing equipment. The British and Canadian troops that landed on Sword, Juno, and Gold on June 6, 1944, quickly pushed inland and joined with parachute regiments previously dropped behind German lines, before encountering fierce resistance at Caen, which did not fall until July 9. Today, the best way to tour this region is by car. Or—since public buses from Bayeux are infrequent—opt for one of the guided bus tours leaving from Caen *(see Tour Options in Normandy Essentials, below).*

★ ⓳   You won't be disappointed by the rugged terrain and windswept sand of **Omaha Beach,** 16 km (10 mi) northwest of Bayeux. Here you can find the **Monument du Débarquement** (Monument to the Normandy Landings) and nearby, in Vierville-sur-Mer, the **U.S. National Guard Monument.** Throughout June 6, Allied forces battled a hailstorm of German bullets and bombs, but by the end of the day they had taken the sector, although they had suffered grievous losses. In Colleville-sur-Mer, overlooking Omaha Beach, is the hilltop **American Cemetery and Memorial,** designed by the landscape architect Markley Stevenson. You can look out to sea across the landing beach from a platform on the north side of the cemetery.

★ ⓴   The most spectacular scenery along the coast is at the **Pointe du Hoc,** 13 km (8 mi) west of St-Laurent. Wildly undulating grassland leads past ruined blockhouses to a cliff-top observatory and a German machine-gun post whose intimidating mass of reinforced concrete merits chilly exploration. Despite Spielberg's cinematic genius, it remains hard to imagine just how Colonel Rudder and his 225 Rangers—only 90 survived—managed to scale the jagged cliffs with rope ladders and capture the German defenses in one of the most heroic and dramatic episodes of the war. A granite memorial pillar now stands on top of a concrete bunker, but the site otherwise remains as the Rangers left it—look down through the barbed wire at the jutting cliffs the troops ascended and see the huge craters left by exploded shells.

㉑   Head west around the coast on N13, pause in the town of **Carentan** to admire its modern marina and the mighty octagonal spire of the Église Notre-Dame, and continue northwest to **Sainte-Mère Église.** At 2:30 AM on June 6, 1944, the 82nd Airborne Division was dropped over Ste-Mère, heralding the start of D-Day operations. After securing their position at Ste-Mère, U.S. forces pushed north, then west, cutting off the Cotentin Peninsula on June 18 and taking Cherbourg on June 26. German defenses proved fiercer farther south, and St-Lô was not liberated until July 19. Ste-Mère's symbolic importance as the first French village to be liberated from the Nazis is commemorated by the Borne 0 (Zero) outside the town hall—a large, domed milestone marking the start of the Voie de la Liberté (Freedom Way), charting the Allies' progress across France.

The **Musée Airborne** *(Airborne Troops Museum),* built behind the church in 1964 in the form of an open parachute, houses documents, maps, mementos, and one of the Waco CG4A gliders used to drop troops. ✉ *Pl. du 6-juin-1944* ☎ *02–33–41–41–35* 🌐 *www.airborne-museum.org* 🎟 *€6* ⏲ *Feb.–mid-Nov., daily 9:30–noon and 2–6.*

★ 22 Head east on D67 from Ste-Mère to **Utah Beach,** which, being sheltered from the Atlantic winds by the Cotentin Peninsula and surveyed by lowly sand dunes rather than rocky cliffs, proved easier to attack than Omaha. Allied troops stormed the beach at dawn and just a few hours later had managed to conquer the German defenses, heading inland to join up with the airborne troops.

OÙ EST PRIVATE RYAN?

The American Cemetery is a moving tribute to the fallen, with its Wall of the Missing, drumlike chapel, and avenues of holly oaks trimmed to resemble open parachutes. The crisply mowed lawns are studded with 9,386 marble tombstones; this is where Stephen Spielberg's fictional hero Captain John Miller was supposed to have been buried in Saving Private Ryan.

4

In **La Madeleine** (✉ *Plage de La Madeleine* ☎ *02–33–71–53–35*) inspect the glitteringly modern **Utah Beach Landing Museum** (✉ *Ste-Marie-du-Mont* ☎ *02–33–71–53–35*), whose exhibits include a W5 Utah scale model detailing the German defenses; it's open April–June, September, and October, daily 9:30–noon and 2–6, and July and August, daily 9:30–6:30. Continue north to the **Dunes de Varreville,** set with a monument to French hero General Leclerc, who landed here. Offshore you can see the fortified **Iles St-Marcouf.** Continue to **Quinéville,** at the far end of Utah Beach, with its **museum** (✉ *Rue de la Plage* ☎ *02–33–95–95–95*) evoking life during the German Occupation; the museum is open April through mid-November, daily 10–7.

WHERE TO STAY & EAT

$$$$ ✕🏨 **La Chenevière.** This grand 18th-century château, inland from Port-en-Bessin and to the east of Omaha Beach, has rooms with modern furnishings, floor-to-ceiling windows, and flowered bedspreads. The restaurant (closed Monday, no lunch Tuesday) serves cuisine appropriate to its surroundings: Dover sole with with artichokes, lobster with wild-mushroom risotto, or roast veal with truffles. ✉ *Les Escures, 14520 Commes* ☎ *02–31–51–25–25* 📠 *02–31–51–25–20* 🌐 *www.lacheneviere.fr* 🛏 *21 rooms* 🛎 *In-room: no a/c, refrigerator, dial-up. In-hotel: restaurant, bar, some pets allowed (fee)* 💳 *AE, DC, MC, V* ⏲ *Closed Jan.–mid-Feb.* 🍽 *MAP.*

$ ✕🏨 **Casino.** You can't get closer to the action than this. The handsome, postwar, triangular-gabled stone hotel, run by the same family since it was built in the 1950s, looks directly onto Omaha Beach. The bar is made from an old life-

THE LONGEST NIGHT

Famously, one parachutist—his name was John Steele—got stuck on the church tower of Sainte-Mère Église (an episode memorably recreated in the 1960 film The Longest Day) one evening; a dummy is strung up each summer to recall the event, and a stained-glass window inside the church honors American paratroopers.

boat, and it's no surprise that seafood and regional cuisine with creamy sauces predominate in Bruno Clemençon's airy sea-view restaurant. ☒*Rue de la Percée, 14710 Vierville-sur-Mer* ☎*02–31–22–41–02* 🖷*02–31–22–41–12* ⌨*12 rooms* ♿*In-room: no a/c. In-hotel: restaurant, bar, no elevator, some pets allowed* ▤*AE, MC, V* ⊘*Closed mid-Nov.–late Mar.* ⊙|*MAP.*

ST-LÔ

㉓ *78 km (49 mi) southeast of Cherbourg, 36 km (22 mi) southwest of Bayeux.*

St-Lô, perched dramatically on a rocky spur above the Vire Valley, was a key communications center that suffered so badly in World War II that it became known as the "capital of ruins." The medieval **Église Notre-Dame** bears mournful witness to those dark days: its imposing, spire-topped west front was never rebuilt, merely shored up with a wall of greenish stone. Reconstruction elsewhere, though, was wholesale. Some of it was spectacular, like the slender, spiral-staircase tower outside Town Hall; the circular theater; or the openwork belfry of the church of Ste-Croix. The town was freed by American troops, and its rebuilding was financed with U.S. support, notably from the city of Baltimore. The **Hôpital Mémorial France–États Unis** (France–United States Memorial Hospital), designed by Paul Nelson and featuring a giant mosaic by Fernand Léger, was named to honor those links.

St-Lô is capital of the Manche *département* (province) and, less prosaically, likes to consider itself France's horse capital. Hundreds of breeders are based in its environs, and the **Haras National** *(National Stud)* was established here in 1886. ☒*Av. du Maréchal-Juin* ☎*02–33–55–29–09* ⊕*www.haras-nationaux.fr* ☒*€4.50* ⊘*Guided tours only, June and Sept. at 4:30, July and Aug. at 11, 2:30, 3:30, and 4:30.*

★ St-Lô's art museum, the **Musée des Beaux-Arts,** is the perfect French provincial museum. Its halls are airy, seldom busy, not too big, yet full of varied exhibits—including an unexpected masterpiece: *Gombault et Macée,* a set of nine silk-and-wool tapestries woven in Bruges around 1600 relating a tale about a shepherd couple, exquisitely showcased in a special circular room. Other highlights include brash modern tapestries by Jean Lurçat; paintings by Corot, Boudin, and Géricault; court miniatures by Daniel Saint (1778–1847); and the Art Deco pictures of Slovenian-born Jaro Hilbert (1897–1995), inspired by ancient Egypt. Photographs, models, and documents evoke St-Lô's wartime devastation. ☒*Centre Culturel, Pl. du Champ-de-Mars* ☎*02–33–72–52–55* ☒*€2.55* ⊘*Wed.–Sun. 2–6.*

MONT-ST-MICHEL

㉔ *44 km (27 mi) south of Granville via D973, N175, and D43; 123 km* **FodorśChoice** *(77 mi) southwest of Caen; 67 km (42 mi) north of Rennes; 325 km* ★ *(202 mi) west of Paris.*

GETTING HERE

There are two routes to Mont-St-Michel, depending on whether you arrive from Caen or from Paris. From Caen you can take either an early-morning or an afternoon train to Pontorson (2 hrs, €22.20), the nearest station; then it's another 15 minutes to the foot of the abbey by bus or taxi. (Both leave from in front of the station.) From Paris, take the TGV from Gare Montparnasse to Rennes, then take a Courriers Bretons bus (☏02–99–19–70–80). The total journey takes 3 hours, 45 minutes (€60). There are three trains daily, but the only one that allows you a full day on the Mont leaves at 7:05 AM and arrives at 10:50 AM. The other options are 8:05 (arriving 1 PM) and 2:05 PM (arriving 7).

EXPLORING

That marvel of French architecture, Mont-St-Michel, is the most visited sight in France after the Eiffel Tower and the Louvre. This beached mass of granite, rising some 400 feet, was begun in 709 and is crowned with the "Marvel," or great monastery, that was built during the 13th century. Fortifications were added 200 years later to withstand attacks from the English. For the historic background and all the information on visiting this spectacular sight, see "A Spire to Greatness: Mont-St-Michel" in this chapter.

WHERE TO STAY & EAT

$$$–$$$$ ✕⚄ **La Mère Poulard.** This legendary hotel consists of adjoining houses with three steep flights of narrow stairs. The restaurant's reputation derives partly from its convenient location (right by the gateway, so don't expect views from atop the Mont), partly from its famous soufflélike omelet, and partly from the talent of chef Michel Bruneau, who established his reputation with his own restaurant in Caen. Room prices start low but ratchet upward according to size; the smallest rooms are bearable for an overnight stay, but not much longer. Walls throughout are plastered with posters and photographs of illustrious guests. You are usually requested to book two meals with the room. Reservations are essential for the restaurant in summer. ✉*Grande-Rue, 50116* ☏*02–33–89–68–68* 🖷*02–33–89–68–69* ⊕*www.mere-poulard.fr* ➷*40 rooms* ⌂*In-room: no a/c, refrigerator. In-hotel: restaurant, bar* ▤*AE, DC, MC, V* ⎱❍⎰*MAP.*

★ $$–$$$ ✕⚄ **Manoir de la Roche Torin.** Run by the Barraux family, this slate-roofed, stone-walled manor set in 4 acres of parkland is a delightful alternative to the high cost of staying on Mont-St-Michel. Rooms are pleasantly old-fashioned, and the bathrooms modern. With walls of Normand stonework and its open fireplace, the restaurant (closed Tuesday, Wednesday, and Saturday lunch) has superb grilled *pré-salé* (salt-meadow lamb). In summer, aperitifs are served in the garden, with a view of Mont-St-Michel. ✉*34 rte. de la Roche-Torin, 9 km (5 mi) from Mont-St-Michel, 50220 Courtils* ☏*02–33–70–96–55* 🖷*02–33–48–35–20* ⊕*www.manoir-rochetorin.com* ➷*15 rooms* ⌂*In-room: no a/c, refrigerator. In-hotel: restaurant, bar, no elevator, some pets allowed (fee)* ▤*AE, DC, MC, V* ⊗*Closed mid-Nov.–mid-Feb.* ❍*MAP.*

$$–$$$ ✕⚄ **Les Terrasses Poulard.** Run by the folks who own the noted Mère Poulard, this ensemble of buildings is clustered around a small garden

Continued on page 291

A SPIRE TO GREATNESS: MONT-ST-MICHEL

A magnetic beacon to millions of travelers each year, this "Wonder of the Western World"—a 264-foot mound of rock topped by a history-shrouded abbey—remains the crowning glory of medieval France.

Wrought by nature and centuries of tireless human toil, this mass of granite surmounted by the soul-lifting silhouette of the **Abbaye du Mont-St-Michel** is Normandy's most enduring image. Its fame stems not just from the majesty of its geographical situation but even more from its impressive history. Perched on the border between Normandy and Brittany, the medieval Mont (or Mount) was a political football between English conquerors and French kings for centuries. Mont-St-Michel was designed to be as much a fortress as it was a shrine, so it looks as tough as it is beautiful.

Legend has it that the Archangel Michael appeared in 709 to Aubert, Bishop of Avranches, inspiring him to build an oratory on what was then called Mont Tombe. The original church was completed in 1144, but further buildings were added in the 13th century to accommodate the hordes of pilgrims—known as *miquelots*—who flocked here even during the Hundred Years' War (1337-1453), when the region was in English hands.

Out of the French rulers' desire to protect Brittany from subjugation by the Normans (whose leader, William the Conqueror, had assumed the English throne in 1066) came the clever strategy of what we would call propaganda. Because of St. Michel's legendary role as dragon slayer and leader of the Heavenly Army, the French lords transformed him, and the Mont, into a major rallying force. During this period the abbey remained a symbol, both physical and emotional, of French independence.

By 1203, King Philippe-Auguste of France had succeeded in wresting the Mont back from the Normans and to shore up French popularity in Normandy he provided funds to restore the abbey. The resulting, greatly expanded, three-level Gothic abbey (1203—1228) became known as *La Merveille* (The Marvel).

During the French Revolution, the abbey was converted into a prison, but shortly after Victor Hugo (of *Hunchback of Notre Dame* fame) declaimed "A toad in a reliquary! When will we understand in France the sanctity of monuments?," the prison was converted into a museum in 1874 and, fittingly, Emmanuel Frémiet's great gilt statute of St. Michael was added to the spire in 1897.

4

CLIMB EVERY MONT

Mont-St-Michel is the result of more than 500 years of construction, from 1017 to 1521, and traces the history of French medieval architecture, from earliest Romanesque to its last flowering, Flamboyant Gothic.

HOW TO TOUR THE MONT

There are two basic options for touring the abbey of Mont-St-Michel: guided tours and exploring on your own (which you can do with the aid of an excellent audioguide tour in English). Realistically, a visit to Mont-St-Michel's abbey and village needs a half a day but an entire day at least is needed if you do several of the museums, go on one of the abbey's guided tours, and fit in a walk on the surrounding expanses of sand.

General admission to the abbey includes an optional hour-long guided tour in English, offered twice a day in high season. A more extensive, two-hour-long guided tour in French costs an extra 4 euros. The English-language tour takes you throughout the spectacular **Église Abbatiale,** the abbey church that crowns the rock, as well as the **Merveille,** a 13th-century, three-story collection of rooms and passageways built by King Philippe-Auguste. The French tour also includes the celebrated **Escalier de Dentelle** (Lace Staircase) and other highlights. Invest in at least one tour while you are here—each of them gets you on top of or into things you can't see alone.

If you do go it alone, stop halfway up Grande-Rue at the church of St-Pierre to admire its richly carved side chapel with its dramatic statue of St. Michael slaying the dragon. The famous **Grand Degré** staircase leads to the abbey entrance, from which a wider flight of steps climbs to the **Saut Gautier Terrace** outside the sober, dignified church. After visiting the arcaded cloisters alongside, you can wander at leisure, and probably get lost, among the maze of vaulted halls.

Grand Degré

② ③

Gardens

MERVEILLE

① ④

⑥

Église St-Pierre ⑤

⑦

Saut Gautier Terrace

Grand-Rue

Gardens

Gardens

⑧

ENTRANCE

DON'T MISS

❶ Église Abbatiale (above). Crowning the mount, the Abbey Church is in two different styles. The main nave and transepts (1020–1135) were built in the Norman Romanesque style; after the collapse of the original chancel in 1421, it was rebuilt in Flamboyant Gothic with seven Rayonnant-style chapels.

❷ La Cloitre de l'Abbatiale (above). The main cloister was the only part of the abbey complex open to "heaven"—the sky. Its southern gallery contains the lavabos (washing stands) of the monks. Look for the column capitals beautifully chiseled with flower and vine motifs.

❸ Salle des Chevaliers (above). Part of the triple-tiered "La Merveille"—the complex of state chambers, refectory, and cloister that surrounds the main church—the Knights' Hall was originally a scriptorium for copying manuscripts. It was the only heated room on the Mont.

❹ Escalier de Dentelle Set atop one of the "flying buttresses" (top right) of the main church, the famous perforated Lace Staircase is a bravura Gothic showpiece of carved stone. It leads to a parapet—adorned with stone gargoyles—390 feet above the sea.

MUSEUMS

Scattered through the Mont are four mini-museums. The most popular is the ❺ **Archéoscope** (Chemin de la Ronde, 02-33-60-14—09) whose sound-and-light show, *L'Eau et La Lumiere* (Water and Light), offers the best introduction to the Mont. Some exhibits use wax figures garbed in the most elegant 15th-century–style clothes. ❻ **The Logis Tiphaine** (02-33-60-23—34) is the home that Bertrand Duguesclin, a general fierce in his allegiance to the cause of French independence, built for his wife Tiphaine in 1365. ❼ **The Musée Historique** (Chemin de la Ronde, 02-33-60-07—01) traces the 1,000-year history of the Mont in one of its former prisons. ❽ **The Musée Maritime** (Grande Rue, 02–33-60-14—09) explores the science of the Mont's tidal bay and has a vast collection of model ships.

INFORMATION

☎ 02-33-89-80-00.

🌐 www.monum.fr; www.ot-montsaintmichel.com.

🎟 €8, with audioguide €12. Guided tour in French: €4. Museums: single ticket, €7, combined ticket €15. The abbey is open May-Aug., daily 9-7; Sept.-Apr., daily 9:30—6. The tourist office is in the Corps de Garde, left of the island gates

4

A SPIRE TO GREATNESS: MONT-ST-MICHEL

WHERE TO EAT & STAY

When day-trippers depart, Mont-St-Michel becomes a completely different experience and a stay overnight—when the island is spectacularly flood-lit—is especially memorable. But if you want to save money—and perhaps your sanity—during the very crowded peak months consider staying nearby at Pontorson, Avranches, Courtils, or day-trip it from St-Malo or Rennes.

La Mère Poulard. With walls plastered with photographs of illustrious guests, Mont-St-Michel's most famous hostelry can be tough to book, thanks to its historic restaurant, birthplace of Mère Poulard's legendary soufflé-like omelet. Chef Michel Bruneau also offers an array of tempting Norman dishes (reservations are essential in summer). Set in adjoining houses, the hotel itself is linked by three steep and narrow stairways. Room prices start low but ratchet upward according to size; the smallest rooms are bearable for an overnight stay, not longer. You are usually requested to book two meals with the room. The hotel's location, right by the main gateway, is most convenient—just don't come expecting any views from atop the Mont.

$$$-$$$$ ✉ Grande-Rue, 50116, ☎ 02–33–89–68–68 🖷 02-33-89-68-69 ⊕ www.mere-poulard.fr ⤶ 40 rooms ♨ In-room: no a/c. In-hotel: restaurant, bar, refrigerator ▤ AE, DC, MC, V

Auberge St-Pierre. This inn is a popular spot thanks to the fact that it's in a half-timber 15th-century building adjacent to the ramparts and has its own garden restaurant that offers seasonal specialties and interesting half-board rates. If you're lucky, you'll wind up in No. 16, which has a view of the abbey. The hotel annex, La Croix Blanche, has another nine rooms (shower only).

$$-$$$ ✉ Grande-Rue, 50170 ☎ 02-33-60-14-03 🖷 02-33-48-59-82 ⊕ www.auberge-saint-pierre.fr ⤶ 21 rooms ♨ In-room: no a/c. In-hotel: restaurant, Internet ▤ AE, MC, V

FOOD WITH A VIEW

Many Mont restaurants don't have views (other than of rooms crammed with diners), so another option is to enjoy a picnic along the *promenade des remparts*, where the vistas will spice up the blandest sandwich.

Les Terrasses Poulard. Run by the folks who own the noted Mère Poulard hotel, this ensemble of buildings is clustered around a small garden in the middle of the Mount. Rooms at this hotel are some of the best—with views of the bay and rustic-style furnishings—and most spacious on the Mount, although many require you to negotiate a labyrinth of steep stairways.

$$-$$$ ✉ Grande-Rue, opposite parish church, 50170 ☎ 02-33-89-02-02 🖨 02-33-60-37-31 ⊕ www.terrasses-poulard.com 🛏 30 rooms ♨ In-room: no a/c. In-hotel: restaurant, refrigerator ▤ AE, DC, MC, V

Manoir de la Roche Torin. Run by the Barraux family, this pretty, slate-roofed, stone-walled manor set in 4 acres of parkland is a delightful alternative to crowded Mont-St-Michel. Rooms are pleasantly old-fashioned, and the bathrooms modern. With walls of Normand stonework and its open fireplace, the restaurant (closed Tuesday, Wednesday, and Saturday lunch) has superb seafood and char-grilled *pré-salé* (salt-meadow lamb). In summer, apéritifs are served in the garden, with a view of Mont-St-Michel.

$$-$$$ ✉ 34 rte. de la Roche-Torin, 9 km (5 mi) from Mont-St-Michel, 50220 Courtils ☎ 02-33-70-96-55 🖨 02-33-48-35-20 ⊕ www.manoir-rochetorin.com 🛏 15 rooms ♨ In-room: no a/c. In-hotel: restaurant, bar, some pets allowed (fee), Internet ▤ AE, DC, MC, V ⊙ Closed mid-Nov.–mid-Feb.

Du Guesclin. The courtesy of the staff, the comfy and clean guest rooms, and a choice of two restaurants make this well-maintained hotel a pleasant option. Downstairs try the casual brasserie for salads and sandwiches; upstairs the panoramic full-service restaurant (closed Wednesday) has a wonderful view of the bay.

$ ✉ Grande-Rue, 50170 ☎ 02-33-60-14-10 🖨 02-33-60-45-81 🛏 10 rooms ♨ In-room: no a/c. In-hotel: 2 restaurants ▤ MC, V ⊙ Closed Nov.–Mar.

NOW YOU SEE IT...

The Mont's choir was rebuilt during the 15th century and it was only then that the heaven-thrusting Gothic spire was added. To step back several centuries, place your hand to block your view of the spire and see the abbey return to its original Romanesque squatness.

TIME AND TIDE WAIT FOR NO MAN

Mont-St-Michel can be washed by the highest tides in Europe, rising up to a crest of 45 feet at times. Dangerously unpredictable, the sea here runs out as far as nine miles before rushing back in—more than a few ill-prepared tourists over the years have drowned. Even when the tide is out, the sandy strand is treacherous because of dangerous quicksands (guided hikes over the strand are available). A 2 km (1 mi) causeway links Mont-St-Michel to the mainland.

Note that the Mont is surrounded by water only at very high tides (99% of visitors see the island "beached" by sand). ■TIP→ To see the rare occurrence of the Mont washed by tides, plan a visit when the moon is full. Occuring only twice a month, the highest tides occur 36 to 48 hours after the full and new moons, with the most dramatic ones during the spring and fall equinoxes (around March 21 and September 23). Experts say the best time to visit is six hours after full or new moons. Time tidetables (posted on the board outside the tourist office) can be accessed on the internet at www.ot-montsaintmichel.com.

TO & FROM

Set across from the mainland village of La Digue, Mont-St-Michel is 44 km (27 mi) south of Granville via D973, N175, and D43; 67 km (42 mi) north of Rennes 123 km (77mi) southwest of Caen; and 325 km (202 mi) west of Paris.

BY CAR Parking lots (€4) at either end of the causeway. The one just outside the Mont's main gate is reserved for hotel users, who access the lot through a pass-key issued by their hotel. The larger parking lot during very high tides is closed to the public, who can then park on the causeway or, if no room is left, in a car park on the mainland about one mile away (a shuttle bus connects the two).

BY TRAIN & BUS Taking the train from Paris to Mont-St-Michel is not easy—the quickest way (3 hrs, 45 mins, €60) is to take the high-speed TGV train from Gare Montparnasse to Rennes (in high season, five departures a day), then a Couriers Breton (02–99–19–70—70) bus transfer to the Mont. The only train that will allow you a full day on the Mont leaves at 7 AM and arrives at 10:50 AM. The other options are 8 (arriving 1 PM) and 2 PM (arriving 7). From Caen you can take either an early morning or late afternoon train to Pontorson (2 hrs, €22), the nearest station to the Mont; then it is another 15 minutes to the foot of the abbey by bus or taxi.

in the middle of the Mont. Rooms are some of the best—with views of the bay and rustic-style furnishings—and most spacious on the Mont, although many require you to negotiate a labyrinth of steep stairways. ✉*Grande-Rue, opposite parish church, 50170* 📠*02–33–89–02–02* 🏠*02–33–60–37–31* ➷*30 rooms* ♿*In-room: no a/c, refrigerator. In-hotel: restaurant* ▤*AE, DC, MC, V* ⑩*MAP.*

$-$$ ✕🖼 **Duguesclin.** The courtesy of the staff, the comfy and clean guest rooms, and a choice of two restaurants make this well-maintained hotel a pleasant option. Downstairs try the casual brasserie for salads and sandwiches; upstairs the panoramic full-service restaurant (closed Wednesday) has a wonderful view of the bay. ✉*Grande-Rue, 50170* 📠*02–33–60–14–10* 🏠*02–33–60–45–81* ➷*10 rooms* ♿*In-room: no a/c. In-hotel: 2 restaurants, no elevator* ▤*MC, V* ⊙*Closed Nov.–Mar.* ⑩*MAP.*

$$$ 🖼 **Auberge St-Pierre.** You won't be overwhelmed with choices on Mont-St-Michel when it comes to accommodations. However, this inn is a popular spot thanks to the fact that it's in a half-timber 15th-century building adjacent to the ramparts. It has its own garden restaurant that offers seasonal specialties and interesting half-board rates. If you're lucky, you'll wind up in No. 16, which has a view of the abbey. The hotel annex, La Croix Blanche, has another nine rooms (shower only). ✉*Grande-Rue, 50170* 📠*02–33–60–14–03* 🏠*02–33–48–59–82* ⊕*www.auberge-saint-pierre.fr* ➷*21 rooms* ♿*In-room: no a/c, dial-up. In-hotel: restaurant, no elevator* ▤*AE, MC, V* ⑩*MAP.*

NORMANDY ESSENTIALS

To research prices, get advice from other travelers, and book travel arrangements, visit www.fodors.com.

TRANSPORTATION

If traveling extensively by public transportation, be sure to load up on information (*Guide Régional des Transports* schedules, the best taxi-for-call companies, etc.) upon arriving at the ticket counter or help desk of the bigger train and bus stations in the area, such as Rouen, Deauville, and Caen.

BY AIR

AIRPORTS
Paris's Charles de Gaulle (Roissy) and Orly airports are the closest intercontinental links with the region. There are flights in summer from London to Deauville, and year-round service between Jersey and Cherbourg, which sits at the northern tip of the Cotentin Peninsular, about 90 minutes' drive from Bayeux. Rouen airport has direct flights to Lyon and Montpellier.

Airport Information Caen (📠02–31–71–20–10). **Cherbourg** (📠02–33–88–57–60). **Deauville** (📠02–31–65–65–65). **Rouen** (📠02–35–79–41–00).

CARRIERS

Air France flies to Caen from Paris. Ryanair flies to Deauville and Dinard (in Brittany, 56 km [35 mi] west of Mont-St-Michel) from London's Stansted airport.

Airlines & Contacts Air France (☏08–02–80–28–02 for information ⊕www. air-france.com). **Ryanair** (⊕www.ryanair.com) for information.

BY BIKE & MOPED

Traveling with your bike is free on all regional trains and many national lines; be sure to ask the SNCF which ones when you're booking.

BY BOAT & FERRY

A number of ferry companies sail between the United Kingdom and ports in Normandy. Brittany Ferries travels between Caen (Ouistreham) and Portsmouth and between Poole/Portsmouth and Cherbourg. The Dieppe-Newhaven route is covered by a daily service from Transmanche.

FARES & SCHEDULES

Boat & Ferry Information Brittany Ferries (☏08–03–82–88–28 ⊕www.brittany-ferries.com). **Transmanche** (☏08–00–65–01–00 ⊕www.transmancheferries.com).

BY BUS

Three main bus systems cover the towns not served by trains. CNA (Compagnie Normande Autobus) runs around Upper Normandy from Rouen to the towns along the Côte d'Alabâtre, including Le Havre. It also services towns outside Rouen, like Caudebec-en-Caux. **Autos-Cars Gris** runs buses from Fécamp to Le Havre, stopping in Étretat along the way. **Bus Verts du Calvados** covers the coast, connecting with Caen and Honfleur, Bayeux, and other towns. It also runs, during July and August, the special D-Day Circuit 44, which allows you to see as many D-Day sights as you can squeeze into one day. These buses depart from the train stations in Bayeux and Caen.

Bus routes connect many towns, including Rouen, Dieppe, Fécamp, Étretat, Le Havre, Caen, Honfleur, Deauville, Trouville, Cabourg, and Arromanches. To get to Honfleur, take a bus from Deauville; from Rouen, train it first to Le Havre, then continue on bus to Honfleur. For Mont-St-Michel, hook up with buses from nearby Pontorson or from Rennes in adjacent Brittany. If you are traveling from Paris to the Mont, take the high-speed TGV train from Gare Montparnasse to Rennes (in high season, five departures a day), then a **Courriers Bretons** bus transfer to the Mont. Many trains depart from Paris's Gare-St-Lazare for Rouen (70 mins). Tourist offices and train stations in Normandy will have printed schedules.

Bus Information Autos-Cars Gris (☏02–35–28–19–88). **Bus Verts du Calvados** (☏08–10–21–42–14 ⊕www.busverts.fr). **CNA (Compagnie Normande d'Autobus** (☏08–25–07–60–27). **Les Courriers Bretons** (☏02–99–19–70–80 ⊕www. lescourriersbretons.com).

BY CAR

From Paris, A13 slices its way to Rouen in 1½ hours (toll €5.20) before forking to Caen (an additional hr, toll €7.50) or Le Havre (45 mins on

A131). N13 continues from Caen to Bayeux in another two hours. At Caen, the A84 forks off southwest toward Mont-St-Michel and Rennes. From Paris, scenic D915 will take you to Dieppe in about three hours. The Pont de Normandie, between Le Havre and Honfleur, effectively unites Upper and Lower Normandy.

BY TRAIN

From Paris (Gare St-Lazare), separate train lines head to Upper Normandy (Rouen and Le Havre or Dieppe) and Lower Normandy (Caen, Bayeux, and Cherbourg, via Évreux and Lisieux). There are frequent trains from Paris to Rouen (70 mins, €19); some continue to Le Havre (2 hrs, €27). Change in Rouen for Dieppe (2 hrs from Paris, €25). The trip from Paris to Deauville (2 hrs, €26) often requires a change at Lisieux. There are regular trains from Paris to Caen (1 hr, 50 mins, €28), some continuing to Bayeux (2 hrs, €31). Taking the train from Paris to Mont-St-Michel is not easy—the quickest way (3 hrs, 45 mins, €60) is to take the TGV from Gare Montparnasse to Rennes, then take the bus. There are three trains daily, but the only one that will allow you a full day on the Mont leaves at 7:05 AM and arrives at 10:50 AM. The other options are 8:05 (arriving 1 PM) and 2:05 PM (arriving 7). From Caen you can take either an early morning or an afternoon train to Pontorson (2 hrs, €22.20), the nearest station to the Mont; then it's another 15 minutes to the foot of the abbey by bus or taxi (buses are directly in front of the station).

Unless you're content to stick to the major towns (Rouen, Le Havre, Dieppe, Caen, Bayeux, Cherbourg), visiting Normandy by train may prove frustrating. You can sometimes reach several smaller towns (Fécamp, Houlgate/Cabourg) on snail-paced branch lines, but the irregular intricacies of what is said to be Europe's most complicated regional timetable will probably have driven you nuts by the time you get there. Other destinations, like Honfleur or Etretat, require train/bus journeys.

Train Information Gare SNCF Rouen (⊠Rue Jeanne d'Arc ☏08–36–35–35–39). **SNCF** (☏08–36–35–35–35 ⊕www.ter-sncf.com/uk/basse-normandie).

CONTACTS & RESOURCES

CAR RENTAL
Local Agencies Avis (⊠44 pl. de la Gare, Caen ☏02–31–84–73–80 ⊠32 av. de Caen, Rouen ☏02–35–72–64–32). **Europcar** (⊠51 quai de Southampton, Le Havre ☏02–35–25–21–95).

EMERGENCIES
Contacts General Ambulance (☏15). **General Fire Department** (☏18). **General Police** (☏17). **Regional hospitals** (⊠Av. de la Côte-de-Nacre, Caen ☏02–31–06–31–06 ⊠29 av. Pierre-Mendès-France, Montivilliers, Le Havre ☏02–32–73–32–32 ⊠1 rue Germont, Rouen ☏02–32–88–89–90).

INTERNET & MAIL
In smaller towns, ask your hotel concierge if there are any Internet cafés nearby.

Internet & Mail Information Cybernet (⊠47 pl. du Vieux-Marché, Rouen ☎02–35–07–73–02). **La Poste (main post office)** (⊠Pl. Gambetta, Caen ☎02–35–07–73–02).

La Poste (main post office) (⊠45 rue Jeanne-d'Arc, Rouen ☎02–35–15–66–73). **Systenium** (⊠130 rue St-Jean, Caen ☎02–31–86–78–06).

MEDIA

Paris-Normandie and *Ouest-France* are the two main newspapers read in Normandy.

TOUR OPTIONS

The firm Cars Périer arranges personalized driving tours with an English-speaking driver.

Fees & Schedules Cars Périer (⊠130 rue Martainville, 76000 Rouen ☎02–35–98–59–00).

BUS TOURS

Cityrama and Paris-Vision run full-day bus excursions from Paris to Mont-St-Michel for €155, meals and admission included. This is definitely not for the faint of heart—buses leave Paris at 6:45 or 7:15 AM and return around 10:30 PM. In Caen, the Mémorial organizes four-hour English-language daily minibus tours of the D-Day landing beaches; the cost is €69, including entrance fees. Normandy Sightseeing Tours runs a number of trips to the D-Day beaches and Mont-St-Michel; a full-day excursion to the D-Day beaches (8:30–6) costs €75.

Fees & Schedules Cityrama (⊠4 pl. des Pyramides, 75001 Paris ☎01–44–55–61–00 ⊕www.cityrama.fr). **Mémorial** (☎02–31–06–06–44 ⊕www.memorial.fr). **Normandy Sightseeing Tours** (⊠618 rte. du Lavoir, 14400 Mosles ☎02–31–51–70–52 ⊕www.normandywebguide.com). **Paris-Vision** (⊠214 rue de Rivoli, 75001 Paris ☎08–00–03–02–14 ⊕www.parisvision.com).

VISITOR INFORMATION

The capital of each of Normandy's *départements*—Caen, Évreux, Rouen, St-Lô, and Alençon—has its own central tourist office. Other major Norman towns with tourist offices are listed below the département offices by name.

Tourist Information Bayeux (⊠Pont St-Jean ☎02–31–51–28–28). **Caen** (⊠Pl. du Canada ☎02–31–27–90–30 🖶02–31–27–90–35). **Deauville** (⊠Pl. de la Mairie ☎02–31–14–40–00 ⊕www.deauville.org). **Dieppe** (⊠Pont Jehan-An ☎02–35–84–11–77 ⊕www.dieppe-tourisme.com). **Évreux** (⊠Bd. Georges-Chauvin ☎02–32–31–51–51 🖶02–32–31–05–98 ⊕www.normandy-tourism.org) for Eure. **Fécamp** (⊠113 rue Alexandre-le-Grand ☎02–35–28–51–01 ⊕www. fecamp.com). **Le Havre** (⊠186 bd. Clemenceau ☎02–32–74–04–04 ⊕www.ville-lehavre.fr). **Honfleur** (⊠9 rue de la Ville ☎02–31–89–23–30). **Lisieux** (⊠11 rue d'Alençon ☎02–31–62–08–41 ⊕www.ville-lisieux.fr). **Mont-St-Michel** (⊠Corps de Garde ☎02–33–60–14–30 ⊕www.ot-montsaintmichel.com). **Rouen** (⊠25 pl. de la Cathédrale ☎02–32–08–32–40 🖶02–32–08–32–44 ⊕www.rouentourisme. com). **St-Lô** (⊠Maison du Département, rte. de Villedieu ☎02–33–05–98–70).

Brittany

Quimper

WORD OF MOUTH

"The Emerald Coast is beautiful, especially around Ploumanach where the rocks are rose-colored and the water green. Along all of the coastline is the 'Sentier des Douaniers,' the historic tax collector's trail which can still be followed on foot today."

—Klondik

WELCOME TO BRITTANY

TOP REASONS TO GO

★ **Waterworld:** Will you prefer the coastal drama of the Granite Coast, with its crazy-shape outcrops, or the rippling waters of the Bay of Morbihan, snuggling in the Gulfstream behind the angry Atlantic?

★ **The Isle Has It:** Venture down the untamed Quiberon Peninsula to boat across to the rugged, unspoiled beauty of Belle-Ile-en-Mer, Brittany's wildest island.

★ **Gauguin's Pont-Aven:** A *cité des artistes,* its colorful folkloric ways helped ignite the painter's interest in Tahiti.

★ **Unidentical Twins:** A ferry ride across the Rance River links two delightfully contrasting towns: ancient, once pirate-ridden St-Malo and grand, genteel, Edwardian Dinard.

★ **Stone Me!:** Muse upon the solemn majesty of row-upon-row of *anciens mehirs* at Carnac, the "French Stonehenge."

1 Northeast Brittany & the Channel Coast. The northern half of Brittany is demarcated by its 240-km (150-mi) Channel Coast, which stretches from Cancale, just west of Mont-St-Michel, to Morlaix, and can be loosely divided into two parts: the **Côte d'Emeraude** (Emerald Coast), with cliffs punctuated by golden, curving beaches; and the **Côte de Granit Rose** (Pink Granite Coast), including the stupefying area around

Trébeurden, where Brittany's granite takes amazing forms glowing an otherworldly pink. On the road heading there are the gateway city of **Rennes; Vitré** and **Dinan—** two beautifully preserved historic towns; the **Château de Combourg,** home of the 19th-century author Chateaubriand; and the great port of **St-Malo,** whose stone ramparts conjure up the days of the great marauding corsairs.

City Walls and Castle Dungeon, St-Malo

GETTING ORIENTED

Bretons like to say they are Celtic, not Gallic, and other French people sometimes feel they are in a foreign land when they visit this jagged triangle perched on the northwest tip of mainland Europe. Two sides of the triangle are defined by the sea. Brittany's northern coast faces the English Channel; its western coast defies the Atlantic Ocean. The north of Brittany tends to be wilder than the south, or Basse Bretagne, where the countryside becomes softer as it descends towards Nantes and the Loire. But wherever you go, "maritime Armor"— the Land of the Sea—is never too far away.

5

1 CÔTE ÉMERAUDE — *Golfe de* — Cap Fréhel — *St-Malo* — St-Malo — St-Brieuc — Dinard — Cancale — Mont-St-Michel — BASSE NORMANDIE — Dinan — N176 — Combourg — N12 — Loudéac — N137 — Fougères — A54 — BRITTANY — Rennes — N24 — N167 — Vitré — Ploërmel — D177 — D166 — N137 — TO NANTES — PAYS DE LA LOIRE

2 **The Atlantic Coast.** Bypassing the lobster-claw of Brittany's **Le Finistere** ("World's End"), this westernmost region allures with folkloric treasures like **Ste-Anne-la-Palud** (famed for its *pardon* festival); **Quimper,** noted for its signature ceramics; and cheerful, riverside villages like **Pont-Aven**, which Gauguin immortalized in many sketches and paintings. Here, the 320-km (200-mi) Atlantic coast zigzags its way east, with frenzied, cliff-bashing surf alternating with sprawling beaches and bustling harbors. The **Belle-Ile** island adorns **Le Morbihan,** the name of the most beautiful stretch of shoreline. Enjoy its away-from-it-all atmosphere, because the bustling city of **Nantes** lies just to the east.

BRITTANY PLANNER

Parlez-Vous Breton?

Most place names in Brittany are Breton; the popular *plou* means parish—this is where the French got the word *plouc,* meaning hick. Other common geographical names are *coat* (forest), *mor* (sea), *aber* or *aven* (estuary), *ster* (river), and *enez* (island). *Ty* and *ti,* like the French *chez,* mean "at the house of." While under the radar screen for the most part during the past decade, the Breton Revolutionary Army is a nationalist group committed to preserving Breton culture against French efforts to repress it. Now that everyone agrees that traditional Breton folkways are a priceless boost to tourism and cultural patrimony, this is a common goal shared by many.

Pardons & Festivals

It has been said that there are as many Breton saints as there are stones in the ground. One of the great attractions of Brittany, therefore, remains its many festivals, pardons, and folklore events: banners and saintly statues are borne in colorful parades, accompanied by hymns, and the entire event is often capped by a feast.

In February, the great Pardon of Terre-Neuve takes place at St-Malo, and in March, Nantes celebrates with a pre-Lenten carnival procession. In mid-May there is a notable pardon of Saint-Yves, patron saint of lawyers, at Tréguier. June is the month of St. John, honored by the ceremonial Feux de Saint-Jean at Locronan and Nantes.

July sees Quimper's Celtic Festival de Cornouaille and the famed pardon in Ste-Anne-d'Auray. August has Lorient's Festival Interceltique, Pont-Aven's Festival of the Golden Gorse, Brest's bagpipe festival, and a big pardon in Ste-Anne-la-Palud. Another pardon held in Le Folgoët during September is one of the most extraordinary, with flocks of bishops, Bretons in traditional costumes, and devout pilgrims.

Making the Most of Your Time

If you have just a few days here, choose your coast— Channel or Atlantic! Cliffs and beaches, boat trips, culture and history…both shorelines offer all these and more. St-Malo makes a good base of you're Channel-bound, handily placed for medieval Dinan; Chateaubriand's home at Combourg; Dinard, the elegant Belle-Epoque resort once favored by British aristocrats; and the lively city of Rennes, the gateway to Brittany set 354 km (220 mi) west of Paris. Pretty Vannes is a good base for exploring the Atlantic coast. Highlights hereabouts include lively Quimper, with its fine cathedral and pottery; the painters' village of Pont-Aven, made famous by Gauguin; the prehistoric menhirs of Carnac; the rugged island of Belle-Ile; and the picturesque Bay of Morbihan. The third side of the Brittany triangle is its verdant, unhurried hinterland. Charming—but forget it unless you're here for the month.

When to Go

The tourist season is short in Brittany season (late June through early September). Long, damp winters keep visitors away, and many hotels are closed until Eastertime.

Brittany is particularly crowded in July and August, when most French people are on vacation, so choose crowd-free June or September, or early October, when autumnal colors and crisp evenings make for an invigorating visit.

If you want to sample local folklore, late summer is the most festive time to come.

Finding a Place to Stay

Outside the main cities (Rennes and Nantes), Brittany has plenty of small, appealing family-run hotels which cater essentially to seasonal visitors. Many close for one or several months between October and March, and booking ahead is strongly advised for the Easter period and in midsummer, when it is routine for prices to be ratcheted up by 30% to 50%.

For luxury hotels Dinard, on the English Channel, and La Baule, on the Atlantic, are the area's two most expensive resorts. Assume that all hotel rooms have air-conditioning, TV, telephones, and private bath, unless otherwise noted.

WHAT IT COSTS

	¢	$	$$	$$$	$$$$
Restaurants	Under €11	€11– €17	€17– €23	€23– €30	Over €30
Hotels	Under €50	€50– €80	€80– €120	€120– €190	Over €190

Restaurant prices are per person for a main course at dinner, including tax (19.6%) and service; note that if a restaurant offers only prix-fixe (set-price) meals, it has been given the price category that reflects the full prix-fixe price. Hotel prices are for a standard double room in high season, including tax (19.6%) and service charge. Hotels operate on the European Plan (EP, with no meal provided) unless we note that they use the Breakfast Plan (BP), or also offer such options as Modified American Plan (MAP, with breakfast and dinner daily, known as demi-pension), or Full American Plan (FAP, or pension complète, with three meals a day). Inquire when booking if these all-inclusive meal plans (which always entail higher rates) are mandatory or optional.

Getting Around

In just over two hours the TGV train from Paris (Gare Montparnasse) whisks you to Rennes, the region's hub.

From Rennes you can continue by TGV to the region's farthest outpoints—Brest (via Morlaix) and Quimper (via Vannes)—or take a branch line to St-Malo or Dinan.

You need to use buses, or a car, to explore the coast between Dinard and Rostoff, and the smaller towns along the Atlantic coast, like Douarnenez, Concarneau, and Pont-Aven.

The A11 expressway leads from Paris to Rennes, continuing as the N12 dual-carriageway to Brest, whence the N165 dual-carriageway heads down the coast toward Nantes.

Roads through the Breton hinterland, on the other hand, are narrow and slow.

5

Introduction by
Nancy Coons
Updated by
Simon Hewitt

YOU FEEL IT EVEN BEFORE the sharp salt air strikes your face from the west—a subliminal rhythm suspended in the mist, a subsonic drone somewhere between a foghorn and a heartbeat, seemingly made up of bagpipes, drums, and the thin, haunting filigree of a tin-whistle tune. This is Brittany, land of the Bretons, where Celtic bloodlines run deep as a druid's roots into the rocky, sea-swept soil. Wherever you wander—along jagged coastal cliffs, through cobbled seaport streets, into burnished-oak cider pubs—you can hear this primal pulse of Celtic music. France's most fiercely and determinedly ethnic people, the Bretons delight in celebrating their primeval culture—circle dancing at street fairs, the women donning starched lace-bonnet *coiffes,* and the men in striped fishermen's shirts at the least sign of a regional celebration. They name their children Erwan and Edwige, carry sacred statues in ceremonial religious processions called *pardons,* pray in hobbit-scale stone churches decked with elfin, moonfaced gargoyles. And scattered over the mossy hillsides stand Stonehenge-like dolmens and menhirs (prehistoric standing stones), eerie testimony to a primordial culture that predated and has long outlived Frankish France.

Similarities in character, situation, or culture to certain islands across the Channel are by no means coincidental. Indeed, the Celts that migrated to this westernmost outcrop of the French landmass spent much of the Iron Age on the British Isles, where they introduced the indigenes to innovations like the potter's wheel, the rotary millstone, and the compass. This first influx of Continental culture to Great Britain was greeted with typically mixed feelings, and by the 6th century is the Saxon hordes had sent these Celtic "Brits" packing southward, to the peninsula that became Brittany. So completely did they dominate their new, Cornwall-like peninsula (appropriately named Finistère, from *finis terrae,* or "land's end") that when in 496 they allied themselves with Clovis, the king of the Franks, he felt as if he'd just claimed a little bit of England. Nonetheless these newly settled Bretons remained independent of France until 1532, only occasionally hiring out as wild and woolly warrior-allies to the Norsemen of Normandy.

Yet the cultural exchange flowed both ways over the Channel. From their days on the British Isles the Britons brought a folklore that shares with England the bittersweet legend of Tristan and Iseult, and that weaves mystical tales of the Cornwall–Cornouaille of King Arthur and Merlin. They brought a language that still renders village names unpronounceable: Aber-Wrac'h, Tronoën, Locmariaquer, Poldreuzic, Kerhornaouen. And, too, they brought a way of life with them: half-timber seaside cider bars, their blackened-oak tables softened with prim bits of lace; stone cottages fringed with clumps of hollyhock, hydrangea, and foxglove, damp woolens and rubber boots set to dry in flagstone entryways; bearded fishermen in yellow oilskins heaving the day's catch into weather-beaten boats, terns and seagulls wheeling in their wake. It's a way of life that feels deliciously exotic to the Frenchman and—like the ancient drone of the bagpipes—comfortably, delightfully, even primally familiar to the Anglo-Saxon.

This cozy regional charm extends inland to Rennes, at 200,000 inhabitants the largest city of Bretagne (to use the French name), as well as to Dinan, Vannes, Quimper, and seaside St-Malo. Though many towns took a beating during the course of the Nazi retreat in 1944, most have been gracefully restored, their sweet whitewashed cottages once again anchoring the soil. And the countryside retains the heather-and-emerald moorscape, framed in forests primeval and bordered by open sea, which first inspired wandering people to their pipes.

EXPLORING BRITTANY

It is useful to know that Brittany is divided into two nearly equal parts—Upper Brittany, along the Channel coast, and Lower Brittany. The latter (called in French Basse-Bretagne or Bretagne Bretonnate) is, generally speaking, the more interesting. But the Channel coast has its share of marvels, including St-Malo and the resort area around Trébeurden, where Perros-Guirec is joined to Ploumanac'h, a curious little beach and town, by a beautiful path through the rocks along the seafront. A big attraction here is the fantastic formation of huge granite rocks along the coast. Consisting of the territory lying west of Saint-Brieuc to the Atlantic coast a short distance east of Vannes, Lower Brittany contains in abundance all things Breton, including many of the pardons and other colorful religious ceremonies that take place hereabouts. As for bright lights, Rennes, the student-fueled mind of Brittany, gives way to poets and painters, bringing a refreshing breeze to the historical heaviness of the region. On the Atlantic coast, Nantes, the working-class heart of Brittany, pumps the economy of the region and provides a bracing swig of daily Breton life. Our chapter splits Brittany in two.

NORTHEAST BRITTANY & THE CHANNEL COAST

Northeast Brittany extends from the city of Rennes to the coast. The rolling farmland around Rennes is strewn with mighty castles in Vitré, Fougères, and Dinan—remnants of Brittany's ceaseless efforts to repel invaders during the Middle Ages and a testimony to the wealth derived from pirate and merchant ships. The beautiful Côte d'Émeraude (Emerald Coast) stretches west from Cancale to St-Brieuc, and the dramatic Côte de Granit Rose (Pink Granite Coast) extends from Paimpol to Trébeurden and the Corniche Bretonne. Follow the coastal routes D786 and D34—winding, narrow roads that total less than 100 km (62 mi) but can take five hours to drive; the spectacular views that unfold en route make the journey worthwhile.

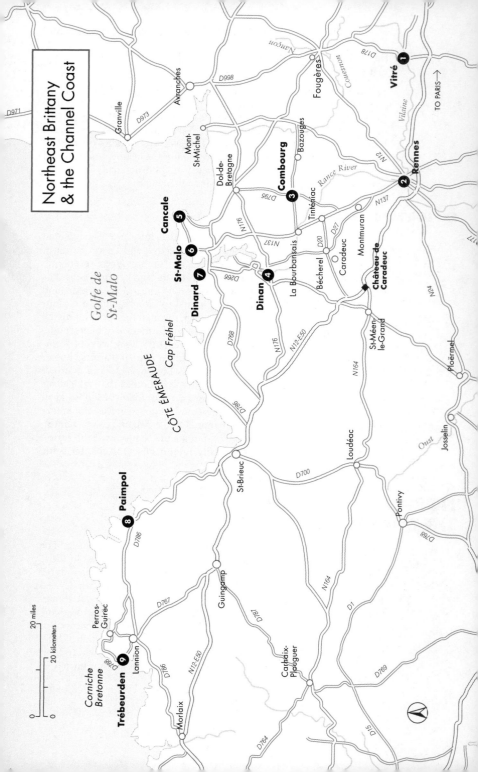

VITRÉ

❶ *32 km (20 mi) south of Fougères via D798 and D178.*

GETTING HERE

Several trains traveling between Paris and Rennes stop daily in Vitré. The trip from Rennes takes 30 minutes. Both SNCF and TIV run a couple of daily buses between Vitré and Fougères (35 mins) but only one round-trip on Sunday.

EXPLORING

There's still a feel of the Middle Ages about the formidable castle, tightly packed half-timber houses, remaining ramparts, and dark alleyways of Vitré (pronounced vee-*tray*). Built high above the Vilaine Valley, the medieval walled town that spreads out from the castle's gates, though small, is the best preserved in Brittany, and utterly beguiling, though you'll have to put on extra-strong fantasy goggles to block out the many tourists who visit here. The castle stands at the west end of town, facing narrow, cobbled streets as picturesque as any in Brittany—Rue Poterie, Rue d'Embas, and Rue Beaudrairie, originally the home of tanners (the name comes from *baudoyers*, or leather workers).

★ Rebuilt in the 14th and 15th centuries to protect Brittany from invasion, the fairy-tale, 11th-century **Château de Vitré**—shaped in an imposing triangle with fat, round towers—proved to be one of the province's most successful fortresses: during the Hundred Years' War (1337–1453), the English repeatedly failed to take it, even when they occupied the rest of the town. It's a splendid sight, especially from the vantage point of Rue de Fougères across the river valley below. Time, not foreigners, came closest to ravaging the castle, which has been heavily though tastefully restored during the past century. The **Hôtel de Ville** (town hall), however, is an unfortunate 1913 accretion to the castle courtyard. Visit the wing to the left of the entrance, beginning with the **Tour St-Laurent** and its museum, which contains 15th- and 16th-century sculptures, Aubusson tapestries, and engravings. Continue along the walls via the **Tour de l'Argenterie**—which contains a macabre collection of stuffed frogs and reptiles preserved in glass jars—to the **Tour de l'Oratoire** (Oratory Tower). ☎02–99–75–04–54 ⊕*www.mairie-vitre.com* 🎫€4 ⊙*May–Sept., Wed.–Mon. 10–noon and 2–6; Oct.–Apr., Mon. and Wed.–Sat. 10–noon and 2–5:30, Sun. 2–5:30.*

Fragments of the town's medieval ramparts include the 15th-century **Tour de la Bridolle** (⊠*Pl. de la République*), five blocks up from the castle.

The church of **Notre-Dame** (⊠*Pl. Notre-Dame*), with its fine, pinnacled south front, was built in the 15th and 16th centuries.

WHERE TO STAY

¢–$ 🏨 **Le Petit Billot.** Carved paneling and faded pastel tones give this small family-run hotel a delightful French provincial air. The hotel has an informal relationship with Le Potager, the restaurant right next door, which serves reliable, though rather unexciting, Breton cuisine (closed Monday, no lunch Saturday, no dinner Sunday). ⊠*5 bis pl. du Général-Leclerc, 35500* ☎02–99–75–02–10 🖨02–99–74–72–96 ⊕*www.petit-*

DINING À L'ARMORICAINE

Brittany is a land of the sea. Surrounded on three sides by water, it's a veritable mine of fish and shellfish. These aquatic delights, not surprisingly, dominate Breton cuisine, starting off with the famed *homard à l'armoricaine* (lobster with cream), a name derived from the ancient name for Brittany—Armorica—and not to be confused with américaine.

Other maritime headliners include *coquilles St-Jacques* (scallops); *cotriade*, a distinctive fish soup with potatoes, onions, garlic, and butter; and langoustines, which are something between a large shrimp and a lobster. Other popular meals include smoked ham and lamb, frequently served with green kidney beans.

The lamb that hails from the farms on the little island of Ouessant, off the coast of Brest, are famed—called *pré-salé*, or "salt meadow," they feed on sea-salted grass, which marinates their meat while their hearts are still pumping, so to speak. Try the regional *ragout de mouton* and you can taste the difference.

Brittany is particularly famous for its crepes (pancakes), served with sweet fillings, or as the heartier *galettes*—thicker, buckwheat pancakes served as a main course and stuffed with meat, fish, or regional lobster. What's the difference between the two? The darker galette has a deeper flavor best paired with savory fillings—like lobster and mushrooms, or the more traditional ham and cheese. A crepe plain and simple is wafer-thin and made with a lighter batter, reserved traditionally for the sweet—strawberries and cream, apples in brandy, or chocolate, for example. Accompanied by a glass of local cider, they are an ideal light, inexpensive meal; as *crepes dentelles* (lace crepes) they make a delicious dessert.

Incidentally, crepes are eaten from the triangular tails up to save the most flavorful buttery part for last. Folklore, however, permits older folks to eat the best part first in case some awful tragedy prevents them from enjoying *"la part de Dieu."*

billot.com ⌨21 rooms, 5 with bath ♿ In-room: no a/c. In-hotel: some pets allowed (fee), no elevator ⊟AE, MC, V ⊗ Closed last wk of Dec. and 1st wk of Jan. ⦿IEP.

RENNES

❷ *36 km (22 mi) west of Vitré via D857 and N157, 345 km (215 mi) west of Paris, 107 km (66 mi) north of Nantes.*

GETTING HERE

The TGV Atlantique travels faster than a speeding bullet from Paris's Gare Montparnasse to Rennes (2¼ hrs, €52), leaving every two hours or so, and through to Brest, while a branch line heads to St-Malo. Rennes's Gare SNCF (Place de la Gare) is about a 20-minute walk from the heart of the city. Trains leaves for Paris (2¼ hrs), Nantes (2 hrs), St-Malo (55 mins), and Bordeaux (6 hrs). The Gare Routière is next to the train station, but it's not the safest place to hang out. Buses go to Nantes (2 hrs), St-Malo (2 hrs), Dinan (1 hr), and Mont-St-Michel

(85 mins). Rennes's city bus system, STAR, will deliver you to almost any destination in town. There are also Ryanair flights to Rennes from England (London Stansted).

EXPLORING

Packed with students during the school year, studded with sterile 18th-century granite buildings, and yet graced with medieval houses, Rennes (pronounced *wren*) is the traditional gateway to Brittany. Since the province was joined to Paris in 1532, Rennes has been the site of squabbles with the national capital, many taking place in the Rennes's Palais de Justice, long the political center of Brittany and the one building that survived a terrible fire in 1720 that lasted a week and destroyed half the city. The remaining cobbled streets and 15th-century half-timber houses form an interesting contrast to the classical feel of the cathedral and Jacques Gabriel's disciplined granite buildings, broad avenues, and spacious squares. Many of the 15th- and 16th-century houses in the streets surrounding the cathedral have been converted into shops, boutiques, restaurants, and crêperies. The cavalier manner in which the French go about running a bar out of a 500-year-old building can be disarming to New Worlders.

The **Parlement de Bretagne** (⊠*Rue Nationale* ⊕*www.parlement-bretagne.com*), the palatial original home of the Breton Parliament and now of the Rennes law courts, was designed in 1618 by Salomon de Brosse, architect of the Luxembourg Palace in Paris. It was the most important building in Rennes to escape the 1720 flames, but in 1994, following a massive demonstration by Breton fishermen demanding state subsidies, a disastrous fire broke out at the building, leaving it a charred shell. Fortunately, much of the artwork—though damaged—was saved by firefighters, who arrived at the scene after the building was already engulfed in flames. It was a case of the alarm that cried "fire" once too often; a faulty bell, which rang regularly for no reason, had led the man on duty to ignore the signal. Restoration has now been completed. Call the tourist office (☎02–99–67–11–66) to book a 90-minute guided tour (€6.10).

The **Musée de Bretagne** *(Museum of Brittany)* reopened in mid-2006 in brand new headquarters designed by superstar architect Christian de Portzamparc and now occupies a vast three-part space that it shares with the Rennes municipal library and Espaces des Sciences. Portzamparc's layout harmonizes nicely with the organization of the museum's extensive ethnographic and archaeological collection, which, chronologically ordered, depicts the everyday life of Bretons from prehistoric times up to the present. There's also a space devoted to the famous Dreyfus Affair; Alfred Dreyfus, an army captain who was wrongly accused of espionage and whose case was championed by Emile Zola, was tried a second time in Rennes in 1899. ⊠*10 cours des Allies* ☎*02–23–40–66–70* ⊕*www.musee-bretagne.fr* 💶*€4 museum, €7 including exhibitions* ⊗*Tues. noon–9, Wed.–Fri. noon–7, weekends 2–7.*

The **Musée des Beaux-Arts** *(Fine Arts Museum)* contains works by Georges de La Tour, Jean-Baptiste Chardin, Camille Corot, Paul Gauguin, and

Maurice Utrillo, to name a few. The museum is particularly strong in French 17th-century paintings and drawings and has an interesting collection of modern French artists. ✉*20 quai Émile-Zola* ☎*02–23–62–17–45* ⊕*www.mbar.org* ✈*€4.30* ⊙*Tues.–Sun. 10–noon and 2–6.*

NEED A BREAK?

Thé au Fourneau (✉*6 rue du Capitaine-Alfred-Dreyfus, near the Fine Arts Museum*) is a cozy tearoom pleasantly cluttered with antiques, which serves chocolate cake, fruit crumble, excellent pastries, snacks, and salads. It's open weekdays 10–6:30.

A late-18th-century building in Classical style that took 57 years to construct, the **Cathédrale St-Pierre** looms above Rue de la Monnaie at the west end of the *Vieille Ville* (Old Town), bordered by the Rance River. Stop in to admire its richly decorated interior and outstanding 16th-century Flemish altarpiece. ✉*Pl. St-Pierre* ⊙*Mon.–Sat. 8:30–noon and 2–5, Sun. 8:30–noon.*

★ Take care to stroll through the lovely **Parc du Thabor** (✉*Pl. St-Melaine*), east of the Palais des Musées. It's a large, formal French garden with regimented rows of trees, shrubs, and flowers, and a notable view of the church of **Notre-Dame-en-St-Melaine.**

WHERE TO STAY & EAT

$ ✗ **Picca.** Around the corner from the Palais de Justice and next to the municipal theater is this oddly named brasserie that serves traditional Breton cuisine. Its huge, sunny terrace is the perfect place to people-watch while downing a half dozen fresh oysters and an aperitif. The prix-fixe menu is €13. ✉*15 Galeries du Théâtre* ☎*02–99–78–17–17* ▭*MC, V.*

★ $$$ ✗▥ **LeCoq-Gadby.** A 19th-century mansion with huge fireplaces and antiques sets the stage for this cozy retreat. Homey guest rooms have four-poster beds and floral covers, while hydrotherapy facilities, a hammam (steam room), a Jacuzzi, and a sauna are all available if you want to be pampered. Jean-Michel Boucault's cuisine must be good—French presidents have dined here on such delicacies as *pigeonneau en cocotte au beurre salé* (pigeon casserole with salted butter). Book way in advance for this popular hotel and restaurant (which does not serve dinner Sunday). ✉*156 rue d'Antrain, 35700* ☎*02–99–38–05–55* ⎙*02–99–38–53–40* ⊕*www.lecoq-gadby.com* ⤶*11 rooms* ⏃*In-room: refrigerator, dial-up, no a/c. In-hotel: restaurant, bar* ▭*AE, DC, MC, V* ⎔*MAP.*

$$–$$$ ▥ **Mercure Rennes Place de Bretagne.** This stately 19th-century hotel is centrally located on a quiet, narrow backstreet close to the cathedral. Rooms overlook the street or a courtyard; all are modern and functional. ✉*6 rue Lanjuinais, 35000* ☎*02–99–79–12–36* ⎙*02–99–79–65–7662* ⊕*www.mercure.com.au* ⤶*48 rooms* ⏃*In-room: dial-up. In-hotel: some pets allowed (fee), bar* ▭*AE, DC, MC, V* ⎔*BP.*

★ $–$$ ▥ **Garden.** This picturesque, central hotel has an age-old wooden gallery overlooking a sunny inner courtyard where breakfast is served. Rooms are small but cheerful, with bright colors and antiques. ✉*3 rue Jean-Marie-Duhamel, 35000* ☎*02–99–65–45–06* ⎙*02–99–65–02–62*

⊕*www.hotel-garden.fr* ↻*25 rooms* ♿*In-room: no a/c. In-hotel: some pets allowed, no elevator* ⊟*AE, MC, V.*

NIGHTLIFE & THE ARTS

The streets around Place Ste-Anne are jammed with popular student bars, most of them housed in fantastic medieval buildings with character to spare. If you feel like dancing the night away, head to **L'Espace** (⊠*45 bd. de la Tour d'Auvergne* ☎*02–99–30–21–95*). For the night owl, the **Pym's Club** (⊠*27 pl. du Colombier* ☎*02–99–67–30–00*), with three dance floors, stays open all night, every night.

Brittany's top classical music venue is the **Opéra de Rennes** (⊠*Pl. de l'Hôtel de Ville* ☎*02–99–78–48–78* ⊕*www.opera-rennes.fr*). All kinds of performances are staged at the **Théâtre National de Bretagne** (⊠*10 av. Louis-Barthou* ☎*02–99–35–27–74*). The famous annual international rock-and-roll festival, **Les Transmusicales** (☎*02–99–31– 12–10 for information*), happens the second week of December in bars around town and at the Théâtre National de Bretagne. The first week of July sees

★ **Les Tombées de la Nuit** (☎*02–99–32–56–56* ⊕*www.lestdnuit.com*), the "Nightfalls" Festival, featuring crowds, Celtic music, dance, and theater performances staged in old historic streets and churches around town.

SHOPPING

A lively **market** is held on Place des Lices on Saturday morning.

COMBOURG

❸ *40 km (25 mi) north of Rennes via D137 and D795.*

The pretty lakeside village of Combourg is dominated by the boyhood home of Romantic writer Viscount René de Chateaubriand (1768–

FodorsChoice 1848), the thick-walled, four-tower **Château de Combourg** *(Cat's Tower)*.

★ Topped with "witches' cap" towers that the poet likened to Gothic crowns, the castle dates mainly from the 14th and 15th centuries. Here, quartered in the tower called "La Tour du Chat," accompanied by roosting birds, a sinister quiet, and the ghost of a wooden-legged Comte de Combourg—whose false leg would reputedly get up and walk by itself—the young René succumbed to the château's moody spell and, in turn, became a leading light of Romanticism. His novel *Atala and René,* about a tragic love affair between a French soldier and a Native American maiden, was an international sensation in the mid-19th century, while his multivolume *History of Christianity* was required reading for half of Europe. The château grounds—ponds, woods, and cattle-strewn meadowland—are suitably mournful and can seem positively desolate when viewed under leaden skies. Its melancholy is best captured in Chateaubriand's famous *Mémoires d'outre-tombe* ("Memories from Beyond the Tomb"). Inside you can view neo-Gothic salons, the Chateaubriand archives, and the writer's severe bedroom up in the "Cat's Tower." ☎*02–99–73–22–95* ⊕*www.combourg.net* ⊠*€5, park only*

€2 ⊘Château (guided tours only) Apr.–Oct., Sun.–Fri. 2–5:30; park Apr.–Oct., Sun.–Fri. 9–noon and 2–6.

OFF THE
BEATEN
PATH
Château de La Ballue. This château, 18 km (11 mi) east of Combourg and dating from 1620, has sophisticated gardens that feature modern sculpture, leafy groves, columns of yew, a fernery, a labyrinth, and a Temple of Diana. To visit the interior, with its gleaming wood paneling and huge granite staircase, you'll have to stay the night—in one of the five large, beautifully decorated, fabric-swathed guest rooms (each with a four-poster bed), and dine with the dynamic English-speaking owners Alain Schrotter and Marie-France Barrère. Reserve well in advance and be sure to specify whether you'll be staying for dinner. Nineteenth-century writers Alfred de Musset, Honoré de Balzac, and Victor Hugo all preceded you as guests. ⊠*Bazouges-la-Pérouse* ☎*02–99–97–47–86* 🖶*02–99–97–47–70* ⊕*www.la-ballue.com* 🖾*Gardens €8* ⊘*May–mid-July and Sept., Fri.–Sun. 1–5:30; mid-July–Aug., daily 1–5:30.*

WHERE TO EAT

★ $ ✕ **L'Écrivain.** Gilles Menier's inventive, light cuisine showcases mussels in flaky pastry flavored with chervil, cod with cream of coriander and a red-berry sauce, and apple crepe with cider butter. Ask for a table in the intimate wood-paneled dining room, with candles on the tables, rather than in the bustling larger hall, and take your *digestif* in the wood-paneled bar with its oil paintings depicting scenes from Chateaubriand's life. Excellent fixed-price menus start at €16. ⊠*1 pl. St-Gilduin* ☎*02–99–73–01–61* ⊕*www.restaurantlecrivain.com* 🖃*MC, V* ⊘*Closed Thurs., 3 wks in Feb., and 2 wks in Oct. No dinner Wed. and Sun.*

DINAN

❹ *35 km (20 mi) west of Combourg.*

Fodor'sChoice
★   ### GETTING HERE
If you come to Dinan by train, you'll arrive in the Art Deco train station (Place du 11-Novembre-1918) but since direct trains are infrequent many travelers opt to train to Rennes and transfer to a SNCF bus (the fare from Rennes is €9). CAT buses also transfer from the train stations in St-Malo (1 hr) and Dinard (45 mins). TAE buses also connect Dinan to Rennes (1¼ hrs) several times a day. No buses run on Sunday.

EXPLORING
During the frequent wars that devastated other cities in the Middle Ages, the merchants who ruled Dinan got rich selling stuff to whichever camp had the upper hand, well aware that loyalty to any side, be it the French, the English, or the Breton, would eventually lead to the destruction of their homes. The strategy worked: today, Dinan is one of the best-preserved medieval towns in Brittany. Although there's no escaping the crowds here in summer, in the off-season or early morning Dinan feels like a time-warped medieval playground.

Like Montmuran, Dinan has close links with warrior-hero Bertrand du Guesclin, who won a famous victory here in 1359 and promptly married a local girl, Tiphaine Raguenel. When he died in the siege of Châteauneuf-de-Randon in Auvergne (central France) in 1380, his body was dispatched home to Dinan. Owing to the great man's popularity, only his heart completed the journey (it rests in the basilica); the rest of him was confiscated by devoted followers along the way.

Along Place des Merciers, Rue de l'Apport, and Rue de la Poissonnerie, take note of the splendid

FAST FORWARD TO THE 1300S

In even years, on the third weekend in July, medieval France is re-created with a market, parade, jousting tournament, and street music for Dinan's Fête des Remparts (Ramparts Festival), one of the largest medieval festivals in Europe.

gabled wooden houses. Rue du Jerzual, which leads down to Dinan's harbor, is also a beautifully preserved medieval street, divided halfway down by the town walls and the massive Porte du Jerzual gateway and lined with restaurants, boutiques, and crafts shops in the converted 15th- and 16th-century warehouses. In summer, boats make the 2-hour, 45-minute trip down the Rance River to St-Malo (€26 round-trip), call ☎08–25–13–81–10 for details; or you can head upstream on a one-hour round-trip on an old longboat, the *Jaman IV,* through a lock to the medieval abbey of St-Magloire, and learn how Napoléon canalized the Rance to enable French boats to cut across to the Atlantic and avoid English warships in the English Channel (€9 round-trip); check ⊕*www.vedettejamaniv.com*. Above the harbor, near Porte St-Malo, is the leafy Promenade des Grands Fossés, the best-preserved section of the town walls, which leads to the castle.

For a superb view of town, climb to the top of the medieval **Tour de l'Horloge** *(Clock Tower).* ⊠*Passage de la Tour de l'Horloge* ☎*02–96–87–58–72* ⌬*€2.50* ☉*Apr.–June, daily 2–6; July–Sept., daily 10–6:30.*

Du Guesclin's heart lies in the north transept of the **Basilique St-Sauveur** (⊠*Pl. St-Sauveur).* The church's style ranges from the Romanesque south front to the Flamboyant Gothic facade and Renaissance side chapels. The old trees in the **Jardin Anglais** (English Garden) behind the church provide a nice frame. More spectacular views can be found at the bottom of the garden, which looks down the plummeting Rance Valley to the river below.

The solidly built, fortresslike **Château,** at the end of the Promenade des Petits Fossés, has a two-story tower, the **Tour du Coëtquen,** and a 100-foot, 14th-century **donjon** (keep) containing a museum with varied displays of medieval effigies and statues, Breton furniture, and locally made lace coiffes (head coverings). ⊠*Porte de Guichet* ☎*02–96–39–45–20* ⊕*armorance.free.fr/dinan5.htm* ⌬*€4* ☉*June–Oct., daily 10–6:30; Nov., Dec., and Feb.–May, daily 1:30–5:30.*

WHERE TO STAY & EAT

$–$$ ✕ **Chablis.** Amid the parade of tourist-trap eateries along the banks of the Rance, this elegant restaurant stands out for its cool, minimalist, black-and-white decor, attentive service, and outstanding wine list, dominated—as the name suggests—by crisp white burgundies that provide the perfect accompaniment to the fish and seafood dishes that come tinge-salt fresh to your crisply linened table. There are also a handful of outdoor tables overlooking the quayside. ⊠ *7 rue du Quai* ☎*02–96–39–40–17* ⊟*MC, V.*

★ **$$–$$$** ⊞ **D'Avaugour.** Set on the town ramparts, with pretty sash windows, mansard roofs, and a Breton stone facade, this hotel has a sunny flower garden, which the best rooms overlook, and where breakfast and afternoon tea are served. Start the day with the full buffet breakfast and a chat with the charming owner, Nicolas Caron, who enjoys speaking English and helping everyone plan day trips. There's a colorful street market opposite the hotel every Thursday. ⊠ *1 pl. du Champ, 22100* ☎*02–96–39–07–49* 🖷*02–96–85–43–04* ⊕*www. avaugourhotel.com* ⇆*21 rooms, 3 suites* ⌂*In-room: dial-up, no a/c. In-hotel: some pets allowed (fee)* ⊟*AE, DC, MC, V* ⊙*Closed mid-Nov.–Dec. 20 and Jan.* ⎟◎⎟*BP.*

¢–$ ⊞ **Arvor.** The cobbled streets of the Vieille Ville are visible from this comfortable 18th-century hotel directly across from the town theater. Now under new management, it offers clean and simple rooms with friendly service. ⊠ *5 rue Auguste-Pavie, 22100* ☎*02–96–39–21–22* 🖷*02–96–39–83–09* ⊕*www.hotel-arvor-dinan.com* ⇆*23 rooms* ⌂*In-room: no a/c. In-hotel: some pets allowed, no elevator* ⊟*MC, V* ⊙*Closed Jan.*

SHOPPING

One of the leading craft havens in France, Dinan has attracted many wood-carvers, jewelers, leather workers, glass specialists, and silk painters, who have set up shop in the medieval houses that line the cobbled, sloping **Rue de Jerzual**. Other delightful studios and artisan boutiques can be found on the nearby **Rue de l'Apport, Place des Merciers,** and **Place des Cordeliers.**

CANCALE

⑤ *46 km (26 mi) northwest of Dinan.*

If you enjoy eating oysters, be sure to get to Cancale (get buses here from St-Malo), a picturesque fishing village renowned for its offshore *bancs d'huîtres* (oyster beds). You can sample the little brutes at countless stalls or restaurants along the quay.

The **Musée de la Ferme Marine** *(Sea Farm Museum)* just south of town explains everything you ever wanted to know about farming oysters and has a display of 1,500 different types of shells. ⊠*Les Parcs St-Kerber, Plage de l'Aurore* ☎*02–99–89–69–99* ⊕*www.ferme-marine.com* 🖅*€7* ⊙*Guided 1-hr tours in English, mid-Feb.–Oct., daily at 2.*

CLOSE UP

No Mean Catch!

To the great surprise of most North Americans, the humble canned sardine is a revered comestible—and justly so—among French *gourmands.* The best brands—Rodel, La Quiberonnaise, Gonidec, and La Belle Illoise—are from Brittany, where the sardine industry was once the backbone of the Breton economy. The sardine tin, in fact, was invented by a Breton named Pierre-Joseph Colin in 1810. The preserved fish immediately made culinary history: Napoléon had thousands loaded into carts and brought to the Russian front where the tasty little fish must have helped soften the blow of France's defeat. The best cans of sardines, usually marked *première catégorie* or *extra*, are treated like bottles of fine wine, carefully dated (some cans are even stamped with the name of the fishing boat credited with the catch), laid away in cellars for up to a decade and lovingly turned every few months for proper aging. Even the vocabulary for aged sardines is borrowed from oenology: one speaks of *grands crus* and *millésimes.* With the current trend toward "limited-edition" canned sardines, the oily fish has acceded to an even more exalted status. Purists take them straight, crushed onto a slice of buttered bread with the back of a fork, with perhaps the tiniest squeeze of lemon to bring out the oily flavors. Whichever way you wolf them down, vintage sardines are tender, delicately flavored, and deeply satisfying as a snack or an entire meal.

WHERE TO STAY & EAT

★ $$$-$$$$ ✕🏨 **Château Richeux.** One of three hotels owned by the famed Roellingers, the Richeux occupies an imposing 1920s waterfront mansion built on the ruins of the Du Guesclin family's 11th-century château, 5 km (3 mi) south of Cancale. Request one of the rooms with large bay windows, which have stunning views of Mont-St-Michel. Readers rave about Le Coquillage, the hotel's small bistro (closed Monday, Tuesday, and Thursday lunch), which specializes in local oysters and seafood platters served up in a relaxed, cozy atmosphere. Some prefer this traditional eaterie over the nouvelle fireworks of the Roellinger place. ✉*Le Point du Jour, St-Méloir des Ondes, 35350* 🕾*02–99–89–64–76* 🖷*02–99–89–18–49* ⊕*www.maisons-de-bricourt.com* 🛏*13 rooms* ⊝*In-room: no a/c. In-hotel: restaurant* ▭*AE, DC, MC, V* ❑❘*BP.*

$$$-$$$$ ✕🏨 **Relais Gourmand Olivier Roellinger.** The name of this place sounds
Fodor'sChoice the trumpet for chef Olivier Roellinger, who grew up in this grand 18th-century, St-Malo-style stone house. Fittingly for the resident of a town named "Oysters," he has mastered the *cuisine marine* of this region to perfection. Even those landlocked lubbers, Parisians, don't think twice about driving here just for dinner. Their 400-km-long (250-mi-long) drive is worth it: glowing

---

WORD OF MOUTH

"The Richeux—a gem of a place—has a sailboat anchored in St-Malo and a 3-hour ride on it is included in the room rate (May–September)! Seeing St-Malo from the sea was a bonus, beautiful and very like Québec city—perhaps not surprising since Jacques Cartier sailed from St-Malo to found Québec."–JuliePA

5

murals, a domed conservatory, stone fireplaces, spotlighted trees, a duck pond, and antique tiles all welcome them in cozily imposing style. But the main attraction is Roellinger's way with seafood, showcased in set menus that start at €97. He leaves *moules à la cancalaise* (mussels with butter)—the basic specialty of the region—in the dust with all sorts of culinary fireworks, such as the spiced consommé of cancalaises and foie gras or the John Dory steamed in seaweed and coconut milk. Luscious desserts all seduce, including farm raspberries with angelica and "churned" milk. The restaurant is closed Tuesday and Wednesday. If you wish to stay the night, attractive rooms (with spectacular views across the oyster beds toward Mont-St-Michel) are available in the luxe **Les Rimains** cottage on Rue des Rimains, a short walk away. ⊠*1 rue Duguesclin, 35260* ☎*02–99–89–64–76* 🖷*02–99–89–88–47* ⊕*www.maisons-de-bricourt. com* 🛏*4 rooms* ♿*In-room: ethernet, no a/c. In-hotel: restaurant* ▤*AE, DC, MC, V* ⊘*Closed mid-Dec.–mid-Mar.* ⦾*BP.*

EN ROUTE Heading north from Cancale, past the attractive beach of Port-Mer, you come to the jagged rock formations rising from the sea at the **Pointe de Grouin,** a magical spot for catching a sunset. From here follow D201 along the coast to St-Malo.

SHOPPING

Sublime tastes of Brittany—salted butter caramels, fruity sorbets, rare honeys, and heirloom breads—are sold in upper Cancale at the Roellingers's **Grain de Vanille** (⊠*12 pl. de la Victoire* ☎*02–23–15–12–70*). Tables beckon so why not sit a spell and enjoy a cup of "Mariage" tea and—Brittany in a bite—some cinnamon-orange-flavor *malouine* cookies?

ST-MALO

❻

Fodor's Choice
★

23 km (14 mi) west of Cancale via coastal D201.

GETTING HERE

The train station (Square Jean-Coquelin) is a 15-minute walk from the walled town—walk straight up Avenue Louis-Martin. Half a dozen trains daily make the 45-mi trip from Rennes St-Malo (€12). Trains connect St-Malo to Dol (15 mins) and Rennes (55 mins); a TGV express from Paris's Gare Montparnassse arrives several times a day in Rennes, where you can transfer. Trains also go to Dinan via Dol (65 mins), but the bus is cheaper and faster. TIV runs buses to Rennes (1¾ hrs), Dinard (40 mins), and Cancale (30 mins). CAT makes the trip to Dinan (35 mins) and Les Courriers Bretons makes the 1¼-hour journey to Mont-St-Michel. Buses leave from the Gare Routière, immediately outside the *intra-muros* Old Town. You can also ferry from here to Dinan and Dinard via Emeraude Lines.

EXPLORING

Thrust out into the sea, bound to the mainland only by tenuous man-made causeways, romantic St-Malo—"the pirates' city"—has built a reputation as a breeding ground for phenomenal sailors. Many were fishermen, but St-Malo's most famous sea dogs were corsairs, pirates paid by the French crown to harass the Limeys across the Channel. Robert Surcouf and Duguay-Trouin were just two of these privateers who helped make this town rich through piratical pillages. Facing Dinard across the Rance Estuary, the stone ramparts of St-Malo have withstood the pounding of the Atlantic since the 12th century, the founding date of the town's main church, the **Cathédrale St-Vincent** (on Rue St-Benoît). The ramparts were considerably enlarged and modified in the 18th century and now extend from the castle for more than 1½ km (1 mi) around the Vieille Ville—known as *intra-muros* (within the walls). The views are stupendous, especially at high tide. The town itself has proved less resistant: a weeklong fire in 1944, kindled by retreating Nazis, wiped out nearly all the old buildings. Restoration work was more painstaking than brilliant, but the narrow streets and granite houses of the Vieille Ville were satisfactorily re-created, enabling St-Malo to regain its role as a busy fishing port, seaside resort, and tourist destination. The ramparts themselves are authentic and the flames also spared houses along the Vieille Ville's Rue de Pelicot. Battalions of tourists invade this quaint part of town in summer, so if you want to avoid crowds, don't come then.

At the edge of the ramparts is the 15th-century **château,** whose great keep and watchtowers command an impressive view of the harbor and coastline. It houses the **Musée d'Histoire de la Ville** (Town History Museum), devoted to local history, and the **Galerie Quic-en-Grogne,** a museum in a tower, where various episodes and celebrities from St-Malo's past are recalled by way of waxworks. ⊠*Hôtel de Ville* ☎*02–99–40–71–11* 🖃*€4.60* ☉*Apr.–Sept., daily 10–12:30 and 2–6; Oct.–Mar., Tues.–Sun. 10–noon and 2–6.*

Five hundred yards offshore is the **Ile du Grand Bé,** a small island housing the somber military tomb of the great Romantic writer Viscount René de Chateaubriand, who was born in St-Malo. The islet can be reached by a causeway at low tide *only.*

The "Bastille of Brittany," the **Fort National,** also offshore and accessible by causeway at low tide only, is a massive fortress with a dungeon constructed in 1689 by that military-engineering genius Sébastien de Vauban. ☎*02–99–85–34–33* ⊕*www.fortnational.com* 🖃*€4* ☉*June–Sept., daily 10:30–6; see Web site at other times* ☞*Times of ½-hr guided tours depend on tides.*

You can pay homage to Jacques Cartier, who set sail from St-Malo in 1535 on a voyage in which he would discover the St. Lawrence River and found Québec, at his tomb in the church of **St-Vincent** (⊠*Grand-Rue*). His statue looks out over the town ramparts, four blocks away, along with that of swashbuckling corsair Robert Surcouf (hero of many daring 18th-century raids on the British navy), eternally wagging an angry finger over the waves at England.

WHERE TO STAY & EAT

$$$ ✕ **Chalut.** The reputation of this small restaurant with nautical decor has grown since chef Jean-Philippe Foucat decided to emphasize fresh seafood. The succinct menus change as frequently as the catch of the

day. Try the sautéed John Dory in wild-mushroom broth or the fresh lobster in lime. ✉ *8 rue de la Corne-de-Cerf* ☎ *02–99–56–71–58* ☰ *AE, MC, V* ⊘ *Closed Mon. No lunch Tues.*

¢–$ ✕ **Café de la Bourse.** Prawns and oysters are downed by the shovelful in this bustling brasserie in the Vieille Ville. Replete with wooden seats, ships' wheels, and posters of grizzled old sea dogs, it's hardly high design. But the large L-shape dining room makes amends with friendly service and a seafood platter for two that includes tanklike crabs flanked by an army of cockles, snails, and periwinkles. ✉ *1 rue de Dinan* ☎ *02–99–56–47–17* ☰ *MC, V* ⊘ *Closed Wed. Nov.–Easter.*

★ $$–$$$ ▦ **Elizabeth.** In a 16th-century town house built into the city wall, the Elizabeth, near the Porte St-Louis, is a little gem of sophistication in touristy St-Malo. North-facing rooms are modern, while the larger, recently renovated suites are tastefully furnished in period style. ✉ *2 rue des Cordiers, 35400* ☎ *02–99–56–24–98* 🖶 *02–99–56–39–24* ⊕ *www.st-malo-hotel-elizabeth.com* ↪ *14 rooms, 3 suites* ⚒ *In-room: no a/c. In-hotel: some pets allowed (fee)* ☰ *AE, DC, MC, V* ⫩*BP.*

$–$$ ▦ **Kyriad.** Formerly the Blue Myriad Atlantis, the view of the sea is magnificent from the hotel's bar, terrace, and breakfast room. Rooms are airy, with modern furnishings; expect to pay around €10 extra for one with a sea view. ✉ *49 chaussée du Sillon, 35400* ☎ *02–99–56–09–26* 🖶 *02–99–56–41–65* ↪ *55 rooms, 14 with bath* ⚒ *In-room: ethernet, no a/c. In-hotel: bar, gym, some pets allowed (fee)* ☰ *AE, MC, V* ⫩*BP.*

NIGHTLIFE & THE ARTS
Bar de l'Univers (✉ *12 pl. Chateaubriand*) is a nice spot to enjoy sipping a drink in a pirate's-lair setting. **La Belle Epoque** (✉ *11 rue de Dinan*) is a popular hangout for all ages until the wee hours. **L'Escalier** (✉ *La Buzardière, Rue de la Tour-du-Bonheur*) is the place for dancing the night away. In summer, performances are held at the **Théâtre Chateaubriand** (✉ *6 rue du Grout-de-St-Georges* ☎ *02–99–40–98–05*). Bastille Day (July 14) sees the **Fête du Clos Poulet,** a town festival with traditional dancing. July and August bring a monthlong religious music festival, the **Festival de la Musique Sacrée.**

SHOPPING
A lively outdoor **market** is held in the streets of Old St-Malo every Tuesday and Friday.

DINARD

❼ *13 km (8 mi) west of St-Malo via Rance Bridge.*

Fodor's Choice
★

GETTING HERE
No trains head here, so you have to train to St-Malo, then transfer to a bus (frequent departures, €3) for the 15-minute ride to Dinard. Buses arrive here from Rennes and other towns in Brittany.

EXPLORING
Dinard is the most elegant resort town on this stretch of the Brittany coast. Its picture-book perch on the Rance Estuary opposite the walled town of St-Malo lured the English aristocracy here in droves toward the

end of the 19th century. What started out as a small fishing port soon became a seaside mecca of lavish Belle Epoque villas (more than 400 still dot the town and shoreline), grand hotels, and a bustling casino. A number of modern establishments punctuate the landscape, but the town still retains something of an Edwardian tone. To make the most of Dinard's beauty, head down to the Pointe de la Vicomté, at the town's southern tip, where the cliffs offer panoramic views across the Baie du Prieuré and Rance Estuary, or stroll along the narrow promenade.

★ The **Promenade Clair de Lune** hugs the seacoast on its way toward the English Channel and passes in front of the small jetty used by boats crossing to St-Malo. In Dinard, the road weaves along the shore and is adorned with luxuriant palm trees and mimosa blooms, which, from July to the end of September, are illuminated at dusk with spotlights; strollers are serenaded with recorded music. The promenade really hits its stride as it rounds the **Pointe du Moulinet** and heads toward the sandy **Plage du Prieuré,** named after a priory that once stood here. River meets sea in a foaming mass of rock-pounding surf: use caution as you walk along the slippery path to the calm shelter of the **Plage de l'Écluse,** an inviting sandy beach bordered by the casino and numerous stylish hotels. The coastal path picks up on the west side of Plage de l'Écluse, ringing the Pointe de la Malouine and the Pointe des Étêtés before arriving at the **Plage de St-Énogat.**

WHERE TO STAY & EAT

$$–$$$ ✕ **La Salle à Manger.** Formerly of Paris's legendary Tour d'Argent, Chef Yannick Lalande serves up inventive Provençal cuisine, broadening its traditional olive oil–tomato-base repertoire to include balsamic vinegar reductions, sesame oil, even wasabi. The seasonal menu emphasizes market-fresh produce and, of course, local seafood. Chef Lalande also came up with the restaurant's home-sweet-home decor: lots of wood, forged iron, a cozy palette of Provençal red, orange, and yellow, and a fireplace. ⊠ *25 bd. Féart* ☎ *02–99–16–07–95* ▤ *MC, V* ⊘ *Closed Mon. and mid-Oct.–mid-Mar. No dinner Sun.*

$–$$ ✕▦ **Printania.** This white-walled, family-run hotel is on the Clair de Lune promenade. Rooms have regional furnishings and pictures of local scenes; the best ones have a balcony and sea view (ask for Room 101, 102, 211, or 311). Seafood and regional dishes are served in the paneled waterfront dining room by waitresses in regional costume. ⊠ *5 av. George-V, 35800* ☎ *02–99–46–13–07* ▦ *02–99–46–26–32* ⊕ *www.printaniahotel.com* ⟿ *56 rooms* ♿ *In-room: no a/c. In-hotel: restaurant, bar* ▤ *AE, MC, V* ⊘ *Closed mid-Nov.–mid-Mar.* ⦿*FAP.*

★ $$$–$$$$ ▦ **Villa Reine-Hortense.** All the Napoléon-III glamour of 19th-century resort France is yours when you stay at this *folie*—a villa built by the Russian Prince Vlassov in homage to his "queen," Hortense de Beauharnais (daughter of Napoléon's beloved Joséphine and mother to Emperor Napoléon III). A magical grand salon topped with a trompe l'oeil treillage, guest rooms with soaring, fairy-tale beds crowned with Empire-style canopies, and glamorous beach views are just some of the delights on tap here. The lucky guest who lands Room 4 will even get to bathe in Queen Hortense's own silver-plated bathtub. ⊠ *19 rue de*

la Malouine, 35800 ☏*02–99–46–54–31* 🖷*02–99–88–15–88* ⊕*www.
villa-reine-hortense.com* ⟲*8 rooms* ♿*In-room: refrigerator, dial-up,
no a/c. In-hotel: bar* ▭*AE, MC, V.*

NIGHTLIFE
During July and August, stretches of the **Clair de Lune** promenade
become a nighttime son-et-lumière wonderland, thanks to spotlights
and recorded music. The main nightlife activity in town is at the **casino**
(✉*4 bd. du Président-Wilson* ☏*02–99–16–30–30*).

SPORTS & THE OUTDOORS
For windsurfing, wander over to the **Wishbone Club** (✉*Digue de
l'Écluse* ☏*02–99–88–15–20*). Boats can be rented from the **Yacht Club**
(✉*Promenade Clair de Lune* ☏*02–99–46–14–32*).

▌**EN
ROUTE**
Forty kilometers (25 mi) west of Dinard along the coast is the **Cap
Fréhel**, where dramatic pink cliffs rise vertically from the sea. The colors are most vivid in the evening, but at any time of day the sight is
formidable. Pick your way through the seagulls and cormorants and, if
you're not afraid of heights, mosey down past the small restaurant for
a vertiginous glimpse of the rocks below. Then climb up to the lighthouse, whose beam can be seen by ships up to 97 km (60 mi) away.

If you've time and are in a martial frame of mind, check out **Fort de Latte**
nearby, a 17th-century fort linked to the mainland by a drawbridge.
Then head west, past fine beaches at Pléhérel and Sables-d'Or–les-Pins,
to pick up D786 and skirt around the Bay of St-Brieuc.

PAIMPOL

❽ *92 km (57 mi) west of Cap Fréhel via D786, 45 km (28 mi) northwest
of St-Brieuc.*

Paimpol is one of the liveliest fishing ports in the area and a good
base for exploring this part of the coast. The town is a maze of narrow streets lined with shops, restaurants, and souvenir boutiques. The
harbor, where fishermen used to unload their catch from far-off seas, is
its main focal point; today most fish are caught in the Channel. From
the sharp cliffs you can see the coast's famous pink-granite rocks. For
centuries, but no longer, Breton fishermen sailed to Newfoundland each
spring to harvest cod—a long and perilous journey. The **Fête des Terres-
Neuves** is a celebration of the traditional return from Newfoundland
of the Breton fishing fleets; it is held on the third Sunday in July. From
Paimpol, trains go to Guingamp, and CAT buses go to St-Brieuc; both
towns are on the Paris–Brest TGV line.

WHERE TO STAY & EAT
★ $$–$$$ ✗▦ **Repaire de Kerroc'h.** Built in the late 18th century by Corouge
Kersau—one of the region's most notorious privateers—this delightful
quayside structure (which looks transplanted from an urban street)
overlooks the harbor and yacht marina. Beyond elegant sash windows
lie rough-hewn stone walls, fireplaces, a lovely Neoclassical dining
nook, while upstairs the spacious guest rooms use their artfully odd

angles to best advantage. Most are decorated in an English style with flowered chintzes and wood accents; a favorite, Les Sept Isles, faces the street and has a view of the boats, whereas the Iles des Gizans double suite (with two bathrooms) is perfect for a large party traveling together. ⊠29 *quai Morand, 22500* 🕾*02–96–20–50–13* 📠*02–96– 22–07–46* ⊕*www.chateauxhotels.com/kerroch* ⟲*13 rooms, 2 suites* ♿*In-room: no a/c. In-hotel: bar, restaurant, public Internet, no elevator* 🚭*AE, DC, MC, V* ⊙*Closed mid-Nov.–mid-Dec.* ⊠*MAP.*

TRÉBEURDEN

❾ *46 km (27 mi) west of Paimpol via D786 and D65, 9 km (6 mi) north-*
Fodor'sChoice *west of Lannion.*
★

GETTING HERE

Trébeurden is just one of the scenic highlights of the Côtes d'Armor, the long stretch of Brittany's northern coast, loosely divided into two parts, the Côte d'Emeraude (Emerald Coast) and the peaceful Côte de Granit Rose (Pink Granite Coast). The main transport hub for this coastline is the resort town of Perros-Guirec. To get to Perros-Guirec you have to go through Lannion, a town 8 km (5 mi) inland and served by train. The trains run from Lannion to Plouaret-Trégor about eight times a day. Plouaret-Trégor is then on the main Paris-Brest train line. CAT runs five buses a day from Lannion to Perros-Guirec, with stop at Trestraou beach and neighboring Ploumanac'h (35 mins). From Lannion, you can get buses to Trébeurden.

EXPLORING

A small, pleasant fishing village that is now a summer resort town, Trébeurden makes a good base for exploring the pink-granite cliffs of the Corniche Bretonne, starting with the rocky point at nearby Le Castel. Take a look at the profile of the dramatic rocks off the coast near Trégastel and Perros-Guirec and use your imagination to see La Tête de Mort (Death's Head), La Tortoise, Le Sentinel, and Le Chapeau de Wellington (Wellington's Hat). The scene changes with the sunlight and the sweep and retreat of the tide, whose caprices can strand fishing boats among islands that were, only hours before, hidden beneath the sea.

★ The famous seaside footpath, the **Sentier des Douaniers** (⊕*www.perros-guirec.com*), starts up at the west end of the Trestraou beach in the resort town of **Perros-Guirec**, 3 km (2 mi) east of Trébeurden; from there this beautifully manicured, fence-lined, and gorgeously scenic path provides a two-hour walk eastward, through fern forests, past cliffs and pink granite boulders to the pretty beach at Ploumanac'h. If you keep your eye out, you might even spot one of the mythical, 900-year-old Korrigans—native sprites with pointed ears, beards, and hoof feet, who come out at night from seaside grottoes to dance around fires. From Perros-Guirec, you can take a boat trip out to the Sept Iles, a group of seven islets that are bird sanctuaries. On a hillside perch above **Ploumanac'h** is the village of La Clarté, home to the little Chapelle Notre Dame de la Clarté (⊠Pl. de la Chapelle), built of local pink granite and decorated with 14 stations of the cross painted by the master of the Pont-Aven school, Maurice Denis. During the **Pardon of la Clarté** (August 15), a bishop preaches an outdoor mass for the Virgin Mary, village girls wear Trégor costumes, and the statue of the Virgin Mary wears a gold crown (she wears a fake one for the rest of the year).

Five kilometers (3 mi) east of Trébeurden is **Cosmopolis,** home to the Radôme: a giant white radar dome, whose 340-ton antenna captured the first live TV satellite transmission from the United States to France in July 1962. Today the sphere houses a museum retracing the history of telecommunications back to the first telegraph in 1792, and spectacular laser shows that employ 200 projectors to bring the history of satellite communication to life. The site also includes one of Europe's largest planetariums (⊕ www.planetarium-bretagne.fr ◳ €7.20), and a children's fun park, Le Village Gaulois (€4). ⊠ *Pleumeur-Bodou* ☏ *02–96–15–80–30* ⊕ *www.leradome.com* ◳ *€7* ⊘ *Apr. and Sept., Mon. and Wed.–Fri. 10–6, weekends 2–6; May–Aug., daily 10–6.*

WHERE TO STAY & EAT

★ $$$–$$$$ ✕⌨ **Manoir de Lan-Kerellec.** The beauty of the Breton coastline is embraced by this Relais & Châteaux hotel, where guest rooms are far more than just comfortable. Set long and cruise-liner-low, this renovated 19th-century Breton manor house has now been outfitted with dramatic windows—plate-glass, round, panoramic—so as to frame stirring vistas of the endless sea and the cliffs of the Côte de Granit Rose. The restaurant, with a wood-beam ceiling inspired by a ship's hull, has a delightful model of the *St-Yves* ship suspended from its ceiling. It mostly serves seafood, but the roast lamb is also good; it does not serve lunch Monday through Thursday, and is closed Monday, October until Easter. ⊠ *11 allée Centrale, 22560* ☏ *02–96–15–00–00* 🖷 *02–96–23–66–88* ☞ *18 rooms* ⚑ *In-room: refrigerator, dial-up. In-hotel: restaurant, tennis court, some pets allowed (fee)* ▤ *AE, DC, MC, V* ⊘ *Closed mid-Nov.–mid-Mar.* ⦿ *MAP.*

THE ATLANTIC COAST

What Brittany offers in the way of the sea handsomely makes up for its shortage of mountain peaks and passes. Its hundreds of miles of saw-tooth coastline reveal the Atlantic Ocean in its every mood and form—from the peaceful cove where waders poke about hunting seashells to the treacherous bay whose waters swirl over quicksands in unpredictable crosscurrents; from the majestic serenity of the breakers rolling across La Baule's miles of golden-sand beaches to the savage fury of the gigantic waves that fling their force against jagged rocks 340 dizzy feet below the cliffs of Pointe du Raz. Brittany's Atlantic coast runs southeast from the down-to-earth port of Brest to the tony city of Nantes, at the mouth of the Loire River. The wild, rugged creeks around the little-visited northwestern tip of Finistère (Land's End) gradually give way to sandy beaches south of Concarneau. Inland, the bent trees and craggy rocks look like they've been bewitched by Merlin in a bad mood.

STE-ANNE-LA-PALUD

10 *136 km (82 mi) southwest of Frébeurden via D767 and D787.*

Fodor's Choice
★

One of the great attractions of the Brittany calendar is the celebration of a religious festival known as a village **pardon,** replete with banners, saintly statues, a parade, bishops in attendance, women in folk costume, a feast, and hundreds of attendees. The seaside village of Ste-Anne-la-Palud has one of the finest and most authentic age-old pardons in Brittany, held on the last Sunday in August.

Another celebrated *pardon* is held in early September some 40 km (35 mi) north of Ste-Anne. Pilgrims come from afar to Le Folgoët, 24 km (15 mi) northeast of Brest, to attend the town's ceremonial procession. Many also drink from the Fontaine de Salaün, a fountain behind the church, whose water comes from a spring beneath the altar. The splendid church, known as the Basilique, has a sturdy north tower that serves as a beacon for miles around and, inside, a rare, intricately carved granite rood screen separating the choir and nave.

WHERE TO STAY & EAT

$$$–$$$$ ✕🏨 **Hôtel de la Plage.** This former private mansion nestles in a cove on a quiet strip of sandy beach on the Bay of Douarnenez—a remote retreat perfect for long, restorative walks. Some of the comfortably furnished rooms face the water, as does the glass-fronted restaurant, where seafood is king and reservations essential. ✉29550 ☎02–98–92–50–12 🖷02–98–92–56–54 ⊕*www.plage.com* ⇆*26 rooms, 4 suites* ⚂*In-hotel: restaurant, tennis court, pool, beachfront, some pets allowed (fee), public Internet* ▤*AE, DC, MC, V* ⊗*Closed Nov.–Apr.* �“❘*MAP.*

DOUARNENEZ

11 *14 km (8 mi) south of Ste-Anne-la-Palud.*

Douarnenez is a quaint old fishing town of quayside paths and zigzagging narrow streets. Boats come in from the Atlantic to unload their catches of mackerel, sardines, and tuna. Just offshore is the Ile Tristan, accessible on foot at low tide (guided tours only, €5.50), and across the Port-Rhu channel is Tréboul, a seaside resort town favored by French families.

☯ One of the three town harbors is fitted out with a unique **Port-Musée** *(Port Museum)* which reopened in May 2006 after an extensive renovation program. Along the wharves you can visit the workshops of boatwrights, sailmakers, and other old-time craftspeople, then go aboard the historic trawlers, lobster boats, Thames barges, and a former lightship anchored alongside. On the first weekend in May you can sail on an antique fishing boat. ✉*Pl. de l'Enfer* ☎02–98–92–65–20 ⊕*www.port-musee.org* ✍*€6.50* ⊗*June–Sept., daily 10–7; Oct., Apr., and May, Tues.–Sun. 10–12:30 and 2–6.*

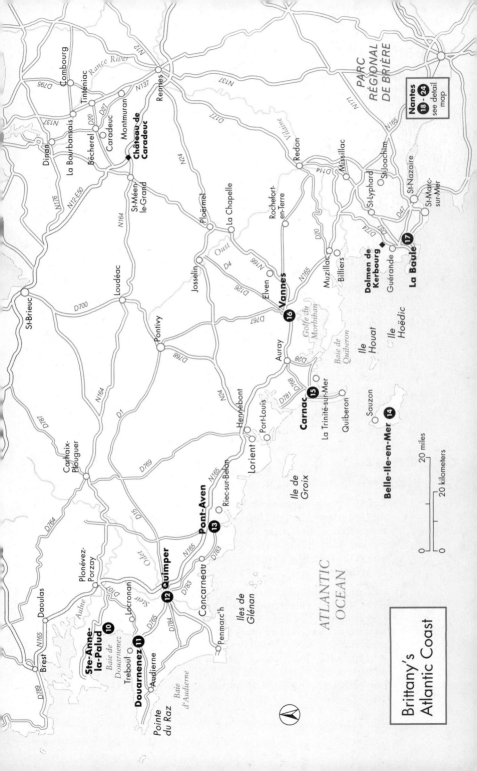

Brittany's Atlantic Coast

WHERE TO STAY & EAT

★ $–$$ ✕⊡ **Manoir de Moëllien.** Surrounded by extensive forested grounds, this textbook 17th-century granite Breton manor house, landmarked by a sturdy tower, and filled with precious antiques, makes an enviable choice. Another plus is the fine restaurant (open to residents only), famous for its local seafood dishes. Sample Bruno Garet's *terrine de poisson chaud* (warm seafood terrine) or the *duo de truites de mer* (poached sea trout). Rooms vary greatly in size, but most have terraces overlooking the peaceful country garden. ⊠*12 km (7 mi) northeast of Douarnenez, 29550 Plonévez-Porzay* ☎*02–98–92–50–40* 🖷*02–98–92–55–21* ⊕*www.moellien.com* ⇥*18 rooms* &*In-room: refrigerator (some), dial-up, no a/c. In-hotel: restaurant, bar, some pets allowed (fee), no elevator* ▤*AE, DC, MC, V* ⊘*Closed Feb–Mar.* ⦅◎⦆*FAP.*

★ $–$$ ✕⊡ **Ty-Mad.** In the 1920s artists and writers such as Picasso and Breton native Max Jacob frequented this small hotel in a quiet residential area near the beach in Tréboul. Under new management, this landmark was completely renovated in 2005. Guest rooms are not large, but 11 of them have great sea views. A garden now adorns the property, and the separate house has been outfitted with a kitchen for larger groups and longer stays. Gérard Tanter's menu, served in the glass-enclosed restaurant, focuses on fresh produce sourced from neighboring farms and fish boats. ⊠*Plage St-Jean, 29100 Treboul* ☎*02–98–74–00–53* 🖷*02–98–74–15–16* ⊕*www.hoteltymad.com* ⇥*17 rooms* &*In-room: no a/c, no TV. In-hotel: restaurant, bar, some pets allowed, no elevator* ▤*MC, V* ⊘*Closed Oct.–Easter* ⦅◎⦆*MAP.*

QUIMPER

⓬ *22 km (14 mi) southeast of Douarnenez via D765.*

GETTING HERE

The twice-daily direct TGV travels 350 mi from Paris Montparnasse to reach Quimper's train station, on the Avenue de la Gare, in 4 hours, 30 minutes (€70). Four trains each day make the 70-minute trip from Quimper to Brest (€14.50) and (sometimes with a change at Redon) the 2-hour, 40-minute trip to Nantes (€30). Buses from the Gare Routière on Place Louis-Armand make infrequent connections to such destinations as Concarneau and Pont-Aven.

EXPLORING

A traditional crowd-puller, the twisting streets and tottering medieval houses of Quimper furnish rich postcard material, but lovers of decorative arts head here because this is the home of Quimperware, one of the more famous variants of French hand-painted earthenware pottery. The techniques were brought to Quimper by Normands in the 17th century, but the Quimperois customized them by painting typical local Breton scenes on the pottery. This lively and commercial town began life as the ancient capital of the Cornouaille province, founded, it's said, by King Gradlon 1,500 years ago. Quimper (pronounced cam-*pair*) owes its strange name to its site at the confluence (*kemper* in Breton) of the Odet and Steir rivers. Stroll along the banks of the Odet and through the **Vieille Ville,** with its cathedral. Then walk along the lively shopping street, Rue Kéréon, and down narrow medieval Rue du Guéodet (note the house with caryatids), Rue St-Mathieu, and Rue du Sallé.

The **Cathédrale St-Corentin** (✉ *Pl. St-Corentin*) is a masterpiece of Gothic architecture and the second-largest cathedral in Brittany (after Dol-de-

ANCIENT EVENINGS

During the second half of July, Quimper hosts the Festival de Cornouaille (☎ 02–98–55–53–53 ⊕ *www.festival-cornouaille.com*), a nine-day Celtic extravaganza. More than 250 artists, dancers, and musicians fill streets already packed with the 4,000 people who come each year to enjoy the traditional street fair.

Bretagne's). Legendary King Gradlon is represented on horseback just below the base of the spires, harmonious mid-19th-century additions to the medieval ensemble. The church interior remains very much in use by fervent Quimperois, giving the candlelighted vaults a meditative air. The 15th-century stained glass is luminous. Behind the cathedral is the stately **Jardin de l'Évêché** (Bishop's Garden).

More than 400 works by such masters as Rubens, Corot, and Picasso mingle with pretty landscapes from the local Gauguin-inspired Pont-Aven school in the **Musée des Beaux-Arts** *(Fine Arts Museum)*, next to the cathedral. Of particular note is a fascinating series of paintings depicting traditional life in Breton villages. ✉ *40 pl. St-Corentin* ☎ *02–98–95–45–20* ⊕ *www.musee-beauxarts.quimper.fr* 🎫 *€4.50* ⊙ *July and Aug., daily 10–7; Sept.–June, Wed.–Mon. 10–noon and 2–6.*

In the mid-18th century Quimper sprang to nationwide attention as a pottery manufacturing center, when it began producing second-rate imitations of Rouen faïence, or ceramics with blue motifs. Today's more colorful designs, based on floral arrangements and marine fauna, are still often hand-painted. To understand Quimper's pottery past with the help of more than 500 examples of "style Quimper," take one of the guided tours at the **Musée de la Faïence** *(Earthenware Museum).* ✉ *14 rue Jean-Baptiste-Bousquet* ☎ *02–98–90–12–72* ⊕ *www.quimper-faiences.com* 🎫 *€4* ⊙ *Mid-Apr.–mid-Oct., Mon.–Sat. 10–6.*

Local furniture, ceramics, and folklore top the bill at the **Musée Départemental Breton** *(Brittany Regional Museum).* ✉ *1 rue du Roi-Gradlon* ☎ *02–98–95–21–60* 🎫 *€3.80* ⊙ *June–Sept., daily 9–6; Oct.–May, Tues.–Sun. 9–noon and 2–5.*

WHERE TO EAT

$$$ ✕ **L'Ambroisie.** This cozy little restaurant has soft-yellow walls, huge contemporary paintings, and different settings at every table. Chef Gilbert Guyon's traditional yet nouvelle menu is seasonal; local products are chosen by hand. Try the buckwheat *galette* crepe stuffed with egg and salmon; the fresh cod, mullet, or sole; the steamed scallops with mushrooms and lemon juice; or the pigeon roasted in apple liqueur

with whipped potatoes and mushrooms. The homemade desserts, like the omelet *norvégienne* with warm chocolate and nougat ice cream in meringue, are delicious. ✉*49 rue Élie-Fréron* ☎*02–98–95–00–02* ⊕*www.ambroisie-quimper.com* ⚓*Reservations essential* ▭*AE, MC, V* ⊘*Closed Mon., early July, and 2 wks in Feb. No dinner Sun. except June–Aug.*

$$ ✕ **Chez Armande.** Concarneau—22 km (14 mi) southwest of Quimper—is a busy town but it's *Ville Close* has a grain of charm. Better yet, the waterfront has some fine seafood restaurants, particularly this one. Specialties include *pot-au-feu de la mer au gingembre* (seafood in a clear ginger broth), *St-Pierre à la fricassée de champignons* (John Dory with fried mushrooms), and *homard rôti en beurre de corail* (roast lobster in coral butter). Try the *tarte de grand-mère aux pommes* (grandma's homemade apple pie) for dessert. ✉*15 bis, av. du Dr-Nicolas* ☎*02–98–97–00–76* ▭*AE, MC, V* ⊘*Closed Tues. and Wed., mid-Nov.–early Dec.*

SHOPPING

Keep an eye out for such typical Breton products as woven and embroidered cloth, woolen goods, brass and wood objects, puppets, dolls, and locally designed jewelry. When it comes to distinctive Breton folk costumes, Quimper is the best place to look. The streets around the cathedral, especially **Rue du Parc**, are full of shops selling woolen goods (notably thick marine sweaters). Faïence and a wide selection of hand-painted pottery can be purchased at the **Faïencerie d'Art Breton** (✉*16 bis, rue du Parc* ☎*02–98–95–34–13* ⊕*www. bretagne-faience.com*).

PONT-AVEN

13 *37 km (23 mi) east of Quimper via D783.*

GETTING HERE

There are no direct trains, so take the rails to nearby Quimperlé and transfer to a bus (30 mins, €2). Buses make the 20-km (12-mi) run from Quimper (1¼ hrs) and Concarneau (30 mins) several times a day. The last buses leave early in the evening, and service is limited on Sunday.

EXPLORING

Long beloved by artists, this lovely village sits astride the Aven River as it descends from the Montagnes Noires to the sea, turning the town's mills along the way (there were once 14; now just a handful remain). Surrounded by one of Brittany's most beautiful stretches of countryside, Pont-Aven (⊕www.pontaven.com) is a former artists' colony where, most famously, Paul Gauguin lived before he headed off to the South Seas. Wanting to break with traditional Western culture and values, in 1888 the lawyer-turned-painter headed to Brittany, a destination almost as foreign to Parisians as Tahiti. Economy was another lure: the Paris stock market had just crashed and, with it, Gauguin's livelihood, so cheap lodgings were also at the top of his list. Before long, Gauguin took to wearing Breton sweaters, berets, and wooden clogs; in his art

Gauguin & the Pont-Aven School

Surrounded by one of Brittany's most beautiful countrysides, Pont-Aven was a natural to become a "cité des artistes" in the heady days of Impressionism and Postimpressionism. It was actually the introduction of the railroad in the 19th century that put travel to Brittany in vogue, and it was here that Gauguin and other like-minded artists founded the noted Pont-Aven school. Inspired by the vibrant colors and lovely vistas to be found here, they created *"synthétisme,"* a painting style characterized by broad patches of pure color and strong symbolism, in revolt against the dominant Impressionist school back in Paris. Gauguin arrived in the summer of 1886, happy to find a place "where you can live on nothing" (Paris's stock market had crashed and cost Gauguin his job). At Madame Gloanec's boardinghouse he welcomed a circle of painters to join him in his artistic quest for monumental simplicity and striking color.

Today Pont-Aven seems content to rest on its laurels. Although it's labeled a "city of artists," the galleries that line its streets display paintings that lack the unifying theme and common creative energy of the earlier works of art. The first Pont-Aven painters were American students who came here in the 1850s. Though Gauguin is not-surprisingly absent (his paintings now go for millions), except for a few of his early zincographs, the exhibit *Hommage à Gauguin* is an interesting sketch of his turbulent life. Also on view in the museum are works by other near-great Pont-Aven artists: Maurice Denis, Emil Bernard, Emil Jordan, and Emmanuel Sérusier.

he began to leave dewy, sunlit Impressionism behind for a stronger, more linear style. The town museum captures some of the history of the Pont-Aven School, whose adherents painted Breton landscapes in a bold yet dreamy style called Syntheticism.

One glance at the Bois d'Amour forest, set just to the north of town (from the tourist office, go left and walk along the river for five minutes), will make you realize why artists continue to come here. Past some meadows, you can find Gauguin's inspiration for his famous painting *The Yellow Christ*—a wooden crucifix inside the secluded **Chapelle de Trémalo** (usually open, per private owners, from 9 to 7) just outside the Bois d'Amour woods. While in Brittany, Gauguin painted many of his earliest masterpieces, now given pride of place in great museums around the world.

> ## BE GAUGUIN
>
> If the spirit of Gauguin inspires you in his former hangout of Pont-Aven, the Maison de la Presse, right next to the bridge at 5 place Paul Gauguin, has boxes of 12 colored pencils and sketchbooks for sale.

The **Musée de Pont-Aven** *(Art Museum)* has a photography exhibition documenting the Pont-Aven School, and works by its participants, such as Paul Sérusier, Maurice Denis, and Emile Bernard. After Gauguin departed for Tahiti, a group of Americans came here to paint, attracted by the light, the landscape, and the reputation. ⊠*Pl. de l'Hôtel-de-Ville* ☎*02–98–06–14–43* ⊡*€4* ⏺*July and Aug., daily 10–7; Feb.–June and Sept.–Dec., daily 10–12:30 and 2–6.*

The crêperies and pizzerias that surround **Place de l'Hôtel-de-Ville** cater to the lazy visitor, just emerging from the tourist office at **No. 5** (☎*02–98–06–04–70*); note the office's helpful list of chambers d'hôte accommodations offered by the residents in town.

Instead, walk the few paces to the **Moulin du Grand Poulguin** (⊠*2 quai Théodore-Botrel* ☎*02–98–06–02–67*), which provides a delightful setting in which to eat a crepe or pizza on a terrace directly on the flowing waters of the Aven River in view of the footbridge.

Those with a sweet tooth can just fill up on the buttery Traou Mad cookies at the **Biscuiterie Traou Mad** (⊠*10 pl. Gauguin* ☎*02–98–06–01–94*); they're baked with the local wheat of the last running windmill in Pont-Aven. After exploring the village, cool off (in summer) with a boat trip down the estuary.

WHERE TO STAY & EAT

$$$$ ✕ **La Taupinière.** On the road from Concarneau, 3 km (2 mi) west of Pont-Aven, is this roadside inn with an attractive garden. Chef Guy Guilloux's open kitchen (with the large hearth he uses to grill above all langoustine, but also crab and fish) turns out local delicacies such as galette crepes stuffed with spider crab and Breton ham specialties. Splurge without guilt on the light homemade rhubarb and strawberry compote. ⊠*Croissant St-André* ☎*02–98–06–03–12* ⊕*www.la-taupiniere.com* ⊲*Reservations essential*Jacket required ▤*AE, MC, V* ⏺*Closed Mon., Tues., plus last 2 wks Mar. and mid-Sept.–mid-Oct.*

$$ ✕▥ **Le Moulin de Rosmadec.** You'll want to set up your easel in a second once you spot this pretty-as-a-picture, 15th-century stone water mill. Set at the end of a quiet street, the Sébilleaus' beloved hostelry sits in the middle of the rushing, rocky Aven River. Inside, atmospheric

Fodor'sChoice ★

beamed ceilings, Breton stone fireplaces, and water views (you can hear the sound of water gently splashing over the stones beneath your window) cast their spell—but who can resist dining on the "island" terrace? Outside or inside, feast on the creations of a serious kitchen: the *sautée de langoustines,* duck in cassis, and lobster *grillé Rosmadec* are all winners. Reservations are essential; the restaurant does not serve dinner Sunday from September to June. If you're very lucky, you'll snag one of the four gently priced guest rooms available. ⊠ *Venelle de Rosmadec, 29930* ☎ *02–98–06–00–22* 🖷 *02–98–06–18–00* ⊕ *www. moulinderosmadec.com* ➩ *4 rooms* ⚲ *In-room: no a/c. In-hotel: restaurant, some pets allowed, no elevator* ⊟ *MC, V* ⊘ *Closed Wed., last 2 wks Feb., and 1st 2 wks Oct.*

$-$$ ⊡ **La Chaumière Roz-Aven.** Built into a rock face on the bank of the Aven, this efficiently run hotel, renovated in 2006 by new owners Valérie and Alain Bodolec, has simple, clean rooms with 18th- and 19th-century-style furnishings. You can choose a room in one of three locations: the 16th-century thatched cottage, the modern annex, or the *maison bourgeoise* with a river or garden view. There's no restaurant, but there's a tearoom and the bar serves tapas and snacks. ⊠ *11 quai Théodore-Botrel, 29930* ☎ *02–98–06–13–06* 🖷 *02–98–06–03–89* ⊕ *www.hotelpontaven.online.fr* ➩ *23 rooms, 2 suites* ⚲ *In-room: no a/c, no TV (some), refrigerator (some). In-hotel: bar, some pets allowed (fee), no elevator* ⊟ *AE, MC, V* ⊘ *Closed Feb.* ⍢ *MAP.*

BELLE-ILE-EN-MER

⓮   *45 mins by boat from Quiberon, 78 km (52 mi) southeast of*
Fodor's Choice *Pont-Aven.*
★

GETTING HERE

Take the 45-minute ferry trip (hourly July–August) to Belle-Ile's Le Palais from Quiberon's Gare Maritime, which can be reached in one hour by bus from Auray train station (on the Quimper–Vannes line) that runs twice daily in summer (€6.50).

EXPLORING

At 18 km (11 mi) long, Belle-Ile is the largest of Brittany's islands. It also lives up to its name: it's indeed beautiful, and less commercialized than its mainland harbor town, Quiberon. Because of the cost and inconvenience of reserving car berths on the ferry, cross over to the island as a pedestrian and rent a car—or, if you don't mind the hilly terrain, a bicycle. Departing from Quiberon—a spa town with pearl-like beaches on the eastern side of the 16-km-long (10-mi-long) Presqu'île de Quiberon (Quiberon Peninsula), a stretch of coastal cliffs and beaches whose dramatic western coast, the Côte Sauvage (Wild Coast), is a mix of crevices and coves lashed by the sea—the ferry lands at **Le Palais,** crushed beneath a monumental Vauban citadel built in the 1680s.

From Le Palais head northwest to **Sauzon,** the prettiest fishing harbor on the island; from here you can see across to the Quiberon Peninsula and the Gulf of Morbihan.

Continue on to the **Grotte de l'Apothicairerie**, which derives its name from the local cormorants' nests, said to resemble apothecary bottles.

At Port Goulphar is the **Grand Phare** (*Great Lighthouse*). Built in 1835, it rises 275 feet above sea level and has one of the most powerful beacons in Europe, visible from 120 km (75 mi) across the Atlantic. If the keeper is available and you are feeling well rested, you may be able to climb to the top.

WHERE TO STAY & EAT

★ $$$$ ✕◨ **Castel Clara.** Perched on a cliff overlooking the surf and the narrow Anse de Goulphar Bay, this '70s-era hotel was François Mitterrand's address when he vacationed on Belle-Ile. The hotel still retains its presidential glamour, with its renowned spa, saltwater pool, and spectacular room views. In the bright, airy restaurant, chef Christophe Hardouin specializes in seafood, caught just offshore. The John Dory baked in sea salt and the grilled sea bream are simple but delicious. Castel Clara's expansive wooden-decked terrace is the perfect lounging spot for cocktails at sundown. ⊠ *Port-Goulphar, 56360 Bangor,* ☎ *02–97–31–84–21* 🖷 *02–97–31–51–69* ⊕ *www.castel-clara.com* ⮐ *33 rooms, 7 suites* ⚲ *In-room: refrigerator, ethernet, no a/c. In-hotel: restaurant, tennis court, pool, spa* ▤ *AE, DC, MC, V* ⊘ *Closed mid-Nov.–mid-Feb.* ⍟ *MAP.*

NIGHTLIFE & THE ARTS

Every year, from the end of July to mid-August, Belle-Ile hosts **Lyrique-en-Mer** (☎ *02–97–31–59–59* ⊕ *www.belle-ile.net*), an ambitious little festival whose heart is opera (the festival was founded by the American bass baritone, Richard Cowan) but which offers up a generous lyric menu of sacred music concerts, gospel, jazz, even the occasional sea chantey and Broadway musical number. Operas and concerts are performed by rising talents from around the world at various romantic locations around the island.

THE OUTDOORS

The ideal way to get around to the island's 90 spectacular beaches is by bike. The best place to rent two-wheelers (and cars—this is also the island's Avis outlet) is at **Roue Libre** (⊠ *Pont Orgo* ☎ *02–97–31–49–81*) in Le Palais.

CARNAC

⑮ *19 km (12 mi) northeast of Quiberon via D768/D781.*

Fodor's Choice At the north end of Quiberon Bay, Carnac is known for its expansive
★ beaches and its ancient stone monuments. Dating from around 4500 "# , Carnac's **menhirs** remain as mysterious in origin as their English contemporary, Stonehenge, although religious beliefs and astronomy were doubtless an influence. The 2,395 megalithic monuments that make up the three *alignements*—Kermario, Kerlescan, and Ménec—form the largest megalithic site in the world and are positioned with astounding astronomical accuracy in semicircles and parallel lines over about 1 km (½ mi). The site, just north of the town, is fenced off for protection, and

you can examine the menhirs up close only October through March; in summer you must join a guided tour (☎02–97–52–29–81); some tours are in English (€4). More can be learned at the **Maison des Mégalithes,** a visitor center explaining the menhirs' history and significance. ✉*Alignements du Ménec* ☎*02–97–52–07–49* ◯*Mid-Feb.–mid-Nov., daily 10–5:30.*

Carnac also has smaller-scale dolmen ensembles and three *tumuli* (mounds or barrows), including the 130-yard-long, 38-foot-high **Tumulus de St-Michel,** topped by a small chapel with views of the rock-strewn countryside. ✉*Chemin du Terminus* ☎*02–97–52–29–81* 🎫*€2* ◯*Easter–Oct.; guided tours of tumulus Apr.–Sept., daily 10, 11, 2, and 3:30.*

VANNES

★ *35 km (20 mi) east of Carnac via D768, 108 km (67 mi) southwest of Rennes.*

GETTING HERE
TGVs from Paris (Gare Montparnasse) leave for Vannes twice daily (€61). Six trains daily (some with a change at Redon) link Vannes to Nantes (1 hr, 20 mins, €19) and trains run every hour or so between Vannes and Quimper (1 hr, 10 mins, €17). The two most useful bus companies are Cariane Atlantique and Transports Le Bayon, with frequent buses to Quiberon and Nantes (3 hrs).

EXPLORING
Scene of the declaration of unity between France and Brittany in 1532, historic Vannes is one of the few towns in Brittany to have been spared damage during World War II. Be sure to saunter through the Promenade de la Garenne, a colorful park, and admire the magnificent gardens nestled beneath the adjacent ramparts. Also visit the medieval wash houses and the cathedral; browse in the small boutiques and antiques shops in the pedestrian streets around pretty place Henri-IV; check out the Cohue, the medieval market hall now used as an exhibition center; and take a boat trip around the scenic Golfe du Morbihan.

The **Cathédrale St-Pierre** boasts a 1537 Renaissance chapel, a Flamboyant Gothic transept portal, and a treasury. ✉*Pl. de la Cathédrale* ◯*Treasury mid-June–mid-Sept., Mon.–Sat. 2–6.*

WHERE TO STAY & EAT
$$$$ ✗ **Régis Mahé.** Step off the train and right into this popular spot, a haven of refinement where seafood reigns. Chef Régis Mahé prefers a small, seasonal menu with local handpicked produce and fish so fresh they nearly swim to the plate. For a local specialty with a twist, try the buckwheat galette crepe filled with lobster and pigeon and served with caramelized leeks. Attention chocolate lovers: save room for the warm chocolate tart with homemade salty caramel ice cream. ✉*24 pl. de la Gare* ☎*02–97–42–61–41* 🖷*02–97–54–99–01* ▭*MC, V* ◯*Closed Sun., Mon., and part of Feb.*

$$$$ ✕▣ **Domaine de Rochevilaine.** *Respirer la mer*—it sounds so much
Fodor'sChoice   more luxurious than "Breathe the sea." At this stunning hotel, you
★   will be able to do that exquisitely and so much more. Set on a magical
presque'île (peninsula) called the Pen Lan point, this enchanting collection of 15th- and 16th-century Breton stone buildings resembles a
tiny village; one, however, that is surrounded by terraced gardens, has a
spectacular spa, and offers grand vistas of the Bay of Vilaine. Once you
step through the "Portail de la Verité"—a monumental 13th-century
stone entryway—the interior allures with a mix of old and new, seen
most elegantly in the restaurant, where Baroque ex-votos, Louis Treize
chairs, rock-face fireplaces, and plate-glass windows make a suitable
backdrop for the delicious cuisine of chef Patrice Caillaut, formerly of
Ledoyen and Troisgros. Delights continue in the guest rooms, asparkle
with checked fabrics, veneered woods, and modern furnishings, while
some have four-poster beds and private terraces. Most rooms face the
ocean, so be sure to specify, especially if you want to call the 270-degree
view from the Admiral's Room your own. To get your toes in the water,
head to the alluring spa, the Aqua Phénica, replete with a full spectrum
of seawater hydrotherapy facilities and gigantic indoor pool. ✉ *Pointe
de Pen-Lan, 30 km (19 mi) southeast of Vannes, at tip of Pointe de Pen-
Lan, 56190 Billiers* ☎ *02–97–41–61–61* 🖶 *02–97–41–44–85* ⊕ *www.
domainerochevilaine.com* ➔ *34 rooms, 5 suites* ⚷ *In-room: refrigerator, dial-up, no a/c. In-hotel: restaurant, pools, some pets allowed (fee),
no elevator* ▤ *AE, DC, MC, V* ¶ *FAP.*

$ ✕▣ **Kyriad.** In an old, rustic building in town, this hotel attracts a var-
ied foreign clientele, drawn by the homey guest rooms—clean, bright,
and simple, with warm yellow walls—and the friendly and efficient
staff. Claude Le Lausque serves a traditional menu in the rustic Image
Sainte-Anne restaurant, with straightforward seasonal specialties like
crab in phyllo pastry, grilled sole, and kidneys flambeed in calvados.
No dinner is served Sunday, November through March. ✉ *8 pl. de la
Libération, 56000* ☎ *02–97–63–27–36* 🖶 *02–97–40–97–02* ⊕ *www.
kyriad-vannes.fr* ➔ *33 rooms* ⚷ *In-room: no a/c (some). In-hotel: restaurant, public Internet* ▤ *AE, DC, MC, V* ¶ *BP.*

LA BAULE

⑰   *72 km (45 mi) southeast of Vannes via N165 and D774.*

Star of the Côte d'Amour coast and gifted with a breathtaking 5-km
(3-mi) beach, La Baule is a fashionable resort town that can make you
pay dearly for your coastal frolics. Though it once rivaled Biarritz,
today tackiness has replaced sophistication, but you still can't beat
that beach, or the lovely, miles-long seafront promenade lined with
hotels. Like Le Touquet and Dinard, La Baule is a 19th-century creation, founded in 1879 to make the most of the excellent sandy beaches
that extend around the broad, sheltered bay between Pornichet and
Le Pouliguen. A pine forest, planted in 1840, keeps the shifting local
sand dunes firmly at bay. All in all, this can offer an idyllic stay for
those who will enjoy a day on the beach, an afternoon at the shops

on Avenue du Général-de-Gaulle and Avenue Louis-Lajarrige, and an evening at the casino.

WHERE TO STAY & EAT

★ ¢–$ ✕ **La Ferme du Grand Clos.** At this lively restaurant in an old farmhouse, 200 yards from the sea, you have to understand the difference between crepe and galette to order correctly, since the menus showcase both in all their forms. Or you can opt for the simple, straightforward menu featuring food the owner likes to call *la cuisine de grand-mère* (grandmother's cooking). Come early for a table; it's a very friendly and popular place. ⬜*52 av. du Maréchal-de-Lattre-de-Tassigny* ☎*02–40–60–03–30* ⊟*MC, V* ⊘*Closed Oct. and Wed., Sept.–June.*

★ $–$$ ✕🖼 **Hôtel de la Plage.** One of the few hotels on the beach in St-Marc-sur-Mer, southeast of La Baule, this comfortable lodging was the setting for Jacques Tati's classic comedy *Mr. Hulot's Holiday*. It has been updated since and, *hélas,* the swinging door to the dining room is no longer there. But the view of the sea and the sound of the surf remain. The restaurant—reserve a beachfront table in advance—serves seasonal fish specialties like the *choucroute de la mer* (sauerkraut with fish). There's also a brasserie for more casual dining. ⬜*37 rue du Commandant-Charcot, 10 km (6 mi) southeast of La Baule, 44600 St-Marc-sur-Mer* ☎*02–40–91–99–01* 🖶*02–40–91–92–00* ⊕*www.hotel-de-la-plage-44.com* ↪*30 rooms* ⚫*In-room: dial-up, no a/c. In-hotel: restaurant* ⊟*MC, V* ⊘*Closed Jan.* ⚟*FAP.*

$$–$$$ 🖼 **Concorde.** This blue-shuttered, white-walled establishment numbers among the least expensive good hotels in pricey La Baule. Rooms are calm, comfortable, modernized but with period furniture, and a short block from the beach (ask for a room with a sea view). ⬜*1 bis, av. de la Concorde, 44500* ☎*02–40–60–23–09* 🖶*02–40–42–72–14* ⊕*www.hotel-la-concorde.com* ↪*47 rooms* ⚫*In-room: dial-up, no a/c* ⊟*AE, MC, V* ⊘*Closed Oct.–mid-Apr.*

NIGHTLIFE

Occasionally you see high stakes on the tables at La Baule's **casino** (⬜*6 av. Pierre-Loti* ☎*02–40–11–48–28*).

NANTES

72 km (45 mi) east of La Baule via N171 and N165, 108 km (67 mi) south of Rennes.

GETTING HERE

TGV trains leave Paris's Gare Montparnasse for Nantes every hour, covering the 387 km (240 mi) in just 2 hours (€54). Trains make the 2-hour, 40-minute run up the coast from Nantes to Quimper (€30) twice daily, stopping at Vannes (1hr, 20 mins, €19). Nantes's train station, at 27 boulevard Stalingrad, is across the street from the Jardin des Plantes and a 10-minute walk from the Vieille Ville. Cariane Atlantique Otages runs four daily buses to Rennes (2 hrs), as well as to other nearby towns.

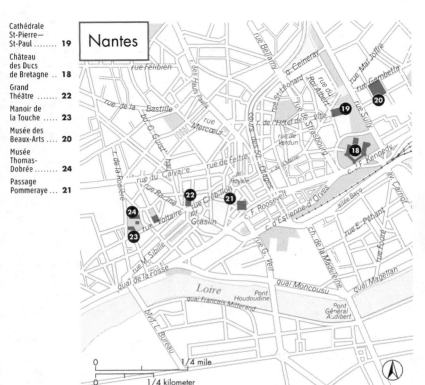

EXPLORING

The writer Stendhal remarked of 19th-century Nantes, "I hadn't taken twenty steps before I recognized a great city." Since then, the river that flowed around the upper-crust Ile Feydeau neighborhood has been filled in and replaced with a rushing torrent of traffic, and now major highways cut through the heart of town. Still, Nantes is more than the sum of its traffic jams. The 15th-century château is still in relatively good shape, despite having lost an entire tower during a gunpowder explosion in 1800. The 15th-century cathedral floats heavenward as well. Its white stones, immense height, and airy interior make it one of France's best. Across the broad boulevard, Cours des 50-Otages, is the 19th-century city. The unlucky Ile Feydeau, surrounded and bisected by highways, still preserves the tottering 18th-century mansion built with wealth from Nantes's huge slave trade. The Loire River flows along the southern edge of the Vieille Ville, making Nantes officially part of the Loire region, although historically it belongs to Brittany. In town you can see many references to Anne de Bretagne, the last independent ruler of Brittany, who married the region away to King Charles VIII of France in 1491. Bretons have never quite recovered from the shock.

Built by the dukes of Brittany, who had no doubt that Nantes belonged in their domain, the **Château des Ducs de Bretagne** is a massive, well-preserved 15th-century fortress with a moat. François II, the duke responsible for building most of it, led a hedonistic life here, surrounded by ministers, chamberlains, and an army of servants. Numerous monarchs later stayed in the castle, where in 1598 Henri IV signed the famous Edict of Nantes advocating religious tolerance. The castle reopened in February 2007 after extensive renovations. ⊠*4 pl. Marc-Elder* ☎*02–51–17–49–00* ⊕*www.chateau-nantes.fr* ⊠*€5* ⊙*Wed.–Mon. 10–6.*

The **Cathédrale St-Pierre–St-Paul** is one of France's last Gothic cathedrals, begun in 1434, well after most other medieval cathedrals had been completed. The facade is ponderous and austere, in contrast to the light, wide, limestone interior, whose vaults rise higher (120 feet) than those of Notre-Dame in Paris. ⊠*Pl. St-Pierre* ☎*02–40–47–84–64* ⊠*Free* ⊙*Crypt Mon.–Sat. 10–12:30 and 2–6, Sun. 2–6:30.*

A fine collection of paintings from the Renaissance period onward, including works by Jacopo Tintoretto, Georges de La Tour, Jean-Auguste-Dominique Ingres, and Gustave Courbet, and 20th-century works is at the **Musée des Beaux-Arts** *(Museum of Fine Arts)*. ⊠*10 rue Georges-Clemenceau* ☎*02–51–17–45–00* ⊠*€3.10* ⊙*Mon., Wed., Fri., and weekends 10–6, Thurs. 10–8.*

Erected in 1843, the **Passage de la Pommeraye** (⊠*Rue Crébillon*) is an elegant shopping gallery in the 19th-century part of town.

The **Grand Théâtre** (⊠*Pl. Graslin*), down the block from the Passage Pommeraye, was built in 1783.

The 15th-century **Manoir de la Touche** (⊠*Rue Voltaire*) was once the abode of the bishops of Nantes.

★ The mock-Romanesque **Musée Thomas-Dobrée** across the way was built by arts connoisseur Thomas Dobrée in the 19th century. On the facade he had chiseled the old Breton saying, ! .. $)!.!& ! 2/' !# $(!./5. ("The Unknown devours me"), and his vast collection offers proof, as it ranges from old-master paintings to tapestries, from medieval manuscripts to Gothic goldwork, including the *coffret* reliquary of the heart of Anne de Bretagne; one room is devoted to the Revolutionary War in Vendée. ⊠*18 rue Voltaire* ☎*02–40–71–03–50* ⊠*€3, free Sun.* ⊙*Tues.–Fri. 1:30–5:30, weekends 2:30–5:30.*

WHERE TO STAY & EAT

$$–$$$ ✕ **La Cigale.** Miniature palm trees, gleaming woodwork, colorful enamel tiles, and painted ceilings have led to the official recognition of La Cigale brasserie (built in 1895) as a *monument historique*. You can savor its Belle Epoque blandishments without spending a fortune—the prix-fixe lunch menus are a good value. But the banks of fresh oysters and well-stacked dessert cart may tempt you to order à la carte. ⊠*4 pl. Graslin* ☎*02–51–84–94–94* ⊕*www.lacigale.com* ⊲*Reservations essential* ▭*MC, V.*

★ $$ ✕ **Villa Mon Rêve.** This cozy, yellow-walled restaurant is in delightful parkland off the D751 east of Nantes. Chef Gérard Ryngel concocts elegantly inventive regional fare (the pike-perch in Anjou red-wine sauce is a good choice), with which you can sample one of more than 50 varieties of Muscadet, the local white wine. Request a table on the terrace when you reserve. ⊠*Levée Divatte, 506 bd. de la Loire, Basse-Goulaine, 8 km (5 mi) east of Nantes* ☎*02–40–03–55–50* ⊕*www.villa-mon-reve.com* ▤*AE, DC, MC, V* ⊗*Closed Tues., part of Feb. and Nov. No dinner Sun.*

$–$$ ✕ **L'Embellie.** Sweet and simple, this spot lures diners with its modern, inventive attitude and friendly service. Chef Yvonnick Briand's "creative regional" cuisine extends to his own smokehouse for salmon and duck, so the foie gras is homemade—he likes to serve it light, atop a mesclun salad. The menu is dependent on Briand's daily trips to markets, so don't hesitate to try any of the fresh fish specials, such as the sea bass steamed in rosemary or other briny delights laced with French West Indian spices. Pineapple *croquant* with rum-laced creole ice cream makes a fitting finale. ⊠*14 rue Armand-Brossard* ☎*02–40–48–20–02* ▤*AE, DC, MC, V* ⊗*Closed Sun., Mon., and 3 wks in Aug.*

$$–$$$ 🏨 **Pérouse.** Bare parquet floors, plain off-white walls, simple high-tech lighting, and minimal contemporary furnishings make rooms feel spacious and have earned the accolade of Europe's Design Hotel of the Year in 1995, just after this white cube of a hotel opened its doors. The amiable staff speak fluent English. A pedestrian zone full of boutiques and restaurants is right outside the door, and Place Royale is 300 yards away. ⊠*3 allée Dusquesne, 44000* ☎*02–40–89–75–00* 🖷*02–40–89–76–00* ⊕*www.hotel-laperouse.fr* ↪*46 rooms* ♿*In-room: refrigerator, ethernet. In-hotel: some pets allowed (fee)* ▤*AE, DC, MC, V* ⊗|*BP.*

NIGHTLIFE & THE ARTS

The informal **Univers** (⊠*16 rue Jean-Jacques-Rousseau* ☎*02–40–73–49–55*) has live-jazz concerts every other week. **Le Tie Break** (⊠*1 rue des Petites-Écuries* ☎*02–40–47–77–00*) is a popular piano bar. The **Théâtre Graslin** (⊠*1 rue Molière* ☎*02–40–69–77–18*) is Nantes's principal concert hall and opera house.

THE OUTDOORS

You can take a 100-minute cruise along the pretty Erdre River, past a string of gardens and châteaux, with the **Bateaux Nantais.** There are also four-course lunch and dinner cruises that last about 2½ hours (€52–€64). ⊠*Quai de la Motte Rouge* ☎*02–40–14–51–14* ⊕*www.bateaux-nantais.fr* 🎫*€10* ⊗*June–Aug., Mon. and Fri. at 3, weekends at 3 and 5; May, Sept., and Oct., weekends at 3.*

SHOPPING

The commercial quarter of Nantes stretches from Place Royale to Place Graslin. Various antiques shops can be found on Rue Voltaire. The Devineau family has been selling wax fruit and vegetables at **Devineau** (⊠*2 pl. Ste-Croix*) since 1803, as well as handmade candles and wildflower honey. For chocolate, head to **Gautier-Debotté** (⊠*9 rue de la Fosse* ⊕*gautier-debotte.com*); try the local Muscadet grapes dipped in brandy and covered with chocolate.

BRITTANY ESSENTIALS

TRANSPORTATION

If traveling extensively by public transportation, be sure to load up on information (*Guide Régional des Transports* schedules, the best taxi-for-call companies, etc.) upon arriving at the ticket counter or help desk of the bigger train and bus stations in the area, such as Rennes and Nantes.

BY AIR

Aéroport de Rennes has domestic flights to and from both Paris airports and Bordeaux, Lyon, Toulouse, Marseille, Strasbourg, and Basle-Mulhouse. **Aéroport de Dinard** hosts flights to the Channel Islands and Ryanair flights to and from London Stansted and to East Midlands airport in the United Kingdom. **Aéroport de Nantes** also hosts Ryanair flights to and from London Stansted. Ryanair also flies from Brest to London Luton.

Air Travel Information Aéroport de Dinard (⊠ *Pleurtuit, south of town* 🕾 *08-25-35-09-00* ⊕ *www.saint-malo.aeroport.fr*). **Aéroport de Nantes** (⊠ *Bouguenais, southwest of city* 🕾 *02-40-84-80-00* ⊕ *www.nantes-aeroport.fr*). **Aéroport de Rennes** (⊠ *St-Jacques de la Lande, southwest of city* 🕾 *02-99-29-60-00* ⊕ *www.rennes.aeroport.fr*).

BY BIKE

Bikes can be rented at most major train stations.

BY BUS

There are many bus routes linking Brittany, serviced by a bewildering number of bus companies. As the region is well-served by train, you do not really need to bother with buses unless you're visiting places not covered in this book. However, a handful of venues cannot be reached by train. These include Carnac (90 mins) and Quiberon (2 hrs), reachable on a Cariane Atlantique bus from Vannes; Dinard (30 mins) with an Ile & Vilaine bus from St-Malo; and Cancale (40 mins, €2), also from St-Malo but with Les Courriers Bretons, which also runs buses between St-Malo and Mont St-Michel (1 hr, 50 mins via Dol, €4.50) and between Rennes and Mont St-Michel (80 mins, €10.50). Pont-Aven can be reached from Quimper via Transports Caoudal. There are many other links, so, as always, check in with the regional tourist office or information window at a big gateway rail or bus station to get printed bus schedules.

Bus Information Cariane Atlantique (🕾 *02-97-47-29-64* ⊕ *www.cariane-atlantique.com*). **Cars du Kreisker** (🕾 *02-98-69-00-93* ⊕ *cars-kreisker.com*). **CAT** (🕾 *02-96-39-21-05*). **Les Courriers Bretons** (🕾 *02-99-19-70-80*). **TIV** (🕾 *02-99-26-11-11*). **Transports Caoudal** (🕾 *02-98-90-88-89*). **Transports Le Bayon** (🕾 *02-97-24-26-20*).

BY CAR

Rennes, the gateway to Brittany, is 310 km (195 mi) west of Paris. It can be reached in about three hours via Le Mans using A81 and A11 (A11 continues southwest from Le Mans to Nantes). Rennes is linked by good roads to Morlaix (E50), Quimper (N24/N165), and Vannes (N24/N166). A car is pretty much essential if you want to see out-of-the-way places.

BY TRAIN

Most towns in this region are accessible by train, though you need a car to get to some of the more secluded spots. The high-speed TGV (Train à Grande Vitesse) departs 15 times daily from Paris (Gare Montparnasse) for Rennes, making this region easily accessible. The trip takes about 2¼ hours (€52). Some trains from Paris branch in Rennes to either Brest or Quimper (4 hrs, 30 mins from Paris, €70), stopping in Vannes (3 hrs from Paris, €61). From Rennes there are frequent regional trains to Dol (35 mins, €10) and St-Malo (50 mins, €13). You can reach Dinan from Dol (20 mins, €5.50). Change at Auray for Quiberon (train service July and August only; otherwise, bus links, 1 hr, €7).

Train Information SNCF (☎ 36–35 €0.34 per minute ⊕ www.voyages-sncf.com). **TGV** (⊕ www.tgv.com).

CONTACTS & RESOURCES

EMERGENCIES

Contacts General Ambulance (☎ 15). **General Fire Department** (☎ 18). **General Police** (☎ 17). **Rennes** (✉ 2 rue Henri-Le-Guilloux, 35000 ☎ 02–99–28–43–21). **Nantes** (✉ 1 pl. Alexis-Ricordeau, 44000 ☎ 02–40–08–33–33).

INTERNET & MAIL

In smaller towns, ask your hotel concierge if there are any Internet cafés nearby.

Internet & Mail Information Cybernet On Line (✉ 22 rue St-Georges, near Pl. du Palais, Rennes ☎ 02–99–36–37–41). **K Point Com** (✉ 15 allée Duguay-Trouin, near Passage de la Pommeraye, Nantes ☎ 02–51–82–27–71).

MEDIA

Ouest France, the biggest-selling regional daily in the country, has several local editions. *Le Télégramme,* based in Brest, covers western Brittany.

SPORTS & THE OUTDOORS

For information on various regional activities such as sailing, hiking, camping, fishing, and daily excursions, contact the Regional Tourist Boards.

Contacts Comité Départemental du Tourisme des Côtes-d'Armor (✉ 7 rue St-Benoît, St-Brieuc ☎ 02–96–62–72–00 🖷 02–96–33–59–10 ⊕ www.cotesdarmor. com). **Comité Départemental du Tourisme de Finistère** (✉ 11 rue Théodore-Le Hars, Quimper ☎ 02–98–76–20–70 🖷 02–98–52–19–19 ⊕ www.finisteretourisme. com). **Comité Départemental du Tourisme de Loire-Atlantique** (✉ 2 allée Baco, Nantes ☎ 02–51–72–95–30 🖷 02–40–20–44–54 ⊕ www.cdt44.com).

TOUR OPTIONS

Information about organized tours of Brittany is available from the very helpful Maison de la Bretagne in Paris.

Fees & Schedules Maison de la Bretagne (✉ *203 bd. St-Germain, 75007 Paris* ☎ *01-53-63-11-50* 🖷 *01-53-63-11-57*).

VISITOR INFORMATION

The principal regional tourist offices are in Nantes and Rennes.

Tourist Information Nantes (✉ *7 rue de Valmy* ☎ *08-92-46-40-44* 🖷 *02-40-89-11-99* ⊕ *www.nantes-tourisme.com*). **Rennes** (✉ *11 rue St-Yves* ☎ *02-99-67-11-11* 🖷 *02-99-67-11-10* ⊕ *en.tourisme-rennes.com*). **La Baule** (✉ *8 pl. de la Victoire* ☎ *02-40-24-34-44* 🖷 *02-40-11-08-10* ⊕ *www.labaule.tm.fr*). **Belle-Ile** (✉ *Quai Bonnelle, Le Palais* ☎ *02-97-31-81-93* 🖷 *02-97-31-81-93* ⊕ *www.belle-ile.com*). **Carnac** (✉ *74 av. des Druides* ☎ *02-97-52-13-52* 🖷 *02-97-52-86-10* ⊕ *www.ot-carnac.fr*). **Dinan** (✉ *9 rue du Château* ☎ *02-96-87-69-76* 🖷 *02-96-87-69-77* ⊕ *www.dinan-tourisme.com*). **Dinard** (✉ *2 bd. Féart* ☎ *02-99-46-94-12* 🖷 *02-99-88-21-07* ⊕ *www.ot-dinard.com*). **Douarnenez** (✉ *2 rue du Dr-Mével* ☎ *02-98-92-13-35* 🖷 *02-98-92-70-47* ⊕ *www.douarnenez-tourisme.com*). **Pont-Aven** (✉ *5 pl. de l'Hôtel de Ville* ☎ *02-98-06-04-70* 🖷 *02-98-06-17-25* ⊕ *www.pontaven.com*). **Quimper** (✉ *7 rue Déesse* ☎ *02-98-53-04-05* 🖷 *02-98-53-31-33* ⊕ *www.quimper-tourisme.com*). **St-Malo** (✉ *Esplanade St-Vincent* ☎ *02-99-56-64-48* 🖷 *02-99-56-67-00* ⊕ *www.saint-malo-tourisme.com*). **Trébeurden** (✉ *Pl. de Crec'h Hery* ☎ *02-96-23-51-64* 🖷 *02-96-15-44-87* ⊕ *www.trebeurden.fr*). **Vannes** (✉ *1 rue Thiers* ☎ *02-97-47-24-34* 🖷 *02-97-47-29-49* ⊕ *www.mairie-vannes.fr*). **Vitré** (✉ *Pl. St-Yves* ☎ *02-99-75-04-46* 🖷 *02-99-74-02-01* ⊕ *www.ot-vitre.fr*).

Champagne Country

WORD OF MOUTH

"I visited the Taittinger cellars in Reims and found them to be very interesting. The cellars are under an old abbey destroyed during the French Revolution. Neat vaulted ceilings, plus you can see where Romans dug out the limestone. And…great Champagne— the tasting at the end of the tour was generous in quantity."

—Michel Paris

WELCOME TO CHAMPAGNE COUNTRY

TOP REASONS TO GO

★ **Champagne—what else!:** Drink it, see the vineyards, visit the cavernous chalk cellars where bottles are stored by the million...

★ **Gothic Glory:** No fewer than 10 Gothic cathedrals dot the region—check out the rivalry between the biggest of them (Amiens) and the tallest (neighboring Beauvais).

★ **Tiny L'Épine:** Set on the Route du Champagne, this cozy village has the superlative Aux Armes de Champagne restaurants, set across from pretty stone-lacework churches.

★ **Laon, "Crowned Mountain":** With its cathedral towers patrolling the hilly horizon, Laon has a site whose grandeur rivals Mont St-Michel (and just as exciting in close-up, with mighty stone oxen guarding the church towers).

★ **The Capital of Bubbly:** Drink now, pray later in Reims, the "Champagne City" and also home to France's great coronation cathedral.

1 Champagne. The region's obsession with Champagne is especially evident in **Reims,** the region's hub, home to the great Champagne houses and site of one of the most historically important cathedrals in France. Once you tally up the 34 VIPs who have been crowned here and toured some Champagne cellars to bone up on the history of this noble beverage, you can head south. Smack dab in the middle of the 28,000 hectares that make up the entire Champagne-producing region, **Épernay** lives and dies for the bubbly brew. Continue on the Route du Champagne to other wine villages.

2 The Cathedral Cities. To the west of Champagne lies a region where the popping of champagne corks is only a distant murmur, and not just because Reims is 161 km (100 mi) away. For here are some of the most gargantuan Gothic hulks of architectural harmony: the cathedrals of **Beauvais,** **Amiens, Laon,** and **Soissons.** Beauvais is positively dizzying from within: with the highest nave in France, you nearly keel over craning your neck back. Laon is still a town with a contemplative air. Amiens is the most colossal church in the land, in places fantastically ornate, while Soissons shows Gothic at its most restrained.

Amiens Cathedral

GETTING ORIENTED

Few drinks in the world have such a pull on the imagination as Champagne, yet surprisingly few tourists visit the pretty vineyards south of Reims. Perhaps it's because the Champagne region is a bit of a backwater, halfway between Paris and Luxembourg. Locals hope the 2007 arrival of the new TGV line serving eastern France and Germany will change all this. Northwest of Laon, the hills of Champagne give way to the plains of Picardy, where only giant cathedrals and giant pyramids of sugar beet in fall break up the skyline.

6

Châlons-en-Champagne

CHAMPAGNE COUNTRY PLANNER

Lift Your Spirits	Traveling "Les Routes du Champagne"

Lift Your Spirits

There's nothing like getting out into Mother Nature to send the spirits soaring and, as it turns out, the flat-as-a-pancake region of Champagne is custom-made for easy and scenic hiking.

Just south of Reims rises the Montagne de Reims, a vast forested plateau on whose slopes grow the Pinot Noir and Pinot Meunier grapes used to make Champagne.

Several sentiers de Grandes Randonnées (long hiking trails; also known as GRs) run across the top of the plateau, burrowing through dense forest and looping around the edges.

For examples, the GR141 and the GR14 form a loop over 50 km (30 mi) long around the plateau's eastern half, passing by several train stations en route.

Super-detailed regional maps are available in Reims at the tourist office.

You can access some of these hiking trails from the Rilly-la-Montagne, Avenay, and Ay stops on the Reims-Epernay rail line.

If you are a serious hiker, make for the Ardennes region, which lies mostly in Champagne.

Traveling "Les Routes du Champagne"

Threading the triangle between Reims, Épernay, and Château-Thierry are the famous **Routes du Champagne** (Champagne Roads), which divy up the region into four fabulous itineraries. These follow the main four "côtes" of the Champagne vineyards.

Northwest of Reims (use the Tinqueux exit) is the **Massif de Saint-Thierry**—a vineyard-rich region once hallowed by kings. Heading south of Reims to Épernay, travel west along the **Vallée de la Marne** through the Hauteurs d'Épernay, traveling west on the right bank of the river and east on the left. To the east of Épernay lies the most beautiful stretch of Champagne Country: the **Montagne de Reims.** To the south of Épernay is the **Côte de Blanc,** the "cradle of Chardonnay." More than 80 producers of Champagne are scattered along these roads, and you can guarantee a better reception if you call the vineyards you'd like to visit in advance.

The two main centers to the Champagne wine road are Reims and Épernay, which are about 64 km (40 mi) apart if you work your way through the wine villages that dot the slopes of the Montagne de Reims. Start in Reims, with its host of major Champagne houses, then make south on N51 and east on D26 through pretty Rilly-la-Montagne, Mailly-Champagne, and Verzy, where you can visit local producers Étienne and Anne-Laure Lefevre at 30 rue de Villers (☎tel. 03–26–97–96–99 ⊕www.Champagne-etienne-lefevre.com). Continue south to Ambonnay, then track back west to Bouzy, Ay, and Hautvillers—where Dom Pérignon is buried in the village church—before crossing the Marne River to Épernay, whose main street is home to several producers. From Épernay, spear south along the Côte de Blanc to Vertus, 19 km (12 mi) away, where Pierre and Sophie Lamandier will sell and tell you all about their organic bio-Champagne at 19 avenue du General-de-Gaulle (☎tel 03–26–52–13–24 ⊕www.larmandier.fr). If you're headed back to Paris, take D1 from Épernay west along the banks of the Marne to Château-Thierry 50 km (30 mi) away. The steep-climbing vineyards hugging the river are the most scenic in Champagne. For information on the Routes du Champagne, see the Web sites listed under Visitor Information at this chapter's end.

Getting Around

As always in France, intercity buses are less frequent than trains, and much slower. There are trains to all the towns and cities mentioned in this chapter, with Reims the natural hub, especially now that it is just 45 minutes from Paris by TGV. Reims is linked to Laon by the A26 expressway, and to Châlons-en-Champagne by the A4 expressway arriving from Paris.

To Whom It May Concern: the west, Amiens and Beauvais are connected by the A16. Épernay, south of Reims, can be reached from Reims by the twisting wine road or quicker N51.

Only Soissons, 20 mi southwest of Laon, is a bit off the beaten track.

Finding a Place to Stay

The Champagne region has a mix of old, rambling hotels, often simple rather than pretentious, and a handful of stylish hostelries catering to jet-set drinks executives.

Be warned, though, that few of the destinations mentioned in this chapter have much in the way of upscale choice, and that the region's most characteristic establishments are in the countryside and need a car to get to.

WHAT IT COSTS

	¢	$	$$	$$$	$$$$
Restaurants	Under €11	€11–€17	€17–€23	€23–€30	Over €30
Hotels	Under €50	€50–€80	€80–€120	€120–€190	Over €190

Restaurant prices are per person for a main course at dinner, including tax (19.6%) and service; note that if a restaurant offers only prix-fixe (set-price) meals, it has been given the price category that reflects the full prix-fixe price. Hotel prices are for a standard double room in high season, including tax (19.6%) and service charge. Hotels operate on the European Plan (EP, with no meal provided) unless we note that they use the Breakfast Plan (BP), or also offer such options as Modified American Plan (MAP, with breakfast and dinner daily, known as demi-pension), or Full American Plan (FAP, or pension complète, with three meals a day). Inquire when booking if these all-inclusive meal plans (which always entail higher rates) are mandatory or optional.

Eating Well

This region is less dependent on tourism than many in France, and most restaurants are open year-round. However, in the largest cities, Reims and Amiens, many restaurants close for two to three weeks in July and August.

Smoked ham, pigs' feet, gingerbread, and Champagne-based mustard are specialties of the Reims area, along with sautéed chicken, kidneys, stuffed trout, pike, and snails.

One particularly hearty dish is *potée champenoise*, consisting of smoked ham, bacon, sausage, and cabbage.

Rabbit (often cooked with prunes) is common, while boar and venison are specialties in fall and winter, when vegetable soups are high on the menu.

In Picardy, the popular *ficelle picarde* is a pancake stuffed with cheese, mushrooms, and ham.

Apart from Champagne, try drinking the region's *hydromel* (mead, made from honey) and ratafia, a sweet apéritif made from grape juice and brandy.

6

Introduction by
Nancy Coons
Updated by
Simon Hewitt

AS YOU HEAD SOUTHEAST TOWARD Reims, the landscape loosens and undulates, and the hills tantalize with vineyards that—thanks to *la méthode champenoise*—produce the world's antidote to gloom. Each year, millions of bottles of bubbly mature in hundreds of kilometers of chalk tunnels carved under the streets of Reims and Epernay, both of which fight for the title "The Champagne City."

Champagne, a place-name that has become a universal synonym for joy and festivity, actually began as a word of humble origin. Like *campagna*, its Italian counterpart, it is derived from the Latin *campus*, which means "open field." In French *campus* became *champ*, with the old language extending this to *champaign*, for "battlefield," and *champaine*, for "district of plains." Today, this vast, endless plain—in the 19th century the famed writer Stendahl bemoaned "the atrocious flat wretchedness of Champagne"—has been the center of Champagne production for more than two centuries, stocking the cellars of its many conquerors—Napoléon, Czar Nicholas I, the Duke of Wellington—as well as those of contemporary case-toting bubblyphiles. Yet long before a drink put it on the map, this area of northern France was marked by great architecture and bloodstained history.

Picardy's monotonous chalk plains are home, in fact, to no fewer than 10 of France's greatest medieval cathedrals, including those of Amiens, Reims, and Laon. These great structures testify to the wealth this region enjoyed thanks to its prime location between Paris and northern Europe. The "flying buttresses" and heaven-seeking spires of these cathedrals remind us that medieval stoneworkers sought to raise radically new Gothic arches to improbable heights, running for cover when the naves failed to stand. Happily, most have stood the test of time (though you might want to hover near the exits at Beauvais, whose nave, the tallest in France, still makes some engineers nervous).

But the region's crossroads status also exacted a heavy toll, and it paid heavily for its role as a battleground for the habitually bickering British, German, and French. From pre-Roman times to the armistice of 1945, some of Europe's costliest wars were fought on northern French soil. World War I and World War II were especially unkind: you can still see trenches near Arras and bullet-pocked buildings in Amiens. These days, of course, the vineyards of Champagne attract tourists interested in less sobering events.

EXPLORING CHAMPAGNE COUNTRY

The province of Champagne is best known for its vineyards, which start just beyond Château-Thierry, 96 km (60 mi) northeast of Paris, and continue along the towering Marne Valley to Épernay. Cheerful villages line the Route du Champagne (Champagne Road), which twines north to Reims, the capital of bubbly. As you head farther northeast, rolling chalk hills give way to the rugged Ardennes Forest, straddling the Belgian border. For a handy Web source for many of the great Champagne houses of the region, log on to ⊕www.umc.fr. Heading back to Paris, many travelers take in an excursion to visit four of

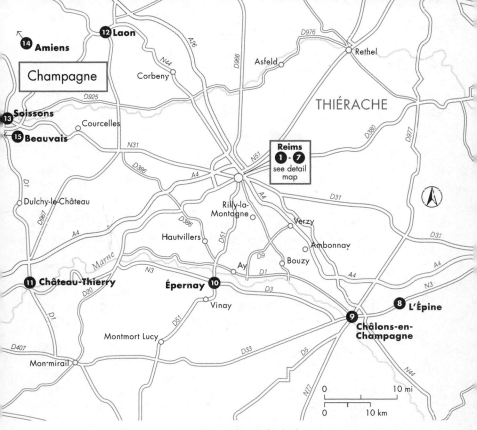

France's most spectacular Gothic cathedrals—Laon, Soissons, Amiens, and Beauvais.

CHAMPAGNE

An uplifting landscape tumbles about Reims and Épernay, perhaps because its inhabitants treat themselves to a regular infusion of the local, world-prized elixir we know and love as Champagne. Each year, millions of bottles mature in endless caves under the towns' streets. But unlike the great vineyards of Bordeaux and Burgundy, there are few country châteaux to go with the fabled names of this region—Mumm, Taittinger, Pommery, and Veuve-Clicquot. Most of the glory is to be found in *caves* and cellars, not to mention the fascinating guided tours offered by the most famous producers.

Despite its glamorous image as the home of Champagne, the region in fact has a laid-back rustic charm where "life in the fast lane" refers strictly to the Paris-bound A4 expressway. On the map, Champagne encompasses Reims and the surrounding vineyards and chalky plains. Picardy, to the south of the region, is traversed by the Aisne and Oise rivers. To the southeast the grapes of Champagne flourish on the steep slopes of the Marne Valley and the Montagne de Reims, really more of a mighty hill than a mountain. Reims is the only city in Champagne. Behind a facade of unwelcoming austerity, it remains one of France's richest tourist sites.

REIMS

144 km (90 mi) northeast of Paris.

GETTING HERE

Big news in 2007: A new TGV (⊕*www.tgv.com*) express train now covers the 170 km (105 mi) from Paris (Gare de l'Est) to Reims in 45 minutes. They depart Paris eight times daily and cost is €28. Regular speed trains from Paris (Gare de l'Est) leave for Reims every 2 hours or so (€22); the 108-mi trip takes around 1 hour, 45 minutes. Several trains daily connect Reims to Épernay (30 mins, €6), and there are four trains a day from Châlons-en-Champagne (40 mins, €9.50), and Laon (40 mins, €8.50). There's one direct train each day from Amiens to Reims (2 hrs, 30 mins, €21) via Laon. STDM Trans-Champagne run three daily buses to Reims from Châlons-en-Champagne (50 mins, €8), while RTA (☎*03–23–50–68–50* ⊕*www.rta02.com*) operates one daily bus between Reims and Laon (2 hrs).

EXPLORING

Although many of Reims's historic buildings were flattened in World War I and replaced by drab, modern architecture, those that do remain are of royal magnitude. Top of the list goes to the city's magnificent cathedral, in which the kings of France were crowned until 1825, while the Musée des Beaux-Arts has a stellar collection, including the famed Jacques-Louis David painting of the murdered Marat in his bath. Reims sparkles with some of the biggest names in Champagne production, and the thriving industry has conferred wealth and sometimes an arrogant reserve on the region's inhabitants. The maze of Champagne cellars constitutes a leading attraction of the city—*see "Champagne Uncorked"* in this chapter for details about visiting Taittinger, Piper-Heidsieck, Mumm, and other fabled Champagne houses. Several of these producers organize visits to their cellars, combining video presentations with guided tours of their cavernous, hewn-chalk underground warehouses.

For a complete list of Champagne cellars, head to the **tourist office** (⊠*2 rue Guillaume-de-Machault* ☎*03–26–77–45–25*) near the cathedral. A handy Web site that lists many of the leading houses is another way to plan your visits: ⊕*www.umc.fr.*

❶ The 11th-century **Basilique St-Rémi** honors the 5th-century saint who gave his name to the city. Its interior seems to stretch into the endless distance, an impression created by its relative murk and lowness. The airy four-story Gothic choir contains some fine original 12th-century stained glass. Like the cathedral, the basilica puts on indoor **son-et-lumière** shows every Saturday evening at 9:30 from late June to early October. They are preceded by a tour of the building and are free. ⊠*53 rue St-Rémi* ☎*03–26–85–31–20* ⊙*Daily 8–7.*

★ ❷ The **Palais du Tau** (formerly the Archbishop's Palace), alongside the cathedral, houses an impressive display of tapestries and coronation robes, as well as several statues rescued from the cathedral facade before they fell off. The second-floor views of the cathedral are terrific. ⊠2 *pl. du Cardinal-Luçon* ☎*03–26–47–81–79* €*6.50* ⊙*July and Aug., Tues.–Sun. 9:30–6:30; Sept.–June, Tues.–Sun. 9:30–12:30 and 2–5:30.*

❸ The **Musée des Beaux-Arts** *(Museum of Fine Arts)*, two blocks southwest of the cathedral, has an outstanding collection of paintings: no fewer than 27 Corots are here, as well as Jacques-Louis David's unforgettable portrait of the revolutionary polemicist Jean-Paul Marat, stabbed to death in his bath by Charlotte Corday in 1793. ⊠*8 rue Chanzy* ☎*03–26–47–28–44* €*3, joint ticket with Musée de la Reddition* ⊙*Wed.–Mon. 10–noon and 2–6.*

❹ The **Cathédrale Notre-Dame** was the age-old setting for the coronations of the French kings. Clovis, king of the Franks in the 6th century, was baptized in an early structure on this site; Joan of Arc led her recalcitrant Dauphin here to be crowned King Charles VII; Charles X's coronation, in 1825, was the last. The east-end windows have stained glass by Marc Chagall. Admire the vista toward the west end, with an interplay of narrow pointed arches. The glory of Reims's cathedral is its facade: it's so skillfully proportioned that initially you have little idea of its monumental size. Above the north (left) door hovers the *Laughing Angel*, a delightful statue whose famous smile threatens to melt into an acid-rain scowl; pollution has succeeded war as the ravager of the building's fabric. With the exception of the 15th-century towers, most of the original building went up in the 100 years after 1211. A stroll around the outside reinforces the impression of harmony, discipline, and decorative richness. The east end presents an idyllic sight across well-tended lawns. A new optical-fiber lighting system, installed fall 2006, illuminates the cathedral exterior every day from dusk until midnight. ⊠*Pl. du Cardinal-Luçon* ⊙*Daily 7:30–7:30.*

Fodor'sChoice

★

6

❺ The Gallo-Roman **Cryptoportique,** an underground gallery and crypt, now a semisubterranean passageway, was constructed around ɪꜱ 200 under the forum of what was Reims's predecessor, the Roman town of Durocortorum. ⊠*Pl. du Forum* ☎*03–26–50–13–74* €*Free* ⊙*Mid-June–mid-Sept., Tues.–Sun. 2–5.*

❻ The **Porte Mars** (⊠*Rue de Mars*), an unlikely but impressive 3rd-century Roman arch adorned by worn bas-reliefs depicting Jupiter, Romulus, and Remus, looms up across from the train station.

❼ The **Musée de la Reddition** *(Surrender Room)*, near the train station, also known as the Salle du 8-Mai-1945, is a well-preserved map-covered room used by General Eisenhower as Allied headquarters at the end of World War II. It was here that General Alfred Jodl signed the German surrender at 2:41 ʜ on May 7, 1945. Fighting officially ceased at midnight the next day. ⊠*12 rue Franklin-Roosevelt* ☎*03–26–47–84–19* €*3, joint ticket with the Musée des Beaux-Arts* ⊙*Wed.–Mon. 10–noon and 2–6.*

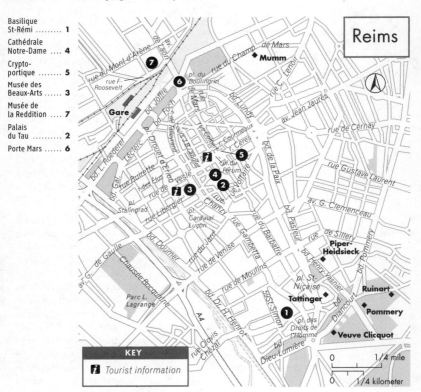

WHERE TO STAY & EAT

$-$$ ✕ **Vigneron.** This little brasserie in a 17th-century mansion is cozy and cheerful, with two tiny dining rooms displaying a jumble of Champagne-related paraphernalia. The food is delightful as well: relatively cheap, distinctly hearty, and prepared with finesse. Try the pigs' feet or andouillettes slathered with delicious mustard made with Champagne. ✉ *1 pl. Paul-Jamot* ☎ *03–26–79–86–86* ▭ *MC, V* ⊘ *Closed weekends, late Dec.–early Jan., and most of Aug.*

★ **$$$$** ✕▦ **Les Crayères.** In a grand park, romantic with towering trees planted by Champagne legend Madame Pommery, this celebrated hotel remains the top showplace of Reims. Not far from the city center (on the A26, take the Saint Rémi exit), the garden estate is centered around its stylish, late-19th-century château, replete with glorious, gilt-trimmed, bouquet-laden interiors. For years, Les Crayères was the redoubt of legendary chef Gérard Boyer. Since his retirement, Didier Elena, who forged his international reputation as head chef at Alain Ducasse's Essex House in New York, has maintained the restaurant's reputation for gastronomic flair with dishes like venison with pumpkin and juniper berries, or sea bass with crab, cress, and a spicy, mustard-based sauce. (Some readers, though, report that standards have become a bit hit-and-miss.) The extensive wine list pays homage to Reims's Champagne heritage. No matter that the restaurant (closed Monday, and no lunch is offered Tuesday; reservations and jacket and tie are all essential) may not hit the heights of Boyer's era—the hotel itself is totally delicious: most guest rooms are bedecked with antiques, boiseries, and couture fabrics. The price tag is decidedly high, but so is the luxe. ⊠*64 bd. Henry-Vasnier, 51100* ☎*03–26–82–80–80* 🖷*03–26–82–65–52* ⊕*www.lescrayeres. fr* ⟿*19 rooms* ⌂*In-room: refrigerator, Wi-Fi. In-hotel: restaurant, bar, tennis court, some pets allowed (fee)* ▤*AE, DC, MC, V* ⊘*Closed late Dec.–mid-Jan.* ⏐◎⏐*BP.*

$$–$$$ ✕▥ **La Paix.** A modern eight-story hotel, a 10-minute walk from the cathedral, La Paix has simple, pastel-color rooms with 18th- and 19th-century reproductions, a pretty garden, and an incongruous chapel. Its brasserie-style restaurant serves mainly grilled meats and seafood. ⊠*9 rue Buirette, 51100* ☎*03–26–40–04–08* 🖷*03–26–47–75–04* ⊕*www. bestwestern-lapaix-reims.com* ⟿*175 rooms* ⌂*In-room: refrigerator. In-hotel: restaurant, bar, pool, some pets allowed (fee)* ▤*AE, DC, MC, V* ⏐◎⏐*BP.*

$–$$$ ✕▥ **Le Cheval Blanc.** This hotel, owned for five generations by the hospitable Robert family, is in the small village of Sept-Saulx, southeast of Reims. Guest rooms overlook a parklike glade on the Vesle River—some are quite small, but the newer suites are larger and have modern furnishings. Restaurant specialties include St-Pierre fish seasoned with Chinese pepper, and partridge with mandarin oranges. There's no lunch on Wednesday. ⊠*Rue du Moulin, 24 km (15 mi) southeast of Reims via D8, 51400 Sept-Saulx* ☎*03–26–03–90–27* 🖷*03–26–03–97–09* ⊕*www.chevalblanc-sept-saulx.com* ⟿*25 rooms* ⌂*In-room: refrigerator, dial-up, no a/c. In-hotel: restaurant, tennis court* ▤*AE, DC, MC, V* ⊘*Closed Tues. Oct.–Mar., and Feb.* ⏐◎⏐*MAP.*

L'ÉPINE

❽ *56 km (35 mi) southeast of Reims via N44 /N3, 7 km (4½ mi) east of Châlons via N3.*

The tiny village of L'Épine is dominated by its church, the twin-towered Flamboyant Gothic **Basilique de Notre-Dame de l'Épine.** The church's facade is a magnificent creation of intricate patterns and spires, and the interior exudes elegance and restraint.

WHERE TO STAY & EAT

★ **$$–$$$** ✕▥ **Aux Armes de Champagne.** The highlight of this cozy former coaching inn (just opposite the town church, so ask for a table with a view) is the restaurant, with its renowned Champagne list and imaginative, often spectacular cuisine by chef Philippe Zeiger. Among his specialties are grilled scallops with cabbage and chestnuts, and artichokes with local goat cheese. (From November through March, the restaurant is closed Monday, and no dinner is served Sunday.) Rooms are furnished with solid, traditional reproductions, wall hangings, and thick carpets. No. 21, with wood beams, is the most atmospheric. ⊠*31 av. du Luxembourg, 51460* ☎*03–26–69–30–30* 🖷*03–26–69–30–36* ⊕*www.aux-armes-de-Champagne.com* ⇋*37 rooms, 2 suites* ⚫*In-room: refrigerator, ethernet, no a/c. In-hotel: restaurant, bar, tennis court* ▤*AE, DC, MC, V* ⊗*Closed Jan.–mid-Feb.* �⏸*BP.*

CHÂLONS-EN-CHAMPAGNE

❾ *7 km (4½ mi) west of L'Epine via N3, 34 km (21 mi) southeast of Épernay via N3.*

GETTING HERE

Trains from Paris (Gare de l'Est) leave for Châlons every 2 hours or so (€22); the 174 km (108-mi) trip takes around 1 hour, 30 minutes. There are four trains a day from Reims to Châlons-en-Champagne (36 mi, 40 mins, €9.50). STDM Trans-Champagne run three daily buses to Châlons from Reims (50 mins, €8) and several buses each day from Épernay (1 hr, €7).

EXPLORING

★ With its twin spires, Romanesque nave, and early Gothic choir and vaults, the church of **Notre-Dame-en-Vaux** bears eloquent testimony to Châlons's medieval importance. The small **museum** beside the excavated cloister contains outstanding medieval statuary. ⊠*Rue Nicolas-Durand* ☎*03–26–64–03–87* 🎫*€5* ⊗*Apr.–Sept., Wed.–Mon. 10–noon and 2–6; Oct.–Mar., Wed.–Fri. 10–noon and 2–5, weekends 10–noon and 2–6.*

The 13th-century **Cathédrale St-Étienne** (⊠*Rue de la Marne*) is a harmonious structure with large nave windows and tidy flying buttresses; the exterior effect is marred only by the bulky 17th-century Baroque west front.

WHERE TO STAY & EAT

$$–$$$ ✕▤ **Angleterre.** Rooms at this stylish spot in central Châlons are elaborate, with marble bathrooms; those in the back are quietest. In the outstanding restaurant (closed Sunday; no lunch Monday or Saturday), chef Jacky Michel's creations include quail with foie gras and red mullet with artichokes, as well as the seasonal dessert *tout-pommes,* featuring five variations on the humble apple. Breakfast is a superb buffet. ⊠*19 pl. Monseigneur-Tissier, 51000* ☎*03–26–68–21–51* 🖷*03–26–70–51–67* ⊕*www.hotel-dangleterre.fr* ⇋*25 rooms* ⚫*In-room: refrigerator. In-hotel: restaurant, bar, some pets allowed (fee), public Wi-Fi* ▤*AE, DC, MC, V* ⊗*Closed mid-July–early Aug. and late Dec.–early Jan.* ⏸*BP.*

EN ROUTE The grapes of Champagne flourish on the steep slopes of the Montagne de Reims—more of a forest-topped plateau than a mountain. From Châlons, take D1 northwest, then turn right on D37 to Ambo-

Continued on page 354

CHAMPAGNE UNCORKED

*"In victory, you deserve Champagne.
In defeat, you need it."*

–Napoléon

*"There comes a time in every woman's life when the
only thing that helps is a glass of Champagne."*

–Bette Davis

6

Dom Pierre Pérignon was the first to discover the secret of Champagne's production by combining the still wines of the region and storing the beverage in bottles. Today, the world's most famous sparkling wine comes from the very same vineyards, along the towering Marne Valley between Épernay and Château-Thierry and on the slopes of the Montagne de Reims between Épernay and Reims.

When you take a Champagne tasting tour, you won't be at the vineyards—it's all done inside the various houses, miles away from where the grapes are grown. Champagne firms–Veuve-Clicquot, Mumm, Pommery, Taittinger, and others—welcome travelers into their chalky, mazelike cellars. Most of the big houses give tours of their *caves* (cellars), accompanied by informative lectures on the Champagne production process. The quality of the tours is inconsistent, ranging from hilarious to despairingly tedious, though a glass of Champagne at the end makes even the most mediocre worth it (some would say). On the tours, you'll discover that Champagne is not made so differently from the way the Dom did it three centuries ago.

BUBBLY BASICS

ALL ABOUT GRAPES

Three types of grape are used to make Champagne: pinot noir, chardonnay, and pinot meunier. The two pinots, which account for 75% of production, are black grapes with white juice. Rosé Champagne is made either by leaving pinot noir juice in contact with the grape skins just long enough to turn it pink, or by mixing local red wine with Champagne prior to bottling. Blanc de Blancs is Champagne made exclusively from white grapes. Blanc de Noirs is made exclusively from black grapes.

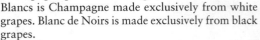

HOW SWEET IT IS

The amount of residual sugar determines the category—ranging from Demi-Sec (literally half-dry, actually sweet) with 33-55 grams of residual sugar per liter, to Extra-Brut (very dry) at less than 6 grams of residual sugar per liter. Classifications in between include Sec at 17 to 35 grams, Extra Dry at 12-20 grams, and Brut, under 15 grams.

VINTAGE VS. NONVINTAGE

Vintage Champagne is named for a specific year, on the premise that the grapes harvested in that year were of extraordinary quality to produce a Champagne by themselves without being blended with wine from other years. Cuvées de Prestige are the finest and most expensive Champagnes that a firm has to offer.

LABEL KNOW-HOW

Along with specific descriptors—such as Blanc de Blancs, Blanc de Noirs, Vintage, etc.—the label carries the following information:

❶ The Champagne appellation
❷ The brand or name of the producer

❸ The level of alcohol volume. Champagne is permitted to vary between 10 and 13%; 12% is common, resulting in classifications like Brut, and Demi-Sec.

THE MERRY WIDOW & THE STARSTRUCK MONK

MADAME CLICQUOT (1777-1866)

WHY THE NICKNAME?
Born Nicole-Barbe Ponsardin and married into the Clicquot family, Madame Clicquot was widowed just seven years after she married François Clicquot (in French, *veuve* means widow).

I'M A HOTSHOT BECAUSE...: After her husband's death, she took over the firm and was one of France's earliest female entrepreneurs and the smartest marketer of the Napoléonic era. During her 60 years in control of the firm, business soared.

GREATEST CONTRIBUTION: She invented the *table de remuage*—the slanted rack used for "riddling," a method for capturing and releasing sediment that collects in the wine—a process that is still used today.

BRAGGING RIGHTS: She persuaded Czar Alexander I to toast Napoléon's demise with Champagne rather than vodka, and other royal courts were soon in bubbly pursuit.

DOM PIERRE PÉRIGNON (1638-1715)

WHY THE NICKNAME?
When Dom Pierre first tasted his creation, he is quoted as saying that he was drinking stars.

I'M A HOTSHOT BECAUSE...: He discovered Champagne when he was about 30 years old while he was the cellarmaster at the Abbey of Hautvillers, just north of Épernay.

GREATEST CONTRIBUTION: He blended wines from different vats and vineyards (now a common practice but then a novelty), reintroduced corks—forgotten since Roman times—and used thicker glass bottles to prevent them from exploding during fermentation.

BRAGGING RIGHTS: Who else can claim the title Father of Champagne?

"Brother, come quickly! I'm drinking stars!"

—Dom Pierre Pérignon

WHAT YOU'LL PAY

Champagne relentlessly markets itself as a luxury product—the sippable equivalent of perfume and haute couture—so it's no surprise that two of the top Champagne brands, Krug and Dom Pérignon, are owned by a luxury goods conglomerate (Louis Vuitton-Moët Hennessy). Sure, at small local producers, or in giant French hypermarkets, you can find a bottle of nonvintage bubbly for $15. But it's more likely to be nearer $40 and, if you fancy something special—say a bottle of vintage Dom Perignon Rose—be prepared to fork out $350. One of the priciest Blanc de Noirs is Bollinger's Vieilles Vignes—tagged at around $400. At the very top of the line is Krug's single-vineyard Clos du Mesnil, with the stellar 1995 vintage retailing at around $750. Just 12,624 bottles were ever produced of this golden elixir.

TOURING THE CELLARS

Experiencing the underground *crayères* is a must for any visit to Champagne. Many firms welcome visitors; for some you need to book in advance (by phone or via Web sites). All tours end with a tasting or three. Don't forget a jacket or sweater—it's chilly down there.

REIMS

CLOSEST TO CITY CENTER

Mumm. Not the most spectacular cellars but a practical option if you have little time: You can walk it from the cathedral and the train station. Mumm exported 1.5 million bottles to America back in 1902, but was confiscated by the French state in World War I because it had always remained in German ownership. Visit starts with 10-minute film and ends with choice of three dégustations: the €18 option includes a rosé and a vintage grand cru.
⊠ 29 rue du Champ-de-Mars, ☎ 03-26-49-59-69, ⊕ www.mumm.com, 🎟 €7.50, ⊙ Weekdays 9:30—10:50 & 2—4:40.

TACKIEST TOUR

Piper-Heidsieck. Disneyland-like electric chariots shunt you through a series of ingenious but at times excruciating tableaux, featuring "Champagne" soap bubbles and a waxwork *Casablanca* Bogart. But for €15 you get the visit plus a great three-glass tasting (Brut, rosé, and Blanc de Blancs) at the elegant bar.
⊠ 51 blvd. Henri-Vasnier, ☎ 03-26-84-43-44, ⊕ www.piper-heidsieck.com 🎟 €7.50 ⊙ Daily Mar.-Dec 9:30-11:45 and 2-5.

FANCIEST ARCHITECTURE

Pommery. This turreted wedding-cake extravaganza on the city outskirts, was designed by Jeanne-Alexandrine Pommery (1819-90), another formidable Champagne widow. The 11 miles of cellars (about a hundred feet underground) are reached by a grandiose 116-step staircase. They include no fewer than 120 chalk pits, several lined with bas-reliefs carved into the rock.
⊠ 5 pl. du General-Gouraud ☎ 03-26-61-62-55 ⊕ www.pommery.com 🎟 €7.50, ⊙ Daily 10-6.

MOST EXPENSIVE VISIT

Ruinart. Founded back in 1729, just a year after Louis XV's decision to allow wine to be transported by bottle (previously it could only be moved by cask) effectively kick-started the Champagne industry. Four of its huge, church-sized 24 chalk galleries are listed historic monuments. This is the costliest visit on offer—and, if you shell out €37, you can taste 1990 vintage rosé as well as the Blanc de Blancs.

✉ 4 rue des Crayères, ☎ 03-26-77-51-21 ⊕ www.champagne-ruinart.fr 🎫 €12 ⊘ Open by appointment.

BEST FOR HISTORY BUFFS

Taittinger. Cavernous chalk cellars, first used by monks for wine storage, house 15 million bottles and partly occupy the crypt of the 13th century abbey that used to stand on the spot. You can see a model of the abbey and its elegant church, both demolished at the Revolution. Especially interesting for lovers of architectural history.

✉ 9 pl. St-Nicaise, ☎ 03-26-85-84-33 ⊕ www.tattinger.com 🎫 €7 ⊘ Mid-Mar.-mid-Nov., daily 9:30-1 & 2-5:30, mid-Nov.-mid-Mar. weekdays only.

ÉPERNAY

BEST MUSEUM

Castellane. Some of the region's deepest cellars—down to 130 feet—and, above ground, a museum with an intriguing display of old tools, bottles, labels and posters. There's also the chance to see the bottling and labeling plant, and climb to the top of a 200-foot tower for a great view over Épernay and the surrounding Marne vineyards.

✉ 57 rue de Verdun ☎ 03-26-51-19-11 ⊕ www.castellane.com 🎫 €7 (incl. museum) ⊘ Daily mid-Mar.-Dec., 10-noon, 2-5:15; Jan.-Feb. weekends 10-noon, 2-5:15.

LADIES' CHOICE

Veuve-Clicquot. The 15-mile chalk galleries here were first excavated in Gallo-Roman times—back in the 3rd century AD! You can see and talk to cellar workers during the visit, and the souvenir shop has the most extensive range of gift ideas of any champagne house. This is Champagne's most feminist firm—named for a woman, and still headed up by a woman today.

✉ 12 rue du Temple ☎ 03-26-89-53-90 ⊕ www.veuve-clicquot.com 🎫 €7.50 ⊘ Open by appointment Apr.-Oct., 10-6, Mon.-Sat.; Nov.-Mar., 10-6 Mon.-Fri.

Veuve Clicquot's President Cecile Bonnefond

BEST HIGH-TECH VISIT

Mercier. Ride an electric train and admire the giant 200,000-bottle oak barrel it took 24 oxen three weeks to cart to the Exposition Universelle in Paris in 1889. An elevator down to (and up from) the cellars is a welcome plus.

✉ 75 av. de Champagne ☎ 03-26-51-22-22 ⊕ www.champagne-mercier.fr 🎫 €7 ⊘ Daily mid-Mar.-mid-Nov., 9:30-11:30 and 2-4:30.

LONGEST CELLAR WALK

Moët & Chandon. Foreign royalty, from Czar Alexander I to Queen Elizabeth II, have been entertained at arguably the most prestigious of all Champagne houses, founded by Charles Moët in 1743. The chalk-cellar galleries run for a mind-blowing 17 miles and house 75 million bottles. The visit includes a glass of Brut Imperial; for €23 you can also taste a couple of vintages.

✉ 18 av. de Champagne ☎ 03-26-51-20-20 ⊕ www.moet.com 🎫 €11 ⊘ Daily Jan.-Nov., Mon.-Fri. 9:30-11:15 and 2-4:15.

nnay to join the famed **Route du Champagne** (sometimes referred to
as the Route du Vin, or Wine Road), a long circuit involving frequent
stops and *dégustations* (tastings) at local Champagne houses, which is
custom-tailored for the car- or cycle-blessed. This winds around the
vine-entangled eastern slopes of the Montagne through such pretty
wine villages as the aptly named Bouzy (known for its fashionable
if overpriced red), Verzy, Mailly-Champagne, Chigny-les-Roses, and
Rilly-la-Montagne. Pick up information at the tourist office in Reims
or other towns and see our section on the Route in "Champagne
Uncorked" in this chapter.

ÉPERNAY

❿ *28 km (18 mi) south of Reims via N51, 35 km (24 mi) west of Châlons-
en-Champagne via N3, 50 km (31 mi) east of Château-Thierry via
D3/N3.*

GETTING HERE
Trains from Paris (Gare de l'Est) leave for Épernay every 2 hours or so
(€19); the 145 km (90-mi) trip takes around 1 hour, 15 minutes. Several
trains daily link Épernay to Reims (20 mi, 30 mins, €6) and Châlons
(20 mi, 15 mins, €7). STDM Trans-Champagne run several buses each
day to Épernay from Châlons (1 hr, €7).

EXPLORING
Although Reims loudly proclaims itself to be the last word in Champagne production, Épernay—set on the south bank of the Marne—is
really the center of the bubbly drink's spirit. It was here in 1741 that
the first full-blown Champagne house, Moët (now Moët et Chandon),
took the lifetime passion of Dom Pérignon and turned it into an industry. Unfortunately, no relation exists between the fabulous wealth of
Épernay's illustrious wine houses and the drab, dreary appearance of
the town as a whole. Most Champagne firms—Moët et Chandon (✉20
av. de Champagne); Mercier (✉70 av. de Champagne); and De Castellane (✉57 rue de Verdun)—are spaced out along the long, straight
Avenue de Champagne, and although their names may provoke sighs
of wonder, their facades are either functional or overdressy. The attractions are underground —see "Champagne Uncorked" in this chapter
for details on guided tours.

To understand how the region's still wine became sparkling Champagne, head across the Marne to **Hautvillers.** Here the monk Dom Pérignon (1638–1715)—upon whom, legend has it, blindness conferred
the gifts of exceptional taste buds and sense of smell—invented Champagne as everyone knows it by using corks for stoppers and blending wines from different vineyards. Dom Pérignon's simple tomb, in
a damp, dreary Benedictine abbey church (now owned by Moët et
Chandon), is a forlorn memorial to the hero of one of the world's most
lucrative drink industries.

WHERE TO STAY & EAT

$$$$ ✗▣ **La Briqueterie.** Épernay is short on good hotels, so it's worth driving south to Vinay to find this luxurious manor. The spacious rooms are modern; ask for one overlooking the extensive gardens. Chef Gilles Goess, who trained at the Paris Ritz, has an inventive touch, witness his lobster with mango mousseline and tarragon jelly. For more regional fare try the Champagne snails with herbed butter and, for dessert, the crepe *soufflée au marc de Champagne* (filled with pastry cream and flavored with brandy). ✉*4 rte. de Sézanne, 6 km (4 mi) south of Épernay, 51530 Vinay* ☎*03–26–59–99–99* 🖷*03–26–59–92–10* ⊕*www.labriqueterie.com* ☎*40 rooms, 2 suites* ᏩIn-room: refrigerator, ethernet. In-hotel: restaurant, bar, pool, gym, some pets allowed (fee)* ▭AE, MC, V ⊘*Closed late Dec.* ⍓|BP.

NIGHTLIFE & THE ARTS

The leading wine festival in the Champagne region is the **Fête St-Vincent** (named for the patron saint of vine growers), held on a Saturday in mid-January. The venue changes from year to year.

CHÂTEAU-THIERRY

⑪ *37 km (23 mi) east of Épernay via N3.*

Built along the Marne River beneath the ruins of a hilltop castle that dates from the time of Joan of Arc, and within sight of the American **Belleau Wood** War Cemetery (open daily 9–5), commemorating the 2,300 American soldiers slain here in 1918, Château-Thierry is best known as the birthplace of the French fabulist Jean de La Fontaine (1621–95). The 16th-century mansion where La Fontaine was born and lived until 1676 is now a museum, the **Musée Jean de La Fontaine,** furnished in the style of the 17th century. It contains La Fontaine's bust, portrait, and baptism certificate, plus editions of his fables magnificently illustrated by Jean-Baptiste Oudry (1755) and Gustave Doré (1868). ✉*12 rue Jean-de-La-Fontaine* ☎*03–23–69–05–60* ☎*€3.30* ⊘*Wed.–Mon. 10–noon and 2–6*

EXCURSION: THE CATHEDRAL CITIES

The hundreds of kilometers of chalk tunnels throughout northern France, some dug by the ancient Romans as quarries, serve as the damp and moldy berth for millions of bottles of Champagne, but they also gave up tons of blocks to create other treasures of the region: the magical and magnificent Gothic cathedrals of the region. We visit five of the most superlative: Amiens, the largest; Beauvais, the tallest; Laon, with the most towers and fantastic hilltop setting; Soissons, beloved by Rodin; and (found in our coverage above) Reims, the most regal. Add in those at St-Omer, St-Quentin, and Châlons-en-Champagne, along with the bijou churches in Rue, St-Riquier, and L'Épine, and aficionados of medieval architecture can follow the development of Gothic architecture from its debut at Noyon to its Flamboyant finale at Abbeville, where, according to the 19th-century English essayist John Ruskin, Gothic "laid down and died."

LAON

⑫ *66 km (41 mi) north of Château-Thierry via D1/N2, 52 km (32 mi) northwest of Reims.*

GETTING HERE
Trains from Paris (Gare du Nord) chug up to Laon, via Soissons, every 2 or 3 hours (€19); the 145 km (90-mi) trip takes around 1 hour, 35 minutes. There are four trains a day from Reims to and Laon (35 mi, 40 mins, €8.50) and three trains daily from Amiens (65 mi, 1 hr 45 mins, €15). RTA (☎03–23–50–68–50 ⊕*www.rta02.com*) operates one daily bus between Reims and Laon (2 hrs).

EXPLORING
Thanks to its awesome hilltop site and the forest of towers sprouting from its ancient cathedral, lofty Laon basks in the title of the "crowned mountain." The medieval ramparts, virtually undisturbed by passing traffic, provide a ready-made itinerary for a tour of old Laon. Panoramic views, sturdy gateways, and intriguing glimpses of the cathedral lurk around every bend. There's even a funicular, which makes frequent trips (except on Sunday in winter) up and down the hillside between the station and the Vieille Ville (Old Town).

Fodor'sChoice The **Cathédrale Notre-Dame,** constructed between 1150 and 1230, is a
★ superb example of early Gothic. The light interior gives the impression of order and immense length, and the first flourishing of Gothic architecture is reflected in the harmony of the four-tiered nave: from the bottom up, observe the wide arcades, the double windows of the tribune, the squat windows of the triforium, and, finally, the upper windows of the clerestory. The majestic towers can be explored during the guided visits that leave from the tourist office, housed in a 12th-century hospital on the cathedral square. Medieval stained glass includes the rose window dedicated to the liberal arts in the left transept, and the windows in the flat east end, an unusual feature for France although common in England. ⊠*Pl. du Parvis* ☏*Guided tours €6, towers €3, audio guide €3* ⊙*Daily 8:30–6:30; guided tours Apr.–Sept., weekends at 4* o- .

The **Musée Muncipal** *(town museum)* has some fine antique pottery and work by the local-born Le Nain brothers, Antoine, Louis, and Mathieu, active in the 17th century and abundantly represented in the Louvre. But its chief draw is the **Chapelle des Templiers** in the garden—a small, octagonal 12th-century chapel topped by a shallow dome. It houses fragments of the cathedral's gable and the chilling effigy of Guillaume de Harcigny, doctor to the insane king Charles VI, whose death from natural causes in 1393 did not prevent his memorializers from chiseling a skeletal portrait that recalls the Black Death. ⊠*32 rue Georges-Ermant* ☎*03–23–20–19–87* ☏*€4* ⊙*June–Sept., Tues.–Sun. 11–6; Oct.–May, Tues.–Sun. 2–6.*

WHERE TO STAY & EAT

$ ✕🖼 **Bannière de France.** In business since 1685, this old-fashioned, uneven-floored hostelry is five minutes from the cathedral. Lieselotte Lefèvre, the German patronne, speaks fluent English. Rooms are cozy and quaint. The restaurant's venerable dining room showcases sturdy cuisine (trout, lemon sole, guinea fowl) and good-value prix-fixe menus. ✉ *11 rue Franklin-Roosevelt, 02000* ☎ *03–23–23–21–44* 🖨 *03–23–23–31–56* ⊕ *www.hoteldelabannieredefrance. com* 🛏 *18 rooms* ♿ *In-room: no a/c. In-hotel: restaurant, bar, no elevator* 🖃 *AE, DC, MC, V* ⊗ *Closed mid-Dec.–mid-Jan.* ℟ *MAP.*

> ### NO STONE LEFT UNTURNED
>
> The filigreed elegance of the five towers is audacious and rare. Look for the 16 stone oxen protruding from the tops, a tribute to the stalwart 12th-century beasts who carted up blocks of stone from quarries far below.

SOISSONS

⑬ *38 km (22 mi) southwest of Laon.*

Although much damaged in World War I, Soissons commands attention for its two huge churches, one intact, one in ruins.

The Gothic **Cathédrale Notre-Dame** was appreciated by Rodin, who famously declared that "there are no hours in this cathedral, but rather eternity." The interior, with its pure lines and restrained ornamentation, creates a more harmonious impression than the asymmetrical, one-towered facade. The most remarkable feature, however, is the rounded two-story transept, an element more frequently found in the German Rhineland than in France. Rubens's freshly restored *Adoration of the Shepherds* hangs on the other side of the transept. ✉ *Pl. Fernand-Marquigny* ⊗ *Daily 9:30–noon and 2:30–5:30.*

The twin-spire facade, arcaded cloister, and airy refectory, constructed from the 14th to the 16th century, are all that is left of the hilltop abbey church of **St-Jean-des-Vignes,** which was largely dismantled just after the Revolution. Its fallen stones were used to restore the cathedral and neighboring homes. But the church remains the most impressive sight in Soissons, its hollow rose window peering out over the town like the eye of some giant Cyclops. ✉ *Cours St-Jean-des-Vignes* 🖃 *Free* ⊗ *Mon.–Sat. 9–noon and 2–6, Sun. 10–12:30 and 1:30–7.*

Partly housed in the medieval abbey of St-Léger, the **Musée de Soissons,** the town museum, has a varied collection of local archaeological finds and paintings, with fine 19th-century works by Gustave Courbet and Eugène Boudin. ✉ *6 rue de la Congrégation* ☎ *03–23–93–30–50* 🖃 *Free* ⊗ *Mon., Tues., Thurs., and Fri., 10–noon and 2–5; weekends 2–5.*

6

Nay, I Know Not the Nave from the Narthex

Consider these architectural terms before passing through Amiens's main medieval portal (front door):

CHANCEL: The space around the altar that's off-limits to everyone but the clergy. It's usually at the east end of the church and is often blocked off by a rail.

CHOIR: The section of the church set off to seat the choir. It's either in the chancel or in a loft in another part of the church.

CLERESTORY: The upper part of the church walls, typically lined with windows (often the stained-glass variety) to bathe the nave with light.

CROCKET: Usually adorning the top of a spire, pinnacle, or gable, this carved ornament often takes the form of foliage, such as acanthus leaves.

CRYPT: An underground chamber usually used as a burial site and often found directly below a church's nave.

GABLE: The triangular upper portion of a wall comprising the area of a pitched roof.

NARTHEX: A hall or small room leading from the main entrance to the nave.

NAVE: The main section of the church that stretches from the chancel to the narthex. This is where worshippers sit during services.

PIER: As opposed to a column, this is a solid masonry support, ranging from a simple square shape to a compound pier often comprised of several sub-distinct shafts.

RIBBED VAULT: A distinct form of Gothic architecture made up of diagonal arches, called ribs, that create a framework projected from the surface to carry the webbed sections in the spaces between the ribs. They thus reduced the masonry used for exterior walls, allowing buildings to be supported by slender piers and the use of wide areas filled with stained-glass windows.

TRANSEPT: The part of the church that extends outward at a right angle from the main body, creating a cruciform (cross-shape) plan.

TYMPANUM: A recessed triangular or semicircular space above the portal, often decorated with sculpture.

WHERE TO STAY & EAT

★ $$$–$$$$ ✕⌂ **Château de Courcelles.** This refined château by the Vesles River is run by easygoing Frédéric Nouhaud. Its pure, classical Louis XIV facade harmonizes oddly with the sweeping brass main staircase attributed to Jean Cocteau. Rooms vary in size and grandeur; the former outbuildings have been converted into large family-size suites. Wind down in the cozy bar next to a roaring fire while anticipating excellent fare, including seasonal game, prepared by chef Thibaut Serin-Moulin and served up in the stately, 18th-century-style dining room, with its white walls and high ceilings. A formal garden and pool are the gateway to 40 acres of parkland and a tree-shaded canal. ⌂ *8 rue du Château, 20 km (12 mi) east of Soissons via N31, 02220 Courcelles-sur-Vesles* ☎ *03–23–74–13–53* 📠 *03–23–74–06–41* ⊕ *www.chateau-de-courcelles.fr* ⟿ *11 rooms, 7 suites* ⌂ *In-room: refrigerator, no a/c.*

In-hotel: restaurant, bar, tennis court, pool, some pets allowed (fee), no elevator ⊟*AE, DC, MC, V* ⦿*MAP.*

AMIENS

⓮ *112 km (70 mi) northwest of Soissons via N31/D935, 58 km (36 mi) north of Beauvais via N1 or A16.*

GETTING HERE

Trains from Paris (Gare du Nord) leave for Amiens every 2 hours or so (€18); the 129 km (80-mi) trip takes 1 hour, 5 minutes. There's one direct train each day from Reims to Amiens (2 hrs, 30 mins, €21) via Laon; three trains daily connect Laon to Amiens (1 hr, 45 mins, €15). Buses run by the CAB'ARO line (☎03–44–48–08–47 ⦿*www.cabaro. info*) run between Beauvais and Amiens six times daily (50 mi, 1 hr, 20 mins, €12).

EXPLORING

Although Amiens showcases some pretty brazen postwar reconstruction, epitomized by Auguste Perret's 340-foot Tour Perret, a soaring concrete stump by the train station, the city is well worth exploring. It has lovely Art Deco buildings in its traffic-free city center, as well as elegant, older stone buildings like the 18th-century Beffroi (belfry) and Neoclassical prefecture. Crowning the city is its great Gothic cathedral, which has survived the ages intact. Nearby is the waterfront quarter of St-Leu—with its small, colorful houses—rivaling the squares of Arras and streets of old Lille as the cutest city district north of Paris.

Fodor's Choice ★ By far the largest church in France, the **Cathédrale Notre-Dame** could enclose Paris's Notre-Dame twice. It may lack the stained glass of Chartres or the sculpture of Reims, but for architectural harmony, engineering proficiency, and sheer size, it's without peer. The soaring, asymmetrical facade has a notable Flamboyant Gothic rose window, and is brought to life on summer evenings when a sophisticated 45-minute light show re-creates its original color scheme. Inside, there is no stylistic disunity to mar the perspective, creating an overwhelming sensation of pure space. Construction took place between 1220 and 1264, a remarkably short period in cathedral-building spans. One of the highlights of a visit here is hidden from the eye, at least until you lift up some of the 110 choir-stall seats and admire the humorous, skillful misericord seat carvings executed between 1508 and 1518. ⊠*Pl. Notre-Dame* ☎03–22–92–03–32 ⊡*Free* ⊗*Access to towers, Wed.–Mon. 3–4:30.*

The **Hôtel de Berny,** near the cathedral, is a steep-roof stone-and-brick mansion built in 1633. It's filled with 18th-century furniture, tapestries, and objets d'art. ⊠*36 rue Victor-Hugo* ☎03–22–97–14–00 ⊡€2 ⊗*Oct.–Mar., Sun. 10–12:30 and 2–6; Apr.–Sept., Thurs.–Sun. 2–6.*

★ Behind an opulent columned facade, the **Musée de Picardie**, built 1855–67, looks like just another pompous offering from the Second Empire. Initial impressions are hardly challenged by its grand staircase lined with monumental frescoes by local-born Puvis de Chavannes, or

its central hall with huge canvases, like Gérôme's 1855 *Siècle
d'Auguste* and Maignon's 1892
Mort de Carpeaux, with flying
muses wresting the dying sculptor from his earthly clay. One step
beyond, though, and you're in a
rotunda painted top to bottom
in modern minimalist fashion by
Sol LeWitt. The basement is filled
with subtly lighted archaeological finds and Egyptian artifacts

> **BEAM ME UP**
>
> If you're a true Verne fan, you
> might want to visit his last resting
> place in the Cimetière de la Mad-
> eleine (⊠2 rue de la Poudrière),
> where he is melodramatically
> portrayed pushing up his tomb-
> stone as if enacting his own sci-fi
> resurrection.

beneath masterly brick vaulting. On the top floor, El Greco leads
the old masters, along with a humorous set of hunting scenes like
Boucher's Rococo-framed *Crocodile Hunt,* from 1736. ⊠*48 rue de la
République* ☎*03–22–97–14–00* ⊕*w2.amiens.com/museedepicardie*
⊠*€4.50* ⊙*Tues.–Sun. 10–12:30 and 2–6.*

Jules Verne (1828–1905) lived in Amiens for the last 35 years of his
life, and his former home, renovated in 2005 to mark the centenary
of his death, is now the **Maison Jules-Verne** (⊠*2 rue Charles-Dubois*
☎*03–22–09–24–30* ⊕*www.jules-verne.net* ⊠*€3* ⊙*Tues.–Sun. 10–
12:30 and 2–6*). It contains some 15,000 documents about Verne's life
as well as original furniture and a reconstruction of the writing studio
where he created his science-fiction classics.

Lovers of science fiction should pay a call on **Espace Imaginaire Jules-
Verne** (⊠*36 rue de Noyon* ☎*03–22–45–37–84* ⊙*Tues.–Fri. 10–7,
Sat.–Mon. 2–7*), which stages exhibitions illustrating his work.

The **Hortillonnages,** on the east side of town, are commercial water
gardens—covering more than 700 acres—where vegetables have been
grown since Roman times. There's an hour-long boat tour of these
aquatic jewels. ⊠*Boats leave from 54 bd. de Beauvillé* ☎*03–22–92–
12–18* ⊠*€6* ⊙*Apr.–Oct., daily 2–6.*

WHERE TO STAY & EAT

★ $$$ ✕ **Les Marissons.** In the scenic St-Leu section of Amiens, beneath the
cathedral, this picturesque waterside restaurant in an elegantly trans-
formed boatbuilding shed serves creative takes on foie gras and regional
ingredients: eel, duck pâté with figs in pastry, turbot with apricots,
rabbit with mint and goat cheese, and pigeon with black currants. To
avoid pricey dining à la carte, order from the prix-fixe menus. ⊠*Pont
de la Dodone, 68 rue des Marissons* ☎*03–22–92–96–66* ⊕*www.les-
marissons.fr* ▤*AE, DC, MC, V* ⊙*Closed Sun. and 3 wks in May. No
lunch Sat.*

$-$$ ✕▥ **Carlton.** This hotel near the train station has a stylish Belle
Epoque facade. In contrast, rooms are sober and functional, though
light and airy, with spacious bathrooms. Foreign guests are common,
and English is spoken. The restaurant, La Brasserie des Capucines,
serves regional, mainly meat dishes. ⊠*42 rue de Noyon, 80000*
☎*03–22–97–72–22* ▤*03–22–97–72–00* ⊕*www.lecarlton.fr* ⟳24

rooms ♿ *In-room: no a/c. In-hotel: restaurant, some pets allowed (fee)* ▤*AE, DC, MC, V* ⦿❘*BP.*

THE ARTS

The **Théâtre de Marionnettes** (✉*31 rue Edouard-David* ☎*03–22–22–30–90*) presents a rare glimpse of the traditional Picardy marionettes, known locally as Chés Cabotans d'Amiens. Shows are performed (in French), usually on Friday evening and Sunday afternoon (daily in August), with plot synopses printed in English.

BEAUVAIS

⓯ *56 km (35 mi) south of Amiens via A16, 96 km (60 mi) west of Soissons.*

GETTING HERE

Trains from Paris (Gare du Nord) leave for Beauvais every hour (€12); the 80-km (50-mi) trip takes around 1 hour, 10 minutes. Buses run by the CAB'ARO line (☎*03–44–48–08–47* ⊕*www.cabaro.info*) run between Amiens and Beauvais six times daily (50 mi, 1 hr, 20 mins, €12).

EXPLORING

Beauvais and its neighbor Amiens have been rivals since the 13th century, when they locked horns over who could build the bigger cathedral. Beauvais lost—gloriously.

Fodor'sChoice
★

A work-in-progress preserved for all time, soaring above the characterless modern blocks of the town center, is the tallest cathedral in France: the **Cathédrale St-Pierre.** You may have an attack of vertigo just gazing up at its vaults, 153 feet above the ground. It may be the tallest, but it's not the largest. Paid for by the riches of Beauvais's wool industry, the choir collapsed in 1284, shortly after completion, and was only rebuilt with the addition of extra pillars. This engineering fiasco proved so costly that the transept was not attempted until the 16th century. It was worth the wait: an outstanding example of Flamboyant Gothic, with ornate rose windows flanked by pinnacles and turrets. It's also still standing—which is more than can be said for the megalomaniacal 450-foot spire erected at the same time. This lasted precisely four years; when it came crashing down, all remaining funds were hurled at an emergency consolidation program, and Beauvais's dream of having the largest church in Christendom vanished forever. Now the cathedral is starting to lean, and cracks have appeared in the choir vaults because of shifting water levels in the soil. No such problems bedevil the **Basse Oeuvre** (Lower Edifice; closed to the public), which juts out impertinently where the nave should have been. It has been there for 1,000 years. Fittingly donated to the cathedral by the canon Étienne Musique, the oldest surviving **chiming clock** in the world—a 1302 model with a 15th-century painted wooden face and most of its original clockwork—is built into the wall of the cathedral. Perhaps Auguste Vérité drew his inspiration from this humbler timepiece when, in 1868, he made a gift to his hometown of the gilded, templelike **astrological clock** (▤€4

⊙Displays at 11:40, 2:40, and 3:40; English audio guide available). Animated religious figurines surrounded by all sorts of gears and dials emerge for their short program at erratic times, although there's a set schedule for visits with commentary. ⊠*Rue St-Pierre* ⊙*May–Oct., daily 9–12:15 and 2–6:15; Nov.–Apr., daily 9–12:15 and 2–5:30.*

From 1664 to 1939 Beauvais was one of France's leading tapestry centers; it reached its zenith in the mid-18th century under the gifted artist Jean-Baptiste Oudry, known for his hunting scenes. Examples from all periods are in the modern **Galerie Nationale de la Tapisserie** *(National Tapestry Museum).* ⊠*22 rue St-Pierre* ☎*03–44–45–09–74* ◪*Free* ⊙*Apr.–Sept., Tues.–Sun. 9:30–12:30 and 2–6; Oct.–Mar., Tues.–Sun. 10–12:30 and 2–5.*

One of the few remaining testaments to Beauvais's glorious past, the old Bishop's Palace is now the **Musée Départemental de l'Oise** *(Regional Museum).* Don't miss the beautifully proportioned attic story, Thomas Couture's epic canvas of the French Revolution, the 14th-century frescoes of instrument-playing sirens on a section of the palace's vaults, or the 1st-century brass *Guerrier Gaulois* (Gallic Warrior). Part of the museum was closed at press time for enlargement and renovation. ⊠*1 rue du Musée* ☎*03–44–11–43–83* ⊕*www.cg60.fr* ◪*€2* ⊙*Wed.– Mon. 10–noon and 2–6.*

WHERE TO STAY & EAT

$ ✕ **Le Zinc Bleu.** This lively brasserie opposite Beauvais cathedral (ask for a table under the glass veranda, or on the sidewalk terrace if the weather's good) offers a choice between sturdy if unadventurous fare (salmon with tagliatelli, duck, various types of steak) and a wide choice of fresh seafood (crab, lobster, Normandy oysters). The Picardy Salada (warm beef with raw vegetables) makes a copious starter. The dining room has light wooden tables and bright modern pictures, but the openwork metal chairs can be a bit tough on the back, so mark this down as a lunch spot more than a place to linger over dinner. ⊠*61 rue St-Pierre* ☎*03–44–48–15–15* ▤*MC, V.*

$–$$ ✕▥ **Chenal Hotel.** There are few hotels in central Beauvais and this foursquare street-corner establishment is perhaps the most convenient of them, close to the train station, a 10-minute walk from the cathedral, and served by a shuttle bus from the airport. Rooms are light and soberly decorated, if on the small side. ⊠*63 bd. Général-de-Gaulle, 60000* ☎*03–44–06–04–60* ☎*03–44–06–04–50* ⊕*chenalhotel.fr* ⊷*29 rooms* ⚙*In-room: no a/c. Bar, some pets allowed (fee)* ▤*MC, V* ▯*BP.*

CHAMPAGNE COUNTRY ESSENTIALS

TRANSPORTATION

If traveling extensively by public transportation, be sure to load up on information ("Guide Régional des Transports" schedules, the best taxi-for-call companies, etc.) upon arriving at the ticket counter or help desk of the bigger train and bus stations in the area, such as Reims and Amiens.

BY AIR

If you're coming from the United States and most other destinations, count on arriving at Paris's Charles de Gaulle or Orly airport. Charles de Gaulle offers easy access to the northbound A16 and A1 for Beauvais and Amiens, and the eastbound A4 for Reims. If coming from the United Kingdom, consider the direct flights to Beauvais from Prestwick, near Glasgow.

BY BOAT & FERRY

Ferry companies travel between northern France and the United Kingdom. P&O Stena and Seafrance ply between Calais and Dover. Speed-Ferries operate a fast catamaran service between Boulogne and Dover, while Norfolk Line operates between Dunkerque and Dover. *For more information, see Boat & Ferry Travel in France Essentials.*

BY BUS

The main bus operator in Picardy is **Courriers Automobiles Picards**; their main hub is the Gare Routière in Amiens. In the Champagne region, services are run by **STDM Trans-Champagne**; the main hub is Châlons-en-Champagne. Their main routes are: three daily buses from Reims to Troyes (2 hrs, 15 mins, €21.50) by way of Châlons-en-Champagne (50 mins, €8) and several buses each day linking Épernay to Châlons (1 hr, €7); **RTA** has one daily bus between Reims and Laon (2 hrs). In Reims, municipal buses run by **Transports Urbains de Reims** depart from the train station (single tickets are €0.90, day-tickets €2.70).

Bus Information Courriers Automobiles Picards (⊠ *B.P. 59, ZAC La Haute Borne, 80136 Rivéry* ☎ *03-22-70-70-70* ⊕ *www.courriersautomobilespicards.com*). **RTA** (⊠ *97 rue Semard, 02430 Gauchy* ☎ *03-23-50-68-50* ⊕ *www.rta02.com*). **STDM** (⊠ *86 rue des Fagnières, 51000 Châlons-en-Champagne* ☎ *03-26-65-17-07* ⊕ *www.stdmarne.fr*). **Transports Urbains de Reims** (⊠ *6 rue Chanzy, Reims* ☎ *03-26-88-25-38* ⊕ *www.tur.fr/english*).

BY CAR

The A4 heads east from Paris to Reims; allow 90 minutes to two hours, depending on traffic. The A16 leads from L'Isle-Adam, north of Paris, up to Beauvais and Amiens. If you're arriving by car via the Channel Tunnel, you'll disembark at Coquelles, near Calais, and join A16 not far from its junction with A26, which heads to Reims (2½ hrs).

BY TRAIN

It's easy to get around the region by train. Most sites can be reached by regular train service, except for the Champagne vineyards, which require a car. There are frequent daily services from Paris (Gare du Nord) to Beauvais; Amiens; and Laon (taking up to two leisurely hours to cover 140 km [87 mi]). A new TGV service, introduced in 2007, now covers the 170 km (105 mi) from Paris (Gare de l'Est) to Reims in 45 minutes. Cross-country services connect Reims to Épernay (20 mins), Châlons (40 mins), and Amiens (2 hrs) via Laon (35 mins).

6

Train Information Gare SNCF Reims (⊠ *Blvd. Joffre* ☏ *03–26–65–17–07*). **SNCF** (☏ *36–35, €0.34 per min* ⊕ *www.voyages-sncf.com*). **TGV** (⊕ *www.tgv.com*).

CONTACTS & RESOURCES

CAR RENTALS

Local Agencies Avis (⊠ *Cour de la Gare, Reims* ☏ *08–20–61–17–05* ⊠ *Gare SNCF, Amiens* ☏ *03–22–91–31–21*). **Europcar** (⊠ *76 bd. Lundy, Reims* ☏ *08–25–04–52–85*).

EMERGENCIES

Contacts Ambulance (☏ *15*). **Regional hospitals** (⊠ *1 pl. Victor-Pauchet, Amiens* ☏ *03–22–66–80–00* ⊠ *American Hospital, 47 rue Cognac-Jay, Reims* ☏ *03–26–78–78–78*).

INTERNET & MAIL

Contacts Clique & Croque (⊠ *27 rue Vesle, Reims* ☏ *03–26–50–58–22*). **Cyber Phone** (⊠ *62 rue St-Leu, Amiens* ☏ *03–22–33–05–36*). **La Poste (main post office)** (⊠ *2 rue Olivier-Métra, Reims* ☏ *03–26–50–58–22*).

MEDIA

Le Courrier Picard (Amiens) covers Picardy, and *L'Union* (Reims) is the newspaper of the Champagne area.

Fees & Schedules Comité Départemental du Tourisme (⊠ *13 bis, rue Carnot, Châlonds-en-Champagne* ☏ *03–26–68–37–52* ⊕ *www.tourisme-en-Champagne.com*).

VISITOR INFORMATION

The Marne Regional Tourist Office is a mine of information about tours and visits in the Champagne region. The principal regional tourist offices in Amiens and Reims are good sources of information about the region. Other, smaller towns also have their own tourist offices, listed below by town. Two main web sites for the region (⊕ *www.tourisme-Champagne-ardenne.com* or ⊕ *www.picardietourisme.com*) are good places for information.

Tourist Information Amiens (⊠ *6 bis, rue Dusevel* ☏ *03–22–71–60–50* ⊕ *www.amiens.fr*). **Beauvais** (⊠ *1 rue Beauregard* ☏ *03–44–15–30–30* ⊕ *www.beauvaistourisme.fr*). **Laon** (⊠ *Pl. du Parvis* ☏ *03–23–20–28–62* ⊕ *www.ville-laon.fr*). **Reims** (⊠ *2 rue Guillaume-de-Machault* ☏ *03–26–77–45–25* ⊕ *www.reims-tourisme.com*). **Soissons** (⊠ *16 pl. Fernand-Marquigny* ☏ *03–23–53–17–37* ⊕ *www.ville-soissons.fr*).

Alsace-Lorraine

Niedermorschwihr

WORD OF MOUTH

"If you happen to be a fan of art and architecture, you'll be in hog heaven in Nancy—both for its 18th-century architecture and for its Art Nouveau treasures of the early 1900s. Stop at the Tourist Office on the Place Stanislas and pick up brochures for walking tours with architectural itineraries of both."

—MaisonMetz

WELCOME TO ALSACE-LORRAINE

Riquewihr, Alsace

TOP REASONS TO GO

★ **The Wine Road:** Ribeauvillé and Riquewihr are at the heart of the Alsatian wine route—two medieval villages filled with Hansel and Gretel houses, cellars bursting with bottles, and wine festivities.

★ **Reborn Colmar:** Although hit by two world wars, Colmar rebuilt itself and the atmospheric maze of cobblestone streets and Petite Venise waterways of the Vieille Ville are pure enchantment.

★ **Nancy's Art Nouveau:** The Art Nouveau capital of France as well as home to Place Stanislas—the most beautiful royal square in Europe—make the hub city of Lorraine an art lover's paradise.

★ **Joan of Arc Country:** If you're a fan of Jeanne d'Arc, then a pilgrimage to her birthplace in Domrémy-la-Pucelle is a must.

★ **Strasbourg, Capital of Alsace:** The symbolic capital of Europe is a cosmopolitan French city rivaled only by Paris in its medieval charms, history, and haute cuisine.

1 **Nancy.** When Stanislas Leszczynski, ex-king of Poland, succeeded in marrying his daughter to Louis XIV, he paid homage to the Sun King by transforming Nancy into another Versailles, embellishing the city with elegant showstoppers like Place Stanislas. Elsewhere in the city, you can sate your appetite for the best Art Nouveau at the Musée Ecole de Nancy and the Villa Majorelle—after all, the style was born here.

2 **Lorraine.** In long-neglected Lorraine, many make the historical pilgrimage to Joan of Arc Country. France's patron saint was born in **Domrémy** in 1411 and in nearby **Vaucouleurs,** the Maid of Orléans arrived to ask the help of the governor. If you listen carefully, you might hear the church bells in which Joan discerned voices challenging her to save France.

European Parliament

3 **Strasbourg.** An appealing combination of medieval alleys, international think tanks, and the European Parliament, this central hub of Alsace is best loved for the villagelike atmosphere of La Petite France, the looming presence of the Cathédrale de Notre-Dame, the rich museums, and the pints of beer sloshing around in the winstubs.

4 Alsace. Tinged with a German flavor, Alsace is a never-ending procession of colorful towns and villages, many fitted out with spires, gabled houses, and storks' nests in chimney pots. Here you can find the Route du Vin, the famous Alsatian Wine Road, with its famous vineyards of Riesling and Traminer. This conveniently heads south to **Colmar,** where the half-timber yellow-and pink-buildings of the *centre ville* seem cut out of a child's coloring book. The town's main treasure is Grünewald's unforgettable 16th-century Issenheim Altarpiece.

GETTING ORIENTED

Bordered by Germany, Alsace-Lorraine has often changed hands between the two countries in the last 350 years. This back-and-forth has left a mark—you'll find Germanic half-timber houses sometimes clash with a very French café scene. Art also pays homage to both nations, as you can see in the museums of Strasbourg, Alsace's main hub. Eastward lies Lorraine, birthplace of Joan of Arc (and the famous quiche). Due west of Strasbourg on the other side of the Vosges Mountains, the main city of Nancy allures with Art Nouveau and elegant 18th-century architecture.

7

LUXEMBOURG
Luxembourg
A31
Thionville
Saarbrücken
0   20 mi
0   20 km
GERMANY
Metz
A4
Bitche
N74
2 LORRAINE
D955
A4   **ALSACE   4**
Hagenau
N4   Saverne   A35
3 Strasbourg
N4
Lunéville
N59   N420
N83
N57   A35
St Dié   *Route de Vin*
Ribeauvillé   Sélestat
Épinal   **GERMANY**
Riquewihr
Colmar   Freiburg
N83
VOSGES
N66
FRANCHE COMTE
A36 Mulhouse
Basel
SWITZERLAND

Half-timber houses in Colmar

ALSACE-LORRAINE PLANNER

Getting Around

Alsace is a small region and is fairly well interconnected with bus routes and train stations, making it possible to travel extensively by public transportation.

If you are, be sure to load up on information (schedules, the best taxi-for-call companies, etc.) upon arriving at the ticket counter or help desk of the bigger train and bus stations in the area, such as Nancy, Strasbourg, and Colmar. In Alsace, trains are the way to go. In Lorraine, you may need to take short bus jaunts to the smaller towns. To find out which towns are on the rail lines, pick up the *Guide Régional des Transports*, a free train and bus guide for both Alsace and Lorraine, at stations and *tabacs* (tobacco shops). Plan ahead if you want to use buses; schedules change frequently.

Making the Most of Your Time

If an overall experience is what you're after, setting up headquarters in Strasbourg or Colmar will give you the best access to the greatest number of sites, either by public transport or car while also residing in one. If wine tasting and vineyards are your priority, setting up in either Riquewihr or Ribeauvillé will put you at the heart of the action. Remember that many of the region's towns and villages, stage summer festivals, including the spectacular pagan-inspired burning of the three pine trees in Thann (late June), the Flower Carnival in Sélestat (mid-August), and the wine fair in Colmar (first half of August). Although Lorraine is a lusterless place in winter, Strasbourg pays tribute to the Germanic tradition with a Christmas fair.

Finding a Place to Stay

Alsace-Lorraine is very well served in terms of accommodations. From the picturesque villages of the Route du Vin, the "Fermes Auberges" of the Vosges to four-star palaces or international-style hotels in the main cities of Nancy and Strasbourg, the range is vast. Since much of Alsace is in the "countryside" there's also a range of *gîtes*, self-catering cottages or houses that provide a base for longer stays (⊕www.gites-de-france.com/gites/uk/rural_gites).

WHAT IT COSTS

	¢	$	$$	$$$	$$$$
Restaurants	Under €11	€11–€17	€17–€23	€23–€30	Over €30
Hotels	Under €50	€50–€80	€80–€120	€120–€190	Over €190

Restaurant prices are per person for a main course at dinner, including tax (19.6%) and service; note that if a restaurant offers only prix-fixe (set-price) meals, it has been given the price category that reflects the full prix-fixe price. Hotel prices are for a standard double room in high season, including tax (19.6%) and service charge. Hotels operate on the European Plan (EP, with no meal provided) unless we note that they use the Breakfast Plan (BP), or also offer such options as Modified American Plan (MAP, with breakfast and dinner daily, known as demi-pension), or Full American Plan (FAP, or pension complète, with three meals a day). Inquire when booking if these all-inclusive meal plans (which always entail higher rates) are mandatory or optional.

A Tippler's Guide to Alsace

Winding south along the eastern foothills of the Vosges from Marienheim to Thann, the Alsatian Wine Route is home to delicious wines and beautiful vineyards. The 121-km (75-mi) Route du Vin passes through small towns, and footpaths interspersed throughout the region afford the opportunity to wander through the vineyards. Buses from Colmar head out to the surrounding towns of Riquewihr, St-Hippolyte, Ribeauvillé, and Eguisheim; pick up brochures on the Wine Route from Colmar's tourist office. Although the route is hilly, bicycling is a great way to take in the countryside and avoid the parking hassle in the towns along this heavily traveled route.

Wine is an object of worship in Alsace, and any traveler down the region's Route du Vin will want to become part of the cult. Just because Alsatian vintners use German grapes, don't expect their wines to taste like their counterparts across the Rhine. German vintners aim for sweetness, creating wines that are best appreciated as an aperitif. Alsatian vintners, on the other hand, eschew sweetness in favor of strength, and their wines go wonderfully with knock-down, drag-out meals. The main wines you need to know about are Gewürztraminer, Riesling, muscat, pinot gris, and sylvaner, all white wines. The only red wine produced in the region is the light and delicious pinot noir.

Gewürztraminer, which in Germany is an ultrasweet dessert wine, has a much cleaner, drier taste in Alsace, despite its fragrant bouquet. It's best served with the richest of Alsace dishes, such as goose. Riesling is the premier wine of Alsace, balancing a hard flavor with certain gentleness. With a grapy bouquet and clean finish, dry muscat does best as an aperitif. Pinot gris, also called tokay, is probably the most full-bodied of Alsatian wines. Sylvaner falls below those grapes in general acclaim, tending to be lighter and a bit dull. You can discover many of these wines as you drive along the Route du Vin.

It's Pronounced Veen-Shtoob

Strasbourg and Nancy may be two of France's more expensive cities, but you wouldn't know it by all their down-to-earth eating spots with down-to-earth prices. Most notably, the regional *winstubs* (*veen*-shtoob), cozier and more wine-oriented than the usual French brasserie, are to be found in most Alsace towns and villages. In Strasbourg and Nancy, as well as the villages along Alsace's wine road, you'll need to arrive early (soon after noon, before 8) to be sure of a restaurant table in July and August. Out of season is a different matter throughout.

How's the Weather?

Alsace is blessed with four distinct seasons and one of the lowest rainfalls in all of France—so anytime at all is the right time to visit, as each season attests. Snow in winter adds magic to the Christmas markets, awaking the child in us that still believes; spring brings forth the scent of burgeoning grape flowers as the world turns green with life; summer can be warm, which rhymes with swarm; autumn is nature's symphony of color as the leaves of tree and vine become a riot of golden yellows and oranges, as the grapes are being bountifully harvested.

7

Introduction by
Nancy Coons

Updated by
Christopher
Mooney

WHO PUT THE HYPHEN IN Alsace-Lorraine? The two regions, long at odds physically and culturally, were bonded when Kaiser Wilhelm sliced off the Moselle chunk of Lorraine and sutured it, à la Dr. Frankenstein, to Alsace, claiming the unfortunate graft as German turf. Though their names to this day are often hyphenated, Alsace and Lorraine have always been two separate territories, with distinctly individual characters. It's only their recent German past that ties them together—it wasn't until 1879, as a concession after France's surrender in 1871, that the newly hyphenated "Alsace-Lorraine" became part of the enemy's spoils. At that point the region was systematically Teutonized—architecturally, linguistically, culinarily (" ... ve haff our own vays of cookink sauerkraut!")—and the next two generations grew up culturally torn. Until 1918, that is, when France undid its defeat and reclaimed its turf. Until 1940, when Hitler snatched it back and reinstated German textbooks in the primary schools. Until 1945, when France once again triumphantly raised the *bleu-blanc-rouge* over Strasbourg.

But no matter how forcefully the French tout its hard-won Frenchness, Alsace's German roots go deeper than the late 19th century, as one look at its storybook medieval architecture will attest. In fact, this strip of vine-covered hills squeezed between the Rhine and the Vosges mountains was called Prima Germania by the Romans, and belonged to the fiercely Germanic Holy Roman Empire for more than 700 years. Yet west of the Vosges, Lorraine served under French and Burgundian lords as well as the Holy Roman Empire, coming into its own under the powerful and influential dukes of Lorraine in the Middle Ages and Renaissance. Stanislas, the duke of Lorraine who transformed Nancy into a cosmopolitan Paris of the East, was Louis XV's father-in-law. Thus Lorraine's culture evolved as decidedly less German than its neighbor to the southeast.

But that's why these days most travelers find Alsace more exotic than Lorraine: its gabled, half-timber houses, ornate wells and fountains, oriels (upstairs bay windows), storks' nests, and carved-wood balustrades would serve well as a stage set for the tale of William Tell and satisfy a visitor's deepest craving for well-preserved old-world atmosphere. Strasbourg, perhaps France's most fascinating city outside Paris, offers all this, and urban sophistication as well. And throughout Alsace, hotels are well scrubbed, with tile bathrooms, good mattresses, and geraniums spilling from every window sill. Although the cuisine leans toward wurst and sauerkraut, sophisticated spins on traditional fare have earned it a reputation—perhaps ironic, in some quarters—as one of the gastronomic centers of France. In fact, it has been crudely but vividly put that Alsace combines the best of both worlds: one dines in France but washes up, as it were, in Germany.

Lorraine, on the other hand, has suffered over the last 20 years, and a decline in its northern industry and the miseries of its small farmers have left much of it tarnished and neglected—or, as others might say, kept it unspoiled. Yet Lorraine's rich caches of verdure, its rolling countryside dotted with *mirabelle* (plum) orchards and crumbling-stucco villages, abbeys, fortresses, and historic cities (majestic Nancy, verdant Metz, war-ravaged Verdun) offer a truly French view of life in the north. Its borders flank Belgium, Luxembourg, and Germany's mellow Mosel (Moselle in French). Home of Baccarat and St-Louis crystal (thanks to limitless supplies of firewood from the Vosges Forest), the birthplace of Gregorian chant, Art Nouveau, and Joan of Arc, Lorraine-the-underdog has long had something of its own to contribute. Although it may lack the Teutonic comforts of Alsace—it subscribes to the more laissez-faire school of innkeeping (concave mattresses, dusty bolsters, creaky floors)—it serves its regional delicacies with flair: *tourte Lorraine* (a pork-and-beef pie), madeleines (shell-shape butter cakes), mirabelle plum tarts, and the famous local quiche.

EXPLORING ALSACE & LORRAINE

These two regions of eastern France border three countries. Alsace, the smaller region, occupies a narrow strip of territory between the Vosges mountains and Germany, across the Rhine River. The capital of Alsace, Strasbourg, is the largest city in the region and one of the most attractive in France. It's a place of such historic and cultural importance that it's worth exploring in depth. Heading southward you can travel Alsace's fabled and photogenic Route du Vin (Wine Road), which links a series of storybook villages and leads down to the historic town of Colmar, home to Grünewald's world-famous altar retable. To the west of Alsace, across the Vosges and sharing a northern frontier with Germany and Luxembourg, is Lorraine. The largest city here, Nancy, also has considerable charm. Westward lies Joan of Arc country, including the much-visted site of her birth in Domrémy-la-Pucelle; eastward is Épinal, home to an historic Vieille Ville (Old Town)as well as the Musée Départemental d'Ar Ancien et Contemporain, a renovated 17th-century structure that is hung with some noted art treasures, including *Job Lectured by his Wife* painted by that muse of Lorraine, Georges de la Tour. Most visitors begin exploring this region to the west—nearest Paris—beginning with Nancy (set 145 km [90 mi] west of Strasbourg).

NANCY

GETTING HERE
The jewel in Lorraine's tourism crown, Nancy, will greatly benefit from the introduction of the record-breaking TGV Est European (⊕*www. tgvesteuropeen.com*) with 10 daily trains almost every hour from Paris's Gare de l'Est, 7:12 to 10:12, all making the run in 90 minutes. The 12:12 and 6:12 will also service Epinal, 45 minutes farther on. Currently, 15 direct TGV and EuroCity trains leave Paris Est almost every half hour with an average travel time of 3 hours. Fares vary from €38.70 to €43.30 depending on the train type. Nancy's train station (⊠*3 pl. Thiers*), a 15-minute walk down Rue Stanislas from the town center, is open 24 hours. Fourteen direct trains to Strasbourg (€26.20) leave every 45 minutes from Nancy and every 10 minutes a train leaves

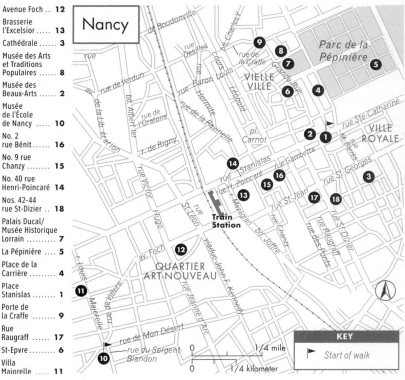

for Metz (€8.90). There are very frequent (every 20 minutes) daily TER services to Luneville (€5.90) and Epinal (€11). The 46 lines of the TED's bus service (☎ *03–83–36–41–14*) cover the entire *département*, leaving from Place de la Republique, for a €1.70 flat rate.

EXPLORING

For architectural variety, few French cities match Nancy, which is in the heart of Lorraine, 300 km (190 mi) east of Paris. Medieval ornamentation, 18th-century grandeur, and Belle Epoque fluidity rub shoulders in the town center, where the bustle of commerce mingles with stately elegance. Its majesty derives from a long history as domain to the powerful dukes of Lorraine, whose double-barred crosses figure prominently on local statues and buildings. Never having fallen under the rule of the Holy Roman Empire or the Germans, this Lorraine city retains an eminently Gallic charm.

The city is at its most sublimely French in its harmoniously constructed squares and buildings, which, as vestiges of the 18th century, have the quiet refinement associated with the best in French architecture. Curiously enough, it was a Pole, and not a Frenchman, who was responsible for much of what is beautiful in Nancy. Stanislas Leszczynski, ex-king of Poland and father of Maria Leszczynska (who married Louis XV of France) was given the Duchy of Lorraine by his royal son-in-law on the understanding that on his death it would revert to France. Stanislas installed himself in Nancy and devoted himself to the glorious embellishment of the city. Today Place Stanislas remains one of the loveliest and most perfectly proportioned squares in the world, with Place de la Carrière—reached through Stanislas's Arc de Triomphe—with its elegant, homogeneous 18th-century houses, its close rival for this honor.

THE HISTORIC CENTER

Concentrated northeast of the train station, this neighborhood—rich in architectural treasures as well as museums—includes classical Place Stanislas and the shuttered, medieval *Vieille Ville*.

THE MAIN ATTRACTIONS

3 Cathédrale. This vast, frigid edifice was built in the 1740s in a ponderous Baroque style, eased in part by the florid ironwork of Jean Lamour. Its most notable interior feature is a murky 19th-century fresco in the dome. The **Trésor** (Treasury) contains minute 10th-century splendors carved of ivory and gold. ⊠*Rue St-Georges, Ville Neuve.*

8 Musée des Arts et Traditions Populaires *(Museum of Folk Arts and Traditions).* Just up the street from the Palais Ducal, this quirky, appealing museum is housed in the **Couvent des Cordeliers** (Convent of the Franciscans, who were known as Cordeliers until the Revolution). It re-creates how local people lived in preindustrial times, using a series of evocative rural interiors. Craftsmen's tools, colorful crockery, somber stone fireplaces, and dark waxed-oak furniture accent the tableaulike settings. The dukes of Lorraine are buried in the crypt of the adjoining **Église des Cordeliers,** a Flamboyant Gothic church; the *gisant* (reclining statue) of Philippa de Gueldra, second wife of René II, executed in limestone in flowing detail, is a moving example of Renaissance portraiture. The octagonal Ducal Chapel was begun in 1607 in the Renaissance style, modeled on the Medici Chapel in Florence. ⊠64 *Grande-Rue, Vieille Ville* ☎03–83–32–18–74 ☞€3.10, €4.60 joint *ticket with Musée Lorrain* ♥ *Wed.–Mon. 10–12:30 and 2–6.*

2 Musée des Beaux-Arts *(Fine Arts Museum).* In a splendid building that now spills over into a spectacular modern wing, a broad and varied collection of art treasures lives up to the noble white facade designed by Emmanuel Héré. Among the most striking are the freeze-the-moment realist tableaux painted by native son Emile Friant at the turn of the 20th century. A sizable collection of Lipschitz sculptures includes portrait busts of Gertrude Stein, Jean Cocteau, and Coco Chanel. You'll also find 19th- and 20th-century paintings by Monet, Manet, Utrillo, and Modigliani; a Caravaggio *Annunciation* and a wealth of old masters from the Italian, Dutch, Flemish, and French schools; and impressive glassworks by Nancy native Antonin Daum. The showpiece is Rubens's massive *Transfiguration.* Good commentary cards in English are available in every hall. ⊠*3 pl. Stanislas, Ville Royale* ☎03–83–85–30–72 ⊕*www.mairie-nancy.fr/culturelle/musee/html/beaux_arts. php* ☞€6 ♥ *Wed.–Mon. 10–6.*

7

Nancy 1900

History has a curious way of having similar events take place at the same time in different places. The creation of the Art Nouveau (New Art) movement is one such event. Simultaneously emerging from Pre-Raphaelite, High Victorian, and the Arts and Crafts movement in England, it was also a synthesis of the Jugenstil (youth style) movement in Germany; the Skonvirke movement in Denmark; the Mloda Polska (Young Poland) style in Poland; Secessionism in Vienna; Modernism in Spain centered in Barcelona and the wild organic architectural flourishes of Gaudi; and the florid poster art of Alfons Mucha in Prague. Its fluid, undulating organic forms drawn from nature, seaweed forms, grasses, flowers, birds, and insects also drew inspiration from Symbolism and Japanese woodcuts.

One of its founding centers was Nancy, which at the time was drawing the wealthy French bourgeoisie of Alsace, recently invaded by Germany, who refused to become German. Proud of their opulence, they had sublime houses built that were entirely furnished, from simple vases and wrought-iron beds to bathtubs in the shape of lily pads, all in the pure Art Nouveau style. All of Nancy paid homage to this style.

Everywhere stylized flowers became the preferred motif. The tree and its leaves, and plants with their flowers, were modified, folded and curled to the artist's demand. Among the main Art Nouveau emblems figure the lily, the iris, morning glory, bracken fern, poppies, peacocks, birds that feed on flowers, ivy, dragonflies, butterflies, and anything that evokes the immense poetry of the seasons. It reveals a world that is as fragile as it is precious.

By giving an artistic quality to manufactured objects, the creators of the Ecole de Nancy accomplished a dream that had been growing since the romantic generation of Victorian England of making an alliance between art and industry. This was a major advance on the bourgeois bad taste for mass-produced imitations inspired by styles of the past and subject to the constraints of mass production. Nancy's great strength was in this collaboration of art and industry.

Among the Ecole de Nancy's most outstanding contributors was Emile Gallé, who worked primarily in glass inventing new, patented techniques, and who brought luxury craftsmanship to a whole range of everyday products, thus reestablishing the link between the ordinary and the exceptional.

As a meeting point for the hopes and interests of artists, intellectuals, industrials, and merchants, the Ecole de Nancy was a thoroughly global phenomenon. From Chicago to Turin, Munich to Brussels, and on to London, the industries of Nancy went on to conquer the world.

★ **❼** **Palais Ducal** *(Ducal Palace).* This palace was built in the 13th century and completely restored at the end of the 15th century and again after a fire at the end of the 19th century. The main entrance to the palace, and the **Musée Lorrain** (Lorraine History Museum), which it now houses, is 80 yards down the street from the spectacularly Flamboyant Renaissance portal. A spiral stone staircase leads up to the palace's most impressive room, the **Galerie des Cerfs** (Stags Gallery). Exhibits here (including pictures, armor, and books) recapture the Renaissance mood of the 16th century—one of elegance and merrymaking, with an undercurrent of stern morality: an elaborate series of huge tapestries, *La Condemnation du Banquet* (Condemnation of the Banquet), expounds on the evils of drunkenness and gluttony. Exhibits showcase Stanislas and his court, including "his" oft-portrayed dwarf; a section on Nancy in the revolutionary era; and works of Lorraine native sons, including a collection of Jacques Callot engravings and a handful of works by Georges de La Tour. ⊠ *64 Grande-Rue, Vieille Ville* ☎ *03–83–32–18–74* ⊠ *€3.10, €4.60 joint ticket with Musée des Arts et Traditions* ⊘ *Wed.–Mon. 10–12:30 and 2–6.*

> ### EVERYONE LOVES A LAMOUR
>
> Fitting showpiece of the southern flank of the square is the 18th-century Hôtel de Ville, Nancy's Town Hall, where the handiwork of Lamour can also be seen to stunning effect on the wrought-iron handrail of the *grand escalier* (grand staircase) leading off the lobby. You can get a closer view when the building is open to the public on summer evenings (July and August, 10:30 to 11 pm) and it's possible to mount the staircase to the Salle des Fêtes and survey the full beauty of Place Stanislas.

★ ▶ **❶** **Place Stanislas.** With its severe, gleaming-white Classical facades given a touch of Rococo jollity by fanciful wrought gilt-iron railings, this perfectly proportioned square, stylishly repaved in honor of its 250th anniversary in 2005, may remind you of Versailles. The square is named for Stanislas Leszczynski, twice dethroned as king of Poland but offered the Duchy of Lorraine by Louis XV (his son-in-law) in 1736. Stanislas left a legacy of spectacular buildings, undertaken between 1751 and 1760 by architect Emmanuel Héré and ironwork genius Jean Lamour. The sculpture of Stanislas dominating the square went up in the 1830s, when the square was named after him. Framing the exit, and marking the divide between the Vieille Ville and the *Ville Neuve* (New Town), is the **Arc de Triomphe**, erected in the 1750s to honor Louis XV. The facade trumpets the gods of war and peace; Louis's portrait is here. ⊠ *Ville Royale.*

ALSO WORTH SEEING

☾ **❺** **La Pépinière.** This picturesque, landscaped city park has labeled ancient trees, a rose garden, playgrounds, a carousel, and a small zoo. ⊠ *Entrance off Pl. de la Carrière, Vieille Ville.*

★ **❹** **Place de la Carrière.** Spectacularly lined with pollarded trees and handsome 18th-century mansions (another successful collaboration between

King Stanislas and Emmanuel Héré), this elegant rectangle leads from Place Stanislas to the colonnaded facade of the **Palais du Gouvernement** (Government Palace), former home of the governors of Lorraine. ⊠ *Vieille Ville.*

❾ Porte de la Craffe. A fairy-tale vision out of the late Middle Ages, this gate is the only remains of Nancy's medieval fortifications. With its twin turrets looming at one end of the Grande-Rue, built in the 14th and 15th centuries, this arch served as a prison through the Revolution. Above the main portal is the Lorraine Cross, comprising a thistle and cross. ⊠ *Vieille Ville.*

❻ St-Epvre. A 275-foot spire towers over this splendid neo-Gothic church rebuilt in the 1860s. Most of the 2,800 square yards of stained glass were created by the Geyling workshop in Vienna; the chandeliers were made in Liège, Belgium; many carvings are the work of Margraff of Munich; the heaviest of the eight bells was cast in Budapest; and the organ, though manufactured by Merklin of Paris, was inaugurated in 1869 by Austrian composer Anton Bruckner. ⊠ *Pl. du Général-de-Gaulle, Vieille Ville.*

ART NOUVEAU NANCY

Fodor's Choice
★   Think *Art Nouveau* and many will conjure up the rich salons of Paris's Maxim's restaurant, the lavender-hue Prague posters of Alphonse Mucha, and the stained-glass dragonflies and opalescent vases that, to this day, remain the darlings of such collectors as Barbra Streisand. All of that beauty was born, to a great extent, in 19th-century Nancy. Inspired and coordinated by the glass master Émile Gallé, the local movement was formalized in 1901 as L'École de Nancy—from there, it spread like wildfire through Europe, from Naples to Monte-Carlo to Prague. The ensuing flourish encompassed the floral *pâte de verre* (literally, glass dough) works of Antonin Daum and Gallé; the Tiffany-esque stained-glass windows of Jacques Gruber; the fluidity of Louis Majorelle's furniture designs; and the sinuous architecture of Lucien Weissenburger, Émile André, and Eugène Vallin. Thanks to these artists, Nancy's downtown architecture gives the impression of a living garden suspended above the sidewalks.

THE MAIN ATTRACTIONS

★ ▶ **❿ Musée de l'École de Nancy** *(School of Nancy Museum).* The only museum in France devoted to Art Nouveau is housed in an airy turn-of-the-last-century garden–town house. It was built by Eugène Corbin, an early patron of the School of Nancy. Re-created rooms and original works of art by local Art Nouveau stars Gallé, Daum, Muller, and Walter all allure. Gallé (1846–1904) was the engine that drove the whole Art Nouveau movement. He called upon artists to resist the imperialism of Paris, follow examples in nature (not those of Greece or Rome), and use a variety of techniques and materials. Many of their gorgeous artifacts are on view here. ⊠ *36 rue du Sergent-Blandan, Quartier Art-Nouveau* ☎ *03–83–40–14–86* ⊕ *www.ecole-de-nancy.com* 🎫 *€4.60* ⊙ *Mon. 2–6, Wed.–Sun. 10:30–6.*

AN ART NOUVEAU WALK

The only museum in France dedicated solely to Art Nouveau, the magical **Musée de l'École de Nancy** ⑩ ☞ is the best place to immerse yourself in this fanciful, highly stylized, and curlicued style that crept into interiors and exteriors throughout Nancy in the early 20th century and then became a sensation around the world. At the museum, pianos ooze, bedsteads undulate; the wood itself of bureaus and armoires, hard and burnished as it is, seems to have melted and re-formed. As you take in the charms of the "New Art" you can learn about the style's foundation at the museum.

In the late 19th century, Nancy was a renaissance city, thanks to a massive immigration due to Alsace's recent annexation, an explosion of the city's powerful chemical industry, and a group of artists who heard the clarion call across the channel from John Ruskin and William Morris that "art must not only be in all, it must be for all." By focusing on the decorative arts—glass, metalwork, furniture—Nancy artisans newly emphasized the alliance between art and industry. No longer would grand collectors and galleries call the shots—the new department stores would make this a truly global style. With a rich regional heritage of Flamboyant Gothic and Rococo in Lorraine itself, it wasn't much of a leap to Art Nouveau, whose floral motifs were richly inspired by the actual field flowers of Lorraine.

Allow a full morning to linger in the Musée de l'École de Nancy and observe the masterworks of Gallé, Daum, Muller, and Walter and then, during the course of about an hour and a half, wander back circuitously

toward the Vieille Ville, stopping to admire Art Nouveau masterworks along the way. To get to the museum from the busy shopping street Rue St-Jean (just up Rue des Dominicains from Place Stanislas), take Bus 5 or 25 uphill and get off at Place Painlevé. From the museum turn left down Rue du Sergent-Blandan and walk about four blocks to **Villa Majorelle** ⑪. This was the first and grandest Art Nouveau mansion to be built (1898) in Nancy, the creation of Louis Majorelle (furniture, boiseries, and metalwork) and the architect Henri Sauvage. The showpiece is the dining room, with its gray stone chimney in the shape of a flame.

Cut east to Place de la Commanderie and head up **Avenue Foch** ⑫ to admire the colorful structures at Nos. 71, 69, and 41. Hike over the Viaduct Kennedy and the *gare* (train station), turn left past the department store Printemps, and follow Rue Mazagran to the **Brasserie l'Excelsior** ⑬. Turn right toward **No. 40 rue Henri-Poincaré** ⑭. Turn right and walk past **No. 9 rue Chanzy** ⑮ (now the Banque Nationale de Paris). Head left to find **No. 2 rue Bénit** ⑯, with its ornate metal structure. Head south to Rue St-Jean; at the corner of **Rue Raugraff** ⑰ are two bay windows, remnants of stores that were once here. Continue down Rue St-Jean and turn right to find **Nos. 42–44 rue St-Dizier** ⑱. Many more Art Nouveau addresses are scattered throughout the city; you can get a detailed map at the tourist office which can also provide an English-language pamphlet on the city's Art Nouveau treasures.

7

★ **⑪** **Villa Majorelle.** This villa was built in 1902 by Paris architect Henri Sauvage for Majorelle himself. Sinuous metal supports seem to sneak up on the unsuspecting balcony like swaying cobras, and there are two grand windows by Gruber: one lighting the staircase (visible from the street) and the other set in the dining room on the south side of the villa (peek around from the garden side). ✉ *1 rue Louis-Majorelle, Quartier Art-Nouveau.*

ALSO WORTH SEEING

⑫ **Avenue Foch.** This busy boulevard lined with mansions was built for Nancy's affluent 19th-century middle class. At No. 69, the occasional pinnacle suggests Gothic influence on a house built in 1902 by Émile André, who designed the neighboring No. 71 two years later. No. 41, built by Paul Charbonnier in 1905, bears ironwork by Majorelle. ✉ *Quartier Art-Nouveau.*

⑬ **Brasserie l'Excelsior.** This bustling brasserie *(see Where to Stay & Eat, below)* has a severely rhythmic facade that is invitingly illuminated at night. Inside, the popular restaurant's fin de siècle decor continues to evoke the Belle Epoque. ✉ *Corner of Rue Mazagran and Rue Henri-Poincaré, Quartier Art-Nouveau.*

⑯ **No. 2 rue Bénit.** This elaborately worked metal exoskeleton, the first in Nancy (1901), exudes functional beauty. The fluid decoration reminds you of the building's past as a seed supply store. Windows were worked by Gruber; the building was designed by Henry-Barthélemy Gutton, while Victor Schertzer conceived the metal frame. ✉ *Quartier Art-Nouveau.*

⑮ **No. 9 rue Chanzy.** Designed by architect Émile André, this lovely structure—now a bank—can be visited during business hours. You can still see the cabinetry of Majorelle, the decor of Paul Charbonnier, and the stained-glass windows of Gruber. ✉ *Quartier Art-Nouveau.*

⑭ **No. 40 rue Henri-Poincaré.** The Lorraine thistle and brewing hops weave through this undulating exterior, designed by architects Émile Toussaint and Louis Marchal. Victor Schertzer conceived this metal structure in 1908, after the success of No. 2 rue Bénit. Gruber's windows are enhanced by the curving metalwork of Majorelle. ✉ *Quartier Art-Nouveau.*

⑱ **Nos. 42–44 rue St-Dizier.** Eugène Vallin and Georges Biet left their mark on this graceful 1903 bank. ✉ *Quartier Art-Nouveau* ☉ *Weekdays 8:30–5:30.*

⑰ **Rue Raugraff.** Once there were two stores here, both built in 1901. The bay windows are the last vestiges of the work of Charles Vallin, Émile André, and Eugène Vallin. ✉ *Corner of rue St-Jean, Quartier Art-Nouveau.*

EATING WELL IN ALSACE-LORRAINE

A bottle of sharp Sylvaner, a pink slab of air-dried ham, a patty of silky Vacherin Mont d'Or melted over potatoes: you don't need pink linens to dine on this primal mountain food, just a hiker's appetite, perhaps whetted by exploring the forested ranges of the region.

Alsace cooking tends to be hearty and influenced by its Germanic origins—*choucroute* (sauerkraut served with ham and sausages) and *baeckeoffe* (a meat-and-potato casserole) are two mainstays—but there's sophistication, too: foie gras accompanied by a glass of *vendanges tardives* (late-harvested) Gewürztraminer, and trout and chicken cooked in Riesling, the classic wine of Alsace. Snails and seasonal game are other favorites,

as are Muenster cheese, salty *bretzel* loaves, and briochelike *kouglof* bread. Geese are very popular, especially if they're stuffed with apples or chestnuts! Carp fried in bread crumbs is a specialty of southern Alsace. Another regional favorite is the *tarte flambée*, a thin-crusted, pizzalike thing, topped with fresh cream, onions, and cheese.

Desserts are also rich, most notably the *Kougelhopf*, a buttery upside-down cake cooked in a round pan and commonly served with kirsch, the local liqueur made from cherries. Lorraine, renowned for quiches, is also famous for its madeleines, *dragées* (almond candies), macaroons, and the lovely little *mirabelle*, a small yellow plum juicy with heady, perfumed nectar.

WHERE TO STAY & EAT

★ $$-$$$ ✕ **Le Capucin Gourmand.** Making the most of Nancy's Art Nouveau pâte de verre, including a giant chandelier and glowing mushroom lamps on the tables, this chic landmark puts its best foot forward under chef Hervé Fourrière. Soigné specialties include a light lobster lasagna with mushrooms, beef marrow served in the bone with truffles and white beans, and a trio of fresh mango desserts. The choice of Toul wines is extensive. ✉ *31 rue Gambetta, Ville Royale* ☎ *03–83–35–26–98* ⏰ *Reservations essential* ▤ *AE, DC, MC, V* ⊗ *Closed Mon. No lunch Sat. No dinner Sun.*

$$ ✕ **Brasserie l'Excelsior.** Above all, you'll want to eat in this 1911 restaurant for its sensational Art Nouveau stained glass, mosaics, Daum lamps, and sinuous Majorelle furniture. But the food is stylish, too, with succulent choices ranging from lamb's tail salad with goat cheese and truffle juice to sea bream with fennel—and don't miss out on the pear and gingerbread crumble. White-aproned waiters exude Parisian chic. ✉ *50 rue Henri-Poincaré, Quartier Art-Nouveau* ☎ *03–83–35–24–57* ⊕ *www.brasserie-excelsior.com* ▤ *MC, V.*

¢–$ ✕ **Le P'tit Cuny.** If you were inspired by the rustic exhibits of the Musée des Arts et Traditions Populaires, cross the street and sink your teeth into authentic Lorraine cuisine in the form of choucroute, *tête de veau* (calf's head), or tangy veal *tourte* (pie). ✉ *95 Grande-Rue, Vieille Ville* ☎ *03–83–32–85–94* ▤ *MC, V* ⊗ *Closed Sun. and Mon.*

★ $$$-$$$$ ✕🔲 **Grand Hôtel de la Reine.** This hotel is every bit as grand as Place Stanislas, on which it stands; the magnificent 18th-century building is officially classified as a historic monument. Rooms are in a suitably regal Louis XV style; the most luxurious overlook the square. The restaurant, Le Stanislas (closed Sunday November–end of March; no lunch Saturday), aglitter with chandeliers and carved-wood boiseries and run with élan by Olivier Hubert, has four- and five-course menus at €50 and €62. Showstoppers here include lobster Bavaroise, duck in Vosges honey, and a supreme of melted chestnuts served with a morel mushroom caramel sauce. ⊠2 pl. Stanislas, Ville Royale, 54000 🕾03–83–35–03–01 🖹03–83–32–86–04 ⊕www.hoteldelareine.com ⤵42 rooms ⚘In-room: refrigerator. In-hotel: restaurant, bar, public Internet, some pets allowed (fee) 🖃AE, DC, MC, V ⟡⃒BP.

$–$$ 🏨 **Guise.** Deep in the shuttered Vieille Ville, this hotel is in an 18th-century nobleman's mansion with a magnificent stone-floor entry. Three and a half years of renovation were completed in 2002 and rooms are now furnished with period pieces. Breakfast on the once-grand main floor and an excellent location make this a good choice if you're a bargain-hunting romantic. Internet access is through the hotel's business center. ⊠18 rue de Guise, Vieille Ville, 54000 🕾03–83–32–24–68 🖹03–83–35–75–63 ⊕www.hoteldeguise.com ⤵42 rooms, 6 junior suites ⚘In-room: no a/c. In-hotel: business services, some pets allowed (fee) 🖃MC, V ⟡⃒BP.

NIGHTLIFE & THE ARTS

Nancy has a rich cultural life that includes ballet, opera, and a highly renowned symphonic orchestra. The **Orchestre Symphonique & Lyrique** (🕾03–83–85–33–11 ⊕www.mairie-nancy.fr) organizes concerts from fall through spring. The **Opéra National de Lorraine** (🕾03–83–85–33–20 ⊕www.mairie-nancy.fr) is the fifth-ranked national regional opera of France with a repertoire ranging from ancient to contemporary music. The **Ballet de Lorraine** (🕾03–83–85–69–01 ⊕www.ballet-de-lorraine. com) was created in 1978 to assume the mission of a national ballet; performances are staged in the Opéra de Nancy in the Place Stanislas.

Les Caves du Roy (⊠9 pl. Stanislas, Ville Royale 🕾03–83–35–24–14) attracts a young upscale crowd that comes to dance. **Le Chat Noir** (⊠63 rue Jeanne-d'Arc, Ville Neuve 🕾03–83–28–49–29) draws a thirtysome-thing crowd to retro-theme dance parties. **HW** (⊠1 ter rue du Général-Hoche, Ville Neuve 🕾03–83–40–25–13) is a popular dance club.

SHOPPING

Ancienne Librairie Dornier (⊠74 Grande-Rue, Vieille Ville 🕾03–83–36–50–62), near the Musée des Arts et Traditions Populaires, is an excellent bookstore that sells engravings as well as old and new books devoted to local history. **Daum Boutique** (⊠14 pl. Stanislas, Vieille Ville 🕾03–83–32–21–65 ⊕www.daum.fr) sells deluxe crystal and examples of the city's traditional Art Nouveau pâte de verre.

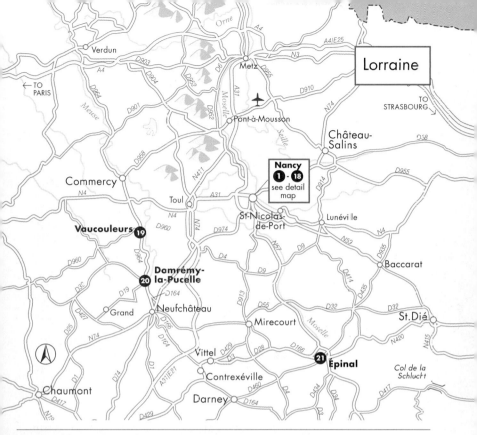

LORRAINE: JOAN OF ARC COUNTRY

Lorraine is the country of France's patron saint, Joan of Arc. Follow D64 that winds between Contrexéville and Void, and you will be on Joan's native soil, almost unchanged since the Middle Ages. In fact, she would probably find much of the countryside today familiar. Various towns bear witness. At Neufchâteau, then a fortified town guarding the region, the inhabitants of Domrémy sought refuge in 1428 from the English armies that menaced their village. It was in Domrémy that Joan was born in 1411, or a year later. Moving on, Vaucouleurs recalls Joan's arrival in May 1428 to ask the help of the governor to see the king to plead for France's cause—and achieve her destiny.

VAUCOULEURS

⓳ *73 km (41 mi) southwest of Nancy on N4 and D964.*

Above the modest main street in the market town of Vaucouleurs, you can see ruins of Robert de Baudricourt's ancient medieval castle and the Porte de France, through which Joan of Arc led her armed soldiers to Orléans. The barefoot Maid of Orléans spent a year within these walls, arriving on May 13, 1428, to ask the help of the governor

Baudricourt. After wheedling an audience with Baudricourt, she then convinced him of the necessity of her mission, learning to ride and to sword-fight. Won over finally by her conviction and popular sentiment, he offered to give her an escort to seek out the king. On February, 23, 1429, clad in page's garb and with her hair cut short, Jeanne d'Arc rode out through the Porte de France. A train route runs to Vaucouleurs from Toul and Nancy.

WHERE TO STAY & EAT

¢ ✕🖼 **Relais de la Poste.** On the main street, this simple hotel has quiet rooms and a pleasant, intimate restaurant (closed Friday–Sunday in November–May). The good regional menu is served noon and night. A friendly family cooks, serves the meals, and checks you in. ⊠ *12 av. André-Maginot, 55140* 🕿*03–29–89–40–01* 🖶*03–29–89–40–93* 🛏*9 rooms* ⚒*In-room: no a/c, dial-up. In-hotel: restaurant, bar* ▤*AE, MC, V* ⊙*Closed last 2 wks Dec.*

DOMRÉMY-LA-PUCELLE

❷⓿ *19 km (12 mi) south of Vaucouleurs on D964.*

GETTING HERE

From Nancy, 32 trains connect with Toul (€5.90); change for Neufchâteau, 39 km (24 mi) southwest of Nancy, for the twice-daily bus connection to Domrémy-la-Pucelle (€3.90), 10 km (6 mi) to the north of Neufchâteau, on the Vaucouleurs line.

EXPLORING

Joan of Arc was born in Domrémy-la-Pucelle in a stone hut in either 1411 or 1412. You can see it as well as the church where she was baptized, the actual statue of St. Marguerite before which she prayed, and the hillside where she tended sheep and first heard voices telling her to take up arms and save France from the English.

Fodor'sChoice   The humble stone-and-stucco **Maison Natale Jeanne d'Arc** *(Joan of Arc's*
★   *Birthplace)* —an irregular, slope-roof, two-story cottage—has been preserved with style and reverence. The modern museum alongside, the **Centre Johannique,** shows a film (French only) while mannequins in period costume present Joan of Arc's amazing story. After she heard mystical voices, Joan walked 19 km (12 mi) to Vaucouleurs. Dressed and mounted like a man, she led her forces to lift the siege of Orléans, defeated the English, and escorted the unseated Charles VII to Reims, to be crowned king of France. Military missions after Orléans failed—

including an attempt to retake Paris—and she was captured at Compiègne. The English turned her over to the Church, which sent her to be tried by the Inquisition for witchcraft and heresy. She was convicted and burned at the stake in Rouen. One of the latest theories is that Jeanne d'Arc was no

A MODERN DAY HERO

As a figure, Joan of Arc remains pivotal to her *époque de transformation:* thanks to her and other leaders, civilization began to evolve from the medieval to the modern.

mere peasant but was distantly connected to France's royal family—a controversial proposal that many historians now discount. ✉ *2 rue de la Basilique* ☎ *03–29–06–95–86* ✉ *€3* ☉ *Apr.–Sept., daily 9–noon and 1:30–6:30; Oct.–Mar., Wed.–Mon. 10–noon and 2–5.*

The ornate late-19th-century **Basilique du Bois-Chenu** *(Bois Chenu Basilica),* high up the hillside above Domrémy, boasts enormous painted and mosaic panels expounding on Joan's legend in glowing Pre-Raphaelite tones. Outside lurk serene panoramic views over the emerald, gently rolling Meuse Valley.

In the nearby forest of Bois-Chenu, perhaps an ancient sacred wood, Jeanne d'Arc gathered flowers. Near the village of Coussy, she danced with other children at country fairs attended by Pierre de Bourlémont, the local seigneur, and his wife Beatrice—the Château of Bourlémont may still be seen. Associated with Coussey and Brixey are Saints Mihiel and Catherine, the two saints who, with the Archangel Saint-Michael, appeared before Joan. In the Chapel of Notre-Dame at Bermont, where Joan vowed to save France, are the statues that existed in her time.

ÉPINAL

㉑ *74 km (44 mi) southeast of Domrémy-la-Pucelle, (44 mi) southeast of Grand, 72 km (45 mi, south of Nancy.*

On the Moselle River at the feet of the Vosges, Épinal, a printing center since 1735, is famous throughout France for boldly colored prints, popular illustrations, and hand-colored stencils.

☺ The **Cité de l'image,** opened in 2003, combines a new public exhibition space with the private museum of the town's most famous printing workshop, l'Imagerie d'Epinal. ✉ *42 quai de Dogneville* ☎ *03–29–81–48–30* ✉ *€7* ☉ *Sept.–June, Mon.–Sat. 9:30–noon and 2–6, Sun. 10–noon and 2–6; July and Aug., Mon.–Sat. 9:30–12:30 and 1:30–6:30, Sun. 10–12:30 and 1:30–6. Open continuously every Fri.*

Fodor'sChoice ★ On an island in the Moselle in the center of Épinal, the spectacular **Musée Départemental d'Art Ancien et Contemporain** *(Museum of Antiquities and Contemporary Art)* is in a renovated 17th-century hospital, whose ancient classical traces are still visible under a dramatic barrel-vaulted skylight. The crowning jewel here is *Job Lectured by His Wife,* one of the greatest works of Georges de la Tour, the painter whose candlelighted scenes constitute Lorraine's most memorable artistic legacy. Other old masters, including works by Rembrandt, Fragonard, and Boucher, are on view, once part of the famous collection of the Princes of Salm. The museum also contains one of France's largest collections of contemporary art, as well as Gallo-Roman artifacts, rural tools, and local faïence. ✉ *1 pl. Lagarde* ☎ *03–29–82–20–33* ✉ *€4.60* ☉ *Wed.–Mon. 10–12:30 and 1:30–6.*

The small but bustling Vieille Ville is anchored by the lovely old **Basilique St-Maurice,** a low gray-stone basilica blending Romanesque and

Gothic styles. Note its sturdy belfry and deep, ornate, 15th-century entry porch. ⊠*Pl. St-Goëry* ☎*03–29–82–58–36.*

STRASBOURG

GETTING HERE

With the advent, in June 2007, of the TGV Est Européen (⊕*www. tgvesteuropeen.com*), the 11 direct trains from Paris, TGV (€51.60) and EuroCity (€46.20), became 16 returns trips a day, taking 2 hours, 20 minutes instead of 4 hours. In addition to the extra-regional links to Nancy, Metz, Sarbrucken, Lyon, and Geneva, Strasbourg's train station (⊠*20 pl. de la Gare*) is at the heart of the regional TER train system and has trains every 30 minutes to Colmar (€10) via Sélestat (€7.10), where you can change for omnibus services to Ribeauvillé (€2.10) and Rosheim/Molseim (for Dambach la Ville, €7.30, and Obernai, €5.10). Call the "on demand" service (☎*08–00–10–09–48*) in Sélestat to arrange transport to Orschwiller (Haut-Koenigsbourg). Buses head out to Obernai and Wangenbourg (connection at Wasselonne for Saverne) from the Gare Routière (☎*03–88–43–23-43*) in Place des Halles. Strasbourg's main train station is across the river from the city center, three-quarters of a mile from the cathedral, in the far west corner of the city.

EXPLORING

Though centered in the heart of Alsace 490 km (304 mi) east of Paris, and drawing appealingly on Alsatian Gemütlichkeit (coziness), the city of Strasbourg is a cosmopolitan French cultural center and the symbolic if unofficial capital of Europe. Against an irresistible backdrop of old half-timber houses, waterways, and the colossal single spire of its red-sandstone cathedral, which seems to insist imperiously that you pay homage to its majestic beauty, Strasbourg is an incongruously sophisticated mix of museums, charming neighborhoods like La Petite France, elite schools (including that notorious hothouse for blooming politicos, the École Nationale d'Administration, or National Administration School), international think tanks, and the European Parliament. The *strasbourgeoisie* have a lot to be proud of.

The Romans knew Strasbourg as Argentoratum before it came to be known as Strateburgum, or City of (Cross) Roads. After centuries as part of the Germanic Holy Roman Empire, the city was united with France in 1681, but retained independence regarding legislation, education, and religion under the honorific title Free Royal City. Since World

BIRD'S-EYE VIEW

Strasbourg's center is an eye-shape island created by the River Ill and canals that connect it to the Rhine. The Cathédrale Notre-Dame lies at the east end of the island, and La Petite France lies at the west end, about ⅓ km (¼ mi) away. Narrow pedestrian streets lined with shops and restaurants connect the two, so that the whole island is just one mesh of Alsatian fare.

War II Strasbourg has become a symbolic city, embodying Franco-German reconciliation and the wider idea of a united Europe. The city center is effectively an island within two arms of the River Ill; most major sites are found here, but the northern districts also contain some fine buildings erected over the last 100 years, culminating in the Palais de l'Europe. You can buy a one-day pass for all the city museums for €6 or a three-day pass for €8.

Note to drivers: the configuration of downtown streets makes it difficult to approach the center via the autoroute exit marked strasbourg centre. Instead, hold out for the exit marked place de l'étoile and follow signs to cathédrale/centre ville. At Place du Corbeau, veer left across the Ill, and go straight to the Place Gutenberg parking garage, a block from the cathedral.

THE HISTORIC HEART

This central area, from the cathedral to picturesque Petite France, concentrates the best of Old Strasbourg, with its twisting backstreets, flower-lined courts, tempting shops, and inviting *winstubs* (wine taverns).

THE MAIN ATTRACTIONS

★ ☺ ☞ ㉒ **Cathédrale Notre-Dame.** Dark pink, ornately carved Vosges sandstone masonry covers the facade of this most novel and Germanic of French cathedrals, a triumph of Gothic art begun in 1176. Not content with the outlines of the walls themselves, medieval builders lacily encased them with slender stone shafts. The off-center **spire,** finished in 1439, looks absurdly fragile as it tapers skyward some 466 feet; you can climb 330 steps to the base of the spire to take in sweeping views of the city, the Vosges Mountains, and the Black Forest.

The interior presents a stark contrast to the facade: it's older (mostly finished by 1275), and the nave's broad windows emphasize the horizontal rather than the vertical. Note Hans Hammer's ornately sculpted pulpit (1484–86) and the richly painted 14th- to 15th-century organ loft that rises from pillar to ceiling. The left side of the nave is flanked with richly colored Gothic windows honoring the early leaders of the Holy Roman Empire—Otto I and II, and Heinrich I and II. The **choir** is not ablaze with stained glass but framed by chunky Romanesque masonry. The elaborate 16th-century **Chapelle St-Laurent,** to the left of the choir, merits a visit; turn to the right to admire the **Pilier des Anges** (Angels' Pillar), an intricate column dating from 1230.

Just beyond the pillar, the Renaissance machinery of the 16th-century **Horloge Astronomique** (Astronomical Clock) whirs into action daily at 12:30 pm (but the line starts at the south door at 11:45 am): macabre clockwork figures enact the story of Christ's Passion. One of the highlights: when the apostles walk past, a likeness of Christ as a rooster crows three times. ⊠*Pl. de la Cathédrale* 🕮*Clock €1, spire platform €3* ☉*Cathedral open daily 7–11:30 and 12:40–7.*

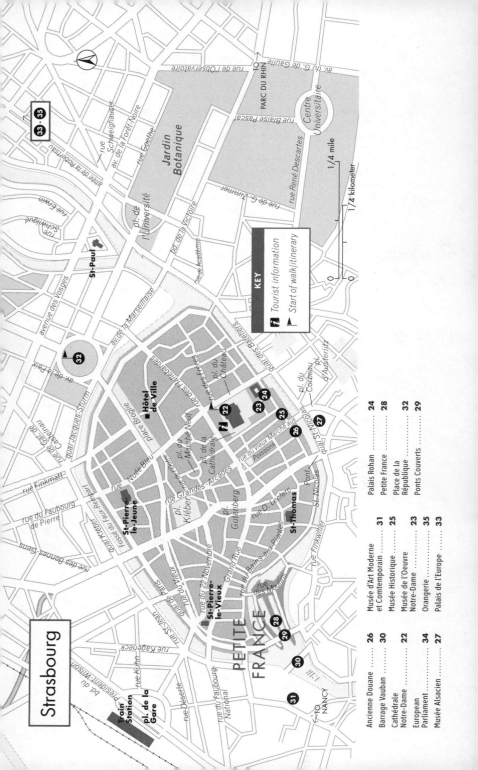

Strasbourg

KEY

🛈 Tourist information

▲ Start of walk/itinerary

0 ———— 1/4 mile

0 ———— 1/4 kilometer

㉗ Musée Alsacien *(Alsatian Museum)*. In this labyrinthine half-timber home, with layers of carved balconies sagging over a cobbled inner courtyard, local interiors have been faithfully reconstituted. The diverse activities of blacksmiths, clog makers, saddlers, and makers of artificial flowers are explained with the help of old-time craftsmen's tools and equipment. ✉ *23 quai St-Nicolas* ☎ *03–88–52–50–01* 💶*€4* 🕐 *Wed.–Mon. 10–6.*

㉛ Musée d'Art Moderne et Contemporain *(Modern and Contemporary Art Museum)*. A magnificent sculpture of a building (designed by architect Adrien Faiensilber) that sometimes dwarfs its contents, this spectacular museum frames a relatively thin collection of new, esoteric, and unsung 20th-century art. Downstairs, a permanent collection of Impressionists and Modernists up to 1950 is heavily padded with local heroes but happily fleshed out with some striking furniture; all are juxtaposed for contrasting and comparing, with little to no chronological flow. Upstairs, harsh, spare works must work hard to live up to their setting; few contemporary masters are featured. Drawings, watercolors, and paintings by Gustave Doré, a native of Alsace, are enshrined in a separate room. ✉ *1 pl. Hans-Jean Arp* ☎ *03–88–23–31–31* 💶*€5* 🕐 *Tues., Wed., Fri., Sat. 11–7, Sun. 10–6, Thurs. noon–10.*

★ **㉓ Musée de l'Oeuvre Notre-Dame** *(Cathedral Museum)*. There's more to this museum than the usual assembly of dilapidated statues rescued from the cathedral before they fell off (you'll find *those* rotting in the Barrage Vauban). Sacred sculptures stand in churchlike settings, and secular exhibits are enhanced by the building's fine old architecture. Subjects include a wealth of Flemish and Upper Rhine paintings, stained glass, gold objects, and massive, heavily carved furniture. ✉ *3 pl. du Château* ☎ *03–88–32–88–17* 💶*€4* 🕐 *Tues.–Sun. 10–6.*

★ **㉔ Palais Rohan** *(Rohan Palace)*. The exterior of Robert de Cotte's massive neoclassical palace (1732–42) may be starkly austere, but there's plenty of glamour inside. Decorator Robert le Lorrain's magnificent ground-floor rooms are led by the great **Salon d'Assemblée** (Assembly Room) and the book- and tapestry-lined **Bibliothèque des Cardinaux** (Cardinals' Library). The library leads to a series of less august rooms that house the **Musée des Arts Décoratifs** (Decorative Arts Museum) and its elaborate display of ceramics. This is a comprehensive presentation of works by Hannong, a porcelain manufacturer active in Strasbourg from 1721 to 1782, dinner services by other local kilns reveal the influence of Chinese porcelain. The **Musée des Beaux-Arts** (Fine Arts Museum), also

---

FREE BEER & PRETZELS

Kronenbourg has free tours of its principal brewery just outside town (⊕ 68 rte. d'Oberhaubergen ☎ 03–88–27–41–58); from Place. Kléber, take Bus No. 7 to Rue Jacob or Tram A to St-Florent, and follow Route d'Oberhausbergen. There are tours weekdays at 10, 11, 2, 3 and 4, but if you show up and the next group isn't filled, you can go along; reservations are required. The hour-long tour culminates in a half-hour tasting session where you can try two beers and eat as many pretzels as you like.

7

in the château, includes master-works of European painting from Giotto and Memling to El Greco, Rubens, and Goya. Downstairs, the **Musée Archéologique** (Archaeology Museum) displays regional archaeological finds, including gorgeous Merovingian treasures. ⊠*2 pl. du Château* ☎*03–88–52–50–00* ☞*€4 each museum, €6 joint ticket* ☉*Wed.–Mon. 10–6.*

28 **Petite France.** With its gingerbread
Fodor'sChoice half-timber houses that seem to
★ lean precariously over the canals of the Ill, its shops, and inviting little restaurants, this is the most magical neighborhood in Strasbourg.

GETTING AROUND

Strasbourg has an extensive tram and bus network; most of the efficient lines of Companie des Transports Strasbourgeois (⊕*www. cts-strasbourg.fr/cts2.html*) leave from the train station at 20 place de la Gare, travel down Rue du Vieux Marché aux Vins, and part ways at Place de la République. Tickets are good for one hour and can also be used on Strasbourg's sleek tram that travels from the train station to Place de l'Homme and out to the burbs.

Historically Alsatian in style, "Little France"—the district is just southwest of the center—is filled with Renaissance buildings that have survived plenty of wars. Wander up and down the tiny streets that connect Rue du Bain-aux-Plantes and Rue des Dentelles to Grand-Rue, and stroll the waterfront promenade.

ALSO WORTH SEEING

26 **Ancienne Douane** *(Old Customs House).* In 2000, a terrible fire ravaged this old customs house set on the Ill River; extensive repairs are expected to continue to 2008. When operational, the airport-hangar scale and flexible walls here lend themselves to enormous expositions of old-master paintings as well as archaeology and history. ⊠*1 rue de Vieux-Marché-aux-Poissons* ☎*03–88–52–50–00* ☞*Call ahead.*

30 **Barrage Vauban** *(Vauban Dam).* Just beyond the Ponts Couverts is the grass-roof Vauban Dam, built by its namesake in 1682. Climb to the top for wide-angle views of the Ponts Couverts and, on the other side, the Museum of Modern Art. Then stroll through its echoing galleries, where magnificent cathedral statuary lies scattered among pigeon droppings. ⊠*Ponts Couverts* ☞*Free* ☉*Mid-Oct.–mid-Mar., daily 9–7; mid-Mar.–mid-Oct., daily 9–8.*

25 **Musée Historique** *(Local History Museum).* This museum, in a step-gabled slaughterhouse dating from 1588, is closed for extensive renovation and not expected to reopen before summer 2008. It contains a collection of maps, armor, arms, bells, uniforms, traditional dress, printing paraphernalia, and two huge relief models of Strasbourg. ⊠*3 pl. de la Grande-Boucherie* ☎*03–88–52–50–00.*

29 **Ponts Couverts** *(Covered Bridges).* These three bridges, distinguished by their four stone towers, were once covered with wooden shelters. Part of the 14th-century ramparts that framed Old Strasbourg, they span the Ill as it branches into four fingerlike canals.

BEYOND THE ILL

If you've seen the center and have time to strike out in new directions, head across the Ill to view two architectural landmarks unrelated to Strasbourg's famous medieval past: Place de la République and the Palais de l'Europe.

SIGHTS TO SEE

34 European Parliament. This sleek building testifies to the growing importance of the governing body of the European Union, which used to make do with rental offices in the Palais de l'Europe. Eurocrats continue to commute between Brussels, Luxembourg, and Strasbourg, hauling their staff and files with them. One week per month, visitors can slip into the hemicycle and witness the tribune in debate, complete with simultaneous translation. ⊠*Behind Palais de l'Europe* ☎*03–88–17–52–85* ⊠*Free* ⊘*Call ahead to verify Parliament in session.*

35 Orangerie. Like a private backyard for the Eurocrats in the Palais de l'Europe, this delightful park is laden with flowers and punctuated by noble copper beeches. It contains a lake and, close by, a small reserve of rare birds, including flamingos and noisy local storks. ⊠*Av. de l'Europe.*

33 Palais de l'Europe. Designed by Paris architect Henri Bernard in 1977, this Continental landmark is headquarters to the Council of Europe, founded in 1949 and independent of the European Union. A guided tour introduces you to the intricacies of its workings and may allow you to eavesdrop on a session. Arrange your tour by telephone in advance; appointments are fixed according to language demands and usually take place in the afternoon. Note: you must provide a *pièce d'identité* (ID) before entering. ⊠*Av. de l'Europe* ☎*03–90–21–49–40 for appointments* ⊠*Free* ⊘*Guided tours by appointment weekdays.*

▶ **32 Place de la République.** The spacious layout and ponderous architecture of this monumental *cirque* (circle) have nothing in common with the Vieille Ville except for the local red sandstone. A different hand was at work here—that of occupying Germans, who erected the former Ministry (1902), the Academy of Music (1882–92), and the Palais du Rhin (1883–88). The handsome neo-Gothic church of **St-Paul** and the pseudo-Renaissance **Palais de l'Université** (University Palace), constructed between 1875 and 1885, also bear the German stamp. Heavy turn-of-the-20th-century houses, some reflecting the whimsical curves of the Art Nouveau style, frame **Allée de la Robertsau**, a tree-lined boulevard that would not look out of place in Berlin.

STRASBOURG BY WATER

Strasbourg is a big town, but the center is easily explored by foot, or, more romantically, by boat. Fluvial Strasbourg (☎*03–88–84–13–13* ⊕*www.strasbourg.port.fr*) organizes 70-minute boat tours along the Ill four times a day in winter and up to every half hour starting at 9:30 during the day from April through October (plus nocturnal tours until 9:30 pm May–September). Boats leave from behind the Palais Rohan; the cost is €7.40.

7

WHERE TO STAY & EAT

$$$$
Fodor'sChoice
★
✕ **Le Buerehiesel.** This lovely Alsatian farmhouse, reconstructed in the Orangerie park, warrants a pilgrimage if you're willing to pay for the finest cooking in Alsace. Antoine Westermann stands in the upper echelon of chefs while remaining true to the ingredients and specialties of his native Alsace: *schniederspaetzle* (onion-perfumed ravioli) with frogs' legs, steamed sea bass served with marinated vegetables, braised goose, and plum tarte tatin with vanilla ice cream. Two smaller salons are cozy, but most tables are set in a modern annex that is mostly glass and steel. In any event, plump European *parlementaires* come on foot; others might come on their knees. ⊠4 *parc de l'Orangerie* ☎03–88–45–56–65 ⊕*www.buerehiesel.fr* ⚑*Reservations essential* ▤*AE, DC, MC, V* ☺ *Closed Sun. and Mon., 3 wks Jan., and 3 wks Aug.*

> ### CROCODILE TEARS
>
> As for Au Crocodile's name, it refers to a stuffed specimen brought back by a Strasbourg general from Napoléon's Egyptian campaign, which took pride of place in a tavern that centuries later became this luxe outpost, today more central than the Buerehiesel and nearly as revered.

★ $$$$
✕ **Au Crocodile.** As one of the temples of Alsatian-French haute cuisine, this has the expected grand salon—asparkle with skylights and a spectacular 19th-century mural showing the *strasbourgeoisie* at a country fair—an exhaustive wine list, and some of the most dazzling dishes around, courtesy of master chef Émile Jung. Fittingly for a restaurant founded in the early 1800s, you'll get a real taste of the-way-Alsace-was here but given a nouvelle spin. Delights include truffle turnover, warmed goose liver with rhubarb, lobster with vermicelli and pink pepper, bitter-chocolate cherry cake, and grapefruit sorbet with a green tea "cigarette." Even more urban finesse is given to the theme menus that are occasionally offered (recent homages include those to the Brothers Goncourt, Goethe, and Gutenberg). The wine cellar is vast and has plenty of tokay pinot gris, Riesling, and other luscious Alsatian vintages to choose from. ⊠10 *rue de l'Outre* ☎03–88–32–13–02 ⊕*www.au-crocodile.com* ⚑*Reservations essential*Jacket and tie ▤*AE, DC, MC, V* ☺*Closed Sun. and Mon., late Dec.–early Jan., and 3 wks in July.*

★ $–$$$
✕ **Chez Yvonne.** Behind red-checked curtains you can find artists, tourists, lovers, and heads of state sitting elbow-to-elbow in this classic winstub, founded in 1873. All come to savor steaming platters of local specialties: watch for duck confit on choucroute, and *tête de veau* (calf's head) in white wine. Warm Alsatian fabrics dress tables and lamps, the china is regional, the photos historic—all making for chic, not kitsch. ⊠10 *rue du Sanglier* ☎03–88–32–84–15 ⚑*Reservations essential* ▤*AE, DC, MC, V.*

$$
✕ **Maison Kammerzell.** This restaurant glories in its richly carved, half-timber 15th-century building—probably the most familiar house in Strasbourg. Fight your way through the tourist hordes on the terrace and ground floor to one of the atmospheric rooms above, with their gleaming wooden furniture and stained-glass windows. Foie gras and choucroute are best bets, though you may want to try the chef's pet discovery, chou-

croute with freshwater fish. ✉*16 pl. de la Cathédrale* ☎*03–88–32–42–14* ⊕*www.maison-kammerzell.com* ⊟*AE, DC, MC, V.*

$ ✗ **Strissel.** This cozy, rustic winstub near the cathedral, in business since the 16th century and in the same family since 1920, finally changed hands in October 2006 and is now owned by Mr. Devalmigere. Happily, he has not changed anything of the charming decor, but only added lights. It has a good choice of Alsace wines and some of the finest choucroute in town (the chef is still the same), often served with pike-perch as a specialty. Try for a room upstairs to admire the stained-glass windows with their tales of life in the vines. ✉*5 pl. de la Grande-Boucherie* ☎*03–88–32–14–73* ⊟*MC, V.*

$$$$ ★ 🏨 **Régent-Petite France.** Opposite the Ponts Couverts and surrounded by canals, this centuries-old former ice factory—replete with noble pediment and mansard roofs—has been transformed into a boldly modern luxury hotel. Delightfully set in the heart of Strasbourg's quaintest quarter, La Petite France, the hotel welcomes you with a spacious marble vestibule, vivid graffiti art, and Le Pont Tournant, an eye-popping modernistic restaurant done up in white, pinks, and reds (enjoy its summer tables over the torrent). Upstairs, Philippe Starck–inspired sculptural room furnishings contrast sharply with the half-timber houses and roaring river viewed from nearly every room. There's no skimping on the amenities—both the beds and the bathrooms are divine. ✉*5 rue des Moulins, 67000* ☎*03–88–76–43–43* 🖷*03–88–76–43–76* ⊕*www.regent-hotels.com* ✈*72 rooms* ♨*In-room: refrigerator. In-hotel: restaurant, bar, public Wi-Fi, some pets allowed (fee)* ⊟*AE, DC, MC, V* ⦿*MAP.*

$$–$$$ 🏨 **Cathédrale.** Expansion and renovation have brought this superbly positioned hotel more than up to par. A sleek marble lobby abuts lounges, a bar, and breakfast room that are rich with ancient beams and sandstone. Rooms feature dark timbers, and most have windows framing a view of the 16th-century half-timber Maison Kammerzell or the cathedral. ✉*13 pl. de la Cathédrale, 67000* ☎*03–88–22–12–12* 🖷*03–88–23–28–00* ⊕*www.hotel-cathedrale.fr* ✈*47 rooms* ♨*In-room: refrigerator, Wi-Fi. In-hotel: bar, some pets allowed (fee)* ⊟*AE, DC, MC, V* ⦿*BP.*

$–$$ 🏨 **Gutenberg.** In a 250-year-old mansion just off Place Gutenberg, this sturdy urban hotel has rooms with fresh, old-fashioned wallpaper, chandeliers, and built-in wood cabinetry. Charming little fifth-floor lofts reveal roof timbers. The skylighted breakfast room is inviting. The location is sweet and just a few blocks from the cathedral. ✉*31 rue des Serruriers, 67000* ☎*03–88–32–17–15* 🖷*03–88–75–76–67* ⊕*www.hotel-gutenberg.com* ✈*42 rooms* ♨*In-room: ethernet* ⊟*MC, V* ⦿*BP.*

$–$$ 🏨 **Rohan.** Across from the cathedral on a picturesque pedestrian street, this modest little hotel has a welcoming air and a marvelous sense of French style, from the Louis XV furniture to the gilt mirrors. Though swagged in rich fabrics, rooms are fully modern, with impeccable all-tile baths. ✉*17 rue Maroquin, 67000* ☎*03–88–32–85–11* 🖷*03–88–75–65–37* ⊕*www.hotel-rohan.com* ✈*36 rooms* ♨*In-room: refrigerator, Wi-Fi (some). In-hotel: parking (fee), some pets allowed (fee), public Wi-Fi* ⊟*AE, DC, MC, V.*

7

NIGHTLIFE & THE ARTS

The annual **Festival Musica** (*Contemporary Music Festival* ✉*1 pl. Dauphine* ☎*03–88–23–46–46* ⊕*www.festival-musica.org*) is held in September and October. The **Opéra National du Rhin** (✉*19 pl. Broglie* ☎*03–88–75–48–23*) has a sizable repertoire. Classical concerts are staged by the **Orchestre Philharmonique** (✉*Palais des Congrès* ☎*03–88–15–09–09*).

The Vieille Ville neighborhood east of the cathedral, along Rue des Frères, is the nightlife hangout for university students and twentysomethings; among its handful of heavily frequented bars is **La Laiterie** (✉*13 rue Hohwald* ☎*03–88–23–72–37* ⊕*www.laiterie.artefact.org*), a multiplex concert hall showcasing art, workshops, and music ranging from electronic to post-rock and reggae. **Le Chalet** (✉*376 rte. de la Wantzenau* ☎*03–88–31–18–31*) is the biggest and most popular disco, but it's some 10 km (6 mi) northeast of the city center.

SHOPPING

The lively city center is full of boutiques, including chocolate shops and delicatessens selling locally made foie gras. Look for warm paisley linens and rustic homespun fabrics, Alsatian pottery, and local wines. Forming the city's commercial heart are **Rue des Hallebardes,** next to the cathedral; **Rue des Grandes Arcades,** with its shopping mall; and **Place Kléber.** An **antiques market** takes place behind the cathedral on Rue du Vieil-Hôpital, Rue des Bouchers, and Place de la Grande Boucherie every Wednesday and Saturday morning.

ALSACE

The Rhine River forms the eastern boundary of both Alsace and France. But the best of Alsace is not found along the Rhine's industrial waterfront. Instead it's in the Ill Valley at the base of the Vosges, southwest of cosmopolitan Strasbourg. Northwest is Saverne and the beginning of the **Route du Vin,** the great Alsace Wine Road, which winds its way south through the Vosges foothills, fruitful vineyards, and medieval villages that would serve well as stage sets for Rossini's *William Tell.* Signs for the road help you keep your bearings on the twisting way south, and you'll find limitless opportunities to stop at wineries and sample the local wares. The Wine Road stretches 170 km (100 mi) between Thann and Marienheim and is easily accessible from Strasbourg or Colmar. Many of the towns and villages have designated "vineyard trails" winding between towns (a bicycle will help you cover a lot of territory). Riquewihr and

WAIFS-TO-GO

The illustrator Waltz Hansi, popular at the turn of the 20th century, created the ubiquitous wide-eyed waifs in Alsatian folk costume that adorn souvenir mugs, dish towels, coasters, and ashtrays on sale around the region; his original work was less cliché.

Ribeauvillé—accessible by bus from Colmar and Séléstat rail stations—are connected by an especially picturesque route. Along the way, stop at any *"Dégustation"* sign for a free tasting and pick up brochures on the "Alsace Wine Route" at any tourist office.

OBERNAI

③ *30 km (19 mi) southwest of Strasbourg via A35/ N422.*

GETTING HERE

Strasbourg's train station (✉*20 pl. de la Gare*) is at the heart of the regional TER train system and has trains every 30 minutes to Colmar (€10)—the city at the southern end of Alsace's Route du Vin—via Séléstat (€7.10), where you can change for omnibus services to Rosheim/ Molsheim (for Obernai, €5.10). Strasbourg also has an extensive tram and bus network that includes buses to Obernai from its Gare Routière in Place des Halles.

EXPLORING

Many visitors begin their saunter down the Route du Vin at Obernai, a thriving, colorful Renaissance market town named for the patron saint of Alsace. Head to the central town enclosed by the ramparts to find some particularly Nikon-friendly sites, including a medieval belfry, Renaissance well, and late-19th-century church.

Place du Marché, in the heart of town, is dominated by the stout, square 13th-century **Kapelturm Beffroi** *(Chapel Tower Belfry)*, topped by a pointed steeple flanked at each corner by frilly openwork turrets added in 1597.

An elaborate Renaissance well near the belfry, the **Puits à Six-Seaux** *(Well of Six Buckets)*, was constructed in 1579; its name recalls the six buckets suspended from its metal chains.

The twin spires of the parish church of **St-Pierre–St-Paul** compete with the belfry for skyline preeminence. They date, like the rest of the church, from the 1860s, although the 1504 Holy Sepulchre altarpiece in the north transept is a survivor from the previous church. Other points of interest include the flower-bedecked **Place de l'Etoile** and the **Hôtel de Ville**, whose council chamber and historic balcony can be viewed.

WHERE TO STAY & EAT

$–$$ ✕▥ **L'Ami Fritz.** White-shuttered, flower-bedecked, with sunny yellow
Fodor'sChoice walls, this welcoming inn combines style, rustic warmth, and three
★   generations of family tradition. Set several miles west of Obernai, the reader-recommended, picture-perfect 18th-century stone house has impeccable guest rooms decked in toile de Jouy and homespun checks (opt for rooms in the main hotel, not in the adjacent annex). Top attraction here is the fine restaurant, where you can feast on Patrick Fritz's sophisticated twists on regional specialties, including featherlight blood sausage in flaky pastry, a delicate choucroute of grated turnips, strudel of black pudding, fillet of zander with beer-flavored choucroute, or the gratinéed freshwater fish braised in Sylvaner. Don't miss the fruity

7

red wine, an Ottrott exclusive, or taking a gander at the town's two medieval castles. The restaurant is closed Wednesday, except for hotel clients. ⊠ *8 rue des Châteaux, 5 km (3 mi) west of Obernai, 67530 Ottrott* ☏ *03–88–95–80–81* 🖷 *03–88–95–84–85* ⊕ *www.amifritz. com* ⟿ *22 rooms* ♿ *In-room: a/c (some), refrigerator, Wi-Fi. In-hotel: restaurant, some pets allowed (fee)* ▤ *AE, DC, MC, V* ⊗ *Closed last 2 wks July, mid-Jan. for 2 wks* ⊖| *MAP.*

$ ⤬⌸ **La Cloche.** Stained glass, dark oak, and Hansi-like murals set the tone in this sturdy half-timber 14th-century landmark on Obernai's market square. Standard local dishes and blackboard specials draw locals on market days. Rooms are well equipped and country-pretty; two double-decker duplex rooms accommodate four. ⊠ *90 rue du Général-Gouraud, 67210* ☏ *03–88–95–52–89* 🖷 *03–88–95–07–63* ⊕ *www.la-cloche.com* ⟿ *20 rooms* ♿ *In-room: a/c (some), dial-up. In-hotel: restaurant, bar, public Wi-Fi* ▤ *MC, V* ⊗ *Closed 2 wks in Jan.* ⊖| *MAP.*

SHOPPING

Dietrich (⊠ *58 and 74 rue du Général-Gouraud* ☏ *03–88–95–57–58* ⊕ *www.dietrich-obernai.fr*) has a varied selection of Beauvillé linens, locally handblown Alsatian wineglasses, and Obernai-patterned china.

MONT-STE-ODILE

★ ③⑦ *12 km (8 mi) southwest of Obernai via Ottrott.*

Mont-Ste-Odile, a 2,500-foot hill, has been an important religious and military site for 3,000 years. The eerie 9½-km-long (6-mi-long) **Mur Païen**, up to 12 feet high and, in parts, several feet thick, rings the summit; its mysterious origins and purpose still baffle archaeologists. The Romans established a settlement here and, at the start of the 8th century Odile, daughter of Duke Etichon of Obernai, who had been born blind, founded a convent on the same spot after receiving her sight while being baptized. The relatively modern convent is now a workaday hostelry for modern pilgrims on group retreats. Odile—the patron saint of Alsace—died here in ad 720; her sarcophagus rests in the 12th-century **Chapelle Ste-Odile.** The spare, Romanesque **Chapelle de la Croix** adjoins Ste-Odile. Various regional bus lines can connect you with Mont-St-Odile.

BARR

③⑧ *11 km (7 mi) southeast of Mont-Ste-Odile, 8 km (5 mi) south of Obernai.*

Surrounded by vineyards that harvest some of the finest vintages of Sylvaner and Gewürztraminer wines, Barr is a thriving, semi-industrial town surrounded by vines, with some charming narrow streets lined with half-timber houses (notably Rue des Cigognes, Rue Neuve, and the tiny Rue de l'Essieu), a cheerful 17th-century Hôtel de Ville, and a decorative arts museum. Most buildings date from after a catastrophic

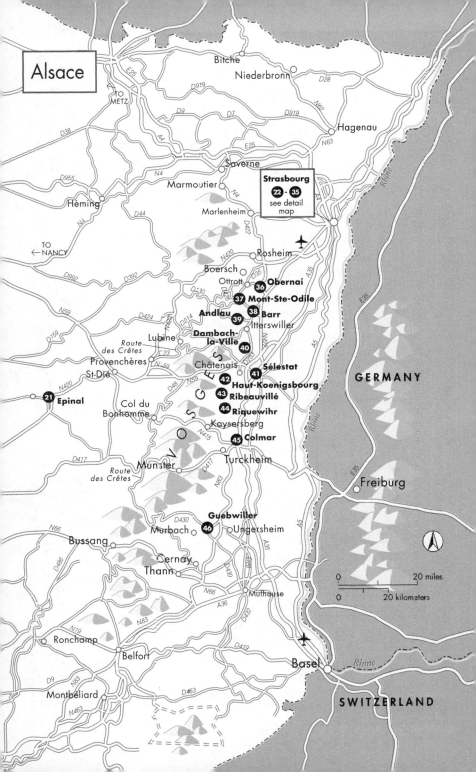

Alsace

Bitche

Niederbronn D28

Hagenau

TO METZ

TO ← NANCY

Strasbourg
22 - **35**
see detail map

Rosheim

Boersch

Ottrott

36 Obernai

37 Mont-Ste-Odile

39 Andlau

38 Barr

Itterswiller

Dambach-la-Ville

40

Châtenois

41 Sélestat

42 Haut-Koenigsbourg

43 Ribeauvillé

44 Riquewihr

Kaysersberg

45 Colmar

Turckheim

21 Epinal

Col du Bonhomme

Münster

Route des Crêtes

Provenchères

St-Dié

Lubine

Route des Crêtes

GERMANY

Freiburg

46 Guebwiller

Murbach

Ungersheim

Bussang

Cernay

Thann

Mulhouse

Ronchamp

Belfort

Montbéliard

Basel

SWITZERLAND

Rhine

0   20 miles

0   20 kilometers

fire in 1678; the only medieval survivor is the Romanesque tower of St-Martin, the Protestant church.

Admire original furniture, local porcelain, earthenware, and pewter at the **Musée de la Folie Marco,** in a mansion built by local magistrate Félix Marco in 1763. One section of the museum explains the traditional process of *schlittage*: sleds, bearing bundles of freshly sawed tree trunks, once slid down the forest slopes over a "corduroy road" made of logs. ⊠*30 rue du Dr-Sultzer* ☎*03–88–08–94–72, 03–88–08–66–65 winter* 🎟*€4* ☉*July–Sept., Wed.–Mon. 10–noon and 2–6; May, June, and Oct., weekends 10–noon and 2–6.*

ANDLAU

39 *3 km (2 mi) southwest of Barr on the Route du Vin.*

Andlau has long been known for its magnificent abbey. Built in the 12th century, the **Abbaye d'Andlau** has the richest ensemble of Romanesque sculpture in Alsace. Sculpted vines wind their way around the doorway as a reminder of wine's time-honored importance to the local economy. A statue of a female bear, the abbey mascot—bears used to roam local forests and were bred at the abbey until the 16th century—can be seen in the north transept. Legend has it that Queen Richarde, spurned by her husband, Charles the Fat, founded the abbey in ad 887 when an angel enjoined her to construct a church on a site to be shown to her by a female bear.

WHERE TO STAY & EAT

$$ ✕🏠 **Arnold.** This yellow-wall, half-timber hillside hotel overlooks the cute wine village of Itterswiller; most rooms have views across the vines. The cheapest rooms, on the top floor, have a shower and no balcony; the priciest have a bath and a balcony facing south. The wood-beam lobby with its wrought-iron staircase has the same quaint charm as the hotel's winstub-style restaurant (no dinner Sunday, closed Monday, May to November) across the street, with its old winepress and local Alsace wines served by the jug; homemade foie gras and venison in cranberry sauce top the menu, along with sauerkraut and *baeckeoffe* (meat-and-potato casserole). ⊠*98 rte. des Vins, 3 km (2 mi) south of Andlau on D253, 67140 Itterswiller* ☎*03–88–85–50–58* 🖨*03–88–85–55–54* ⊕*www.hotel-arnold.com* ⇆*29 rooms* ♿*In-room: no a/c, refrigerator, ethernet. In-hotel: restaurant, some pets allowed (fee), public Wi-Fi* ▤*AE, MC, V* ⸂⊙⸃*MAP.*

DAMBACH-LA-VILLE

40 *8 km (5 mi) southeast of Andlau via Itterswiller.*

GETTING HERE

Strasbourg's train station (⊠*20 pl. de la Gare*) is at the heart of the regional TER train system and has trains every 30 minutes to Colmar (€10)—the city at the southern end of Alsace's Route du Vin—via Sélestat (€7.10), where you can change for omnibus services to Rosheim/ Molseim (for Dambach la Ville, €7.30).

EXPLORING

One of the prettiest villages along the Alsace Wine Road, Dambach-la-Ville is a fortified medieval town protected by ramparts and three powerful 13th-century gateways. It's particularly rich in half-timber, high-roof houses from the 17th and 18th centuries, clustered mainly around **Place du Marché** (Market Square). Also on the square is the 16th-century **Hôtel de Ville** (Town Hall). As you walk the charming streets, notice the wrought-iron signs and roof-top oriels.

WHERE TO STAY & EAT

¢ ✕⌃ **Le Raisin d'Or.** Set around the corner from the village church and halfway up the street that climbs straight into the vineyards, this unpretentious hotel is where you'll get a down-to-earth welcome and a hearty meal in a typical Alsace dining room (closed Monday and Tuesday) with heavy wooden tables and checked tablecloths. Hearty fare like sauerkraut, sausage meat, and potatoes will make you feel like the cook is one of those geese-stuffers. Rooms are on the small side, with functional dark-wood furnishings, but the best have balconies overlooking the street. ⌂28 bis, rue Clemenceau, 67650 ⌂03–88–92–48–66 ⌂03–88–92–61–42 ⊕www.au-raisin-dor.com ⌿8 rooms ⌂In-room: no a/c, refrigerator. In-hotel: restaurant, bar ⊟DC, MC, V ⊗Closed mid-Dec.–early Jan. ⁌⊖MAP.

SÉLESTAT

④ 9 km (5½ mi) southeast of Dambach via D210 and N422, 47 km (29 mi) southwest of Strasbourg.

GETTING HERE

Strasbourg's train station (⌂20 pl. de la Gare) is at the heart of the regional TER train system and has trains every 30 minutes to Colmar via Sélestat, €7.10.

EXPLORING

Sélestat, midway between Strasbourg and Colmar, is a lively, historic town with a Romanesque church and a library of medieval manuscripts (and, important to note, a railway station with trains to and from Strasbourg). Head directly to the Vieille Ville and explore the quarter on foot.

The church of **St-Foy** (⌂Pl. du Marché-Vert) dates from between 1155 and 1190; its Romanesque facade remains largely intact (the spires were added in the 19th century), as does the 140-foot octagonal tower over the crossing. Sadly, the interior was mangled over the centuries, chiefly by the Jesuits; their most inspired legacy is the Baroque pulpit of 1733 depicting the life of St. Francis Xavier. Note the Romanesque bas-relief next to the baptistery, originally the lid of a sarcophagus.

Among the precious medieval and Renaissance manuscripts on display at the **Bibliothèque Humaniste** *(Humanist Library)*, a major library founded in 1452 and installed in the former Halle aux Blés, are a 7th-century lectionary and a 12th-century Book of Miracles. There's also a town register from 1521, with the first-ever recorded reference to a

> **FLOWER POWERED**
>
> The colorful Corso Fleuri Flower Carnival takes place on the second Sunday in August, when Sélestat decks itself—and the floats in its vivid parade—with a magnificent display of dahlias.

Christmas tree! ⊠*1 rue de la Bibliothèque* ☎*03–88–58–07–20* ⊠*€3.70* ⊙*Sept.–June, Mon. and Wed.–Fri. 9–noon and 2–6, Sat. 9–noon; July and Aug., Mon. and Wed.–Fri. 9–noon and 2–6, weekends 2–5.*

HAUT-KOENIGSBOURG

㊷ *11 km (7 mi) west of Sélestat via D159.*

One of the most popular spots in Alsace is the romantic, crag-top castle of Haut-Koenigsbourg, originally built as a fortress in the 12th century.

Fodor'sChoice ★ ☺ The ruins of the **Château du Haut-Koenigsbourg** were presented by the town of Sélestat to German emperor Wilhelm II in 1901. The château looked just as a kaiser thought one should, and he restored it with some diligence and no lack of imagination—squaring the main tower's original circle, for instance. The site, panorama, drawbridge, and amply furnished imperial chambers may lack authenticity, but they are undeniably dramatic. Call the "on demand" service (☎*08–00–10–09–48*) in Sélestat to arrange transport to Orschwiller (Haut-Koenigsbourg). ☎*03–88–82–50–60* ⊠*€7.50* ⊙*Nov.–Feb., daily 9:45–noon and 1–5; Mar. and Oct., daily 9:45–5; Apr., May, and Sept., daily 9:30–5:30; June–Aug., daily 9:30–6:30.*

RIBEAUVILLÉ

㊸ Fodor'sChoice ★ *13 km (8 mi) south of Haut-Koenigsbourg via St-Hippolyte, 16 km (10 mi) southwest of Sélestat.*

GETTING HERE

Strasbourg's train station (⊠*20 pl. de la Gare*) is at the heart of the regional TER train system and has trains every 30 minutes to Colmar (€10) via Sélestat (€7.10), where you can change for omnibus services to Ribeauvillé (€2.10).

EXPLORING

The beautiful half-timber town of Ribeauvillé, surrounded by rolling vineyards and three imposing châteaux, produces some of the best wines in Alsace. (The Trimbach family has made Riesling and superb Gewürztraminer here since 1626.) The town's narrow main street, crowded with winstubs, pottery shops, bakeries, and wine sellers, is bisected by the 13th-century **Tour des Bouchers,** a clock-belfry completed (gargoyles and all) in the 15th century. Storks' nests crown several towers in the village, while streets are adorned with quaint shop signs, fairy-tale turrets, and tour guides herding the crowds with directions in French and German. Make for the Place de la Marie and its Hôtel de Ville to see its famous collection of silver-gilt 16th-century tankards and chalices.

WHERE TO STAY & EAT

¢–$ ✕ **Zum Pfifferhüs.** This is a true-blue winstub, with yellowed murals, glowing lighting, and great local wines available by the glass. The cooking is pure Alsace, with German-scale portions of choucroute, ham hock, and fruit tarts. No smoking here. ✉14 Grand-Rue 🕾03–89–73–62–28 ⚓Reservations essential ▱MC, V ◷Closed Wed. and Thurs., Feb., and 2 wks in July.

> ### MINSTREL SHOW
>
> In Ribeauvillé, Place de la Marie is a great place to perch come every first Sunday in September, when the town hosts a grand parade to celebrate the Jour des Ménétriers (Fête of the Minstrels), a day when at least one fountain here spouts free Riesling. Headlined by medieval musicians, the party begins mid-afternoon while the best street seats go for €8 each. Contact the tourist office for info.

$$$$ ✕▦ **L'Auberge de l'Ill.** England's late Queen Mother, Marlene Dietrich,
Fodor's Choice and Montserrat Caballé are just a few of the famous who have feasted
★ at this culinary temple, but, oddly, the place has never been as famous as it should be, the long trek from Paris to the half-timber village of Illhaeusern perhaps the reason. Still, you need to book weeks in advance (closed Monday and Tuesday) to snare a table in this classic yet casual dining room. Master chef Paul Haeberlin marries grand and Alsatian cuisine, with the emphasis on proper marriage, not passionate love. The results are wonderful enough: salmon soufflé, lamb chops in dainty strudel, and showstoppers like *le homard Prince Vladimir*, or lobster with shallots braised in champagne and crème fraîche. Germanic-Alsatian flair is particularly apparent in such dishes as the truffled *baeckeoffe* (baker's oven), a casserole-terrine of lamb and pork with leeks. The kitchen's touch is incredibly light, so you'll have room to savor such master desserts as white peaches served in a chocolate "butterfly" with champagne sabayon sauce. If you want to enjoy the pleasant surroundings of the auberge, with its terraced lawns and romantic trees beside the Ill, opt for an overnight in one of the guest rooms in the new **Hôtel des Berges,** set behind the restaurant and designed to evoke an Alsatian tobacco barn, replete with Havanese woods, rooms named after famous cigars, and a lulling and lovely country-luxe decor. ✉2 rue de Collonges-au Mont d'Or, 10 km (6 mi) east of Ribeauvillé, 68970 Illhœusern 🕾03–89–71–89–00 🖷03–89–71–82–83 ⊕www. auberge-de-l-ill.com ⌨12 rooms ⚘In-room: refrigerator. In-hotel: restaurant, public Wi-Fi, some pets allowed (fee) ▱AE, DC, MC, V ◷Closed 1st wk Jan. and Feb.

$$–$$$ ▦ **Seigneurs de Ribeaupierre.** On the edge of Ribeauvillé's old quarter, this gracious half-timber inn offers a warm regional welcome with a touch of flair. It has exposed timbers in pastel tones, sumptuous fabrics, and slick bathrooms upstairs, as well as a fire crackling downstairs on your way to the generous breakfast. ✉11 rue du Château,

7

68150 ☎03–89–73–70–31 🖹03–89–73–71–21 ⌨10 rooms ᗑIn-room: no a/c, no TV. In-hotel: bar ☰AE, MC, V ⊘Closed Jan. and Feb. †⊙IBP.

$–$$ ⊞ **Tour.** In the center of Ribeauvillé and across from the Tour des Bouchers, this hotel, with an ornate Renaissance fountain outside its front door, is a good choice for experiencing the atmospheric town by night. Rooms and amenities are modern; those on the top floor have exposed timbers and wonderful views of ramshackle rooftops. ⊠1 rue de la Mairie, 68150 ☎03–89–73–72–73 🖹03–89–73–38–74 ⊕www.hotel-la-tour.com ⌨31 rooms ᗑIn-room: no a/c. In-hotel: bar, public Wi-Fi ☰AE, DC, MC, V ⊘Closed early Jan.–mid-Mar.

RIQUEWIHR

④④ *5 km (3 mi) south of Ribeauvillé.*

Fodor's Choice
★

With its dormer windows fit for a Rapunzel, hidden cul-de-sacs home to Rumpelstiltskins, and unique once-upon-a-timeliness, Riquewihr is the showpiece of the Wine Route and a living museum of the quaint architecture of old Alsace. Its steep main street, ramparts, and winding back alleys have scarcely changed since the 16th century, and could easily serve as a film set. Merchants cater to the sizable influx of tourists with a plethora of kitschy souvenir shops; bypass them to peep into courtyards with massive wine presses, to study the woodwork and ornately decorated houses, to stand in the narrow old courtyard that was once the Jewish quarter, or to climb up a narrow wooden stair to the ramparts. You would also do well to settle into a winstub to sample some of Riquewihr's famous wines. Just following your nose down the heavenly romantic streets will reward your eye with bright blue, half-timber houses, storybook gables, and storks'-nest towers. The facades of certain houses dating from the late Gothic period take pride of place, including the Maison Kiener (1574), the Maison Priess (1686), and the Maison Liebrich (1535), but the Tower of Thieves and the Postal Museum, ensconced in the château of the duke of Württemberg, are also fascinating.

WHERE TO STAY & EAT

★ **¢–$$** ✗ **Au Tire-Bouchon.** "The Corkscrew" is the best winstub in town to feast on Alsatian varieties of choucroute garni, including some rare delights like the *verte* (or green, flavored with parsley) version and the blowout "Choucroute Royale." There are also fine Muscats, great breads, and fragrant onion tarts to savor. With communal tables and kind service, this is heartily recommended. If booked up, try the nearby Auberge

---

THE BUTLER DID IT

At the restaurant Au Tire-Bouchon, the famous "Choucroute Royale" is garnished with seven different kinds of wursts and meats and served with a half bottle of mulled champagne plopped in the center of a mound of sauerkraut. The contents of the bottle is then poured by the waitress, with great flourish, over the entire dish.

CLOSE UP

Sauerkraut & Choucroute

To embark on a full gastronomic excursion into the hearty, artery-clogging terrain of Alsatian cuisine, your tour should probably start with *flammekueche*—a flat tart stuffed with bacon, onions, cream cheese, and heavy cream. The next stop is *baeckeoffe*, marinated pork, mutton, and beef simmered in wine with potatoes and onions, sometimes with a round of creamy Muenster cheese melted on top. And to finish up, land with a thud on a hefty slice of *Kougelhopf*, a butter-rich ring-shape brioche cake with almonds and raisins.

If, however, you have neither the constitution nor the inclination for such culinary heft, there is one dish that sums up the whole of Alsatian cuisine: *choucroute garnie*. Borrowed from the Germans, who call it sauerkraut, the base definition of choucroute is cabbage pickled in brine. In more elaborate terms, this means *quintal d'Alsace*, a substantial variety of local white cabbage, shredded and packed into crockery and left to ferment with salt and juniper berries for at least two months. Beyond this, any unanimity regarding the composition of *choucroute garnie* breaks down. The essential ingredients, however, seem to be sauerkraut, salted bacon, pork sausages, juniper berries, white wine, onions, cloves, black peppercorns, garlic, lard or goose fat, potatoes, and salt pork—pig's knuckles, cheeks, loin, shanks, feet, shoulder, and who knows what else? No matter—the taste is unforgettable.

7

du Schoenebourg. ⊠*29 rue du Général-de-Gaulle* ☎*03–89–47–91–61* 🚬*AE, MC, V.*

$ ✕🖼 **Sarment d'Or.** This cozy little hotel by the city walls, near the Dolder belfry, blends irreproachable modern comforts with bare-stone walls and dark-timber ceilings. The restaurant downstairs offers firelight romance and delicious cuisine—foie gras, frogs' legs in garlic cream, and breast of duck in pinot noir; it's closed Monday and does not serve dinner Sunday or lunch Tuesday. ⊠*4 rue du Cerf, 68340* ☎*03–89–86–02–86* 🖨*03–89–47–99–23* ⊕*www.riquewihr-sarment-dor.com* 🛏*9 rooms* ♿*In-room: no a/c. In-hotel: restaurant, no elevator* 🚬*MC, V* ⊗*Closed Jan.–mid-Feb. and 1st 2 wks of July* ⧖*MAP.*

★ $–$$ 🖼 **Hôtel de la Couronne.** Like an illustration out of the Brothers Grimm, this hotel is set in a 16th-century house with central tower and side wings. Its steep mansard roof, country shutters, and rusticated stone trim beautifully blend into the heart of medieval Riquewihr—the only modern note will be your car (allowed to drive to the hotel even though the town center is pedestrianized). Inside, several rooms have grand timber beams and folkloric wall stencils, making this a truly charming base to tour a truly charming town. ⊠*5 rue de la Couronne, 68340* ☎*03–89–49–03–03* 🖨*03–89–49–01–01* ⊕*www.hoteldelacouronne.com* 🛏*40 rooms* ♿*In-room: no a/c. In hotel: public Internet, no elevator* 🚬*AE, DC, MC, V.*

COLMAR

★ *13 km (8 mi) southeast of Riquewihr via D3/D10, 71 km (44 mi) southwest of Strasbourg.*

GETTING HERE

In June 2007, the sole direct Paris Est to Colmar (€52) train, which currently takes over 5 hours, was complemented by three TGV high-speed return trips taking 2 hours, 50 minutes. Otherwise, 13 semi-direct hourly trains connect through Strasbourg or Mulhouse, both being within easy reach on the frequent regional network. The last of the five Sélestat (€4)-bound trains/buses to stop at Ribeauvillé (€2.10) is at 1:06 and the 16 trains to Metzeral (€4.20) can deliver wine and cheese at Turckheim and Munster (€3.30). Turckheim can also be reached by bus (TRACE) three times a day from Colmar's main railway station. The LK Groupe (⊕ *www.l-k.fr*) has regular bus services from the Gare SNCF to towns throughout the region, including Ribeauvillé (seven daily). Colmar's train station on Rue de la Gare is in the far southwestern corner of town; from here, walk 15 minutes down Avenue de la République for the tourist office, or take municipal TRACE buses (buy ticket from driver).

EXPLORING

Forget that much of Colmar's architecture is modern (because of the destruction wrought by World Wars I and II): its Vieille Ville (Old Town) heart—an atmospheric maze of narrow streets lined with candy-color, half-timber Renaissance houses hanging over cobblestone lanes in a disarmingly ramshackle way—outcharms Strasbourg. Wander along the calm canals that wind through **La Petite Venise** (*Little Venice*), an area of bright Alsatian houses with colorful shutters and window boxes that's south of the center of town. Here, amid weeping willow trees that shed their tears into the eddies of the Lauch River and half-timber houses gaily bedecked with geraniums and carnations, you have the sense of being in a tiny village. Elsewhere, the Vieille Ville streets fan out from the beefy towered church of **St-Martin.** Each shop-lined backstreet winds its way to the 15th-century customs house, the **Ancienne Douane,** and the square and canals that surround it.

The **Maison Pfister** *(⌧11 rue Mercière)*, built in 1537, is the most striking of Colmar's many old dwellings. Note its decorative frescoes and medallions, carved balcony, and ground-floor arcades.

Up the street from the Ancienne Douane on the Grand'Rue, the **Maison aux Arcades** *(Arcades House)* was built in 1609 in High Renaissance style with a series of arched porches (arcades) anchored by two octagonal towers.

> ### "HALLUCINOGENIC"
>
> That's the adjective often used by art historians to describe the proto-Expressionist power of Grünewald's tortured faces, which made a direct appeal to the pain-racked victims dying at the convent, often from their illness brought on by the ingestion of fungus-ridden grains.

Fodor's Choice ★ The cultural highlight of Colmar is the **Musée d'Unterlinden,** once a medieval Dominican convent and hotbed of Rhenish mysticism, and now an important museum. Its star attraction is one of the greatest altarpieces of the 16th century, the *Retable Issenheim* (1512–16), by Matthias Grünewald, majestically displayed in the convent's Gothic chapel. Originally painted for the convent at Issenheim, 22 km

(14 mi) south of Colmar, the multipanel altarpiece is framed with two-sided wings, which unfold to reveal the Crucifixion and Incarnation; the side panels illustrate the Annunciation and the Resurrection. Other panels depict the life of St. Anthony, notably the Temptation. Grünewald's altarpiece, replete with its raw realism (note the chamber pots, boil-covered bellies, and dirty linen), was believed to have miraculous healing powers over ergotism, a widespread disease in the Middle Ages. Produced by the ingestion of fungus-ridden grains, the malady caused its victims to experience delusional fantasies. Arms and armor, stone sculpture, ancient winepresses and barrels, and antique toys cluster around the enchanting 13th-century cloister. Upstairs are fine regional furnishings and a collection of Rhine Valley paintings from the Renaissance, including Martin Schongauer's opulent 1470 altarpiece painted for Jean d'Orlier. ⊠*1 rue Unterlinden* ☎*03–89–20–15–50* ⊕*www.musee-unterlinden.com* 🎟*€7* ⊗*May–Oct., daily 9–6; Nov.–Apr., Wed.–Mon. 9–noon and 2–5.*

★ The **Église des Dominicains** *(Dominican Church)* houses the Flemish-influenced *Madonna of the Rosebush* (1473), by Martin Schongauer (1445–91), the most celebrated painting by the noted 15th-century German artist. This work, stolen from St-Martin's in 1972 and later recovered and hung here, has almost certainly been reduced in size from its original state but retains enormous impact. The grace and intensity of the Virgin match that of the Christ child; yet her slender fingers dent the child's soft flesh (and his fingers entwine her curls) with immediate intimacy. Schongauer's text for her crown is: me carpes genito tuo o santissima virgo ("Choose me also for your child, o holiest Virgin"). ⊠*Pl. des Dominicains* ☎*03–89–24–46–57* 🎟*€1.50* ⊗*Apr.–Dec., daily 10–1 and 3–6.*

The **Musée Bartholdi** *(Bartholdi Museum)* is the birthplace of Frédéric-Auguste Bartholdi (1834–1904), the local sculptor who designed the Statue of Liberty. Exhibits of Bartholdi's works claim the ground floor; a reconstruction of the artist's Paris apartments and furniture are upstairs; and, in adjoining rooms, the creation of Lady Liberty is explored. ⊠*30 rue des Marchands* ☎*03–89–41–90–60* ⊕*www.musee-bartholdi.com* 🎟*€4.30* ⊗*Mar.–Dec., Wed.–Mon. 10–noon and 2–6.*

WHERE TO STAY & EAT

★ $$$–$$$$ ✕ **Au Fer Rouge.** If you want a delicious feast of Old Colmar, head to this cobblestone square to find an adorable 17th-century Alsatian *colombage* (dovecote) mansion, replete with carved timber beams, oil paintings, stained glass, leaded windows, copper tankards, and flower window boxes. Even better, the kitchen is manned by a chef happy to leapfrog from yesteryear to tomorrow by offering nouvelle versions of classic standards. Patrick Fulgraff's salads are *"gourmandise d'oie"* (garnished with goose), his *croustillant au camembert* is topped with aspics and creams, his rabbit sausage comes with grilled polenta, and his wine list has one foot in Alsace and the other in France. He has also introduced gourmet tapas-style dishes called "Les Férettes" for light meals in the newly renovated salon. For the restaurant be sure to sit in the main floor salon and avoid the lackluster basement room. All in all, very much the best restaurant in Colmar. ✉ *52 Grand'rue* ☎ *03–89–41–37–24* ⊕ *www.au-fer-rouge.com* ☱ *AE, MC, V* ⊘ *Closed Sun. dinner and Mon.*

$–$$ ✕ **Chez Hansi.** Named for the Rockwell-like illustrator whose beclogged folk children adorn most of the souvenirs of Alsace, this hypertraditional beamed tavern in the Vieille Ville serves excellent down-home classics such as choucroute and pot-au-feu, prepared and served with a sophisticated touch despite the waitresses' dirndls. ✉ *23 rue des Marchands* ☎ *03–89–41–37–84* ☱ *MC, V* ⊘ *Closed Wed., Thurs., and Jan.*

¢–$ ✕ **Au Koïfhus.** Not to be confused with the shabby little Koïfhus on Rue des Marchands, this popular landmark (the name means customs-house) serves huge portions of regional standards, plus changing specialties: roast quail and foie gras on salad, game stews with spaetzle (dumplings), and freshwater fish. Choose between the big, open dining room, glowing with wood and warm fabric, and a shaded table on the broad, lovely square. ✉ *2 pl. de l'Ancienne-Douane* ☎ *03–89–23–04–90* ☱ *MC, V.*

$$–$$$ ✕🖾 **Le Maréchal.** A maze of narrow, creaky corridors connects the series of Renaissance houses that make up this romantic riverside inn. Built in 1565 in the fortified walls that encircle the Vieille Ville, the Maréchal has rooms that are small but lavished with extravagant detail, from glossy rafters to rich brocades to four-poster beds (and even Jacuzzis)—ask for the Wagner or Bach rooms. A vivid color scheme—scarlet, sapphire, candy pink—adds to the Vermeer atmosphere. This is not a high-tech luxury hotel: it's an endearing, quirky, lovely old place hanging over a Petite Venise canal. The gastronomic restaurant, A l'Echevin, offers such dishes as terrine of rouget, leeks, truffles, and pigeon breast and foie gras crisped in pastry. Dine in salons or on a terrace perched over the river. ✉ *4 pl. des Six-Montagnes-Noires, 68000* ☎ *03–89–41–60–32* 🖨 *03–89–24–59–40* ⊕ *www.hotel-le-marechal.com* 🛏 *30 rooms* ⌂ *In-room: refrigerator, Wi-Fi (some). In-hotel: restaurant, public Wi-Fi, some pets allowed (fee)* ☱ *AE, DC, MC, V* ⦿ *MAP.*

FodorsChoice
★

$$ ✕🖾 **Rapp.** In the Vieille Ville, just off the Champ de Mars, this solid, modern hotel has business-class comforts, a professional and welcom-

ing staff, and a good German-scale breakfast. There's even an extensive indoor-pool complex, including sauna, steam bath, and workout equipment—all included in the low price. The restaurant is closed Friday, and does not serve dinner Thursday or lunch Saturday. ⊠ *1–3–5 rue Weinemer, 68000* ☎*03–89–41–62–10* 🖷*03–89–24–13–58* ⊕*www.hotel-rapp-colmar.com* ⟐*38 rooms* ⟐*In room: Wi-Fi. In-hotel: restaurant, bar, pool, gym* ▤*AE, DC, MC, V* ⊗*Closed July and 2 wks in Jan.*

SPORTS & THE OUTDOORS

A guide to bicycling in the Lorraine is available from the Comité Départemental de Cyclisme. For a list of signposted trails in the Vosges foothills, contact the Sélestat Tourist Office. **Loisirs Accueil Haut-Rin** (⊠*1 rue Schlumberger, 68000 Colmar* ☎*03–89–20–10–62* ⊕*www.tourisme-alsace.com*) is a helpful association for bicyclists in the Colmar area.

GUEBWILLER

★ ㊻ *26 km (16 mi) southwest of Colmar via N83/D3.*

Despite its admirable churches, fine old buildings, and pleasantly authentic feeling, Guebwiller is often overlooked.

The **Église St-Léger** (⊠*Pl. St-Léger*), built in 1180–1280, is one of the most harmonicus Romanesque churches in Alsace, though its original choir was replaced by the current Gothic one in 1336. The bare, solemn interior is of less interest than the three-tower exterior. The towers match—almost: the one on the left has small turrets at the base of its steeple, while the one on the right is ringed by triangular gables. The octagonal tower over the crossing looms above them both, topped by a seldom-visited stork's nest. The surrounding square has a lively weekly market.

The **Église Dominicaine** (⊠*Rue de l'Hôpital*) has an unmistakable silhouette thanks to the thin, lacy lantern that sticks out of its roof like an effeminate chimney. Its large 14th-century nave is adorned with frescoes and contains a fine rood screen.

★ Guebwiller's largest church, **Notre-Dame** (⊠*Rue de la République*), has a Baroque grandeur that would not be out of keeping in Paris—a reflection of the wealth of the Benedictine abbey in nearby Murbach, whose worldly friars, fed up with country life, opted for the comparatively brighter lights of Guebwiller in the mid-18th century. The monks—who needed a noble pedigree of four generations to qualify for the cloth—outmaneuvered church authorities by pretending to take temporary exile in Guebwiller while "modernizing" Murbach Abbey, thus circumventing the need for papal permission before abbeys could move. As a token gesture, the crafty clerics smashed the nave of Murbach Abbey, then failed to replace it and refused to budge from their "temporary" home. Instead, they commissioned Louis Beuque to design this church in Guebwiller (1762–85). The interior is majestic without being overbearing—apart, perhaps, from the trick 3-D–effect stucco *Assumption,* which puffs its way out a half-open coffin behind the gold-and-marble altar before erupting over the walls and balcony and making for the roof.

OFF THE
BEATEN
PATH

Ecomusée de Haute-Alsace. Great for kids, this open-air museum near Ungersheim, southeast of Guebwiller (via D430), is really a small village created from scratch in 1984, including 70 historic peasant houses and buildings typical of the region. The village is crisscrossed by donkey carts and wagons, and behind every door lie entertaining demonstrations of the old ways. An off-season visit is a study in local architecture; in high season the place comes alive. Small restaurants, snack bars, a playground, and a few amusement rides are scattered about for breaks. You can lodge on-site in traditional-style Alsace houses. ☎*03–89–74–44–74* ⊠*€6.50 July and Aug., €9.50 Sept.–June* ⊕*www.ecomusee-alsace.fr* ۞*July and Aug., daily 9–7; Apr.–June and Sept., daily 9:30–6; Mar. and Oct., daily 10–5; Nov.–Feb., daily 10:30–5.*

The **Musée du Florival** is in one of the 18th-century canons' houses alongside Notre-Dame. It has a fine collection of ceramics designed by Théodore Deck (1823–91), a native of Guebwiller who was director of the renowned Sèvres porcelain factory near Paris. It also contains archaeological treasures, artifacts from everyday life, and religious sculpture. ⊠*1 rue du 4-Février* ☎*03–89–74–22–89* ⊠*€4* ۞*Mon. and Wed.–Fri. 2–6, weekends and holidays 10–noon and 2–6.*

ALSACE-LORRAINE ESSENTIALS

TRANSPORTATION

If traveling extensively by public transportation, be sure to load up on information (schedules, the best taxi-for-call companies, etc.) upon arriving at the ticket counter or help desk of the bigger train and bus stations in the area, such as Nancy, Strasbourg, and Colmar.

BY AIR

There are regular flights from London, Amsterdam, Copenhagen, Casablanca, Madrid, and Paris arriving at Entzheim, near Strasbourg, whose airport shuttle bus Navette Routière leaves the city center every half hour, stopping at the regular city bus stop at Place de la Gare and Place de l'Homme de Fer.

Air Travel Information Aéroport International Strasbourg (⊠*Rte. de Strasbourg, 15 km [9½ mi] southwest of city, Entzheim* ☎*03–88–64–67–67* ⊕*www. strasbourg.aeroport.fr*).

BY BUS

The two main bus companies are **Les Rapides de Lorraine,** based in Nancy, and **Compagnie des Transports Strasbourgeois,** based in Strasbourg. Nancy, Strasbourg, and Colmar all have city buses, many lines run by Rapides de Lorraine. In Strasbourg, most of the 15 efficient lines leave from the train station; bus tickets can also be used on the city trams. Nancy is fairly spread out, but the central area is manageable on foot. **Allô Bus** runs buses through the city, most stopping on Rue St-Jean.

Bus Information Compagnie des Transports Strasbourgeois (⊠ *14 rue de la Gare-aux-Marchandises, 67200 Strasbourg* ☎ *03-88-77-70-70* ⊕ *www.cts-strasbourg.fr/cts2 html*).

Les Rapides de Lorraine (⊠ *52 bd. d'Austrasie, 54000 Nancy* ☎ *03-83-32-34-20* ✍ *cftirdlnancy@aol.com* ☎ *03-83-32-34-20 Agence Ted for ticket information and tariffs*).

BY CAR

A4 heads east from Paris to Strasbourg, via Verdun, Metz, and Saverne. It's met by A26, descending from the English Channel, at Reims. A31 links Metz to Nancy, continuing south to Burgundy and Lyon.

N83/A35 connects Strasbourg, Colmar, and Mulhouse. A36 continues to Belfort and Besançon. A4, linking Paris to Strasbourg, passes through Lorraine via Metz, linking Lorraine and Alsace. Picturesque secondary roads lead from Nancy and Toul through Joan of Arc country and on to Épinal. Several scenic roads climb switchbacks over forested mountain passes through the Vosges, connecting Lorraine to Alsace; a quicker alternative is the tunnel *under* the Vosges at Ste-Marie-aux-Mines, linking Sélestat to Lunéville and Épinal. Alsace's Route du Vin, winding from Marlenheim, in the north, all the way south to Thann, is the ultimate in scenic driving.

BY TRAIN

Main-line trains leave Paris (Gare de l'Est) every couple of hours for the four-hour, 500-km (315-mi) journey to Strasbourg. Some stop in Toul, and all stop in Nancy, where there are connections for Épinal. By 2008 a new TGV service is slated to link Paris to Strasbourg in 2 hours, 20 minutes, stopping near Verdun and Nancy.

Several local trains a day run between Strasbourg and Colmar (40 mins distant), stopping in Sélestat (bus link to Ribeauvillé). There's also a snail-pace daily service from Strasbourg to Obernai, Barr, and Dambach-la-Ville. But you'll need a car to visit smaller villages.

Train Information Gare SNCF Colmar (⊠ *Rue de la Gare* ☎ *36-35*). **Gare SNCF Nancy** (⊠ *3 pl. Thiers* ☎ *36-35*). **Gare SNCF Strasbourg** (⊠ *20 pl. de la Gare* ☎ *36-35*). **SNCF** (☎ *36-35, €0.34 per min* ⊕ *www.voyages-sncf.com*). **TGV** (⊕ *www.tgv.com*).

CONTACTS & RESOURCES

CAR RENTAL

Local Agencies Avis (⊠ *Pl. de la Gare, Strasbourg* ☎ *03-88-32-30-44*). **Europcar** (⊠ *18 rue de Serre, Nancy* ☎ *03-83-37-57-24*). **Hertz** (⊠ *1 pl. Thiers, Nancy* ☎ *03-83-32-13-14*).

EMERGENCIES

Contacts **Ambulance** (🕾15). **Hôpital Central** (✉29 av. du Mal-de-Lattre-de-Tassigny, 54000 Nancy 🕾03-83-85-85-85). **Hôpital Civil** (✉1 pl. de l'Hôpital, 67000 Strasbourg 🕾03-88-11-67-68).

TOUR OPTIONS

Walking tours of Strasbourg's Vieille Ville are directed by the tourist office *(see Visitor Information, below)* for €6 and depart at 2:30 every Saturday afternoon in low season, daily at 10:30 in July and August; minitram tours €6 leave from Place du Château, by the cathedral. For Colmar and its enchanting environs, take a highly recommended van tour with Les Circuits d'Alsace—castles, villages, and vineyards make for an exhilarating itinerary.

Contacts **Les Circuits d'Alsace** (✉8 pl. de la Gare, 68000 Colmar 🕾03-89-41-90-88 ⊕ www.alsace-travel.com). **Strasbourg minitram tours** (🕾03-88-77-70-03).

VISITOR INFORMATION

The principal regional tourist offices are in Nancy and Strasbourg. Other tourist offices are listed by town after the principal offices.

Tourist Information **Nancy** (✉14 pl. Stanislas 🕾03-83-35-22-41 ⊕ www.ot-nancy.fr). **Strasbourg** (✉17 pl. de la Cathédrale 🕾03-88-52-28-28 ⊕ www.ot-strasbourg.fr ✉4 pl. de la Gare 🕾03-88-32-51-49); there's also a city tourist office at the train station. **Colmar** (✉4 rue Unterlinden 🕾03-89-20-68-92 ⊕ www.ville-colmar.fr). **Obernai** (✉Pl. du Beffroi 🕾03-88-95-64-13 ⊕ www.obernai.fr). **Sélestat** (✉10 bd. du Mal-Leclerc 🕾03-88-58-87-20 ⊕ www.ville-selestat.fr).

Burgundy

8

WORD OF MOUTH

"Beaune is a classic wine town a little north on the train. Though heavily used by tourists it has some incredible glazed-tile roofs to see, two or three nice museums, and wine, wine, wine."

—IndyTravel

WELCOME TO BURGUNDY

TOP REASONS TO GO

★ **Wine is a Wonderful Thing:** Burgundy vineyards are among the world's best, so take the time to stroll through Clos de Vougeot and really get a feel for the "terroir."

★ **Dijon, Burgundy's Hub:** One of France's prettiest cities, with colorful banners and polished storefronts along narrow medieval streets, Dijon is perpetually being dolled up for a street fair.

★ **Relish the Romanesque:** Burgundy is home to a knee-weakening concentration of Romanesque churches and Vézelay's Basilique has the region's greatest 12th-century sculptures.

★ **Beaune, Capital of Caves:** Famed for its wine caves and its 15th-century, Flemish-style Hospices, Beaune lets you get both your cultural and viticultural fill.

★ **Cluny, "Light of the World":** Once center of a vast Christian empire and today a ruin, this Romanesque abbey still inspires by the sheer volume of what it once was.

1 **Northwest Burgundy.** The northern part of Burgundy came under the sway of the medieval Paris-based Capetian kings, and the mighty Gothic cathedrals they built are still much in evidence, notably St-Etienne at **Sens.** Twenty miles to the north is **Troyes,** its charming half-timber houses adding to the appeal of a town overlooked by most air-conditioned bus tours. Southeast lies **Auxerre,** beloved for its steep, crooked streets and magnificent churches; the wine village of **Chablis;** and two great Renaissance châteaux, **Tanlay** and **Ancy-le-Franc.** Closer to Dijon are the great Cistercian abbey at **Fontenay** and the noted Romanesque basilica at **Vézelay,** with a delightful hilltop setting.

2 **Dijon.** Burgundy's only real city, **Dijon** became the capital of the duchy of Burgundy in the 11th century and acquired most of its important architecture and art treasures during the 14th and 15th centuries under four Burgundian dukes. The churches, the ducal palace, and one of the finest art museums in France are evidence of the dukes' patronage of the arts. Other treasures are culinary, including the world's best *boeuf bourguignon.*

François Rude Square, Dijon

3 Wine Country. South of Dijon, follow the Côte d'Or, one of the most famous wine routes, south as it heads past the great wine villages of **Clos de Vougeot** and **Nuits-St-Georges** to **Beaune,** the hub of Burgundy's wine region. At the Hospices take in the great Rogier van der Weyden *Last Judgment* and the intimate Cour d'Honneur, the perfect postcard setting. Continuing south you'll find **Autun,** with famous Roman ruins, and the Romanesque landmark of **Cluny**, once the largest Christian church until Rome's St. Peter's was built.

GETTING ORIENTED

Having done its duty by producing a wealth of what many consider the world's greatest wines, Burgundy—Bourgogne to the French—deserves to be rolled on the palate and savored like a glass filled with Clos de Vougeot. Surrounded by hedgerowed countryside, fabled vineyards, and magnificent Romanesque abbeys, all the sights here—from the medieval sanctuary of Cluny to the wine village of Beaune—invite the wanderer to tarry and partake of their mellow splendor. At the center of it all is Dijon, once ruled by dukes more powerful than kings, which retains something of the opulence it acquired in the late Middle Ages.

Abbey of Cluny

8

BURGUNDY PLANNER

Getting Around

Burgundy, whose northern perimeter begins 75 km (50 mi) from Paris, is one of the largest regions in France. It's sliced in half by the north–south A6. (As all roads lead to Paris, it's generally quicker to move in this direction than from west to east or vice versa.) But a vast network of secondary roads makes travel from city to city or even village to village both practical and picturesque. While the area has a highly advanced network of roads, its public trains and buses do not have a wide network—you'll have to plan accordingly when visiting some notable villages or historic sites.

Finding a Place to Stay

Burgundy is perhaps one of the best-served regions of France in terms of accommodations. The vast range has everything from simple *gîtes d'étape* (bed-and-breakfasts) to four-star châteaux. Especialy in summer, Burgundy is often overrun with tourists, so finding accommodations can be a problem. It's wise to make advance reservations, especially in the wine country (from Dijon to Beaune).

Making the Most of Your Time

France's prime preoccupations with food and wine are nowhere better celebrated than in Burgundy. Though it might sound glib, the best way to see Burgundy is to stay for as long as possible. If you're simply passing through, then there's entirely too much to see and do in one trip.

If you want to go bike riding, then the obvious place to set up is Beaune. If, on the other hand, you're an amateur medieval art historian or are interested in the lesser known wines of Irancy, Chitry, and Tonnerre, basing yourself at Auxerre or Vézelay in northern Burgundy would allow you to focus on these pursuits while also visiting vineyards, the cathedral of Sens, and the once-proud Abbaye de Pontigny. If the conveniences of modern cities are your preference but you also want a taste of medieval Burgundy, then Dijon, Burgundy's capital, offers you the best of both worlds. Dijon has all the charm of another era and all the functionality of a major metropolis. It's the gateway to the Côte d'Or as well as being the perfect place to set off for exploring the back roads of Burgundy.

WHAT IT COSTS

	¢	$	$$	$$$	$$$$
Restaurants	Under €11	€11– €17	€17– €23	€23– €30	Over €30
Hotels	Under €50	€50– €80	€80– €120	€120– €190	Over €190

Restaurant prices are per person for a main course at dinner, including tax (19.6%) and service; note that if a restaurant offers only prix-fixe (set-price) meals, it has been given the price category that reflects the full prix-fixe price. Hotel prices are for a standard double room in high season, including tax (19.6%) and service charge. Hotels operate on the European Plan (EP, with no meal provided) unless we note that they use the Breakfast Plan (BP), or also offer such options as Modified American Plan (MAP, with breakfast and dinner daily, known as demi-pension), or Full American Plan (FAP, or pension complète, with three meals a day). Inquire when booking if these all-inclusive meal plans (which always entail higher rates) are mandatory or optional.

Eating Well in the Region

Tonton Moutarde (Uncle Mustard) is what one young Parisian sophisticate affectionately used to call her Dijon relative, who was actually in the mustard business. For many French people, mention of Burgundy's capital conjures up images of round, rosy, merry men enjoying large suppers of boeuf à la Bourguignonne and red wine. And admittedly, chances are that in any decent restaurant you can find at least one *Dijonnais* true to the stereotype. These days, however, Dijon is not quite the wine-mustard capital of the world it used to be, but the happy fact remains that mustard finds its way into many regional specialties, including the sauce that usually accompanies andouillettes (chitterling sausages).

Dijon ranks with Lyon as the gastronomic capital of France and Burgundy's hearty traditions help explain why. It all began in the early 15th century when Jean, Duc de Berry, arrived here, built a string of castles, and proceeded to make food, wine, and art top priorities for his courtiers. Today, Parisian gourmands consider a three-hour drive a small price to pay for the cuisine of Joigny's Jean Michel Lorain or Vézelay's Marc Meneau.

Game, freshwater trout, coq au vin, *poulet au Meursault* (chicken in white wine sauce), snails, and, of course, boeuf à la Bourguignonne (incidentally, this dish is only called boeuf bourguignon when you are *not* in Burgundy) number among the region's specialties. The queen of chickens is the *poulet de Bresse,* which hails from east of the Côte d'Or and can be as pricey as a bottle of fine wine. Sausages—notably the *rosette du Morvan* and others served with a potato puree—are great favorites. Ham is a big item, especially around Easter, when garlicky *jambon persillé*—ham boiled with pig's trotters and served cold in jellied white wine and parsley (no wonder it's now found throughout the summer months) often tops the menu. Also look for *saupiquet des Amognes*—a Moravian delight of hot braised ham served with a spicy cream sauce. *Pain d'épices* (gingerbread) is the dessert staple of the region. Like every other part of France, Burgundy has its own cheeses. The Abbaye de Cîteaux, birthplace of Cistercian monasticism, has produced its mild cheese for centuries. Chaource and hearty Époisses also melt in your mouth—as do Bleu de Bresse and Meursault.

How's the Weather?

Whenever it's gray and cloudy in Paris, chances are the sun is shining in Burgundy. Situated in the heart of France, Burgundy has warm and dry summers. The climate in spring and fall isn't quite as idyllic, with a mixture of sun and scattered showers. The winter months vary from year to year, and although snow is not common, freezing temperatures mean the bare vines and trees are covered with a soft white hue. Layers of clothing are always advisable, as you're ready for cooler mornings and hotter afternoons. Waterproof outer layers are wise on longer day trips if the weather forecast is changeable. May in Burgundy is lovely, as are September and October, when the sun is still warm on the shimmering golden trees and the grapes, now ready for harvesting, are scenting the air with anticipation. This is when the vines are colorful and the *caves* (cellars) are open for business. Many festivals also take place around this time.

8

Introduction by
Nancy Coons

Updated by
Christopher
Mooney

DRAIN TO THE DREGS BURGUNDY'S full-bodied vistas: rolling hill-sides carpeted in emerald green, each pasture crosshatched with hedge-rows, patterned with cows, quilted with vineyards. Behind a massive quarried-stone wall, a château looms, seemingly untouched by time, the only signs of human habitation the featherbeds airing from case-ment windows and a flock of sheep mowing the grounds. In the vil-lages, tightly clustered houses—with roofs of slate from the days when they protected against brigands—circle the local church, its spire a lightning rod for the faithful. On a hilltop high over the patchwork of green rises a patrician edifice of white rock, a Romanesque church whose austerity and architectural purity hark back to the early Roman temples on which it was modeled. And deep inside a musty *cave* or perhaps a wine cellar redolent of cork and soured grapes, a row of glasses gleams like a treasured necklace, their garnet contents waiting to be swirled, sniffed, and savored.

Although you may often fall under the influence of extraordinary wine during a sojourn in Burgundy—in French, Bourgogne—the beauty sur-rounding you will be no boozy illusion. Passed over by revolutions, both political and industrial, left unscarred by world wars, and rela-tively inaccessible thanks to necessarily circuitous country roads, the region still reflects the pastoral prosperity it enjoyed under the Capetian dukes and kings.

Those were the glory days—when self-sufficient Burgundy held its own against the creeping spread of France and the mighty Holy Roman Empire—a period characterized by the expanding role of the dukes of Bourgogne. Consider the Capetians, history-book celebrities all: there was Philippe le Hardi (the Bold), with his power-brokered marriage to Marguerite of Flanders. There was Jean sans Peur (the Fearless), who murdered Louis d'Orléans in a cloak-and-dagger affair in 1407 and was in turn murdered, in 1419, on a dark bridge while negotiating a secret treaty with the future Charles VII. There was Philippe le Bon (the Good), who threw in with the English against Joan of Arc, and then Charles le Téméraire, whose temerity stretched the boundaries of Burgundy—already bulging with Flanders, Luxembourg, and Picardy—to include most of Holland, Lorraine, Alsace, and even parts of French-speaking Switzerland. He met his match in 1477 at the Battle of Nancy, where he and his boldness were permanently parted. Nonetheless, you can still see Burgundian candy-tile roofs in Fribourg, Switzerland, his easternmost conquest.

Yet the Capetians in their acquisitions couldn't hold a candle to the "light of the world": the great Abbaye de Cluny, founded in 910, grew to such overweening ecclesiastical power that it dominated the European Church on a papal scale for some four centuries. It was Urban II himself who dubbed it *"la Lumière du Monde."* And like the Italian popes, Cluny, too, indulged a weakness for worldly luxury and knowledge, both sacred and profane. In nearby Clairvaux, St-Bernard himself vented his outrage, chiding the monks who, although sworn to chastity and poverty, kept mistresses, teams of horses, and a library of unfathomable depth that codified classical and Eastern lore for all posterity—that is, until it was destroyed in the Wars of Religion, its wisdom lost for all time. The abbey itself met a similar fate, its wealth of quarry stone ransacked after the French Revolution.

Neighboring abbeys, perhaps less glorious than Cluny but with more humility than hubris, fared better. The stark geometry of the Cistercian abbeys—Clairvaux, Cîteaux—stand in silent rebuke to Cluny's excess. The basilicas at Autun, Vézelay, and Paray le Monial remain today in all their noble simplicity, yet manifest some of the finest Romanesque sculpture ever created; the tympanum at Autun rejects all time frames in its visionary daring. Anchored between Autun and Vézelay rises the broad massif of the Morvan, its dewy green flanks densely wooded in oak and beech. Hidden streams, rocky escarpments, dark forests, and meadows alive with falcons and hoopoes—a hiker's dream—are protected today by the Parc Naturel Régional du Morvan.

It's almost unfair to the rest of France that all this history, all this art, all this natural beauty comes with delicious refreshments. As if to live up to the extraordinary quality of its Chablis, its Chassagne-Montrachet, its Nuits-St-Georges, its Gevrey-Chambertin, Burgundy flaunts some of the best good, plain food in the world. Two poached eggs in savory wine sauce, a slab of ham in aspic, a dish of beef stew, a half dozen earthy snails—no frills needed—just the pleasure of discovering that such homely material could resonate on the tongue, and harmonize so brilliantly with the local wine. This is simplicity raised to Gallic heights, embellished by the poetry of one perfect glass of pinot noir paired with a licensed and diploma'd *poulet de Bresse* (Bresse chicken), sputtering in unvarnished perfection on your white-china plate. Thus you may find that food and drink entries take up as much space in your travel diary as the sights you see. And that's as it should be in such well-rounded, full-bodied terrain.

EXPLORING BURGUNDY

Arriving in Burgundy from Paris by car, we suggest you grand-tour it from Sens to Autun, with rewarding detours to the town of Troyes, in Champagne to the east, and the hilly forests of the Morvan, in the west. In northern Burgundy, the accents are thinner than around Dijon, and sunflowers cover the countryside instead of vineyards. Near Auxerre, many small, unheard-of villages boast a château or a once-famous abbey; they happily see few tourists, partly because public transportation is more than a bit spotty. Highlights of northern Burgundy include Sens's great medieval cathedral, historic Troyes, Auxerre's Flamboyant Gothic cathedral, the great Romanesque sculptures of the basilica at Vézelay and cathedral at Autun, and the lakes of the Morvan Regional Park.

Go next to the wine country in the southeast of Burgundy, which begins at Dijon, home to three noted churches and some fine museums, including the Chartreuse de Champmol and its great *Well of Moses* sculpture, and stretches south down the Saône Valley through charming Beaune to Mâcon. The area includes the prestigious Côte de

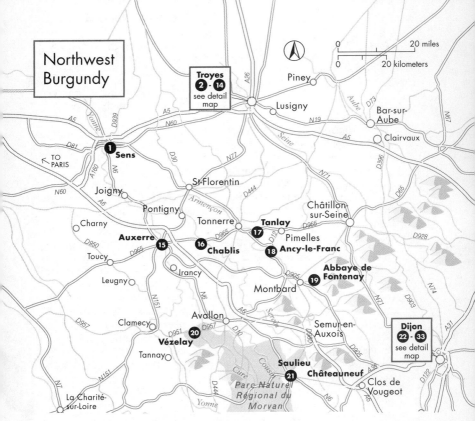

Nuits and Côte de Beaune, where great wines are produced from the pinot noir and chardonnay grapes. Next comes the Côte Chalonnaise, around Mercurey, then, still farther south, around Mâcon, the fine white wines of St-Véran and Pouilly-Fuissé. Throughout this killer countryside, small towns with big wine names draw tourists to their cellars. Farther south, fruity gamay (red) heralds neighboring Beaujolais, while Cluny and Tournus add more spice to Burgundy's reputation for tasty church architecture.

NORTHWEST BURGUNDY

In the Middle Ages, Sens, Auxerre, and Troyes (officially in the neighboring Champagne region) came under the sway of the Paris-based Capetian kings, who erected mighty Gothic cathedrals in those towns. Outside these major centers of northwest Burgundy, countryside villages are largely preserved in a rural landscape that seems to have remained the same for centuries. Here "life in the fast lane" is considered a reference to the Paris-bound A6 expressway. If you're driving down from Paris, we suggest you take the A6 into Burgundy (or alternatively the A5 direct to Troyes) before making a scenic clockwise loop around the Parc du Morvan.

SENS

① *112 km (70 mi) southeast of Paris on N6.*

GETTING HERE

It makes sense for Sens to be your first stop in Burgundy, since it's only 90 minutes by car from Paris on the N6, a fast road that hugs the pretty Yonne Valley south of Fontainebleau. Training in and out of Sens is a breeze as it is on a major train route with 15 TER trains (€16.30) leaving the Paris Gare de Lyon train station weekdays and 12 on weekends. The picturesque railway station is a portal to the region's rail network (Transport Express Regional) and frequent trains, around 15 daily, can take you to Auxerre (€9.80), Dijon (€25.40), Beaune (€29), and many points between. Avallon (€16.80) can be reached directly twice daily at 8:09 am and 7:38 pm. The regional TransYonne bus network, in conjunction with Les Rapides de Bourgogne (☎03–86–64–83–91), runs a noon link from the SNCF station to Auxerre on Wednesday and on demand on Saturday (☎0800–303–309 for information and to reserve). There is no public airport, but you could conceivably arrive by boat from practically any side of France as Sens is very prettily set on the Yonne River with links to the Burgundy Canal and the Seine.

EXPLORING

Fodor's Choice
★

Historically linked more with Paris than with Burgundy, Sens was for centuries the ecclesiastical center of France and is still dominated by its **Cathédrale St-Étienne,** once the French sanctuary for Thomas à Becket and a model for England's Canterbury Cathedral. You can see the cathedral's 240-foot south tower from way off; the highway forges straight past it. The pompous 19th-century buildings lining the narrow main street—notably the meringuelike Hôtel de Ville—can give you a false impression if you're in a hurry: the streets leading off it near the cathedral (notably Rue Abelard and Rue Jean-Cousin) are full of half-timber medieval houses. On Monday the cathedral square is crowded with merchants' stalls, and the beautiful late-19th-century market hall—a distant cousin of Baltard's former iron-and-glass Halles in Paris—throbs with people buying meat and produce. A smaller market is held on Friday morning.

Begun around 1140, the cathedral once had two towers; one was topped in 1532 by an elegant though somewhat incongruous Renaissance campanile that contains two monster bells; the other collapsed in the 19th century. Note the trefoil arches decorating the exterior of the remaining tower. The gallery, with statues of former archbishops of Sens, is a 19th-century addition, but the statue of St. Stephen, between the doors of the central portal, is thought to date from late in the 12th century. The vast, harmonious interior is justly renowned for its stained-glass windows; the oldest (circa 1200) are in the north transept and include the stories of the Good Samaritan and the Prodigal Son; those in the south transept were manufactured in 1500 in Troyes and include a much-admired *Tree of Jesse*. Stained-glass windows in the north of the chancel retrace the story of Thomas à Becket: Becket fled to Sens from England to escape the wrath of Henry II

8

before returning to his cathedral in Canterbury, where he was murdered in 1170. Below the window (which shows him embarking on his journey in a boat, and also at the moment of his death) is a medieval statue of an archbishop said to have come from the site of Becket's home in Sens. Years of restoration work have permitted the display of Becket's *aube* (vestment) in the annex to the Palais Synodal. ⊠ *Pl. de la République.*

The roof of the 13th-century **Palais Synodal** *(Synodal Palace)*, alongside Sens's cathedral, is notable for its yellow, green, and red diamond-tile motif—incongruously added in the mid-19th century by medieval monument restorer Viollet-le-Duc.

Its six grand windows and vaulted Synodal Hall are outstanding architectural features; the building now functions as an exhibition space. Annexed to the Palais Synodal is an ensemble of Renaissance buildings with a courtyard offering a fine view of the cathedral's Flamboyant Gothic south transept, constructed by master stonemason Martin Chambiges at the start of the 16th century (rose windows were his specialty, as you can appreciate here). Inside is a museum with archaeological finds from the Gallo-Roman period, including the *trésor de Villethierry,* a cache of bronze jewelry unearthed during the construction of the A5 highway; exceptional stelae depicting various trades; and the remains of Roman baths discovered in situ 20 years ago. The cathedral treasury, now on the museum's second floor, is one of the richest in France, comparable to that of Conques. It contains a collection of miters, ivories, the shrouds of St. Sivard and St. Loup, and sumptuous reliquaries. But the star of the collection is Thomas à Becket's restored brown-and-silver-edged linen robe. His chasuble, stole, and sandals are too fragile to display. ☎ *03–86–64–46–22* ⊡ *€5* ⊙ *June–Sept., Wed.–Mon. 10–noon and 2–6; Oct.–May, Wed. and weekends 10–noon and 2–6, Mon., Thurs., and Fri. 2–6.*

WHERE TO STAY & EAT

$$–$$$ ✕ **Clos des Jacobins.** With its lemon-yellow walls and exceptional fish specialties, this restaurant in the center of town strikes a happy balance between elegant and casual. Try the €28 lunch *menu du marché,* which may include *matelotte d'oeufs pochés à l'Irancy* (poached eggs in wine sauce) and *blanc de turbot au Noilly-Prat* (turbot with dry vermouth). ⊠ *49 Grande-Rue* ☎ *03–86–95–29–70* ⊕ *www.restaurantlesjacobins. com* ⊟ *AE, MC, V* ⊙ *Closed Wed. No dinner Sun. or Tues.*

★ $$–$$$ ✕⊞ **La Lucarne aux Chouettes.** There's nothing Hollywoodesque about actress Leslie Caron's charmingly rustic riverside hotel and restaurant, the "Owl's Nest," set in four 17th-century buildings. The lovely white-wash-brick dining room, with its ingenious twisted rope chandeliers, has a homey-meets-elegant feel, as do the rooms: the "Loft" is an enormous wood-beamed aerie atop the house (the bathroom is in the room itself, just as it was in the rip-roaring days of the 1680s), while "The Suite" glows with a portrait of Sarah Bernhardt. The legendary hostess (the beloved Lili-Gigi-Fanny of everyone's memories) is often on hand to extend a warm greeting, although she does still depart for rare film shoots. In summer enjoy the terrace over the Yonne. The town itself, a *bastide* (fortified town, built on a grid pattern), is entered and exited via sturdy, angular 13th- and 14th-century gateways. ⊠ *7 quai Bretoche, 12 km (7 mi) south of Sens on N6, 89500 Villeneuve-sur-Yonne* ☎ *03–86–87–18–26* 🖷 *03–86–87–22–63* ⊕ *www.lesliecaron-auberge. com* 🖃 *4 rooms* ⟁ *In-room: no a/c. In-hotel: restaurant, no elevator* ▤ *AE, MC, V* ⊙ *Closed Mon. No dinner Sun. Sept.–June.*

$–$$$ ✕▥ **Paris & Poste.** Owned for the last several decades by the Godart family, the modernized Paris & Poste—which began life as a canon's house in 1776 before becoming a post house in 1796—is a convenient and pleasant stopping point. Rooms are clean, spacious, and well equipped; most open onto a patio (No. 42 is especially nice). But it's the traditional red-and-gold restaurant, which serves great home-smoked salmon (closed Monday, no dinner Sunday); the padded, green leather armchairs in the lounge; and the little curved wooden bar that give this place its comfy charm. Better, the dishes of chef-owner Phillipe Godard, available in a broad range of prix-fixe menus, exhibit real flair. ⊠ *97 rue de la République, 89100* ☎ *03–86–65–17–43* 🖷 *03–86–64–48–45* ⊕ *www.hotel-paris-poste.com* 🖃 *30 rooms* ⟁ *In-room: no a/c (some). In-hotel: restaurant, no elevator, parking (no fee)* ▤ *AE, DC, MC, V.*

★ $$$ ▥ **Château de Prunoy.** Though it's a little out of the way, this château and park—built by one of Louis XVI's finance ministers—is spectacular enough to be worth the trip. Grand public rooms are a stylish blend of Louis Seize gilt-trimmed antiques and grandmother's knickknackery, although many of the guest rooms seem to be the suave result of an elegant decorator (but do avoid the one designed as a Japanese teahouse). Quirky flea-market finds help make it all very *chez soi*, right down to the presence of the owner's friendly Labradors. Dinner is not especially grand but the dining salon itself is country-adorable. ⊠ *40 km (25 mi) southwest of Sens, 40 km (25 mi) northwest of Auxerre on N6 to D943 to D18, 89120 Prunoy* ☎ *03–86–63–66–91* 🖷 *03–86–63–77–79* 🖃 *14 rooms, 5 suites* ⟁ *In-room: no a/c. In-hotel: restaurant, tennis court, pool, gym, no elevator* ▤ *AE, DC, MC, V.*

TROYES

★   *64 km (40 mi) east of Sens, 150 km (95 mi) southeast of Paris.*

The inhabitants of Troyes would be dismayed if you mistook them for Burgundians. Troyes is the historic capital of the counts of Champagne. It was also the home of the late-12th-century writer Chrétien (or Chrestien) de Troyes who, in seeking to please his patrons Count

8

Henry the Liberal and Marie de Champagne, penned the first Arthurian legends. Few, if any, other French town centers contain so much to see. In the Vauluisant and St-Jean districts, a web of enchanting pedestrian streets with timber-frame houses, magnificent churches, fine museums, and a wide choice of restaurants makes the Old Town— Vieux Troyes—especially appealing. Troyes is divided by the Boulevard Dampierre, a broad, busy thoroughfare. On one side is the quiet cathedral quarter, on the other the more upbeat commercial part. Keep your eyes peeled, instead, for the delightful architectural accents that make Troyes unique: *essentes,* geometric chestnut tiles that keep out humidity and are fire resistant; and sculpted *poteaux* (in Troyes they are called *montjoies*), carvings at the joint of corner structural beams. There's a lovely one of Adam and Eve next door to the Comtes de Champagne hotel. Along with its neighbors Provins and Bar-sur-Aube, Troyes was one of Champagne's major fair towns in the Middle Ages. The wool trade gave way to cotton in the 18th century, and today Troyes draws busloads of shoppers from all over Europe to scour for bargains at its outlet clothing stores.

The dynamic **tourist office** (⊠*16 bd. Carnot* 🕾*03–25–82–62–70* ⊕*www.tourism-troyes.com*) has information and sells €12 passes that admit you to the town's major museums, with a free audio guide and champagne tasting thrown in.

❷ Although Troyes is on the Seine, it's the capital of the Aube *département* (province) administered from the elegant **Préfecture** behind its gleaming gilt-iron railings.

❸ Across the Bassin de la Préfecture, an arm of the Seine, is the **Hôtel-Dieu** *(hospital),* fronted by superb 18th-century wrought-iron gates topped with the blue-and-gold fleurs-de-lis emblems of the French monarchy. Around the corner is the entrance to the **Apothicairie de l'Hôtel-Dieu,** a former medical laboratory, the only part of the Hôtel-Dieu open to visitors. Inside, time has been suspended: floral-painted boxes and ceramic jars containing medicinal plants line the antique shelves. ⊠*Quai des Comtes-de-Champagne* 🕾*03–25–80–98–97* 🖾*€2* ☉*July and Aug., Tues.–Sun. 9–5; Sept.–June, Tues.–Sun. 9–noon and 1–5.*

★ ❹ The **Musée d'Art Moderne** *(Modern Art Museum)* is housed in the 16th- to 17th-century bishop's palace. Its magnificent interior, with a wreath-and-cornucopia carved oak fireplace, ceilings with carved wood beams, and a Renaissance staircase, now contains the Lévy Collection—one of the finest provincial collections in France, including Art Deco glassware, tribal art, and an important group of Fauve paintings by André Derain and others. ⊠*Palais Épiscopal, Pl. St-Pierre* 🕾*03–25–76–26–80* ⊕*www.ville-troyes.fr/premiere.htm* 🖾*€5* ☉*Tues.–Sun. 10–1 and 2–6.*

❺ Noted monument of Flamboyant Gothic—a style regarded as the last gasp of the Middle Ages—the **Cathédrale St-Pierre–St-Paul** dominates the heart of Troyes; note the incomplete single-tower west front, the small Renaissance campaniles on top of the tower, and the artistry of Martin Chambiges, who worked on Troyes's facade (with its characteristic

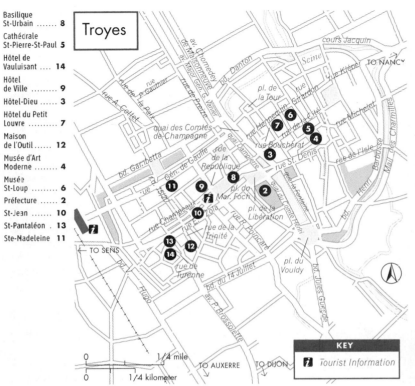

Troyes

large rose window and flamboyant flames) around the same time as he did the transept of Sens. At night the floodlighted features burst into dramatic relief. The cathedral's vast five-aisle interior, refreshingly light thanks to large windows and the near-whiteness of the local stone, dates mainly from the 13th century. It has fine examples of 13th-century stained glass in the choir, such as the *Tree of Jesse* (a popular regional theme), and richly colored 16th-century glass in the nave and west front rose window. The choir stalls and organ were requisitioned from Clairvaux Abbey. One of the chapels contains black-basalt tombstones marking the remains of Count Henry I of Champagne, carved in 1792 after the count's palace was destroyed, and the cathedral treasury displays such curiosities as a piece of St. Bernard of Clairvaux's skull. The arcaded triforium above the pillars of the choir was one of the first in France to be glazed rather than filled with stone. Across the street from the cathedral, behind an iron fence, is an unusual, lopsided, late-medieval **grange aux dîmes** (tithe barn) with a peaked roof. It's used as a warehouse by the winemaker next door. ⊠*Pl. St-Pierre* ☎*03–25–76–98–18* ☎*Free* ☉*July–mid-Sept., daily 10–7; mid-Sept.–June, daily 9–noon and 1–5; Sun. 10–noon and 2–5.*

★ ❻ The former 18th-century abbey of St-Loup to the side of the cathedral now houses the **Musée St-Loup,** an arts and antiquities museum noted for its superlative collection of old-master paintings. Exhibits are devoted to natural history, with impressive collections of birds and meteorites; local archaeological finds, especially gold-mounted 5th-century jewelry and a Gallo-Roman bronze statue of Apollo; medieval statuary and gargoyles; and paintings from the 15th to the 19th century, including works by Rubens, Anthony Van Dyck, Antoine Watteau, François Boucher, and Jacques-Louis David. ⊠*1 rue Chrestien-de-Troyes* ☎*03–25–76–21–68* ⊠€*4* ⊙*Tues.–Sun. 9–noon and 2–5.*

❼ The **Hôtel du Petit Louvre** (⊠*Rue Boucherat*) is a handsome, 16th-century former coaching inn.

★ ❽ The **Basilique St-Urbain** was built between 1262 and 1286 by Pope Urban IV, who was born in Troyes. St-Urbain is one of the most remarkable churches in France, a perfect culmination of the Gothic quest to replace stone walls with stained glass. Its narrow porch frames a 13th-century *Last Judgment* tympanum, whose highly worked elements include a frieze of the dead rising out of their coffins (note the grimacing skeleton) and an enormous crayfish, a testament to the local river culture. Inside, a chapel on the south side houses the *Vièrge au Raisin* (*Virgin with Grapes*), clutching Jesus with one hand and a bunch of champagne grapes in the other. ⊠*Pl. Vernier* ☎*03–25–73–37–13* ⊠*Free* ⊙*Daily 9:30–noon and 2–5:30.*

❾ Place du Maréchal-Foch, the main square of central Troyes, is flanked by cafés, shops, and the delightful facade of the **Hôtel de Ville** *(Town Hall).* In summer the square is filled with people from morning to night.

❿ The clock tower of the church of **St-Jean** is an unmistakable landmark. England's warrior king Henry V married Catherine of France here in 1420. The church's tall 16th-century choir contrasts with the low nave, constructed earlier. ⊠*Pl. du Marché au Pain* ☎*03–25–73–06–96* ⊠*Free.*

⓫ **Ste-Madeleine,** the oldest church in Troyes, is best known for its elaborate triple-arched stone rood screen separating the nave and the choir. Only six other such screens still remain in France—most were dismantled during the French Revolution. This filigreed Flamboyant Gothic beauty was carved with panache by Jean Gailde between 1508 and 1517. ⊠*Rue de la Madeleine* ☎*03–25–73–82–90* ⊠*Free* ⊙*Daily 9:30–12:30 and 2–5:30.*

↺ ⓬ There's a practical reason why the windows of the **Maison de l'Outil** *(Tool and Craft Museum)* are filled with bizarre and beautiful outsize models—like a winding staircase and a globe on a swivel. It's the display venue for the "showpieces" created by apprentice Compagnons

A TOWN MADE FOR WALKERS

The tourist literature is quick to tell you that Troyes's Old Town resembles a champagne cork: the Seine flows around what would be the top half and the train station is at the bottom. Though large for a cork, Troyes is small for a town; everything is accessible by foot—although you can hop on Le Bus to get around if you wish.

de Devoir, members of the national craftsmen's guild whose school is in Troyes. The museum, in the 16th-century Hôtel de Mauroy, also contains a collection of paintings, models, and tools relevant to such traditional wood-related trades as carpentry, clog making, and barrel making—including a medieval anvil, called a *bigorne.* ⊠*7 rue de la Trinité* 🕾*03–25–73–28–26* 🖃*€6.50* 🕙*Daily 10–6.*

⓭ The 16th- to 18th-century church of **St-Pantaléon** primarily serves the local Polish community. A number of fine canopied stone statues, many of them the work of the Troyen Dominique le Florentin, decorator to François I, are clustered around its pillars. ⊠*Rue de Turenne* 🕾*03–25–73–06–99* 🖃*Free* 🕙*Daily 9:30–12:30 and 2–5:30.*

🌣 ★ ⓮ The charmingly turreted 16th- to 17th-century **Hôtel de Vauluisant** houses two museums: the **Musée Historique** (History Museum) and the **Musée de la Bonneterie** (Textile Museum). The former traces the development of Troyes and southern Champagne, with a particularly magnificent selection of religious sculptures and paintings of the late-Gothic era; the latter outlines the history and manufacturing procedures of the town's 18th- to 19th-century textile industry. ⊠*4 rue Vauluisant* 🕾*03–25–42–33–33* 🌐*www.ville-troyes.fr/premiere.htm* 🖃*Joint ticket for both museums €3* 🕙*Tues.–Sun. 9–noon and 1–5.*

WHERE TO STAY & EAT

The pleasure of Troyes is its historic town center, Le Vieux Troyes. This is where you want your hotel to be—or at least within walking distance of it. If you want to dine informally, it's also the area to find a restaurant, especially along Rue Champeaux.

¢–$ ✗ **La Taverne de l'Ours.** This popular, convivial brasserie has faux Art Nouveau and neo-Gothic furbelows, brass globe lamps, and plushy seating alcoves. It also has delicious, hearty cuisine, such as roast *cochon de lait* (suckling pig) straight off the spit. The €19 lunch menu is a good value, and even tastier when accompanied by the grapey, dark pink rosé *des Riceys* from the Champagne–Burgundy border. Happily, this place is open year-round. ⊠*2 rue Champeaux* 🕾*03–25–73–22–18* 🖃*MC, V.*

$$–$$$$ 🛏 **Le Champ des Oiseaux.** "There are places like moments; those which FodorśChoice permanently imprint memories," is the hotelier's description of this ★ *chic et charmant* lodging. Le Champ comes through on that promise. Idyllically situated in ancient Troyes and named after the city's centuries-old roosting haunts of storks, this ensemble of three vine-clad pink-and-yellow 15th- and 16th-century houses (their bright colors are part of a town campaign to "medievalize" half-timber facades) seem ready to receive Manon Lescaut on the run. A daub-and-wattle facade abuzz with the pattern of timbered logs and a storybook courtyard, graced with a fairy-tale staircase, overhanging porch, and cobblestone patio, all set the scene for the charm within. Tin chandeliers, Nantes silks and calico hangings, 15th-century scrollwork panels, beamed roofs right out of the *Return of Martin Guerre,* and more traditional luxe touches make the interiors a joy. The guest salon is set in a vaulted cave-wine cellar fitted out with the latest in soigné

8

furniture. The biggest guest room, the Suite Médiévale, is under the oak-beam eaves, while the Salle Bleue (Blue Room) looks worthy of the cover of *Maison Française*. Downstairs is a lovely breakfast room with a stone fireplace. ⊠*20 rue Linard-Gonthier, 10000* ☎*03–25–80–58–50* 🖶*03–25–80–98–34* ⊕*www.champdesoiseaux.com* 🛏*9 rooms, 3 suite* ♿*In-room: no a/c. In-hotel: room service, no elevator, public Wi-Fi* ⊟*AE, DC, MC, V.*

$$–$$$ 🖼 **Relais St-Jean.** This half-timber hotel, in the pedestrian zone near the church of St-Jean, has good-size rooms with modern decor, white-and-pastel-color walls, and floral-pattern curtains. Some rooms are connected by a path running through the second floor's tree-filled atrium. Black-leather chairs and mirrored walls in the bar contrast rudely with the wicker and plants of an adjoining room, but have a drink here anyway, and good-natured owner Pierre Rinaldi will gladly stop to chat. The hotel has no restaurant, but just down the street is the friendly **Valentino** (⊠*35 rue Paillot-de-Montabert* ☎*03–25–73–14–14*), which has dining in its courtyard. ⊠*49 rue Paillot-de-Montabert, 10000* ☎*03–25–73–89–90* 🖶*03–25–73–88–60* ⊕*www.relais-st-jean.com* 🛏*25 rooms* ♿*In-room: refrigerator. In-hotel: bar, no elevator, public Wi-Fi* ⊟*AE, DC, MC, V.*

¢–$ 🖼 **Comtes de Champagne.** In Vieux Troyes's former mint, a topsy-turvy 16th-century building, this bargain hotel has a quaint inner courtyard with large vines, a philodendron, and refurbished rooms with iron bedsteads. Ask for the largest room, on the second floor, one of the few with its own bath. The two couples who comanage, the Gribourets and the Picards, are friendly folks. ⊠*56 rue de la Monnaie, 10000* ☎*03–25–73–11–70* 🖶*03–25–73–06–02* ⊕*www.comtesde-champagne.com* 🛏*35 rooms, 8 with bath* ♿*In-hotel: bicycles, no elevator* ⊟*MC, V.*

SHOPPING

If there's an ideal place for a shopping spree, it's Troyes. Many clothing manufacturers are just outside town, clustered together in two large suburban malls: **Marques Avenue,** in St-Julien-les-Villas (take N71 toward Dijon); and **Marques City** and the American outlet store **McArthur Glen,** in Pont-Ste-Marie (take N77 toward Chalons-sur-Marne). Ralph Lauren and Calvin Klein at McArthur Glen face off with Laura Ashley at Marques Avenue and Doc Martens at Marques City, to name a few of the shops. The malls are open Monday 2–7, Tuesday–Friday 10–7, and Saturday 9:30–7.

OFF THE BEATEN PATH

Clairvaux. Although much of it has been replaced by a sprawling 19th-century prison, the Abbaye de Clairvaux, 64 km (40 mi) east of Troyes via N19, was once the Cistercian mother abbey of Champagne and northern Burgundy. St. Bernard, a native of Fontaine-les-Dijon, founded Clairvaux (meaning "bright valley") only two years after his entry into Cîteaux, in 1115, and three years before establishing the community of Fontenay, in 1118. Subsequently known as Bernard of Clairvaux, he went on to condemn the behavior of Pierre Abélard, preach the Second Crusade in Vézelay, and decry the lavish pomp of Cluny. The 12th-century vaulted halls of the lay brothers' dormitory remain, as do parts of the once-flourishing 18th-century abbey. Guided tours cost €6.50. ⊠ *Off N19, watch for signs* ☎ *03–25–27–88–17* ⊕ *abbaye-clairvaux. barsuraube.net* ✉ *Free* ⊘ *Mid-Mar.–mid-Nov., Wed.–Sun.*

AUXERRE

⑮

Fodor's Choice
★

21 km (13 mi) southwest of Pontigny, 58 km (36 mi) southeast of Sens.

GETTING HERE

Auxerre is quite easily reached by rail from Gare de Lyon by one of eight trains, with a change at Laroche Migennes, and three direct trains from Paris-Bercy daily (at 7:10 am, 14:38 pm and 6:36 pm). The fare is €22.40. Five trains a day put Sermizelles-Vézelay (€6.90) just one hour away, where you can take either a taxi (☎ 03–86–32–31–88) during the week or the noon-only Saturday bus service to connect to Vézelay proper. Next stop Avallon provides six daily connections to Saulieu (€13.70) and Autun (€19.20). Twelve daily trains link Auxerre to Montbard (€14.80) with Dijon at the end of the line (€22.70). The TransYonne bus network (Les Rapides de Bourgogne) links Auxerre to Sens, Avallon, and Tonnerre with a daily service. Chablis can be reached twice daily, at 11:45 am and 5:15 pm by bus from the SNCF station. If you are driving, Auxerre is served by several major arteries including the A6 autoroute (Autoroute of the Sun) and the N6 (National 6). Auxerre has its own private airport, but no regular passenger service. Built on the Yonne River, it can also be reached by boat, though we suspect few of you will be traveling by boat.

EXPLORING

Auxerre is a beautifully evocative town with three imposing and elegant churches perched above the Yonne River. Its steep, undulating streets are full of massively photogenic, half-timber houses in every imaginable style and shape. Yet this harmonious, architecturally interesting town is underappreciated, perhaps because of its location, midway between Paris and Dijon.

Fanning out from Auxerre's main square, **Place des Cordeliers** (just up from the cathedral), are a number of venerable, crooked, steep streets lined with half-timber and stone houses. The best way to see them is to start from the riverside on the Quai de la République, where you find the tourist office (and can pick up a handy local map), and continue along the Quai de la Marine. The medieval arcaded gallery of the **Ancien Evêché** (Old Bishop's Palace), now an administrative building, is just visible on the hillside beside the tourist office. At **9 rue de la Marine** (which leads off one of several riverside squares) are the two oldest houses in Auxerre, dating from the end of the 14th century. Continue up the hill to Rue de l'Yonne, which leads into the **Rue Cochois**. Here, at No. 23, is the appropriately topsy-turvy home and shop of a *maître verrier* (lead-glass maker). Closer to the center of town, the most beautiful of Auxerre's many *poteaux* (the carved tops of wooden corner posts) can be seen at **8 rue Joubert**: the building dates from the late 15th century and its Gothic tracery windows, acorns, and oak leaves are an open-air masterpiece.

8

The town's dominant feature is the ascending line of three magnificent churches—St-Pierre, St-Étienne, and St-Germain—and the **Cathédrale St-Étienne,** in the middle, rising majestically above the squat houses around it. The 13th-century choir, the oldest part of the edifice, contains its original stained glass, dominated by brilliant reds

and blues. Beneath the choir, the frescoed 11th-century Romanesque crypt keeps company with the treasury, which has a panoply of medieval enamels, manuscripts, and miniatures. A 75-minute son-et-lumière show focusing on Roman Gaul is presented every evening from June to September. ✉ *Pl. St-Étienne* ☎ *03–86–52–23–29* 🖂 *Crypt €3, treasury €1.90* ⊗ *Easter–mid-Nov., Mon.–Sat. 9–6, Sun. 2–6; mid-Nov.–Apr., Mon.–Sat. 10–5.*

North of Place des Cordeliers is the former **Abbaye de St-Germain,** which stands parallel to the cathedral some 300 yards away. The church's earliest aboveground section is the 12th-century Romanesque bell tower, but the extensive underground crypt was inaugurated by Charles the Bald in 859 and contains its original Carolingian frescoes and Ionic capitals. It's the only monument of its kind in Europe—a labyrinth retaining the plan of the long-gone church built above it—and was a place of pilgrimage until Huguenots burned the remains of its namesake, a Gallo-Roman governor and bishop of Auxerre, in the 16th century. Several hundred years of veneration had already seen the burial of 33 bishops of Auxerre as close to the central tomb of St-Germain as they could physically get. The frescoes are a testimony to the brief artistic sophistication of the Carolingian Renaissance: witness St. Stephen running from a stone-hurling crowd toward the disembodied hand of God, a date-bearing palm tree, and the reversed images of a young bishop and an old one teaching each other. ✉ *Pl. St-Germain* ☎ *03–86–18–05–50* 🖂 *€4.40* ⊗ *Tours Oct.–Apr., daily at 10, 11, and 2–5; May–Sept., daily every ½ hr between 10 and 5:30.*

WHERE TO STAY & EAT

$$–$$$$ ✕ **Le Jardin Gourmand.** As its name implies, this restaurant in a former manor house has a pretty garden (*jardin*) where you can dine on summer evenings. There's also an organic vegetable garden producing fresh herbs, gorgeous greens, and other foods that wind up on the table. The interior is accented by sea-green and yellow panels and is equally congenial and elegant. The menu, which changes eight times a year, shows both flair and invention. The staff is discreet and friendly. ✉ *56 bd. Vauban* ☎ *03–86–51–53–52* ⊕ *www.lejardingourmand.com* ▭ *MC, V* ⊗ *Closed Tues. and Wed.*

$–$$ 🏠 **Normandie.** Set in a rather grand 19th-century mansion, the vine-covered Normandie is in the center of Auxerre, just a short walk from the cathedral. Rooms are unpretentious and clean. There's a billiard room, and the terrace is a nice place to relax after a long day of sightseeing. ⊠*41 bd. Vauban, 89000* ☎*03–86–52–57–80* 🖷*03–86–51–54–33* ⊕*www.hotelnormandie.fr* ⇆*47 rooms* ⟁*In-hotel: bar, gym, no elevator, public Wi-Fi* ⊟*AE, DC, MC, V.*

★ $ 🏠 **Château de Ribourdin.** Retired farmer Claude Brodard began building his *chambres d'hôte* (bed-and-breakfast) in an old stable eight years ago, and the result is cozy, comfortable, and reasonably priced. Château de la Borde is the smallest, sunniest, and most intimate room, but they all overlook Monsieur Brodard's fields. Homemade preserves—cassis, quince, and carrot—are served at breakfast. ⊠*8 rte. de Ribourdin, 8 km (5 mi) southwest of Auxerre on D1, 89240 Chevannes* ☎*03–86–41–23–16* ⇆*5 rooms* ⟁*In-room: no a/c, no phone, no TV. In-hotel: pool, no elevator* ⊟*No credit cards* ⊙*BP.*

FLIGHT CRU

If Burgundy looks sublime from the ground, have you ever wondered what it looks like from the air? Wonder no longer: put a little wind beneath your wine-soaked wings. The **France Montgolfière Balloon Company** (☎*03–80–97–38–61* ⊕*www.franceballoons.com*) can float you for hours over Chablis and the Morvan region. **Montgolfières Air Escargot** (☎*03–85–87–12–30* ⊕*www.air-escargot.com*) features some dandy flights over the châteaux of Burgundy. The price may be stratospheric, but so is the experience.

CHABLIS

🔟 *16 km (10 mi) east of Auxerre.*

8

The pretty village of Chablis nestles amid the towering vineyards that produce its famous white wine on the banks of the River Serein and is protected, perhaps from an ill wind, by the massive, round, turreted towers of the Porte Noël gateway. Although in America Chablis has become a generic name for cheap white wine, it's not so in France: there it's a bone-dry, slightly acacia-tasting wine of tremendous character, with the premier cru and grand cru wines standing head to head with the best French whites. Prices in the local shops tend to be inflated, so your best bet is to buy directly from a vineyard; keep in mind that most are closed Sunday.

The town's **Maison de la Vigne et du Vin** can provide information on nearby cellars where you can take tours and taste wine. ⊠*1 rue de Chichae* ☎*03–86–42–42–22* ⊕*www.vins-bourgogne.fr.*

WHERE TO STAY & EAT

★ $–$$ ✗🏠 **Hostellerie des Clos.** The simple yet comfortable rooms at this moderately priced inn have floral curtains and wicker tables with chairs. But most of all, come here for chef Michel Vignaud's cooking, some of the best in the region. He uses Chablis as a base for sauces to accompany his bream with shellfish or fried veal kidneys. ⊠*18 rue Jules-Rathier, 89800* ☎*03–86–42–10–63* 🖷*03–86–42–17–11* ⊕*www.hostellerie-des-clos.fr* ⇆*26 rooms, 10 suites* ⟁*In-room: refrigerator. In-hotel: restaurant, public Wi-Fi* ⊟*AE, MC, V* ⊙*Closed late Dec.–mid-Jan.* ⊙*MAP.*

TANLAY

⑰ *26 km (16 mi) east of Chablis.*

Fodor'sChoice
★ A masterpiece of the French early Baroque, the **Château de Tanlay,** built around 1550, is a miraculous survivor due to the fact that, unlike most aristos who fled the countryside to take up the royal summons to live at Versailles, the Marquis and Marquise de Tanlay opted to live here among their village retainers. Spectacularly adorned with rusticated obelisks, pagodalike towers, the finest in French Classicist ornament, and a "grand canal," the château is centered around a typical *cour d'honneur.* Inside, the Hall of Caesars vestibule, framed by wrought-iron railings, leads to a wood-panel salon and dining room filled with period furniture. A graceful staircase climbs to the second floor, which has the showstopper—a gigantic gallery frescoed in Italianate trompe l'oeil. A small room in the tower above was used as a secret meeting place by Huguenot Protestants during the 1562–98 Wars of Religion; note the cupola with its fresco of scantily clad 16th-century religious personalities. ☎03–86–75–70–61 ☒€2.50, *guided tours €8.50 ☉Apr.–Oct., tours Wed.–Mon. at 10, 11:30, 2:15, 3:15, 4:15, and 5:15.*

ANCY-LE-FRANC

⑱ *14 km (9 mi) southeast of Tanlay.*

It may be strange to find a textbook example of the Italian Renaissance in Ancy-le-Franc, but in mid-16th-century France the court had taken up this import as the latest rage. So, quick to follow the fashion and gain kingly favor, the Comte de Tonnerre decided to create a family seat using all the artists François I (1515–47) had imported from Italy to his court at Fontainebleau.

Fodor'sChoice
★ Built from Sebastiano Serlio's designs, with interior blandishments by Primaticcio, the **Château d'Ancy-le-Franc** is an important example of Italianism, less for its plain, heavy exterior than for its sumptuous rooms and apartments, many—particularly the magnificent Chambre des Arts (Art Gallery)—with carved or painted walls and ceilings and original furnishings. Here, Niccolo dell'Abate and other court artists created rooms filled with murals depicting the signs of the zodiac, the Battle of Pharsala, and the motif of Diana in Her Bath (much favored by Diane de Poitiers, sister of the Comtesse de Tonnerre). Such grandeur won the approval of the Sun King, Louis XIV, no less, who once stayed in the Salon Bleu (Blue Room). ☒*Pl. Clermont-Tonnerre* ☎03–86–75–14–63 ⊕*www. chateau-ancy.com* ☒€8 ☉*Early Apr.–June and Sept., tours Tues.–Sun. at 10:30, 11:30, 2, 3, 4, and 5; July and Aug., tours Tues.–Sun. at 9:30, 10:30, 11:30, 2, 3, 4, and 5; Oct.–mid-Nov., tours Tues.–Sun. at 10:30, 11:30, 2, 3, and 4.*

Continued on page 434

GRAPE EXPECTATIONS
A BURGUNDY WINE PRIMER

From the steely brilliance of *Premier Cru Chablis* in the north to the refined *Pouilly-Fuissés* in the south, Burgundy—*Bourgogne* to the French—is where you can sample deep-colored reds and full-flavored whites as you amble from one fabled vineyard to another along the **Route des Grands Cru**.

8

An oenophile's nirvana, Burgundy is accorded almost religious reverence, and with good reason: its famous chardonnays and pinot noirs, and the "second-tier" gamays and aligotés, were perfected in the Middle Ages by the great monasteries of the region.

The specific character of a Burgundy wine is often dependent on the individual grower or négociant's style. There are hundreds of vintners and merchants in this region, many of them producing top wines from surprisingly small parcels of land.

Adding to the complexity is France's century-old *appellation controllée*, or AOC, wine classification system. In Burgundy, it specifies vineyard, region, and quality. The most expensive, top-tiered wines are called *monopole* and *grand cru*, followed by *premier cru*, *village*, and generic *Bourgogne*. Although there are 100 different AOC wines in the area, the thicket of labels and names is navigable once you learn how to read the road signs; and the payoff is tremendous, with palate-pleasing choices for all budgets.

GEOGRAPHY + CLIMATE = *TERROIR*

Soil, weather conditions, grapes, and savoir-faire are the basic building blocks of all great wines, but this is particularly true in Burgundy, where grapes of the same variety, grown a few feet apart, might have different names and personalities, as well as varying prices.

CHABLIS

Chablis' famous chardonnays are produced along both banks of the Serein River. The four appellations, in ascending order of excellence, are Petit Chablis AOC, Chablis AOC, Chablis Premier Cru AOC, and Chablis Grand Cru AOC. Flinty and slightly acidic, with citrus, pineapple, and green apple flavors and aromas, they age well (except the Petit Chablis, which are best drunk young) and are typically less intense than other burgundy whites, due to their colder northern climate.

CÔTE DE NUITS

The northernmost area, the Côte de Nuits, sometimes called the "Champs-Elysées of Burgundy," is the land of the unparalleled Grand Cru. Deep and ruby rich in color, full of flesh coupled with a great "nose," the powerful pinot noir reds develop wonderfully with age, and are perfect matches for hearty Burgundian beef and game dishes.

The 30-mile long Côte d'Or contains two of the most gorgeous and distinguished wine regions. The best wines here come from Gevrey-Chambertin, Chambolle-Musigny, Morey-St-Denis, Vougeot, Echézeaux, Vosne-Romanée, Romanée-Conti, Nuits-St-Georges, and Prémeaux. Marsannay produces a pale pink, mouth-watering rosé, by far the best in Burgundy.

CÔTE DE BEAUNE

The Côte de Beaune, just to the south, is known for both full-bodied reds and some of the world's best dry whites. Delicately flavored, the reds mature faster than those to the north and are best in Aloxe-Corton, Beaune, Pommard, Volnay, and Santenay. Whites are dry, crisp, and pale, with a delicate bouquet and a "fat" buttery quality. Search out Corton-Charlamagne in Aloxe-Corton, then head south for the storied Montrachets. Green-gold in color and aromatically complex, they are the universal standard for dry whites.

CÔTE CHALONNAISE

Farther south is the Côte Chalonnaise. Although not as famous, it produces chardonnays almost as rich as its northern neighbors. Pinot noirs with *villages* appellations Rully, Givry, and Mercurey are well-structured, with body, bouquet, and a distinction very similar to Côte de Beaune reds. Montagny and Rully whites are dry, light, well balanced, and fruity– much ends up in sparkling Crémant de Bourgogne. Bourgogne Aligoté de Bouzeron are worth a stop, too. Named after its grape, it is the fresh and lively white wine traditionally mixed with Crème de Cassis to make a Kir, but is just as delicious on its own.

CÔTE MAÇONNAISE

Next is the Côte Maçonnaise, the largest of the four Côtes, which brings its own quality dry whites to the market, particularly the distinctive and refined Saint Vérans, Virés and the more famous Pouilly-Fuissés. With lightly oaked aromas of toast and hazel-nuts, these are three of France's best wines for seafood. Macon *villages* light and fruity reds are drinkable but hardly worth a detour. The best are found between Hurigny and Viré and, like the whites, should be drunk young while they still have their freshness.

LABEL KNOW–HOW

SOCIÉTÉ CIVILE DU DOMAINE DE LA ROMANÉE-CONTI
PROPRIÉTAIRE A VOSNE-ROMANÉE (COTE-D'OR) FRANCE

❷ **MONTRACHET**
APPELLATION MONTRACHET CONTROLÉE

❸ *1708 Bouteilles Récoltées*

❹ BOUTEILLE N° 01201
ANNÉE 1995

❺ *Mise en bouteille au domaine*

❶ The name and address of the proprietor.
❷ This wine was produced in the Montrachet region
❸ Number of bottles made
❹ Bottle number 1,201 and Vintage
❺ 'Made and bottled on the estate'– a great signifier of quality

FOR THE VINE INSPIRED

If you're going to spend a fortune on a bottle of Romanée-Conti and want to know how to savor it, sign up for one of the wine classes offered by the Ecole des Vins de Bourgogne, sponsored by the Bureau Interprofessionel des Vins de Bourgogne (B.I.V.B.; 6 rue du 16éme Chasseur, 03-80-26-35-10, www.bivb.com). They offer several choices, ranging from a two-hour intro to a full weekend jammed with trips to vineyards and cellars in Maçon and Chablis.

TOURING AND TASTING

To navigate Burgundy's wine roads, you can travel by car or go by bus with a tour company. The *Route des Grands Crus* travels north to south from Dijon to Beaune and Santenay.

Cote de Nuits, Burgundy

There are a countless number of vineyards here, but these are a few of our favorites. Vineyards accept drop-ins but it's best to reserve by phone or e-mail. General tastings are almost always free, but buying a bottle is in good form. By-appointment tour prices vary with number of attendees and wines tasted. If you're not up for a drive you can taste many of these wines in town cellars or local restaurants.

Antonin Rodet

Makers of fine wines since 1875, Antonin Rodet's delivers a complete range of high quality but reasonably priced Burgundies. Six house-labeled wines can be tasted. Rodet has acquired a number of château wineries all over the region, but a visit to Château de Rully (Hautes Côtes de Beaune) or Domaine des Perdrix (Côte de Nuits), is an unforgettable experience. ☏ *03-85-98-12-12* ✉ *rodet@rodet.com* ⊕ *www.rodet.com*

Bouchard Père et Fils Château de Beaune

Bouchard is one of the major domaines and négociants in Beaune. Its unparalleled legacy of 50,000 bottles from the Côte de Beaune and Côte de Nuits appellations includes a unique collection of rare vintages dating back to the 19th century. The museum and 15th-century cellar is accessible year round (8–12; 2–5) but the personalized tour and extensive tasting is by appointment only. ☏ *03-80-24-80-24* ✉ *bpf@bouchard-pereetfils.com* ⊕ *http://www.bouchard-pereetfils.com*

Château De Chorey Les Beaune

This magnificent 17th-century château, with 13th-century moat and towers, has been in the Germain family for five generations. The wines are frequently found in cellars of France's top restaurants and though drop-in tastings are possible, a stay in one of the chambres d'hôtes, combined with the cellar visit and comprehensive tasting (3 reds and 3 whites) of the estate's wines, is a rare and exceptional experience. The château is open from Easter to end of October, up to 16 people can be accommodated overall in the luxurious five bedrooms (€160-€210) and suites (€220) overlooking the vineyard, park or tower. English is spoken and pets are welcome. ☏ *03-80-22-06-05* ✉ *Contact@Chateau-De-Chorey-Les-Beaune.fr* ⊕ *www.chateau-de-chorey-les-beaune.fr*

∎TIP➔ Late summer is the most popular time to visit—which is reason enough to avoid it. Visit in spring, or the fall, just before the October harvests. Harvest time is exciting, but with everyone out in the fields, you're less likely to find anyone in the cellars to open a bottle for you to sample–unless you pitch in and help bring in the crop.

Château de Meursault

This elegant well-visited château has been producing a miraculous Meursault since the 7th century. Walk up the recently opened Allée des Maronniers, through the vines to the château's *cour d'honneur.* Cellars dating from the 14th and 16th centuries and an art gallery are included in the twice-daily guided tour, 9:30–12; 2:30–6, with a sommelier-aided tasting. €15 per person. English is spoken. ☎ 03-80-26-22-75 ✉ chateau.meursault@kriter.com

Château de Santenay

This majestic 9th–16th century castle is also the former residence (1302-1404) of Philippe le Hardi, son of the king of France. The estate has a total of 237 acres of vines, one of the largest in Burgundy. The château is open year round, seven days a week, a visit to the gardens and surrounding park culminates in a wine-tasting with bottles available for purchase. The award-wining Saint-Aubin 'En Vesvau', matured and aged in wooden casks, is a must-try as is the Château Philippe le Hardi AOC Aloxe-Corton "Les Brunettes et Planchots". The tour and wine tasting is €6 per person. English is spoken. ☎ 03-80-20-61-87 ✉ contact@chateau-de-santenay.com ⊕ www.chateau-de-santenay.com

The 74-km (50-mi) **Route des Grands Crus,** which meanders through every wine town, is known as D122. Less scenic is A31 from Dijon to Beaune and N74.

CÔTE DE NUITS

CÔTE DE BEAUNE

GRAPE EXPECTATIONS

8

ABBAYE DE FONTENAY

⑲ *32 km (20 mi) southeast of Ancy-le-Franc.*

Fodor's Choice
★

The best preserved of the Cistercian abbeys, the Abbaye de Fontenay was founded in 1118 by St. Bernard. The same Cistercian criteria applied to Fontenay as to Pontigny: no-frills architecture and an isolated site—the spot was especially remote, for it had been decreed that these monasteries could not be established anywhere near "cities, feudal manors, or villages." The monks were required to live a completely self-sufficient existence, with no contact whatsoever with the outside world. By the end of the 12th century the buildings were finished, and the abbey's community grew to some 300 monks. Under the protection of Pope Gregory IX and Hughes IV, duke of Burgundy, the monastery soon controlled huge land holdings, vineyards, and timberlands. It prospered until the 16th century, when religious wars and administrative mayhem hastened its decline. Dissolved during the French Revolution, the abbey was used as a paper factory until 1906. Fortunately, the historic buildings emerged unscathed. The abbey is surrounded by extensive, immaculately tended gardens dotted with the fountains that gave it its name. The church's solemn interior is lightened by windows in the facade and by a double row of three narrow windows, representing the Trinity, in the choir. A staircase in the south transept leads to the wood-roofed dormitory (spare a thought for the bleary-eyed monks, obliged to stagger down for services in the dead of night). The chapter house, flanked by a majestic arcade, and the scriptorium, where monks worked on their manuscripts, lead off from the adjoining cloisters. ⊠*Marmagne* 🕾*03–80–92–15–00* ⊕*www.abbayedefontenay. com* 🎟€*8.90* 🕙*Apr.–mid-Nov., daily 10–6; mid-Nov.–Mar., daily 10–noon and 2–5.*

VÉZELAY

⑳ *48 km (30 mi) west of Abbaye de Fontenay.*

In the 11th and 12th centuries one of the most important places of pilgrimage in the Christian world, hilltop Vézelay today is a picturesque, somewhat isolated, village. Its one main street, Rue St-Étienne, climbs steeply and stirringly to the summit and its medieval basilica, world-famous for its Romanesque sculpture. In summer you have to leave your car at the bottom and walk up. Off-season you can drive up and look for parking in the square.

It's easy to ignore this tiny village, but don't: hidden under its narrow *ruelles* (small streets) are Romanesque cellars that once sheltered pilgrims and are now opened to visitors by home owners in summer. Sections of several houses have arches and columns dating from the 12th and 13th centuries: don't miss the hostelry across from the tourist office and, next to it, the house where Louis VII, Eleanor of Aquitaine, and the king's religious supremo Abbé Suger stayed when they came to hear St. Bernard preach the Second Crusade in 1146.

In the 11th and 12th centuries the celebrated **Basilique Ste-Madeleine** was one of the focal points of Christendom. Pilgrims poured in to see the relics of St. Mary Magdalene (in the crypt) before setting off on the great trek to the shrine of St. James at Santiago de Compostela, in northwest Spain. Several pivotal church declarations of the Middle Ages were made from here, including St. Bernard's preaching of the Second Crusade (which attracted a huge French following) and Thomas à Becket's excommunication of English king Henry II. By the mid-13th century the authenticity of St. Mary's relics was in doubt; others had been discovered in Provence. The basilica's decline continued until the French Revolution, when the basilica and adjoining monastery buildings were sold by the state. Only the basilica, cloister, and dormitory escaped demolition, and were falling into ruin when ace restorer Viollet-le-Duc, sent by his mentor Prosper Merimée, rode to the rescue in 1840 (he also restored the cathedrals of Laon and Amiens and Paris's Notre-Dame).

FEAST THE EYES & THE SOUL

The faithful have been making the pilgrimage to Vézelay since the 12th century when it was the departure point for the Second and Third Crusades. All marvel at the feast of sculptural details of the Basilique Ste-Madeleine, complete with biblical scenes, Christ figures, and a tongue-flailing demon bearing a strange resemblance to Jim Morrison in concert. Just behind the basilica is a park that's great for picnics and views of the Parc du Morvan.

Today the UNESCO-listed basilica has recaptured much of its glory and is considered to be one of France's most prestigious Romanesque showcases. The exterior tympanum was redone by Viollet-le-Duc (have a look at the eroded original as you exit the cloister), but the narthex (circa 1150) is a Romanesque masterpiece. Note the interwoven zodiac signs and depictions of seasonal crafts along its rim, similar to those at both Troyes and Autun. The pilgrims' route around the building is indicated by the majestic flowers over the left-hand entrance, which metamorphose into full-blown blooms on the right; an annual procession is still held on July 22. Among the most beautiful scenes on the nave capitals is one of Moses grinding grain (symbolizing the Old Testament) into flour (the New Testament), which St. Paul collects in a sack.

The basilica's exterior is best seen from the leafy terrace to the right of the facade. Opposite, a vast, verdant panorama encompasses vines, lush valleys, and rolling hills. In the foreground is the Flamboyant Gothic spire of St-Père-sous-Vézelay, a tiny village 3 km (2 mi) away that is the site of Marc Meneau's famed restaurant. ⊠*Pl. de la Basilique* ☎*03–86–33–39–50* ⊕*www.vezelaytourisme.com* ☎*Free, €3.20 for guided tour* ☉*Mon.–Sat. 8–12:30 and 1:15–6, Sun. 11–12:15.*

WHERE TO STAY & EAT

$ ✕ **Bougainville.** One of the few affordable restaurants in this well-heeled town is in an old house with a fireplace in the dining room and the requisite Burgundian color scheme of brown, yellow, and ocher. Philippe

8

Guillemard presides in the kitchen, turning out such regional favorites as hare stew, crayfish, escargot ragout in chardonnay sauce, and venison with chestnuts. He has also devised a vegetarian menu—a rarity in Burgundy—with deeply satisfying dishes like terrine of Époisses cheese and artichokes. ⊠*26 rue St-Étienne* ☎*03–86–33–27–57* ☰*MC, V* ⊘*Closed Tues., Wed., and mid-Nov.–mid-Feb.*

★ **$$$–$$$$** ✕⊡ **L'Espérance.** Heading one of the greatest kitchens in Burgundy, chef Marc Meneau is justly renowned for his original creations, such as roast veal in a bitter caramel-based sauce and turbot in a salt-crust *croûte.* The setting—by a stream and a large, statue-filled garden with Vézelay in the background—is exquisite. Note that the restaurant is closed Tuesday and there's no lunch Monday or Wednesday. Accommodations, which vary in price, come in a trinity of delights: charming rooms overlooking the garden; full suites in a renovated mill by the trout stream; and rooms in the annex, the Pré des Marguerites, done up in a cozy *style anglais.* ⊠*St-Père-en-Vézelay, 89450 St-Père* ☎*03–86–33–39–10* 🖶*03–86–33–26–15* ⊕*www.marc-meneau.com* ⚖*Reservations essential* ✒*31 rooms* ♿*In-room: no a/c (some), refrigerator. In-hotel: restaurant, pool, no elevator, public Wi-Fi* ☰*AE, DC, MC, V* ⊘*Closed Feb.* ⴲ|*MAP.*

$–$$ ✕⊡ **Poste & Lion d'Or.** On a small square in the lower part of town is this rambling hotel, completely renovated in a traditional style in 2006. A terrace out front welcomes you; the good-size rooms have traditional chintzes. The comfortable restaurant is a popular spot with locals, who come for the regional fare, such as roast partridge in blackcurrant sauce and rabbit casserole. ⊠*Pl. du Champ de Foire, 89450* ☎*03–86–33–21–23* 🖶*03–86–32–30–92* ⊕*www.laposte-liondor.com* ✒*37 rooms, 1 suite* ♿*In-hotel: restaurant, bar, no elevator* ☰*AE, MC, V* ⊘*Closed mid-Nov.–end-Feb.* ⴲ|*MAP.*

$$–$$$ ⊡ **Pontot.** With Vézelay's limited lodging you would do well to book ahead, especially for this historic fortified house with sumptuous little rooms and a lovely garden. Another advantage is the hotel's location in the center of the village halfway up the hill. ⊠*Pl. du Pontot, 89450* ☎*03–86–33–24–40* 🖶*03–86–33–30–05* ✒*10 rooms* ♿*In-room: no a/c, no TV. In-hotel: no elevator* ☰*V* ⊘*Closed mid-Nov.–May.*

SAULIEU

㉑ *48 km (30 mi) southeast of Vézelay.*

Saulieu's reputation belies its size: it's renowned for good food (Rabelais, that roly-poly 16th-century man of letters, extolled its gargantuan hospitality) and Christmas trees (a staggering million are packed and sent off from the area each year).

The town's **Basilique St-Andoche** (⊠*Pl. du Docteur Roclore*) is almost as old as that of Vézelay, though less imposing and much restored. Note the Romanesque capitals.

The **Musée François-Pompon,** adjoining the basilica, is a museum partly devoted to the work of animal-bronze sculptor Pompon (1855–1933), whose smooth, stylized creations seem contemporary but predate World War II. The museum also contains Gallo-Roman funeral stones, sacred art, and a room devoted to local gastronomic lore. ✉ *Rue Sallier* ☎ *03–80–64–19–51* 🖾 *€4* ⊘ *Apr.–Sept., Wed.–Mon. 10–12:30 and 2–6; Oct.–Mar., Wed.–Mon. 10–12:30 and 2–5:30.*

WHERE TO STAY & EAT

$$$$
Fodor'sChoice
★

✕🖾 **Relais Bernard Loiseau.** Originally a historic coaching auberge, this is now one of the region's finest hotels and restaurants. The setting is exquisite: a chapel-like wood-beam dining room with a lush flower garden radiating around it. Guest rooms combine exposed beams and glass panels with cheerful traditional furnishings; a newer annex has the most comfortable (and air-conditioned) rooms, while the more stylish accommodations (styles range from Louis XVI to Empire) are in the main house. Some are tiny (one is complete with porthole window), some are luxurious (one has a comfy balcony overlooking the countryside)—no matter which you book, try to get a room facing the garden courtyard. In the restaurant, chef Patrick Bertron continues to turn out a featherlight nouvelle version of rich Burgundian fare pioneered by Bernard Loiseau, one of France's culinary superstars, who died in 2003. ✉ *2 rue d'Argentine, off N6, 21210 Saulieu* ☎ *03–80–90–53–53* 🖾 *03–80–64–08–92* ⊕ *www.bernard-loiseau.com* 🛏 *33 rooms* ♿ *In-room: no a/c (some). In-hotel: restaurant, gym, no elevator, public Internet* ▭ *AE, DC, MC, V* ⊘ *Closed Tues.* ⫦ *BP.*

$

✕🖾 **Chez Camille.** Small, quiet, and friendly sum up this hotel in a 16th-century house with an exterior so ordinary you might easily pass it by. But within, rooms have period furniture and original wooden beams. Ask for No. 22 or No. 23, the most dramatic, with a beamed ceiling that looks like spokes in a wheel. Traditional Burgundian fare—duck and boar are specialties—makes up the menu in the glass-roof restaurant with its green wicker chairs. ✉ *1 pl. Édouard-Herriot, on N6 between Saulieu and Beaune, 21230 Arnay-le-Duc* ☎ *03–80–90–01–38* 🖾 *03–80–90–04–64* ⊕ *www.chez-camille.fr* 🛏 *11 rooms* ♿ *In-room: no a/c. In-hotel: restaurant, no elevator, public Internet* ▭ *AE, DC, MC, V* ⫦ *MAP.*

$$

🖾 **Château les Roches.** The village of Mont-St-Jean, about 15 kms (10 mi) from Saulieu, is renowned for its *vide-grenier*, or garage sale, that takes place every August. This charming B&B, built early in the 20th century by a Parisian judge for his mistress, has half a dozen spacious and luxuriously furnished rooms. Each is different, but all have carefully chosen furnishings and modern, well-appointed bathrooms. The American–Swedish and German owners serve delicious dinners in the dining room on Friday and Saturday. In the warmer months, breakfast is served on the terrace overlooking the valley. ✉ *Rue de Glanot, 21320 Mont-St-Jean* ☎ *03–80–84–32–71* ⊕ *www.lesroches-burgundy.com* 🛏 *6 rooms* ♿ *In-room: no a/c. In-hotel: tennis court, bicycles, public Internet* ▭ *AE, DC, MC, V* ⫦ *MAP.*

8

DIJON

38 km (23 mi) northeast of Châteauneuf, 315 km (195 mi) southeast of Paris.

GETTING HERE

As the administrative capital of Burgundy, Dijon has most everything a city has to offer, including fast TGV train service. There are 17 TGV trains leaving Paris daily and 14 on weekends (€51.70), so getting to Dijon by train is perhaps the most efficient way of arriving on Burgundy's doorstep. Once here the extensive TER network (Express Regional Transport) can take you almost anywhere within the region with frequent connections to Sens (€25.40), Nevers (€26.20), Beaune (€6.40) and Auxerre (€22.70). Right next to the Dijon Ville train station is the Gare Routière from which the regional TRANSCO (☎03–80–42–11–00) bus company operates 32 regular shared school/public bus routes that crisscross the Côte d'Or. For wine lovers, the No. 44 (Dijon–Chalon) represents the logical choice with an itinerary that reads like an oenologist's wish list. The 12:15 pm will get you to the cellar(s) of your choice in time for an early afternoon tasting. Price is based on the number of sections traveled and at €0.90 per section the trip to Beaune will cost you €6.30.

EXPLORING

The erstwhile wine-mustard center of the world, site of an important university, and studded with medieval art treasures, Dijon is the age-old capital of Burgundy. Throughout the Middle Ages, Burgundy was a duchy that led a separate existence from the rest of France, culminating in the rule of the four "Grand Dukes of the West" between 1364 and 1477—Philippe le Hardi (the Bold), Jean Sans Peur (the Fearless), Philippe le Bon (the Good), and the unfortunate Charles le Téméraire (the Foolhardy, whose defeat by French king Louis XI at Nancy spelled the end of Burgundian independence). A number of monuments date from this period, including the Palais des Ducs (Ducal Palace), now largely converted into an art museum. The city has magnificent half-timber houses and *hôtels particuliers,* some rivaling those in Paris. There's also a striking trio of central churches, built one following the other for three distinct parishes—St-Bénigne, its facade distinguished by Gothic galleries; St-Philibert, Dijon's only Romanesque church (with Merovingian vestiges); and St-Jean, an asymmetrical building now used as a theater.

Dijon's fame and fortune outlasted its dukes, and the city continued to flourish under French rule from the 17th century on. It has remained the major city of Burgundy—and the only one with more than 150,000 inhabitants. Its site, on the major European north–south trade route and within striking

> ## DO YOU GREY POUPON?
>
> Dijon's legendary Maille mustard shop at 32 rue de la Liberté (⊕www.maille.com), established in 1777, still sells Grey Poupon in painted ceramic pots at outrageous prices, along with a myriad selection of oils, vinegars, and spices.

distance of the Swiss and German borders, has helped maintain its economic importance. It's also a cultural center—just a portion of its museums are mentioned below. And many of the gastronomic specialties that originated here are known worldwide, although unfortunately the Dijon traditions have largely passed into legend. They include snails (now, shockingly, mainly imported from the Czech Republic), mustard (the handmade variety is a lost art), and cassis (a black-currant liqueur often mixed with white wine—preferably Burgundy Aligoté—to make *kir*, the popular aperitif).

THE HISTORIC CENTER

WHAT TO SEE

㉙ Cathédrale St-Bénigne. The chief glory of this comparatively austere cathedral is its atmospheric 11th-century crypt—a forest of pillars surmounted by a rotunda. ⊠ *Pl. St-Bénigne.*

㉔ Chambre des Métiers. This stately mansion with Gallo-Roman stelae incorporated into the walls (a quirky touch) was built in the 19th century. ⊠ *Rue Philippe-Pot.*

★ **㉝ Chartreuse de Champmol.** All that remains of this former charterhouse—a half-hour walk from Dijon's center and now surrounded by a psychiatric hospital—are the exuberant 15th-century gateway and the *Puits de Moïse* (*Well of Moses*), one of the greatest examples of late-medieval sculpture. The well was designed by Flemish master Claus Sluter, who also created several other masterpieces during the late 14th and early 15th centuries, including the tombs of the dukes of Burgundy. If you closely study Sluter's six large sculptures, you will discover the Middle Ages becoming the Renaissance right before your eyes. Representing Moses and five other prophets, they are set on a hexagonal base in the center of a basin and remain the most compellingly realistic figures ever crafted by a medieval sculptor.

㉘ Hôtel de Vogüé. This stately 17th-century mansion has a characteristic red, yellow, and green Burgundian tile roof—a tradition whose disputed origins lie either with the Crusades and the adoption of Arabic tiles or with Philip the Bold's wife, Marguerite of Flanders. ⊠ *Rue de la Chouette.*

㉚ Musée Archéologique (*Antiquities Museum*). This museum, in the former abbey buildings of the church of St-Bénigne, traces the history of the region through archaeological finds. ⊠ *5 rue du Dr-Maret* ☎ *03–80–30–88–54* 🆓 *Free* 🕙 *Mid-May–Sept., Wed.–Mon. 8:55–6; Oct.–mid-May, Wed.–Sun. 9–12:30 and 1:35–6.*

㉛ Musée de la Vie Bourguignonne & d'Art Sacré (*Museum of Burgundian Traditions & Religious Art*). Housed in the former Cistercian convent, one museum contains religious art and sculpture; the other has crafts and artifacts from Burgundy, including old storefronts saved from the streets of Dijon that have been reconstituted, in Hollywood moviemaking style, to form an imaginary street. ⊠ *17 rue Ste-Anne* ☎ *03–80–44–*

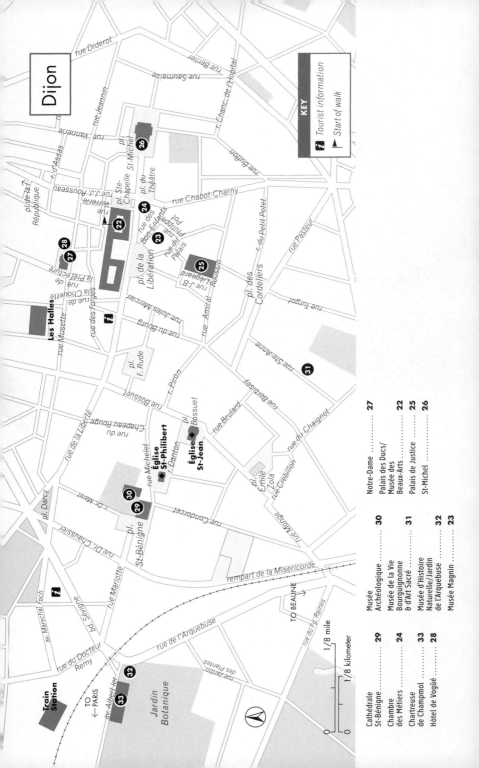

Dijon

KEY

🛈 *Tourist information*

▲ *Start of walk*

Burgundy Big Time

With no city larger than the capital Dijon (population 150,000), Burgundy seems the sleepy epitome of La France Profonde. Yet Dijon is one of the richest cities in France, and top European medieval painter Rogier van der Weyden stars down the road in Beaune. How come? Because, from 1369 to 1477, Burgundy hit the big time as an independent European power. In 1369, Philip II of Burgundy married Marguerite de Flandre. She brought Nevers, Franche-Comté, and French Flanders with her as dowry. Burgundy prospered. In 1435, the Peace of Arras, signed with France, recognized Burgundy's further claims to Belgium, Picardy, and the Netherlands. Burgundy's capital moved from Dijon to Brussels where, in 1436, Van der Weyden was appointed official city painter. In 1443 the art-loving

Burgundian Chancellor Nicolas Rolin commissioned the Last Judgment from Van der Weyden that still hangs in Beaune's Hôtel Dieu. Everything in the vineyard looked rosy, but there was just one problem: the northern and southern ends of Burgundy remained asunder, with Lorraine in between. When Charles the Bold succeeded Philip the Good in 1467, conquering Lorraine was top priority. Charles snatched part of Lorraine in 1475, but was slain two years later laying siege to Nancy. French King Louis XI seized the chance to invade Burgundy to annex it for the French crown. Charles's daughter Mary married Maximilian of Habsburg, taking Flanders and Holland with her. The Duchy of Burgundy had passed into the wine-vat of history.

12–69 ☒Free ⊙May–Sept., Wed.–Mon. 9–6; Oct.–Apr., Wed.–Mon. 9–noon and 2–6.

8

🕳 **Musée d'Histoire Naturelle** (*Natural History Museum*). The museum is in the impressive botanical garden, the **Jardin de l'Arquebuse**, a pleasant place to stroll amid the wide variety of trees and tropical flowers. ☒*1 av. Albert-Ier ☎03–80–76–82–76 museum, 03–80–76–82–84 garden* ☒*Free ⊙Museum Wed.–Fri. and Mon. 9–noon and 2–6, weekends 2–6; garden daily 7:30–6; until 8 o- in summer.*

🕳 **Musée Magnin.** In a 17th-century mansion, this museum showcases a private collection of original furnishings and paintings from the 16th to the 19th century. ☒*4 rue des Bons-Enfants* ☎03–80–67–11–10 ☒*€3.50 ⊙Tues.–Sun. 10–noon and 2–6.*

🕳 **Notre-Dame.** One of the city's oldest churches, Notre-Dame stands out with its spindlelike towers, delicate arches gracing its facade, and 13th-century stained glass. Note the windows in the north transept tracing the lives of five saints, as well as the 11th-century Byzantine cedar Black Virgin. ☒*Rue de la Préfecture.*

🕳 **Palais des Ducs** (*Ducal Palace*). The elegant, classical exterior of the former palace can best be admired from the half-moon Place de la Libération and the Cour d'Honneur. The **kitchens** (circa 1450), with their six huge fireplaces and (for its time) state-of-the-art aeration funnel in the ceiling, and the 14th-century **chapter house** catch the eye, as does the

Fodor's Choice
★

15th-century **Salle des Gardes** (Guard Room), with its richly carved and colored tombs and late-14th-century altarpieces. The palace now houses one of France's major art museums, the **Musée des Beaux-Arts** (Fine Arts Museum). Here are displayed the magnificent tombs sculpted by celebrated artist Claus Sluter for dukes Philip the Bold and his son John the Fearless—note their dramatically moving mourners, hidden in shrouds. These are just two of the highlights of a rich collection of medieval objects and Renaissance furniture gathered here as testimony to Marguerite of Flanders, wife of Philip the Bold, who brought to Burgundy not only her dowry, the rich province of Flanders (modern-day Belgium), but also a host of distinguished artists—including Rogier van der Weyden, Jan van Eyck, and Claus Sluter. Their artistic legacy can be seen in this collection, as well as at several of Burgundy's other museums and monuments. Among the paintings are works by Italian old masters and French 19th-century artists, such as Théodore Géricault and Gustave Courbet, and their Impressionist successors, notably Édouard Manet and Claude Monet. ⊠ *Rue Rameau* 🕾 *03–80–74–52–70* ⧦ *Free* ⊘ *Wed.–Mon. 10–5.*

㉕ Palais de Justice. The meeting place for the old regional Parliament of Burgundy serves as a reminder that Louis XI incorporated the province into France in the late 15th century. ⊠ *Rue du Palais.*

㉖ St-Michel. This church, with its chunky Renaissance facade, fast-forwards 300 years from Notre-Dame. ⊠ *Pl. St-Michel.*

WHERE TO STAY & EAT

As a culinary capital of France, Dijon has many superb restaurants, with three areas popular for casual dining. One is around Place Darcy, a square catering to all tastes and budgets: choose from the bustling Concorde brasserie, the quiet bar of the Hôtel de la Cloche, the underground Caveau de la Porte Guillaume wine-and-snack bar, or—for your sweet tooth—the Pâtisserie Darcy. For a really inexpensive meal, try the cafeteria Le Flunch on Boulevard de Brosses (near Place Darcy). Two other areas for casual dining in the evening are Place Émile-Zola and the old market (Les Halles), along Rue Bannelier.

★ $$$$ ✕ **Stéphane Derbord.** From starters like crawfish tails with anise or duck foie gras with gingerbread, to entrées like sizzling Charolais beef with ham and onions, to desserts such as rice pudding topped with caramelized spices, the talented Derbord, the city's rising gastronomic star, ensures dinner in this Art Deco restaurant is an elegantly refined affair. Tempting prix-fixe menus go from €25 to €85. ⊠ *10 pl. Wilson* 🕾 *03–80–67–74–64* ⊕ *www.restaurantstephanederbord.fr* ⧆ *Reservations essential* ⧮ *AE, DC, MC, V* ⊘ *Closed Sun., early Jan., 1 wk in Feb. and 1st 2 two wks Aug. No lunch Mon. or Tues.*

★ $$$–$$$$ ✕ **Le Pré aux Clercs.** This bright and beautiful Napoléon III–style restaurant is the perfect showcase for chef Jean-Pierre Billoux's golden touch, which can turn the lowliest farmyard chicken into a palate-plucking pièce de résistance. Most house specialties are inventive, like the langoustines with sherry vinaigrette or, to finish with, the roast pear with spices. The welcome is always convivial, and the wine list reads like a who's who of the region's best—but not necessarily best-known—winemakers. The €36 lunch menu (including wine) is a startling introduction to modern Burgundian cuisine. ⊠*13 pl. de la Libération* ☎*03–80–38–05–05* ⚠*Reservations essential* ▭*AE, MC, V* ⊘*Closed Mon. No dinner Sun.*

★ $$–$$$ ✕ **La Dame d'Aquitaine.** In a happy marriage between two of France's greatest gastronomic regions, chef Monique Saléra, from Pau, and her Dijonnais husband create a wonderful blend of regional cuisines. The foie gras and duck, in confit or with cèpes, come from Saléra's native region; the coq au vin, snails, and *lapin à la moutarde* (rabbit with mustard) from her husband's Burgundy; the *magret de canard aux baies de cassis* (duck breast with black currants) is a hybrid. The moderate prix-fixe menus, starting at €15 for lunch and €29 for dinner, offer succulent value. ⊠*23 pl. Bossuet* ☎*03–80–30–45–65* ⚠*Reservations essential* ▭*AE, DC, MC, V* ⊘*Closed Sun. No lunch Mon.*

$–$$$ ✕ **Les Oenophiles.** A collection of superbly restored 17th-century buildings belonging to the Burgundian Company of Wine Tasters forms the backdrop to this pleasant restaurant. It's lavishly furnished but also quaint (candles sparkle in the evening). The food is good, especially the roast pheasant with mushrooms, the langoustines with ginger, and the nougat-and-honey dessert. After dinner you can visit the small wine museum in the cellar. ⊠*18 rue Ste-Anne* ☎*03–80–30–73–52* ⚠*Reservations essential* ▭*AE, DC, MC, V* ⊘*Closed Sun.*

$ ✕ **Le Bistrot des Halles.** Of the many restaurants in the area, this one is the best value. Well-prepared dishes range from escargots to boeuf bourguignon with braised endive. Dine either at the sidewalk tables or inside, where traditional French decor—mirrors and polished wood—predominates. ⊠*10 rue Bannelier* ☎*03–80–49–94–15* ▭*MC, V* ⊘*Closed Sun. and Mon.*

$$$–$$$$ ✕▥ **Hostellerie du Chapeau Rouge.** A piano player in the bar and an elegant staircase give this hotel a degree of charm that the rooms, though clean and well appointed, lack. The restaurant, renowned as a haven of classic regional cuisine, serves snails cooked in basil and stuffed pigeon. Owner William Frachot and his staff are attentive. ⊠*5 rue Michelet, 21000* ☎*03–80–50–88–88* 📠*03–80–50–88–89* ⊕*www. chapeau-rouge.fr* ⇆*26 rooms, 4 suites* ♿*In-hotel: restaurant, bar, no elevator, public Internet* ▭*AE, DC, MC, V.*

$$$–$$$$ ▥ **La Cloche.** In use since the 19th century, La Cloche is a successful cross between a luxury chain and a grand hotel. The entry hall is imposing, and the gleaming bar has smart leather chairs. Rooms are large and plush; try to get one overlooking the tiny, tranquil back garden and its reflecting pool. The garden is also the backdrop for the stylish restaurant, Les Jardins de la Cloche. ⊠*14 pl. Darcy, 21000* ☎*03–80–30–12–32* 📠*03–80–30–04–15* ⊕*www.hotel-lacloche.com* ⇆*53 rooms, 15 suites* ♿*In-room: refrigerator. In-hotel: restaurant, bar, gym, no-smoking rooms, public Wi-Fi* ▭*AE, DC, MC, V.*

$–$$ ▥ **Wilson.** This hotel's "bones" are 17th century, set as it is in a fetching timber-frame post house, but inside rooms are modern, airy, light, and accented with wooden beams and Louis Treize chairs. Another

8

plus: the hotel is near Stéphane Derbord's noted restaurant. ⊠*Pl. Wilson, 21000* ☏*03–80–66–82–50* 🖷*03–80–36–41–54* ⊕*www.wilsonhotel.com* 🛏*27 rooms* ⚲*In-room: no a/c (some). In-hotel: parking (fee), no elevator, public Wi-Fi* 🟰*AE, MC, V.*

¢–$ 🏨 **Le Jacquemart.** In old Dijon, in a neighborhood known for its antiques shops, the recently refurbished Le Jacquemart is housed in an 18th-century building with a steep staircase, high-ceilinged rooms of variable comfort, and rustic furniture. It's a quiet, restful spot and thus very popular, so make sure you book well in advance. ⊠*32 rue Verrerie, 21000* ☏*03–80–60–09–60* 🖷*03–80–60–09–69* ⊕*www.hotellejacquemart.fr* 🛏*31 rooms* ⚲*In-room: no a/c. In-hotel: no elevator, public Wi-Fi* 🟰*AE, MC, V.*

NIGHTLIFE & THE ARTS

Dijon stages **L'Été Musical** *(Musical Summer)*, a predominantly classical music festival in June; the tourist office can supply the details. For three days in June the city hosts **Arts in the Streets** (☏*03–80–65–91–00 for information*), an event at which dozens of painters exhibit their works. During the **Bell-Ringing Festival,** in mid-August, St-Bénigne's bells chime and chime. In September Dijon puts on the **Festival International de Folklore.** November in Dijon is the time for the **International Gastronomy Fair.**

Bar Messire (⊠*3 rue Jules-Mercier* ☏*03–80–30–16–40*) attracts an older crowd.**Central Perk** (⊠*15 bis rue du Général Fauconnet* ☏*03–80–71–42–74*) is a popular disco. **Eden Bar** (⊠*12 rue des Perrieres* ☏*03–80–41–48–64*) caters to a broad clientele.

SHOPPING

The auction houses in Dijon are good places to prospect for antiques and works of art. Tempting food items—mustard, snails, and candy (including snail-shape chocolates–*escargots de Bourgogne*) can easily be found in the pedestrian streets in the heart of Dijon.

WINE COUNTRY

Burgundy—Bourgogne to the French—has given its name to one of the world's great wines. Although many people will allow a preference for Bordeaux, others for Alsace, Loire, or Rhône wines, some of the leading French gourmets insist that the precious red nectars of Burgundy have no rivals, and treat them with reverence. So for some travelers a trip to Burgundy's Wine Country takes on the feel of a spiritual pilgrimage. East of the Parc du Morvan, the low hills and woodland gradually open up, and vineyards, clothing the contour of the land in orderly beauty, appear on all sides. The vineyards' steeply banked hills stand in contrast to the region's characteristic gentle slopes. Burgundy's most famous vineyards run south from Dijon through Beaune to Mâcon along what has become known as the Côte d'Or (*or* doesn't mean gold here, but is an abbreviation of *orient,* or east). Here you can go from vineyard to vineyard tasting the various samples (both the powerfully tannic young reds and the mellower older ones). Purists will remind you that you're not supposed to drink them but simply taste them, then spit them into the little buckets discreetly provided. But who wants to be a purist?

The Côte d'Or is truly golden for wine lovers, branching out over the countryside in four great vineyard-*côtes* (slopes or hillsides) in southern Burgundy. The northernmost, the Côte de Nuits, sometimes called the "Champs-Élysées of Burgundy," is the land of the unparalleled grand cru reds from the pinot noir grape. The Côte de Beaune, just to the south, is known for both full-bodied reds and some of the best dry whites in the world. Even farther south is the Côte Chalonnaise. Although not as famous, it produces bottle after bottle of chardonnay almost as rich as its northern neighbors. Finally, the Côte Mâconnaise, the largest of the four côtes, brings its own quality whites to the market. There are hundreds of vintners in this region, many of them producing top wines from surprisingly small parcels of land. To connect these dots, consult the regional tourist offices for full information of the noted wine routes of the region. The 74-km (50-mi) Route des Grands Crus ranges from Dijon to Beaune and Santenay. You can extend this route southward by the Route Touristique des Grands Vins, which travels some 98 km (60 mi) in and around Chalon-sur-Saône. Coming from the north, you can tour the areas (covered above) around Auxerre and Chablis on the Route des Vignobles de l'Yonne.

CLOS DE VOUGEOT

36 *16 km (10 mi) south of Dijon.*

The reason to come to Vougeot is to see its *grange viticole* (winemaking barn) surrounded by its famous vineyard—a symbolic spot for all Burgundy aficionados.

Fodor'sChoice The **Château du Clos de Vougeot** was constructed in the 12th century by ★ Cistercian monks from neighboring Cîteaux—who were in need of wine for mass and also wanted to make a diplomatic offering—and completed during the Renaissance. It's best known as the seat of Burgundy's elite company of wine lovers, the Confrérie des Chevaliers du Tastevin, who gather here in November at the start of an annual three-day festival, Les Trois Glorieuses. Josephine Baker slurped here once. You can admire the château's cellars, where ceremonies are held, and ogle the huge 13th-century grape presses, uncertain marvels of medieval engineering. ☎03–80–62–86–09 ⊕*www.tastevin-bourgogne.com* €3.70 ⊙*Apr.–Sept., daily 9–6:30; Oct.–Mar., daily 9–11:30 and 2–5:30.*

Near Clos de Vougeot at St-Nicolas-lès-Cîteaux is the **Abbaye de Cîteaux,** where the austere Cistercian order was founded in 1098 by Robert de Molesmes. The abbey has housed monks for more than 900 years. From D996, follow signs that point the way along a short country road that breaks off from the road to Château de Gilly, a four-

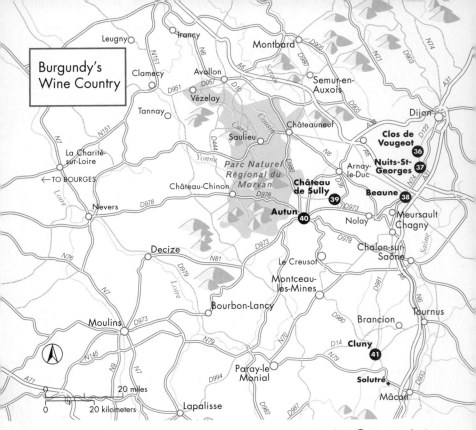

star hotel. ⊠ *Off D996* ☎*03–80–61–32–58* 💷*€7* 🕐*May–early Oct., Tues.–Sat. 9:15–noon and 1:45–4:45; Sun. after 10:30 mass* ✆*Guided tours available.*

WHERE TO STAY & EAT

$$$–$$$$ ✕⊡ **Château de Gilly.** Considered by some an obligatory stop on their tour of Burgundy's vineyards, this château, 3 km (2 mi) from Vougeot, has almost become too popular for its own good (an on-site conference center doesn't help things). Formerly an abbey and a government-run avant-garde theater, the château does show some glorious vestiges worthy of its Relais & Châteaux parentage: painted ceilings, a gigantic vaulted crypt-cellar (now the dining room), suits of armor. Guest rooms have magnificent beamed ceilings and lovely views, though the least expensive have standard-issue fabrics, reproduction furniture, and ordinary bathrooms. The restaurant's menu includes pastries made with Cîteaux's famous handmade cheese and perch with a *pain d'épices* (gingerbread) crust. An "elegant form of dress" is requested for dinner. ⊠*Gilly-lès-Cîteaux, 21640* ☎*03–80–62–89–98* 🖷*03–80–62–82–34* ⊕*www.chateau-gilly.com* 🛏*37 rooms, 11 suites* ⚥*In-room: no a/c. In-hotel: restaurant, tennis court, pool, public Wi-Fi* ▤*AE, DC, MC, V* ¶⊙*MAP.*

NUITS-ST-GEORGES

㊲ *21 km (13 mi) south of Dijon, 5 km (3 mi) south of Clos de Vougeot.*

Wine has been made in Nuits-St-Georges since Roman times; its "dry, tonic, and generous qualities" were recommended to Louis XIV for medicinal use. But this is also the heart of currant country, where crops yield up the wonderfully delicious ingredient known as cassis (the signature taste of the famous kir cocktail). The **Cassisium,** in a sparkling glass and steel building, explores the world of cassis using films, interactive displays, guided tours of Védrenne's liqueur production, and even a "slot" fruit machine. A cassis tasting is the final stop. ✉ *Rue des Frères Montgolfier* ☎ *03–80–62–49–70* 💶 *€6.80* ⏱ *Apr.–late Nov., daily 10–1, 2–7; late Nov.–Mar., Tues.–Sat. 10:30–1, 2–5:30.*

WHERE TO STAY & EAT

$ ✕ **La Toute Petite Auberge.** Vosne-Romanée, the greatest wine village on the côte, also entices with one of the most charming restaurants in Burgundy. No surprises on the menu (jambon persillé, coq au vin, crème brûlée), but everything is excellent and prices are more than reasonable. As you would expect, the wine list is top-notch. ✉ *Vosne-Romanée, on the N74, 2 km (1 mi) north of Nuits-St-Georges* ☎ *03–80–61–02–03* ⚑ *Reservations essential* ▬ *MC, V* ⏱ *Closed Wed. No dinner Tues.*

¢–$ ✕ **Au Bois de Charmois.** About 3 km (2 mi) out of Nuits-St-Georges, on the way toward Meuilley, is this marvelous little inn serving local fare at tasty prices—a three-course lunch (sample the huge plate of garlicky frog legs) is a finger-lickin' €16. An even less-expensive menu is available at lunch on weekdays. It's especially pleasant to sit in the courtyard under the ancient trees, though on chilly, gray days the small dining room is full of good cheer. ✉ *Rte. de la Serrée* ☎ *03–80–61–04–79* ▬ *MC, V* ⏱ *Closed Mon.*

★ $$–$$$ 🏨 **Domaine Comtesse Michel de Loisy.** Comtesse Christine de Loisy is an institution unto herself in the Nuits-St-Georges area: an internationally traveled, erudite *dame d'un certain âge,* who is also a well-known oenologist and local historian. Rooms in her eclectic *hôtel particulier* are furnished with fine antiques, tapestries, chintz-covered walls, and Oriental carpets and memorably temper grandeur with old-fashioned charm. Four of the five have a view of the flower-filled courtyard or the magnificent winter garden. Happily, the domain offers an optional two-day program of wine tastings, Burgundy-focused meals, and vineyard excursions. ✉ *28 rue du Général-de-Gaulle, 21700* ☎ *03–80–61–02–72* 🖷 *03–80–61–36–14* 🌐 *www.domaine-de-loisy.com* 🛏 *3 rooms, 2 suites* ⚑ *In-room: no a/c, no TV. In-hotel: no elevator* ▬ *AE, MC, V* ⏱ *Closed end-Dec.–early-Jan.* ⵔ *BP.*

$ 🏨 **Albizzia.** The Dufouleur family, Burgundian wine growers since the 16th century, run this charming chambre d'hôte in the small village of Quincey, just outside Nuits-St-Georges. Facing the night-lighted church in the village square, the B&B is in an old stone farmhouse, entirely renovated, with two very cozy double rooms. Breakfast in summer is served in the beautiful garden, and wine tastings (with local cheeses)

8

are held year-round in the Dufouleur cellar. ✉ *Grande Rue, Quincey, 4 km (2½ mi) south of Nuits-St-Georges, 21700* ☎ *03–80–61–13–23* 🖷 *03–80–61–13–23* ➲ *4 rooms* ⚄ *In-room: no a/c, no TV. In-hotel: no elevator, no-smoking rooms* ▤ *No credit cards* ⦿ *BP.*

BEAUNE

③⑧
Fodor'sChoice
★

19 km (12 mi) south of Nuits-St-Georges, 40 km (25 mi) south of Dijon, 315 km (197 mi) southeast of Paris.

GETTING HERE

The wine capital of Burgundy is also one of the most visited towns in the region. Though there are only 2 direct TGV trains leaving Paris Gare de Lyon daily (at 7:14 am and 5:44 pm), there are 12 in all, with changes at Dijon, and 10 on weekends. Travel time is just under three hours and the peak fare is €55.40. Beaune is only 20 minutes from Dijon (€6.40) and gets plenty of train traffic from the through lines to Lyon (€21) and Nevers (€22.80). For those heading farther north, trains to Laroche Migennes (Auxerre €26.10) and the 8:24 to Sens (€29) are available. Beaune also benefits from the broad regional TRANSCO bus network and buses, which depart from the SNCF station, run to Dijon via Nuits St. Georges (60 mins on the No. 44 wine-lovers line), and to Saulieu (Fri. only at 6 pm) with the No. 72. Access by car is facilitated by its position at the confluence of the A6 (Paris to the Côte d'Azur), the A31 (North to Dijon and Nancy), and the A36 (connecting with Alsace and Germany), as well as being served by the N74.

EXPLORING

Beaune is sometimes considered the wine capital of Burgundy because it's at the heart of the region's vineyards, with the Côte de Nuits to the north and the Côte de Beaune to the south. In late November, Les Trois Glorieuses, a three-day wine auction and fête at the Hospices de Beaune, pulls in connoisseurs and the curious from France and abroad. Despite the hordes, Beaune remains one of France's most attractive provincial towns, teeming with art above ground and wine barrels down below.

Some of the region's finest vineyards are owned by the **Hospices de Beaune** (better known to some as the Hôtel-Dieu), founded in 1443 as a hospital to provide free care for men who had fought in the Hundred Years' War. A visit to the Hospices (across from the tourist office) is one of the highlights of a stay in Beaune; its tiled roofs and Flemish architecture have become icons of Burgundy, and the same glowing colors and intricate patterns are seen throughout the region. The interior looks medieval but was repainted by 19th-century Gothic restorer Viollet-le-Duc. Of special note are the **Grand' Salle,** more than 160 feet long, with the original furniture, a great wooden roof, and the picturesque **Cour d'Honneur.** The Hospices carried on its medical activities until 1971—its nurses still wearing their habitlike uniforms—and the hospital's history is retraced in the museum, whose wide-ranging collections contain some weird medical instruments from the 15th century. You can also see a collection of tapestries that belonged to the repentant founder of the Hospices, ducal chancellor Nicolas Rolin, who hoped charity would relieve him of his sins—one of which was collecting wives. Outstanding are both the tapestry he had made for Madame Rolin III, with its repeated motif of "my only star," and one relating the legend of St. Eloi and his miraculous restoration of a horse's leg. But the star of the collection is Rogier Van der Weyden's stirring, gigantic 15th-century masterpiece *The Last Judgment,* commissioned for the hospital by Rolin. The intense colors and mind-tripping imagery were meant to scare the illiterate patients into religious submission. Notice the touch of misogyny; more women are going to hell than to heaven, while Christ, the judge, remains completely unmoved. A son-et-lumière show is presented every evening April through October. ⊠*Rue de l'Hôtel-Dieu* ☎*03–80–24–45–00* ⊕*www.hospices-de-beaune.tm.fr* ⊡*€6* ☉*Late Mar.–mid-Nov., daily 9–6:30; mid-Nov.–late Mar., daily 9–11:30 and 2–5:30.*

A series of tapestries relating the life of the Virgin hangs in Beaune's main church, the 12th-century **Collégiale Notre-Dame.** ⊠*Just off Av. de la République.*

★ To many, the liquid highlight of a visit to Burgundy is a visit to the **Marché aux Vins** *(Wine Market)* where, in flickering candlelight, and armed with your own *tastevin* (which you get to keep as a souvenir), you can taste a tongue-tingling, mind-spinning array of regional wines in the atmospheric setting of barrel-strewn cellars and vaulted passages. The selection runs from young Beaujolais to famous old Burgundies and there's no limit on how much you drink. Other Beaune tasting houses include Cordelier on the Rue de l'Hôtel-Dieu and the Caves Patriarche on the Rue du Collège. ⊠*Rue Nicolas-Rolin* ☎*03–80–25–08–20* ⊡*€10* ☉*Daily 9:30–noon and 2–6.*

<table>
<tr><td>**NEED A BREAK?**</td><td>For a break and a snack of handmade pain d'épices (gingerbread) in all shapes and incarnations, stop by Mulot & Petitjean (⊠*Pl. Carnot*). This famed pastry shop has a 200-year history.</td></tr>
</table>

WHERE TO STAY & EAT

★ $$$$ ✕ **Bernard Morillon.** This famous restaurant, in a stylish 18th-century town house that shares a courtyard (where you can dine in summer) with the neighboring Cep Hotel, is considered by many critics to be the best table in Beaune. Soft-spoken chef Bernard Morillon lets his cooking do the talking. Warm oyster soup with poached quail eggs, fillet of local Charolais beef with foie gras, and poulet de Bresse (that famous succulent regional chicken) simmered in red wine, are among Bernard's mouthwatering delights. Service is as polished as the gleaming silverware, and as warmhearted as the Burgundy wine list. ⊠*31 rue Maufoux* ☎*03–80–24–12–06* ⚖*Reservations essential* ⊟*AE, DC, MC, V* ☉*Closed Mon., and Feb. No lunch Tues. and Sat.*

$$–$$$ ✕ **L'Écusson.** Don't be put off by its unprepossessing exterior: this is a comfortable, friendly, thick-carpeted restaurant with good-value prix-fixe menus. Showcased is chef Jean-Pierre Senelet's sure-footed culinary mastery with dishes like boar terrine with dried apricot and juniper berries, and roast crayfish with curried semolina and ratatouille. ⊠*2 rue*

8

du Lieutenant-Dupuis ☎*03–80–24–03–82* ⚄*Reservations essential* ▤*AE, DC, MC, V* ☉*Closed Wed., Sun., and Feb.*

$–$$ ✕ **La Grilladine.** Chef Jean-Marc Jacquel's cuisine, though not elaborate, is good, hearty Burgundy fare: boeuf bourguignon and *oeufs en meurette* (eggs with onions and wine sauce on toast). The prix-fixe menus are extremely reasonable. Warm and cheerful, the room allures with rose-pink tablecloths, exposed stone walls, and an ancient beam supporting the ceiling. ✉*17 rue Maufoux* ☎*03–80–22–22–36* ⚄*Reservations essential* ▤*MC, V* ☉*Closed Mon. and mid-Dec.–mid-Jan.*

★ $$$–$$$$ ✕▦ **Hostellerie de Levernois.** An idyllically elegant and gracious country manor, this Relais & Châteaux property, smartly run by Jean-Louis and Susanne Bottigliero, gleams with light from its large picture windows. The cuisine, under chef Vincent Maillard, who previously worked at the Carlton in Cannes and the Louis XV in Monaco, is of the highest standard. The lodgings in the modern annex overlooking the landscaped garden are the most up to date. Meals are occasions to be savored, but they are also expensive; prix-fixe menus begin at €65 and may spotlight duck with foie gras and truffles or langoustines with mustard vinaigrette. The bistro offers more reasonably priced menus at €28 and €32, but is only open for lunch weekdays. ✉*Rte. de Verdun-sur-le-Doubs, 3 km (2 mi) east of Beaune, 21200 Levernois* ☎*03–80–24–73–58* 🖷*03–80–22–78–00* ⊕*www.levernois.com* ⟋*15 rooms, 1 suite, 2 apartments* ⚄*In-room: refrigerator. In-hotel: 2 restaurants, no elevator, public Wi-Fi* ▤*AE, DC, MC, V* ☉*Closed Feb.–mid-Mar.* ⑂*MAP.*

$–$$ ✕▦ **Hôtel Central.** This well-run establishment with modern rooms, just 100 yards from the Hospices de Beaune, lives up to its name. The stone-walled restaurant (closed late November to late January) is cozy—some might say cramped—and the consistently good cuisine is popular with locals, who come to enjoy oeufs en meurette and coq au vin. Service is efficient, if a little hurried. ✉*2 rue Victor-Millot, 21200* ☎*03–80–24–77–24* 🖷*03–80–22–30–40* ⟋*20 rooms, 10 with bath* ⚄*In-room: no a/c (some), refrigerator. In-hotel: restaurant, no elevator* ▤*MC, V.*

★ $$$–$$$$ ▦ **Hôtel Le Cep.** This venerable town-center hotel might be considered the shining showpiece among Beaune's myriad hostelries. It's actually an ensemble of buildings spanning the 14th to the 16th century, oozing history from every arcade of its Renaissance courtyard, yet all rooms—named for different Burgundy wines—have been luxuriously modernized, and decorated with crystal chandeliers and individual panache; some have wood beams, others canopied or four-poster beds. Those on the top story offer views over Beaune's famed multicolored tile roofs. Breakfast is served in a vaulted cellar; there's no hotel restaurant as such, but the lip-smackerous Bernard Morillon operates right next door. ✉*27 rue Maufoux, 21200* ☎*03–80–22–35–48* 🖷*03–80–22–76–80* ⊕*www.hotel-cep-beaune.com* ⟋*40 rooms, 22 suites* ⚄*In-room: refrigerator. In-hotel: bar, parking (fee), public Wi-Fi* ▤*AE, DC, MC, V.*

$$$ ⛨ **Château de Chorey.** To really soak up the flavor of the vineyards, stay at this family winery about 2 km (1 mi) north of Beaune. Guest rooms are up a circular stone staircase; furnishings are from the attic. Though it's a bit rustic and casual, it's the kind of place where you can open the windows and let the country air, perfumed by grapes, waft in. A good breakfast is served, but no other meals; try their wine before going out to eat in Beaune. ⊠*2 rue Jacques-Germain, 21200 Chorey-les-Beaune* ☎*03–80–22–06–05* 📠*03–80–24–03–93* 🛏*3 rooms, 2 suite* ♿*In-room: no a/c, refrigerator. In-hotel: no elevator* ▤*MC, V* ⊘*Closed Nov.–mid-Apr.* ⎟⊙⎟*BP.*

$–$$ ⛨ **Hôtel de la Cloche.** In a 15th-century residence in the heart of town, this hotel has rooms furnished with care by owners Monsieur and Madame Lamy, both of whom are always on hand to assist. The best rooms, those with a full bath, are more expensive; the smaller yet delightful attic rooms, each with a shower and separate toilet, are less so. Breakfast is served on the garden terrace in summer. Recent renovations and the addition of eight new rooms overlooking the courtyard have given this dependable address a welcome face-lift—and the price is right. ⊠*42 pl. Madeleine, 21200* ☎*03–80–24–66–33* 📠*03–80–24–04–24* 🛏*29 rooms, 2 suites* ♿*In-room: refrigerator. In-hotel: public Internet* ▤*AE, MC, V* ⎟⊙⎟*MAP.*

THE ARTS

In July Beaune celebrates its annual **International Festival of Baroque Music,** which draws big stars of the music world. On the third Sunday in November at the Hospices is Beaune's famous wine festival, **Les Trois Glorieuses** (⊕*www.bourgogne.net/vente/1vente.html*). For both festivals, contact **Beaune's Office de Tourisme** (⊠*1 rue de l'Hôtel-Dieu* ☎*03–80–26–21–30* 📠*03–80–25–04–81* ⊕*www.beaune-burgundy.com*).

8

CHÂTEAU DE SULLY

㊴ *35 km (19 mi) west of Beaune.*

"The Fontainebleau of Burgundy" was how Madame de Sévigné described this turreted Renaissance château, proclaiming the inner court, whose Italianate design was inspired by Sebastiano Serlio, as the latest in chic. The building is magnificent, landmarked by four lantern-topped corner towers that loom over a romantic moat filled with the waters of the River Drée. Originally constructed by the de Rabutin family and once owned by Gaspard de Saulx-Tavannes—an instigator of the St. Bartholomew's Day Massacre, August 24, 1572, he reputedly ran through Paris's streets yelling, "Blood, blood! The doctors say that bleeding is as good for the health in August as in May!"—the château was partly reconstructed in elegant Régence style in the 18th century. Maurice de MacMahon, the Irish-origin president of France from 1873 to 1879, was born here in 1808. ☎*03–85–82–09–86* ⊕*www.chateaudesully.com* 💶*€3.50, €7.30 for guided tour* ⊙*Daily 10–noon and 2–6.*

AUTUN

 20 km (12 mi) southwest of Sully, 48 km (30 mi) west of Beaune.

Fodor'sChoice
★

One of the most richly endowed *villes d'art* in Burgundy, Autun is a great draw for fans of both Gallo-Roman and Romanesque art. The name derives from Augustodonum—city of Augustus—and it was Augustus Caesar who called it "the sister and rival of Rome itself." You can still see traces of the Roman occupation—dating from when Autun was much larger and more important than it is today—in its well-preserved archways, Porte St-André and Porte d'Arroux, and the Théâtre Romain, once the largest arena in Gaul. Parts of the Roman walls surrounding the town also remain and give a fair indication of its size in those days. The significance of the curious Pierre (or "stone") de Couhard, a pyramidlike Roman construction, baffles archaeologists. Logically enough, this Roman outpost became a center for the new 11th-century style based on Roman precedent, the Romanesque, and its greatest sculptor, Gislebertus, left his precocious mark on the town cathedral. Several centuries later, Napoléon and his brother Joseph studied here at the military academy.

★ Autun's principal monument is the **Cathédrale St-Lazare,** a Gothic cathedral in Classical clothing. It was built between 1120 and 1146 to house the relics of St. Lazarus; the main tower, spire, and upper reaches of the chancel were added in the late 15th century. Lazarus's tricolor tomb was dismantled in 1766 by canons: vestiges of exquisite workmanship can be seen in the neighboring Musée Rolin. The same canons also did their best to transform the Romanesque-Gothic cathedral into a Classical temple, adding pilasters and other ornaments willy-nilly. Fortunately, the lacy Flamboyant Gothic organ tribune and some of the best Romanesque stonework, including the inspired nave capitals and the tympanum above the main door, emerged unscathed. Jean Ingres's painting *The Martyrdom of St. Symphorien* has been relegated to a dingy chapel in the north aisle of the nave. The *Last Judgment* carved in stone above the main door was plastered over in the 18th century, which preserved not only the stylized Christ and elongated apostles but also the inscription ▨,%▨%▨ 4▨3 ▨▨ ▨%▨▨ (Gislebertus did this). Christ's head, which had disappeared, was found by a local canon shortly after World War II. Make sure to visit the cathedral's **Salle Capitulaire,** which houses Gislebertus's original capitals, distinguished by their relief carvings. The cathedral provides a stunning setting for **Musique en Morvan,** a festival of classical music held in July. ✉*Pl. St-Louis.*

The **Musée Rolin,** across from the cathedral, was built by Chancellor Nicholas Rolin, an important Burgundian administrator and famous art patron (he's immortalized in one of the Louvre's greatest paintings, Jan van Eyck's *Madonna and the Chancellor Rolin*). The museum is noteworthy for its early Flemish paintings and sculpture, including the magisterial *Nativity* painted by the Maître de Moulins in the 15th century. But the collection's star is a Gislebertus masterpiece, the *Temptation of Eve,* which originally topped one of the side doors of the cathedral.

Try to imagine the missing elements of the scene: Adam on the left and the devil on the right. ⊠*5 rue des Bancs* ☎*03–85–52–09–76* ✉*€3.50* ⊙*Oct.–Mar., Wed.–Sat. 10–noon and 2–5, Sun. 10–noon and 2:30–5; Apr.–Sept., Wed.–Mon. 9:30–noon and 1:30–6.*

The **Théâtre Romain,** at the edge of town on the road to Chalon-sur-Saône, is a historic spot for lunch. Pick up the makings for a picnic in town and eat it on the stepped seats, where as many as 15,000 Gallo-Roman spectators perched during performances 2 millennia ago. In August a Gallo-Roman performance—the only one of its kind—is put on by locals wearing period costumes. The peak of a Gallo-Roman pyramid can be seen in the foreground. Elsewhere on the outskirts of town are the remains of an ancient Roman Temple of Janus.

CIRCLING THE WAGONS À LA FRANÇAISE

On Friday and Saturday nights in early August, Augustodunum comes to life. Unique in France, Augustodunum draws 600 people to Autun's ancient Roman theater where they bring Celtic and Gallo-Roman times to life in a Busby Berkeley-esque extravaganza featuring Celtic fairies, Roman gladiators, and chariot races. Log on to ⊕ www.ville-autun.fr/distrair_spect_murcie.php for all the details.

WHERE TO STAY & EAT

$–$$$ ✕▦ **Les Ursulines.** Placed above the Roman ramparts of the old city, this converted 17th-century convent offers spacious, well-kept rooms overlooking a geometric, French-style garden. The restaurant, adorned with plush green carpets, floral-patterned curtains, and cane-backed Louis XV–style chairs, is worth a trip in itself, especially for the escargots with dried tomatoes and garlic confit. Some guest rooms have fine views of the surrounding Morvan hills, and breakfast is served in the historic chapel area. ⊠*14 rue Rivault, 71400* ☎*03–85–86–58–58* 🖶*03–85–86–23–07* ⊕*www.hotelursulines.fr* ⇄*36 rooms, 7 suites* ♿*In-room: no a/c (some), refrigerator. In-hotel: no-smoking rooms, no elevator, public Wi-Fi* ▭*AE, DC, MC, V.*

$–$$ ✕▦ **Hostellerie du Vieux Moulin.** In a calm setting near the center of town, this former mill sits in a tree-lined garden with a pond. The spacious rooms—some with views of the river, others looking out over the countryside—are done in a cozy country style. The restaurant has a rustic feel with a great stone fireplace, wooden beams, wrought-iron trim, and well-chosen antiques. The theme is carried over into the kitchen, where the refined and innovative dishes are inspired by traditional Burgundian specialties like *oeufs en meurette* (eggs poached in red wine). Pastries are the chef's specialty, so don't forget dessert. Lunch and dinner are served in the garden in the warmer months. ⊠*Porte d'Arroux, 71400* ☎*03–85–52–10–90* 🖶*03–85–86–32–15* ⇄*16 rooms* ♿*In-room: no TV (some). In-hotel: no elevator, public Wi-Fi* ▭*MC, V.*

8

CLUNY

41   *77 km (46 mi) southeast of Autun.*

GETTING HERE

Getting to Cluny is quite easy as there are seven trains leaving Paris Gare de Lyon Monday to Saturday and six on Sunday (€69), though travel times vary from three to five hours depending on the connection. The fastest combine TGV and a 30-minute bus liaison from Mâcon that can also take you to Chalon-sur-Saone, three times a day (at 8:31 am, 1:42 pm, and 6:11 pm), for connections to Dijon at 1:07 pm, Laroche Migennes (Auxerre) at 1:26 pm, Montchanin at 3 pm, Autun at 4:14 pm, Etang at 4:42 pm, and Sens at 8:02 pm. TRANSDEV (Les Rapides de Saône et Loire: www.r-s-l.fr) have regular buses that also link Cluny to Chalon-sur-Saone, where you can connect to Mâcon, Autun, and Le Creusot TGV railway station. Driving to Cluny is a delight as the surrounding countryside of the Mâconnais is among the most beautiful of France, with rolling fields and picturesque villages reminding one of why it is so easy to fall in love with France.

EXPLORING

The village of Cluny is legendary for its medieval abbey, once the center of a vast Christian empire and today one of the most towering of medieval ruins. Although most of the complex was destroyed by the mobs of the French Revolution, one soaring transept of this church remains standing, today one of the most magnificent sights of Romanesque architecture. Looming as large as Cluny does, art historians have written themselves into knots tracing the fundamental influence of its architecture in the development of early Gothic style. Founded in the 10th century, the **Ancienne Abbaye** was the largest church in Europe until the 16th century, when Michelangelo built St. Peter's in Rome. Cluny's medieval abbots were as powerful as popes; in 1098 Pope Urban II (himself a Cluniac) assured the head of his old abbey that Cluny was the "light of the world." That assertion, of dubious religious validity, has not stood the test of time—after the Revolution the abbey was sold as national property and much of it used as a stone quarry. Today Cluny stands in ruins, a reminder of the vanity of human grandeur. The ruins, however, suggest the size and gorgeous super-romantic glory of the abbey at its zenith, and piecing it back together in your mind is part of the attraction.

Fodor'sChoice
★

In order to get a clear sense of what you are looking at, start at the **Porte d'Honneur,** the entrance to the abbey from the village, whose classical architecture is reflected in the pilasters and Corinthian columns of the **Clocher de l'Eau-Bénite** (a majestic bell tower), crowning the only remaining part of the abbey church, the south transept. Between the two are the reconstructed monumental staircase, which led to the portal of the abbey church, and the excavated column bases of the vast narthex. The entire nave is gone. On one side of the transept is a national horse-breeding center (*haras*) founded in 1806 by Napoléon and constructed with materials from the destroyed abbey; on the other is an elegant pavilion built as new monks' lodgings in the 18th century. The gardens in front of it once contained an ancient lime tree (destroyed by a 1982 storm) named after Abélard, the controversial philosopher who sought shelter at the abbey in 1142. Off to the right is the 13th-century *farinier* (flour mill), with its fine oak-and-chestnut roof and collection of exquisite Romanesque capitals from the vanished choir. The **Musée Ochier,** in the abbatial palace, contains Europe's foremost Romanesque lapidary museum. Vestiges of both the abbey and the village constructed around it are conserved here, as well as part of the Bibliothèque des Moines (Monks' Library). 🕾 *03–85–59–15–93* ⊕ *www.monum.fr* 🖭 *€6.50* ☺ *Sept.–Apr., daily 9:30–noon and 1:30–5; May–Aug., daily 9:30–6:30.*

The village of Cluny was built to serve the abbey's more practical needs, and several fine Romanesque houses around the Rue d'Avril and the Rue de la République, including the so-called **Hôtel de la Monnaie** *(Abbey Mint,* ⊠ *6 rue d'Avril* 🕾 *03–85–59–25–66),* are prime examples of the period's different architectural styles.

Parts of the town ramparts, the much-restored 11th-century defensive **Tour des Fromages** (⊠ *6 rue Mercière* 🕾 *03–85–59–05–34),* now home to the tourist office, and several noteworthy medieval churches also remain.

WHERE TO STAY & EAT

$$ ✕⬚ **Hôtel Bourgogne.** This old-fashioned hotel was built in 1817, exactly where parts of the abbey once stood. It has a small garden and an atmospheric restaurant with a sober pink palette and comfort cuisine, such as *sandre cuit à la plancha* (grilled pike-perch). The evening meal is mandatory in July and August, and the restaurant is closed Tuesday and Wednesday. ⊠ *Pl. de l'Abbaye, 71250* 🕾 *03–85–59–00–58* 🖷 *03–85–59–03–73* ⊕ *www.hotel-cluny.com* 🖙 *13 rooms, 3 suites* ⏦ *In-room: no a/c (some). In-hotel: restaurant, bar, no elevator* ▤ *AE, DC, MC, V* ☺ *Closed Dec. and Jan., Tues. and Wed. in Feb.* ℿ ⬚*MAP.*

THE ARTS

The ruined abbey of Cluny forms the backdrop of the **Grandes Heures de Cluny** (🕾 *03–85–59–05–34 for details),* a classical music festival held in August.

BURGUNDY ESSENTIALS

To research prices, get advice from other travelers, and book travel arrangements, visit www.fodors.com.

TRANSPORTATION

If traveling extensively by public transportation, be sure to load up on information (schedules, the best taxi-for-call companies, etc.) upon arriving at the ticket counter or help desk of the bigger train and bus stations in the area, such as Troyes, Dijon, and Beaune.

BY AIR

AIRPORTS

Dijon Airport serves domestic flights between Paris and Lyon.

Airport Information Dijon Airport (☎ *03–80–67–67–67* ⊕ *www.dijon.aeroport.fr*).

BY BIKE & MOPED

Details about recommended bike routes and where to rent bicycles (train stations are a good bet) can be found at most tourist offices. La Peurtantaine arranges bicycle tours of Burgundy.

Bike Tours La Peurtantaine (⊠ *Morvan Découverte, Le Bourg, 71550 Anost* ☎ *03–85–82–77–74*).

BY BUS

Local bus services are extensive; where the biggest private companies, **Les Rapides de Bourgogne** and **TRANSCO,** do not venture, the national SNCF routes often do. TRANSCO's No. 44 bus travels through the Côte d'Or wine region, connecting Dijon to Beaune (1 hr, €6.30) via Vougeot (40 mins, €2.70) and Nuits-St-Georges (47 mins, €3.60). The buses of Les Rapides de Bourgogne connect Auxerre to Chablis (20 mins), Pontigny (20 mins), and Sens (90 mins) with all trips costing €2.50. The No. 7 bus from Chalon-sur-Saône's train station takes you over to Cluny. It's hard to reach Vézelay: the best bet may be to train to nearby Sermizelles, then catch the one bus on Saturday at noon. To get to Avallon and Saulieu, take a train to Montbard, a TGV station stop, and then get a bus to either town. **Cars Taboreau** operate in the Parc du Morvan and go as far as Montsauche-les-Settons, close to the Lac des Settons; Autun is a good place to catch buses going to the southern reaches of the Morvan. Always inquire at the local tourist office for timetables and ask your hotel concierge for information.

Bus Information Cars Taboreau (⊠ *Matrat, Gouloux* ☎ *03–86–78–71–90*). **Les Rapides de Bourgogne** (⊠ *3 rue des Fontenottes, Auxerre* ☎ *03–86–94–95–00*). **TRANSCO** (⊠ *Gare Routière, Cour de la Gare, Dijon* ☎ *03–80–42–11–00*).

BY CAR

Although bus lines do service smaller towns and scenic byways, traveling through Burgundy by car allows you to explore its meandering country roads at leisure. A6 is the main route through the region; it heads southeast from Paris through Burgundy, past Sens, Auxerre, Chablis, Avallon, Saulieu, and Beaune, continuing on to Mâcon, Lyon, and the south. A38 links A6 to Dijon, 290 km (180 mi) from Paris; the trip takes around three hours, depending on traffic. A31 heads down from Dijon to Beaune, a distance of 45 km (27 mi). N74 is the slower, more scenic route of the two, but if it's scenery you want, D122 is the Route des Grands Crus, which reads like a wine list as it meanders through every wine town and village and the thick of the grape-growing fields. The uncluttered A5 links Paris to Troyes, where the A31 segues south to Dijon.

BY TRAIN

The TGV zips out of Paris (Gare de Lyon) to Dijon (1½ hrs, €30 to €60) 20 times a day, Mâcon (1½ hrs, €51), and on to Lyon (2 hrs, €59). Trains run frequently, though the fastest Paris–Lyon trains do not stop at Dijon or go anywhere near it. Some TGVs stop at Le Creusot, between Chalon and Autun, 90 minutes from Paris—from there, you can hop on a bus for a 45-minute ride to Autun. There's also TGV service directly from Roissy Airport to Dijon (1 hr, 50 mins). Beaune is well serviced by trains, with many arriving from Dijon, Lyon, and Paris. Sens is on a main-line route from Paris (45 mins). The region has two local train routes: one linking Sens, Joigny, Montbard, Dijon, Beaune, Chalon, Tournus, and Mâcon and the other connecting Auxerre, Avallon, Saulieu, and Autun. If you want to get to smaller towns or to vineyards, use bus routes or opt for the convenience of renting a car.

Train Information SNCF (☎ *36–35, €0.34 per min*) ⊕ *www.voyages-sncf.com*).
TGV (⊕ *www.tgv.com*).

CONTACTS & RESOURCES

CAR RENTAL
Local Agencies Avis (✉ *SNCF Railway Station, Dijon* ☎ *08–20–61–16–63*). **Europcar** (✉ *SNCF Railway Station, Dijon* ☎ *08–21–80–58–07*). **Hertz** (✉ *78 cours de la Gare, Dijon* ☎ *03–80–53–14–00*).

EMERGENCIES
For basic information, see this section in the Essentials chapter. In most cases, contact the town Comissariat de Police.

Emergencies Police (✉ *11 rue de Metz, Dijon* ☎ *03–80–69–17–99 or 17*). **General hospital** (✉ *3 rue du Faubourg Raines, Dijon* ☎ *03–80–29–30–31 or 15*).

INTERNET & MAIL
In smaller towns, ask your hotel concierge if there are any Internet cafés nearby.

Internet & Mail Information Cybersp@ce 21 (✉ *46 rue Monge Jeanne, Dijon* ☎ *08–72–77–66–99*). **Net Games** (✉ *17 rue de Laurencin, Sens* ☎ *03–86–64–30–33*). **La Poste main post office** (✉ *Pl. Grangier, Dijon* ☎ *03–80–50–62–19*). **La Poste main post office** (✉ *95 rue Republique, Sens* ☎ *03–86–83–10–00*).

MEDIA
Le Bien Public (Dijon) is one of France's oldest and most respected regional dailies and is widely available throughout the region.

Lyonne–Republicaine (Auxerre) includes a useful weekly cultural supplement covering Dijon and Beaune.

TOUR OPTIONS
For general information on tours in Burgundy, contact the regional tourist office, the Comité Régional du Tourisme. Tours of Beaune with a guide and a wine tasting can be arranged in advance through the

8

Beaune tourist office. Gastronomic weekends, including wine tastings, are organized by Bacchus Wine Tours.

Contacts Beaune tourist office (⊠*Rue de l'Hôtel-Dieu* ☎*03–80–26–21–30*). **Bacchus Wine Tours** (⊠*6 rempart St-Jean, 21200 Beaune* ☎*03–80–24–79–12* ⊕ *www.route-des-grands-crus-de-bourgogne.com*). **Comité Régional du Tourisme** (⌂*5 av. Garibald, 21000 Dijon* ☎*03–80–28–02–80*).

VISITOR INFORMATION
Following are principal regional tourist offices, listed by town, as well as addresses of other tourist offices in towns mentioned in this chapter.

Tourist Information Autun (⊠*2 av. Charles-de-Gaulle* ☎*03–85–86–80–38* ⊕ *www.autun.com*). **Auxerre** (⊠*1 quai de la République* ☎*03–86–52–06–19* ⊕ *www.ot-auxerre.fr*). **Avallon** (⊠*4 rue Bocquillot* ☎*03–86–34–14–19*). **Beaune** (⊠*Rue de l'Hôtel-Dieu* ☎*03–80–26–21–30* ⊕ *www.beaune-burgundy.com*). **Cluny** (⊠*6 rue Mercière* ☎*03–85–59–05–34*). **Dijon** (⊠*34 rue des Forges* ☎*03–80–44–11–44* ⊕ *www.ot-dijon.fr*). **Mâcon** (*Principal regional tourist office* ⊠*1 pl. St-Pierre* ☎*03–85–21–07–07*). **Sens** (⊠*Pl. Jean-Jaurès* ☎*03–86–65–19–49*). **Tournus** (⊠*2 pl. Carnot* ☎*03–85–51–13–10*). **Troyes** (⊠*16 bd. Carnot* ☎*03–25–82–62–70* ⊕ *www.ot-troyes.fr* ✉ *Rue Mignard* ☎*03–25–73–36–88*). **Vézelay** (⊠*Rue St-Pierre* ☎*03–86–33–23–69*).

Lyon & the Alps

Lyon

WORD OF MOUTH

"With the best of all worlds intersecting there—Alps, Mediterranean, Massif Central, and Beaujolais wine country—Lyon has an
endless energy and cultural richness that would inspire me to stay
forever. Just remember that this is the realm of Paul Bocuse and
Marc Veyrat—you may wind up spending more time in restaurants
than in museums."

—Cheyne

WELCOME TO LYON & THE ALPS

TOP REASONS TO GO

★ **Vieux Lyon:** Frolic all day the Renaissance way touring Lyon's picturesque Old Town *traboules,* or passageways, and its 16th-century courtyards.

★ **Le Beaujolais Nouveau est arrivé!:** The third Thursday of November is a party like no other in France, when wine celebrations in honor of the new Beaujolais harvest go around the clock.

★ **The Mont Blanc Resorts:** Whether you après-ski the day away in Chamonix or enjoy the high life of Megéve, you'll be singing "Ain't No Mountain High Enough" once you see France's tallest peak.

★ **Grenoble's Market Day:** Sunday mornings offer a chance to walk miles through myriad markets, from haberdashery to food products of every flavor under the sun.

★ **Epic Epicureanism:** There is no possible way to cite the Lyon-Rhône Alps without mentioning Paul Bocuse, Marc Veyrat, and all the four-star chefs in between.

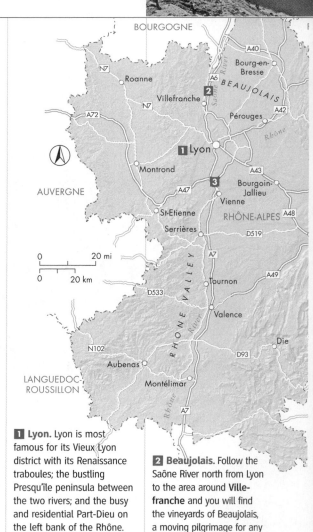

1 Lyon. Lyon is most famous for its Vieux Lyon district with its Renaissance traboules; the bustling Presqu'île peninsula between the two rivers; and the busy and residential Part-Dieu on the left bank of the Rhône. The city's historic industrial power has generated ample cultural resources and the energy to create first-rate music, cinema, theater, opera, dance, and cuisine.

2 Beaujolais. Follow the Saône River north from Lyon to the area around **Villefranche** and you will find the vineyards of Beaujolais, a moving pilgrimage for any wine lover. Diminutive villages materialize as if by magic from rolling vine-covered hillsides, with the major hub being **Bourg-en-Bresse,** famed for its church and its chickens.

GETTING ORIENTED

Lyon is France's natural hub, where the rivers Rhône and Saône meet and the mountainous Massif Central leans toward the lofty Alps. Lyon—France's "second city"—is a magnet for the surrounding region, including the vineyards of Beaujolais. South of Lyon, is the quaint Rhône Valley. Along the southeastern border of France rises a mighty barrier of mountains that provides some of the most spectacular scenery in Europe: the French Alps, soaring to their climax in Europe's highest peak, Mont Blanc.

9

4 Grenoble & the Alps. Grenoble, in the Dauphiné, is the gateway to the Alps and is set at the nexus of rivers and highways connecting Marseille, Valence, Lyon, Geneva, and Turin. Culture hounds will love its Stendahl Itinerary and its art-filled Musée. To the east, rustic towns announce the Alps, none more jewel-like than **Annecy,** thanks to its blue lake, covered lanes, and quiet canals. The region's natural Alpine splendors are on view in **Chamonix** and **Megève,** ski resorts, which are most active from December to April.

3 The Rhône Valley. Like platonic lovers, the masculine Rhône River joins the feminine Saône and become a fluvial force rolling south to the Mediterranean. Their bounty includes hundreds of steep vineyards and small-town wine-makers tempting you with samples. The ancient Roman ruins of **Vienne** and the Romanesque relics of **Valence** reflect the Rhône's importance as a trade route.

The Quai de la Saone, Lyon

LYON & THE ALPS PLANNER

How's the Weather?

Lyon and the Rhône-Alps are so diverse in altitude and climate that the weather will depend mostly on where you are and when, and which way the wind blows.

Freezing gales have been known to turn late September's dance festival into a winter carnival, with icy blasts from the Massif Central sweeping down the Saône.

As a rule, however, Lyon may be rainy and misty, but not especially cold, whereas Grenoble and the Alps can be bitter cold any time of year, though especially from December to April.

The Beaujolais wine region is generally temperate, though a November Nouveau Beaujolais fest a few years ago froze vines and revelers alike.

South of Lyon along the Rhône the sun beats down on the vineyards in full summer (Côte-Rotie really does mean "roast hillside").

But keep in mind that the winds howl in winter. Come prepared for rain and snow. Adding a festive warmth to the season is, happily, Lyon's Christmas lights display.

Making the Most of Your Time

Lyon merits an exploration of several days, at least two, for its ample range of architecture, food, and culture. The wine country of the Beaujolais up the river Saône is another two-day visit, unless a drive-through directly to Bourg-en-Bresse is the best solution that time constraints will allow.

Medieval Pérouges is another good day's browse with time for a late afternoon and evening drive into the Alps to Annecy where the Vieille Ville (Old Town) is an eyeful by day or night. Talloires, around the lake, is another lovely visit to plan time for, as is that legendary culinary shrine, La Maison de Marc Veyrat, in Veyrier-du-Lac.

The mountain resort of Megève is a place to either settle in for a few days or blow through on your way to Chambéry and the abbey of Grande Chartreuse. Grenoble offers opportunities for perusing masterpieces in its superb museum or following Stendhal's footsteps through the old quarter.

From Grenoble, Valence via the autoroute is a quick transfer to admire the cathedral and the art museum. From there, see the limestone wonder of the Ardèche Gorge on your way to Provence or, if you're headed back to Lyon, stop at Vienne for its Roman sites.

WHAT IT COSTS

	¢	$	$$	$$$	$$$$
Restaurants	Under €11	€11– €17	€17– €23	€23– €30	Over €30
Hotels	Under €50	€50– €80	€80– €120	€120– €190	Over €190

Restaurant prices are per person for a main course at dinner, including tax (19.6%) and service; note that if a restaurant offers only prix-fixe (set-price) meals, it has been given the price category that reflects the full prix-fixe price. Hotel prices are for a standard double room in high season, including tax (19.6%) and service charge. Hotels operate on the European Plan (EP, with no meal provided) unless we note that they use the Breakfast Plan (BP), or also offer such options as Modified American Plan (MAP, with breakfast and dinner daily, known as demi-pension), or Full American Plan (FAP, or pension complète, with three meals a day). Inquire when booking if these all-inclusive meal plans (which always entail higher rates) are mandatory or optional.

Getting Around

Lyon is best explored on foot, with the occasional tramway or subway connection to get you across town in a hurry. Boat tours around the Presqu'île give you another perspective on this riverine metropolis while Velo'V bike rentals can also be handy. A car is the best way to get around the Beaujolais wine country and the rest of Rhône-Alpes. Regional roads are fast and well maintained, though smaller mountain routes are slower and passes may be closed in winter. Lyon is an important rail hub, with two in-town train stations and a third at Lyon-Saint-Exupéry airport. Trains from the Part-Dieu train station connect easily with Villefranche-sur-Saône in the middle of the Beaujolais country, while the Gare de Perrache serves points south such as Valence and Vienne. The main train stations in this chapter are in Lyon, Annecy, and Grenoble but most small towns along the way have train stations, too, or, more accurately, a building with a few wooden seats along the tracks. So one of the best ways to explore the Alps is to keep your eye out for a stop that looks interesting and abandon ship. Buses from Lyon and Grenoble also efficiently serve the region's smaller towns. Unfortunately, you can't get to many small towns without passing through major towns, even if it means backtracking many kilometers and many euros. Many ski centers, such as Chamonix, have shuttle buses that connect them with surrounding villages. Tourist destinations, such as Annecy, have convenient bus links with Grenoble, while Satobus links Lyon's Saint-Exupéry airport with all major ski stations in the Alps.

Finding a Place to Stay

Hotels, inns, bed-and-breakfasts, *gîtes d'étapes* (hikers' way stations), and *tables d'hôte* run the gamut from grande luxe to spartanly rustic in this multifaceted region embracing non-plus-ultra-urban chic in Lyon as well as ski huts in the Alps. Lyon accommodations range from *péniches* (riverboats) to panoramic guest rooms high in the hilltop Croix Rousse district. The Alps, of course, are well endowed with top hotels, especially in Grenoble and the time-honored ski resorts such as Chamonix and Megève. Many hotels expect you to have at least your evening meal there, especially in summer; in winter they up the ante and hope travelers will take all three meals. Assume that all hotel rooms have air-conditioning, TV, telephones, and private bath, unless otherwise noted.

How to Be Suave About Mooching Free Wine

Wine tasting is a thirsty budget traveler's godsend. You just walk into a cellar, tell them you want a dégustation, and walk out with a wealth of knowledge (and a little buzz) all for the price of one bottle.

The Beaujolais region has hundreds of village *caves*—cellars where wine is made, stored, and sold—from big-time tourist operators to mom-and-pop stops. Make sure the ones you pick have dégustation signs out front. Signs that say vente en direct (sold directly from the property) and vente au détail (sold by the bottle) are also good indicators.

Look for the town's co-op *caveau* (wine cellar), where you can pay a few euros to taste all the wine you want.

Those who are completely shameless have been known to heavily imbibe and then pretend they absolutely love everything they've tried, so the vintners aren't so offended when no sale is made (a bike can come in handy here—just point to it and tell them there's no way to carry any wine home but that you'll be back later with the car).

If you want to feel no pain, head for the bottles marked "Supérieur AOC"—they have a slightly higher alcohol content (10%) than other Beaujolais wines.

9

Introduction by
Nancy Coons

Updated
by George
Semler

AS THE NOBLE RHÔNE COURSES down from Switzerland, flowing out of Lake Geneva and being nudged west and south by the flanking Jura Mountains and the Alps, it meanders through France at its bracing best. Here you can find the pretty towns and fruity purple wines of Beaujolais, the brawny, broad shoulder cuisine of Lyon (and its nouvelle adaptions), the extraordinary beauty of the Alps, and friendly wine villages sitting high on the steep hills bordering the Rhône as it flows to the Mediterranean. To the west, deep gorges cut grooves through a no-man's-land of ragged stone and pine: the Ardèche. History is to be found here, but the kind that treads lightly: the ruins at Vienne mark, with more grace than pomp, the region's Gallo-Roman roots, while Lyon's gigantic amphitheater and intimate Odéon confirm Roman Lugdunum's 2,000 years of bright cultural history.

So relax and dig into the *terroir,* the earth. Strike up a flirtation with saucy Beaujolais, the region's pink-cheeked country lass-in-a-glass, blushing modestly next to Burgundy, its high-toned neighbor. The very names of Beaujolais's robust wines conjure up a wildflower bouquet: Fleurie, Chiroubles, Juliénas, St-Amour. Glinting purple against red-checked linens in a Lyonnais *bouchon* tavern, they flatter every delight listed on the blackboard menu: a salty chew of sausage, a crunch of bacon, a fat boudin noir bursting from its casing, a tangle of country greens in a tangy mustard vinaigrette, or a taste of crackling roast chicken.

If you are what you eat, then Lyon itself is real and hearty, as straightforward and unabashedly simple as a *poulet de Bresse.* Yet the refinements of world-class opera, theater, and classical music also happily thrive in Lyon's gently patinated urban milieu, one strangely reminiscent of 1930s Paris—lace curtains in painted-over storefronts, elegant bourgeois town houses, deep-shaded parks, and low-slung bridges lacing back and forth over the broad, lazy Saône and Rhône rivers. Far from the madding immensity of Paris, immerse yourself in what feels, tastes, and smells like the France of yore.

When you've had your fill of this, pack a picnic of victuals to tide you over and take to the hills. If you head west, the Gorges de l'Ardèche will land you in a craggy world of stone villages; if you head northeast, you'll ease into the Alps, a land of green-velvet slopes and icy mists, ranging from the modern urban hub of Grenoble and the crystalline lake of Annecy to the state-of-the-art ski resorts of Chamonix and Megève. The grand finale: awe-inspiring Mont-Blanc, at 15,700 feet Western Europe's highest peak. End your day's exertions on the piste or the trail with a bottle of gentian-perfumed Suze, repair to your fir tree–enclosed chalet, and dress down for a hearty mountain-peasant supper of raclette, fondue, or cheesy *ravioles,* all in the company of a crackling fire.

Grouped together in this guide solely for geographic convenience, Lyon and the Alps are as alike as chocolate and broccoli. Lyon is fast, congested, and saturated with culture (and smog). It may be the gateway to the Alps, but otherwise the two halves of the region could be on different continents. While in the bustling city, it's hard to believe the pristine Alps are only an hour's train ride away from this rich metropolis. Likewise, while in a small Alpine village you could almost forget that France has any large cities at all—much less one of the biggest and noisiest just on the other side of the mountains. When leaving Lyon, few travelers can resist paying a call on the Alps. Everything you imagine when you hear their name—soaring snowcaps, jagged ridges, crystalline lakes—is true. Their major outpost—Grenoble—buzzes with Alpine talk, propelling visitors away from city life and into the great Alpine high.

EXPLORING LYON & THE ALPS

East-central France can be divided into two areas: the Alps and "not the Alps." The second area includes Lyon—a magnet for the surrounding region, including the vineyards of Beaujolais—and the area south of Lyon, dominated by the mighty Rhône as it flows toward the Mediterranean. This chapter is divided into four chunks: Lyon, France's "second city"; Beaujolais and La Dombes—where hundreds of wine *caves* alternate with glacier-created lakes and towns built of *pierres dorées*, soft, golden-tone stones that come from the local hillsides; the Rhône Valley, studded with quaint villages and hilltop castles; and Grenoble and the Alps, where you can often find down-home friendliness on tap at sky-high ski resorts.

LYON

GETTING HERE

A total of three stations—two in-town and a third at the airport—make Lyon a major transportation hub. The Gare de La Part-Dieu (⊠ *Bd. Vivier-Merle*) is used for the TGV (⊕ *www.tgv.com*) routes and links Lyon with many other cities, including Montpellier and Marseilles, along with Grenoble (1 hr 32 mins, €18), and Bordeaux, with four trains a day taking 6 (TGV) to 8½ hours. The Lyon–Grenoble line on TER-SNCF (⊕ *www.ter-SNCF.com/rhone-alpes*) connects Grenoble to Lyon's Part-Dieu train station in 1 hour, 17 minutes for €17.30. SNCF (⊕ *www.sncf.fr*) links Lyon Part-Dieu with the Beaujolais and local towns such as Villefranche-sur-Saône (19 mins, €6). On the other side of town, the *centre ville* station at Gare de Perrache (⊠ *Cours de Verdun, Pl. Carnot* ☎ *04–72–56–95–30*) services the *centre ville*—many trains stop at both stations. The third station, Ároport-Lyon-Saint-Exupéry, is the main TGV station. Six TGV trains daily connect this airport station with Grenoble (1 hr, €26.40). Satobus Alpes (☎ *04–72–68–72–17* ⊕ *www.satobus-alpes.altibus.com*) connects Lyon-Saint-Exupéry airport with Grenoble (1 hr, € 18), Annecy (2 hrs, €30), and the Alps year-round.

EXPLORING

Lyon and Marseille each claim to be France's "second city." In terms of size and industrial importance, Marseille probably deserves that title. But for tourist appeal, Lyon, 462 km (287 mi) southeast of Paris, is the clear winner. Easily accessible by car or by train, Lyon's speed and scale are human in ways that Paris may have lost forever. Lyon has its share of historic buildings and quaint *traboules* (from the Latin *transambulare,* or walk-through), which are the passageways under and through town houses dating from the Renaissance (in Vieux Lyon) and the 19th century (in La Croix Rousse). Originally designed as dry, high-speed shortcuts for silk weavers delivering their wares, these passageways were used by the French Resistance during World War II to elude German street patrols. The city's setting at the confluence of the Saône and the Rhône is a spectacular riverine landscape overlooked from the heights to the west by the imposing Notre-Dame de Fourvière church and from the north by the hilltop neighborhood of La Croix Rousse. Meanwhile, the Confluence Project at the southern tip of the Presqu'île, or peninsula, the land between the Saône and the Rhône, has reclaimed (from the rivers) nearly a square mile of center-city real estate that will gradually open 2007–2009 as a complex of parks, business, and cultural facilities. Another attraction is Lyon's extraordinary dining scene—the city has more good restaurants per square mile than any other European city except Paris.

Lyon's development owes much to its riverside site halfway between Paris and the Mediterranean, and within striking distance of Switzerland, Italy, and the Alps. Lyonnais are proud that their city has been important for more than 2,000 years: Romans made their Lugdunum (the name means "hill or fortress of Lug," the supreme deity of Celtic mythology"), the second largest Roman city after Rome itself, capital of Gaul around 43 bc. The remains of the Roman theater and the Odéon, the Gallo-Roman music hall, are among the most spectacular Roman ruins in the world. In the middle of the city is the Presqu'île, a fingerlike peninsula between the rivers, only half a dozen blocks wide and about 10 km (6 mi) long (though, thanks to the Confluence Project, it is growing), where modern Lyon throbs with shops, restaurants, museums, theaters, and a postmodern Jean Nouvel–designed opera house. West of the Saône is Vieux Lyon (Old Lyon), with its peaceful Renaissance charm and lovely traboules and patios; above it is the old Roman district of Fourvière. To the north is the hilltop Croix Rousse District, where Lyon's silk weavers once operated their looms in lofts designed as workshop dwellings, while across the Rhône to the east is a mix of older residential areas, the famous Halles de Lyon market, and the ultramodern Part-Dieu business and office district with its landmark *gratte-ciel* (skyscraper) beyond.

All in all, Lyon is a city of ups and downs: from the Presqu'île to the top of the Croix Rousse or from Vieux Lyon to the top of the Roman Fourvière, from a simple bouchon with checked tablecloths to a stunningly haute-cuisine establishment such as Paul Bocuse or Leon de Lyon. Consider taking advantage of the Lyon City Card, a one-, two-, or three-day pass to museums with discounts at boutiques, restaurants, and cultural events costing, respectively, €20, €30, and € 40.

VIEUX LYON & FOURVIÈRE

Vieux Lyon—one of the richest groups of urban Renaissance dwellings in Europe—has narrow cobblestone streets, 15th- and 16th-century mansions, lovely *traboules* (passageways) and patios, small museums, and the cathedral. When Lyon became an important silk weaving town in the 15th century, Italian merchants and bankers built dozens of Renaissance-style town houses. Officially cataloged as national monuments, the courtyards and passageways are open to the public during the morning. The excellent Renaissance Quarter map of the traboules and courtyards of Vieux Lyon, available at the tourist office and in most hotel lobbies, offers the city's most gratifying exploring (use the silver buttons at the top of entryway door-buzzer panels to gain access). Above Vieux Lyon, in hilly Fourvière, are the remains of two Roman theaters and the Basilique de Notre-Dame, visible from all over the city.

THE MAIN ATTRACTIONS

⓫ **Basilique de Notre-Dame-de-Fourvière.** The rather pompous late-19th-century basilica, at the top of the ficelle (funicular railway), is—for better or worse—the symbol of Lyon. Its mock-Byzantine architecture and hilltop site make it a close relative of Paris's Sacré-Coeur. Both were built to underline the might of the Roman Catholic Church after the Prussian defeat of France in 1870 gave rise to the birth of the anticlerical Third Republic. The excessive gilt, marble, and mosaics in the interior underscore the Church's wealth, although they masked its lack of political clout at that time. One of the few places in Lyon where you can't see the basilica is the adjacent terrace, whose panorama reveals the city—with the cathedral of St-Jean in the foreground and the glass towers of the reconstructed Part-Dieu business complex glistening behind. For a yet more sweeping view, climb the 287 steps to the basilica observatory. ⊠ *Pl. de Fourvière, Fourvière* ✆ *Observatory €2.50* ☉ *Observatory Easter–Oct., daily 10–noon and 2–6; Nov.–Easter, weekends 2–6. Basilica daily 8–noon and 2–6.*

❽ **Cathédrale St-Jean.** Solid and determined—having withstood the sieges of time, revolution, and war—the cathedral's stumpy facade is stuck almost bashfully onto the nave. Although the mishmash inside has its moments—the fabulous 13th-century stained-glass windows in the choir and the varied window tracery and vaulting in the side chapels—the interior lacks drama and harmony. Still, it's an architectural history lesson. The cathedral dates from the 12th century, and the chancel is Romanesque, but construction on the whole continued over three centuries. The 14th-century astronomical clock, in the north transept, is a marvel of technology very much worth seeing. It chimes a hymn to St. John on the hour at noon, 2, 3, and 4 as a screeching rooster and other automatons enact the Annunciation. To the right of the Cathédrale St-Jean stands the 12th-century **Manécanterie** (choir school). ⊠ *70 rue St-Jean, Vieux Lyon* ☎ *04–78–92–82–29.*

⓮ **Hôtel Bullioud.** This Renaissance mansion, close to the Hôtel Paterin, is noted for its courtyard, with an ingenious gallery (1536) built by Phi-

9

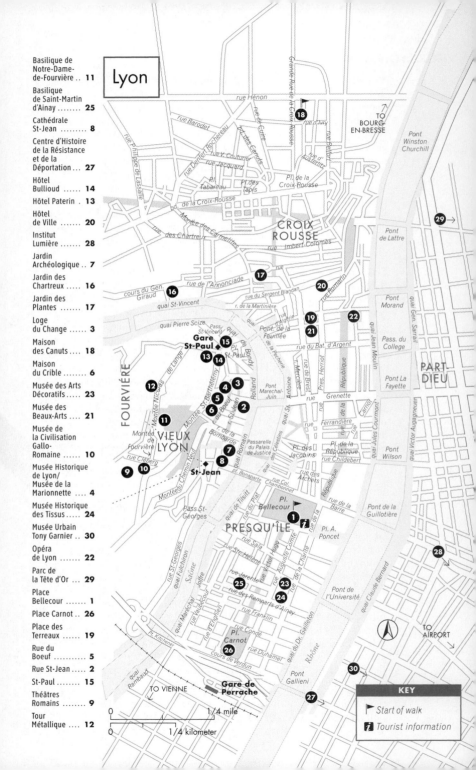

GETTING AROUND

Lyon's squeaky-clean and efficient subway gets you from one end of town to another in 5 to 10 minutes, even though missing the rich display of sights and scenes aboveground seems criminal. Four métro lines and three tramway lines crisscross the city. A single ticket costs €1.60, and a 10-ticket book is €12.50. A day "Liberté" pass for bus and métro is €4.30 (available from bus drivers and the automated machines in the métro). Lyon's TCL buses are another efficient form of travel. One way to have the best of both worlds is the tramway system that glides peacefully through the city. The bicycle rental program, VéloV (⊕ www.velov. grandlyon.com) is another handy transport option with 3,000 bicycles for rent at 250 points around town (first 30 mins free, 90 mins €.5, next hour €2). For open-air taxis at bus prices, the Cyclopolitain (⊕ www. cyclopolitain.com), electric tricycles driven by young "Cyclonautes," is green as a Granny Smith and cheap (from €1 per person).

libert Delorme, one of France's earliest and most accomplished exponents of Classical architecture. He also worked on several spectacular châteaux in central France, including those at Fontainebleau and Chenonceaux. ⊠8 *rue Juiverie, off pl. St-Paul, Vieux Lyon.*

❻ Maison du Crible. This 17th-century mansion is one of Lyon's oldest. In the courtyard you can glimpse a charming garden and the original Tour Rose—an elegant pink tower. The higher the tower in those days, the greater the prestige—this one was owned by the tax collector—and it's not so different today. ⊠*16 rue du Boeuf, off Pl. du Petit-Collège, Vieux Lyon* ⌑*Free* ⊙*Daily 10–noon and 2–6.*

❿ Musée de la Civilisation Gallo-Romaine *(Gallo-Roman Civilization Museum).* Since 1933, systematic excavations have unearthed vestiges of Lyon's opulent Roman precursor. The statues, mosaics, vases, coins, and tombstones are excellently displayed in this semisubterranean museum next to the Roman theaters. The large, bronze Table Claudienne is inscribed with part of Emperor Claudius's address to the Roman Senate in ad 48, conferring senatorial rights on the Roman citizens of Gaul. ⊠*17 rue Clébert, Fourvière* ☎*04–72–38–81–90* ⊕*www.musees-gallo-romains.com* ⌑*€4* ⊙*Tues.–Sun. 10–5.*

❹ Musée Historique de Lyon *(Lyon Historical Museum).* This museum is housed in the city's largest ensemble of Renaissance buildings, the Hôtel de Gadagne, built between the 14th and the 16th century. Medieval sculpture, furniture, pottery, paintings, and engravings are on display. Also housed here is the **Musée de la Marionnette** (Puppet Museum), tracing the history of marionettes, beginning with Guignol and Madelon (Lyon's Punch

ISN'T IT ROMANTIC?

History majors will want to know that in 1600 Henri IV came to Lyon to meet his Italian fiancée, Marie de' Medici, en route from Marseille; he took one look at her, gave her the okay, and they were married immediately in this cathedral.

9

and Judy, created by Laurent Mourguet in 1795). ⊠ *1 pl. du Petit-Collège, Vieux Lyon* ☏*04-78-42-03-61* ⟐*€4* ⊙ *Wed.–Mon. 10:45–6.*

▶❶ **Place Bellecour.** Shady, imposing Place Bellecour is one of the largest squares in France and is Lyon's fashionable center, midway between the Saône and the Rhône. Classical facades erected along its narrower sides in 1800 lend architectural interest. The large, bronze equestrian statue of Louis XIV, installed in 1828, is the work of local sculptor Jean Lemot. On the south side of the square is the **tourist office** (☏*04-72-77-69-69*). ⊠*Presqu'île.*

❺ **Rue du Boeuf.** Like the parallel Rue St-Jean, Rue du Boeuf has lovely
Fodor's Choice traboules, courtyards, spiral staircases, towers, and facades. The tra-
★ boule at No. 31 Rue du Boeuf hooks through and out onto Rue de la Bombarde. No. 36 has a notable courtyard. At No. 19 is the standout Maison de l'Outarde d'Or, so named for the great bustard, a goose-like game bird, depicted in the coat of arms over the door. The late-15th-century house and courtyard inside have spiral staircases in the towers, which were built as symbols of wealth and power. The Hotel Tour Rose at No. 22 has, indeed, a beautiful *tour rose* (pink tower) in the inner courtyard. At the corner of Place Neuve St-Jean and Rue du Boeuf is the famous sign portraying the bull for which Rue du Boeuf is named, the work of the Renaissance Italy–trained French sculptor Jean de Bologne. No. 18 contains Antic Wine, the emporium of English-speaking Georges Dos Santos, "the flying sommelier," who is a wealth of information (throw away this book and just ask Georges). No. 20 conceals one of the rare open-shaft spiral staircases allowing for a view all the way up the core. At No. 16 is the Maison du Crible, and No. 14 has another splendid patio. ⊠*Vieux Lyon.*

❷ **Rue St-Jean.** Once Vieux Lyon's major thoroughfare, this street leads north from Place St-Jean to Place du Change, where money changers operated during medieval trade fairs. Many area streets were named for their shops, still heralded by intricate iron signs. The elegant houses along the street were built for illustrious Lyonnais bankers and Italian silk merchants during the French Renaissance. The traboule at No. 54 leads all the way through to Rue du Boeuf No. 27. Beautiful Renaissance courtyards can be visited at No. 50, No. 52, and No. 42. At No. 27 rue St-Jean an especially lovely traboule winds through to No. 6 rue des 3 Maries. No. 28 has a pretty courtyard; No. 24, the Maison Laurencin, has another; Maison Le Viste at No. 21 has a splendid facade. The courtyard at No. 18 merits a close look. The houses at No. 5 place du Gouvernement and No. 7 and No. 1 rue St-Jean also have facades you won't want to miss. ⊠*Vieux Lyon.*

❾ **Théâtres Romains** (*Roman Theaters*). Two ruined, semicircular Roman-built theaters are tucked into the hillside, just down from the summit of Fourvière. The **Grand Théâtre**, the oldest Roman theater in France, was built in 15 bc to seat 10,000. The smaller **Odéon**, with its geometric flooring, was designed for music and poetry performances. Lyon International Arts Festival performances are held here each September. ⊠*Colline Fourvière, Fourvière* ⟐*Free* ⊙ *Daily 9–dusk.*

ALSO WORTH SEEING

⑬ Hôtel Paterin. This is a particularly fine example of the type of splendid Renaissance mansion found in the area. ⊠*4 rue Juiverie, off pl. St-Paul, Vieux Lyon.*

❼ Jardin Archéologique *(Archaeological Garden).* This garden contains the excavated ruins of two churches that succeeded one another on this site. The foundations of the churches were unearthed during a time when apartment buildings—constructed here after churches had been destroyed during the Revolution—were being demolished. One arch still remains and forms part of the ornamentation in the garden. ⊠*Entrance on Rue de la Bombarde, Vieux Lyon.*

> ## LYON'S TRABOULES
>
> Lyon is famous for its historic *traboules* (from the Latin *transambulare*, or walk-through), which are the passageways under and through town houses dating from the Renaissance (in Vieux Lyon) and the 19th century (in La Croix Rousse). They were originally built to protect silk from the elements as the local weavers carried it around the city. While some are simple alleys, others lead to beautiful Renaissance courtyards.

⑯ Jardin des Chartreux. This garden is just one of several small, leafy parks in Lyon. It's a peaceful place to take a break while admiring the splendid view of the river and Fourvière Hill. ⊠*Entrance on Quai St-Vincent, Presqu'île.*

⑰ Jardin des Plantes *(Botanical Garden).* In the peaceful, luxurious Botanical Garden are remnants of the once-huge **Amphithéâtre des Trois Gauls** (Three Gauls Amphitheater), built in ad 19. ⊠*Entrance on Rue de la Tourette, Vieux Lyon* ⊙*Dawn–dusk.*

❸ Loge du Change. Originally a center for the money-changing activities that took place here in the late 15th and 16th centuries, the building was constructed by Simon Gourdet in the mid-16th century and completely redesigned in 1747 by Jean-Baptiste Roche, using plans supplied by his famous colleague Jacques-Germain Soufflot, the architect of Paris's Panthéon. After serving as an inn during the French Revolution, the Loge became a Protestant church in 1803, and is now one of Vieux Lyon's prime concert venues. ⊠*Pl. du Change, Vieux Lyon.*

⑮ St-Paul. The 12th-century church of St-Paul is noted for its octagonal lantern, its frieze of animal heads in the chancel, and its Flamboyant-Gothic chapel. ⊠*Pl. St-Paul, Vieux Lyon.*

⑫ Tour Métallique *(Metal Tower).* Beyond Fourvière Basilica is this skeletal metal tower built in 1893 and now a television transmitter. The stone staircase, the **Montée Nicolas-de-Lange**, at the foot of the tower, is a direct but steep route from the basilica to the St-Paul train station. ⊠*Colline Fourvière, Fourvière.*

9

PRESQU'ÎLE & THE CROIX ROUSSE DISTRICT

Presqu'île, the peninsula flanked by the Saône and the Rhône, is Lyon's modern center, with fashionable shops, a trove of restaurants and museums, and squares graced by fountains and 19th-century buildings. This is the core of Lyon, where you'll be tempted to wander the streets from one riverbank to the other and to explore the entire stretch from the Gare de Perrache railroad station to the Place Bellecour and up to Place des Terreaux.

The hillside and hilltop district north of Place des Terreaux, the Croix Rousse District, is flanked by the Jardins des Plantes on the west and the Rhône on the east. It once resounded to the clanking of looms churning out the exquisite silks and other cloth that made Lyon famous. By the 19th century more than 30,000 *canuts* (weavers) worked on looms on the upper floors of the houses. So tightly packed were the buildings that the only way to transport fabrics was through the traboules, which had the additional advantage of protecting the fine cloth in poor weather.

THE MAIN ATTRACTIONS

OFF THE BEATEN PATH

Les Halles de Lyon. For a sensory feast you won't soon forget, walk over west of the Rhône to Les Halles de Lyon, the city's main produce market, especially on Saturday, Sunday, or a holiday morning when the place crackles with excitement. On the left bank of the Rhône on Part-Dieu's Cours Lafayette, the market offers everything from pristine lettuce to wild mushrooms to poulet de Bresse to caviar, from 150 kinds of cheese at the Alain Martinet stand to the *Rolls de l'huitre* (Rolls-Royce of oysters) at Chez Georges. The *salons de dégustation* (tasting rooms) are in fact raging restaurants with a joie de vivre hard to surpass in Lyon, or anywhere else. Maison Monestir, le Jardin des Halles, Chez Léon, Au Patio are all good, but Maison Rousseau, with its raised platforms amid the produce for serving oysters and snails with marvelous bread, St-Marcellin cheese, and a white Côtes du Rhône, stands out.

㉔ Hôtel de Ville *(Town Hall).* Architects Jules Hardouin-Mansart and Robert de Cotte redesigned the very impressive facade of the Town Hall after a 1674 fire. The rest of the building dates from the early 17th century. ⌧ *Pl. des Terreaux, Presqu'île.*

㉘ Institut Lumière. On the site where the Lumière brothers invented the first cinematographic apparatus, this museum has daily showings of early films and contemporary movies as well as a permanent exhibit about the Lumières. Researchers may access the archives, which contain numerous films, books, periodicals, director and actor information, photo files, posters, and more. ⌧ *25 rue Premier-Film, Part-Dieu* ☎ *04–78–78–18–95* ⊕ *www.institut-lumiere.org* ⌧ *€6* ⊙ *Tues.–Fri. 9–12:30 and 2–6, weekends 2–6.*

★ **㉑ Musée des Beaux-Arts** *(Fine Arts Museum).* In the elegant 17th-century Palais St-Pierre, once a Benedictine abbey, this museum has one of France's largest collections of art after that of the Louvre, including Rodin's *Walker,* Byzantine ivories, Etruscan statues, and Egyptian arti-

IN & AROUND LYON: A WALK

Start your walk armed with free maps from the Lyon tourist office on Presqu'île's Place Bellecour ❶ ➤.

Cross the square and head north along lively Rue du Président-Herriot; turn left onto Place des Jacobins and explore Rue Mercière and the small streets off it.

Cross the Saône on the Passerelle du Palais de Justice (Palace of Justice Footbridge); now you are in Vieux Lyon.

Facing you is the old Palais de Justice. Turn right and then walk 200 yards along Quai Romain Rolland to No. 17, where there's a traboule that leads to No. 9 rue des Trois Maries.

Take care, a right to get to small Place de la Baleine. Exit the square on the left (north) side and then go right on historic Rue St-Jean ❷.

All along Rue St-Jean are traboules and patios leading into lovely courtyards with spiral staircases and mullioned windows.

Head up to cobblestoned Place du Change; on your left is the Loge du Change ❸ church.

Take care, Rue Soufflot and turn left onto Rue de Gadagne. The Hôtel de Gadagne now houses two museums: the Musée Historique de Lyon ❹, with medieval sculpture and local artifacts, and the Musée de la Marionnette, a puppet museum.

Walk south along Rue du Boeuf ❺, parallel to Rue St-Jean, with its many traboules, courtyards, and spiral staircases.

Just off tiny Place du Petit-Collège, at No. 16, is the Maison du Crible ❻, with its pink tower.

Cut through the traboule at 31 rue du Boeuf into Rue de la Bombarde and go left to get to the Jardin Archéologique ❼, a small garden with two excavated churches.

Alongside the gardens is the solid Cathédrale St-Jean ❽, itself an architectural history lesson. The ficelle (funicular railway) runs from the cathedral to the top of Colline de Fourvière (Fourvière Hill).

Take care, the Montée de Fourvière to the Théâtres Romains ❾, the well-preserved remnants of two Roman theaters.

Overlooking the theaters is the semi-subterranean Musée de la Civilisation Gallo-Romaine ❿, a repository for Roman finds.

Continue up the hill and take the first right to the mock-Byzantine Basilique de Notre-Dame-de-Fourvière ⓫.

Return to Vieux Lyon via the Montée Nicolas-de-Lange, the stone stairway at the foot of the metal tower, the Tour Métallique ⓬.

You will emerge alongside the St-Paul train station. Venture onto Rue Juiverie, off Place St-Paul, to see two splendid Renaissance mansions, the Hôtel Paterin ⓭, at No. 4, and the Hôtel Bullioud ⓮, at No. 8.

9

facts. Amid old master, Impressionist, and modern paintings are works by the tight-knit Lyon School, characterized by exquisitely rendered flowers and overbearing religious sentimentality. Note Louis Janmot's *Poem of the Soul*, immaculately painted visions that are by turns heavenly, hellish, and downright spooky. A recent legacy has endowed the museum with a new trove of treasures including works by Manet, Monet, Degas, Bacon, Braque, and Picasso. ⊠*Palais St-Pierre, 20 pl. des Terreaux, Presqu'île* ☎*04–72–10–17–40* ⊕*www.mba-lyon.fr* ⌨*€6* ⊗*Wed.–Mon. 10:30–6.*

For an adorable perch over the Rhône and a perfect sunset observation point, **Pieds Humides** (⊠*15 quai Victor Augagneur, Part-Dieu)*—literally, "damp feet"—is a nonpareil little kiosk for a coffee, a *pot de vin*, or a passable *plat du jour*.

㉔ Musée Historique des Tissus *(Textile History Museum)*. On display is a fascinating exhibit of intricate carpets, tapestries, and silks, including Asian tapestries from as early as the 4th century, Turkish and Persian carpets from the 16th to the 18th century, and 18th-century Lyon silks, so lovingly depicted in many portraits of the time and still the star of many costume exhibits mounted throughout the world today. ⊠*34 rue de la Charité, Presqu'île* ☎*04–78–38–42–00* ⊕*www.musee-des-tissus.com* ⌨*€6, joint ticket with Musée des Arts Décoratifs* ⊗*Tues.–Sun. 10–5:30.*

㉚ Musée Urbain Tony Garnier *(Tony Garnier Urban Museum)*. Known also as the Cité de la Création (City of Creation), this project was France's first attempt at low-income housing. Over the years, tenants have tried to bring some art and cheerfulness to their environment: 22 giant murals depicting the work of Tony Garnier, the turn-of-the-20th-century Lyon architect, were painted on the walls of these huge housing projects, built in 1920 and 1933. Artists from around the world, with the support of UNESCO, have added their vision to the creation of the ideal housing project. To get there, take the métro from Place Bellecour to Monplaisir-Lumière and walk 10 minutes south along Rue Antoine. ⊠*4 rue Serpollières, Part-Dieu* ☎*04–78–75–16–75* ⊕*www. museeurbaintonygarnier.com* ⌨*€6* ⊗*Daily 2–6.*

㉒ Opéra de Lyon. The barrel-vaulted Lyon Opera, a reincarnation of a moribund 1831 building, was designed by star French architect Jean Nouvel and built in the early 1990s. It incorporates a columned exterior, soaring glass vaulting, Neoclassical public spaces, an all-black interior down to and including the bathrooms and toilets, and the latest backstage magic. High above, looking out between the heroic statues lined up along the parapet, is a small restaurant, Les Muses. ⊠*Pl. de la Comédie, Presqu'île* ☎*04–72–00–45–00, 04–72–00–45–45 for tickets* ⊕*www.opera-lyon.com.*

⑲ Place des Terreaux. The four majestic horses rearing up from a monumental 19th-century fountain in the middle of this large square are by Frédéric-Auguste Bartholdi, who sculpted New York Harbor's Statue of Liberty. The 69 fountains embedded in the wide expanse of the square are illuminated by fiber-optic technology at night. The notable

Continued on page 482

LYON: FRANCE'S CULINARY CAULDRON

No other city in France teases the taste buds like Lyon, birthplace of traditional French cuisine. Home to both the workingman's *bouchons* (taverns)—irresistible in their cozy checked-tablecloth atmosphere— and celeb chefs, the capital of the Rhône-Alpes region has become the engine room of France's modern cooking canon.

If you are what you eat, then Lyon is both simple *and* sophisticated—as unabashedly straightforward as a stew of buttery *poulet de Bresse* and as glamorous as black-truffle soup in pastry. Birthplace of France's original comfort food, Lyon reinvented itself in the 1970s when native chef Paul Bocuse helped launch the Nouvelle Cuisine revolution. Since then, the buzz factor has been revved up even higher by the "molecular gastronomy" fashioned by the new megastar of nearby Annecy, Marc Veyrat. This philosopher-chef has rocketed French food another step into the ozone with cuisine as light and lofty as the natural Alpine environment that produces it. His headline-making creations—caramelized frogs with wild licorice, anyone?—are the talk of foodies everywhere.

IT'S A FAR, FAR BUTTER THING...

What is most amazing is that Bocuse and Veyrat have done this fine-tuning of French haute cuisine in the Rhône-Alpes region, long known as a paradise for traditional trencherman's fare. For it was here in Lyon that the time-honored *cuisine de grand-mère* (grandmother's cooking) was first whipped up by a battery of women— Lyon's famous *mères*—in the late 19th century. Dining at their marble-counter *bouchons* took guts, literally. Based on animal "discards"—of necessity, served swimming in butter or camouflaged in rich sauces—dishes such as *sabodet* (a sausage made of pig's head), *gâteau de foie de volaille* (chicken liver pudding), and sturdy tripe stews were not for the fainthearted. Designed to sustain 19th-century pony riders, stagecoach drivers, and field laborers, this was home-cooking magnified to the nth degree.

CROSSROADS OF CUISINES

Inspired by the rapid acceleration of modern life, however, Bocuse took the heretical step of removing the bulk from bouchon fare. Recognizing that Lyon was at the heart of a crossroads of cuisines—the Mediterranean olive oil–based cuisine to the south; the mountain products and traditions of the Alps to the east; the Massif Central beef trust to the west; and the butter belt of northern France—he concluded that no ingredients had to be imported from any distance. Consequently, the new attributes of freshness and *authentique* taste came to the fore.

A NEW GENERATION

Not surprisingly, cooks in and around Lyon have long been finding ways to make the best of this cornucopia. A Michelin road map of the region's top dining establishments reveals a Rhône-Alpes galaxy totaling more than 60 stars, 19 of which are grouped around the city of Lyon. Marc Veyrat leads a new generation of chefs, among them Nicolas Le Bec, Christian Têtedoie, and Mathieu Viannay—each holding forth in an eponymous Lyon restaurant—as well as a growing list of upcoming contenders (Alain Alexanian, Christophe Ansanay-Alex, Sonia Ezsgulian, Philippe Gauvreau, Guy Lassausaie, Manuel Viron). All are blowing the lid off old Lyon.

Soupe aux truffes

Black pudding

Gâteau de foie de volaille

Escargots

Poulet de Bresse

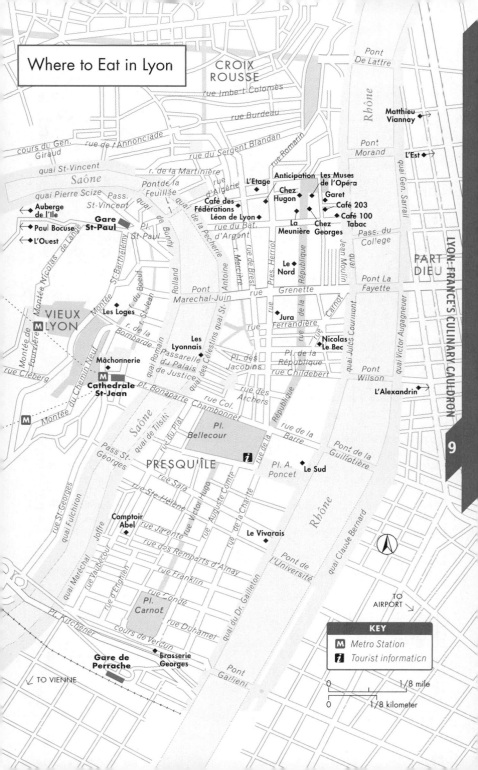

FINDING THE FEAST

Bouchons draw diners to their outdoor tables in summer.

LES BOUCHONS

Set with tile walls, homey wooden benches, and zinc counters, Lyon's iconic **bouchons** (taverns or eating houses) were the medieval equivalent of today's truck stops. Named for the bundles of straw hung over the door, indicating the availability of food and drink for horses as well as stagecoach drivers, these family-run taverns were customarily run by legendary figures such as Mère Brazier, Mère Fillioux, and dozens of other Lyonnais female chefs. Bouchon dishes rely heavily on pig parts (*cochonailles*), but it is most noted for their daunting use of "discards," such as **museau vinaigrette** (pickled ox muzzle) and **tête de veau** (calf's head). Unfortunately, the bouchon tradition has led to a host of modern-day fakes, so look for a little plaque at the door showing Gnafron, a Grand Guignol character, for the real thing. Lyon's best bouchons are just off Place Bellecour behind the Town Hall, and include **Café des Fédérations, Chez Hugon,** and **Comptoir Abel.**

PULL UP THOSE SLEEVES: IT'S TIME TO EAT!

Andouillettes (veal and pork tripe sausage)

Bavette (skirt steak with shallots)

Blanquette de veau (veal stewed in cream, egg yolks, onions, and mushrooms)

Boudin noir (black sausage)

Bugnes (beignets of fried pork fat)

Frisée aux lardons (salads of frilly endives, eggs, and bacon)

Gâteau de foies blonds de volaille (chicken liver mousse)

Gras double (tripe)

Paillasson (fried hashed potatoes)

Pot-au-feu (vegetable and meat stew, a winter favorite)

(left) Downtown city market
(top right) Great goat cheeses at Les Halles

SHOPPING AROUND

A fifteen-minute walk east of the Rhône brings one to **Les Halles de Lyon**—the city's fabled food hall—the place to whet an appetite, especially on weekend mornings when everyone from Paul Bocuse to Pierre Chavent gathers to inspect the produce on display. After admiring exquisite lettuces, wild mushrooms, raspberries, sea bass, poulets de Bresse, or the 300 varieties of goat, sheep, and cow cheese at the **Alain Martinet** stand, it will become impossible not to notice the throng of people crowded around **Maison Rousseau**, shellfish emporium supreme since 1906. Elevated trivets offer spectacular displays of oysters, mussels, garlic-stuffed snails, and other tempting gastropods. Jean-Louis Lemmens and his wife Alexandra run this happy place, serving dishes from Tues.—Sat. 7:30—10:30 and Sunday from 7:30—2:00 during the shellfish months, that is, months with an "r" in them: September through April. (Closed May—August.) Les Halles has many other *salons de dégustations* (tasting rooms).

Pots de Lyon (wine flagons, heavy-bottomed bottles originally conceived to satirize government attempts to limit silk workers' wine consumption in favor of increased labor productivity)	with black truffles, thus "half in mourning")	**Sabodet** (pig's head sausage)
	Poulet de Bresse (the celebrated, free-range Bresse chicken)	**Saucissons chauds** (slices of warm sausage with potatoes drizzled with oil and vinegar)
Poularde demi-deuil (hen	**Quenelles** (pike dumplings)	
	Rosette (a garlicky pork sausage)	**Tablier de sapeur** (breaded, fried tripe)

TASTE-OFF!: PAUL BOCUSE

Born: February 11, 1926, in Collonges-au-Mont d'Or, outside Lyon, France

Personality Profile: Perfectionist, polygamous, public relations genius.

Trademark: Towering white toque.

Favorite pastime: L'Amour—with a happy 60-year marriage, and mistresses of 50 and 35 years duration, Monsieur is a busy man in the kitchen and d'ailleurs.

Claim to Fame: Leader of the Nouvelle Cuisine movement.

Bocuse at his Best: Based since 1959 at his eponymous res-

taurant outside Lyon in Collonges-au-Mont d'Or, he also owns four brasseries in town—Le Nord, L'Est, L'Ouest, and Le Sud.

Best-Known Dish: Soupe aux truffes noires VGE (black-truffle soup in pastry named for former French president Valéry Giscard d'Estaing).

Quote: "Food and sex have much in common. We consummate a union, devour a lover with our eyes, hunger for one another."

For forty years, Paul Bocuse has played Daniel in Lyon's den. Not only did he daringly remake French cooking in one of its most tradition-bound centers, but he became one of the first great male chefs in a city long famous for its *cuisine des femmes.* Born in 1926, he began working at a restaurant in Lyon in 1942, butchering an occasional piglet on the side (the only way to really bring home the bacon back then). Under the aegis of the legendary Fernand Point at La Pyramide in Vienne, just south of Lyon, he moved away from the richness of *la grande cuisine* and introduced a lighter, fresher way of cooking, using sauces thickened without flour and vegetables harvested young and in season. By 1965 he had won his third Michelin star.

By the early 1970s, Bocuse had become the leading ambassador for Nouvelle Cuisine, which emphasized natural sauces, barely cooked baby vegetables, a parsimonious use of dressings, and artful yet simple presentation. He often traveled the world as a Nouvelle evangelist while, back home, his 60-cook staff continued to thrive under his eagled-eyed wife, Raymonde.

These days, Bocuse's once-revolutionary Nouvelle has matured into *cuisine classique.* "It's not nouvelle cuisine anymore," he said recently; "it's now *ancienne* cuisine [old cuisine]." But because Bocuse's touch remains so sublime celebrities still think nothing of hopping the TGV from Paris to dine chez Paul.

Paul Bocuse

TASTE-OFF!: MARC VEYRAT

Born: May 8, 1950, in Annecy in the Haute-Savoie, French Alps.

Personality Profile: Epicurean and poetic but a Savoyard to the core.

Trademark: Black farmer's *sapé* hat, ever-present when he greets diners at his Maison de Marc Veyrat in Veyrier-du-Lac (outside Annecy).

Favorite pastime: Wandering Alpine trails in search of new herbs, nuts, and spices for his recipes.

Claim to Fame: The only chef in history to simultaneously rack up six Michelin stars (three for each of his two restaurants) and a 20/20 Gault Millau rating.

Mentor: Himself. Marc Veyrat is an autodidact who never graduated from cooking school.

Best-Known Dish: *Escalope de foie chaud au pain d'épice aux huit arômes* (warm breaded liver with spice bread and eight herbal aromas).

Quote: "My cuisine is a marriage between nature and the cultures of the world, while never forgetting my roots."

French cooking's revolutionary baton has now been passed to Annecy's poet-chef, Marc Veyrat. Reservations at La Maison de Marc Veyrat are France's hardest to get despite it being considered La Republique's most expensive restaurant. A dynamo of culinary creativity, Veyrat lives in his trademark Savoyard farmer's hat—a symbol of his anti-chef-royalty, anti-classical roots. Alternately described as enfant terrible and wunderkind at 57, he is the product of 11 generations of peasant farmers, has a fascination with Alpine flora that began during childhood hikes. In 1985, Veyrat opened La Maison in a traditional lakeside villa that he renovated brilliantly in a sleek-cum-rustic style featuring wooden beams and paneling.

Veyrat is to Bocuse what Bocuse is to Escoffier. He has eliminated all flour, oil, butter, and cream in favor of dietetic wild plants, which he manipulates using modern biochemical culinary techniques, such as cooking at low temperatures. Whereas Bocuse peeled back centuries of baroque culinary art in an effort to return to the true essences of ingredients, Veyrat's *cuisine du terroir* redefines "haute" via a postmodern "Alpine" bent. Witness his fir-sap soup; bass cooked on slate; eggs infused with lichen and nutmeg; and lobster with lovage and licorice root. But some foodies carp that Alpine haute cuisine is at best merely a question of distance above sea level, and at worst an oxymoron.

A Veyrat trademark dessert, five types of crème brûlée.

buildings on either side are the Hôtel de Ville and the Musée des Beaux-Arts. ⊠*Presqu'île.*

ALSO WORTH SEEING

㉕ Basilique de Saint-Martin d'Ainay. The abbey church of one of Lyon's most ancient monasteries, this fortified church dates back to a 10th-century Benedictine abbey and a 9th-century sanctuary before that. The millenary, circa-1,000-year energy field is palpable around this hulking structure, especially near the rear of the apse where the stained-glass windows glow richly in the twilight. One of the earliest buildings in France to be classified a national monument, in 1844, its interior murals and frescoes are disappointingly severe compared to the quirky, rough exterior. ⊠*Pl. de l'Abbaye d'Ainay, Presqu'île* ☎*04–78–72–10–03* ☜*Free* ☉*Daily 9–1 and 4–7.*

㉗ Centre d'Histoire de la Résistance et de la Déportation (*Museum of the History of the Resistance and the Deportation*). During World War II, especially after 1942, Lyon played an important role in the Resistance movement against the German occupation of France. Displays include equipment, such as radios and printing presses, photographs, and exhibits recreating the clandestine lives and heroic exploits of Resistance fighters. ⊠*14 av. Berthelot, Part-Dieu* ☎*04–78–72–23–11* ☜*€4* ☉*Wed.–Sun. 9–5:30.*

Ⓒ ▶ **⑱ Maison des Canuts** (*Silk Weavers' Museum*). Despite the industrialization of silk and textile production, old-time Jacquard looms are still in action at this historic house in the Croix Rousse. The weavers are happy to show children how to operate a miniature loom. ⊠*10–12 rue d'Ivry, La Croix Rousse* ☎*04–78–28–62–04* ☜*Free* ☉*Tues.–Sat. 10–6:30; guided tours by appointment 11 and 3:30.*

★ **㉓ Musée des Arts Décoratifs** (*Decorative Arts Museum*). Housed in an 18th-century mansion, the museum has fine collections of silverware, furniture, objets d'art, porcelain, and tapestries. ⊠*34 rue de la Charité, Presqu'île* ☎*04–78–38–42–00* ⊕*www.lesartsdecoratifs.fr* ☜*€6, joint ticket with the nearby Musée Historique des Tissus* ☉*Tues.–Sun. 10–5:30.*

Ⓒ **㉙ Parc de la Tête d'Or** (*Golden Head Park*). On the bank of the Rhône, this 300-acre park encompasses a lake, pony rides, and a small zoo. It's ideal for an afternoon's outing with children. Take the métro from Perrache train station to Masséna. ⊠*Pl. du Général-Leclerc, Quai Charles-de-Gaulle, Cité Internationale* ⊕*www.parc-tete-dor.com* ☜*Free* ☉*Dawn–dusk.*

㉖ Place Carnot. Spread out in front of the Perrache train station built in 1857, this bustling square holds an excellent Christmas market from early December through New Year's. The two main monuments represent La République and (the seated figure) the City of Lyon. The Brasserie Georges, dating from 1836, has hosted legendary personalities from Mistinguet to Jacques Brel and Johnny Halliday. ⊠*Presqu'île.*

WHERE TO STAY & EAT

★ $$$$ ✗ **Auberge de l'Île.** For a pretty one-hour walk up the river Saône's right bank and a return down the other, the Ile Barbe is a lush and leafy enclave to keep in mind. Alex Ansanay's lovely restaurant, whether outside on the terrace or inside the graceful former 17th-century monastery refectory, serves smart, contemporary cuisine based on fresh market products prepared with originality. Look for game in fall and winter. The wine list is strong in local Côtes du Rhône and Macon treasures. ✉ *L'Île Barbe, Collonges au Mont-D'Or* ☎ *04–78–83–99–49* ⚑ *Reservations essential* 🗖 *AE, MC, V* ⊘ *Closed Sun., Mon., and Aug. 1–24.*

★ $$$$ ✗ **Léon de Lyon.** Chef Jean-Paul Lacombe's innovative uses of the region's butter, cream, and foie gras put this restaurant at the forefront of the city's gastronomic scene. Dishes such as fillet of veal with celery and leg of lamb with fava beans are memorable; suckling pig comes with foie gras, onions, and a truffle salad. Alcoves and wood paneling in this 19th-century house add charm to the mix. Evening prix-fixe menus are €115 and €170, with a lunch menu at €61. ✉ *1 rue Pléney, Presqu'île* ☎ *04–72–10–11–12* ⚑ *Reservations essential* Jacket required 🗖 *AE, DC, MC, V* ⊘ *Closed Sun., Mon., and 1st 3 wks Aug.*

$$$$ ✗ **Les Loges.** This lovely dining room, lavishly appointed with mahogany chairs, modern art, and a giant medieval hearth, serves a range of culinary delights that deliciously represent the New Lyon cooking. Chef Anthony Bonnard's *poitrine de veau* (breast of veal) with asparagus and essence of almonds or his *foie gras poêlé au coing* (sautéed duck or goose liver with quince) are two specialties to look for, though the menu is in constant flux according to markets and seasons. ✉ *6 rue du Boeuf, Vieux Lyon* ☎ *04–72–77–44–44* 🗖 *AE, DC, MC, V* ⊘ *Closed Aug. 4–26. No dinner Sun.*

★ $$$$ ✗ **Matthieu Viannay.** This bright young star in Lyon's dining scene has attracted the attention and admiration of this demanding gastronomical city's food critics and cuisine cognoscenti with daring new recipes combining originality, conceptual simplicity, and authenticity of ingredients. His escargots in bone-marrow croquette are as spare and novel as the stripped stone-and-wood decor of this contemporary enclave, set in the upper Brotteaux district (east of the Rhône and upriver from Pont Morand behind the Opera). ✉ *47 av. Foch, Les Brotteaux* ☎ *04–78–89–55–19* ⚑ *Reservations essential* 🗖 *AE, MC, V* ⊘ *Closed weekends except holidays; Aug.; and Dec. 29–Jan. 5.*

$$$$
Fodor's Choice
★
✗ **Nicolas Le Bec.** Ever since walking off with the 2002 Gault-Millau Chef of the Year honors, Nicolas Le Bec has been hot as a pistol, whether at his past spot, Les Loges, or here in this cozy hideaway near Place Bellecour. With a constantly changing menu responding to the seasons, the market, and the chef's abundant curiosity, there's always a new take on anything from artichokes to risotto in this postmodern culinary antithesis of traditional Lyonnais bouchon cooking. Le Bec's past triumphs include his duck foie gras with black figs and his roast crayfish with purple artichokes, and fans keep packing this place to see what new wonders he has up his sleeve. ✉ *14 rue Grolée, Presqu'île*

9

☎04–78–42–15–00 ⊕*www.nicolaslebec.com* ☒*Reservations essential* ▤*AE, MC, V* ⊘*Closed Sun., Mon., and 1st 2 wks Aug.*

$$$$ ✗ **Paul Bocuse.** Parisians hop the TGV to dine at this culinary shrine
Fodor'sChoice in Collonges-au-Mont-d'Or, then snooze back to the capital. Whether
★   Bocuse—who kick-started the "new" French cooking back in the 1970s
and became a superstar in the process—is here or not, the legendary
black-truffle soup in pastry crust he created in 1975 to honor President
Giscard d'Estaing will be. So will the frogs'-leg soup with watercress,
the green bean–and–artichoke salad with foie gras, or the Bresse wood-
pigeon "tripled": drumstick in puff pastry with young cabbage, breast
roasted and glazed in cognac, and an aromatic dark pâté of the innards.
For a mere €158 for two, the *volaille de Bresse truffée en vessie "Mere
Fillioux"* (Bresse hen cooked in a pig bladder with truffles) comes to the
table looking something like a basketball—the bladder is removed and
discarded revealing a poached chicken within. Like the desserts, the
grand dining room is done in traditional style. Call ahead if you want
to find out whether Bocuse will be cooking, and book far in advance.
For more on Bocuse, *see "Lyon: France's Culinary Cauldron"* in this
chapter. ☒*50 quai de la Plage, Collonges-au-Mont-d'Or, Pont de Collonges Nord* ☎04–72–42–90–90 ⊕*www.bocuse.fr* ☒*Reservations
essential*Jacket required ▤*AE, DC, MC, V.*

$$–$$$$ ✗ **L'Alexandrin.** Chef Alex Alexanian's take on nouvelle cuisine is every-
thing to every mouth. If succulent game is your weakness, this is the
place, especially during hunting season. If you're tired of oversaturated
Lyonnais cuisine, try the special *fruits et légumes* menu, a creative feast
of fresh goodies selected each morning from Les Halles market, just
around the corner. Whether a dish is based on veal, rabbit, or sole,
Alexanian's touch is always light on calories and heavy on flavor. ☒*83
rue Moncey, Part-Dieu* ☎04–72–61–15–69 ▤*MC, V* ⊘*Closed Sun.,
Mon., and July 29–Aug. 20.*

$–$$$$ ✗ **Le Nord.** Should you want to keep some change in your pocket and
still sample cooking by Paul Bocuse–trained-and-supervised chefs, four
Bocuse bistros are distributed around Lyon's cardinal points. Le Nord
specializes in Eastern cuisine, with specialties including dishes cooked
over coals and excellent fish and seafood. The decor is classical turn-
of-the-20th-century brasserie with wooden benches and paneled walls.
For cooking from around Mediterranean amid bright sun-drenched
colors, **Le Sud** (☒*11 pl. Antonin-Poncet, Presqu'île* ☎04–72–77–80–
00) is the Bocusian homage to southern Europe. The rollicking **L'Est**
(☒*Gare des Brotteaux 14, Les Brotteaux* ☎04–37–24–25–26) is set
in the old 19th-century Brotteaux train station and cooks up a travel
theme, thanks to a menu that includes dishes from all over the planet
and a decor flavored with railroad memorabilia, paraphernalia, and a
soupçon of nostalgia. **L'Ouest** (☒*Quai du Commerce 1, Villefranche*
☎04–78–35–63–13) exults in a Postmodern wood-and-steel design, a
fitting setting for Bocuse's maritime culinary adventures in the islands
of the Atlantic, Caribbean, and the South Seas. ☒*18 rue Neuve,
Presqu'île* ☎04–72–10–69–69 ▤*AE, DC, MC, V.*

★ **$$–$$$**   ✗ **L'Étage.** Hidden over Place des Terreaux, this semisecret upstairs
dining room prepares some of Lyon's finest new cuisine. A place at the

window (admittedly hard to come by), overlooking the facade of the Beaux Arts academy across the square, is a moment to remember, especially if it's during the December 8 Festival of Lights. ⊠ *4 pl. des Terreaux, Presqu'île* ☎*04–78–28–19–59* ▤*AE, DC, MC, V* ☉*Closed Feb., July 23–Aug. 23, Sun., and Mon.*

$–$$$ ✕ **Anticipation.** Light, creative dishes using the region's famed specialties (such as poulet de Bresse) are carefully prepared here by John Rosiak, a former cook at Georges Blanc. The cheery, homey feel makes it a place where you can settle in for an evening of good fare and fun. ⊠*8 rue Chavanne, Presqu'île* ☎*04–78–30–91–92* ▤*AE, MC, V* ☉*Closed Mon. No dinner Sun.*

$–$$$ ✕ **Café des Fédérations.** For 80 years this sawdust-strewn café with homey red-check tablecloths has reigned as one of the city's leading bouchons. It may have overextended its stay, however, by trading on past glory. Some readers report a desultory hand in the kitchen, and native Lyonnais seem to head elsewhere. Others say Raymond Fulchiron not only serves deftly prepared local classics like *boudin blanc* (white-meat sausage) but also stops by to chat with you, making you feel at home. ⊠*8 rue du Major-Martin, Presqu'île* ☎*04–78–28–26–00* ▤*AE, DC, MC, V* ☉*Closed weekends and July 23–Aug. 23.*

$–$$$ ✕ **Chez Hugon.** This typical bouchon-tavern with red-check tablecloths is behind the Musée des Beaux-Arts and is one of the city's top-rated insider spots. Practically a club, it's crowded with regulars, who keep busy trading quips with the owner while Madame prepares the best *tablier de sapeur* (tripe marinated in wine and fried in bread crumbs) in town. Whether you order the hunks of homemade pâté, the stewed chicken in wine vinegar sauce, or the plate of *ris de veau* (sweetbreads), your dinner will add up to good, inexpensive food and plenty of it. ⊠*12 rue Pizay, Presqu'île* ☎*04–78–28–10–94* ▤*MC, V* ☉*Closed weekends and Aug.*

★ $–$$$ ✕ **Les Muses de l'Opéra.** High up under the glass vault of the Opéra de Lyon designed by Jean Nouvel, this small restaurant looks out past the backs of sculptures of the eight Muses over the Hôtel de Ville. The quality and variety of the creative contemporary cuisine make it hard to decide between the choices offered, but the salmon in butter sauce with watercress mousse is a winner. ⊠*Pl. Comédie, Opéra de Lyon, 7th fl., Presqu'île* ☎*04–72–00–45–58* ⌕*Reservations essential* ▤*AE, MC, V* ☉*No dinner Sun.*

$–$$ ✕ **Comptoir Abel.** This charming 400-year-old house is one of Lyon's most frequently filmed and photographed taverns. Simple wooden tables in wood-paneled dining rooms, quirky art on every wall, heavy-bottomed *pot lyonnais* wine bottles: every detail is obviously pampered and lovingly produced. The *salade lyonnaise* (green salad with

Fodor's Choice
★

9

homemade croutons and sautéed bacon, topped with a poached egg) or the *rognons madère* (kidneys in a madeira sauce) are standouts. ⊠*25 rue Guynemer, Presqu'île* ☎*04–78–37–46–18* ☰*AE, DC, MC, V* ⊘*Closed Sat., Sun., and Dec. 22–Jan. 2.*

$–$$ ✗ **Jura.** The rows of tables, the 1934 mosaic-tile floor, and the absence of anything pretty gives this place the feel of a men's club. The mustachioed owner, looking as if he stepped out of the turn-of-the-20th-century prints on the walls, acts gruffly but with a smile, as his wife rushes around. The game and steak dishes are robust, as is the *cassoulet des escargots* (stew of beans, mutton, and snails). For dessert, stick with the fine cheese selection. ⊠*25 rue Tupin, Presqu'île* ☎*04–78–42–20–57* ☰*MC, V* ⊘*Closed weekends May–Sept., Sun. and Mon. Sept.–Apr.*

$–$$ ✗ **Les Lyonnais.** This popular brasserie, decorated with photographs of local celebrities, is particularly animated. The simple food—chicken simmered for hours in wine, meat stews, and grilled fish—is served on bare wood tables. A blackboard announces plats du jour, which are less expensive than items on the printed menu. Try the *caille aux petits legumes* (quail with vegetables) for a change from heavier bouchon fare such as *la quenelle* (pike dumpling) or *l'andouillette* (sausage). ⊠*1 rue Tramassac, Vieux Lyon* ☎*04–78–37–64–82* ☰*AE, DC, MC, V* ⊘*Closed Aug. and 1st wk Jan.*

★ $–$$ ✗ **Mâchonnerie.** The word *mâchon* comes from the morning snack of the silk weaver or *canut*, and has come to mean the typical food of the Lyon region. This is one of Lyon's most respected popular bistros, under the *ficelle*, the funicular up to the Fourvière hill. Try the *andouillettes* (sausage). ⊠*36 rue Tramassac, Vieux Lyon* ☎*04–78–42–24–62* ☰*AE, DC, MC, V* ⊘*No lunch weekdays. Closed Sun.*

$–$$ ✗ **Le Vivarais.** Robert Duffaud's simple, tidy restaurant is an outstanding culinary value. Don't expect napkins folded into flower shapes—the excitement is on your plate, with dishes like *lièvre royale* (hare rolled and stuffed with foie gras and a hint of truffles). ⊠*1 pl. du Dr-Gailleton, Presqu'île* ☎*04–78–37–85–15* ⬗*Reservations essential* ☰*AE, MC, V* ⊘*Closed Sun., and July 24–Aug. 22.*

¢–$ ✗ **Brasserie Georges.** This inexpensive brasserie at the south end of Rue de la Charité next to the Perrache train station is one of the city's largest and oldest, founded in 1836 but now in a palatial 1925 Art Deco building. Meals range from hearty veal stew or sauerkraut and sausage to more refined fare. The kitchen could be better—stick with the great standards, such as *saucisson brioché* (sausage in brioche stuffed with truffled foie gras)—but the ambience is as delicious as it comes. ⊠*30 cours Verdun, Perrache* ☎*04–72–56–54–54* ☰*AE, DC, MC, V.*

★ ¢–$ ✗ **Café 203/Café 100 Tabac.** These two clever sister bistros near the opera are young, hot, and happening. One is named for the Peugeot 203 (an antique model of which is parked outside), and the other is a play on "100/sans" (100%–without) tobacco—yes, you read it here: smoke-free. Open from dawn to after midnight (but no Sunday breakfast), the Italianate cuisine is fresh and original, fast, inexpensive, and delicious. For a quick pre- or post-opera meal, this is the spot. ⊠*9 rue du Garet, Presqu'île* ⊠*23 rue de l'Arbre Sec, Presqu'île* ☎*04–78–28–65–66* ☰*AE, DC, MC, V.*

$$$$ ✕▦ **La Cour des Loges.** King Juan Carlos of Spain, Celine Dion, and the
Fodor'sChoice Rolling Stones have all graced this most eye-popping of Lyon hotels.
★ Spectacularly renovated around a glassed-in Renaissance courtyard,
this former Jesuit convent is now an extravaganza of glowing fireplaces, Florentine crystal chandeliers, Baroque credenzas, high-beamed
ceilings, mullioned windows, guest rooms swathed in Venetian red and
antique Lyon silks, suites that are like artist ateliers, and Phillipe Starck
bathrooms. The restaurant, **Les Loges,** is one of Lyon's most graceful
dining rooms, with, in addition, a cellar-level wine bar and a café-
épicerie with a lovely vaulted ceiling. ✉ *6 rue du Boeuf, Vieux Lyon
69005* ☎*04–72–77–44–44* 🖷*04–72–40–93–61* ⊕*www.courdesloges.
com* 📞*52 rooms* ♿*In-room: refrigerator, Wi-Fi. In-hotel: restaurant,
bar, pool, gym, public Wi-Fi, parking (fee)* ▤*AE, DC, MC, V.*

★ **$$$$** ✕▦ **La Tour Rose.** Philippe Chavent's silk-swathed Vieux Lyon hotel
occupies a Renaissance-period convent set around a gorgeous Floren-
tine-style courtyard under a rose-washed tower. The glass-roof restaurant occupies a former chapel and offers views of the hanging garden
overhead. Each guest room is named for a famous silk-weaving concern
and decorated in its goods; taffetas, plissés, and velvets cover walls,
windows, and beds in daring, even startling styles. The signature specials here—smoked-duck soup, skate in oyster coulis, hibiscus sorbet—
are well worth all the extra louis d'or. Six apartments with kitchenettes
in an adjacent annex provide excellent value for longer stays. ✉*22 rue
du Boeuf, Vieux Lyon, 69005* ☎*04–78–92–69–10* 🖷*04–78–42–26–
02* ⊕*www.tour-rose.com* 📞*11 rooms, 8 suites* ♿*In-room: refrigerator, Wi-Fi. In-hotel: restaurant, bar, public Wi-Fi, parking (fee), some
pets allowed* ▤*AE, DC, MC, V.*

★ **$$$$** ✕▦ **Villa Florentine.** High above the *Vieille Ville* (Old Town), near the
Roman theaters and the basilica, this pristine hotel was once a 17th-
century convent—and everyone knows the sisters always enjoyed the
best real estate in town. Glowing in its ocher-yellow exterior, it has
beamed and vaulted ceilings, terraces, and particularly marvelous
views, which are seen to best advantage from the pool and the excellent restaurant, Les Terrasses de Lyon—an extravaganza complete
with glassed-in winter garden and tomato-red salons. Throughout,
in time-warp fashion, 17th-century Italianate architectural details are
contrasted with the latest in bright postmodern Italian furnishings.
✉*25–27 montée St-Barthélémy, Fourvière, 69005* ☎*04–72–56–56–
56* 🖷*04–72–40–90–56* ⊕*www.villaflorentine.com* 📞*20 rooms, 8
suites* ♿*In-room: refrigerator, ethernet, Wi-Fi. In-hotel: restaurant,
bar, pool, parking (fee), some pets allowed (fee), public Wi-Fi* ▤*AE,
DC, MC, V.*

$$$–$$$$ ▦ **Boscolo Grand Hôtel.** This Belle Epoque hotel off Place de la Répub-
lique has a courteous and efficient staff. Rooms have high ceilings,
mostly modern furnishings, and one special piece such as an armoire
or writing desk. Erté prints try hard to set a stylish tone in the guest
rooms, the Rhône is just across the street, and tour groups are kept
happy and content. ✉*11 rue Grôlée, Presqu'île, 69002* ☎*04–72–40–
45–45* 🖷*04–78–37–52–55* ⊕*www.boscolohotels.com* 📞*140 rooms*

♿ *In-room: Wi-Fi. In-hotel: restaurant, bar, public Wi-Fi, parking (fee), some pets allowed (fee)* ▤*AE, DC, MC, V* ⭐*◯IBP.*

$$$　🏨 **Phénix Hotel.** This little hotel in Vieux Lyon is a winning combi-
Fodor's Choice nation of location, charming staff, tastefully decorated rooms, and
★ moderate prices. Overlooking the Saône at the upstream edge of Vieux
Lyon, the hotel's modern design and decor is gracefully juxtaposed
with its 16th-century ceiling beams and Renaissance facade. Some
rooms have fireplaces, and the smallish upper floor rooms are charm-
ingly built into the eaves and rooftop dormers. ✉ *7 quai Bondy, Vieux
Lyon, 69005* ☎*04–78–28–24–24* 🖷*04–78–28–62–86* ⊕*www.hotel-
le-phenix.fr* ⬦*36 rooms* ♿*In-room: Wi-Fi. In-hotel: restaurant, bar,
public Wi-Fi, parking (fee), some pets allowed (fee)* ▤*AE, DC, MC,
V* ⭐*◯IBP.*

$$–$$$　🏨 **Collèe.** A faithful reproduction of the owner Laurent Phelip's school-
Fodor's Choice boy days in Vieux Lyon, this charmingly nostalgic theme hotel ("… tak-
★ ing us back to our dreams," as the owner puts it) offers public spaces
decorated as antique classrooms complete with polished wooden desks
with inkwells and geography maps. The breakfast room is a study hall.
Guest rooms range from simple "undergraduate" quarters to "postgrad-
uate" suites—they are challenging in their stark-white mimimal decor but
most of them come with splendid views over the Saône and Lyon. ✉ *5 pl.
St-Paul, Vieux Lyon, 69005* ☎*04–72–10–05–05* 🖷*04–78–27–98–84*
⊕*www.college-hotel.com* ⬦*39 rooms* ♿*In-hotel: bar, public Wi-Fi,
parking (fee), some pets allowed (fee)* ▤*AE, DC, MC, V* ⭐*◯IBP.*

$$　🏨 **Hôtel des Artistes.** This intimate hotel on an elegant square opposite the Théâtre des Célestins has long been popular among stage and
screen artists; black-and-white photographs of actors and actresses
adorn lobby walls. Rooms are smallish but modern and comfortable,
and the friendly reception and great location appeal to all comers. ✉ *8
rue Gaspard-André, Presqu'île, 69002* ☎*04–78–42–04–88* 🖷*04–78–
42–93–76* ⊕*www.hoteldesartistes.fr* ⬦*45 rooms* ♿*In-room: no a/c,
refrigerator. In-hotel: public Wi-Fi.* ▤*AE, DC, MC, V.*

$–$$　🏨 **Citôtel Dubost.** This little gem is a lot better than a first glance might
indicate. Rooms are small but impeccable; the art hanging around
the walls is generic but good; the breakfast bread, croissant, and coffee is uniformly excellent, and the staff is friendly and helpful. The
one-minute walk to Lyon's slick subway line at Gare Perrache can
be handy in rain or in haste, though the walk to the other end of
Presqu'île is an entertaining 45-minute gallop not to miss. ✉ *19 pl.
Carnot, Presqu'île, 69002* ☎*04–78–42–00–46* 🖷*04–72–40–96–66*
⊕*www.hotel-dubost.com* ⬦*56 rooms* ♿*In-hotel: some pets allowed*
▤*AE, DC, MC, V.*

★ $　🏨 **Hôtel du Théâtre.** The friendly and enthusiastic owner is sufficient
reason to recommend this small hotel. But its location and reasonable
prices make it even more commendable. Rooms are simple but clean;
those overlooking Place des Célestins not only have a theatrical view
but also a bathroom with a tub. Those facing the side have a shower
only. Breakfast is included. ✉ *10 rue de Savoie, Presqu'île, 69002*
☎*04–78–42–33–32* 🖷*04–72–40–00–61* ⊕*www.hotel-du-theatre.fr*

Lyon's Dance Blowout

Lyon's Biennale de la Dance throws France's second city into perpetual motion for nearly three weeks every other September (on even-numbered years). Brainchild of Lyon choreographer Guy Darmet, each year celebrates a different theme: 2004 brought together dance companies from Eastern Europe and 2006 was entitled "The World of Cities, Cities of the World," celebrating great cities around the globe. The result, no matter which even year you choose, is a nonpareil dance blowout at the confluence of the Saône and Rhône rivers. At each biennale, in addition to the more than 100 performances scheduled in the city's finest venues

such as the Jean Nouvel opera house, the Maison de la Danse, and the cookie box–like Théâtre des Célestins, popular highlights include the tumultuous 4,500-dancer street parade that roars down the left bank of the Rhône on the festival's first Sunday, and the three Saturday night dance galas held in the graceful Brotteaux train station, the Halle Tony Garnier, or the Place des Terreaux. Collective dance classes for thousands and spontaneous outbursts of tango, salsa, or nearly any other genre of rhythmic movement, pop up all over town, while newspaper front pages feature little else. For details: ⊕ *www.biennale-de-lyon.org*.

⌨24 rooms ⌂In-room: no a/c. In-hotel: bar, parking (fee) ☰AE, DC, MC, V.

★ $ ⊡ **Lyon Guesthouse.** This spectacular location overlooking all of Lyon from atop the promontory of La Croix Rousse is an art gallery and bed-and-breakfast run by an enterprising art historian, Françoise Besson. Ninety-two stairs are the only way up to this fourth-floor crow's nest, so travel light and stay fit. ⊠6 montée du Lieutenant Aliouche, La Croix Rousse, 69001 ☎04–78–29–62–05 ⊕www.lyonguesthouse.com ⌨3 rooms ⌂In-room: no a/c. In-hotel: no elevator ☰AE, DC, MC, V.

$ ⊡ **Péniche El Kantara.** For a friendly host and an unusual sleep on the
Fodor's Choice Saône river, Dominique Abafourd takes good care of her guests aboard
★   her river barge. With an indoor pool, a cozy midriver terrace, and gorgeous wood-paneled cabins, this is a cruise you will not forget. ⊠13 quai Rambaud, Presqu'île, 69002 ☎04–78–42–02–75 ✎dominique. abafourd@tiscali.fr ⌨2 rooms ⌂In-room: no a/c. In-hotel: bar, pool ☰AE, DC, MC, V.

NIGHTLIFE & THE ARTS

Lyon is the region's liveliest arts center; check the weekly *Lyon-Poche*, published on Wednesday and sold at newsstands, for cultural events and goings-on at the dozens of discos, bars, and clubs.

For darts and pints and jazz on weekends, head to the **Albion Public House** (⊠12 rue Ste-Catherine, Presqu'île ☎04–78–28–33–00), where they even accept British pounds. The low-key chic **L'Alibi** (⊠13 quai Romain-Roland, Vieux Lyon ☎04–78–42–04–66) has a laser show along with the music. Romantics rendezvous at the **Bar de la Tour Rose** (⊠22 rue du Boeuf, Vieux Lyon ☎04–78–37–25–90). **Le Boudoir**

9

(✉*13 pl. Jules Ferry, Les Brotteaux* ☎*04–72–74–04–41*) is a popular saloon in the old Brotteaux train station. **Bouchon aux Vin** (✉*64 rue Mercière, Presqu'île* ☎*04–78–42–88–90*) is a wine bar with 30-plus vintages. **Café Cuba** (✉*19 pl. Tolozan, Presqu'île* ☎*04–78–28–35–77*) provides interesting tapas, cocktails, and Havana cigars until 1 am near the Jean Nouvel opera house.

Café-Théâtre de L'Accessoire (✉*26 rue de l'Annonciade, Presqu'île* ☎*04–78–27–84–84*) is a leading café-theater where you can eat and drink while watching a review. **La Cave des Voyageurs** (✉*7 pl. St-Paul– St-Barthélémy, Vieux Lyon* ☎*04–78–28–92–28*), just below the St-Paul train station, is a cozy place to try some top wines. Computer jocks head into cyberspace at **Le Chantier** (✉*18–20 rue Ste-Catherine, Presqu'île* ☎*04–78–39–05–56*), while their friends listen to jazz and nibble on tapas. Caribbean and African music pulses at **Le Club des Iles** (✉*1 Grande-Rue des Feuillants, Presqu'île* ☎*04–78–39–16–35*). **Le Complexe du Rire** (✉*7 rue des Capucins, Presqu'île* ☎*04–78–27–23– 59*) is a lively satirical and comic review above Place des Terreaux. **Edyn's Club** (✉*3 rue Terme, Presqu'île* ☎*04–78–30–02–01*) rocks on weekends and holiday eves.

The café-theater **Espace Gerson** (✉*1 pl. Gerson, Vieux Lyon* ☎*04– 78–27–96–99*) presents revues in conjunction with dinner. Live jazz is played in the stone-vaulted basement of **Hot Club** (✉*26 rue Lanterne, Presqu'île* ☎*04–78–39–54–74*). For the young, 30 and under, **Quai Ouest** (✉*40 quai Pierre Scize, Presqu'île* ☎*04–78–28–20–40*) offers surefire nocturnal action on the banks of the Saône. A gay crowd is found among the 1930s blandishments at **La Ruche** (✉*22 rue Gentil, Presqu'île* ☎*04–78–39–03–82*). For the hottest English pub in Lyon, the **Smoking Dog** (✉*16 rue Lainerie, Vieux Lyon* ☎*04–78–37–25–90*) is the place to head. **Villa Florentine** (✉*25 Montée St-Barthélémy, Four-vière* ☎*04–72–56–56–56*) is a quiet spot for sipping a drink to the strains of a harpist, who plays on Friday and Saturday.

Center stage for Lyon's amazing arts scene, the **Opéra de Lyon** (✉*1 pl. de la Comédie, Presqu'île* ☎*04–72–00–45–45* ⊕*www.opera-lyon. org*) presents plays, concerts, ballets, and opera from October to June. Lyon's Société de Musique de Chambre performs at **Salle Molière** (✉*18 quai Bondy, Vieux Lyon* ☎*04–78–28–03–11*).

Early fall sees the unforgettably spectacular **Biennale de la Danse** *(Dance Biennial)*, which takes place in even-numbered years. *See "Lyon's Dance Blowout" Close-Up Box* (⊕www.biennale-de-lyon.org) for the full scoop. September is the time for the **Foire aux Tupiniers** (☎*04–78–37– 00–68*), a pottery fair. October brings the **Festival Bach** (☎*04–78–72– 75–31*). The **Biennale d'Art Contemporain** *(Contemporary Art Biennial,* ☎*04–78–30–50–66*) is held in even-numbered years in late September. The **Festival du Vieux Lyon** (☎*04–78–42–39–04*) is a music festival in November and December. On December 8—the Fête de La Immaculée Conception (Feast of the Immaculate Conception)—startling lighting creations transform the city into a fantasy for the marvelous **Fête de Lumière,** Lyon's Festival of Lights.

SHOPPING

Lyon remains France's silk-and-textile capital, and all big-name designers have shops here. The 19th-century **Passage de l'Argue** (between Rue du Président Édouard-Herriot and Rue de la République in the center of town) is lined with traditional shops. The **Carré d'Or** district has more than 70 luxury shops between Place Bellecour and Cordeliers. **Passage Thiaffait** (⊕www.passagethiaffait.fr) on the Croix Rousse hillside is home to the Creators' Village, with young designers offering original one-of-a-kind creations.

Lyon's biggest shopping mall is the **Part-Dieu Shopping Center** (⊠*Rue du Dr-Bouchut, Part-Dieu* ☎*04–72–60–60–62*), where there are 14 movie theaters and 250 shops. France's major department stores are well represented in Lyon. **Galeries Lafayette** (⊠*In Part-Dieu Shopping Center, Part-Dieu* ☎*04–72–61–44–44* ⊠*6 pl. des Cordeliers, Presqu'île* ☎*04–72–40–48–00* ⊠*200 bd. Pinel, Villeurbanne* ☎*04–78–77–82–12*) has always brought Parisian flair to its outlying branches. **Printemps** (⊠*42 rue de la République, Presqu'île* ☎*04–72–41–29–29*) is the Lyon outpost of the big Paris store.

Captiva (⊠*10 rue de la Charité, Perrache* ☎*04–78–37–96–15*) is the boutique of a young designer who works mainly in silk. **Zilli** (⊠*4 Président Carnot, Presqu'île* ☎*04–78–42–10–27*) designs and sells exclusively men's clothing. **Nicolas Faffiotte** (⊠*4 rue E. Herriot, Presqu'île* ☎*04–78–37–36–25*) specializes in wedding dresses and high-end evening wear. **Les Gones** (⊠*33 rue Leynaud, La Croix Rousse* ☎*04–78–28–40–78*), in the Croix Rousse, is a boutique carrying the work of several young designers. The workshop of **Monsieur Georges Mattelon** (⊠*Rue d'Ivry, Presqu'île* ☎*04–78–28–62–04*) is one of the oldest silk-weaving shops in Lyon. Lyonnais designer **Clémentine** (⊠*18 rue Émile-Zola, Presqu'île*) is good for well-cut, tailored clothing. **Étincelle** (⊠*34 rue St-Jean, Vieux Lyon*) has trendy outfits for youngsters.

For antiques, wander down **Rue Auguste-Comte** (⊠*From Pl. Bellecour to Perrache*). **Image en Cours** (⊠*26 rue du Boeuf, Vieux Lyon*) sells superb engravings. **La Maison des Canuts** (⊠*10–12 rue d'Ivry, La Croix Rousse*) carries local textiles. Fabrics can also be found at the **Boutique des Soyeux Lyonrais** (⊠*3 rue du Boeuf, Vieux Lyon*).

For arts and crafts there are several places where you can find irresistible objects. Look for Lyonnais puppets on **Place du Change.** For new art, try the **Marché des Artistes** (*Artists' Market*) ⊠*Quai Romain-Rolland, Vieux Lyon*) every Sunday morning from 7 to 1. Held on Sunday morning is another **Marché des Artisans** (*Crafts Market*) ⊠*Quai Fulchiron, Vieux Lyon*). A **Marché aux Puces** (*Flea Market,* ⊠*Take Bus 37, 1 rue du Canal, Villeurbanne*) takes place on Thursday and Saturday mornings 8–noon and on Sunday 6–1. For **secondhand books** try the market along Quai de la Pêcherie near Place Bellecour, held every Saturday and Sunday 10–6.

Food markets are held from Tuesday through Sunday on Boulevard de la Croix-Rousse, at Les Halles on Cours Lafayette, on Quai Victor

9

Augagneur, and on Quai St-Antoine. For up-to-the-minute information on food, restaurants, and great wines, don't miss the (prize-winning and English-speaking) "flying sommelier," Georges Dos Santos at **Antic Wine** (✉*18 rue du Boeuf, Vieux Lyon* ☎*04–78–37–08–96*). A wineshop with an excellent selection is **À Ma Vigne** (✉*18 rue Vaubecour, Presqu'île* ☎*04–78–37–05–29*). **Cave de la Côte** (✉*5 rue Pleney, Presqu'île* ☎*04–78–42–93–20*) also has good wines. For chocolates head to **Bernachon** (✉*42 cours Franklin-Roosevelt, Les Brotteaux*); some say it's the best *chocolaterie* in France. For fragrances, photos, furniture, philosophy, and comprehensive Oriental tea culture, **Cha Yuan** (✉*7–9 rue des Remparts d'Ainay, Presqu'île*) is the best boutique in Lyon, with more than 300 varieties of tea on sale from all over the world. **Eléphant des Montagnes** (✉*43 rue Auguste Comte, Presqu'île*), not far from Perrache station, has treasures from Nepal, Afghanistan, India, and the Himalayas, lovingly retrieved by Pierre Chavanne. **La Boîte à Dessert** (✉*1 rue de l'Ancienne-Préfecture, Presqu'île*) makes luscious peach turnovers. For culinary variety, shop **Les Halles** (✉*102 cours Lafayette, Part-Dieu*). **Pignol** (✉*17 rue Émile-Zola, Presqu'île*) is good for meats and sandwich makings. **Reynon** (✉*13 rue des Archers, Presqu'île*) is the place for charcuterie.

BEAUJOLAIS & LA DOMBES

North of Lyon along the Saône are the vineyards of Beaujolais, a thrill for any oenophile. In the area around Villefranche, small villages—perhaps comprising a church, a bar, and a boulangerie—pop up here and there out of the rolling vine-covered hillsides. Lyon's tourist office has a decent map of the Beaujolais region; even better is the "Vignobles de Beaujolais" map, available in Villefranche's tourist office. Beaujolais wine is made exclusively from the *gamay noir à jus blanc* grape. The region's best wines are all labeled "Grands Crus," a more complex version of the otherwise light, fruity Beaujolais. Although the region's wines get better with age, many Beaujolais wines are drunk nearly fresh off the vine; every third Thursday in November marks the arrival of the Beaujolais Nouveau, a bacchanalian festival that also showcases regional cuisine.

Probably the easiest way to get to the vineyards is by car, but biking is another alternative. Although getting to the vineyards by bike is not easy from Villefranche-sur-Saône, this is the place to rent one and then take a train to a small town, bike around for the day, and come back.

East of the Saône is the fertile land of La Dombes, where ornithologists flock to see migratory birdlife. North of La Dombes and east of the Beaujolais wine villages is Bourg-en-Bresse, famous for its marvelous church and a breed of poultry that delights gourmands; it makes a good base after Lyon. South toward the Rhône, the great river of southern France, is the well-preserved medieval village of Pérouges.

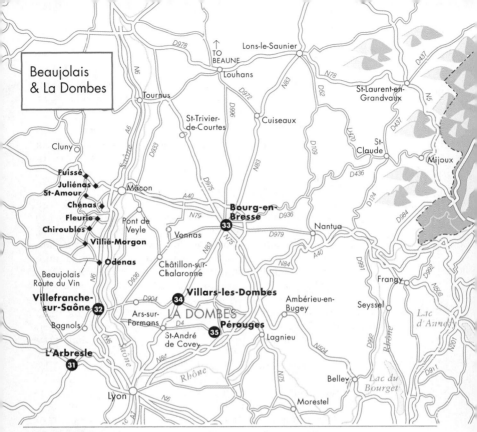

L'ARBRESLE

③ 16 km (10 mi) northwest of Lyon.

If you love modern architecture, don't miss Éveux, outside L'Arbresle. Here the stark, blocky Dominican convent of **Ste-Marie de la Tourette** protrudes over the hillside, resting on slender pillars that look like stilts and revealing the minimalist sensibilities of architect Le Corbusier, who designed it in 1957–59. ☎04–74–01–01–03 ⬛€5 ⊙July and Aug., daily 9–noon and 2–6; Sept.–June, weekends 2–6.

VILLEFRANCHE-SUR-SAÔNE

③ 22 km (14 mi) north of L'Arbresle, 31 km (19 mi) north of Lyon.

GETTING HERE

SNCF (⊕www.sncf.fr) trains links Lyon Part-Dieu with Villefranche-sur-Saône (19 mins, €6). Satobus (☎04–72–68–72—17 ⊕www.satobus.com) connects Lyon-Saint-Exupéry airport with Villefranche-sur-Saône (25 mins, €7). In addition, Autocars du Rhône (lines 161 and 164) connects Lyon with Villefranche-sur-Saône with multiple connections to surrounding towns.

EXPLORING

The lively industrial town of Villefranche-sur-Saône is the capital of the Beaujolais region and is known for its *vin nouveau* (new wine). Thanks to marketing hype, this youthful, fruity red wine is eagerly gulped dwn around the world every year on the third Thursday of November.

The town really has only one sight: the 13th-century church of **Notre-Dame des Marais** (⊠*49 rue Roland, off Rue de la Gare*). Also check out **Rue Nationale,** lined with photogenic, authentic examples of Renaissance architecture, courtyards, and alleyways.

WHERE TO STAY & EAT

$–$$ ✗ **Juliénas.** This simple little restaurant delivers what other, pricier restaurants in town don't, won't, or can't: bistro fare that does honor to traditional Beaujolais cookery. All the all-stars are here: andouillette, hot sausage, pork with tarragon, and, for dessert, a luscious *île flottante* ("Floating Island" meringue). The prix-fixe menu, served lunch and dinner, is one of the best deals in the region. ⊠*236 rue d'Anse* ☎*04–74–09–16–55* ▤*AE, MC, V* ✆*Closed Sun. No lunch Sat.*

$$$$ ✗▥ **Château de Bagnols.** A destination in itself, Lady Hamlyn's cel-
Fodor'sChoice ebrated (and very pricey) castle-hotel is one of the glories of the Beau-
★ jolais region. Don't be put off by the severe and fortresslike exterior: inside, all is trompe l'oeil frescoes, colored marbles, and sumptuous fabrics. The Grand Salon matches the grandest of Paris's 17th-century showpieces, while guest rooms in the main château evoke the 18th century—many are covered with historic frescoes done by a Baroque school of artists inspired by the "Grand Fabrique," Lyon's famed brocade makers. These lilies are then gilded with period glassware, porcelain, and antique furniture. Elsewhere, rooms in La Résidence—the converted stables and carriage houses—are rustic-contemporary, some with amazing wood-beam trim and calico drapes. Set with silver candelabra, giant bouquets, and a wall-wide fireplace, the massive Salle des Gardes is now the setting for the high-style restaurant, while wine tastings are occasionally held in the beautiful stone *cuvage* (wine-pressing room). ⊠*15 km (9 mi) southwest of Villefranche on D38 to Tarare, 69620 Bagnols* ☎*04–74–71–40–00* ▤*04–74–71–40–49* ⊕*www.bagnols. com* ⤿*16 rooms, 5 apartments* ⚅*In-room: refrigerator, Wi-Fi. In-hotel: restaurant, bar, pool, public Wi-Fi, some pets allowed* ▤*AE, DC, MC, V* ✆*Closed Jan.–Mar.*

BEAUJOLAIS ROUTE DU VIN

Fodor'sChoice *16 km (10 mi) north of Villefranche-sur-Saône, 49 km (30 mi) north*
★ *of Lyon.*

GETTING HERE

For the Beaujolais wine country, most people train to the station on the Place de la Gare in Villefranche-sur-Saône (*see above*) where trains to smaller towns are available.

EXPLORING

Not all Beaujolais wine is promoted as *vin nouveau,* despite the highly successful marketing campaign that has made Beaujolais Nouveau synonymous with French wine and the new grape harvest from Tokyo to Timbuktu (celebrated in full force on the third Thursday of November annually around the world). Wine classed as "Beaujolais Villages" is higher in alcohol and produced from a clearly defined region northwest of Villefranche. Beaujolais is made from one single variety of grape, the *gamay noir à jus blanc.* However, there are 12 different appellations: Beaujolais, Beaujolais Villages, Brouilly, Chénas, Chiroubles, Côte de Brouilly, Fleurie, Juliénas, Morgon, Moulin à Vent, Régnié, and St-Amour. The Beaujolais Route du Vin (Wine Road), a narrow strip 23 km (14 mi) long, is home to nine of these deluxe Beaujolais wines, also known as *grands crus.*

The **École Beaujolaise des Vins** (*Beaujolais School of Wine,* ✉ *Villefranche* 🕿 *04–74–02–22–18* 📠 *04–74–02–22–19* ✺ *www.beaujolais.com*) organizes lessons in wine tasting and on creating your own cellar.

In the southernmost and largest *vignoble* (vineyard) of the Beaujolais crus is **Odenas,** producing Brouilly, a soft, fruity wine best consumed young. In the vineyard's center is towering Mont Brouilly, a hill whose vines produce a tougher, firmer wine classified as Côte de Brouilly.

From Odenas take D68 via St-Lager to **Villié-Morgon,** in the heart of the Morgon vineyard; robust wines that age well are produced here.

At Monternot, east of Villié-Morgon, you can find the 15th-century **Château de Corcelles,** noted for its Renaissance galleries, canopied courtyard well, and medieval carvings in its chapel. The guardroom is now an atmospheric tasting cellar. ✉ *Off D9 from Villié-Morgon* 🕿 *04–74– 66–72–42* ⊙ *Mon.–Sat. 10–noon and 2:30–6:30.*

From Villié-Morgon D68 wiggles north through several more wine villages, including **Chiroubles,** where a rare, light wine best drunk young is produced. The wines from **Fleurie** are elegant and flowery. Well-known **Chénas** is favored for its two crus: the robust, velvety, and expensive Moulin à Vent and the fruity and underestimated Chénas. The wines of **Juliénas** are sturdy and a deep color; sample them in the cellar of the town church (closed Tuesday and lunchtime), amid bacchanalian decor. **St-Amour,** west of Juliénas, produces light but firm reds and a limited quantity of whites. The famous white Pouilly-Fuissé comes from the area around **Fuissé.**

BOURG-EN-BRESSE

❸❸ *30 km (18 mi) east of St-Amour on N79, 81 km (49 mi) northeast of Lyon.*

GETTING HERE

SNCF (✺ *www.sncf.fr*) trains link Lyon Perrache station with Bourg-en-Bresse (1 hr, 5 mins, €10). In addition, Satobus (🕿 *04–72–68–72–*

9

NOT JUST GLORIFIED GRAPE JUICE

The act of wine making can be summed up in 25 words or less: Crush grapes; let 'em sit around for a while; wait for the stuff to ferment; put wine in bottle; add cork. Wine making the art—now that would take a tome or two to describe. The Beaujolais vintner is the quintessential artiste. Wineries in this region employ teams of microbiologists and chemists to run tests and control acidity and add sulfites and pull every scientific string known to enology. But, still, the vintner is guardian of a millennia-old tradition and practitioner of a craft that depends heavily on the vagaries of sun, winds, water, time, black magic, superstition, and plain good luck. The infinite complexities of wine can shift thanks to details as small as the weight of the grape crusher, the species of wood in the aging barrel, the elasticity of the cork, and the size of the bottle. Vintners argue over whether mechanical grape crushers are too hard on the grape, and long for the days when six men would strip naked, hop in the crushing barrel, and split the grape skins with warm flesh and bone rather than cold, ugly metal.

17 ⊕*www.satobus.com*) connects Lyon-Saint-Exupéry airport with Bourg-en-Bresse (1 hr, 15 mins, €33).

EXPLORING

Cheerful Bourg-en-Bresse is esteemed among gastronomes for its fowl—striking-looking chickens, the *poulet de Bresse,* with plump white bodies, bright blue feet, and red combs (adding up to France's *tricolore,* or national colors). The town's southeasternmost district, Brou, is its most interesting and the site of a singular church. This is a good place to stay before or after a trip along the Beaujolais Wine Road.

The **Église de Brou,** a marvel of the Flamboyant Gothic style, is no longer in religious use. The church was built between 1506 and 1532 by Margaret of Austria in memory of her husband, Philibert le Beau, Duke of Savoy, and their finely sculpted tombs highlight the rich interior. **Son-et-lumière** shows—on Easter and Pentecost Sunday and Monday, and on Thursday, Saturday, and Sunday from May through September—are magical. A massive restoration of the roof has brought it back to its 16th-century state with the same gorgeous, multicolor, intricate patterns found throughout Burgundy. The museum in the nearby **cloister** stands out for its paintings: 16th- and 17th-century Flemish and Dutch artists keep company with 17th- and 18th-century French and Italian masters, 19th-century artists of the Lyon School, Gustave Doré, and contemporary local painters. ⊠*63 bd. de Brou* ☎*04–74–22–83–83* ☎*€5* ⊙*Apr.–Sept., daily 9–12:30 and 2–6:30; Oct.–Mar., daily 9–noon and 2–5.*

WHERE TO STAY & EAT

★ $-$$$$ ✕ **L'Auberge Bressane.** Overlooking the Brou church, the modern, polished dining room and chef Jean-Pierre Vullin's cuisine are a good combination. Frogs' legs and Bresse chicken with wild morel–cream sauce are specialties; also try the *quenelles de brochet* (poached-fish dumplings). Jean-Pierre wanders through the dining room ready for a chat while his staff provides excellent service. Don't miss the house aperitif, a champagne cocktail with fresh strawberry puree. The wine list has 300 vintages. ⊠*166 bd. de Brou* 🕾*04–74–22–22–68* ⚓*Reservations essential* ⊟*AE, DC, MC, V* ☻*Closed Tues. except holidays.*

$$–$$$ ✕ **La Petite Auberge.** This cozy flower-decked inn is in the countryside on the outskirts of town. Madame Bertrand provides games for children. Chef Philippe Garnier has a subtle way with mullet (he grills it in saffron butter) and Bresse chicken (browned in tangy cider vinegar). ⊠*St-Just, Rte. de Ceyzeriat* 🕾*04–74–22–30–04* ⊟*AE, DC, MC, V* ☻*Closed Jan. and Tues. No dinner Mon.*

$$$–$$$$ ✕▦ **Georges Blanc.** Set in the village of Vonnas and one of the great
Fodor'sChoice culinary addresses in all Gaul, this simple 19th-century inn full of
★ antique country furniture makes a fine setting for poulet de Bresse, truffles, and lobster, all featured on its legendary menu. The wizard here is Monsieur Blanc, whose culinary DNA extends back to innkeepers dating from the French Revolution. He made his mark in the 1980s with a series of cookbooks, notably *The Natural Cuisine of Georges Blanc.* Today, he serves up his traditional-yet-nouvelle delights in a vast dining room (closed Monday and Tuesday; no lunch Wednesday), renovated—overly so, some might say—in a stately manner replete with Louis Treize–style chairs, fireplace, and floral tapestries. Wine connoisseurs will go weak in the knees at the cellar here, overflowing with 130,000 bottles. The 30 guest rooms range from (relatively) simple to luxurious. It's worth the trip from Bourg-en-Bresse, but be sure you bring deep pockets. However, a block south you can also repair to Blanc's cheaper and more casual restaurant, **L'Ancienne Auberge,** most delightfully set in a 1900s "Fabrique de Limonade" soda-water plant and now festooned with antique bicycles and daguerrotypes. ⊠*Pl. du Marché, 23 km (14 mi) from Bourg-en-Bresse, 01540 Vonnas* 🕾*04–74–50–90–90* 🖷*04–74–50–08–80* ⊕*www.georgesblanc. com* ⚓*Reservations essential* ⇆*38 rooms* ♿*In-room: refrigerator, Wi-Fi. In-hotel: restaurant, tennis court, pool, public Wi-Fi, some pets allowed* ⊟*AE, DC, MC, V* ☻*Closed Jan.*

$–$$ ✕▦ **Hôtel de France.** This centrally located and impeccably renovated hotel offers comfortable rooms equipped with the full range of the most modern amenities, from hair dryers to minibars. The adjoining restaurant, Chez Blanc, has been taken over by Georges Blanc and, as expected, is rising to the top of local gastronomical charts. ⊠*19 pl. Bernard, 01000* 🕾*04–74–23–30–24* 🖷*04–74–23–69–90* ⊕*www.grand-hoteldefrance.com* ⇆*42 rooms, 2 suites* ♿*In-room: no a/c, refrigerator. In-hotel: restaurant, some pets allowed* ⊟*AE, DC, MC, V.*

VILLARS-LES-DOMBES

❸❹ *29 km (18 mi) south of Bourg-en-Bresse, 37 km (23 mi) north of Lyon.*

Villars-les-Dombes is the unofficial capital of La Dombes, an area once covered by a glacier. When the ice retreated, it left a network of lakes and ponds that draws anglers and bird-watchers today.

9

The 56-acre **Parc des Oiseaux,** one of Europe's finest bird sanctuaries, is home-sweet-home to 400 species of birds (some 2,000 individuals from five continents); 435 aviaries house species from waders to birds of prey; and tropical birds in vivid hues fill the indoor birdhouse. Allow two hours. Admission fees, which vary according to season, are most expensive from May through October. ⊠ *Off N83* ☎ *04–74–98–05–54* ⊕ *www.parc-des-oiseaux.com* ⊠ *€8–€12* ⊙ *Daily 9:30–dusk.*

PÉROUGES

★ ㉟   *21 km (13 mi) southeast of Villars-les-Dombes, 36 km (22 mi) northeast of Lyon.*

Wonderfully preserved (though a little too precious), hilltop Pérouges, with its medieval houses and narrow cobbled streets surrounded by ramparts, is 200 yards across. Hand-weavers first brought it prosperity; the industrial revolution meant their downfall, and by the late 19th century the population had dwindled from 1,500 to 12. Now the government has restored the most interesting houses, and a potter, bookbinder, cabinetmaker, and weaver have given the town a new lease on life. A number of restaurants make Pérouges a good lunch stop.

Encircling the town is **Rue des Rondes**; from this road you can get fine views of the countryside and, on clear days, the Alps. Park your car by the main gateway, **Porte d'En-Haut,** alongside the 15th-century fortress-church. Rue du Prince, the town's main street, leads to the **Maison des Princes de Savoie** (Palace of the Princes of Savoy), formerly the home of the influential Savoie family that once controlled the eastern part of France. Note the fine watchtower. **Place de la Halle,** a pretty square with great charm, around the corner from the Maison des Princes de Savoie, is the site of a lime tree planted in 1792.

The **Musée du Vieux Pérouges** *(Old Pérouges Museum),* to one side of the Place de la Halle, contains local artifacts and a reconstructed weaver's workshop. The medieval **garden** is noted for its array of rare medicinal plants. ⊠ *Pl. du Tilleul* ☎ *04–74–61–00–88* ⊠ *€5* ⊙ *May–Sept., daily 10–noon and 2–6.*

WHERE TO STAY & EAT

★ $$$-$$$$ ✕ 🏠 **L'Ostellerie du Vieux Pérouges.** "The Old Man of Pérouges" is uniquely comprised of four medieval stone residences set around its main showpiece—an extraordinary corbelled, 14th-century timber-frame house now home to the inn's restaurant. Here, regional delights are served up on pewter plates by waitresses in folk costumes, recipes handed down from the days of Charles VII inspire the cook, and everybody partakes of the famous "pancake of Pérouges" dessert. The sweet taste will linger in your guest room, thanks to some time-burnished accents, such as antiques, gigantic stone hearths, and glossy wood floors and tables. Rooms in the geranium-decked 15th-century Au St-Georges

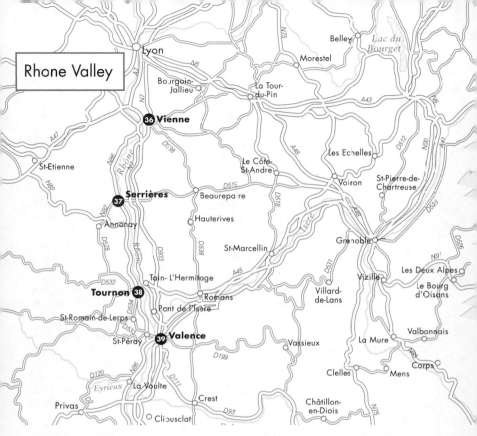

Rhone Valley

Lyon · Belley · Lac du Bourget · Morestel · Bourgoin-Jallieu · La Tour-du-Pin · St-Etienne · **36 Vienne** · Le Côte-St-Andre · Les Echelles · St-Pierre-de-Chartreuse · Voiron · **37 Serrières** · Beaurepaire · Annonay · Hauterives · Grenoble · St-Marcellin · Les Deux Alpes · Tain- L'Hermitage · Vizille · Le Bourg d'Oisans · **Tournon 38** · Romans · Villard-de-Lans · St-Romain-de-Lerps · Pont de l'Isère · Valbonnais · St-Péray · **39 Valence** · Vassieux · La Mure · Corps · Clelles · Mens · Eyrieux · La Voulte · Privas · Crest · Châtillon-en-Diois · Cliousclat

et Manoir manor are more spacious than—but also nearly twice the cost of—those in Le Pavillon (aka "L'Annexe") and have marble bathrooms and period furniture (one or two rooms even have their own garden). At the lower end of the scale, however, the rooms are fairly simple and threadbare. ⊠ *Pl. du Tilleul, 01800 Pérouges* 🕾 *04-74-61-00-88* 🖷 *04-74-34-77-90* ⊕ *www.ostellerie.com* 📑 *28 rooms* ♨ *In-room: no a/c, refrigerator. In-hotel: restaurant, bar, no elevator, public Wi-Fi, some pets allowed* ⊟ *AE, DC, MC, V.*

THE RHÔNE VALLEY

At Lyon, the Rhône, joined by the Saône, truly comes into its own, plummeting south in search of the Mediterranean. The river's progress is often spectacular, as steep vineyards conjure up vistas that are more readily associated with the river's Germanic cousin, the Rhine. All along the way, small-town vintners invite you to sample their wines. Early Roman towns like Vienne and Valence reflect the Rhône's importance as a trading route. To the west is the rugged, rustic Ardèche *département* (province), where time seems to have slowed to a standstill.

VIENNE

36

★

27 km (17 mi) south of Lyon via A7.

GETTING HERE

SNCF trains (⊕*www.sncf.fr*) links Lyon-Perrache or Lyon-Part-Dieu stations with Vienne (21 mins, €5.80). In addition, Satobus (☎*04–72–68–72–17* ⊕*www.satobus.com*) connects Lyon-Saint-Exupéry airport with Vienne (1 hr, 15 mins, €33).

EXPLORING

One of Roman Gaul's most important towns, Vienne became a religious and cultural center under its count-archbishops in the Middle Ages and retains considerable historic charm despite being a major road and train junction. The tourist office anchors Cours Brillier in the leafy shadow of the Jardin Public (Public Garden). The €7 Passport admits you to most local monuments and museums; it's available at the tourist office or at the first site that you visit.

On Quai Jean-Jaurès, beside the Rhône, is the church of **St-Pierre.** Note the rectangular 12th-century Romanesque bell tower with its arcaded tiers. The lower church walls date from the 6th century.

Although religious wars deprived the cathedral of **St-Maurice** of many of its statues, much original decoration is intact; the portals on the 15th-century facade are carved with Old Testament scenes. The cathedral was built between the 12th and the 16th century, with later additions, such as the splendid 18th-century mausoleum to the right of the altar. A frieze of the zodiac adorns the entrance to the vaulted passage that once led to the cloisters but now opens onto Place St-Paul.

★ Place du Palais is the site of the remains of the **Temple d'Auguste et de Livie** *(Temple of Augustus and Livia)*, accessible via Place St-Paul and Rue Clémentine; they probably date in part from Vienne's earliest Roman settlements (1st century bc). The Corinthian columns were walled in during the 11th century, when the temple was used as a church; in 1833 Prosper Mérimée intervened to have the temple restored.

The last vestige of the city's sizable Roman baths is a **Roman gateway** (⊠*Rue Chantelouve*) decorated with delicate friezes.

★ The **Théâtre Romain** *(Roman Theater)*, on Rue de la Charité, is one of the largest in Gaul (143 yards across). It held 13,000 spectators and is only slightly smaller than Rome's Theater of Marcellus. Rubble buried Vienne's theater until 1922; excavation has uncovered 46 rows of seats, some marble flooring, and the frieze on the stage. Concerts take place here in summer. ⊠*7 rue du Cirque* ☎*04–74–85–39–23* ☎*€6, includes Cité Gallo-Romaine and St-André-le-Bas museums* ☉*Apr.–Aug., daily 9–12:30 and 2–6; Sept.–mid-Oct., Tues.–Sun. 9–12:30 and 2–6; mid-Oct.–Mar., Tues.–Sat. 9:30–12:30 and 2–5, Sun. 1:30–5:30.*

Rue des Orfèvres (off Rue de la Charité) is lined with Renaissance facades and distinguished by the church of **St-André-le-Bas,** once part of a powerful abbey. If possible, venture past the restoration now in progress to see the finely sculpted 12th-century capitals (made of Roman stone) and the 17th-century wood statue of St. Andrew. It's best to see the cloisters during the music festival held here and at the cathedral from June through August. ⊠ *Cour St-André* ☎ *04–74–85–18–49* ⌨ *€6, includes Cité Gallo-Romaine and Théâtre Romain museums* ☉ *Apr.–mid-Oct., Tues.–Sun. 9:30–1 and 2–6; mid-Oct.–Mar., Tues.–Sat. 9:30–12:30 and 2–5, Sun. 2–6.*

Across the Rhône from the town center is the excavated **Cité Gallo-Romaine** *(Gallo-Roman City),* covering several acres. Here you can find villas, houses, workshops, public baths, and roads, all built by the Romans. ⌨ *€6, includes Théâtre Romain and St-André-le-Bas museums* ☉ *Daily 9–6.*

WHERE TO STAY & EAT

$$-$$$$ ✕ **Le Bec Fin.** With its understatedly elegant dining room and an inexpensive weekday menu, this unpretentious enclave opposite the cathedral is a good choice for lunch or dinner. Red meat, seafood, and freshwater fish are well prepared here. Try the turbot cooked with saffron. ⊠ *7 pl. St-Maurice* ☎ *04–74–85–76–72* ⚄ *Reservations essential* ☰ *AE, DC, MC, V* ☉ *Closed Dec. 24–Jan. 12, and Mon. No dinner Sun. or Wed.*

★ $$$-$$$$ ✕⌨ **La Pyramide.** Back when your grandmother's grandmother was making the grand tour, La Pyramide was *le must*—Fernand Point had perfected haute cuisine for a generation and became the first superstar chef, teaching a regiment of students who went on to glamorize French dining the world over. Many decades later, La Pyramide has dropped its museum status and now offers contemporary classics by acclaimed chef Patrick Henriroux, accompanied by a peerless selection of wines featuring local stars from the nearby Côte Rôtie and Condrieu vineyards. Both classical and avant-garde dishes triumph here, from *crème soufflée de crabe au croquant d'artichaut* (cream crab soufflé with crunchy artichoke) to the *veau de lait aux légumes de la vallée* (suckling veal with vegetables from the Drôme Valley). Guest rooms are graceful and comfortable in this relaxed setting. ⊠ *14 bd. Fernand-Point, 38200* ☎ *04–74–53–01–96* ⊟ *04–74–85–69–73* ⊕ *www.relaischateaux.com/pyramide* ⇥ *21 rooms* ⚄ *In-room: refrigerator, Wi-Fi. In-hotel: restaurant, bar, public Wi-Fi, some pets allowed, no elevator* ☰ *AE, DC, MC, V.*

SERRIÈRES

㊲ *32 km (20 mi) south of Vienne, 59 km (37 mi) south of Lyon.*

Riverboats traditionally stop at little Serrières, on the Rhône's west bank. Life on the water is depicted at the **Musée des Mariniers du Rhône** *(Boatmen's Museum),* in the wooden-roof Gothic chapel of St-Sornin. ☎ *04–75–34–01–26* ⌨ *€6* ☉ *July and Aug., weekends 3–6.*

WHERE TO STAY & EAT

★ $-$$ ✕⌨ **Schaeffer.** Guest rooms here are decorated in contemporary style, but the real draw is the dining room (closed Monday; no dinner Sunday), where chef Bernard Mathé invents variations on traditional French dishes: smoked duck cutlet in lentil stew or lamb with eggplant in anchovy butter. The number of desserts is overwhelming, but pistachio cake with bitter chocolate is the clear winner. Reservations are essential for the restaurant. Menus run from €40 to €60. ✉ *Rte. Nationale 86, 07340* ☎ *04–75–34–00–07* 🖷 *04–75–34–08–79* ⊕ *www.hotel-schaeffer.com* 📞 *11 rooms* ♿ *In-room: refrigerator. In-hotel: restaurant, bar, some pets allowed, no elevator* ▤ *AE, DC, MC, V* ⊘ *Closed Jan., 1st weekend in Nov., Sun. dinner and Mon. Sept.– June, Tues. July and Aug., no lunch Sat. year-round.*

TOURNON

38 *36 km (20 mi) south of Serrières, 59 km (37 mi) south of Vienne.*

Tournon is on the Rhône at the foot of granite hills. Its hefty **Château,** dating from the 15th and 16th centuries, is the chief attraction. The castle's twin terraces have wonderful views of the Vieille Ville, the river, and—towering above Tain-l'Hermitage across the Rhône—the steep vineyards that produce Hermitage wine, one of the region's most refined—and costly—reds. In the château is a museum of local history, the **Musée Rhodanien** (or du Rhône). ✉ *Pl. Auguste-Faure* ☎ *04–75– 08–10–23* 💶 *€4* ⊘ *June–Aug., Wed.–Mon. 10–noon and 2–6; Apr., May, Sept., and Oct., Wed.–Mon. 2–6.*

☾ A ride on one of France's last steam trains, the **Chemin de Fer du Vivarais,** makes an adventurous two-hour trip 33 km (21 mi) along the narrow, rocky Doux Valley to Lamastre and back to Tournon. ✉ *Departs from Tournon station* ☎ *04–78–28–83–34* 💶 *Round-trip €20* ⊘ *June–Aug., daily 10 am ; May and Sept., weekends 10 am .*

WHERE TO STAY & EAT

$$$ ✕🖾 **Michel Chabran.** This modern interpretation of Drôme-style stone-and-wood design has floral displays, airy picture windows over the garden, and guest rooms with a touch of contemporary Danish influence. Next to the main road, sleeping with the windows open can make for a noisy night—though the air-conditioning largely solves that. The restaurant is known for its truffle menu served from December to March and imaginative and light fare such as mille-feuille de foie gras with artichokes and lamb from Rémuzat. ✉ *29 av. du 45e Parallèle, on left (east) bank of Rhône, 10 km (6 mi) south of Tournon via N7 and 7 km (4½ mi) north of Valence, 26600 Pont de l'Isère* ☎ *04–75–84–60– 09* 🖷 *04–75–84–59–65* ⊕ *www.chateauxhotels.com/chabran* 📞 *12 rooms* ♿ *In-room: refrigerator. In-hotel: restaurant, pool, public Wi-Fi, some pets allowed, no elevator* ▤ *AE, DC, MC, V* ⊘ *Closed Wed. No lunch Thurs. No dinner Sun. Oct.–Mar.* ❢❢ *MAP.*

EN ROUTE

From Tournon's Place Jean-Jaurès, slightly inland from the château, follow signs to the narrow, twisting **Route Panoramique;** the views en route to the old village of **St-Romain-de-Lerps** are breathtaking. In good weather the panorama at St-Romain includes 13 départements, Mont Blanc to the east, and arid Mont Ventoux to the south. D287 winds down to St-Péray and Valence; topping the **Montagne de Crussol**, 650 feet above the plain, is the ruined 12th-century **Château de Crussol**.

VALENCE

 17 km (11 mi) south of Tournon, 92 km (57 mi) west of Grenoble, 127 km (79 mi) north of Avignon.

GETTING HERE

SNCF trains (⊕*www.sncf.fr*) link Lyon Part-Dieu station with Valence by TGV (36 mins, €29.80). Lyon-Perrache to Valence on the local train is a better connection (1 hr, €14.70). In addition, Satobus (☎04–72–68–72–17 ⊕*www.satobus.com*) connects Lyon-Saint-Exupéry airport with Valence (1 hr, 15 mins, €33).

EXPLORING

Valence, the Drôme département capital, is the region's market center. Steep-curbed alleyways called *côtes* extend into the Vieille Ville from the Rhône. At the center of the Vieille Ville is the cathedral of **St-Apollinaire**. Although begun in the 12th century in the Romanesque style, it's not as old as it looks: parts of it were rebuilt in the 17th century, with the belfry rebuilt in the 19th.

The **Musée des Beaux-Arts** *(Fine Arts Museum)*, next to the cathedral of St-Apollinaire, in the former 18th-century bishops' palace, displays excellent Gallo-Roman mosaics, sculpture, and the famous Sanguines, red-hue pastel drawings by landscapist Hubert Robert (1733–1808). ⊠*Pl. des Ormeaux* ☎04–75–79–20–80 ⊕*www.musee-valence.org* ⌨€3 ⊙*Oct.–mid-June, Tues.–Sun. 2–5:45; mid-June–Sept., Tues.–Sat. 10–noon and 2–6:45.*

WHERE TO STAY & EAT

$$$$
Fodor'sChoice
★

✕⌨ **Pic.** Kubla Khan would have decamped from Xanadu in a minute for this Drôme pleasure palace. The Maison Pic has been a culinary landmark for decades, although its (too?) glossy Relais & Château makeover into a full-scale hotel has nearly obliterated any traces of its time-stained past. Not that you will complain—much of the decor is to die for: vaulted white salons, red-velvet sofas, 18th-century billiard tables, gigantic Provençal (that's where the Pic family came from) armoires, lovely gardens, and an eye-popping pool make this a destination in itself. The famous restaurant (closed Monday; no dinner Sunday) is going stronger than ever—try the truffle-flavored *galettes* (pancakes) with asparagus or bass with caviar (served either "avec modération" or "passionnément") to see how Anne-Sophie, great-granddaughter of the founding matriarch, is continuing the family legacy. Dine in the cardinal-red dining room seated on Louis Seize–style bergères or, in summer, on the shaded terrace, then retire upstairs to the guest rooms, done in a mix of rustic antiques and high-style fabrics. A café, the Auberge du Pin, also entices (with much lower prices). ⊠*285 av. Victor-Hugo, 26000* ☎04–75–44–15–32 ⊟04–75–40–96–03 ⊕*www.pic-valence.com* ⇆*12 rooms, 3 apartments* ⌂*In-room: refrigerator,*

9

Wi-Fi. In-hotel: restaurant, bar, pool, public Wi-Fi, some pets allowed ⊟*AE, DC, MC, V.*

GRENOBLE & THE ALPS

This is double-treat vacationland: in winter some of the world's best skiing is found in the Alps; in summer chic spas, shimmering lakes, and hilltop trails offer additional delights. The Savoie and Haute-Savoie départements occupy the most impressive territory; Grenoble, in the Dauphiné, is the gateway to the Alps and the area's only city, occupying the nexus of highways from Marseille, Valence, Lyon, Geneva, and Turin.

This is the region where Stendhal was born and where the great 18th-century philosopher Jean-Jacques Rousseau lived out his old age. So, in addition to natural splendors, the traveler should also expect worldly pleasures: incredibly charming Annecy, set with arcaded lanes and quiet canals in the old quarter around the lovely 16th-century Palais de l'Isle; the old-master treasures on view at Grenoble's Musée; and the fashionable lakeside promenades of spa towns like Aix-les-Bains are just some of the civilized enjoyments to be discovered here.

As for *le skiing*, the season for most French resorts runs from December 15 to April 15. By late December resorts above 3,000 feet usually have sufficient snow. January is apt to be the coldest—and therefore the least popular—month; in Chamonix and Megève, this is the time to find hotel bargains. At the high-altitude resorts the skiing season lasts until May. In summer the lake resorts, as well as the regions favored by hikers and climbers, come into their own.

GRENOBLE

104 km (65 mi) southeast of Lyon, 86 km (52 mi) northeast of Valence.

GETTING HERE

Paris Gare de Lyon dispatches four trains daily (2 direct and 2 via Lyon Part-Dieu) to Grenoble (3 hrs, 10 mins; 3 hrs, 50 mins via Lyon). Six TGV trains daily connect Lyon-Saint-Exupéry airport with Grenoble (1 hr, €26.40). Satobus (⊕*www.satobus.com*) connects Lyon-Saint-Exupéry with Grenoble in 65 minutes every hour on the half hour. Altibus (⊕*www.altibus.com*) connects Grenoble with 60 ski stations and towns throughout the Alps. Grenoble's Gare Routière is right next to the train station and is the place to catch VFD buses to Annecy (1 hr, 40 mins, €8), Alpe d'Huez (1 hr, 30 mins, €7), and Chamrousse (1 hr, 15 mins, €6).

EXPLORING

Capital of the Dauphiné (Lower Alps) region, Grenoble sits at the confluence of the Isère and Drac rivers and lies within three *massifs* (mountain ranges): La Chartreuse, Le Vercors, and Belledonne. This cosmopolitan city's skyscrapers seem intimidating by homey French standards. But along with the city's nuclear research plant, they bear

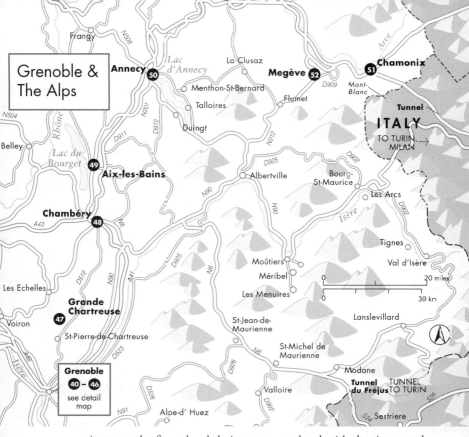

witness to the fierce local desire to move ahead with the times, and it's not surprising to find one of France's most noted universities here. Grenoble's main claim to fame is as the birthplace of the great French novelist Henri Beyle (1783–1842), better known as Stendhal, author of *The Red and the Black* and *The Charterhouse of Parma*. The heart of the city forms a crescent around a bend of the Isère, with the train station at the western end and the university all the way at the eastern tip. As it fans out from the river toward the south, the crescent seems to develop a more modern flavor. The hub of the city is **Place Victor Hugo,** with its flowers, fountains, and cafés, though most sights and nightlife are near the Isère in Place St-André, Place de Gordes, and Place Notre-Dame; Avenue Alsace-Lorraine, a major pedestrian street lined with modern shops, cuts right through it.

Near the center curve of the River Isère is a **téléphérique** (cable car), starting at Quai St-Stéphane-Jay, which whisks you over the River Isère and up to the hilltop and its **Fort de la Bastille,** where there are splendid views and a good restaurant. Walk back down via the footpath through the Jardin Dauphinoise. 🎫€6 *round-trip* ⊘*Apr.–Oct., daily* 9 am *–midnight; Nov., Dec., Feb., and Mar., daily 10–6.*

On the north side of the River Isère is Rue Maurice-Gignoux, lined with gardens, cafés, mansions, and a 17th-century convent that con-

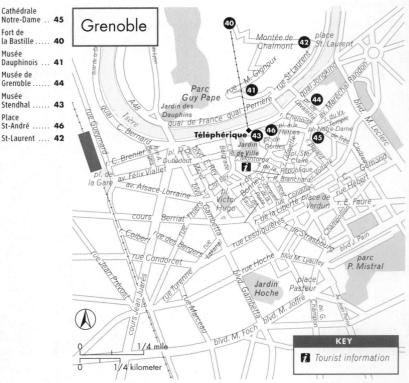

Grenoble

⓪ tains the **Musée Dauphinois,** featuring the history of mountaineering and skiing. The Premiers Alpins section explores the evolution of the Alps and its inhabitants. The museum restaurant is one of Grenoble's best. ⊠ *30 rue Maurice-Gignoux* ☎ *04–76–85–19–01* ⌧ *Free* ⊙ *Nov.–Apr., Wed.–Mon. 10–6; May–Oct., Wed.–Mon. 10–7.*

④ The church of **St-Laurent,** near the Musée Dauphinois, has a hauntingly ancient 6th-century crypt—one of the country's oldest Christian monuments—supported by a row of formidable marble pillars. A tour of the church traces the emergence of Christianity in the Dauphiné. ⊠ *2 pl. St-Laurent* ☎ *04–76–44–78–68* ⌧ *Free* ⊙ *Wed.–Mon. 8–noon and 2–6.*

On the south side of the River Isère and nearly opposite the cable-car stop is the Jardin de Ville—an open space filled with

GETTING AROUND

Grenoble's layout is maddening: your only hope lies in the big, illuminated maps posted throughout town or the free map from the tourist office. Use the mountains for orientation: the sheer Vercors plateau is behind the train station; the Chartreux, topped by the Bastille and *téléphérique* (cable car), are on the other side of the Isère River; and the distant peaks of the Belledonne are behind the park. TAG runs 21 bus and tram routes, many starting at Place Victor Hugo.

immense plane trees—where a handsome conical tower with slate roof marks the **Palais Lesdiguières.** This was built by the right hand of King Henri IV, the Duc de Lesdiguières (1543–1626), and possibly the prototype for Stendhal's voraciously egoistic protagonists (as Constable of France, the duke

had a reign of terror, marrying his young lover Marie Vignon—31 years his junior—after having her husband assassinated). A master urbanist, Lesdiguières did much to establish the Grenoble you see today, so it ❹❸ may only be apt his palace is now the **Musée Stendhal,** where family portraits trace the life of Grenoble's greatest writer amid elegant wooden furniture turned out by the Hache family dynasty of famous woodworkers. Copies of original manuscripts and major memorabilia will please fans, who will wish to then pay a call to the **Maison Stendhal,** at 20 Grande Rue, Stendhal's grandfather's house and the place where the author spent the "happiest days of his life"; you can also take a stroll back over to the **Jardin de Ville,** where the author met his first "love" (basically unrequited), the actress Virginie Kubly.

Fodor'sChoice The city tourist office distributes a **"Stendhal Itinerary"** that also includes ★ the author's birthplace, at 14 rue Hébert, now a repository for memorabilia on the Resistance and deportations of World War II. ⊠ *1 rue Hector-Berlioz* ☎*04–76–54–44–14* ⊕*www.armance.com/tourisme. html* ⊠*Free* ⊙*Oct.–June, Tues.–Sun. 2–6; July–Sept., Tues.–Sun. 9–noon and 2–6.*

Several blocks east of the Musée Stendhal is Place de Lavalette, on the south side of the river where most of Grenoble is concentrated, ★ ❹❹ and site of the **Musée de Grenoble,** formerly the Musée de Peinture et de Sculpture (Painting and Sculpture Museum). Founded in 1796 and since enlarged, it's one of France's oldest museums and the first to concentrate on modern art (Picasso donated his *Femme Lisant* in 1921); a modern addition incorporates the medieval Tour de l'Isle (Island Tower), a Grenoble landmark. The collection includes 4,000 paintings and 5,500 drawings, among them works from the Italian Renaissance, Rubens, Flemish still lifes, Zurbaran, and Canaletto; Impressionists such as Renoir and Monet; and 20th-century works by Matisse (*Intérieur aux Aubergines*), Signac, Derain, Vlaminck, Magritte, Ernst, Miró, and Dubuffet. Modern-art lovers should also check out the **Centre National d'Art Contemporain** (⊠*155 cours Berriat* ☎*04–76–21–95–84*). Behind the train station in an out-of-the-way district, it is noted for its distinctive warehouse museum and cutting-edge collection. ⊠*5 pl. de Lavalette* ☎*04–76–63–44–44* ⊕*www.museedegrenoble.fr/* ⊠*€5* ⊙*Wed. 11–10, Thurs.–Mon. 11–7.*

❹❺ Despite its 12th-century exterior, the 19th-century interior of the **Cathédrale Notre-Dame** is somewhat bland. But don't miss the adjoining bishop's house, now a museum on the history of Grenoble; the main treasure is a noted 4th-century baptistery. ⊠*Pl. Notre-Dame* ⬛*Free* ⊙*Museum: Wed.–Mon. 10–noon and 2–5.*

㊻ **Place St-André** is a medieval square, now filled with umbrella-shaded tables and graced with the **Palais de Justice** on one side and the **Église St-André** on the other. For a tour of Grenoble's oldest and most beautiful streets, wander the area between Place aux Herbes and the **Halles Ste-Claire,** the splendid glass-and-steel-covered market in Place Ste-Claire, several blocks southeast. Facing the market's spouting fish fountain, at the end of the street is the Baroque Lyçee Stendhal entryway. A tour of Grenoble's **four Sunday markets** begins at L'Estacade food and flea market around the intersection of Avenue Jean Jaurès and the train tracks, followed by Les Halles, Place aux Herbes, and Place St-André.

WHERE TO STAY & EAT

★ $$$-$$$$ ✕ **L'Auberge Napoléon.** Frédéric Caby's culinary haven in a meticulously restored town house (once inhabited by Napoléon Bonaparte himself) is where chef Agnès Chotin, one of France's top *cuisinières* (lady chefs) puts together the best table in Grenoble. Specializing in *terroir* (that is, unique to the region) creations ranging from *daube de sanglier en aumonière croustillante* (wild boar stewed in port wine with lemon crust) to *crème de potiron* (cream of squash soup), Mlle. Chotin proposes a foie gras menu that is nearly as wicked and wonderful as her regional *cru* chocolate dessert offering. ⊠*7 rue Montorge* ☎*04–76–87–53–64* ⊕*www.auberge-napoleon.fr* ⊟*AE, DC, MC, V* ⊙*Closed Sun., and 1st wk May, last wk Aug., 1st wk Sept., and Jan. 2–7. No lunch.*

¢-$ ✕ **Café de la Table Ronde.** The second-oldest café in France, junior only to the Procope in Paris, this was a favorite haunt of Henri Beyle (aka Stendhal) as well as the spot where Choderlos de Laclos sought inspiration for (or perhaps a rest from) his 1784 *Liaisons Dangereuses.* Traditionally known for gatherings of *les mordus* (literally the "bitten," or passionate ones), the café still hosts poetry readings and concerts and serves dinner until nearly midnight. ⊠*7 pl. St-André* ☎*04–76–44–51–41* ⊟*AE, DC, MC, V.*

★ $$$$ ✕⊡ **Park Hôtel Grenoble.** Grenoble's finest hotel, with spacious corner rooms over the leafy Parc Paul Mistral, is more than comfortable. This smoothly run establishment attends to your every need with skill and good cheer, from recommendations around town to dinner in front of a roaring fire in Le Parc, the excellent restaurant. Try the sumptuous *foie gras de canard poêlé aux figues* (duck liver sautéed with figs) and the *tournedos de charolais aux morilles* (Charolais beef with morels) with a Château Fombrauge, Saint Emilion '95 grand cru. ⊠*10 pl. Paul Mistral, 38000* ☎*04–76–85–81–23* ☎*04–76–46–49–88* ⊕*www.park-hotel-grenoble.com* ⇆*34 rooms, 16 apartments* ⚷*In-room: refrigerator, Wi-Fi. In-hotel: restaurant, bar, parking (fee), public Wi-Fi, some pets allowed (fee)* ⊟*AE, DC, MC, V.*

★ $$$ ✕⊡ **Chavant.** Dining under the watchful eye of the charming Danièle Chavant is a pleasure at this ivy-covered mansion—note that the dining room is closed Saturday lunch, Sunday dinner, and Monday—in Bresson, a 15-minute drive south of town (out Avenue J. Perrot to

Avenue J. Jaurès, which becomes Route D269). The lobster smothered in truffles is wonderfully wicked and wholly delicious, while the *civet de biche en robe d'automne* (venison with apples, potatoes, and turnips in a daube sauce) is unforgettable. Rooms are elegant and spacious, overlooking meadows and forests beyond the lush garden and pool. ⊠*Rue Bresson, 8 km (5 mi) south of Grenoble, 38320 Bresson* ☎*04–76–25–25–38* 🖳*04–76–62–06–55* ⊕*www.chateauxhotels.com* 🛏*5 rooms, 2 suites* ⚒*In-room: no a/c, refrigerator. In-hotel: restaurant, pool, public Wi-Fi, some pets allowed (fee)* ▤*AE, DC, MC, V* ⊗*Closed Christmas wk.*

$ 🏨 **Europe.** This modest hotel, the town's oldest, at the edge of old Grenoble on a corner of Place Grenette is handy for its central location. As it's an easy walk from the river, the Jardin de Ville, and the city museums, once you're ensconced here, you're set to explore the town. Rooms are adequate and the staff is helpful. ⊠*22 pl. Grenette, 38000* ☎*04–76–46–16–94* 🖳*04–76–43–13–65* ⊕*www.hoteleurope. fr* 🛏*45 rooms* ⚒*In-room: refrigerator. In-hotel: gym, parking (fee)* ▤*AE, DC, MC, V.*

NIGHTLIFE & THE ARTS

Look for the monthly *Grenoble-Spectacles* for a list of events around town. **La Soupe aux Choux** (⊠*7 rte. de Lyon*) is the spot for jazz. **Barberousse** (⊠*3 rue Bayard*), near Place Notre-Dame, is an always popping, pirate ship–like rum mill. **Cinq Jours de Jazz** is just that—five days of jazz—in February or March. In summer, classical music characterizes the **Session Internationale de Grenoble-Isère.**

GRANDE CHARTREUSE

㊼ *23 km (14 mi) north of Grenoble; head north on D512 and fork left 8 km (5 mi) on D520-B just before St-Pierre-de-Chartreuse.*

St. Bruno founded this 12-acre monastery in 1084; it later spawned 24 other charterhouses in Europe. Burned and rebuilt several times, it was stripped of possessions during the French Revolution, when the monks were expelled. On their return they resumed making their sweet liqueur, Chartreuse, the 132-plant–based formula that is today known to only a few monks. Sold worldwide, Chartreuse is a main source of income for the monastery. Enclosed by wooded heights and limestone crags, the monastery is austere and serene. Although it is not open to visitors, you can see the road that goes to it (and get a inside peak thanks to *In Great Silence*, the Philip Gröning documentary film, which was released to great acclaim around the world in 2007).

The **Musée de la Grande Chartreuse–La Correrie,** near the road to the monastery, has exhibits on monastic life and sells the monks' distillation. ☎*04–76–88–60–45* ⊠*€5* ⊗*Apr.–Nov., daily 10–noon and 2–6.*

9

CHAMBÉRY

48 *44 km (27 mi) northeast of Voiron, 40 km (25 mi) north of St-Pierre-de-Chartreuse, 55 km (34 mi) north of Grenoble.*

As for centuries—when it was the crossroads for merchants from Germany, Italy, and the Middle East—elegant old Chambéry remains the region's shopping hub. Townspeople congregate for coffee and people-watching on pedestrians-only **Place St-Léger.**

The town's highlight is the 14th-century, mammoth **Château des Ducs de Savoie,** fitted out with one of Europe's largest carillons. Its Gothic **Ste-Chapelle** has good stained glass and houses a replica of the Turin Shroud. Elsewhere, the city allures with a Vieille Ville festooned with historic houses—from medieval to Premier Empire—a Musée des Beaux-Arts, and the Fountain of the Elephants. ⊠ *Rue Basse du Château* 📷 *No phone* 💶 *€5* 🕐 *Guided tours May, June, and Sept., daily at 10:30 and 2:30; July and Aug., daily at 10:30, 2:30, 3:30, 4:30, and 5:30; Mar., Apr., Oct., and Nov., Sat. at 2:15, Sun. at 3:30.*

WHERE TO STAY & EAT

★ **$$$–$$$$** ✕🏨 **Château de Candie.** If you wish to experience "la vie Savoyarde" in all its pastel-hue, François Boucher–charm, head to this towering 14th-century manor on a hill east of Chambéry. Its large restaurant is famous for its wedding feasts but anyone can delight in its special treats, such as the rabbit terrine with shallot compote and an *escalope de fruits de mer,* where the copious seafood is arranged in the shape of a lobster. Even more delicious are the guest rooms, which range from blowout magnificent—the chandeliered nuptial chamber has a canopied red-velvet bed—to rooms done up in sweet peasant-luxe furnishings. Owner Didier Lhostis, an avid antiques collector, spent four years renovating, so rooms feature an array of delights—antique panels of boiserie, honey-gold beams, a grandfather clock, carved armoires, a 19th-century "psyché" mirror, and glorious regional fabrics. Better yet are views ranging over the neighboring Chartreuse monastery and villages. So who can blame you for lingering over the lavish breakfast? ⊠ *Rue du Bois de Candie, 6 km (4 mi) east of Chambéry, 73000 Chambéry-le-Vieux* 📷 *04–79–96–63–00* 📠 *04–79–96–63–10* 🌐 *www.chateaudecandie.com* 🛏 *15 rooms, 5 apartments* ♿ *In-room: no a/c, refrigerator. In-hotel: restaurant, bar, pool, public Wi-Fi, some pets allowed (fee)* 🚫 *AE, MC, V* 🍴*MAP.*

AIX-LES-BAINS

49 *14 km (9 mi) north of Chambéry, 106 km (65 mi) east of Lyon.*

The family resort and spa town of Aix-les-Bains takes advantage of its position on the eastern side of **Lac du Bourget,** the largest natural freshwater lake in France, with a fashionable lakeshore esplanade. Although the lake is icy cold, you can sail, fish, play golf and tennis, or picnic on the 25 acres of parkland at the water's edge. (Try to avoid it on weekends, when it gets really crowded.) The main town of Aix is 3 km (2 mi) inland from the lake itself. Its sole reason for being is its thermal waters. Many small hotels line the streets, and streams of the weary take to the baths each day; in the evening, for a change of pace, they play the slot machines at the casino or attend tea dances.

The Roman Temple of Diana (2nd to 3rd century ad) now houses the **Musée Archéologique** *(Archaeology Museum)*; enter via the tourist office on Place Mollard.

The ruins of the original Roman baths are underneath the present **Thermes Nationaux** *(National Thermal Baths)*, built in 1934. ⊙ *Guided tours only Apr.–Oct., Mon.–Sat. at 3; Nov.–Mar., Wed. at 3.*

OFF THE BEATEN PATH **Abbaye de Hautecombe.** You can tour this picturesque 12th-century monastery, a half-hour boat ride from Aix-les-Bains, every day but Tuesday; mass is celebrated in French daily at noon and at 6 pm. ☎ *04–79–54–26–12* ⊕ *www.chemin-neuf.org/hautecombe* ☎ *€3.50* ⊙ *Departures from Le Grand Port, Mar.–June, Sept., and Oct., daily at 2:30; July and Aug., daily at 9:30, 2, 2:30, 3, 3:30, and 4:30.*

ANNECY

⑤⓪
Fodor'sChoice
★

33 km (20 mi) north of Aix-les-Bains, 137 km (85 mi) east of Lyon, 43 km (27 mi) southwest of Geneva.

GETTING HERE

Satobus Alpes (☎ *04–72–68–72–17* ⊕ *satobus-alpes.altibus.com*) connects Lyon-Saint-Exupéry airport with Annecy (2 hrs, €30) and the main winter sport stations in the Alps year-round. There's a direct TGV train connection from Lyon-Saint-Exupéry airport to Annecy (1 hr, 51 mins, €22.80). TGV connects Paris Gare de Lyon to Annecy (3 hrs, 46 mins, €84.40). Annecy Haute-Savoie Airport (⊕ *www.annecy. aeroport.fr*) receives flights from other French and some European destinations.

EXPLORING

Jewel-like Annecy is on crystal-clear **Lac d'Annecy** (Annecy Lake), surrounded by snow-tipped peaks. Though the canals, flower-decked bridges, and cobbled pedestrian streets are filled on market days—Tuesday and Friday—with shoppers and tourists, the town is still tranquil. Does it seem to you that the River Thiou flows backward, that is, out of the lake? You're right: it drains the lake, feeding the town's canals. Most of the Vieille Ville is now a pedestrian zone lined with half-timber houses. Here is where the best restaurants are, so you'll probably be back in the evening.

★ Meander through the Vieille Ville, starting on the small island in the River Thiou, at the 12th-century **Palais de l'Isle** *(Island Palace)*, once site of courts of law and a prison, now a landmark. Like a stone ship, the small islet perches in midstream, surrounded by cobblestone quais and it remains one of France's most picturesque (and photographed) sites. It houses the **Musée d'Histoire d'Annecy** and is where tours of the old prisons and cultural exhibitions begin. ☎04–50–33–87–30 ☑€5 ⊘June–Sept., daily 10–6; Oct.–May, Wed.–Mon. 10–noon and 2–6.

★ Crowning the city is one of the most picturesque castles in France, the medieval **Château d'Annecy.** Set high on a hill opposite the Palais and bristling with stolid towers, the complex is landmarked by the Tour Perrière, which dominates the lake, and the Tour St-Paul, Tour St-Pierre, and Tour de la Reine (the oldest, dating from the 12th century), which overlook the town. All give storybook views over the town and countryside. Dwellings of several eras line the castle courtyard, one of which contains a small museum on Annecy history and how it was shaped by the Nemeurs and Savoie dynasties. ☎04–50–33–87–31 ☑€5 ⊘June–Sept., daily 10–6; Oct.–May, Wed.–Mon. 10–noon and 2–6.

A drive around Lake Annecy—or at least along its eastern shore, which is the most attractive—is a must; set aside a half day for the 40-km (25-mi) trip. Picturesque **Talloires,** on the eastern side, has many hotels and restaurants.

Just after Veyrier-du-Lac, keep your eyes open for the privately owned medieval **Château de Duingt.**

Fodor's Choice

★ Continue around the eastern shore to get to the magnificently picturesque **Château de Menthon-St-Bernard.** The exterior is the stuff of fairy tales; the interior is even better. The castle's medieval rooms—many adorned with tapestries, Romanesque frescoes, Netherlandish sideboards, and heraldic motifs—have been lovingly restored by the owner, who can actually trace his ancestry directly back to St. Bernard. All in all, this is one of the loveliest dips into the Middle Ages you can make in eastern France. You can get a good view of the castle by turning onto the Thones road out of Veyrier. ☎04–50–60–12–05 ☑€5 ⊘July and Aug., daily 2–4:30; May, June, and Sept., Tues., Thurs., and weekends 2–4:30; Oct.–Apr., Thurs. and weekends 2–4:30.

WHERE TO STAY & EAT

$-$$ ✕ **L'Étage.** This small second-floor restaurant serves inexpensive local fare—from cheese and beef fondue to grilled freshwater fish from Lake Annecy, and raclette made from the local Reblochon cheese. Minimal furnishings and plain wooden tables give it a rather austere look, but the often lively crowd makes up for it by creating true bonhomie. ⊠13 rue du Pâquier ☎04–50–51–03–28 ⊟AE, DC, MC, V.

$$$$ ✕☒ **L'Impérial Palace.** Though the Palace, across the lake from the town center, is Annecy's leading hotel, it lacks depth of character. In contrast to its Belle Epoque exterior, the spacious, high-ceiling guest rooms are done in the subdued colors so loved by contemporary designers. The better rooms face the public gardens on the lake; waking up to breakfast on the terrace is a great way to start the day. Service is professional, but you pay for it. Fine cuisine is served in the stylish La Voile; the food in Le Jackpot Café, in the casino, is acceptable and less costly. ⊠Allée de l'Impérial, 74000 ☎04–50–09–30–00 🖷04–50–09–33–33 ⊕www. hotel-imperial-palace.com ↩91 rooms, 8 suites ⚒In-room: refrigerator, Wi-Fi. In-hotel: 2 restaurants, bar, gym, public Wi-Fi ⊟AE, DC, MC, V ⦿MAP.

$$$$
Fodor'sChoice
★
✕▣ **La Maison de Marc Veyrat.** One of Europe's latter-day culinary shrines, this elegant Third Empire mansion has become packed with critics and millionaires fighting to pay top dollar to taste the creations of the new culinary messiah, Marc Veyrat. His domain offers guest rooms with spectacular views of Lake Annecy, but most everyone will be too knocked out by the dining room fireworks. Veyrat's miracles are wrought with local Alpine produce, most

> **SAVE THOSE PENNIES**
>
> At his house-mortgaging prices, Marc Veyrat's food had better be sublime. The molasses sorbet is €60 while his Degreased Kidneys with Goutweed and Wild Lovage flavored with Coffee Bonbons is €110, the average rate for many of his main courses. So just keep repeating: If I don't go first class, my heirs will.

of which the self-taught shepherd handpicks himself during daily treks through the idyllic mountain pastures that surround the hotel. The resulting meals are once-in-a-lifetime events. To wit: his hot-and-cold Foie Gras with Fig Purée, Bitter Chocolate, and Bitter Orange Juice; or his Crayfish and Roquefort Sabayon with Queen of the Meadow Froth; or his Roasted Langoustines with Hogweed Semolina; or his amazing desserts, such as his sublime molasses sorbet. Warning: appetizers are around €70, main courses, €110, and desserts €60; the popular tasting menus run €270 and €360. The restaurant is closed Monday and Tuesday (but open Tuesday for dinner in July and August); there is no lunch served weekdays. Upstairs, super-expensive guest rooms and suites—many done in a luxe-châlet style—await those who just want to retire and digest the feast. For more on Veyrat's *cuisine d'auteur*, see "Lyon: France's Culinary Cauldron" in this chapter. ⊠*13 Vieille rte. des Pensières, 5½ km (3½ mi) from Annecy on D909, Veyrier-du-Lac 74290* ☎*04–50–60–24–00* 🖷*04–50–60–23–63* ⊕*www.marc-veyrat. com* ⇘*9 rooms, 2 suites* ♿*In-room: refrigerator, Wi-Fi. In-hotel: restaurant, bar, public Wi-Fi, some pets allowed (fee)* ▤*AE, DC, MC, V* ⊙*Closed Dec.–mid-Apr.*

$$–$$$
Fodor'sChoice
★
▣ **Hôtel du Palais de l'Isle.** Steps away from the lake, in the heart of Old Annecy, and directly overlooking one of the most enchanting corners of the town (if not Europe) is this delightful small hotel. Happily, some of the hotel rooms directly look out on the "prow" of the magical stone Palais. Without destroying the building's ancient feel, rooms have a cheery, contemporary look and Philippe Starck furnishings; some have a view of the Palais de l'Isle. Rates reflect the size of the room. Breakfast is served. Though the area is pedestrian-only, you can drive up to unload luggage. ⊠*13 rue Perrière, 74000* ☎*04–50–45–86–87* 🖷*04–50–51–87–15* ⊕*www.hoteldupalaisdelisle.com* ⇘*33 rooms* ♿*In-room: no a/c. In-hotel: public Wi-Fi, some pets allowed (fee)* ▤*AE, MC, V.*

SPORTS & THE OUTDOORS

Bikes can be rented at the **train station** (⊠*Pl. de la Gare*). Mountain bikes are available from **Loca Sports** (⊠*37 av. de Loverchy* ☎*04–50–45–44–33*). **Sports Passion** (⊠*3 av. du Parmelan* ☎*04–50–51–46–28*) is a convenient source for cyclists. From April through October you can take an hour-long cruise around Lake Annecy on the **M.S.** *Libellule* (⊠*Compagnie des Bateaux du Lac d'Annecy, 2 pl. aux Bois* ☏*04–50–51–08–40*) for €9.

CHAMONIX-MONT-BLANC

⑤¹ *94 km (58 mi) east of Annecy, 83 km (51 mi) southeast of Geneva.*

GETTING HERE

Alpybus (⊕*www.alpybus.com*) transfers passengers from Geneva to Chamonix (1 hr, 10 mins, €19.50). Satobus Alpes (☏*04–72–68–72–17* ⊕*satobus-alpes.altibus.com*) connects Lyon-Saint-Exupéry airport with Annecy (2 hrs, €30) and the main winter sport stations in the Alps year-round. The direct TGV connection from Lyon-Saint-Exupéry airport (⊕*www.sncf.fr*) to Annecy takes 1 hour, 51 minutes (€22.80). TGV connects Paris Gare de Lyon to Annecy (3 hrs, 46 mins, €84.40). The required train ride from St-Gervais-Les-Bains to Chamonix is in itself an incredible trip, up the steepest railway in Europe. You'll feel your body doing strange things to adjust to the pressure change.

EXPLORING

Chamonix is the oldest and biggest of the French winter-sports resort towns. It was the site of the first Winter Olympics, held in 1924. As a ski resort, however, it has its limitations: the ski areas are spread out, none is very large, and the lower slopes often suffer from poor snow conditions. On the other hand, some runs are extremely memorable, such as the 20-km (12-mi) run through the **Vallée Blanche** or the off-trail area of **Les Grands Montets.** And the situation is getting better: many lifts have been added, improving access to the slopes as well as lessening lift lines. In summer it's a great place for hiking, climbing, and enjoying outstanding views. If you're heading to Italy via the Mont Blanc Tunnel, Chamonix will be your gateway.

Chamonix was little more than a quiet mountain village until a group of Englishmen "discovered" the spot in 1741 and sang its praises far and wide. The town became forever tied to mountaineering when Horace de Saussure offered a reward for the first Mont Blanc ascent in 1760. Learn who took home the prize at the town's **Musée Alpin,** which documents the history of mountaineering; exhibits include handmade skis, early sleds, boots, skates, Alpine furniture, and geological curios and mementos from every area of Alpine climbing lore. ⊠*89 Av. Michel Groz* ☏*04–50–53–25–93* 🎫*€5* ⊙*Daily 2–7.*

Nowadays the valley's complex transportation infrastructure takes people up to peaks like the Aiguille du Midi and past freeway-size glaciers like La Mer de Glace via *téléphériques, télécabines* (gondolas), *télésièges* (chairlifts), and narrow-rail cars. **Aiguille du Midi** is a 12,619-foot granite peak topped with a needlelike observation tower. The world's highest cable car soars 12,000 feet up the Aiguille du Midi, providing positively staggering views of 15,700-foot **Mont**

Blanc, Europe's loftiest peak. Be prepared for a lengthy wait, both going up and coming down—and wear warm clothing. *€37 round-trip, €3 extra for elevator to summit; €55 for Télécabine Panoramic Mont-Blanc, which includes Plan de l'Aiguille, Aiguille du Midi, and Pointe Helbronner ⊙ May–Sept., daily 8–4:45; Oct.– Apr., daily 8–3:45.*

The **Mer de Glace** (literally, the "sea of ice") glacier can be seen up close and personal from the Train du Montenvers *€20 one-way*), a cogwheel mountain train that leaves from behind the SNCF train station. The hike back down is an easy two-hour ramble. From the top of the train you can mount yet another transportation device—a mini-*téléphérique* that suspends you over the glacier for five minutes.

UP, UP & AWAY

Some of the most popular modes of transportation in the Alps are the gondolas and chairlifts that can take you as far as Italy and Switzerland. In summer and winter, téléphériques (gondolas), télécabines (big, luxurious gondolas), and télésièges (chairlifts) give you immediate access to the virgin land up high for a price that would make a gigolo blush.

WHERE TO STAY & EAT

★ $$$–$$$$ ✕⌂ **Hameau Albert 1er.** At Chamonix's most desirable hotel, rooms are furnished with elegant reproductions, and most have balconies. Many, such as No. 33, have unsurpassed views of Mont Blanc. Choose between rooms in the original building or Alpine lodge–style accommodations—with touches of contemporary rustic elegance—in the complex known as le Hameau. The dining room also has stupendous Mont Blanc views. Pierre Carrier's cuisine is perfectly prepared and presented classical fare based on exquisite ingredients—from white truffles in season to impeccable game or seafood delicacies—with minimal interest in originality, surprise, or artifice. ⊠ 119 impasse du Montenvers, 74400 ☎ 04–50–53–05–09 🖷 04–50–55–95–48 ⊕ www.hameaualbert.fr ⇄ 21 rooms, 3 chalets, 12 rooms in farmhouse ⌂ In-room: refrigerator, Wi-Fi. In-hotel: 2 restaurants, bar, pool, gym, public Wi-Fi, parking (fee), some pets allowed (fee) ☰ AE, DC, MC, V ⊙ Closed 2 wks in May, 3 wks in Nov. ⊙ FAP.

$$$–$$$$ ✕⌂ **Mont-Blanc.** In the center of town, this Belle Epoque hotel has catered to the rich and famous since 1878. Family owned, it is permeated by a sense of well-being; the staff is warm and efficient. High ceilings give guest rooms a majestic feel, accentuated by warm, pale colors, and period pieces. Most rooms look onto Mont Blanc or Mont Brevant. Dining on chef Morand's creations in the restaurant, Le Matafan, is a refined pleasure. Besides classic French dishes (try the succulent crayfish with shallots and chanterelle mushrooms), many foods available only locally are served, such as a delicious lake fish known as *fera*. ⊠ 62 allée Majestic, 74400 ☎ 04–50–53–05–64 🖷 04–50–55–89–44 ⊕ www.chamonixhotels.com ⇄ 32 rooms, 8 apartments ⌂ In-room: refrigerator. In-hotel: restaurant, bar, tennis courts, pool, parking (fee), some pets allowed (fee) ☰ AE, DC, MC, V ⊙ Closed Nov. ⊙ MAP.

9

$$ 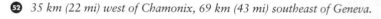 **L'Auberge Croix-Blanche.** In the heart of Chamonix, this small inn has modest and tidy rooms, each with a good-size bathroom—from one you can even lie in the tub and look out the window at Mont Blanc. Make sure you ask for one of the newly renovated rooms. The hotel has no restaurant, but right next door is the Brasserie de L'M, where reasonably priced Savoie specialties are served. The hotel shuttle bus can take you to the slopes. ✉*87 rue Vallot, 74404* ☎*04–50–53–00– 11* 🖷*04–50–53–48–83* ✐croix-blanche@chamonixhotels.com ➦*31 rooms, 4 suites* ♿*In-room: no a/c, refrigerator. In-hotel: bar* 🖃*AE, DC, MC, V* ⊘*Closed May 2–June 11.*

NIGHTLIFE

Chamonix après-ski begins at the saloons in the center of town: the Chamouny, the Brasserie du Rond Point, or, in spring, the outdoor tables. Argentière's L'Office is an Anglo refuge, while Francophones head for the Savoie. Le Jeckyll, next to the Hotel Des Aiglons, is a hard-core party headquarters, along with Cantina and Le Pub, although Wild Wallabies Bar may be the wildest of all. **Chambre Neuf** (✉*272 av. Michel Croz* ☎*04–50–55–89–81*) is once again hot, while **No Escape** (✉*27 rue de la Tour* ☎*04–50–93–80–65*) is a trendy newcomer. The **Casino** (✉*Pl. de Saussure* ☎*04–50–53–07–65*) has a bar, a restaurant, roulette, and blackjack. Entrance to the casino is €12, though entry is free to the slot machine rooms.

SPORTS & THE OUTDOORS

Contact the **Chamonix Tourist Office** for information on skiing in the area. Want to try bobsledding? Two approximately 3,000-foot-long runs are open winter and summer at **Parc de Loisirs des Planards** (☎*04– 50–53–08–07*). Chamonix's indoor **skating rink** (☎*04–50–53–12–36*) is open year-round, Thursday–Tuesday 3–6 and Wednesday 3–11. The **Sports Centre Olympide** (☎*04–50–53–09–07*) has an indoor-outdoor Olympic-size pool.

MEGÈVE

52 *35 km (22 mi) west of Chamonix, 69 km (43 mi) southeast of Geneva.*

GETTING HERE

Satobus Alpes (☎*04–72–68–72–17* ⊕*satobus-alpes.altibus.com*) con-nects Lyon-Saint-Exupéry airport with Megéve (2 hrs, €30) and the main winter sport stations in the Alps year-round. SNCF rail connec-tions (⊕*www.sncf.fr*) to Megéve are routed to Sallanches (12 km [8 mi] away). Megève Airport takes flights from French and European destinations.

EXPLORING

The smartest of the Mont Blanc stations, idyllic Alpine Megève is not only a major ski resort but also a chic winter watering hole that draws royalty, celebrities, and fat wallets from all over the world (many will fondly recall Cary Grant bumping into Audrey Hepburn here in the opening scenes of the 1963 thriller *Charade*). The après-ski amusements tend to submerge the skiing here because the slopes are comparatively easy, and beginners and skiers of only modest ability will find Megève more to their liking than Chamonix. This may account for Megève's having one of France's largest ski schools. Ski passes purchased here cover the slopes not only around Megève but also in Chamonix. In summer the town is a popular spot for golfing and hiking. From Megève the drive along N212 to Albertville goes along one of the prettiest little gorges in the Alps.

WHERE TO STAY & EAT

$$$$ ✕▦ **Les Fermes de Marie.** By reassembling four Alpine chalets brought down from the mountains and decorating rooms with old Savoie furniture (shepherds' tables, sculptured chests, credenzas), Jocelyne and Jean-Louis Sibuet have created a luxury hotel with a delightfully rustic feel. Both a summer and winter resort, it has shuttle-bus service to ski lifts in season and a spa providing a wide range of services in this most tranquil of settings. In the kitchen, chef Christophe Côte creates fine cuisine based on local products. ✉*Chemin de Riante Colline, 74120* ☎*04–50–93–03–10* ☐*04–50–93–09–84* ⊕*www.fermesdemarie.com* ⌖*61 rooms, 7 suites, 3 duplex apartments* ♿*In-room: no a/c, refrigerator, Wi-Fi. In-hotel: 3 restaurants, bar, pool, gym, spa, public Wi-Fi, some pets allowed (fee)* ☰*AE, DC, MC, V* ⊗*Closed Apr., May, Oct., and Nov.* ⎮◎⎮*MAP.*

$$$$ ▦ **Hôtel Mont-Blanc.** Each guest room at this hotel in the heart of Megève's pedestrian-only zone has a different theme, from Austrian to English to Haute Savoie; half have a small balcony overlooking the courtyard—an ideal spot for summer breakfasts and evening cocktails. Wood predominates, as does artwork collected from all over Europe. Public areas are comfortable, from the lounge with huge easy chairs to the leather-bound library that doubles as a tearoom and bar. ✉*Pl. de l'Église, 74120* ☎*04–50–21–20–02* ☐*04–50–21–45–28* ⌖*40 rooms* ♿*In-room: no a/c, refrigerator, Wi-Fi. In-hotel: bar, pool, public Wi-Fi, some pets allowed (fee)* ☰*AE, DC, MC, V* ⊗*Closed May 1–June 10* ⎮◎⎮*EP.*

$$ ▦ **Les Cîmes.** This tiny, reasonably priced hotel run by an English couple offers small, neat rooms and a pleasant little restaurant. Simple food is served, such as roast lamb or grilled fish. Breakfast is included in room rates. The hotel's only drawback is its location on a main street entering Megève, which can be a little noisy. ✉*341 av. Charles Feige, 74120* ☎*04–50–21–11–13* ☐*04–50–58–70–95* ⊕*www.hotellescimes.com* ⌖*8 rooms* ♿*In-room: no a/c, refrigerator. In-hotel: restaurant, parking (fee)* ☰*AE, DC, MC, V* ⎮◎⎮*BP, FAP, MAP.*

SPORTS & THE OUTDOORS

For information about skiing in the area, contact the **Megève Tourist Office.** In summer you can play at the 18-hole **Megève Golf Course** (✉*Golf du Mont d'Arbois* ☎*04–50–21–29–79*).

9

LYON & THE ALPS ESSENTIALS

TRANSPORTATION

BY AIR

AIRPORTS

The region's international gateway airport is Aéroport-Lyon-Saint-Exupéry, 26 km (16 mi) east of Lyon, in Satolas. There are domestic airports at Grenoble, Valence, Annecy, Chambéry, and Aix-les-Bains.

To get between the Aéroport-Lyon-Saint-Exupéry and downtown Lyon take the Satobus, a shuttle bus that goes to the city center between 5 am and 9 pm and to the train station between 6 am and 11 pm; journey time is 35–45 minutes, and the fare is €8.50. There's also a bus from Satolas to Grenoble; journey time is just over an hour, and the fare is €20. A taxi into Lyon costs about €30. Taking a taxi from the small Grenoble airport to downtown Grenoble is expensive, but it may be your only option.

Airport Information Aéroport-Lyon-Saint-Exupéry (☎ 08–26–80–08–26 from within France, 33-426-007-007 from abroad). **Satobus** (☎ 04–72–68–72–17).

BY BUS

Where there's no train service, SNCF often provides bus transport. Buses cover the entire region, but Lyon and Grenoble are the two main bus hubs for long-distance (national and international) routes. The Grenoble–Lyon connection on TER-SNCF (⊕ www.ter-SNCF.com/rhone-alpes) will get you from Grenoble to Lyon's Part-Dieu train station in 1 hour, 17 minutes for €17.30. Buses from Lyon and Grenoble thoroughly and efficiently serve the region's smaller towns. Many ski centers, such as Chamonix, have shuttle buses connecting them with surrounding villages. Tourist destinations, such as Annecy, have convenient bus links with Grenoble.

Grenoble's Gare Routière is right next to the train station and is the place to catch VFD buses to Annecy (1 hr, 40 mins, €6.50), Alpe d'Huez (1 hr, 30 mins, €5), and Chamrousse (1 hr, 15 mins, €4). All buses leave Annecy from the Gare Routière right next to the train station on the Place de la Gare. From it, Voyages Crolard has routes around the Lac d'Annecy. Autocars Francony has buses to Chamonix. As for Alpine villages, regional buses head out from the main train stations at Annecy, Chambéry, Megève, and Grenoble.

Bus Information Gare Routière Centre d'Échanges de Lyon-Perrache (⊠ Pl. Carnot s/n ☎ 04–72–56–95–30 ⊕ www.intercars.fr). **Gare Routière Grenoble** (⊠ 11 pl. de la Gare ☎ 04–76–87–90–31 ⊕ www.transisere.fr).

BY CAR

Regional roads are fast and well maintained, though smaller mountainous routes can be difficult to navigate and high passes may be closed in winter. A6 speeds south from Paris to Lyon (463 km [287 mi]). The Tunnel de Fourvière, which cuts through Lyon, is a classic hazard, and at peak times you may sit idling for hours. Lyon is 313 km (194 mi) north of Marseille on A7. To get to Grenoble (105 km [63 mi] south-east) from Lyon, take A43 to A48. Coming from the south, take A7 to Valence and then swing east on A49 to A48 to Grenoble. Access to the Alps is easy from Geneva or Italy (via the Tunnel du Mont Blanc at Chamonix or the Tunnel du Fréjus from Turin). Another popular route into the Alps, especially coming north from Provence, is from Sisteron via N85, La Route Napoléon.

BY TRAIN

The high-speed TGV (Train à Grande Vitesse) to Lyon leaves Paris (from Gare de Lyon) hourly and arrives in just two hours. There are also six TGVs daily between Paris's Charles de Gaulle Airport and Lyon. Two in-town train stations and a third at the airport (Lyon-Saint-Exupéry) make Lyon a major transportation hub. The Gare de La Part-Dieu is used for the TGV routes. On the other side of town, the *centre-ville* station at Gare de Perrache is the more crowded option and serves all the sights of the *centre-ville*—many trains stop at both stations. The TGV station at Ároport-Lyon-Saint-Exupéry serves, as well as Paris, Grenoble, Avignon, Arles, Valence, Annecy, Aix-les-Bains, Chambéry, Turin, and Milan. Sample trips: Ároport-Lyon-Saint-Exupéry TGV to Grenoble (1 hr. 8 mins, €27); Lyon Part-Dieu to Grenoble (1 hr, 32 mins, €18); Lyon Part-Dieu TGV to Montpellier (1 hr, 50 mins, € 43); Lyon Part-Dieu TGV to Marseille (1 hr, 35 mins, €44).

The TGV also has less frequent service to Grenoble, where you can connect to local SNCF trains headed for villages in the Alps. South of Lyon the TGV goes to Avignon and then splits and goes either to Marseille or Montpellier. The trips from Lyon to Marseille and Lyon to Montpellier take about 1½ hours. Major rail junctions include Grenoble, Annecy, Valence, Chambéry, and Lyon, with frequent train service to other points. Major routes include: Grenoble to Lyon (1¼ hrs), Annecy (2½ hrs), and Chamonix (4 hrs). For the Beaujolais wine country, most people train to Villefranche-sur-Saône's station on the Place de la Gare; trains run to smaller towns from here.

Train Information Gare SNCF Lyon–Perrache (⊠ *Cours de Verdun, Pl. Carnot*). **Gare SNCF Grenoble** (⊠ *Pl. de la Gare*). **Gare SNCF Annecy** (⊠ *Pl. de la Gare*). **SNCF** (☎ *36–35, €0.34 per min* ⊕ *www.voyages-sncf.com*). **TGV** (⊕ *www.tgv.com*).

TGV Lyon—Part-Dieu (⊠ *Blvd. Vivier-Merle*).

CONTACTS & RESOURCES

CAR RENTAL

Local Agencies Avis (⊠ *1 av. du Dr-Desfrançois, Chambéry* ☎ *04–79–33–58–54* 🖷 *04–79–15–13–53* ⊠ *In Aéroport-Lyon-Saint-Exupéry* ☎ *04–72–22–75–43*). **Hertz** (⊠ *16 rue Émile-Gueymard, Grenoble* ☎ *04–76–43–12–92* 🖷 *04–76–47–97–26* ⊠ *11 rue Pasteur, Valence* ☎ *04–75–44–39–45* 🖷 *04–75–44–76–88*).

9

EMERGENCIES

In case of an emergency, call the fire department or the police. Samu, in Lyon, provides emergency medical aid and ambulance service. Lyon has several all-night pharmacies. One of the largest is Pharmacie Blanchet. In Grenoble contact Europ'ambulance.

Contacts General Ambulance (☎15). **General Fire Department** (☎18). **General Police** (☎17). **Europ'ambulance** (☎04–76–33–10–03 Grenoble). **Pharmacie Blanchet** (✉5 pl. des Cordeliers ☎04–78–37–81–31 Lyon). **Samu** (☎04–72–33–15–15 Lyon).

TOUR OPTIONS

BOAT TOURS

Navig-Inter arranges daily boat trips from Lyon along the Saône and Rhône rivers.

Fees & Schedules Navig-Inter (✉13 bis, quai Rambaud, 69002 Lyon ☎04–78–42–96–81).

BUS TOURS

Philibert runs bus tours of the region from April to October starting in Lyon.

Fees & Schedules Philibert (✉24 av. Barthélémy-Thimonier, B.P. 16, 69300 Caluire ☎04–72–23–10–56 🖶04–72–27–00–97).

WALKING TOURS

The Lyon tourist office organizes walking tours of the city in English.

Fees & Schedules Lyon Tourist Office (✉Pl. Bellecour ☎04–72–77–69–69).

VISITOR INFORMATION

Contact the Comité Régional du Tourisme Rhône-Alpes for information on Lyon and the Alps. The Maison du Tourisme deals with the Isère département and the area around Grenoble. Local tourist offices for towns mentioned in this chapter are listed by town below.

Tourist Information Comité Régional du Tourisme Rhône-Alpes (✉78 rte. de Paris, 69260 Charbonnières-les-Bains ☎04–72–59–21–59 🖶04–72–59–21–60 ⊕www.rhonealpes-tourisme.com). **Maison du Tourisme** (✉14 rue de la République, B.P. 227, 38019 Grenoble ☎04–76–42–41–41 🖶04–76–00–18–98 ⊕www.grenoble-isere-tourisme.com). **Annecy** (✉Centre Bonlieu, 1 rue Jean-Jaurès ☎04–50–45–00–33 ⊕www.lac-annecy.com). **Bourg-en-Bresse** (✉6 av. d'Alsace-Lorraine ☎04–74–22–49–40 ⊕www.bourg-en-bresse.org). **Chambéry** (✉24 bd. de la Colonne ☎04–79–33–42–47 ⊕www.chambery-tourisme.com). **Chamonix** (✉85 pl. du Triangle de l'Amitié ☎04–50–53–00–24 ⊕www.chamonix.com). **Évian-les-Bains** (✉Pl. d'Allinges ☎04–50–75–04–26 ⊕www.evian.fr). **Grenoble** (✉14 rue de la République ☎04–76–42–41–41 ⊕www.ville-grenoble.fr ✉Train station ☎04–76–54–34–36). **Lyon** (✉Pl. Bellecour ☎04–72–77–69–69 ⊕www.lyon-france.com ✉Av. Adolphe Max near cathedral ☎04–72–77–69–69 ✉Perrache train station). **Megève** (✉Rue Monseigneur Conseil ☎04–50–21–27–28 ⊕www.megeve.com). **Valence** (✉Parvis de la Gare ☎08–92–70–70–99 ⊕www.tourisme-valence.com). **Vienne** (✉Cours Brillier ☎04–74–53–80–30 ⊕www.vienne-tourisme.com).

Provence

Gordes

WORD OF MOUTH

"While in Gordes, be sure to visit the Abbaye de Sénanque. It's surrounded by the most amazing lavender fields in bloom in July."

—Mamc

"We loved the Camargue, with the beautiful grasses, flamingos, and storks, and the wild horses and bulls—we spent a full day there, having dinner in Aigues Mortes (which actuclly was, for us, c disappointment)."

—IkraKauer

www.fodors.com/forums

WELCOME TO PROVENCE

TOP REASONS TO GO

★ **Vincent van Gogh's Arles:** Ever since the fiery Dutchman immortalized Arles in all its chromatic drama, this town has had a starring role in museums around the world.

★ **Provence Unplugged:** The famous lagoons of the Camargue will swamp you with their strange beauty once you catch sight of their white horses, pink flamingoes, and black bulls.

★ **Scent-sational Lavender:** Get hip-deep in purple by touring the Lavender Route starting at the Abbaye de Sénanque (near Gordes) and follow a wide, blue-purple swath that ranges across the Drôme and the Vaucluse.

★ **Go fishing for Marseille's best bouillabaisse:** The version at Chez FonFon will make your taste buds stand up and sing "La Marseillaise".

★ **Paul Cézanne, Superstar:** Tour Cézanne Country in the area around Mont Ste-Victoire, located near the artist's hometown of Aix-en-Provence.

1 Arles & the Camargue. Still haunted by the genius of Van Gogh, **Arles** remains fiercely Provençal and is famed for its folklore events. A bus ride away and bracketed by the towns of **Aigues-Mortes** and **Stes-Maries-de-la-Mer**, the vast Camargue nature park is one of France's most remarkable terrains, famed for its cowboys, horseback rides, and exclusive *mas* (converted farmhouse) hotels.

2 Avignon & the Vaucluse. This area is the heart of Provençal delights. Presided over by its medieval Palais des Papes, **Avignon** is an ideal gateway to explore the nearby ancient Roman ruins of **Orange.** About 16 km (10 mi) east of Avignon is the Sorgue Valley, where everybody goes "flea"-ing in the famous antiques market at **L'Isle-sur-la-Sorgue.** Just east are the Luberon's famed hilltop villages (made chic by Peter Mayle), such as picture-perfect **Gordes.** South lies **Roussillon,** set like a ruby in its red cliffs.

3 Aix-en-Provence & the Mediterranean Coast. For one day, join all those fashionable folk for whom café-squatting, people-watching, and boutique-shopping are a way of life in **Aix-en-Provence** (one of France's 10 richest towns). Enjoy the elegant 18th-century streets, then track the spirit of Cézanne at his famous studio and nearby muse, **Mont Ste-Victoire.** Head south to become a Calanques castaway before diving into **Marseille,** one of France's most vibrant and colorful cities.

Remoulins

Nîmes

D999   Beaucaire

Tarascon

A9

LANGUEDOC ROUSSILLON

A54

Arles

D979

1

Aigues-Mortes

D570

THE CAMARGUE

Etang de Vaccarès

BOUCHES-DU-RHÔNE

Stes-Maries-de-la-Mer

Orange

Carpentras

D31

Avignon

2

L'Isle-sur-
la-Sorgue

Gordes

Châteaurenard

Roussillon

N570

N7

St-Rémy-
de-Provence

A7

Cavaillon

Apt

D99

MONTAGNE DU LUBERON

A L P I L L E S **4**

D°73

Les Baux-
de-Provence

PROVENCE-ALPES-
CÔTE D'AZUR

VAUCLUSE

Salon-de-
Provence

N7

A54

N568

D10

Aix-en-
Provence

Istres

N113

A8

*Etang de
Berre*

A7

3

Fos-sur-Mer

TO →
ST-TROPEZ,
CANNES
& NICE

Port-St-Louis-
du-Rhône

A51

A7

A52

*Golfe
de Fos*

10

M e d i t e r r a n e a n   S e a

Marseille

A50

Cassis

Les Calanques

Vincent Van Gogh's bedroom.,
St-Rémy-de-Provence.

GETTING ORIENTED

What many visitors remember best about Provence is the light. The sunlight here is vibrant and alive, bathing the vineyards, olive groves, and fields full of lavender and sunflowers with an intensity that captivated Cézanne and Van Gogh. Bordering the Mediterranean and flanked by the Alps and the Rhône River, Provence attracts hordes of visitors. Fortunately, many of them are siphoned off to the resorts along the Riviera, which is part of Provence but whose jet-set image doesn't fit in with the tranquil charm of the rest of the region.

4 The Alpilles. These spiky mountains guard treasures like **Les Baux-de-Provence**—be bewitched by its *ville morte* ("dead town") and its luxurious L'Oustau de la Baumanière inn. Nearby is ritzy **St-Rémy-de-Provence**, Van Gogh's famous retreat.

0   7.5 mi

0   7.5 km

PROVENCE PLANNER

How's the Weather?

Surprisingly enough it does rain (and has even snowed)—for about four weeks out of the year. Otherwise it's mostly hot and dry. It does get chilly at night, so it's wise to bring warm clothing for those evening strolls through the lavender fields; in winter, it can be fleece-jacket-mitts-and-scarf cold. Be prepared for four distinct seasons, there's a summer, a fall, a winter, and a spring, and it's best to find out what the temperature is before you disembark.

Finding a Place to Stay

Provence is more about charming bed-ane-breakfasts and lovely expensive hideaways than big hotels, so space is at a premium, especially in summer. Book as far in advance as possible, especially if you're considering coming in the high season, but even if you're here in low season, think to call ahead first. Many return visitors book their next year's stay at the end of this year's visit.

Making the Most of Your Time

The rugged, unpredictable charm of Provence catches the imagination and requires long, thoughtful savoring—like a fine wine over a delicious meal. Come here in any season except November or January, when most of the hotels close and all of Provence seems to be on holiday. The area's best in late spring, summer, or early fall, when the temperature rises and you can eat outdoors after sunset. The best place to start your trip is in Avignon. It's on a fast train link from Paris, but even if you arrive in record time, it's at exactly this moment that you need to slow down. As you step off the train and are confronted with all that magnificent architecture and art, breathe deeply. Provence is about lazy afternoons and spending "just one more day," and Avignon is a good place to have a practice run: it's cosmopolitan enough to the most energetic visitor occupied, while old and wise enough to teach the value of time. From here you can access every part of Provence easily, either by train, by bus, or by car.

Getting Around

Public transport is well organized in Provence, with most towns accessible by train or by bus. It's best to plan on combining the two—often smaller Provençal towns won't have their own train station, but a local bus connection to the train station at the nearest town over. Driving is also a good option, although for the first-time visitor, driving on the highways in Provence can be a scary experience. It is fast...regardless of the speed limit. Off the highway, however, on the national roads, or the district roads, driving can be the best and most relaxing way to get around. People are friendly, and long stretches of empty road lead to new adventures in color and beauty. Depending on the season you could find yourself bathed in swaths of purple lavender, surrounded by silvery olive trees, or stumbling into an ancient cobbledstoned village. Get a good map, as the road signs (and the local accents) can be confusing.

Black Diamonds

Sheer ugliness makes the black truffle an unlikely candidate for a gourmet delicacy, but the elusive *rcbasse de Provence*, dubbed the *diamant noire* (black diamond) by gastronome Brillat-Savarin in 1826, is firmly placed as one of (if not *the*) culinary stars of France. Local lore has it that the truffle was a gift from Zeus, born of a bolt of lightning, and a plateful was the price for strangers to win citizenship into ancient Athens. The Romans quickly figured out that it was an aphrodisiac, and later Napoléon, hungry for an heir, was advised to feed his wife, the Empératrice Marie-Louise, dozens. Such refined history comes at a price: the truffle is now a precious rarity, retailing on average at €450 per kg and peaking at a record €1,060 per kg. Local Provençal producers will give you truffle hunting demonstrations and a tasting if you kindly agree to buy their goods. Most can be found in small towns near Orange or Vaison-la-Romaine. Visit Joel Barthelemy every Sunday in Suze-la-Rousse (☎04–75–04–87–13) cr the Domaine de Bramarel south of Grignan (☎04–75–46–52–20).

WHAT IT COSTS

	¢	$	$$	$$$	$$$$
Restaurants	Under €11	€11–€17	€17–€23	€23–€30	Over €30
Hotels	Under €50	€50–€80	€80–€120	€120–€190	Over €190

Restaurant prices are per person for a main course at dinner, including tax (19.6%) and service; note that if a restaurant offers only prix-fixe (set-price) meals, it has been given the price category that reflects the full prix-fixe price. Hotel prices are for a standard double room in high season, including tax (19.6%) and service charge. Hotels operate on the European Plan (EP, with no meal provided) unless we note that they use the Breakfast Plan (BP), or also offer such options as Modified American Plan (MAP, with breakfast and dinner daily, known as demi-pension), or Full American Plan (FAP, or pension complète, with three meals a day). Inquire when booking if these all-inclusive meal plans (which always entail higher rates) are mandatory or optional.

Treasure Hunting

On a Sunday morning in the middle of the high season, l'Isle sur la Sorgue is assuredly the busiest place in France. Idle tourists fill the cafés, the squares buzz with eager conversations, and the more serious market strollers adjust reading glasses and study notebocks crammed with hastily jotted remarks. All this anticipation is with good reason: this is the antiques mecca of the region. Dealers began settling here in the 1960s and slowly acquired a reputation; these days there are an estimated 300 concentrated in picturesque booths along the main streets. Merchandise ranges from high-quality antiques and garden statuary to quirky collectibles, while the buyers could be big-name designers or first-time visitors with more money than sense. Beware, the dealers know how to sniff out the unprepared and the unwary: *do not* hesitate to bargain. There are also architectural salvage specialists offering old zinc bars, bistro fittings, and hotel reception booths. Should you succumb, there are transport firms to ship your chosen items around the world.

10

Introduction by
Nancy Coons
Updated by
Sarah Fraser

AS YOU APPROACH PROVENCE THERE'S a magical moment when you finally leave the north behind: cypresses and red-tile roofs appear; you hear the screech of cicadas and breathe the scent of wild thyme and lavender. Along the highway, oleanders bloom on the center strip against a backdrop of austere, sun-filled landscapes, the very same that inspired the Postimpressionists.

This is Provence, a disarming culture of *pastis* (an anise-based aperitif), *pétanque* (lawn bowling), and shady plane trees, where dawdling is a way of life. You may sit yourself at a sidewalk café, wander aimlessly down narrow cobbled alleyways, heft melons in the morning marketplace and, after a three-hour lunch, take an afternoon snooze in the cool shade of a 500-year-old olive tree.

Ever since Peter Mayle abandoned the London fog and described with sensual relish a life of unbuttoned collars and espadrilles in his bestselling *A Year in Provence,* the world has beaten a path here. Now Parisians are heard in the local marketplaces passing the word on the best free-range rabbit, the purest olive oil, the lowest price on a five-bedroom *mas* (farmhouse) with vineyard and pool. And a chic *bon-chic-bon-genre* city crowd languishes stylishly at the latest country inn and makes an appearance at the most fashionable restaurant. Ask them, and they'll agree: ever since Princess Caroline of Monaco moved to St-Rémy, Provence has become the new Côte d'Azur.

But chic Provence hasn't eclipsed idyllic Provence, and it's still possible to melt into a Monday-morning market crowd, where blue-aproned *paysannes* scoop fistfuls of mesclun into willow baskets, matron-connoisseurs paw through bins containing the first Cavaillon asparagus, a knot of *pépés* in workers' blues takes a pétanque break...welcoming all into the game.

Relax and join them—and plan to stay around a while. There are plenty of sights to see: some of the finest Roman ruins in Europe, from the Pont du Gard to the arenas at Arles and Nîmes; the pristine Romanesque abbeys of Senanque and de Montmajour; bijou chapels and weathered mas; the monolithic Papal Palace in old Avignon; and everywhere vineyards, pleasure ports, and sophisticated city museums. Between sights, allow yourself time to feel the rhythm of modern Provençal life, to listen to the pulsing *breet* of the insects, smell the *parfum* of a tiny country path, and feel the air of a summer night on your skin....

EXPLORING PROVENCE

Bordered to the west by the Languedoc and melting to the south and east into the blue waters of the Mediterranean, Provence falls easily into four areas. The Camargue is at the heart of the first, its hypnotic plane of marsh grass stretching to the sea, interrupted only by an occasional explosion of flying flamingos or a modest stampede of stocky bulls led by latter-day cowboys, and flowing out in waves of earthy color to Nîmes and Van Gogh's picturesque Arles to the east. Northeast of Arles, the rude and rocky Alpilles jut upward, their hillsides green with orchards and olive groves; here you can find feudal Les Baux and the Greco-Roman enclave of St-Rémy, now fashionable with the Summer People. The third area, which falls within the boundaries of the Vaucluse, begins at Avignon and extends north to Orange and Vaison-la-Romaine, then east to the forested slopes of the Luberon, where you can find hilltop towns like Ménerbes, Roussillon, and Gordes, which are the jewels in a landscape studded with blue-black forests, sun-bleached rocks, and golden perched villages. The fourth area encompasses Cézanne country, east of the Rhône, starting in Aix-en-Provence, then winding southward to big-city Marseille—tough, gorgeous, and larger than life—and east along the Mediterranean coast to the idyllic Iles d'Hyères. Note: a very handy Web resource to all the villages of Provence is ⊕ *www.provencebeyond.com/villages.*

ARLES & THE CAMARGUE

Sitting on the banks of the Rhône River, with a *Vieille Ville* (Old Town) where time seems to have stood still since 1888—the year Vincent van Gogh immortalized the city in his paintings—Arles remains both a vibrant example of Provençal culture and the gateway to the Camargue, a wild and marshy region that extends south to the Mediterranean. Arles, in fact, once outshone Marseille as the major port of the area before sea gave way to sand. Today it competes with nearby Nîmes for the title "Rome of France," thanks to its magnificent Roman theater and Arènes (amphitheater). Just west and south of these landmarks, the Camargue is a vast watery plain formed by the sprawling Rhône delta and extending over 800 square km (300 square mi)—its landscape remains one of the most extraordinary in France.

ARLES

36 km (22 mi) south of Avignon, 31 km (19 mi) east of Nîmes, 92 km (57 mi) northwest of Marseille, 720 km (430 mi) south of Paris.

10

GETTING HERE
If you are arriving by plane, note that Arles is roughly 20 km (12 mi) from the Nîmes-Arles-Camargue airport (☎04-66-70-49-49). The easiest way from the landing strip to Arles is by taxi (about €30). Buses run between Nîmes and Arles three times daily on weekdays and twice on Saturday (not at all on Sunday), and four buses weekdays between Arles and Stes-Maries-de-la-Mer, through Cars de Camargue (☎04-90-96-36-25). The SNCF (☎08-92-35-35-35) runs three buses Monday -Saturday from Avignon to Arles, and Cartreize (☎08-00-19-94-13 ⊕www.lepilote.com) runs a service between Marseille and Arles. Arles is along the main coastal train route, and you can take the TGV (trains à grands vitesses) to Avignon from Paris and jump on the local connection to Arles. For all train information, check out www.voyages-sncf.com, or call 08-36-35-35-35.

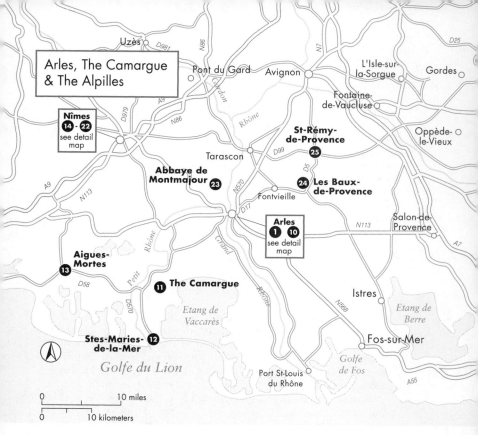

Arles, The Camargue & The Alpilles

Uzès D981
Pont du Gard
Avignon
L'Isle-sur-la-Sorgue
Gordes
Nîmes ⑭ - ㉒ see detail map
Fontaine-de-Vaucluse
St-Rémy-de-Provence ㉕
Tarascon
Oppède-le-Vieux
Abbaye de Montmajour ㉓
Les Baux-de-Provence ㉔
Fontvieille
Arles ① ⑩ see detail map
Salon-de-Provence
Aigues-Mortes ⑬
The Camargue ⑪
Istres
Etang de Vaccarès
Etang de Berre
Stes-Maries-de-la-Mer ⑫
Fos-sur-Mer
Golfe du Lion
Port St-Louis du Rhône
Golfe de Fos
Rhône
Grand Rhône
Petit Rhône

0 ————— 10 miles
0 ————— 10 kilometers

EXPLORING

If you were obliged to choose just one city to visit in Provence, lovely little Arles would give Avignon and Aix a run for their money. It's too chic to become museumlike yet has a wealth of classical antiquities and Romanesque stonework, quarried-stone edifices and shuttered town houses, and graceful, shady Vieille Ville streets and squares. Throughout the year there are pageantry, festivals, and cutting-edge arts events. Its panoply of restaurants and small hotels makes it the ideal headquarters for forays into the Alpilles and the Camargue.

A Greek colony since the 6th century BC, little Arles took a giant step forward when Julius Caesar defeated Marseille in the 1st century BC. The emperor-to-be designated Arles a Roman colony and lavished funds and engineering know-how on it. It became an international crossroads by sea and land and a market to the world, with goods from Africa, Arabia, and the Far East. The emperor Constantine himself moved to Arles and brought Christianity with him.

The remains of this golden age are reason enough to visit Arles today, yet its character nowadays is as gracious and low-key as it once was cutting-edge. Seated in the shade of the plane trees on Place du Forum or strolling the rampart walkway along the sparkling Rhône, you can see what enchanted Gauguin and drove Van Gogh frantic with inspiration.

Though it's a hike from the center, a good place to set the tone and context for your exploration of Arles is at the state-of-the-art **Musée de l'Arles et de la Provence Antiques** *(Museum of Ancient Arles and Provence)*. The bold, modern triangular structure (designed by Henri Ciriani) lies on the site of an enormous Roman *cirque* (chariot-racing stadium). The permanent collection includes jewelry, mosaics, town plans, and 4th-century carved sacophagi from *Les Alyscamps*. You can learn all about Arles in its heyday, from the development of its monuments to details of daily life in Roman times. Ask for the English-language guidebook. ⊠*Presqu'île du Cirque Romain* ☎*04–90–18–88–88* ⊕*www.arles-antique.org* ⊠*€5.50, free 1st Sun. of every month* ⊙*Apr.–Dec., daily 9–7; Jan.–Mar., daily 10–5.*

SAVING MONEY ON SITES

If you plan to visit many of the monuments and museums in Arles, buy a *visite generale* ticket for €12. This covers the entry fee to the Musée de l'Arles et de la Provence Antiques and any and all of the other museums and monuments (except the independent Museon Arlaten, which charges €4). The ticket is good for the length of your stay.

A good way to plunge into post-Roman Arles is through the quirky old **Museon Arlaten** *(Museum of Arles).* Created by the father of the Provençal revival, turn-of-the-20th-century poet Frédéric Mistral, it enshrines a seemingly bottomless collection of regional treasures ranging from 18th-century furniture and ceramics to a mixed-bag collection of toothache-prevention cures. Following Mistral's wishes, women in full Arlésienne costume oversee the labyrinth of lovely 16th-century halls. ⊠*29 rue de la République* ☎*04–90–93–58–11* ⊠*€4, free 1st Sun. of every month* ⊙*Apr., May, and Sept., daily 9:30–12:30 and 2–6; June–Aug., daily 9:30–1 and 2–6:30; Oct.–Mar., Tues.–Sun. 9:30–12:30 and 2–5.*

At the entrance to a 17th-century Jesuit college you can access the ancient underground galleries called the **Cryptoportiques.** Dating from 30 BC to 20 BC, this horseshoe of vaults and pillars buttressed the ancient forum from below ground. Used as a refuge for Resistance members in World War II, these galleries still have a rather ominous atmosphere. Yet openings let in natural daylight, and artworks of considerable merit and worth were unearthed here, adding to the mystery of the original function of these passages. ⊠*Rue Balze* ☎*04–90–49–36–74* ⊠*€3.50* ⊙*May–Sept., daily 9–noon and 2–7; Oct., daily 9–noon and 2–6; Nov.–Feb., daily 10–noon and 2–5; Mar. and Apr., weekends, 9–noon and 2–6.*

Van Gogh immortalized many everyday objects and captured particular views still seen today, but his famous painting of the **Pont Van Gogh.** (Langois Bridge) seems to touch a particular cord among Arles residents. For years rumors circulated in favor of restoration (after it was bombed in World War II) but with no immediate response. Persistence paid off and it's now resplendent, restored to its former glory on the southern outskirts of Arles. ⊠*Rte. de Port St-Louis.*

10

In the Footsteps of Van Gogh

It was the light that drew Vincent van Gogh to Arles. For a man raised under the iron-gray skies of the Netherlands and the gaslight pall of Paris, Provence's clean, clear sun was a revelation. In his last years he turned his frenzied efforts toward capturing the resonance of "… golden tones of every hue: green gold, yellow gold, pink gold, bronze or copper colored gold, and even from the yellow of lemons to the matte, lusterless yellow of threshed grain." Arles, however, was not drawn to Van Gogh. Though it makes every effort today to make up for its misjudgment, Arles treated the artist very badly during the time he passed here near the end of his life—a time when his creativity, productivity, and madness all reached a climax.

Van Gogh began working in Arles in 1888 with an intensity and tempestuousness that first drew, then drove away his companion Paul Gauguin, with whom he had dreamed of founding an artists' colony. Astonishingly productive—he applied a pigment-loaded palette knife to some 200 canvases in that year alone—he nonetheless lived in intense isolation, counting his sous, and writing his visions in lengthy letters to his long-suffering, infinitely patient brother Theo. Often heavy-drinking, occasionally whoring, Vincent alienated his neighbors, driving them to distraction and ultimately goading them to action.

The people of Arles circulated a petition to have him evicted just a year after he arrived, a shock that left him more and more at a loss to cope with life and led to his eventual self-commitment to an asylum in nearby St-Rémy. The houses he lived in are no longer standing, though many of his subjects remain as he saw them (or are restored to a similar condition). Happily, the city has provided helpful markers and a numbered itinerary to guide you between landmarks. You can stand on the Place Lamartine, where his famous Maison Jaune stood until it was destroyed by World War II bombs. Starry Night may have been painted from the Quai du Rhône just off Place Lamartine, though another was completed at St-Rémy. The Café La Nuit on Place Forum is an exact match for the terrace platform, scattered with tables and bathed in gaslight under the stars, from the painting Terrace de café le Soir; Gauguin and Van Gogh used to drink here.

Both the Arènes and Les Alyscamps were featured in paintings, and the hospital where he broke down and cut off his earlobe is now a kind of shrine, its garden reconstructed exactly as it figured in Le Jardin de l'Hôtel-Dieu. The drawbridge in Le pont de Langlois aux Lavandières has been reconstructed outside of town, at Port-de-Bouc, 3 km (2 mi) south on D35.

About 25 km (16 mi) away is St-Rémy-de-Provence, where Van Gogh retreated to the asylum St-Paul-de-Mausolée. Here he spent hours in silence, painting the cloisters and nearby orchards, vineyards, and star-spangled crystalline skies—the stuff of inspiration.

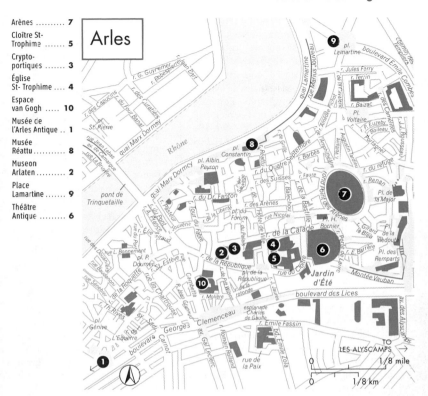

Classed as a world treasure by UNESCO, the extraordinary Roman-
★ ❹ esque **Église St-Trophime** (⊠*Pl. de la République*) alone would justify a
visit to Arles, though it's continually upstaged by the antiquities around
it. Its transepts date from the 11th century and its nave from the 12th;
the church's austere symmetry and ancient artworks (including a stunning Roman-style 4th-century sarcophagus) are fascinating in themselves. But it's the church's superbly preserved Romanesque sculpture
on the 12th-century portal—its entry facade—that earns international
respect. Particularly remarkable is the frieze of the Last Judgment with
chain-bound souls being dragged off to Hell or, on the contrary, being
lovingly delivered into the hands of the saints.

❺ Tucked discreetly behind St-Trophime is a peaceful haven, the **Cloître St-
Trophime** *(St-Trophime Cloister).* A Romanesque treasure worthy of the
church, it's one of the loveliest cloisters in Provence. A sturdy walkway
above offers up good views of the town. ☎*04–90–49–36–74* ✉*€3.50*
☉*May–Sept., daily 9–7; Oct., Mar., and Apr., daily 9–6; Nov.–Feb.,
daily 10–5.*

Directly up Rue de la Calade from Place de la République are the pictur-
❻ esque ruins of the **Théâtre Antique** *(Ancient Theater),* built by the Romans
under Augustus in the 1st century BC. It's here that the noted Venus of Arles
statue, now in the Louvre, was dug up and identified. Now overgrown

10

and a pleasant, parklike retreat, it was once an entertainment venue that held 20,000 people. Today it's a concert stage for the Festival d'Arles, in July and August, and site of the Recontres Internationales de la Photographie (Photography Festival), from early July to mid-September. ⊠*Rue de la Calade* ☎*04–90–49–36–74* ⊕*www.rip-arles.org* 🎫*€3* ⊘*May–Sept., daily 9–6:30; Oct., Mar., Apr., daily 9–noon and 2–6; Nov.–Feb., daily 10–noon and 2–5.*

❼ Rivaled only by the even better-preserved version in Nîmes, the **Arènes** *(Arena)* dominates old Arles. It was built in the 1st century AD to seat 21,000 people, with large tunnels through which wild beasts were forced to run into the center arena. Before being

> ### WHISPERS ABOUT VAN GOGH'S EAR
>
> Ill-received and ostracized in Arles, Van Gogh was packed off to an asylum in nearby St-Rémy after he cut off the lobe of his left ear on December 23, 1888. Theories abound, but historians believe he made the desperate gesture in homage to Gauguin, who had arrived to set up a "Studio of the South." Following the fashion in Provençal bullrings for a matador to present his lady love with an ear from a dispatched bull, Vincent wielded the knife after arguing with Gauguin, whom he had come to idolize.

plundered in the Middle Ages, it had three stories of 60 arcades each; its four medieval towers are testimony to its transformation from classical sports arena to feudal fortification. Complete restoration began in 1825 and today it holds nearly as many as it once did. It's primarily a venue for the traditional spectacle of the corridas, or bullfights, which take place annually during the *féria pascale,* or Easter festival. The less bloodthirsty local variant *Course Carmarguaise* (in which the bull is not killed), also takes place here. Nearby is the **Fondation Van Gogh** (⊠*24 bis rond point des Arènes* ☎*04–90–93–08–08* 🎫*€7* ⊘*May–Sept., daily 10–7; Oct. –Apr., daily 10–6*), where you can savor works by various modern and contemporary artists, including Francis Bacon and Doisneau, inspired by Van Gogh. ⊠*Rond Point des Arènes* ☎*04–90–49–36–74* ⊕*www.fondationvangogh.arles.org* 🎫*€7* ⊘*May–Sept., daily 9:30–6:30; Oct., Mar., Apr., daily 9–noon and 2–6, Nov.–Feb., daily 10–noon and 2–5.*

❽ The **Musée Réattu** lavishes three rooms on local painter Jacques Réattu's turn-of-the-19th-century ephemera but redeems itself with a decent collection of 20th-century art including some daubs by Dufy and Gauguin. There's also an impressive 57 drawings done by Picasso in 1971, including one delightfully tongue-in-cheek depiction of noted muse and writer Lee Miller in full Arles dress. The best thing about the Réattu may be the building itself, a Knights of Malta priory dating from the 15th century. ⊠*Rue Grand Prieuré* ☎*04–90–49–38–34* 🎫*€4* ⊘*Apr.–Sept., daily 10–12:30 and 2–7:30; Oct.–Mar., daily 1–5.*

You'll have to go to Amsterdam to view Van Goghs, but Arles has provided helpful markers and a numbered itinerary to guide you from one landmark to another—many of them recognizable from his ❾ beloved canvases. You can stand on **Place Lamartine** (between the rail station and the ramparts), which is the site of his residence here, the now-famous Maison Jaune (Yellow House); it was destroyed by bombs in 1944. The artist may have set up his easel on the Quai du Rhône, just off Place Lamartine, to capture the view that he transformed into his legendary *Starry Night*. Eight other sites are included on the city's "Promenade Vincent van Gogh" (⊕int.tourisme.ville-arles.fr/uk/a4/a4.htm), linking sight to canvas, including the Place du Forum; the Trinquetaille bridge; Rue Mireille; the Summer Garden on the Boulevard des Lices; and the road along the Arles à Bouc canal.

> ### YOU OUGHTA BE IN PICTURES
>
> In July, Arles's famous photography festival, Les Rencontres Internationales de la Photographie (⊠10 Rond Point des Arènes ☎04-90-96-76-06 ⊕ www. rencontres-arles.co) brings movers and shakers in international photography into the Théâtre Antique for five days of highly specialized colloquiums and homages. Ordinary folks can profit, too, by attending the photography exhibits displayed in some 17 venues in Arles, open to the public throughout July and August.

The most strikingly resonant site, impeccably restored and landscaped to match one of Van Gogh's paintings, is the courtyard garden of what is now the **Espace van Gogh**. This was the hospital to which the tortured artist repaired after cutting off his earlobe. Its cloistered grounds have become something of a shrine for visitors and there are photo plaques comparing the renovation to some of the master's paintings, including *Le Jardin de la Maison de Santé*. The exhibition hall is open for temporary exhibitions; the garden is always on view. For more about Van Gogh, check out shows of contemporary art inspired by "Vince" at the nearby Fondation Vincent Van Gogh, at 24 bis Rond-point des Arènes. *For more information about Van Gogh, see our Close-Up Box, "Van Gogh in Arles and St-Rémy."* ⊠*Pl. Dr. Félix Rey* ☎*04–90–49–39–39* ⊕*www.ville-arles.fr* ☞*Free.*

OFF THE BEATEN PATH

Les Alyscamps. Though this romantically melancholy Roman cemetery lies 1 km (½ mi) southeast from the Vieille Ville, it's worth the hike—certainly, Van Gogh thought so, as several of his famous canvases prove. This long necropolis amassed the remains of the dead from antiquity to the Middle Ages. Greek, Roman, and Christian tombs line the long shady road that was once the entry to Arles—the Aurelian Way. The trail leads you to further mysteries—take time to explore the Romanesque tower and ruined church of St. Honorat and locate the spot where (legend has it) St. Trophimus fell to his knees when God spoke to him. ☎*04–90–49–36–74* ☞*€3.50* ۞*May–Sept., daily 9–11:30 and 2–5:30; Mar., Apr., and Oct., daily 9–11:30 and 2–5; Nov.–Feb., daily 10–11:30 and 2–4:30.*

WHERE TO STAY & EAT

$$$$

Fodor's Choice

★

✕ **La Chassagnette.** Sophisticated yet down-home comfortable, this restaurant is the fashionable address in the area (14 km [8 mi] south of Arles). Reputedly the only registered "organic" restaurant in Provence, this spot is fetchingly designed and has a dining area that extends outdoors,

10

where large family-style picnic tables can be found under a wooden slate canopy overlooking the extensive gardens. The menu is based around Camarguais "tapas"—you might hit as many as 30 tapas tastes in one meal. Using ingredients that are certified organic and grown right on the property, innovative master chef Luc Rabanel also serves up open-rotisserie-style prix-fixe menus that are a refreshing mix of modern and classic French-country cuisine. ⊠*Rte. du Sambuc, 14 km (8 mi) south of Arles on D36* ☎*04–90–97–26–96* ☖*Reservations essential* ☰*MC, V* ☉*Closed Tues. and Nov.–mid-Dec. No lunch Wed.*

$$$ ✕ **L'Affenage.** A vast smorgasbord of Provençal hors d'oeuvres draws loyal locals to this former fire-horse shed. They come here for heaping plates of grilled vegetables, tapenade, chickpeas in cumin, and a slab of ham carved off the bone. In summer you can opt for just the first-course buffet and go back for thirds; reserve a terrace table out front. ⊠*4 rue Molière* ☎*04–90–96–07–67* ☖*Reservations essential* ☰*AE, MC, V* ☉*Closed Sun. and 3 wks in Aug. No lunch Mon.*

$–$$$ ✕ **Brasserie Nord-Pinus.** With its tile-and-ironwork interior, tastefully framed black-and-white photos, crisp white tablecloths, and its terrace packed with all the right people, this cozy-chic retro brasserie showcases light and unpretentious cooking: zucchini-flower risotto with fresh goat cheese, oven-cooked bass, or wild king prawns sautéed with pepper and cognac are some signature dishes. ⊠*Pl. du Forum* ☎*04–90–93–44–44* ☰*AE, DC, MC, V* ☉*Closed Feb. and Wed. in Nov.–Mar.*

$–$$$ ✕ **Le Cilantro.** With so many typical and rather ho-hum Provençal menus around, it's delightfully refreshing to find modern, innovative cooking, dished up by chef Jerome Laurent. He seems determined to bring Arles gastronomy into the 21st century, and menus include red tuna Rossini with fois gras, green asparagus and artichokes, or rack of lamb roasted in almond milk and braised carrots. Reserve in advance and save room for desert. ⊠*29/31 rue Porte de Laure* ☎*04–90–18–25–05* ☰*AE, DC, MC, V.*

$–$$$ ✕ **La Gueule du Loup.** Serving as hosts, waiters, and chefs, the ambitious couple that owns this restaurant tackles serious cooking—lamb with eggplant and red-pepper puree, monkfish and squid in saffron, or chestnut mousse perfumed with almond milk top the delights here. Jazz music and vintage magic-act posters add color and warmth to the old Arles stone-and-beam rooms. ⊠*39 rue des Arènes* ☎*04–90–96–96–69* ☖*Reservations essential* ☰*MC, V* ☉*Closed Sun. and Mon. Oct.–Mar.; Sun. Apr.–Sept. No lunch Mon.*

$$$$ ☷ **L'Hôtel Particulier.** Once owned by the Baron of Chartrouse, this extraordinary 18th-century *hôtel particulier* (mansion) is delightfully intimate and carefully discreet behind a wrought-iron gate. Decor is sophisticated yet charmingly simple: stunning gold-framed mirrors, white-brocaded chairs, marble writing desks, artfully hung curtains, and hand-painted wallpaper. Rooms look out onto a beautifully landscaped garden; even if you take the five-minute walk into the center of town you can come back, stretch out by the pool, and listen to the birds chirp. ⊠*4 rue de la Monnaie, 13200* ☎*04–90–52–51–40* 🖶*04–90–96–16–70* ⊕*www. hotel-particulier.com* ⇥*8 rooms* ☖*In-room: dial-up. In-hotel: pool, some pets allowed (fee), parking (fee)* ☰*AE, DC, MC, V.*

$$$–$$$$ 🏨 **Jules César.** Once a Carmelite convent but styled like a Roman palace, this pleasant landmark anchors the lively (sometimes noisy) Boulevard des Lices. Don't be misled by the rather imposing lobby as this place turns out to be a friendly, traditional hotel. Rooms have high arched ceilings and massive Provençal armoires softened by plush carpets and burnished reds and oranges. Some windows look over the pool; others over the pretty cloister, where breakfast is served under a vaulted stone arcade. The restaurant, unexpectedly intimate for its size, has a lovely terrace, and nice, simply prepared dishes—try the lobster risotto or the grilled steak. A meal plan is available with a minimum stay of three nights. ⊠*Bd. des Lices, 13200* ☎*04–90–52–52–52* 🖷*04–90–52–52–53* ⊕*www.hotel-julescesar.fr* ⇄*53 rooms, 5 suites* ⟐*In-room: Wi-Fi, refrigerator. In-hotel: restaurant, pool, parking (fee), some pets allowed (fee)* ⊟*AE, MC, V* ⟐*BP, MAP.*

★ **$$$–$$$$** 🏨 **Nord-Pinus.** Picasso felt right at home at this eclectic and quintessentially Mediterranean hotel on Place du Forum. The salon is dramatic with angular wrought iron, heavy furniture, colorful ceramics, and a standing collection of Peter Beard's black-and-white photographs. Rooms are individually decorated: wood or tiled floors, large bathrooms, handwoven rugs, and tasteful (if somewhat exotic) artwork are cleverly set off to stylish art director–chic advantage. Although it's hard to beat the low-key and accommodating service, this hotel may not be for everyone: traditionalists should head for the more mainstream luxuries of the Jules César. As the hotel fronts the busy Place du Forum, ask for a room in the back if noise bothers you. ⊠*Pl. du Forum, 13200* ☎*04–90–93–44–44* 🖷*04–90–93–34–00* ⊕*www.nord-pinus. com* ⇄*26 rooms* ⟐*In-room: dial-up, refrigerator (some). In-hotel: bar, parking (fee), some pets allowed* ⊟*AE, DC, MC, V.*

¢–$ 🏨 **Le Cloître.** Built as a private home, this grand old medieval building has luckily fallen into the hands of a couple devoted to making the most of its historic details—with their own bare hands. They've chipped away plaster from pristine quarry-stone walls, cleaned massive beams, restored tile stairs, and mixed natural chalk and ocher to plaster the walls. ⊠*16 rue du Cloître, 13200* ☎*04–90–96–29–50* 🖷*04–90–96–02–88* ⊕*www.hotelcloitre.com* ⇄*30 rooms* ⟐*In-room: no a/c (some), no TV (some). In-hotel: parking (fee), some pets allowed, public Internet* ⊟*AE, MC, V* ⟐*Closed Nov.–mid-Mar.*

★ **¢–$** 🏨 **Muette.** With 12th-century exposed stone walls, a 15th-century spiral staircase, weathered wood, and an Old Town setting, a hotelier wouldn't have to try very hard to please. But the couple that owns this place does: hand-stripped doors, antiques, sparkling blue-and-white-tile baths, hair dryers, good mattresses, Provençal prints, and fresh sunflowers in every room show they care. ⊠*15 rue des Suisses, 13200* ☎*04–90–96–15–39* 🖷*04–90–49–73–16* ⊕*www.hotel-muette. com* ⇄*18 rooms* ⟐*In-hotel: parking (fee), some pets allowed, public Internet* ⊟*AE, MC, V* ⟐*Closed last 2 wks in Feb.*

NIGHTLIFE & THE ARTS

To find out what's happening in and around Arles (even as far away as Nîmes and Avignon), the free weekly *Le César* lists films, plays, cabarets, and jazz and rock events. It's distributed at the tourist office and

10

in bars, clubs, and cinemas. In high season the cafés stay lively until the wee hours; in winter the streets empty out by 11. **Le Cargo de Nuit** (✉ 7 av. Sadi-Carnot ☎ 04–90–49–55–99 ⊕ www.cargodenuit.com) is the main venue for live jazz, reggae, and rock, with a dance floor next to the stage. A meal allows you reduced entry to see the show. Though Arles seems to be one big sidewalk café in warm weather, the place to tipple is the hip bar **Le Cintra,** in the Hôtel Nord-Pinus.

THE CAMARGUE

⑪   *19 km (12 mi) east of Aigues-Mortes, 15 km (9 mi) south of Arles.*

Fodor's Choice
★

Stretching to the horizon for about 800 square km (309 square mi), the vast alluvial delta of the Rhône known as the Camargue is an austere, unrelievedly flat marshland, scoured by the mistral and swarmed over by mosquitoes. Between the endless flow of sediment from the Rhône and the erosive force of the sea, its shape is constantly changing. Even the Provençal poet Frederic Mistral described it in bleak terms: *"Ni arbre, ni ombre, ni âme"* ("Neither tree, nor shade, nor a soul.")

Yet its harsh landscape harbors a concentration of exotic wildlife unique in Europe, and its isolation has given birth to an ascetic and ancient way of life that transcends national stereotype. This strange region is worth discovering, slowly, either on foot or on horseback—especially as its wildest reaches are inaccessible by car. People find the Camargue intriguing, birds find it irresistible. Its protected marshes lure some 400 species, including more than 160 in migration.

As you drive the scarce roads that barely crisscross the Camargue, you can usually be within the boundaries of the **Parc Regional de Camargue** (⊕ www.parc-camargue.fr). Unlike state and national parks in the United States, this area is privately owned and utilized following regulations imposed by the French government. The principal owners are the *manadiers* (the Camargue equivalent of small-scale ranchers) and their *gardians* (a kind of open-range cowboy), who keep it for grazing their wide-horn bulls and their dappled-white horses. When it's not participating in a bloodless bullfight (mounted players try to hook a red ribbon from its horns), a bull may well end up in the wine-rich regional stew called *gardianne de taureau*. Riding through the marshlands in leather pants and wide-rimmed black hats and wielding long prongs to prod their cattle, the gardians themselves are as fascinating as the wildlife. Their homes—tiny and whitewashed—dot the countryside.

The easiest place to view birdlife is in a private reserve just outside the regional park called the **Parc Ornithologique du Pont de Gau** *(Pont du Gau Ornithological Park)*. On some 150 acres of marsh and salt lands, birds are welcomed and protected (but in no way confined); injured birds are treated and kept in large pens, to be released if and when able to survive. A series of boardwalks (including a short, child-friendly inner loop) snakes over the wetlands, the longest leading to an observation blind, where a half hour of silence, binoculars in hand, can reveal unsuspected satisfactions. ☎ 04–90–97–82–62 ⊕ www.parcornithologique.

com €6.50 Apr.–Sept., daily 9–7; Oct.–Mar., daily 9–sunset.

WHERE TO STAY & EAT

★ $$$$ ✕⊡ **Le Mas de Peint.** In a 17th-century farmhouse on roughly 1,250 acres of Camargue ranch land, this quietly sophisticated jewel of a hotel may just be the ultimate mas (traditional rural Provençal house) experience. A study in country elegance, the rooms have beautifully preserved 400-year-old wood beams, carefully polished stone floors, and creamy linen fabrics all tastefully complemented by brass beds, claw-foot bathtubs, and natural, soft Provençal colors. The small restaurant (reservations essential), charmingly decorated with checked curtains, paysan chairs, and fresh roses on every table, is worth the trip even if you can't stay the night. The prix-fixe menu (€37–€49), changing daily, features sophisticated specialties often using homegrown ingredients, such as roasted tuna flank with escargots à la provençale, or grilled game hen with roasted baby potatoes and exquisite cinnamon-flavor beets. A meal plan is available with a minimum stay of three nights. ✉ *Le Sambuc, 20 km (12 mi) south of Arles, 13200* ☎ *04–90–97–20–62* 🖶 *04–90–97–22–20* ⊕ *www.masdepeint. com* ⇨ *8 rooms, 3 apartments* △*In-hotel: restaurant, pool, some pets allowed, no TV, no elevator* ▤*AE, DC, MC, V* ⊙*Closed mid-Nov.– mid-Mar.* ⏏*MAP.*

> **DEEP IN THE HEART OF…PROVENCE?**
>
> Although the thought might give pause to Texans, historians tell us that the American cowboy is descended from the French *gardian*, the Provençal cowboy. In the early 19th century, Camargue ranchers shipped out to the French colony of New Orleans, then fanned out across America as the first bronc-stompers. They brought along their black felt hats, string ties, and *bleus de travail*, or "jeans" (invented in the Provence city of Nîmes). Their festival wear, including traditional velvet vests— is seen in full glory during the Fête des Gardians in Arles in May.

STES-MARIES-DE-LA-MER

⑫ *18 km (10 mi) south of the Camargue, 129 km (80 mi) west of Marseille, 39 km (24 mi) south of Arles.*

The principal town within the confines of the Parc Régional de Camargue, Stes-Maries is a beach resort with a fascinating history. Provençal legend has it that around AD 45 a band of the very first Christians were rounded up and set adrift at sea without provisions in a boat without a sail. Their stellar ranks included Mary Magdalene, Martha, and Mary Salome, mother of apostles James and John; Mary Jacoby, sister of the Virgin; and Lazarus, not necessarily the one risen from the dead. Joining them in their fate was a dark-skinned servant girl named Sarah. Miraculously, their boat washed ashore at this ancient site, and the grateful Marys built a chapel in thanks.

Two extraordinary festivals (⊕*www.saintesmariesdelamer.com*) celebrating the Marys take place every year in Stes-Maries, one on May

24–25 and the other on the Sunday nearest October 22. In addition, the town honors the arrival of the Marys with its *navette,* a small pastry baked in the shape of the boat. But pilgrims attracted to Stes-Maries aren't only lighting candles to the two St. Marys: Sarah has been adopted as an honorary saint by the Gypsies of the world.

★ What is most striking to a visitor entering the damp, dark, and forbidding fortress-church, **Église des Stes-Maries,** is its novel character. Almost devoid of windows, its tall, barren single nave is cluttered with florid and sentimental ex-votos (tokens of blessings, prayers, and thanks) and primitive and sentimental artworks depicting the famous trio. Another oddity brings you back to the 21st century: a sign on the door forbids visitors from entering *torso nu* (topless). Outside its otherworldly role Stes-Maries is first and foremost a beach resort: dead flat, whitewashed, and more than a little tacky. Unless you've made a pilgrimage here for the sun and sand, don't spend much time in the town center, except to visit the quirky

Museé Baroncelli. ☎ *04–90–97–87–60* ✉ *rue Victor-Hugo* 🎫 *€3* ⊙ *Apr.–Sept., Mon.–Sat. 9–noon and 2–6; Oct.–Mar., Mon.–Sat. 9–noon and 2–5.*

On display are wonderful exhibits on Camargue traditions, plus a very odd-looking stuffed flamingo donated to the museum by its namesake, a 19th-century marquis who gave up all his creature comforts to become a real salt-of-the-earth cowboy.

WHERE TO STAY

★ $$–$$$ 🍴 **Mas de Cacharel.** A haven for nature lovers, this quiet, laid-back retreat is nestled in the middle of 170 acres of private marshland. The Wild West–like ranch setting is enhanced by simple whitewashed buildings and rather sparse decor; rooms are furnished

> **STAYING OUT OF TOWN**
>
> If you've chosen Stes-Maries as a base for viewing the Camargue, stay in one of the discreet mas set outside its city limits.

with terra-cotta tiles, jute rugs, and white cotton throws, and large picture windows gaze out over hauntingly beautiful stretches of rose-color reeds. The cavernous dining hall with Provençal chairs and an enormous hand-carved fireplace is a gathering place for sharing stories, local wine, and a hearty €17 plate of selected meats, fresh tomatoes, and regional goat cheese. ✉ *4 km (2½ mi) north of town on D85, 13460* ☎ *04–90–97–95–44* 🖷 *04–90–97–87–97* ⊕ *www.hotel-cacharel.com* 🛏 *16 rooms* ⚐ *In-room: no a/c, no TV. In-hotel: bar, pool, some pets allowed, no elevator* 💳 *MC, V.*

AIGUES-MORTES

⓭ *16 km (10 mi) northwest of Stes-Maries-de-la-Mer, 41 km (25 mi) south of Nîmes, 48 km (30 mi) southwest of Arles.*

Like a tiny illumination in a medieval manuscript, Aigues-Mortes is a precise and perfect miniature fortress-town contained within symmetrical crenellated walls, its streets laid out in geometric grids. Now awash in a flat wasteland of sand, salt, and monotonous marsh, it was once a major port town from which no less than St-Louis himself (Louis IX) set sail in the 13th century to conquer Jerusalem. In 1248 some 35,000 zealous men launched 1,500 ships toward Cyprus, engaging the infidel on his own turf and suffering swift defeat; Louis was briefly taken prisoner. A second launching in 1270 led to more crushing loss, and he succumbed to the plague.

Louis's state-of-the-art **fortress-port** remains astonishingly well preserved. Its stout walls now contain a small Provençal village filled with tourists, but the visit is more than justified by the impressive scale of the original structure ⊠*Porte de la Gardette* ☎*04–66–53–61–55* 🎫*€6.50* ☾*May–Aug., daily 10–7; Sept.–Apr., daily 10–1 and 2–4:30.*

It's not surprising that the town within the rampart walls has become tourist oriented, with the usual stream of gift shops and postcard stands. But **Place St-Louis,** where a 19th-century statue of the father of the fleur-de-lis reigns under shady pollards, has a mellow village feel. The pretty, bare-bones **Église Notre-Dame des Sablons,** on one corner of the square, has a timeless air (the church dates from the 13th century, but the stained glass is ultramodern).

WHERE TO STAY & EAT

★ **$$–$$$** ✕🏨 **Les Arcades.** Long a success as an upscale seafood restaurant, this beautifully preserved 16th-century house now has large, airy rooms, some with tall windows overlooking a green courtyard. Pristine whitestone walls, color-stained woodwork, and rubbed-ocher walls frame antiques and lush fabrics. Classic cooking includes lotte (monkfish) in saffron and poached turbot in hollandaise, and the house specialty: hot oysters in a creamy herbed-butter sauce. Breakfast is included in the hotel price. ⊠*23 bd. Gambetta, 30220* ☎*04–66–53–81–13* 🖶*04–66–53–75–46* ⊕*www.les-arcades.fr* 🛏*9 rooms* ♿*In-room: dial-up. In-hotel: restaurant, pool, some pets allowed (fee)* ▤*AE, DC, MC, V* ☾*Closed 1st 3 wks of Mar., last 2 wks of Oct.* ⊙|*BP.*

NÎMES

35 km (20 mi) north of Aigues-Mortes, 43 km (26 mi) south of Avignon, 121 km (74 mi) west of Marseille.

GETTING HERE

On the Paris-Avignon-Montpellier train line, Nîmes has a direct rail link to and from Paris (about a 3-hour ride). For TGV and train information go to: www.voyages-sncf.com, or call 08–36–35–35–35. The Nîmes gare routière (bus station) is just behind the train station. Cars de Camargue (04–90–96–36–25) runs several buses to and from Arles (four daily Mon.–Sat., two Sun.). STD Gard (04–66–29–27–29) has several buses (daily except Sun.) between Avignon and Nîmes and Uzès and Nîmes. Some Uzès buses stop at Remoulins for the Pont du Gard and a few continue on to St-Quentin-la-Poterie. Note that although all the sites in Nîmes are walkable, the useful La Citadine bus (TNC 04–

10

66–38–15–40) runs a good loop from the station and passes by many of the principal sites along the way €1.30.

EXPLORING

If you've come to the south seeking Roman treasures, you need look no farther than Nîmes (pronounced *neem*): the Arènes and Maison Carrée are among continental Europe's best-preserved antiquities. But if you've come in search of a more modern mythology—of lazy, graceful Provence—give Nîmes a wide berth. It's a feisty, run-down rat race of a town, with jalopies and Vespas roaring irreverently around the ancient temple. Its medieval Vieille Ville has none of the gentrified grace of those in Arles or St-Rémy. Yet its rumpled and rebellious ways trace directly back to its Roman incarnation, when its population swelled with newly victorious soldiers flaunting arrogant behavior after their conquest of Egypt in 31 BC.

Already anchoring a fiefdom of pre-Roman *oppida* (elevated fortresses) before ceding to the empire in the 1st century BC, this ancient city grew to formidable proportions under the Pax Romana. Its next golden age bloomed under the Protestants, who established an anti-Catholic stronghold here and wreaked havoc on iconic architectural treasures—not to mention the papist minority. Their massacre of some 200 Catholic citizens in 1567 is remembered as the Michelade; many of those murdered were priests sheltered in the *évêché* (bishop's house), now the Museum of Old Nîmes.

★ ⑭ The **Arènes** *(Arena)* is considered the best-preserved Roman amphitheater in the world. A miniature of the Colosseum in Rome (note the small carvings of Romulus and Remus—the wrestling gladiators—on the exterior and the intricate bulls' heads etched into the stone over the entrance on the north side), it stands more than 520 feet long and 330 feet wide, and has a seating capacity of 24,000. Bloody gladiator battles and theatrical wild-boar chases drew crowds to its bleachers. Nowadays its most colorful use is the **corrida,** the bullfight that transforms the arena (and all of Nîmes) into a sangria-flushed homage to Spain. Concerts (check Web site below) are held year-round thanks to a new high-tech glass-and-steel structure that covers the arena for winter use. ⊠ *Bd. Victor-Hugo* ☎ *04–66–21–82–56* ⊕ *www.culturespaces. com* ✑ *€7.70; joint ticket to Arènes, Tour Magne, and Maison Carée €9.50* ☉ *Apr., May, and Sept., daily 9–6; Oct. and Nov., daily 9–5:30, Dec.–Mar., daily 9–4:30.*

⑮ The **Musée des Beaux-Arts** *(Fine Arts Museum)* has now been beautifully restored by architect Jean-Michel Wilmotte. Centerpieces of this early-20th-century building are the skylighted atrium and a vast ancient Roman mosaic of a marriage ceremony that provides intriguing insights into the Roman aristocratic lifestyle. Exhibitions (such as the seven paintings devoted to Cleopatra by Nîmes-born painter Natoire) offer fascinating glimpses into history, but it is the varied collection of Italian, Flemish, and French paintings (notably Rubens's *Portrait of a Monk*) that is the particularly interesting mainstay of

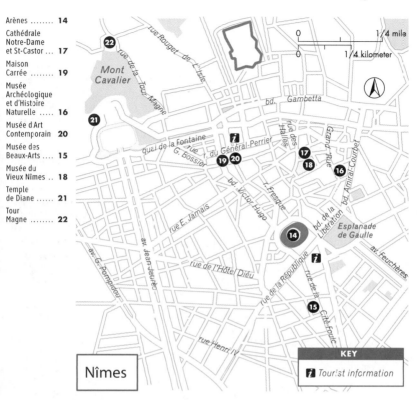

the collection. ⊠ *Rue de la Cité-Foulc* 🕾 *04–66–67–38–21* 💳 *€4.60*
🕙 *Tues.–Sun. 10–6.*

⑯ The **Musée Archéologique et d'Histoire Naturelle** *(Museum of Archaeology and Natural History)* is housed in an old Jesuit college and has a
wonderful collection of local archaeological finds, including sarcophagi
and beautiful pieces of Roman glass. A treasure trove of statues, busts,
friezes, tools, coins, and pottery complete the collection. ⊠ *Bd. de
l'Admiral-Courbet* 🕾 *04–66–76–74–80* 💳 *Free* 🕙 *Tues.–Sun. 10–6.*

Destroyed and rebuilt in several stages, with particular damage by rampaging Protestants who slaughtered eight priests from the neighboring
⑰ évêché, the **Cathédrale Notre-Dame et St-Castor** (⊠ *Pl. aux Herbes*) still
shows traces of its original construction in 1096. A remarkably preserved Romanesque frieze portrays Adam and Eve cowering in shame,
the gory slaughter of Abel, and a flood-wearied Noah. Inside, look for
the 4th-century sarcophagus (third chapel on the right) and a magnificent 17th-century chapel (in the apse).

⑱ The **Musée du Vieux Nîmes** *(Museum of Old Nîmes)*, in the 17th-century
bishop's palace opposite the cathedral, has embroidered garments in
exotic and vibrant displays. Look for the 14th-century jacket made of
blue serge de Nîmes, the famous fabric from which Levi-Strauss first

fashioned blue jeans. ⊠*Pl. aux Herbes* ☎*04–66–76–73–70* ⊡*Free* ⊙*Tues.–Sun. 10–6.*

★ ⑲ Lovely and forlorn in the middle of a busy downtown square, the exquisitely preserved **Maison Carrée** *(Square House)* strikes a timeless balance between symmetry and whimsy, purity of line and richness of decor. Modeled on the Temple to Apollo in Rome, adorned with magnificent marble columns and elegant pediment, it remains one of the most noble surviving structures of ancient Roman civilization anywhere. Built around 5 BC and dedicated to Caius Caesar and his grandson Lucius, it has survived subsequent use as a medieval meeting hall, an Augustine church, a storehouse for Revolutionary archives, and a horse shed. Temporary art and photo exhibitions are held here, and there's a display of photos and drawings of ongoing archaeological work. Most notably, there's a splendid ancient Roman fresco of Cassandra (being dragged by her hair by a hunter) that was discovered in 1992 and has been carefully restored. As lovely as it is inside, however, the building's center of town location has incurred some serious traffic pollution, and, sadly, the facade could do with a cleanup. ⊠*Bd. Victor-Hugo* ☎*04–66–36–26–76* ⊕*www.culturespaces. com* ⊡*€4.50; joint ticket to Arènes, Tour Magne, €9.50* ⊙*Apr., May, and Sept., daily 9–6; Oct.–Nov., daily 9–5:30, Dec.–Mar., daily 9–4:30.*

The glass-fronted Carré d'Art (directly opposite the Maison Carrée) was designed by British architect Sir Norman Foster as its neighbor's stark contemporary mirror: it literally reflects the Maison Carrée's creamy symmetry and figuratively answers it with a featherlight deconstructed colonnade. Homages aside, it resembles an airport terminal. It now ⑳ houses the **Musée d'Art Contemporain** *(Contemporary Art Museum)*, featuring art from 1960 onward by artists such as Arman, and temporary exhibitions of newer works by artists like Javier Perez. The chic café on the top floor serves good coffee and has great views—stop here before heading off to the public library section, which has a great collection of old manuscripts. ⊠*Pl. de la Maison Carrée* ☎*04–66–76–35–70* ⊕*www.musees.nimes.fr* ⊡*€4.90* ⊙*Tues.–Sun. 10–6.*

㉑ The shattered Roman ruin known as the **Temple de Diane** *(Temple of Diana)* dates from the 2nd century BC. The temple's function is unknown, though it's thought to have been part of a larger Roman complex that is still unexcavated. In the Middle Ages Benedictine nuns occupied the building before it was converted into a church. Destruction came during the Wars of Religion.

㉒ The **Tour Magne** *(Magne Tower)*, at the far end of the Jardin de la Fontaine, is all that remains of a tower the emperor Augustus had built on Gallic foundations; it was probably used as a lookout post. Despite a loss of 30 feet in height over the course of time, it still provides fine views of Nîmes for anyone energetic enough to climb the 140 steps. ⊠*Quai de la Fontaine* ☎*04–66–67–65–56* ⊡*Tour Magne €2.70, joint ticket to Arènes, Maison Carrée, €9.50* ⊙*Apr., May, and Sept., daily 9–6; Oct. and Nov., daily 9–5:30, Dec.–Mar., daily 9–4:30.*

WHERE TO STAY & EAT

$$$-$$$$ ✕ **Alexandre.** Rising star chef Michel Kayser adds a personal touch to local specialties at this *à la mode* modern restaurant. Wild Camargue rice soufflé with shellfish, lemon pulp, and local olive oil, or rich bull steak roasted in its own juice served with panfried mashed potatoes and anchovy *beignets* are headliners, but the menu changes by the season and by the chef's creative whimsy. Decor is elegantly spare with a bent for luscious purples, burnt siennas, stone walls, and large bay windows. The gardens are extensive, and often stray apricots and peaches plucked from the overhanging branches will appear on your plate, magically transformed into some delicious goody. ✉ *2 rue Xavier Tronc* ☎ *04–66–70–08–99* ⊕ *www.michelkayser.com* ⌖ *Reservations essential* ▭ *AE, DC, MC, V* ⊗ *Closed Mon., and no lunch Wed. and Sun. in Sept.–June Closed Sun. and Mon. in July–Aug.*

$$$-$$$$ ✕ **Magister.** Garnering a reputation for top, perfectly executed cooking, this high-end hot spot is a must. The wine list is filled with good local vintage choices; the service is smooth, and the atmosphere warm. Highlights include the stuffed pigeon or the lamb braised in red wine and mint. ✉ *5 rue Nationale* ☎ *04–66–76–11–00* ▭ *AE, MC, V* ⊗ *No dinner Sun.*

$$-$$$ ✕ **Le Jardin d'Hadrien.** This chic enclave, with its quarried white stone, ancient plank-and-beam ceiling, and open fireplace, would be a culinary haven even without its lovely hidden garden, a shady retreat for summer meals. Fresh cod crisped in salt and olive oil, zucchini flowers filled with *brandade* (the creamy, light paste of salt cod and olive oil), and a frozen parfait perfumed with licorice all show chef Alain Vinouze's subtle skills. Prix-fixe menus are €18 and €28. ✉ *11 rue Enclos Rey* ☎ *04–66–22–07–01* ⌖ *Reservations essential* ▭ *AE, MC, V* ⊗ *Closed Wed. No dinner Tues. Closed Sun. and no lunch Mon. in July and Aug.*

$$-$$$ 🏨 **New Hotel La Baume.** In the heart of scruffy Vieux Nîmes, this noble 17th-century *hôtel particulier* has been reincarnated as a stylish hotel with an architect's eye for mixing ancient detail with modern design. The balustraded stone staircase is a protected historic monument, and stenciled beamed ceilings, cross vaults, and archways counterbalance hot ocher tones, swags of raw cotton, leather, and halogen lighting. ✉ *21 rue Nationale, 30000* ☎ *04–66–76–28–42* 🖷 *04–66–76–28–45* ⊕ *www. new-hotel.com* ⇆ *34 rooms* ⌕ *In-room: dial-up, refrigerator. In-hotel: parking (fee), some pets allowed (fee)* ▭ *AE, DC, MC, V* ⧯*CP.*

SHOPPING

In Nîmes's *Vieille Ville* you can find the expected rash of chain stores mixed with fabulous interior-design boutiques and fabric shops selling the Provençal cottons that used to be produced here en masse (Les Indiennes de Nîmes, Les Olivades, Souleiado). Antiques and collectibles are found in tiny shops throughout the city's backstreets, but there's a concentration of them in the Old Town. The fashionable shopper may want to check out Nîmes-founded Fashion group **Cacharel** (✉ *2 pl. de la Maison Carrée* ☎ *04–66–21–82–82*). The only commercial maker of authentic brandade, Nîmes's signature salt-cod-and-olive-oil paste, is **Raymond** (✉ *24 rue Nationale* ☎ *04–66–67–20–47*). It's paddled fresh into a plastic carton or sold in sealed jars so you can take it home.

10

L'Huilerie (✉ *10 rue des Marchands* ☎*04–66–67–37–24*) is a delightful treasure house of teas and spices that shows off great gift ideas, including smartly packaged mustards, honeys, and olive oils.

THE ALPILLES

The low mountain range called the Alpilles (pronounced ahl-*pee*-yuh) forms a rough-hewn, rocky landscape that rises into nearly barren limestone hills, the surrounding fields silvered with ranks of twisted olive trees and alleys of gnarled *amandiers* (almond trees). There are superb antiquities in St-Rémy and feudal ruins in Les Baux.

ABBAYE DE MONTMAJOUR

㉓   *35 km (20 mi) southeast of Nîmes, 5 km (3 mi) northeast of Arles*

This magnificent Romanesque abbey looming over the marshlands north of Arles stands in partial ruin. Begun in the 12th century by a handful of Benedictine monks, it grew according to an ambitious plan of church, crypt, and cloister. Under the management of corrupt lay monks in the 17th century, it grew more sumptuous; when those lay monks were ejected by the Church, they sacked the place. After the Revolution it was sold to a junkman, and he tried to pay the mortgage by stripping off and selling its goods. A 19th-century medieval revival spurred its partial restoration, but its 18th-century portions are still in ruins. Ironically, because of this mercenary history, what remains is a spare and beautiful piece of Romanesque architecture. The **cloister** rivals that of St-Trophime in Arles for its balance, elegance, and air of mystical peace: Van Gogh was drawn to its womblike isolation and came often to the abbey to paint and reflect. The interior, renovated by Rudi Ricciotti, is now used for temporary art exhibitions. ☎*04–90–54–64–17* ✑*€6.50* ⊙*Apr.–Sept., daily 9–6:30; Oct.–Mar., Wed.–Mon. 10–1 and 2–5.*

LES BAUX-DE-PROVENCE

★ **㉔**   *17 km (10 mi) west of Montmajour, 18 km (11 mi) northeast of Arles, 29 km (18 mi) south of Avignon.*

When you first search the craggy hilltops for signs of Les Baux-de-Provence (pronounced lay-*bo*), you may not quite be able to distinguish between bedrock and building, so naturally does the ragged skyline of towers and crenellations blend into the sawtooth jags of stone. This tiny château-village ranks as one of the most visited tourist sites in France with its natural scenery and medieval buildings of astonishing beauty. From this intimidating vantage point, the lords of Les Baux ruled throughout the 11th and 12th centuries over one of the largest fiefdoms in the south. In the 19th century Les Baux found new purpose: the mineral bauxite, valued as an alloy in aluminum production, was discovered in its hills and named for its source. A profitable industry sprang up that lasted into the 20th century before fading into history.

Today Les Baux offers two faces to the world: its beautifully preserved medieval village and the ghostly ruins of its fortress, once referred to as the *ville morte* (dead town). In the village, lovely 12th-century stone houses, even their window frames still intact, shelter the shops, cafés, and galleries that line the steep cobbled streets. At the edge of the village is a cliff that offers up a stunning view over the Val d'Enfer (Hell's Valley) said to have inspired Dante's *Inferno*. Farther along is the **Cathédrale d'Images** (⊠ *Val d'Enfer, petite route de Mailliane* 🕾 *04–90-54-38-65* 🎫*€7.50* 🕑*Mar., daily 10–6, Apr.–Sept., daily 10–7; Oct.–mid-Jan, daily 10–6*). The setting is a vast old bauxite quarry, with 66-foot-high stone walls, which makes a dramatic setting for the thousands of images projected onto its walls.

Up above, the 17-acre cliff-top sprawl of ruins is contained under the umbrella name the **Château des Baux.** At the entry, the Tour du Brau contains the **Musée d'Histoire des Baux,** a small collection of relics and models. Its exit gives access to the wide and varied grounds, where Romanesque chapels and towers mingle with skeletal ruins. The tiny **Chapelle St-Blaise** shelters a permanent music-and-slide show called "*Van Gogh, Gauguin, Cézanne au Pays de l'Olivier*," which features artworks depicting olive orchards in their infinite variety. In July and August there are fascinating medieval exhibitions: people dressed up in authentic costumes, displays of medieval crafts, and even a few jousting tournaments with handsome knights carrying fluttering silk tokens of their beloved ladies. 🕾*04–90-54-55-56* ⊕*www.chateau-baux-provence.com* 🎫*€7.50 with audioguide* 🕑*Mar.–May, Sept., and Oct., daily 9–6:30; June–Aug., daily 9–8; Nov. and Feb., daily 9–6; Dec. and Jan., daily 9–5.*

WHERE TO STAY & EAT

$$$$

Fodor'sChoice ★

✕🔲 **L'Oustau de la Baumanière.** Sheltered by rocky cliffs below the village of Les Baux, this long-famous hotel, with its formal landscaped terrace and broad swimming pool, has a guest book studded with names like Winston Churchill, Elizabeth Taylor, and Pablo Picasso. The interior is luxe-Provençal chic, thanks to tile floors, arched stone ceilings, and brocaded settees done up in Canovas and Halard fabrics. Guest rooms—breezy, private, and beautifully furnished with antiques—have a contemporary flair, but the basic style remains archetypal Baux. These rooms are set in three buildings on broad landscaped grounds; the best are in the enchanting Le Manoir. As for the famed Baumanière restaurant (reservations essential), chef Jean-André Charial's hallowed reputation continues to attract culinary pilgrims (too many, it would appear from the noisy crowds that drive up the nearby road to the hotel). You can't blame them: the Oustau legacy is a veritable museum of Provençal tradition, but one that has been given a nouvelle face-lift—lobster cooked in Châteauneuf-du-Pape and set on a bed of polenta is a typical dazzler. Note that from November through December and in March the restaurant is closed Wednesday and doesn't serve lunch Thursday; during January and February both the hotel and restaurant are closed. ⊠*13520 Les-Baux-de-Provence* 🕾*04–90-54-33-07* 🖨*04–90-54-40-46* ⊕*www.oustaudebaumaniere.com* 🛏*15 rooms, 12 suites* ♿*In-room: Wi-Fi,*

10

refrigerator. In-hotel: restaurant, tennis courts, pool, some pets allowed (fee) ☰AE, DC, MC, V ⊘*Closed Jan. and Feb.* ℺⼁MAP.

$–$$ ✕⼁ **La Reine Jeanne.** At this modest inn majestically placed right at the entrance to the village, you can stand on balconies and look over rugged valley views worthy of the château up the street. Rooms are small, simple, and—despite the white vinyl–padded furniture— lovingly decorated. Reserve in advance for one of the two rooms with a balcony, though even one of the tiny interior rooms gives you the chance to spend an evening in Les Baux after the tourists have drained away. Good home-style cooking is served in the restaurant, which has views both from inside and outside on the pretty terrace. ✉*Grande Rue Baux, 13520* ☏*04–90–54–32–06* ⎙*04–90–54–32–33* ⊕*www.la-reinejeanne.com* ⇌*9 rooms* &*In-room: dial-up. In-hotel: restaurant, some pets allowed* ☰*MC, V* ⊘*Closed mid-Nov.–Dec. and mid–Jan.–1st wk of Feb.*

> ### A BUDGET BAUMANIÈRE
>
> You can try a less expensive, though still stylish, Oustau experience a km (½ mi) away at La Cabro d'Or (☏04–90–54–33–21 or 04–90–54–45–98 ⊕www.lacabrodor.com). Run by the same owners, it's cheaper (€170–€240), more rustic, more private, and don't be surprised to see a billy goat wander by your room window. It'sclosed November–mid-December.

ST-RÉMY-DE-PROVENCE

㉕
Fodor'sChoice
★

8 km (5 mi) north of Les Baux, 24 km (15 mi) east of Arles, 19 km (12 mi) south of Avignon.

There are other towns as pretty as St-Rémy-de-Provence, and others in more dramatic or picturesque settings. Ruins can be found throughout the south, and so can authentic village life. Yet something felicitous has happened in this market town in the heart of the Alpilles—a steady infusion of style, of art, of imagination—all brought by people with a respect for local traditions and a love of Provençal ways. Here, more than anywhere, you can meditate quietly on antiquity, browse redolent markets with basket in hand, peer down the very row of plane trees you remember from a Van Gogh, and also enjoy urbane galleries, cosmopolitan shops, and specialty food boutiques. An abundance of chic choices in restaurants, mas, and even châteaux awaits you; the almond and olive groves conceal dozens of stone-and-terra-cotta gîtes, many with pools. In short, St-Rémy has been gentrified through and through, and is now a sort of arid, southern Martha's Vineyard or, perhaps, the Hamptons of Provence.

First established by an indigenous Celtic-Ligurian people who worshiped the god Glan, the village Glanum was adopted and gentrified by the Greeks of Marseille in the 2nd and 3rd centuries BC. Under the Pax Romana there developed a veritable city, with temples and forum, luxurious villas, and baths. The Romans (and Glanum) eventually fell, but a village grew up next to their ruins, taking its name from their protectorate, the Abbey St-Remi, which was based in Reims. St-Rémy de Provence grew to be an important market town, and wealthy families built fine mansions in its center—among them the de Sade family (whose black-sheep relation held forth in the Lubéron at Lacoste). Another famous native son was the eccentric doctor, scholar, and astrologer Michel Nostradamus (1503–66), who is credited by some as having predicted much of the modern age. Perhaps the best known of St-Rémy's residents was the ill-fated Vincent van Gogh. Shipped unceremoniously out of Arles at the height of his madness (and creativity), he committed himself to the asylum St-Paul-de-Mausolée.

A visit to St-Rémy should start from the outskirts inward. To visit Glanum you must park in a dusty roadside lot on D5 south of town (toward Les Baux).

But before crossing, you'll be confronted with two of the most miraculously preserved classical monuments in France, simply called **Les Antiques.** Dating from 30 BC, the **Mausolée** (mausoleum), a wedding-cake stack of arches and columns, lacks nothing but its finial on top, yet it's dedicated to a Julian (as in Julius Caesar), probably Caesar Augustus. A few yards away stands another marvel: the **Arc Triomphal,** dating from AD 20.

Across the street from Les Antiques and set back from D5, a slick visitor center prepares you for entry into the ancient village of **Glanum** with scale models of the site in its various heydays. A good map and an English brochure guide you stone by stone through the maze of foundations, walls, towers, and columns that spread across a broad field; helpfully, Greek sites are noted by numbers, Roman ones by letters. ⊠ *Off D5, direction Les Baux* ☎ *04–90–92–23–79* ⊠ *€6.10; €7.50 includes entry to Hôtel de Sade* ⊙ *Apr.–Sept., daily 9–7; Oct.–Mar., daily 10:30–noon and 2–5.*

★ You can cut across the fields from Glanum to **St-Paul-de-Mausolée,** the lovely, isolated asylum where Van Gogh spent the last year of his life (1889–90). But enter it quietly: it shelters psychiatric patients to this day—all of them women. You're free to walk up the beautifully manicured garden path to the church and its jewel-box Romanesque **cloister,** where the artist found womblike peace. ⊠ *Rte. des Baux; next to Glanum, off D5, direction Les Baux* ☎ *04–90–92–77–00* ⊠ *€3.80* ⊙ *Apr.–Oct., daily 9:30–7; Nov.–Mar., daily 10:15–4:45.*

Within St-Rémy's fast-moving traffic loop, a labyrinth of narrow streets leads you away from the action and into the slow-moving inner sanctum of the **Vieille Ville.** Here trendy, high-end shops mingle pleasantly with local life, and the buildings, if gentrified, blend in unobtrusively.

Make your way to the **Hôtel de Sade,** a 15th- and 16th-century private manor now housing the treasures unearthed from the ruins of Glanum. The de Sade family built the house around remains of 4th-century baths and a 5th-century baptistery, now nestled in its courtyard. At this writing, it was closed indefinitely for restoration; call for details. ⊠ *Rue du Parage* ☎ *04–90–92–64–04.*

10

WHERE TO STAY & EAT

★ $$–$$$$ ✕ **L'Assiette de Marie.** Marie Ricco is a collector, and she's turned her tiny restaurant into a bower of attic treasures. Seated at an old school desk, you choose from the day's specials, all made with Marie's Corsican-Italian touch—marinated vegetables with tapenade, a cast-iron casserole of superb pasta, and satiny *panetone* (flan). ⊠*1 rue Jaume Roux* ☎*04–90–92–32–14* ♨*Reservations essential* ▤*MC, V* ⊘*Closed Thurs., and Nov.–Mar.*

$$–$$$$ ✕ **La Gousse d'Ail.** It may have moved to larger premises around the corner, but thankfully, this intimate, indoor Vieille Ville hideaway and family-run bistro remains fundamentally the same. It continues to live up to its name (the Garlic Clove), serving robust, highly flavored southern dishes in hearty portions. Try the house specialties: grilled bull steak with creamed garlic or a powerful garlic-almond pesto. Aim for Wednesday night, when there's Gypsy music and jazz. ⊠*6 bd. Marceau* ☎*04–90–92–16–87* ▤*AE, DC, MC, V* ⊘*Closed mid-Nov.–mid-Mar. No lunch Thurs. and Sat.*

$$–$$$$ ✕ **La Maison Jaune.** This modern retreat in the Vieille Ville draws crowds of summer people to its pretty roof terrace, with accents of sober stone and lively contemporary furniture both indoors and out. The look reflects the cuisine: with vivid flavors and a cool, contained touch, chef François Perraud prepares grilled sardines with crunchy fennel and lemon confit, and veal lightly flavored with olives, capers, and celery. ⊠*15 rue Carnot* ☎*04–90–92–56–14* ♨*Reservations essential* ▤*MC, V* ⊘*Closed Mon., and Jan. and Feb. No dinner Sun. No lunch Tues.*

$$$–$$$$ ✕▥ **Bistrot d'Eygalières.** Belgian chef Wout Bru's understated restaurant in nearby Eygalières is quickly gaining a reputation (and stars) for its
Fodor'sChoice ★   elegant, light, and subtly balanced cuisine, like sole with goat cheese, lobster salad with candied tomatoes, and foie-gras carpaccio with summer truffles. The wine list is both eclectic and thorough, though prices are a bit on the high side. Guest rooms are very chic, very comfortable; Wout's wife, Suzy, has a wonderful eye and a welcoming disposition. Book well ahead. ⊠*Rue de la République,10 km (6 mi) southeast of St-Rémy-de-Provence on D99 then D24, 13810* Eygalières ☎*04–90–90–60–34* ☐*04–90–90–60–37* ⊕*www.chezbru.com* ♨*Reservations essential* ⋙*2 rooms, 2 suites* ♿*In-room: Wi-Fi, refrigerator. In-hotel: restaurant, some pets allowed, no elevator* ▤*AE, MC, V* ⊘*Closed mid-Nov.–mid-Mar. Restaurant closed Mon. No dinner Sun. in Oct. and Nov. No lunch Tues. in May–Sept.*

$$$–$$$$ ✕▥ **Domaine de Valmouriane.** In this genteel mas-cum-resort, peacefully isolated within a broad park, overstuffed English-country furniture mixes cozily with cool Provençal stone and timber. The grounds are impressive, with picture-perfect cypress trees; inside, much has been restored, so all is comfort and ease, if not the height of authenticity. The restaurant offers up fresh game, herbs from the garden, seafood, local oils, and truffles, but it's the personal welcome from Philippe and Martin Capel that makes you feel like an honored guest. The pool, surrounded by a slate walk and delightful gardens, is most inviting. ⊠*Petite rte. des Baux, D27, 13210* ☎*04–90–92–44–62* ☐*04–90–92–37–32* ⊕*www. valmouriane.com* ⋙*13 rooms* ♿*In-room: dial-up. In-hotel: restaurant,*

tennis court, pool, parking (no fee), some pets allowed (fee) =AE, DC, MC, V ☻*Closed mid-Nov.–mid–Dec.* ¶O¶*FAP, MAP.*

$$$–$$$$ 🖬 **Mas de Cornud.** An American stewards the wine cellar and an Egyptian runs the kitchen, but the attitude is pure Provence: David and Nito Carpita have turned their fairly severe, stone, black-shuttered farmhouse just outside St-Rémy, into a B&B filled with French country furniture and objects from around the world. The welcome is so sincere you'll feel like one of the family in no time. Table d'hôte dinners, cooking classes, and tours can be arranged. Breakfast is included and the minimum stay is two nights. ⊠*Rte. de Mas-Blanc, 13210* ☎*04–90–92–39–32* 📠*04–90–92–55–99* ⊕*www.mascornud.com* ⛌*5 rooms, 1 suite* ⚘*In-room: no a/c, dial-up. In-hotel: restaurant, pool, parking (no fee), some pets allowed (fee), no elevator* =*No credit cards* ☻*Closed Jan. and Feb.* ¶O¶*BP, MAP.*

★ $$–$$$ 🖬 **Mas des Carassins.** A textbook example of a Provençal mas, this rambling 19th-century farmhouse is done with an impressive amount of style. Guest rooms have stonework walls and wrought-iron canopy beds but you may wish to sleep under the stars because the mas is beautifully surrounded with thyme bushes, pots of lemon and orange trees, fountains, pools, and centuries-old olive trees. *Bien sûr,* you'll want to enjoy the copious lunch outside at a shady and intimate table. Breakfast is included in the price. ⊠*1 chemin Gaulois, 13810* ☎*04–90–92–15–48* 📠*04–90–92–63–47* ⊕*www.hoteldescarassins.com* ⛌*14 rooms* ⚘*In room: Wi-Fi, refrigerator. In-hotel: restaurant, pool, parking, some pets allowed (fee)* =*MC, V* ☻*Closed Jan. and Feb.* ¶O¶*BP.*

★ $–$$ 🖬 **Château de Roussan.** In a majestic park shaded by ancient plane trees, this yellow-stone 18th-century château (once the property of Nostradamus's brother) is a helter-skelter of brocantes (antiques) and bric-a-brac, and the bathrooms have an afterthought air about them. Cats outnumber the staff. Yet if you're the right sort for this place—backpackers, romantic couples on a budget, lovers of atmosphere over luxury—you can blossom in this three-dimensional costume-drama scene. Meal plans are available with a two-night minimum stay. ⊠*D99, rte. de Tarascon, 13210* ☎*04–90–92–11–63* 📠*04–90–92–50–59* ⊕*www.chateau-de-roussan.com* ⛌*19 rooms* ⚘*In-room: dial-up. In-hotel: restaurant, some pets allowed (fee), parking, no elevator* =AE, DC, MC, V ¶O¶*MAP.*

SHOPPING

Every Wednesday morning St-Rémy hosts one of the most popular **markets** in Provence, during which Place de la République and narrow Vieille Ville streets overflow with fresh produce and herbs, as well as fabrics and brocantes (antiques). With all the summer people, it's little wonder that food shops and *traiteurs* (take-out caterers) do the biggest business in St-Rémy. Olive oils are sold like fine old wines, and the breads heaped in boulangerie windows are as knobby and rough-hewn as they should be. The best food shops are concentrated in the Vieille Ville. Local goat cheeses are displayed like jewels and wrapped like fine pastries at **La Cave aux Fromages** (⊠*1 pl. Joseph-Hilaire* ☎*04–90–92–32–45*). At **Chocolaterie Joel Durand** (⊠*3 bd. Victor-Hugo* ☎*04–90–92–38–25*), the chocolates are numbered to indicate the various flavors, from rose petal to Camargue saffron.

10

AVIGNON & THE VAUCLUSE

Anchored by the magnificent papal stronghold of Avignon, the Vaucluse spreads luxuriantly east of the Rhône. Its famous vineyards—Gigondas, Vacqueyras, Beaumes-de-Venise—seduce connoisseurs, and its Roman ruins in Orange and Vaison-la-Romaine draw scholars and arts lovers. Arid lowlands with orchards of olives, apricots, and almonds give way to a rich and wild mountain terrain around the formidable Mont Ventoux and flow into the primeval Luberon, made a household name by Peter Mayle. The hill villages around the Luberon—Gordes, Roussillon, Oppède, Bonnieux—are as lovely as any you'll find in the south of France.

AVIGNON

82 km (51 mi) northwest of Aix-en-Provence, 95 km (59 mi) northwest of Marseille, 224 km (140 mi) south of Lyon.

GETTING HERE

Taxi Radio Avignonnais (⊠Pl. Pie ☎ 04-90-82-20-20) is the easiest way to get into town. The main bus station is on Avenue Monteclar (☎04-90-82-07-35) next to the train station. Buses run to and from Avignon, Arles (45 mins, €6), Carpentras (45 mins, €4), Cavaillon (1 hr, €4), Nîmes (1½ hrs, €9), or farther afield to Orange, Isle sur la Sorgue, Marseille, Nice, and Cannes. There are a number of different bus agencies, try: Autocars Barlatier (☎04-90-38-15-58), Autocars Sumian (☎04-90-71-03-00), Cars Lieutaud (☎04-90-86-36-75), Les Express de la Durance (☎04-90-71-03-00), or Voyages Arnaud (☎04-90-38-15-58). Town buses and services to the TGV station are run by TCRA (☎04-32-74-18-32 ⊕ www.tcra.fr). Avignon is at the junction of the Paris–Marseille and Paris–Montpellier lines. The Gare Centre Ville has frequent links to Arles, Nîmes, Orange, Toulon, and Carcassonne. The Gare TGV (☎08-92-35-35-35 ⊕www.tgv.com) is 4 km (2½ mi) south of Avignon. Train information can be found at www.voyages-sncf.com, or call 08-36-35-35-35. A bus service leaves from the station at the arrival of each train and takes passengers to the Centre Ville station, and leaves from the Centre Ville station to the TGV station every 15 minutes.

EXPLORING

Avignon is anything but a museum; it surges with modern ideas and energy and thrives within its ramparts as it did in the heyday of the popes—and, like those radical church lords, it's sensual, cultivated, and cosmopolitan, with a taste for worldly pleasures. Avignon remained papal property until 1791, and elegant mansions bear witness to the

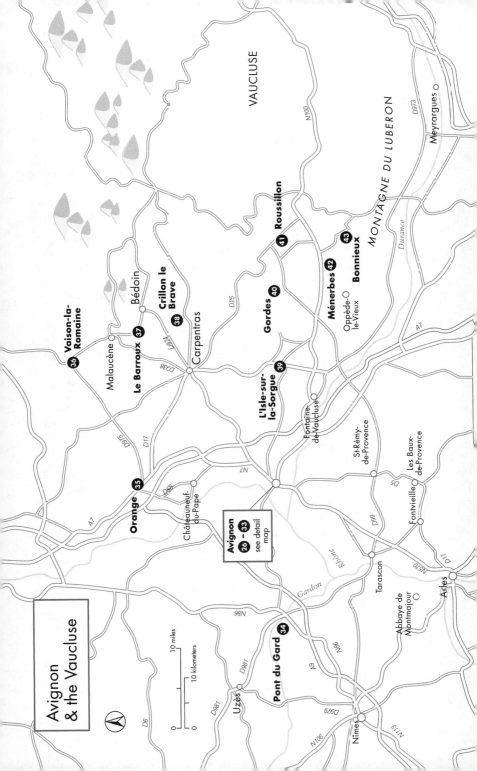

Avignon & the Vaucluse

VAUCLUSE

MONTAGNE DU LUBERON

36 Vaison-la-Romaine

37 Le Barroux

38 Crillon le Brave

Bédoin

Malaucène

Carpentras

D974

D938

D17

D25

D975

35 Orange

Châteauneuf-du-Pape

A7

D68

N7

40 Gordes

41 Roussillon

42 Ménerbes

43 Bonnieux

Oppède-le-Vieux

39 L'Isle-sur-la-Sorgue

Fontaine-de-Vaucluse

N100

Durance

D973

Meyrargues

A7

St-Rémy-de-Provence

Fontvieille

Les Baux-de-Provence

D5

D99

D570

D17

Tarascon

Arles

Rhône

Gardon

Avignon
26 – 33
see detail map

34 Pont du Gard

N86

Abbaye de Montmajour

Uzès

D981

D981

D981

D6

N86

A9

D979

Nîmes

N113

N106

Rhône

10 miles

10 kilometers

0

0

town's 18th-century prosperity. From its famous Palais des Papes (Papal Palace), where seven exiled popes camped between 1309 and 1377 after fleeing from the corruption and civil strife of Rome, to the long, low bridge of childhood-song fame stretching over the river, you can beam yourself briefly into 14th-century Avignon, so complete is the context, so evocative the setting.

★ ❷ The colossal **Palais des Papes** creates a disconcertingly fortresslike impression, underlined by the austerity of its interior. Most of the original furnishings were returned to Rome with the papacy, others were lost during the French Revolution. Some imagination is required to picture its earlier medieval splendor, awash with color and with worldly clerics enjoying what the 14th-century Italian poet Petrarch called "licentious banquets." On close inspection, two different styles of building emerge at the palace: the severe **Palais Vieux** (Old Palace), built between 1334 and 1342 by Pope Benedict XII, a member of the Cistercian order, which frowned on frivolity, and the more decorative **Palais Nouveau** (New Palace), built in the following decade by the artsy, lavish-living Pope Clement VI. The Great Court, entryway to the complex, links the two.

The main rooms of the Palais Vieux are the **Consistory** (Council Hall), decorated with some excellent 14th-century frescoes by Simone Martini; the **Chapelle St-Jean** (original frescoes by Matteo Giovanetti); the **Grand Tinel,** or Salle des Festins (Feast Hall), with a majestic vaulted roof and a series of 18th-century Gobelin tapestries; the **Chapelle St-Martial** (more Giovanetti frescoes); and the **Chambre du Cerf,** with a richly decorated ceiling, murals featuring a stag hunt, and a delightful view of Avignon. The principal attractions of the Palais Nouveau are the **Grande Audience,** a magnificent two-nave hall on the ground floor, and, upstairs, the **Chapelle Clémentine,** where the college of cardinals once gathered to elect the new pope. ⊠ *Pl. du Palais* ☎ *04–90–27–50–00* ⊕ *www.palais-des-papes.com* ☖ *€9.50 entry includes choice of guided tour or individual audioguide; €11.50 includes audioguided tour to pont St-Bénézet* ⊙ *Oct.–Mar., daily 9:30–5:45; Apr.–Nov., daily 9–8; July, during theater festival, daily 9–9.*

❷ The **Cathédrale Notre-Dame-des-Doms,** first built in a pure Provençal Romanesque style in the 12th century, was quickly dwarfed by the extravagant palace that rose beside it. It rallied in the 14th century with the addition of a cupola—which promptly collapsed. As rebuilt in 1425, it's a marvel of stacked arches with a strong Byzantine flavor and is topped nowadays with a gargantuan Virgin Mary lantern—a 19th-century afterthought—whose glow can be seen for miles around. ⊠ *Pl. du Palais* ☎ *04–90–86–81–01* ⊙ *Mon.–Sat. 8–6, Sun. 9–7.*

❷ The **Petit Palais**—the former residence of bishops and cardinals before Pope Benedict built his majestic palace—has a large collection of oldmaster paintings. The majority are Italian works from the early-Renaissance schools of Siena, Florence, and Venice—styles with which the Avignon popes would have been familiar. Later key works to seek out include Sandro Botticelli's *Virgin and Child* and Venetian paintings by Vittore

Carpaccio and Giovanni Bellini. ⌂*Pl. du Palais* ☎*04–90–86–44–58* ⊕*www.petit-palais.org* 🎫*€6* ⊙*Oct.–May, Wed.–Mon. 9:30–1 and 2–5:30; June–Sept., Wed.–Mon. 10–1 and 2–6.*

★ ㉙ The **Pont St-Bénézet** *(St. Bénézet Bridge)* is the subject of the famous children's song: *"Sur le pont d'Avignon on y danse, on y danse..."* ("On the bridge of Avignon one dances, one dances..."). Unlike London Bridge, this one still stretches its arches across the river, but only partway: half was washed away in the 17th century. Its first stones allegedly laid with the miraculous strength granted St-Bénézet in the 12th century, it once reached all the way to Villeneuve. ⌂*Port du Rochre* ⊕*www.avignon-tourisme.com* 🎫*€3* ⊙*Apr.–Oct., daily 9–8; Nov.–Mar., daily 9–5:45.*

㉚ From the entrance to the Pont St-Bénézet, walk along the ramparts to a spiral staircase leading to the hilltop garden known as **Rocher des Doms**

Fodor'sChoice *(Rock of the Domes)*. Set with grand Mediterranean pines, this park on
★ a bluff above town offers extraordinary views of the palace, the rooftops of Old Avignon, the Pont St-Bénézet, and formidable Villeneuve across the Rhône. On the horizon loom Mont Ventoux, the Luberon, and Les Alpilles. Often called the "cradle of Avignon," the rock's grottoes were among the first human habitations in the area. Today, the park also has a fake lake, home to some swans. ⌂*Montée du Moulin off pl. du Palais* ⊕*www.avignon-et-provence.com.*

㉛ The **Place de l'Horloge** *(Clock Square)* is the social nerve center of Avignon, where the concentration of bistros, brasseries, and restaurants draws swarms of locals to the shade of its plane trees.

㉜ Housed in a pretty little Jesuit chapel on the main shopping street, the **Musée Lapidaire** gathers a collection of classical sculpture and stonework from Gallo-Roman times, as well as pieces from the Musée Calvet's collection of Greek and Etruscan works. There's a notable depiction of *Tarasque of Noves*—the man-eating monster immortalized by Alphonse Daudet—but most items are haphazardly labeled and insouciantly scattered throughout the noble chapel, itself slightly crumbling but awash with light. ⌂*27 rue de la République* ☎*04–90–85–75–38* 🎫*€2* ⊙*Wed.–Mon. 10–1 and 2–6.*

㉝ Worth a visit for the beauty and balance of its architecture alone, the fine old **Musée Calvet** contains a rich collection of antiquities and classically inspired works. Acquisitions include Neoclassical and Romantic and are almost entirely French, including works by Manet, Daumier, and David. The main building itself is a Palladian-style jewel in pale Gard stone dating from the 1740s; the garden is so lovely that it may distract you from the paintings. ⌂*65 rue Joseph-Vernet* ☎*04–90–86–33–84* 🎫*€6* ⊙*Wed.–Mon. 10–1 and 2–6.*

WHERE TO STAY & EAT

$$–$$$$ ✕ **Brunel.** Stylishly decorated in a hip, contemporary retro-bistro style with urbane shades of gray (look for the Philippe Starck chairs), this Avignon favorite entices with the passionate Provençal cooking of Avignon-born and -bred chef Roger Brunel. This is down-home bistro

10

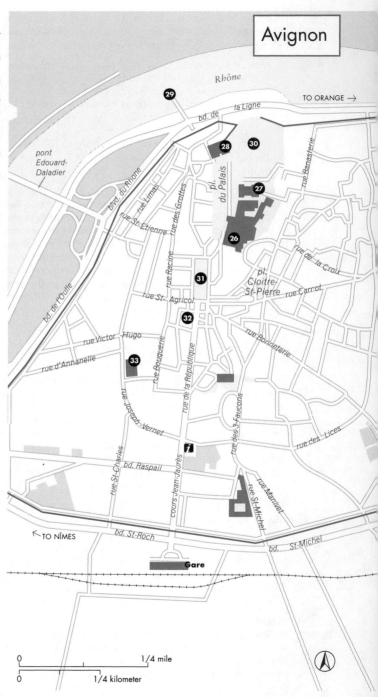

Avignon

fare based on a sophisticated larder: parchment-wrapped mullet with eggplant, peppers, and tomatoes; pigeon roasted with basil; and caramelized apples in tender pastry. The prix-fixe menu is €38. ⊠*46 rue de la Balance* ☎*04–90–85–24–83* ⚄*Reservations essential* ⊟*MC, V* ⊙*Closed Sun. and Mon.*

$$–$$$$ ✕ **La Compagnie des Comptoirs.** Glassed into the white stone cloister of the trendy complex called Le Cloître des Arts is the culinary haven of the celebrated Porcel twins of Le Jardin de Sens fame (in Montpellier). Contemporary decorator Imaad Rahmouni did the interior, bringing together classic simplicity with modern elegance: in summer the 15th-century walls are artfully draped with Indian fabrics. Menu selections are beautifully presented and offer flavor mixtures from India, Italy, and Morocco: who can resist chicken breast wrapped in hazelnuts, baked with prunes and *trompette des morts* mushrooms, or the dessert of cubed banana and pineapple served on softened fresh vanilla ice cream? ⊠*83 rue Joseph-Vernet* ☎*04–90–85–99–04* ⚄*Reservations essential* ⊟*AE, MC, V* ⊙*Closed Sun. and Mon. in Oct.–Apr.*

★ **$–$$$** ✕ **Le Grand Café.** Behind the Papal Palace and set in a massive former army supply depot—note the carefully preserved industrial decay—this urban-chic entertainment complex combines an international cinema, a bar, and this popular bistro. Gigantic 18th-century mirrors and dance-festival posters hang against crumbling plaster and brick, and votive candles half-light the raw metal framework—an inspiring environment for intense film talk and a late supper of apricot lamb on a bed of semoule, goat cheese, or marinated artichokes. The prix-fixe dinner menu is €30. ⊠*La Manutention, Cours Maria Casares* ☎*04–90–86–86–77* ⊟*AE, MC, V* ⊙*Closed Jan. and Sun. and Mon.*

¢–$ ✕ **Maison Nani.** Crowded inside and out with trendy young professionals, this pretty lunch spot serves stylish home cooking in generous portions without the fuss of multiple courses. Choose from heaping salads sizzling with fresh meat, enormous kebabs, and a creative quiche du jour. It's just off Rue de la République. ⊠*29 rue Théodore Aubanel* ☎*04–90–82–60–90* ⊟*No credit cards* ⊙*Closed Sun. No dinner Mon.–Thurs.*

★ **$$$$** ✕▥ **Hôtel de la Mirande.** A designer's dream of a hotel, this *petit palais* permits you to step into 18th-century Avignon, thanks to painted coffered ceilings, sumptuous antiques, and other superb *grand siècle* touches (those rough sisal mats on the floors were the height of chic back in the Baroque era). The central lounge is a skylighted and jazz-warmed haven. Upstairs, guest rooms are both gorgeous and comfy, with extraordinary baths and even more extraordinary handmade wall coverings. The costume-drama dining room is the perfect setting for the restaurant's sophisticated cuisine, one of the best in Avignon under chef Sébastien Aminot. Look for friendly Tuesday- and Wednesday-night cooking classes (€85) from guest chefs in the massive downstairs "country" kitchen. ⊠*Pl. de la Mirande, 84000* ☎*04–90–85–93–93* ⊞*04–90–86–26–85* ⊕*www.la-mirande.fr* ➥*19 rooms, 1 suite* ♿*In-room: Wi-Fi, refrigerator. In-hotel: restaurant, bar, parking (fee), some pets allowed (fee)* ⊟*AE, DC, MC, V.*

10

$$$-$$$$ ✗⊡ **Hôtel d'Europe.** Once host to Victor Hugo, Napoléon Bonaparte, and Emperor Maximilian, this vine-covered 16th-century home is regally discreet and classic. Beyond the walled court shaded by trees, the splendor continues inside with Aubusson tapestries, porcelains, and Provençal antiques. Guest rooms are mostly emperor-size, with two suites overlooking the Papal Palace. The highly acclaimed restaurant, La Vieille Fontaine, is certainly one of Avignon's finest; during the festival period, tables in the courtyard are highly coveted and are top places to preen while enjoying such delights as hot duck foie gras with peaches. ⊠*12 pl. Crillon, 84000* ☎*04–90–14–76–76* 🖷*04–90–14–76–71* ⊕*www.heurope.com* ⟿*41 rooms, 3 suites* ⚒*In-room: Wi-Fi, refrigerator. In-hotel: restaurant, parking (fee), some pets allowed (fee)* ⊟*AE, DC, MC, V.*

$$-$$$ ⊡ **La Banasterie.** Hidden away on a side street by the Palais des Papes, this new upmarket B&B offers up one of the most warmly elegant welcomes in Avignon. The Parisian couple who own it ask for little more than to share their passion: *chocolat*. The handful of warmly and luxuriously decorated bedrooms all bear the names of different kinds of chocolate; the gracious hosts offer you a hot cup of sinfully rich cocoa before bed, and the most scrumptious chocolates appear nightly on your pillow. ⊠*11 rue de la Banasterie, 84000* ☎*04–32–76–30–78* 🖷*04–32–76–30–78* ⊕*www.labanasterie.com* ⟿*2 rooms, 3 suites* ⚒*In-room: Wi-Fi, refrigerator. In-hotel: no parking* ⊟*MC, V.*

$$ ⊡ **Du Palais des Papes.** Despite its mere two-star rating, this is a remarkably solid, comfortable hotel, just off the Place du Palais. With chic ironwork furniture and rich fabrics, the exposed-stone-and-beam decor fulfills fantasies of a medieval city—but one with good tile baths. ⊠*1 rue Gérard-Philippe, 84000* ☎*04–90–86–04–13* 🖷*04–90–27–91–17* ⊕*www.hotel.avignon.com* ⟿*26 rooms, 2 suites* ⚒*In-room: dial-up, no a/c (some). In-hotel: restaurant, bar, cable TV, pets allowed (fee)* ⊟*AE, MC, V.*

NIGHTLIFE & THE ARTS

Held annually in July, the Avignon festival, known officially as the **Festival Annuel d'Art Dramatique** (*Annual Festival of Dramatic Art,* ☎*04–90–27–66–50 tickets and information*), has brought the best of world theater to this ancient city since 1947. Some 300 productions take place every year; the main performances are at the Palais des Papes.

Within its fusty old medieval walls, Avignon teems with modern nightlife well into the wee hours. Having recently joined the masses near Place Pie, the **Red Lion** (⊠*21 rue St-Jean-les-Vieux* ☎*04–90–86–40–25*) serves Guinness, Stella, and Beck on tap and is hugely popular with students and the English-speaking crowd. At **AJMI** (*Association Pour le Jazz et la Musique Improvisée,* ⊠*4 rue Escaliers Ste-Anne* ☎*04–90–86–08–61*), in La Manutention, you can hear live jazz acts of some renown. Avignon's trendy twenty- and thirtysomethings come to dance at the **Red Zone** (⊠*25 rue Carnot* ☎*04–90–27–02–44*). Just beyond the Ramparts by the Rhone lies the converted barn and full-blooded disco **Le Bokao's** (⊠*9 bis quai St Lazare* ☎*04–90–82–47–95*), playing pumping disco, house and techno. On Wednesday, the ladies are invited to run the bar. At the cabaret **Dolphin Blues** (⊠*Chemin de L'île Piot*

☎04–90–82–46–96), a hip mix of comedy and music dominates the repertoire, and there's children's theater as well. **Le Rouge Gorge** (⊠*10 bis, rue Peyrollerie, behind palace* ☎*04–90–14–02–54*) presents a dinner show and after-dinner dancing every Friday and Saturday night.

SHOPPING

Avignon has a cosmopolitan mix of French chains, youthful clothing shops (it's a college town), and a few plummy shops. **Rue St-Agricole** is where to find Parisian designers Lacroix and Hermès, and **Rue des Marchands** off Place Carnot is another, more mainstream shopping stretch. But **Rue de la République** is the main artery, with chic street fashion names like Zara.

PONT DU GARD

③④
Fodor'sChoice
★

22 km (13 mi) southwest of Avignon, 37 km (23 mi) southwest of Orange, 48 km (30 mi) north of Arles.

No other architectural sight in Provence rivals the Pont du Gard, a mighty, three-tier aqueduct nearly midway between Nîmes and Avignon. Erected some 2,000 years ago as part of a 48-km (30-mi) canal supplying water to the Roman settlement of Nîmes, it's astonishingly well preserved. In the early morning the site offers an amazing blend of natural and classical beauty—the rhythmic repetition of arches resonates with strength, bearing testimony to an engineering concept relatively new in the 1st century AD, when it was built under Emperor Claudius. Later in the day crowds become a problem, even off-season. At the **Public Information Centre** (☎*04–66–37–50–99* ⊠€*10* ⊙*May–Sept., daily 9:30–6:30; Oct.–Dec. and Feb. –Apr., daily 10–5*), a film and a multimedia display detail the history of the aqueduct; in addition, there is a nifty children's area and an interactive exhibition about life in Roman times, archaeology, nature, and water You can approach the aqueduct from either side of the Gardon River. If you choose the south side (Rive Droite), the walk to the *pont* (bridge) is shorter and the views arguably better (and the tour buses seem to stay on the Rive Gauche). Note there have been reports of break-ins in the parking area, so get a spot close to the booth. Although access to the spectacular walkway along the top of the aqueduct is now off-limits, the bridge itself is still a breathtaking experience. If you're only interested in taking a look at the bridge, it'll only cost €5 to park. ⊠*Concession Pont-du-Gard* ☎*04–66–37–50–99* ⊠€*10, including parking* ⊙*Oct.–Apr., daily 10–6; May–Sept., daily 9:30–7.*

WHERE TO STAY & EAT

$–$$ ✕⊡ **La Garbure.** With eight rooms decked out in soft pastel ruffles and a low-price *menu terroir* (prix-fixe menu of regional specialties), this pretty inn aims to please. Look for potted quail in Carpentras truffles and stuffed rabbit with subtle thyme sauce (the restaurant is closed Sunday, October through June, and does not serve Sunday lunch in season, July through September). ⊠*3 rue Joseph-Ducos, 84230* ☎*04–90–83–75–08* 🖷*04–90–83–52–34* ⊕*www.la-garbure.com* ⤏*8 rooms* ⊕*In-room: dial-up, refrigerator. In-hotel: restaurant, some pets allowed*

10

⊟*MC, V* †⊙†*MAP* ⊗*Closed last 3 wks of Nov.*

$–$$ ✕⊞ **La Sommellerie.** This inspired regional restaurant serves local ingredients in deliciously inventive ways. Arguably the best in the area, it's often full with locals and tourists alike (book ahead). There are some extremely comfortable rooms available to sleep off all that great wine, too. ⊠*4 km (2½ mi) down D17* ☏*04–90–83–50–00* ⊕*www.la-sommellerie.fr* ⮑*12 rooms, 2 suites* ⚲*In-hotel: restaurant, pool, parking, some pets allowed (fee), public Wi-Fi* ⊟*AE, MC, V* †⊙†*MAP.*

> ### GETTING TO THE PONT DU GARD
>
> The Pont du Gard is a 40-minute ride from Nîmes's bus station on Rue Ste-Félicité; you're dropped off 1 km (½ mi) from the bridge at Auberge Blanche.

ORANGE

⑤ *31 km (19 mi) north of Avignon, 193 km (121 mi) south of Lyon.*

Even less touristy than Nîmes and just as eccentric, the city of Orange (pronounced oh-*rawnzh*) nonetheless draws thousands every year to its ★ spectacular **Théâtre Antique,** a colossal Roman theater built in the time of Caesar Augustus. Its vast stone stage wall, bouncing sound off the facing hillside, climbs four stories high—a massive sandstone screen that Louis XIV once referred to as the "finest wall in my kingdom." The niche at center stage contains the original statue of Augustus, just as it reigned over centuries of productions of classical plays. Today this theater provides a backdrop for world-class theater and opera. ⊠*Pl. des Frères-Mounet* ☏*04–90–51–17–60* ⊡*€7.70 with audioguide and entry to Espace Culturel* ⊗*Apr., May, and Sept., daily 9–6; June–Aug., daily 9–7; Mar. and Oct, daily 9:30–5:30.*

Privatization required that the small Musée Municipal (Town Museum) change its name. As the **Espace Culturel** *(Cultural Space)*, it's now a joint venture with the Théâtre Antique. A touristy boutique offers theater figurines and books; the displays include antiquities unearthed around Orange, including three detailed marble *cadastres* (land-survey maps) dating from the 1st century AD. Upstairs are Provençal fabrics manufactured in local mills in the 18th century and a collection of faience pharmacy jars. ⊠*Pl. des Frères-Mounet* ☏*04–90–51–18–24* ⊡*€7.50, joint ticket to Théâtre Antique €7.70 with audioguide and entry to Espace Culturel* ⊗*Mar.–Oct., daily 9:30–5:30; Apr., May, and Sept., daily 9–6, June–Aug., 9–7.*

North of the city center is the **Arc de Triomphe,** which once straddled the Via Agrippa between Lyon and Arles. Three arches support a heavy double attic (horizontal top) floridly decorated with battle scenes and marine symbols, references to Augustus's victories at Actium. The arch, which dates from about 20 BC, is superbly preserved, particularly the north side, but to view it on foot, you'll have to cross a roundabout seething with traffic. ⊠*North of center on Av. de l'Arc, in direction of Gap.*

Continued on page 567

Just exactly where does Provence's famous Lavender Route begin? Any number of towns have fields gloriously carpeted with the purple flower, but chances are this particular journey starts back home with your first sight of a travel poster showing hills corduroyed with rows of lilac, amethyst, and mauve. Or when that vial of essence of *Lavandula vera* is passed under your nose and

BLUE GOLD: THE LAVENDER ROUTE

you inhale the wild, pure-blood ancestor of the incense-intense aroma that characterizes all those little folkloric potpourris. Sated with the strong scent of gift-shop soaps and sachets, you develop a longing for the real thing: the fragrance of meadowsoft, mountain-fresh lavender. Well, let your nostrils flare, for your lavender lust is about to be requited.

OUR LAVENDER MAGICAL MYSTERY TOUR

If you want to have a peak lavender experience—literally—detour 18 km (10 mi) to the northwest and take a spectacular day's drive up the winding road to the **summit of Mont Ventoux** (follow signs from Sault to see the lavender-filled valleys below).

Have your Nikon ready for the beautifully preserved Cistercian simplicity of the **Abbaye Notre-Dame de Sénanque**, a perfect foil for the famous waving fields of purple around it.

No shrinking violet, the hilltop village of **Gordes** is famous for its luxe hotels, restaurants, and lavender-stocked shops.

Get a fascinating A to Z tour—from harvesting to distilling to production—at the **Musée de la Lavande** near Coustellet.

KEY

🝆 *Distillery*
⬭ *Lavender field*

Provence is threaded by the "Routes de la Lavande" (the Lavender Routes), a wide blue-purple swath that connects over 2,000 producers across the Drôme, the plateau du Vaucluse, and the Alpes-de-Haute-Provence, but our itinerary is lined with some of the prettiest sights—and smells—of the region. Whether you're shopping for artisanal bottles of the stuff (as with wine, the finest lavender carries its own Appellation d'Origine Contrôlée), spending a session at a lavender spa, or simply wearing hip-deep purple as you walk the fields, the most essential aspect on this trip is savoring a magical world of blue, one we usually only encounter on picture postcards.

To join the lavender-happy crowds, you have to go in season, which runs from

Purple haze

Gordes

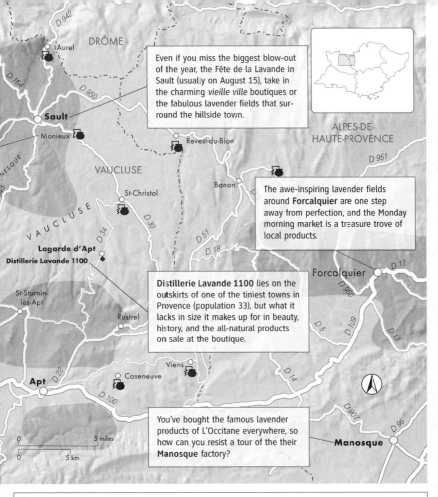

Even if you miss the biggest blow-out of the year, the Fête de la Lavande in Sault (usually on August 15), take in the charming *vieille ville* boutiques or the fabulous lavender fields that surround the hillside town.

The awe-inspiring lavender fields around **Forcalquier** are one step away from perfection, and the Monday morning market is a treasure trove of local products.

Distillerie Lavande 1100 lies on the outskirts of one of the tiniest towns in Provence (population 33), but what it lacks in size it makes up for in beauty, history, and the all-natural products on sale at the boutique.

You've bought the famous lavender products of L'Occitane everywhere, so how can you resist a tour of the their **Manosque** factory?

ALPES-DE-HAUTE-PROVENCE

DRÔME
Aurel
Sault
Monieux
Revest-du-Bion
VAUCLUSE
Banon
St-Christol
VAUCLUSE
Lagarde d'Apt
Distillerie Lavande 1100
St-Sturnin-les-Apt
Rustrel
Forcalquier
Viens
Apt
Caseneuve
Manosque
5 miles
5 km

10

June to early September. Like Holland's May tulips, the lavender of Haute-Provence is in its true glory only once a year: the last two weeks of July, when the harvesting begins—but fields bloom throughout the summer months for the most part. Below, we wind through the most generous patches of lavender. Drive the colorful gambit southeastward (Coustellet, Gordes, Sault, For-calquier, and Manosque), which will give you good visiting (and shopping) time in a number of the villages that are fou de la lavande (crazy for lavender). And for the complete scoop on the hundreds of sights to see in lavender land, contact: **Les Routes de la Lavande** ✉ *2 av. de Venterol, 26111 Nyons* ☎ *04–75–26–65–91* 🖷 *04–75–26–32–67* ⊕ *www.routes-lavande.com.*

Lavender Harvest Festival, Sault

Monday Morning Market, Forcalquier

Abbaye Notre-Dame de Sénanque

DAY 1

SÉNANQUE:
A Picture-Perfect Abbey

An invisible Master of Ceremonies for the Lavender Route would surely send you first to the greatest spot for lavender worship in the world: the 12th-century Cistercian **Abbaye Notre-Dame de Sénanque**, which in July and August seems to float above a sea of lavender, a setting immortalized in a thousand travel posters. Happily, you'll find it via the D177 only 4 km (2½ mi) north of Gordes, among the most beautiful of Provence's celebrated perched villages. An architecture student's dream of neat cubes, cylinders, and pyramids, its pure Romanesque form alone is worth contemplating in any context. But in this arid, rocky setting the gray stone building seems to have special resonance—ancient, organic, with a bit of the borie about it. Along with the abbeys of Le Thornet and Silvacane, this is one of the trio of "Three Sisters" built by the Cistercian order in this area. Sénanque's **church** is a model of symmetry and balance. Begun in 1150 and completed at the start of the 13th century, it has no decoration but still touches the soul with its chaste beauty. The adjoining **cloister,** from the 12th century, is almost as pure, with barrel-vaulted galleries framing double rows of discreet, abstract pillars (you'll find no child-devouring demons or lurid biblical tales here). Next door, the enormous vaulted **dormitory** and the **refectory** shelter a display on the history of Cistercian abbeys. The few remaining monks here now preside over a cultural center that presents concerts and exhibitions. The bookshop is one of the best in Provence, with a huge collection of Provençaliana (lots in English). ☎ 04–90–72–05–72 ✉ €5 ⏱ *1-hour guided tours of the abbey (in French only) by reservation. Bookshop open Feb.–Oct., Mon.–Sat. 10–6, Sun. 2–6; Nov.–Feb., daily 2–6.*

THE ESSENCE OF THE MATTER

Provence and lavender go hand in hand—but why? The flower is native to the Mediterranean, and grows so well because the pH balance in the soil is naturally perfect for it (pH 6–8). But lavender was really put on the map here when ancient Romans arrived to colonize Provence and used the flower to disinfect their baths and perfume their laundry (the word comes from Latin *lavare,* "to wash"). From a small grass-roots industry, lavender proliferated over the centuries until the first professional distillery opened in Provence in the 1880s to supply oils for southern French apothecaries. After World War I, production boomed to meet the demand of the perfumers of Grasse (the perfume center of the world). Once described as the "soul of Haute-Provence," lavender is now farmed in England, India, and the States, but the harvest in the South of France remains the world's largest.

After spending the morning getting acquainted with the little purple flower at Sénanque, drive south along the D2 (or D177) back to **Gordes**, through a dry, rocky region mixed with deep valleys and far-reaching plains. Wild lavender is already omnipresent, growing in large tracts as you reach the entrance of the small, unspoiled hilltop village, making for a patchwork landscape as finely drawn as a medieval illumination. A cluster of houses rises above the valley in painterly hues of honey gold, with cobbled streets winding up to the village's picturesque Renaissance château, making it one of the most beautiful towns in Provence. Gordes has a great selection of hotels, restaurants, and B&Bs to choose from (see our listings under Gordes, *above*). Spend the early afternoon among tasteful shops that sell lovely Provençal crafts and produce, much of it lavender-based, and then after lunch, head out to Coustellet.

COUSTELLET:
A Great Lavender Museum
Set 2 mi south of Gordes, Coustellet is noted for its **Musée de la Lavande** (take the D2 southeast to the outskirts of Coustellet). Owned by one of the original lavender families, who have cultivated and distilled the flower here for over five generations, this museum lies

ON THE CALENDAR

If you plan to be at the Musée de la Lavande between July 1 and August 25 you can work up a sweat cutting your own swath of lavender with a copper scythe, then make your own distillation in the museum's lab.

on the outskirts of more than 80 acres of prime lavender-cultivated land.

Not only can you visit the well-organized and interesting museum (note the impressive collection of scythes and distilling apparatus), you can buy up a storm in the boutique, which offers a great selection of lavender-based products at very reasonable prices. ☎ *04–90–76–91–23* ⊕ *www.museedela-lavande.co* ✉ *€5* ☉ *Daily July–Aug., daily 9–7; Sept.–Dec., Mar.–June, daily 9–noon, 2–6.*

There are four main species. True lavender (*Lavandula angustifolia*) produces the most subtle essential oil and is often used by perfume makers and laboratories. Spike lavender (*Lavandula latifolia*) has wide leaves and long floral stems with several flower spikes. Hybrid lavender (*lavandin*) is obtained from pollination of true lavender and spike lavender, making a hybrid that forms a highly developed large round cluster. French lavender (*Lavandula stoechas*) is wild lavender that grows throughout the region and is collected for the perfume industry. True lavender thrives in the chalky soils and hot, dry climate of higher altitudes of Provence. It was picked systematically until the end of the 19th century and used for most lavender-based products. But as the demand for this remarkable flower grew, so did the need for a larger production base. By the beginning of the 20th century, the demand for the flower was so great that producers planted fields of lavender at lower altitudes, creating the need for a tougher, more resistant plant: the hybrid *lavandin*.

Lavender Harvest Festival, Sault

DAY 2

LAGARDE D'APT:
A Top Distillerie

On the second day of your lavender adventure, begin by enjoying the winding drive 34 km (21 mi) east to the town of **Apt**. Aside from its Provençal market, busy with all the finest food products of the Luberon and Haute Provence, Apt itself is unremarkable (even actively ugly from a distance) but is a perfect place from which to organize your visits to the lavender fields of Caseneuve, Viens, and Lagarde d'Apt. Caseneuve (east exit from Apt onto the N100 and then northwest on the D35) and Viens (12 km/7 mi east from Apt on the D209) are small but charming places to stop for a quick bite along the magnificent drive through the rows upon rows of lavender, but if you have to choose between the three, go to the minuscule village of Lagarde d'Apt (12 km/7 mi east from Apt on the D209) and visit the **Distillerie Lavande 1100** (follow signs on the D34). As one of the most important distilleries in the region, this heavenly domain, planted by Maurice

Fra at 1,100 meters altitude, produces primarily lavender but also delves into the realms of other aromatic plants. The picture-perfect stone building rises up like a lighthouse, surrounded by waves of color; aside from admiring the views, you can tour the distillery, learn more about how to cultivate lavender and take your time to browse among the all-natural products that line the shelves of the shop. ☎ 04–90–75–01–42 ✉ Free July 25–Aug. 25 ◷ Daily 9am–7pm.

SAULT:
The Biggest Festival

To enjoy a festive overnight, continue northwest from Lagarde d'Apt to the village of **Sault**, 16 km (10 mi) to the northeast. Beautifully perched on a rocky outcrop overlooking the valley that bears its name, Sault is one of the key stops along the Lavender Route. There are any number of individual distilleries, producers, and fields to visit—to make the most of your visit, ask the Office du Tourisme (☎ 04–90–64–01–21, ⊕ www.tourism. fr/office-du-tourisme/sault.html) for a list of events. Make sure to pop into the **Centre de Découverte de la Nature** et du Patrimoine Cynégétique (✉ Av. de l'Oratoire ☎ 04–90–64–13–96 ✉ €8) to see the exhibitions on the natural history of the region, including some on lavender. Aim to be in Sault for the not-to-be-missed **Fête de la Lavande** (✉ along the D950 at the Hippodrome le Defends ⊕ www.fetedelalavande.com), a day-long festival entirely dedicated to lavender, the best in the region, and usually held around August 15. Village folk dress in traditional Provençal garb and parade on bicycles, horses leap over barrels of fragrant bundles of hay, and local producers display their wares at the market—all of which culminates in a communal Provençal dinner (€17) served with lavender-based products.

DAY 3

FORCALQUIER:
The Liveliest Market

On your third day, the drive from Sault over 35 km (23 mi) east to Forcalquier is truly spectacular. As you approach the village in late July, you will see endless fields of *Lavandula vera* (true wild lavender) broken only by charming stone farmhouses or discreet distilleries. The epicenter of Haute-Provence's lavender cultivation, **Forcalquier** boasts a lively Monday morning market with a large emphasis on lavender-based products, and it is a great departure point for walks, bike rides, horse rides, or drives into the lavender world that surrounds the town. In the 12th century, Forcalquier was known as the capital city of Haute-Provence and was called the *Cité des Quatre Reines* (City of the Four Queens) because the four daughters (Eleanor of Aquitaine among them) of the ruler of this region, Raimond Béranger V, all married royals. Relics of this former glory can be glimpsed in the Vieille Ville of Forcalquier, notably its Cathédrale Notre-Dame and the Couvent des Cordeliers. However, everyone heads here to marvel at the

MAKING SCENTS

BLOOMING:

Lavender fields begin blooming in late June, depending on the area and the weather, with fields reaching their peak from the first of July to mid-October. The last two weeks in July are considered the best time to catch the fields in all their glory.

HARVESTING:

Lavender is harvested from July to September, when the hot summer sun brings the essence up into the flower. Harvesting is becoming more and more automated; make an effort to visit some of the older fields with narrow rows—these are still picked by hand. Lavender is then dried for two to three days before being transported to the distillery.

DISTILLING:

Distillation is done in a steam alembic, with the dry lavender steamed in a double boiler. Essential oils are extracted from the lavender by water vapor, which is then passed through the cooling coils of a retort.

BLUE GOLD: THE LAVENDER ROUTE

10

lavender fields outside town. Contact Forcalquier's Office du Tourisme (⊠ 13 pl. Bourguet ☎ 04–92–75–25–30 ⊕ www.forcalquier.com) for information on the lavender calendar, then get saddled up on a bicycle for a trip into the countryside at the town's Moulin de Sarret. Plan on enjoying a fine meal and an overnight stay (reserve way in advance) at the town's most historic inn, the **Hostellerie des Deux Lions** (⊠ 11 pl. du Bourguet ☎ 04–92–75–25–30). For a workshop on lavender, meet **Monique Claessens** (☎ 04–92–73–06–76) in the village of Mane but found often at her stand in Forcalquier's Monday market (8 AM–NOON).

MANOSQUE:
Love That L'Occitane
Fifteen mi (9 km) south of Forcalquier is Manosque, home to the **L'Occitane** factory. You can get a glimpse of what the Luberon was like before it became so hip—Manosque is certainly not a tourist epicenter—but a trip here is worth it for a visit to the phenomenally successful cosmetics and skin care company that is now the town's main employer. Once you make a reservation, you can take a two-hour tour of the production site, view a documentary film, get a massage with oils, then rush into the shop where you can stock up on L'Occitane products for very reasonable prices. From Manosque you can head back to Apt and the Grand Luberon area or turn south about 52 km (30 mi) to Aix-en-Provence. ⊠ *Z. I. St-Maurice* ☎ *04–92–70–19–00* ⊕ *www.loccitane.com* ☺ *Weekdays 10–noon and 2:30–4:30.*

BRINGING IT HOME

Yes, you've already walked in the pungent-sweet fields, breathing in the ephemeral scent that is uniquely a part of Provence. Visually, there is nothing like the waving fields rising up in a haze of bees. But now it's time to shop! Here are some top places to head to stop and smell the lavender element in local wines, honey, vinegar, soaps, and creams. A fine place to start is the **Ferme Lavanicole Château du Bois** (⊠ Les Espanols, Lagarde d'Apt ☎ 04–90–76–91–23). The **Distillerie Lavande 1100** (⊠ follow signs on the D34, Lagarde d'Apt ☎ 04–90–75–01–42), open daily from July 25 to August 25, offers a nice selection of natural products, skin care, and creams. In Gordes and Sault there are lovely Provençal markets that have a wide range of lavender-based products, from honey to vinegar to creams. A great selection of the finest essential oils is available at **Distillerie du Vallon** (⊠ Rte. des Michouilles, Sault ☎ 04–90–64–14–83). **L'Occitane** (⊠ Z.I. St-Maurice, Manosque ☎ 04–92–70–19–00) is the mother store. In nearby Volx you can hit the **Maison aux Huiles Essentiels** (⊠ Z.I. La Carretière, Volx ☎ 04–92–78–46–77) for aromatherapy in all its glory.

SCENT-SATIONAL

WHERE TO STAY & EAT

$-$$$ ✘ **La Yaka.** At this intimate, unpretentious bistro you are greeted by the beaming owner, who is also your host and waiter, then pampered with specialties that are emphatically *style grandmère* (like Grandma used to make: rabbit stew, *caillette*, or pork-liver meat loaf, and even canned peas with bacon). It's all served up in charming stone-and-beam rooms. ✉*24 pl. Sylvain* ☎*04–90–34–70–03* ▬*MC, V* ☉*Closed Wed. and Nov. No dinner Tues.*

$-$$$ ☷ **Arène.** On a quiet square in the Vieille Ville center, this comfortable old hotel has attentive owners and a labyrinth of rooms done in rich colors and heavy fabrics. The nicest ones look out over the square. As it's built of several fine old houses strung together, there's no elevator, but a multitude of stairways compensates. ✉*Pl. de Langues, 84100* ☎*04–90–11–40–40* 📠*04–90–11–40–45* ⊕*www.hotel-arene.fr* ➷*30 rooms* ♿*In-room: dial-up, refrigerator. In-hotel: parking (fee), some pets allowed, no elevator* ▬*AE, DC, MC.*

VAISON-LA-ROMAINE

③⑥ *27 km (17 mi) northeast of Orange, 30 km (19 mi) northeast of Avignon.*

This ancient town thrives as a modern market center yet retains an irresistible Provençal charm, with medieval backstreets, lively squares lined with cafés, and, as its name implies, the remains of its Roman past. Vaison's well-established Celtic colony joined forces with Rome in the 2nd century BC and grew to powerful status in the empire's glory days. No gargantuan monuments were raised, yet the luxurious villas surpassed even those of Pompeii.

There are two broad fields of **Roman ruins,** both in the center of town: before you pay entry at either of the ticket booths, pick up a map (with English explanations) at the **Maison du Tourisme et des Vins** (☎*04–90–36–02–11*), which sits between them; it's open July and August, daily 9–12:30 and 2–6:45; September–June, Monday–Saturday 9–noon and 2–5:45. Like a tiny Roman forum, the **Maison des Messii** (Messii House) spreads over the field and hillside in the heart of town. Its skeletal ruins of villas, landscaped gardens, and museum lie below the ancient theater, and are accessed next to the booth across from the tourist office. Closest to the entrance, the foundations of the Maison des Messii retain the outlines of its sumptuous design. A formal garden echoes similar landscaping in ancient times; wander under its cypresses and flowering shrubs to the **Musée Archéologique Théo-Desplans** (Théo-Desplans Archaeology Museum). In this streamlined venue the accoutrements of Roman life have been amassed and displayed by theme: pottery, weapons, representations of gods and goddesses, jewelry, and sculpture. Cross the park behind the museum to climb into the bleachers of the 1st-century **theater,** which is smaller than Orange's but is still used today for concerts and plays. Across the parking lot is the **Quartier de la Villasse,** where the remains of a lively market town evoke images of main-street shops, public gar-

10

dens, and grand private homes, with floor mosaics. The most evocative image of all is in the area of the *thermes* (baths): a neat row of marble-seat toilets. In July and August guided nocturnal visits (€5, start 10 PM) are a must and have eerie backlighting and clever narration. ✉ *Av. Général-de-Gaulle at Pl. du 11 Novembre* ☎ *04–90–36–02–11* 🖥 *Ruins, museum, and Nazareth cloister €7; €5 each* ⊘ *Museum June–Sept., daily 9:30–6; Mar.– May and Oct., daily 10–12:30 and 2:30–6; Nov.–Feb., daily 10–11:30 and 2–4. Villasse June– Sept., daily 9:30–noon and 2–6; Mar.–May and Oct., daily 10– 12:30 and 2–6; Nov.–Feb., daily 10–noon and 2–4:30.*

> ### TRUFFLING MATTERS
>
> While Vaison has centuries-old attractions, the most popular for Americans may well now be Patricia Wells's Cooking Classes (⊕ www.patriciawells.com). A living monument of Provence, the celebrated food critic first made her name known through posh food columns and *The Food Lover's Guide to France*. Firsthand, she now introduces people to the splendors of French cooking in her lovely farmhouse near Vaison through weeklong cooking seminars—definitely luxe ($3,000 a student, eight students only), and set over Madame Wells's own Chanteduc vineyards.

Take the time to climb up into the **Haute Ville,** a medieval neighborhood perched high above the river valley. Its 13th- and 14th-century houses owe some of their beauty to stone pillaged from the Roman ruins below, but their charm is from the Middle Ages.

If you're in a medieval mood, stop into the sober Romanesque **Cathédrale Notre-Dame-de-Nazareth,** based on recycled fragments and foundations of a Gallo-Roman basilica. Its richly sculpted **cloister** is the key attraction. ✉ *Av. Jules-Ferry* ⊘ *June–Sept., daily 9:30–noon and 2–5:30; Mar.– May and Oct., daily 10–noon and 2–5:30; Nov.–Feb., daily 10–noon and 2–4.*

One last highlight: the remarkable single-arch **Pont Romain** *(Roman Bridge)*, built in the 1st century, stands firm across the Ouvèze River.

WHERE TO STAY & EAT

$$$$ ✕ **Le Moulin à Huile.** Innovative chef Robert Bardot shows off his superb culinary talents by mixing creative regional cuisine with a touch of the exotic—top creations include the veal marinated in spiced milk, ginger, and cloves, or the unusual roasted peach with strawberry coulis. His impressive prix-fixe menus are served in an old, beautifully restored *moulin* (mill) by the Pont Romain, with a lovely garden terrace and a fairly spectacular view over the old city. Recent additions include three tastefully decorated rooms, which book up fast so reserve well in advance. ✉ *Rte. de Malaucene* ☎ *04–90–36–20–67* ⊕ *www.moulin-huile.com* ⚒ *In-hotel: parking, some pets allowed (fee)* ▭ *AE, MC, V* ⊘ *Closed Mon. No dinner Sun.*

★ **$$–$$$** ✕🖼 **Le Beffroi.** Crowned with a centuries-old stone clock tower and set on a cliff top in the Vieille Ville, this elegant grouping of 16th-century homes makes a fine little hotel. The extravagant salon decked out in period style leads to the sizable rooms with beams and antiques; the big corner rooms have breathtaking views. From April through October, dine on local specialties under the fig tree in the intimate enclosed garden court. The hotel restaurant, La Fontaine, has real flair—as one taste of their foie gras ravioli or duck in lavender honey will prove. By day you can enjoy a simple salad on the garden terrace or take a dip in the rooftop pool. Meal plans are available only with a two-night minimum stay. ⊠*Rue de l'Évêché, 84110* ☎*04–90–36–04–71* 🖷*04–90–36–24–78* ⊕*www.le-beffroi.com* ⇆*22 rooms* ♿*In-room: no a/c, dial-up. In-hotel: restaurant, pool, parking (fee), some pets allowed (fee)* ▤*AE, DC, MC, V* ⊗*Closed Feb. and Mar.* ⦿|*MAP.*

$–$$$ 🏠 **Évêché.** In the medieval part of town, this turreted 16th-century former bishop's palace has just four small rooms. The warm welcome and rustic charm—delicate fabrics, exposed beams, wooden bedsteads—have garnered a loyal following among travelers who prefer B&B character over modern luxury. Room rates include breakfast. ⊠*Rue de l'Évêché, 84110* ☎*04–90–36–13–46* 🖷*04–90–36–32–43* ⊕*eveche. free.fr* ⇆*4 rooms, 2 suites* ♿*In-hotel: some pets allowed, public Internet, no elevator* ▤*No credit cards* ⦿|*BP.*

LE BARROUX

③⑦
Fodor'sChoice
★

16 km (10 mi) south of Vaison-la-Romaine, 34 km (21 mi) northeast of Avignon.

Of all the marvelous hilltop villages stretching across the south of France, this tiny ziggurat of a town may be unique: it's 100% boutique-and-gallery-free and has only one tiny old *épicerie* (small grocery) selling canned goods, yellowed postcards, and today's *Le Provençal*. You are forced, therefore, to look around you and listen to the trickle of the ancient fountains at every labyrinthine turn.

The **château** is its main draw, though its perfect condition reflects a complete restoration after a World War II fire. Grand vaulted rooms and a chapel date from the 12th century, and other halls serve as venues for contemporary art exhibits. ☎*04–90–62–35–21* 🎟*€4* ⊗*Apr.–June, weekends 10–7; July–Sept., daily 10–7; Oct., daily 2–6.*

10

WHERE TO STAY & EAT

$ ✕🏠 **Les Géraniums.** Though it has simple, pretty rooms, many with views sweeping down to the valley, this family-run auberge emphasizes its restaurant. A broad garden terrace stretches along the cliff side, where you can sample herb-roasted rabbit, a truffle omelet, and local cheeses. New rooms in the annex across the street take in panoramic views, and half-pension is strongly encouraged. ⊠*Pl. de la Croix, 84330* ☎*04–90–62–41–08* 🖷*04–90–62–56–48* ⇆*22 rooms* ♿*In-hotel: restaurant, bar, parking* ▤*AE, DC, MC, V* ⊗*Closed mid-Nov.–Dec. 1 and Jan.–mid-Mar.* ⦿|*MAP.*

CRILLON LE BRAVE

38 *12 km (7 mi) southeast of Le Barroux, 21 km (13 mi) southeast of Vaison-la-Romaine.*

The main reason to come to this tiny village, named after France's most notable soldier-hero of the 16th century, is to stay or dine at its hotel, the Hostellerie de Crillon le Brave. But it's also pleasant— perched on a knoll in a valley shielded by Mont Ventoux, with the craggy hills of the Dentelles in one direction and the hills of the

Luberon in another. Today the village still doesn't have even a *boulangerie* (bakery), let alone a souvenir boutique.

WHERE TO STAY & EAT

$$$$ ✕🖫 **Hostellerie de Crillon le Brave.** The views from the interconnected hilltop houses of this Relais & Châteaux property are as elevated as its prices, but for this you get a rarefied stage-set of medieval luxury. A cozy-chic southern touch informs book-filled salons and brocante-trimmed guest rooms, some with terraces looking out onto infinity. In the stone-vaulted dining room, stylish French cuisine is served. Wine tastings and regional discovery packages encourage longer stays. ⊠*Pl. de l'Église, 84410* ☎*04–90–65–61–61* 🖷*04–90–65–62–86* ⊕*www.crillonlebrave. com* 🛏*32 rooms* ♻*In-room: no a/c (some), Wi-Fi, refrigerator. In-hotel: restaurant, tennis court, pool, parking, some pets allowed (fee)* ▤*AE, DC, MC, V* ☉*Closed Nov.–mid-Mar.*

L'ISLE-SUR-LA-SORGUE

39 *28 km (17 mi) southwest of Crillon le Brave, 41 km (25 mi) southeast*
Fodor's Choice *of Orange, 26 km (16 mi) east of Avignon.*
★

Crisscrossed with lazy canals and alive with moss-covered waterwheels that once drove its silk, wool, and paper mills, this old valley town retains a gentle appeal—except, that is, on Sunday, when it transforms itself into a Marrakech of marketeers, its streets crammed with antiques and brocantes, its cafés swelling with crowds of bargain seekers making a day of it. There are also street musicians, food stands groaning under mounds of rustic breads, vats of tapenade, cloth-lined baskets of spices, and miles of café tables offering ringside seats to the spectacle. On a nonmarket day life returns to its mellow pace, with plenty of antiques dealers open year-round, as well as fabric and interior design shops, bookstores, and food stores for you to explore.

The token sight to see is L'Isle's 17th-century church, the **Collégiale Notre-Dame-des-Anges,** extravagantly decorated with gilt, faux marble, and sentimental frescoes. Its double-colonnaded facade commands the center of the Vieille Ville.

WHERE TO STAY & EAT

$$$–$$$$ ✗ **La Prévôté.** With all the money you saved bargaining on that chipped Quimper vase, splurge on lunch at this discreet, pristine spot hidden off a backstreet courtyard. The cuisine has won top awards for chef Roland Mercier—try his cannelloni stuffed with salmon and goat cheese, or tender duckling with lavender honey. The prix-fixe menus start at €25 and top out at €65. ⊠ *4 bis, rue Jean-Jacques-Rousseau* ☎ *04–90–38–57–29* ⬧ *Reservations essential* ☰ *MC, V* ⊘ *Closed Tues. and Wed. in Dec.–June, Tues. in July and Aug.*

$–$$$ ✗ **Lou Nego Chin.** In winter you sit shoulder to shoulder in the cramped but attractive dining room (chinoiserie linens, brightly hued tiles), but in summer tables are strewn across the quiet street, on a wooden deck along the river. Ask for a spot at the edge so you can watch the ducks play, then order the inexpensive house wine and the menu du jour, often a hearty omelet Provençal, goat-cheese salad, or a good, garlicky stew. ⊠ *12 quai Jean Jaurès* ☎ *04–90–20–88–03* ⬧ *Reservations essential* ☰ *DC, MC, V* ⊘ *Closed Wed. No dinner Tues. in Oct.–Apr.*

★ **$–$$** ✗☷ **Le Mas de Cure-Bourse.** This graceful old 18th-century post-coach stop is well outside the fray, snugly hedge-bound in the countryside amid 6 acres of fruit trees and fields. Rooms are freshly done in Provençal prints and painted country furniture, and you can be served sophisticated home cooking with a local touch. Half-pension is strongly encouraged, although the restaurant is closed for the month of November and on Monday, and lunch is not served Tuesday. ⊠ *Rte. de Caumont, 84800* ☎ *04–90–38–16–58* ⊟ *04–90–38–52–31* ⊕ *www. masdecurebourse.com* ⬧ *13 rooms* ⬧ *In-room: no a/c, dial-up. In-hotel: restaurant, pool, parking (no fee)* ☰ *MC, V* ⏽ *MAP.*

$ ✗☷ **La Gueulardière.** After a Sunday glut of antiquing along the canals, you can dine and sleep just up the street in a hotel full of collectible finds, from the school posters in the restaurant to the oak armoires and brass beds that furnish the simple lodgings. Each room has French windows that open onto the enclosed garden courtyard, a nice spot to enjoy a private breakfast in the shade. ⊠ *1 cours René Char, 84800* ☎ *04–90–38–10–52* ⊟ *04–90–20–83–70* ⬧ *5 rooms* ⬧ *In-room: no a/c. In-hotel: restaurant, parking (no fee), some pets allowed* ☰ *MC, V* ⊘ *Closed mid-Dec.–mid-Jan.*

SHOPPING

The famous **L'Isle-sur-la-Sorgue Sunday morning flea market** takes place from the Place Gambetta up the length of Avenue des Quatre Otages. Of the dozens of antiques shops in L'Isle, one conglomerate concentrates some 40 dealers under the same roof: **L'Isle aux Brocantes** (⊠ *7 av. des Quatre Otages* ☎ *04–90–20–69–93*); it's open Saturday–Monday. Higher-end antiques are concentrated next door at the twin shops of **Xavier Nicod et Gérard Nicod** (⊠ *9 av. des Quatre Otages* ☎ *04–90–38–35–50 or 04–90–38–07–20*). **Maria Giancatarina** (⊠ *4 av. Julien Guigue, across from train station* ☎ *04–90–38–58–02*) showcases beautifully restored linens, including *boutis* (Provençal quilts). A major group of antiquaires are found at **Hôtel Dongler** (⊠ *9 esplanade Robert Vasse* ☎ *04–90–38–63–63*). A tempting selection is on view at **Le Quai de la Gare** (⊠ *4 av. Julien Guigue* ☎ *04–90–20–73–42*). A popu-

10

lar source is **Village des Antiquaires de la Gare** (✉2 *bis, av. de l'Égalité* ☎*04–90–38–04–57).*

GORDES

40
Fodor's Choice
★

16 km (10 mi) southeast of Fontaine-de-Vaucluse, 35 km (22 mi) east of Avignon.

Gordes was once merely an unspoiled hilltop village; it's now a famous unspoiled hilltop village surrounded by luxury vacation homes, modern hotels, restaurants, and B&Bs. No matter: the ancient stone village still rises above the valley in painterly hues of honey gold, and its mosaiclike cobbled streets—lined with boutiques, galleries, and real-estate offices—still wind steep and narrow to its Renaissance château—making this certainly one of the most beautiful towns in Provence.

The only way to see the interior of the **château** is to view its ghastly collection of photo paintings by pop artist Pol Mara, who lived in Gordes. It's worth the price of admission just to look at the fabulously decorated stone fireplace, created in 1541. ☎*04–90–72–02–75* ✉*€4* ☉*Daily 10–noon and 2–6.*

Just outside Gordes, on a lane heading north from D2, follow signs to the **Village des Bories.** Found throughout this region of Provence, the bizarre and fascinating little stone hovels called *bories* are concentrated some 20 strong in an ancient community. Their origins are provocatively vague: built as shepherds' shelters with tight-fitting, mortarless stone in a hivelike form, they may date to the Celts, the Ligurians, even the Iron Age—and were inhabited or used for sheep through the 18th century. ☎*04–90–72– 03–48* ✉*€5.50* ☉*Daily 9–sunset or 8, whichever comes earlier.*

If you've dreamed of Provence's famed lavender fields, head to a wild valley some 4 km (2½ mi) north of Gordes (via D177) to find the beautiful 12th-century Romanesque

Fodor's Choice
★

Abbaye de Sénanque, which floats above a redolent sea of lavender (in full bloom in July and August; *for more information, see the Close-Up Box, "Blue Gold: The Lavender Route" in this chapter).* Begun in 1150 and completed at the dawn of the 13th century, the **church** and adjoining **cloister** are without decoration, but still touch the soul with their chaste beauty. In this orbit, the gray-stone buildings seem to have special resonance—ancient, organic, with a bit of the borie about them. Next door, the enormous vaulted **dormitory** contains an exhibition on the abbey's construction, and the **refectory** shelters a display on the history of Cistercian abbeys. ☎*04–90–72–05–72* ✉*€6* ☉*Mar.–Oct., Mon.–Sat. 10–noon and 2–6, Sun. 2–6; Nov.–Feb., daily 2–5; call ahead for reservations.*

WHERE TO STAY & EAT

$–$$$$ ✕ **Les Cuisines du Château.** Across from the château, this tiny but deluxe bistro has daily *aioli,* a smorgasbord of fresh cod and lightly steamed vegetables crowned with the garlic mayonnaise. Evenings are reserved for intimate, formal indoor meals à la carte—roast Luberon lamb, beef with truffle sauce. The '30s-style bistro tables and architectural lines are a relief from Gordes's ubiquitous rustic-chic. ☒ *Pl. du Château* ☎ *04–90–72–01–31* ⌂ *Reservations essential* ▤ *MC, V* ⊗ *Closed Wed., no dinner on Tues., Sept.–May. No dinner Tues., mid-Jan.–mid-Mar. Closed Nov.–mid-Dec.*

$$$–$$$$ ✕▥ **La Bastide de Gordes.** Spectacularly perched on Gordes's hilltop, the newly renovated Bastide is big, yet intimately scaled, with architectural origins going back to the 16th century. The hotel, with its superb restaurant (and impressive, 20,000-bottle wine cellar), is surrounded by manicured lawns and a broad, elegantly appointed shaded terrace. Guest rooms are traditional and comfortable, with a few *haut Provençal* accents. The clientele is increasingly upscale and international, attracted by the new and luxe three-level Daniel Jouvance spa, which includes a Roman-style steam room, Japanese baths, and a chromatic pool with breathtaking views of the Vallée de Gordes. ☒ *Le Village, 84220* ☎ *04–90–72–12–12* 🖷 *04–90–72–05–20* ⊕ *www.bastide-de-gordes.com* ⟿ *39 rooms, 6 suites* ⌂ *In-room: Wi-Fi, refrigerator. In-hotel: restaurant, bar, pools, spa, some pets allowed (fee), parking* ▤ *AE, MC, V* ⊗ *Closed Jan. and 1st 2 wks of Feb.*

$$–$$$ ✕▥ **La Ferme de la Huppe.** This 17th-century stone farmhouse just outside Gordes has several sweet touches, including a courtyard and rooms furnished with secondhand finds. Dine poolside on three styles of roast lamb, prepared by the proprietors' son, Gerald Konings, but reserve ahead: the restaurant (closed Thursday) is as popular as the hotel. Breakfast is included in the price and meal plans are available with a minimum stay of three nights. ☒ *Les Pourquiers, 3 km (2 mi) east of Gordes, R.D.156, 84220* ☎ *04–90–72–12–25* 🖷 *04–90–72–01–83* ⊕ *www.lafermedelahuppe.com* ⟿ *9 rooms* ⌂ *In-room: Wi-Fi, refrigerator. In-hotel: restaurant, pool, some pets allowed (fee), parking, no elevator* ▤ *AE, MC, V* ⊗ *Closed end Nov.–Mar.* ⦿ MAP.

$$$–$$$$ ▥ **Les Romarins.** At this small hilltop inn on the outskirts of Gordes you can gaze at the town across the valley while having breakfast on a sheltered terrace in the morning sun. Rooms are clean, well lighted, and feel spacious—ask for either No. 1, in the main building, which has a seemingly limitless view, or the room with a terrace in the atelier. Oriental rugs, antique furniture, and a pool add to your contentment. ☒ *Rte. de Sénanque, 84220* ☎ *04–90–72–12–13* 🖷 *04–90–72–13–13* ⊕ *www. hoteldesromarins.com* ⟿ *13 rooms* ⌂ *In-room: Wi-Fi, refrigerator. In-hotel: pool, parking, some pets allowed (fee), no elevator* ▤ *MC, V.*

10

ROUSSILLON

❹ *10 km (6 mi) east of Gordes, 45 km (28 mi) east of Avignon.*

Fodor's Choice
★

In shades of deep rose and russet, this quintessential and gorgeous hilltop cluster of houses blends into the red-ocher cliffs from which its stone was quarried. The ensemble of buildings and jagged, hand-cut slopes is equally dramatic, and views from the top look out over a landscape of artfully eroded bluffs that Georgia O'Keeffe would have loved. Unlike neighboring hill villages, there's little of historic architectural detail here; the pleasure of a visit lies in the richly varied colors that change with the light of day, and in the views of the contrasting countryside, where dense-shadowed greenery sets off the red stone with Cézannesque severity. There are pleasant *placettes* (tiny squares) to linger in nonetheless, and a Renaissance fortress tower crowned with a clock in the 19th century; just past it, you can take in expansive panoramas of forest and ocher cliffs. A **Sentier des Ocres** *(Ocher Trail)* starts out from the town cemetery and takes 45 minutes to wend its way through a magical, multicolored "palette de pierres" (palette of rocks) replete with eroded red cliffs and chestnut groves. 🖾€2, €6 *includes entry to the Usine Mathieu Rousillon* ⊙*July and Aug., daily 10–5:30; Sept.–mid-Nov. and Mar.–June, daily 9–noon and 1–5; mid-Nov.–Feb., Wed.–Mon. 9–noon and 1–5.*

The area's famous vein of natural ocher, which spreads some 25 km (16 mi) along the foot of the Vaucluse plateau, has been mined for centuries, beginning with the ancient Romans, who used it for their pottery. You can visit the old **Usine Mathieu de Roussillon** *(Roussillon's Mathieu Ocher Works)* to learn more about ocher's extraction and its modern uses. There are explanatory exhibits, ocher powders for sale, and guided tours in English on advance request. ✉*On D104 southeast of town* ☎*04–90–05–66–69* 🖾*Tour: €5 for guided tour, €6 includes entry to Sentier des Ocres* ⊙*Mar.–Nov., Wed. –Mon. 10–7.*

WHERE TO STAY & EAT

★ $$$ ✗🖾 **Mas de Garrigon.** An exquisite hotel, tastefully decorated in classic Provençal style, the Garrigon has spacious rooms, a cozy library, and views of the surrounding ocher cliffs. It also has the best restaurant (by far) in Roussillon—which is a good thing, as the management takes it very personally if you pass on their demi-pension offer. So don't: the food is superb—monkfish in salt crust, straw-baked lamb with rosemary jus, inventive vegetable courses, plus wonderful desserts. And the family welcome is warm and genuine. ✉*Rte. de St-Saturnin-d'Apt, 3 km (2 mi) north on D2, 84220* ☎*04–90–05–63–92* 🖾*04–90–05–70–01* ⊕*www.masdegarrigon-provence.com* ⟋*8 rooms, 1 suite* ⚿*In-room: dial-up, refrigerator. In-hotel: pool, parking (no fee)* ⊟*AE, DC, MC, V* ⅥⓄⅠMAP.*

$–$$$ 🖾 **Ma Maison.** In the valley 4 km (2½ mi) below Roussillon, this isolated 1850 mas has been infused with a laid-back, cosmopolitan style by its artist-owners. Wicker-backed chairs mix with Oriental rugs, wrought iron, and fluffy white bedspreads. There's a big saltwater pool, a massive country kitchen, and a garden with lovely breakfast tables romantically set under sprawling, shady branches. Breakfast is included. ✉*Quartier Les Devens, 84220* ☎*04–90–05–74–17* 🖾*04–90–05–74–63* ⊕*www.mamaison-provence.com* ⟋*3 rooms, 2 suites* ⚿*In-room: dial-up, no a/c. In-hotel: pool, some pets allowed (fee), no elevator* ⊟*MC, V* ⊙*Closed mid-Oct.–mid-Mar.* ⅥⓄⅠBP.*

MÉNERBES

42 *30 km (19 mi) southeast of Avignon.*

Famous as the former home base of *A Year in Provence* author Peter Mayle (he has since moved on to another town in the Luberon), the town of Ménerbes clings to a long, thin hilltop over this sought-after valley, looming over the surrounding forests like a great stone ship. At its prow juts the **Castellet**, a 15th-century fortress. At its stern looms the 13th-century **Citadelle**. These redoubtable fortifications served the Protestants well during the 16th-century Wars of Religion—until the Catholics wore them down with a 15-month siege.

A campanile tops the Hôtel de Ville (Town Hall) on pretty **Place de l'Horloge** *(Clock Square)*, where you can admire the delicate stonework on the arched portal and mullioned windows of a Renaissance house. Just past the tower on the right is an overlook taking in views toward Gordes, Roussillon, and Mont Ventoux.

Seven kilometers (4 mi) east of Ménerbes is the eagle's-nest village of Lacoste, presided over by the once-magnificent Château de Sade, erstwhile retreat to the notorious Marquis de Sade (1740–1814) when he wasn't on the run from authorities. For some years, the wealthy Paris couturier Pierre Cardin has been restoring the castle wall by wall and under his generous patronage the **Festival Lacoste** takes place here throughout the months of July and August. A lyric, musical, and theatrical extravaganza, events (and their dates) change yearly, ranging from outdoor poetry recitals to ballet to colorful operettas. ⊠*Carrières du Château, Lacoste* ☎*04–90–75–93–12* ⊕*www.lacoste-84.com* ⊠*€20–€140.*

WHERE TO STAY

★ $$$–$$$$ ⌂ **Hostellerie Le Roy Soleil.** In the imposing shadow of the Luberon, this luxurious country inn has pulled out all stops on comfort and decor: marble and granite bathrooms, wrought-iron beds, and coordinated fabrics. But the integrity of its 17th-century building, with thick stone walls and groin vaults and beams, keeps it just short of pretentiousness and makes it a lovely place to escape to. ⊠*Rte. des Beaumettes, 84560* ☎*04–90–72–25–61* 🖶*04–90–72–36–55* ⊕*www.roy-soleil.com* ⇄*10 rooms, 9 suites, 3 apartments* ♿*In-hotel: restaurant, bar, pool, parking (no fee), some pets allowed (fee), public Wi-Fi* ⊟*AE, MC, V* ⊗*Closed last 3 wks of Jan.–late Feb.* ⍩*FAP.*

BONNIEUX

★ ❸ 11 km (7 mi) south of Roussillon, 45 km (28 mi) north of Aix-en-Provence.

The most impressive of the Luberon's villages, Bonnieux rises out of the arid hills in a jumble of honey-color cubes that change color subtly as the day progresses. The village is wrapped in crumbling ramparts and dug into bedrock and cliff. Most of its sharply raked streets take in wide-angle valley views, though you can get the best view from the pine-shaded grounds of the 12th-century church, reached by stone steps that wind past tiny niche houses.

WHERE TO STAY & EAT

$$$–$$$$ ✕ **Le Fournil.** In an old bakery in a natural grotto deep in stone, lighted by candles and arty torchères, this restaurant would be memorable even without its trendy look and stylishly presented Provençal cuisine.

10

Try the adventurous dishes such as the crisped pigs'-feet *galette* (patty) and check out the informed wine list. ✉ *5 pl. Carnot* ☏*04–90–75–83–62* ⚐*Reservations essential* ▤*MC, V* ⊘*Closed Mon. and Tues., late Nov.–mid-Dec., and mid-Jan.–mid-Feb. No lunch Sat.*

★ $$$ ✗ **Auberge de la Loube.** The chef's inclusion in a Peter Mayle book hasn't gone to his toque: for simple, unpretentious Provençal food perfectly prepared, nothing beats this restaurant in the neighboring hamlet of Buoux. Meals are served on a covered terrace out back. The gargantuan starters are famous and fabulous, as are house specialties like scrambled eggs with truffles and roasted leg of lamb. Sunday lunch is a feast worthy of Pagnol. ✉*Quartier la Loube–Buoux* ☏*04–90–74–19–58* 🖷*04–90–74–19–58* ⚐*Reservations essential* ▤*No credit cards* ⊘*Closed Wed., Thurs., and Jan.*

★ $–$$ 🏨 **Hostellerie du Prieuré.** Not every hotel has its own private chapel, but this gracious inn occupies an 18th-century abbey, right in the village center. A pleasantly warm glow quietly surrounds you from the fire-lit salon to the dining room burnished with Roussillon ocher. Summer meals and breakfasts are served in the enclosed garden oasis. Rooms have plush carpets and antiques. The Coutaz family has been in the hotel business since Napoléon III, and it shows. ✉*In center of village, 84480* ☏*04–90–75–80–78* 🖷*04–90–75–96–00* ⊕*www.esprit-de-france.com* ⌨*10 rooms* ⚐*In-room: no a/c. In-hotel: restaurant, tennis court, parking (no fee), some pets allowed (fee), no elevator* ▤*MC, V* ⊘*Closed Nov.–Mar.* ⏴*FAP, MAP.*

AIX-EN-PROVENCE & THE MEDITERRANEAN COAST

The southeastern part of this area of Provence, on the edge of the Côte d'Azur, is dominated by two major towns: Aix-en-Provence, considered the main hub of Provence and the most cultural town in the region; and Marseille, a vibrant port town that combines seediness with fashion and metropolitan feistiness with classical grace. For a breathtaking experience of the dramatic contrast between the azure Mediterranean sea and the rocky, olive tree–filled hills, take a trip along the coast east of Marseille and make an excursion to the Iles d'Hyères.

AIX-EN-PROVENCE

★ *48 km (29 mi) southeast of Bonnieux, 82 km (51 mi) southeast of Avignon, 176 km (109 mi) west of Nice, 759 km (474 mi) south of Paris.*

GETTING HERE

The center of Aix is best explored by foot, but there is a municipal bus service that serves the entire town and the outlying suburbs. Most leave from La Rotonde in front of the tourism office (☏*04–42–26–37–28*), where you can also buy tickets (€1.30 one way) and ask for a bus route map. The Aix TGV station is 10 km (6 mi) west of the city and is served by regular shuttle buses. The old Aix station is on the slow Marseille–

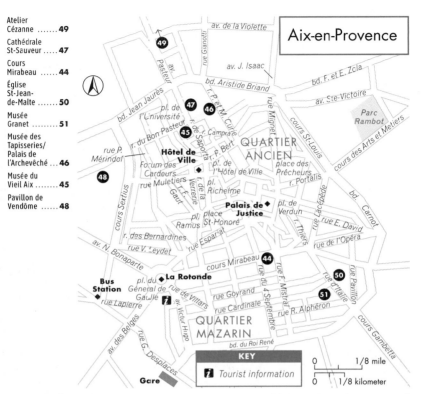

Aix-en-Provence

to–Sisteron line, with trains arriving roughly every hour from Marseille St Charles.

EXPLORING

Gracious, posh, cultivated, and made all the more cosmopolitan by the presence of some 30,000 international university students, the lovely old town of Aix (pronounced *ex*) was once the capital of Provence. The vestiges of that influence and power—fine art, noble architecture, and graceful urban design—remain beautifully preserved today. That and its thriving market, vibrant café life, and world-class music festival make Aix vie with Arles and Avignon as one of the towns in Provence that shouldn't be missed.

Romans were first drawn here by mild thermal baths, naming the town Aquae Sextiae (Waters of Sextius) in honor of the consul who founded a camp near the source in 123 BC. Just 20 years later some 200,000 Germanic invaders besieged Aix, but the great Roman general Marius pinned them against the mountain known ever since as Ste-Victoire. Marius remains a popular local first name to this day. Under the wise and generous guidance of Roi René (King René) in the 15th century, Aix became a center of Renaissance arts and letters. At the height of its political, judicial, and ecclesiastic power in the 17th and 18th centuries, Aix profited from a surge of private building, each grand *hôtel*

10

particulier (mansion) vying to outdo its neighbor. Its signature *cours* (courtyards) and *places* (squares), punctuated by grand fountains and intriguing passageways, date from this time.

It was into this exalting elegance that artist Paul Cézanne (1839–1906) was born, though he drew much of his inspiration from the raw countryside around the city and often painted Ste-Victoire. A schoolmate of Cézanne's made equal inroads: the journalist and novelist Émile Zola (1840–1902) attended the Collège Bourbon with Cézanne and described their friendship as well as Aix itself in several of his works. You can still sense something of the ambience that nurtured these two geniuses in the streets of modern Aix.

44 Under the deep shade of tall plane trees whose branches interlace over the street (when not seasonally pollarded back), **Cours Mirabeau** prevails as the city's social nerve center. One side of the street is lined with dignified 18th-century hôtels particuliers; you can view them from a comfortable seat in one of the dozen or so cafés and restaurants that spill onto the sidewalk on the other side.

45 In the **Musée du Vieil Aix** *(Museum of Old Aix)*, an eclectic assortment of local treasures resides in a 17th-century mansion, from faience to *santons* (terra-cotta figurines) to ornately painted furniture. The building itself is lovely, too. ⊠ *17 rue Gaston-de-Saporta* ☎ *04-42-21-43-55* ⊠ *€4* ⊘ *Apr.–Oct., Tues.–Sun. 10–noon and 2:30–6; Nov.–Mar., Tues.–Sun. 10–noon and 2–5.*

46 The **Musée des Tapisseries** is housed in the 17th-century **Palais de l'Archevêché** (Archbishop's Palace) and showcases a sumptuous collection of tapestries that once decorated the walls of the bishops' quarters. Their taste was excellent: there are 17 magnificent hangings from Beauvais and a series on the life of Don Quixote from Compiègne. Temporary exhibitions offer interesting sneak peeks into contemporary textile art. The main opera productions of the Festival International d'Art Lyrique take place in the broad courtyard here. ⊠ *Pl. de l'Ancien-Archevêché* ☎ *04-42-23-09-91* ⊠ *€2.50* ⊘ *Oct.–Dec., and Feb.–Apr., Wed.–Mon. 1:30–5; Apr.–Oct., Wed.–Mon. 10–6.*

★ **47** The **Cathédrale St-Sauveur** (⊠ *Rue Gaston de Saporta*) juxtaposes so many eras of architectural history, all clearly delineated and preserved, it's like a survey course in itself. It has a double nave—Romanesque and Gothic side by side—and a Merovingian (5th-century) **baptistery,** its colonnade mostly recovered from Roman temples built to honor pagan deities. Shutters hide the ornate 16th-century carvings on the **portals,** opened by a guide on request. The guide can also lead you into the tranquil Romanesque **cloister** next door, so that you can admire its carved pillars and slender columns. As if these treasures weren't enough, the cathedral also has an extraordinary 15th-century triptych painted by Nicolas Froment in the heat of inspiration following his travels in Italy and Flanders. Called the *Triptyque du Buisson Ardent* (*Burning Bush Triptych*), it depicts the generous art patrons King René and Queen Jeanne kneeling on either side of the Virgin, who is poised above a burning bush. These days, to avoid light damage, it's only opened for viewing on Tuesday from 3 to 4.

48 **Pavillon de Vendôme.** This extrava-
FodorsChoice gant Baroque villa was first built
★ in 1665 as a "country" house for
the Duke of Vendome; its position
just outside the city's inner circle
allowed the duke to commute discreetly from his official home on
the Cours Mirabeau to this love
nest, where his mistress, La Belle du
Canet, was comfortably installed.

Though never officially inhabited, it was expanded and heightened in
the 18th century to draw attention to the classical orders—Ionic, Doric,
and Corinthian—in its parade of neo-Grecian columns. Inside its cool,
broad chambers you can find a collection of Provençal furniture and
artworks. ⊠*13 rue de la Molle* ☎*04–42–21–05–78* ✆*€2* ☉*Mar.–mid-
Sept., Wed.–Mon. 10–6; mid-Sept.–Dec. and Feb., Wed.–Mon. 1:30–5.*

★ **49** Just north of the Vieille Ville loop is the **Atelier Cézanne** *(Cézanne Studio).* After the death of his mother forced the sale of the painter's
beloved country retreat, known as Jas de Bouffan, he had this studio
built just above the town center. In the upstairs work space Cézanne
created some of his finest paintings, including *Les Grandes Baigneuses*
(The Large Bathers). But what is most striking is its collection of simple
objects that once featured prominently in the portraits and still-lifes he
created—redingote, bowler hat, ginger jar—all displayed as if awaiting his return. ⊠*9 av. Paul-Cézanne* ☎*04–42–21–06–53* ⊕*www.
atelier-cezanne.com* ✆*€5.50* ☉*Apr.–Sept., daily 10–noon and 2–6;
Oct.–Mar., daily 10–noon and 2–5.*

50 The 12th-century **Église St-Jean-de-Malte** (⊠*Intersection of Rue Cardinale and Rue d'Italie*) served as a chapel of the Knights of Malta, a medieval order of friars devoted to hospital care. It was Aix's first attempt
at the Gothic style. It was here that the counts of Provence were buried throughout the 18th century; their tombs (in the upper left) were
attacked during the Revolution and have been only partially repaired.

10

**NEED A
BREAK?**
For an excellent cup of inexpensive fresh roasted coffee, wander in to La
Brûlerie Richelme (⊠*Pl. Richelme*). Comfy chairs and lively student patron-
age make this place super-casual, and the light snacks are just the thing.

51 In the graceful Quartier Mazarin, the **Musée Granet** is set below the
Cours Mirabeau. Once the Ecole de Dessin (Art School) that granted
Cézanne a second prize in 1856, this former priory of the Eglise St-Jean-
de-Malte is now an art museum. There are eight of Cézanne's paintings
upstairs as well as a nice collection of his watercolors and drawings.
You can also find works by Rubens, David, and a group of sentimental works by the museum's founder, François Granet. At this writing,
the museum was closed for an ambitious renovation project that will
eventually double the exhibition area. The newly renovated museum
reopened its doors in summer 2006 for a major show on "Cézanne
in Provence" and will unveil its other renovated salons through the-

beginning of 2007. ⊠*13 rue Cardinale* ☎*04–42–26–88–32* ⊕*www.*
cezanne-2006.com ⊠*€2* ⊘ *Wed.–Mon. 10–noon and 2–6.*

OFF THE
BEATEN
PATH

Jas de Bouffon. To honor the 100th anniversary of Cézanne (1839–1906),
his hometown mounted a special "Saison Cézanne" in 2006 to honor the
centenary of his death. Besides bringing a summer blockbuster exhibition of "Cézanne in Provence" to the Musée Granet, the town opened to
the public for the first time the famed Jas de Bouffon. Cézanne's father
bought this lovely estate—whose name translates as "the sheepfold"—in
1859 to celebrate his rise from hatmaker to banker. The budding artist
lived here until 1899 and painted his first images of Mont Ste-Victoire—
the founding seeds of 20th-century art—from here. Today its salons are
empty but the grounds are full of his spirit, especially the Allée des Mar-
ronniers out front. The Jas is a mile south of the center of town and can
only be visited on tour by booking a minibus seat through the town's
central tourist office. ☎*04–42–16–10–91* ⊕*www.aixenprovencetour-
ism.com* ⊠*€5.50* ⊘*Daily 10–6 for reserved tours.*

WHERE TO STAY & EAT

★ **$$$$** ✕ **Le Clos de la Violette.** Whether you dine under the chestnut trees or in
the airy, pastel dining room, you can get to experience the cuisine of one
of the south's top chefs, Jean-Marc Banzo. He spins tradition into gold,
from poached crab set atop a humble white-bean-and-shrimp salad to
grilled red mullet with squid-stuffed cabbage. The restaurant isn't far
from the Atelier Cézanne, outside the Vieille Ville ring. Some feel that
the service can be erratic, and the welcome a little cool. ⊠*10 av. de la
Violette* ☎*04–42–23–30–71* ⊕*www.closdelaviolette.fr* ⚐*Reservations
essential*Jacket required ☰*AE, MC, V* ⊘*Closed Sun. and Mon.*

$–$$$ ✕ **Antoine Coté Cour.** Filled with trendy insiders and fashion-conscious
Aixois, this lively Italian restaurant has floor-to-ceiling windows that
give almost every table a view of the plant-filled courtyard. Delicious
smells wafting out from the open kitchen make this place literally hum
in hungry anticipation. Pastas are superb; try the mushroom and pro-
sciutto fettuccine or the gnocchi à la Provençal. ⊠*19 cours Mirabeau*
☎*04–42–93–12–51* ☰*DC, MC, V* ⊘*Closed Sun. No lunch Mon.*

★ **$–$$$** ✕ **Le Passage.** This is an edgy, urban brasserie from chef Franck
Dumond, who has created a wildly popular setting in which to eat
good, affordable food. In a sleekly converted former candy factory in
the center of town, the complex also has a bookstore, cooking workshop, and a small wine store and épicerie all arranged around a sunny
atrium. Its New York vibe runs from the Andy Warhol reproductions
in the main dining room to the menu: roasted beef fillet with thick-cut
fries and a terrific raspberry crème brûlée with fig chutney. ⊠*10 rue
Villars* ☎*04–42–37–09–00* ⚐*Reservations essential* ☰*AE, MC, V.*

★ **¢–$$** ✕ **Brasserie Les Deux Garçons.** Cézanne and Émile Zola used to chow
down here back when, so who cares if the food is rather ordinary. Eat-
ing isn't what you came for. Instead, revel in the exquisite gold-ivory
style Consulate decor, which dates from the restaurant's founding in
1792. It's not so hard to picture the greats—Mistinguett, Churchill,
Sartre, Picasso, Delon, Belmondo, and Cocteau—enjoying their demi-
tasse under these mirrors. Better, savor the linen-decked sidewalk tables

that look out to the Cours Mirabeau, the fresh flowers, and the white-swathed waiters serving espressos in tiny gilt-edge cups. In winter at night, the upstairs turns into a cozy, dimly lighted piano bar buzzing with an interesting mix of local jazz lovers, tourists, and students. ⊠ *53 cours Mirabeau* ☎ *04-42-26-00-51* ▤ *AE, MC, V.*

$$$$ **Le Pigonnet.** Cézanne painted Ste-Victoire from what is now the
Fodor'sChoice large flower-filled garden terrace of this enchanting abode, and the
★ likes of Princess Caroline, Iggy Pop, and Clint Eastwood have spent a few nights under the luxurious roof of the family-owned, old-world, country-style hotel. Spacious and filled with light, each room is a marvel of decoration: baby-soft plush rugs, beautifully preserved antique furniture, rich colors of burnt reds, autumn yellows, and delicate oranges. The restaurant's terrace spills out onto a sculpted green, but the inside dining salon is equally pleasant on a rainy day, thanks to its softly draped yellow curtains and large picture windows. For sheerest Provençal luxe, this place can't be beat. ⊠ *5 av. du Pigonnet, 13100* ☎ *04-42-59-02-90* 🖷 *04-42-59-47-77* ⊕ *www.hotelpigonnet.com* 🛏 *52 rooms, 1 apartment* ⌂ *In-room: Wi-Fi, refrigerator. In-hotel: restaurant, pool, parking* ▤ *AE, MC, V.*

$$$$ **Villa Gallici.** Perched on a hill overlooking the pink roofs of Aix, this former archbishop's palace was transformed into a homage to *le style provençal* thanks to the wizardry of three designers, Gilles Dez, Charles de Montemarco, and Daniel Jouvre. Hued in the lavenders and blues, ochers and oranges of Aix, rooms swim in the most gorgeous Souleiado and Rubelli fabrics and trim. This hilltop garden retreat stands serenely apart from the city center on the outskirts of town (offering great views), and that means the shops of Cours Mirabeau are a 15-minute walk away. All this noted, some say the food needs work. ⊠ *Av. de la Violette, 13100* ☎ *04-42-23-29-23* 🖷 *04-42-96-30-45* ⊕ *www.villagallici.com* 🛏 *18 rooms, 4 suites, 3 duplexes* ⌂ *In-room: Wi-Fi, refrigerator. In-hotel: restaurant, pool, parking (no fee)* ▤ *AE, DC, MC, V* ⊗ *Closed Jan.*

$$-$$$ **Nègre-Coste.** Its prominent Cours Mirabeau position and its lavish public areas make this 18th-century town house a popular hotel. Provençal decor and newly tiled bathrooms live up to the lovely ground-floor salons. Large windows open up to the Cours Mirabeau, perfect for people-watching with a morning cup of coffee; quieter ones at the back look over the rooftops to the cathedral. ⊠ *33 cours Mirabeau, 13100* ☎ *04-42-27-74-22* 🖷 *04-42-26-80-93* ⊕ *www.hotelnegre-coste.com* 🛏 *36 rooms, 1 suite* ⌂ *In-room: Wi-Fi, refrigerator. In-hotel: parking (fee)* ▤ *AE, MC, V.*

$$ **St-Christophe.** With so few mid-price *hôtels de charme* in Aix and a distinct shortage of regional style, you might as well opt for this glossy Art Deco–style hotel, where the comfort and services are remarkable for the price. Rooms are slickly done in deep jewel tones, and the top-floor rooms have artisanal tiles in the bathrooms. Meal plans are available with a three-night minimum stay. ⊠ *2 av. Victor-Hugo, 13100* ☎ *04-42-26-01-24* 🖷 *04-42-38-53-17* ⊕ *www.hotel-saintchristophe.com* 🛏 *53 rooms, 10 suites* ⌂ *In-room: dial-up. In-hotel: restaurant, parking (fee), some pets allowed (fee)* ▤ *AE, MC, V* ⊙*BP, MAP.*

10

★ $-$$ ⊡ **Quatre Dauphins.** In the quiet Mazarin quarter, this modest but impeccable lodging inhabits a noble hôtel particulier. Its pretty, comfortable little rooms have been spruced up with *boutis* (Provençal quilts), Les Olivades fabrics, quarry tiles, jute carpets, and hand-painted furniture. The house-proud but unassuming owner-host bends over backward to please. ⊠*55 rue Roux-Alphéran, 13100* ☎*04–42–38–16–39* 🖷*04–42–38–60–19* 🖙*13 rooms* ♿*In-room: dial-up. In-hotel: some pets allowed (fee)* ⊟*MC, V.*

NIGHTLIFE & THE ARTS

To find out what's going on in town, pick up a copy of the events calendar *Le Mois à Aix* or the bilingual city guide *Aix la Vivante* at the tourist office. **Le Scat Club** (⊠*11 rue de la Verrerie* ☎*04–42–23–00–23*) is the place for live soul, funk, reggae, rock, blues, and jazz. **Le Divino** (⊠*Mas des Auberes, Rte. de Venelles, 5 km [3 mi], from town* ☎*04–42–99–37–08*) is New York stylish and draws the hip, young, and beautiful people. The **Bistrot Aixois** (⊠*37 cours Sextius* ☎*04–42–27–50–10*) is newly renovated and still the hottest student nightspot, with young yuppies lining up to get in. The **Red Clover** (⊠*30 rue de la Verrerie* ☎*04–42–23–44–61*) is a friendly, boisterous Irish pub. Don't expect to speak any French here. For a night of playing roulette and the slot machines, head for the **Casino Municipal** (⊠*2 bis, av. N.-Bonaparte* ☎*04–42–26–30–33*).

Every July during the **Festival International d'Art Lyrique** *(International Opera Festival,* ☎*04–42–17–34–00 for information),* you can see world-class opera productions in the spectacular courtyard of the Palais de l'Archevêché.

SHOPPING

Aix is a market town, and a sophisticated **food and produce market** sets up every morning on Place Richelme; just up the street, on Place Verdun, is a good high-end *brocante* (collectibles market) Tuesday, Thursday, and Saturday mornings. A famous Aixois delicacy is *calissons,* a blend of almond paste and glazed melon in almond shapes. The most picturesque shop specializing in calissons is **Bechard** (⊠*12 cours Mirabeau).* **Leonard Parli** (⊠*35 av. Victor-Hugo),* near the train station, also offers a lovely selection of calissons.

In addition to its old-style markets and jewel-box candy shops, Aix is a modern shopping town—perhaps the best in Provence. The winding streets of the Vieille Ville above Cours Mirabeau—centered around **Rue Clemenceau, Rue Marius Reinaud, Rue Espariat, Rue Aude,** and **Rue Maréchal Foch**—have a head-turning parade of goods.

MARSEILLE

31 km (19 mi) south of Aix-en-Provence, 188 km (117 mi) west of Nice, 772 km (483 mi) south of Paris.

GETTING HERE

The main train station is the Gare St-Charles on the TGV line, with frequent trains from Paris, the main coast route (Nice/Italy), and Arles. For train and ticket information, go to www.voyages-sncf.com, or call

08–36–35–35–35. Handy to note that inside the train station, SOS Voyageurs (☎04–91–62–12–80 ⊙Mon.–Sat. 9–7) helps with children, the elderly, and lost luggage. The Gare Routière (bus station) is on Place Victor Hugo (☎04–91–08–16–40). Here you will find Cartrieze (☎08–00–19–94–13 ⊕www.lepilote.com) controlling the routes into and from the Bouches du Rhone; Eurolines (☎04–91–50–57–55 ⊕www.eurolines.fr) operating coaches between Marseille, Avignon, and Nice via Aix-en-Provence. Marseille also has a métro system, most of the lines service the suburbs, but several stop in the city center (including Gare St-Charles, Colbert, Vieux Port, and Notre Dame; tickets €1.60) and can help you get around quickly.

EXPLORING

Marseille may sometimes be given a wide berth by travelers in search of a Provençal idyll, but it's their loss. Miss it and you miss one of the vibrant, exciting cities in France. With its Cubist jumbles of white stone rising up over a picture-book seaport, bathed in light of blinding clarity and crowned by larger-than-life neo-Byzantine churches, the city's neighborhoods teem with multiethnic life, its souklike African markets reek deliciously of spices and coffees, and its labyrinthine Vieille Ville is painted in broad strokes of saffron, cinnamon, and robin's-egg blue. Feisty and fond of broad gestures, Marseille is a dynamic city, as cosmopolitan now as when the Phoenicians first founded it, and with all the exoticism of the international shipping port it has been for 2,600 years. Vital to the Crusades in the Middle Ages and crucial to Louis XIV as a military port, Marseille flourished as France's market to the world—and still does today.

The heart of Marseille is clustered around the Vieux Port—immortalized in all its briny charm in the 1961 Leslie Caron film version of *Fanny*. The hills to the south of the port are crowned with mega-monuments, such as Notre-Dame de la Garde and Fort St-Jean. To the north lies the ramshackle hilltop Vieille Ville known as Le Panier. East of the port you can find the North African neighborhood and, to its left, the famous thoroughfare called La Canebière. South of the city, the cliff-top waterfront highway leads to obscure and colorful ports and coves.

10

One of many museums devoted to Marseille's history as a shipping port is ❷ the **Musée de la Marine et de l'Economie de Marseille** *(Marine and Economy Museum)*. Inaugurated by Napoléon III in 1860, this impressive building houses both the museum and the city's Chamber of Commerce. The front entrance and hallway are lined with medallions celebrating the ports of the world with which the city has traded, or trades still. The museum charts the maritime history of Marseille from the 17th century onward with paintings and engravings. It's a model-lover's dream with hundreds of steamboats and schooners, all in miniature.

GETTING AROUND

Marseille has a métro system, but it mostly services the suburbs. However, the two main lines have several stops in the center city, which can help you get around quickly, including the main stops at Gare St-Charles, Colbert, Vieux Port, and Notre-Dame. A ticket costs €1.60.

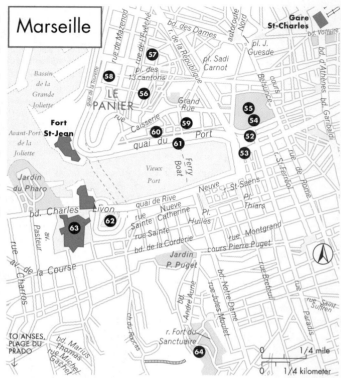

⊠*Palais de la Bourse, 7 La Canebière, La Canebière* ☎*04–91–39–33–33* 🎫*€2* ⊙*Daily 10–6.*

53 With more than 3,000 outfits and accessories, the **Musée de la Mode de Marseille** *(Marseille Fashion Museum)* has well-displayed and ever-changing exhibitions about fashion, dating from the 1920s to the present. Thematic shows also highlight new and cutting-edge designers like Fred Sathel. ⊠*11 La Canebière, La Canebière* ☎*04–96–17–06–00* 🎫*€2* ⊙*June–Sept., Tues.–Sun. 11–6; Oct.–May, Tues.–Sun. 10–5.*

★ **54** The modern, open-space **Musée d'Histoire de Marseille** *(Marseille History Museum)* illuminates Massalia's history by mounting its treasure of archaeological finds in didactic displays and miniature models of the city as it appeared in various stages of history. There's a real Greek-era wooden boat in a hermetically sealed display case. ⊠*Centre Bourse, entrance on Rue de Bir-Hakeim, Vieux Port* ☎*04–91–90–42–22* 🎫*€3 includes entry into Jardin des Vestiges* ⊙*June–Sept., Mon.–Sat. 10–7; Oct.–May., Tues.–Sun. 10–5.*

> **TRIP TIP**
>
> If you plan on visiting many of the museums in Marseille buy a museum "passport" for €8 at the tourism office. It covers the entry fee into all the museums in Marseille.

⑤ The **Jardin des Vestiges** *(Garden of Remains)*, just behind the Marseille History Museum, stands on the site of Marseille's classical waterfront and includes remains of the Greek fortifications and loading docks. It was discovered in 1967 when roadwork was being done next to the Bourse (Stock Exchange). ⊠*Centre Bourse, Vieux Port* ☏*04–91–90–42–22* ☞*€3 includes entry to Museum of History* ⊙*Mon.–Sat. noon–7.*

★ ⑤ **Le Panier** is the old heart of Marseille, a maze of high shuttered houses looming over narrow cobbled streets, *montées* (stone stairways), and tiny squares. Long decayed and neglected, it's the principal focus of the city's efforts at urban renewal. Wander this neighborhood at will, making sure to stroll along Rue du Panier, the montée des Accoules, Rue du Petit-Puits, and Rue des Muettes.

★ ⑤ At the top of the Panier district, the **Centre de la Vieille Charité** *(Center of the Old Charity)* is a superb ensemble of 17th- and 18th-century architecture designed as a hospice for the homeless by Marseillais artist-architects Pierre and Jean Puget. Even if you don't enter the museums, walk around the inner court, studying the retreating perspective of triple arcades and admiring the Baroque chapel with its novel egg-peaked dome. Of the complex's two museums, the larger is the **Musée d'Archéologie Méditerranéenne** (Museum of Mediterranean Archaeology), with a sizable collection of pottery and statuary from classical Mediterranean civilization, elementally labeled (for example, "pot"). There's also a display on the mysterious Celt-like Ligurians who first peopled the coast, cryptically presented with emphasis on the digs instead of the finds themselves. The best of the lot is the evocatively mounted Egyptian collection, the second largest in France after the Louvre's. There are mummies, hieroglyphs, and gorgeous sarcophagi in a tomblike setting. Upstairs, the **Musée d'Arts Africains, Océaniens, et Amérindiens** (Museum of African, Oceanic, and American Indian Art) creates a theatrical foil for the works' intrinsic drama: the spectacular masks and sculptures are mounted along a pure black wall, lighted indirectly, with labels across the aisle. ⊠*2 rue de la Charité, Le Panier* ☏*04–91–14–58–80* ☞*€2 per museum* ⊙*May–Sept., Tues.–Sun. 11–6; Oct.–Apr., Tues.–Sun. 10–5.*

NEED A BREAK?

With handsome decor and pale green walls, the pretty 1901 Café Parisien (⊠1 pl. Sadi Carnot, Le Panier ☏04–91–90–05–77) is always buzzing. It's where the club scene comes for breakfast while locals and tourists stop by later in the day. It opens at 4:30 AM and serves until around midnight.

⑤ A gargantuan, neo-Byzantine 19th-century fantasy, the **Cathédrale de la Nouvelle Major** (⊠*Pl. de la Major, Le Panier*) was built under Napoléon III—but not before he'd ordered the partial destruction of the lovely 11th-century original, once a perfect example of the Provençal Romanesque style. You can view the flashy decor—marble and rich red porphyry inlay—in the newer of the two churches; the medieval one is being restored.

⑤ The **Musée du Vieux Marseille** *(Museum of Old Marseille)* is set in the 16th-century **Maison Diamantée** (Diamond House)—so named for its diamond-faceted Renaissance facade—built in 1570 by a rich mer-

10

chant. Focusing on the history of Marseille, the newly reopened, painstakingly renovated museum features santons, crèches, and furniture, offering a glimpse into 18th-century Marseille life. ⊠*Rue de la Prison, Vieux Port* ☎04–91–55–28–69 ⊡€2 ⊙*June–Sept., Tues.–Sun. 10–6; Oct.–May, Tues.–Sun. 10–5.*

In 1943 Hitler destroyed the neighborhood along the Quai du Port—some 2,000 houses—displacing 20,000 citizens. This act of brutal urban renewal, ironically, laid the ground open for new discoveries. When Marseille began to rebuild in 1947, they dug up remains of a Roman shipping warehouse full of the terra-cotta jars and amphorae that once lay in the bellies of low-slung ships. The **Musée des Docks Romains** (*Roman Docks Museum*) created around it demonstrates the scale of Massalia's shipping prowess. ⊠*2 pl. de Vivaux, Vieux Port* ☎04–91–91–24–62 ⊡€2 ⊙*Oct.–May, Tues.–Sun. 10–5; June–mid-Sept., Tues.–Sun. 11–6.*

㉖ Departing from the Quai below the Hôtel de Ville, the **Ferry Boat** is
Fodor'sChoice a Marseille treasure. To hear the natives pronounce "fer-ry bo-at"
★ (they've adopted the English) is one of the joys of a visit here. For a pittance you can file onto this little wooden barge and chug across the Vieux Port. ⊠*Pl. des Huiles on Quai de Rive Neuve side and Hôtel de Ville on Quai du Port, Vieux Port* ⊡€1.

Founded in the 4th century by St-Cassien, who sailed into Marseille's port full of fresh ideas on monasticism acquired in Palestine and Egypt,
★ **㉒** the **Abbaye St-Victor** grew to formidable proportions. With its Romanesque design, this church would be as much at home in the Middle East as its founder was. By far the best reason to come is the **crypt**, St-Cassien's original, which lay buried under the medieval church's new structure. In evocative nooks and crannies you can find the 5th-century sarcophagus that allegedly holds the martyr's remains. Upstairs, look for the reliquary containing what's left of St. Victor himself, who was ground to death between millstones, probably by Romans. ⊠*3 rue de l'Abbaye, Rive Neuve* ⊡*Crypt entry €2* ⊙*Daily 8:30–6:30.*

㉓ The twin **Fort St-Nicolas and Fort St-Jean** flank the entrance to the Vieux Port. In order to keep the feisty, rebellious Marseillais under his thumb, Louis XIV had the fortresses built with the guns pointing *toward* the city. The Marseillais, whose local identity has always been mixed with a healthy dose of irony, are quite proud of this display of the king's (later justified) doubts about their allegiance. To view them, climb up to the Jardin du Pharo.

Towering above the city and visible for miles around, the preposter-
㉔ ously overscaled neo-Byzantine monument called **Notre-Dame-de-la-Garde** was erected in 1853 by the ever-tasteful Napoléon III. Its interior is a Technicolor bonanza of red-and-beige stripes and glittering mosaics. The gargantuan *Madonna and Child* on the steeple (almost 30 feet high) is covered in real gold leaf. The boggling panoply of naive ex-votos, mostly thanking the Virgin for deathbed interventions and shipwreck survivals, makes the pilgrimage worth it. ⊹*On foot, climb up Cours Pierre Puget, cross Jardin Pierre Puget, cross bridge to Rue Vauvenargues, and hike up*

to Pl. Edon. Or catch Bus 60 from Cours Jean-Ballard ☎*04–91–13–40–80* 🕑*May–Sept., daily 7 AM–8 PM; Oct.–Apr., daily 7–7.*

<table>
<tr><td>OFF THE
BEATEN
PATH</td><td>**Château d'If.** François I, in the 16th century, recognized the strategic advantage of an island fortress surveying the mouth of Marseille's vast harbor, so he had one built. Its effect as a deterrent was so successful that it never saw combat, and was eventually converted into a prison.</td></tr>
</table>

★ It was here that Alexandre Dumas locked up his most famous character, the Count of Monte Cristo. Though he was fictional, the hole Dumas had him escape through is real enough, and is visible in the cells today. Video monitors playing relevant scenes from dozens of Monte Cristo films bring each tower and cell to life. On the other hand, the real-life Man in the Iron Mask, whose cell is still being shown, was not actually imprisoned here. The boat ride (from the Quai des Belges, €10, for information call 04–91–46–54–65) and the views from the broad terrace alone are worth the trip. ☎*04–91–59–02–30* ⊕*www. monuments-france.fr* ✉*Château €4.60* 🕑*Apr.–Sept., daily 9:30–6:30; Oct.–Mar., Tues.–Sun. 9:30–5.*

WHERE TO STAY & EAT

$$$$ ✕ **Chez Fonfon.** Tucked into the filmlike tiny fishing port Vallon des Auffes, this Marseillais landmark has one of the loveliest settings in greater Marseille. A variety of fresh seafood, impeccably grilled, steamed, or roasted in salt crust are served in two pretty dining rooms with picture windows overlooking the fishing boats that supply your dinner. Try classic bouillabaisse served with all the bells and whistles—broth, hot-chili rouille, and flamboyant table-side filleting. ✉*140 rue du Vallon des Auffes, Vallon des Auffes* ☎*04–91–52–14–38* ⊕*www. chez-fonfon.com* ⌕*Reservations essential* 🟰*AE, DC, MC, V* 🕑*Closed Sun. and 1st 2 wks in Jan. No lunch Mon.*

★ $$$$ ✕ **L'Epuisette.** Artfully placed on a rocky, fingerlike cliff surrounded by the sea, this seafood restaurant offers gorgeous views of crashing surf on one side and the port of Vallon des Auffes on the other. Chef Guillaume Sourrieu has acquired a big reputation (and Michelin stars) for sophisticated cooking—mullet fillets on a bed of peppers and eggplant, sauced with peppery rouille, or sea bass baked in a salt crust, are some top delights—all matched with a superb wine list. Save room for dessert. ✉*Anse du Vallon des Auffes, Vallon des Auffes* ☎*04–91–52–17–82* 🟰*AE, MC, V* 🕑*Closed Sun. and Mon.*

$$$$ ✕ **Mets de Provence.** Climb the oddly slanted wharf-side stairs and enter a cosseted Provençal world. With boats bobbing out the window and a landlubbing country decor, this romantic restaurant makes the most of Marseille's split personality. Classic Provençal hors d'oeuvres—tapenade, brandade, aioli—lead into seafood (dorado roasted with fennel and licorice) and meats (rack of lamb in herb pastry). The four-course lunch (€40, including wine) is marvelous. ✉*18 quai de Rive-Neuve, Vieux Port* ☎*04–91–33–35–38* 🟰*MC, V* 🕑*Closed Sun. No lunch Sat. No dinner Mon.*

$$$$ ✕ **Le Peron.** Chic and stylishly modern with its dark-wood interior and large windows overlooking the sea, this restaurant is a magnet for hip young professionals. The staff are efficient and friendly; meals are well

10

presented and tasty—try grilled garlic scallops in a puree of purple potatoes or the lobster risotto—and the prix-fixe lunch menu at €49 is worth the splurge. The view is one of the best in the city. ⊠*56 corniche J.-F.-Kennedy, Endoume* ☎*04–91–52–15–22* ⊟*AE, DC, MC, V.*

$$–$$$$ ✕ **Baie des Singes.** On a tiny rock-ringed lagoon as isolated from the nearby city as if it were a desert island, this cinematic corner of paradise was once a customs house under Napoléon III. You can rent a mattress and lounge chair, dive into the turquoise water, and shower off for the only kind of food worthy of such a locale: fresh fish. It's all served at terrace tables overlooking the water. ⊠*Anse des Croisettes, Les Goudes* ☎*04–91–73–68–87* ⊟*MC, V* ⊘*Closed Oct.–Mar.*

$–$$$$ ✕ **Les Arcenaulx.** At this book-lined, red-wall haven in the stylish book-and-boutique complex of a renovated arsenal, you can have a sophisticated regional lunch—and read while you're waiting. Look for mussels in saffron with buckwheat crepes, carpaccio of cod with crushed olives, or rabbit with garlic confit. The terrace (on the Italian-scale Cours d'Estienne d'Orves) is as pleasant as the interior. ⊠*25 cours d'Estienne d'Orves, Vieux Port* ☎*04–91–59–80–30* ⊟*AE, DC, MC, V* ⊘*Closed Sun.*

★ ¢–$$ ✕ **Etienne.** This historic Le Panier hole-in-the-wall has more than just good fresh-anchovy pizza from a wood-burning oven. There are also fried squid, eggplant gratin, a slab of rare-grilled beef big enough for two, and the quintessential *pieds et paquets,* Marseille's earthy classic of sheeps' feet and stuffed tripe. Be warned: pizza is considered an appetizer here and main courses are huge. ⊠*43 rue de la Lorette, Le Panier* ☎*No phone* ⊟*No credit cards.*

¢–$$ ✕ **Au Petit Naples.** With huge portions, a convivial atmosphere, and a small, busy beachfront location, this restaurant is jammed with locals and savvy tourists from every walk of life. Some connoisseurs say that the pizza here is even better than at Marseille's noted Etienne. ⊠*14 plage de l'Estaque, L'Estaque* ☎*04–91–46–05–11* ⊟*No credit cards* ⊘*Closed Sun. No lunch Sat.*

★ $$$$ ✕⌂ **Le Petit Nice.** On a rocky promontory overlooking the sea, this fantasy villa was bought from a countess in 1917 and converted to a hotel–restaurant. The Passédat family has been getting it right ever since, with father and son manning the exceptional kitchen (one of the coast's best), creating truffled brandade, sea-anemone beignets, fresh fish roasted whole, and licorice soufflé (the restaurant is closed Sunday and Monday for lunch in summer, and Sunday and Monday for lunch and dinner in winter; prix-fixe menus are €110 and €139). Most rooms are sleek and minimalist, with some Art Deco–cum–postmodern touches, while outside the fetching pool is illuminated at night by antique gaslight fixtures. ⊠*Anse de la Maldormé, Corniche J.-F.-Kennedy, Endoume, 13007* ☎*04–91–59–25–92* ⎙*04–91–59–28–08*

FISHY TREAT

When bouillabaisse is presented properly, the broth is served first, with croutons and rouille, a creamy garlic sauce that you spoon in to suit your taste. The fish comes separately, and the ritual is to put pieces into the broth after having a go at the soup on its own.

⊕*www.petitnice-passedat.com* ⟿*13 rooms, 3 suites* ⌂*In-room: Wi-Fi, refrigerator. In-hotel: restaurant, pool, parking (no fee), some pets allowed (fee)* ▤*AE, DC, MC, V* ⦿|*MAP.*

$$$–$$$$ 🖭 **Mercure Beauvau Vieux Port.** Chopin spent the night and George Sand kept a suite in this historic hotel overlooking the Vieux Port. It recently underwent a complete overhaul—even closing for more than a year—but its loyal clientele were not disappointed when the doors finally reopened. Public rooms still have real antiques, burnished woodwork, Provençal-style decor, and plush carpets, all comprising a convincing part of this intimate urban hotel's genuine old-world charm. Guest rooms are in the same style but have been updated to include all the modern comforts. Harbor-view rooms, with balconies high over the fish market, more than justify the splurge. ⊠*4 rue Beauvau, Vieux Port, 13001* ☏*04–91–54–91–00, 800/637–2873 for U.S. reservations* 🖷*04–91–54–15–76* ⊕*www.mercure.com* ⟿*73 rooms* ⌂*In-room: Wi-Fi, refrigerator. In-hotel: bar, some pets allowed (fee)* ▤*AE, DC, MC, V.*

$ 🖭 **Alizé.** On the Vieux Port, its front rooms taking in postcard views, this straightforward lodging has been modernized to include tight double-pane windows, slick modular baths, and a laminate-and-all-weather carpeted look. Public spaces have exposed stone and historic details, and a glass elevator whisks you to your floor. It's an excellent value and location for the price. ⊠*35 quai des Belges, Vieux Port, 13001* ☏*04–91–33–66–97* 🖷*04–91–54–80–06* ⊕*www.alize-hotel.com* ⟿*39 rooms* ⌂*In-room: Wi-Fi. In-hotel: some pets allowed (fee)* ▤*AE, DC, MC, V.*

NIGHTLIFE & THE ARTS

With a population of more than 800,000, Marseille is a big city by French standards, with all the nightlife that entails. Arm yourself with *Marseille Poche,* a glossy monthly events minimagazine; the monthly *In Situ,* a free guide to music, theater, and galleries; *Sortir,* a weekly about film, art, and concerts in southern Provence; or *TakTik,* a hip weekly on theater and art. They're all in French. Rock, jazz, and reggae concerts are held at the **Espace Julien** (⊠*39 cours Julien, Préfecture* ☏*04–91–24–34–10*). **Le Trolleybus** (⊠*24 quai de Rive Neuve, Bompard* ☏*04–91–54–30–45*) is the most popular disco in town, with a young, *branché* (hip) crowd. The **Red Lion** (⊠*231 av. Pierre Mendès France, Vieux Port* ☏*04–91–25–17–17*) is a mecca for English-speakers; they even pour onto the sidewalk, pints in hand, pub-style. There's happy hour daily (5 to 8) and live music Wednesday. **Le Moulin** (⊠*47 bd. Perrin, St-Just* ☏*04–91–06–33–94*) is a converted cinema that has become one of Marseille's best live-music venues for visiting French and international music stars.

Classical music concerts are given in the **Abbaye St-Victor** (☏*04–91–05–84–48 for information*). Operas and orchestral concerts are held at the **Opéra Municipal** (⊠*2 rue Molière, Vieux Port* ☏*04–91–55–21–24*).

SPORTS & THE OUTDOORS

Marseille's waterfront position makes it easy to swim and sunbathe within the city sprawl. From the Vieux Port, Bus 83 or Bus 19 will take you to the vast green spread of reclaimed land called the **Parc**

10

Balnéaire du Prado. Its waterfront is divided into beaches, all of them public and well equipped. The beach surface varies between sand and gravel. Marseille is a mecca for diving (*plongée*), with several organizations offering *baptêmes* (baptisms, or first dives) to beginners. The coast is lined with rocky inlets, grottoes, and ancient shipwrecks, not to mention thronging with aquatic life. For general information contact the **Association Plongez Marseille** (⊠ *Port de la Pointe Rouge, 13008* ☎ *06–20–49–47–12*). **Océan 4** (⊠ *83 av. de la Pointe-Rouge, Vieux Port* ☎ *04–91–73–91–16*) is an English-speaking company that offers initiations and day trips, and has equipment, showers, and storage.

SHOPPING

Savon de Marseille (Marseille soap) is a household standard in France, often sold as a satisfyingly crude and hefty block in odorless olive-oil green. But its chichi offspring are dainty pastel guest soaps in almond, lemon, vanilla, and other scents.

The locally famous bakery **Four des Navettes** (⊠ *136 rue Sainte, Garde Hill* ☎ *04–91–33–32–12*), up the street from Notre-Dame-de-la-Garde, makes orange-spice, shuttle-shape navettes. These cookies are modeled on the little boat in which Mary Magdalene and Lazarus washed up onto Europe's shores.

CASSIS

⑥⑤

Fodor'sChoice
★

30 km (19 mi) east of Marseille, 42 km (26 mi) west of Toulon.

Surrounded by vineyards and monumental cliffs, guarded by the ruins of a medieval castle, and nestled around a picture-perfect fishing port, Cassis is the prettiest coastal town in Provence. Stylish without being too recherché, it's where pleasure-boaters come to spend the night, restock their galleys at its market, replenish their nautical duds in its boutiques, and relax with a bottle of cassis and a platter of sea urchins in one of its numerous waterfront cafés. Pastel houses set at Cubist angles frame the port, and the mild rash of parking-garage architecture that scars its outer neighborhoods doesn't spoil the general effect, one of pure and unadulterated charm. The **Château de Cassis** has loomed over the harbor since the invasions of the Saracens in the 7th century, evolving over the centuries into a walled enclosure crowned with stout watchtowers. It's private property today and best viewed from a portside café.

You can't visit Cassis without touring the **calanques,** the fjordlike finger bays that probe the rocky coastline. Either take a sightseeing cruise or hike across the cliff tops, clambering down the steep sides to these barely accessible retreats. Or you can combine the two, going in by boat and hiking back; make arrangements at the port. The calanque closest to Cassis is the least attractive: **Port Miou** was a stone quarry until 1982, when the calanques became protected sites. Now this calanque

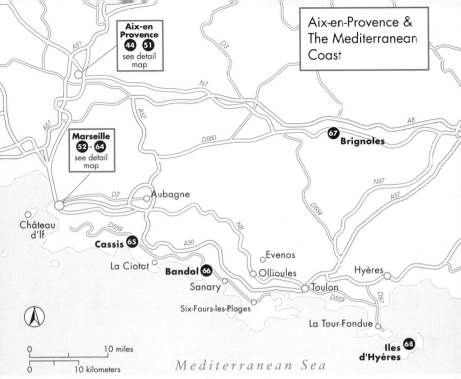

Aix-en-Provence &
The Mediterranean
Coast

Aix-en-Provence
44 51
see detail
map

Marseille
52 - 64
see detail
map

67 **Brignoles**

Château
d'If

Cassis 65

La Ciotat   **Bandol** 66

Sanary

Six-Fours-les-Plages

Aubagne

Evenos

Ollioules

Toulon

Hyères

La Tour-Fondue

Iles 68
d'Hyères

0   10 miles

0   10 kilometers

M e d i t e r r a n e a n   S e a

is an active leisure and fishing port. **Calanque Port Pin** is prettier, with wind-twisted pines growing at angles from the white-rock cliffs. But

★ it's the third calanque that's the showstopper: the **Calanque En Vau** is a castaway's dream, with a tiny beach at its root and jagged cliffs looming overhead. The series of massive cliffs and calanques stretches all the way to Marseille. Note that boats make round-trips several times a day to the Calanques de Cassis from Marseille's Quai des Belges. Here, boat tours to the Calanques are organized by the **Groupement des Armateurs Côtiers Marseillais** (⊠*1 quai des Belges* ☎*04–91–55–50–09* ⊕*www. answeb.net/gacm*); otherwise, contact the tourism office and they will give the right numbers to call, or they will help you organize a tour.

WHERE TO STAY & EAT

$$–$$$ ✕ **Chez Nino.** This is the best of the many restaurants lining the harbor, with top-notch Provençal food and wine and a spectacular terrace view. The owners, Claudie and Bruno, are extremely hospitable as long as you stick to the menu—don't ask for sauce on the side—and you are as passionate about fish and seafood as they are. The sardines in *escabeche* are textbook perfect, as are the grilled fish and the bouillabaisse. And if you want to indulge, there are now two suites (€700) and one room (€300) available for the night, beautifully decorated with views of the sea. ⊠*2 quai Barthélémy* ☎*04–42–01–74–32* ⊟*AE, DC, MC, V* ⊗*Closed Mon. No dinner Sun. off-season.*

$$–$$$$ 🏨 **Les Roches Blanches.** First built as a private home in 1887, this cliff-side villa takes in smashing views of the port and the Cap Canaille, both from the best rooms and from the panoramic dining hall. The beautifully landscaped terrace is shaded by massive pines, and the horizon pool appears to spill into the sea. Yet the aura is far from snooty or deluxe; it's friendly, low-key, and pleasantly mainstream. ⊠ *Rte. des Calanques, 13260* 🕾*04–42–01–09–30* 🖷*04–42–01–94–23* ⊕*www. roches-blanches-cassis.com* ⇆*19 rooms, 5 suites* ⚭*In-room: Wi-Fi, refrigerator. In-hotel: 2 restaurants, bar, pool, parking (fee), some pets allowed (fee)* ⊟*AE, MC, V* ⊗*Closed Nov.–Mar.* �†◎†*MAP*

SPORTS & THE OUTDOORS

To go on a **boat ride** to Les Calanques, get to the port around 10 AM or 2 PM and look for a boat that's loading passengers. Round-trips should include visits to at least three calanques and average €10. To **hike** the calanques, gauge your skills: the GR98 (marked with red-and-white bands) is the most scenic, but requires scrambling to get down the sheer walls of En Vau. The alternative is to follow the green markers and approach En Vau from behind. If you're ambitious, you can hike the length of the GR98 between Marseille and Cassis, following the coastline.

█ **EN ROUTE**   From Cassis head east out of town and cut sharply right up the **Route des Crêtes.** This road takes you along a magnificent crest over the water and up to the very top of **Cap Canaille.** Venture out on the vertiginous trails to the edge, where the whole coast stretches below.

BANDOL

⑥⑥   *25 km (16 mi) southeast of Cassis, 15 km (9 mi) west of Toulon.*

Although its name means wine to most of the world, Bandol is also a popular and highly developed seaside resort town. It has seafood snack shacks, generic brasseries, a harbor packed with yachts, and a waterfront promenade. Yet the east end of town conceals lovely old villas framed in mimosas, bougainvillea, and pine. And a port-side stroll up the palm-lined Allée Jean-Moulin feels downright Côte d'Azur. But be warned: the sheer concentration of high-summer crowds cannot be exaggerated. If you're not a beach lover, pick up an itinerary from the tourist office and visit a few Bandol vineyards just outside town.

█ **OFF THE BEATEN PATH**   **La Cadiere d'Azur.** Set 6 km (4 mi) north of Bandol, La Cadiere is one of Provence's secrets: a beautiful, sleepy medieval town perched on a limestone hill overlooking the majestic vineyards of Bandol. Van Gogh and French painter Favory passed through here, as did several writers and poets. Small, generations-old shops selling local pottery and produce line the main street today. An added attraction is the special trip-worthy Hostellerie Bérard.

WHERE TO EAT

$$$$ ✕ **Auberge du Port.** This is a fish-first-and-foremost establishment, with a terrace packed night and day—and not because of the splendid view it offers of Ile Bandor. Going off menu for a daily catch special can be costly, but worth it if a memorable fish-dish experience has so far eluded you on the trip. Otherwise, try the excellent *friture* of small fish fried with lemon or the classic fish stew *bourride*. Get here early for something especially fresh and savory. And book ahead. ⊠ *9 allée Jean-Moulin* ☎ *04–94–29–42–63* ♨ *Reservations essential* 🗖 *AE, DC, MC, V.*

★ $$–$$$$ ✕🖽 **Hostellerie Bérard.** Master Chef René Bérard is as celebrated for his haute cuisine as he is for his elegant country inn. The rooms, decorated in handsome Provençal style, are scattered throughout a cluster of beautifully restored old buildings, including an 11th-century monastery. In the airy and window-filled restaurant, delicious Mediterranean-inspired Provençal meals emphasizing local seafood and fresh produce grace the tables. Try the ravioli stuffed with goat cheese, sorrel, and Parmesan in a lemon chicken broth; the lightly grilled red mullet wrapped in seaweed and topped with peas and fresh rosemary is another winner. If you want to attempt similar gastronomic heights at home, Chef Bérard, cheerfully sympathetic to all cooking woes, has weeklong culinary getaways; otherwise you can soak your troubles away in the new aromatherapy spa downstairs. ⊠ *La Cadière d'Azur 83740* ✛ *6 km (4 mi) north of Bandol* ☎ *04–94–90–11–43* 🖷 *04–94–90–01–94* ⊕ *www. hotel-berard.com* ⤴ *41 rooms, 3 suites* ♿ *In-room: dial-up, refrigerator. In-hotel: restaurant, pool, some pets allowed (fee), parking (fee)* 🗖 *AE, DC, MC, V* ☉ *Closed early Jan.–mid-Feb.* 🍴 *MAP.*

BRIGNOLES

67 *86 km (47 mi) northwest of Bandol, 70 km (39 mi) north of Toulon.*

This rambling backcountry hill town, crowned with a medieval château, is the market center for the wines of the Var and the crossroads of this green, ungentrified region—until now, that is. With a Ducasse restaurant now in the region, real estate has rocketed, and le tout Paris whispers that this little corner of nowheresville is *the* next Luberon. The main point of interest in the region is the **Abbaye de La Celle,** a 12th-century Benedictine abbey that served as a convent until the 17th century. There's a refectory and a ruined cloister; the simple Romanesque chapel still serves as the parish church.

WHERE TO STAY & EAT

$$$$ ✕🖽 **Hostellerie de l'Abbaye de La Celle.** Superchef Alain Ducasse put this
Fodor'sChoice country inn—buried in the unspoiled backcountry north of Toulon and
★ just south of Brignoles—back on the map a decade ago. Up the road from the town's royal abbey, this beautifully restored 18th-century *bastide* (country house)—a dream in ocher-yellow walls, Arles green shutters, and white stone trim—was once part of the convent where future queens of Provence were raised. Guest rooms mix Louis XVI and regional accents; half are split-level with their own gardens, some with views of vineyards, others of a park thick with chestnut and mulberry trees. Beds are enormous—none more so than those of the Charles de Gaulle suite (where the great man once stayed). Wherever you bed down, the scent of fresh thyme and lemon basil wafts through the win-

dows from the gardens. Today, the formidable kitchen is headed up by Chef Benoît Witz, whose seemingly magical creations find a superb balance (and a Michelin star) between taste and texture: velouté of crawfish gently covering a bruschetta topped with tomatoes and garden herbs, or duck breast with polenta and cherries. ⊠ *Pl. du Général-de-Gaulle, 83170 La Celle* ☎ *04–98–05–14–14* 🖷 *04–98–05–14–15* ⊕ *www.abbaye-celle.com* 🛏 *9 rooms, 1 suite, 3 duplexes* 🕭 *In-room: Wi-Fi, refrigerator. In-hotel: restaurant, pool* ☰ *AE, DC, MC, V.*

ILES D'HYÈRES

68 *32 km (20 mi) off coast south of Hyères. To get to islands, follow narrow Giens Peninsula to La Tour-Fondue, at its tip. Boats (leaving every half hour in summer, every 60 or 90 mins rest of year, for €12 roundtrip) make a 20-min beeline to Porquerolles. For Port-Cros and Levant, you depart from Port d'Hyères at Hyères-Plages.*

Off the southeastern point of France's star and spanning some 32 km (20 mi), this archipelago of islands could be a set for a pirate movie; in fact, it has been featured in several, thanks to a soothing microclimate and a wild and rocky coastline dotted with palms. And not only film pirates made their appearance: in the 16th century the islands were seeded with convicts to work the land. They soon ran amok and used their adopted base to ambush ships heading into Toulon. A more wholesome population claims the islands today, which are made up of three main areas. **Port-Cros** is a national park, with both its surface and underwater environs protected. **Levant** has been taken over, for the most part, by nudists.

★ **Porquerolles** is the largest and best of the lot—and a popular escape from the modern world. Off-season, it's a castaway delight of pine forests, sandy beaches, and vertiginous cliffs above rocky coastline. Inland, its preserved pine forests and orchards of olives and figs are crisscrossed with dirt roads to be explored on foot or on bikes; except for the occasional jeep or work truck, the island is car-free. In high season (April to October), day-trippers pour off the ferries and surge to the beaches. For information on the islands, contact the tourism office of Hyères.

WHERE TO STAY & EAT

$$$$ ✕⊡ **Les Glycines.** In soft shades of yellow-ocher and sky-blue, this sleekly modernized little bastide has an idyllic enclosed courtyard. Back rooms look over a jungle of mimosa and eucalyptus. Public salons have Provençal chairs and fabrics. The restaurant, where food is served on the terrace or in the garden, proffers port-fresh tuna and sardines. The inn is just back from the port in the village center. Prices include breakfast and dinner. ⊠ *Pl. d'Armes, 83400 Ile de Porquerolles* ☎ *04–94–58–30–36* 🖷 *04–94–58–35–22* ⊕ *www.aubergedesglycines. com* 🛏 *8 rooms, 3 suites* 🕭 *In-room: Wi-Fi. In-hotel: restaurant, bar* ☰ *AE, MC, V* ⧖ *MAP.*

★ $$$$ ✕⊡ **Mas du Langoustier.** A fabled forgetaway, the Langoustier comes with a lobster-orange building, pink bougainvillea, and a secluded spot at the westernmost point of the Ile de Porquerolles, 3 km (2 mi) from the harbor. Manager Madame Richard—who may pick you up at the port in her Dodge—knows a thing or two about the island: her grandmother was given the island as a wedding gift. Choose between big California-modern rooms and charming old-style Provençal. Chef Joël Guillet creates inspired, spectacular southern French cuisine, to be accompanied by the rare island rosé (note that prices include breakfast and dinner). ⊠*Pointe du Langoustier, 83400 Ile de Porquerolles* ☎*04–94–58–30–09* 🖷*04–94–58–36–02* ⊕*www.langoustier.com* ⇥*50 rooms* ⅋*In-room: Wi-Fi, refrigerator. In-hotel: restaurant, tennis court, beachfront* ⊟*DC, MC, V* ⊗*Closed Nov.–Apr.* ⧖*MAP.*

THE OUTDOORS
You can rent a mountain bike (*velo tout-terrain*, or VTT) for a day to pedal the paths and cliff-top trails of Porquerolles at **Cycle Porquerol** (⊠*Rue de la Ferme* ☎*04–94–58–30–32*). **L'Indien** (⊠*Pl. d'Armes* ☎*04–94–58–30–39*) offers a wide variety of bikes. **Locamarine 75** (⊠*On port* ☎*04–94–58–35–84*) rents motorboats to amateurs with or without license.

PROVENCE ESSENTIALS

To research prices, get advice from other travelers, and book travel arrangements, visit www.fodors.com.

TRANSPORTATION

If traveling extensively by public transportation, be sure to load up on information (schedules, the best taxi-for-call companies, etc.) upon arriving at the ticket counter or help desk of the bigger train and bus stations in the area, such as Avignon, Aix-en-Provence, and Marseille.

BY AIR
Marseille has one of the largest airports in France, the Aéroport de Marseille Provence in Marignane, about 20 km (12 mi) northwest of the city center. Regular flights come in daily from Paris and London. In summer Delta Airlines flies direct from New York to Nice (about 190 km [118 mi] from Marseille and about 150 km [93 mi] from Toulon). Airport shuttle buses to Marseille center leave every 20 minutes 5:30 AM–10:50 PM daily (€8). Shuttles to Aix leave hourly 8 AM–11:10 PM (€7.30).

Air Travel Information Aéroport de Marseille Provence in Marignane (☎*04-42-14-14-14* ⊕ *www.marseille.aeroport.fr*).

BY BIKE & MOPED
Bikes can be rented from the train stations in Aix-en-Provence, Arles, Avignon, Marseille, Nîmes, and Orange at a cost of about €10 per day. Contact the Comité Départemental de Cyclotourisme for a list of scenic bike routes in Provence.

Bike Maps Comité Départemental de Cyclotourisme (⊠*Les Passadoires, 84420 Piolenc* ☎*04-90-29-64-80*).

10

BY BUS

A moderately good network of bus services—run by a perplexing number of independent bus companies (for best advice on schedules, consult the town tourist office or your hotel concierge)—links places not served, or poorly served, by train. If you plan to explore Provence by bus, Avignon, Marseille, Aix-en-Provence, and Arles are good bases. Avignon is also the starting point for excursion-bus tours and boat trips down the Rhône. In most cases, you can buy bus tickets on the bus itself.

Aix-en-Provence: One block west of La Rotonde, the station (⊠Rue Lapierre) is crowded with many bus companies—to/from destinations include Marseille (1 hr, every ½ hr, €5), Arles (1½ hrs, 2 to 5 daily, €10), and Avignon (1½ hrs, 2 to 4 daily, €12). C.A.P. (Compagnie Autocars de Provence) makes daily forays from 2 to 7 into Marseille, the Calanques by Cassis, Les Baux, the Luberon, and Arles, leaving from in front of the tourist office, at the foot of Cours Mirabeau. **Arles:** Arles is one of the largest hubs, serviced out of the *Gare Routière* (bus station) on Avenue Paulin-Talabot, opposite the train station; within the city, bus stations are mainly on Boulevard G. Clémenceau. You can travel from Arles to such stops as Nîmes (1 hr, 4 daily, €6) and Avignon (45 mins, 10 daily, €7); four buses daily head out to Aix-en-Provence and Marseille (only 2 run on weekends). Out of Arles, Les Cars de Camargue and Ceyte Tourisme Méditerranée can take you on round-trip excursions to the Camargue's Stes-Marie-de-la-Mer (1 hr, 3 daily, €5), Mas du Pont de Rousty, Pont de Gau, as well as stops in the Alpilles area, including Les Baux-des-Provence and St-Rémy-de-Provence (neither of which have train stations). **Avignon:** The bus station is right by the rail station on Boulevard St-Roch; lines connect to nearby towns such as Fontaine-de-Vaucluse. St-Rémy-de-Provence is 40 minutes from Avignon by bus. **Les Baux:** Buses here head from Avignon or Arles. **Marseille:** The station (⊠3 pl. Victor Hugo) is next to the train station and offers myriad connections to cities and small towns. **Nîmes:** The bus station (⊠Rue Ste-Félicité) connects with Montpellier, Pont du Gard, and many other places. **Orange:** The station is on Cours Pourtoules, on the eastern edge of the city, and offers links to Avignon, Vaison-la-Romaine, and Marseille. **Stes-Maries-de-la-Mer:** As the gateway to the Camargue region (in which there is little or no public transportation), buses head here from Arles, Nîmes, and Aigues-Mortes. **St-Rémy-de-Provence:** You can reach its bus station on Place de la République by frequent buses from Avignon (45 mins, €6).

As for the Luberon villages, a bewildering number of bus companies feature routes with (infrequent) buses. You can get to **Gordes** on the two-to-four buses daily run by Les Express de la Durance. Voyages Arnaud has routes that include **L'Isle-sur-la-Sorgue, Fontaine-de-Vaucluse,** and **Bonnieux.** Autocars Barlatier runs buses that stop in Bonnieux. For a complete list of bus Web sites for Provence, log on to ⊕*www.provence-jouques.com/fr/venir/venir15.html.* One Web site that provides in-depth info on bus travel is ⊕*www.beyond.fr.*

Bus Information Aix-en-Provence's Gare Routière (⊠*Av. de la Europe* ☎*04-42-91-26-80).* **Avignon's Gare Routière** (⊠*58 bd. St-Roch* ☎*04-90-82-07-35).*

Marseille's Gare Routière (⊠ *3 pl. Victor-Hugo* ☎ *04–91–08–16–40*). **Autocars Barlatier** (☎ *04–90–38–15–58*). **Les Cars de Camargue** (⊠ *1 rue Jean-Mathieu Artaud, Arles* ☎ *04-90-96-36-25* ⊕ *www.carsdecamargue.com*). **Cars Fort** (⊠ *27 av. Jean Jaurès, Nîmes* ☎ *04-66-36-60-80*). **Cars Lieutaud** (☎ *04-90-36-05-22* ⊕ *www.cars-lieutaud.fr*). **Ceyte Tourisme Méditerranée** (⊠ *14 bd. Georges Clemenceau, Arles* ☎ *04-90-18-96-33* ⊕ *www.autocars-ctm.com*). **Les Express de la Durance** (☎ *04-90-71-03-00*). **Voyages Arnaud** (☎ *04-90-38-15-58*).

BY CAR

A6–A7 (a toll road) from Paris, known as the Autoroute du Soleil—the Highway of the Sun—takes you straight to Provence, where it divides at Orange, 659 km (412 mi) from Paris; the trip can be done in a fast five or so hours.

After route A7 divides at Orange, A9 heads west to Nîmes (723 km [448 mi] from Paris) and continues into the Pyrénées and across the Spanish border. Route A7 continues southeast from Orange to Marseille, on the coast (1,100 km [680 mi] from Paris), while A8 goes to Aix-en-Provence (with a spur to Toulon) and then to the Côte d'Azur and Italy.

BY TRAIN

The high-speed TGV *Méditerranée* line ushered in a new era in Trains à Grande Vitesse travel in France; the route means that you can travel from Paris's Gare de Lyon to Avignon (first class, one-way tickets cost about €90) in 2 hours, 40 minutes, with a mere 3-hour trip to Nîmes, Aix-en-Provence, and Marseille. Not only is the idea of Provence as a day trip now possible (though, of course, not advisable), you can even whisk yourself there directly upon arrival at Paris's Charles de Gaulle airport.

After the main line of the TGV divides at Avignon, the westbound link heads to Nîmes and points west; heading east, the line connects with Orange. The southeast-bound link takes in Marseille, Toulon, and the Côte d'Azur. Montpellier is the stop after Nîmes, with other links at Béziers and Narbonne. There is also frequent service by daily local trains to other towns in the region from these main TGV stops. With high-speed service now connecting Nîmes, Avignon, and Marseille, travelers without cars will find a Provence itinerary much easier to pull off. For full information on the TGV *Méditerranée*, log onto the TGV Web site; you can purchase tickets on this Web site or through RailEurope, and you should always buy your TGV tickets in advance.

Aix-en-Provence: The station (⊠ Pl. Victor Hugo) is a five-minute walk from Place du Général-de-Gaulle and offers many connections, including Marseille (30 mins, 12 to 20 trains daily, €6), Nice (3½ hrs, 8 trains daily, €28), and Cannes (3½ hrs, eight trains daily, €26), along with other destinations; note that the TGV station for Aix is about 16 km (10 mi) west of the city—a shuttle bus connects it with the town station. **Arles:** Only one TGV train from Paris arrives daily; from the gare centrale station (⊠ Av. Paulin Talabot) you can connect to Nîmes (30 mins, €7), Marseille (1 hr, €12), Avignon Centre (1 hr, €6), and Aix-en-Provence (2 hrs with connection, €24). **Avignon:** The Gare Avignon

TGV station is located a few miles southwest of the city in the district of Courtine (a *navette* shuttle bus connects with the train station in town); other trains (and a few TGV) use the Gare Avignon Centre station located at 42 boulevard. St-Roch, where you can find trains to Orange (20 mins, €5), Arles (20 mins, €6), L'Isle-sur-la-Sorgue, Nîmes, Marseille, and Aix-en-Provence. **Marseille:** The station (esplanade St-Charles) serves all regions of France and is at the northern end of center city, a 20-minute walk from the Vieille Ville. Marseille has train routes to Aix-en-Provence (30 mins, 12 to 20 trains daily, €6), Avignon (1 hr, hourly, €16), Nîmes (1½ hrs, €22), Arles (1 hr, €12), and Orange (1½ hrs, €20). Once in Marseille, you can link up with the coastal train route, which links all the resort towns lining the coast eastward to Monaco and Menton, along with trains to Cassis, Bandol, and Toulon. **Nîmes:** There are eight TGV trains daily on the four-hour trip from Paris; frequent trains connect with Avignon Centre (45 mins, €8) and Arles (30 mins, €7), along with Montpellier and Marseille; to reach the Vieille Ville from the station, walk north on Avenue Fauchères. **Orange:** The center city is a 15-minute walk from the train station—walk from Avenue Frédéric Mistral to Rue de la République, then follow signs.

Aix-en-Provence's *Gare SNCF (Train station,* ✉*Av. Victor Hugo* ☎*04–91–08–16–40).* **Marseilles's** *Gare St-Charles (*☎*04–91–08–16–40).* **SNCF** (☎*36–35, €0.34 per min* ⊕*www.voyages-sncf.com).* **TGV** (☎*877/284–8633* ⊕*www.tgv.com).* **www.beyond.fr** (⊕*www.beyond.fr).*

CONTACTS & RESOURCES

CAR RENTAL

Local Agencies Avis (✉*11 bd. Gambetta, Aix* ☎*04–42–21–64–16* ✉*At train station, Avignon* ☎*04–90–27–96–10* ✉*At train station, Marseille* ☎*04–91–64–71–00* ✉*19 av. Charles de Gaulle, Orange* ☎*04–90–34–11–00).* **Budget** (✉*Bd. St-Roch, Avignon* ☎*04–90–27–94–95* ✉*42 bd. Edouard Daladier, Orange* ☎*04–90–34–00–34).* **Hertz** (✉*43 av. Victor Hugo, Aix* ☎*04–42–27–91–32* ✉*2A av. Monclar, Avignon* ☎*04–90–14–26–90* ✉*At train station, Marseille* ☎*04–91–90–14–03).*

EMERGENCIES

For basic information, see this section in the Essentials chapter. In most cases, contact the town Comissariat de Police.

Emergencies Police (✉*Pl. B. Niollon, Aix-en-Provence* ☎*17 for police, 15 for medical assistance).* **Police** (✉*Pl. de la Préfecture, Marseille* ☎*04–91–39–00–00).* **Hôpital de la Timone** (✉*264 rue St-Pierre, Marseille* ☎*04–91–49–91–91).*

INTERNET & MAIL

In smaller towns, ask your hotel concierge if there are any Internet cafés nearby.

Internet & Mail Information Ad'Art Informative (✉*32 rue de la Balance, Avignon* ☎*04–90–86–68–70).* **Cyber Sal@delle** (✉*17 rue de la République, Arles* ☎*04–90–93–13–56).* **Esc@lia** (✉*3 rue Coutelleine, Marseille* ☎*04–91–91–65–10).* **Hub Lot Cybercafé** (✉*15 rue Paul Bert, Aix-en-Provence* ☎*04–42–21–37–31).* **La Poste main post office** (✉*Sq. Mattéi, Aix-en-Provence).* **La Poste main post office**

(✉ *5 bd. des Lices. Arles*). La **Poste** main post office (✉ *Cours Président Kennedy, Avignon*). La **Poste** main post office (✉ *1 pl. de l'Hôtel des Postes, Marseille*)

LODGING

APARTMENT-VILLA RENTALS

Properties for rent in Provence are listed by the national house-rental agency, Gîtes de France. Regional offices are in Bouches-du-Rhône, Gard, Var, and Vaucluse. In addition, each of the tourist offices in towns in the region usually publishes lists of independent rentals (*locations meublés*), many of them inspected and classified by the tourist office itself.

Local Agents Bouches-du-Rhône (✉ *Domaine du Vergon, B.P. 26, 13370 Mallemort* ☎ *04-90-59-49-40* 🖷 *04-90-59-16-75*). **Gard** (✉ *3 pl. des Arènes, B.P. 59, Cedex 4, 30007 Nîmes* ☎ *04-66-27-94-94* 🖷 *04-66-27-94-95*). **Var** (✉ *1 bd. Maréchal Foch, Draguignan* ☎ *04-94-50-93-93* 🖷 *04-94-50-93-90*). **Vaucluse** (✉ *Pl. Campana, B.P. 164, Cedex 1, 84008 Avignon* ☎ *04-90-85-45-00*).

BED & BREAKFASTS

Gîtes de France, the French national network of vacation lodging, rates participating B&Bs for comfort and lists them in a catalog. For chambres d'hôtes regulated by this national network, contact the local branches, divided by *départements* (administrative regions).

MEDIA

La Provence (published in Marseille) is one of the South's leading regional dailies and widely available. The *International Herald Tribune* is the only English language daily to reliably hit newstands on the day of publication while provence.angloinfo.com is a local-based Web site that daily lists articles (in English) from a selection of newspapers from around the world.

TOUR OPTIONS

PRIVATE GUIDES

Bus tours through the Camargue, departing from Avignon with a passenger pickup in Arles (behind the tourism office, in front of the Atrium hotel, 9:45 AM) are offered by Self-Voyages Provence for about €45. Ask about the optional riverboat trip down the Rhône. Taxis T.R.A.N. can take you round-trip from Nîmes to the Pont du Gard (ask the taxi to wait while you explore for 30 minutes).

Contacts Self Voyages Provence (✉ *42 bd. Raspail, 84000 Avignon* ☎ *04-90-14-70-00* 🌐 *www.self-voyages.fr*). **Taxis T.R.A.N** (☎ *04-66-29-40-11*).

WALKING TOURS

The tourist offices in Arles, Nîmes, Avignon, Aix-en-Provence, and Marseille all organize a full calendar of walking tours (some in summer only).

VISITOR INFORMATION

Regional tourist offices prefer written queries only. The mother lode of general information is the Comité Regional du Tourisme de Provence-Alpes-Côte d'Azur. For information specific to one département, contact

10

the following: Comité Départemental du Tourisme des Bouches-du-Rhône, Comité Départemental du Tourisme du Var, Comité Départemental du Tourisme de Vaucluse. Local tourist offices for major towns covered in this chapter can be phoned, faxed, or addressed by mail.

Regional Tourist Offices Comité Regional du Tourisme de Provence-Alpes-Côte d'Azur (✉12 pl. Joliette, 13002 Marseille ☎04–91–56–47–00 🖷04–91–56–47–01 ⊕www.crt-paca.fr/fre/accueil_flash.jsp). **Comité Départemental du Tourisme des Bouches-du-Rhône** (✉13 rue Roux de Brignole, 13006 Marseille ☎04–91–13–84–13 🖷04–91–33–01–82 ⊕ www.visitprovence.com). **Comité Départemental du Tourisme du Var** (✉1 bd. Maréchal Foch, 83300 Draguignan ☎04–94–50–55–50 🖷04–94–50–55–51 ⊕www.tourismevar.com). **Comité Départemental du Tourisme de Vaucluse** (🖃 B.P. 147, Cedex 1, 84008 Avignon ☎04–90–80–47–00 🖷04–90–86–86–08).

Local Tourist Offices Aigues-Mortes (✉Pl. St. Louis, 30220 ☎04–66–53–73–00 🖷04–66–53–65–94 ⊕www.ot-aiguesmortes.fr). **Aix** (✉2 pl. du Général-de-Gaulle, B.P. 160, Cedex 1, 13605 ☎04–42–16–11–61 🖷04–42–16–11–62 ⊕www.aixenprovencetourism.com). **Arles** (✉35 pl. de la République, 13200 ☎04–90–18–41–21 🖷04–90–93–17–17 ⊕ www.ville-arles.fr). **Avignon** (✉41 cours Jean-Jaurès, 84000 ☎04–90–82–65–11 🖷04–90–82–95–03 ⊕www.ot-avignon.fr). **Le Barroux** (✉2 pl. du Général-de-Gaulle, B.P. 160, Cedex 1, 13605 ☎04–42–16–11–61 🖷04–42–16–11–62 ⊕ www.aixenprovencetourism.com). **Camargue** (✉1 pl. Frederic Mistral,13800 St-Gilles du Gard ☎04–66–87–33–75 🖷04–66–87–16–28 ⊕www.ot-saint-gilles.fr). **Cassis** (✉Quai des Moulins, 13260 ☎04–08–92–25–98–92 🖷04–92–01–28–31 ⊕ www.cassis.fr). **Fontaine-de-Vaucluse** (✉Chem de la Fontaine, 84800 ☎04–90–20–32–22 🖷04–90–20–21–37 ⊕www.oti-delasorgue.fr). **Gordes** (✉Le Chateau, 84220 ☎04–90–72–02–75 🖷04–90–72–02–26 ⊕www.gorges-village.com). **Hyères** (✉3 av. Ambroise Thomas, 83400 ☎04–94–01–84–50 🖷04–94–01–84–51 ⊕ www.ot-hyeres.fr). **L'Isle-sur-la-Sorgue** (✉Pl. de l'Église, 84800 ☎04–90–38–04–78 🖷04–90–38–35–43 ⊕ot-islessurlasorgue.fr). **Les-Baux-de-Provence** (✉Maison du Roi, 13520 ☎04–90–54–34–39 🖷04–90–54–51–15 ⊕www.lesbauxdeprovence.com). **Marseille** (✉4 la Canebière, 13001 ☎04–91–13–89–00 🖷03–91–13–89–20 ⊕www.destination-marseille.com). **Nîmes** (✉6 rue Auguste, 30000 ☎04–66–67–29–11 🖷04–66–21–81–04 ⊕www.ot-nimes.fr). **Orange** (✉5 cours Aristide Briand, 84110 ☎04–90–34–70–88 🖷04–42–16–11–62 ⊕ www.ville-orange.fr). **Roussillon** (✉2 pl. de la Poste, 84220 ☎04–90–05–60–25 🖷04–90–05–63–31 ⊕www.roussillon-provence.com). **Stes-Maries-de-la-Mer** (✉5 av. Van Gogh, 13700 ☎04–90–97–82–55 🖷04–90–97–71–15 ⊕www.saintesmaries.com). **St-Rémy** (✉Pl. Jean-Jaurès, 13210 ☎04–90–92–05–22 🖷04–90–92–38–52 ⊕www.saintremy-de-provence.com). **Vaison la Romaine** (✉Pl. Chanoene Sautel, 84110 ☎04–90–36–02–11 ⊕ www.vaison-la-romaine.com).

The French Riviera

Beaulieu-Sur-Mer

WORD OF MOUTH

"The best way to stay on the Riviera is to stay in the small towns.
For example, Villefranche-sur-Mer is minutes by train from Nice;
Antibes is minutes by train from Cannes. Both towns have darling
seaside cafés and restaurants. If you need a more extensive scene,
simply hop the frequent, easily accessible trains to the Riviera's
big cities."

—Amelia

WELCOME TO
THE FRENCH RIVIERA

Old port, St. Tropez

TOP REASONS TO GO

★ **Monaco, toy kingdom:** Yes, Virginia, you can afford to visit Monte Carlo—that is, if you avoid its casinos and head for its tropical gardens.

★ **Picasso & Company:** Because artists have long loved the Côte d'Azur, it's blessed with superb art museums, including the Fondation Maeght in St-Paul and the Musée Picasso in Antibes.

★ **Èze, island in the sky:** The most perfectly perched of the coast's villages perchés, Èze has some of the most breathtaking views this side of a NASA space capsule.

★ **St-Tropez à go-go:** Brave the world's most outlandish fishing port in high summer and soak up the scene. Just don't forget the fake tan lotion.

★ **Nice, Queen of the Riviera:** With its bonbon-color palaces, blue Baie des Anges, time-stained Old Town, and Musée Matisse, this is one of France's most colorful cities.

Old Town Cannes

1 St-Tropez to Antibes. Put on the map by Brigitte Bardot, **St-Tropez** remains one of France's ritziest vacation spots. Happily, the town has managed to stay small and laid-back, thanks to the lack of train service and chain hotels. Conspicuous consumption characterizes the celluloid city of **Cannes** when its May film fest turns it into Oscar-goes-to-the-Mediterranean but the Louis Vuitton set enjoys this city year-round. But for the utmost in Riviera charm, head up the coast to Antibes: once Picasso's home, it is set with a harbor and Old Town so dreamy it will have you reaching for your paintbrush.

ITALY

Menton
Monte-Carlo
MONACO
St-Jean-
Cap-Ferrat
Villefranche-
sur-Mer
Vence
St-Paul-
de-Vence
Cagnes-sur-Mer
Nice
Baie des Anges
EASTERN CÔTE d'AZUR
Antibes
Cap d'Antibes
Cannes
N202
Eze
N7
A8
N7
A8

Mediterranean Sea

2

3

4

Villefranche-sur-Mer, near Nice

GETTING ORIENTED

The French Rivera can supply the visitor with everything his heart desires—and his purse can stand. Home to sophisticated resorts beloved by billionaires, remote hill villages colonized by artists, Mediterranean beaches, and magnificent views, the Côte d'Azur (to use the French name) stretches from Marseille to Menton. Thrust out like two gigantic arms, divided by the Valley of the Var at Nice, the Alpes-Maritimes peaks throw their massive protection, east and west, the length of that favored coast from St-Tropez to the Italian frontier. Some talk about how great the Riviera used to be. In our opinion, it still is *la crème de la crème.*

3 Nice. Walking along the seaside Promenade des Anglais is one of the iconic Riviera experiences. Add in top-notch museums, a charming old quarter, scads of ethnic restaurants, and a raging nightlife, and Nice is a must-do.

4 The Eastern Côte d'Azur. The 24-karat sun shines most brightly on the fabled glamour ports of **Villefranche-sur-Mer** (hi there, Bill Gates!) and **St-Jean-Cap-Ferrat.** If you want to kiss the sky, head up to the charming, mountaintop village of **Èze.** To the east of glittering **Monaco**—looking more like Manhattan every day—lies **Menton**, an enchanting Italianate resort where winters are so mild that lemon trees bloom in January.

2 The Hill Towns. High in the hills overlooking Nice are the medieval walled villages of **St-Paul-de-Vence** and **Vence**, invaded by waves of artists in the 20th century. Today, you can hardly turn around without bumping into a Calder mobile, and top sights include the famous inn La Colombe d'Or, Matisse's sublime Chapelle du Rosaire, and the Fondation Maeght—probably the best museum this side of the Louvre.

THE FRENCH RIVIERA PLANNER

Finding a Place to Stay

Certain areas of the Riviera book up faster than others, but all hit overload from June to September. It's essential to book in advance; up to half a year for the summer season is not unheard of, and is, in fact, much appreciated. Festivals, good weather, and strikes (it *is* France) will also affect your chances. If you arrive without a reservation, try the tourist information centers, which can usually be of help. Smaller villages often have tiny, charming hotels or bed-and-breakfasts, which translates to fewer than 10 rooms, and which also means they fill up fast, even out of season in some places. If you're really out of luck, do *not* try sleeping on the beach; as romantic as it sounds, it is not tolerated and strictly controlled. Worst-case scenario is a string of cheap motels on the outskirts of most major city centers, which cost €25–€65. Assume that all hotel rooms have air-conditioning, TV, telephones, and private bath, unless otherwise noted.

Making the Most of Your Time

Come to the Riviera in spring, summer, or early fall. In winter it rains, many places close, and public transport is more limited.

If you're setting into one town and making day trips, it's best to divide your time by visiting west and then east of Nice. Parallel roads along the Corniches allow for access into towns with different personalities. The A8 main *autoroute* (keep spare change at the ready, as it costs €2.40 to use this road between Cannes and Nice), as well as the coastal train, makes zipping up and down from Monaco to Fréjus–St-Raphael a breeze.

Visit different resort towns, but make sure you tear yourself away from the coastal *plages* (beaches) to visit the perched villages that the region is famed for. Venturing farther north to reach these villages, east or west, either by the Route Napoléon (RN 98), the D995, or on the Corniche roads, plan on at least one overnight.

Food plays a crucial role here and some of the best restaurants aren't so easy to access; make sure to include taxi money in your budget to get to some of the more remote restaurants, or plan on renting a car. Try to come in truffle, lavender, or olive season.

Parlez-Vous English?

After struggling through several weeks of searching through your well-worn English-French dictionary, let your brain slide into the peaceful lanes of full comprehension. Riviera Radio 106.5 is the Riviera's English-language radio station, with news, weather, traffic, and wisecracking DJs programmed to do just that. Many hotels, *tabacs*, and the local tourism office carry the *Herald*, which is the international English paper, and the *Riviera Times*, which is for local English Riviera news. There are also a few English-language bookstores along the coast, namely Heidi's Books in Antibes (⌂24 rue Aubernon ☎04–93–34–74–11). The English community tends to flock to any of the many Irish pubs along the coast, most notorious for not speaking French at all—try Morrison's in Cannes (⌂10 rue Tesseire ☎04–92–98–16–17).

Feeling Festive?

Every month of the year there's a festival somewhere on the Riviera, catering to all manner of tastes and pastimes. The queen of all festivals is of course the International Film Festival in Cannes, where all the stars of today and yesterday play for 10 jam-packed days in May, but there's every other type of festival imaginable, too. To give you a small taste: in May there's the Monaco Grand Prix; in June there's the Advertising festival in Cannes, as well as both the Nice and Juan-les-Pins jazz festivals; in July, the lavender festivals; in August, the fireworks festivals; in February, the Fête du Citron (Citrus festival) in Menton, and Carnival in Nice. Check with your local tourism office to see what's happening when in whatever area you happen to be in. Information is also available online at www.cr-paca.fr. Tickets can be bought at local tourist offices, FNAC branches (⊕www.fnac.fr), or through agencies like France Billet (☎08-92-69-26-94 ⊕www.francebillet.com) or Globaltickets (☎01-42-81-88-98 ⊕www.globaltickets.com).

How's the Weather?

Sexy south of France may be reputed for many steamy things, but it's not at all humid. It is, in fact, hot and dry for most of the year. Recent high season temperatures have gone up to 105°F, while spring and fall still see highs of 68°F. Summer wear usually boils down to a bikini and light wrap. Rainfall between March and October cools things off. According to the locals, winter (November–early March) is cold, rainy, miserable—which may be relative, as the area's famous for having more than 340 days of sunshine per year.

Getting Around

The less-budget-conscious can consider jetting around by helicopter (heliports in Monaco, Nice, Cannes, St-Tropez, and some of the hill towns) or speedboat (access to all resort towns), but affordable public transport along the Riviera boils down to the train, the bus, or renting a car. The train accesses all major coastal towns, and most of the *gares* (train stations) are in town centers. Note that only a handful of hill towns have train stations. The bus network between towns is fantastic. Renting a car is a good option, and the network of roads here are well marked and divided nicely into slow and very curvy (Bord de Mer Coast Road), faster and curvy (Route National 98), and fast and almost straight (Autoroute A8). Make sure you leave extra time if you're driving or taking the bus, as traffic is always heavy.

WHAT IT COSTS

	¢	$	$$	$$$	$$$$
Restaurants	Under €11	€11–€17	€17–€23	€23–€30	Over €30
Hotels	Under €50	€50–€80	€80–€120	€120–€190	Over €190

Restaurant prices are per person for a main course at dinner, including tax (19.6%) and service; note that if a restaurant offers only prix-fixe (set-price) meals, it has been given the price category that reflects the full prix-fixe price. Hotel prices are for a standard double room in high season, including tax (19.6%) and service charge. Hotels operate on the European Plan (EP, with no meal provided) unless we note that they use the Breakfast Plan (BP), or also offer such options as Modified American Plan (MAP, with breakfast and dinner daily, known as demi-pension), or Full American Plan (FAP, or pension complète, with three meals a day). Inquire when booking if these all-inclusive meal plans (which always entail higher rates) are mandatory or optional.

Introduction by
Nancy Coons

Updated by
Sarah Fraser

WITH THE ALPS AND PRE-ALPS PLAYING bodyguard against inland winds and the sultry Mediterranean warming the breezes, the French Riviera—or, to use the French term for the region, the Côte d'Azur—is pampered by a nearly tropical climate. This is where the dreamland of azure waters and indigo sky begins, where balustraded white villas edge the blue horizon, the evening air is perfumed with jasmine and mimosa, and parasol pines are silhouetted against sunsets of ripe apricot and gold. As emblematic as the sheet-music cover for a Jazz Age tune, the French Riviera seems to epitomize happiness, a state of being the world pursues with a vengeance.

But the Jazz Age dream confronts modern reality: on the hills that undulate along the blue water, every cliff, cranny, gully, and plain bristles with cubes of hot-pink cement and balconies of ironwork, each skewed to catch a glimpse of the sea and the sun. Like a rosy rash, these crawl and spread, outnumbering the trees and blocking each other's views. Their owners and renters, who arrive on every vacation and at every holiday—Easter, Christmas, Carnival, All Saints' Day—choke the tiered highways with bumper-to-bumper cars, and on just about any day in high summer the traffic to the beach—slow-moving at any time—coagulates and blisters in the hot sun.

There has always been a rush to the Côte d'Azur (or Azure Coast), starting with the ancient Greeks, who were drawn eastward from Marseille to market their goods to the natives. From the 18th-century English aristocrats who claimed it as one vast spa, to the 19th-century Russian nobles who transformed Nice into a tropical St. Petersburg, to the 20th-century American tycoons who cast themselves as romantic sheiks, the beckoning coast became a blank slate for their whims. Like the modern vacationers who followed, they all left their mark—villas, shrines, Moroccan-fantasy castles-in-the-air—temples all to the sensual pleasures of the sun and the sultry sea breezes. Artists, too, made the French Riviera their own, as museumgoers who have studied the sunny legacy of Picasso, Renoir, Matisse, and Chagall will attest. Today's admirers can take this all in, along with the Riviera's textbook points of interest: animated St-Tropez; the Belle Epoque aura of Cannes; the towns made famous by Picasso—Antibes, Vallauris, Mougins; the urban charms of Nice; and a number of spots where the per-capita population of billionaires must be among the highest on the planet: Cap d'Antibes, Villefranche-sur-Mer, and Monaco. The latter, once a Belle Epoque fairyland, has for some time been known as the Hong Kong of the Riviera, a bustling community where the sounds of drills tearing up the ground for new construction has mostly replaced the clip-clop of the horse-drawn fiacres. The ghosts of Grace Kelly and Cary Grant must have long since gone elsewhere.

Veterans of the area know that the beauty of the French Riviera coastline is only skin deep, a thin veneer of coddled glamour that hugs the water and hides a more ascetic region up in the hills. These low-lying mountains and deep gorges are known as the *arriére-pays* (backcountry) for good cause: they are as aloof and isolated as the waterfront resorts are in the swim. Medieval stone villages cap rocky hills and play out scenes of Provençal life—the game of boules, the slowly savored *pastis* (the anise-and-licorice-flavored spirit mixed slowly with water), the farmers' market—as if the ocean were a hundred miles away. Some of them—Èze, St-Paul, Vence—have become virtual Provençal theme parks, catering to busloads of tourists day-tripping from the coast. But just behind them, dozens of hill towns stand virtually untouched, and you can lose yourself in a cobblestone maze.

You could drive from St-Tropez to the border of Italy in three hours and take in the entire Riviera, so small is this renowned stretch of Mediterranean coast. Along the way you'll undoubtedly encounter the downside: jammed beaches, insolent waiters serving frozen seafood, traffic gridlock. But once you dabble your feet off the docks in a picturesque port full of brightly painted boats, or drink a Lillet in a hilltop village high above the coast, or tip your face up to the sun from a boardwalk park bench and doze off to the rhythm of the waves, you—like the artists and nobles who succumbed before you—will very likely be seduced to linger.

EXPLORING THE FRENCH RIVIERA

You can visit any spot between St-Tropez and Menton in a day trip; the hilltop villages and towns on the coastal plateau are just as accessible. Thanks to the efficient raceway, A8, you can whisk at high speeds to the exit nearest your destination up or down the coast; thus, even if you like leisurely exploration, you can zoom back to your home base at day's end. The lay of the land east of Nice is nearly vertical, as the coastline is one great cliff, a corniche terraced by three parallel highways—the **Basse Corniche,** the **Moyenne Corniche,** and the **Grande Corniche**—that snake along its graduated crests. The lowest (*basse*) is the slowest, following the coast and crawling through the main streets of resorts—including downtown Monte Carlo, Cap-Martin, Beaulieu, and Villefranche-sur-Mer. The highest (*grande*) is the fastest, but its panoramic views are blocked by villas, and there are few safe overlooks. The middle (*moyenne*) runs from Nice to Menton and offers views down over the shoreline and villages—it passes through a few picturesque towns, most notably Èze. Above the autoroutes, things slow down considerably, but you'll find exploring the winding roads and overlooks between villages an experience in itself.

ST-TROPEZ TO ANTIBES

Flanked at each end by subtropical capes and crowned by the red-rock Estérel, this stretch of the coast has a variety of waterfront landmarks. St-Tropez first blazed into fame when it was discovered by painters like Paul Signac and writers like Colette, and since then it has never looked back. It remains one of the most animated stretches of territory on the French Riviera, getting flooded at high season with people who like to roost at waterfront cafés to take in the passing parade. St-Tropez vies with Cannes for name recognition and glamour, but the more modest

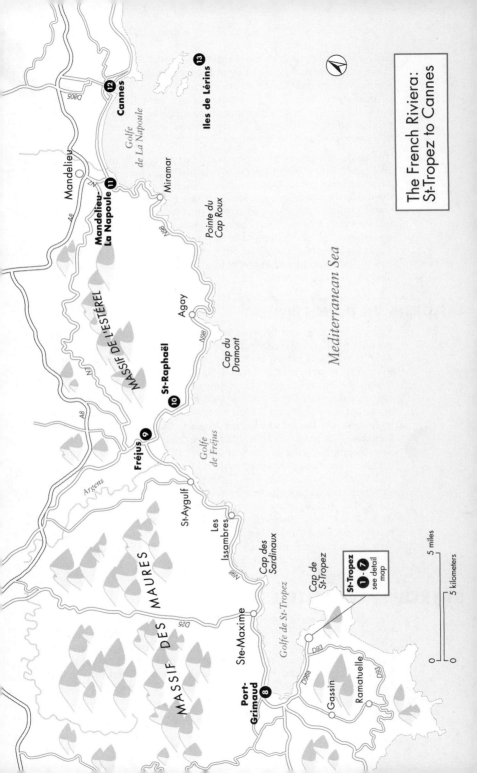

The French Riviera: St-Tropez to Cannes

Mediterranean Sea

Cannes 12

Iles de Lérins 13

Golfe de La Napoule

Mandelieu

Mandelieu-La Napoule 11

Miramar

Pointe du Cap Roux

MASSIF DE L'ESTÉREL

Agay

Cap du Dramont

St-Raphaël 10

Fréjus 9

Golfe de Fréjus

Argens

St-Aygulf

Les Issambres

Cap des Sardinaux

MASSIF DES MAURES

Golfe de St-Tropez

Ste-Maxime

Port-Grimaud 8

Cap de St-Tropez

St-Tropez 1 – 7 see detail map

Gassin

Ramatuelle

D805

A8

N7

N1

N98

D25

N98

D98a

D93

0 — 5 miles

0 — 5 kilometers

resorts—Ste-Maxime, Fréjus, and St-Raphaël—offer a more affordable Riviera experience. Historic Antibes and jazzy Juan-les-Pins straddle the subtropical peninsula of Cap d'Antibes.

ST-TROPEZ

35 km (22 mi) southwest of Fréjus, 66 km (41 mi) northeast of Toulon.

GETTING HERE

Keep in mind that while St-Tropez can be heaven, getting there can be hellish. Out on a limb, scorned by any train route, you can only get to St-Trop by car, bus, or boat (from nearby ports like St-Raphaël). Driving a car can test anyone's mettle, thanks to the crowds, the narrow roads, and the Parking du Port parking lot (opposite the bus station on Avenue du Général de Gaulle, with shuttle bus into town mid-March to October) or the new Parc des Lices (beneath the Place des Lices) in the center of town and their fees: a staggering €5 an hour in peak season. A train-bus connection can be made if you are leaving from Nice center: Take the train (direction St-Raphael) from the center city Gare SNCF station (⊠ *Av. Thiers* ☎ *04–92–14–80–80* ⊕ *www.voyages-sncf. com*), which costs €9.20 one way; from St-Raphael, there is a daily bus service with Sodetrav (☎ *08–25–00–06–50* ⊕ *www.sodetrav.fr*), with one way costing €10.10. Make sure you get to St-Raphaël's bus station early or you'll be elbowed out of a seat by aggressive bronzed ladies and forced to stand the whole way. Travel time from St-Raphael to St-Tropez is 1½ hours. The other option is to take a boat from the Nice harbor with Trans Côte d'Azur (☎ *04–92–00–42–30* ⊕ *www.trans-cote-azur.com*), which has daily trips from June to September. If you decide to rent a car, take the N98 coast road (the longest route but also the prettiest, with great picnic stops along the way). Car rental agencies abound—check with your hotel or the tourism office. If you want to save time and make a bit of a splash, you can get here by helicopter as well. There are a number of lines, including Heli Air Monaco (⊕ *www. heliairmonaco.com*); prices and times vary according to season.

EXPLORING

At first glance, St-Tropez really doesn't look all that lovely: there's a moderately pretty port full of bobbing boats, a picturesque *Vieille Ville* (Old Town) in candied-almond hues, sandy beaches, and old-fashioned squares with plane trees and *pétanque* (lawn bowling) players. So what made St-Tropez a household name? In two words: Brigitte Bardot. When this *pulpeuse* (voluptuous) teenager showed up in St-Tropez on the arm of the late Roger Vadim in 1956 to film *And God Created Woman*, the world snapped to attention. Neither the gentle descriptions of writer Guy de Maupassant (1850–93) nor the water-color tones of Impressionist Paul Signac (1863–1935), nor even the stream of painters who followed him (including Matisse and Bonnard) could focus the world's attention on this seaside hamlet as could this one luscious female, in head scarf, Ray-Bans, and capri pants. With the film world following in her steps, St-Tropez became the hot spot it—to some extent—remains. What makes it worthwhile is if you get

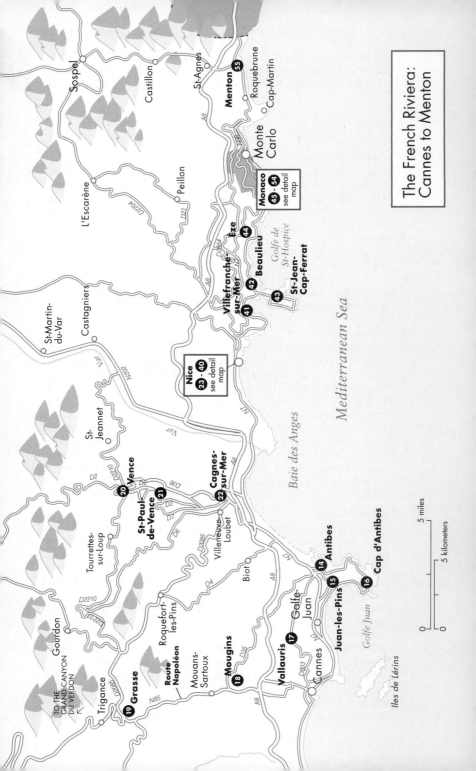

The French Riviera: Cannes to Menton

Menton 55

Roquebrune
Cap-Martin

St-Agnes

Castillon

Monte Carlo

Monaco 45 - 54
see detail map

Éze 44

Beaulieu 42

Golfe de St-Hospice

Villefranche-sur-Mer 41

St-Jean-Cap-Ferrat 43

Peillon

L'Escarène

Sospel

Nice 23 - 40
see detail map

St-Martin-du-Var

Castagniers

St-Jeannet

Vence 20

St-Paul-de-Vence 21

Cagnes-sur-Mer 22

Villeneuve-Loubet

Tourrettes-sur-Loup

Biot

Gourdon

TO THE GRAND CANYON DU VERDON

Trigance

Grasse 19

Route Napoléon

Mouans-Sartoux

Mougins 18

Roquefort-les-Pins

Vallauris

Cannes

Golfe-Juan 17

Juan-les-Pins 15

Antibes 14

Cap d'Antibes 16

Golfe Juan

Baie des Anges

Mediterranean Sea

Iles de Lérins

5 miles

5 kilometers

up early (before the 11 o'clock breakfast rush at Le Gorille Café and other port-side spots lining Quai Suffern and Quai Jean-Jaurès) and wander the medieval backstreets and waterfront by yourself; you can experience what the artists found to love: its soft light, warm pastels, and the scent of the sea wafting in from the waterfront.

Anything associated with the distant past seems almost absurd in St-Tropez. Still, the place has a history that predates the invention of the string bikini, and people have been finding reasons to come here since ad 68, when a Roman soldier from Pisa named Torpes was beheaded for professing his Christian faith in front of Emperor Nero, transforming this spot into a place of pilgrimage. Since then people have come for the sun, the sea, and, more recently, the celebrities. The latter—ever since St-Tropez became "hot" again, there have been Elton, Barbra, Oprah, Jack, and Uma sightings—stay hidden in villas, so the people you'll see are mere mortals, lots of them, many intent on displaying the best, and often the most, of their youth, beauty, and wealth. Still, if you take an early morning stroll along the harbor or down the narrow medieval streets—the rest of the town will still be sleeping off the Night Before—you can see just how charming St-Tropez is. There's a weekend's worth of boutiques to explore and many cute cafés where you can sit under colored awnings and watch the spectacle that is St-Trop (*trop* in French means "too much") saunter by.

Start your St-Trop tour at the *nouveau bassin* (new harbor) for private pleasure boats. There's a large parking lot and the bus station here. With the sea on your left, walk around to the Vieux Port (old harbor), enjoying the life of the quays and the views around the bay as you go.

❶ The **Vieux Port,** bordered by the Quai de l'Epi, the Quai Bouchard, the Quai Peri, the Quai Suffren, and the Quai Jean-Jaurès, is the nerve center of this famous yachting spot, a place for strolling and looking over the shoulders of artists daubing their versions of the view on easels set up along the water's edge, surreptitiously looking out for any off-duty celebs. For it is here, from folding director's chairs at the famous port-side cafés Le Gorille (named for its late exceptionally hirsute manager), Café de Paris, and Sénéquier's—which line Quai Suffren and Quai Jean-Jaurès—that the cast of St-Tropez's living theater plays out its colorful roles.

★ ❷ Just inland from the southwest corner of the Vieux Port stands the extraordinary **Musée de l'Annonciade** *(Annunciation Museum)*, where the legacy of the artists who loved St-Tropez has been lovingly preserved. This 14th-century chapel, converted to an art museum, alone merits a visit to St-Tropez. Cutting-edge temporary exhibitions keep visitors on their toes while works stretching from Pointillists to Fauves to Cubists line the walls of the permanent collection. Signac, Matisse, Signard, Braque, Dufy, Vuillard, Rouault: many of them painted in (and about) St-Tropez, tracing the evolution of painting from Impressionism to Expressionism. The museum also hosts temporary exhibitions every summer, from local talent to up-and-coming international artists. ✉*Quai de l'Épi/Pl. Georges Grammont* ☎*04–94–17–84–10*

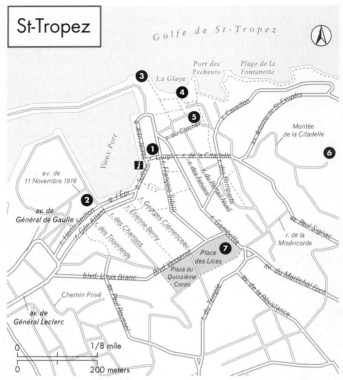

St-Tropez

💌*€5 regularly, €6 special exhibits* 🕑*June–Sept., Wed.–Mon. 10–1
and 3–7; Oct. and Dec.–May, Wed.–Mon. 10–noon and 1–6.*

Head back past the Quai Suffern to the Mole Jean Réveille, the harbor
wall, for a good view of Ste-Maxime across the sparkling bay, the hills
of Estérel and, on a clear day, the distant Alps. Retrace your steps along

❸ the mole and quayside to the 15th-century **Tour du Portalet.** Head past it

❹ to the old fisherman's quarter, the **Quartier de la Ponche,** just east of the
Quai Jean-Jaurès. Complete with gulf-side harbor, this Old Town maze
of backstreets and old ramparts is daubed in shades of gold, pink, ocher,
and sky-blue. Trellised jasmine and wrought-iron birdcages hang from
the shuttered windows, and many of the tiny streets dead-end at the sea.
Here you can find the **Port des Pécheurs** (Fishermen's Port), on whose
beach Bardot did a star-turn in *And God Created Woman*. Twisting,
narrow streets, designed to break the impact of the mistral, open to tiny
squares with fountains. The main drag here, Rue de la Ponche, leads
into Place l'Hôtel de Ville, landmarked by a **mairie** (town hall) marked
out in typical Tropezienne hues of pink and green. Head up Rue Guich-

❺ ard to the Baroque **Église de St-Tropez,** to pay your respects to the bust
and barque of St. Torpes, every day but May 17th, when they are carried
aloft in the Bravade parade honoring the town's namesake saint.

Head up Rue de la Citadelle to
6 the 16th-century **Citadelle,** which
stands in a lovely hilltop park; its
ramparts offer a fantastic view of
the town and the sea. Although
it's hard to imagine St-Tropez as
a military outpost amid today's
bikini-clad sun worshippers, inside
the Citadelle's conjon the **Musée
Naval** (Naval Museum) displays
ship models, cannons, maps, and
pictures of St-Tropez from its days
as a naval port. At press time the
museum was closed for renovations, expected to reopen in late
2008. It's likely that the theme of
the museum will change, but until

> **YOU CAN NEVER
> BE TOO RICH, TOO
> THIN, OR TOO TAN**
>
> You can see plenty of Brigitte
> Bardot wannabes (not all of them
> female) who strut along the
> quaint streets in skintight leopard
> skin, toting leopard-collared
> terriers, mixing in with a
> "BCBG"—"bon-chic-bon-genre,"
> or "well-bred yuppie"—crowd in
> nautical togs and Gap shirts, with
> only golden retrievers or dalma-
> tians, please.

that decision is made you can still see some of the navy models in the
Citadelle, as well as a series of temporary art exhibitions. ⊠ *Rue de la
Citadelle* ☎ *04–94–97–59–43* 🖃 *Citadelle €2.50* ☉ *Oct.–Mar., daily
10–12:30 and 1:30–5:30; Apr.–Sept., daily 10–12:30 and 1–6:30.*

Descend from the Citadelle using the Montée G.-Ringrave to the social
7 center of the Old Town, the **Place des Lices** (also called the Place Carnot).
Here, you can hear pétanque balls—a southern version of boules—
clicking in the sand square. The square's symmetrical forest of plane
trees (what's left of them) provides shade to rows of cafés and restaurants, skateboarders, children, and the grandfatherly pétanque players. Enjoy a time-out in the town "living room," Le Café (not be be
confused with the nearby Café des Arts). The square becomes a moveable feast (for both eyes and palate) on market days—Tuesday and
Saturday—while at night a café seat is as hotly contested as a quayside
seat during the day. Just as Deborah Kerr and David Niven once did in
Bonjour Tristesse, watch the boule players under the glow of hundreds
of electric bulbs. Heading back to the Vieux Port area, take in the boutiques lining Rues Sibilli, Clemenceau, or Gambetta to help accessorize
your evening look—you never know when that photographer from *Elle*
will be snapping away at the trendoisie.

WHERE TO STAY & EAT

A word of warning: if you're planning to stay in St-Tropez in high season, make sure you book literally months in advance.

$$–$$$$ ✕ **Le Café.** The busy terrace here often doubles as a stadium for differ-
ent factions cheering on favorite local *pétanque* players in the Place des
Lices. You, too, can play—borrow some *boules* from the friendly bar
staff (and get your *pastis* bottle at the ready: you'll need it to properly
appreciate the full *pétanque* experience). Note that hilarious "begin-
ner" *pétanque soirees* are on tap Saturday nights in summer. A great
way to really sink into the local culture, it's an even bigger bonus that
the food is as good as the setting. Try the beef carpaccio with olive tap-

enade or the large prawns flambéed with Pastis à la Provençal. ⊠*5 pl. des Lices* ☎*04–94–97–44–69* ⊕*www.lecafe.fr* ⊟*AE, MC, V.*

$$–$$$$ ✕ **Le Girelier.** Fish, fish, and more fish—sea bass, salmon, sole, sardines, monkfish, lobster, crayfish, fish eggs spread on a thin slice of toast—they're painted on the walls, sizzling on the grill, trying to jump for their lives as the boats come into the Old Port. Will they make it? Not if chef Yves Rouet gets to them first, with a little thyme or perhaps a whisper of olive oil and garlic. Like his father before him, chef Yves makes an effort to prepare Mediterranean-only fish for his buffed and bronzed clientele, who enjoy the casual sea-shanty space and the highly visible Vieux Port terrace tables. Grilling is the order of the day, with most fish sold by weight (beware the check), but this is also a stronghold for bouillabaisse. There's beef on the menu, too, in case you're a fish-phobe. The €38 set menu is one of the best bargains in town. ⊠*Quai Jean-Jaurès* ☎*04–94–97–03–87* ⊟*AE, DC, MC, V* ⊘*Closed Nov.–Mar. and Mon. No lunch July and Aug.*

$$–$$$$ ✕ **Lei Mouscardins.** Breton-born chef Laurent Tarridec's spectacular seaside locale offers 180-degree sea views, just on the edge of St-Tropez's Vieille Ville, and is one of the most respected restaurants in town. His cooking favors the sophisticated tradition of upscale seasonal Provençal cuisine: opt for a frothy mullet soup, hearty rabbit stew, tender, long-simmered veal, or, for the more ambitious diner, the surprisingly tasty green olive soup lightly seasoned with almond milk. Fixed-price menus are €67, €109, and €130. ⊠*Tour du Portalet* ☎*04–94–97–29–00* ⊕*www.lei-mouscardins.com* ⊟*AE, MC, V* ⊘*Closed mid-Nov.–mid-Dec. and mid-Feb.*

$$–$$$$ ✕ **La Table du Marché.** With an afternoon tearoom and a summer deli–sushi bar, this charming bistro from celebrity chef Christophe Leroy offers up a mouthwatering spread of regional specialties in a surprisingly casual atmosphere. Sink into one of the overstuffed armchairs in the upstairs dining room, cozy with chic Provençal accents and antique bookshelves, and, for a light snack, try the tomato pistou tart. Hungry guests can happily dive into a nicely balanced €18 or €26 set lunch menu while perusing the good wine list. ⊠*38 rue Georges Clemenceau* ☎*04–94–97–85–20* ⊕*www.christophe-leroy.com* ⊟*AE, MC, V.*

$$–$$$$ ✕ **Villa Romaná.** Bruce Willis, George Clooney, and other lotharios have made this the latest paparazzi favorite. The decor is "Tropezienne"— an over-the-top orgy of neo-Pompeian murals, leopard-skin banquettes, overstuffed chairs, and red-velvet tassels. Food is not quite the raison d'être—along with the usual tuna and veal numbers, you can get everything from caviar to pizzas to a chocolate blowout called "Halicarnasse"—since the partying crowd seems to be more interested in the luscious bonbons sitting at the next table rather than those on the dessert trolley. Open in the evenings only, this spot closes on certain weeknights in low season, when it also opens for Sunday lunch. ⊠*Chemin des Conquettes* ☎*04–94–97–15–50* ⊕*www.villa-romana.com* ⊟*AE, DC, MC, V.*

$$$$ ✕▦ **Le Byblos.** Arranged like a toy Mediterranean village, fronted with stunning red, rust, and yellow facades, and complete with ocher-stucco cottagelike suites grouped around courtyards landscaped with palms, olive trees, and lavender, this longtime fave of the glitterati began life as a "Phoenician-style" resort (the name means Bible) dreamed up by a Lebanese millionaire. Decades later, it has seen the jet set *jet, jet, jet.* Guest rooms are *à la provençale,* but modern in comfort. Chef Georges Pelissier creates artful dinner classics in the Bayader restaurant: sea bass roasted with salsify and garlic chips or rib-sticking beef tournedos with foie gras. Opt for more nouvelle Med fireworks (try the excellent sweet-and-sour tuna with wok vegetables) on offer at **Spoon Byblos** (✉*Entrance on Av. du Maréchal-Foch* ☎04–94–56–68–20 ⊕*www. spoonbyblos.fr* ⊘*No lunch*). Another outpost of superstar chef Alain Ducasse, it boasts a client list that includes the likes of George Clooney, Naomi Campbell, and Jack Nicholson. Sit on the designer terrace and play with the fun *nouveau concept* menu—pick one ingredient (chicken), match it up with three different sauces (satay, citrus vinaigrette, balsamic), and one of three vegetable choices. It's tasty, too. As evening falls, all head to the hotel's Caves du Roy—a gigantic disco extravaganza where squillionaires have been seen buying champagne by the carton for the crowd. Paparazzi-free, it's virtually impossible to get in unless you get there early or reserve a table in advance (be aware that very impressive-looking security guards will turn away anyone not dressed appropriately). ✉*Av. Paul-Signac, 83990* ☎04–94–56–68–00 🖷04–94–56–68–01 ⊕*www.byblos.com* ⇙*52 rooms, 43 suites* ♿*In-room: refrigerator, Wi-Fi. In-hotel: 2 restaurants, pool, gym, spa, parking (no fee), some pets allowed (fee)* ⊟*AE, DC, MC, V* ⊘*Closed mid-Oct.–Easter.*

$$$$ ✕⊡ **La Résidence de la Pinède.** Perhaps the most opulent of St-Tropez's luxe hangouts, this balustraded white villa and its broad annex sprawl elegantly along a private waterfront, wrapped around an isolated courtyard and a pool shaded by parasol pines. Louis XVI bérgères, a beam here and there, gilt frames, indirect spots, and oh-so-comfy beds make for an alluring if somewhat homogenized interior. Pay extra for a seaside room, where you can lean over the balcony and take in broad coastal views and the large seafront restaurant; the chef has a celebrated reputation, and you'll understand why after one taste of his truffled ravioli. Rates including half board are available. ✉*Plage de la Bouillabaisse, 83991* ☎04–94–55–91–00 🖷04–94–97–73–64 ⊕*www.residencepinede.com* ⇙*35 rooms, 4 suites* ♿*In-room: refrigerator, Wi-Fi. In-hotel: restaurant, bar, pool, parking (no fee), some pets allowed (fee)* ⊟*AE, DC, MC, V* ⊘*Closed mid-Oct.–mid-Apr.* ⊧*MAP.*

$$$ ⊡ **Ermitage.** Surrounded by mimosas and lemon trees, this big, old-fashioned, tangerine-hue hotel is on a hill above town and from its back rooms commands striking sea views. Once a 19th-century private villa, it still has some of its former glory: the beautiful walled garden is a lovely summer retreat and the wood-burning fireplace and cozy "colonial"-rattan bar make for solid elegance. The guest rooms are simply decorated, light-bathed in soft pastels. Owner Annie Bolloreis's friendly welcome makes this a real charmer. ✉*Av. Paul-Signac, 83990* ☎04–94–97–52–33 🖷04–94–97–10–43 ⇙*27 rooms* ♿*In-room: no a/c (some). In-hotel: bar, parking (no fee), some pets allowed (fee), public Internet* ⊟*MC, V* ⊘*Closed mid-Nov.–Mar.*

$$–$$$ ✕⊡ **Ferme Ladouceur.** Set on the road to the pretty and historic village of Ramatuelle (which is about 11 km [7 mi] southwest of St-Tropez), surrounded by vineyards, and not far from the talcum-powder beach of Pampelonne is this *naïf* farmhouse. The domain of Constance Ladouceur (whose paintings adorn the hallways) is a big draw because of its restaurant, which brings in many budget-minded locals. Quirky, simple, affordable, with breakfast included in the price—little wonder you need to book here far in advance. ⊠*Quartier la Rouillère, 83350* ☎*04–94–79–24–95* 🖷*04–94–79–12–14* ⌨*7 rooms* ♿*In-room: no a/c, no phone, no TV. In-hotel: restaurant, some pets allowed* ▤*AE, MC, V* ⊘*Closed Nov.–Mar.* ❛⊙❜*BP.*

★ **$–$$**   ⊡ **Lou Cagnard.** Inside an enclosed garden courtyard, this pretty little hotel is unaffected and friendly. Five ground-floor rooms open onto the lovely manicured garden, where breakfast is served in the shade of a fig tree. Lovingly decorated rooms have regional tiles and Provençal fabrics. ⊠*18 av. Paul Roussel, 83900* ☎*04–94–97–04–24* 🖷*04–94–97–09–44* ⊕*www.hotel-lou-cagnard.com* ⌨*19 rooms* ♿*In-hotel: parking (fee), public Internet* ▤*MC, V* ⊘*Closed Nov.–late Dec.*

NIGHTLIFE & THE ARTS

Costing the devil and often jammed to the scuppers, **Les Caves du Roy** (⊠*Av. Paul-Signac* ☎*04–94–97–16–02*), a disco in the Byblos Hotel, is *the* place to see and be seen; it's filled with svelte model types and their wealthy, silver-haired fans. You, too, may be sprayed with Moët during one of those champagne-spraying parties (so many bottles are set off, waiters are given football helmets). Virtually impossible to get into unless you book long in advance, there's a horrific door policy during high season; don't worry, it's *not* you. Every July and August, classical music concerts are given in the gardens of the **Château de la Moutte** (⊠*Rte. des Salins* ☎*04–94–97–45–21 information* ⊕*www. music-lamoutte.com* ✉*€23*). For ticket information inquire at the tourist office. Swanky **Octave Café** (⊠*Pl. de la Garonne* ☎*04–94–97–22–56*) is a piano bar (obligatory drinks) with soft seating and sleek black tables. Although not a bar listed among the "big players," stars like Liza Minnelli and Johnny Hallyday have been known to get up and sing a song or two here. The **VIP Room** (⊠*Residence du Nouveau Port* ☎*04–94–97–14–70* ⊕*www.viproom.fr*) draws flashy, gilded youths with deep pockets—although some question the "VIP" in the club's name.

SHOPPING

Designer boutiques may be spreading like wild mushrooms all over St-Tropez, but the main fashionista strutting platform is along **Rue Gambetta** or **Rue Allard**. For those who balk at spending a small fortune on the latest strappy sandal, **Rue Sibilli**, behind the Quai Suffren, is lined with all kinds of trendy boutiques. The **Place des Lices** overflows with produce, regional foods, clothing, and *brocantes* (collectibles) on Tuesday and Saturday mornings. Don't miss the picturesque little fish market that fills up **Place aux Herbes** every morning.

PORT-GRIMAUD

11

⑧ *7 km (4½ mi) west of St-Tropez.*

Although much of the coast has been targeted with new construction of extraordinary ugliness, this modern architect's version of a Provençal fishing village works. A true operetta set and only begun in 1966, it has grown gracefully over the years, and offers hope for the pink concrete–scarred coastal landscape. It's worth parking and wandering up the village's Venice-like canals to admire its Old Mediterranean canal-tile roofs and pastel facades, already patinated with age. Even the church, though resolutely modern, feels Romanesque. There is, however, one modern touch some might appreciate: small electric tour boats (get them at Place du Marché) that carry you for a small charge from bar to shop to restaurant throughout the complex of pretty squares and bridges.

FRÉJUS

⑨ *37 km (23 mi) northeast of St-Tropez.*

GETTING HERE

Fréjus-Ville has a small train station on Rue Marin Bidouré, seconds away by rail from the larger one in St-Raphaël. If you're traveling from any of the towns on the St-Raphaël-Ventimiglia line, you have to get off in St-Raphaël and take a train going farther west toward Toulon or Marseille to reach Fréjus-Ville. Fréjus's bus station, on the north side of the city center, has buses connecting with St-Tropez and St-Raphaël.

EXPLORING

Don't be turned off if you begin with a stroll on the sandy curve along the tacky, overcommercial Fréjus-Plage (Fréjus Beach). Just turn your back on modern times and head uphill to Fréjus-Centre. Here you can enter a maze of narrow streets lined with small shops barely touched by the cult of the lavender sachet. The farmers' market (Monday, Wednesday, and Saturday mornings) is as real and lively as any in Provence, and the cafés encircling the fountains and squares nourish an easygoing social scene.

Yet Fréjus (pronounced fray-*zhooss*) also has the honor of owning some of the most important historic monuments on the coast. Founded in 49 bc by Julius Caesar himself and named Forum Julii, this quiet town was once a thriving Roman city of 40,000 citizens. Today you can see the remains.

Just outside the Vieille Ville is the Roman **Théâtre Antique;** its remaining rows of arches are mostly intact, and much of its stage works are still visible at its center.

The **Arènes** (often called the Amphithéâtre) is still used today for concerts and bullfights, and can still seat up to 10,000. Back down on the coast, a big French naval base occupies the spot where ancient Roman galleys once set out to defeat Cleopatra and Mark Anthony at the Battle of Actium. ⊠*Rue Henri Vadon* 🕾*04–94–51–34–31* 🖾*€2* ⊘*Nov.–Mar., Tues.–Sun. 9:30–12:30 and 2–4:45; Apr.–Oct., Tues.– Sun. 9:30–12:30 and 2–5:45.*

★ Fréjus is also graced with one of the most impressive religious monuments in Provence: called the **Groupe Épiscopal,** it's made up of an early Gothic **cathedral,** a 5th-century Roman-style **baptistery,** and an early Gothic **cloister,** its gallery painted in sepia and earth tones with a phantasmagoric assortment of animals and biblical characters. Off the entrance and gift shop is a small museum of finds from Roman Fréjus, including a complete mosaic and a sculpture of a two-headed Hermès. ⊠*58 rue de Fleury* 🕾*04–94–51–26–30* 🖾*Cathedral free; cloister, museum, and baptistery €4.60* ⊘*Cathedral daily 8:30–noon and 2–6. Cloister, museum, and baptistery June.–Sept., daily 9–6:30; Oct.–Mar., Tues.–Sun. 9–noon and 2–5.*

★ Set 5 km (2½ mi) north of Fréjus on the RN7 is the eccentric **La Chapelle Notre Dame de Jérusalem.** Designed by Jean Cocteau as part of an artists' colony that never happened, it is unusual not only for its octagonal shape, stained glass, and frescoes depicting the mythology of the first Crusades, but also because the tongue-in-cheek painting of the apostles above the front door boasts the famous faces of Coco Chanel, Jean Marais, and poet Max Jacob. ⊠*Av. Nicolaï, la Tour de la Mare* 🕾*04–94–53–27–06* 🖾*€4.60* ⊘*June.–Sept., daily 9–6:30; Oct.–Mar., Tues.–Sun. 9–noon and 2–5.*

☾ Families with children will be delighted with the **Parc Zoologique.** Its interactive 20-acre safari-like park has a number of colorful and exotic animals to tantalize the senses. Look for the ruffed lemur and spotted leopard. ⊠*Zone au Capitau, just off A8* 🕾*04–98–11–37–37* ⊕*www. zoo-frejus.com* 🖾*€12* ⊘*June.–Aug., daily 10–6; Mar.–May, daily 2–5; Nov.–Feb., daily 10:30–4.*

☾ On hot summer days, why not head to the **Aqualand** waterpark? It contains the biggest wavepool in Europe. ⊠*RN98* 🕾*04–94–51–82–51* ⊕*www.aqualand.fr* 🖾*€23, includes minigolf* ⊘*June–Sept., daily 9–8.*

ST-RAPHAËL

❿ *1 km (½ mi) southeast of Fréjus, 41 km (25½ mi) southwest of Cannes.*

GETTING HERE
St-Raphaël-Valescure is the name of St-Raphaël's train station (⊠*Pl. de la Gare*). St-Raphaël is the western terminus of the TER line that runs along the Riviera. To get to towns farther west, you have to take a bus from just behind the train station; various companies connect with Cannes, Fréjus, and St-Tropez. Popular ferries leave from St-Raphaël's Vieux Port from St-Tropez, the Iles-de-Lérins, and the Calanques de l'Esterel.

EXPLORING

Right next door to Fréjus, with almost no division between, is St-Raphaël, a sprawling resort town with a busy downtown anchored by a casino. It's also a major sailing center, has five golf courses nearby, and draws the weary and indulgent to its seawater-based thalassotherapy. It serves as a major rail crossroads, the closest stop to St-Tropez. The port has a rich history: Napoléon landed at St-Raphaël on his triumphant return from Egypt in 1799; it was also from here in 1814 that he cast off for Elba in disgrace.

Worth the bother of penetrating dense city traffic and cutting inland past the train station is St-Raphaël's **Vieille Ville** *(Old Town)*, a tiny enclave of charm crowned by the 12th-century **Église St-Pierre-des-Templiers**, a miniature-scale Romanesque church, and the intimate little **Musée Archéologique Marin** (Marine Archaeology Museum), both located on Rue–des Templiers.

WHERE TO STAY & EAT

★ $$$–$$$$ ✕ **La Bouillabaisse.** Enter through the beaded curtain covering the open doorway to a wood-paneled room decked out with starfish and the mounted head of a swordfish: this classic hole-in-the-wall has a brief, straightforward menu inspired by the fish markets. You might have the half lobster with spicy *rouille* (peppers and garlic whipped with olive oil), the seafood-stuffed paella, or the generous house bouillabaisse. ⊠*50 pl. Victor-Hugo* ☎*04–94–95–03–57* ▤*AE, MC, V* ☉*Closed Mon.*

★ $ 🏠 **Le Thimothée.** The owners of this bargain lodging are throwing themselves wholeheartedly into improving an already attractive 19th-century villa. They've also restored the garden, with its grand palms and pines shading the walk leading to a pretty little swimming pool. Though it's tucked away in a neighborhood far from the waterfront, the two top-floor rooms have poster-perfect sea views. ⊠*375 bd. Christian-Lafon, 83700* ☎*04–94–40–49–49* 🖷*04–94–19–41–92* ⊕*www.thimothee. com* ➮*12 rooms* ♿*In-room: refrigerator, dial-up, no a/c (some). In-hotel: pool, parking (fee), some pets allowed (fee)* ▤*AE, MC, V.*

EN
ROUTE

The rugged **Massif de l'Estérel,** between St-Raphaël and Cannes, is a hiker's dream. Made up of rust-red volcanic rocks (porphyry) carved by the sea into dreamlike shapes, the harsh landscape is softened by patches of lavender, scrub pine, and gorse. By car, take N7, the mountain route to the north, and lose yourself in the desert landscape far from the sea.

Or keep on N98, the **Corniche de l'Estérel** (the coastal road along the dramatic corniche), and drive past little coves dotted with sunbathers, tiny calanques, and sheer rock faces plunging down to the waves. Try to leave early in the morning, as tempers tend to fray when the route gets congested with afternoon traffic.

MANDELIEU–LA NAPOULE

⑪ *32 km (20 mi) northeast of St-Raphaël, 8 km (5 mi) southwest of Cannes.*

Offering both train and bus stations that offer frequent connections between Cannes and St-Raphaël, La Napoule is the small, old-fashioned port village, Mandelieu the big-fish resort town that devoured it. You can visit Mandelieu for a golf-and-sailing retreat—the town is replete with many sporting facilities and hosts a bevy of sporting events, including sailing regattas, windsurfing contests, and golf championships (there are two major golf courses in Mandelieu right in the center of town overlooking the water). By the sea, a yacht-crammed harbor sits under the shadow of some high-rise resort hotels. La Napoule, on the other hand, offers the requisite quaintness, ideal for a port-side stroll, casual meal, beach siesta, or visit to its peculiar castle.

★ Set on Pointe des Pendus (Hanged Man's Point), the **Château de la Napoule,** looming over the sea and the port, is a spectacularly bizarre hybrid of Romanesque, Gothic, Moroccan, and Hollywood cooked up by the eccentric American sculptor Henry Clews (1876–1937). Working with his architect-wife, he transformed the 14th-century bastion into something that suited his personal expectations and then filled the place with his own fantastical sculptures. The couple reside in their tombs in the tower crypt, its windows left slightly ajar to permit their souls to escape and allow them to "return at eventide as sprites and dance upon the windowsill." Today the château's foundation hosts visiting writers and artists, who set to work surrounded by Clews's gargoyle-ish sculptures. ⊠*Av. Henry Clews* ☎*04–93–49–95–05* ⊕*www.chateaulanapoule.com* ⟗*€6, gardens only €3.50* ☉*Feb.–Oct., daily 10–6; guided visits at 11:30, 2:30, 3:30, and 6:30; Nov.–Jan., daily 2–5; guided visits at 2:30, 3:30, and 4:30.*

WHERE TO STAY & EAT

$$$$ ✕ **L'Oasis.** Long famed as a culinary landmark, this Gothic villa by the sea is home to Stéphane Raimbault, a master of Provençal cuisine and a great connoisseur of Asian techniques and flavorings. The combination creates unexpected collisions—Jabugo ham with anise, lobster, and ginger, or Thai-spiced crayfish with squid-ink ravioli—most but not all entirely successful. Still, few can quibble with the beauty of the famous garden terrace shadowed by gorgeous palm trees. ⊠*Rue J. H. Carle* ☎*04–93–49–95–52* ⊕*www.oasis-raimbault.com* ⊟*AE, MC, V* ☉*Closed 1 wk mid-Feb. No dinner Sun. and no lunch Mon. May–Sept.*

★ **$$$–$$$$** ✕ **Le Boucanier.** The low-ceiling dining room is upstaged by wraparound plate-glass views of the marina and château at this waterfront favorite. Locals gather here for mountains of oysters and whole fish, grilled simply and served with a drizzle of fruity olive oil, a pinch of rock salt, or a brief flambé in pastis. ⊠*Port de La Napoule* ☎*04–93–49–80–51* ⊟*AE, DC, MC, V.*

$$$–$$$$ ✕▥ **L'Ermitage du Riou.** A smart Florentine-style hotel, with elegant marble columns and lovely ceiling frescos, this dainty treasure also has a deeply atmospheric restaurant where you can sit out on the dock over the water and eat lobster salad with mixed citrus fruits followed by a scrumptious mushroom risotto. Meal plans are available with a minimum three-night stay. ⊠*Av. Henri Clews, 06210* ☎*04–93–49–95–56* 🖷*04–92–97–69–06* ⊕*www.ermitage-du-riou.fr* ⇆*40 rooms* ⌂*In-room: refrigerator, Wi-Fi. In-hotel: pool, parking (fee), some pets allowed (fee)* ▤*AE, DC, MC, V* ⊗*Closed Jan.*

SPORTS

The **Golf Club de Cannes-Mandelieu** (⊠*Rte. du Golf* ☎*04–92–97–32–00* ⊕*www.golfoldcourse.com*) is one of the most beautiful in the south of France; it is bliss to play on English turf, under Mediterranean pines with mimosa blooming here and there in spring. The club has two courses—one with 18 holes (par 71) and one with 9 (par 33).

CANNES

⑫ *6 km (4 mi) east of Mandelieu-La Napoule, 73 km (45 mi) northeast of St-Tropez, 33 km (20 mi) southwest of Nice.*

GETTING HERE

Cannes has one central train station, the *Gare SNCF* (⊠*Rue Jean Jaures* ⊕*www.voyages-sncf.com*). All major trains pass through here—check out the SNCF Web site for times and prices—but many of the trains run the St-Raphaël-Ventimiglia route. You can also take the TGV directly from Paris (6½ hrs). Cannes's main bus station, which is on Place de l'Hôtel-de-Ville by the port, serves all coastal destinations. Rapides Côtes d'Azur runs most of the routes out of the central bus station on Place Bernard Gentille, including Nice (1½ hrs, €6), Mougins (20 mins, €2), Grasse (45 mins, €4), and Vallauris (30 mins, €3). Within Cannes, Bus Azur runs the routes, with a ticket costing €1.30 (a weekly ticket is available). The bus line RCA (☎*04–93–85–64–44* ⊕*www.rca.tm.fr*) goes to Nice along the coast road, stopping in all villages along the way, and to the Nice airport, every 30 minutes, Monday–Saturday, for a maximum ticket price of €13.70 round-trip. From the *Gare SNCF*, RCA goes to Grasse every 30 minutes Monday–Saturday and every hour Sunday, via Mougins. The other option is any of the Transport Alpes Maritimes (TAM) buses (☎*08–10–06–10–06* ⊕*www.lignedazur.com*), which service the same destinations and are now cheaper thanks to a government initiative towards communal transport and are a bargain basement €1.30 to all destinations along the coast (but, be patient, you may not get a seat). For the big spender, Cannes also has a heliport, with a free shuttle to the center of town. Heli Air Monaco helicopters (⊕*www.heli-airmonaco.com*) leave from the airport in Nice, the ride takes about 20 minutes, and costs around €80 depending on the season.

EXPLORING

A tasteful and expensive breeding ground for the upscale, Cannes is a sybaritic heaven for those who believe that life is short and sin has something to do with the absence of a tan. Backed by gentle hills and flanked to the southwest by the Estérel, warmed by dependable sun but kept bearable in summer by the cool Mediterranean breeze, Cannes is pampered with the luxurious climate that has made it one of the most popular and glamorous resorts in Europe. The cynosure of sun worshippers since the 1860s, it has been further glamorized by the modern success of its film festival.

Its bay served as nothing more than a fishing port until 1834, when an English aristocrat, Lord Brougham, fell in love with the site during an

> ### THAT SUNKISSED GLOW...
>
> Vacationing in summer only became fashionable after Chanel (whose first shop was on Cannes's Croisette, at No. 5, *mais naturellement*) decreed suntans chic.

emergency stopover with a sick daughter. He had a home built here and returned every winter for a sun cure—a ritual quickly picked up by his peers. With the democratization of modern travel, Cannes has become a tourist and convention town; there are now 20 compact Twingos for every Rolls-Royce. But glamour—and the perception of glamour—is self-perpetuating, and as long as Cannes enjoys its ravishing climate and setting, it will maintain its incomparable panache. If you're a culture-lover of art of the noncelluloid type, however, you should look elsewhere—there are only two museums here: one is devoted to history, the other to a collection of dolls. Still, as his lordship instantly understood, this is a great place to pass the winter.

Pick up a map at the tourist office in the **Palais des Festivals,** the scene of the famous Festival International du Film, otherwise known as the Cannes Film Festival. As you leave the information center, follow the Palais to your right to see the red-carpeted stairs where the stars ascend every year. Set into the surrounding pavement, the **Allée des Etoiles** (Stars' Walk) enshrines some 300 autographed imprints of film stars' hands—of Départieu, Streep, and Stallone, among others.

The most delightful thing to do is to head to the famous mile-long waterfront promenade, **La Croisette,** which starts at the western end by the Palais des Festivals, and allow the *esprit de Cannes* to take over. This is precisely the sort of place for which the verb *flâner* (to dawdle, saunter) was invented, so stroll among the palm trees and flowers and crowds of poseurs (fur coats in tropical weather, cell phones on Rollerblades, and sunglasses at night). Head east past the broad expanse of private beaches, glamorous shops, and luxurious hotels (such as the wedding-cake Carlton, famed for its see-and-be-seen terrace-level brasserie). The beaches along here are almost all private, though open for a fee—each beach is marked with from one to four little life buoys, rating their quality and expense.

If you need a culture fix, check out the modern art and photography exhibitions (varying admission prices) held at the **Malmaison,** a 19th-century mansion that was once part of the Grand Hotel. ⊠ *47 La Croisette, La Croisette* ☎ *04–93–06–44–90* ☼ *Sept.–June, Tues.–Sun. 10:30–12:30 and 2–6:30; July and Aug., Tues.–Sun. 10:30–12:30 and 2–7.*

Head down the Croisette and fight for a spot at **Le 72 Croisette** (⊠ *72 La Croisette* ☎ *04–93–94–18–30*), the most feistily French of all the Croisette bars. It offers great ringside seats for watching the rich and famous enter the Martinez hotel next door, and it's open 24 hours a day.

Two blocks behind La Croisette lies **Rue d'Antibes,** Cannes's main high-end shopping street. At its western end is **Rue Meynadier,** packed tight with trency clothing boutiques and fine food shops. Not far away is the covered **Marché Forville,** the scene of the animated morning food market.

Climb up Rue St-Antoine into the picturesque Vieille Ville neighborhood known as **Le Suquet,** on the site of the original Roman *castrum.* Shops proffer Provençal goods, and the atmospheric cafés give you a chance to catch your breath; the pretty pastel shutters, Gothic stonework, and narrow passageways are lovely distractions.

The hill is crowned by the 11th-century château, housing the **Musée de la Castre,** and the imposing four-sided **Tour du Suquet** (Suquet Tower), built in 1385 as a lookout against Saracen-led invasions. ⊠*Pl. de la Castre, Le Suquet* ☎*04–93–38–55–26* ☎*€3* ☉*Apr.–June, Tues.–Sun. 10–1 and 2–6; July and Aug., daily 10–7; Sept., Tues.–Sun.10–1 and 2–6.*

WHERE TO STAY & EAT

★ $$$–$$$$ ✕ **La Villa des Lys.** Superstar decorator Jacques Garcia only works for art-collecting billionaires, high-style industrialists, and the most-talked-about restaurants. Into that latter category falls the Villa des Lys, home to the culinary wizard Bruno Oger, who produces stunning menus that leave discerning palates craving more. Inspired by the Belle-Epoque-meets-the-Parthenon style of the Villa Kerylos (up the coast in Beaulieu), Garcia has garnished these luxe rooms with Homeric chandeliers, Mycenaean doorways, egg-and-dart moldings, a retractable ceiling, and fabrics that smolder with ancient terra-cotta hues. No matter: Oger's creations take center stage. How can they not with such delights as warm duck foie gras with truffle and peanut tapenade in a braised Jerusalem artichoke (€38, yes for an appetizer); or purple urchin soup with crabmeat, accompanied by a mincemeat crepe with coral, or turbot marinière with lemon bread crumbs, confit shallots, and creamy arborio risotto, or Breton lobster with black truffles and creamed macaroni? Save room for dessert: the stuffed orange au suprême caramélisé is a little slice of heaven. ⊠*10 La Croisette, La Croisette* ☎*04–92–98–77–41* ⚇*Reservations essential* ▤*AE, DC, MC, V* ☉*Closed Sun., Mon., and mid-Nov.–mid-Dec.*

$–$$$$ ✕ **Astoux et Brun.** Deserving of its reputation for impeccably fresh *fruits de mer,* this restaurant is a beacon to all fish lovers. Well-trained staff negotiate cramped quarters to lay down heaping seafood platters, shrimp casseroles, or piles of oysters shucked to order. Astoux is noisy, cheerful, and always busy, so arrive early to get a table and avoid the line. ⊠*27 rue Felix Faure, La Croisette* ☎*04–93–39–21–87* ▤*AE, MC, V.*

$–$$$$ ✕ **La Mère Besson.** This long-standing favorite continues to please a largely foreign clientele with its regional specialties such as sweet-and-sour sardines *à l'escabèche* (marinated), monkfish Provençal (with tomatoes, fennel, and onion), and roast lamb with garlic puree. The formality of the damask linens and still-life paintings is moderated by clatter from the open kitchen. Dinner prix-fixe menus are €28 and €35. ⊠*13 rue des Frères-Pradignac, La Croisette* 🖀*04–93–39–59–24* ▤*AE, DC, MC, V* ⊘*Closed Sun. Sept.–June. No lunch except during festivals.*

\$–\$\$\$ ✕ **Le Petit Lardon.** Popular and unpretentious, this tiny bistro is feisty and fun. Watch for a great mix of seasonal Provençal and Burgundian flavors: escargot served with butter and garlic, roast rabbit *au jus* stuffed with raisins, and melt-in-your-mouth lavender crème brûlée. Busy, bustling and friendly, it's ideal for a casual meal, but it's tiny, so reserve well in advance. ⊠*Rue de Batéguier, La Croisette* 🖀*04–93–39–06–28* ▤*AE, MC, V* ⊘*Closed Sun.*

¢–\$\$\$ ✕ **La Pizza.** Sprawling up over two floors and right in front of the old port, this busy Italian restaurant serves steaks, fish, and salads, but go there for what they're famous for: gloriously good right-out-of-the-wood-fire-oven pizza in hungry-man-size portions, and they have an outpost in Nice as well. ⊠*3 quai St-Pierre, La Croisette* 🖀*04–93–39–22–56* ▤*AE, MC, V.*

★ \$\$\$\$ 🏨 **Carlton InterContinental.** As one of the turn-of-the-19th-century pioneers of this resort town, this deliciously pompous Neoclassical landmark quickly staked out the best position: La Croisette seems to radiate symmetrically from its figurehead waterfront site. Almost sharing star billing with Grace Kelly and Cary Grant in Alfred Hitchcock's *To Catch a Thief,* the Carlton still hosts many film festival banquets in its gilt-and-marble Grand Salon (along with, alas, business conferences year-round). Seven deluxe suites on the top floor, each with unsurpassed sea views and every comfort imaginable, as well as snazzy seafront rooms add to its cache; those at the back compensate for the lack of a sea view with cheery Provençal prints. The top-floor suites have been recently renovated and are a glory of burnished wood and rich creams, and the health and fitness center, although small, has every luxe item imaginable. The restaurant is good, the brasserie swank, and the Bar des Célébrités lives up to its name during the film festival. ⊠*58 bd. de la Croisette, La Croisette, 06414* 🖀*04–93–06–40–06* 🖷*04–93–06–40–25* ⊕*www.interconti.com* ⤏*338 rooms, 36 suites* ⓐ*In-room: refrigerator, Wi-Fi. In-hotel: 3 restaurants, bars, gym, parking (fee), no-smoking rooms, some pets allowed (fee).*

★ \$\$\$\$ 🏨 **Le Cavendish Boutique Hotel.** Lovingly restored by friendly owners Christine and Guy Welter, this giddily opulent former residence of English Lord Cavendish is a true delight. Rooms—designed by Christopher Tollemar of JoJo Bistro in New York fame—are done in bright swaths of color ("wintergarden" greens, "incensed" reds) that play up both contemporary decor and 19th-century elegance. Beauty, conviviality, even smells—sheets are scented with lavender water and fresh flowers line the entryway—all work together in genuine harmony. The downstairs bar is cozy for a nightcap and the copious buffet breakfast is simply excellent. ⊠*11 bd. Carnot, St-Nicolas, 06400* 🖀*04–97–06–26–00* 🖷*04–97–06–26–01* ⊕*www.cavendish-cannes.com* ⤏*34 rooms* ⓐ*In-room: refrigerator, Wi-Fi. In-hotel: bar, parking (fee), some pets allowed (fee)* ▤*AE, MC, V.*

$$–$$$ 🏨 **Molière.** Plush, intimate, and low-key, this hotel, a short stroll from the Croisette, has pretty tile baths and small rooms in cool shades of peach, indigo, and white-waxed oak. Nearly all overlook the vast, enclosed front garden, where palms and cypresses shade terrace tables, and where breakfast, included in the price, is served most of the year. ✉ *5 rue Molière, La Croisette, 06400* ☎ *04–93–38–16–16* 📠 *04–93–68–29–57* ⊕ *www.hotel-moliere.com* ↪ *24 rooms* ⬥ *In-room: Wi-Fi. In-hotel: bar, some pets allowed (fee)* ☰ *AE, MC, V* ⊗ *Closed mid-Nov.–late Dec.* ⭗ *BP.*

$ 🏨 **Albert Ier.** In a quiet residential area above the Forville market—a 10-minute walk uphill from La Croisette and the beach—this neo-Deco mansion has pretty rooms in pastels, as well as tidy tile baths and an enclosed garden. You can have breakfast on the flowered, shady terrace or in the family-style salon. ✉ *68 av. de Grasse, Le Suquet, 06400* ☎ *04–93–39–24–04* 📠 *04–93–38–83–75* ⊕ *www.hotelalbert1ercannes. com* ↪ *11 rooms* ⬥ *In-room: refrigerator, Wi-Fi, no a/c. In-hotel: parking (no fee), some pets allowed, no elevator* ☰ *MC, V* ⊗ *Closed last wk of Nov., 1st 2 wks of Dec.*

NIGHTLIFE & THE ARTS

The Riviera's cultural calendar is splashy and star-studded, and never more so than during the **International Film Festival** in May. The film screenings are not open to the public, so unless you have a pass, your stargazing will be on the streets or in restaurants (though if you hang around in a tux, a stray ticket might come your way).

As befits a glamorous seaside resort, Cannes has two casinos. The famous **Casino Croisette** (✉ *In Palais des Festivals, La Croisette* ☎ *04–92–98–78–00*) draws more crowds to its slot machines than any other casino in France. The **Palm Beach Casino Club** (✉ *Pl. Franklin-Roosevelt, Point de la Croisette, La Croisette* ☎ *04–97–06–36–90*) manages to retain an exclusive atmosphere even though you can show up in jeans. The biggest player to date in the Cannes nightlife scene is **Le Baoli** (✉ *Port Pierre Canto, La Croisette* ☎ *04–93–43–03–43* ⊕ *www. lebaoli.com*), where the likes of Leonardo DiCaprio and Ivana Trump have been known to stop by; it's usually packed until dawn even outside of festival time. To make the correct entrance at the popular **La Discotheca** (✉ *22 rue Macé, La Croisette* ☎ *04–93–99–94–86*) have yourself whisked by limo from the steak house Le Farfalla in front of the Palais des Festivals. If you're craving something a little less French, the most English of pubs in Cannes, **Morrison's Irish Pub** (✉ *10 rue Teisseire, La Croisette* ☎ *04–92–98–16–17* ⊕ *www.morrisonspub.com*), has live music every Wednesday and Thursday and a plethora of Irish-English staff. At **Jimmy'z** (✉ *Palais des Festivals, La Croisette* ☎ *04–92–98–78–78*) the cabaret shows are legendary. The stylish and the beautiful flock to **Les Coulisses** (✉ *29 rue de Commandant André, La Croisette* ☎ *04–92–99–17–17*). The hip Latin bar **Caliente** (✉ *84 bd. de la Croisette, La Croisette* ☎ *04–93–94–49–59*) is jammed in summer until dawn with salsa-dancing regulars.

THE OUTDOORS

Most of the **beaches** along La Croisette are owned by hotels and/or restaurants, though this doesn't necessarily mean the hotels or restaurants front the beach. It does mean they own a patch of beachfront bearing their name, where they rent out chaise longues, mats, and umbrellas to the public and hotel guests (who also have to pay). Public beaches are between the color-coordinated private beach umbrellas and offer simple open showers and basic toilets. Sailboats can be rented at either port or at some of the beachfront hotels.

> **STAR-GAZING?**
>
> Remember, the film screenings are *not* open to the public and the stars themselves no longer grace cafés, beaches, or the morning market; they hide in the privacy of the Hôtel du Cap–Eden Roc on the Cap d'Antibes. Your best bet is behind the barriers set up on the Croisette to watch the red-carpet events at the Palais des Festivals.

ILES DE LÉRINS

⑬ *15–20 mins by ferry off the coast of Cannes.*

When you're glutted on glamour, you may want to make a day trip to the peaceful Iles de Lérins (Lérins Islands); boats depart from Cannes's Vieux Port. Allow at least a half day to enjoy either of the islands; you can fit both in only if you get an early start. Access to the ferry is across the large parking in front of the Sofitel hotel, southwest from the Palais des Festivals. You have two options: to go to Isle St-Honorat take

Compangie Planaria (✉ *Quai Lauboeuf, port of Cannes, La Croisette, Cannes* ☎ *04–92–98–71–38)*

or, for Isle St-Margueritte, the **Trans Cote D'Azur** (✉ *Quai Lauboeuf, port of Cannes, La Croisette, Cannes* ☎ *04–92–98–71–30).*

It's a 15-minute, €11 round-trip (summer) or €5 round-trip (winter) to **Ile Ste-Marguerite.** Its **Fort Royal,** built by Richelieu and improved by Vauban, offers views over the ramparts to the rocky island coast and the open sea.

Behind the prison buildings is the **Musée de la Mer** *(Marine Museum),* with a Roman boat dating from the 1st century bc and a collection of amphorae and pottery recovered from ancient shipwrecks. It's more famous, however, for reputedly being the prison of the Man in the Iron Mask. Inside you can see his cell and hear his story, and although the truth of his captivity is not certain, it is true that many Huguenots were confined here during Louis XIV's religious scourges. ☎ *04–93–43–18–17* 🖃€3 ☉ *Oct.–Mar., Tues.–Sun. 10:30–1:15 and 2:15–4:45; Apr.–mid-June, Tues.–Sun. 10:30–1:15 and 2:15–5:45; mid-June–mid-Sept., daily 10:30–5:45, mid-Sept.–end-Sept., Tues.–Sun. 10:30–1:15 and 2:15–5:45.*

Ile St-Honorat can be reached in 20 minutes (€11 round-trip) from the Vieux Port. Smaller and wilder than Ste-Marguerite, it's home to an

11

active monastery and the ruins of its 11th-century predecessor. Oddly enough, the monks are more famous in the region for their non-religious activity: manufacturing and selling a rather strong liqueur called Lerina.

ANTIBES

14 **Fodor's**Choice ★

11 km (7 mi) northeast of Cannes, 15 km (9 mi) southeast of Nice.

GETTING HERE

Antibes has one central train station, the *Gare SNCF* (⊠*Pl. Pierre-Semard* ⊕*www.voyages-sncf.com*), which is at the far end of town but still within walking distance of the Vieille Ville and only a block or so from the beach. Local trains are frequent, coming from Nice (20 mins, €4), Juan-les-Pins, Biot, Cannes (10 mins, €3), and almost all other coastal towns. There are also high-speed TGVs (Trains at Great Speed) that depart from Antibes. Bus service, available at Antibes's Gare Routière (bus station) (⊠*1 pl. Guynemer*) is supplied by both the RCA lines (☎*04–93–85–64–44* ⊕*www.rca.tm.fr*) and the TAM lines (☎*04–93–85–61–81* ⊕*www.lignedazur.com*). One example is the No. 200 RCA bus between Cannes and Antibes, which runs every 20 minutes and costs €€1.30. To get to Cannes, Nice, Cagnes-sur-Mer, Juan-les-Pins, or to catch local buses—including one that threads the big Cap d'Antibes peninsula—wait at the different posts on Place du Général-de-Gaulle; most lines run every 20 minutes.

EXPLORING

No wonder Picasso once called this home—Antibes (pronounced Awn-*teeb*) is a stunner. With its broad stone ramparts scalloping in and out over the waves and backed by blunt medieval towers and a skew of tile roofs, it remains one of the most romantic old towns on the Mediterranean coast. As gateway to the Cap d'Antibes, Antibes's Port Vauban harbor has some of the largest yachts in the world tied up at its berths—their millionaire owners won't find a more dramatic spot to anchor, with the tableau of the snowy Alps looming in the distance and the formidable medieval block towers of the Fort Carré guarding entry to the port. Stroll Promenade Amiral-de-Grasse along the crest of Vauban's sea walls, and you can understand why the views inspired Picasso to paint on a panoramic scale. Yet a few steps inland you can enter a souklike maze of old streets that are relentlessly picturesque and joyously beautiful.

To visit Old Antibes, pass through the **Porte Marine,** an arched gateway in the rampart wall. Follow Rue Aubernon to **Cours Masséna,** where the little sheltered market sells lemons, olives, and hand-stuffed sausages, and the vendors take breaks in the shoe-box cafés flanking one side.

★ From Cours Masséna head up to the **Eglise de l'Immaculée-Conception** (⊠*Pl. de la Cathédrale*), which served as the region's cathedral until the bishopric was transferred to Grasse in 1244. The church's 18th-century facade, a marvelously Latin mix of classical symmetry and fantasy, has been restored in shades of ocher and cream. Its stout medieval watchtower was built in the 11th century with stones "mined" from Roman structures. Inside is a Baroque altarpiece painted by the Niçois artist Louis Bréa in 1515.

Next door to the cathedral, the ★ medieval **Château Grimaldi** rises high over the water on a Roman foundation. Famed as rulers of Monaco, the Grimaldi family lived here until the Revolution, but this fine old castle was little more than a monument until in 1946 its curator offered use of its vast chambers to Picasso, at a time when that extraordinary genius was enjoying a period of intense creative energy. The result is now housed in the **Musée Picasso**, a bounty of exhilarating paintings, ceramics, and lithographs inspired by the sea and by Greek mythology—all very Mediterranean. Even those who are not great Picasso fans should enjoy his vast paintings on wood, canvas, paper, and walls, alive with nymphs, fauns, and centaurs. The museum houses more than 300 works by the artist, as well as pieces by Miró, Calder, and Léger. At this writing, the museum was closed for renovations, with plans to reopen for winter 2008. ⊠ *Pl. du Château* ☎ *04–92–90–54–20* ⚿ *€6 (may change)* ⊘ *June–Sept., Tues.–Sun. 10–6; Oct.–May, Tues.–Sun. 10–noon and 2–6 (may change).*

Fodor'sChoice A few blocks south of the Château Grimaldi is the **Commune Libre du** ★ **Safranier** *(Free Commune of Safranier)*, a magical little 'hood with a character all its own. Here, not far off the seaside promenade and focused around the Place du Safranier, tiny houses hang heavy with flowers and vines and neighbors carry on conversations from window to window across the stone-stepped Rue du Bas-Castelet. It is said that Place du Safranier was once a tiny fishing port; now it's the scene of this subvillage's festivals.

The Bastion St-André, a squat Vauban fortress, now contains the **Musée Archéologique** *(Archaeology Museum)*. Its collection focuses on Antibes's classical history, displaying amphorae and sculptures found in local digs as well as salvaged from shipwrecks from the harbor. ⊠ *Av. Général-Maizières* ☎ *04–92–90–54–35* ⚿ *€3* ⊘ *Oct.–May, Tues.–Sun. 10–noon and 2–6; June–Sept., Tues.–Sun. 10–noon and 2–8.*

WHERE TO STAY & EAT

$$–$$$$ ✕ **La Jarre.** You can dine under the beams or the ancient fig tree at **Fodor'sChoice** this lovely little garden hideaway, just off the ramparts and behind the ★ cathedral on one of Antibes's dreamiest back alleys. It has an ambitious menu of Provençal specialties filtered through an international lens: lobster sushi with butter and basil, roasted sea bass with creamed soya and green asparagus, grilled pepper steak, sweet-and-sour duck breast, and coconut crème brûlée are all headliners here. ⊠ *14 rue St-Esprit* ☎ *04–93–34–50–12* ⚌ *AE, MC, V* ⊘ *Closed Wed. Sept.–mid-June, and mid June–Aug. No lunch Mon.–Wed.*

★ **$-$$$$** ✕ **Le Brûlot.** Set one street back from the market, this bistro remains one of the most popular in Antibes. Burly chef Christian Blancheri hoists anything from pigs to apple pies in and out of his roaring wood oven, and it's all delicious. Watch for the duck and crispy chips, sardines *à l'escabèche* (in a tangy sweet-sour marinade), sizzling lamb chops, or grilled fresh fish. ✉ *3 rue Frédéric Isnard* ☎ *04–93–34–17–76* ▭ *MC, V* ☉ *Closed Sun. No lunch Tues. and Wed.*

$$-$$$ ✕⊡ **L'Auberge Provençale.** Overlooking the largest square in Antibes's Old Town, this onetime abbey now has six rooms complete with exposed beams, canopy beds, and lovely antique furniture. The dining room and the arbored garden are informed with the same impeccable taste; the menu allures with fresh seafood inventions such as *rascasse* (rock fish) sausage with mint, as well as bouillabaisse and duck grilled over wood coals. The restaurant is closed Monday and for Tuesday lunch. ✉ *61 pl. Nationale, 06600* ☎ *04–93–34–13–24* ⊟ *04–93–34–89–88* ⇨ *7 rooms* ⚲ *In-room: dial-up. In-hotel: restaurant, some pets allowed (fee), no elevator* ▭ *MC, V.*

NIGHTLIFE

La Siesta (✉ *Rte. du Bord de Mer, Antibes* ☎ *04–93–33–31–31* ⊕ *www. lasiesta.fr*) is an enormous summer entertainment center with seven dance floors (some on the beach), bars, slot machines, and roulette.

THE OUTDOORS

Antibes and Juan together claim 25 km (15½ mi) of coastline and 48 **beaches** (including Cap d'Antibes). In Antibes you can choose between small sandy inlets—such as **La Gravette,** below the port; the central **Place de Ponteil;** and **Plage de la Salis,** toward the Cap—rocky escarpments around the Vieille Ville; or the vast stretch of sand above the Fort Carré.

JUAN-LES-PINS

⑮ *5 km (3 mi) southwest of Antibes.*

If Antibes is the elderly, historic parent, then Juan-les-Pins is the jazzy younger-sister resort town that, with Antibes, bracelets the wrist of the Cap d'Antibes. The scene along Juan's waterfront is something to behold, with thousands of international sunseekers flowing up and down the promenade or lying flank to flank on its endless stretch of sand. The **Plage de Juan-les-Pins** is made up of sand, not pebbles, and ranks among the Riviera's best (rent a beach chair from the nearby hotel concessions, the best of which is Les Belles Rives). Along with these white-powder wonders, Juan is famous for the quality—some pundits say quantity—of its nightlife. There are numerous nightclubs where you can do everything but sleep, ranging from casinos to discos to strip clubs. If all this sounds like too much hard work, wait for July's jazz festival—one of Europe's most prestigious—or simply repair to the Juana or Les Belles Rives; if you're lucky enough to be a guest at either hotel, you'll understand why F. Scott Fitzgerald set his *Tender Is the Night* in "Juantibes," as both places retain the golden glamour of the Riviera of yore. These hotels are surrounded by the last remnants of the pine forests that gave Juan its name. Elsewhere, Juan-les-Pins suffers from a plastic feel and you might get more out of Antibes.

WHERE TO STAY & EAT

★ $$$$ ✕⊡ **Les Belles Rives.** If "living well is the best revenge," then vacationers at this landmark hotel should know. Not far from the onetime villa of Gerald and Sara Murphy—those Roaring '20s millionaires who devoted their life to proving this maxim—the Belles Rives became the home-away-from-home for literary giant F. Scott Fitzgerald and his wife Zelda (chums of the Murphys). Lovingly restored to 1930s glamour, the public salons and piano bar prove that what's old is new again: France's stylish young set now make this endearingly *neoclassique* place one of their favorites. The gastronomic restaurant's cuisine is innovative; the fixed menu is good value. Dine on the terrace on a fine summer night, with the sea lapping below and stars twinkling in the velvety Mediterranean sky. There's no pool, but happily the recently renovated private beach is just steps away. ⊠*Bd. Baudoin, 06160* 🕾*04–93–61–02–79* 🖶*03–93–67–43–51* ⊕*www.bellesrives.com* 🛏*44 rooms* ⚐*In-room: refrigerator, Wi-Fi. In-hotel: 2 restaurants, bar, beachfront, parking (no fee), some pets allowed (fee)* ⊟*AE, V.*

$$–$$$ ⊡ **Le Mimosa.** The fabulous setting, in an enclosed hilltop garden studded with tall palms, mimosas, and tropical greenery, makes up for the hike down to the beach. Rooms are small and modestly decorated in Victorian florals, but ask for one with a balcony: many look over the garden and sizable pool. Rates can include half board. ⊠*Rue Pauline, 06160* 🕾*04–93–61–04–16* 🖶*04–92–93–06–46* 🛏*34 rooms* ⚐*In-hotel: pool, parking (no fee), some pets allowed (fee), public Wi-Fi* ⊟*AE, MC, V* ⊙*Closed Oct.–Apr.* ⑩*MAP.*

NIGHTLIFE & THE ARTS

The glassed-in complex of the **Eden Casino** (⊠*Bd. Baudoin, Juan-les-Pins* 🕾*04–92–93–71–71*) houses restaurants, bars, dance clubs, and a casino. By far the most popular club in the town—and rumored to be the favorite haunt of Oasis's Noel Gallagher—is **The Village** (⊠*Pl. de la Nouvelle Orléans, 1 bd. de la Pinède, Juan-les-Pins* 🕾*04–92–93–90–00* ⊙*Closed Sun.–Thurs.*). Every July the **Festival International Jazz à Juan** (🕾*04–97–23–11–10*) challenges Montreux for its stellar lineup and romantic venue under ancient pines. This place hosted the European debut performances of such stars as Meels Dah-*vees* (Miles Davis) and Ray Charles.

CAP D'ANTIBES

⑯ *2 km (1 mi) south of Antibes.*

This extravagantly beautiful peninsula, protected from the concrete plague infecting the mainland coast, has been carved up into luxurious estates shaded by thick, tall pines. Since the 19th century its wild greenery and isolation have drawn a glittering guest list of aristocrats, artists, literati, and the merely fabulously wealthy: Guy de Maupassant, Anatole France, Claude Monet, the Duke and Duchess of Windsor, the Greek shipping tycoon Stavros Niarchos, and the cream of the Lost Generation, including Ernest Hemingway, Gertrude Stein, and Scottie and Zelda Fitzgerald. Now the most publicized focal point is the Hotel Eden Roc, rendezvous and weekend getaway of film stars. The Cap is about 6 km (4 mi) long so don't consider it a gentle stroll from downtown Antibes. Happily, the 2A or 2A bis municipal bus (€1.30 ⊕www.envibus.fr) often connects the two. You can sample a little of what draws famous people to the site by walking up the Chemin de Calvaire from the Plage de la Salis in Antibes (about 1 km [½ mi]) and taking in the extraordinary views (spectacular at night) from the hill that supports the old lighthouse, the **Phare de la Garoupe** *(Garoupe Lighthouse)*. Next to the lighthouse, the 16th-century double chapel of **Notre-Dame-de-la-Garoupe** contains ex-votos and statues of the Virgin, all in memory and for the protection of sailors. 04–93–67–36–01 ⊙ *Easter–Sept., daily 9:30–noon and 2:30–7; Oct.–Easter, daily 10–noon and 2:30–5.*

To fully experience the Riviera's heady hothouse exoticism, visit the ★ glorious **Jardin Thuret** *(Thuret Garden)*, established by botanist Gustave Thuret in 1856 as a testing ground for subtropical plants and trees. Thuret was responsible for the introduction of the palm tree, forever changing the profile of the French Riviera. On his death the property was left to the Ministry of Agriculture, which continues to dabble in the introduction of exotic species. The Jardin is in the middle of the Cap; from the Port du Croûton head up Chemin de l'Aureto, then Chemin du Tamisier, and turn right on the Boulevard du Cap. ⊠62 *bd. du Cap* 04–93–67–88–66 ⊕*jardin-thuret.antibes.inra.fr* Free ⊙ *Oct.–May, weekdays 8:30–5:30; June–Sept., weekdays 8–6.*

Bordering the Cap's zillion-dollar hotels and fabled estates runs one of Fodor'sChoice the most spectacular footpaths in the world: the **Sentier Tirepoil**, which ★ runs about 1½ km (1 mi) along the outermost tip of the peninsula. It begins gently enough at the pretty Plage de la Garoupe (where Cole Porter and Gerard Murphy used to hang out), with a paved walkway and dazzling views over the Baie de la Garoupe and the faraway Alps. Round the far end of the cap, however, and the paved promenade soon gives way to a boulder-studded pathway that picks its way along 50-foot cliffs, dizzying switchbacks, and thundering breakers *(Attention Mort*—"Beware: Death"—read the signs, reminding you this path can be very dangerous in stormy weather). On sunny days, with exhilarating winds and spectacular breakers coming in from the sea, you'll have company (families, even), although for most stretches all signs of civilization completely disappear—except for a yacht or two. The walk is long, and takes about two hours to complete, but it may prove two of the more unforgettable hours of your life (especially if you tackle it at sunset).

The Sentier Tirepoil passes below (but unfortunately does not access) Fodor'sChoice the **Villa Eilenroc,** designed by Charles Garnier, who created the Paris ★ Opéra—which should give you some idea of its style. It commands the tip of the peninsula from a grand and glamorous garden. You may tour the grounds freely, but, during high season, the house remains closed (unless the owners, on a good day, choose to open the first floor to visitors). But from September to June visitors are allowed to wander through the reception salons, which retain the Louis Seize–Trianon feel of the noble facade. The Winter Salon still has its 1,001 Nights ceiling mural painted by Jean Dunand, the famed Art Deco designer; display cases are filled with memorabilia donated by Caroline Groult-Flaubert (Antibes resident and goddaughter of the great author); while the boudoir has boiseries from the Marquis de Sévigné's Paris mansion. As you leave, be sure to detour to La Rosaerie, the rose garden of the estate—in the distance you can spot the white portico of the Château de la Cröe, another legendary villa (now reputedly owned by a syndicate of Russian billionaires). Whether or not the Eilenroc is haunted by Helene Beaumont, the rich singer who built it, or King Leopold II of Belgium, King Farouk of Egypt, Aristotle Onassis, and Greta Garbo—who all rented here—only you will be able to tell. ⊠ *At peninsula's tip* ☏ *04–93–67–74–33* ⊕ *www.antibes-juanlespins.com* ☞ *Free* ⊘ *House: mid-Sept.–June, Wed. 9–noon and 1:30–5; Gardens: mid-Sept.–June, Tues. and Wed. 9–5.*

Across the Bay of Millionaires from the Villa Eilenroc (and just down the road from the posh Hôtel du Cap–Eden Roc) is a picturesque mini-peninsula, landmarked by an ancient battery tower that now contains the **Musée Napoléonien** *(Napoleonic Museum)*. Here, you can peruse a collection of watercolors of Antibes, platoons of lead soldiers, and scale models of military ships. ⊠ *Batterie du Grillon, Av. Kennedy* ☏ *04–93–61–45–32* ☞ *€3* ⊘ *Mid-Sept.–mid-June, Tues.–Sat. 10–4:30; mid-June–mid-Sept., Tues.–Sat. 10–6.*

WHERE TO STAY & EAT

★ $$$$ ✕ **Restaurant de Bacon.** Since 1948, under the careful watch of the Sordello brothers, this has been *the* spot for seafood on the French Riviera. The catch of the day may be minced in lemon seviche, floating in a top-of-the-line bouillabaisse, or simply grilled with fennel, crisped with hillside herbs. The warm welcome, discreet service, sunny dining room, and dreamy terrace over the Baie des Anges, with views of the Antibes ramparts, justify extravagance. Many of the à la carte fish dishes are pricey, with many going for €60 or €70 apiece (the luxe lobster version of their bouillabaisse soars to €130) but, happily, fixed-menu prices are €50 and €80. ⊠ *Bd. de Bacon* ☏ *04–93–61–50–02* ⊕ *www.restaurant-debacon.com* ⚏ *Reservations essential* ▭ *AE, DC, MC, V* ⊘ *Closed Mon. and Nov.–Jan. No lunch Tues.*

★ $$$$ 🏨 **Hôtel du Cap–Eden Roc.** In demand by celebrities from De Niro to Madonna (perhaps understandably, since their bills are picked up by Paramount Pictures and other film giants when they fly in for the Cannes film festival—don't even try to book a room in early May), this extravagantly expensive hotel has long catered to the world's fantasy of a subtropical idyll on the French Riviera. First opened in 1879, the Villa Soleil, as this retreat for ailing artists was then called, joined forces and facilities with the neighboring Eden Roc tearoom in 1914, and expanded its luxuries to include a swimming pool blasted into seaside bedrock. After the Great War, two stylish American intellectuals, Sara and Gerald Murphy, rented the entire complex and invited all their friends, a stellar lot ranging from the Windsors to Rudolf Valentino and Marlene Dietrich. Their most frequent guests were Zelda and F. Scott Fitzgerald, who used it as the model for Hôtel des Etrangers in his *Tender Is the Night*. Today its broad, sun-drenched rooms, thickly carpeted and furnished with antiques in the main Second Empire mansion, look out on 22 acres of immaculate tropical gardens bordered by rocky shoreline. Down by the water is the Pavillon Eden Roc wing, more modern but with sheer-horizon views. Everyone dresses stylishly for dinner. Credit cards are not accepted (rumor has it that this may change soon); the hotel can arrange for a bank transfer. And if you're not a celebrity, tip big to keep the staff interested. ⊠*Bd. Kennedy, 06160* ☎*04-93-61-39-01* 🖷*04-93-67-76-04* ⊕*www.edenroc-hotel.fr* ⬛*121 rooms, 9 suites* ⌂*In-room: Wi-Fi. In-hotel: restaurant, bar, tennis courts, pool, gym* ▭*No credit cards* ⊘*Closed mid-Oct.–Mar.*

$$–$$$ 🏨 **Hôtels La Garoupe and La Gardiole.** Cool, simple, and accessible to non–movie stars, this pair of partnered hotels offers a chance to sleep on the hallowed peninsula and bike or walk to the pretty Garoupe beach. A sizable pool, framed by high walls and tall pines, offers cool-down time. Rooms are comfortably furnished in both buildings, with the Garoupe offering modern decor and the Gardiole rustic Provençal design. ⊠*60–74 chemin de la Garoupe, 06160* ☎*04-92-93-33-33* 🖷*04-93-67-61-87* ⊕*www.hotel-lagaroupe-gardiole.com* ⬛*40 rooms* ⌂*In-room: safe, refrigerator, Wi-Fi. In-hotel: restaurant, pool* ▭*AE, MC, V.*

$$ 🏨 **Hôtel La Jabotte.** A few steps from a sandy beach, this adorable guesthouse is built around a central courtyard, where guests relax over a breakfast (included in the room price) of croissants, baguette, fresh juice, and homemade jam. Rooms are tastefully decorated with motifs of birds, flowers, or calligraphy, and the owner is as charming as the setting. ⊠*13 av. Max-Maurey, 06160* ☎*04-93-61-45-89* 🖷*04-93-67-61-87* ⊕*www.jabotte.com* ⬛*10 rooms* ⌂*In-room: no a/c. In-hotel: bar, some pets allowed* ▭*AE, MC, V* ⦿*BP.*

THE HILL TOWNS: ON THE TRAIL OF PICASSO & MATISSE

The hills that back the French Riviera are often called the *arrière-pays*, or backcountry. This particular wedge of backcountry—behind the coast between Cannes and Antibes—has a character all its own: deeply, unselfconsciously Provençal, with undulating fields of lavender watched over by villages perched on golden stone. Many of these villages look as if they do not belong to the last century—but they do, since they played the muse to some of modern art's most famous exemplars, notably Paolo Picasso and Henri Matisse. A highlight here is the Maeght Foundation, in St-Paul de Vence (also home to the incomparable inn, La Colombe d'Or), one of France's leading museums of modern art. The town's neighbor, Vence, has the Chapelle du Rosaire, entirely designed and decorated by Matisse. It's possible to get a small taste of this backcountry on a day trip out of Fréjus, Cannes, or Antibes; even if you're vacationing on the coast, you may want to settle in for a night or two. Of course, you'll soon discover the stooped, stone row houses that are now galleries and boutiques offering everything from neo–Van Gogh sofa art to assembly-line lavender sachets, and everywhere you can hear the gentle *breet-breet* of mechanical souvenir *cigales* (cicadas). So if you're at all allergic to souvenir shops and middlebrow art galleries, aim to visit off-season or after hours, when the stone-paved alleys are emptied of tourists and the scent of strawberry potpourri is washed away by the natural perfume of bougainvillea and jasmine wafting from terra-cotta jars.

VALLAURIS

⑰ *6 km (4 mi) northeast of Cannes, 6 km (4 mi) west of Antibes.*

In the low hills over the coast, dominated by a blocky Renaissance château, this ancient village was ravaged by waves of the plague in the 14th century, then rebuilt in the 16th century by 70 Genoese families imported to repopulate the abandoned site. They brought with them a taste for Roman planning—hence the grid format in the Old Town—but, more important in the long run, a knack for pottery making, as well. Their skills and the fine clay of Vallauris proved to be a marriage made in heaven, and the village thrived as a pottery center for hundreds of years.

In the 1940s Picasso found inspiration in the malleable soil and settled here in a simple stone house, creating pottery art with a single-minded passion. But he returned to painting in 1952 to create one of his masterworks in the château's Romanesque chapel, the vast multi-panel oil-on-wood composition called *La Guerre et la Paix* (*War and*

★ *Peace*). The chapel is part of the **Musée National Picasso** today, where several of Picasso's ceramic pieces are displayed. ⊠*Pl. de la Libération* ☎*04–93–64–71–83* ⊕*www.musee-picasso-vallauris.fr* ☜*€3.20* ☉*June–Sept., Wed.–Mon. 10–12:15 and 2–6; Oct.–May, Wed.–Mon. 10–12:15 and 2–5.*

MOUGINS

⑱ *6 km (4 mi) north of Valluris, 8 km (5 mi) north of Cannes, 11 km (7 mi) northwest of Antibes.*

Passing through Mougins, a popular summerhouse community convenient to Cannes and Nice and famously home to a group of excellent restaurants, you may perceive little more than suburban sprawl. But in 1961 Picasso found much to admire and settled into a *mas* (farmhouse) that verily became a pilgrimage spot for artists and art lovers; he died here in 1973.

You can find Picasso's final home and see why, of all spots in the world, he chose this one, by following D35 2 km (1 mi) south of Mougins to the ancient ecclesiastical site of **Notre-Dame-de-Vie** (⊠*Chemin de la Chapelle*). This was the hermitage, or monastic retreat, of the Abbey of Lérins, and its 13th-century bell tower and arcaded chapel form a pretty ensemble. Approached through an allée of ancient cypresses, the house Picasso shared with his wife, Jacqueline, overlooks the broad bowl of the countryside (now blighted with modern construction). Unfortunately, the residence—the former priory—is closed to the public. The chapel is only open during Sunday mass at 9 am. Elsewhere in town are a small **Musée Municipal,** set in the 17th-century St-Bernardin Chapel, and a huge **Musée de l'Automobile,** with 100 vintage cars, in a modern structure on the Aire des Bréguières.

WHERE TO STAY & EAT

$$–$$$$ ✕ **Le Bistrot de Mougins.** In a 15th-century stable with high, curved brick ceilings, this restaurant plays up to its historical past. Rustic chairs and flowered tablecloths offer a real picnic-in-the-country feel. Simple, Provençal-style dishes are hard to beat: escargots in butter and herbs, steak with a green peppercorn sauce, or sea bass grilled with fennel are top choices. ⊠*Pl. du Village* ☎*04–93–75–78–34* ▭*AE, MC, V* ⊗*No lunch Wed. and Sat.*

★ $$–$$$$ ✕ **Le Feu Follet.** In a beautiful period-house setting right in the center of the village, new chef Didier Chouteau is causing quite a stir: from the homemade foie gras to the hand-smoked salmon to mouthwatering basics like roasted scampi with lemon and basil. The best seats are on the enclosed terrace by the quietly tinkling fountain looking out into the mayor's flower garden, but the cozy rooms inside are atmospheric, too. Try to save room for dessert—the lighter-than-the-clouds crème brûlée is truly outstanding. ⊠*Pl. du Commandant Lamy* ☎*04–93–90–15–78* ▭*AE, MC, V* ⊗*Closed Mon. No dinner Sun.*

$$–$$$ ✕ **La Terrasse à Mougins.** Perfectly situated, this friendly little restaurant is casual, country, and chic. The dapper yellow, white, and pastel blue walls fade into insignificance before the panoramic views that look out on the edge of the Vieille Ville. The service is excellent, the restaurant menu varied, although its decor is nothing to write home about and its windows are plate glass (we are in rural France, are we not?). In any event, an after-dinner drink on the terrace looking out over the valley should constitute a moment of sheer, unadulterated pleasure. ⊠*1 bd. Courteline, 06250* ☎*04–92–28–36–20* ⊕*www.la-terrasse-a-mougins. com* ▭*AE, DC, MC, V.*

$$$$ ✕▦ **Le Mas Candille.** Nestled in a huge private park, this 19th-century *mas* has been cleverly transformed into an ultraluxurious hotel. Rooms—all cool colors and country chic—are very refined: a profusion of pillows, heated towels, and all the hidden electrical hookups you could possibly need. Antique wallpapers, "reissued" vintage furniture, and too many other high-gloss touches make this place *Elle Decor*-worthy, if not really authentic to the locale. The opulent, saffron-hue restaurant is the well-ordered domain of chef Serge Gouloumes whose impressive resume includes stints at Ma Maison in Beverly Hills and the Poisson d'Or in Saint Martin. His succulent menus are causing quite a stir in gastronomic circles; watch for items like wild bass in a rosemary tempura clay crust or foie gras tartin with Armagnac. In addition to the main house and the gourmet restaurant, there's a *bastide* (villa) and a Shiseido spa. ⊠*Bd. Clément-Rebuffel, 06250* ☎*04–92–28–43–43* 🖷*04–92–28–43–40* ⊕*www.lemascandille.com* ⇖*39 rooms, 1 suite*

Continued on page 642

CUISINE OF THE SUN

Why do colors seem more intense in Provence, flavors more vivid? It could be the hot, dry climate, which concentrates the essence of fruit and vegetables, or the sun beaming down on the market stalls. Or perhaps you are just seeing the world through rosé-tinted (wine) glasses. Whatever the reason, the real story of Provençal food is one of triumph over the elements. Here's how to savor its *incroyable* flavor.

FROM HOT TO HAUTE

As you bite into a honey-ripe Cavaillon melon or a snow-white, fennel-perfumed sea bass fillet, you might think that nature has always been kind to Provence. Not so. On the wind-battered coast of Marseille, fishermen salvaged the boniest rock fish to create a restorative soup—bouillabaisse—that would become legendary worldwide. In the sun-blasted mountains north of Nice, impoverished farmers developed a repertoire of dishes found nowhere else in France, using hardy Swiss chard, chickpea flour, and salt cod (shipped in from Scandinavia to compensate for a scarcity of fresh fish). Camargue cowboys tamed the wild bull to create their own version of *daube*, a long-simmered stew that transforms tough cuts of meat into a gourmet marvel. Olive oil, the very symbol of Provençal food, is only now overcoming a 1950s frost that entirely wiped out France's olive groves—the local production is tiny compared to that of Spain or Italy but of exceptionally high quality. Even the tomato has a relatively short history here, having been introduced in the 1820s and at first used only in cooked dishes.

FISH TALES

If Provençal cooking is united by a common struggle against the very conditions that give its ingredients their intensity—brilliant sunshine, arid soil, fierce wind, infrequent, pounding rain—it is divided by the area's dramatically changing landscapes. In the Vaucluse alone, scorched plains punctuated by ocher cliffs give way to remarkably lush, orchard-lined mountains and gently sloped vineyards. The wild Calanques of Marseille—source of spiky sea urchins and slithering octopuses—ease into

AIL DE PROVENCE

An indispensable ingredient in Provençal cooking, these garlic bulbs can be white, pink, or purplish; the darker the color, the stronger the flavor.

OLIVES DE NICE

True Niçois olives are not uniformly black but come in delicate shades of green and deep violet.

the more tranquil waters of St-Tropez, home to gleaming bream and sea bass. Everywhere you will find sun-ripened fruit dripping provocatively with nectar and vegetables so flavor-packed that meat might seem a mere accessory. The joy of visiting this region lies in discovering these differences, which might be subtle (as in a local version of boullabaisse or fish soup) or unmistakable (as in the powerful scent that signals truffle season in Carpentras).

POTS, PANS & PICKS

The best Provençal chefs remain fiercely proud of the dishes that define their region or their village, even while injecting their own identities and ideas into

the food. Thanks to its ports, Provence has always been open to outside influences, yet the wealth of readily available ingredients prevents chefs from straying too far from their roots—when the local basil is so headily perfumed, why use lemongrass? If menus at first seem repetitive, go beyond the words *(tapenade, ratatouille, pistou)* to notice how each chef interprets the dish: this is not a land of printed recipes but of spontaneity inspired by the seasons and the markets. Don't expect perfect food every time, but with the help of this book, seek out those who love what they do enough to make *la cuisine de soleil* even more dazzling than the sunshine.

LA VIE EN ROSE

One sip and you'll agree: rosé wine tastes wonderful in the south of France, particularly along the coast. Some experts claim that the sea air enhances the aroma, which might explain why a bottle of Côtes de Provence rosé loses some of its holiday magic at home. French rosés are generally dry, thirst-quenching, and best served chilled. They are considered easy-drinking holiday wines, and quality is constantly improving. Be sure to try a Bandol at least once; the rest of the time, you can't go wrong with a good local rosé.

THE TOP TEN DISHES

AÏOLI

The name for both a dragon's-breath mayonnaise made with helpings of garlic and also a complete recipe of salt cod, potatoes, hard-boiled eggs, and vegetables, aïoli pops up all over Provence, but seems most beloved of the Marseillais. Not an indigenous food, salt cod arrived on the French coast in the Middle Ages from Scandinavia. In keeping with Catholic practice, some restaurants serve it only on Fridays. And it's a good sign if they ask that you place your order at least a day in advance. A grand aïoli is a traditional component of the Niçois Christmas feast.

BOUILLABAISSE

Originally a humble fisherman's soup made with the part of the catch that nobody else wanted, bouillabaisse—the famous fish stew—consists of four or five kinds of fish: the villainous-looking rascasse (red scorpion fish), grondin (sea robin), baudroie (monkfish), congre (conger eel), and rouget (mullet). Snobs add lobster. The whole lot is simmered in a stock of onions, tomatoes, garlic, olive oil, and saffron, which gives the dish its golden color. When presented properly, the broth is served first, with croutons and rouille, a creamy garlic sauce that you spoon in to suit your taste. The fish comes separately, and the ritual is to put pieces into the broth after having a go at the soup on its own.

Bourride

BOURRIDE

This poached fish dish owes its anise kick to pastis and its garlic punch to aïoli. The name comes from the Provençal bourrido, which translates less poetically as "boiled." Monkfish—known as baudroie in Provence and lotte in the rest of France—is a must, but chefs occasionally dress up their bourride with other species and shellfish.

DAUBE DE BOEUF

To distinguish their prized beef stew from boeuf bourguignon, Provençal chefs make a point of not marinating the meat, instead cooking it very slowly in tannic red wine that is often flavored with orange zest. In the Camargue, daube is made with the local taureau (bull's meat), while the Avignon variation uses lamb. In Nice, try ravioli à la daube.

FOUGASSE

The Provençal answer to Italian focaccia, this soft flatbread is distinguished by holes that give it the appearance of a lacy leaf. It can be made savory—flavored with olives, anchovy, bacon, cheese, or anything else the baker has on hand—or sweet, enriched with olive oil and dusted with icing sugar. When in Menton, don't miss the sugary fougasse mentonnaise.

LES PETITS FARCIS

The Niçois specialty called les petits farcis are prepared with tiny summer vegetables (usually zucchini, tomatoes, peppers, and onions) that are traditionally stuffed with veal or leftover daube (beef stew). Enjoy them warm (not hot); this is the best temperature to appreciate their flavors. Like so many Niçois dishes, they make great picnic food.

Fougasse, the Provençal answer to Italian focacia

RATATOUILLE

At its best, ratatouille is a glorious thing—a riot of eggplant, zucchini, bell peppers, and onions, each sautéed separately in olive oil and then gently combined with sweet summer tomatoes. A well-made ratatouille, to which a pinch of saffron has been added to heighten its flavor, is also delicious served chilled.

SOCCA

You'll find socca vendors from Nice to Menton. but this chickpea pancake cooked on a giant iron platter in a wood-fired oven is really a Niçois phenomenon, born of sheer poverty at a time when wheat flour was scarce. After cooking, it is sliced into finger-lickin' portions with an oyster knife. Enjoy it with a glass of pointu, chilled rosé.

SOUPE AU PISTOU

Provençal's answer to pesto, pistou consists of the simplest ingredients—garlic, olive oil, fresh basil, and Parmesan—ideally pounded together by hand in a stone mortar with an olivewood pestle. Most traditionally it brings a potent kick to soupe au pistou, a kind of French minestrone made with green beans, white beans, potatoes, and zucchini.

TIAN DE LÉGUMES

A tian is both a beautiful earthenware dish and one of many vegetable gratins that might be cooked in it. Again showing the thrifty use of ingredients in Provençal cooking, the tian makes a complete meal of seasonal vegetables. eggs, and a little cheese. Swiss chard is a favorite ingredient in winter, while eggplant and tomato are best bets in summer.

THE ITALIAN CONNECTION

The most distinctive food on the Riviera comes from Nice. It's a curious mixture of Parisian, Provençal, and Italian cuisine, pungent with garlic, olives, anchovies, and steaming shellfish. Among the specialties here: pissaladière, an onion tart laced with black olive purée and anchovies; pan bagnat, a French loaf—a baguette—split down the middle, soaked in olive oil, and garnished with tomatoes, radishes, peppers, onions, hard-boiled eggs, black olives, and a sprig of basil; and l'estocaficada, a ragout of stockfish (air-dried unsalted fish, often cod). soaked in water before being cooked and served with potatoes, tomatoes, and zucchini.

THE TASTEMAKERS

It is not entirely surprising that some of France's best chefs now work in Provence and on the Riviera. It was here—in Ville-neuve-Loubet, outside Cannes—that **Auguste Escoffier**, the legendary founding father of haute cuisine, was born (his villa is now a museum). Today, Escoffier's heirs are forging new paths in the "new Mediterranean cuisine" in all its costly splendor. Everybody knows the name of Alain Ducasse, whose luxurious cuisine moderne is on show at Monaco's Le Louis XV. Here are the newer stars that are making gastronomes genuflect today.

Alain Llorca

Former Negresco chef **Alain Llorca**—whose name reveals his Basque roots—has found the perfect setting for his Spanish-influenced style in the freshly renovated, plum-and-white dining room of the Moulin de Mougins, the famous culinary temple put on the map years ago by Roger Vergé. No matter how simple or complex the dish, Llorca makes each ingredient sing—a crisp-skinned farmer's chicken breast proves tender enough to cut with a fork, its accompanying spring vegetables straight from his own potager (vegetable garden). Llorca's sense of humor comes through in his ronde des tapas—look for such whimsical nibbles as foie gras bonbons, goat cheese croque-monsieur, and bouillabaisse-style octopus.

Antique dealers feel at home at Le Jardin du Quai in L'Isle-sur-la-Sorgue, which jovial young chef **Daniel Hébet** runs like an open house. In summer, regulars linger on the garden patio reading the paper and chatting, while in winter the high-ceiling bistro-style dining room exudes the same welcoming vibe. Shrugging off the constraints of haute cuisine with a no-choice set menu at lunch and dinner, Hébet still makes clever use of techniques, serving vivid green, individually skinned broad beans in a frothy sauce with barely cooked chanterelles and artfully peeled fat white asparagus. Don't miss his quinoa-crusted cod.

After an illustrious haute cuisine career, **Jacques Maximin** has found contentment in running a convivial country auberge near Vence. The name, La Table d'Amis, speaks volumes about his approach—here the chef treats customers like old friends, occasionally even relieving them of decision-making by serving what he has decided they should eat. Even if you're not so lucky, you can hardly go wrong with a menu that reveals his long experience and a renewed joie de vivre—Catalan-style scallops with risotto are just one perfect example of his openness to other southern cooking styles.

The summer tomato menu has become a much-anticipated annual tradition at **Christian Etienne**'s restaurant next to the Palais des Papes in Avignon, where each year he celebrates the versatility of this vegetable with a tasting extravaganza that might include tartare of three varieties with oil from the Bleu Argent olive mill in Provence, foie gras with Roma tomato petals, and tomato macaroon with lime sorbet. Etienne is one of the long-established masters of Provençal cooking, and if his cooking sometimes makes generous use of butter (rather than uniquely olive oil), his customers aren't complaining.

Christian Etienne

TO MARKET, TO MARKET

Marché aux poissons, Marseille

Markets define Provençal living, from the see-and-be-seen Cours Saleya in Nice to villages that spring to life once or twice a week as the trucks bearing goat cheese or sunny-yolked farmers' eggs pull up to the main square. Below are a few of the best; all are open Tuesday through Sunday except Cotignac.

Cours Saleya, Nice – The coast's most colorful market, as much for the people as for the goods on display (it's liveliest on weekends). Local producers cluster in Place Pierre Gauthier.

Marché Forville, Cannes – Though not the best-known market on the Côte d'Azur, Forville has an extraordinary selection, from the small producers who line the center aisle to the small fish market, which is usually sold out by late morning.

Marché Richelme, Aix-en-Provence – This market is legendary, and rightly so, for its lovely setting in the Old Town and its eye-popping range of goods. No wonder Cézanne immortalized such apples and pears.

Marché aux poissons, Marseille – You'll understand the wonder of bouillabaisse once you've visited this market on the Vieux Port: colorful fishing boats pull up to the quay and fill blue plastic tubs with still-leaping fish and lively octopuses.

Cotignac market (Tuesday) – One of dozens of small markets in Provence, Cotignac has retained a real village atmosphere and provides the perfect excuse to visit this seductive town.

TRUFFES DE CARPENTRAS

This town in the Vaucluse is the center of the "black diamond" trade, thanks to its Saturday truffle market, held from November to March.

♿ *In-room: refrigerator, Wi-Fi. In-hotel: 2 restaurants, golf course, pools, spa, some pets allowed (fee)* ═AE, DC, MC, V.

★ $$$-$$$$ ✕▦ **Le Moulin de Mougins.** Housed in a 16th-century olive mill on a hill above the coastal fray, this sophisticated inn houses one of the most famous restaurants in the region (reservations essential). Culinary wizard Roger Vergé sold it lock, stock, and barrel to brilliant young chef Alain Llorca, and the loyal clientele watched in wary anticipation as the proud new owner initiated a radical face-lift for the much-loved institution. They were not disappointed. Local design guru Jaqueline Morabito achieves marvels in white, pink, and plum tones with remarkable silver and gold Baroque chandeliers. Sculptures by César, Arman, and Folon stand beside the signatures of the restaurant's famous guests—Sharon Stone, Elizabeth Taylor—and the chairs are plush comfort. The menu underwent a full overhaul, too; the result is sun-drenched Mediterranean cuisine that is truly excellent. Try the Italian risotto with fresh garden peas, grated truffles, olive oil, and veal, or the Mediterranean sea bass steamed with seaweed, white coco beans, and shellfish. The chocolate-and-orange cake is a slice of heaven; in summer dine outside under the awnings. Guest rooms are elegant; the apartments small but deluxe. ✉*Notre-Dame-de-Vie, 06250* ☎*04–93–75–78–24* 🖶*04–93–90–18–55* ⊕*www.moulin-mougins.com* ➥*3 rooms, 4 apartments* ♿*In-room: refrigerator, Wi-Fi. In-hotel: restaurant, some pets allowed (fee), no elevator* ═*AE, DC, MC, V* ⊘*Closed mid-Nov.–mid-Jan. Restaurant closed Mon.*

> **CUISINE DU COEUR**
>
> Roger Vergé, mastermind of Provençal sun-kissed cuisine, retired from being a superchef in 2003 and handed both his famed Moulin de Mougins and his Ecole de Cuisine du Soleil to the famed Alain Llorca. The cooking school (✉Pl. du Commandante Lamy ☎04-93-75-78-24), one of the best on the French Rivera, is in Mougins and offers two-hour courses daily (in the morning and afternoon) for €58 each. The menu changes for each session and students eat their creations at the end of the course. A booklet of five tickets for five different sessions costs €264.

GRASSE

⑲ *10 km (6 mi) northwest of Mougins, 17 km (10½ mi) northwest of Cannes, 22 km (14 mi) northwest of Antibes, 42 km (26 mi) southwest of Nice.*

High on a plateau over the coast, this busy, modern town is usually given a wide berth by anyone who isn't interested in its prime tourist industry, the making of perfume. But its unusual art museum features works of the 18th-century artist Fragonard, and the picturesque back-streets of its very Mediterranean Vieille Ville round out a pleasant day trip from the coast. You can't visit the laboratories where the great blends of Chanel, Dior, and Guerlain are produced, but to accommodate the crowds of tourists who come here wanting to know more, Grasse has three functioning perfume factories that create simple blends and demonstrate production techniques for free.

Fragonard (⊠20 bd. Fragonard ☎04-83-36-44-65 ⊕www.fragonard.com) operates in a factory built in 1782 that is open daily to the public.

Galimard (⊠73 rte. de Cannes ☎04-93-09-20-00 ⊕www.galimard.com) traces its pedigree back to 1747, and is open daily.

Molinard (⊠60 bd. Victor-Hugo ☎04-93-36-01-62 ⊕www.molinard.com) was established in 1849, and is open weekdays.

The **Musée International de la Parfumerie** (International Museum of Perfume), not to be confused with the museum in the Fragonard factory, traces the 3,000-year history of perfume making. At this writing, the museum was closed for renovations, occasionally open for special exhibitions. ⊠8 pl. du Cours ☎04-93-36-80-20 ⊠€4 ⊙June–Sept., daily 10–7; Oct.–May, Wed.–Sun. 10–12:30 and 2–5:30.

The **Musée Fragonard** headlines the work of Grasse's most famous son, Jean-Honoré Fragonard (1732–1806), one of the great French artists of his day. The lovely villa contains a collection of drawings, engravings, and paintings by the artist. Other rooms in the mansion display works by Fragonard's son Alexandre-Evariste and his grandson, Théophile. ⊠23 bd. Fragonard ☎04-93-36-02-71 ⊠€3.50 ⊙June–Sept., daily 10–12:30 and 1:30–6:30; Oct. and Dec.–May, Wed.–Sun. 10–12:30 and 2–5:30.

The **Musée d'Art et d'Histoire de Provence** (Museum of the Art and History of Provence), just down from the Fragonard perfumery, has a large collection of faïence from the region, including works from Moustiers, Biot, and Vallauris. ⊠2 rue Mirabeau ☎04-93-36-80-20 ⊠€2 ⊙June–Sept., daily 10–12:30 and 2–6:30; Oct and Dec.–May, Wed.–Sun. 10–12:30 and 2–5:30.

Continue down Rue Mirabeau and lose yourself in the dense labyrinth of the **Vieille Ville** (Old Town), its steep, narrow streets thrown into shadow by shuttered houses five and six stories tall.

WHERE TO STAY & EAT

$–$$$ ✕ **Le Gazan.** A local institution, this cozy and crowded restaurant serves consistently good food. Try the succulent house specialty: steak fillet grilled to a nice turn with a violet-infused *jus* served with seasonal vegetables. For a lighter snack, indulge in delicious *girolles* (wild mushrooms) panfried with garlic, parsely, and butter. ⊠10 pl. de la Foux ☎04-93-36-44-88 ═AE, DC, MC, V.

$–$$ ✕ **Arnaud.** Just off Place aux Aires, this easygoing corner bistro serves up inventive home cooking under a vaulted ceiling decorated with stenciled grapevines. Choose from an ambitious and sophisticated menu of à la carte specialties—three kinds of fish in garlic sauce, *pieds et paquets* (pigs' feet and tripe), or a hearty *confit de canard* (preserved duck). ✉ *10 pl. de la Foux* ☎ *04–93–36–44–88* ▤ *AE, DC, MC, V.*

★ $$$$ ✕ **La Bastide Saint-Antoine.** The cicadas live better than most humans at this picture-perfect 18th-century estate overlooking the Estéval. Once home of an industrialist who hosted Kennedys and Rolling Stones, now the domain of celebrated chef Jacques Chibois, it welcomes you with old stone walls, shaded walkways, an enormous pool, and a mouthwatering ocher-hue and blue-shutter mansion draped with red trumpetflower begonia and purple bougainvillea. The guest rooms glossily mix Louis Seize–style chairs, Provençal embroidered bedspreads, and hightech delights (massaging showers). The restaurant is exceedingly excellent and expensive—try the extraordinary truffle, cream, and foie gras soup or the lobster with a black-olive fondue and beet juice. Happily, lunch is a bargain €55. ✉ *48 av. Henri-Dunant, 06130* ☎ *04–93–70–94–94* 🖷 *04–93–70–94–95* ⊕ *www.jacques-chibois.com* ➥ *9 rooms, 7 suites* ⟁ *In-room: refrigerator, Wi-Fi. In-hotel: restaurant, pool* ▤ *AE, DC, MC, V.*

VENCE

🔟 *20 km (12 mi) west of Grasse, 4 km (2½ mi) north of St-Paul, 22 km (14 mi) north of Nice.*

GETTING HERE

No trains run to Vence or St-Paul-de-Vence. Nos. 400 or 94 buses of Compagnie SAP frequently make the hour-long run to and from Nice for about €5 a ticket; frequent buses also connect Vence and St-Paul-de-Vence with Cagnes-sur-Mer's train station, about 10 km (6 mi) from Vence. Or inquire at that station about taxi service (and don't be surprised to have a Mercedes pull up and your female chauffeur garbed in a pink Chanel suit!).

EXPLORING

Encased behind stone walls inside a thriving modern market town is **la Vieille Ville,** the historic part of Vence, which dates from the 15th century. Though crowded with boutiques and souvenir shops, it's slightly more conscious of its history than St-Paul—plaques guide you through its historic squares and *portes* (gates). Leave your car on Place du Grand Jardin and head to the gate to the Vieille Ville, passing Place du Frêne, with its ancient ash tree planted in the 16th century, and then through the Portail du Peyra to the Place du Peyra, with its fountains. Ahead lies the former cathedral on Place Clemenceau, also address to the ocher-color Hôtel de Ville (town hall). A flea market is held on the square on Wednesday; backstreets and alleys hereabouts have been colonized by craft stores and "art galleries."

In the center of the Vieille Ville, the **Cathédrale de la Nativité de la Vierge** *(Cathedral of the Birth of the Virgin, on Place Godeau)* was built on the Romans' military drilling field and traces bits and pieces to Carolingian and even Roman times. It's a hybrid of Romanesque and Baroque styles, expanded and altered over the centuries. Note the rostrum added in 1499—its choir stalls are carved with particularly vibrant and amusing scenes of daily life back when. In the baptistery is a ceramic mosaic of Moses in the bulrushes by Chagall.

Fodor'sChoice
★ On the outskirts of "new" Vence, toward St-Jeannet, the **Chapelle du Rosaire** (*Chapel of the Rosary*) and better known to the world-at-large as the Matisse Chapel, was decorated with beguiling simplicity and clarity by Matisse between 1947 and 1951—the chapel was the artist's gift to nuns who had nursed him through illness. It reflects the reductivist style of the era: walls, floor, and ceiling are gleaming white, and the small stained-glass windows are cool greens and blues. "Despite its imperfections I think it is my masterpiece…the result of a lifetime devoted to the search for truth," wrote Matisse, who designed and dedicated the chapel when he was in his eighties and nearly blind. ⊠ *Av. Henri-Matisse* ☎ 04–93–58–03–26 ⊠€2.80 ☉*Mid-Dec.–mid-Nov., Tues. and Thurs. 10–11:30 and 2–5:30; Mon., Wed., and Sat. 2–5:30.*

WHERE TO STAY & EAT

★ $$$$ ✕ **Table d'Amis de Jacques Maximin.** This temperamental legend and superchef has found peace of mind in a gray-stone farmhouse covered with wisteria—his home and his own country restaurant. Here he devotes himself to creative country cooking superbly prepared and unpretentiously priced—salad of artichoke hearts, squid, Parmesan, and penne, Mediterranean fish grilled in rock salt and olive oil, and candied-eggplant sorbet. The yellow dining room is airy and uncluttered; the garden is a palm-shaded delight. Reserve way in advance. ⊠ 689 *chemin de la Gaude* ☎ 04–93–58–90–75 ⚫*Reservations essential* ▤*AE, MC, V* ☉*Closed mid-Nov.–mid-Dec. No dinner Sun. No lunch Mon. and Tues. mid-Dec.–May, or Fri. and Sat. Oct.–June.*

$$–$$$$ ✕ **La Farigoule.** A long, beamed dining room that opens onto a shady terrace casts an easygoing spell and serves as an hors d'oeuvre for some sophisticated Provençal cooking. Watch for tangy *pissaladières* (pizza-like tarts) with sardines marinated in ginger and lemon, salt-cod ravioli, lamb with olive polenta, and a crunchy parfait of honey and hazelnuts. Fixed-menu dinners are €28 and €45. ⊠ 15 *rue Henri-Isnard* ☎ 04–93–58–01–27 ▤*MC, V* ☉*Closed Tues., Sun., and no lunch Wed. Oct.–Easter; closed Tues., no lunch Sat. and Wed., June–Sept.*

★ $$$$ ✕▦ **Château du Domaine St. Martin.** Exuding an expensive charm, this famous domain occupies the ancient site of a fortress of the Knights Templars. Sitting on a hilltop perch and surrounded by acres of greenery designed by Jean Mus, the mansion welcomes you with public salons that are light, airy, and a bit too sleek for some tastes. All guest rooms are, luxuriously, junior suites, except for six *bastides* (two- and three-bedroom villas) accented with beautiful antiques. **La Commanderie** restaurant is perhaps the best reason to come here, thanks to its stunning walls adorned with china, chef Philippe Guérin's superb creations, and one of the most panoramic terraces around—the views over Old Vence to the Baie des Anges are eye-popping. ⊠ *Av. des Templiers, 06142* ☎ 04–93–58–02–02 ⊟ 04–93–24–08–91 ⊕*www.chateau-st-martin. com* ⌸ 38 *rooms* ⚫*In-room: refrigerator, Wi-Fi. In-hotel: 2 restau-*

rants, bar, tennis courts, pool, parking (no fee), some pets allowed (fee), public (Wi-Fi ⊟AE, MC, V ⊘Closed mid-Oct.–mid-Feb. ⱺ|MAP.

★ $–$$ ✕⊡ **L'Auberge des Seigneurs et du Lion d'Or.** Dating back to the 15th century and the only hotel set within Vence's ancient walls, this time-stained inn has rustic, medieval charm. Downstairs is the restaurant, all copper pots, wood trim, and *ambience à la François Premier.* Upstairs, surprisingly, guest rooms are airy and bright; drapes, bedspreads, and bureau runners are all in matching hues—*de provence.* Some rooms have great views; try to get one in the back, as the front street can be noisy. The kitchen here specializes in roast meats—the chicken prepared on a spit of vines instead of wood is *magnifique;* the place is very popular, especially in winter, so be sure to book well in advance. ⊠*Pl. du Frêne, 06140* ☎*04–93–58–04–24* ⊜*04–93–24–08–01* ⇎*6 rooms* &*In-room: refrigerator, dial-up. In-hotel: restaurant, some pets allowed (fee), no elevator* ⊟*AE, MC, V* ⊘*Closed Nov.–mid-Mar.*

ST-PAUL-DE-VENCE

㉑   4 km (2½ mi) south of Vence, 18 km (11 mi) north of Nice.

Fodor's Choice
★

The famous medieval village of St-Paul-de-Vence can be seen from afar, standing out like its companion, Vence, against the skyline. In the Middle Ages St-Paul was basically a city-state, and it controlled its own political destiny for centuries. But by the early 20th century St-Paul had faded to oblivion, overshadowed by the growth of Vence and Cagnes—until it was rediscovered in the 1920s when a few penniless artists began paying for their drinks at the local auberge with paintings. Those artists turned out to be Signac, Modigliani, and Bonnard, who met at the Auberge de la Colombe d'Or, now a sumptuous inn, where the walls are still covered with their ink sketches and daubs. Nowadays art of a sort still dominates in the myriad tourist traps that take your eyes off the beauty of St-Paul's old stone houses and its rampart views. The most commercially developed of Provence's hilltop villages, St-Paul is nonetheless a magical place when the tourist crowds thin. Artists are still drawn to St-Paul's light, its pure air, its wraparound views, and its honey-color stone walls, soothingly cool on a hot Provençal afternoon. Film stars continue to love its lazy yet genteel ways, lingering on the garden-bower terrace of the Colombe d'Or and challenging the locals to a game of pétanque under the shade of the plane trees. Even so, you have to work hard to find the timeless aura of St-Paul; get here early in the day to get a jump on the cars and tour buses, which can clog the main D36 highway here by noon, or plan on a stay-over. Either way, do consider a luncheon or dinner beneath the Picassos at the Colombe d'Or, even if the menu prices seem almost as fabulous as the collection. (For public transport info, *see* Getting There *under* Vence, *above.*)

★   Many people come to St-Paul just to visit the **Fondation Maeght,** founded in 1964 by art dealer Aimé Maeght and set on a wooded cliff top high above the medieval town. It's not just a small modern art museum but an extraordinary marriage of the arc-and-plane architecture of José Sert; the looming sculptures of Miró, Moore, and Giacometti; and a humbling hilltop perch of pines, vines, and flowing planes of water.

On display is an intriguing and ever-varying parade of the work of modern masters, including the wise and funny late-life masterwork *La Vie (Life)*, by Chagall. On the extensive grounds, the fountains and impressive vistas help to beguile even those who aren't into modern art. ☎ *04–93–32–81–63* 🌐 *www.fondation-maeght.com* 🎟 *€11* 🕑 *July–Sept., daily 10–7; Oct.–June, daily 10–12:30 and 2:30–6.*

WHERE TO STAY & EAT

$$$$ Fodor's Choice ★ **La Colombe d'Or.** Considered by many to be the most beautiful inn in France, "the golden dove" occupies a lovely, rose-stone Renaissance mansion set just outside the walls of St-Paul. Walk into the dining room and you'll do a double take—yes, those are real Mirós, Bonnards, and Légers on the walls, given in payment in hungrier days when this inn was known as the heart of St-Paul's artistic revival. Back then, it was the cherished retreat of Picasso and Chagall, Maeterlinck and Kipling, Yves Montand and Simone Signoret (who met and married here). Today, a ceramic Léger mural still lords it over the famous fig-tree luncheon terrace, a Calder stabile soaks in the giant pool, and there's even a Braque in the bar. The food is yumptious if not as four-star as the crowd (this is one of the very few places where movie stars enjoy being recognized). Upstairs, the guest rooms are bewitching, replete with Louis XIII armoires, medieval four-posters, wood beams, Provençal borders, and painted murals (even rooms in the two annexes are flawless in taste). Henri Matisse once called La Colombe "a small paradise," and who are we to argue? Simply put: If you haven't visited La Colombe, you really haven't been to the French Riviera. ✉ *Pl. Général-de-Gaulle, 06570* ☎ *04–93–32–80–02* 📠 *04–93–32–77–78* 🌐 *www.la-colombe-dor.com* 🛏 *16 rooms, 10 suites* *In-room: no a/c (some), refrigerator. In-hotel: restaurant, bar, pool, some pets allowed, public Wi-Fi, no elevator* 💳 *AE, DC, MC, V* 🕑 *Closed Nov.–mid-Dec. and 2 wks in Jan.* 🍽 *MAP.*

¢–$$ **Hostellerie les Remparts.** With original stone walls, coved ceilings, light-color fabrics, a warm welcome, and perfect location in the center of the Vieille Ville, this small medieval hotel is an uncut gem. Its restaurant serves good regional specialties. In summer expect to book at least two months in advance, and at least 10 days in advance for a table in the restaurant. ✉ *72 rue Grande, 06570* ☎ *04–93–32–09–88* 📠 *04–93–32–09–88* 🌐 *www.hotel-les-remparts.net* 🛏 *9 rooms* *In-room: no a/c, no TV, refrigerator. In-hotel: restaurant, some pets allowed, no elevator* 💳 *AE, MC, V.*

HAUT-DE-CAGNES

22 Fodor's Choice ★ *6 km (4 mi) south of St-Paul-de-Vence, 21 km (13 mi) northeast of Cannes, 10 km (6 mi) north of Antibes, 14 km (9 mi) southwest of Nice.*

GETTING HERE

Cagnes-sur-Mer is the station stop on the main Marseilles–Ventimiglia coastal train line. More than two dozen trains pull into the station at Avenue de la Gare in the commercial sector called Cagnes-Ville. Sample trips: from Nice (13 mins, €5) and from Cannes (23 mins, €6). A free shuttle bus (navette) connects Place du Général-du-Gaulle in the center of Cagnes-Ville (turn right out of train station and walk about 10 blocks) to Haut-de-Cagnes at least once an hour; if the navette isn't running in low season, there's also a municipal bus that goes to the hilltop village from a stop across the street from the station about three blocks to the west (ask at the train station). Les Collettes, Renoir's villa, is walkable from Place du Général-du-Gaulle.

EXPLORING

Although from N7 you may be tempted to give wide berth to **Cagnes-sur-Mer**—with its congested sprawl of freeway overpasses, tacky tourist-oriented stores, beachfront pizzerias, and train station—don't. Just follow the brown signs inland touting Bourg Médiéval and up into one of the most beautiful *villages perchés* (perched villages) along the Riviera: Haut-de-Cagnes. Alice, of Wonderland fame, would adore this steeply cobbled Old Town, honeycombed as it is with tiny little piazzas, return-to-your-starting-point-twice alleys, and winding streets that abruptly change to stairways. Anyone would find it a pleasure to wander these old byways, some with cobbled steps, others passing under vaulted arches draped with bougainvillea. Many of the pretty residences are dollhouse-size (especially the hobbit houses on Rue Passebon) and most date from the 14th and 15th centuries. There is nary a shop, so the commercial horrors of Mougins or St-Paul-de-Vence are left far behind. It's little wonder the rich and literate—Soutine, Modigliani, and Simone de Beauvoir, among them—have long kept Haut-de-Cagnes a secret forgetaway. Or almost: enough cars now arrive that a garage (Parking du Planastel) has been excavated out of the hillside, while a free *navette* shuttle bus links Haut-de-Cagnes with the bus station of Cagnes-sur-Mer (about an eight-block walk from the town train station, which lies on the main coastal rail route).

Haut-de-Cagnes's steep-cobbled Vieille Ville is crowned by the fat, crenellated **Château Grimaldi,** built in 1310 by the Grimaldis (who now rule ★ over Monaco) and reinforced over the centuries. You are welcomed inside the Château Grimaldi by a grand Renaissance courtyard nearly filled with the branches of its mammoth, 200-year-old pepper tree—a spectacular sight.Within are vaulted medieval chambers, a vast Renaissance fireplace, a splendid 17th-century trompe-l'oeil fresco of the fall of Phaëton from his sun-chariot, and three small specialized collections dealing with the history of the olive; memorabilia of the cabaret star Suzy Solidor; and a collection of modern Mediterranean artists, including Cocteau and Dufy. ⊠*Pl. Grimaldi* ☎*04–92–02–47–30* 🎟€3, €4.50 joint ticket with Musée Renoir ☉Oct and Dec..–Apr., Wed.– Mon. 10–noon and 2–5; May–Sept., Wed.–Mon. 10–noon and 2–6.

After staying up and down the coast, Auguste Renoir (1841–1919) settled in a house in Les Collettes, just east of the Vieille Ville, now ★ the **Musée Renoir.** Here, he passed the last 12 years of his life, painting the landscape around him, working in bronze, and rolling his wheelchair through the luxuriant garden, tiered with roses, citrus groves, and some of the most spectacular olive trees along the coast. You can view this sweet and melancholic villa as it has been preserved by Renoir's children, and admire 11 of his last paintings. Although up a steep hill, Les Collettes is walkable from Place du Général-du-Gaulle in central Cagnes-Ville. ✉*Av. des Collettes* ☎*04–93–20–61–07* 💶*€3, €4.50 joint ticket with Château Grimaldi* 🕐*Oct. and Dec.–Apr., Wed.–Mon. 10–noon and 2–5; May–Sept., Wed.–Mon. 10–noon and 2–6. Guided tours in English, Thurs. July and Aug.*

WHERE TO STAY & EAT

$$$–$$$$

Fodor's Choice
★

✕🏨 **Hôtel Le Cagnard.** Housed in a 14th-century residence built on the outer walls of the Grimaldi castle, this lovely hideaway is a modern escape to a medieval world. Faithful to old-world style in antiques-abounding decor, the rooms are

very elegant but it's the ceiling of the restaurant that is truly remarkable: covered in Renaissance-style murals, it can be retracted to show off the night sky. The lavish menu (closed Thursday; no lunch Monday and Tuesday; reservations essential) lives up to the surrounding splendor with dishes like foie gras cooked with figs, peaches, apricots, and rosemary, or—*Dieu!*—the black truffle lasagna. Portions are generous, but try to resist and wait for dessert—the caramelized apple pie is a little slice of heaven. The word "Cagnard" means "very warm sun" in the Provençal dialect, and we can only say that everyone here will enjoy basking in the warmth of Jean-Marc and Françoise Laroche's welcome. If you're arriving on the town square by the shuttle bus, the hotel's *voiturier* will be sent to pick up your luggage; there's also an alley where cars can drop off guests. ✉*54 rue Sous Barri* ☎*04–93–20–73–21* 📠*04–93–22–06–39* 🌐*www.le-cagnard.com* 🛏*15 rooms, 11 suites* ♿*In-room: refrigerator, dial-up. In-hotel: restaurant, bar, parking (no fee), some pets allowed (fee)* ▭*AE, MC, V* 🕐*Closed Nov.–mid-Dec.*

NICE

GETTING HERE

Nice is the main point of entry into the French Riviera region. It's home to the second-largest airport in France, which sits on a peninsula between Antibes and Nice, the Aéroport Nice-Côte d'Azur (☎*08–20–42–33–33* 🌐*www.nice.aeroport.fr)*), which is 7 km (4 mi) south of the city. From the airport, you can take a bus to almost anywhere. There are a few options: RCA (☎*04–93–85–64–44* 🌐*www.rca.tm.fr)*), which is more comfortable and more expensive (💶*€6*) to Nice or the Transport Alpes Maritimes (TAM) buses (☎*08–10–06–10–06* 🌐*www.lignedazur.com)*), which service the same destinations and are cheaper at (💶*€1.30*) thanks to a new government initiative to encourage communal transport, but not as luxurious—you may not get a seat or have a place to put your bags. To go to the center of Nice, take the No. 98 bus from the airport (☎€1.30), which will take you to the main *Gare Routière*, or bus station (⊠5 bd. Jean Jaures ☎04–93–85–61–81) and from here you can transfer on to any number of lines that spider the city (ask for directions at the station's information center). If you plan on heading on via train, take the No. 99 bus from the airport (☎€1.30), which will take you to the main *Gare SNCF* train station (⊠*Av. Thiers* ☎04–92–14–80–80). From here you can access all coastal major cities by train. For departure time and train prices to most destinations in this chapter, check out: (☎08–36–35–35–35 ⊕*www.voyages-sncf. com*). The other option from the airport is a taxi (☎04–93–13–78–78), although this is a far more expensive choice, costing €10 to Nice and €70 to Cannes. For information on the various bus and train lines that connect Nice with other towns on the French Riviera, *see Transportation in French Riviera Essentials* at the end of this chapter.

EXPLORING

As the fifth-largest city in France, this distended urban tangle is sometimes avoided, but that decision is one to be rued: Nice's waterfront, paralleled by the famous Promenade des Anglais and lined by grand hotels, is one of the noblest in France. It's capped by a dramatic hilltop château, below which the slopes plunge almost into the sea and at whose base a bewitching warren of ancient Mediterranean streets unfolds.

It was in this old quarter, now Vieux Nice, that the Greeks established a market-port in the 4th century bc and named it Nikaia. After falling to the Saracen invasions, Nice regained power and developed into an important port in the early Middle Ages. In 1388, under Louis d'Anjou, Nice, along with the hill towns behind, effectively seceded from the county of Provence and allied itself with Savoie as the Comté de Nice (Nice County). It was a relationship that lasted some 500 years and added rich Italian flavor to the city's culture, architecture, and dialect.

Nowadays Nice strikes an engaging balance between historic Provençal grace, port-town exotica, urban energy, whimsy, and high culture. You could easily spend your vacation here, attuned to Nice's quirks, its rhythms, its very multicultural population, and its Mediterranean tides. The high point of the year falls in mid-February when the city hosts one of the most spectacular Carnival celebrations in France (⊕www. nicecarnival.com).

VIEUX NICE

Framed by the "château"—really a rocky promontory—and Cours Saleya, Nice's Vieille Ville is its strongest drawing point and, should you only be passing through, the best place to capture the city's historic atmosphere. Its grid of narrow streets, darkened by houses five and six stories high with bright splashes of laundry fluttering overhead and jewel-box Baroque churches on every other corner, creates a magic that seems utterly removed from the French Riviera fast lane.

THE MAIN ATTRACTIONS

㉗ Cathédrale Ste-Réparate. An ensemble of columns, cupolas, and symmetrical ornaments dominates the Vieille Ville, flanked by its own 18th-century bell tower and capped by its glossy ceramic-tile dome. The cathedral's interior, restored to a bright palette of ocher, golds, and rusts, has elaborate plasterwork and decorative frescoes on every surface. ✉ *Rue Ste-Réparate, Vieux Nice.*

㉔ Chapelle de l'Annonciation. This 17th-century Carmelite chapel is a classic example of pure Niçoise Baroque, from its sculpted door to its extravagant marble work and the florid symmetry of its arches and cupolas. ✉ *Rue de la Poissonerie, Vieux Nice.*

㉕ Chapelle de la Miséricorde. A superbly balanced *pièce-montée* (wedding cake) of half domes and cupolas, this chapel is decorated within an inch of its life with frescoes, faux marble, gilt, and crystal chandeliers. A magnificent Bréa altarpiece crowns the ensemble. ✉ *Cours Saleya, Vieux Nice.*

★ ㉓ Cours Saleya. This long pedestrian thoroughfare, half street, half square, is the nerve center of Old Nice, the heart of the Vieille Ville and the stage-set for the daily dramas of marketplace and café life. Framed with 18th-century houses and shaded by plane trees, the long, narrow square bursts into a fireworks-show of color Tuesday through Sunday, when flower-market vendors roll armloads of mimosas, irises, roses, and orange blossoms into *cornets* (paper cones) and thrust them into the arms of shoppers. Cafés and restaurants, all more or less touristy, fill outdoor tables with onlookers who bask in the sun. At the far-east end, antiques and *brocantes* (collectibles) draw avid junk-hounds every Monday morning. At this end you can also find Place Félix. Little wonder the great painter Matisse lived (from 1921 to 1938) in the imposing yellow stone building that looms over the square. Indeed, you don't need to visit the city's famous Musée Matisse to understand this great artist: simply stand in the doorway of his former apartment (at 1 Place Charles Félix) and study the Place de l'Ancien Senat 10 feet away—it's a golden Matisse pumped up to the nth power.

Choose from a fantastic array of colorful sorbets, gelati, and ice creams and settle in to do some serious people-watching at one of the patio tables overlooking the fountain at **Fennocchio** (✉ 2 *pl. Rossetti, Vieux Nice* ☎ 04–93–80–72–25).

㉚ Musée d'Art Moderne. The assertive contemporary architecture of the Modern Art Museum makes a bold and emphatic statement regarding Nice's presence in the modern world. The art collection inside focuses intently and thoroughly on contemporary art from the late 1950s onward, but pride of place is given to sculptor Nikki de Saint Phalle's recent donation of more than 170 exceptional pieces. ✉ *Promenade des Arts, Vieux Nice* ☎ 04–97–13–42–01 ⊕ *www.mamac-nice.org* 🎫 €4. Free 1st and 3rd Sun. of every month ⊙ *Tues.–Sun. 10–6.*

㉘ Palais Lascaris. The aristocratic Lascaris Palace was built in 1648 for Jean-Baptiste Lascaris-Vintimille, *marechal* to the duke of Savoy. The

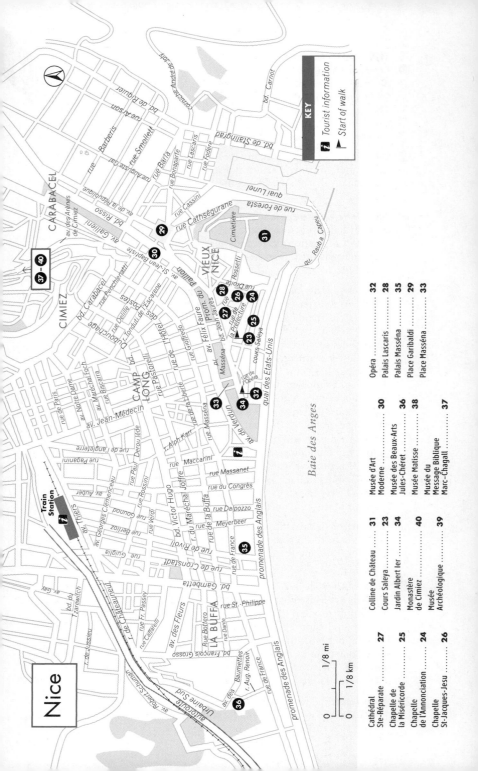

Nice

KEY

🚺 Tourist information

► Start of walk

Baie des Anges

0 ___ 1/8 mi
0 ___ 1/8 km

IN & AROUND THE VIEILLE VILLE

First, head for the morning flower market on the **Cours Saleya** ㉓ ☞. At the center of Cours Saleya is the florid, Baroque **Chapelle de la Miséricorde** ㉔. Thread your way into the Vieille Ville maze to the extravagant **Chapelle de l'Annonciation** ㉕. Continue up Poissonerie to Rue de la Place Vieille, then head right to Rue Droite; the **Chapelle St-Jacques-Jesu** ㉖ looms large and spare. Turn left on Rue Rossetti and cross the square to the **Cathédrale Ste-Réparate** ㉗. Now take a break from the sacred, doubling back up Rue Rossetti and continuing left up narrow Rue Droite to the magnificent **Palais**

Lascaris ㉘. Head next to Boulevard Jean-Jaurès, which empties onto the grand, arcaded **Place Garibaldi** ㉙; one of its five street spokes points straight to the **Musée d'Art Moderne** ㉚. From Place Garibaldi and Boulevard Jean-Jaurès, wind your way up to the ruins of the castle, now a park called the **Colline de Château** ㉛.

Timing

Aim for morning on this walk, so you can see the market on Cours Saleya at its liveliest. If you include a visit to the Palais Lascaris, this could make a full day's outing.

magnificent vaulted staircase, with its massive stone balustrade and niches filled with classical gods, is surpassed in grandeur only by the Flemish tapestries (after Rubens) and the extraordinary trompe-l'oeil fresco depicting the fall of Phaëthon. The first floor houses faïence displays from the Musée Masséna until the latter's renovations are finally completed. ✉15 *rue Droite, Vieux Nice* ☎04–93–62–72–40 ☜*Free; €3 guided tour, including Vieille Ville* ⊘ *Wed.–Mon. 10–6.*

ALSO WORTH SEEING

㉖ **Chapelle St-Jacques-Jesu.** If the Vieille Ville's other chapels are jewel boxes, this 17th-century chapel is a barn: broad, open, and ringing hollow, this church seems austere by comparison, but that's only because the theatrical decoration is spread over a more expansive surface. ✉*Corner of Rue Droite and Rue Gesu, Vieux Nice.*

㉛ **Colline de Château** *(Château Hill).* Though nothing remains of the once-massive medieval stronghold but a few ruins left after its 1706 dismantling, this park still bears its name. From here take in extraordinary views of the Baie des Anges, the length of the Promenade des Anglais, and the red-ocher roofs of the Vieille Ville. ⊘*Daily 7–7.*

㉙ **Place Garibaldi.** Encircled by grand vaulted arcades stuccoed in rich yellow, the broad pentagon of this square could have been airlifted out of Turin. In the center, the shrinelike fountain sculpture of Garibaldi seems to be surveying you as you stroll under the arcades and lounge in its cafés.

ALONG THE PROMENADE DES ANGLAIS

Nice takes on a completely different character west of Cours Saleya, with broad city blocks, vast Neoclassical hotels and apartment houses, and a series of inviting parks dense with palm trees, greenery, and splashing fountains. From the Jardin Albert Ier, once the delta of the Paillon River, the famous Promenade des Anglais stretches the length of the city's waterfront. The original promenade was the brainchild of Lewis Way, an English minister in the then-growing community of British refugees drawn to Nice's climate. Nowadays it's a wide multilane boulevard thick with traffic—in fact, it's the last gasp of the N98 coastal highway. Beside it runs its charming parallel, a wide, sun-washed pedestrian walkway with intermittent steps leading down to the smooth-rock beach. A daily parade of *promeneurs*, rollerbladers, joggers, and sun baskers strolls its broad pavement, looking out over the hypnotic blue expanse of the sea. Only in the wee hours is it possible to enjoy the waterfront stroll as the cream of Nice's international society once did, when there was nothing more than hoofbeats to compete with the roar of the waves.

GETTING AROUND

In Nice, the Sunbus is a convenient way to cut across town; a day pass costs €4, and a one-way ticket is €1.30. Get tickets at neighborhood tabacs (tobacconists) or at their ticket office at 10 avenue Félix Faure or their Station Centrale on Square Général Leclerc. Their main routes include No. 12, from train station to Promenade des Anglais, and No. 30, from train station to Vieux Nice. The Sunbus station is on Square Général Leclerc (☏ 08–10–06–10–06 ⊕ www.slignedazur.com.com).

SIGHTS TO SEE

㉞ Jardin Albert Ier *(Albert I Garden).* Along the Promenade des Anglais, this luxurious garden stands over the delta of the River Paillon, underground since 1882. Every kind of flower and palm tree grows here, thrown into exotic relief by night illumination.

★ **㊱ Musée des Beaux-Arts Jules-Chéret** *(Jules-Chéret Fine Arts Museum).* Although the collection here is impressive, it's the 19th-century Italianate mansion that houses it that remains the showstopper. Originally built for a member of Nice's Old Russian community, the Princess Kotschoubey, this was a Belle Epoque wedding cake, replete with one of the grandest staircases on the coast, salons decorated with Neo-Pompéienne frescoes, an English-style garden, and white columns and balustrades by the dozen. After the *richissime* American James Thompson took over and the last glittering ball was held here, the villa was bought by the municipality as a museum in the 1920s. Unfortunately, much of the period decor was sold but, in its place, now hang paintings by Degas, Boudin, Monet, Sisley, Dufy, and Jules Chéret, whose posters of winking *damselles* distill all the *joie* of the Belle Epoque. From the Negresco Hotel area the museum is about a 15-minute walk up a gentle hill. ✉ *33 av. des Baumettes, Centre Ville* ☎ *04–92–15–28–25* ⊕ *www.musee-beaux-arts-nice.org* ☏ *€4* ⊗ *Tues.–Sun. 10–6.*

32 **Opéra.** A half block west of the Cours Saleya stands a flamboyant Italian-style theater designed by Charles Garnier, architect of the Paris Opéra. It's home today to the Opéra de Nice, with a permanent chorus, orchestra, and ballet corps. The season runs from mid-November to mid-June, and operas cost anywhere from €8 to €85. ⊠*4 rue St-François-de-Paule, Vieux Nice/Port* ☎*04–92–17–40–79.*

★ **35** **Palais Masséna** *(Masséna Palace).* This spectacular Belle Epoque building, housing the **Musée d'Art et d'Histoire** (Museum of Art and History), is undergoing a complete (and lengthy) renovation and was scheduled to reopen sometime in late 2006, but that date was being pushed forward to 2008 at this writing. Call 04–93–88–11–34 for more information. In the meantime, visit the free palace gardens; set with towering palm trees, a marble bust of the handsome General Masséna, and backdropped by the wedding-cake trim of the Hotel Negresco, this is one of Nice's most imposing oases. ⊠*Entrance at 65 rue de France, Centre Ville* ☎*04–93–88–11–34.*

33 **Place Masséna.** As Cours Saleya is the heart of the Vieille Ville, so this broad square is the heart of the city as a whole. It's framed by an ensemble of Italian-style arcaded buildings first built in 1815, their facades stuccoed in rich red ocher. On the west flank sits the city's Belle Epoque icon, the Hôtel Negresco.

CIMIEZ

Once the site of the powerful Roman settlement Cemenelum, the hilltop neighborhood of Cimiez—4 km (2½ mi) north of Cours Saleya—is Nice's most luxurious quarter (use Bus 15 from Place Masséna or Avenue Jean-Médecin to visit its sights).

SIGHTS TO SEE

40 **Monastère de Cimiez.** This fully functioning monastery is worth the pilgrimage. You can find a lovely **garden,** replanted along the lines of the original 16th-century layout; the **Musée Franciscain,** a didactic museum tracing the history of the Franciscan order; and a 15th-century **church** containing three works of remarkable power and elegance by Bréa. ⊠*Pl. du Monastère, Cimiez* ☎*04–93–81–00–04* ⊠*Free* ⊗*Mon.–Sat. 10–noon and 3–6.*

39 **Musée Archéologique** *(Archaeology Museum).* This museum, next to the Matisse Museum, has a dense and intriguing collection of objects extracted from the digs around the Roman city of Cemenelum, which flourished from the 1st to the 5th century. ⊠*160 av. des Arènes-de-Cimiez, Cimiez* ☎*04–93–81–59–57* ⊠*€4, €3 for a guided tour Thurs. at 3:30* ⊗*Wed.–Mon. 10–6.*

38 **Musée Matisse.** In the '60s the city of Nice bought this lovely, light-bathed **FodorśChoice** 17th-century villa, surrounded by the ruins of Roman civilization, and ★ restored it to house a large collection of Henri Matisse's works. Matisse settled in Nice in 1917, seeking a sun cure after a bout with pneumonia, and remained here until his death in 1954. During his years on the French Riviera, Matisse maintained intense friendships and artistic liaisons with

Renoir, who lived in Cagnes, and with Picasso, who lived in Mougins and Antibes. Settling first along the waterfront, he eventually moved up to the rarefied isolation of Cimiez and took an apartment in the Hôtel Regina (now an apartment building), where he lived out the rest of his life. Matisse walked often in the parklands around the Roman remains and was buried in an olive grove outside the Cimiez cemetery. The collection of artworks includes several pieces the artist donated to the city before his death; the rest were donated by his family. In every medium and context—paintings, gouache cutouts, engravings, and book illustrations—it represents the evolution of his art, from Cézanne-like still lifes to exuberant dancing paper dolls. Even the furniture and accessories speak of Matisse, from the Chinese vases to the bold-printed fabrics with which he surrounded himself. A series of black-and-white photographs captures the artist at work, surrounded by personal—and telling—details. At this writing, the museum was closed for renovations until June 2007. ⊠*164 av. des Arènes-de-Cimiez, Cimiez* 🕾*04–93–81–08–08* 🖂*€4* ☉ *Wed.–Mon. 10–6.*

> ### STROKES OF GENIUS
>
> What Tahiti was to Gauguin, Nice was to Matisse. Its flower marketplaces, palaces, palm trees soothed and, together with the constantly changing show of light—so different from the relentless glare of St-Tropez (which helped him invent Fauvism)—inspired him. By 1919, ailing with bronchitis, he settled in Nice, where he started to paint images of unrivaled voluptuousness: seminude odalisques inspired by Delacroix, the siren call of these "poster girls" was potent; many artists, like Picasso, soon relocated to the South of France for good.

★ ㉟ **Musée du Message Biblique Marc-Chagall** (*Marc Chagall Museum of Biblical Themes*). This museum has one of the finest permanent collections of Chagall's (1887–1985) late works. Superbly displayed, 17 vast canvases depict biblical themes, each in emphatic, joyous colors. ⊠*Av. du Dr-Ménard, head up Av. Thiers, then take a left onto Av. Malausséna, cross railway tracks, and take first right up Av. de l'Olivetto, Cimiez* 🕾*04–93–53–87–20* 🖂*€6.70* ☉*July–Sept., Wed.–Mon. 10–6; Oct–June, Wed.–Mon. 10–5.*

WHERE TO STAY & EAT

★ $$$$ ✕ **Le Parcours.** Chef Marc Delacourt left the prestigious kitchens of the Château Chevre d'Or hotel to set up this sleek, streamlined restaurant in Falicon, a small perched village on the outskirts of Nice. Decor tends to Zen with a modern twist; there are even TV screens showing what's happening in the kitchen if you can drag your eyes away from the spectacular window views for long enough to watch. Most main courses are delicious, the wine list is short but well thought out, and the €30 lunch menu is a bargain. ⊠*1 pl. Marcel Eusebi, Falicon Village: 15 mins outside Nice, in direction of Sospel* 🕾*04–93–84–94–57* ⌖*Reservations essential* ▤*MC, V* ☉*Closed Mon. No dinner Sun. or Tues.*

$$–$$$$ ✕ **Don Camillo.** In a complete turnabout, the once fading Don Camillo has shed its staid, old maid–ish decor and introduced a swanky, modern look. The food, always good, is now even better with just a touch more inspiration; chef Stephane Vano reinvents Niçois classiques that are as tasty as they are affordable. ⊠ *5 rue des Ponchettes, Vieux Nice* ☎ *04–93–85–67–95* ⚑ *Reservations essential* ▭ *AE, DC, MC, V* ⊘ *Closed Sun. No lunch Mon.*

$$–$$$$ ✕ **Indyana.** Targeting hip twenty- to thirtysomethings, enterprising brothers Christophe and Pascal Ciamos have come up with a stylish, swanky place that fills nightly with an intriguing mix of young entrepreneurs, artsy types, and the fashion-forward. Intimate lighting and an eclectic combination of loft-meets-Art-Deco-Moroccan decor is matched by a fusion cuisine menu that ranges from sushi to traditional beef platters with potato-zucchini gratin. ⊠ *11 rue Gustave Deloye, Vieux Nice* ☎ *04–93–80–67–69* ⚑ *Reservations essential* ▭ *AE, DC, MC, V* ⊘ *No lunch Sun. and Mon.*

$–$$$$ ✕ **Grand Café de Turin.** Whether you squeeze onto a banquette in the dark, low-ceiling bar or win a coveted table under the arcaded porticoes on Place Garibaldi, this is *the* place to go for shellfish in Nice: sea snails, clams, plump *fines de claires,* and salty *bleues* oysters, and urchins by the dozen. It's packed noon and night, so don't be too put off by the sometimes brusque reception of the waiters. ⊠ *5 pl. Garibaldi, Vieux Nice* ☎ *04–93–62–29–52* ▭ *AE, DC, MC, V.*

★ $$$ ✕ **La Mérenda.** The back-to-bistro boom climaxed here when Dominique Le Stanc retired his crown at the Negresco to take over this tiny, unpretentious landmark of Provençal cuisine. Now he and his wife work in the miniature open kitchen, creating the ultimate versions of stuffed sardines, pistou, and slow-simmered *daubes* (beef stews). To reserve entry to the inner sanctum, you must stop by in person (there's no telephone). The dinner menu is €25 to €30. ⊠ *4 rue de la Terrasse, Vieux Nice* ☎ *No phone* ▭ *No credit cards* ⊘ *Closed weekends, last wk July, and 1st 2 wks Aug.*

$$–$$$ ✕ **Terres de Truffes.** Celebrity chef Bruno Clément opened this stylish bistrot-deli in an effort to bring the exquisite but expensive taste of truffles to the masses. He has succeeded. Truffles come with everything, from caramelized truffle ice cream to truffle-infused baked Brie; and even the most budget-conscious can afford to indulge. ⊠ *11 rue St-Francois-de-Paule, Vieux Nice* ☎ *04–93–62–07–68* ▭ *AE, MC, V.*

¢–$ ✕ **Chez René/Socca.** This back-alley landmark is the most popular dive in town for socca, the chickpea-pancake snack food unique to Nice. Rustic olive-wood tables line the street, and curt waiters splash down your drink order. For the food, you get in line at the Socca, choose your €3 plate (or plates), and carry it steaming to the table yourself. It's off Place Garibaldi on the edge of the Vieille Ville, across from the *Gare Routière* (bus station). ⊠ *2 rue Miralheti, Vieux Nice* ☎ *04–93–92–05–73* ▭ *No credit cards* ⊘ *Closed Mon.*

★ $$$$ ✕▭ **Hôtel Negresco.** One of those names, like the Pierre or Claridges, which is synonymous with "Grand Hotel," the Negresco is a white-stucco slice of old-fashioned Riviera extravagance. Still the icon of Nice, it has hosted everyone from the Beatles to the Burtons. Built by

Henri Negresco in 1912 as a wedding cake of plaster busts, marble columns, and gilded ceilings, it is the very epitome of La Belle Epoque. Yes, the main hall is a bit forlorn but its Gustave Eiffel glass ceiling still awes, as does its *qualité du Louvre* collection of old-master paintings. Upstairs, each floor lobby is devoted to an era from French history (Napoléon III on the fifth, etc.). Happily, most guest rooms are traditionally elegant, replete with swagged drapes and fine antiques (plus a few unfortunate "with-it" touches like those plastic-glitter bathtubs). Downstairs, Le Chantecler ranks among the very finest restaurants in France, while the Carrousel Room—complete with merry-go-round horses and Folies Bérgère chandelier—is an over-the-top setting for your breakfast. For a touch of the Old Riviera, repair to the historic walnut-and-velour bar for a champagne cocktail. ⊠ *37 promenade des Anglais, Promenade des Anglais, 06000* ☎*04–93–16–64–00* 📠*04–93–88–35–68* ⊕*www.hotel-negresco-nice.com* ↩*145 rooms* ⚲*In-room: refrigerator, Wi-Fi. In-hotel: 2 restaurants, bar, beachfront, some pets allowed* ⊟*AE, DC, MC, V.*

★ **$$$$** ✕🏠 **La Perouse.** Just past the Vieille Ville, at the foot of the château, this hotel is a secret treasure cut into the cliff (an elevator takes you up to the reception). Some of the best rooms (including Raoul Dufy's favorite) not only have views of the azure sea but also look down into an intimate garden with lemon trees and a cliff-side pool. The excellent restaurant serves meals in the candlelight garden May–September. ⊠*11 quai Rauba-Capeau, Le Château, 06300* ☎*04–93–62–34–63* 📠*04–93–62–59–41* ⊕*www.hotel-la-perouse.com* ↩*63 rooms* ⚲*In-room: refrigerator, Wi-Fi. In-hotel: restaurant, pool, gym, some pets allowed* ⊟*AE, DC, MC, V.*

★ **$$–$$$** 🏠 **Windsor.** This is a memorably eccentric hotel with a vision: most of its white-on-white rooms either have frescoes of mythological themes or are works of artists' whimsy. But the real draw of this otherworldly place is its astonishing city-center garden—a tropical oasis of lemon, magnolia, and palm trees. You can breakfast or dine here by candlelight. ⊠*11 rue Dalpozzo, Vieux Nice, 06000* ☎*04–93–88–59–35* 📠*04–93–88–94–57* ⊕*www.hotelwindsornice.com* ↩*57 rooms* ⚲*In-room: no a/c (some), refrigerator. In-hotel: restaurant, bar, gym, parking (fee), public Wi-Fi* ⊟*AE, DC, MC, V* ⦿*MAP.*

$–$$ 🏠 **Felix.** On popular, pedestrian Rue Masséna and a block from the beach, this tiny hotel is owned by a hardworking couple (both fluent in English) who make you feel welcome. Rooms are compact but neat and bright, so they don't feel as small, and four have tiny balconies providing a ringside seat over the pedestrian thoroughfare. ⊠*41 rue Masséna, Vieux Nice, 06000* ☎*04–93–88–67–73* 📠*04–93–16–15–78* ↩*14 rooms* ⚲*In-room: refrigerator, dial-up* ⊟*AE, DC, MC, V.*

NIGHTLIFE & THE ARTS

The **Casino Ruhl** (⊠*1 promenade des Anglais, Vieux Nice* ☎*04–97–03–12–22*), gleaming neon-bright and modern, is a sophisticated Riviera landmark. With sleek decor, a piano bar, and live bands, the **Dizzy Club** (⊠*26 quai Lunel, Vieux Nice* ☎*04–93–26–54–79*) is consistently popular. Pretty people throng to the predominantly gay **La Suite du Comptoire** (✉2 *rue Bréa, Vieux Nice* ☎04–93–92–92–91) to dance to blues and soul music amid splendid Baroque decor. If you're all dressed up and have just won big, invest in a drink in the intimate walnut-and-velour **Bar Le Relais** (✉37 *promenade des Anglais, Vieux Nice* ☎04–93–16–64–00), in the landmark Hôtel Negresco.

In July the **Nice Jazz Festival** (☎08–92–70–74–07) draws performers from around the world. Classical music and ballet performances take place at Nice's convention center, the **Acropolis** (✉*Palais des Congrès, Esplanade John F. Kennedy, Centre Ville* ☎04–93–92–83–00). The season at the **Opéra de Nice** (✉4 *rue St-François-de-Paul, Vieux Nice* ☎04–92–17–40–40) runs from September to June.

THE OUTDOORS

Nice's **beaches** extend all along the Baie des Anges, backed full length by the Promenade des Anglais. Public stretches alternate with posh private beaches that have restaurants—and bar service, mattresses and parasols, waterskiing, parasailing, windsurfing, and jet-skiing. One of the handiest private beaches is the **Beau Rivage** (☎04–92–47–82–82), set across from the Opéra. The sun can also be yours for the basking at **Ruhl** (☎04–93–87–09–70), across from the Casino.

SHOPPING

Olive oil by the gallon in cans with colorful, old-fashioned labels is sold at tiny **Alziari** (✉14 *rue St-François-de-Paule, Vieux Nice*). A good source for crystalized fruit, a Nice specialty, is the **Confiserie du Vieux Nice** (✉14 *quai Papacino, Vieux Nice*), on the west side of the port. The venerable **Henri Auer** (✉7 *rue St-François-de-Paule, Vieux Nice*) has sold crystallized fruit since 1820. For fragrances, linens, and pickled-wood furniture, head to **Boutique 3** (✉3 *rue Longchamp, Vieux Nice*), run by three Niçoise women of rare talent and taste.

For every sort of hat imaginable, from the basic beret to huge creations with many a flower and ostrich plume, check out **La Chapellerie** (✉36 *cours Saleya, Vieux Nice*).

Seafood of all kinds is sold at the **fish market** (✉*Pl. St-François, Vieux Nice*) every morning except Monday. At the daily **flower market** (✉*Cours Saleya, Vieux Nice*) you can find all kinds of plants and fruits and vegetables. The **antiques and brocante market** (✉*Pl. Robilante, Vieux Nice*), by the old port, is held Tuesday through Saturday.

THE EASTERN FRENCH RIVIERA

You may build castles in Spain or picture yourself on a South Sea island, but when it comes to serious speculation about how to spend that first $10 million and slip easily into the life of the idle rich, most people head for France and the stretch of coast that covers the eastern Côte d'Azur. Here, backed by the mistral-proof Alps and coddled by mild Mediterranean breezes, waterfront resorts—Villefranche and Menton—draw energy from the thriving city of Nice, while jutting tropical peninsulas—Cap Ferrat, Cap Martin—frame the tiny principality of Monaco. Here the corniche highways snake above sparkling waters, their pink-and-white villas turning faces toward the sun. Cliffs bristle with palm trees and parasol pines, and a riot of mimosa, bougainvillea, jasmine, and even cactus blooms in the hothouse climate. Crowded with sunseekers, the Riviera still reveals quiet corners with heart-stopping views of sea, sun, and mountains—all within one memorable frame.

VILLEFRANCHE-SUR-MER

④ *10 km (6 mi) east of Nice.*

Fodor'sChoice
★

GETTING HERE

Villefranche is a major stop on the Marseilles–Ventimiglia coastal train route, with more than 20 arrivals every day from Nice (30 mins). Buses connect with Nice and Monaco via Sun Bus's No. 100.

EXPLORING

Nestled discreetly along the deep scoop of harbor between Nice and Cap Ferrat, this pretty watercolor of a fishing port seems surreal, flanked as it is by the big city of Nice and the assertive wealth of Monaco. The town is a somewhat overbuilt stage-set of brightly colored houses—the sort of place where Pagnol's *Fanny* could have been filmed. Genuine fishermen actually skim up to the docks here in weathered-blue *barques,* and the streets of the Vieille Ville flow directly to the waterfront, much as they did in the 13th century. Some of the prettiest spots in town are around Place de la Paix, Rue du Poilu, and Place du Conseil, which looks out over the water. The deep harbor, in the caldera of a volcano, was once preferred by the likes of Onassis and Niarchos and royals on their yachts (today, unfortunately, these are usually replaced by warships as a result of the presence of a nearby naval base). The character of Villefranche was subtly shaped by the artists and authors who gathered at the Hôtel Welcome—Diaghilev and Stravinsky, taking a break from the Ballet Russe in Monaco; Somerset Maugham and Evelyn Waugh; and, above all, Jean Cocteau, who came here to recover from the excesses of Paris life.

So enamored was Jean Cocteau of this painterly fishing port that he decorated the 14th-century **Chapelle St-Pierre** with images from the life of St. Peter and dedicated it to the village's fishermen. ✉*Pl. Pollanais* 📞*04–93–76–90–70* 💶*€2* ☉*Mid-June–mid-Sept., Tues.–Sun. 4–8:30; mid-Sept.–mid-Apr., Tues.–Sun. 10–noon and 2–6:30; mid-Apr.–mid-June, Tues.–Sun. 10–noon and 3–7.*

Running parallel to the waterfront, the extraordinary 13th-century **Rue Obscure** *(literally, Dark Street)* is entirely covered by vaulted arcades; it sheltered the people of Villefranche when the Germans fired their parting shots—an artillery bombardment—near the end of World War II.

The stalwart 16th-century **Citadelle St-Elme**, restored to perfect condition, anchors the harbor with its broad, sloping stone walls. Beyond its drawbridge lie the city's administrative offices and a group of minor gallery-museums, with a scattering of works by Picasso and Miró. Whether or not you stop into these private collections of local art (all free of charge), you're welcome to stroll around the inner grounds and to circle the imposing exterior.

WHERE TO STAY & EAT

$ ✕ **La Grignotière.** Tucked down a narrow side street just a few steps away from the marketplace, this small and friendly local restaurant offers up top-quality, inexpensive dishes. The homemade lasagna is excellent, as is the spaghetti pistou. ⊠*3 rue du Poilu* ☎*04–93–76–79–83* ☐*MC, V* ⊗*No lunch.*

★ $$$–$$$$ ⊞ **Hôtel Welcome.** When Villefranche harbored a community of artists and writers, this waterfront landmark was their adopted headquarters. Somerset Maugham holed up in one of the tiny crow's-nest rooms at the top, and Jean Cocteau lived here while writing *Orphée.* Elizabeth Taylor and Richard Burton used to tie one on in the bar (now nicely renovated). It's comfortable and modern, with the best rooms brightened with vivid colors and stenciled quotes from Cocteau; some have spectacular views. ⊠*Quai Courbet, 06230* ☎*04–93–76–27–62* ☐*04–93–76–27–66* ⊕*www.welcomehotel.com* ⤸*34 rooms, 2 suites* ⚁*In-room: refrigerator, Wi-Fi. In-hotel: bar, some pets allowed (fee)* ☐*AE, DC, MC, V* ⊗*Closed mid-Nov.–mid-Dec.*

$–$$ ⊞ **Hôtel Provençal.** Within walking distance of the port, this inexpensive hotel may not look like much from the outside but is friendly and accommodating. The rooms are large and humbly decorated with deep blue carpets, green velour chairs, and white bedspreads. About half of the rooms have a sea view; the other half look out over colorful rooftops. ⊠*Av. Maréchal Joffre, 06360* ☎*04–93–76–53–53* ☐*04–93–76–96–00* ⊕*www.hotelprovencal.com* ⤸*45 rooms* ⚁*In-room: refrigerator, dial-up. In-hotel: restaurant, bar, some pets allowed* ☐*MC, V* ⊗*Closed Nov.–Dec 24.*

BEAULIEU

42 *4 km (2½ mi) east of Villefranche, 14 km (9 mi) east of Nice.*

GETTING HERE
With frequent arrivals and departures, Beaulieu is a main stop on the main Marseille–Ventimiglia coastal train line. From Beaulieu's train station, hourly buses, for €2 a ticket, connect with neighboring St-Jean-Cap-Ferrat

EXPLORING
With its back pressed hard against the cliffs of the corniche and sheltered between the peninsulas of Cap Ferrat and Cap Roux, this once-grand resort basks in a tropical microclimate that earned its central neighborhood the name *Petite Afrique.* The town was the pet of 19th-century society, and its grand hotels welcomed Empress Eugénie, the Prince of Wales, and Russian nobility. It's still a posh address, but if

you're a picky atmosphere-hunter, you may find the town center too built-up with apartment buildings.

One manifestation of Beaulieu's Belle Epoque excess is the eye-knocking **Villa Kerylos,** a mansion built in 1902 in the style of classical Greece (to be exact, of the villas that existed on the island of Delos in the 2nd century bc). It was the dream house of the amateur archaeologist Théodore Reinach, who originally hailed from a super-rich family from Frankfurt, helped the French in their excavations at Delphi, and became an authority on ancient Greek music. He commissioned an Italian architect from Nice, Emmanuel Pontremoli, to surround him with Grecian delights: cool Carrara marble, rare fruitwoods, and a dining salon where guests reclined to eat *à la grecque.* Don't miss this—it's one of the most unusual houses in the south of France. Not far from the house is the **Promenade Maurice Rouvier,** an enchanting coastal path that leads to St-Jean-Cap-Ferrat. ⊠ *Rue Gustave-Eiffel* ☎ *04–93–01–01–44* ⊕ *www.villa-kerylos.com* ✉ *€8, €14.50 to visit both Villa Kerylos and Villa Ephrussi de Rothschild in same wk* ⊘ *Mid-Feb.–June and Sept.–mid-Nov., daily 10–6; July and Aug., daily 10–7; mid-Dec.–mid-Feb., weekdays 2–6, weekends 10–6.*

WHERE TO STAY & EAT

★ $$$$ ✕▦ **La Reserve.** The first impression of old-world grandeur given by the handsome pastel pink building and beautifully proportioned lobby is carried through to every corner of this opulent and sophisticated hideaway. Rooms tend to expensive cream and peach tones highlighted with some truly glorious antiques, while large beautiful bouquets of fresh flowers add a welcoming touch. Not to be outdone by the discreet sophistication of the hotel, the Michelin-starred restaurant is a marvel of light and color. Chef Olivier Brulard creates original recipes from fresh Mediterranean products, and rarely disappoints. The view is specatacular, the service discreet, and the wine just so. Reserve well in advance during the summer season. ⊠ *5 bd. General Leclerc, 06160* ☎ *04–93–01–00–01* 🖷 *04–93–01–28–99* ⊕ *www.reservebeaulieu.com* ⇄ *41 rooms* ♿ *In-room: refrigerator, Wi-Fi. In-hotel: restaurant, bar, pool, beachfront, some pets allowed (fee), parking (fee)* ▭ *AE, DC, MC, V* ⊘ *Closed Nov.–mid-Dec.* ¶◎¶ *FAP, MAP.*

ST-JEAN-CAP-FERRAT

㊸ *2 km (1 mi) south of Beaulieu on D25.*

This luxuriously sited pleasure port moors the peninsula of Cap Ferrat; from its port-side walkways and crescent of beach you can look over the sparkling blue harbor to the graceful green bulk of the corniches. Yachts purr in and out of port, and their passengers scuttle into cafés for take-out drinks to enjoy on their private decks. Unfortunately, Cap Ferrat is a vast peninsula and hides its secrets—except for the Villa Ephrussi, most fabled estates are hidden behind iron gates and towering hedges—particularly well.

★ Between the port and the mainland, the floridly beautiful **Villa Ephrussi de Rothschild** stands as witness to the wealth and worldly flair of the baroness who had it built. Constructed in 1905 in neo-Venetian style (its flamingo-pink facade was thought not to be in the best of taste by the local gentry), the house was baptized "Ile-de-France" in homage to the Baroness Bétrice de Rothschild's favorite ocean liner (her staff used to wear sailing costumes and her ship travel-kit is on view in her bedroom). Precious artworks, tapestries, and furniture adorn the salons—in typical Rothschildian fashion, each room is given over to a different 18th-century "époque." Upstairs are the private apartments of Madame la Baronne, which can only be seen on a guided tour offered around noon. The grounds are landscaped with no fewer than seven theme gardens and topped off with a Temple of Diana (no less); be sure to allow yourself time to wander here, as this is one of the few places on the coast where you'll be allowed to experience the lavish pleasures characteristic of the Belle Epoque Côte d'Azur. Tea and light lunches are served in a glassed-in porch overlooking the grounds and spectacular views of the coastline. ⊠*Av. Ephrussi* ☎*04–93–01–33–09* 🖃*Access to ground floor and gardens €9.50, €14.50 joint ticket for Villa Kerylos to be used in same wk, guided tour upstairs €3 extra* ☉*Mid-Feb.–June and Sept.–mid-Nov., daily 10–6; July and Aug., daily 10–7; mid-Dec.–mid-Feb., weekdays 2–6, weekends 10–6.*

While Cap Ferrat's villas are sequestered for the most part in the depths of tropical gardens, you can nonetheless walk its entire **coastline promenade** if you strike out from the port; from the restaurant Capitaine Cook, cut right up Avenue des Fossés, turn right on Avenue Vignon, and follow the Chemin de la Carrière. The 11-km (7-mi) walk passes through rich tropical flora and, on the west side, over white cliffs buffeted by waves. When you've traced the full outline of the peninsula, veer up the Chemin du Roy past the fabulous gardens of the **Villa des Cèdres,** owned by King Leopold II of Belgium at the turn of the last century. The king owned several opulent estates along the French Riviera, undoubtedly paid for by his enslavement of the Belgian Congo. His African plunder also stocked the private zoo on his villa grounds, today the town's **Parc Zoologique** (⊠*Bd. du Général-de-Gaulle* ☎*04–93–76–07—60* 🖃*€14* ☉*Mid-June–mid-Sept., daily 9:30–7; mid-Sept.–mid-June, daily 9:30–5:30*). Past the gardens, you can reach the **Plage de Passable,** from which you cut back across the peninsula's wrist. A shorter loop takes you from town out to the **Pointe de St-Hospice,** much of the walk shaded by wind-twisted pines. From the port climb Avenue Jean Mermoz to Place Paloma and follow the path closest to the waterfront. At the point are an 18th-century prison tower, a 19th-century chapel, and unobstructed views of Cap Martin.

WHERE TO STAY & EAT

$$–$$$ ✕ **Le Sloop.** This sleek port-side restaurant caters to the yachting crowd and sailors who cruise into dock for lunch. The focus is fish, of course: *soupe de poisson* (fish soup), *St-Pierre* (John Dory) steamed with asparagus, roasted whole sea bass. Its outdoor tables surround a tiny "garden" of potted palms. The fixed menu is €28. ⊠*Port de Plai-*

sance ☎04–93–01–48–63 ▤MC,
V ✆Closed Wed. mid-Sept.–mid-
Apr., no lunch Tues. and Wed.
mid-Apr.–mid-Sept.

★ **$$$**   📷 **Brise Marine.** With a glowing
Provençal-yellow facade, bright
blue shutters, and balustraded sea
terrace, this lovely vision fulfills
most desires for that perfect, pic-
turesque Cap Ferrat hotel. Pretty pastel guest rooms feel like bedrooms
in a private home—many offer window views of the gorgeous peninsula
stunningly framed by statuesque palms. ✉58 av. Jean Mermoz, 06230
☎04–93–76–04–36 ☏04–93–76–11–49 ⊕www.hotel-brisemarine.
com ⌨18 rooms ♿In-room: refrigerator, Wi-Fi. In-hotel: bar, park-
ing (fee), some pets allowed ▤AE, DC, MC, V ✆Closed Nov.–Jan.

$$–$$$ 📷 **Clair Logis.** With soft pastels, antique furniture, and large picture
windows, this converted villa is perfectly framed by a sprawling gar-
den park. The main house offers up subtle bourgeois elegance; for the
budget-conscious there are other simpler, airy rooms scattered over
several small buildings. Most have charming balconies looking out over
gently swaying palms. There's no pool, but breakfast on the cobble-
stone terrace is lovely, and it's a good way to gear up for the 15-minute
walk down to the beach. ✉12 av. Centrale, point de St-Jean, 06230
☎04–93–76–51–81 ☏04–93–76–51–82 ⊕www.hotel-clair-logis.fr
⌨18 rooms ♿In-room: refrigerator. In-hotel: parking (no fee), some
pets allowed (fee), no elevator ▤AE, MC, V.

ÈZE

🏵 **44**   2 km (1 mi) east of Beaulieu, 12 km (7 mi) east of Nice, 7 km (4½ mi)
Fodor'sChoice   west of Monte Carlo.
★

GETTING HERE

Èze is one of the most visited perched villages in France and is fairly
easy to gain access via public transporation. Take the train from Nice's
Gare SNCF (✉Av. Thiers ☎04–92–14–80–80 ⊕www.voyages-sncf.
com) to the village by the sea, Èze-bord-de-Mer. From the station
there take bus No. 83 run by Lignes d'Azur bus (☎08–10–06–10–06
⊕www.lignedazur.com) for a shuttle (frequent departures) between the
station and the sky-high village of Èze, which runs about every hour
year-round and costs €1.30. Note that if you're rushing to make a train
connection that this shuttle trip has many switchbacks up the steep
mountainside and takes a full 15 minutes. If you want to avoid the train
entirely and are traveling on a budget, from the Nice Gare Routière
(✉5 bd. Jean Jaures ⊕www.rca.tm.fr)you can take the Transport
Alpes Maritimes's 100 TAM bus (☎04–93–85–61–81 ⊕www.cg06.
fr/transport/transports-tam.html) which will take you directly to Èze-
bord-de-Mer along the lower Corniche and costs €1.30, where you can
then transfer to the No. 83 shuttle listed above. Otherwise, you can
take the RCA bus No. 112 at Nice's Gare Routière, which goes from
Nice to Beausoleil and stops at Èze Village. By car, you should arrive

using the Moyenne Corniche, which deposits you near the gateway to Èze Village; buses (from Nice and Monaco) also use this highway.

EXPLORING

Towering like an eagle's nest above the coast and crowned with ramparts and the ruins of a medieval château, preposterously beautiful Èze (pronounced *ehz* is unfortunately the most accessible of all the perched villages—this means crowds, many of whom head here to shop in the boutique-lined staircase-streets (happily most shops here are quite stylish, and there's a nice preponderance of bric-a-brac and vintage fabric dealers). But most come here to drink in the views, for no one can deny that this is the most spectacularly sited of all coastal promontories; if you can manage to shake the crowds and duck off to a quiet overlook, the village commands splendid views up and down the coast, one of the draws that once lured fabled visitors—lots of crowned heads, Georges Sand, Friedrich Nietzsche—and residents: Consuelo Vanderbilt, when she was tired of being duchess of Marlborough, traded in Blenheim Palace for a custom-built house here.

From the crest-top **Jardin Exotique** *(Tropical Garden)*, full of rare succulents, you can pan your videocam all the way around the hills and waterfront. But if you want a prayer of a chance of enjoying the magnificence of the village's arched passages, stone alleyways, and ancient fountains, come at dawn or after sunset—or (if you have the means) stay the night—but spend the midday elsewhere. The church of **Notre-Dame**, consecrated in 1772, glitters inside with Baroque retables and altarpieces. Èze's tourist office, on Place du Général-de-Gaulle, can direct you to the numerous footpaths—the most famous being the **Sentier Friedrich Nietzsche**—that thread Èze with the coast's three corniche highways. Note that Èze Village is the famous hilltop destination, but Èze extends down to the coastal beach and the township of Èze-sur-Mer. By car, you should arrive using the Moyenne Corniche, which deposits you near the gateway to Èze Village; buses (from Nice and Monaco) also use this highway. By train, you'll arrive at the station in Èze-sur-Mer, where (most months) a navette shuttle bus takes you up to hilltop Èze, a trip which, with its 1,001 switchbacks up the steep mountainside, takes a full 15 minutes.

WHERE TO STAY & EAT

$$–$$$$ ✗ **Troubadour.** Amid the clutter and clatter, this is a wonderful find: comfortably relaxed, this old family house proffers pleasant service and excellent dishes like roasted scallops with chicken broth and squab with citrus zest and beef broth. Full-course menus range from €38 to €50. ⊠*4 rue du Brec* ☎*04–93–41–19–03* ▤*AE, DC, MC, V* ⊗*Closed Sun. No lunch Mon., mid-Nov.–mid-Dec.*

¢–$ ✗ **Loumiri.** Classic Provençal and regional seafood dishes are tastily prepared and married with decent, inexpensive wines at this cute little bistro near the entrance to the Vieille Ville. The best bet is to order *à l'ardoise*—that is, from the blackboard listing of daily specials. The lunch menu prix-fixe (€15) is the best deal in town. Prix-fixe dinner menus start at €23. ⊠*Av. Jardin Exotique* ☎*04–93–41–16–42* ▤*MC, V* ⊗*Closed Mon. and mid-Dec.–mid-Jan. No dinner Wed.*

$$$$
Fodor's Choice
★

✕▣ Château de la Chèvre d'Or. Giving substance to Riviera fairy tales, this extraordinary xanadu seems to sit just below cloud level like a Hilton penthouse, medieval-style. The "château of the Golden Goat" is actually an entire stretch of the village, streets and all, bordered by gardens that hang to the

WORD OF MOUTH

"The Château de la Chèvre d'Or is expensive, but worth it for the truly amazing setting—nothing beats lunch there on a sunny day."
–tulipsMC1

mountainside in nearly Babylonian style. The fanciest guest rooms come replete with stone boulder walls, peasant-luxe fireplaces, faux 15th-century panel paintings, and chandeliered rock-grotto bathrooms, but nearly all have exposed stone and exposed beams (even the cheapest have views over Èze's charming tile roofs). No fewer than three restaurants, ranging from the nicely affordable grill to the *haute gastronomique* grand dining room with its panoramic view, spoil you for choice. Children are just plain spoiled with the hotel's fabulous Chicken in Coca-Cola sauce (€30). The swimming pool alone, clinging like a swallow's nest to the hillside, may justify the investment, as do the liveried footmen who greet you at the village entrance to wave you, VIP-style, past the cattle drive of tourists, or the breakfast on the spectacular terrace, which seems to levitate over the bay. ⊠*Rue du Barri, 06360* ☎*04–92–10–66–66* 🖷*04–93–41–06–72* ⊕*www.chevre-dor.com* 🛏*23 rooms, 9 suites* ♿*In-room: refrigerator, Wi-Fi. In-hotel: 3 restaurants, bar, tennis court, pool, some pets allowed* 🖃*AE, DC, MC, V* ⊗*Closed Dec.–Feb.*

★ $$$$
✕▣ Château Eza. Vertiginously perched on the edge of a cliff 3,000 feet above the crouching tiger of St-Jean-Cap-Ferrat, this former residence of Prince William of Sweden is one of the most dramatic, romantic, and expensive inns on the entire Mediterranean coast. Surprisingly, the public salons are cool, sleek, and modern, almost letting you think you're wandered into Soho. But the guest rooms—there are only 10—are spread among a cluster of striking Romanesque 13th-century buildings on cobblestone streets too narrow for cars. Most have private entrances and all are luxed out to the max: canopy beds, costly objets d'art and antiques, exquisite carpets and tapestries, wood-burning fireplaces and unbelievable views. If you're not staying the night, the views from the panoramic restaurant and outdoor terrace (gasp—everyone does) are just as good. The wine list is one of the best on the Riviera, though the food has slipped a notch and service can be haughty. ⊠*Rue de la Pise, 06360* ☎*04–93–41–12–24* 🖷*04–93–41–16–64* ⊕*www.chateaueza.com* 🛏*7 rooms, 3 suites* ♿*In-room: refrigerator, Wi-Fi. In-hotel: restaurant* 🖃*AE, DC, MC, V* ⊗*Closed Oct.–Mar.*

★ $$$
▣ La Bastide aux Camelias. There are only four bedrooms in this lovely B&B, each individually decorated with softly draped fabrics and polished antiques. Close to Èze Village, set in the nearby Grande Corniche Park, it offers up the usual run of breathtaking views, but also has inviting, less precipitous ones of garden greenery. Have the complimentary breakfast on the picture-perfect veranda, indulge in a cooling drink by the gorgeous pool, or stretch out on the manicured lawn. There's even

a spa, hamman, and Jacuzzi included in the price. It's gentle hospitality that's much in demand, however, so reserve well in advance. ⊠*Rte. de l'Adret, 06360* ☎*04–93–41–13–68* ➔*04–93–41–13–68* ⊕*www. bastideauxcamelias.com* ➔*4 rooms* ⌂*In-room: refrigerator. In-hotel: pool, parking (no fee), some pets allowed (fee), public Internet, no elevator* ⦿*BP.*

MONACO

7 km (4½ mi) east of Èze, 21 km (13 mi) east of Nice.

GETTING HERE

From the Nice airport, there is a direct bus service from Compagnie des Autobus de Monaco (☎*377/97–70–22–22* ⊕*www.cam.mc*) to the Place du Casino (in front of the Monte Carlo casino); it takes 50 minutes and costs €12.50. This company also runs a bus line that threads the avenues of Monaco. Both buses and trains connect Nice with Monaco. RCA (☎*04–93–85–64–44* ⊕*www.rca.tm.fr*) has buses connecting with Nice's center-city bus station (⊠*Gare routière, 5 bd. Jean Jaures* ☎*04–93–85–61–81*); tickets cost €15.50. The 100TAM bus (Transport Alpes Maritimes) (☎*08–10–06–10–06* ⊕*www.lignedazur. com*) costs €1.30 and leaves from the main bus station in Nice, but be prepared as it takes about two hours to get there. From Nice's train station (⊠*Gare SNCF, Av. Thiers* ☎*04–92–14–80–80* ⊕*www.voyages-sncf.com*), Monaco is serviced by regular trains along the Cannes–Ventimiglia line; Monaco's train station is on Avenue Prince Pierre. From Nice, the journey costs €3.50 one-way and takes 20 minutes. You can also helicopter your way in, leaving from the Nice airport to Monaco. Heli Air Monaco (⊕*www.heliairmonaco.com*) takes about 20 minutes and costs around €80 depending on the season. A taxi (☎*04–93–13–78–78*) from Nice will cost around €100 depending on the season and the time of day.

EXPLORING

It's positively feudal, the idea that an ancient dynasty of aristocrats could still hold fast to its patch of coastline, the last scrap of a once-vast domain. But that's just what the Grimaldi family did, clinging to a few acres of glory and maintaining their own license plates, their own telephone area code (377—don't forget to dial this when calling Monaco from France or other countries), and their own highly forgiving tax system. Yet the Principality of Monaco covers just 473 acres and would fit comfortably inside New York's Central Park or a family farm in Iowa. And its 5,000 pampered citizens would fill only a small fraction of the seats in Yankee Stadium. The harbor district, known as **La Condamine,** connects the new quarter, officially known as **Monte Carlo,** with the Vieille Ville, officially known as **Monaco-Ville** (or Le Rocher). Have no fear that you'll need to climb countless steps to get to the Vieille Ville, as there are plenty of elevators and escalators climbing the steep cliffs.

Prince Rainier III, the family patriarch who famously wed Grace Kelly and brought Hollywood glamour to his toy kingdom, passed away in

April 2005; his son, the eminently responsible Prince Albert, took over as head of the family and principality. Albert traces his ancestry to Otto Canella, who was born in 1070. The Grimaldi dynasty began with Otto's great-great-great-grandson, Francesco Grimaldi, also known as Frank the Rogue. Expelled from Genoa, Frank and his cronies disguised themselves as monks and in 1297 seized the fortified medieval town known today as Le Rocher (the Rock). Except for a short break under Napoléon, the Grimaldis have been here ever since, which makes them the oldest reigning family in Europe.

It's the tax system, not the gambling (actually, the latter helps pay for the former), that has made Monaco one of the most sought-after addresses in the world. It bristles with gleaming glass-and-concrete corncob-towers 20 and 30 stories high and with vast apartment complexes, their terraces, landscaped like miniature gardens, jutting over the sea. You now have to look hard to find the Belle Epoque grace of yesteryear. But if you repair to the town's great 1864 landmark Hôtel de Paris—still a veritable crossroads of the buffed and befurred Eurogentry—or enjoy a grand bouffe at its famous Louis XV restaurant, or attend the Opéra, or visit the ballrooms of the Casino (avert your eyes from the flashy gambling machines), you may still be able to conjure up Monaco's elegant past and the much-missed spirit of Princess Grace.

★ ㊺ Place du Casino is the center of Monte Carlo, and the **Casino** is a must-see, even if you don't bet a sou. Into the gold-leaf splendor of the Casino, the hopeful traipse from tour buses to tempt fate beneath the gilt-edge Rococo ceiling (but do remember the fate of Sarah Bernhardt, who lost her last 100,000 francs here). Jacket and tie are required in the back rooms, which open at 3 pm. Bring your passport (under-18s not admitted). Note that there are special admission fees to get into many of the period gaming rooms—only the Salle des Jeux Americains is free. ⊠*Pl. du Casino* ☎*377/92–16–20–00* ⊕*www.sbm.mc* ☉*Daily noon–4* AM .

㊻ In the true spirit of the town, it seems that the **Opéra de Monte-Carlo** (⊠*Pl. du Casino* ☎*377/98–06–28–28* ⊕*www.opera.mc*), with its 18-ton gilt-bronze chandelier and extravagant frescoes, is part of the Casino complex. The grand theater was designed by Charles Garnier, who also built the Paris Opéra. Its main auditorium, the Salle Garnier, was inaugurated by Sarah Bernhardt in 1879.

㊼ Some say the most serious gamblers play at **Sun Casino,** in the Monte Carlo Grand Hotel, by the vast convention center that juts over the water. ⊠*12 av. des Spélugues* ☎*377/92–16–21–23* ☉*Tables open weekdays at 5* PM *and weekends at 4* PM ; *slot machines open daily at 11* AM .

㊽ From Place des Moulins an elevator descends to the Larvotto Beach complex, artfully created with imported sand, and the **Musée National Automates et Poupées,** housed in a Garnier villa within a rose garden. It has a beguiling collection of 18th- and 19th-century dolls and automatons. ⊠*17 av. Princesse Grace* ☎*377/93–30–91–26* ⊠*€6* ☉*Easter–Aug., daily 10–6:30; Sept.–Easter, daily 10–12:15 and 2:30–6:30.*

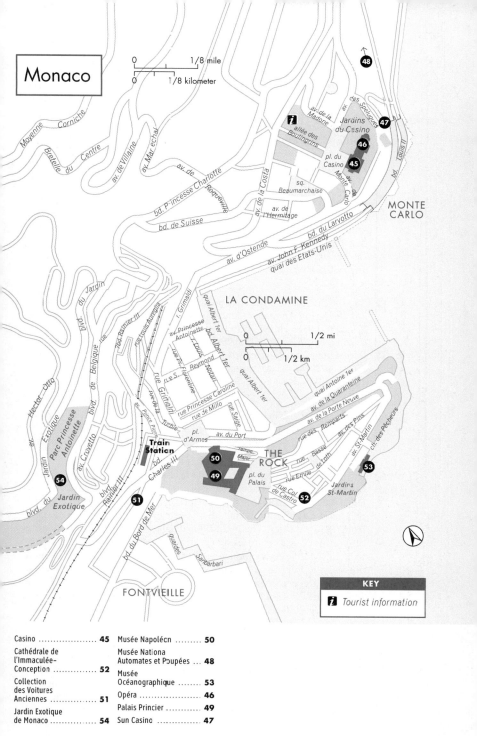

Monaco

0 — 1/8 mile
0 — 1/8 kilometer

MONTE CARLO

LA CONDAMINE

0 — 1/2 mi
0 — 1/2 km

THE ROCK

Train Station

Parc Princesse Antoinette

Jardin Exotique

FONTVIEILLE

KEY

Tourist information

49 West of Monte Carlo stands the famous Rock, crowned by the **Palais Princier,** where the royal family resides. A 40-minute guided tour (summer only) of this sumptuous chunk of history, first built in the 13th century and expanded and enhanced over the centuries, reveals an extravagance of 16th- and 17th-century frescoes, as well as tapestries, gilt furniture, and paintings on a grand scale. Note that the **Relève de la Garde** (Changing of the Guard) is held outside the front entrance of the palace most days at 11:55 am . ⊠ *Pl. du Palais* 🕾 *377/93–25–18–31* 🖾 *€6, joint ticket with Musée Napoléon €9* ⊙ *Apr., daily 10:30–6:30; May–Sept., daily 9:30–6:30; Oct., daily 10–5:30* ⊙ *Closed Nov.–Mar.*

One wing of the Palais Princier, open throughout the year, is taken up **50** by the **Musée Napoléon,** filled with Napoleonic souvenirs—including that hat and a tricolor scarf—and genealogical charts. ⊠ *In Palais Princier* 🕾 *377/93–25–18–31* 🖾 *€4, joint ticket with palace apartments €9* ⊙ *Apr., daily 10:30–6:30; May–Sept., daily 9:30–6:30; Oct., daily 10–5:30; Dec., daily 10:30–5.*

On the Terrasses de Fontvieille are two remarkable sights (opened in ᗇ **51** 2003): the **Collection des Voitures Anciennes** *(Collection of Vintage Cars)* and the **Jardin Animalier** (Animal Garden). The former is a collection of Prince Rainier's vintage cars from a De Dion Bouton to a Lamborghini Countach; the latter, a minizoo housing the Rainier family's animal collection, an astonishing array of wild beasts including monkeys and exotic birds. ⊠ *Terrasses de Fontvieille* 🕾 *377/92–05–28–56 or 377/93–25–18–31* 🖾 *€6 Voitures; €4 Animalier* ⊙ *June–Sept., daily 10–6.*

Follow the flow of crowds down the last remaining streets of medieval **52** Monaco to the **Cathédrale de l'Immaculée-Conception** (⊠ *Av. St-Martin*), an uninspired 19th-century version of the Romanesque style. Nonetheless, it harbors a magnificent altarpiece, painted in 1500 by Bréa, and the tomb of Princess Grace.

ᗇ ★ **53** At the prow of the Rock, the grand **Musée Océanographique** *(Oceanography Museum)* perches dramatically on a cliff. It's a splendid Edwardian structure, built under Prince Albert I to house specimens collected on amateur explorations. Jacques Cousteau (1910–97) led its missions from 1957 to 1988. The main floor displays skeletons and taxidermy of enormous sea creatures; early submarines and diving gear dating from the Middle Ages; and a few interactive science displays. The main draw is the famous **aquarium,** a vast complex of backlighted tanks containing every imaginable species of fish, crab, and eel. ⊠ *Av. St-Martin* 🕾 *377/93–15–36–00* ⊕ *www.oceano.mc* 🖾 *€11* ⊙ *July and Aug., daily 9:30–7:30; Apr.–June, daily 8:30–7; Sept., daily 9:30–7; Oct.–Mar., daily 10–6.*

Carved out of the rock face and one of Monte Carlo's most stunning **54** escape hatches, the **Jardin Exotique de Monaco** *(Monaco Exotic Gar-* **Fodor's**Choice *den)* is studded with thousands of succulents and cacti, all set along ★ promenades, belvederes over the sea, and even framing faux boulders (actually hollow sculptures). There are rare plants from Mexico and Africa, and the hillside plot, threaded with bridges and grottoes, can't be beat for coastal splendor. Thanks go to Prince Albert I, who started it all. Also on the grounds, or actually under them, are the **Grottes de l'Observatoire**—spectacular grottoes and caves a-drip with stalagmites and spotlighted with fairy lights. The largest cavern is called "La Grande Salle" and looks like a Romanesque rock cathedral. Traces of Cro-Magnon civilization have been found here so the grottoes now bear the official name of the **Musée d'Anthropologie Préhistorique.** ✉*Bd. du Jardin Exotique* ☎*377/93–15–29–80* 💰*€6.90* 🕐*Mid-May–mid-Sept., daily 9–7; mid-Sept.–mid-Nov. and mid-Dec.–May, daily 9–6.*

WHERE TO STAY & EAT

$$$$
Fodor's Choice
★

✗ **Le Louis XV.** Louis Quinze to the initiated, this extravagantly showy restaurant stuns with neo-Baroque details, yet it manages to be upstaged by its product: the superb cuisine of Alain Ducasse, one of Europe's most celebrated chefs. With too many tokens on his Monopoly board, Ducasse jets between his other, ever-growing interests leaving the Louis XV kitchen, for the most part, in the more-than-capable hands of chef Franck Cerutti, who draws much of his inspiration from the Cours Saleya market in Nice. Ducasse's absence is no great loss. Glamorous iced lobster consommé with caviar, and risotto perfumed with Alba white truffles slum happily with stockfish (stewed salt cod) and tripe. There are sole sautéed with tender baby fennel, salt-seared foie gras, milk-fed lamb with hints of cardamom, and dark-chocolate sorbet crunchy with ground coffee beans or hot wild strawberries on an icy mascarpone sorbet—in short, a panoply of delights using the sensual flavors of the Mediterranean. The decor is magnificent—a surfeit of gilt, mirrors, and chandeliers—and the waitstaff seignorial as they proffer a footstool for madame's handbag. In Ducasse fashion, the Baroque clock on the wall is stopped just before 12. Cinderella should have no fears. If your wallet is a chubby one, this is a must (menus run from €190 to €210). ✉*Hôtel de Paris, Pl. du Casino* ☎*377/98–06–88–64* 🌐*www.alain-ducasse.com* 🔲*AE, DC, MC, V* 🕐*Closed late Nov.–late Dec., late Feb.–mid-Mar., and Tues. and Wed., except Wed. evenings, late June–late Aug.*

$$–$$$$

✗ **Castelroc.** With its tempting pine-shaded terrace just across from the entrance to the palace, this popular local lunch spot serves up specialties of cuisine Monegasque, ranging from anchoïade to stockfish. The fixed-price menus: lunch €21.50, dinner €44 are a bargain. ✉*Pl. du Palais* ☎*377/93–30–36–68* 🔲*AE, MC, V* 🕐*Closed weekends and Dec. and Jan.*

$–$$$$

✗ **Zebra Square.** An offshoot of its sister hot spot in Paris, this trendy bar–restaurant atop the Grimaldi Forum serves impeccable modern-Provençal cuisine on a lovely terrace looking out to the sea. Better yet, it turns into a late-night lounge after midnight and its low lighting and great selection of music are easy to *groove* to. ✉*10 av. Princess Grace* ☎*377/93–99–25–50* 🔲*AE, MC, V* 🕐*Closed Sun. and Dec. and Jan. No lunch Sat.*

$$–$$$

✗ **Café de Paris.** This landmark Belle Epoque brasserie, across from the Casino, offers the usual classics (shellfish, steak tartare, matchstick frites, and fish boned table-side). Supercilious, super-pro waiters fawn gracefully over titled preeners, gentlemen, jet-setters, and tourists alike.

Happily, there's good hot food until 2 am . ⊠*Pl. du Casino* ☎*377/92–16–20–20* ▭*AE, DC, MC, V.*

$$$$ ✕▣ **Hôtel Metropole.** With its wonderfully impressive entrance, this fine Belle Epoque palace just underwent a multimillion-dollar face-lift with spectacular results. From the moment you walk through the colossal neo-Roman arch, down the cypress-studded lane, and into the cozy Jacques Garcia–designed lounge, you're swept away into Rothschild-Renaissance-meets-contemporary style: the clever trompe-l'oeil bookcase in the bar is actually the door to the bathroom, for example. Guest rooms are luxe and tastefully decorated in creams and beiges, but the main attraction here, especially for those with a healthy respect for creative and top-notch cuisine, is the restaurant. Headed up by much acclaimed chef Joël Robuchon, the menu varies from season to season but never fails to delight. The garden has also been transformed into an urban oasis, now harboring some 3,000 species of plants. Guests can choose from a number of chauffeur-driven half-day and day trips, plus children's programs and—*mais, oui*—dogs' programs. ⊠*4 av. de la Madonne, 98000* ☎*377/93–15–15–15* ⊟*377/93–25–24–44* ⊕*www.metropole.com* ⇆*146 rooms, 10 suites* ♿*In-room: refrigerator, Wi-Fi. In-hotel: restaurant, bar, pool, gym, parking (fee), some pets allowed (fee)* ▭*AE, DC, MC, V* ⦿*MAP.*

$$$ ▣ **Alexandra.** The friendly proprietress, Madame Larouquie, makes you feel right at home at this central, comfortable spot just north of the Casino. Though the color schemes clash and the bedrooms are spare, bathrooms are spacious and up-to-date, and insulated windows keep traffic noise out. Breakfast is included in the price. ⊠*35 bd. Princesse-Charlotte, 98000* ☎*377/93–50–63–13* ⊟*377/92–16–06–48* ⇆*56 rooms* ♿*In-room: refrigerator, Wi-Fi* ▭*AE, DC, MC, V* ⦿*BP.*

NIGHTLIFE & THE ARTS

There's no need to go to bed before dawn in Monte Carlo when you can go to the **casinos.** Monte Carlo's spring arts festival, **Printemps des Arts,** takes place from early April to mid-May and includes the world's top ballet, operatic, symphonic, and chamber-music performers (☎*377/93–25–58–04*). Year-round, opera, ballet, and classical music can be enjoyed at the magnificently sumptuous Salle Garnier auditorium of the **Opéra de Monte-Carlo** (⊠*Pl. du Casino* ☎*337/98–06–28–28* ⊕*www.opera.mc*), the main venue of the Opéra de Monte-Carlo and the Orchestre Philharmonique de Monte-Carlo, both worthy of the magnificent hall.

SPORTS

Held at the beautiful Monte Carlo Country Club, the **Monte Carlo Open Tennis Masters Series** (☎*377/97–98–70–00* ⊕*montecarlo.masters-series.com/1005*) is held during the last two weeks of April every year. When the tennis stops, the auto racing begins: the **Grand Prix de Monaco** (☎*377/93–15–26–00 for information* ⊕*www.grand-prix-monaco.com*) takes place in mid-May.

MENTON

Fodor's Choice
★

55 *9 km (5½ mi) east of Monaco.*

GETTING HERE

RCA Menton (☎08–20–42–33–33 ⊕*www.rca.tm.fr*) runs a regular daily bus service from Menton's main bus station (✉*Gare routière, Av. de Sospel* ☎04–93–35–93–60). This bus route runs along the Basse Corniche to the Nice bus station at 5 boulevard Jean Jaures and tickets cost €17.50. Local trains on the Nice–Ventimiglia line (⊕*www.voyages-sncf.com*) are very regular and you can take them from any one of the 15 stations along the route, including Nice, a trip that takes 36 minutes and costs €4.20. The Menton Gare SNCF train station is within walking distance of the sea and the center of town.

EXPLORING

Menton, the most Mediterranean of the French resort towns, rubs shoulders with the Italian border and owes its balmy climate to the protective curve of the Ligurian shore. Its picturesque harbor skyline seems to beg artists to immortalize it, while its Cubist skew of terracotta roofs and yellow-ocher houses, Baroque arabesques capping the church facades, and ceramic tiles glistening on their steeples all evoke the villages of the Italian coast. Also worth a visit are the many exotic gardens set in the hills around the town. Menton is the least pretentious of the French Riviera resorts and all the more alluring for its modesty.

The **Basilique St-Michel** (✉*Parvis St-Michel*), a majestic Baroque church, dominates the skyline of Menton with its bell tower. Beyond the beautifully proportioned facade—a 19th-century addition—the richly frescoed nave and chapels contain several works by Genovese artists and a splendid 17th-century organ.

Just above the main church, the smaller **Chapelle de l'Immaculée-Conception** answers St-Michel's grand gesture with its own pure Baroque beauty, dating from 1687. Between 3 and 5 you can slip in to see the graceful trompe l'oeil over the altar and the ornate gilt lanterns early penitents carried in processions.

Two blocks below the square, **Rue St-Michel** serves as the main commercial artery of the Vieille Ville, lined with shops, cafés, and orange trees.

Between the lively pedestrian Rue St-Michel and the waterfront, the marvelous **Marché Couvert** (*Covered Market*) sums up Menton style with its Belle Epoque facade decorated in jewel-tone ceramics. Inside, it's just as appealing, with merchants selling chewy bread, mountain cheeses, oils, fruit, and Italian delicacies in Caravaggesque disarray.

On the waterfront opposite the market, a squat medieval bastion crowned with four tiny watchtowers houses the **Musée Jean-Cocteau.** Built in 1636 to defend the port, it was spotted by the artist-poet-filmmaker Jean Cocteau (1889–1963) as the perfect site for a group of his works. There are bright, cartoonish pastels of fishermen and wenches in love, and a fantastical assortment of ceramic animals in the

Paradise Found: The Magnificent Gardens of Menton

The French Riviera is famed for its panoply of grand villas and even grander gardens built by Victorian dukes, Spanish exiles, Belgian royals, and American blue bloods.

Although its hothouse crescent blooms everywhere with palm and lemon trees and jungle flowers, nowhere else does it bloom so extravagantly than in Menton, famous for its temperate climes and 24-karat sun.

With a temperate microclimate created by its southeastern and sunny exposure (the Alps are a natural buffer against cold winds), Menton attracted a great share of wealthy hobbyists during the 1920s and 1930s, including Major Lawrence Johnston, a gentleman gardener best known for his Cotswolds wonderland, Hidcote Manor.

Fair-haired and blue-eyed, this gentle American wound up buying a choice estate in the village of Gorbio—one of the loveliest of all perched seaside villages, set 10 km (6 mi) west of Menton—and spent two decades making the **Serre de la Madone** one of the horticultural masterpieces of the coast.

He brought back exotica from his many trips to South Africa, Mexico, and China, and planted them in a series of terraces, accented by little pools, vistas, and stone steps.

Although most of his creeping plumbago, pink belladonna, and night-flowering cacti are now gone, his garden has been reopened by the municipality.

It's best to call for a reservation at the Serre de la Madone; car facilities are very limited but the garden can also be reached from Menton via bus No. 7 (get off at Mers et Monts stop).

Back in Menton, green-thumbers will also want to visit the town's Jardin Botanique, the **Val Rahmeh Botanical Garden** (⊠ Av. St-Jacques), planted by Maybud Campbell in the 1910s, much prized by connoisseurs, bursting with rare ornamentals and subtropical plants, and adorned with water-lily pools and fountains.

The tourist office can also give you directions to other gardens around Menton, including the Fontana Rosa, the Villa Maria Serena, and the Villa Les Colombières, as well as issue Heritage Passports for select garden visits; log onto www.menton.com.

⊠ *Serre de la Madone: 74 rte. de Gorbio* ☎ *04–93–57–73–90* ⊕ *www. serredelamadone.com* 🖾 *€8 for Serre, €4 for Val Rahmeh* ⊙ *Tours only: Feb. 20–Apr., Fri. 9:30 and Tues.–Sun. 3; May–Oct., Tues.–Sun. 9:30 and 3.*

wrought-iron vitrines he designed. ⊠ *Vieux Port* ☎ *04–93–57–72–30* 🖾 *€3* ⊙ *Wed.–Mon. 10–noon and 2–6.*

The 19th-century Italianate **Hôtel de Ville** conceals another Cocteau treasure: it was he who decorated the **Salle des Mariages** (Marriage Room), in which civil marriages take place, with vibrant allegorical scenes. ⊠ *17 av. de la République* 🖾 *€2* ⊙ *Weekdays 8:30–12:30 and 1:30–5.*

At the far west end of town stands the 18th-century **Palais Carnolès** *(Carnolès Palace)* in vast gardens luxuriant with orange, lemon, and grapefruit trees. It was once the summer retreat of the princes of Monaco; nowadays it contains a sizable collection of European paintings from the Renaissance to the present day plus some interesting temporary exhibits. ⊠ *3 av. de la Madone* ☎ *04–93–35–49–71* 🖾 *Free* ⊙ *Wed.–Mon. 10–noon and 2–6.*

WHERE TO STAY & EAT

★ $$–$$$ ✕🖾 **Aiglon.** Sweep down the curving stone stairs to the terrazzo mosaic lobby of this truly lovely 1880 garden villa for a drink or a meal by the pool, or settle onto your little balcony overlooking the grounds and a tiny wedge of sea. There's a room for every whim, all soft-edged, comfortable, and romantic, although you will be loath to leave the grand salon, a picture-perfect confection of 19th-century elegance that wouldn't shame some of the nobler houses in Paris. The poolside restaurant, Le Riaumont, serves candlelight dinners of fresh, local fish lightly steamed and sauced with a Provençal accent; breakfast is served in a shady garden shelter. It's a three-minute walk from the beach. Half-board prices are available. ⊠ *7 av. de la Madone, 06502* ☎ *04–93–57–55–55* 🖷 *04–93–35–92–39* ⊕ *www.hotelaiglon.net* ➪ *28 rooms, 2 apartments* ⬥ *In-room: no TV. In-hotel: restaurant, bar, pool, some pets allowed (fee), public Internet* 🖃 *AE, DC, MC, V* ⊙ *Restaurant closed mid-Nov.–mid-Dec.* ⦙◎⦙ *MAP.*

NIGHTLIFE & THE ARTS

In August the **Festival de Musique de Chambre** *(Chamber Music Festival)* (☎ *04–92–41–76–95*) takes place on the stone-paved plaza outside the church of St-Michel. The **Fête du Citron** *(Lemon Festival)* (☎ *04–92–41–76–76*) at the end of February, celebrates the lemon with floats and sculptures like those of the Rose Bowl Parade, all made of real fruit.

FRENCH RIVIERA ESSENTIALS

TRANSPORTATION

If traveling extensively by public transportation, be sure to load up on information (schedules, the best taxi-for-call companies, etc.) upon arriving at the ticket counter or help desk of the bigger train and bus stations in the area, such as Nice, Monaco, and St-Raphaël.

AIRPORTS

The Nice–Côte d'Azur Airport sits on a peninsula between Antibes and Nice.

Airport Information Nice–Côte d'Azur Airport (⊠ *7 km [4½ mi] from Nice* ☎ *04-93-21-30-30).*

BY AIR

There are frequent flights between Paris and Nice on EasyJet, AOM, and Air France, as well as direct flights on Delta Airlines from New York. The flight time between Paris and Nice is about one hour.

BY BOAT

Considering the congestion buses and cars confront on the road to St-Tropez, the best way to get to that resort is to train to St-Raphaël, then hop on one of the four boats each day (between April and October) that leave from the Gare Maritime de St-Raphaël on Rue Pierre-Auble. The trip takes about an hour and costs €9. Transports Maritimes MMG also offers a shuttle boat linking St-Tropez and Ste-Maxime April to October; tickets are €6 and the ride is a half hour. Once in St-Tropez, stay on the water for a one-hour boat ride tour offered by MMG of the Baie des Cannebiers (nicknamed the "Bay of Stars") to see some celebrity villas.

Boat Travel Information Transports Maritimes MMG (⊠ *Quai L.-Condroyer, Ste-Maxime* ☎ *04–94–96–51–00*). **Transports Maritimes Raphaelois** (⊠ *St-Raphaël* ☎ *04–94–95–17–46*).

BY BUS

If you want to penetrate deeper into villages and backcountry spots not on the rail line, you can take a bus out of Cannes, Nice, Antibes, or Menton to the most frequented spots. Note that the quickest way to get around by public transportation is the great coastal train line that connects the main cities and a lot of villages from Cannes to Menton *(see By Train, below)*. In addition to town bus stations, you can hook up with buses heading to most destinations in this chapter using the bus station at the Nice airport (next to Terminal 1). Rapides Côte d'Azur runs Bus No. 100, which departs every 15 minutes (between 6 am and 8 pm) and stops at all the villages between Nice and Menton along the Corniche Inférieure. A trip to Beaulieu, for instance, costs €1.80 round-trip and takes eight minutes from Nice. For the villages set on the Moyenne Corniche, take Bus No. 112, which departs Nice six times a day (three on Sunday). A trip to Èze, for instance, costs €2.50 and takes 20 minutes. Fewer villages are found on the Grande Corniche, the highest highway, but some, such as La Turbie, are serviced by Rapides Côte d'Azur No. 116. From Menton's bus station, you can take buses back to Monaco and Nice. Many hotels and excursion companies organize day trips into St-Paul and Vence.

Monaco's buses help stitch together the principality's widely dispersed neighborhoods. Take a bus from Antibes bus station to Vallauris (every 30 mins, €3) or one running from the train station in Golfe-Juan. Antibes bus station is by Rue de la République, and has buses connecting with Nice (every half hr, €5), Cagnes-sur-Mer (20 mins, €2.50), Biot (25 mins, €1), Cannes (30 mins, €2). Cagnes-sur-Mer is one of the coastal towns served by train, but you can easily connect with adjacent St-Paul-de-Vence and Vence using Bus. No. 400, with departures every 30 minutes from Cagnes Ville's bus station on Place du Général de Gaulle. Note that you can take a free navette shuttle bus from here up to the hill town of Haut-de-Cagnes June–December. The bus station in Cagnes Ville is about eight blocks away from the train station (but municipal buses can help you make this trip—ask at Cagnes's bus station).

St-Tropez's Gare Routière (bus station) is on Avenue du Général de Gaulle and has bus routes run by Sodetrav to/from St-Raphaël (1½ hrs, 10 daily, €9), the town with the nearest railway station, with stops in Grimaud and Port Grimaud, Ste-Maxime, and Fréjus (1 hr, €9). Note that in high season, the traffic jam to St-Tropez can lead to two-plus–hour bus rides, so if you arrive in St-Raphaël, it may be best to hop on the shuttle boats that connect the two ports. Buses also link up with Ramatuelle and Gassin (both are 25 mins, 3 daily in peak season, €4). Bus drivers give change and hand you a ticket, which must be stamped (*composté*) in the ticket validator.

Bus Information A.pes-Maritimes Bus Services—RCA Transport (Rapides Côte d'Azur) (⊠ *5 bd. Jean Jaurès, Nice* ☎ *04-93-85-64-44* ⊕ *www.rca.tm.fr*). **Cannes Gare routière** (*bus station,* ⊠ *Pl. Bernard Cornut Gentille* ☎ *04-93-45-20-08*). **Compagnie des Autobus de Monaco** (⊠ *2 av. du pdt J.F. Kennedy, Monaco* ☎ *377/97-70-22-22* ⊕ *www.cam.mc*).

Menton gare routière (⊠ *12 promenade Maréchal Leclerc* ☎ *04-93-28-43-27*). **Nice Gare Routière** (⊠ *5 bd. Jean Jaurès* ☎ *04-93-85-61-81*). **Phocéens Santa Azur (Voyages)** (⊠ *4 pl. Massena, Nice* ☎ *04-93-13-18-20* ⊠ *5 sq. Mérimée, Cannes* ☎ *04-93-39-79-40* ⊠ *8 pl. de Gaul, Antibes* ☎ *04-93-34-15-98*). **Rapides Côte d'Azur** (☎ *04-93-85-64-44* ⊕ *www.rca.tm.fr*). **SAP (Société Auto-mobile de Provence)** (☎ *04-93-58-37-60*). **SNCF** (☎ *08-36-35-35-35* ⊕ *www.ter-sncf.com/uk/paca*). **Société des Cars Alpes-Littoral** (☎ *04-92-51-06-05*). **Sodetrav** (☎ *0825/000-650* ⊕ *www.sodetrav.fr*). **Transports Alpes-Maritimes** (☎ *04-93-89-41-45*).

BY CAR

The best way to explore the secondary sights in this region, especially the backcountry hill towns, is by car. It also allows you the freedom to zip along A8 between the coastal resorts and to enjoy the tremendous views from the three corniches that trace the coast from Nice to the Italian border. N98, which connects you to coastal resorts in between, can be extremely slow, though scenic. A8 parallels the coast from above St-Tropez to Nice to the resorts on the Grand Corniche; N98 follows the coast more closely. From Paris the main southbound artery is A6/A7, known as the Autoroute du Soleil; it passes through Provence and joins the eastbound A8 at Aix-en-Provence.

BY TRAIN

Nice is the major rail crossroads for trains arriving from Paris and other northern cities and from Italy, too. To get from Paris to Nice (with stops in Cannes and other resorts along the coast), you can take the TGV, though it only maintains high speeds to Valence before returning to conventional rails and rates. Night trains arrive at Nice in the morning from Paris, Metz, and Strasbourg.

You can easily move along the coast between Cannes, Nice, and Ventimiglia by train on the slick double-decker Côte d'Azur line, a dramatic and highly tourist-pleasing branch of the SNCF lines that offers panoramic views as it rolls from one famous resort to the next, with more than two dozen trains running a day. This line is called Marseille-Vintimille (Ventimiglia, in Italy) heading east to Italy and Vintimille-Marseille in the west direction. Some main stops on this line are: Antibes (30 mins, €4), Cannes (40 mins, €6), Menton (30 mins, €4), and Monaco (25 mins, €3); other stops include Villefranche-sur-Mer, Beaulieu, Cap-Martin, St-Jean-Cap-Ferrat, and Èze-sur-Mer. But train travelers will have difficulty getting up to St-Paul, Vence, Peillon, and other backcountry villages; that you must accomplish by bus or car.

As for the western parts of the French Riviera, catch trains at Fréjus's main station on Rue Martin-Bidoure and St-Raphaël's Gare de St-Raphaël on Rue Waldeck-Rousseau, where the rail route begins its scenic crawl along the coast to Italy, stopping in La Napoule and Cannes. St-Raphaël is the main train hub, on the coastal rail line between Menton and Marseille (it's about 2 hrs from the latter by rail, with hourly trains costing €20). The resort port of Mandelieu-La Napoule is on the main rail line between St-Raphaël and Cannes. There's no rail access to St-Tropez; St-Raphaël and Fréjus are the nearest stops.

Train Information Gare Cannes Ville (*Train station,* ⊠ *Rue Jean Jaurès*). **Gare Nice Ville** (⊠ *Av. Thiers* 🕾 *08–36–35–35–35*). **SNCF** (🕾 *36–35, €0.34 per min* ⊕ *www.voyages-sncf.com*). **TGV** (🕾 *877/2848633* ⊕ *www.tgv.com*). **www.beyond. fr** (⊕ *www.beyond.fr*).

CONTACTS & RESOURCES

CAR RENTAL

Most likely you'll want to rent your car at one of the main rail stops, either St-Raphaël, Nice, Monaco, or Menton, or at the airport in Nice, where all major companies are represented.

Local Agencies Avis (⊠ *2 av. des Phocéens, Nice* 🕾 *04–93–80–63–52* ⊠ *Nice Airport* 🕾 *04–93–21–42–80* ⊠ *190 pl. Pierre Coullet, St-Raphaël* 🕾 *04–94–95–60–42*). **Budget** (⊠ *23 rue de Belgique, Nice* 🕾 *04–93–16–24–16* ⊠ *Nice Airport* 🕾 *04–93–21–36–50* ⊠ *40 rue Waldeck–Rousseau, St-Raphaël* 🕾 *04–94–82–24–44*). **Europcar** (⊠ *3 av. Gustave V, Nice* 🕾 *04–92–14–44–50* ⊠ *Nice Airport* 🕾 *04–93–21–43–54* ⊠ *47 av. de Grande-Bretagne, Monaco* 🕾 *377/93–50–74–95* ⊠ *54 pl. Pierre Coullet, St-Raphaël* 🕾 *04–94–95–56–87*). **Hertz** (⊠ *1 promenade des Anglais, Nice* 🕾 *04–93–87–11–87* ⊠ *Nice airport* 🕾 *04–93–21–36–72* ⊠ *32 rue Waldeck–Rousseau, St-Raphaël* 🕾 *04–94–95–48–68* ⊠ *27 bd. Albert I, Monaco* 🕾 *377/93–50–79–60*).

EMERGENCIES

For basic information, see this section in the Essentials chapter. In most towns, contact the Comissariat de Police or Gendarmerie.

Emergencies Police (⊠ *1 av. Maréchal Foch, Nice* 🕾 *04–92–17–22–22, 17 for police, 15 for medical assistance*). **Police** (⊠ *2 quai Saint-Pierre, Cannes* 🕾 *04–97–06–42–85*). **Police** (⊠ *Rue François Sibilli, St-Tropez* 🕾 *17*).

INTERNET & MAIL

In smaller towns, ask your hotel concierge whether there are any Internet cafés nearby.

Internet & Mail Information Kreatik Café (⊠ *17 av. du Général Leclerc, St-Tropez* 🕾 *04–94–97–40–61*). **Panini & Web** (⊠ *25 promenade des Anglais,*

Nice ☎ *04–93–88–72–75*). **La Poste main post office** (✉ *22 rue Biovouac Napoléon, Cannes*). **La Poste main post office** (✉ *23 av. Thiers, Nice*). **La Poste main post office** (✉ *Pl. Celli, St-Tropez*).**Web Center** (✉ *24 rue Hoche, Cannes* ☎ *04–93–68–72–37*).

LODGING

APARTMENT & VILLA RENTALS

The tourist offices of individual towns often publish lists of *locations meublés* (furnished rentals), sometimes vouched for by the tourist office and rated for comfort. Gîtes de France is a nationwide organization that rents *gîtes ruraux* (rural vacation lodgings) by the week, usually outstanding examples of a region's character. The headquarters for the regions covered in this chapter are listed below. Write or call for a catalog, then make a selection and reservation.

Local Agents Gîtes de France des Alpes-Maritimes (✉ *55 promenade des Anglais, B.P. 1602, Cedex 01, 06011 Nice* ☎ *04–92–15–21–30* 📠 *04–93–86–01–06* ⊕ *www.gites-de-france-alpes-maritimes.com*).

Gîtes de France Var (✉ *Rond-Point du 4 Décembre 1974, B.P. 215, 83006 Draguignan Cedex* ☎ *04–94–50–93–93* 📠 *04–94–50–93–90*).

MEDIA

The *Nice Matin* (published in Nice) is the leading regional daily along the coast. The *International Herald Tribune* is the only English-language daily to reliably hit newsstands on the day of publication while *www.angloinfo.com* is a local Web site that daily lists articles (in English) from a selection of newspapers from around the world.

TOUR OPTIONS

BUS TOURS

Santa Azur organizes all-day or half-day bus excursions to sights near Nice, including Monaco, Cannes, and nearby hill towns, either leaving from its offices or from several stops along the Promenade des Anglais, mainly in front of the big hotels. In Antibes, Phocéens Voyages organizes similar bus explorations of the region.

Fees & Schedules Phocéens Voyages (✉ *8 pl. de Gaulle, Antibes* ☎ *04–93–34–15–98*). **Santa Azur** (✉ *11 av. Jean-Médecin, Nice* ☎ *04–93–85–46–81*).

TOUR GUIDES

The city of Nice arranges individual guided tours on an à la carte basis according to your needs. For information contact the Bureau d'Accueil and specify your dates and language preferences.

Contacts Bureau d'Accueil (☎ *04–93–14–48–00*).

VISITOR INFORMATION

For information on travel within the department of Var (St-Tropez to La Napoule), write to the Comité Départemental du Tourisme du Var. The Comité Régional du Tourisme Riviera Côte d'Azur provides information on tourism throughout the department of Alpes-Maritimes, from Cannes to the Italian border. For information on the Belle Epoque splendors of the region, log on to the helpful Comité Régional

Web site ⊕ *www.guideriviera.com* and click on "Belle Epoque." Local tourist offices (*Office du Tourisme*) in major towns discussed in this chapter are listed below by town.

Tourist Information **Antibes/Juan-les-Pins** (✉ *11 pl. de Gaulle, 06600 Antibes* ☎ *04-92-90-53-00* 🖷 *04-92-90-53-01*). **Cannes** (✉ *Palais des Festivals, Esplanade G. Pompidou, B.P. 272, 06403* ☎ *04-93-39-24-53* 🖷 *04-92-99-84-23* ⊕ *www.cannes-on-line.com*). **Comité Départmental du Tourisme du Var** (✉ *1 bd. Maréchal Foch, 83300 Draguignan* ☎ *03-94-50-55-50* 🖷 *04-94-50-55-51* ⊕ *www.ville-Draguignan.fr*). **Comité Régional du Tourisme Riviera Côte d'Azur** (✉ *55 promenade des Anglais, B.P. 1602, Cedex 1, 06011 Nice* ☎ *04-93-37-78-78* ⊕ *www.crt-riviera.fr*). **Èze** (✉ *Pl. du Général de Gaulle, 06360* ☎ *04-93-41-26-00* 🖷 *04-93-41-04-80* ⊕ *www.eze-riviera.com*). **Fréjus** (✉ *325 rue Jean-Jaurès, B.P. 8, 83601* ☎ *04-94-51-83-83* 🖷 *04-94-51-00-26* ⊕ *www.ville-frejus.fr*). **Grasse** (✉ *Palais des Congrès, 22 Cours Honoré Cresp, 06130* ☎ *04-93-36-66-66* 🖷 *04-93-36-86-36* ⊕ *www.grasse-riviera.com*). **Menton** (✉ *Palais de l'Europe, Av. Boyer, 06500* ☎ *04-92-41-76-76* 🖷 *04-92-41-76-78* ⊕ *www.villedementon. com*). **Monaco** (✉ *2a bd. des Moulins, 98000 Monte Carlo* ☎ *377/92-16-61-66* 🖷 *377/92-16-60-00* ⊕ *www.monaco-tourism.com*). **Nice** (✉ *5 promenade des Anglais, 06000* ☎ *04-92-14-48-00* 🖷 *04-92-14-48-03* ⊕ *www.nicetourism.com*) or in person at the train station or airport. **St-Jean-Cap-Ferrat** (✉ *59 av. Denis Semeria, 06230* ☎ *04-93-76-08-90* 🖷 *04-93-76-16-67* ⊕ *www.ville-saint-jean-cap-ferrat.fr*). **St-Paul-de-Vence** (✉ *2 rue Grande, 06570* ☎ *04-93-32-86-95* 🖷 *04-93-32-60-27*). **St-Raphaël** (✉ *Rue Waldeck-Rousseau, 83700* ☎ *04-94-19-52-52* 🖷 *04-94-83-85-40* ⊕ *www.saint-raphael.com*). **St-Tropez** (✉ *Quai Jean-Jaurès, B.P. 183, 83992* ☎ *04-94-97-45-21* 🖷 *04-94-97-82-66* ⊕ *www. ot-saint-tropez.com*). **Vence** (✉ *Pl. du Grand Jardin, 06140* ☎ *04-93-58-06-38* 🖷 *04-93-58-91-81* ⊕ *www.ville-vence.fr*).

The Midi-Pyrénées & Languedoc-Roussillon

Carcassonne

WORD OF MOUTH

"Set about 40 km (20 mi) from the Mediterranean, Céret is a truly delightful little town. It has a distinctly Catalan air as opposed to French; people still dance the Sardana in this valley and it's not an affectation for tourists but a real part of their cross-border Catalan cultural heritage."

—DrDoGood

WELCOME TO THE MIDI-PYRÉNÉES & LANGUEDOC-ROUSSILLON

TOP REASONS TO GO

★ **Matisse Madness:** Captivating Collioure, the main town of the Côte Vermeille, was where Matisse and Derain went mad with color and created the Fauvist art movement in the early 20th century.

★ **Fairy–tale Carcassone:** With storybook towers, turrets, and battlements, medieval Carcassonne is the greatest sand castle ever built that didn't wash away.

★ **Tumultuous Toulouse:** With rosy roofs and red-brick mansions, the "pink city" of Toulouse is a place where high culture is an evening at an outdoor café, an art form perfected by the 80,000 students who make this city tick.

★ **Albi's Toulouse-Lautrec:** Presided over by its fortress-like Cathédrale Ste-Cécile, Albi honors its most famous native son, Toulouse-Lautrec, with the largest museum of his works.

★ **Cordes in the Sky:** This picture-postcard refuge built for the Counts of Toulouse in the Middle Ages redefines the idea of a *village perché* in a startling situation.

1 Toulouse. Now the center of Europe's high-tech aviation industry (Airbus is here), the city sees itself as the modern gateway to the south. Happily, Toulouse's new high-tech attitude hasn't infringed on the well-preserved *centre ville*, a veritable museum of mansions, where the brick-paved streets make you feel like you're in a small town and aerospace engineers own Renaissance houses.

Outdoor market in Toulouse

2 Albi & the Gers. Some 75 km (47 mi) northeast of Toulouse is **Albi**, set along the Tarn River and once a major center of the Cathars; the huge Cathédrale Ste-Cécile was a symbol of the church's victory of these heretics. Day-trip to the west to **Cordes-sur-Ciel**—the oldest and best preserved of the Renaissance *bastides* (planned towns)—and **Moissac**, where art lovers can relish the Romanesque at the abbey church of St-Pierre.

12

GETTING ORIENTED

Spend some time in the Midi-Pyrénées, the country's largest region, and the term "the south of France" takes on new meaning. This western half of France's south is less glamorous (and much less expensive) than the Riviera and Provence but has an array of must-sees, beginning with lively Toulouse. South lies Languedoc, a province of contrasts—of rolling sun-baked plains around storybook Carcassonne, of stone-and-shrub-covered hills spiked with ruins of ancient civilizations. Stretching east to the Mediterranean is the southernmost province of Roussillon, so called from the red color of the earth and home to that artists' paradise, the Vermillion Coast.

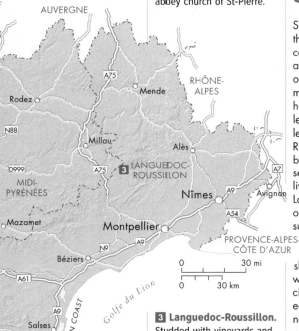

3 Languedoc-Roussillon. Studded with vineyards and art treasures, Languedoc is a vast province that ranges from Toulouse in the Pyrenean hills eastward to aristocratic **Montpellier** set on the Mediterranean. In between are famous sights like **Carcassonne**—the largest medieval town extant—and *le littoral languedocien* (the Languedoc coast), where France's "second Riviera" draws both artists and sunworshippers to **Collioure** and other towns along the **Côte Vermeille**.

Place de la Comedie, Montpellier

MIDI-PYRÉNÉES & LANGUEDOC-ROUSSILLON PLANNER

How's the Weather?

You can expect pleasantly warm weather as early as April and as late as October, but be prepared for rainstorms and/or heat waves at almost any time.

The weather is especially unpredictable in the Pyrénées: a few passing clouds can rapidly turn into a full-blown storm.

Needless to say, during July and August towns high on tourist lists—like Albi, Carcassonne, and Collioure—are packed.

So perhaps opt for April and May, which are delightful months on the Côte Vermeille, and it is also the time when the Pyrenean flowers are at their best.

June and September (grape-picking season, or *vendange*) are equally good for the inland points. As October draws near, the chilly winds of winter begin to appear and frenzied mushroom hunters ferret amid the chestnut and pine trees.

No matter what the season, there is plenty to occupy the outdoorsman here, whether it be hiking the Grandes Randonnées (GRs) paths, scaling lofty peaks, or skiing sun-dappled snow fields.

The Grand Tour

The Midi-Pyrénées and Languedoc-Roussillon form the main body of France's traditional southwestern region. Sports-and nature-lovers flock here to enjoy the natural attributes of the area, of which Toulouse—a university town of rosy pink brick—is the cultural star. Here, too, are Albi and its wonderful Toulouse-Lautrec Museum; Moissac and its famous Romanesque cloister; the once-upon-a-timeliness of Carcassonne; and the relatively undiscovered city of Montpellier. And when you see picturesque Collioure's stunning Mediterranean setting, you can understand why Matisse went color-berserk. Getting to know this vast region would take several weeks, or even years. But it's possible to sample all its finest offerings in nine days, if that's all the time you have.

Begin by practicing your "Olé's" in Spanish-soul Toulouse; then head west to the Gers département and take in the famous Romanesque sculptures of the abbey church at Moissac.

On Day 3 head east to Cordes-sur-Ciel, a fortified village, for a wonderful dip in the Middle Ages. Spend the night in Albi, and take a virtual art class with Toulouse-Lautrec at the famous museum here devoted to his masterworks. On the fourth day head some 112 km (70 mi) south to storybook Carcassonne to introduce your kids to the Puss in Boots fantasy of this castellated wonder. After a night filled with medieval history and glamour, head south on Day 5 to Céret, a town of rocky ridges and red rooftops immortalized by Picasso.

On Day 6, pack your crayons for a trip to Matisse Country on the Vermilion Coast and head to Roussillon's most picturesque coastal town, Collioure, to channel the spirits of the famous Fauve painters. Then on Day 7, drive north to Perpignan, the historic hub city of the Roussillon, and head out of the region to discover the sights of Narbonne.

On Day 8, make a detour to Minerve, a medieval hilltop village, then head back northeast past the Languedoc frontier to spend your last night in Montpellier; on Day 9 tour this city's fascinating Vieille Ville, steeped in culture, history, and young blood (a famous university is based here).

Finding a Place to Eat

As a rule, the closer you get to the Mediterranean coast, the later you dine and the more you pay for your seafood platter and that bottle of iced rosé. The farther you travel from the coast, the higher the altitude, the more rustic the setting you'll find yourself in, and the more reasonable the prices will be. During the scorching summer months in sleepy mountain villages, lunches are light, interminable, and *bien arrosé* (French for "with lots of wine"). Here you can also find that small personal restaurant where the chickens roasting on spits above the open fire have first names and the cheese comes from the hippie couple down the road who came here in the '60s and love their mountains, their goats, and the universe in general.

Finding a Place to Stay

Hotels range from Mediterranean modern to medieval baronial to Pyrenean chalet; most are small and cozy rather than luxurious and sophisticated. Toulouse has the usual range of big-city hotels; make reservations well in advance if you plan to visit in spring or fall. Look for *gîtes d'étape* (hikers' way stations) and *table d'hôtes* (bed-and-breakfasts), which offer excellent value and a chance to meet local and international travelers and sample life on the farm, as well as the delights of *cuisine du terroir* (country cooking). As for off-season—if there is such a thing, since chic Parisians often arrive in November in their SUVs with a hunger for the authentic—call ahead and double-check when hotels close for their annual hibernation (which usually starts sometime in winter, either before, or right after, the Christmas holidays). Assume that all hotel rooms have air-conditioning, TV, telephones, and private bath, unless otherwise noted.

WHAT IT COSTS

	¢	$	$$	$$$	$$$$
Restaurants	Under €11	€11–€17	€17–€23	€23–€30	Over €30
Hotels	Under €50	€50–€80	€80–€120	€120–€190	Over €190

Restaurant prices are per person for a main course at dinner, including tax (19.6%) and service; note that if a restaurant offers only prix-fixe (set-price) meals, it has been given the price category that reflects the full prix-fixe price. Hotel prices are for a standard double room in high season, including tax (19.6%) and service charge. Hotels operate on the European Plan (EP, with no meal provided) unless we note that they use the Breakfast Plan (BP), or also offer such options as Modified American Plan (MAP, with breakfast and dinner daily, known as demi-pension), or Full American Plan (FAP, or pension complète, with three meals a day). Inquire when booking if these all-inclusive meal plans (which always entail higher rates) are mandatory or optional.

Introduction
by George
Semler

Updated by
John Fanning

LIKE THE MOST CELEBRATED DISH of this area, cassoulet, the southwestern region of France is a feast of diverse ingredients. Just as it would be a gross oversimimplification to refer to cassoulet merely as a dish of baked beans, southwestern France is much more than just Toulouse, the peaks of the Pyrénées, and the fairy-tale ramparts of Carcassonne. Rolling, sunbaked plains and rock- and shrub-covered hills dotted with ruins of ancient civilizations parallel the burning coastline; the fortifications and cathedrals of once-great cities like Béziers and Narbonne rise like ghosts from the Mediterranean haze; and Collioure and the famed Côte Vermeille, immortalized by Matisse and Derain, nestle colorfully just north of the border with Spain. Nevertheless, the city of Toulouse remains the cultural and human hub of this rich corner of France. Serving as gateway to the region, alive with music, sculpture, and architectural gems, and vibrant with students, Toulouse is all that more famous regional capitals would like to have remained, or to become. Sinuously spread along the romantic banks of the Garonne as it meanders north and west from the Catalan Pyrénées on its way to the Atlantic, "La Ville Rose"—so called for its redbrick buildings—has a Spanish sensuality unique in all Gaul, a feast for eyes and ears alike. Toulouse was the ancient capital of the province called Languedoc, so christened when it became royal property in 1270, meaning the country where *oc*—instead of the *oil* or *oui* of northeastern France—meant yes.

Outside Toulouse, the terrain of the Midi-Pyrénées and Languedoc-Roussillon is studded with highlights, like so many raisins sweetening up a spicy stew. Albi, with its Toulouse-Lautrec legacy, is a star attraction, while each outlying town—from Moissac to Cordes-sur-Ciel—has artistic and architectural treasures waiting to be uncovered. Besides Albi's Toulouse-Lautrec Museum, other art museums await, including Céret's Musée d'Art Moderne, which is packed with Picassos, Braques, and Chagalls.

Céret, in fact, is the gateway to an "open-air museum" prized by artists and poets: the Côte Vermeille, or Vermilion Coast, centered around the fishing village of Collioure, where Matisse, Derain, and the Fauvists committed chromatic mayhem in the early years of the 20th century. They were called the Fauves, or "wild beasts," partly because their colors were taken from the savage tones found in Mother Nature hereabouts. Where Matisse, Derain, Picasso, Gris, and Braque first vacationed and painted, thousands soon followed. A town of espadrille merchants, anchovy packers, and lateen-rigged fishing boats in the shadow of its 13th-century Château Royal, Collioure is now as much a magnet for tourists as it once was and still is a lure for artists. Today, the town—set with narrow, cobbled streets and pink-and-mauve houses—is a living museum, as you can discover by touring its Route du Fauvisme, where 20 points along a route through town compare reproductions of noted Fauvist canvases with the actual scenes that were depicted in them (view-finder picture frames let you see how little has changed in eight decades).

The view of the fabled Côte Vermeille from the Alberes mountain range reveals a bright-yellow strand of beach curving north and east toward the Camargue wetlands. From the vineyards above Banyuls-sur-Mer to the hills once traversed by Hannibal and his regiment of elephants, this storied coast retains a Spanish tinge, reminding us that the province of Roussillon was once part of Catalonia (just over the border to the south) and the veritable crown of Aragon's medieval Mediterranean empire. The Mediterranean smooth and opalescent at dawn; villagers dancing Sardanas to the music of the raucous and ancient woodwind *flavioles* and *tenores*; the flood of golden light so peculiar to the Mediterranean...everything about this fabled vacation region seems to be asking to be immortalized in oil on canvas.

EXPLORING THE MIDI-PYRÉNÉES & LANGUEDOC-ROUSSILLON

France's largest region, Midi-Pyrénées spreads from the Dordogne in the north to the Spanish border along the Pyrénées. Radiating out from Toulouse to the surrounding towns of Albi and Moissac, and up through the Ariège Valley into the Pyrénées Orientales, the central and southern parts of the Midi-Pyrénées are rich in history, natural resources, art, and architecture. Languedoc-Roussillon extends west to east from Carcassonne to the Mediterranean. South to north, it ranges from Collioure through Perpignan, Narbonne, Beziers, and Montpellier, all once part of "French Catalonia." Montpellier is at the dead center of the Mediterranean coastline, a five-hour train ride from Paris and Nice, as well as from Barcelona.

This chapter divides the region into three sections. The first covers the lively city of Toulouse. The second encompasses the area to the north and west of Toulouse, including the Gers *département,* Albi, the Lot Valley, and verdant Gascony. The third extends southeast into Languedoc-Roussillon and up the Mediterranean coast to the now-inland crossroads of Narbonne.

TOULOUSE: LA VILLE ROSE

GETTING HERE

If you train to Toulouse you arrive at its Gare Matabiau (☎05–61–10–11–04), which is right beside the Toulouse Gare Routiere (bus station), on Boulevard Pierré-Sémard. The Gare Routière (☎05–61–61–67–67) is also where the airport shuttle—every 20 minutes (⊕*www.navetteviatoulouse.com*)—leaves you off from Blagnac Airport (☎08–25–38–00–00), about 7 mi to the northwest. If you want the TGV (⊕*www.tgv.com*) there are around nine a day from Paris at about €75 a go.

EXPLORING

The ebullient city of Toulouse is the capital of the Midi-Pyrénées and the fourth-largest city in France. Just 100 km (60 mi) from the border with Spain, Toulouse's flavor is in many ways closer to southern European Spanish than to northern European French. Weathered redbrick buildings line sidewalks, giving the city its nickname, "La Ville Rose" (the Pink City). Downtown, the sidewalks and restaurants pulse late into the night with tourists, workers, college students, and technicians from the giant Airbus aviation complex headquartered outside the city.

Toulouse was founded in the 4th century bc and quickly became an important part of Roman Gaul. In turn, it was made into a Visigothic and Carolingian capital before becoming a separate county in 843. Ruling from this Pyrenean hub— one of the great artistic and literary capitals of medieval Europe—the counts of Toulouse held sovereignty over nearly all of the Languedoc and maintained a brilliant court known for its fine troubadours and literature. In the early 13th century Toulouse was attacked and plundered by troops representing an alliance between the northern French nobility and the papacy, ostensibly to wipe out the Albigensian heresy (Catharism), but more realistically as an expansionist move against the power of Occitania, the French southwest. The counts toppled, but Toulouse experienced a cultural and economic rebirth thanks to the *woad* (dye) trade; consequently, wealthy merchants' homes constitute a major portion of Toulouse's architectural patrimony.

> **GETTING AROUND**
>
> For the most part, Toulouse's hotels, restaurants, and sights are within walking distance of one another. The main square of the *centre ville* (town center) is Place du Capitole, a good 15-minute walk from the train station but only a few blocks away from the city's other focal points—Place Wilson, Place Esquirol, and Basilique St-Sernin. The métro still has only one line but conveniently connects the Gare Matabiau with Place du Capitole and Place Esquirol. The Servat bus system is efficient, too.

Toulouse, at the intersection of the Garonne and the Canal du Midi, midway between the Massif Central and the Pyrénées, became an important nexus between Aquitania, Languedoc, and the Roussillon. Today Toulouse is France's second-largest university town after Paris and the center of France's aeronautical industry.

OLD TOULOUSE

The area between the boulevards and the Garonne forms the historic nucleus of Toulouse. Originally part of Roman Gaul and later the capital for the Visigoths and then the Carolingians, by ad 1000 Toulouse was one of the artistic and literary centers of medieval Europe. Despite its 13th-century defeat by the lords of northern France, Toulouse quickly reemerged as a cultural and commercial power and has remained so ever since. Religious and civil structures bear witness to this illustrious past, even as the city's booming student life mirrors a dynamic present. This is the heart of Toulouse, with Place du Capitole at its center.

The huge garage beneath Place du Capitole is a good place to park, and offers easy walking distance to all the major sites. If you leave your car in another garage, you can take the subway that runs north–south to central Toulouse; it costs €1.30.

THE MAIN ATTRACTIONS

⑤ **Basilique St-Sernin.** Toulouse's most
Fodor'sChoice famous landmark and the world's
★ largest Romanesque church once belonged to a Benedictine abbey, built in the 11th century to house pilgrims on their way to Santiago de Compostela in Spain. Inside, the aesthetic high point is the magnificent central apse, begun

TRIP TIP

If you intend to see a lot of Toulouse's sights then you should invest in a "City Pass" (Carte Privilegé). It's €10 and allows you half price on all the sites. Also, go to www.toulouse-tourisme. com for details on the City Pass program for reduced bookings on selected hotels.

12

in 1080, glittering with gilded ceiling frescoes, which date from the 19th century. When illuminated at night, St-Sernin's five-tier octagonal tower glows red against the sky. Not all the tiers are the same: the first three, with their rounded windows, are Romanesque; the upper two, with pointed Gothic windows, were added around 1300. The ancient crypt contains the relics and reliquaries of 128 saints, but the most famous item on view is a thorn that legend says is from the Crown of Thorns. ⊠ *Pl. Saint-Sernin* ☎ *05–61–21–80–45* ⛫ *Crypt €3* ☉ *Daily 8:30–11:45 and 2–5:45.*

② **Capitole/Hôtel de Ville** *(Capitol/Town Hall).* The 18th-century Capitole is home to the Hôtel de Ville and the city's highly regarded opera company. The reception rooms are open to the public when not in use for official functions or weddings. Halfway up the **Grand Escalier** (Grand Staircase) hangs a large painting of the *Jeux Floraux*, the "floral games" organized by a literary society created in 1324 to promote the local Occitanian language, Langue d'Oc. The festival continues to this day: poets give public readings here each May, and the best are awarded silver- and gold-plated violets, one of the emblems of Toulouse. At the top of the stairs is the **Salle Gervaise**, a hall adorned with a series of paintings inspired by the themes of love and marriage. The mural at the far end of the room portrays the Isle of Cythères, where Venus received her lovers, alluding to a French euphemism for getting married: *embarquer pour Cythères* (to embark for Cythères). More giant paintings in the **Salle Henri-Martin,** named for the artist (1860–1943), show the passing seasons set against the eternal Garonne. Look for Jean Jaurès (1859–1914), one of France's greatest socialist martyrs, in *Les Rêveurs* (*The Dreamers*); he's wearing a boater-style hat and a beige coat. At the far left end of the elegant **Salle des Illustres** (Hall of the Illustrious) is a large painting of a fortress under siege, portraying the women of Toulouse slaying Simon de Montfort, leader of the Albigensian crusade against the Cathars, during the siege of Toulouse in 1218. ⊠ *Pl. du Capitole* ☎ *05–61–22–34–12* ⛫ *Free* ☉ *Weekdays 9–7.*

★ **⑧** **Église des Jacobins.** An extraordinary structure built in the 1230s for the Dominicans (renamed Jacobins in 1216 for their Parisian base in Rue St-Jacques), the church is dominated by a single row of seven columns running the length of the nave. The easternmost column (on the far

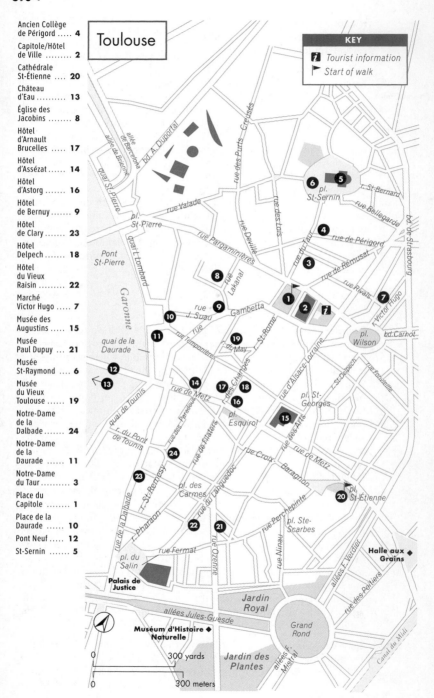

Toulouse

KEY

i Tourist information

▶ Start of walk

right) is one of the finest examples of palm-tree vaulting ever erected, the much-celebrated *Palmier des Jacobins*, a major masterpiece of Gothic art. Fanning out overhead, its 22 ribs support the entire apse. The original refectory site is used for temporary art exhibitions. The cloister is one of the city's aesthetic

PAR AVION

It was from Toulouse that Antoine de St-Exupéry—famed author of *The Little Prince*—pioneered mail flights to Africa and over the Atlantic to South America.

12

and acoustical gems and in summer hosts piano and early music concerts. ⊠*Rue Lakanal s/n* ☎*05–61–22–21–92* 🖃*Church free, cloister €3* ☉*Daily 10–7.*

⓮ **Hôtel d'Assézat.** Built in 1555 by Toulouse's top Renaissance architect, Nicolas Bachelier, this mansion, considered the city's most elegant, has arcades and ornately carved doorways. It's now home to the **Fondation Bemberg,** an exceptional collection of paintings ranging from Tiepolo to Toulouse-Lautrec, Monet, and Bonnard. ⊠*Rue de Metz* ☎*05–61–12–06–89* 🖃*€4.60* ☉*Tues.–Sun. 10–12:30 and 1:30–6.*

❾ **Hôtel de Bernuy.** Now part of a school, this mansion, around the corner from the Église des Jacobins, was built for Jean de Bernuy in the 16th century, the period when Toulouse was at its most prosperous. De Bernuy made his fortune exporting woad, the dark-blue dye that brought unprecedented wealth to 18th-century Toulouse. De Bernuy's success is reflected in the use of stone, a costly material in this region of brick, and by the octagonal stair tower. You may wander freely around the courtyard. ⊠*Rue Gambetta* ☉*Weekdays 8–6:30.*

★ ⓯ **Musée des Augustins** *(Augustinian Museum).* In this former medieval Augustinian convent, the museum uses the sacristy, chapter house, and cloisters for displaying an outstanding array of Romanesque sculpture and religious paintings. Built in Mediterranean-Gothic style, the architectural complex is vast and holds a collection rich with treasures and discoveries. ⊠*21 rue de Metz* ☎*05–61–22–21–82* 🖃*Museum €3, museum and special exhibits €5.50; museum free 1st Sun. of month* ☉*Daily 10–6.*

❻ **Musée St-Raymond.** The city's archaeological museum, next to the basilica of St-Sernin, has an extensive collection of imperial Roman busts, as well as ancient coins, vases, and jewelry. ⊠*Pl. St-Sernin* ☎*05–61–22–31–44* 🖃*€3* ☉*Daily 10–6.*

⓳ **Musée du Vieux Toulouse** *(Museum of Old Toulouse).* This museum is worthwhile for the building itself as much as for its collection of Toulouse memorabilia, paintings, sculptures, and documents. Be sure to note the ground-floor fireplace and wooden ceiling. ⊠*7 rue du May* ☎*05–62–27–11–50* 🖃*€2.20* ☉*Mid-May–mid-Oct., Mon.–Sat. 2–6.*

▶ ❶ **Place du Capitole.** This vast, open square in the city center, lined with shops and cafés, is a good spot for getting your bearings or for soaking up some spring or winter sun. A parking lot is conveniently underneath.

❿ Place de la Daurade. On the Garonne, this is one of Toulouse's nicest squares. A stop at the Café des Artistes is almost obligatory. The corner of the quai offers a romantic view of the Garonne, the Hôtel Dieu across the river, and the Pont Neuf.

⬛ NEED A BREAK? A 10-minute walk from the Basilique St-Sernin, you will find one of the oldest cafés in Toulouse, Le Concorde (⊠*17 rue de la Concorde*). This is the perfect place to sip a glass of Banyuls or a *demi* (glass of draft beer) and listen to an evening accordion concert of classic French cabaret.

ALSO WORTH SEEING

❹ Ancien Collège de Périgord *(Old Périgord College).* The wooden gallery-like structure on the street side of the courtyard is the oldest remnant of the 14th-century residential college. ⊠*56–58 rue du Taur.*

⓭ Château d'Eau. This 19th-century water tower at the far end of the Pont Neuf, once used to store water and build water pressure, is now used for photography exhibits (it was built in 1822, the same year Nicéphore Nièpce created the first permanent photographic images). ⊠*1 pl. Laganne* ☎*05–61–77–09–40* ⊠€*2.50* ⊙*Tues.–Sun. 1–7.*

⓱ Hôtel d'Arnault Brucelles. One of the tallest and best of Toulouse's 49 towers can be found at this 16th-century mansion. ⊠*19 rue des Changes.*

⓰ Hôtel d'Astorg et St-Germain. This 16th-century mansion is notable for its lovely Romanesque wooden stairways and galleries and for its top-floor *mirande*, a wooden balcony. ⊠*16 rue des Changes.*

⓲ Hôtel Delpech. Look for the 17th-century biblical inscriptions carved in Latin in the stone under the windows. ⊠*20 rue des Changes.*

❼ Marché Victor Hugo *(Victor Hugo Market).* This hangarlike indoor market is always a refreshing stop. Consider eating lunch at one of the seven upstairs restaurants. **Chez Attila,** just to the left at the top of the stairs, is the best of them. ⊠*Pl. Victor-Hugo.*

⓫ Notre-Dame de la Daurade. Overlooking the Garonne is this 18th-century church. The name *Daurade* comes from *doré* (gilt), referring to the golden reflection given off by the mosaics decorating the 5th-century temple to the Virgin Mary that once stood on this site. ⊠*1 pl. de la Daurade.*

❸ Notre-Dame du Taur. Built on the spot where St. Saturnin (or Sernin), the martyred bishop of Toulouse, was dragged to his death in ad 250 by a rampaging bull, this church is famous for its *cloche-mur,* or wall tower. The wall looks like an extension of the facade and has inspired many similar versions throughout the region. ⊠*Rue du Taur.*

⓬ Pont Neuf *(New Bridge).* Despite its name, the graceful span of the Pont Neuf opened to traffic in 1632. The remains of the old bridge—one arch and the lighter-color outline on the brick wall of the **Hôtel-Dieu** (hospital)—are visible across the river. The 16th-century hospital was used for pilgrims on their way to Santiago de Compostela. Just over the bridge, on a clear day in winter, the snowcapped peaks of the Pyrénées are often visible in the distance, said to be a sign of imminent rain.

SOUTH OF RUE DE METZ

South of Rue de Metz you'll discover the cathedral of St-Étienne, the antiques district along Rue Perchepinte, and town houses and palaces along the way on Rue Ninau, Rue Ozenne, and Rue de la Dalbade—all among the top sights in Toulouse.

A TAXING MATTER

At the intersection of Rue des Changes and Rue des Temponiéres you can find a building with trompe l'oeil windows. These bricked-in apertures are a reminder of the window tax that all citizens of Toulouse struggled so mightily to avoid centuries ago.

12

SIGHTS TO SEE

20 **Cathédrale St-Étienne.** The cathedral was erected in stages between the 11th and the 17th century, though the nave and choir languished unfinished because of a lack of funds. A fine collection of 16th- and 17th-century tapestries traces the life of St. Stephen. In front of the cathedral is the city's oldest fountain, dating from the 16th century. ⊠*Pl. St-Étienne* ☎*05–61–21–27–60* ⊙*Mon.–Sat. 8–7, Sun. 9–7.*

23 **Hôtel de Clary.** This mansion, known as the Hôtel de Pierre because of its unusually solid *pierre* (stone) construction—at the time considered a sign of great wealth—is one of the finest 16th-century mansions on the street. The ornately sculpted stone facade was designed by Nicolas Bachelier in the 16th century. ⊠*25 rue de la Dalbade.*

22 **Hôtel du Vieux Raisin.** Officially the Hôtel Beringuier Maynier, named for the original owner, the house became the Vieux Raisin (Old Grape) after the early name of the street and even earlier inn. Built in the 15th and 16th centuries, the mansion has an octagonal tower, male and female figures on the facade, and allegorical sculptures of the three stages of life—infancy, maturity, and old age—over the windows to the left. ⊠*36 rue de Languedoc.*

21 **Musée Paul Dupuy.** This museum, dedicated to medieval applied arts, is housed in the Hôtel Pierre Besson, a 17th-century mansion. ⊠*13 rue de la Pleau* ☎*05–61–14–65–50* ⊠*€3* ⊙*Daily 10–5.*

24 **Notre-Dame de la Dalbade.** Originally Sancta Maria de Ecclesia Alba, in Langue d'Oc (Ste-Marie de l'Église Blanche, in French, or St. Mary of the White Church—*alba* meaning "white"), the name of the church evolved into "de Albata" and later "Dalbade." Ironically, one of its outstanding features today is the colorful 19th-century ceramic tympanum over the Renaissance door. ⊠*Pl. de la Dalbade.*

WHERE TO STAY & EAT

$$$–$$$$ ✕ **Cosi Fan Tutte.** Just steps from Rue Perchepinte and the Musée Paul Dupuy, this Italian specialist might be a welcome change from the web-footed deluge of southwestern French cuisine. *Saint-Jacques poêlés* (scallops) are the cry from mid-January to mid-April, while truffles and

EATING WELL

Dining in France's Southwest is a rougher, heartier, and more rustic version of classic Mediterranean cooking—the peppers are sliced thick, the garlic and olive oil used with a heavier hand, the herbs crushed and served au naturel.

Expect *cuisine de marché*, market-based cooking, savory seasonal dishes based on the culinary trinity of the south—garlic, onion, and tomato—straight from the village market. Languedoc is known for powerful and strongly seasoned cooking.

Garlic and goose fat are generously used in traditional recipes. Be sure to try some of the renowned foie gras (goose or duck liver) and *confit de canard* (preserved duck). The most famous regional dish is cas-

soulet, a succulent white-bean stew with *confit d'oie* (preserved goose), duck, lamb, or, a mixture of all three.

Keep your eyes open for festive *cargolades*—huge communal barbecues starting off with thousands of buttery-garlic snails roasted on open grills and eaten with your fingers, followed by cured bacon and lamb cutlets and vats (and vats) of local wine. In the Roussillon and along the Mediterranean coast from Collioure up through Perpignan to Narbonne, the prevalent Catalan cuisine features olive oil–based cooking and sauces such as the classic *aioli* (crushed and emulsified garlic and olive oil). When you're on the coast, it's fish of course, often cooked over wood coals.

pigeon also find their way onto a menu that changes constantly with the market. ⊠*8 rue Mage* ☎*05–61–53–07–24* ☰*MC, V* ⊘*Closed Sun., Mon., Aug. 1–22, and Dec. 22–30.*

$$$–$$$$ ✕ **Jardins de l'Opéra.** Stephan Tourne's elegant restaurant next to the Grand Hôtel de l'Opéra is a perennial favorite. Intimate rooms and a covered terrace around a little pond make for undeniable charm, though some will find the grand flourishes—glass ceilings and mammoth chandeliers—a little, too, well, operatic, and might prefer the adjacent brasserie, Grand Café de l'Opéra. The food is gastronomique local fare, with seductive nouvelle or Gascon touches such as the ravioli stuffed with foie gras and truffle sauce. ⊠*1 pl. du Capitole* ☎*05–61–23–07–76* ⚐*Reservations essential* ☰*AE, MC, V* ⊘*Closed Sun., Mon., and Aug.*

$$$–$$$$ ✕ **Le 19.** Centrally placed across the street from the Hôtel Garonne and next to the Pont Neuf, this lovely former 16th-century fish market has vaulted ceilings that will take your breath (but not your appetite) away. Sleek contemporary design and international cuisine combine happily here. ⊠*19 descente de la Halle aux Poissons* ☎*05–34–31–94–84* ☰*AE, DC, MC, V* ⊘*Closed Sun., May 1–8, Aug. 5–22, and Dec. 24–Jan. 6. No lunch Sat. or Mon.*

$$$–$$$$ ✕ **Michel Sarran.** This clean-lined post-nouvelle haven for what is argu-
Fodor'sChoice ably Toulouse's finest dining departs radically from traditional stick-to-
★ your-ribs southwest France cuisine in favor of Mediterranean formulas suited to the rhythms and reasons of modern living. Foie-gras soup with belon oysters and *liègeois du bar* (sea perch) are two examples of Michel Sarran's light but flavorful cuisine. ⊠*21 bd. A. Duportal*

☎05–61–12–32–32 ⚑*Reservations essential* 🟰*AE, DC, MC, V* ⊘*Closed weekends, July 30–Aug., and Jan. No lunch Wed.*

$$–$$$ ✕ **L'Empereur de Huê.** This sleek-lined contemporary space, open for dinner only, produces traditional Vietnamese cuisine at attractive prices. Soup dumplings and pea shoots are always excellent here, as are the duck-based dishes, without exception. ✉*17 rue Couteliers* ☎*05–61–53–55–72* 🟰*AE, DC, MC, V* ⊘*No lunch.*

★ $–$$$ ✕ **Brasserie Flo "Les Beaux Arts."** Overlooking the Pont Neuf, this elegant brasserie is the place to be at sunset, as painters Ingres and Matisse knew all too well. Watch the colors change over the Garonne from a quayside window or a sidewalk table while enjoying delicious seafood, including four varieties of oysters. The house white wine, a local St-Lannes from the nearby Gers region, is fresh and fruity yet dry, and the service is impeccable. ✉*1 quai de la Daurade* ☎*05–61–21–12–12* 🟰*AE, MC, V.*

$–$$ ✕ **Au Bon Vivre.** This intimate restaurant lined with tables with red-check tablecloths fills up at lunch and dinner every day. Quick, unpretentious, and always good, the house specialties include such dishes as cod, venison, and cassoulet. ✉*15 pl. Wilson* ☎*05–61–23–07–17* 🟰*AE, DC, MC, V.*

★ $–$$ ✕ **La Corde.** This little hideaway is worth taking the time to find. Built into a lovely 15th-century corner tower hidden in the courtyard of the 16th-century Hôtel Bolé, La Corde claims the distinction of being the oldest restaurant in Toulouse. Try the *effiloché de canard aux pêches* (shredded duck with caramelized peach). ✉*4 rue Jules-Chalande* ☎*05–61–29–09–43* 🟰*AE, DC, MC, V* ⊘*Closed Sun. No lunch Mon.*

★ $$$–$$$$ 🏨 **Grand Hôtel de l'Opéra.** In a former 17th-century convent, this downtown doyen has an old-world feel with 21st-century amenities. Little wonder the likes of Deneuve, Pavarotti, and Aznavour favored this place. Grandeur is the keynote in the lobby, complete with soaring columns and Second Empire bergères and sofas of tasseled velvet. Guest rooms are plush, with rich fabrics, painted headboards, and the most *chaleureuse* (cozy and warm) colors, with the best overlooking the grand square outside. Even though you're on busy Place du Capitole, this hotel is a tranquil oasis. ✉*1 pl. du Capitole, 31000* ☎*05–61–21–82–66* 🖨*05–61–23–41–04* ⊕*www.grand-hotel-opera.com* ⇆*57 rooms* ⌂*In-room: refrigerator, Wi-Fi (some). In-hotel: 2 restaurants, bar, gym, parking (fee)* 🟰*AE, DC, MC, V.*

$$$ 🏨 **Hôtel Garonne.** In the thick of the most Toulousain part of town,
Fodor'sChoice next to the Pont Neuf and the former fish market, this is a small but
★ hyper-stylish spot. Modern guest rooms are strikingly done up in bold reds and blacks with rich wood trims; the best suite has a view of the Garonne. The restaurant, Le 19, is spectacular, set in a vast hemispherical brick-laid room, with soigné seating, high-art lighting, and nouvelle versions of regional dishes. A final plus: the staff is cheery and helpful. ✉*22 descente de la Halle aux Poissons, 31000* ☎*05–34–31–94–80* 🖨*05–34–31–94–81* ⊕*www.hotelsdecharmetoulouse.com* ⇆*14 rooms* ⌂*In-room: refrigerator, ethernet. In-hotel: parking (fee)* 🟰*AE, DC, MC, V.*

$–$$ ⊡ **Grand Hôtel d'Orléans.** This picturesque former stagecoach relay station was built in 1867 and still retains a certain 19th-century charm. Four floors of wooden balustrades overhung with plants look down over a central patio. Guest rooms are small and cozy. ⊠*72 rue Bayard, near Matabiau railroad station, 31000* ☎*05–61–62–98–47* 🖷*05–61–62–78–24* ⊕*www.grand-hotel-orleans.fr* ⇖*56 rooms* ⚲*In-room: Wi-Fi. In-hotel: restaurant, parking (fee), some pets allowed (fee)* ▭*AE, MC, V.*

$–$$ ⊡ **Hôtel Albert I.** The building may seem undistinguished and the reception hall is no Versailles, but the rooms are cheerful and spacious (especially the older ones with giant fireplaces and mirrors). The extremely warm and personable owner, Madame Hilaire, is on hand to give suggestions of all kinds. A continental breakfast is served, and nearby parking can be arranged by the hotel. ⊠*8 rue Rivals, 31000* ☎*05–61–21–17–91* 🖷*05–61–21–09–64* ⊕*www.hotelalbert1.com* ⇖*48 rooms* ⚲*In-room: ethernet. In-hotel: parking (fee), some pets allowed (fee)* ▭*AE, MC, V.*

NIGHTLIFE & THE ARTS

For a schedule of events, contact the city tourist office. If you want to stay up late—as many do in Toulouse—a complete list of clubs and discos can be found in the annual *Toulouse Pratique (⊕www. leguidetoulousepratique.com)*, available at any newsstand. As for cultural highlights, so many opera singers perform at the **Théâtre du Capitole** and the **Halle aux Grains** that the city is known as the *capitale du bel canto*. The opera season lasts from October until late May, with occasional summer presentations as well. A wide variety of dance companies perform in Toulouse: the **Ballet du Capitole** stages classical ballets; **Ballet-Théâtre Joseph Russillo** and **Compagnie Jean-Marc Matos** put on modern-dance performances. The **Centre National Choréographique de Toulouse** welcomes international companies each year in the St-Cyprien quarter.

The most exciting music venue in Toulouse is the auditorium-in-the-round **Halle Aux Grains** (⊠*Pl. Dupuy* ☎*05–61–63–13–13*). **Théâtre du Capitole** (⊠*Pl. du Capitole* ☎*05–61–22–31–31*) is the orchestra, opera, and ballet specialist. **Théâtre Daniel Sorano** (⊠*35 allée Jules-Guesde* ☎*05–61–25–66–87*) stages dramatic productions and concerts. **Théâtre de la Digue** (⊠*3 rue de la Digue* ☎*05–61–42–97–79*) is a theater and dance venue.

Begin your night on the town at **Père Louis** (⊠*45 rue des Tourneurs* ☎*05–61–21–33–45*), an old-fashioned winery (and restaurant), with barrels used as tables plus vintage photographs. **Bar Basque** (⊠*7 pl. St-Pierre* ☎*05–61–21–55–64*) is one of the many good watering holes around Place St-Pierre. **Chez Ton Ton** (⊠*16 pl. St-Pierre* ☎*05–61–21–89–54*), always a brawl, is another appealing Place St-Pierre dive. **Le Bistro Etienne** (⊠*5 rue Riguepels* ☎*05–61–25–20–41*), near the Cathedral of St-Étienne, is a hot spot for the third-Thursday-in-November Beaujolais Nouveau blowout. Brazilian guitarists perform at **La Bonita**

(⊠*112 Grand-Rue St-Michel* ☎*05–62–26–36–45*). Be sure to stop by the top jazz spot **Le Mandala** (⊠*23 rue des Aminodiers* ☎*05–61–21–10–05*) for a bit of the bubbly and some of the best jazz in town. **Melting Pot** (⊠*26 bd. de Strasbourg* ☎*05–61–62–82–98*) lives up to its title, with young people from around the world crowding the bar and dance floor.

12

Puerto Habana (⊠*12 port St-Étienne* ☎*05–61–54–45–61*) is the place for salsa music. **Le Purple** (⊠*2 rue Castellane* ☎*05–62–41–81–20*) is a hot multispace disco. Outside town is **Villa Garden** (⊠*157 av. de Lespinet* ☎*05–62–17–38–80*), which is tricky to find but worth checking out. **La Cinecita** (⊠*5 rue Labeda* ☎*05–61–22–47–25*) is always a lively spot. **Le Teatro** (⊠*1 pl. St-Cyprien* ☎*05–61–59–50–00*) is frequented by Toulousains looking for everything: food, drink, and action.

If you're looking for a pretty terrace for lunch or a late dinner (until 10:30), head to **Les Terrasses de Saint-Rome** (⊠*39 rue St-Rome* ☎*05–62–27–06–06*). Local glitterati and theater stars go to **Ubu** (⊠*16 rue St-Rome* ☎*05–61–23–26–75*), the city's top nightspot for 20 years. For a midnight dinner over the Garonne, **Brasserie Flo "Les Beaux Arts"** (⊠*1 quai de la Daurade* ☎*05–61–21–12–12*) is the place to be.

SHOPPING

Toulouse is a chic design outlet for clothing and artifacts of all kinds. **Rue St-Rome, Rue Croix Baragnon, Rue des Changes,** and **Rue d'Alsace-Lorraine** are all good shopping streets.

ALBI & THE GERS

Along the banks of the Tarn to the northeast of Toulouse is Albi, Toulouse's rival in rose colors. West from Albi, along the river, the land opens up to the rural Gers *département*, home of the heady brandy Armagnac and heart of the former dukedom of Gascony. Studded with châteaux—from simple medieval fortresses to ambitious classical residences—and with tiny, isolated villages, the Gers is an easy place to fall in love with, or in.

ALBI

★ **㉕** *75 km (47 mi) northeast of Toulouse.*

GETTING HERE

About 12 trains daily (1 hr, €14.45) run between Toulouse and Albi's main station on Place Stalingrad (set in a somewhat isolated part of town). In summer months, you can catch infrequent buses to adjoining towns, including Cordes-sur-Ciel (1 hr) from the bus station on Place Jean Jaurès.

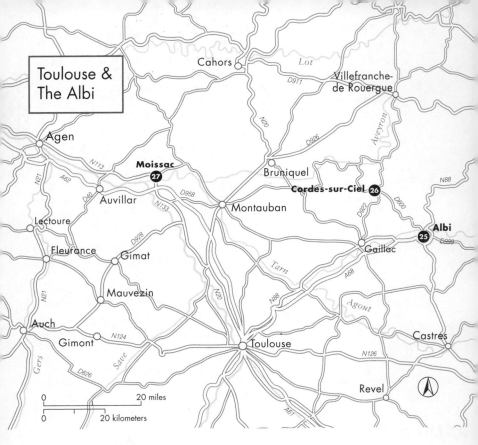

Toulouse &
The Albi

EXPLORING

Toulouse-Lautrec's native Albi is a well-preserved and busy provincial market town. In its heyday, Albi was a major center for the Cathars, members of a dualistic and ascetic religious movement critical of the hierarchical and worldly ways of the Catholic Church. Pick up a copy of the excellent visitor booklet (in English) from the **tourist office** (✉ *Pl. Ste-Cécile* ☎ *05–63–49–48–80* ⊕ *www.albi-tourisme.fr*), and follow the walking tours—of the *Vieille Ville* (Old City), the old ramparts, and the banks of the River Tarn.

Fodor's Choice
★ One of the most unusual and dazzling churches in France, the huge **Cathédrale Ste-Cécile,** with its intimidating clifflike walls, resembles a cross between a castle and an ocean liner. It was constructed as a symbol of the Church's return to power after the 13th-century crusade that wiped out the Cathars. The interior is an astonishingly ornate contrast to the massive austerity of the outer walls. Maestro Donnelli and a team of 16th-century Italian artists (most of the Emilian school) covered every possible surface with religious scenes and brightly colored patterns—it remains the largest group of Italian Renaissance paintings in a French church. On the west wall you can find one of the most splendid organs in the world, built in 1734 and outfitted with 3,500 pipes, which loom over a celebrated fresco of the Last Judgment. ✉ *Pl.*

Ste-Cécile ☎05–63–38–47–40 ☉June–Sept., daily 9–6:30; Oct.–May, daily 9–noon and 2–6:30.

Fodor'sChoice
★

The **Musée Toulouse-Lautrec** occupies the landmark **Palais de la Berbie** (Berbie Palace), set between the cathedral and the Pont Vieux (Old Bridge) in a garden designed by the famed André Le Nôtre (creator of the "green geometries" at Versailles). Built in 1265 as a residence for Albi's archbishops, the fortresslike structure was transformed in 1922 into a museum to honor Albi's most famous son, Belle Epoque painter Henri de Toulouse-Lautrec (1864–1901). Toulouse-Lautrec left Albi for Paris in 1882, and soon became famous for his colorful and tumultuous evocations of the lifestyle of bohemian glamour found in and around Montmartre. Son of a wealthy and aristocratic family (Lautrec is a village not far from Toulouse), the young Henri suffered from a genetic bone deficiency and broke both legs as a child, which stunted his growth. The artist's fascination with the decadent side of life led to an early grave at the age of 37 and Hollywood immortalization in the 1954 John Huston film *Moulin Rouge*. A 10-year renovation was completed in 2004, with vast new infrastructure and loan exhibition rooms excavated under the building. Upstairs, the collection of artworks (with more than a thousand, the world's largest Toulouse-Lautrec corpus) has been deftly organized into theme rooms, including ones devoted to some of his greatest portraits and scenes from Paris's maisons closées (brothels), with paintings stylishly hung amid the palace's brick ogival arches. There are other masterworks here, including paintings by Georges de la Tour and Francesco Guardi. ⊠*Palais de la Berbie, just off Pl. Ste-Cécile ☎05–63–49–48–70 ☜€5, guided tour €8.50, gardens free ☉June and Sept., daily 9–noon and 2–6; July and Aug., daily 9–6; Oct.–Mar., Wed.–Sun. 10–noon and 2–5; Apr. –May, daily 10–noon and 2–6.*

From the central square and parking area in front of the Palais de la Berbie, walk to the 11th- to 15th-century college and **Cloître de St-Salvy** (⊠*Rue Ste-Cécile*).

Next, take a look at Albi's finest restored traditional house, the **Maison du Vieil Albi** *(Old Albi House, ⊠Corner of Rue de la Croix-Blanche and Puech-Bérenguer).*

If you're a real fan of Toulouse-Lautrec, you might view his birthplace, the **Maison Natale de Toulouse-Lautrec** (⊠*14 rue Henri de Toulouse-Lautrec*), although there are no visits to the house, the Hôtel du Bosc, which remains a private residence.

Rue de l'Hôtel de Ville, two streets west of the Maison Natale, leads past the Mairie (City Hall), with its hanging globes of flowers, to

MY WAY OR THE HIGHWAY

Beneath the church's organ is an impressive 15th-century mural depicting appropriate punishments for the seven deadly sins in the Last Judgment. The scenes of torture and hellfire give an indication of how the Vatican kept its Christian subjects in line during the crusade against the Cathars and subsequent Inquisition trials.

Albi's main square, **Place du Vigan**. Take a break in one of the two main cafés, Le Pontie or Le Vigan.

WHERE TO STAY & EAT

$$-$$$$ ✕ **Le Jardin des Quatre Saisons.** A good-value menu and superb fish dishes are the reasons for this restaurant's excellent reputation. Chef-owner Georges Bermond's house specialties include mussels baked with leeks and *suprême de sandre* (a freshwater fish cooked in wine), and change with *les saisons.* ✉*19 bd. de Strasbourg* 🕾*05–63–60–77–76* ▱*AE, MC, V* ⊘*Closed Mon. No dinner Sun.*

$-$$ ✕🏨 **Hôtel Chiffre.** A former stagecoach inn, this centrally located town house has impeccable rooms overlooking a cozy garden. The restaurant serves hearty regional cuisine such as excellent foie gras and magret de canard (breast of duck) and lamb in a parsley-and-garlic sauce. ✉*50 rue Séré-de-Rivières, 81000* 🕾*05–63–48–58–48* 🖷*05–63–38–11–15* ⊕*www.hotelchiffre.com* ◿*38 rooms* ♿*In-room: refrigerator, dial-up. In-hotel: restaurant, parking (fee)* ▱*AE, MC, V* ⦿*MAP.*

$$-$$$ 🏨 **Hostellerie St-Antoine.** Founded in 1734, this hotel in the center of town is one of the oldest in France. It's been run by the same family for five generations, a lineage attested to by the display of Toulouse-Lautrec sketches given to the owner's great-grandfather, a friend of the painter. Modern renovations have made it eminently comfortable. Room 30 has a pleasing view of the garden; pristine white furnishings give it a spacious feel. ✉*17 rue St-Antoine, 81000* 🕾*05–63–54–04–04* 🖷*05–63–47–10–47* ⊕*www.saint-antoine-albi.com* ◿*44 rooms* ♿*In-room: refrigerator, Wi-Fi. In-hotel: parking (fee)* ▱*AE, DC, MC, V.*

¢-$ 🏨 **La Régence—George V.** This little in-town B&B is near the cathedral and the train station. Each room is unique, and the garden makes for a pleasant retreat in summer. ✉*27–29 av. Maréchal-Joffre, 81000* 🕾*05–63–54–24–16* 🖷*05–63–49–90–78* ⊕*www.laregence-georgev. fr* ◿*22 rooms* ♿*In-room: no a/c. In-hotel: restaurant, some pets allowed (fee)* ▱*AE, MC, V.*

SHOPPING

Around **Place Ste-Cécile** are numerous clothing, book, music, and antiques shops. The finest foie gras in town is found at **Albi Foie Gras** (✉*29 rue Mariès*). **L'Artisan Chocolatier** (✉*4 rue Dr-Camboulives, on Pl. du Vigan* 🕾*05–63–38–95–33*) is famous for its chocolate. Albi has many **produce markets**: one takes place Tuesday through Sunday in the market halls near the cathedral; another is held on Sunday morning on Place Ste-Cécile. A Saturday-morning **flea and antiques market** (✉*Pl. du Castelviel*) is held in the Halle du Castelviel.

CORDES-SUR-CIEL

26
Fodor's Choice
★   *25 km (15 mi) northwest of Albi, 80 km (50 mi) northeast of Toulouse.*

GETTING HERE

In July and August, a bus runs the 25 km (16 mi) from Albi's bus station on Place Jean Jaurès to the bottom of Cordes twice daily. At other times of the year, you'll have to take the train to Cordes-Vindrac, where is frequently served from Toulouse (1¼ hrs) and Albi (1 hr);

CLOSE UP

Crusading Cathars

Scorched by the southern heat, the dusty ruins perched high atop cliffs in southern Languedoc were once the refuges of the Cathars, the notoriously ascetic religious group persecuted out of existence by the Catholic church in the 12th and 13th centuries. The Cathars inhabited an area ranging from present-day Germany all the way to the Atlantic Ocean. Adherents to this dualistic doctrine of material abnegation and spiritual revelation abstained from fleshly pleasures in all forms—forgoing procreation and the consumption of animal products. In some cases, they even committed suicide by starvation; diminishing the amount of flesh in the world was the ultimate way to foil the forces of evil. However, not thrilled by a religion that did not "go forth and multiply" (and that saw no need to pay taxes to the church), Pope Innocent III launched the Albigensian Crusade (Albi was one of the major Cathar strongholds), and Pope Gregory IX rounded up the stragglers during a period of inquisi-

tion starting in 1233. All these forces had been given scandalously free rein by the French court, who allowed dukes and counts from northern France to build fortified bastide (fortified) towns through the area to entrap the peasantry.

The counts were more than happy to oblige the pope with a little hounding, an inquisition or two, and some burnings at the stake. Forthwith, entire towns were judged to be guilty of heresy and inhabitants were thrown by the dozens to their deaths from high town walls. The persecuted "pure" soon took refuge in the Pyrénées mountains, where they survived for 100 years. Now all that remains of this unhappy sect are their former hideouts, with tour groups visiting the vacant stone staircases and roofless chapels of haunted places like Peyrepertuse and Quéribus. For more information (in French), log on to ⊕ www.cathares.org or go hiking with medievalist Ingrid Sparbier (sp.ingrid@wanadoo.fr).

12

---

from Cordes-Vindrac, it is 3 km (1½ mi) to Cordes via bike, taxi, or footpower. Note that traffic is banned in the upper town in summer and parking nearby is virtually impossible.

EXPLORING

A must-stop for all travelers, the picture-book hilltop village of Cordes-sur-Ciel, built in 1222 by Count Raymond VII of Toulouse, is one of the most impressively preserved *bastides* (fortified medieval towns built along a strict grid plan) in France. When mists steal up from the Cérou Valley and enshroud the hillside, Cordes appears to hover in midair, hence its nickname, Cordes-sur-Ciel (Cordes-in-the-Sky/Heaven). Named after Andalusian Cordoba, it was built as a redoubt after the Occitan wars waged against the region's Cathars; its conical hill is studded with caves once used as graineries during times of siege. When peace arrived in the 15th century, the town thrived as a center for leather and fabric makers and many rich residents built pink-sandstone Gothic-style houses, a sizable number of which still line the main street, Grande-Rue Haute (also called rue Droite). Today, many are now occupied by painters, sculptors, weavers, leatherworkers, and even creators of illuminated manuscripts, whose ateliers and stores lure the summer crowds. The annual blow-out is the Fêtes Médiévales du Grand Fauconnier (named after the town's most historic abode; www.grandfauconnier.com), a three-day festival held around July 15, replete with an artisanal fair and costumed Bal Médiéval. The village's 14th-century St-Michel church and the venerable covered market, supported by 24 octagonal stone pillars, are also noteworthy, as is the nearby well, which is more than 300 feet deep. The small Musée Charles-Portail has relics from the town's medieval past while closer to the Haut de la Cité is the two-room Musée de la Sucre (Sugar), which showcases the works of the noted chef, Yves Thuriès, who presides over the town's famous inn and restaurant, Le Grand Écuyer.

WHERE TO STAY & EAT

$$–$$$$ ✕ **Les Saveurs d'Ingres.** Cyril Paysserand's *cuisine d'auteur* is some of the best fare in the area, served in a graceful vaulted dining room in midtown Montauban, just a few doors up from the Ingres Museum. Not unlike Ingres himself, Paysserand sticks with the classical canons prepared in novel and sensual ways. If you've maxed out on cassoulet and web-footed fare in general, try the frogs' legs here or the *bécasse* (woodcock) in season for a welcome change of pace. ⊠ *13 rue de l'Hôtel de Ville* 🕾 *05–63–91–26–42* 🗖 *AE, DC, MC, V* ⊘ *Closed Sun., Mon., Aug. 7–29, and Dec. 24–Jan. 6.*

$$$–$$$$ ✕🖾 **Le Grand Écuyer.** The dramatic hilltop setting of this hotel suits
Fodor's Choice   it well—it's a perfectly preserved Gothic mansion, built as a hunt-
★   ing lodge for the count of Toulouse, Raymond VII, and now fitted out with time-burnished ancestral portraits, suits of armor, and four-poster beds. The best guest rooms—Planol, Horizon, and Ciel—have views of the rolling countryside, while the Raymond VII salon was a favorite of novelist Albert Camus ("In Cordes everything is beautiful, even regret"). Yves Thuriès is one of the region's best chefs and chocolatiers and his table has drawn such celebrities as King Juan Carlos of Spain and England's queen mother. Menus begin at €59 and culminate in a seven-course "rotating" gourmet extravaganza that costs €84. Delights includes the codfish "demi-sel" with chickpea puree, the pan-seared Brittany lobster with roasted pear and pink grapefruit emulsion, and the white-chocolate-and-pistachio-marbled "velouté." Thuriès also owns the town's stylish L'Hostellerie du Vieux Cordes, which takes over (at nicely lower prices) when Le Grand closes from fall to early spring every year. ⊠ *Haute de la Cité, 81170* 🕾 *05–63–53–79–50* 🖨 *05–63–53–79–51* ⊕ *www.thuries.fr* 🗗 *12 rooms, 1 suite* ⚭ *In-room: refrigerator, Wi-Fi (some). In-hotel: restaurant, bar, some pets allowed (fee)* 🗖 *AE, DC, MC, V* ⊘ *Closed mid-Oct.–early Apr.* ꪘ *MAP.*

$$ 🖾 **Hôtel du Midi–Mercure.** The Hôtel du Midi combines old-world elegance with modern comforts. A plaque on the hotel's facade attests that Manuel Azaña, last president of the Second Spanish Republic (1931–36), died here in exile in 1940. ⊠ *12 rue Notre-Dame, 82000* 🕾 *05–63–63–17–23* 🖨 *05–63–66–43–66* ⊕ *www.accorhotels.com*

⟲44 *rooms* ⟐ *In-room: refrigerator. In-hotel: restaurant, bar, parking (fee), some pets allowed (fee)* ☰*AE, DC, MC, V.*

★ $ ✕⟨⟩ **L'Hostellerie du Vieux Cordes.** Sister hotel to Le Grand Écuyer, this lovely 13th-century house is built around a spectacular courtyard dotted with tiny white tables and shaded by a magnificent 300-year-old wisteria. Guest rooms are stylish decorated with tone-on-tone color schemes and antique accents. Downstairs, the restaurant Tonin'ty has a 19th-century vibe, with delicious menus crafted around salmon and duck by famed chef Yves Thuriès (the restaurant is closed in January and on Monday from November to Easter). ✉*Rue St-Michel, 81170* ☎*05–63–53–79–20* 🖷*05–63–56–02–47* ⊕*www.thuries.fr* ⟲*19 rooms* ⟐*In-room: no a/c, refrigerator, Wi-Fi (some). In-hotel: restaurant* ☰*AE, DC, MC, V* ⊘*Closed Jan.* ⦿*MAP.*

MOISSAC

㉗ *16 km (25 mi) west Cordes-sur-Ciel, 72 km (45 mi) northwest of Toulouse.*

Moissac has both the region's largest (and most beautiful) Romanesque cloisters and one of its most remarkable abbey churches. The port—at the confluence of the lateral canal and the Aveyron and Garonne rivers—is a surprising sight so far from the sea. For a spectacular view over this Mississippi-like riverine expanse, France's widest, head to the lookout point at Boudou, 2 km (1 mi) west of Moissac off Route N113. Moissac has a train station but rail service is infrequent; a trip from Montauban takes about 20 minutes.

Fronted by a magnificent Romanesque sculpted portal that depicts in stone Book 4 of the Apocalypse, the **Abbaye St-Pierre** was founded in the 7th century by Saint Didier, bishop of Cahors, and bears traces of many settlers of the region, from Arabs to Normans to Magyars. Little is left of the original abbey, and subsequent religious wars laid waste to its 11th-century replacement. Today's abbey, dating mostly from the 15th century, narrowly escaped demolition early in the 20th century when the Bordeaux-Sète railroad was rerouted within feet of the cloisters. Each of the 76 capitals has a unique pattern of animals, geometric motifs, and religious or historical scenes. Look for the Cain and Abel story on the 12th column to the right of the entry point. The 63rd column (fourth back from the northeast corner) shows St-Sernin being dragged to his death by a bull. On the famed Apocalypse south portal, carved in the 12th century, the representation of a sweetly mournful Jeremiah (author of the Old Testament Book of Lamentations), on the lower part of the door, is especially noteworthy. The **Musée des Arts et Traditions Populaires** (Folk Art Museum), in the abbey, contains regional treasures and a roomful of local costumes. ✉*6 bis, rue de l'Abbaye* ☎*05–63–04–05–73* 🎫*Cloisters and museum €5* ⊘*Apr.– June, Sept., and Oct., daily 9–noon and 2–6; July and Aug., daily 9–7; Nov.–Mar., daily 10–noon and 2–5.*

★

12

WHERE TO STAY & EAT

★ ¢–$　✕🏨 **Le Pont Napoléon.** One of France's rising culinary stars, Michel Dussau, who trained with Alain Ducasse (and others), is a master of refined simplicity and innovative combinations of regional products. Try fois gras *pôelé* (sautéed goose liver) and anything made with Moissac's *chasselas* grapes (the restaurant is closed Sunday, Monday, and Wednesday). Guest rooms are furnished with elegant, authentic antiques; some have lovely views of the Tarn and the bridge. ✉2 allées Montebello, 82200 ☎05–63–04–01–55 🖶05–63–04–34–44 ⊕www. le-pont-napoleon.com ➟12 rooms ♿In-hotel: restaurant, bar ⊟AE, DC, MC, V ⊙Closed Jan. 2–20 ⏏MAP.

LANGUEDOC-ROUSSILLON

A region immortalized by Matisse and Picasso, Languedoc-Roussillon extends along the southern Mediterranean coast of France to the Pyrénées. Draw a line between Carcassonne and Narbonne: the area to the south down to the Pyrénées, long dominated by the House of Aragón, the ruling family of adjacent Catalonia, is known as the Roussillon. Inland, the area, with its dry climate, is virtually one huge vineyard. The Canal du Midi flows through the region to **Le Littoral Languedocien** (the Languedoc Coast). Beaches stretch down the coast to Cerbère at the Spanish border. This strip is known as the Côte Vermeille (Vermilion Coast) and attracts droves of European sun worshippers even though the beaches are rocky. The farther south you go, the stronger the Spanish influence. Heading northward, Languedoc begins around Narbonne and extends to the region's hub, the elegant city of Montpellier. All in all, Languedoc-Roussillon is one of the most idyllic regions in France. Life here—even in such urban centers as Béziers or Perpignan—is distinctly relaxed and friendly. You'll probably be taking afternoon *siestes* (naps) before you know it.

CARCASSONNE

❷❽　*88 km (55 mi) southeast of Toulouse, 105 km (65 mi) south of Albi.*

Fodor's Choice
★　### GETTING HERE

The shuttle to Salvaza Airport from the train station (beside the Canal du Midi on Avenue du Maréchal Joffre) also links you up with the Cité and Place Gambetta. Ryanair (⊕*www.ryanair.com*) has daily flights to Stansted and Dublin. Due to the high volume of visitors, many trains arrive Carcassone's train station—17 trains to Narbonne and 24 to Toulouse alone. Cars Tessier (⊕*www.tessier.fr*) will bus you to all the same places as the trains, and at times a lot faster, too.

EXPLORING

Set atop a hill overlooking lush green countryside and the Aude River, Carcassonne is a spectacular medieval town that looks lifted from the pages of a storybook—literally, perhaps, as its circle of towers and battlements (comprising the longest city walls in Europe) is said to be the setting for Charles Perrault's classic tale *Puss in Boots*. The

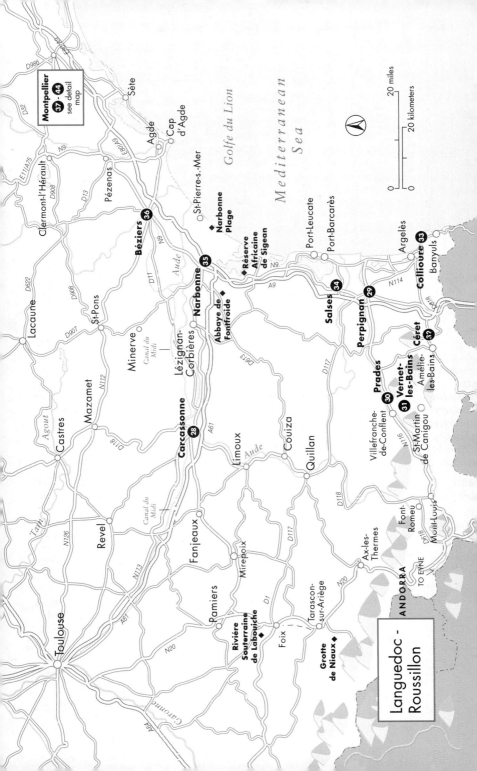

Languedoc-Roussillon

Montpellier **37** - **44**
see detail map

Golfe du Lion

Mediterranean Sea

20 miles

20 kilometers

Sète

Agde

Cap d'Agde

St-Pierre-s.-Mer

Narbonne Plage

Béziers 36

Réserve Africaine de Sigean

Narbonne 35

Abbaye de Fontfroide

Port-Leucate

Port-Barcarès

Argelès

Collioure 33

Banyuls

Salses 34

Perpignan 29

Céret 32

Lézignan-Corbières

Clermont-l'Hérault

Pézenas

Minerve

St-Pons

Mazamet

Lacaune

Castres

Revel

Carcassonne 28

Canal du Midi

Limoux

Couiza

Quillan

Prades 30

Vernet-les-Bains 31

Villefranche-de-Conflent

St-Martin de Canigou

Amélie-les-Bains

Font-Romeu

Mont-Louis

EYNE

Fanjeaux

Mirepoix

Ax-les-Thermes

ANDORRA

TO EYNE

Toulouse

Pamiers

Rivière Souterraine de Labouiche

Foix

Tarascon-sur-Ariège

Grotte de Niaux

oldest sections of the walls (northeast sector), built by the Romans in the 1st century ad , were later enlarged, in the 5th century, by the Visigoths. Legend has it that Charlemagne once set siege to the settlement in the 9th century, only to be outdone by one Dame Carcas, a clever woman who boldly fed the last of the city's wheat to a pig in full view of the conqueror; Charlemagne, thinking this indicated endless food supplies, promptly decamped, and the exuberant townsfolk named their city after her. During the 13th century, Louis IX (St. Louis) and his son Philip the Beautiful strengthened Carcassonne's fortifications—so much so that the town came to be considered inviolable by marauding armies and was duly nicknamed "the virgin of Languedoc."

**THE POSTCARD
COMES TO LIFE**

Carcassonne usually goes medieval in mid-August with Les Médiévales (⊕ www.carcassonne-tourisme.com), a festival of troubadour song, rich costumes, and jousting performances (some years the event isn't held; check with the tourist office). And don't forget the Bastille Day fireworks over La Cité—spectacular!

A town that can never be taken in battle is often abandoned, however, and for centuries thereafter Carcassonne remained under a Sleeping Beauty spell. It was only awakened during the mid-19th-century craze for chivalry and the Gothic style, when, in 1835, the historic-monument inspector (and poet) Prosper Mérimée arrived. He was so appalled by the dilapidated state of the walls that he commissioned the architect, painter, and historian Viollet-le-Duc (who found his greatest fame restoring Paris's Notre-Dame) to restore the town. Today the 1844 renovation is considered almost as much a work of art as the medieval town itself. No matter if the town is more Viollet than authentic medieval, it still remains one of the most romantic sights in France.

The town is divided by the river into two parts—La Cité, the fortified upper town, and the lower, newer city (the *ville basse*), known simply as Carcassonne. Unless you are staying at a hotel in the upper town, you are not allowed to enter it with your car; you must park in the lot (fee by the hour) across the road from the drawbridge. Be aware that the train station is in the lower town, which means either a cab ride, a 30-minute walk up to La Cité, or a ride on the *navette* shuttle bus. Plan on spending at least a couple of hours exploring the walls and peering over the battlements across sun-drenched plains toward the distant Pyrénées. Once inside the walls of the upper town, a florid carousel announces that 21st-century tourism is about to take over. The streets are lined with souvenir shops, crafts boutiques, restaurants, and tiny "museums" (i.e., a Cathars Museum, a Hat Museum), all out to make a buck and rarely worth that. Staying overnight within the ancient walls lets you savor the timeless atmosphere after the daytime hordes are gone.

The 12th-century **Château Comtal** is the last inner bastion of Carcassonne. It has a drawbridge and a museum, the **Musée Lapidaire,** where stone sculptures found in the area are on display. ☎04–68–11–70–77 ✉€6.50 ⊗June–Sept., daily 9:30–6; Oct.–May, daily 9–noon and 2–5.

The real draw in the ville basse, built between the Aude and the Canal du Midi, is the **Musée des Beaux-Arts** *(Fine Arts Museum)*. It houses a nice collection of porcelain, 17th- and 18th-century Flemish paintings, and works by local artists—including some stirring battle scenes by Jacques Gamelin (1738–1803). ✉1 rue Verdun ☎04–68–77–73–70 ✉Free ⊗Nov.–June, Tues.–Sat. 10–noon and 2–6; July and Aug., daily 9–6.

WHERE TO STAY & EAT

$–$$$ ✕ **Le Languedoc.** This restaurant in the ville basse (whose owners also own the Montségur just down the road) serves up tempting versions of the region's specialties, from confit to game. In summer the flowery patio is a perfect spot for a long evening dinner. Be sure to try the quail with foie gras, if available. ✉32 allée d'Iéna ☎04–68–25–22–17 ▤AE, DC, MC, V ⊗Closed mid-Dec.–mid-Jan. and Mon. No dinner Sun. July–Oct.

★ ¢–$$ ✕ **Sire de Cabaret.** Nestled beneath the château of Roquefére, an unspoiled *village fleuri* in the Cabardés region of the Montagne Noire, this regional favorite serves up amazing steaks *à la Languedocienne*. Cooked over chestnut wood fires, they are accompanied by mushrooms picked from nearby mountains by the genial chef Patrick Malea and served by his wife, Carmen (and a famously droll waiter, Jean-Pierre). With charcuterie *fait maison* (homemade sausages, pâtés, rillettes, and cured meats), this is a place worth visiting as much for its rustic charm as for its great food. In warm weather, ask for a table on the terrace and enjoy your *poisson à la plancha* (fish on a plank) beneath olive trees amid hills cloaked with green oaks and chestnut trees. They also have a lovely B&B cottage next door, but make sure to reserve well in advance as it is nearly always booked. ✉Roquefére, 25 km (11 mi) north of Carcassonne,11380 ☎04–68–26–31–89 ☒04–68–26–31–89 ⊕www.gites-de-france-aude.com ⏴2 rooms ▤MC, V ⊗Closed Jan. and Feb. 1–14. No dinner Wed. and Sun. Sept.–June.

$$$$ ✕▥ **Hôtel de la Cité.** Set within the walled upper town, this is *the* spot for celebrities in Carcassonne. The ivy-covered former episcopal palace offers creature comforts the ascetic Cathars would have hated. Afternoon tea is in the library bar or rotunda lounge with its antique-tile floors, detailed woodwork, and leaded windows (with storybook views). Dining in the sumptuous La Barbacane restaurant—all double-vaulted ceiling, ogival windows, and light tea-brown walls—is an event. For more casual fare, enjoy the charmingly cobbled square as you sip a pastis at the brasserie Chez Saskia. A pool, set like a sapphire in the garden, beckons on hot days. ✉Pl. August-Pierre Pont, 11000 La Cité de Carcassonne ☎04–68–71–98–71 ☒04–68–71–50–15 ⊕www.hoteldelacite.orient-express.com ⏴53 rooms, 8 suites ⌂In-room: refrigerator, Wi-Fi. In-hotel: 2 restaurants, pool, parking (fee) ▤AE, DC, MC, V ⊗Closed Dec. and Feb. ▮⊙|MAP.

★ $$$–$$$$ ✕⊞ **Domaine d'Auriac.** This elegant 19th-century manor house southwest of Carcassonne offers an environment of superb grace and comfort. Room prices vary according to size and view; the largest look out onto a magnificent park and vineyards. Next to a terrace planted with mulberry trees, the restaurant, famed as one of the best in the area, offers superlative Languedoc cuisine; enjoy the Provençal-style salon festooned with copper pots while savoring truffled pigeon, John Dory in blueberry wine, and game dishes, in season, accompanied by rare regional vintages. ⊠*Rte. de St-Hilaire, 4 km (2½ mi) southwest of Carcassonne, 11000 Carcassonne* ☎*04–68–25–72–22* 🖨*04–68–47–35–54* ⊕*www.domaine-d-auriac.com* ⤶*24 rooms* ⚶*In-room: Wi-Fi. In-hotel: restaurant, bar, golf course, tennis court, pool* ⊟*AE, DC, MC, V* ⊘*Closed Jan., Apr. 27–May 5, and Nov. 16–25* ⦵*MAP.*

$$$–$$$$ ⊞ **Château de Garrevaques.** With a florid Roussillon-ocher facade and set equidistant (50 km [31 mi]) from Toulouse, Carcassonne, and Albi, this retreat makes a particularly apt base camp for exploring the region, the more so since the current châtelaines are the 16th generation to call this home. Marie-Christine and Claude Combes receive guests with a friendly welcome amid family heirlooms. The only salon in truly baronial style is the main living room graced with a dazzling Zuber suite of *grisaille* (gray-and-white) hand-painted wallpaper panels depicting scenes of the Psyché and Cupid legend. Guest rooms are graced with period accents, stolid antiques, paisley fabrics, and some fetching 19th-century color schemes. The table d'hôte dinner is a good chance to sample the local country cooking and meet invariably interesting fellow guests. Check out the **Pavillon du Château,** occupying the former stables (complete with heavy wooden beams) with 15 rooms, two restaurants, and a spa. Chocolate massage (yes, massage, this is not dessert) is the house specialty, along with a hammam and hot-stone treatments. ⊠*5 km (3 mi) northwest of Revel, 81700 Garrevaques* ☎*05–63–75–04–54* 🖨*05–63–70–26–44* ⊕*www.garrevaques.com* ⤶*23 rooms, 1 suite* ⚶*In-room: Wi-Fi. In-hotel: 2 restaurants, tennis court, pool, spa* ⊟*AE, DC, MC, V* ⦵*BP.*

$–$$ ⊞ **Hôtel Montségur.** With its ville basse location, this hotel is especially convenient. Rooms on the first two floors have Louis XV and Louis XVI furniture, some of it genuine; those above are more romantic, with gilt-iron bedsteads under sloping oak beams. ⊠*27 allée d'Iéna, 11000* ☎*04–68–25–31–41* 🖨*04–68–47–13–22* ⊕*www.hotelmontsegur.com* ⤶*21 rooms* ⚶*In-room: Wi-Fi. In-hotel: parking, some pets allowed (fee)* ⊟*AE, DC, MC, V* ⊘*Closed Dec. 20–Feb. 3.*

THE ARTS

Carcassonne hosts a major arts festival in July, with dance, theater, classical music, and jazz; for details, contact the town's **Poleculturel** (⌖*10 rue de la Republic* ☎*04–68–11–59–15* ⊕ *www.festivaldec-arcassonne.com*).

PERPIGNAN

㉙ *118 km (71 mi) southeast of Carcassonne, 27 km (17 mi) northwest of Collioure.*

GETTING HERE

Ryanair (⊕*(www.ryanair.com)*) has a daily flight from Perpignan as does Flybe (⊕*www.flybe.com*). The airport has navettes (shuttles) from the train station (⊠At end of Av. du Général de Gaulle) an hour before each takeoff. The TGV from Paris takes about six hours for about €75. The bus station is to the north of town on Avenue Général Leclerc (☎04–68–35–29–02).

EXPLORING

Salvador Dalí once called Perpignan's train station "the center of the world." That may not be true, but the city is certainly the capital hub of the Roussillon. Although it's big, you need stray no farther than the few squares of the *centre ville* (town center) grouped near the quays of the Basse River; this is the place to be for evening concerts and casual tapas sessions—you might even succumb to the "cosmological ecstasy" Dalí said he experienced here. In medieval times Perpignan was the second city of Catalonia (after Barcelona), before falling to Louis XIV's French army in 1659. The Spanish influence is evident in Perpignan's leading monument, the fortified **Palais des Rois de Majorque** *(Kings of Majorca Palace)*, begun in the 13th century by Jacques II of Majorca. Highlights here are the majestic **cour d'Honneur** (Courtyard of Honor), the two-tier Flamboyant Gothic chapel of **Ste-Croix Marie-Madelene,** and the **Grande Salle** (Great Hall) with its monumental fireplaces. ⊠*Rue des Archers* ☎04–68–34–48–29 ☜€4 ☉*Oct.–May, daily 9–5; June–Sept., daily 10–6.*

Perpignan's centre ville is sweet and alluring, lined with blooming rosemary bushes and landmarked by a medieval monument, the 14th-century **Le Castillet,** with its tall, crenellated twin towers. Originally this hulking brick building was the main gate to the city; later it was used as a prison. Now the **Casa Pairal,** a museum devoted to Catalan art and traditions, is housed here. ⊠*Pl. de Verdun* ☎04–68–35–42–05 ☜€4 ☉*Wed.–Mon. 11–5:30.*

The **Promenade des Plantanes,** across Boulevard Wilson from Le Castillet, is a cheerful place to stroll among flowers, plane trees, and fountains.

To see other interesting medieval buildings, walk along the **Petite Rue des Fabriques d'En Nabot**—near Le Castillet, and to the adjacent Place de la Loge, the town's nerve center.

Note the frilly wrought-iron campanile and dramatic medieval crucifix on the **Cathédrale St-Jean** (⊠*Pl. Gambetta*).

WHERE TO STAY & EAT

★ **$–$$** ╳ **Les Antiquaires.** With traditional Rousillon cooking served up in a rustic setting in a corner of old Perpignan, this friendly spot lives up to its title as a refuge for things antique. Duck à l'orange, a house favorite, has been on the menu here for 32 years, by popular demand. Foie gras in a Banyuls sauce is another staple in this pretty spot known for unpretentious yet refined cuisine. ⊠*Pl. Desprès* ☎*04–68–34–06–58* ⊟*AE, DC, MC, V* ⊙*Closed Mon., July 1–23 and mid-Jan. –Feb 1. No dinner Sun.*

\$–\$\$ ✕ **Le France.** In the center of Perpignan in a 15th-century former stock market with exposed beams and arcades, this café-restaurant is perfect for a light meal or a glass of iced champagne under the parasols as you watch the world go by. The menu changes every three months, but try the light appetizers such as scallop salad, or a foie gras with green beans and raisins. Grilled duck breast with apples or the *tagine de lotte* (monkfish stew) and big plates of tapas are also served. ⊠*1 pl. de la Loge* ☎*04–68–51–61–71* ⊟*MC, V.*

\$\$–\$\$\$ ✕🖼 **La Villa Duflot.** In a large park filled with olive and cypress trees, this hotel–restaurant complex serves some of the best meals in one of the calmest, prettiest settings in the city—too bad reports filter in about rude and snobbish hotel staff. Try to request a room with a view over the park—they're airy and comfortable with warm creamy colors; the rooms overlooking the patio aren't nearly as nice although they are a bit more economical. Much of the finesse is saved for the food and the food is *good*. The gastronomic restaurant popular with haute Perpignan serves light Mediterranean specialties around the pool—try the *parillade*, an assortment of the freshest catch of the day grilled to perfection and served with tangy aioli. ⊠*Rond Pont Albert Donnezan, 66000* ☎*04–68–56–67–67* 🖨*04–68–56–54–05* ⤶*32 rooms* 🛇*In-room: refrigerator, Wi-Fi. In-hotel: restaurant, bar, some pets allowed* ⊟*AE, DC, MC, V.*

SHOPPING

Rue des Marchands, near Le Castillet, is thick with chic shops. **Maison Quinta** (⊠*Rue Louis Blanc*) is a top design and architectural artifacts store. Excellent local ceramics can be found at the picturesque **Sant Vicens Crafts Center** (⊠*Rue Sant Vicens, off D22 east of town center*).

PRADES

㉚   *45 km (27 mi) west of Perpignan.*

Once home to famed Catalan cellist Pablo Casals, the market town of Prades is famous for its annual summer music festival (from late July to mid-August), the **Festival Pablo Casals.** Founded by Casals in 1950,
★ the music festival is primarily held at the medieval **Abbaye de St-Michel de Cuxa.** One of the gems of the Pyrénées, the abbey's sturdy, crenellated bell tower is visible from afar. If the remains of the cloisters here seem familiar, it may be because you have seen the missing pieces in New York City's Cloisters Museum. The 10th-century pre-Romanesque church is the biggest in France and a superb aesthetic and acoustical venue for the summer cello concerts. The six-voice Gregorian vespers service held (somewhat sporadically—call to confirm) at 7 pm in the monastery next door is hauntingly simple and medieval in tone and texture. (⊠*3 km [2 mi] on D27 south of Prades and Codalet* ☎*04–68–96–15–35* ⊕*www.prades-festival-casals.com* 💶*€4* ⊙*May–Sept., Mon.–Sat. 9:30–11:30 and 2–6; Oct.–Apr. 9:30–11:30 and 2–5*)

WHERE TO STAY & EAT

★ ¢–$ ✕ **Le Jardin d'Aymeric.** Locals swear by this semisecret gem, a charming little place that serves excellent cuisine du terroir in a relaxed and rustic setting. The menu changes seasonally and the market rules supreme. On the walls you can find a changing show by local artists, as only befits this slightly bohemian refuge. ⊠ 3 av. Général de Gaulle ☎ 04–68–96–53–38 ▭ MC, V ⊙ Closed June 25–July 8, Feb., and Mon. No dinner Wed. and Sun.

¢–$ ✕▭ **Les Glycines.** This flower-wreathed, traditional hotel in the middle of Prades offers small but charming rooms of impeccable cleanliness and simplicity. After a healthy hike to St-Michel-de-Cuxa, you can come to its rambling restaurant to savor fine home cooking and plenty of friendly good cheer. ⊠ 129 av. Général de Gaulle, 66100 ☎ 04–68–96–51–65 ▤ 04–68–96–45–57 ⇱ 19 rooms ⟁ In-room: no a/c, Wi-Fi. In-hotel: restaurant, parking (fee) ▭ MC, V.

> ## THE LITTLE TRAIN THAT COULD
>
> Le petit train jaune ("Little Yellow Train") is a fun way to see some of the most spectacular countryside in the Pyrénées. This life-size toy train makes the 63-km (40-mi) three-hour trip from Villefranche to La Tour de Carol about five times a day. When the weather is nice, ride in one of the open-air cars. For information about hours and prices, contact the Villefranche tourist office (☎ 04–68–96–22–96) or the SNCF Web site (⊕ www.traintouristique-ter.com/train-jaune.htm).

12

VERNET-LES-BAINS

③① 12 km (7 mi) southwest of Prades, 55 km (34 mi) west of Perpignan.

English writer Rudyard Kipling came to take the waters in Vernet-les-Bains, a long-established spa town that is dwarfed by imposing Mont Canigou. The celebrated medieval abbey, **Abbaye St-Martin du Canigou,** is a steep 30-minute climb up from the parking area in Casteil, 2 km (1 mi) south of Vernet-les-Bains. One of the most photographed abbeys in Europe thanks to its sky-kissing perch atop a triangular promontory at an altitude of nearly 3,600 feet, it was constructed in 1009 by Count Guifré of Cerdagne. St-Martin du Canigou's breathtaking (literally) mountain perch was due, in part, to an effort to escape the threat of marauding Saracens from the Middle East. Damaged by earthquake in 1428 and abandoned in 1783, the abbey was (perhaps too) diligently restored by the bishop of Perpignan early in the 20th century. Parts of the cloisters, along with the higher (and larger) of the two churches, date from the 11th century. The lower church, dedicated to Notre-Dame-sous-Terre, is even older. Rising above is a stocky, fortified bell tower. Although the hours vary, masses are sung daily; call ahead to confirm. Easter mass here is especially joyous and moving. Note the abbey is closed January and also on Tuesday from October to May. ☎ 04–68–05–50–03 ▦ €4 ⊙ Oct.–May, tours daily at 10, 11, 2, 3, 5; June–Sept., tours daily at 10, 11, 12, 2, 3, 4, 5; and Sun. no visits at 11.

Fodor's Choice
★

CÉRET

★ *68 km (41 mi) southeast of Prades, 35 km (21 mi) west of Collioure,*
31 km (19 mi) southwest of Perpignan.

The "Barbizon of Cubism," Céret achieved immortality when leading artists found this small Catalan town irresistible at the beginning of the 20th century. Here in this medieval enclave set on the
banks of the Tech River, Picasso and Gris developed a vigorous new
way of seeing that would result in the fragmented forms of Cubism,
a thousand years removed from the Romanesque sculptures of the
Roussillon chapels and cloisters. Adorned by cherry orchards—the
town famously grows the first and finest crop in France—the town
landscapes have been captured in paintings by Picasso, Gris, Dufy,
Braque, Chagall, Masson, and others. Some of these are on view in
② the fine collection of the **Musée d'Art Moderne** *(Modern Art Museum).*
Fodor's Choice ✉*8 bd. Maréchal-Joffre* ☎*04–68–87–27–76* ⊕*www.musee-ceret.*
★ *com* ✉*€5.50* ⊗*July–mid-Sept., daily 10–7; mid-Sept.–June, daily*
10–6 (closed Tues. Oct. 1–Apr. 30).

The heart of town is, not surprisingly, the Place Picasso. Like the Span-
ish roots of this artist, Céret is proud of its Catalan heritage and it often
hosts sardana dances. Be sure to stroll through pretty **Vieux Céret** *(Old*
Céret): find your way through **Place et Fontaine de Neuf Jets** (Nine
Fountains Square), around the church, and out to the lovely fortified
Porte de France gateway. Then walk over the single-arched **Vieux Pont**
(Old Bridge).

WHERE TO STAY & EAT

★ **$$-$$$** ✕▦ **Les Feuillants.** One of the top restaurants in the area (closed Monday;
no dinner Sunday), this elegant address offers refined Mediterranean
and international cuisine, a good wine list, traditional-contemporary
design, and paintings by Michel Becker. Dishes, such as panfried cuttle-
fish, are showpieces of the region and often come with flowers, herbs,
cherries (the town emblem), and a hint of Catalonian *cuisine d'auteur*
thrown in. Touches of creativity—seared foie gras with cherry and raisin chutney, a violet artichoke heart cooked tempura style—are often
in evidence. Guest rooms, though few, are gems. ✉*1 bd. Lafayette,*
66400 ☎*04–68–87–37–88* 🖶*04–68–87–44–68* ➷*3 rooms, 3 apart-*
ments ♿*In-hotel: restaurant, no elevator* ▭*MC, V* ⊗*Closed 2 wks in*
Feb. and 2 wks in Nov. ⦿*MAP.*

★ **¢-$** ▦ **Les Arcades.** This comfortable spot in mid-Céret looks, smells, and
feels exactly the way an inn ensconced in the heart of a provincial French
town should. That the world-class collection of paintings of the Musée
d'Art Moderne and the top-rated Les Feuillants restaurant are both just
across the street puts it over the top. ✉*1 pl. Picasso, 66400* ☎*04–68–*
87–12–30 🖶*04–68–87–49–44* ⊕*www.hotel-arcades-ceret.com* ➷*30*
rooms ♿*In-room: dial-up. In-hotel: parking (fee)* ▭*MC, V.*

COLLIOURE

33

35 km (21 mi) east of Céret, 27 km (17 mi) southeast of Perpignan.

GETTING HERE

Collioure has about a dozen trains (☎04–68–82–05–89) and many buses that make the trip to and from Perpignan (20 mins away). The train station is at the end of Avenue Aristide Maillol and buses leave year-round from the car parks at Place du 8 Mai and Place Jean Jaurés. For specific times: ⊕*www.voyages-sncf.com.*

EXPLORING

The heart of Matisse Country, this pretty seaside fishing village with a sheltered natural harbor has become a summer magnet for tourists (beware the crowds in July and August). Painters such as Henri Matisse, André Derain, Henri Martin, and Georges Braque—who were dubbed Fauves for their "savage" (*fauve* means "wild animal") approach to color and form—were among the early discoverers of Collioure. The view they admired remains largely unchanged today: to the north, the rocky Îlot St-Vincent juts out into the sea, a modern lighthouse at its tip, whereas inland the Albères mountain range rises to connect the Pyrénées with the Mediterranean. The town harbor is a painting unto itself, framed by a 12th-century royal castle and a 17th-century church fortified with a tower.

Matisse set up shop in summer of 1905 and was greatly inspired by the colors of the town's terra-cotta roofs (*see "Matisse Country" below*). The information center, behind the Plage Boramar, has an excellent map that points out the main sites once favored by the Fauve painters, which have now been organized into a pedestrian trail called the *Chemin du Fauvisme* (originating at the Espace Fauve at the Quai de l'Amirauté). In the streets behind the Vieux Port you can see former fishermen's stores now occupied by smart boutiques and restaurants. To find tomorrow's Matisses and Derains, head to the streets behind the Place du 18-Juin and to the old quarter of Le Mouré, set under Fort Miradou—the studios here are filled with contemporary artists at work. Today, the most prized locales are the café-terraces overlooking the main beach or the fashionable Rue Camillle Pelletan by the harbor, where you can feast on Collioure's tender, practically boneless anchovies and the fine Rivesaltes and other local wines from the impeccably cultivated vineyards surrounding the town. Although nearby villages are apparently only rich in quaintness, Collioure is surprisingly prosperous, thanks to the cultivation of *primeurs,* early ripe fruit and vegetables, shipped to the markets of northern France.

At the end of Boulevard du Boramar is the 17th-century church of **Notre-Dame-des-Anges** (⊠*Pl. de l'Église*). It has exuberantly carved, gilded Churrigueresque altarpieces by celebrated Catalan master Joseph Sunyer and a pink-dome bell tower that doubled as the original lighthouse.

A slender jetty divides the Boramar Beach, beneath Notre-Dame-des-Anges, from the small landing area at the foot of the **Château Royal,**

12

Matisse Country

The little coastal village of Collioure continues to play the muse to the entire Côte Vermeille—after all, it gave rise to the name of the Vermilion Coast because the great painter Henri Matisse daringly painted Collioure's yellow-sand beach using a bright red terra-cotta hue. For such artistic daredevilry, he was branded a "wild beast"—or Fauve—and then rewrote the history of art in the process. Considered, along with Picasso, one of the most influential artists of the modern period, Matisse (1869–1954), along with fellow painter and friend André Derain (1880–1954), discovered "Fauvism" en vacances in Collioure in 1905. In search of inspiration, he and Derain holed up there during that summer, seduced by its pink and mauve houses, ocher rooftops, and the dramatic combination of sea, sun, and hills. Back then, the final touches of color were added by the red and green fishing boats. With nature's outré palette at hand, Matisse was inspired to passionate hues and a brash distortion of form.

At summer's end, Matisse made the trip to Paris to show his Collioure works at the Salon d'automne, the season's biggest art event. Because the canvases of Matisse, Derain, Vlaminck, and Marquet were so shockingly hued, they were made to hang their paintings in a back room, Room 7. The public jeered at their work, saying they were primitive, coarse, and extreme. Room 7 became known as "the cage." Before long, they were being called Fauves—a name made up by a somewhat sympathetic critic—and their sucess de scandale quickly won them new adherents, including the painters Rouault, Van Dongen, Braque, and Dufy. Fauvism became the rage

from 1905 to 1908; by 1909 Matisse was famous all around the world.

Today, Matisse's masterpieces grace the walls of the greatest museums in the world. In a sense, Collioure has something better: a host of virtual Matisses, 3-D Derains, and pop-up Dufys. Realizing this, the mayor decided to create the "Chemin du Fauvisme" (The Fauvist Way) a decade ago, erecting 20 reproductions of Matisse's and Derain's works on the very spots where they were painted. Matisse could return today and find things little changed: the Château Royal still perches over the harbor, the Fort Saint-Elme still makes a striking perspectival point on its hilltop, and the Plage Boramar still looks like a 3-acre "Matisse." Pick up the Chemin's trail at the town's Espace Fauve by going to Avenue Camille Pelletan (☎04–68–98–07–16) or check out their Web site at www.collioure.net/fenetre.asp for more information.

a 13th-century castle, once the summer residence of the kings of Majorca (from 1276 to 1344), and remodeled by Vauban 500 years later. ☎04–68–82–06–43 ☜€4 ⊘June–Sept. daily 10–5:15; Oct.–May, daily 9–4:15.

No Matissses hold pride of place at the town's **Musée d'Art Moderne Fonds Péské** but the collection of 180 works deftly sums up the influence the painter had on this cité des peintures. Works by Cocteau, Valtat, and other artists are impressively housed in a picturesque villa (built by Senator Gaston Pams) on a beautiful hillside site. ⊠Rte. de Porte-Vendres ☎04–68–82–10–19 ☜€2 ⊘July and Aug., daily, 10–noon and 2–7; Sept.–June, Mon.–Sat. 10–noon and 2–6.

> **OLÉ!**
>
> If you're around Collioure's Place du 18-Juin on the weekends from April to June and during September, you can enjoy a festival of Catalan dance and music. Contact the town tourist office (☎04–68–82–15–47) for full information. Throughout the region, in neighboring towns like Céret, other Sardane events are also held during this time of year.

WHERE TO STAY & EAT

$$$–$$$$ ✕⌑ **Relais des Trois Mas.** The vistas are priceless, and the rooms very pricey indeed at the Relais. Overlooking the harbor from the cliffs south of town, this hotel enjoys a perfect perch. Inside are small but interestingly furnished rooms—headboards, for example, are made from delightful wooden motifs. Rooms are named for painters whose work appears on the bathroom tiles. Below is a pebbled beach, though you may prefer the small pool (hewn from rock) or the huge Jacuzzi. Dine at the restaurant, La Balette, on the terrace or in one of the two small dining rooms overlooking the harbor. ⊠Rte. de Port-Vendres, 66190 ☎04–68–82–05–07 🖷04–68–82–38–08 ➷19 rooms, 4 suites ♿In-room: refrigerator. In-hotel: restaurant, pool, beachfront, public Internet ▤AE, MC, V ⊘Closed Jan. ¶◎¶FAP.

$ ✕⌑ **Les Templiers.** Universally considered the "soul" of Collioure, this
Fodor'sChoice place merits a visit on every itinerary. Way back when, Matisse, Maillol,
★ Dalí, Picasso, and Dufy used to hang out here. Today, owner Jojo Pous, son of the force behind Collioure's art colony, is proud to show off the more than 2,500 original works hanging from every nook and cranny (including the ceiling and stairs)—one of the most glorious sights in Languedoc-Roussillon. The bar itself is a work of art, curved like the hull of a skiff and ending with a wood sculpture of a mermaid suckling an infant sailor. Collioure is Catalan in all senses but cartographically, so the food here is mostly Catalan and usually excellent; be sure to try dishes that feature the town's fabled anchovies. The rooms overlooking the château are cozy, but be sure yours is not in the annex. ⊠12 quai de l'Amirauté, 66190 ☎04–68–98–31–10 🖷04–68–98–01–24 ⊕www.hotel-templiers.com ➷46 rooms ♿In-room: no a/c, Wi-Fi. In-hotel: restaurant, bar ▤AE, DC, MC, V ⊘Closed Jan. and 1st wk Feb. ¶◎¶FAP.

12

$$–$$$ ⊞ **Casa Pairal.** An idyllic, palm-shaded 19th-century town house surrounded by a leafy garden, this small oasis is a handy address in often tumultuous (for all its idyllic reputation) Collioure. The main house is more charming than the annex but all rooms are comfortable and tastefully appointed. A five-minute walk to the water's edge, the hotel is comfortingly traditional, while the alluring courtyard, garden, and pool are relaxing and intimate. ⊠ *Impasse des Palmiers, 66190* ☎ *04–68–82–05–81* 🖷 *04–68–82–52–10* ⊕ *www.hotel-casa-pairal. com* ⇋ *27 rooms* �ċ *In-room: Wi-Fi. In-hotel: pool, parking (fee)* ⊟ *AE, DC, MC, V.*

SALSES

➌➍ *16 km (10 mi) north of Perpignan, 48 km (30 mi) south of Narbonne.*

Salses has a history of sieges. History relates that Hannibal stormed through the town with his elephants on his way to the Alps in 218 bc, though no trace of his passage remains.

The colossal and well-preserved **Fort de Salses,** built by Ferdinand of Aragon in 1497–1504 and equipped for 300 horses and 1,500 soldiers, fell finally to the French under Cardinal Richelieu in 1642 after three sieges. Bulky round towers ring the rectangular inner fort, and the four-story keep, with its narrow corridors, was designed to keep the fort's governor safe to the last. ☎ *04–68–38–60–13* ⛫ *€6.50* ◷ *Oct.–May, daily 10–12:30 and 2–5; June–Sept., daily 9:30–7.*

NARBONNE

➌➎ *59 km (37 mi) north of Sales, 60 km (37 mi) east of Carcassonne, 94 km (58 mi) south of Montpellier.*

GETTING HERE

Narbonne is an important rail junction of the region. The train station is on Boulevard Frédéric Mistral, north of the city center and adjacent to the Gare Routiere (bus station) on Avenue Carnot. Via train, it takes nearly an hour to get from Perpignan and Montpellier and an hour and a half from Toulouse. There are many connections: about six a day to Perpignan, as well as many others along the coast to the north and south. If you're coming from Paris on the TGV (⊕ *www.tgv.com*) to Perpignan, and then on the regular train to Narbonne, it'll cost you about €90 one-way.

EXPLORING

In Roman times, bustling, industrial Narbonne was the second-largest town in Gaul (after Lyon) and an important port, though today little remains of its Roman past. Until the sea receded during the Middle Ages, Narbonne prospered.

The town's former wealth is evinced by the 14th-century **Cathédrale St-Just-et-St-Pasteur** (⊠ *Rue Armand-Gauthier*); its vaults rise 133 feet from the floor, making it the tallest cathedral in southern France. Only Beauvais and Amiens, in Picardy, are taller, and as at Beauvais, the nave at Narbonne was never built. The "Creation" tapestry is the cathedral's finest treasure.

Richly sculpted cloisters link the cathedral to the former **Palais des Archevêques** *(Archbishops' Palace)*, now home to **museums** of archaeology, art, and history. Note the late-13th-century keep, the Donjon Gilles-Aycelin; climb the 180 steps to the top for a view of the region and the town. ⊠*Palais des Archevêques* ☎*04–68–90–30–30* ⊠*€7.50, includes all town museums* ⊗*May–Sept., daily 9–noon and 2–6; Oct.– Apr., Tues.–Sun. 10–noon and 2–5.*

On the south side of the Canal de la Robine is the **Musée Lapidaire** *(Sculpture Museum)*, in the handsome 13th-century former church of **Notre-Dame de la Mourguié.** Classical busts, ancient sarcophagi, lintels, and Gallo-Roman inscriptions await you. ⊠*Pl. Lamourguier* ☎*04–68– 65–53–58* ⊠*€7.50, includes all town museums* ⊗*May–Sept., daily 9–noon and 2–6; Oct.–Apr., Tues.–Sun. 10–noon and 2–5.*

WHERE TO STAY & EAT

$$–$$$ ✕⊡ **Le Relais du Val d'Orbieu.** This pretty spot 14 km (8 mi) west of town is a viable solution to Narbonne's scarcity of good hotels. Owner Jean-Pierre Gonzalvez speaks English and is extremely helpful. Grouped around a courtyard, most rooms are reached through covered arcades. The better ones are pleasantly simple, with bare tile floors and large French doors leading onto terraces; the standard ones are slightly smaller and do not have terraces or views. The prix-fixe menu restaurant (no lunch) lacks intimacy, but is more than serviceable. ⊠*14 km (8 mi) west of Narbonne, D24, 11200 Ornaisons* ☎*04–68–27–10–27* ⊟*04–68–27–52–44* ⊕*www.relaisduvaldorbieu.com/anglais/suite.htm* ⊅*13 rooms, 5 apartments* ⌂*In-room: no a/c, refrigerator, dial-up. In-hotel: restaurant, tennis court, pool* ⊟*AE, DC, MC, V* ⊗*Closed Dec. and Jan.* ⍩*MAP.*

$–$$ ⊡ **Hotel La Résidence.** One block from the Canal de la Robine and another single block from the Place Salengro and the cathedral, this traditional favorite has housed France's artistic crème de la crème from Georges Brassens to Michel Serrault. The 19th-century building is charming, while rooms combine old-fashioned warmth with modern comforts. ⊠*6 rue Premier Mai, 11100* ☎*04–68–32–19–41* ⊟*04– 68–65–51–82* ⊅*26 rooms* ⌂*In-hotel: parking (fee), public Internet* ⊟*AE, DC, MC, V* ⊗*Closed mid-Jan.–mid-Feb.*

BÉZIERS

36 *25 km (12 mi) northeast of Narbonne, 65 km (33 mi) southwest of Montpellier.*

The Languedoc's wine capital, or *capital du vin*—crowds head here for tastings during the October wine harvest festival—and centerpiece of the Canal du Midi, Béziers owes its reputation to the genius of native son and royal salt-tax collector Pierre-Paul Riquet (that's his statue presiding over the Allées Paul Riquet). He was a visionary at a time when roads were in deplorable shape and grain was transported on the backs of mules. Yet he died a pauper in 1680, a year before the canal's completion (it was begun by the ancient Romans) and the revolutionizing of commerce in the south of France. Few would have predicted much of a future for Béziers in July of 1209, after Simon de Montfort, leader of the crusade against the Cathars, scored his first major victory here, massacring hundreds. Today the Canal du Midi hosts mainly pleasure cruisers, and Béziers sits serenely on its perch overlooking the distant Mediterranean and the foothills of the Cévennes Mountains. Early August sees the four-day *féria*—a festival with roots in Spain and replete with gory bull-fighting (you've been warned).

> **NO SOUR GRAPES**
>
> As in most other wine-producing regions of France, visiting the wine cellars around Béziers is easiest with a car. Luckily, the villages are clustered relatively close together, and buses are frequent enough that it is possible to do some serious wine sipping without a car. To insure a fine day out, stop at Béziers Oenopole (⊠1 allée Paul Riquet ☎04–67–76–20–20) and find out about the best Minervois and Faugères appellations. The tourist office has a complete list of vineyards (and even posts jobs for grape-stomping and other vine-related tasks during the September harvest).

The heavily restored **Église de la Madeleine** (⊠*Off Rue de la République*), with its distinctive octagonal tower, was the site of the beginning of the 1209 massacre. About 7,000 townspeople who had sought refuge from Simon de Montfort in the church were burned alive before he turned his attention to sacking the town; the event is known as *le grand mazel* ("the great bonfire"). Restoration work means that you may only be able to admire the crenellations, gargoyles, floral frieze, and crooked arches of the late-11th-century pentagonal apse.

Béziers's late-19th-century **Halles** *(Market Hall)* was done in the style of the architect Baltard, who built the original Les Halles in Paris. This is a particularly beautiful example, with large stone cabbages gracing the entrance like urns. ⊠*Entrances on Rue Paul Riquet, Pl. Pierre Sémard* ⊙*Daily 6:30 am–1 pm.*

The **Ancienne Cathédrale St-Nazaire** (⊠*Plan des Albigeois*) was rebuilt over several centuries after the sack of Béziers. Note the medieval wall along Rue de Juiverie, which formed the limit between the cathedral precincts and the Jewish quarter of town. The western facade resembles a fortress for good reason: it served as a warning to would-be invaders. Look for the magnificent 17th-century walnut organ and the frescoes about the lives of St. Stephen and others.

Adjoining the cathedral are a 14th-century cloister and the **Jardin des Evêques** *(Bishops' Garden)*, a terraced garden descending to the banks of the Orb. The views from here, which take in Béziers's five bridges, are magnificent. ⊠*Plan des Albigeois* ⊙*Oct.–Apr., daily 10–noon and 2–5:30; May–Sept., daily 10–7.*

WHERE TO STAY & EAT

$$–$$$ ✕⊡ **Château de Lignan.** Set in its own park, this elegant estate northwest of Béziers has two slender tile-roof towers, lending a vaguely Italianate air to the austere stucco facade. Pity that rooms have little to distinguish them from standard chain hotels except their size and louvered windows, but the restaurant is exceptional. The octagonal sprawl of the skylighted dining room is cheery and welcoming. Simple, streamlined fare such as strongly flavored *loup en papillote* (sea bass cooked in foil) makes a perfect prelude to the vanilla ice cream–filled baked pears. ⊠*Pl. de l'Église, 6 km (4 mi) northwest of Béziers, 34490 Lignan-sur-Orb* ☎*04–67–37–91–47* 🖷*04–67–37–99–25* ⊕*www.qdinet. fr* ➬*49 rooms* ⌂*In-room: refrigerator, Wi-Fi. In-hotel: restaurant, pool* ☐*AE, MC, V* ⎢⎝*MAP.*

THE OUTDOORS

Daylong excursions on the Canal du Midi include passage over the canal bridge spanning the Orb and through the nine locks. Some companies working the Canal de Midi have extensive routes, some as far as the Mediterranean resort town of Agde, 21 km (14 mi) away. **Les Bâteaux du Soleil** (⊠*6 rue Chassefière, 34300 Agde* ☎*04–67–94–08–79* 🖷*04–67–21–28–38*) has some wide-ranging excursions.

■
OFF THE
BEATEN
PATH

Minerve. Set 37 km (25 mi) west of Béziers in the limestone gorges of the Vallée de la Cesse, Minerve is a quintessential Cathar medieval hilltop village. It sheltered many heretics during the Albigensian Crusade but proved no match for Simon de Montfort's siege in July 1210—180 Cathar *Perfecti* (elite Cathari) were burned after the army had blocked the village access with a catapult called La Malvoisine (the Evil Neighbor), now reconstructed. The austere, Romanesque Église St-Étienne has one of the oldest altar tables in Europe, dating from ad 456. The Musée Hurepel re-creates the events of the Albigensian Crusade in a series of figurine-populated dioramas. Around Minerve are a number of *ponts naturels* (natural bridges), enormous tunnels in the rock cut by the path of the Cesse River, prehistoric grottoes, and dolmens. For information about Minerve (and many Minervois vineyards) contact the tourist office (⊠*9 rue des Martyrs* ☎*04–68–91–81–43*).

MONTPELLIER

62 km (35 mi) northeast of Béziers, 42 km (26 mi) southwest of Nîmes.

GETTING HERE

British Airways and Air France fly out of the Airport Montpellier-Méditerranée (☎*04–67–20–85–00*), set southeast of Montpellier. Shuttles leave the bus station about every hour for the airport from Place du Bicentenaire. The TGV takes 4 hours, 40 minutes from Paris for about €85 and there are direct trains as far afield as Avignon, Nice, and Marseille. If you're trying to get to the sea, hail Bus No. 17 (which passes every half hour for Palavas).

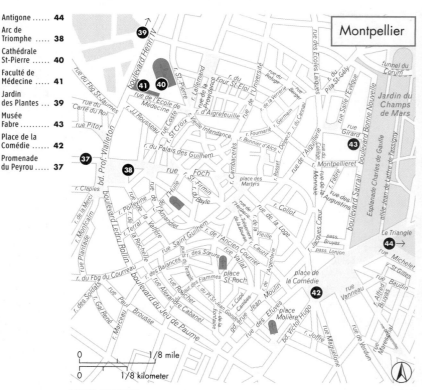

EXPLORING

Vibrant Montpellier (pronounced monh-pell-*yay*), capital of the Languedoc-Roussillon region, has been a center of commerce and learning since the Middle Ages, when it was a crossroads for pilgrims on their way to Santiago de Compostela, in Spain, and an active shipping center trading in spices from the East. With its cargo of exotic luxuries, it also imported Renaissance learning, and its university—founded in the 13th century—has nurtured a steady influx of ideas through the centuries. Though the port silted up by the 16th century, Montpellier never became a backwater, and as a center of commerce and conferences it keeps its focus on the future. An imaginative urban planning program has streamlined the 17th-century Vieille Ville, and monumental perspectives dwarf passersby on the 17th-century Promenade du Peyrou. An even more utopian venture in urban planning is the Antigone district: a vast, harmonious 100-acre complex designed in 1984 by Barcelona architect Ricardo Bofill. A student population of some 75,000 keeps things lively, especially on the Place de la Comédie, the city's social nerve center. The Old Town is a pedestrian paradise, and you can travel around the entire city on the excellent bus system (the Gare Routière station is by the train terminal on Rue Jules Ferry).

★ ③⑦ Montpellier's grandest avenue is the **Promenade du Peyrou,** built at the end of the 17th century and dedicated to Louis XIV.

③⑧ The Peyrou's centerpiece is the enormous **Arc de Triomphe,** designed by d'Aviler in 1689 and finished by Giral in 1776; it looms majestically over the peripheral highway that loops around the city center. Together, the noble scale of these harmonious stone constructions and the sweeping perspectives they frame make for an inspiring stroll through this posh stretch of town. At the end of the park is the **Château d'Eau,** a Corinthian temple and the terminal for **les Arceaux,** an 18th-century aqueduct; on a clear day the view from here is spectacular, taking in the Cévennes Mountains, the sea, and an ocean of red-tile roofs (it's worth it to come back here at night to see the entire promenade lighted up).

Boulevard Henri IV runs north from the Promenade du Peyrou to
③⑨ France's oldest botanical garden, the **Jardin des Plantes,** planted on order of Henri IV in 1593. An exceptional range of plants, flowers, and trees grows here. ✉*Free* ◷*Gardens Tues.–Sat. 9–noon and 2–5. Greenhouses weekdays 9–noon and 2–5, Sat. 9–noon.*

After taking in the broad vistas of the Promenade de Peyrou, cross over into the Vieille Ville and wander its maze of narrow streets full of pretty shops and intimate restaurants. At the northern edge of the
④⓪ Vieille Ville, visit the imposing **Cathédrale St-Pierre** (✉*Pl. St-Pierre*), its fantastical and unique 14th-century entry porch alone worth the detour: two cone-topped towers—some five stories high—flank the main portal and support a groin-vaulted shelter. The interior, despite 18th-century reconstruction, maintains the formal simplicity of its 14th-century origins.

④① Next door to the cathedral, peek into the noble **Faculté de Médecine,** on Rue de l'École de Médecine, one of France's most respected medical schools, founded in the 13th century and infused with generations of international learning—especially Arab and Jewish scholarship.

From the medical school follow Rue Foch, which slices straight east. The number of bistros and brasseries increases as you leave the Vieille Ville to cross Place des Martyrs; veering right down Rue de la
④② Loge, you spill out onto the festive gathering spot known as **Place de la Comédie.** Anchored by the Neoclassical 19th-century Opéra-Comédie, this broad square is a beehive of leisurely activity, a cross between Barcelona's Ramblas and a Roman *passeggiata* (afternoon stroll, en masse). Brasseries, bistros, fast-food joints, and cinemas draw crowds, but the pleasure is getting there and seeing who came before, in which shoes, and with whom.

From Place de la Comédie, Boulevard Sarrail leads north past the shady
★ ④③ Esplanade Charles de Gaulle to the **Musée Fabre.** Renovated in 2006, the museum is a mixed bag of architectural styles (a 17th-century *hôtel,* a vast Victorian wing with superb natural light, and a remnant of a Baroque Jesuit college). This rich art museum has a surprisingly big collection, thanks to its namesake. François-Xavier Fabre, a native of

Montpellier, was a student of the great 18th-century French artist David, who established roots in Italy and acquired a formidable collection of masterworks—which he then donated to his hometown, supervising the development of this fine museum. Among his gifts were the *Mariage Mystique de Sainte Catherine,* by Veronese, and Poussin's coquettish *Venus et Adonis.* Later contributions include a superb group of 17th-century Flemish works (Rubens, Steen), a collection of 19th-century French canvases (Géricault, Delacroix, Corot, Millet) that inspired Gauguin and Van Gogh, and a growing group of 20th-century acquisitions that buttress a legacy of paintings by early Impressionist Frédéric Bazille. ⊠*39 bd. Bonne Nouvelle* ☎*04–67–14–83–00* ☜€*6* ⊗*Tues., Thurs., Fri. 10–5, Wed. 3–9, weekends 11–6.*

> ### GETTING AROUND
>
> Montpellier's historic *centre ville* is a pedestrian's paradise, with a labyrinth of stone paths and alleys leading from courtyard to courtyard. Hotels, restaurants, and sights are all within walking distance of Place de la Comédie, but the town also has a comprehensive bus system, SMTU, which starts out from the Gare Routière on Place du Bicentenaire. With thousands of college students in town, bike rentals are another easy way to get around.

NEED A BREAK?   Enjoy a 15-minute stroll from the Musée Fabre to the lively café-bar Bar du Musée (⊠*3 rue Montpellieret* ☎*04–67–60–45–65*). Pop in for an aperitif and a look at the ever-changing exhibit of local artists—and trendy Montpellierains nibbling olives.

④④ At the far-east end of the city loop, Montpellier seems to transform itself into a futuristic ideal city, all in one smooth, low-slung postmodern style. This is the **Antigone** district, the result of city planners' efforts (and local industries' commitment) to pull Montpellier up out of its economic doldrums. It worked. This ideal neighborhood, designed by the Catalan architect Ricardo Bofill, covers 100-plus acres with plazas, esplanades, shops, restaurants, and low-income housing, all constructed out of stone-color, prestressed concrete. Be sure to visit Place du Nombre d'Or—symmetrically composed of curves—and the 1-km-long (½-mi-long) vista that stretches down a mall of cypress trees to the glass-fronted **Hôtel de Region** (⊠*Rue de Pompegnane*).

WHERE TO STAY & EAT

$$$$ ✕ **Le Jardin des Sens.** Blink and look again: twins Laurent and Jacques
Fodor'sChoice Pourcel, trained under separate masters, combine forces here to achieve
★   a quiet, almost cerebral cuisine based on southern French traditions. At every turn are happy surprises: foie gras crisps, dried-fruit risotto, and lamb sweetbreads with *gambas* (prawns). A modest lunch menu (in the $$ category) lets you indulge on a budget. Decor is minimal stylish, with steel beams and tables on three tiers. Truth is, the restaurant is in a rather *delabré* working-class neighborhood and from the outside looks like an anonymous warehouse. ⊠*11 av. St-Lazare, 34000* ☎*04–99–*

58–38–38 🖥*04–99–58–38–39* ⊕*www.jardindessens.com* ☰*AE, DC, MC, V* ⊘*Closed Jan. and Sun. No lunch Mon. and Wed.*

★ **$$$$** ✕ **L'Olivier.** For a great taste of Provence right in the heart of Montpellier, this is the place to go. The decor is nothing to write home about—spartan Provençal feel, even with the odd splash of a painting on the wall—but the cuisine proves a very satisfying gastronomic surprise. You come to L'Olivier for the good food. The *filet de sole aux homard et morilles* (sole and lobster in a wild mushroom sauce) and the slow-cooked *Costières du Gard pigeon aux cepes* (regional pigeon in a wild mushroom sauce) might not equal the three-star extravaganzas served up at Jardin des Sens but they are well worth the price. ✉*12 rue Aristide Olivier* ☎*04–67–92–86–28* ☰*AE, MC, V* ⊘*Closed Mon. and last wk Aug.*

$$–$$$ ✕ **Le Chat Perché.** People flock here for the warm bistro ambience, the terrace overlooking the square below, the carefully selected regional wines, and the traditional dishes served with flair. The cuisine varies with the seasons, the markets, and the humor of the chef. *Everything here is homemade and reasonably priced.* ✉*10 rue collège Duvergier, Place de la Chapelle Neuve* ☎*04–67–60–88–59* ⚠*Reservations essential* ☰*MC, V* ⊘*Closed Sun. and Jan. No lunch Mon.*

★ **$$–$$$** ✕ **Le Petit Jardin.** On a quiet Vieille Ville backstreet, this simple restaurant lives up to its name: you dine looking over (or seated in) a lovely, deep-shaded garden with views of the cathedral. A simple omelet with pepper sauce, fresh foie gras in a rhubarb sauce, or hearty osso buco (veal shanks in saffron-tomato sauce) mirrors the welcome, which is warm and unpretentious. ✉*20 rue Jean-Jacques Rousseau* ☎*04–67–60–78–78* ☰*AE, MC, V* ⊘*Closed Jan. and Mon.*

$ ✕ **Chez Mémé.** This ever-popular restaurant is the perfect spot for a traditional dinner reminiscent of *cuisine de Mémé* (Grandma's cooking), serving grilled trout with almonds, ratatouille, and warm apple tart with a dollop of cream. The portions are ample, the atmosphere is fast, fun, and friendly with local musicians playing for their soup, *and* it's ever so light on the pocket. *Yippee!* ✉*18 rue Ecoles Laïques* ☎*04–67–02–43–26* ☰*MC, V* ⊘*Closed Sun. No lunch.*

★ **$$–$$$** 🏨 **Le Guilhem.** On the same quiet backstreet as the restaurant Le Petit Jardin, this jewel of a *hôtel de charme* is actually a series of 16th-century houses. Rebuilt from ruins to include an elevator and state-of-the-art white-tile baths, it nonetheless retains original casement windows (many overlooking the extraordinary old garden), slanting floors, and views toward the cathedral. Soft yellows and powder blues add to its *temps perdu* gentleness. Tiny garret-style rooms at the top are great if you're traveling alone; if not, ask for the largest available. ✉*18 rue Jean-Jacques-Rousseau, 34000* ☎*04–67–52–90–90* 🖥*04–67–60–67–67* ⊕*www.leguilhem.com* ⇨*35 rooms* ⚙*In-room: Wi-Fi. In-hotel: parking (fee)* ☰*AE, DC, MC, V.*

NIGHTLIFE & THE ARTS

Concerts are performed in the very imposing **Opéra Comédie de Montpellier** (✉*11 bd. Victor Hugo* ☎*04–67–60–19–99*). The resident **Orchestre National de Montpellier** is a young and energetic group of some reputation, performing regularly in the Opéra Berlioz in the Corum conference complex.

MIDI-PYRÉNÉES & LANGUEDOC-ROUSSILLON ESSENTIALS

TRANSPORTATION

If traveling extensively by public transportation, be sure to load up on information (schedules, the best taxi-for-call companies, etc.) upon arriving at the ticket counter or help desk of the bigger train and bus stations in the area, such as Toulouse, Carcassonne, and Montpellier.

BY AIR

AIRPORTS

All international flights for Toulouse arrive at Blagnac Airport, 8 km (5 mi) northwest of the city. The airport shuttle (⊕*www.navetteviatoulouse.com*) runs every 20 minutes between 7:35 am and 12:15 pm from the airport to the bus–train station in Toulouse (fare €4). From the Toulouse bus station to the airport, buses leave every 20 minutes 5 am–8:20 pm.

Airport Information Airport Montpellier-Méditerranée (☎*04-67-20-85-00*). **Airport Carcassonne-Salvaza** (☎*04-68-71-96-46*). **Airport International, Perpignan** (☎*04-68-35-36-36*). **Airport Béziers-Vias** (☎*04-67-80-90-09*). **Blagnac Airport** (☎*08-25-38-00-00*).

CARRIERS

Air France has regular flights between Paris and Toulouse; Montpellier is served by frequent flights from Paris and London. In addition, be sure to check out Ryanair, EasyJet, and Flybe, who offer surprisingly cheap flights to Perpignan, Montpellier, Carcassonne, or Toulouse—often as low as €30 one-way.

Airlines & Contacts Air France (☎*08-20-82-08-20* ⊕ *www.airfrance.com*). **EasyJet** (☎*08-25-08-25-08* ⊕ *www.easyjet.com*). **Flybe** (☎*44-13-92-26-85-00 in U.K.*). **Ryanair** (☎*04-68-71-96-65* ⊕ *www.ryanair.com*).

BY BUS

As in most rural regions in France, there's an array of bus companies (in addition to SNCF buses, Intercars, Semvat, Courriers de la Garonne, Salt Autocars, Transnod, among others) threading the Midi-Pyrénées countryside. Toulouse's bus links include Albi (1½ hrs, €13), Auch, Castres, Foix (1 hr, € 8), Carcassonne (2 hrs, €12), and Montauban; Albi connects with Cordes-sur-Ciel (summer only; other times take train to Cordes-Vindrac, 5 km [3 mi] away) and Montauban; Montauban with Moissac (20 mins, € 4), and Auch; Montpellier with Béziers and Narbonne. For Courriers Catalans, Cars Capeille, and Car Inter 66 buses to the Côte Vermeille, Collioure, Céret, Prades, and Font-Romeu depart from Perpignan. The train to Carcassonne is scenic and romantic, although buses (cheaper and faster) go there as well.

Bus Information Gare Routière Carcassonne (✉ *Bd. De Varsovie, Ville Basse*). **Gare Routière Montpellier** (✉ *Pl. du Bicentenaire* ☎ *04-67-58-57-59*). **Gare Routière Perpignan** (✉ *Av. du Général Leclerc s/n* ☎ *04-68-35-29-02*). **Gare Routière Toulouse** (✉ *64 bd. Pierre Sémard* ☎ *05-61-61-67-67*).

BY CAR

The fastest route from Paris to Toulouse (677 km [406 mi] south) is via Limoges on A20, then A62; the journey time is about six hours. If you choose to head south over the Pyrénées to Barcelona, the Tunnel du Puymorens saves half an hour of switchbacks between Hospitalet and Porta, but in good weather and with time to spare the drive over the Puymorens Pass is spectacular. Plan on taking three hours between Toulouse and Font-Romeu and another three to Barcelona. The fastest route from Toulouse to Barcelona is the under-three-hour, 391-km (235-mi) drive via Carcassonne and Perpignan on A61 and A9, which becomes AP7 at Le Perthus.

A62/A61 slices through the region on its way through Carcassonne to the coast at Narbonne, where A9 heads south to Perpignan. At Toulouse, where A62 becomes A61, various highways fan out in all directions: N124 to Auch; A64 to St-Gaudens, Tarbes, and Pau; A62/A20 to Montauban and Cahors; N20 south to Foix and the Ariège Valley; A68 to Albi and Rodez. A9 (La Languedocienne) is the main highway artery that connects Montpellier with Beziers to the south and Nîmes to the north.

BY TRAIN

Most trains for the southwest leave from Paris's Gare d'Austerlitz. There are direct trains to Toulouse and Montauban. Carcassonne connects with either Toulouse or Montpellier. Four trains leave Paris (Gare de Lyon) daily for Narbonne and one for Perpignan, although others connect with Montpellier. Most of these trips take between six and seven hours. Note that at least three high-speed TGV (Trains à Grande Vitesse) per day leave Paris (Gare Montparnasse) for Toulouse; the journey time is five hours. A TGV line also serves Montpellier four times a day (departing Paris's Gare de Lyon).

The regional French rail network in the southwest provides regular service to many towns, though not all. Within the Midi-Pyrénées region, Toulouse is the biggest hub, with a major line linking Carcassonne (45 mins, €15), Béziers, Narbonne (1½ hrs, €21) (change here for Perpignan), and Montpellier (2 hrs, €32); trains also link up with Albi (1 hr, €11), Foix (1 hr, €12), Ax-les-Thermes (2 hrs, €15), and Montauban (30 mins, € 8); the latter connects with Moissac. Toulouse trains also connect with Biarritz (4 hrs, € 35), Pau (2 hrs, €33), and Bordeaux (3 hrs, €39). Montpellier connects with Carcassonne (1 hr, €12), Perpignan (2 hrs, €28), Narbonne, Béziers, and other towns. Béziers is linked by train to Carcassonne, Perpignan, Narbonne, and Montpellier, as well as Paris. From Perpignan, take one of the dozen or so daily trains to Collioure (20 mins, €6).

Train Information Gare SNCF Carcassonne (✉ *Quai Riquer s/n* ☎ *08-92-35-35-35*). **Gare SNCF Montpellier** (✉ *Rue Jules Ferry* ☎ *08-86-92-35-35 (or*

35–36)). **Gare SNCF Perpignan** (✉ *Av. du Général de Gaulle* ☎ *35–36*). **SNCF** (☎ *36–35, €0.34 per min* ⊕ *www.voyages-sncf.com*). **SNCF Toulouse-Matabiau** (✉ *64 bd. Pierre Semard* ☎ *05–61–10–11–04*). **TGV** (⊕ *www.tgv.com*).

CONTACTS & RESOURCES

CAR RENTAL

Local Agencies **Avis** (✉ *13 bd. Conflent, Perpignan* ☎ *04–68–34–26–71* ✉ *Blagnac Airport, Toulouse* ☎ *05–34–60–64–00*). **Europcar** (✉ *Aeroport Salvaza, Carcassonne* ☎ *04–68–72–23–69*). **Hertz** (✉ *Rue St. Jean, Montpellier train station* ☎ *04–67–06–87–90* ✉ *33 bd. Omer Sarrant, Carcassonne* ☎ *04–68–25–41–26*)

EMERGENCIES

For basic information, see this section in the Essentials chapter. In most cases, contact the town Comissariat de Police.

Emergencies **Police** (✉ *Av. Dr. Correlles, Toulouse* ☎ *17*). **Police** (✉ *Pl. de la Comédie, Montpellier* ☎ *04–67–34–71–00*). **Police** (✉ *23 bd. de l'Embouchure, Perpignan* ☎ *04–68–66–30–70*). **Hospital La Peyronie** (✉ *371 av. du Doyen Gaston Giraud, Montpellier* ☎ *04–67–33–70–32*).**Purpan Hospital** (✉ *Pl. du Dr. Joseph Baylac, Toulouse* ☎ *05–61–77–22–33*).

INTERNET & MAIL

In smaller towns, ask your hotel concierge if there are any Internet cafés nearby.

Internet & Mail Information **Alerte Rouge** (✉ *73 rue de Verdun, Carcassonne* ☎ *04–68–25–20–39*). **Alerte Rouge** (✉ *21 pl. St-Sernin, Toulouse* ☎ *05–61–34–99–38*). **Clicnet** (✉ *9 rue Verdun, Montpellier* ☎ *04–67–06–90–21*). **Net and Games** (✉ *45 bis, av. Gen. Leclerc, Perpignan* ☎ *04–68–35–36–29*). **La Poste main post office** (✉ *15 rue Rondelet, Montpellier* ☎ *04–67–34–50–00*).

La Poste main post office (✉ *9 rue Lafayette, Toulouse* ☎ *05–34–45–70–82*).

MEDIA

Le Dépeche du Midi is the local newspaper of Toulouse, carrying listings and regional news items. *L'Indépendant* (published in Perpignan) is one of the Roussillon's leading regional dailies and widely available across southern France. *Midi Libre* (Perpignan) is a popular local paper from Montpellier south to the Spanish border, up into the Pyrénées Orientales and along the Côte Vermeille.

TOUR OPTIONS

Contact the Toulouse tourist office for information about walking tours and bus tours in and around Toulouse. Ask for the English-speaking, encyclopedic, and superbly entertaining Gilbert Casagrande for a nonpareil tour of Toulouse. The Comité Régional du Tourisme has a brochure, "1,001 Escapes in the Midi-Pyrénées," with descriptions of weekend and short organized package vacations.

In addition to publishing map itineraries that you can follow yourself, the **Montpellier tourist office** (☎ *04–67–60–60–60*) provides guided walking tours of the city's neighborhoods and monuments daily in summer and on Wednesday and Saturday during the school year (roughly,

September–June). They leave from the Place de la Comédie. A small **tourist train** (☎ *04–67–51–27–37 information*) with broadcast commentary leaves from the Esplanade Charles de Gaulle between 2 and 9, Monday through Saturday.

Contacts Comité Régional du Tourisme Midi-Pyrénées (*CRT,* ✉ *54 bd. de l'Embouchure, 31200 Toulouse* ☎ *05–61–13–55–55*). **Montpellier tourist office** (✉ *30 allée Jean de Lattre de Tassigny, Esplanade Comédie* ☎ *04–67–60–60–60*). **Toulouse tourist office** (✉ *Donjon du Capitole* ☎ *05–61–11–02–22* ⊕ *www. toulouse-tourisme.com*).

VISITOR INFORMATION

The regional tourist office for the Midi-Pyrénées is the Comité Régional du Tourisme. For Pyrénées-Roussillon information, contact the Comité Départemental de Tourisme du Pyrénées-Roussillon. For Languedoc-Roussillon contact the Comité Régional du Tourisme du Languedoc-Roussillon. Local tourist offices are listed by town below. Other handy Web sites for the regions in this chapter include ⊕*www.audetourisme. com* and ⊕*www.tourisme-tarn.com.*

Tourist Information Comité Régional du Tourisme (*CRT,* ✉ *54 bd. de l'Embouchure, 31200 Toulouse* ☎ *05–61–13–55–55*). **Comité Départemental de Tourisme du Pyrénées-Roussillon** (✉ *Quai de Lattre de Tassigny, B.P. 540, 66005 Perpignan* ☎ *04–68–34–29–94*). **Comité Régional du Tourisme du Languedoc-Roussillon** (✉ *20 rue de la République, 34000 Montpellier* ☎ *04–67–22–81–00* 🖶 *04–67–58–06–10* ⊕ *www.sunfrance.com*).

Albi (✉ *Pl. Ste-Cécile* ☎ *05–63–49–48–80* ⊕ *www.albi-tourisme.com*). **Béziers** (✉ *Palais des Congrès, 29 av. St-Saëns* ☎ *04–67–76–84–00*). **Carcassonne** (✉ *28 rue de Verdun* ☎ *04–68–10–24–30* ⊕ *www.carcassonne-tourisme.com*). **Céret** (✉ *1 av. Clemenceau* ☎ *04–68–87–00–53* ⊕ *www.ot-ceret.fr*). **Collioure** (✉ *Pl. 18-juin* ☎ *04–68–82–15–47* ⊕ *www.collioure.com*). **Cordes-sur-Ciel** (✉ *Maison Fonpeyrouse* ☎ *05–63–56–00–52*). **Moissac** (✉ *6 pl. Durand de Bredon* ☎ *05–63–04–01–85*). **Montpellier** (✉ *30 allée Jean de Lattre de Tassigny, Esplanade Comédie* ☎ *04–67–60–60–60* ⊕ *www.ot-montpellier.fr*). **Narbonne** (✉ *Pl. Roger-Salengro* ☎ *04–68–90–30–66*). **Perpignan** (✉ *Quai de Lattre de Tassigny* ☎ *04–68–66–31–63*). **Prades** (✉ *4 rue des Marchands* ☎ *04–68–05–41–02*). **Toulouse** (✉ *Donjon du Capitole* ☎ *05–61–11–02–22* ⊕ *www.toulouse.fr*). **Ville-franche-de-Conflent** (✉ *Pl. de l'Eglise* ☎ *05–62–64–00–00*).

The Basque Country, Gascony & Hautes-Pyrénées

Ossau Valley

WORD OF MOUTH

"St-Jean-de-Luz in the extreme southwest corner is lovely, and the Basque countryside is as well. Farther east is Pau, a less-touristy city with nice restaurants and a château worthy of a visit (the birthplace of Henry IV). Any of the roads into the mountain passes of the Pyrénées is worth a trip for the gorgeous mountain scenery."

—Bob14

WELCOME TO THE BASQUE COUNTRY, GASCONY & HAUTES-PYRÉNÉES

TOP REASONS TO GO

★ **Biarritz, Big Sur à la mode:** Today, Biarritz is Europe's surf capital, a far cry from its beginnings as the favorite watering place of Empress Eugénie, but, face it, this is one party everyone is invited to.

★ **Basque Chic:** Ainhoa, Sare, and St-Jean-de-Luz are three of the prettiest villages that show off the colorful, asymmetric architecture of the Basques.

★ **Michel Guérard's Les Prés de Eugénie:** Not quite the *dernier cri* he used to be, the father of nouvelle cuisine still creates glorious meals in tucked-away Eugénie-les-Bains.

★ **Gorgeous Gavarnie:** Victor Hugo called the 1,400-foot-high waterfall here "the greatest architect's greatest work."

★ **Pretty Pau:** Set with a panoramic view of the Pyrénées, Pau is the historic capital of Béarn (as in béarnaise sauce)—its regal monuments recall its royal past as the birthplace of King Henri IV.

1 The Atlantic Pyrénées. From the first important height at the 2,969-foot La Rhune, towering over the edge of the Atlantic, the Basque Pyrénées rise eastward through picturesque valleys and villages to the Iparla Ridge above Bidarrai and the range's first major peak at the 6,617-foot Orhi peak. The hills cosset cozy villages like **Sare, Ainhoa,** and **Bidarray** (Alain Ducasse's luxury Basque inn is here). The colorful architecture and flower balconies help preserve **St-Jean-Pied-de-Port**'s charm. Gateway to the Pyrénées, **Pau** is the most culturally vibrant city in Gascony, with elegant *hôtels particuliers* and a royal château.

2 Hautes-Pyrénées. The Hautes-Pyrénées include the highest and most spectacular natural wonders in the cordillera. Although mountain peaks soar in this region, they have always attracted notable cultural luminaries including Victor Hugo, Montaigne, and Rossini, who came to marvel at the legendary **Cirque de Gavarnie,** a natural mountain amphitheater. Millions others venture here to holy **Lourdes.**

3 **The Basque Coast.** Fine sand beaches in tawny yellows and red, green, and blue fishing villages keep your eyes busy with their competing palettes on the lush Basque Coast, with world-class chefs making the most of local produce. **Bayonne** as the graceful French provincial city, **Biarritz** as the imperial beach domain, and **St-Jean-de-Luz** as the colorful fishing port all play their parts to perfection along this southwestern coastline backed by the soft green pastures of the Basque hills.

GETTING ORIENTED

13

The most southwestern corner of France's sprawling "Southwest," the rolling hills of the French Basque provinces stretch from the Atlantic beaches of glittering Biarritz to the first Pyrenean heights: the hills and highlands of Gascony around the city of Pau. These are mere stepping-stones compared to the peaks of the Hautes-Pyrénées, which lie to the east and sit in the center of the towering barrier historically separating the Iberian Peninsula from continental Europe.

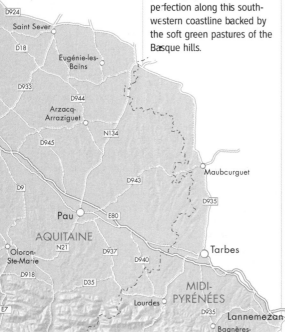

Lourdes, Hautes-Pyrénées

Sare, Pyrénées Atlantiques

BASQUE COUNTRY, GASCONY & HAUTES-PYRÉNÉES PLANNER

Making the Most of Your Time

Unless you prefer rising with the sun, traveling west to east, with the sun behind you as the shadows lengthen, is the best way to approach this part of the Pyrénées.

Bayonne is the natural starting point, at the mouth of the Atlantic Pyrenean watershed, with the Basque Museum as an instructive primer for the culture of the villages you are about to go through.

Biarritz and St-Jean-de-Luz offer opportunities for beach time and glamour. The picturesque villages of Sare, Ainhoa, and Bidarrai all guide you into the mountains and valleys, threaded by rivers flowing into the Nive.

St-Jean-Pied-de-Port is a Pyrenean hub from which Eugénie-les-Bains, Sauveterre de Bearn, and Navarrenx are short detours before continuing east to Pau, the Hautes-Pyrénées, and their crowning glory, Gavarnie.

Wherever you head, make haste slowly: this region's proximity to Spain comes to life in its architecture, in the expressive Midi accent, which turns the word *demain* (tomorrow) into "demaing," and the slow-paced lifestyle.

Getting Around

A car is the best way of getting around the Basque Coast and the Pyrénées. Train and bus connections will get you from Bayonne to Biarritz and Hendaye and up to St-Jean-Pied-de-Port easily, but less pivotal destinations will entail much waiting and loss of valuable time. The roads are good, albeit slow, and you shouldn't plan on doing much better than 60 km–70 km an hour on average. For walking the hills or long distance hikes across the GR10 or the Haute Randonnée Pyrénéenne along the crest of the cordillera, bus and trains such as the SNCF Bayonne to St-Jean-Pied-de-Port connection will drop you off and pick you up at trail heads such as the one at Bidarrai's Pont d'Enfer. Bus lines from St-Jean-Pied-de-Port will take you east to Larrau, Mauleon, and Pau. From Pau there are SNCF connections up into the Pyrénées, with subsequent SNCF buses to points such as Gavarnie.

Finding a Place to Stay

From palatial beachside splendor in Biarritz to simple mountain auberges in the Basque Country to Pyrenean refuges in the Hautes-Pyrénées, the gamut of lodging in southwest France is conveniently broad. Upland lodging need not be considered less opulent than coastal options with Bidarrai's Alain Ducasse hotel, Ostapé, or Firmin Arrambide's Les Pyrénées on call for top comfort at altitude. For top value and camaraderie, look for *gîtes* or *tables d'hôtes* (rustic bed-and-breakfasts and way stations for hikers and skiers), where all guests dine together. Be sure to book summertime lodging on the Basque coast well in advance, particularly for August. In the Hautes-Pyrénées only Gavarnie during its third-week-of-July music festival presents a potential booking problem. An even better approach is to make it up as you go: the surprises that come along are usually very pleasant. Assume that all hotel rooms have air-conditioning, TV, telephones, and private bath, unless otherwise noted.

Getting on Top of Things

Supping on the hearty regional cuisine makes perfect sense after a day of hiking along the gorges and into the mountains of the Pyrénées, which are best explored on foot.

Day trips to promontories such as the La Rhune overlooking Biarritz and the Basque Coast or the walk up to Biriatou from the beach at Hendaye are great ways to get to know the countryside intimately.

Hiking the Pyrénées from one end to the other is a 43-day enterprise. Shorter outings tailored to time available and fitness may be preferable (and leave you closer to finer dining options).

The GR (Grande Randonnée) 10, a trail signed by discreet red-and-white paint markings, runs all the way from the Atlantic at Hendaye to Banyuls-sur-Mer on the Mediterranean, through villages and up and down mountains. Placed along the way are mountain refuges.

The HRP (Haute Randonnée Pyrénéenne, or High Pyrenean Hike) stays closer to the border crest, following the terrain in both France and Spain irrespective of national borders. Local trails are also well indicated, usually with blue or yellow markings.

Some of the classic walks in the Basque Pyrénées include the Iparla Ridge walk between Bidarrai and St-Etienne-de-Baïgorry, the Santiago de Compostela Trail's dramatic St-Jean-Pied-de-Port to Roncesvalles walk over the Pyrénées, and the Holçarté Gorge walk between Larrau and Ste-Engrâce. Trail maps are available from local tourist offices.

WHAT IT COSTS

	¢	$	$$	$$$	$$$$
Restaurants	Under €8	€8–€12	€12–€17	€17–€25	Over €25
Hotels	Under €50	€50–€80	€80–€120	€120–€180	Over €180

Restaurant prices are per person for a main course at dinner, including tax (19.6%) and service; note that if a restaurant offers only prix-fixe (set-price) meals, it has been given the price category that reflects the full prix-fixe price. Hotel prices are for a standard double room in high season, including tax (19.6%) and service charge. Hotels operate on the European Plan (EP, with no meal provided) unless we note that they use the Breakfast Plan (BP), or also offer such options as Modified American Plan (MAP, with breakfast and dinner daily, known as demi-pension), or Full American Plan (FAP, or pension complète, with three meals a day). Inquire when booking if these all-inclusive meal plans (which always entail higher rates) are mandatory or optional.

How's the Weather?

The Basque Country is known for its wet climate, but, when the skies clear, the hillsides are so green and the air so clear that the rain gods are immediately forgiven. Late fall and winter are generally rainier than the early autumn or late spring. The Pyrenean heights such as Brèche de Roland and Gavarnie, on the other hand, may only be approached safely in mid-summer. Treacherous ice and snow plaques can be present even in mid-June and summer blizzards are never impossible. Global warming may be shrinking glaciers and extending the Pyrénées' safety period, but freak conditions, the reverse side of the same coin, may be creating even more unpredictable and dangerous conditions. Beach weather is from May through September and sometimes lasts until mid-October's *veranillo de San Martin* (Indian Summer). Skiing conditions are reliable from December through March and, on occasion, into April.

13

Introduction
by George
Semler

Updated
by George
Semler

A PELOTA-PLAYING MAYOR IN THE province of Soule recently welcomed a group of travelers with the following announcements: that the Basque Country is the most beautiful place in the world; that the Basque people were very likely direct descendants of Adam and Eve via the lost city of Atlantis; that his own ancestors fought in the Crusades; and that Christopher Columbus was almost certainly a Basque. There, in brief, was a composite picture of the pride, dignity, and humor of the Basques. And if Columbus was not a Basque (a claim very much in doubt), at least historians know that whalers from the regional village of St-Jean-de-Luz sailed as far as America in their three-masted ships and that Juan Sebastián Elkano, from the Spanish Basque village of Guetaria, commanded the completion of Magellan's voyage around the world after Magellan's 1521 death in the Philippines. The distinctive culture—from berets and pelota matches to Basque cooking—of this little "country" has cast its spell over the corners of the earth. And continues to do so—just witness the enduring fame of Mark Kurlansky's 1999 *The Basque History of the World*.

The most popular gateway to the entire region is Biarritz, the queen of France's Atlantic coast, whose tony refinements once lured the crowned heads of Europe. It was Empress Eugénie who gave Biarritz its coming-out party, transforming it, in the era of Napoléon III, from a simple bourgeois town into an international favorite. Today, after a round of sightseeing, you can still enjoy the Second Empire trimmings from a perch at the roulette table in the town's casino. Then work on your suntan at Biarritz's famous beach or, a few miles away, really bask under the Basque sun at the picturesque port of St-Jean-de-Luz. As for the entire Pays Basque (Basque Country), it is happily compact: the ocher sands along the Bay of Biscay are less than an hour from the emerald hills of St-Jean-Pied-de-Port in the Basque Pyrénées.

Heading eastward toward the towering peaks of the central Pyrenean cordillera lies the Béarn region, with its splendid capital city of Pau, while northward lies a must detour for lovers of the good life: Eugénie-les-Bains, where you can savor every morsel of a Michel Guérard feast at one (or all) of his magnificently stylish restaurants and hotels. East through the Aubisque Pass, at the Béarn's eastern limit, is the heart of the Hautes-Pyrénées, where the mountains of Vignemale and Balaïtous compete with the Cirque de Gavarnie, the world's most spectacular cirque (or natural amphitheater), centered around a 1,400-foot waterfall. Whether you finish up with a vertiginous Pyrenean hike or choose to pay your respects to the religious shrine at Lourdes, this region always winds up lifting your spirits.

EXPLORING THE BASQUE COUNTRY, GASCONY & HAUTES-PYRÉNÉES

From the lazy, sandy sea level around Bayonne, Biarritz, and St-Jean-de-Luz, this southwest tag end of the Pyrénées hops suddenly up to La Rhune (3,000 feet) and from there it's ever higher, through lush green hills of the inland Basque and Béarn countries past the 6,617-foot Pic d'Orhy to the 6,700-foot Vignemale peak just west of Gavarnie and

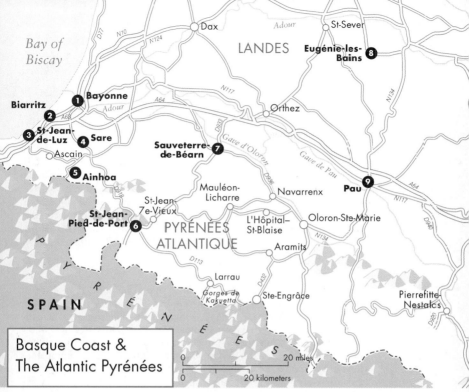

Bay of
Biscay

LANDES

Dax   Adour   St-Sever

Eugénie-les-
Bains **8**

Biarritz   **Bayonne** **1**
2   Adour
3 **St-Jean-
de-Luz**   **4** **Sare**
Ascain

Orthez

**Sauveterre-
de-Béarn** **7**

Gave d'Oloron

Gave de Pau

5 **Ainhoa**

Mauléon-
Licharre   Navarrenx   **Pau** **9**

St-Jean-
St-Jean-   7e-Vieux
Pied-de-Port **6**   **PYRÉNÉES
ATLANTIQUE**

L'Hôpital–
St-Blaise   Oloron-Ste-Marie

Aramits

P   Larrau
Y

R   Gorges de
Kakuetta   Ste-Engrâce   Pierrefitte-
Nestalès

SPAIN   N
É
E
S

Basque Coast &
The Atlantic Pyrénées

0   20 miles
0   20 kilometers

its historically famous Cirque. Bayonne and Pau are the urban and
cultural centers anchoring and connecting these lofty highlands to the
rest of France, while the Basque, Béarn, Gascon, and Bigorre cultures
offer linguistic as well as culinary variety as you meander eastward and
upward from the Basque coast. Gascony is the realm bordered by the
Bay of Biscay to the west, the Pyrénées to the south, and the Garonne
River to the north and east—pretty Pau is the main city in the region,
which sweeps south past Lourdes to Cauterets. Trans-Pyrenean hikers
(and drivers) generally prefer moving from west to east for a number
of reasons, especially the excellent light prevailing in the late afternoon
and evening during the prime months of May to October.

THE BASQUE COAST

La Côte Basque—a world unto itself with its own language, sports, and
folklore—occupies France's southwesternmost corner along the Spanish
border. Inland, the area is laced with rivers: the Bidasoa River border
with Spain marks the southern edge of the region, and the Adour River,
on its northern edge, separates the Basque country from the neighboring Les Landes. The Nive River flows through the heart of the verdant
Basque littoral to join the Adour at Bayonne, and the smaller Nivelle
River flows into the Bay of Biscay at St-Jean-de-Luz. Bayonne, Biarritz,
and St-Jean-de-Luz are the main towns along the coast, all less than
40 km (25 mi) from the first peak of the Pyrénées.

BAYONNE

❶ *48 km (30 mi) southwest of Dax, 184 km (114 mi) south of Bordeaux, 295 km (183 mi) west of Toulouse.*

GETTING HERE

SNCF connects Bayonne with Paris (5 hrs, €70) with four trains daily; in addition high-speed trains (TGVs, Trains à Grande Vitesse) cover the 800 km (500 mi) from Paris in 4½ hours. Train connections from Bayonne include St-Jean-de-Luz (25 mins), St-Jean-Pied-de-Port (1 hr, €8), Toulouse (4 hrs), Bordeaux (2 hrs), Pau (2 hrs, €16); trains make the short jaunt to Biarritz frequently in summer; in winter, take a bus. The bus company STAB, or Société Transports en comun de l'Agglomération de Bayonne (☎*05–59–14–15–16* ⊕*www.bus-stab.com*) connects Bayonne with towns on the French Basque coast, notably Biarritz (15 mins, €2) and Pau. The STAB shuttle connects the airport with Biarritz, Bayonne, and the surfing mecca of Anglet (20 mins, €1.20).

EXPLORING

At the confluence of the Adour and Nive rivers, Bayonne, France's most indelibly Basque city, was in the 4th century a Roman fort, or *castrum*, and for 300 years (1151–1451) a British colony. The city gave its name to the bayonet blade (from the French *baïonnette*), invented here in the 17th century, but today's Bayonne is more famous for its ham (*jambon de Bayonne*) and for the annual Basque pelota world championships held in September. Even though the port is spread out along the Adour estuary some 5 km (3 mi) inland from the sea, the two rivers and five bridges lend this small gem of a city a definite maritime feel. The houses fronting the quay, the intimate Place Pasteur, the Château-Vieux, the elegant 18th-century homes along Rue des Prébendés, the 17th-century ramparts, and the cathedral are some of the town's not-to-be-missed sights. Les Halles market in the Place des Halles on the left bank of the Nive is also a must visit.

The **Cathédrale** (called both Ste-Marie and Notre-Dame) was built mainly in the 13th century, and is one of France's southernmost examples of Gothic architecture. Its 13th- to 14th-century cloisters are among its best features.

The airy, modernized **Musée Bonnat**, in itself reason enough to visit Bayonne, has a notable treasury of 19th-century paintings collected by French portraitist and historical painter Léon Bonnat (1833–1922). ⊠*5 rue Jacques-Lafitte* ☎*05–59–59–08–52* ⊕*www.musee-bonnat. com* ☒*€5.50* ⊙*May–Oct., Wed.–Mon. 10–6; Nov.–Apr., Wed.–Mon. 10–12:30 and 2–6.*

The handsomely designed and appointed **Musée Basque** on the right bank of the Nive offers an ethnographic history of the Basque country and culture. ⊠*37 quai des Corsaires* ☎*05–59–46–61–90* ☒*€5.50* ⊙*Tues.–Sun. 10–12:30 and 2–6; ticket window closes 1 hr before closing time.*

WHERE TO STAY & EAT

★ $$$-$$$$ ✕ **L'Auberge du Cheval Blanc.** This innovative Basque establishment in the Petit Bayonne quarter near the Musée Bonnat serves a combination of *cuisine du terroir* (home-style regional cooking) and original concoctions in contemporary surroundings. Jean-Claude Tellechea showcases fresh fish as well as upland specialties from the Basque hills, sometimes joining the two in groundbreaking dishes such as the *merlu rôti aux oignons et jus de volaille* (hake roasted in onions with essence of poultry). The local Irouléguy wines offer the best value on the wine list. ✉ *68 rue Bourgneuf* ☎ *05–59–59–01–33* ☰ *AE, DC, MC, V* ⊗ *Closed Mon., and July 3–July 11, Aug. 2–7. No lunch Sat. or dinner Sun., except Aug.*

$$-$$$ ☷ **Le Grand Hôtel.** Just down the street from the Château-Vieux, this central spot has pleasant, comfortable rooms with an old-world feel. ✉ *21 rue Thiers, 64100* ☎ *05–59–59–62–00* 🖶 *05–59–59–62–01* ⊕ *www.bw-legrandhotel.com* ⟿ *54 rooms* ♿ *In-room: refrigerator. In-hotel: bar, parking (fee), public Internet and Wi-Fi, some pets allowed (fee)* ☰ *AE, DC, MC, V* ⫶⊘*BP.*

BIARRITZ

❷   *8 km (5 mi) south of Bayonne, 190 km (118 mi) southwest of Bordeaux,*
FodorsChoice   *50 km (31 mi) north of San Sebastián, 115 km (69 mi) west of Pau.*
★

GETTING HERE

At 18 allée Moura, Biarritz's La Négresse train station (3 km [2 mi] is southeast of the *centre ville (city center)*, so hop on Bus No. 2 to reach the centrally located Hôtel de Ville near the main beach) has trains connecting with St-Jean-de-Luz (15 mins, €3), Bordeaux (2 hrs, €26), and many other places, including San Sebastián, Spain (30 mins, €2). From Bayonne airport, bus No. 6 runs hourly to the Biarritz city center from 6 am to 7 pm. Up to 10 trains arrive from Bayonne (8 mins, €2), a hub for trains connecting with Paris and other big cities in France. Most buses to Bayonne and Anglet run from the STAB bus booth (Rue Louis Barthous), near the main tourist office. Tickets cost €1.20 for a single ride, €4.75 for a five-ride card. The ATCRB bus has regular service to other Basque towns, including St-Jean-de-Luz. SNCF connects Biarritz with Paris by TGV (6 hrs, €81.60) with six trains daily.

EXPLORING

Once a favorite resort of Charlie Chaplin, Coco Chanel, and exiled Russian royals, Biarritz first rose to prominence when rich and royal Carlist exiles from Spain set up shop here in 1838. Unable to visit San Sebastián just across the border on the Basque coast, they sought a summer watering spot as close as possible to their old stomping ground. Among the exiles was Eugénie de Montijo, soon destined to become empress of France. As a child, she vacationed here with her family, fell in love with the place, and then set about building her own palace once she married Napoléon III. During the 14 summers she spent here, half the crowned heads of Europe—including Queen Victoria and Edward VII—were her guests in Eugénie's villa, a gigantic wedding-cake edifice, now the **Hôtel du Palais**, set on the main sea promenade of town, the **Quai de la Grande**

Plage, where the fashionable set used to stroll in Worth gowns and picture hats. Whether you consider Napoléon III's bombastic architectural legacies an eyesore or an eyeful, they at least have the courage of their convictions. Biarritz may no longer lay claim to the title "the resort of kings and the king of resorts"; however, today there's no shortage of deluxe hotel rooms or bow-tie gamblers ambling over to the casino. The old, down-to-earth charm of the former fishing village has been thoroughly trumped by Biarritz's glitzy Second Empire aura, and you won't find the bathing beauties and high-rollers here complaining.

Though nowhere near as drop-dead stylish as it once was, the town is making a comeback as a swank surfing capital with its new casino and convention center. If you want to rediscover yesteryear Biarritz, start by exploring the narrow streets around the cozy 16th-century church of **St-Martin.** Adjacent to the Grand Plage are the set-pieces of the Hôtel du Palais and the **Eglise Orthodoxe Russe,** a Byzantine-style church built by the White Russian community that considered Biarritz their 19th-century Yalta-by-the-Atlantic. The duchesses often repaired to the terraced restaurants of the festive **Place Ste-Eugénie,** still considered the

★ social center of town. A lorgnette view away is the harbor of the **Port des Pêcheurs** (Fishing Port), which provides a tantalizing glimpse of the Biarritz of old. Biarritz's beaches attract crowds—particularly the fine, sandy beaches of **La Grande Plage** and the neighboring **Plage Miramar,** both set amid craggy natural beauty. A walk along the beach promenades gives a view of the foaming breakers that beat constantly upon the sands, giving the name Côte d'Argent (Silver Coast) to the length of this part of the French Basque coast.

★ If you wish to pay your respects to the Empress Eugénie, visit **La Chapelle Impériale,** which she had built in 1864 to venerate a figure of a Mexican Black Virgin from Guadelupe (and perhaps to expiate her sins for furthering her husband's tragic folly of putting Emperor Maximilian and Empress Carlotta on the "throne" of Mexico). The style is a charming hybrid of Roman-Byzantine and Hispano-Mauresque. ⊠*Rue Pellot* ☉*Mid-Apr.–mid-July and mid-Sept.–mid-Oct., Mon., Tues., and Sat. 3–7; mid-July–mid-Sept., Mon.–Sat. 3–5; mid-Oct.–Dec., Sat. 3–5.*

WHERE TO STAY & EAT

$$$-$$$$ ✕ **Les Platanes.** Bruno Locatelli offers an eclectic cuisine filled with surprises in this lovely Basque house and cozy dining room. Reaching far beyond—though not neglecting—his Béarn roots and Basque surroundings, this talented and courageous young chef has made a name for himself with classics like foie gras de canard mi-cuit (barely cooked duck liver) and innovative combinations such as roast, boned pigeon in green cardamom. ⊠*32 av. Beau Soleil* ☎*05–59–23–13–68* ▭*AE, DC, MC, V* ☉*Closed Mon., Tues. No lunch July and Aug. and Sat. Sept.–June.*

$$-$$$$ ✕ **Chez Albert.** In summer it's nearly impossible to find a place on the terrace of this easygoing and popular seafood restaurant. Views of the fishing port and the salty harborside aromas of things maritime make the hearty fish and seafood offerings all the more irresistible here. ⊠*Port des Pêcheurs s/n* ☎*05–59–24–43–84* ▭*AE, DC, MC, V* ☉*Closed Nov. 28–Dec. 12, Jan. 4–Feb. 9, and Wed. except in July and Aug.*

Continued on page 743

BASQUE SPOKEN HERE

Bilbao
Bilbo

Saint-Sébastien
Donostia

BISCAYE

LABOURD

GUIPEÚZLOA

(FRANCE)

BASSE-
NAVARRE

ÁLAVA

Vitoria
Gasteiz

(SPAIN)

SOULE

Pampelune
Irunea

NAVARRE

13

Basque solar cross

While the Basque Country's future as an independent nation-state has yet to be determined, the quirky, fascinating culture of the Basque people is not restricted by any borders. Experience it for yourself in the food, history, and sport.

The cultural footprints of this tiny corner of Europe, which straddle the Atlantic end of the border between France and Spain, have already touched down all over the globe. The sport of jai-alai has come to America. International magazines give an ecstatic thumbs-up to Basque cooking. Historians are pointing to Basque fishermen as the true discoverers of North America. And bestsellers, not without irony, proclaim *The Basque History of the World*. As in the ancient 4 + 3 = 1 graffiti equation, the three French (Labourd, Basse Navarre, and Soule) and the four Spanish (Guipúzcoa, Vizcaya, Alava, and Navarra) Basque provinces add up to a single people with a shared history. Although nationless, Basques have been Basques since Paleolithic times.

Stretching across the Pyrénées from Bayonne in France to Bilbao in Spain, the New Hampshire-sized Basque region retains a distinct culture, neither expressly French nor Spanish, fiercely guarded by its three million inhabitants. Fables stubbornly connect them with Adam and Eve, Noah's Ark, and the lost city of Atlantis, but a leading genealogical theory points to common bloodlines with the Celts. The most tenable theory is that the Basques are descended from aboriginal Iberian peoples who successfully defended their unique cultural identity from the influences of Roman and Moorish domination.

It was only in 1876 that Sabino Arana—a virulent anti-Spanish fanatic—proposed the ideal of a "pure" Basque independent state. That dream was crushed by Franco's dictatorial reign (1939–75, during which many Spanish Basques emigrated to France) and was immortalized in Pablo Picasso's *Guernica*. This famous painting, which depicts the catastrophic Nazi bombing of the Basque town of Guernika stands not only as a searing indictment of all wars but as a reminder of history's brutal assault upon Basque identity.

"THE BEST FOOD YOU'VE NEVER HEARD OF"

So said *Food & Wine* magazine.

It's time to get filled in.

An old saying has it that every soccer team needs a Basque goaltender and every restaurant a Basque chef. Traditional Basque cuisine combines the fresh fish of the Atlantic and upland vegetables, beef, and lamb with a love of sauces that is rare south of the Pyrénées. Today, the *nueva cocina vasca* (new Basque cooking) movement has made Basque food less rustic and much more nouvelle. And now that pintxos (the Basque equivalent of tapas) have become the rage from Barcelona to New York City, Basque cuisine is being championed by foodies everywhere. Even superchef Alain Ducasse has gotten in on the action by opening his Ostapé inn in Bidarray in the heart of the Pays Basque.

WHO'S THE BEST CHEF?

Basques are so naturally competitive that meals often turn into comparative rants over who is better: Basque chefs based in France or in Spain. Some vote for Bayonne's Jean-Claude Tellechea (his L'Auberge du Cheval Blanc is famed for groundbreaking surf-and-turf dishes like hake roasted in onions with essence of poultry) or St-Jean-Pied-de-Port's Firmin Arrambide (based at his elegant Les Pyrénées inn). Others prefer the postmodern lobster salads found over the border in San Sebastián and Bilbao, created by master chefs José María Arzak and Martin Berasategui (at their eponymously named restaurants).

SIX GREAT DISHES

Angulas. Baby eels, cooked in olive oil and garlic with a few slices of guindilla pepper.

Bacalao al pil-pil. Cod cooked at a low temperature in an emulsion of olive oil and fish juices, which makes a unique pinging sound as it sizzles.

Besugo. Sea bream, or besugo, is so revered that it is a traditional Christmas dish. Enjoy it with sagardo, the signature Basque apple cider.

Marmitako. This tuna stew with potatoes and pimientos is a satisfying winter favorite.

Ttoro. Typical of Labourd fishing villages such as St-Jean-de-Luz, this peppery Basque bouillabaisse is known as *sopa de pescado* (fish soup) south of the French border.

Txuleta de buey. The signature Basque meat is ox steaks marinated in parsley and garlic and cooked over coals.

BASQUE SPORTS: JAI-ALAI TO OXCART-LIFTING

Sports are core to Basque society, and virtually none are immune from the Basque passion for competing, betting, and playing.

Over the centuries, the rugged physical environment of the Basque hills and the rough Cantabrian sea traditionally made physical prowess and bravery valued attributes. Since Basque mythology often involved feats of strength, it's easy to see why today's Basques are such rabid sports fans.

PELOTA

A Basque village without a frontón (pelota court) is as unimaginable as an American town without a baseball diamond. "The fastest game in the world," pelota is called *jai-alai* in Basque (and translated officially as "merry festival").

With rubber balls flung from hooked wicker gloves at speeds up to 150 mph—the impact of the ball is like a machine-gun bullet—jai-alai is mesmerizing. It is played on a three-walled court 175 feet long and 56 feet wide with 40-foot side walls.

Whether singles or doubles, the object is to angle the ball along or off of the side wall so that it cannot be returned. Betting is very much part of pelota and courtside wagers are brokered by bet makers as play proceeds. While pelota is the word for "ball," it also refers to the game. There was even a recent movie in Spain entitled *La Pelota Vasca*, used metaphorically to refer to the greater "ball game" of life and death.

HERRIKIROLAK

Herrikirolak (rural sports) are based on farming and seafaring. Stone lifters (*harrijasotzaileak* in Euskera) heft weights up to 700 pounds. *Aizkolari* (axe men) chop wood in various contests, *Gizon proba* (man trial) pits three-man teams moving weighted sleds; while *estropadak* are whale-boat rowers who compete in spectacular regattas (culminating in the September competition off La Concha beach in San Sebastián). *Sokatira* is tug of war, and *segalariak* is a scything competition. Other events include oxcart-lifting, milk-can carrying, and ram fights.

SOCCER

When it comes to soccer, Basque goaltenders have developed special fame in Spain, where Bilbao's Athletic Club and San Sebastián's Real Sociedad have won national championships with budgets far inferior to those of Real Madrid or FC Barcelona. Across the border, Bayonne's rugby team is a force in the French national competition; the French Basque capital is also home to the annual French pelota championship.

PARLEZ-VOUS EUSKERA?

Although the Basque people speak French north of the border and Spanish south of the border, they consider Euskera their first language and identify themselves as the *Euskaldunak* (the "Basque speakers"). Euskera remains one of the great enigmas of linguistic scholarship. Theories connect it with everything from Sanskrit to Japanese to Finnish.

What is certain is where Euskera did not come from, namely the Indo-European family of languages that includes the Germanic, Italic, and Hellenic language groups. Currently used by about a million people in northern Spain and southwestern France, Euskera sounds like a consonant-ridden version of Spanish, with its five pure vowels, rolled "r," and palatal "n" and "l." Basque has survived two millennia of cultural and political pressure and is the only remaining language of those spoken in southwestern Europe before the Roman conquest.

The Euskaldunak celebrate their heritage during a Basque folk dancing festival.

A BASQUE GLOSSARY

Aurresku: The high-kicking *espata danza* or sword dance typically performed on the day of Corpus Christi in the Spanish Basque Country.

Akelarre: A gathering of witches that provoked witch trials in the Pyrénées. Even today it is believed that *jenti-lak* (magic elves) inhabit the woods and the Olentzaro (the evil Basque Santa Claus) comes down chimneys to wreak havoc—a fire is kept burning to keep him out.

Boina: The Basque beret or *txapela,* thought to have developed as the perfect protection from the siri-miri, the perennial "Scotch mist" that soaks the moist Basque Country.

Eguzki: The sun worship was at the center of the pagan religion that, in the Basque Country, gave way only slowly to Christianity. The Basque solar cross is typically carved into the east-facing facades of ancient *caserios* or farmhouses.

Espadrilles: Rope-soled canvas Basque shoes, also claimed by the Catalans, developed in the Pyrénées and traditionally attached by laces or ribbons wrapped up the ankle.

Etxekoandre: The woman who commands all matters spiritual, culinary, and practical in a traditional Basque farmhouse. Basque matriarchal inheritance laws remain key.

Fueros: Special Basque rights and laws (including exemption from serving in the army except to defend the Basque Country) originally conceded by the ancient Romans and abolished at the end of the Carlist Wars in 1876 after centuries of Castilian kings had sworn to protect Basque rights at the Tree of Guernika.

  Ikurriña: The Basque flag, designed by the founder of Basque nationalism, Sabino Arana, composed of green and white crosses over a red background and said to have been based on the British Union Jack.

Lauburu: Resembling a four-leaf clover, lau (four) buru (head) is the Basque symbol.

Twenty: Basques favor counting in units of twenty (*veinte duros*—20 nickels—is a common way of saying a hundred pesetas, for example).

Txakolí: A slightly fizzy young wine made from grapes grown around the Bay of Biscay, this fresh, acidic brew happily accompanies tapas and fish.

EATING WELL IN THE PAYS BASQUE

As with expensive bottles of wine, the point of diminishing returns in Basque dining arrives in a hurry, the local cuisine nearly always more satisfying in simple environments where the fare is better than it has any right to be. Once described as "essentially the art of cooking fish," the Basque coast's traditional fresh seafood is unsurpassable every day of the week except Monday, the fleet having stayed in port on Sunday. The inland Basque country and upland Béarn is famous for game in fall and winter and lamb in spring In the Hautes-Pyrénées, the higher altitude makes power dining attractive and thick bean soups and wild boar stews come into their own.

Dining in the regions of the Basque country is invariably a feast, whether it's on seafood or the famous migra-

tory palombes (wood pigeons). Dishes to keep in mind include ttoro (hake stew), pipérade (tomatoes and green peppers cooked in olive oil, and often scrambled eggs), bakalao al pil-pil (cod cooked in oil "al pil-pil"—the bubbling sound the fish makes as it creates its own sauce), marmitako (tuna and potato stew), and zikiro (roast lamb). Home of the eponymous sauce bérnaise, Béarn is also famous for its garbure, thick vegetable soup with confit de canard (preserved duck) and fèves (broad beans). Civets (stews) made with isard (wild goat) or wild boar are other specialties. La Bigorre and the Hautes-Pyrénées are equally dedicated to garbure, though they may call their version soupe paysanne bigourdane (Bigorran peasant soup) to distinguish it from that of their neighbors.

13

★ $$$$ ✕☒ **Château de Brindos.** Take Jazz Age glamour, Spanish Gothic and Renaissance stonework, and the luxest of guest rooms and you have this Pays Basque Xanadu—a large, rambling, white-stone manor topped with a Spanish belvedere tower set 4 km (2½ mi) east of Biarritz in Anglet. This was originally the home of Sir Reginald Wright, whose great soirées held here in the 1920s and '30s are conjured up in the saloon, now presided over by that premier mixologist, bartender Marc Pony. In recent years, interiors have been lovingly restored by Serge Blanco, who has managed to honor the mansion's history while installing state-of-the-art technology and comfort. Tapestries, wrought-iron Spanish wall sconces, Louis XIV–style armchairs, and dramatic stone fireplaces all dazzle the eye, as do views of the estate's private lake from guest rooms rife with quilted fabrics and overstuffed chaise longues. In summer dine out under the willows at the edge of the water at the grand restaurant (closed Monday, no dinner Sunday). Chef Antoine Antunès has trained with the best, from Guérard to Arrambide, and offers a guarantee of creative dining. ☒*1 allée du Château, 64600* ☎*05–59–23–89–80* 🖷*05–59–23–89–81* ⊕*www.chateaudebrindos. com* ⟿*24 rooms, 5 suites* ⚙*In-room: refrigerator, Wi-Fi (some). In-hotel: restaurant, bar, pool, parking (fee), public Internet and Wi-Fi, some pets allowed (fee)* ☰*AE, DC, MC, V* ☉*Closed Nov 28.–Dec. 11 and Jan. 3–16* ⫴*MAP.*

★ $$$$ ✕☒ **Hôtel du Palais.** Set on the beach, this majestic, colonnaded redbrick hotel with an immense driveway, lawns, and a grand semicircular dining room, still exudes an opulent, aristocratic air, no doubt imparted by Empress Eugénie when she built it in 1855 as her Biarritz palace. Napoleonic frippery is everywhere in the public areas, but don't go looking for it in the more standard guest rooms, none of which have sea views. Still, the lobby alone may be worth the price of admission. The three restaurants— Hippocampe (where lunch is served beside the curved pool above the Atlantic), the regal dinner spot Villa Eugénie, and the La Rotonde (with its spectacular soaring columns, gilt trim, and sea views)—are all creatively directed by star chef Jean-Marie Gautier. Don't miss out on his lobster gazpacho. ⊠*1 av. de l'Impératrice, 64200* ☎*05–59–41–64–00* 📠*05–59–41–67–99* ⊕*www.hotel-du-palais.com* ⤳*124 rooms, 30 suites* &*In-room: refrigerator, Wi-Fi (some). In-hotel: 3 restaurants, bar, pool, public Internet and Wi-Fi, parking (fee), some pets allowed (fee)* ☰*AE, DC, MC, V* ⊗*Closed Feb. 11–21* ⫿⊙⫿*MAP.*

> ## ROCK OF AGES
>
> Leading off the Port des Pêcheurs is the Plateau de l'Atalaye, where you can head through a tunnel to a Gustave Eiffel–designed footbridge—actually, a leftover piece from the Eiffel Tower—and the Rocher de la Vierge (Rock of the Virgin). Her sculpted figure has blessed sailors in the Bay of Biscay since 1865. Enjoy the spectacular vista of the coast from the Rocher, then return to town.

$$–$$$ ✕⊞ **Windsor.** This hotel, built in the 1920s, is close to the casino and the beach. Rooms are modern and cozy; those with sea views cost about twice as much as the ones facing the inner courtyard and street. The restaurant, Le Galion, serves up a fine terrine de foie gras with Armagnac, and ravioli stuffed with crab. ⊠*19 bd. du Général-de-Gaulle, 64200* ☎*05–59–24–08–52* 📠*05–59–24–98–90* ⊕*www. hotelwindsorbiarritz.com* ⤳*48 rooms* &*In-room: no a/c. In-hotel: restaurant, bar, public Internet, parking (fee), some pets allowed (fee)* ☰*AE, DC, MC, V.*

$–$$ ⊞ **Hôtel La Romance.** This tiny, early-19th-century villa on a quiet alley near the Hippodrome des Fleurs racetrack is an intimate refuge, and just a 10-minute walk from downtown Biarritz. Madame Subra takes patient care of everyone here, while the minuscule garden becomes a dappled oasis of serenity during the midsummer Biarritz maelstrom. Quarters are tight but homey. ⊠*6 allée des Acacias, 64200* ☎*05–59–41–25–65* 📠*05–59–41–25–65* ⊕*www.touradour.com/hotels/fr/ hotels-biarritz.asp* ⤳*10 rooms* &*In-room: no a/c. In-hotel: public Internet* ☰*AE, MC, V* ⊗*Closed mid-Jan.–Mar.*

$–$$ ⊞ **Maïtagaria.** This typical Basque town house is a handy and comfortable family operation that makes you feel more like a guest in a private home than a hotel client. The lush patio makes a fine breakfast spot in summer. Rooms are efficient and well equipped. ⊠*34 av. Carnot, 64200* ☎*05–59–24–26–65* 📠*05–59–24–27–37* ⊕*www.hotel-maitagaria.com* ⤳*17 rooms* &*In-room: no a/c, Wi-Fi (some). In-hotel: public Internet and Wi-Fi, some pets allowed (fee)* ☰*AE, DC, MC, V* ⊗*Closed Dec. 1–15.*

CLOSE UP

Le Surfing

The area around Biarritz has become Europe's hot-cool surfing center. The season kicks off big time every summer with the Roxy Jam long-board world women's championship (usually held July 1–8, ⊕ *www.roxy.com*). For more real action head to the coast north of Biarritz and the towns of Anglet and Hossegor. La Barre beach in the north doubles as the hangout for dedicated surfers who live out of their vans.

On the southern end (by the Anglet-Biarritz border) are surf shops, snack bars, and one boulangerie. These give the main beach drag, Chambre d'Amour, a decidedly California flair. If you're coming by train, get off in Bayonne or Biarritz and transfer to a STAB bus to Anglet.

The main tourist office (⊠ 1 av. de la Chambre d'Amour ☎ 05–59–03–77–01 ⊕ *www.ville-anglet.fr*) is closed off-season. Hossegor, 20 km (12 mi) north of Bayonne, hosts the RipCurl Pro and the International Surf Championships every August.

13

NIGHTLIFE & THE ARTS

September, the three-week **Le Temps d'Aimer** festival presents dance performances, from classical to hip-hop, in a range of venues throughout the city. They are often at the Théâtre Gare du Midi, a renovated railway station. Troupes such as the Ballets Biarritz, Les Ballets de Monte-Carlo, and leading étoiles from other companies take to the stage in an ambitious schedule of events. At the **Casino de Biarritz** (⊠ *1 av. Edouard-VII* ☎ *05–59–22–77–77*) you can play the slots or blackjack, or go dancing at the Flamingo. **Le Caveau** (⊠ *4 rue Gambetta* ☎ *05–59–24–16–17*) is a mythical Biarritz dance club with guaranteed action every night. **Le Copa** (⊠ *24 av. Édouard-VII* ☎ *05–59–24–65–39*) is a popular bar-restaurant-disco complex near the center of town. **Ibiza** (⊠ *1 rue de la Poste* ☎ *05–59–22–33–10*) stays open late and, like its namesake Balearic island, rocks. **Newquay** (⊠ *20 pl. Georges Clemenceau* ☎ *05–59–22–19–90*) is a midtown hub of nocturnal activity. **Le Playboy** (⊠ *s/n Rue Monbau* ☎ *05–59–24–38–46*) fills with the surfing crowd in season. **Le Queen's Bar** (⊠ *25 pl. Clemenceau* ☎ *05–59–24–70–65*) is a comfortable hangout both day and night.

SPORTS & THE OUTDOORS

France's Atlantic Coast has become one of the hottest surfing destinations in the world. The "Endless Summer" arrives in Biarritz every year in late July for the **Roxy Jam** championships and concludes with other events in August *(see Le Surfing box)*. **Désertours Aventure** (⊠ *65 av. Maréchal-Juin* ☎ *05–59–41–22–02*) organizes rafting trips on the Nive River and four-wheel-drive-vehicle tours through the Atlantic Pyrénées. **Golf de Biarritz** (⊠ *2 av. Edith-Cavell* ☎ *05–59–03–71–80*) has an 18-hole, par-69 course. **Pelote Basque: Biarritz Athletic-club** (⊠ *Parc des Sports d'Aguilera* ☎ *05–59–23–91–09*) offers instruction in every type of Basque pelota including *main nue* (bare-handed), *pala* (paddle), *chistera* (with a basketlike racquet), and *cesta punta* (another game played with the same curved basket).

On Wednesday and Saturday at 9 pm in July, August, and September, you can watch pelota games at the **Parc des Sports d'Aguilera** (☎05–59–23–91–09).

ST-JEAN-DE-LUZ

❸
Fodor's Choice
★

23 km (16 mi) southwest of Bayonne, 24 km (18 mi) northeast of San Sebastián, 54 km (32 mi) west of St-Jean-Pied-de-Port.

GETTING HERE

The train station (✉Av. de Verdun) has frequent service to Biarritz (15 mins, €3) and Bayonne (25 mins, €5). Regional ATCRB buses (☎05–59–26–06–99) leave from Place Maréchal Foch by the tourist office. They're slower but cheaper than the train and give you more beachtown options, including Bayonne (40 mins, €2) and Biarritz (35 mins, €1.50).

EXPLORING

Back in 1660, Louis XIV chose this tiny fishing village as the place to marry the Infanta Maria Teresa of Spain. Ever since, travelers have journeyed here to enjoy the unique coastal charms of St-Jean. Situated along the coast between Biarritz and the Spanish border, it remains memorable for its colorful harbor, old streets, curious church, and elegant beach. Its iconic port shares a harbor with its sister town Ciboure, on the other side of the Nivelle River. The glorious days of whaling and cod fishing are long gone, but some historic multihue houses around the docks are evocative enough.

The tree-lined **Place Louis-XIV**, alongside the Hôtel de Ville (Town Hall), with its narrow courtyard and dainty statue of Louis XIV on horseback, is the hub of the town. In summer, concerts are offered on the square, as well as the famous "Toro de fuego" festival, which honors the bull with a parade and a papier-mâché beast. Take a tour of the twin-towered **Maison Louis-XIV**. Built as the Château Lohobiague, it housed the French king during his nuptials and is austerely decorated in 17th-century Basque fashion. *✉Pl. Louis XIV* ☎*05–59–26–01–56* *✆€5.50* *☉June–Sept., daily 10–noon and 2:30–6; Oct.–May by appointment.*

The marriage of the Sun King and the Infanta took place in 1660 in the church of **St-Jean-Baptiste** (*✉Pl. des Corsaires*). The marriage tied the knot, so to speak, on the Pyrénées Treaty signed by Mazarin on November 7, 1659, ending Spanish hegemony in Europe. Note the church's unusual wooden galleries lining the walls, creating a theaterlike effect. Fittingly, St-Jean-Baptiste hosts a "Musique en Côte Basque" festival of early and Baroque music during the first two weeks of September. The church is open daily from 9 to 6, with a three-hour closure for lunch.

Of particular note is the Louis XIII–style **Maison de l'Infante** *(Princess's House)*, between the harbor and the bay, where Maria Teresa of Spain, accompanied by her mother, Queen Anne of Austria and a healthy entourage of courtiers, stayed prior to her marriage to Louis XIV. *✉Quai de l'Infante.*

WHERE TO STAY & EAT

$$$–$$$$ ✗ **Chez Dominique.** A walk around the picturesque fishing port to the Ciboure side of the harbor will take you past the house where Maurice Ravel was born (No. 27), and to this rustic maritime eatery. The simple, home-style menu here is based on what the fishing fleet caught that morning; in cold weather, try the hearty *marmitako* (tuna stew). The views over the harbor are unbeatable. ⊠*15 quai M. Ravel* ☎*05–59–47–29–16* ☰*AE, DC, MC, V* ⊙*Closed Mon., Tues. (except mid-June–Aug.), and mid-Feb.–mid-Mar. No dinner Sun.*

$$–$$$$ ✗ **Chez Pablo.** The catch of the day determines the daily offering here. Long tables covered with red-and-white tablecloths, benches, and plaster walls give off a casual vibe, but the dishes are often excellent. ⊠*Rue Mme. Etxeto* ☎*05–59–26–37–81* ☰*No credit cards* ⊙*Closed Sun.*

$$–$$$ ✗ **La Taverne Basque.** This well-known midtown standard is one of the old-faithful local dining emporiums, specializing in Basque cuisine with a pronounced maritime emphasis. Try the *ttoro* (a rich fish, crustacean, potato, and vegetable soup). ⊠*5 rue République* ☎*05–59–26–01–26* ☰*AE, DC, MC, V* ⊙*Closed Mon. and Tues. (except July and Aug.), and Mar.*

$$–$$$ ✗ **Txalupa.** The name is Basque for "skiff" or "small boat," and you can feel like you're in one when you're this close to the bay—yachts and fishing vessels go about their business just a few yards away. This well-known haunt with a terrace over the port serves the famous *jambon de Bayonne* (Bayonne ham) in vinegar and garlic sauce, as well as fresh fish and natural produce such as wild mushrooms. ⊠*Pl. Louis-XIV* ☎*05–59–51–85–52* ☰*AE, DC, MC, V.*

$$$$ ✗▣ **Le Grand Hôtel.** Traditionally famed as St-Jean-de-Luz's premier hotel, this elegant spot originally built in the 1920s offers panoramic ocean views, intimacy, and a sense of being where the action is. Rooms have been redesigned in colorful pastels, wood, and marble, and the unbeatable location at the northern end of the St-Jean-de-Luz beach will make you feel like the Sun King himself. ⊠*43 bd. Thiers, 64500* ☎*05–59–26–35–36* 🖷*05–59–51–99–84* ⊕*www.luzgrandhotel.fr* 🛏*50 rooms* ⚭*In-room: refrigerator, Wi-Fi (some). In-hotel: restaurant, bar, pool, gym, public Internet and Wi-Fi, some pets allowed (fee)* ☰*AE, DC, MC, V* ⊙*Closed Nov. 27–Dec. 18.*

THE ATLANTIC & HAUTES-PYRÉNÉES

The Atlantic Pyrénées extend eastward from the Atlantic to the Col du Pourtalet, and encompass Béarn and the mountainous part of the Basque Country. Watching the Pyrénées grow from rolling green foothills in the west to jagged limestone peaks to glacier-studded granite massifs in the Hautes-Pyrénées makes for an exciting experience. The Atlantic Pyrénées' first major height is at La Rhune (3,000 feet), known as the Balcon du Côte Basque (Balcony of the Basque Coast). The highest Basque peak is at Orhi (6,700 feet); the Béarn's highest is Pic d'Anie (8,510 feet). Not until Balaïtous (10,321 feet) and Vignemale (10,321 feet), in the Hautes-Pyrénées, does the altitude surpass the 10,000-foot mark. Starting east from St-Jean-de-Luz up the Nivelle River, a series of villages—including Ascain, Sare, Ainhoa, and Bidarrai—are picturesque stepping-stones leading up to St-Jean-Pied-de-Port and the Pyrénées.

This journey ends in Pau, in the Béarn region, far from the Pays Basque. The Béarn is akin in temperament to the larger region which enfolds it, Gascony. Gascony may be purse-poor, but is certainly rich in scenery and lore. Its proud and touchy temperament is typified in literature by the character d'Artagnan in Dumas's *The Three Musketeers* and in history by the lords of the château of Pau. An inscription over the château's entrance, touchez-y, si tu l'oses—"Touch this if you dare"—was left by the golden-haired Gaston Phoebus (1331–91), 11th count of Foix and viscount of Béarn, a volatile arts lover with a nasty temper who murdered his brother and his only son.

Farther east, past Lourdes, the Hautes-Pyrénées include the highest and most spectacular natural wonders in the cordillera: the legendary Cirque de Gavarnie (natural mountain amphitheater), the Vignemale and Balaïtous peaks, and the Brèche de Roland are the star attractions.

SARE

❹ *14 km (8 mi) southeast of St-Jean-de-Luz, 9 km (5½ mi) southwest of Ainhoa on D118: take first left.*

GETTING HERE
Les Autocards Basques Bondissants buses leave from the train station in St-Jean-de-Luz and go to Sare and some neighboring villages.

EXPLORING
The gemlike village of Sare is built around a large fronton, or backboard, where a permanent pelota game rages around the clock. Not surprisingly, the Hôtel de Ville (town hall) offers a permanent exhibition on Pelote Basque (☉ July and Aug., daily 9–1 and 2–6:30; Sept.–June, daily 3–6). Sare was a busy smuggling hub throughout the 19th century. Its chief attractions are colorful wood-beam and whitewashed Basque architecture, the 16th-century late-Romanesque church with its lovely triple-decker interior, and the **Ospitale Zaharra** pilgrim's hospice behind the church. More than a dozen tiny chapels sprinkled around Sare were built as ex-votos by seamen who survived Atlantic storms.

Up the Sare Valley are the panoramic Col de Lizarrieta and the **Grottes de Sare,** where you can study up on Basque culture and history at a **Musée Ethnographique** (Ethnographic Museum) and take a guided tour (in five languages) for 1 km (½ mi) underground and see a son-et-lumière (sound and light) show. ☎ 05–59–54–21–88 🎟 €7 ☉ Feb.–Dec., Tues.–Sun. 11–7.

Fodor'sChoice West of Sare on D4, at the Col de St-Ignace, take the **Petit Train de la**
★ **Rhune,** a tiny wood-panel cogwheel train that reaches the less-than-
⟳ dizzying speed of 5 mph while climbing up La Rhune peak. The views of the Bay of Biscay, the Pyrénées, and the grassy hills of the Basque farmland are wonderful. Most round trips last 90 minutes. ☎ 05–59–

13

54–20–26 ⊕*www.rhune.com* ✉*€13* ⊙*Easter vacation, May and June, daily 10 and 3; July–Sept., daily every 35 mins.*

WHERE TO STAY & EAT

★ $ ✕▣ **Baratxartea.** This little inn 1 km (½ mi) from the center of Sare is one of the town's prettiest and most ancient *quartiers* is a find. Monsieur Fagoaga's family-run hotel and restaurant occupy a 16th-century town house complete with *colombiers* (pigeon roosts), and surrounded by some of the finest rural Basque architecture in Labourd. ✉*Quartier Ihalar, 64310* ☎*05-59-54-20-48* 🖷*05-59-47-50-84* ⊕*www.hotelbaratxartea.com* ⇆*14 rooms* ⚇*In-room: no a/c. In-hotel: restaurant, some pets allowed (fee)* ▭*AE, DC, MC, V* ⊙*Closed mid-Nov.–mid-Mar.* ⦿⊙*MAP.*

AINHOA

❺ *9 km (5½ mi) east of Sare, 23 km (14 mi) southeast of St-Jean-de-Luz,*
Fodor'sChoice *31 km (19 mi) northwest of St-Jean-Pied-de-Port.*
★

The Basque village of Ainhoa is officially registered among the villages selected by the national tourist ministry as the prettiest in France. A town that best represents the Labourd region, it was established in the 13th century by Juan Perex de Bastan. Today, the streets are lined with lovely 16th- to 18th-century houses graced with whitewashed walls, flower-filled balconies, brightly painted shutters, and carved master beams. The Romanesque church of **Notre-Dame de l'Assomption** has a traditional Basque three-tier wooden interior with carved railings and ancient oak stairs. Explore Ainhoa's little streets, dotted with artisanal ateliers and art galleries. Unfortunately, you'll need your own wheels to get to Ainhoa.

WHERE TO STAY & EAT

$$$$ ✕▣ **Ostapé.** The celebrated Alain Ducasse opened this luxury address
Fodor'sChoice 6 km (4 mi) southeast of Ainhoa in 2003. Though the master is seldom
★ seen here, his touch is palpable in the style, the ultracontemporary equipment and accoutrements, and, especially, in the regional Basque cuisine with international accents orchestrated by chef Alain Souliac. Within a 100-acre park, Ostapé's Basque-style villas surround a 17th-century farmhouse where the restaurant is placed in what were once the quarters for livestock. While some of the complex is modern and cold, various rooms and suites remain lovely settings for Basque woodwork, regional textiles, and sleek sculptures. The landscape is superlatively Basque and the nearby Iparla Ridge hike—one of the greatest in the Pyrénées—will keep appetites primed for fine dining here or at Ducasse's adjacent restaurant Auberge Iparla (☎*05-59-37-77-21* iparla2@wanadoo.fr), set in the upper part of Bidarray. ✉*Chahatoa, 3 km (1½ mi) west of Bidarray, 64780* ☎*05-59-37-91-91* 🖷*05-59-37-91-92* ⊕*www.ostape.com* ⇆*14 suites, 8 duplex apartments* ⚇*In-room: refrigerator, Wi-Fi (some). In-hotel: restaurant, bar, pool, gym, public Internet and Wi-Fi, some pets allowed (fee)* ▭*AE, DC, MC, V* ⊙*Closed Nov. 15–Mar. 31* ⦿⊙*MAP.*

★ $$$ ✕⊞ **Ithurria.** This is a registered historic monument, once a staging post on the fabled medieval pilgrims' route to Santiago de Compostela. If you're doing a modern version of the pilgrims' journey or just need a stopover on your way deeper into the mountains, the Ithurria—set in a 17th-century building in the prevailing Basque style and surrounded by a garden—will give you a fine atmospheric night. The rustic dining room (no lunch Thursday, except in July and August) is the gemstone here, with fare to match, combining inland game and fresh seafood from the Basque coast in creative ways. Guest rooms are modern, comfortable, and tastefully decorated. ⊠ *Rue Principale, 64250* ☎ *05–59–29–92–11* ⊟ *05–59–29–81–28* ⊕ *www.ithurria.com* ⇥ *27 rooms* ⚭ *In-room: no a/c, refrigerator. In-hotel: restaurant, bar, pool, gym, public Internet, some pets allowed (fee)* ⊟ *AE, DC, MC, V* ⊙ *Closed Nov.–Mar.*

> ## AGAINST THE ELEMENTS
>
> The Pays Basque has a very moist climate, due in large part to the strong Atlantic winds from the west hitting the Pyrénées' valleys. As a result, traditional Basque houses—whitewashed buildings with red and green trim—have a protective outer wall on the west side to guard them against the fierce wind and rain.

$ ✕⊞ **Oppoca.** This 17th-century *relais*, or stagecoach relay station, on Ainhoa's main square and pelota court remains one of the loveliest Basque houses in town. Rooms are small but adequate and the owners are a jolly group, always ready to share their knowledge about the locals and the locale. The restaurant serves creditable upland Basque specialties. ⊠ *Pl. du Fronton s/n, 64250* ☎ *05–59–29–90–72* ⊟ *05–59–29–81–03* ⊕ *www.oppoca.com* ⇥ *12 rooms* ⚭ *In-room: no a/c. In-hotel: restaurant, bar, public Internet, some pets allowed (fee), no elevator* ⊟ *AE, DC, MC, V* ⊙ *Closed mid-Nov.–mid-Dec.* ⍾ *MAP.*

ST-JEAN-PIED-DE-PORT

❻ *54 km (33 mi) east of Biarritz, 46 km (28 mi) west of Larrau.*

GETTING HERE

SNCF trains from Bayonne to St-Jean-Pied-de-Port (1 hr, €8) depart six times daily in each direction. The bus company STAB (☎ *05–59–14–15–16* ⊕ *www.bus-stab.com*) connects Bayonne with St-Jean-Pied-de-Port and towns in between.

EXPLORING

St-Jean-Pied-de-Port, a fortified town on the Nive River, got its name from its position at the foot (*pied*) of the mountain pass (*port*) of Roncevaux (Roncesvalles). The pass was the setting for *La Chanson de Roland* (*The Song of Roland*), the 11th-century epic poem considered the true beginning of French literature. The bustling town center, a major stop for pilgrims en route to Santiago de Compostela, seems, after a tour through the Soule, like a frenzied metropolitan center—even in winter. In summer, especially around the time of Pamplona's San Fermin blowout (the running of the bulls, July 7–14), the place is filled to the gills and is somewhere between exciting and unbearable.

Walk into the old section of town through the Porte de France, just behind and to the left of the tourist office; climb the steps on the left up to the walkway circling the ramparts, and walk around to the stone stairway down to the Rue de l'Église. The church of **Notre-Dame-du-Bout-du-Pont** *(Our Lady of the End of the Bridge)*, known for its magnificent doorway, is at the bottom of this cobbled street.

13

The church is a characteristically Basque three-tier structure, designed for women to sit on the ground floor, men to be in the first balcony, and the choir in the loft above.

From the **Pont Notre-Dame** *(Notre-Dame Bridge)* you can watch the wild trout in the Nive (also an Atlantic salmon stream) as they pluck mayflies off the surface. Note that fishing is *défendu* (forbidden) in town. Upstream, along the left bank, is another wooden bridge. Cross it and then walk around and back through town, crossing back to the left bank on the main road.

On **Rue de la Citadelle** are several sights of interest: the **Maison Arcanzola** (Arcanzola House), at No. 32 (1510); the **Maison des Évêques** (Bishops' House), at No. 39; and the famous **Prison des Évêques** (Bishops' Prison), next door to it.

Continue up along Rue de la Citadelle to get to the **Citadelle**, a classic Vauban fortress, now occupied by a school. The views from the Citadelle, complete with maps identifying the surrounding heights and valleys, are panoramic.

WHERE TO STAY & EAT

$$–$$$ ✕ **Chez Arbillaga.** Tucked inside the citadel ramparts, this lively bistro is a sound choice for lunch or dinner. The food represents what the Basques do best: simple cooking of excellent quality, such as *agneau de lait à la broche* (roast lamb), in winter, or *coquilles St-Jacques au lard fumé* (scallops with bacon), in summer. ⊠*8 rue de l'Église* ☎*05–59–37–06–44* ▤*AE, DC, MC, V* ⊘*Closed 1st 2 wks of June and Oct. and Wed. Jan.–May.*

$$$–$$$$ ✕▥ **Les Pyrénées.** A former stagecoach inn on the route to Santiago de
Fodor'sChoice Compostela now houses the best restaurant in the Pyrénées, directed
★ by renowned master chef Firmin Arrambide. Specializing in contemporary *cuisine d'auteur,* Arrambide's flair is characterized by refined interpretations of Pays Basque cooking based on local Pyrenean delicacies, such as wine sauces from the nearby Irouléguy vineyards, the famous *fromage de brebis* sheep's milk cheese, and the best sweet and spicy bell peppers in France. Add in luxury—*saumon frais de l'Adour grillé à la bearnais* or his dishes featuring wood pigeon, langoustines,

and truffles—and you know why everyone is talking. The desserts are almost more fabulous: Arrambide's recipe for Gâteau Basque has circled the world. The restaurant is closed Tuesday from late September to end of June; no dinner Monday November to March. Guest rooms are Relais-&-Château-modern and vary in size; four have balconies. ✉ *19 pl. Charles de Gaulle, 64220* ☎ *05–59–37–01–01* 🖷 *05–59–37–18–97* ⊕ *www.relais-chateaux.com/pyrenees* ⇥ *14 rooms, 4 suites* ♨ *In-room: refrigerator, Wi-Fi (some). In-hotel: restaurant, bar, pool, public Internet and Wi-Fi, some pets allowed (fee)* 🖃 *AE, DC, MC, V* ⊘ *Closed Jan. 5–28 and Nov. 20–Dec. 22* ⦿*MAP.*

$–$$ ✕⌖ **Central Hôtel.** Get the best quality for price in town at this family-run hotel and restaurant (no dinner Monday; closed Tuesday March to June) over the Nive, where trout could be literally—though illegally—caught from certain rooms. The wonderfully musical 200-year-old oak staircase is another memorable detail. The owners speak Basque, Spanish, French, English, and some German, so communicating is rarely a problem. The cuisine is superb, especially the lamb and *magret de canard* (duck breast). ✉ *1 pl. Charles de Gaulle, 64220* ☎ *05–59–37–00–22* 🖷 *05–59–37–27–79* ⇥ *14 rooms* ♨ *In-room: no a/c. In-hotel: restaurant, public Internet, no elevator* 🖃 *AE, DC, MC, V* ⊘ *Closed Dec.–Feb.* ⦿*MAP.*

SAUVETERRE-DE-BÉARN

❼ *39 km (23 mi) northeast of St-Jean-Pied-de-Port.*

Fodor'sChoice
★

Make your first stop the terrace next to the church: the view from here takes in a postcard-perfect group of buildings—the Gave d'Oloron, the fortified 12th-century drawbridge, the lovely Montréal Tower, along with the Pyrénées rising romantically in the distance.

The bridge, known both as the **Vieux Pont** *(Old Bridge)* and the Pont de la Légende (Bridge of the Legend), is associated with the legend of Sancie, widow of Gaston V de Béarn. Accused of murdering a child after her husband's death in 1170, Sancie was subjected to the "Judgment of God" and thrown, bound hand and foot, from the bridge by order of her brother, the king of Navarre. When the river carried her safely to the bank, she was deemed exonerated of all charges.

WHERE TO STAY & EAT

$–$$ ✕⌖ **La Maison de Navarre.** This charming town house in the Saint Marc quarter of Sauveterre-de-Béarn is imbedded in a lush garden a five-minute walk from the *gave* (river). The cuisine is Béarnais with cosmopolitan touches and the rooms are cozy and colorful. ✉ *Rte. Départementale 933, 64390* ☎ *05–59–38–55–28* 🖷 *05–59–38–55–71* ⊕ *www.lamaisondenavarre.com* ⇥ *7 rooms* ♨ *In-room: refrigerator. In-hotel: restaurant, public Internet, no elevator* 🖃 *AE, DC, MC, V* ⊘ *Closed Nov. 3–10 and Feb. 14–Mar. 1* ⦿*MAP.*

EUGÉNIE-LES-BAINS

❽ *92 km (53 mi) northeast of Sauveterre-de-Bérn, 56 km (34 mi) north of Pau, 140 km (87 mi) south of Bordeaux.*

13

GETTING HERE

For transport to Eugénie-les-Bains from Pau, CITRAM Pyrénées (☎*05–59–27–22–22* ⊕*www.annuaire-des-autocaristes.com*) dispatches three daily buses from Pau to the town of Aire-sur-l'Adour (1 hr, 15 mins, €11). For transport from Aire-sur-l'Adour to Eugénie-les-Bains, RDTL (Réseau Départementale des Transports des Landes) (☎*05–58–56–80–80* ⊕*www.rdtl.fr*) offers regular bus connections (20 mins, €6). For transport to Eugénie-les-Bains via Dax (71 km), SNCF (⊕*www.sncf.com*)) offers 20 trains daily from Bayonne to Dax (35 mins, €8.20). For transport from Dax to Eugénie-les-Bains, contact RDTL (☎*05–58–56–80–80* ⊕*www.rdtl.fr*)). The Dax to Hagetmau bus connects with the Hagetmau to Aire-sur-l'Adour line which stops in Eugénie-les-Bains (1 hr, 30 mins, €13).

EXPLORING

Empress Eugénie popularized Eugénie-les-Bains at the end of the 19th century, and in return the villagers renamed the town after her. Michel and Christine Guérard brought the village back to life in 1973 by putting together one of France's most fashionable thermal retreats, which became the birthplace of nouvelle cuisine, thanks to the great talents of chef Michel. Their little kingdom now includes two restaurants, two hotels, a cooking school, and a spa. The 13 therapeutic treatments address everything from weight loss to rheumatism. Two springs are certified by the French Ministry of Health: L'Impératrice and Christine-Marie, whose 39°C (102°F) waters come from nearly 1,300 feet below the surface.

WHERE TO STAY & EAT

★ $$$$ ╳⌂ **La Ferme aux Grives.** With four superb rooms for the lucky first-comers, Michel Guérard's delightfully re-created old coaching inn, set at one end of their Prés d'Eugénie fiefdom, is meant to be a more rustic alternative to their main flagship restaurant. Nature's bounty is the theme: a banquet table is laid out with vegetables and breads, darkened beams cast romantic shadows, and hunting paintings cover the walls. Grandmother's food is given a nouvelle spin, and nearly everything is *authentique*: even the suckling pig turns on a spit in the fireplace. ⌂*40320 Eugénie-les-Bains* ☎*05–58–05–05–06* 🖷*05–58–51–10–10* 🛏*1 room, 3 suites*

> ### WHAT'S GOOD FOR THE GOOSE IS NOT FOIE GRAS
>
> Gascony is France's largest producer of fois gras, the luxurious restaurant specialty. Foie gras de canard is duck liver pâté and foie gras d'oie is goose liver pâté. Neither is very popular with animal rights activists and lovers. To produce these "delicacies," the ducks or geese are mechanically force-fed with tubes in order to enlarge their livers before they're dispatched at about three months of age. The duck variety is more common, less expensive, but probably more delicious.

♿ *In-room: no a/c, refrigerator, Wi-Fi (some). In-hotel: restaurant, bar, public Internet and Wi-Fi, some pets allowed (fee), no elevator* ☰*AE, DC, MC, V* ⊘*Closed Jan. 4–Feb. 12* ❘⊚❘*MAP.*

$$$$ ✕⊞ **Les Prés d'Eugénie.** Ever since Michel Guérard's eponymous restau-
Fodor's Choice rant fired the first shots of the nouvelle revolution in the late 1970s, the
★ excellence of this suave culinary landmark has been a given (so much
so that the breakfast here outdoes dinner at most other places). Thanks
to Guérard's signature flair, *cuisine minceur*—the slimmer's dream—
collides with the lusty fare of the Landes region (langoustines garnished
with foie gras and mesclun greens, lobster with confetti-ed calf's head).
In the lovely Second Empire–style hotel, set in a fine garden, grandeur prevails and rooms are formal. However, rooms in the "annex"—
the former 18th-century **Couvent des Herbes**—have an understated
luxe and look out over the herb garden. To top it all off, the complex includes an excellent spa, dance studio, two pools, and a 9-hole
golf course, while "theme" weeks are devoted to cooking, perfumes,
wines, or gardening. ✉*40320, Eugénie-les-Bains* ☎*05–58–05–06–07,
05–58–05–05–05 restaurant reservations* 🖷*05–58–51–10–10* ⊕*www.
michelguerard.com* ⤴*22 rooms, 6 suites* ♿*In-room: no a/c, refrigerator, Wi-Fi (some). In-hotel: restaurant, bar, golf course, tennis courts,
pools, gym, public Internet and Wi-Fi, some pets allowed (fee)* ☰*AE,
DC, MC, V* ❘⊚❘*MAP.*

★ **$$$–$$$$** ✕⊞ **La Maison Rose.** A (relatively) low-cost, low-calorie alternative to
Les Prés d'Eugénie, Michel and Christine Guérard's newest hotel beck-
ons with a sybaritically simple spa approach. Set in a renovated, super-
stylish 18th-century farmhouse adorned with old paintings hung with
ribbons, rustic antiques, and Pays Basque handicrafts, this is a retreat
that would have delighted the sober Madame de Maintenon—if she
had wanted to lose weight, that is. This is a serious spa, complete with
slimming cures and the most stylish relaxation room in France (oh,
those Provençal-style chaises longues). No room service—everyone eats
in the main dining room, a two-story, beam-ceiling delight. The kitch-
en's touch remains an inventive benediction to local produce. ✉*40320
Eugénie-les-Bains* ☎*05–58–05–06–07* 🖷*05–58–51–10–10* ⊕*www.
michelguerard.com* ⤴*26 rooms, 5 studios* ♿*In-room: no a/c, kitchen,
refrigerator, Wi-Fi (some). In-hotel: restaurant, pool, gym, public Inter-
net and Wi-Fi, some pets allowed (fee)* ☰*AE, DC, MC, V* ❘⊚❘*MAP.*

PAU

⑨ *66 km (36 mi) southeast of Eugénie-les-Bains, 106 km (63 mi) east of
Bayonne and Biarritz.*

GETTING HERE

Set 12 km (7 mi) north of Pau, the Pau-Pyrénées airport (✉*Aéro-
port Pau-Pyrénées, Uzein* ☎*05–59–33–33–00* ⊕*www.pau.aeroport.
fr*) receives daily flights from Paris, London, Lyon, and Amsterdam,
among other points. SNCF connects Pau with Paris (5 hrs, €70) with
four trains daily. Trains connect with Biarritz (1½ hrs, €16) five times
daily. In addition, you can take the train to Lourdes (1 hr, 15 mins, €4),
Bayonne (2 hrs, €16), Biarritz (1½ hrs), and Toulouse (3 hrs). STAP

buses (☎05–59–14–15–16 ⊕*www.bus-stap.com*) connects Pau with Bayonne and Toulouse. To reach the center of Pau from the train station on Avenue Gaston-Lacoste, cross the street and take the funicular up the hill to Place Royale.

EXPLORING

The stunning views, mild climate, and elegance of Pau—the historic capital of Béarn, a state annexed to France in 1620—make it a lovely place to visit and a convenient gateway to the Pyrénées. The birthplace of King Henri IV, Pau was "discovered" in 1815 by British officers returning from the Peninsular War in Spain, and it soon became a prominent winter resort town. Fifty years later English-speaking inhabitants made up one-third of Pau's population, many believing in the medicinal benefits of mountain air (later shifting their loyalties to Biarritz for the sea air). They started the Pont-Long Steeplechase, still one of the most challenging in Europe, in 1841; created France's first golf course here in 1856; introduced fox hunting to the region; and founded a famous British tea shop where students now smoke strong cigarettes while drinking black coffee.

Fodor's Choice ★ Pau's regal past is commemorated at its **Musée National du Château de Pau,** begun in the 14th century by Gaston Phoebus, the flamboyant count of Béarn. The building was transformed into a Renaissance palace in the 16th century by Marguerite d'Angoulême, sister of François I. A woman of diverse gifts, her pastorales were performed in the château's sumptuous gardens. Her bawdy *Heptameron*—written at age 60—furnishes as much sly merriment today as it did when read by her doting kingly brother. Marguerite's grandson, the future king of France Henri IV, was born in the château in 1553. Exhibits connected to Henri's life and times are displayed regularly, along with portraits of the most significant of his alleged 57 lovers and mistresses. His cradle, a giant turtle shell, is on exhibit in his bedroom, one of the sumptuous, tapestry-lined royal apartments. ⊠*Rue du Château* ☎05–59–82–38–00 ⊕*www.musee-chateau-pau.fr* ⊠*€5, free 1st Sun. of month* ⊗*Apr.–Oct., daily 9:30–11:30 and 2–5:45; Nov.–Mar., daily 9:30–11:30 and 2–4:30.*

To continue on your royal path, follow the **Sentiers du Roy** (King's Paths), a marked trail just below the Boulevard des Pyrénées. When you reach the top, walk along until the sights line up with the mountain peaks you see. For some man-made splendors instead, head to the **Musée des Beaux-Arts** and feast on works by El Greco, Degas, and Rodin. ⊠*Rue Mathieu-Lalanne* ☎05–59–27–33–02 ⊕*musee.ville-pau.fr* ⊠*€3* ⊗*Tues.–Sun. 10–noon and 2–6.*

WHERE TO STAY & EAT

$$$$ **Fodor's**Choice ★ ✕ **Chez Ruffet.** Well worth the short drive (or, even better, a 2-km [1-mi] hike) out to Jurançon, this 18th-century farmhouse with its classically lovely dovecot and ancient beams, floorboards, and fireplace is the best restaurant in or near Pau. Chef Stéphane Carrade has imbibed deeply from the masters—Bocuse, Guérard, Troisgros—and promptly taken off in all directions, mostly his own. Fascinated with worldwide prod-

ucts and preparations, Carrade unabashedly rolls out his *agneau d'Aragón clouté au lomo Ibérico et badigeonné au miso et gingembre* (lamb from Aragón with Ibérico fillet daubed with miso and ginger), combining Aragonese, Andalusian, Japanese, and Moorish flavors. His *fois frais de canard cuit à l'étouffé aux feuilles de citronnier et sarments de vignes* (fresh foie stewed with lemon leaves and grapevine cuttings) is another signature offering. ✉*3 av. Ch. Touzet, 64001 Jurançon* 🕾*05–59–06–25–13* ⊕*www. restaurant-chezruffet.com* ▤*AE, DC, MC, V* ⊘*Closed Sept. 12–19 and Dec. 20–Jan. 14. No dinner Sun. No lunch Wed. or Sat.*

$$-$$$ ✘ **Henri IV.** On a quiet pedestrian street near the Château, this dining room with its open fire is a cozy find for a wet and freezing night in winter, while the terrace is a shady place to cool off in summer. Traditional Béarn cooking here stars *magret de canard* (breast of duck) cooked over coals and *cuisses de grenouille* (frogs' legs), made dry and crunchy in parsely and garlic. ✉*18 rue Henri IV* 🕾*05–59–27–54–43* ▤*AE, DC, MC, V.*

$-$$ ▦ **Hôtel de Gramont.** Five minutes from the château, this 17th-century stagecoach stop is Pau's oldest inn and a cozy and convenient base. Ask for one of the *chambres mansardées* (dormered bedrooms) under the eaves overlooking the Hédas. ✉*3 pl. de Gramont, 64000* 🕾*05–59–27–84–04* 🖷*05–59–27–62–23* ⇦*33 rooms* ⅋*In-room: no a/c* ▤*AE, DC, MC, V.*

NIGHTLIFE & THE ARTS

During the music and arts **Festival de Pau,** theatrical and musical events take place almost every evening from mid-July to late August, nearly all of them gratis. Nightlife in Pau revolves around the central Triangle area (surrounded by Rue Lespy, Rue Émile Garet, and Rue Castetnau). The streets around Pau's imposing château are sprinkled with cozy pubs and dining spots, although the **casino** (✉*Parc Beaumont* 🕾*05–59–27–06–92*) offers racier entertainment.

> **TOUT SWEET**
>
> While in Pau, enjoy some of life's sweetest pleasures at Confiserie Francis Miot (✉48 rue Joffre 🕾05–59–27–69–51) with his signature delicacies, "Les Coucougnettes du Vert Galant"—small, red, tender bonbons made from almond paste. Their name is Occitanian argot for testicles (in Catalan *cullons,* in Spanish, *cojones*) and why not? Henri IV—aka le Vert Galant ("the swordsman")—was famed for his 57 lovers. At the gates of Pau in the village of Uzos, Miot has his own Musée des Arts Sucrés (✉Rte. de Nay, Uzos 🕾05–59–35–05–56 ⊕www. feerie-gourmande.com 🎟€5 ⊘Mon.–Sat. 10–noon and 2–5).

LOURDES

❿ *41 km (27 mi) southeast of Pau, 19 km (12 mi) southwest of Tarbes.*

GETTING HERE

Lourdes's train station on the Avenue de la Gare is one of the busiest in the country. So many pilgrim trains arrive between Easter and October

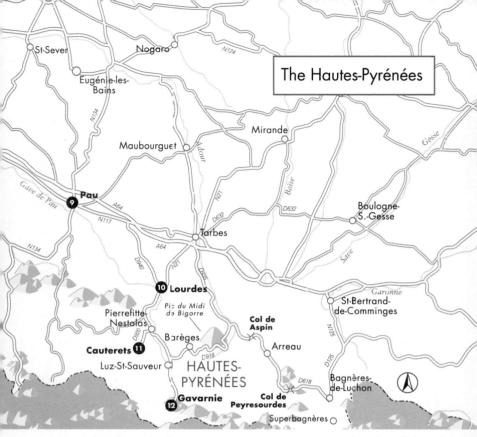

The Hautes-Pyrénées

that the station has a separate entrance to accommodate the religious masses. From the train station, local buses take anxious visitors to the grotto every 20 minutes (Easter–October). Trains go directly to Pau (25 mins, €8), Bayonne (1½ hrs, €18), and Toulouse (2 hrs).

EXPLORING

Five million pilgrims flock to Lourdes annually, many in quest of a miraculous cure for sickness or disability.It all started in February 1858 when Bernadette Soubirous, a 14-year-old miller's daughter, claimed she saw the Virgin Mary in the **Grotte de Massabielle,** near the Gave de Pau (in all, she had 18 visions). Bernadette dug in the grotto, releasing a gush of water from a spot where no spring had flowed before. From then on, pilgrims thronged the Massabielle rock for the water's supposed healing powers, though church authorities reacted skeptically. It took four years for the miracle to be authenticated by Rome and a sanctuary erected over the grotto. In 1864 the first organized procession was held. Today there are six official annual pilgrimages between Easter and All Saints' Day, the most important on August 15. In fall and winter there are much fewer visitors, but that will be a plus for those in search of peace and tranquillity.

Lourdes celebrated the centenary of Bernadette Soubirous's visions by building the world's largest underground church, the **Basilique Souter-**

raine St-Pie X, with space for 20,000 people—more than the town's permanent population. The Basilique Supérieure (1871), tall and white, hulks nearby

The **Pavillon Notre-Dame,** across from St-Pie X, houses the **Musée Bernadette** (Museum of Stained-Glass Mosaic Religious Art), with mementos of Bernadette's life and an illustrated history of the pilgrimages. In the basement is a collection devoted to religious gem-work relics. ✉ *72 rue de la Grotte* ☎ *05–62–94–13–15* ⊠ *Free* ◷ *July–Nov., daily 9:30–11:45 and 2:30–6:15; Dec.–June, Wed.–Mon. 9:30–11:45 and 2:30–5:45.*

Across the river is the **Moulin de Boly** *(Boly Mill),* where Bernadette was born on January 7, 1844. ✉ *12 rue Bernadette-Soubirous* ⊠ *Free* ◷ *Easter–mid-Oct., daily 9:30–11:45 and 2:30–5:45.*

The **cachot,** a tiny room where, in extreme poverty, Bernadette and her family took refuge in 1856, can also be visited. ✉ *15 rue des Petits-Fossés* ☎ *05–62–94–51–30* ⊠ *Free* ◷ *Easter–mid-Oct., daily 9:30–11:45 and 2:30–5:30; mid-Oct.–Easter, daily 2:30–5:30.*

The **château** on the hill above town can be reached by escalator, by 131 steps, or by the ramp up from Rue du Bourg (from which a small Basque cemetery with ancient discoidal stones can be seen). Once a prison, the castle now contains the

Fodor's Choice **Musée Pyrénéen,** one of France's best provincial museums, devoted to
★ the popular customs, arts, and history of the Pyrénées. ✉ *25 rue du Fort* ☎ *05–62–94–02–04* ⊠ *€5* ◷ *Easter–mid-Oct., daily 9–noon and 2–7, last admission at 6; mid-Oct.–Easter, Wed.–Mon. 9–noon and 2–7, last admission at 6.*

WHERE TO STAY & EAT

$ ✕▨ **Hôtel Albret/La Taverne de Bigorre.** The Moreau family's popular establishment serves traditional French mountain cooking such as hearty garbure. Rooms are clean and comfortable, with a personal touch that is very welcome in Lourdes. ✉ *21 pl. du Champ Commun, 65100* ☎ *05–62–94–75–00* 🖷 *05–62–94–78–45* ⊕ *www.lourdes-hotelalbret. com* ↪ *26 rooms* △ *In-room: no a/c. In-hotel: restaurant, bar, public Internet, parking (fee)* ☰ *AE, DC, MC, V* ◷ *Closed Jan.*

CAUTERETS

⑪ *30 km (19 mi) south of Lourdes, 49 km (30 mi) south of Tarbes.*

GETTING HERE

Unless you're coming to Cauterets from a hiking path, only one road leads into town, on which SNCF buses travel to and from Lourdes several times a day (50 mins).

EXPLORING

Cauterets (which derives from the word for hot springs in the local *bigourdan* dialect) is a spa and resort town (for long-term treatments) high in the Pyrénées. It has been revered since Roman times for thermal baths thought to cure maladies ranging from back pain to female sterility. Novelist Victor Hugo (1802–85) womanized here; Lady Aurore Dudevant—better known as the writer George Sand (1804–76)—is said to have discovered her feminism here. Other famous visitors include Gastón Phoébus, Chateaubriand, Sarah Bernhardt, King Edward VII of England, and Spain's King Alfonso XIII.

EN ROUTE
Two kilometers (1 mi) south of Cauterets is the parking lot for the thermal baths, where the red-and-white-marked GR10 *Sentier des Cascades* (Path of the Waterfalls) departs for Pont d'Espagne. This famous walk (three hrs round-trip) features stunning views of the waterfalls and abundant *marmottes* (Pyrenean groundhogs). From **Pont d'Espagne,** to which you can also drive, continue on foot or by chairlift to the plateau and a view over the bright blue **Lac de Gaube,** fed by the river of the same name. Above is **Le Vignemale** (10,817 feet), France's highest Pyrenean peak. Return via Cauterets to Pierrefitte-Nestalas and turn right on D921 up Luz-St-Sauveur and Gavarnie.

GAVARNIE

⑫ *30 km (19 mi) south of Cauterets on D921, 50 km (31 mi) south of Lourdes.*

GETTING HERE

From Lourdes SNCF buses connect to Luz-St-Sauveur (34 mins, € 3.50; Gavarnie is 20 km (12 mi) south of Luz-St-Sauveur by taxi or Capou bus service (30 mins, €3).

EXPLORING

Fodor's Choice ★
A spectacular natural amphitheater, the **Cirque de Gavarnie** has been dubbed the "Colosseum of nature" and inspired many writers, including Victor Hugo. At its foot is the village of Gavarnie, a good base for exploring the mountains in the region. The Cirque is a Cinerama wall of peaks that is one of the world's most remarkable examples of glacial erosion and a daunting challenge to mountaineers. Horses and donkeys, rented in the village, are the traditional way to reach the head of the valley (though walking is preferable), where the Hôtel du Cirque has hosted six generations of visitors. When the upper snows melt, numerous streams tumble down from the cliffs to form spectacular waterfalls; the greatest of them, Europe's highest, is the **Grande Cascade,** dropping nearly 1,400 feet.

Geologists point to the Cirque de Gavarnie as one of the world's most formidable examples of the effects of glacial erosion; the cliffs were worn away by the advancing and retreating ice sheets of the Pleistocene epoch. Seeing it, one can understand its irresistible appeal for mountain climbers—there is a statue of one of the first of these, Lord Russell, in the village.

Another dramatic sight is 12 km (7 mi) west of the village of Gavarnie. Take D921 up to the Col de Boucharo, where you can park and walk five hours up to the **Brèche de Roland** glacier (you cross it during the last two hours of the hike). For a taste of mountain life, have lunch high up at the Club Alpin Français's **Refuge de Sarradets ou de la Brèche.** This is a serious climb, only feasible from mid-June to mid-September, for which you need (at least) good hiking shoes and sound physical conditioning. Crampons and ice axes are available for rent in Gavarnie; check with the **Gavarnie tourist office** (✉ *Pl. de la Bergère* ☎ *05–62–92–49–10*) for weather reports and for information about guided tours.

WHERE TO STAY & EAT

★ $$–$$$ ✕ **Hôtel du Cirque.** With its legendary views of the Cirque de Gavarnie, this spot is magical at sunset. Despite its name it's just a restaurant, but not just any old eating establishment: the *garbure* here is as delicious as the sunset is grand. Seventh-generation owner Pierre Vergez claims his recipe using water from the Cirque and *cocos de Tarbes,* or *haricots tarbais* (Tarbes broad beans) is unique. ✉ *1-hr walk above village of Gavarnie* ☎ *05–62–92–48–02* ▭ *MC, V* ⊗ *Closed mid-Sept.–mid-June.*

$–$$ ✕🏨 **Hôtel Marboré.** This multigabled house over a rushing mountain brook offers all the history and tradition of Gavarnie along with delightful creature comforts. Rooms are bright and pleasant and look out onto lush hillside meadows. The kind and lively owner-manager Roselyne Fillastre attends to all with great warmth and vivacity. The restaurant, too, is excellent: look forward to fine cuisine prepared with the freshest ingredients. ✉ *Village de Gavarnie, 65120* ☎ *05–62–92–40–40* 📠 *05–62–92–40–30* 🌐 *www.lemarbore.com* *24 rooms* *In-room: no a/c. In-hotel: restaurant, bar, no elevator* ▭ *MC, V* ⊗ *Closed Nov. 4–Dec. 20* 🍽 *MAP.*

NIGHTLIFE & THE ARTS

Every July Gavarnie holds an outdoor ballet and music performance, **La Fête des Pyrénées** (☎ *05–62–92–49–10 information*), using the Cirque de Gavarnie as a backdrop; showtime is at sunset. For information contact the tourist office.

BASQUE COUNTRY, GASCONY & HAUTES-PYRÉNÉES ESSENTIALS

TRANSPORTATION

If traveling extensively by public transportation, be sure to load up on information (schedules, the best taxi-for-call companies, etc.) upon arriving at the ticket counter or help desk of the bigger train and bus stations in the area, such as Bayonne, Biarritz, and Pau.

AIRPORTS

Biarritz-Anglet-Bayonne Airport serves the southwesternmost corner of France and has several daily flights to and from Paris and several weekly to London, Marseille, Geneva, Lyon, Nice, and Pau. Pau-Pyrénées International Airport has 10 flights daily to and from Paris as well as flights to Nantes, Lyon, Marseille, Nice, Biarritz, Madrid, Rome, Venice, Milan, and Geneva.

Airport Information Aéroport Biarritz-Anglet-Bayonne (☎ 05–59–43–83–83). Aéroport Pau-Pyrénées (✉ 64230, Uzein ☎ 05–59–33–33–00 ⊕ www. pau.aeroport.fr).

BY AIR

CARRIERS

Air France flies to Pau, Bayonne, and Biarritz from Paris and from other major European destinations. Air Littoral flies between Biarritz, Pau, Toulouse, Nice, and Marseille.

Airlines & Contacts Air France (☎ 05–59–33–34–35). Air Littoral (☎ 05–59–33–26–64).

BY BUS

Various private bus concerns—STAB (serving the Bayonne–Anglet–Biarritz metropolitan areas) and ATCRB (up and down the coast and inland to many Basque towns, such as Bayonne, Biarritz, St-Jean-de-Luz, and Bidart)—service the region. Where they don't, the trusty SNCF national bus lines can occasionally come to the rescue. Other bus companies also thread the area. T.P.R. Buses head out from Pau to Lourdes (1 hr, 15 mins, €4) six times a day. From Lourdes, SNCF buses go to Cauterets and to Luz-St-Sauveur, from where you can grab one of two daily buses for the 20-km (12-mi), 40-minute (€3) ride up the valley to Gavarnie. Les Autocars Basques Bondissants buses leave from the train station in St-Jean-de-Luz and go to villages like Sare (no public transport goes to Ainhoa). Beware of peak-hour traffic on roads in summer, which can mean both delays in transport time and few seats on buses. Check in with the local tourist office for handy schedules or ask your hotel concierge for the best advice.

Bus Information STAB–Biarritz (✉ Rue Louis Barthou, Biarritz ☎ 05–59–24–26–53). ATCRB (☎ 05–59–26–06–99). Transports Basques Associés (✉ Pl. St-André, Bayonne, 05–59–59–49–00). R.D.T.L. Buses (✉ Pl. des Basques, Bayonne ☎ 05–59–35–17–59).

BY CAR

A64 connects Pau and Bayonne in less than an hour, and A63 runs up and down the Atlantic coast. N117 connects Hendaye with Toulouse via Pau and Tarbes. N134 connects Bordeaux, Pau, Oloron-Ste-Marie, and Spain via the Col de Somport and Jaca. The D918 from Bayonne through Cambo and along the Nive River to St-Jean-Pied-de-Port is a pretty drive, continuing on (as D919 and D920) through the Béarn country to Oloron-Ste-Marie and Pau.

ROAD CONDITIONS

Roads are occasionally slow and tortuous in the more mountainous areas, but valley and riverside roads are generally quite smooth and fast. D132, which goes between Arette and Pierre-St-Martin, can be snowed in between mid-November and mid-May, as can N134 through the Valley d'Aspe and the Col de Somport into Spain.

BY TRAIN

High-speed trains (TGVs, Trains à Grande Vitesse) cover the 800 km (500 mi) from Paris to Bayonne in 4½ hours. Biarritz's La Négresse train station (3 km [2 mi] southeast of the town center) has trains connecting with Bayonne, Bordeaux, St-Jean-de-Luz, and many other places. Bayonne and Toulouse are connected by local SNCF trains via Pau, Tarbes, and Lourdes. You can take the train from Pau run to Lourdes, Bayonne, and Biarritz. From Bayonne, trains connect with many destinations, including St-Jean-de-Luz, St-Jean-Pied-de-Port, Toulouse, Bordeaux, Pau. Local trains go between Bayonne and Biarritz and from Bayonne into the Atlantic Pyrénées, a slow but picturesque trip. A local train runs along the Nive from Bayonne to St-Jean-Pied-de-Port. Hendaye is connected to Bayonne and to San Sebastián via the famous *topo* (mole) train, so called for the number of tunnels it passes through.

Train Information **Gare Ville Bayonne** (⊠ *Quartier St-Esprit* ☎ *08–36–35–35–35*). **Gare Ville Biarritz La Négresse** (⊠ *18 allée Moura* ☎ *05–59–23–04–84*). **SNCF** (☎ *36–35 €0.34 per minute* ⊕ *www.voyages-sncf.com*). **TGV** (⊕ *www.tgv.com*).

CONTACTS & RESOURCES

CAR RENTAL

Local Agencies Avis (⊠ *Biarritz-Parme Airport, Biarritz* ☎ *05–59–23–67–92* ⊠ *107 bd. Général-de-Gaulle, Hendaye* ☎ *05–59–20–79–04* ⊠ *Pau-Pyrénées International Airport, Pau* ☎ *05–59–33–27–13* ⊠ *Train station, St-Jean-de-Luz* ☎ *05–59–26–76–66*). **Budget** (⊠ *Biarritz-Parme Airport, Biarritz* ☎ *05–59–23–58–62* ⊠ *Pau-Pyrénées International Airport, Pau* ☎ *05–59–33–77–45*). **Eurodollar** (⊠ *Biarritz-Parme Airport, Biarritz* ☎ *05–59–41–21–12*). **Europcar** (⊠ *Train station, Bayonne* ☎ *05–59–55–38–20* ⊠ *Biarritz-Parme Airport, Biarritz* ☎ *05–59–23–90–68* ⊠ *Pau-Pyrénées International Airport, Pau* ☎ *05–59–33–24–31*). **Hertz** (⊠ *Biarritz-Parme Airport, Biarritz* ☎ *05–59–43–92–92* ⊠ *Pau-Pyrénées International Airport, Pau* ☎ *05–59–33–16–38*).

EMERGENCIES

For basic information, see this section in the Essentials chapter. In most cases, contact the town Comissariat de Police.

Emergencies Commissariat de Police (⊠ *9 rue de Marhum, Bayonne* ☎ *05–59–46–22–22, 17 general emergency number*). **Commissariat de Police** (⊠ *Rue O'Quin, Pau* ☎ *05–59–98–22–22, 17 general emergency number*). **Centre Hospitalier de la Côte Basque** (⊠ *13 av. Interne Jacques Loeb, Bayonne* ☎ *05–59–44–35–35*). **Hospital François Miterrand** (⊠ *Bd. Hautes Rives, Pau* ☎ *05–59–92–48–48*).

INTERNET & MAIL

In smaller towns, ask your hotel concierge if there are any Internet cafés nearby.

Internet & Mail Information C. Cyber (⊠ *9 rue Lamothe, Pau* ☎ *05–59–82–89–40*). **Cyber Net Café** (⊠ *9 pl. de la République, Bayonne* ☎ *05–59–50–85–10*). **Formatique** (⊠ *15 av. de la Marne, Biarritz* ☎ *05–59–22–12–79*). **La Poste main post office** (⊠ *17 rue de la Poste, Biarritz* ☎ *05–59–22–41–10*).

MEDIA

Le Sud-Ouest (published in Bayonne) is the southwest corner of France's leading regional daily and available throughout the Basque Coast and inland to Saint-Jean-Pied-de-Port. *La République des Pyrénees* (Pau) covers the central and Hautes Pyrenees.

TOUR OPTIONS

In Biarritz, Aitzin organizes tours of Bayonne, Biarritz, the Basque coast, and the Basque Pyrénées. The Association des Guides, in Pau, arranges guided tours of the city, the Pyrénées, and Béarn and Basque Country. The Bayonne tourist office gives guided tours of the city. La Guild du Tourisme des Pyrénées-Atlantiques offers information on and organizes visits and tours of the Basque Country and the Pyrénées. Guides Culturels Pyrénéens, in Tarbes, arranges many tours, including explorations on such themes as cave painting, art and architecture, Basque sports, hiking, and horseback riding.

Contacts Aitzin (☎ *05–59–24–36–05*). **Association des Guides** (☎ *05–59–30–44–01*). **Bayonne tourist office** (☎ *05–59–46–01–46*). **Guides Culturels Pyrénéens** (☎ *05–62–44–15–44*). **La Guild du Tourisme des Pyrénées-Atlantiques** (☎ *05–59–46–37–05*).

VISITOR INFORMATION

Tourist Information Ainhoa (✉ *Mairie* ☎ *05–59–29–92–60*). **Bayonne** (✉ *Pl. des Basques* ☎ *05–59–46–01–46* ⊕ *www.ville-bayonne.fr*). **Biarritz** (✉ *1 sq. Ixelles* ☎ *05–59–22–37–10* ⊕ *www.biarritz.fr*). **Cauterets** (✉ *15 Cauterets* ☎ *05–62–92–50–27*). **Gavarnie** (✉ *In center of village* ☎ *05–62–92–49–10* ⊕ *www.gavarnie.com*). **Lourdes** (✉ *Fl. Beyramalu* ☎ *05–62–42–77–40* ⊕ *www.lourdes-france.com*). **Pau** (✉ *Pl. Royale* ☎ *05–59–27–27–08* ⊕ *www.ville-pau.fr*). **St-Jean-de-Luz** (✉ *Pl. Foch* ☎ *05–59–26–03–16* ⊕ *www.saint-jean-de-luz.com*). **St-Jean-Pied-de-Port** (✉ *14 pl. Charles-de-Gaulle* ☎ *05–59–37–03–57*). **Sare** (✉ *Mairie* ☎ *05–59–54–20–14*). **Sauveterre-de-Béarn** (✉ *Mairie* ☎ *05–59–38–58–65* ⊕ *www.tourisme.fr/office-de-tourisme/sauveterre-de-bearn.htm*).

13

Bordeaux &
the Wine Country

Medoc

WORD OF MOUTH

"As a red wine fan, I can suggest a procedure that I followed a couple of years ago with great results. We booked into the Hotel Burdigala in central Bordeaux after the fall harvest, when things in the vineyards had calmed down a bit. The concierge at the hotel arranged individual guided tours at First Growth vineyards like Lafite, Mouton-Rothchild, and Château Margaux. Needless to say, those were memorable experiences. And rumour has it that most of the region's better hotels also arrange these tours."

—Gradyghost224

www.fodors.com/forums

WELCOME TO BORDEAUX & THE WINE COUNTRY

Riding through vineyards near St-Émilion

TOP REASONS TO GO

★ **La Route de Medoc:** With eight *appellations* alone in this one small area and names like Rothschild, Latour, and Margaux on the bottles, this is one itinerary that leaves no sour grapes.

★ **Bordeaux, Wine Mecca:** Flourishing around the banks of the Gironde estuary, Bordeaux's great wine shippers gave their city center a nearly royal 18th-century elegance.

★ **Buy a Rothschild:** While the family's Château Lafite is often locked, the arms are wide open to oenophiles at Château Mouton-Rothschild, thanks to its visitor center and museum.

★ **St-Émilion, Medieval Jewel:** With its 13th-century ramparts, cobblestoned streets, and rock-face hermitage, this fortified hilltop town is one of the Bordeaux country's richest wine districts.

★ **Bordeaux Bacchanal:** Don't miss the four-day wine extravaganza at the end of June where the *appellations* come to party on Bordeaux's biggest square.

1 **Bordeaux.** Dominated geographically by the nearby Atlantic Ocean and historically by great wine merchants and shippers, **Bordeaux** has long ranked among France's largest cities. There is considerable, if concentrated, affluence, which hides behind dour 18th-century facades. Showing off may not be a regional trait but, happily, the city fathers did provide cultural riches, including the spectacular Place de la Bourse, the Grand Théâtre, and the Musée des Beaux-Arts.

2 **The Médoc.** Northwest of Bordeaux, this triangulated peninsula extends from the Garonne River to the Atlantic coast. Dutch engineers drained this marshy landscape in the 18th century to expose the gravelly soil that is excellent for growing grapes and, today, the Médoc is fabled as the home of several of the *grands crus* classés, including Château Margaux, Château Latour, Château Lafite-Rothschild, and Château Mouton-Rothschild. Public buses run here but stops are often in the middle of nowhere—a car, bike, or guided tour may be the best option.

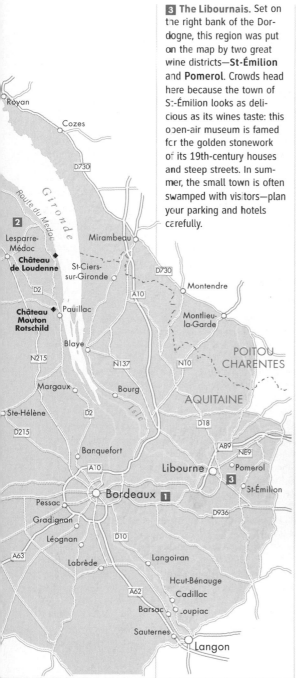

3 **The Libournais.** Set on the right bank of the Dordogne, this region was put on the map by two great wine districts—**St-Émilion** and **Pomerol.** Crowds head here because the town of St-Émilion looks as delicious as its wines taste: this open-air museum is famed for the golden stonework of its 19th-century houses and steep streets. In summer, the small town is often swamped with visitors—plan your parking and hotels carefully.

GETTING ORIENTED

Along with Burgundy and the Loire, Bordeaux is one of the great wine regions of France. As the capital of the Gironde *département* and of the historic province of Aquitaine, the city of Bordeaux is both the commercial and cultural center of southwest France and an important transportation hub. It's smack dab in the middle of one of the finest wine-growing areas in the world: Sauternes lies to the south, flat and dusty Médoc to the west, and Pomerol and St-Émilion to the east.

14

Chateau Margaux, Médoc.

BORDEAUX & THE WINE COUNTRY PLANNER

Getting Around

Bordeaux is one of France's main transportation hubs. However, once you get out into the surrounding Gironde—the "Wine Country"—you can find its seven regions (divided according to geography and the types of wine produced) difficult to reach without a car. Public buses run frequently through the countryside, but stops often appear in the middle of nowhere and schedules are irregular. Get very specific information from Bordeaux's main tourist office and from the bus ticket window on the Esplanade des Quinconces, before boarding a bus. If you have access to a car, you can find life much easier, particularly if you purchase a Michelin map (from the train-station *tabac*). Map number 234 covers a large portion of the southwest. Another option is to go on a bus tour organized by the Bordeaux tourist office.

The Grape Escape

Baron Philippe de Rothschild, legendary owner of Bordeaux's famed Mouton-Rothschild vineyard, was known for his custom of drinking *vin ordinaire* at most lunches and dinners. Indeed, any French person knows you can't enjoy fine vintages at every meal. Still, if you're traveling to Bordeaux, you're going to want to enjoy some of the region's celebrated liquid fare. With more than 1,000 square kilometers of wine-growing country, more than 5,000 châteaux (also refered to as *crus, clos,* and *domaines*), and more than 100,000 vineyards producing around 70 million annual gallons of wine, you'll find it hard not to resist sampling this ample liquid bounty—but where do you start?

Best bet is to head north for the Route des Châteaux (also called the Route de Médoc or the Route des Grands-Crus), stocked with maps and pointers from the very helpful Bordeaux tourist office (the *Le tourisme de viticole* desk is the place for this)—they can be found at 12 cours du 30-Juillet in the city center. Or check out the "Wine Tours" section of the Bordeaux tourist Web site before you travel: www.bordeaux-tourisme.com. A map is essential, as signage is poor and many "châteaux" are small manors hidden in the hills.

Northwest of Bordeaux city is the most famous wine district. All along the west coast of the Gironde estuary south, until you hit the meeting point of the Dordogne and Garonne rivers just north of the city, you can encounter the Médoc wine region. The farthest north is the Médoc *appellation* itself with, to the south of it, the Paulliac appellation, which surrounds the Saint-Estèphe and Saint-Julien appellations, nearer to the estuary. Nearer Bordeaux and just south of the Pauillac region is the conglomeration of the Listrac, Moulis, Margaux, and (nearest to the city along the Garonne) the Haut-Médoc appellations. The D2, or Route des Châteaux, to the north of the city cuts northwest through the majority of the wine country along the Gironde all the way to Talais, and the N215 farther west runs through the other side of the region passing through appellations like Listrac and Moulis that the D2 bypasses. If you head in the other direction, toward the Libournais and St-Émilion regions, use Libourne as your main transportation (train) hub.

Bordelais Banquet

Restaurants in the Médoc region are surprisingly few. However, Bordeaux city is jammed with restaurants (especially around Place du Parlement), with dazzingly fresh seafood showcased because of the proximity to the Atlantic. Bordeaux's student population means lots of cafés (in the Quartier St-Pierre especially) and bars (Place de la Victoire and Cours de la Somme). For a pique-nique, hit the market behind the Cours de l'Intendance and don't forget the hundreds of artisanal cheeses at Jean d'Alos Fromager-Affineur (⊠4 rue Montesquieu). When in St-Émilion don't forget those mouth-melting macaroons, invented here by the town's Ursuline nuns in the 17th century.

Finding a Place to Stay

Apart from cosmopolitan Bordeaux, this region of south-west France can seem pretty sleepy outside the summer months. Needless to say, if traveling in the Médoc region book in advance because there is a scarcity of hotels, so much so that your strategy might be to stay in Bordeaux city. There's more accommodation there (especially between October and March when many countryside places are closed). Too bad the city is decidedly lacking in charming hotels. Wherever you stay, reserve ahead for the crowded summer months. Prices off-season (October–May) often drop as much as 20%. Assume that all hotel rooms have air-conditioning, TV, telephones, and private bath, unless otherwise noted.

WHAT IT COSTS

	¢	$	$$	$$$	$$$$
Restaurants	Under €11	€11– €17	€17– €23	€23– €30	Over €30
Hotels	Under €50	€50– €80	€80– €120	€120– €180	Over €180

Restaurant prices are per person for a main course at dinner, including tax (19.6%) and service; note that if a restaurant offers only prix-fixe (set-price) meals, it has been given the price category that reflects the full prix-fixe price. Hotel prices are for a standard double room in high season, including tax (19.6%) and service charge. Hotels operate on the European Plan (EP, with no meal provided) unless we note that they use the Breakfast Plan (BP), or also offer such options as Modified American Plan (MAP, with breakfast and dinner daily, known as demi-pension), or Full American Plan (FAP, or pension complète, with three meals a day). Inquire when booking if these all-inclusive meal plans (which always entail higher rates) are mandatory or optional.

How's the Weather?

West-coast weather—even as close to southern France as this—can have bad storms even in summer because of the nearby Atlantic, but this is the case with a lot of the south of France. Happily, storms or bad days don't hang around for long. The thing to keep in mind is *when* you come. French people usually vacation within their own national borders so that means mid-July to the end of August is when you'll have company, and lots of it, especially in the more famous destinations. Spring and fall are the best times to visit—there aren't as many tourists around, and the weather is still pleasant. The *vendanges* (grape harvests) usually begin about mid-September in the Bordeaux region (though you can't visit the wineries at this time), and two weeks later in the Cognac region, to the north.

14

Introduction by
Nancy Coons

Updated by
John Fanning

IF YOU'RE LOOKING FOR THE good life, your search may be ended. Few other regions of France pack such a concentration of fine wine, extraordinary spirits, and gustatory delights ranging from exquisite cuisine to the most rib-sticking of country cooking. The countryside will enchant you without your quite knowing why: what the French call *la douceur de vivre* (the sweetness of living) may have something to do with it. To the east, extending their lush green rows to the rising sun, the fabled vineyards of the Route de Médoc entice visitors to discover such enchanting medieval wine towns as St-Émilion. To the north, the Atlantic coast offers elite enclaves of white-sand beach. In between is the metropolis of Bordeaux, replete with 18th-century landmarks and 20-year-old college students. Some complain that Bordeaux is like Paris without the good stuff. If you're a wine lover, however, it is still the doorway to paradise.

The history, economy, and culture of Bordeaux have always been linked to the production and marketing of wine. The birth of the first Bordeaux winery is said to have occurred between ad 37 and 68, when the Romans called this land Burdigala. By the Middle Ages, a steady flow of Bordeaux wines was headed to England, where it's still dubbed "claret," after *clairet,* a light red version from earlier days. During these centuries, the region was also put on the tourist radar because it had become a major stopping-off point on the fabled Santiago de Compostela pilgrimage road. "Souvenirs" from that era are Bordeaux's Cathedral St-André and the basilicas of St. Seurin (where by legend Charlemagne laid down Roland's ivory horn after the defeat of Ronceveaux) and St. Michel—all so important they have been listed as World Heritage sites by UNESCO.

With all these allurements, it's no wonder the English fought for it so determinedly throughout the Hundred Years' War. This coveted corner of France became home to Eleanor of Aquitaine, and when she left her first husband, France's Louis VII, to marry Henry II of Normandy (later king of England), both she and the land came under English rule. Henry Plantagenet was, after all, a great-grandson of William the Conqueror, and the Franco-English ambiguity of the age exploded in a war that defined much of modern France and changed its face forever. Southwestern France was the stage upon which much of the war was conducted—hence the region's many castles and no end of sturdy churches dedicated to the noble families' cause.

What they sought, the world still seeks. The wines of Bordeaux set the standard against which other wines are measured, especially the burgeoning worldwide parade of Cabernets. From the grandest *premiers grands crus*—the Lafite-Rothschilds, the Margaux—to the modest *supérieur* in your picnic basket, the rigorously controlled Bordeaux commands respect. Fans and oenophiles come from around the world to pay homage; to gaze at the noble symmetries of estate châteaux, whose rows of green-and-black vineyards radiate in every direction; to lower a nose deep into a well-swirled glass to inhale the heady vapors of oak and almond and leather; and, finally, to reverently pack a few bloodline labels into a trunk or a suitcase for home.

The rest you will drink on-site, from the mouthful of golden Graves that eases the oysters down to the syrupy sip of Sauternes that civilizes the smooth gaminess of the foie gras to the last glass of Médoc paired with the salt-marsh lamb that leads to pulling the cork on a Pauillac—because there is, still to come, the cheese tray.... With a smorgasbord of 57 wine appellations (areas) to choose from, a spanking new Bordeaux—courtesy of France's former prime minister, Alain Juppé, who became mayor of the city—and the wine country that surrounds it with a veritable army of varietals, the entire region of Bordeaux intoxicates with good taste and tastes.

EXPLORING BORDEAUX & THE WINE COUNTRY

14

If there's a formula for enjoying this region, it would include cultural highlights and relaxing by the sea, but above all tasting wine and indulging in the joys of Bordelais cuisine. The world-famous vineyards of Médoc, Sauternes, Graves, Entre-Deux-Mers, Pomerol, and St-Émilion surround the elegant 18th-century city of Bordeaux, set on the southwest edge of the region near the foot of the Gironde Estuary. As the gateway to marvelous Margaux and superlative Sauternes, Bordeaux—best entered from the south by the river—is 580 km (360 mi) southwest of Paris, 240 km (150 mi) northwest of Toulouse, and 190 km (118 mi) north of Biarritz.

BORDEAUX: CITY OF WINE

Bordeaux as a whole, rather than any particular points within it, is what you'll want to visit in order to understand why Victor Hugo described it as Versailles plus Antwerp, and why, when he was exiled from his native Spain, the painter Francisco de Goya chose it as his last home (he died here in 1828). The capital of southwest France and the region's largest city, Bordeaux remains synonymous with the wine trade: wine shippers have long maintained their headquarters along the banks of the Garonne, while buyers from around the world arrive for the huge biannual Vinexpo show (held in odd years). An aura of 18th-century elegance permeates downtown Bordeaux, where fine shops invite exploration. To the south of the city center are old docklands undergoing gradual renewal—one train station has now been transformed into a big multiplex cinema—but the area is still a bit shady. As a whole, Bordeaux is a less exuberant city than many others in France. That noted, lively and stylish elements are making a dent in the city's conservative veneer, and the cleaned-up riverfront is said by some, after a bottle or two, to exude an elegance redolent of St. Petersburg. A multibillion-euro tramway system is scheduled for completion in 2008. To get a feel for the historic port of Bordeaux, take the 90-minute boat trip that leaves Quai Louis-XVIII every weekday afternoon, or the regular passenger ferry that plies the Garonne between Quai Richelieu and the Pont d'Aquitaine in summer. A nice time to stroll around the city center is the first Sunday of the month, when it's pedestrian-only and cars are banned.

Red Gold: The Wines of Bordeaux

Everyone in Bordeaux celebrated the 2000 vintage as the "crop of the century," a wine that comes along once in a lifetime.

But bringing everything down to earth are some new sour grapes: the increasingly loud whispers that Bordeaux may be "over."

In this world of nouvelle cuisine and uncellared wines, some critics feel the world has moved away from pricey, rich, red wines and more people are opting for lighter choices from other lands.

Be that as it may, if you have any aspirations to being a wine connoisseur, Bordeaux will always remain the top of the pyramid, the bedrock of French viticulture.

It has been considered so ever since the credentials of Bordeaux wines were traditionally established in 1787.

That year, Thomas Jefferson went down to the region from Paris and splurged on bottles of 1784 Château d'Yquem and Château Margaux, for prices that were, he reported, "indeed dear."

Jefferson knew his wines: in 1855, both Yquem and Margaux were officially classified among Bordeaux's top five.

And two centuries later, some of his very bottles fetched upward of $50,000 when offered in a high-flying auction in New York City.

As it turns out, Bordeaux's reputation dates from the Middle Ages. From 1152 to 1453, along with much of what is now western France, Bordeaux belonged to England. The light red wine then produced was known as *clairet*, the origin of our word "claret."

Today no other part of France has such a concentrated wealth of top-class vineyards.

The versatile Bordeaux region yields sweet and dry whites and fruity or full-bodied reds from a huge domain extending on either side of the Gironde (Blaye and Bourg to the north, Médoc and Graves to the south) and inland along the Garonne (Sauternes) and Dordogne (St-Émilion, Fronsac, Pomerol) or in between these two rivers (Entre-Deux-Mers).

At the top of the government-supervised scale—which ranks, from highest to lowest, as Appelation d'Origine Contrôlée (often abbreviated AOC); Vin Délimité de Qualité Supérieur (VDQS—a level that represents about 10% of French wines); Vins de Pays, and Vin de Table—are the fabled vintages of Bordeaux, leading off with Margaux.

Sadly, vineyards of Margaux are among the ugliest in France, lost amid the flat, dusty plains of Médoc.

Bordeaux is better represented at historic St-Émilion, with its cascading cobbled streets, or at Sauternes, where the noble rot (a fungus that sucks water from the grapes, leaving them sweeter) steals up the riverbanks as autumn mists vanish in the summer skies. The harvests, or *vendanges,* begin in September and can last into December.

GETTING HERE

If you're taking a train you'll arrive at one of France's major hubs, the Gare de Bordeaux, St-Jean (☎05–47–47–10–00 ⊕*www.ter-sncf. com/uk/aquitaine*), located about 3 km (2 mi) from the city center. Bordeaux's urban buses (Nos. 7 and 8) will take you from the train station into the city center for less than €1.50 one-way. Citram Aquitaine (⊠*8 rue de Corneille* ☎05–56–43–68–43 ⊕*www.citram.com*) is the main bus operator for farther afield in the Gironde, and even to other nearby *départements* (provinces). You can get here by train in about three hours from Paris, and even faster (about 90 mins)—at least 16 times a day—if you hop on a TGV (⊕*www.tgv.com*) for about €55 one-way. Every 35 minutes (weekdays) you can get to the airport from the train station for €6.50; it takes about 45 minutes. The Aéroport de Bordeaux-Mérignac (☎05–56–34–50-50 ⊕*www.bordeaux.aeroport. fr*) is 10 km (7 mi) west of the city center in Mérignac.

EXPLORING

▶ ❶ For a view of the picturesque quayside, stroll across the Garonne on the **Pont de Pierre,** built on the orders of Napoléon between 1810 and 1821 and until 1965 the only bridge across the river.

❷ Return to the left bank and head north to **Place de la Bourse,** an open square (built 1729–33) ringed with large-windowed buildings designed by the era's most esteemed architect, Jacques Gabriel, father of the architect Jacques-Ange Gabriel (who went on to remodel Paris's Place de la Concorde).

A few blocks to the southeast of Place de la Bourse is **Place du Parlement,** also ringed by elegant 18th-century structures and packed with lively outdoor cafés.

❸ Just north of the Esplanade des Quinconces, a sprawling square, is the two-story **Musée d'Art Contemporain** *(Contemporary Art Center),* imaginatively housed in a converted 19th-century spice warehouse, the Entrepôt Lainé. Many shows here showcase cutting-edge artists who invariably festoon the huge expanse of the place with hanging ropes, ladders, and large video screens. ⊠*7 rue Ferrère* ☎05–56–00–81–50 ⊠*Free* ۞*Tues.–Sun. 11–6, Wed. 11–8.*

The trendy **museum café,** next to the art library on the top floor of the Musée d'Art Contemporain, offers a good choice of beverages and snacks, and fine views over the Bordeaux skyline. It's open Tuesday through Sunday, 11–6. ⊠*7 rue Ferrère.*

★ ❹ Turn back along the Garonne and cross Esplanade des Quinconces to tree-lined Cours du XXX-Juillet and the **Maison du Vin,** run by the CIVB (Conseil Interprofessionnel des Vins de Bordeaux), the headquarters of the Bordeaux wine trade (note that the city tourist office is just across the street). Before you set out to explore the regional wine country, stop at the Maison to gain clues from the person at the Tourisme de Viticole desk (English-speaking), who has helpful guides on all the various wine regions. More important, tasting a red (like Pauillac or St-Émilion), a dry white (like an Entre-Deux-Mers, Graves, or Côtes

14

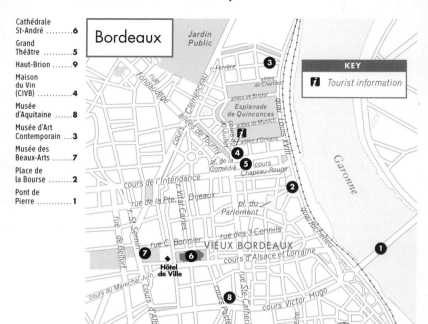

de Blaye), and a sweet white (like Sauternes or Loupiac) will help you decide which of the 57 wine appellations (areas) to explore. You can also make purchases at the **Vinothèque** opposite. ⊠*8 cours du XXX-Juillet* ☎*05–56–52–32–05* ⊕*www.la-vinotheque.com* ☜*Free* ☉*Mon.–Sat. 10–7:30.*

⑤ One block south is the city's leading 18th-century monument: the **Grand Théâtre,** designed by Victor Louis and built between 1773 and 1780. It's the pride of the city, with an elegant exterior ringed by graceful Corinthian columns and a dazzling foyer with a two-winged staircase and a cupola. The theater hall has a frescoed ceiling with a shimmering chandelier composed of 14,000 Bohemian crystals. ⊠*Pl. de la Comédie* ☎*05–56–00–85–95* ⊕*www.opera-bordeaux.com* ☜*€5* ☞*Contact tourist office for guided tours.*

Continue south on Rue Ste-Catherine, then turn right on Cours d'Alsace
⑥ et Lorraine to reach the **Cathédrale St-André** (⊠*Pl. Pey-Berland*). This hefty edifice isn't one of France's finer Gothic cathedrals, but the intricate 14th-century chancel makes an interesting contrast with the earlier nave. Excellent stone carvings adorn the facade. You can climb the 15th-century, 160-foot **Tour Pey-Berland** for a stunning view of the city; cost is €5, and it's open Tuesday–Sunday 10–12:30 and 2–5:30.

❼ The nearby **Musée des Beaux-Arts,** across tidy gardens behind the ornate Hôtel de Ville (town hall), has a collection of works spanning the 15th to the 21st century, with important paintings by Paolo Veronese (*St. Dorothy*), Camille Corot (*Bath of Diana*), and Odilon Redon (*Apollo's Chariot*), and sculptures by Auguste Rodin. ⊠*20 cours d'Albret* ☏*05–56–10–20–56* ▱*Free* ⊙ *Wed.–Mon. 11–6.*

> **BORDEAUX'S BIG WINE BLOWOUT**
>
> The four-day Fête du Vin (Wine Festival) at the end of June sees glass-clinking merriment along the banks of the Garonne. The city's grandest square gets packed with workshops, booths, and thousands of wine lovers. Log on to ⊕ *www.bordeaux-tourisme.com* for all the heady details.

Two blocks south of the Cathédrale **❽** St-André is the **Musée d'Aquitaine,** an excellent museum that takes you on a trip through Bordeaux's history, with emphases on Roman, medieval, Renaissance, port-harbor, colonial, and 20th-century daily life. The detailed prehistoric section almost saves you a trip to Lascaux II, which is reproduced here in part. ⊠*20 cours Pasteur* ☏*05–56–01–51–00* ▱*Free* ⊙ *Tues.–Sun. 11–6.*

One of the region's most famous wine-producing châteaux is actually within the city limits: follow N250 southwest from central Bordeaux **❾** for 3 km (2 mi) to the district of Pessac, home to **Haut-Brion,** producer of the only non-Médoc wine to be ranked a *premier cru* (the most elite wine classification). It's claimed the very buildings surrounding the vineyards create their own microclimate, protecting the precious grapes and allowing them to ripen earlier. The white château looks out over the celebrated pebbly soil. The wines produced at **La Mission–Haut Brion (Domaine Clarence Dillon),** across the road, are almost as sought-after. ⊠*133 av. Jean-Jaurès, Pessac* ☏*05–56–00–29–30* ⊕*www.haut-brion.com* ▱*Free 1-hr visits by appointment, weekdays only, with tasting* ⊙ *Closed mid-July–mid-Aug.*

WHERE TO STAY & EAT

$$$$
Fodor's Choice
★

✕ **Le Chapon-Fin.** With all the laurels and stars thrown at Thierry Marx, the culinary wizard ensconced at Pauillac's Château Cordeillan-Bages, it was just a matter of time before he would swoop in and give Bordeaux's own landmark restaurant an all-out reenergizing shot in the arm. It needed one: founded in 1825, favored by such VIPs as Sarah Bernhardt, Toulouse-Lautrec, and Edward VII, and graced with an extraordinary decor (half winter-garden, half rococo-grotto), the Chapon-Fin had hardened with age. These days the chef in charge is Nicolas Frion, who trained with Marx and has a winning moderne touch. Try his veal sweetbreads studded with cloves and accompanied by creamed leeks, truffles, and pecans, or his fried and stuffed squid served with a cuppucino of fennel. You haven't really been to Bordeaux until you've been here—so book now. ⊠*5 rue Montesquieu, 33000* ☏*05–56–79–10–10* 🖷*05–56–79–09–10* ⊕*www.chapon-fin.com* ⚏*Reservations essential* ▤*AE, MC, V* ⊙ *Closed Sun., Mon., 1 wk in Feb., last wk July, first 2 wks Aug.*

14

EATING WELL IN BORDEAUX

The Bordeaux region might be reknowned worldwide for its quality wines but that doesn't mean Bordelais cuisine has to take a back seat on your gustatory travels. The regional wine is used to great effect as a base for many of the region's famous food specialties. Lamprey, a good local fish, is often served in a red wine sauce as lamproie à la Bordelaise and another, in a white wine, as esturgeon à la Libournaise, or sturgeon cooked Libourne-style. But don't stop there, for there's also caviar from the Gironde, scallops, chipiron (squid), cod, shad, eel, pibale (elver), rouget (a type of goatfish), and sole and oysters from Arcachon. Of course the lamb from Pauillac and the beef from Bazas and Aquitaine are rightly famous, too, as is the grenier médocain (medoc andouillette) for the not so faint of heart. Don't miss the fattened capons from Grignols or anything on the menu that says palombe, as it means you could be lucky enough to eat some wood pigeon.

Local vegetables to accompany all these many meats are the famous cêpe mushrooms of Bordeaux with their nutty flavor, artichokes from Macau, and young garlic shoots called aillet. In addition to all this, if Bordeaux is one of the few French regions that does not make its own cheese, it more than makes up for it with its array of desserts and candies: fanchonnette bordelaise (puff pastry in custard covered by meringues); niniche de Bordeaux (soft chocolate caramel); Cannelé de Bordeaux (small cakes made in fluted molds that can only be found here); cruchade bordelaise (a cornflour cake); gâteau des rois bordelais (literally, king's cake, made after Christmas and topped with candied fruit); and of course, those famous macaroons from Saint-Émilion.

And why not wash it all down with a Bordelais anisette or Lillet (you have the choice of either red or white)— never mind the 57 wine regions surrounding you to choose from!

★ $$$–$$$$ ✕ **La Tupina.** With much glory stolen by its noble cellars, Bordeaux has struggled mightily against its reputation as a culinary backwater. Happily, earthy spins on *cuisine de terroir* are served up at this lovely restaurant (the name means kettle) on one of Bordeaux's oldest streets, under the eye of flamboyant owner Jean-Pierre Xiradakis. Dried herbs hang from the ceiling, a Provençal grandfather clock ticks off the minutes, and an antique fireplace sports a grill bearing sizzling morsels of duck and chicken. Like the room itself, the menu aspires to the *"nostalgie des anciennes menus,"* and it succeeds. On the same street (No. 34) is the owner's fetching—and cheaper—Bar Cave de la Monnaie bistro. ⊠ *6 rue Porte-de-la-Monnaie* ☎ *05–56–91–56–37* ⊕ *www.latupina. com* ⚕ *Reservations essential* ▭ *AE, DC, MC, V.*

$$ ✕ **L'Estacade.** *Le tout Bordeaux* now congregates at this fashionable spot, spectacularly set in a pierlike structure right on the Garonne River. Enormous bay windows allow you to drink in a beautiful panorama of the 18th-century Place de la Bourse on the opposite bank. The cuisine

is creative (prawn risotto, mullet with trout roe); the wine list has few selections to offer other than young Bordeaux, but that seems only fitting. ✉*Quai de Queyries* ☎*05–57–54–02–50* 🖷*05–57–54–02–51* ⊕*www.lestaquade.com* ▤*AE, MC, V.*

$$ ✕ **Gravelier.** Anne-Marie, daughter of Pierre Troisgros of Roanne, married Yves Gravelier, and they combine their culinary talents here. In sparse decor, full of light and openness, imaginative cuisine is served: fillets of *rouget* (red mullet) with foie gras, and pigeon potpie with Chinese cabbage. The €24 lunch menu is a good deal. ✉*114 cours de Verdun* ☎*05–56–48–17–15* ▤*AE, DC, MC, V* ⊗*Closed Sun. and 3 wks in Aug.*

$–$$ ✕ **Café Français.** For more than 30 years, Madame Jouhanneau has presided over this venerable bistro in the heart of the Vieille Ville (Old Town) hard by the Cathédrale St-André. The interior, with large mirrors and plush curtains, is sober, the mood busy. But it's the food, solidly based on fresh regional specialties, that counts, and, for solid sustenance at reasonable prices, it's hard to beat. Try for a table on the terrace: the view over Place Pey-Berland is never less than diverting. ✉*5–6 pl. Pey-Berland* ☎*05–56–52–96–69* ▤*AE, DC, MC, V.*

$$$$ ✕🏨 **Burdigala.** Of the three luxury hotels in Bordeaux, Burdigala (Latin for "Bordeaux") is the only one within walking distance of the center of town. Although the modern exterior is unappealing, the inside is comfortable, with guest rooms crammed with smart modern furniture, fancy bedspreads, and comfy seats. The soundproof rooms are neat; No. 416 is especially quiet and sunny. Deluxe rooms have marble bathrooms with whirlpool baths. The Jardin du Burdigala restaurant serves nouvelle cuisine. ✉*115 rue Georges-Bonnac, 33000* ☎*05–56–90–16–16* 🖷*05–56–93–15–06* ⊕*www.burdigala.com* ⇄*67 rooms, 4 suites* ♿*In-room: refrigerator, Wi-Fi. In-hotel: restaurant, some pets allowed (fee)* ▤*AE, MC, V* ⍾*MAP.*

$$–$$$ 🏨 **Quality Hotel Sainte-Catherine.** This fully modernized hotel is in a 19th-century building in the old part of town. Service is limited, but the reception staff is helpful. The compact, pastel-tone rooms are decorated with light floral fabrics. ✉*27 rue du Parlement-Ste-Catherine, 33000* ☎*05–56–81–95–12* 🖷*05–56–44–50–51* ⊕*www.quality-hotel-sainte-catherine-bordeaux.federal-hotel.com* ⇄*84 rooms* ♿*In-room: refrigerator, dial-up. In-hotel: bar, some pets allowed (fee), public Internet* ▤*AE, DC, MC, V* ⍾*BP.*

$–$$ 🏨 **Des Quatre Soeurs.** In an elegant 1840 town house near the Grand Théâtre, this hotel has sober, well-kept rooms of varying sizes, all with air-conditioning. It's changed a bit since Richard Wagner stayed here. ✉*6 cours du XXX-Juillet, 33000* ☎*05–57–81–19–20* 🖷*05–56–01–04–28* ⊕*/4soeurs.free.fr* ⇄*29 rooms, 5 suites* ♿*In-hotel: some pets allowed (fee)* ▤*AE, MC, V* ⍾*MAP.*

NIGHTLIFE & THE ARTS

L'Aztécal (✉*61 rue Pas-St-Georges* ☎*05–56–44–50–18*) is a comfortable spot for a drink. **Comptoir du Jazz** (✉*59 quai Paludate* ☎*05–56–49–15–55*), near the station, is the place for jazz. Neighboring **Le**

Touring the Wineries

There are certain rules that are known wide and far for the traveler to Bordeaux's wine country. For instance, when paying a call on the region's vineyards and châteaux, remember to respect etiquette. If you're planning on visiting any of the more famous growers (but this also includes other vineyards), make sure to call ahead of time and arrange a dégustation (wine tasting) —many of the labels are "by appointment only" because they are too small to have full-time guides. Even the famous Château Mouton-Rothschild—visited by thousands—requires reservations, at least a week in advance for a regular tour and several weeks for a tour that includes the cellars.

Everyone knows that the staff at Bordeaux's tourist office can help with questions. And since many vineyards are inaccessible without a car or bike, the easiest way to tour those of the Route de Médoc and Gironde is to join one of the nearly daily bus tours sponsored by the city's tourist office (☎05–56–00–22–88 ⊕ www.bordeaux-tourisme.com). Here's the main scoop. These tours depart from (and return to) the Office du Tourisme at 12 cours XXX Juillet. In low season, reservations can be had by the day; in high season, make them in advance. There are one-day trips and also half-day trips (usually, 2 to 6 in the afternoon). In high season, there is a tour every day; in low, just a few a week. Most tours stop at two chateaux only—for instance, in the Médoc, you can visit the Château Palmer (Troisième Cru Classé) and the Château Lanessan (Cru Bourgeois) —but there are so many different tours you can go on a different one each day for a week and not see the same domains. Tours are offered in several languages, including English, and usually a bus holds 40 participants.

Sénéchal (✉ *57 bis, quai Paludate* ☎*05–56–85–54–80*) is the place to dance the night away.

★ Arguably one of the most beautiful historic theaters in Europe, the **Grand Théâtre** (✉*Pl. de la Comédie* ☎*05–56–00–85–95* ⊕*www.opera-bordeaux.com*) puts on performances of French plays and occasionally operas. The theater (which can be visited on guided tours) is an 18th-century showpiece studded with marble muses.

SHOPPING

Between the cathedral and the Grand Théâtre are numerous pedestrian streets where stylish shops and clothing boutiques abound— Bordeaux may favor understatement but there's no lack of elegance. For an exceptional selection of cheeses, go to **Jean d'Alos Fromager-Affineur** (✉*4 rue Montesquieu* ☎*05–56–44–29–66*). The **Vinothèque** (✉*8 cours du XXX-Juillet* ☎*05–56–52–32–05*) sells top-ranked Bordeaux wines. **La Maison des Millésimes** (✉*37 rue Esprit-des-Lois* ☎*05–56–44–03–92*) has a wide range of great wines and will deliver to anywhere in the world.

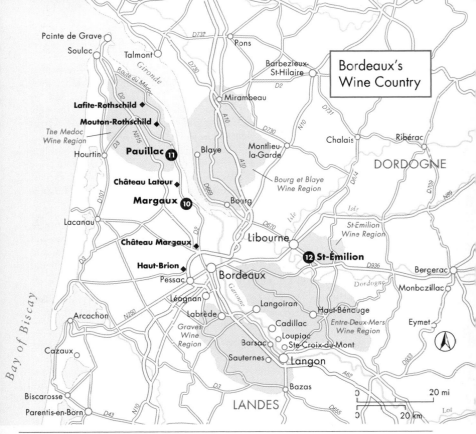

ROUTE DU MÉDOC & THE WINE COUNTRY

The Médoc wine region, which accounts for eight of the most famous appellations of the wine country that surrounds Bordeaux, is north and northwest of Bordeaux, along the Gironde estuary. However, the medieval region of St-Émilion, 35 km (36 mi) to the east of the city, has vineyards that are family owned and relatively small, with on average 7 hectares to each property—they are divided into two appellations, St-Émilion and St-Émilion Grand Cru.

GETTING HERE

If you're heading north you'll have to make your way to or through Pauillac (try to ignore the oil refinery). The buses of Citram Aquitaine (☎05–56–43–68–43) operates in this region as well as the more unreliable SNCF buses. It takes about 50 minutes from Bordeaux to Pauillac. Citram Aquitaine also connects Bordeaux with Margaux (90 mins) and as far north as Point de Grave (150 mins). The train will drop you off at the Gare de Pauillac on 2 bis place Verdun. You can also train it around four times a day as far as Soulac (9 km below Point de Grave), by changing at Lesparre for around €15 one way. If you want to get into the Medoc from Bordeaux by car make sure to get off the road that encircles Bordeaux (the "Rocade") using Sortie (exit) 7.

EXPLORING

North of Bordeaux, the Route du Médoc wine road (D2)—sometimes called the Route des Châteaux—winds through the dusty Médoc Peninsula, past the townships of Margaux, St-Julien, Pauillac, and St-Estèphe. Even the vines in Médoc look dusty, and so does the ugly town of **Margaux,** the area's unofficial capital, 27 km (17 mi) northwest of Bordeaux. Yet **Château Margaux** (☎05–57–88–83–83 ⊕*www. chateau-margaux.com*), housed in a magnificent Neoclassical building from 1810, is recognized as a producer of premiers crus, whose wine qualifies with Graves's Haut-Brion as one of Bordeaux's top five reds. As with most of the top Bordeaux châteaux, visits to Château Margaux are by appointment only.

The well-informed, English-speaking staff at the tourist office (☎05–56–00–66–00) can direct you to other châteaux such as **Lascombes** and **Palmer,** which have beautiful grounds, reasonably priced wines, and are open without reservations. In nearby Cussac, visit the winery and carriage museum at **Château Lanessan.**

★ ⓫ Some 90 km (56 mi) north of Bordeaux on highway D2 is **Pauillac,** home to the three wineries—Lafite-Rothschild, Latour, and Mouton-Rothschild—that produce Médoc's other top reds.

★ Renowned **Château Latour** (☎05–56–73–19–80 ⊕*www.chateau-latour. com*) sometimes requires reservations a month in advance for its wine-tastings (weekdays only). If the posh prices of these fabled *grands crus* are not for you, rent a bike in Pauillac at **Sport Nature** (☎05–57–75–22–60), and visit any of the slightly less-expensive nearby wineries. Of all the towns and villages in the Médoc, Pauillac is the prettiest; you may want to stroll along the riverfront and stop for refreshments at one of its restaurants. A train line connects Pauillac to Bordeaux, running several times daily in summer.

★ **Lafite-Rothschild** is among the most resonant names of the wine world. Even by the giddy standards of the Médoc, Lafite—owned by the Rothschild family since 1868 (but first recorded as making wine as early as 1234)—is a high temple of wine making at its most memorable. Prices may be sky high but no one fortunate enough to sample one of the château's classic vintages will forget the experience in a hurry. Too bad you can't visit the family château on the grounds—its rooms are the defining examples of *le style Rothschild,* one of the most opulent styles of 19th-century interior decoration. ⊠*33250 Pauillac* ☎*05–56–59–26–83* ⊕*www.lafite.com* ✉*Free* ☉*By appointment only at 2 and 3:30, reserve at least 2 wks in advance; closed Aug.–Oct.*

Most of the great vineyards in this area are strictly private (although the owners are usually receptive to inquiries about visits from bona fide wine connoisseurs). One vineyard, however, has long boasted a welcoming visitor center: **Mouton-Rothschild,** whose eponymous wine was brought to perfection in the 1930s by that flamboyant figure Baron Philippe de Rothschild, whose wife, Pauline, was a great style-setter of the 1950s. The baron's daughter, Philippine, continues to lavish money and love on this growth, so wine lovers flock here for either the one-hour visit,

A Bordeaux Baedeker

How to find the best vineyards if you are based in Bordeaux? Easy—just head in any direction. The city is at the hub of a patchwork of vineyards: the Médoc peninsula to the northwest; Bourg and Blaye across the estuary; St-Émilion inland to the east; then, as you wheel around clockwise, Entre-Deux-Mers, Sauternes, and Graves.

The nearest vineyard to Bordeaux itself is, ironically, one of the best: Haut-Brion, on the western outskirts of the city, and one of the five châteaux to be officially recognized as a premier cru, or first growth.

There are only five premiers crus in all, and Haut-Brion is the only one not in the Médoc (Château Mouton-Rothschild, Château Margaux, Château Latour, and Château Lafite-Rothschild complete the list). The Médoc is subdivided into various appellations, wine-growing districts with their own specific characteristics and taste.

Pauillac and Margaux host premiers crus; St-Julien and St-Estèphe possess many domaines of almost equal quality, followed by Listrac and Moulis; wines not quite so good are classed as Haut-Médoc or, as you move farther north, Médoc, pure and simple.

Wines from the Médoc are made predominantly from the cabernet sauvignon grape, and can taste dry, even austere, when young. The better ones often need 15 to 25 years before "opening up" to reveal their full spectrum of complex flavors.

When considering lighter reds for earlier consumption, serious connoisseurs prefer to head southeast beyond Libourne to the stunning Vieille Ville of St-Émilion. The surrounding vineyards see the fruity merlot grape in

control, and wines here often have more immediate appeal than those of the Médoc. There are several small appellations apart from St-Émilion itself, the most famous being Pomerol, whose Château Pétrus is the world's most expensive wine.

South of St-Émilion is the region known as Entre-Deux-Mers ("between two seas"—actually two rivers, the Dordogne and Garonne), whose dry white wine is particularly flavorsome.

The picturesque villages of Loupiac and Sainte-Croix du Mont are sandwiched between the Garonne River and hillside vineyards producing sweet, not dry, white wine.

But the best sweet wine produced hereabouts—some would say in the world—comes from across the Garonne and is made at Barsac and Sauternes.

Nothing in the grubby village of Sauternes would suggest that mind-boggling wealth lurks amid the picturesque vine-laden slopes and hollows. The village has a wineshop where bottles gather dust on rickety shelves, next to handwritten price tags demanding small fortunes.

Making Sauternes is a tricky business. Autumn mists steal up the valleys to promote Botrytis cinerea, a fungus known as pourriture noble or noble rot, which sucks moisture out of the grapes, leaving a high proportion of sugar. Heading back north toward Bordeaux you encounter the vineyards of the Graves region, so called because of its gravelly soil. *Santé!*

14

which includes a tour of the cellars, *chai* (wine warehouse), and museum, or the slightly longer visit that tops off the tour with a tasting. ⊠ *Le Pouyalet, 33250 Pauillac* ☎ *05–56–73–21–29* ⊕ *www. bpdr.com* ⊠ *€5; with tasting, €13* ⊙ *Mon.–Thurs. 9:30–11 and 2–4, Fri. 9:30–11 and 2–3, by appointment only, reserve at least 2 wks in advance.*

At the tip of the Gironde peninsula, near a memorial commemorating the landing of U.S. troops in 1917, is the Pointe de Grave, where you can take the *bac (ferry,* ☎ *05– 56–73–37–73)* across the Gironde from Le Verdon to Royan; it runs at least six times daily and costs €20.80 per car and €3 per passenger. During the 20-minute crossing, keep an eye out for the **Phare de Cordouan** on your left, a lighthouse that looks as if it's emerging from the sea (at low tide, its base is revealed to rest on a sandbank).

WHERE TO STAY & EAT

★ $$$$ ✕▦ **Château Cordeillan-Bages.** This stone-face, single-story 17th-century "chartreuse" just outside Pauillac is surrounded by the vines that produce its own *cru bourgeois.* Paris-trained Thierry Marx is considered the highest-rated chef in the region, no mean accolade in a part of France where food can take second place to world-class wine. His fortes range from local salt-meadow lamb and "liquid" quiche lorraine to spaghetti with an oxtail, truffle, and cêpe sauce. Of course, who will be able to resist the accompaniment of one of the 1,000-plus Bordeauxs from the cellars? (The restaurant is closed Monday and Tuesday; there's no lunch Saturday.) The dining room is cookie-cutter-château, but the guest rooms are cozy, comfortable, and Relais-&-Châteaux stylish. The hotel features cooking classes and also offers courses in affiliation with the Ecole du Bordeaux Wine School. ⊠ *Rte. des Châteaux, 1½ km (1 mi) south of town, 33250 Pauillac* ☎ *05–56–59–24–24* ⊟ *05–56– 59–01–89* ⊕ *www.cordeillanbages.com* ⇌ *26 rooms, 2 suites* ⌂ *In-room: refrigerator, Wi-Fi. In-hotel: restaurant, bar* ⊟ *AE, DC, MC, V* ⊙ *Closed Dec.–mid-Feb.* ¶◎¶MAP.

$ ▦ **France & Angleterre.** A convenient choice if you wish to explore Pauillac's winding streets, this low-key spot offers some doubles overlooking the quaint waterfront. The restaurant serves grilled bass with fennel and entrecote with cêpes and is closed Sunday lunch October to March. ⊠ *3 quai Albert-Pichon, 33250 Pauillac* ☎ *05–56–59–01– 20* ⊟ *05–56–59–02–31* ⊕ *www.hoteldefrance-angleterre.com* ⇌ *29* *rooms* ☝*In-room: dial-up, no a/c. In-hotel: restaurant, public Wi-Fi* ☰*AE, DC, MC, V* ☽*Closed mid-Dec.–mid-Jan.* ❢❍❙*MAP.*

ST-ÉMILION

⓬ 74 km (41 mi) *southeast of Pauillac, 35 km (23 mi) east of Bordeaux.*

Fodor'sChoice
★

GETTING HERE

To take a train to St-Émilion you first need to head to Libourne—a 10-minute ride away. There are two direct trains from Paris to Libourne and another three that connect with Angouleme to Libourne. Trains from Bordeaux (40 mins) run three times a day for about €7 and twice a day on weekends and holidays. Citram Aquitaine (⊕*www.citram. com*) will bus you to St-Émilion five times a day, the trip being a two-pronged affair: 45 minutes to Libourne for around €6, and from there on a Marachesseau bus (10 mins) to St-Émilion for €2.

EXPLORING

Suddenly the sun-fired flatlands of Pomerol break into hills and send you tumbling into St-Émilion. This jewel of a town has old buildings of golden stone, ruined town walls, well-kept ramparts offering magical views, and a church hewn into a cliff. Sloping vineyards invade from all sides, and thousands of tourists invade down the middle, many thirsting for the red wine and macaroons that bear the town's name. The medieval streets, delightfully cobblestoned (though often very steep), are filled with wine stores (St-Émilion reaches maturity earlier than other Bordeaux reds and often offers better value for the money than Médoc or Graves), crafts shops, bakeries, cafés, and restaurants.

The **Office de Tourisme** *(Tourist Office,* ⊠*Pl. des Créneaux* ☎*05-57-55-28-28* ⊕*www.saint-emilion-tourisme.com)* hires out bikes (€14 per day) and organizes tours of the pretty local vineyards—the fabled **Château Angelus** and **Château Belair,** among others—including wine tastings and train rides through the vineyards. Note that it's best to hit the road on a weekday, when more châteaux are open.

A stroll along the 13th-century ramparts takes you to the **Château du Roi** *(King's Castle).* To this day nobody knows whether it was Henry III of England or King Louis VIII of France who chose the site and ordered its building.

From the castle ramparts, cobbled steps lead down to **Place du Marché,** a leafy square where cafés remain open late into the balmy summer night. Beware of the inflated prices charged at the café tables.

The **Église Monolithe** *(Monolithic Church)* is one of Europe's largest underground churches, hewn out of the rock face between the 9th and the 12th century. The church was built by monks faithful to the memory of St-Émilion, an 8th-century hermit and miracle worker. Its spire-topped *clocher* (bell tower) rises out of the bedrock, dominating the center of town. ⊠*Pl. du Marché* ☎*€6.30* ☽*Tours leave from tourist office, daily 10–noon and 2–5.*

I Heard It Through the Grapevine

Many tips, advisos, and bits of Bordeauxiana can be yours if you log on to the Talk Forums at www.fodors.com. Here's a vintage sampler of helpful contributions.

"Our last full day in Bordeaux we drove north up the wine road for another day of vineyard tours. In the morning we drove through Margaux to have a look, but continued north to Pauillac where we had a tour and tasting at Mouton-Rothschild.

This may be the most disappointing wine tour I've ever had. Compared to the other big three, this was a complete disaster. First, the tour and tasting cost 24 euros each, which isn't that big a deal, but considering the other three vineyards we went to were free, we were kind of expecting something special.

Second, the whole tour was geared around the Rothschild family and their success; not about the vineyard, the employees, or more importantly, the wine itself.

Granted, Baron Phillippe was a revolutionary in the wine world, but the whole tour was geared around him and his daughter so we found it to be a bit much.

Last, the tasting was of three barrel samples. Wine is one of my most favorite things in the world to talk about, taste, travel for, or to learn about but I don't pretend to be Robert Parker.

I have no idea how they can taste a wine and determine the future potential based on a 'barrel sample'—it is so tanic and unpleasant to drink.

I suppose with years of practice, but for 48 euros we would have preferred a glass of something that had at least finished barrel-aging." —JMWF

"For some of the other smaller châteaux, there are no tours, but just tastings. However, do note that almost all châteaux are closed from 12 noon to 2 pm for lunch." —at

"I would highly recommend that you write for appointments at Château Latour and Château Margaux.

My husband and I had a private tour at Latour. Tour guide was a French woman who had studied at Berkeley and spoke English beautifully.

First saw a movie, then tour of the château, then to the wine tasting—tasted 3 or 4 glasses. Everything was first class—especially the wine! Lasted almost 3 hours.

Margaux was larger (10 folks), but the tour guide spoke English. Tasted some old vintages. Saw wine cave with vintages back to 1890s. About 2 hours.

We also made same-day reservations at Pichon-Longeville (beautiful château) and Lynch-Bages." —oforparis!

Just south of the town walls is **Château Ausone,** an estate that is ranked with Château Angelus as a producer of St-Émilion's finest wines.

WHERE TO STAY & EAT

$-$$ ✕ **Chez Germaine.** Family cooking and regional dishes are the focus at this central St-Émilion eatery. The candlelighted upstairs dining room and the terrace are both pleasant places to enjoy the reasonably priced set menus. Grilled meats and fish are house specialties; for dessert, go for the almond macaroons. ⊠ *13 pl. du Clocher* ☎ *05–57–74–49–34* ▤ *AE, DC, MC, V* ⊗ *Closed Dec.–Feb.*

$$$$ ✕▤ **Grand Barrail.** This turn-of-the-20th-century luxury hotel just outside St-Émilion, flanked by a lake and vineyards, may seem a little stiff and heavy, but rooms are unusually large and smartly furnished. Talented chef Christophe Rhomer serves various succulent selections of fresh foie gras seared in ever changing sauces, in the Belle Epoque dining room (no dinner Sunday, no lunch Tuesday, closed Monday in January and February). St-Émilions constitute at least 60% of the impressive wine list. ⊠ *Rte. Lebourne, 4 km (2½ mi) northwest of St-Émilion on D243, 33330* ☎ *05–57–55–37–00* ▤ *05–57–55–37–49* ⊕ *www.grand-barrail.com* ⇦ *33 rooms, 9 suites* ⌂ *In-room: refrigerator. In-hotel: restaurant, bar, pool, some pets allowed (fee), public Wi-Fi* ▤ *AE, DC, MC, V* ⊗ *Closed 3 wks Feb. and late Nov.–mid-Dec.* ⏀ *MAP.*

$$$$ ✕▤ **L'Hostellerie de Plaisance.** Part of the Relais & Châteaux group,
Fodor'sChoice this sumptuous hotel has long been considered the top and most pricey
★ address in St.-Émilion. Set next to the tourist office in the upper part of town and housed in a stunningly elegant limestone mansion, it's just across the way from the town's famous stone Église Monolithe. Guest rooms are warm and appealing and many come with terraces overlooking the tile roofs of the town; some have excellent views of the vineyards. Dinner is best accompanied by St-Émilion wines (the owners also possess two grand cru vineyards). You can enjoy picking and choosing from chef Philippe Etchebest's exotic menu; the crab stuffed with cabbage, pork with mango chutney, or the truffled bananas are all winners. ⊠ *3 pl. du Clocher, 33330* ☎ *05–57–55–07–55* ▤ *05–57–74–41–11* ⊕ *www.hostelleriedeplaisance.com* ⇦ *28 rooms, 3 suites* ⌂ *In-room: refrigerator, Wi-Fi. In-hotel: restaurant, some pets allowed (fee)* ▤ *AE, DC, MC, V* ⊗ *Closed mid-Dec.–Feb.* ⏀ *MAP.*

★ $$$–$$$$ ▤ **Château Lamothe du Prince Noir.** Magically set on a circular moat, fitted out with a storybook turret, and covered in an ambuscade of ivy, this manor house is one of the region's most charming accommodations. Set halfway between St-Émilion and Bordeaux, it has interiors graced with colorful fabrics and fine antiques. The spacious guest rooms have large four-poster beds with soft cotton sheets; you may find them a little too frilly, but they're comfortable. Owner Jacques Bastide speaks English and is extremely helpful with suggestions. ⊠ *6 rte. du Stade, 25 km (16 mi) west of St-Émilion, 20 km (12 mi) northeast of Bordeaux, 33450 St-Sulpice-et-Cameyrac* ☎ *05–56–30–82–16* ▤ *05–56–30–88–33* ⊕ *www.chateaux-france.com* ⇦ *5 suites* ⌂ *In-room: no a/c, Wi-Fi. In-hotel: pool* ▤ *MC, V* ⊗ *Closed Nov.–Apr.* ⏀ *BP.*

14

$$-$$$ ⊞ **Auberge de la Commanderie.** Close to the ramparts, this 19th-century two-story hotel has a gorgeous, white-shuttered facade that beautifully blends in with St-Émilion's fabled stonework. Public rooms overlook some vineyards. As for guest rooms, they range from tiny and barebones to large and decorated with colorful prints; some have exposed historic stonework. Try for Room 2, 3, 7, or 8, as they overlook the small garden. ⊠ *Rue des Cordeliers, 33330* ☎ *05–57–24–70–19* 🖷 *05–57– 74–44–53* ⊕ *www.aubergedelacommanderie.com* ⇘ *17 rooms* ⚑ *In-room: no a/c (some), Wi-Fi* ▬ *MC, V* ☉ *Closed mid-Dec.–mid-Feb.*

BORDEAUX & WINE COUNTRY ESSENTIALS

TRANSPORTATION

If traveling extensively by public transportation, be sure to load up on information (*Le Guide Régional des Transports* schedules, the best taxi-for-call companies, etc.) upon arriving at the ticket counter or help desk of the bigger train and bus stations in the area, such as Bordeaux.

AIRPORTS

Frequent daily flights on Air France link Bordeaux and the domestic airport at Limoges with Paris. Flybe has six direct flights a week from Southampton to Bordeaux and Ryanair flies into Pau and Biarritz farther south.

Airport Information Aéroport de Bordeaux-Mérignac (☎ *05–56–34–50–50* ⊕ *www.bordeaux.aeroport.fr*).

BY AIR

Airlines & Contacts Air France (☎ *08–02–80–28–02* ⊕ *www.airfrance.fr*). **Flybe** (☎ *0044/1392–268529* ⊕ *www.flybe.com*). **Ryanair** (☎ *0353/1249–7791* ⊕ *www. ryanair.com*).

BY BUS

The regional bus operator is Citram Aquitaine; the main Gare Routière (bus terminal) in Bordeaux is on Allées de Chartres (by Esplanade des Quinconces), near the Garonne River. Citram Aquitaine buses cover towns in the wine country and beach areas not well served by rail (for instance, one or two buses run daily to St-Émilion and Pauillac). If you want to get to the ocean or airport there's also Cars de Bordeaux. Their buses leave for the airport leave every 45 minutes from Bordeaux's railway station.

Bus Information Cars de Bordeaux (⊠ *6 quai Souys, Bordeaux* ☎ *05–57–77– 58–78* ⊕ *www.groupe-sera.com*).**Citram Aquitaine** (⊠ *8 rue de Corneille, Bordeaux* ☎ *05–56–43–68–43* ⊕ *www.citram.com*).

BY CAR

As the capital of southwest France, Bordeaux has superb transport links with Paris, Spain, and even the Mediterranean (A62 express-way via Toulouse links up with the A61 to Narbonne). The A10, the Paris–Bordeaux expressway, passes close to Poitiers and Saintes before continuing toward Spain as A63. The A20 south is the main route from Paris to just before Cahors. The A20 also connects with the N21 at Limoges which brings you down to Bordeaux.

BY TRAIN

The superfast TGV (Train à Grande Vitesse) Atlantique service links Paris (Gare Montparnasse) to Bordeaux—585 km (365 mi) in 3½ hours—with stops at Poitiers and Angoulême. Trains link Bordeaux to Lyon (6 hrs) and Nice (8½ hrs) via Toulouse. Five trains daily make the 3½-hour, 400-km (250-mi) trip from Paris to Limoges.

> ## MÉDOC MARATHON
>
> The Médoc Marathon (⊕ www. marathondumedoc.com), on the first or second Saturday of September, is more than just a 42-km (26-mi) race through the vineyards: 52 groups of musicians turn out to serenade the runners, who can indulge in no fewer than 22 giant buffets en route, and drink free wine from 21 estates along the way. Speed is not exactly of the essence for most taking part in the competition; 2008 sees the 24th running of this hybrid athletic-alcoholic event.

14

Bordeaux is the region's major train hub. Around five trains a day leave from Bordeaux for St-Émilion taking anywhere from 30 to 55 minutes depending on when you leave. If you're heading north to Paulliac then there are at least three trains (around 80 mins) a day from Bordeaux. Training it to Pointe de Grave, though, means planning ahead, as it takes more than two hours and there are usually only two connecting trains a day.

Train Information SNCF (☎ 08-36-35-35-35 ⊕ www.ter-sncf.com/uk/aquitaine). **Gare de Bordeaux** (✉ St-Jean ☎ 05-47-47-10-00).

CONTACTS & RESOURCES

CAR RENTAL
Local Agencies Avis (✉ Gare St-Jean, Bordeaux ☎ 05-56-91-65-50). **Hertz** (✉ Gare St-Jean, Bordeaux ☎ 05-57-59-05-95) (✉ Aéroport Bordeaux-Mérignac, Mérignac ☎ 08-25-00-24-00 ⊕ www.hertz.fr).

EMERGENCIES
Contacts Ambulance (☎ 15). **Hôpital St-André** (✉ 1 rue Jean-Burguet, 33075 Bordeaux ☎ 05-56-79-56-79 ⊕ www.chu-bordeaux.fr).

INTERNET & MAIL
In smaller towns, ask your hotel concierge if there are any Internet cafés nearby.

Internet & Mail Information Art Obas (✉ 7 rue Maucoudinat, Bordeaux ☎ 05-56-44-26-30). **Cyberstation** (✉ 23 cours Pasteur, south of cathedral, Bordeaux ☎ 05-56-01-15-15). **Net Tel Com** (✉ 26 cours de la Marne, Bordeaux ☎ 05-56-31-94-08). **La Poste (main post office)** (✉ 8 cours du Chapeau Rouge, Bordeaux ☎ 05-56-48-45-80).

MEDIA

Sud Ouest, published in Bordeaux, is the regional daily of southwest France. If you're looking for an English newspaper while in France your best bet is the International Herald Tribune, especially good on the weekends. *USA Today* can also be found from the same newsagents who carry the *New York Times*, but it's always best to stock up on foreign newspapers at the bigger train stations.

TOUR OPTIONS

The Office de Tourisme in Bordeaux organizes daylong coach tours of the surrounding vineyards every Wednesday and Saturday afternoon. The office has information on other wine tours and tastings, and on local and regional sights; a round-the-clock phone service in English is available.

Fees & Schedules Office de Tourisme (✉ *12 cours du XXX-Juillet, 33080 Bordeaux cedex* ☎ *05–56–00–66–00).*

VISITOR INFORMATION

Tourist Information Bordeaux (✉ *12 cours du XXX-Juillet* ☎ *05–56–00–66–00* ⊕ *www.bordeaux-tourisme.com).* **Pauillac** (✉ *La Verrerie* ☎ *05–56–59–03–08* ⊕ *www.pauillac-Medoc.com).* **St-Émilion** (✉ *15 rue du Clocher* ☎ *05–57–55–28–28* ⊕ *www.saint-emilion-tourisme.com).*

The Dordogne

Sarlat-la-Canéda

WORD OF MOUTH

"It was amazing to hear that Lascaux's prehistoric cave dwellers are considered artists as they used the natural curves of the walls to create the most realistic depictions of muscles possible. Guides use laser pointers to outline objects for you and, at one point, they turn off the lights and light a candle—it gives you goose bumps to see the paintings come to life when the flame flickers."

—Wendy

WELCOME TO THE DORDOGNE

TOP REASONS TO GO

★ **Fantastic Food:** Périgord truffles, foie gras, walnuts, plums, and myriad species of mushrooms jostle for attention on restaurant menus here—and the goose liver pâté is as good as it gets.

★ **Rock Stars:** Lascaux is the "Louvre" of Paleolithic man and millions have witnessed prehistory writ large on its spectacularly painted cave walls.

★ **Religious Rocamadour:** Climb toward heaven up the towering cliff to Place St-Amadour's seven chapels and you might be transported to a better place.

★ **Sarlat's Cité Médiévale:** Feast your eyes on Sarlat's honey-color houses and 16th-century streets and then just feast at the hundred or so wine and foie gras shops.

★ **Versailles in the Sky:** Set 400 feet above the Dordogne River, the ancestral garden of the Marquises de Marqueyssac is a 3-km (2 mi) maze of topiaries, parterres, and hedges.

1 Western Dordogne to Rocamadour. With a "Walt Disney" look, the Western Dordogne countryside is studded with Renaissance castles, like those at **Monbazillac** and **Biron**. Surrounded by lands cultivated by peasant farmers for centuries, *bastide* towns such as **Monpazier** were once heavily fortified. Heading southeast, the Lot Valley welcomes travelers with the lively town of **Cahors,** noted for its Romanesque cathedral in the Aquitaine domed style, and **St-Cirq-Lapopie,** a Renaissance-era time machine. Have your Nikon ready for **Rocamadour**'s sky-touching Cité Religieuse, one of France's most famous pilgrimage shrines.

Detail from Lascaux

15

GETTING ORIENTED

Just northeast of Bordeaux, the region of Périgord is famed for its prehistoric art, truffle-rich cuisine, and once-upon-a-timefied villages. The best of these delights are found in the beloved *département* called the Dordogne. Part of the Aquitaine region, this living postcard is threaded by the Dordogne River, which, after its descent from the mountainous Massif Central, weaves westward past prehistoric sites like Lascaux. Astounding, too, are the medieval cliff-hewn villages like Rocamadour—provided that you manage to peer through the crowds in high season.

2 Eastern Périgord to Brantôme. You'll have a fight on your hands figuring out which sector of the Dordogne is the most beautiful, but many give the prize to the Périgord Noir. Immerse yourself in the past at **Sarlat-la-Canéda**, the golden-stone regional capital so beautifully preserved film crews flock here for its 16th- and 17th-century turrets and towers. Nearby is the prehistoric grotto at **Domme**, the riverside village of **La Roque-Gageac**, and the hilltop castle at **Beynac**. To the north is the Vézère Valley, the prehistoric capital of France, home to fabled **Lascaux**. Beyond lies the thriving city of **Périgueux**.

Market day in Sarlat-la-Caneda

THE DORDOGNE PLANNER

Taken to Cask

To the world, Cognac is not a place but a drink. That's cool with the locals of Cognac, who are perfectly content to take a back seat to the liquor that is lovingly aged in their cellar casks and pumps their economy.

A trip 49 km (56 mi) northwest of Brantôme makes a fitting finale to a tour of the Dordogne's countryside. Heading up into the Poitou-Charentes region, the black-wall town of Cognac seems an unlikely home for one of the world's most celebrated drinks.

Cognac owed its development to the transport of salt and wine along the Charente River. When 16th-century Dutch merchants discovered that the local wine was both tastier and easier to transport when distilled, the town became the heart of the brandy industry. From Apr.–Sept., most cognac houses organize visits of their premises and *chais*, the local name for cognac warehouses. Otard wins the history prize for being housed in the Château de Cognac, where King François I was born in 1494. Wherever you decide to go, you'll be inhaling the atmosphere of cognac: 3% of the caskbound liquid evaporates every year. It's known as *la part des anges*, the angels' share.

Saying Hi to the Flintstone Clan

Perhaps the most famous cultural sights in the Dordogne are the prehistoric caves and grottos, such as Lascaux II, Grotte du Pech-Merle, the Domme grottoes, and Grotte du Grand-Roc. Lascaux can take up to 2,000 people a day, but others—such as the Grotte des Combarelles in Les Eyzies-de-Tayac—only take 6 people on a tour at any given time (guaranteeing an intimate look).

Either because demand far outstrips supply, or because tickets are so limited, it's recommended you call or e-mail to prebook ticket reservations in advance. For places like Lascaux, as far as possible (up to a year); for less popular sights, you may only need a reservation a couple of days in advance, or you can sign up for a tour as early in the morning as possible.

The main tourist offices in the region, such as the one at Les Eyzies-de-Tayac, have the lowdown on all the caves and prehistoric sights in the area. If you were not able to call ahead for tickets, it's worth stopping by the cave of your choice even if the office says tickets are sold out—space often opens up.

Be forewarned: you might get signed onto a tour that starts in a couple of hours, leaving you with time to kill, so have a game plan handy for other places to visit nearby.

WHAT IT COSTS

	¢	$	$$	$$$	$$$$
Restaurants	Under €11	€11–€17	€17–€23	€23–€30	Over €30
Hotels	Under €50	€50–€80	€80–€120	€120–€190	Over €190

Restaurant prices are per person for a main course at dinner, including tax (19.6%) and service; note that if a restaurant offers only prix-fixe (set-price) meals, it has been given the price category that reflects the full prix-fixe price. Hotel prices are for a standard double room in high season, including tax (19.6%) and service charge. Hotels operate on the European Plan (EP, with no meal provided) unless we note that they use the Breakfast Plan (BP), or also offer such options as Modified American Plan (MAP, with breakfast and dinner daily, known as demi-pension), or Full American Plan (FAP, or pension complète, with three meals a day). Inquire when booking if these all-inclusive meal plans (which always entail higher rates) are mandatory or optional.

Making the Most of Your Time

From a practical perspective perhaps staying in Sarlat or thereabouts would be your best plan of attack for getting to really appreciate this divergent and wonderful region. Not only is this historic town a great place to enjoy, but it's also near the caves with Lascaux and Montignac to its north, Les Eyzies de Tayac to its west, Beynac et Cazenac, La Roque-Gageac, and Domme immediately to its south, and Rocamadour a little farther afar to the southeast. Also, Sarlat is just off the A20 highway, which brings you right into Cahors to the south and north to the regional airport in Brive La Gaillarde (the Bergerac airport to the east on the D703/D660 is a little bit farther afield). After getting yourself situated, the first thing to do is eat, because even before enjoying those awe-inspiring views from Rocamadour and La Roque-Gageac, there's the important task of foie gras and truffles to savor. After all, scenery and history are not the only things the Dordogne is famous for!

If you prefer solitude, you won't have any trouble finding it in the vast, underpopulated spaces stretching inland and eastward in the rolling countryside of the Dordogne, chock-full of storybook villages, riverside châteaux, medieval chapels, and prehistoric sites. Best bet is to get out of the overpopulated places such as Périgueux and Bergerac and head for the hills, literally. The cathedral in Périgueux is something to see, but the châteaux and villages that sprinkle this region like so much historical and cultural confetti (in places such as Biron, Hautefort, Beynac, and the awe-inspiring Rocamadour) are sites you'll kick yourself for not seeing before the attractions of the big towns.

À la périgourdine

If you're traveling in the Dordogne between October and March it's essential to call restaurants ahead of time to avoid disappointment, as some shut for the slow season.

Closing times, too, can be variable, but when you do sit down somewhere don't leave without tasting the regional delicacies of foie gras, truffles, walnuts, and chestnuts. When you snag your table, hone in on the menu's listing for dishes *à la périgourdine*.

These delights usually mean you're about to enjoy truffles or foie gras, or, heaven forbid, both!

15

Finding a Place to Stay

Advance booking is particularly desirable in the highly popular Dordogne, where hotels fill up quickly, in midsummer.

Many country or small-town hotels expect you to have at least one dinner with them, and if you have two meals a day with your lodging and stay several nights, you can save money. Prices off-season (October–May) often drop as much as 20% but note that a number of hotels are closed from the end of October through March.

Assume that all hotel rooms have air-conditioning, TV, telephones, and private bath, unless otherwise noted.

Introduction by
John Fanning

Updated by
John Fanning

WANT TO SMILE HAPPILY EVER after? Discover a picture-postcard fantasy of fairy-tale castles, cliff-top châteaux, geese flocks, storybook villages, and prehistoric wonders? Join the club. Since the 1990s, the Dordogne region has become one of the hottest destinations in France. Formerly one of those off-the-beaten-path areas, it's now in danger of getting four-starred, boutiqued, and postcarded to death. But scratch the surface and you can find one of the most authentic and appealing regions of rural France (no need to take our word: busloads of people from northern France vacation here). What's more, and unlike the Loire Valley, for example, where attractions are often many miles apart, you can discover romantic riverside château after château with each kilometer traveled. Then factor in four troglodyte villages, numerous natural gouffres (chasms), the sky-kissing perched village of Rocamadour, and the most famous prehistoric sights in the world, and you can see why all these attractions have not gone unnoticed: in July and August even the smallest village hereabouts is often packed with sightseers.

With abundant vegetation to please your eye and soul, the region is marked by rich, luxuriant valleys through which flow clearwater rivers, such as the Dordogne, Isle, Dronne, Vézére, and the Lot. Separating the valleys are rugged plateaus of granite and limestone, sharp outcroppings of rock, and steep, sheer cliffs. Happily, the 10-km (6-mi) stretch of the Dordogne River from Montfort to Beynac is easily accessible by car, bike, canoe, or on foot, and shouldn't be missed, especially when fields of sunflowers line the banks in season. Offering a nice contrast to the region's rugged physiognomy and nature sauvage (wilderness) are medieval châteaux perched high above valleys and hyper-picturesque villages, such as La Roque-Gageac, wedged between rocky cliffs and the Dordogne River. The region is centered around Sarlat, whose impeccably restored medieval buildings make it a great place to use as a base. Even better, the area around Sarlat is honeycombed with dozens of grottes (caves) filled with Paleolithic drawings, etchings, and carvings. Just north of Sarlat is Lascaux, the "Louvre" of Cro-Magnon man and perhaps the most notable sight ever created by the Flintstone clan.

Fast-forward 30,000 years. The modern era dawns as the regions comes under Merovingian rule in the 9th century. Divided up later by the dukes of Aquitaine, the region later went to England and then around 1370 was returned to the French crown. The crown complicated matters still further by giving the area to the house of Bourbon in 1574, which meant Henry of Navarre inherited it. Henry became Henry IV, king of France, in 1589, and so the region returned to the crown again. Well, history is repeating itself, at least from an English perspective, as over the last several decades the British have moved back here in droves. They see the Dordogne as the quintessential French escape—and now the rest of the world is following in their footsteps.

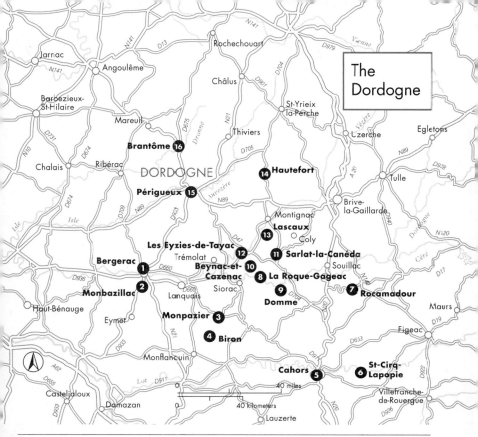

EXPLORING THE DORDOGNE

The Dordogne départment (province) is in the Aquitaine region of the southwest of France where, above the river valleys, oak and chestnut forests crowd in on about 1,200 castles and châteaux, most of them from the 13th and 14th centuries. The Dordogne region, so named for the river that bisects the area after it leaves Bordeaux (through Bergerac and onto the beautiful picture postcard town of Sarlat), is a spread-out place. To the east of Bordeaux city and a little farther north you can first encounter Cyrano's town of Bergerac and Monbazillac to its south (with its amazing views). To the east of Bergerac is Sarlat with Les Eyzies de Tayac, Montignac, and Lascaux to its north and Beynac et Cazenac, Domme, and La Roque-Gageac to its south. Midway between Bergerac and Sarlat and much farther north is Périgueux, with Brantome to its northeast on the D939. To the south is the Lot Valley, with Rocamadour to the southeast of Sarlat, Cahors directly south, and St-Cirq-Lapopie to its east.

WESTERN DORDOGNE TO ROCAMADOUR

From a bird's-eye view the geographic area we treat in this chapter is known in France by four colors: the Périgord Noir, Blanc, Poupre, and Vert. Sarlat and its environs are known as the Périgord Noir, or Black Périgord; Périgueux to the north is based in the Périgord Blanc (white) region; Bergerac to the southwest is the Périgord Poupre (purple); and Brantôme in the far north is in the Périgord Vert (green) region. With more than 2 million visitors every year, the Périgord Noir is the most frequented. But the entire Dordogne relies heavily on travelers so, thankfully, the local tourist offices have plenty of informative guides and maps to help you enjoy whatever "color" you choose. Many first opt for "purple," since Bergerac is the main hub for flights (after Bordeaux). Thus we kick things off in Western Dordogne and then head southwest down to the lovely Lot Valley, where dramatic Rocamadour lures a million and a half tourists and pilgrims every year.

BERGERAC

❶ *57 km (36 mi) east of St-Émilion via D936, 88 km (55 mi) east of Bordeaux.*

GETTING HERE

About 5 km south of town, Aéroport Bergerac-Perigord-Dordogne (☎05–53–22–25–25) has more than 20 Ryanair and Flybe flights a week. Unfortunately, there is yet no train or bus service to the airport so you have to taxi (☎05–53–23–32–32) into the town center. Transports Urbains Bergeracois (TUB, ☎05–53–57–17–10) is the urban bus service and costs €1 a ticket. Three bus operators leave the town for the surrounding region, with Les Cars Bleus (☎05–53–23–81–92) going to Eymet on two alternating routes through Sigoules or Issigeac; Boullet (☎05–53–61–00–46) heading to Lalinde; and C.F.T.A. Perigueux (☎05–53–08–43–13) traveling to Bergerac. Every trip costs €2. Bordeaux has five trains (taking anywhere from 1 hr, 15 mins to nearly 2 hrs) daily that run through Bergerac and hook up with Sarlat (1 hr, 15 mins); the rail station (☎05–53–63–53–80) is on Avenue du 108e.

EXPLORING

Yes, this is the Bergerac of Cyrano de Bergerac fame—but not exactly. The real satirist and playwright Cyrano (1619–55) who inspired playwright Edmond Rostand's long-nosed swashbuckler, was born in Paris and never set foot anywhere near this town. That hasn't prevented his legend from being preempted by the town fathers, who have plastered his schnoz all over the town's promotional materials and erected an exceedingly ugly statue of him. They shouldn't have bothered; Bergerac's gorgeous old half-timber houses, narrow alleys, riverside setting, and gastronomic specialties are more than enough to attract tourists staying in Bordeaux or Sarlat, both less than 100 km (62 mi) away. In the 14th century the English moved in but in 1450 the French took over and, in time, Bergerac became a Protestant bastion. Today, it's a lively farm trade town with colorful markets held Wednesday and Saturday (the larger of the two).

Guided walking tours of the Vieille Ville (Old Town) in English (75–90 mins, €4.50) leave from the **tourist office** (✉ *97 rue Neuve d'Argenson* ☎ *05–53–57–03–11* ⊕ *www.bergerac-tourisme.com*).

There are also hour-long cruises along the Dordogne at 11, 2, 3, and 4, daily Easter through October (€7) in old wooden sailboats with **Périgord Gabarres** (☎ *05–53–24–58–80*).

The **Cloître des Récollets,** a former convent, is in the wine business. The convent's stone-and-brick buildings range in date from the 12th to the 15th century and include galleries, a large vaulted cellar, and a cloister where the **Maison des Vins** (Wine Center) provides information on, and samples of, local vintages of sweet whites and fruity young reds. ✉ *1 rue des Récollets* ☎ *05–53–63–57–57* ☜ *Free* ⊙ *Sept.–Dec. and Feb.–May, Sun.–Mon. 9–12:30 and 2–6; June–Aug., daily 9–7.*

Along with its historical nuances Bergerac also has some unusual entities in its environs: its tobacco institute and museum. The history of tobacco growing—from its pre-Columbian origins to its spread worldwide—is outlined at the **Musée du Tabac** *(National Tobacco Museum).* The exhibits will please both aficionados and enemies of the nicotine weed—nonsmokers can revel in the gory descriptions of the way they used to torture smokers in ancient Persia. It's housed in the 17th-century Renaissance Maison Peyrarède (famous as Henry IV's château), near the quayside. ✉ *Pl. du Feu* ☎ *05–53–63–04–13* ☜ *€3.50* ⊙ *Tues.–Fri. 10–noon and 2–6, Sat. 10–noon and 2–5, Sun. 2:30–6:30. Closed weekends mid-Nov.–mid-Mar.*

WHERE TO STAY & EAT

$$–$$$ ✕ **L'Imparfait.** In business in the heart of old Bergerac, this characterful restaurant has beamed ceilings, openwork stone and brick walls, large lamps and tall, cane-back chairs. The lunch menu at €19 is good value and for €40 in the evening you can start with warm oysters with saffron or a skewer of langoustine with honey and rosemary, then move on to ravioli in a citron sauce. ✉ *6–10 rue des Fontaines* ☎ *05–53–57–47–92* ▭ *AE, MC, V* ⊙ *Closed late Dec.–Feb.*

$ 🛏 **Bordeaux.** In business since 1855, the Bordeaux has contemporary furnishings and neat rooms. Request one on the garden courtyard or No. 22, which is slightly more spacious. The owner, Monsieur Manant, is very helpful. ✉ *38 pl. Gambetta, 24100* ☎ *05–53–57–12–83* 🖶 *05–53–57–72–40* ⊕ *www.hotel-bordeaux-bergerac.com* 🛏 *40 rooms* ⚒ *In-room: no a/c, Wi-Fi. In-hotel: pool, some pets allowed (fee)* ▭ *AE, DC, MC, V* ⊙*FAP.*

MONBAZILLAC

❷ *6 km (4 mi) south of Bergerac via D13.*

From the hilltop village of Monbazillac are spectacular views of the sweet wine–producing vineyards tumbling toward the Dordogne. The

storybook corner towers of the beautifully proportioned 16th-century
★ gray-stone **Château de Monbazillac** pay tribute to the fortress tradition
of the Middle Ages, but the large windows and sloping roofs reveal a
Renaissance influence. Regional furniture and an ornate early-17th-
century bedchamber enliven the interior. A wine tasting is included
to tempt you into buying a case or two of the famous but expensive
bottles. ☎*05–53–63–65–00 weekdays, 05–53–61–52–52 weekends*
⊕*www.chateau-monbazillac.com* ✆*€5.90* ⊙*June–Sept., daily 10–7;
Feb.–May and Oct.–Dec., Tues.–Sun. 10–noon and 2–5.*

MONPAZIER

❸ *45 km (28 mi) southeast of Bergerac via D660.*

Fodor'sChoice
★
Monpazier, on the tiny Dropt River, is one of France's best-preserved
and most photographed bastide (fortified) towns. It was built in ocher-
color stone by English king Edward I in 1284 to protect the southern
flank of his French possessions. The bastide has three stone gateways (of an original six), a large central square, and the church of **St-
Dominique,** housing 35 carved-wood choir stalls and a would-be relic
of the True Cross.

Opposite the church is the finest medieval building in town, the **Maison
du Chapître** *(Chapter House),* once used as a barn for storing grain. Its
wood-beam roof is constructed of chestnut to repel insects.

WHERE TO STAY & EAT

¢ ✕⊡ **France.** Once an outbuilding on the estates of the Château de
Biron, the Hôtel de France has never capitalized on its 13th-century
heritage or its 15th-century staircase. Instead, it has remained a small,
modest family-run hotel that caters less to tourists than to locals at its
bar and restaurant, serving rich regional food. Rooms are a clutter of
old furniture (with a plastic-cabinet shower and toilet squeezed into the
corner); some are quite large. ⊠*21 rue St-Jacques, 24540* ☎*05–53–
22–66–01* 䑓*05–53–22–07–27* ⤙*10 rooms* ♿*In-room: no a/c, no TV.
In-hotel: restaurant, bar* ☰*MC, V* ⊙*Closed Nov.–Feb.* ⋈*MAP.*

BIRON

❹ *8 km (5 mi) south of Monpazier via D2/D53.*

★ Stop in Biron to see its massive hilltop castle, the **Château de Biron.**
Highlights of the château, which with its keep, square tower, and
chapel dates from the Renaissance, include monumental staircases,
Renaissance-era apartments, the kitchen with its huge stone-slab floor,
and a gigantic dungeon, replete with a collection of scarifying torture instruments. The classical buildings were completed in 1760. The
Gontaut-Biron family—whose ancestors invented great typefaces centuries ago—have lived here for 14 generations. ☎*05–53–63–13–39*
✆*€5.70* ⊙*Apr.–June, Sept., Oct., and Nov., Tues.–Sun. 10–12:30 and
2–6; July and Aug., daily 10–7.*

CAHORS

 60 km (38 mi) southeast of Monpazier via D811.

GETTING HERE

If you're taking a train to Cahors you'll arrive at the station (☎ *05–65–23-33–57*) on Place Jouinot Gambetta from Paris's Gare d'Austerlitz in around five hours for about €60 one-way. Trains run frequently between Toulouse and Cahors and the shuttle (€5) between Toulouse Airport and Toulouse Bus Station (next door to the railway station) run every 20 minutes. So maybe you're better off flying into Toulouse as opposed to Bergerac, from where it is difficult to reach Cahors, or even into the regional airport of Brive La Gaillarde (⊕ *www.airlinair*) and then heading south to Cahors. Buses leave from the train station and, as with the rest of the Dordogne, can be erratic, even if they are only €2 a trip.

15

EXPLORING

Less touristy and populated than most of the Dordogne, the Lot Valley has a subtler charm. The cluster of towns along the Lot River and the smaller rivers that cut through the dry, vineyard-covered plateau have a magical, abandoned feel. Just an hour north of southwestern France's main city, Toulouse, Cahors is the Lot area's largest town, hosts the helpful regional information center (⊠ *107 quai Cavaignac* ☎ *05–65–35–07–09* ⊕ *www.tourisme-lot.com*), and makes a fine base from which to explore the Lot River valley, a 50-km (31-mi) gorge punctuated by medieval villages. Here and on other routes—notably the GR46, which spans the interior of the Lot region, with breathtaking views of the limestone plateaus and quiet valleys between Rocamadour and St-Cirq-Lapopie—*cyclotourisme* (biking) rules supreme.

Modern Cahors encircles its *Ville Antique* (Old Town), which dates from 1 bc. Once an opulent Gallo-Roman town, Cahors, sitting snugly within a loop of the Lot River, is famous for its vin de Cahors, a tannic red wine known to the Romans as "black wine." It was the Romans who introduced wine to Cahors, and Caesar is said to have brought Cahors wine back to Rome, but perhaps the region's biggest booster was the former bishop of Cahors who went on to become Pope John XXII. This second Avignon pope of the 14th-century made sure his hometown wine became the communion wine of the Avignon church. Malbec is the most common grape used, which produces, according to recent studies, one of the most potent anticarcinogenic and antiaging wines on the planet—Madiran. There's also a growing amount of merlot in the region and the local jurançon noir grape to be tasted. Many of the small estates in the area offer tastings and the town tourist office on Place François-Mitterrand (☎*05–65–53–20–65*) can point you in the direction of some of the more notable vineyards, including the Domaine de Lagrezette (in Caillac) and the Domaine de St-Didier (in Parnac).

Cahors was also an early episcopal see and the capital of the old region of Quercy. Ruled by bishops until the 14th century, the university here was founded by Pope John XXII in 1322. The old parts of the town are interesting from an architectural perspective.

Fodor's Choice
★

The town's finest sight is the 14th-century **Pont Valentré**, a bridge with three elegant towers that constitutes a spellbinding feat of medieval engineering.

Also look for the fortresslike **Cathédrale St-Étienne** (⊠*Off Rue du Maréchal-Joffre*), with its Byzantine style and cloisters connecting to the courtyard of the archdeaconry, which is awash with Renaissance decoration and thronged with townsfolk who come to view art exhibits.

WHERE TO STAY & EAT

$$$–$$$$ ✕🖫 **Château de Mercuès.** The former home of the count-bishops of Cahors, on a rocky spur just outside town, has older rooms in baronial splendor (ask for one of these), as well as unappealing modern ones (which tend to attract midges). One of the best is "Tour," with a clever ceiling that slides back to expose the turret. Duck, lamb, and truffles reign in the restaurant, but the high prices lead you to expect more creativity from chef Philippe Combet than is delivered. The restaurant is closed Monday, and there's no lunch Tuesday–Thursday. ⊠*8 km (5 mi) northwest of Cahors on road to Villeneuve-sur-Lot, 46090 Mercuès* ☎*05–65–20–00–01* 🖶*05–65–20–05–72* ⊕*www.chateaudemercues. com* 🔄*24 rooms, 8 suites* ⚐*In-room: no a/c, refrigerator, dial-up. In-hotel: restaurant, tennis courts, pool, some pets allowed (fee), public Internet* ▤*AE, DC, MC, V* ⊙*Closed Nov.–Easter* ⎢⍥⎢*MAP.*

ST-CIRQ-LAPOPIE

❻   *32 km (20 mi) east of Cahors via D653, D662, and D40.*

Fodor's Choice
★

GETTING HERE

The easiest way to reach St-Cirq-Lapopie from Cahors's train station is to take the SNCF bus bound for Figeac (40 mins); St-Cirq is a 25-minute walk from where the bus drops you. From the bus stop Tour de Faure, go back to the D181 (sign says "St-Cirq 2 KM"), cross the bridge, and walk uphill. It's a haul, but worth the hike.

EXPLORING

Perched on the edge of a cliff 330 feet up, the beautiful 13th-century village of St-Cirq (pronounced san-*sare*) looks as though it could slide right into the Lot River. Filled with artisans' workshops and not yet renovated à la Disney, the town has so many dramatic views you may end up spending several hours. Traversing steep paths and alleyways among flower-filled balconies, you'll realize it deserves its description as

CLOSE UP

Nobody Knows the Truffles I've Seen

The Dordogne is a land of foie gras and cognac so travelers get to eat (and quaff) like the kings (and queens) who once disputed this coveted corner, staking it out with châteaux-forts and blessing it with Romanesque churches.

Begin by following the winding sprawl of the Dordogne River into duck country. This is the land of the *gavée* goose, force-fed extravagantly to plump its liver into one of the world's most renowned delicacies.

Duck or goose fat glistens on potatoes, on salty confits, and on *rillettes d'oie*, a spread of potted duck that melts on the tongue as no mere butter ever could.

Wild mushrooms and truffles (referred locally to as "black diamonds") weave their musky perfume through dense game pâtés.

Although truffle production is nothing like it used to be, this subterranean edible fungus has been beguiling oils, chefs, and foodies for centuries.

The truffle forms a symbiotic relationship with the roots of certain trees (in the Périgord region they are mainly found growing from green oaks) and plants to form a part that is technically known as the ascoma, the fruiting body of a fungus.

Mysteriously appearing anywhere from November to February in the forests of Périgord (and other areas of western Europe), the more famous truffles are black but they can be white.

The Périgord truffes (truffles) have been highly respected since the 15th century. Their taste is savory, zesty, and extremely aromatic, and because of this they have been glorified as a delicacy in recipes for thousands of years (if we are to believe old Greek and Roman writings on the subject).

They can be canned for export and are traditionally hunted for by pigs, but are now commonly discovered by dogs, who can be taught to point for truffles.

Also, as the dogs don't eat the truffles when they find them they make for much better hunters than the avaricious piglets.

Cultivation of the famous fungus has had success, too. It means inoculating the roots of a host plant seedling with fungal spores, but for all its success it's still thought to taste inferior to the ones found in the forests. There are hundreds of species of truffle, too.

To stand up to such an onslaught of earthy textures and flavors, the best Dordogne wines, such as Bergerac and Cahors, are known as coarser brews.

However, since the 1970s the winegrowers around Cahors have succeeded in mellowing those coarser edges.

And to round it all off? A snifter of amber cognac—de rigueur for the digestion.

Dining thus, in a vine-covered stone *ferme auberge* deep in the green wilds of Dordogne, replete with a feast of pâtés, truffles, and cognacs, you begin to see what the Plantagenets were fighting for.

15

one of the most beautiful villages in France. A mostly ruined 13th-century château can be reached by a stiff walk along the path that starts near the Hôtel de Ville. Stop by the tourist office (⊠ *Pl. du Sombral* ☎ 05–65–31–29–06) in the center of town for information on other points of interest in town. Morning hikes in the misty gorges in the valley are beyond beautiful.

★ Discovered in 1922, the **Grotte du Pech-Merle** displays 4,000 square feet of prehistoric drawings and carvings. Particularly known for its peculiar polka-dot horses, impressions of the human hand, and footprints, this is the most impressive "real-thing" prehistoric cave that is open to the public in France. The admission charge includes a 20-minute film, an hour-long tour, and a visit to the adjacent museum. Take a great bike ride here from St-Cirq-Lapopie or the SNCF bus from Cahors—getting off at Conduché (before St-Cirq) and walking the 7 km (4 mi) along D41—or just drive (from Cahors take D653 7 km (4 mi) to the right turn by Vers). On peak summer days, tickets are at a premium so book them in advance. ⊠ *10 km (6 mi) north of St-Cirq-Lapopie, 3 km (2 mi) west of Cabrerets* ☎ *05–65–31–27–05* ⊕ *www.pechmerle.com* ☎ *€7.50* ⊙ *mid-Apr.–Oct., daily 9:30–noon and 1:30–5.*

WHERE TO STAY

$$–$$$ 🏨 **Pélissaria.** This intimate 16th-century hotel is small and simple but chock-full of atmosphere. The best rooms look out across the village or the valley and river; some rooms in the garden have less grand views (Nos. 3 and 4 are very small). The lounge is a snug place to relax in front of the fire in the evening. ⊠ *Le Bourg, 46330 St-Cirq-Lapopie* ☎ *05–65–31–25–14* ⊕ *perso.wanadoo.fr/hoteldelapelissaria* ↻ *10 rooms* ⌂ *In-room: no a/c. In-hotel: pool, some pets allowed (fee)* ▭ *MC, V* ⊙ *Closed Nov.–Apr.* ⊙| *MAP.*

ROCAMADOUR

➐ *72 km (45 mi) north of St-Cirq via Labastide-Murat.*

GETTING HERE

Bergerac airport (⊕ *www.bergerac.aeroport.fr*) could seem a bit far to travel to get to this famous village, but there's always the regional supplier Airlinair (⊕ *www.airlinair.com*), which flies from Paris into nearby Brive La Gaillarde directly north of Rocamadour (for as little as €40 one-way two times a day during the week and once on Sunday) or the Toulouse airport. If you're getting here by train—direct connections available to Toulouse (1½ hrs) and Brive (40 mins, €7)—you'll want to have your walking shoes on because the Rocamadour-Padirac station (☎*05–65–33–63–05*) is a shared affair with the neighboring village of Padirac and is 4 km (3 mi) away from the village. Walking takes about an hour, biking 15 minutes. A handy taxi-cab firm is: Taxi Pascal Herbert (☎*05–65–50–14–82, 06–81–60–14–60 cell*).

EXPLORING

Rocamadour is a medieval village that seems to defy the laws

> **GOD'S VIEW**
>
> On the uppermost plateau of the Cité Réligieuse stands the Château de Rocamadour, a private residence of the church fathers. Open to the public for an admission fee are its ramparts, which have spectacular views of the gorge. However, you can enjoy the same views for free just by walking the Chemin de la Croix up to the castle.

of gravity; it surges out of a cliff 1,500 feet above the Alzou River gorge—an awe-inspiring sight that makes this one of the most-visited tourist spots in France. The town got its name after the discovery in 1166 of the 1,000-year-old body of St. Amadour "quite whole." The body was moved to the cathedral, where it began to work miracles. Legend has it that the saint was actually a publican named Zacheus, who, after the honor of entertaining Jesus in his home, came to Gaul after the crucifixion and, under the name of Amadour, established a private chapel in the cliff here. Pilgrims have long flocked to the site, climbing the 216 steps to the church on their knees. Making the climb on foot is a sufficient reminder of the medieval penchant for agonizing penance; today two elevators lift weary souls. Unfortunately, the summer influx of a million tourists has brought its own blight, judging by the dozens of tacky souvenir shops. Cars are not allowed; park in the lot below the town.

The town is split into four levels joined by steep stairs. The lowest level is occupied by the village of Rocamadour itself, and mainly accessed through the centuries-old Porte du Figuier (Fig Tree Gate). Past this portal, the **Cité Médiévale,** or the **Basse Ville,** though in parts grotesquely touristy, is full of beautifully restored structures, such as the 15th-century **Hôtel de Ville,** near the Porte Salmon, which houses the **tourist office** (☎*05–65–33–22–00*) and an excellent collection of tapestries. ⌨*€2* ⊙*Mon.–Sat. 10–noon and 2–5.*

The Basse Ville's Rue Piétonne, the main pedestrian street, is lined with crêperies, tea salons, and hundreds of tourists, many of whom are heading heavenward by taking the **Grand Escalier** staircase or elevator (fee) from Place de la Carreta up to the **Cité Religieuse,** set halfway up the cliff. If you walk, pause at the landing 141 steps up to admire the fort. Once up, you can see tiny Place St-Amadour and its seven chapels: the basilica of **St-Sauveur** opposite the staircase; the **St-Amadour crypt** beneath the basilica; the chapel of **Notre-Dame,** with its statue of the Black Madonna, to the left; the chapels of **John the Baptist, St-Blaise,** and **Ste-Anne** to the right; and the Romanesque chapel of **St-Michel** built into an overhanging cliff. St-Michel's two 12th-century

Fodor's Choice
★

15

frescoes—depicting the Annunciation and the Visitation—have survived in superb condition.

> **DELICIEUX!**
>
> Delicious is Château de la Treyne's spectacular storybook terrace set with tables overlooking the river. Here you can feast on fried scallops on chestnut galettes with a cappuccino of mushrooms, just one of the dishes featured in the hotel's special Menu St. Jacques de Compostelle, which honors the castle's history as a way station for pilgrims on the ancient Compostela route to Spain.

WHERE TO STAY & EAT

$$$$ Fodor's Choice ★ **Château de la Treyne.** Certainly the most spectacular château-hotel in the Dordogne, this Relais & Châteaux outpost sits in splendor in enchantingly Baroque gardens that are perched over the Dordogne River. Set in Lacave, 6 km (3½ mi) northwest of Rocamadour, La Treyne was nearly destroyed in the 16th-century Wars of Religion but happily reconstructed under Louis XIII. Today, the Great Lounge restaurant (closed for lunch Tuesday to Friday) is a symphony of chandeliers, oak panels, and Louis Treize chairs, but the much-photographed dining terrace always seduces in warm weather. The adjacent Music Lounge allures with its gigantic fireplace and old-master paintings. Guest rooms are astonishingly stylish, ranging from the Prison Doreé, or "Golden Prison" (set atop the castle tower, replete with centuries-old stone walls and panoramic views) to the hyper-charming "Soleil Levant" (the former chapel, now glowing in historic limes and yellow). The smallest, such as the Vendages, still cost a pretty penny (rooms here range from €180 to €660) *but* they do include breakfast and dinner for two. As for modern luxe, delights range from Jacuzzis to minibars. For taste in every sense of the word, La Treyne is tops. *La Treyne, 21 km (13 mi) northwest of Rocamadour, 46200 Lacave 05-65-27-60-60 05-65-27-60-70 www.chateaudelatreyne.com 17 rooms, 4 suites In-room: refrigerator, dial-up (some). In-hotel: restaurant, tennis court, bar, pool, some pets allowed (fee), public Internet AE, DC, MC, V Closed mid-Nov.–Christmas, and Jan.–Apr. MAP.*

$$–$$$$ ★ **Château de Roumégouse.** With a beautiful flowered terrace overlooking the Rocamadour cliff face, this forested Relais & Châteaux beauty is on the road between Rocamadour and Gramat. The gorgeous castellated structure has a history going back to the 10th century and is reputedly haunted by the medieval folk heroine Resplendine de Rignac (if so, she probably has moved into the 19th-century fairy-tale tower that looms over the château). Inside, three air-conditioned dining salons beckon with luxurious evening meals (lunch is only served Sunday). The first is neo-baronial with an impressive historic fireplace; the second is "Louis" in style and brightened with light linens and pleasant paintings; the third is the covered veranda, used for breakfast and flaunting great views of the surrounding valleys. As for the guest rooms, they are delightfully done up in soothing colors with very soigné furniture accents and antiques. At the end of a long day of sightseeing,

the castle's 12-acre park is the perfect restorative. ⊠*Rte. de Rocamadour, Rignac 46500 Gramat* ☎*05–65–33–63–81* 🖷*05–65–33–71–18* ⊕*www.chateauderoumegouse.com* ⇆*13 rooms, 2 suites* 🕭*In-room: no a/c, Wi-Fi. In-hotel: restaurant, pool, some pets allowed, no elevator* ⊟*AE, MC, V* ☉*Closed Jan.–Apr.*

$–$$$ ╳🖾 **Grand Hôtel Beau Site.** This is the best of the few Vieille Ville hotels in Rocamadour. The charm of the ancient beams, exposed stone, and open hearth in the foyer ends, however, as you climb the stairs; rooms are modern and functional. The modern, large-window Jehan de Valon restaurant overlooks the canyon, serving foie gras, local lamb, and walnut gâteau. Best of all, you can park inside Rocamadour if you stay here. ⊠*Cité Médiévale, 46500* ☎*05–65–33–63–08* 🖷*05–65–33–65–23* ⊕*www.bw-beausite.com* ⇆*40 rooms, 3 suites* 🕭*In-hotel: restaurant, bar, some pets allowed (fee), public Internet* ⊟*AE, DC, MC, V* ☉*Closed mid-Nov.–mid-Feb.* ⑂*MAP.*

¢–$ 🖾 **Lion d'Or.** In the center of Rocamadour, this simple, bargain-priced, family-run hotel has a panoramic restaurant with views of the valley, where genial owner Dominique Duclos serves up delicious truffle omelets and homemade foie gras au Noilly. ⊠*Cité Médiévale, 46500* ☎*05–65–33–62–04* 🖷*05–65–33–72–54* ⊕*www.liondor-rocamadour. com* ⇆*35 rooms* 🕭*In-room: no a/c, Wi-Fi (some). In-hotel: restaurant* ⊟*MC, V* ☉*Closed Nov.–Easter* ⑂*FAP.*

15

EASTERN PERIGORD TO BRANTÔME

Entering the Perigord Noir, a trifeca of top Dordogne sights awaits: the cliff-face village of La Roque-Gageac, the prehistoric grottoes of Domme, and the storybook castle at Beynac. Just eastward lies Sarlat, the regional center and a town famed for its half-timber pastorale and medieval vibe. Northward lies the Vézère Valley, the prehistoric capital of France, celebrated for its locales settled by primitive man, such as Lascaux. Continuing north the traveler arrives at the bustling city of Périgueux and numerous riverside towns, including historic Brantôme. For three centuries during the Middle Ages, this entire region was a battlefield in the wars between the French and the English. Of the castles and châteaux dotting the area, those at Hautefort and Beynac are among the most spectacular. Robust Romanesque architecture is more characteristically found in this area than the airy Gothic style in view elsewhere in France, and can be admired at Périgueux Cathedral and in countless village churches.

LA ROQUE-GAGEAC

⑧ *55 km (36 mi) west of Rocamadour via Payrac, 10 km (6 mi) southwest*
Fodor'sChoice *of Sarlat via D703.*
★
Across the Dordogne from Domme, in the direction of Beynac, romantically huddled beneath a cliff, is strikingly attractive La Roque-Gageac, one of the best-restored villages in the valley. Crafts shops

line its narrow streets, dominated by the outlines of the 19th-century mock-medieval Château de Malartrie and the Manoir de Tarde, with its cylindrical turret. If you leave the main road and climb one of the steep cobblestone paths, you can check out the medieval houses on their natural perches and even hike up the mountain for a view down to the village.

WHERE TO STAY & EAT

$–$$ ✕🍴 **La Plume d'Oie.** This small inn overlooks the river and the limestone cliffs. Rooms, in light fabrics and wicker furniture, vary in size and price—the best overlook the Dordogne. La Plume d'Oie's major raison d'être, however, is the stone-walled restaurant, at which you are expected to have at least one meal. Chef–owner Marc-Pierre Walker prepares classic regional cuisine, such as roasted duckling in a pepper shallot sauce and the ever popular panfried foie gras (the restaurant is closed Monday and does not serve lunch Tuesday; reservations are essential). ✉24250 La Roque-Gageac ☎05–53–29–57–05 🖨05–53–31–04–81 🛏4 rooms ⚇In-room: no a/c. In-hotel: restaurant ☰MC, V ⊗Closed Christmas–Feb.

DOMME

9 *5 km (3 mi) east of La Roque-Gageac.*

The historic cliff-top village of Domme is famous for its **grottoes,** where prehistoric bison and rhinoceros bones have been discovered. You can visit the 500-yard-long illuminated galleries, which are lined with stalactites. ✉Pl. de la Halle 🎫€6 ⊗Apr.–Sept., daily 10–noon and 2–6; Mar. and Oct., daily 2–6.

BEYNAC-ET-CAZENAC

10 *11 km (7 mi) west of La Roque-Gageac via D703.*

One of the most enchanting sights in the Dordogne is the medieval castle that sits atop the wonderfully restored town of Beynac. Perched atop a sheer cliff face beside an abrupt bend in the Dordogne River, the muscular 13th-century **Château de Beynac** has unforgettable views from its battlements. During the Hundred Years' War this castle often faced off with forces massed directly across the way at the fort of Castenaud. Star of many films, Beynac was last featured in Luc Besson's 1999 life of Joan of Arc, *The Messenger.* Tours of the castle are in English for groups by reservation. ☎05–53–29–50–40 🎫€7 ⊗May–Sept., daily 10–6:30; Oct.–Apr., daily 10–6.

With a fabulous mountaintop setting, the now-ruined castle of **Castlenaud** (☎05–53–31–30–00), containing a large collection of medieval arms, is just upstream from Beynac across the Dordogne; it's open February–May and September and October, daily 10–6; July and August, daily 9:30–7. Admission is €7.20.

★ Five kilometers (3 mi) from Castlenaud is the turreted **Château des Milandes** (☎ *05–53–59–31–21* ⊕ *www.milandes.com*), open April to October, daily 10–6:15 (€7.80). Built around 1489 in Renaissance style, it has lovely terraces and gardens and was once owned by the American-born cabaret star of Roaring '20s Paris, Josephine Baker. Here she housed her "rainbow family," a large group of adopted children from many countries. Today, there's a museum devoted to her memory and, from April to October, falconry displays. From here D53 (via Belvès) leads southwest to Monpazier.

> ## VERSAILLES IN THE SKY
>
> Perched on their cliff top, the topiaries of Marqueyssac seem like a mirage. This style of garden first made its mark at Versailles, where the king's eye could stretch along nearly 3 km (2 mi) of manicured gardens before finally coming up against a wall of trees, resulting in the feeling that the entire world was within his grasp. Here, on the contrary, gorgeous views extend miles over the Dordogne Valley below.

15

Fodor's Choice
★

One of the most regal yet picturesque sights in the Périgord Noir is the garden of the **Château de Marqueyssac,** set in Vézac, about 3 km (1½ mi) south of Beynac-et-Cazenac. The park was founded in 1682 and its design, including an enchanting parterre of cut topiaries, was greatly influenced by the designs of André le Nôtre, the "green geometer" of Versailles. Shaded paths bordered by 150,000 hand-pruned boxwoods are graced with breathtaking viewpoints, rock gardens, waterfalls, and verdant glades. From the belvedere 400 feet above the river, there's an exceptional view of the Dordogne valley, with its castles and beautiful villages such as Beynac, Fayrac, Castelnaud, Roque-Gageac, and Domme. A tea salon is open from March to mid-November and is just the place to drink in the panoramic views from the parterre terrace. To get a dazzling preview, log on to the Web site. ⊠ *Belvédère de la Dordogne, Vézac, 9 km (5 mi) southwest of Sarlat* ☎ *05–53–31–36–36* ⊕ *www.marqueyssac.com* ☎ *€6.80* ⊗ *July and Aug., daily 9–8; Feb., Mar., and Oct.–mid-Nov. daily 10–6; mid-Nov.–Jan. daily 2–5; Apr., May, June, and Sept. 10–7.*

WHERE TO EAT & STAY

¢–$ ✕▥ **Pontet.** A few blocks from the Dordogne River and within the shadow of cliff-top Château de Beynac, this is one of the hotel mainstays of the adorably Dordognesque town of Beynac. Guest rooms are sweet and simple, and a short hike down to the river will bring you to the hotel's Hostellerie Maleville, a big riverside restaurant, where you'll want to forgo a table in the modern, wood-beamed dining room for a blissfully magical perch on the riverbank itself. Here, umbrellas and willow trees shade diners happily tucking into such fare as goose neck stuffed with truffles and Beynacoises potatoes. ⊠ *24220 Beynac-et-Cazenac* ☎ *05–53–29–50–06* 🖷 *05–53–28–28–52* ➴ *12 rooms* ⟡ *In-room: no a/c. In-hotel: restaurant* ▤ *AE, MC, V.*

SARLAT-LA-CANÉDA

① *10 km (6 mi) northeast of Beynac via D57, 74 km (46 mi) east of*
Fodor'sChoice *Bergerac.*
★

GETTING HERE

Flying here usually means coming into Bergerac airport (⊕ *www. bergerac.aeroport.fr*) but there's also the regional supplier, Airlinair, which flies from Paris into nearby Brive La Gaillarde to the north (for as little as €40 one-way two times a day during the week and once on Sunday). A half-hour walk out of town, Sarlat train station (⊠ *Rue de la Gare* ☎05–53–59–00–21) on the northeast of town is badly linked with the rest of the Dordogne. For trains to Les Eyzies (1 hr) and Périgueux (1½ hrs) you'll need to change at Le Buisson. There are trains to Sarlat from Bordeaux twice a day. To get to Paris you have to change at Souillac and the trip takes about 5½ hours for about €70 one-way. Buses, again minimal, are operated by Effia Transports Belmon (☎05–56–33–03–80) on the Souillac route and Périgord Voyages/Cheze (☎05–53–59–01–48) on the Périgueux one. Don't get off at the train station but at the stops at Place Pasteur or Rue de la République.

EXPLORING

Sarlat (as it is usually known) defines enchantment. If you're planning a trip to the many prehistoric caves and the amazing perched villages near this gorgeous town then this capital of the Périgord Noir is the place to stay. It's ideally located, with Les Eyzies de Tayac, Montignac, and Lascaux to its north and Beynac et Cazenac, Domme, and La Roque-Gageac just to its south. Even Rocamadour, to the southeast on the D704, which connects with the D673 isn't all that far from here and Cahors is a straight shot south on the A20 peage (paid road) or the more scenic (and longer) N20.

Tucked among hills adorned with corn and wheat, Sarlat is a beautiful, well-preserved medieval town that, despite attracting huge numbers of visitors, has managed to retain some of its true character. With its storybook streets, Sarlat's **Cité Médiévale** is filled most days with tour groups, and is especially hectic on Saturday, market day: all the geese on sale are proof of the local addiction to foie gras. To do justice to the town's golden-stone splendor, wander through its medieval streets in the later afternoon or early evening, aided by the tourist office's walking map. The tourist office (⊠ *Rue Tourny* ☎05–53–31–45–45) also organizes walking tours, which for €5 give you an in-depth look at the town's medieval buildings.

The end of the Hundred Years' War (1453) favored the construction of beautiful urban architecture in the Dordogne but Sarlat was especially favored: when the region was handed back to the French king by the English, he rewarded the town with royal privileges for its loyalty to his crown. Before long, a new merchant class sprang up, building gabled and golden-stoned mansions in the latest French Renaissance style. It's no surprise to learn that only Nice and Paris have had more films shot in their locales than Sarlat; Lasse Hallstrom's *Chocolat* (2000) and

Luc Besson's *The Messenger* (1998) are some of the more recent and better known of the more than 45 movies that have used the town as a backdrop. Also, every year in November the town actually has its own film festival with comedians, film stars, producers, and film technicians arriving to host an informational get-together for 500 students. In addition, there's also a theater festival here mid-July to the end of August.

Sarlat's Cité Médiévale has many beautiful photo-ops. Of particular note is Rue de la Liberté, which leads to **Place du Peyrou**, anchored on one corner by the steep-gabled Renaissance house where writer-orator Étienne de la Boétie (1530–63) was born.

The elaborate turreted tower of the **Cathédrale St-Sacerdos** (⊠*Pl. du Peyrou*), begun in the 12th century, is the oldest part of the building and, along with the choir, all that remains of the original Romanesque structure.

The sloping garden behind the cathedral, the **Jardin des Enfers,** contains a strange, conical tower known as the Lanterne des Morts (Lantern of the Dead), which was occasionally used as a funeral chapel.

Running the length of the Enfer gardens is the **Rue Montaigne,** where the great 16th-century philosopher, Michel de Montaigne, once lived— some of the half-timber houses that line this street cast a fairy-tale spell. Rue d'Albusse, adjoining the garden behind the cathedral, and Rue de la Salamandre are narrow, twisty streets that head to Place de la Liberté and the 18th-century **Hôtel de Ville.**

Opposite the town hall is the rickety Gothic church of **Ste-Marie,** with its picturesque gargoyles overlooking Place du Marché aux Oies.

Ste-Marie points the way to Sarlat's most interesting street, **Rue des Consuls.** Among its medieval buildings are the Hôtel Plamon, with broad windows that resemble those of a Gothic church, and, opposite, the 15th-century Hôtel de Vassal.

WHERE TO STAY & EAT

★ $$ ✕▦ **Hostellerie La Couleuvrine.** Sarlat is not overly blessed with beautiful historic hotels so this one is a true standout. Topped with a massive crenellated tower and built into the town's ancient ramparts, this imposing structure once held off besieging forces during the Wars of Religion thanks to its tower *couleuvrines* ("long cannons"). Inside, the atmosphere is richest in the medieval restaurant (closed January): a vast half-timber, 13th-century stone hall where the town council once presided. Today, the giant fireplace remains but you'll also be warmed up by rich Louis Treize armchairs, pink bouquets, and the room's Renaissance wood trim. Even more delicious is the food, such as the brick-pressed duck with artichokes and the fresh-fruit kebab with Sauternes zabaglione. Guest rooms are simply but elegantly furnished; the showpiece is the tower room complete with a crenellated Cinerama view out the windows. While not in Sarlat's Cite Médiévale, it is just a few blocks to the east—check out the photo map on the hotel's Web site for a nifty visual tour of the town. This is great value for the money. ⊠*1 pl. de la Bouquerie, 24200* ☎*05–53–59–27–80* 🖷*05–53–31–26–83*

⊕www.la-couleuvrine.com ⟿24 *rooms* ☒*In-room: no a/c, Wi-Fi. In-hotel: restaurant* ⊟*AE, MC, V* �ⓄⅠ*EP, MAP.*

$–$$ ✕🏠 **Hôtel de la Madeleine.** This sturdy stone 19th-century building just to the north of the Old Town has small but cozy pastel-color bedrooms with floral quilts; three have a balcony. The restaurant (closed mid-November to mid-March; no lunch Monday and Tuesday except in July and August), with its crisp white table-cloths, showcases the slurpable talent of owner-chef Philippe Melot and his cream of lentil with truffles, burbot with orange, and goose either stewed in Cahors wine or roasted with fried potatoes and cèpe fricassee. Apple tart with caramel and rum-and-raisin ice cream

is de rigueur to finish the meal. ✉*1 pl. de la Petite-Rigaudie, 24200* 🕾*05-53-59-10-41* 🖶*05-53-31-03-62* ⊕*www.hoteldelamadeleine-sarlat.com* ⟿*39 rooms* ☒*In-hotel: restaurant, some pets allowed (fee), public Wi-Fi* ⊟*AE, DC, MC, V* ⊘*Closed Jan.–mid-Feb.* ⓄⅠ*MAP.*

$ 🏠 **Hôtel des Recollects.** One of Sarlat's time-burnished hotels, this is in the southern section of the town's Cité Médiévale, side by side with the 17th-century Chapelle des Recollects and its convent. Today, the hotel—blessed with a golden-stone facade—is centered around the convent's ancient cloister, which makes an exquisite setting for breakfast. Guest rooms are extremely simple, befitting the rates, which also include such pluses as air-conditioning, minibars, and the nice location. ✉*1 pl. de la Bouquerie, 24200* 🕾*05-53-31-36-00* 🖶*05-53-30-32-62* ⊕*www.hotel-recollets-sarlat.com* ⟿*18 rooms* ☒*In-room: refrigerator, Wi-Fi. In-hotel: private parking* ⊟*AE, MC, V* ⓄⅠ*EP.*

EN ROUTE The road between Sarlat and Les Eyzies (twisty D47) goes past the elegant **Château de Puymartin** (🕾*05-53-59-29-97*); it's open April–October, daily 10–noon; admission is €5.

LES EYZIES-DE-TAYAC

⑫ *21 km (13 mi) northwest of Sarlat via D47.*

Sitting comfortably under a limestone cliff, Les Eyzies is the doorway to the prehistoric capital of France. Early Homo sapiens (the species to which humans belong) lived about 40,000 years ago and skeletal remains and other artifacts of this Aurignacian culture were first found here in 1868. Many signs of Cro-Magnon man have been discovered in this vicinity; a number of excavated caves and grottoes, some with wall paintings, are open for public viewing, including the Grotte-Font-de-Gamme, just south of the town, with very faint drawings to be seen on a tour, and the Grotte des Combarelles. Stop by the town tourist office for the lowdown on all the caves in the area—the office also sells tickets for most sites and you should reserve here because a surprising number of tours sell out in advance (sometimes there are only six people allowed at any one time in a cave).

Amid the dimness of the **Grotte du Grand-Roc** you can view weirdly shaped crystalline stalactites and stalagmites—not for the claustrophobic. At the nearby **Abri Préhistorique de Laugerie**, you can visit caves once home to prehistoric man. ⊠ *Rte. du Périgueux* ☎ *05–53–06–92–70* ⊕ *www.grandroc.com* ✉ *€7.50* ⊙ *Apr.–Oct., daily 10–6 (July and Aug., daily 9:30–7).*

To truly enhance your understanding of the paintings at Lascaux and other caves in the Dordogne, visit the **Musée National de Préhistoire** *(National Museum of Prehistory)*, which attracts large crowds to its renowned collection of prehistoric artifacts, including primitive sculpture, furniture, and tools. You can also get ideas at the museum about excavation sites to visit in the region. ⊠ *1 rue du Musée* ☎ *05–53–06–45–45* ⊕ *www.musee-prehistoire-eyzies.fr* ✉ *€5* ⊙ *July and Aug., daily 9:30–6:30; Sept.–June, Wed.–Mon. 9:30–12:30 and 2:30–5:30.*

As you head north from Les Eyzies-de-Tayac toward Lascaux, stop off 7 km (4 mi) north of Les Eyzies near the village of Tursac to discover the enchanting troglodyte "lost village" of **La Madeleine**, found hidden in the Valley of Vézère at the foot of a ruined castle and overlooking the Vézère River. Human settlement here dates back to 15,000 bc, but what is most eye-catching now is its picturesque cliff-face chapel—seemingly half Cro-Magnon, half Gothic, it was constructed during the Middle Ages. The "Brigadoon" of the Dordogne, La Madeleine was abandoned in the 1920s. Guided visits tour the site (call ahead, English available). ⊠ *Tursac, 7 km (4 mi) north of Les Eyzies-de-Tayac* ✉ *€5.50* ⊙ *July and Aug., daily 10–8, Sept.–June, daily 10–6.*

Fodor's Choice
★

WHERE TO STAY & EAT

$$$–$$$$ ✕🏨 **Le Centenaire.** Though it's also a stylish, modern Relais & Châteaux hotel, Le Centenaire is known foremost as a restaurant. Chef Roland Mazère adds flair to the preparation of local delights: risotto with truffles or snails with ravioli and gazpacho. The dining room's golden stone and wood beams retain local character (on Thursday and on weekends, the restaurant serves lunch only; a jacket is required). ⊠ *24620 Les Eyzies-de-Tayac* ☎ *05–53–06–68–68* 🖷 *05–53–06–92–41* ⊕ *www.hotelducentenaire.fr* ⇄ *19 rooms* ⚫ *In-room: refrigerator, Wi-Fi. In-hotel: restaurant, pool, gym, some pets allowed (fee)* ▭ *AE, DC, MC, V* ⊙ *Closed Nov.–Apr.* ⦿ *MAP.*

★ $$$–$$$$ ✕🏨 **Le Vieux Logis.** Built around the most gorgeous dining room in the Dordogne, this vine-clad manor house in Trémolat remains one of the best hotels of the region. The warm guest rooms vary in size; most face the well-tended garden and a rushing brook. The best have terra-cotta tile floors, stone walls, and suitelike bathrooms. The lounge is très chic,

15

with exposed beams, Louis Treize–style exposed beams, and mounted faience plates over the fireplace. Be sure to enjoy a meal in the restaurant, a stunning vision in half-timber and pink and red paisley fabrics. For dinner, the five-course Menu Vieux Logis (€49) might include the chef's forte, pigeon in a walnut wine sauce. Cheaper fare is available from a second restaurant, Le Bistrot, which is wildly popular and set in a house at the gates to the property. ⊠ *Le Bourg, 24 km (15 mi) west of Les Eyzies, 24510Trémolat* 🕾*05–53–22–80–06* 🖷*05–53–22–84–89* ⊕*www. vieux-logis.com* 🗗*27 rooms, 9 apartments* ♿*In-room: refrigerator. In-hotel: 2 restaurants, pool, some pets allowed (fee), public Wi-Fi* ▭*AE, DC, MC, V* ¶◎|*MAP.*

THE ROCKY ROAD TO LASCAUX

Reaching Lascaux II is a major production without a car. If driving from Sarlat, head to Montignac, 26 km (16 mi) north on Route D704; Lascaux II is 1 km (½ mi) south of Montignac on Route D704. If using public transport, get yourself to Montignac by bus from Sarlat (on the Bordeaux-Brive line), the nearest town with a train station. Sarlat has early-morning buses (7, 9 am), which leave from Place de la Petite Rigandie. In Montignac, you can buy tickets for Lascaux II next to the tourist office on Place Bertran.

LASCAUX

⓭ *27 km (17 mi) northeast of Les Eyzies via D706.*

Fodor'sChoice ★ Set just south of Montignac, the famous **Grotte de Lascaux** *(Lascaux Caves)* contain hundreds of prehistoric wall paintings—between 15,000 and 20,000 years old, making them the oldest known paintings in the world. The undulating horses, cow, black bulls, and unicorn on their walls were discovered by chance by four schoolkids looking for their dog in 1940. Unfortunately, the original Lascaux caves began to deteriorate due to the carbon dioxide exhaled by thousands of visitors. To make the colorful mosaic of animals accessible to the general public, the French authorities built Lascaux II, a formidable feat in itself. They spent 12 years perfecting the facsimile, duplicating every aspect of two of the main caves to such a degree that the result is equally awesome. Painted in black, purple, red, and yellow, the powerful images of stags, bison, and oxen are brought to life by the curve of the stone walls; many of them appear pregnant, and historians think these caves were shrines to fertility (not living quarters—no tool implements were ever found). Unlike caves marked with authentic prehistoric art, Lascaux II is completely geared toward visitors, and you can watch a fancy presentation about cave art or take a 40-minute tour in the language of your choice. This is one of the most visited sights in the Dordogne and, in summer, tickets can be at a premium. To be sure of admittance, arrive early as tickets can sell out by midday. During the winter season, you are permitted to purchase tickets at the site but from April to October, tickets are available only at a booth beside the tourist office in Montignac (⊠Pl. Place Bertran-de-Born). Even better, make reservations via e-mail as soon as you know you're heading to the Dordogne. ☒*Rte. de la Grotte de Lascaux* ☎*05–53–51–95–03* ⊕*www.semitour. com* ☜*€8.20* ◷*Feb. 7–Mar., daily 10–noon and 2–5:30; Apr.–June, Sept. and Oct., 9–noon and 2–5:30; July and Aug., 9–7.*

WHERE TO STAY & EAT

$$–$$$$ ✗⌂ **Manoir d'Hautegente.** This old, ivy-covered manor (originally a forge) enjoys a pastoral nook by the Coly River. Inside, the modernized rooms have beige-fabric wall coverings, and the colorful curtains match the bedspreads. Four duplexes can be found in the old miller's home nearby. Chef Ludovic Lavud's specialties include foie gras carmelized in pecans and goose breast in a truffle sauce. The restaurant is closed Monday through Wednesday and there's no lunch Thursday. ☒*Haute Gente, 12 km (7 mi) east of Lascaux, 24120 Coly* ☎*05–53–51–68–03* ☐*05–53–50–38–52* ⊕*www.manoir-hautegente.com* ⌁*11 rooms, 6 suites* ⌂*In-room: no a/c (some), refrigerator. In-hotel: restaurant, pool, public Internet* ▭*DC, MC, V* ◷*Closed Nov.–Easter.*

15

HAUTEFORT

⓮ *25 km (15½ mi) north of Lascaux via D704.*

The reason to come to Hautefort is its castle, which presents a disarmingly arrogant face to the world.

★ The silhouette of the **Château de Hautefort** bristles with high roofs, domes, chimneys, and cupolas. The square-lined Renaissance left wing clashes with the muscular, round towers of the right wing, and the only surviving section of the original medieval castle—the gateway and drawbridge—plays referee in the middle. Adorning the inside are 17th-century furniture and tapestries. ☒*Hautefort* ☎*05–53–50–51–23* ⊕*www.chateau-hautefort.com* ☜*€8.50* ◷*Apr. and May, daily 10–12:30 and 2–6:30; June–Sept., daily 9:30–7; Mar., Oct., and Nov., weekends 2–6.*

PÉRIGUEUX

⓯ *46 km (27 mi) west of Hautefort via D5, 120 km (75 mi) northeast of Bordeaux.*

GETTING HERE

As opposed to using the Bergerac airport (⊕*www.bergerac.aeroport. fr*), set to the southwest, to get to Périgueux you can try the regional supplier, Airlinair (⊕www.airlinair.com), which flies from Paris to Brive la Gaillarde, to the west of Périgueux (for as little as €40 one-way two times a day during the week and once on Sunday). The bus station on Rue Denis Papin houses C.F.T.A. Périgueux (☎*05–53–08–43–13*), which is part of the Transpérigord bus system. Bus lines (1, 1A, 2, 3, 10) leave here for Angouleme, Brantôme, and Bergerac for €2 a trip. Peribus (☎*05–53–53–30–37*) on Place Montaigne is where you can catch a city bus. The train station is also on Rue Denis Papin. It takes 4½ hours to get here from Paris's Gare d'Austerlitz, connecting in Bordeaux and will cost you around €60. If you're training it to Cahors from Perigueux you'll have to travel the 50 minutes east first to Brive La Gaillard and then head south to Cahors which is another hour, all for around €25 one way. It'll take you less time to get to Bergerac (70 mins) to the southeast, but you'll still have to connect at Le Buisson.

EXPLORING

For anyone tired of the bucolic delights of the Périgord, even a short visit to this thriving city may prove a welcome reimmersion in classy urban ways, the whole in a stage-set setting. With more than 2,000 years of history, from its Gallo-Roman cité to its medieval town, Périgueux is best known for its weird-looking cathedral because of its association with the routes of Santiago de Compostela. Finished in 1173 (although certain archaeologists date it as early as 984) and fully and fancifully restored in the 19th century, the **Cathédrale St-Front** looks like it might be on loan from Istanbul, given its shallow-scale domes and elongated conical cupolas sprouting from the roof like baby minarets. You may be struck by similarities with the Byzantine-style Sacré-Coeur in Paris; that's no coincidence—architect Paul Abadie (1812–84) had a hand in the design of both. Mandatory visit to the cathedral over, you can make for the cluster of tiny pedestrian-only streets that run through the heart of Périgeux. As this is a commercial center for the region and a transportation nexus, the shops are stylish and sophisticated—some consider them the best reason for visiting this thriving town. Specialty-food shops proliferate (patés are the town's chief export), as do dimly lighted cafés and elegant fashion haunts.

Don't forget the open-air markets in the heart of the medieval cité though, as this is the capital of the Périgord and that means one of the capitals of produce. Farmers' markets are held every day from eight in the morning to one in the afternoon on the Place du Coderc. Every Wednesday and Saturday you can catch the big markets, which spill over from the Place du Coderc to the front of the Mairie town hall. And for those of you who love your gras (fat) as the locals do, then you'll have to witness, every Wednesday and Saturday from November to March, one of the many marchés de gras!

BRANTÔME

⑯ *27 km (17 mi) north of Périgueux via D939.*

Fodor's Choice
★

When the reclusive monks of the abbey of Brantôme decided the inhabitants of the village were getting too nosy, they dug a canal between themselves and the villagers, setting the *brantômois* adrift on an island in the middle of the River Dronne. How happy for them, or at least for us. Brantôme has been unable to outgrow its small-town status and remains one of the prettiest villages in France. Today it touts itself as the "Venice of Périgord." Enjoy a walk along the river or through the old, narrow streets. The meandering river follows you wherever you stroll. Cafés and small shops abound.

At night the **Abbaye Benedictine** is romantically floodlighted. Possibly founded by Charlemagne in the 8th century, it has none of its original buildings left, but its bell tower has been hanging on since the 11th century (the secret of its success is that it is attached to the cliff rather than the abbey, and so withstood waves of invaders). Fifth-century hermits carved out much of the abbey and some rooms have sculpted reliefs of the Last Judgment. Also here is a small museum devoted to the 19th-century painter Fernand-Desmoulin. ⊠*Bd. Charlemagne* ☎*05–53–05–80–63* ✆*€4* ☉*July and Aug., daily 10–7; Sept. and June, daily 10–6; Apr. and May, daily 10–12:30 and 2–6; Oct.–Dec. and Feb.–Mar. 10–noon and 2–5.*

WHERE TO STAY & EAT

★ $$$$ ✕⌨ **Le Moulin de l'Abbaye.** Storybook-perfect and set in the heart of Brantôme, this ivy-covered, turquoise-shuttered stone building looks directly over the placid waters of the Dronne, making this the ideal place to sample the watery charms of this little town. All the lovely and stylish rooms—named after wine châteaux—are individually decorated. Both Château Montrose and Château Cheval-Blanc have four-poster beds. The restaurant, presided over by chef Bernard Villain, has eight magnificent arched windows with views of the river—a truly memorable setting for delights such as white and green asparagus in morel sauce, sautéed *maigret de canard,* and chocolate "velvet" with toasted sesame nougatine and orange-anise. The food is so good, you'll probably want to splurge on the half-board rates (which raises the tab here considerably), but set some time aside for feasts at the nearby fishermen's bistro, Au Fil de l'Eau, which has an exquisite riverside terrace. For even more luxe and prettier guest rooms, explore the owner's other Brantôme hostelries, set nearby—the riverbank Maison de l'Abbé and the cliff-side Maison du Meunier, which has an eye-dazzling, two-story drawing room. ⊠*1 rte. des Bourdeilles, 24310* ☎*05–53–05–80–22* ☎*05–53–05–75–27* ⊕*www.moulin-abbaye.com* ⇗*19 rooms* ⅃*In-room: Wi-Fi. In-hotel: 3 restaurants, some pets allowed* ▭*AE, DC, MC, V* ☉*Closed Nov.–Apr* ⎁*BP.*

DORDOGNE ESSENTIALS

TRANSPORTATION

If traveling extensively by public transportation, be sure to load up on information (*Guide Régional des Transports* schedules, the best taxi-for-call companies, etc.) upon arriving at the ticket counter or help desk of the bigger train and bus stations in the area, such as Rocamadour.

AIRPORTS

Frequent daily flights on Air France link Bordeaux and the domestic airport at Limoges with Paris (from several provincial airports) but if you're not interested in making the trip from Bordeaux then there's also Bergerac airport, which has about 28 flights a week from such diverse English cities as Southampton, Leeds Bradford, Edinburgh, Exeter, and Birmingham on Flybe and on Ryanair (London Stansted, East Midlands, and Liverpool). Also, there's the regional supplier, Airlinair (www.airlinair.com), which flies from Paris into nearby Brive La Gaillarde two times a day during the week and once on Sunday.

Airport Information **Aéroport de Bergerac-Périgord-Dordogne** (☎ *05–53–22–25-25* ⊕ *www.bergerac.aeroport.fr*). **Aéroport de Bordeaux-Mérignac** (☎ *05–56–34–50-50* ⊕ *www.bordeaux.aeroport.fr*).

BY AIR

Airlines & Contacts **Air France** (☎ *08–02–80–28–02* ⊕ *www.airfrance.com*). **Airlinair** (⊕ *www.airlinair.com*). **Flybe** (⊕ *www.flybe.com*). **Ryanair** (⊕ *www.ryanair.com*)

BY BUS

The regional bus operator in the Dordogne is the Trans-Périgord network. It connects the main towns in the Dordogne with 13 bus lines, operated by eight different outfits. Since September 2006 the local French authorities have made the maximum fare €2 and have reduced rates for people who buy 10 passes for €14, so traveling by bus in the Dorgdogne could save you a lot of money. The Périgueux to Angouleme route is operated by C.F.T.A Périgueux (☎ *05–53–08–43–13*) and the Périgueux to Hautefort one by Périgord Voyages/Cheze (☎ *05–53–59–01–48*). For urban transport in Périgueux town use Peribus and in Bergerac use TUB (Transports Urbains Bergeracois).

Bus Information **C.F.T.A. Périgueux** (✉ *Gare Routière, 19 rue Denis-Papin, 24000 Périgueux* ☎ *05–53–08–43–13*). **Peribus** (✉ *Pl. Montaigne Périgueux, Périgueux* ☎ *05–53–53–30–37*). **Périgord Voyages** (✉ *Lafeuillade, 24200 Carsac* ☎ *05–53–59–01–48* ⊕ *www.perigord-voyages.com*). **Trans-Périgord** (✉ *Carbanat, 24250 Veyrines-de-Domme* ☎ *05–53–28–52–20*).

BY CAR

As the capital of southwest France, Bordeaux has superb transport links with Paris, Spain, and even the Mediterranean (A62 expressway via Toulouse links up with the A61 to Narbonne). The A20 is the main route from Paris to just before Cahors. It connects with the N21 at Limoges, which brings you down into Périgueux and Bergerac. N89 links Bordeaux to Périgueux and D936 runs along the Dordogne Valley from Libourne to Bergerac continuing as D660 toward Sarlat.

BY TRAIN

The superfast TGV (Train à Grande Vitesse) Atlantique service links Paris (Gare Montparnasse) to Bordeaux—585 km (365 mi) in 3½ hours—with stops at Poitiers and Angoulême. Trains link Bordeaux to Lyon (6 hrs) and Nice (8½ hrs) via Toulouse. Five trains daily make the 3½-hour, 400-km (250-mi) trip from Paris to Limoges.

Bordeaux is the region's major train hub. Trains run regularly from Bordeaux to Bergerac (80 mins), with occasional stops at St-Émilion, and four times daily to Sarlat (nearly 3 hrs). At least six trains daily make the 90-minute journey from Bordeaux to Périgueux, and four continue to Limoges (2½ hrs).

A handy hint is to go to the Raileurope Web site ⊕ *www.raileurope. com* and hit the drop-down menu for "Train Tickets & Schedules" on the left hand side and then just enter your desired destination. Remember that these train tickets are much cheaper in France, but the site makes for a great preparation search tool instead of the exceedingly labor-intensive SNCF site, which is replete with complex details and short on basis facts.

Train Information SNCF (☎ *08-36-35-35-35* ⊕ *www.ter-sncf.com/uk/aquitaine).*

CONTACTS & RESOURCES

CAR RENTAL
Local Agencies Avis (✉ *26 cours Alsace Lorraine, Bergerac* ☎ *05-53-57-69-83* ⊕ *www.avis.fr).* **Avis** (✉ *18 rue Président Wilson, Périgueux* ☎ *05-53-53-39-02* ⊕ *www.avis.fr).* **Budget** (✉ *32 av. 108, Bergerac* ☎ *05-53-74-20-00* ⊕ *www.budget. fr).* **Budget** (✉ *12 rue Denis Papin, Périgueux* ☎ *05-53-35-94-76* ⊕ *www.budget.fr).* **Hertz** (✉ *1 av. Henri Babusse, Périgueux* ☎ *05-53-54-61-80* ⊕ *www.hertz.fr).* **Rent A Car** (✉ *163 av. Mal Juin, Périgueux* ☎ *05-53-05-00-50* ⊕ *www.rentacar.fr).*

EMERGENCIES
Contacts Ambulance (☎ *15).* **Centre Hospitalier de Périgueux** (✉ *80 av. Georges Pompidou, Périgueux* ☎ *05-53-45-25-25* ⊕ *www.hopitalperigueux.com).* **Centre Hospitalier Samuel Pozzi** (✉ *9 av. Prof Albert Calmette, Bergerac* ☎ *05-53-63-88-88).* **Hôpital** (✉ *Le Pouget, Sarlat* ☎ *005-53-31-75-75* ⊕ *www.ch-sarlat.fr).*

INTERNET & MAIL
In smaller towns, ask your hotel concierge if there are any Internet cafés nearby.

Internet & Mail Information Clic & Surf Cybercafe (✉ *17 av. Gambetta, Sarlat* ☎ *05-53-30-80-77* ⊕ *www.clicetsurf.com).* **La Poste (main post office)** (✉ *9 rue du Quatre-Septembre, Périgueux* ☎ *05-53-03-61-12).*

MEDIA
The English-language monthly *French News* is published in Périgueux and largely devoted to the Dordogne. Your best bet for a more global English newspaper while in France is the *International Herald Tribune* (especially good on the weekends). *USA Today* can also be found from the same newsagents but it's always best to stock up on foreign newspapers at the local train stations in the bigger towns.

TOUR OPTIONS
The Office de Tourisme in Sarlat offers general guided tours of the town in English every Wednesday from June to September at 2 pm and from July to August at 11 am every Wednesday. The guided tours in French are much more frequent and the cost is €5.

If it's truffles you're after then you should go on a guided tour of the truffle groves in Sorges (a picturesque village to the northeast of Périgueux) every Tuesday and Thursday in July and August. The tours can be arranged and leave from the Sorges Truffle Museum (☎ *05-53-46–*

15

71–43) at 3:30 and last around an hour. The rest of the year, reservations can be made to go on guided tours for more than 20 people.

Fees & Schedules **Office de Tourisme** (✉ *Ecomusée de la Truffe, 24420 Sorges* ☎ *05-53-46-71-43*).

VISITOR INFORMATION

Tourist Information **Bergerac** (✉ *97 rue Neuve d'Argenson* ☎ *05-53-57-03-11* ⊕ *www.bergerac-tourisme.com*). **Beynac et Cazenac** (✉ *La Balme* ☎ *05-53-29-43-08* ⊕ *www.cc-perigord-noir.fr*). **Brantôme** (✉ *Bd. Charlemagne* ☎ *05-53-05-80-52* ⊕ *www.tourisme.fr/office-de-tourisme/brantome*). **Cahors** (✉ *Pl. François Mitterand* ☎ *05-65-53-20-65* ⊕ *www.mairie-cahors.fr*). **Les Eyzies de Tayac** (✉ *19 rue de la Préhistoire* ☎ *05-53-06-97-05* ⊕ *www.leseyzies.com*). **Montignac (Lascaux)** (✉ *Pl. Bertran-de-Born* ☎ *05-53-51-82-60* ⊕ *www.bienvenue-montignac.com*). **Périgueux** (✉ *25 rue du Président-Wilson* ☎ *05-53-35-50-24*). **Rocamadour** (✉ *Maison du Tourisme* ☎ *05-65-33-22-00* ⊕ *www.rocamadour.com*). **Sarlat** (✉ *Rue Tourny* ☎ *05-53-31-45-45* ⊕ *www.ot-sarlat-perigord.fr*). **St-Cirque Lapopie** (✉ *Pl. du Sombral* ☎ *05-65-31-29-06* ⊕ *www.saint-cirqlapopie.com*).

VOCABULARY

One of the trickiest French sounds to pronounce is the nasal final *n* sound (whether or not the *n* is actually the last letter of the word). You should try to pronounce it as a sort of nasal grunt—as in "huh." The vowel that precedes the *n* will govern the vowel sound of the word, and in this list we precede the final *n* with an *h* to remind you to be nasal.

Another problem sound is the ubiquitous but untransliterable *eu*, as in *bleu* (blue) or *deux* (two), and the very similar sound in *je* (I), *ce* (this), and *de* (of). The closest equivalent might be the vowel sound in "put," but rounded. The famous rolled *r* is a glottal sound. Consonants at the ends of words are usually silent; when the following word begins with a vowel, however, the two are run together by sounding the consonant. There are two forms of "you" in French: *vous* (formal and plural) and *tu* (a singular, personal form). When addressing an adult you don't know, *vous* is always best.

English	French	Pronunciation

Basics

English	French	Pronunciation
Yes/no	Oui/non	wee/nohn
Please	S'il vous plaît	seel voo play
Thank you	Merci	mair-**see**
You're welcome	De rien	deh ree-**ehn**
Excuse me, sorry	Pardon	pahr-**don**
Good morning/afternoon	Bonjour	bohn-**zhoor**
Good evening	Bonsoir	bohn-**swahr**
Goodbye	Au revoir	o ruh-**vwahr**
Mr. (Sir)	Monsieur	muh-**syuh**
Mrs. (Ma'am)	Madame	ma-**dam**
Miss	Mademoiselle	mad-mwa-**zel**
Pleased to meet you	Enchanté(e)	ohn-shahn-**tay**
How are you?	Comment allez-vous?	kuh-mahn-tahl-ay **voo**
Very well, thanks	Très bien, merci	tray bee-ehn, mair-**see**
And you?	Et vous?	ay voo?

Numbers

English	French	Pronunciation
one	un	uhn
two	deux	deuh
three	trois	twah
four	quatre	**kaht**-ruh

five	cinq	sank
six	six	seess
seven	sept	set
eight	huit	wheat
nine	neuf	nuf
ten	dix	deess
eleven	onze	ohnz
twelve	douze	dooz
thirteen	treize	trehz
fourteen	quatorze	kah-torz
fifteen	quinze	kanz
sixteen	seize	sez
seventeen	dix-sept	deez-**set**
eighteen	dix-huit	deez-**wheat**
nineteen	dix-neuf	deez-**nuf**
twenty	vingt	vehn
twenty-one	vingt-et-un	vehnt-ay-**uhn**
thirty	trente	trahnt
forty	quarante	ka-**rahnt**
fifty	cinquante	sang-**kahnt**
sixty	soixante	swa-**sahnt**
seventy	soixante-dix	swa-sahnt-**deess**
eighty	quatre-vingts	kaht-ruh-**vehn**
ninety	quatre-vingt-dix	kaht-ruh-vehn-**deess**
one hundred	cent	sahn
one thousand	mille	meel

Colors

black	noir	nwahr
blue	bleu	bleuh
brown	brun/marron	bruhn/mar-**rohn**
green	vert	vair
orange	orange	o-**rahnj**
pink	rose	rose
red	rouge	rouge
violet	violette	vee-o-**let**
white	blanc	blahnk
yellow	jaune	zhone

Days of the Week

Sunday	dimanche	dee-**mahnsh**
Monday	lundi	luhn-**dee**
Tuesday	mardi	mahr-**dee**
Wednesday	mercredi	mair-kruh-**dee**
Thursday	jeudi	zhuh-**dee**
Friday	vendredi	vawn-druh-**dee**
Saturday	samedi	sahm-**dee**

Months

January	janvier	zhahn-vee-**ay**
February	février	feh-vree-**ay**
March	mars	marce
April	avril	a-**vreel**
May	mai	meh
June	juin	zhwehn
July	juillet	zhwee-**ay**
August	août	ah-**oo**
September	septembre	sep-**tahm**-bruh
October	octobre	awk-**to**-bruh
November	novembre	no-**vahm**-bruh
December	décembre	day-**sahm**-bruh

Useful Phrases

Do you speak English?	Parlez-vous anglais?	par-lay **voo** **ahn**-glay
I don't speak . . . French	Je ne parle pas . . . français	zhuh nuh parl pah frahn-**say**
I don't understand	Je ne comprends pas	zhuh nuh kohm-**prahn** pah
I understand	Je comprends	zhuh kohm-**prahn**
I don't know	Je ne sais pas	zhuh nuh say **pah**
I'm American/ British	Je suis américain/ anglais	zhuh sweez a-may-ree-**kehn**/ ahn-**glay**
What's your name?	Comment vous appelez-vous?	ko-mahn voo za-pell-ay-**voo**
My name is . . .	Je m'appelle . . .	zhuh ma-**pell** . . .
What time is it?	Quelle heure est-il?	kel air eh-**teel**

How?	Comment?	ko-**mahn**
When?	Quand?	kahn
Yesterday	Hier	yair
Today	Aujourd'hui	o-zhoor-**dwee**
Tomorrow	Demain	duh-**mehn**
Tonight	Ce soir	suh **swahr**
What?	Quoi?	kwah
What is it?	Qu'est-ce que c'est?	kess-kuh-**say**
Why?	Pourquoi?	**poor**-kwa
Who?	Qui?	kee
Where is . . .	Où est . . .	oo ay
the train station?	la gare?	la gar
the subway station?	la station de métro?	la sta-**syon** duh may-**tro**
the bus stop?	l'arrêt de bus?	la-**ray** duh **booss**
the post office?	la poste?	la post
the bank?	la banque?	la bahnk
the . . . hotel?	l'hôtel . . .?	lo-**tel**
the store?	le magasin?	luh ma-ga-**zehn**
the cashier?	la caisse?	la **kess**
the . . . museum?	le musée . . .?	luh mew-**zay**
the hospital?	l'hôpital?	lo-pee-**tahl**
the elevator?	l'ascenseur?	la-sahn-**seuhr**
the telephone?	le téléphone?	luh tay-lay-**phone**
Where are the restrooms? (men/women)	Où sont les toilettes? (hommes/femmes)	oo sohn lay twah-**let** (**oh**-mm/**fah**-mm)
Here/there	Ici/là	ee-**see**/la
Left/right	A gauche/à droite	a goash/a draht
Straight ahead	Tout droit	too drwah
Is it near/far?	C'est près/loin?	say pray/lwehn
I'd like . . .	Je voudrais . . .	zhuh voo-**dray**
a room	une chambre	ewn **shahm**-bruh
the key	la clé	la clay
a newspaper	un journal	uhn zhoor-**nahl**
a stamp	un timbre	uhn **tam**-bruh
I'd like to buy . . .	Je voudrais acheter . . .	zhuh voo-**dray** **ahsh**-tay
cigarettes	des cigarettes	day see-ga-**ret**
matches	des allumettes	days a-loo-**met**
soap	du savon	dew sah-**vohn**
city map	un plan de ville	uhn plahn de **veel**
road map	une carte routière	ewn cart roo-tee-**air**

magazine	une revue	ewn reh-**vu**
envelopes	des enveloppes	dayz ahn-veh-**lope**
writing paper	du papier à lettres	dew pa-pee-**ay** a **let**-ruh
postcard	une carte postale	ewn cart pos-**tal**
How much is it?	C'est combien?	say comb-bee-**ehn**
A little/a lot	Un peu/beaucoup	uhn peuh/bo-**koo**
More/less	Plus/moins	plu/mwehn
Enough/too (much)	Assez/trop	a-say/tro
I am ill/sick	Je suis malade	zhuh swee ma-**lahd**
Call a . . .	Appelez un . . .	a-play uhn
doctor	docteur	dohk-**tehr**
Help!	Au secours!	o suh-**koor**
Stop!	Arrêtez!	a-reh-**tay**
Fire!	Au feu!	o fuh
Caution!/Look out!	Attention!	a-tahn-see-**ohn**

Dining Out

A bottle of . . .	une bouteille de . . .	ewn boo-**tay** duh
A cup of . . .	une tasse de . . .	ewn tass duh
A glass of . . .	un verre de . . .	uhn vair duh
Bill/check	l'addition	la-dee-see-**ohn**
Bread	du pain	dew pan
Breakfast	le petit-déjeuner	luh puh-**tee** day-zhuh-**nay**
Butter	du beurre	dew burr
Cheers!	A votre santé!	ah vo-truh sahn-**tay**
Cocktail/aperitif	un apéritif	uhn ah-pay-ree-**teef**
Dinner	le dîner	luh dee-**nay**
Dish of the day	le plat du jour	luh plah dew zhoor
Enjoy!	Bon appétit!	bohn a-pay-**tee**
Fixed-price menu	le menu	luh may-**new**
Fork	une fourchette	ewn four-**shet**
I am diabetic	Je suis diabétique	zhuh swee dee-ah-bay-**teek**
I am vegetarian	Je suis végé-tarien(ne)	zhuh swee vay-zhay-ta-ree-**en**
I cannot eat . . .	Je ne peux pas manger de . . .	zhuh nuh **puh** pah mahn-**jay** deh

I'd like to order	Je voudrais commander	zhuh voo-**dray** ko-mahn-**day**
Is service/the tip included?	Est-ce que le service est compris?	ess kuh luh sair-**veess** ay comb-**pree**
It's good/bad	C'est bon/mauvais	say bohn/ mo-**vay**
It's hot/cold	C'est chaud/froid	say sho/frwah
Knife	un couteau	uhn koo-**toe**
Lunch	le déjeuner	luh day-zhuh-**nay**
Menu	la carte	la cart
Napkin	une serviette	ewn sair-vee-**et**
Pepper	du poivre	dew **pwah**-vruh
Plate	une assiette	ewn a-see-**et**
Please give me . . .	Donnez-moi . . .	doe-nay-**mwah**
Salt	du sel	dew sell
Spoon	une cuillère	ewn kwee-**air**
Sugar	du sucre	dew **sook**-ruh
Waiter!/Waitress!	Monsieur!/ Mademoiselle!	muh-**syuh**/ mad-mwa-**zel**
Wine list	la carte des vins	la cart day vehn

MENU GUIDE

French	English

General Dining

Entrée	Appetizer/Starter
Garniture au choix	Choice of vegetable side
Plat du jour	Dish of the day
Selon arrivage	When available
Supplément/En sus	Extra charge
Sur commande	Made to order

Petit Déjeuner (Breakfast)

Confiture	Jam
Miel	Honey
Oeuf à la coque	Boiled egg
Oeufs sur le plat	Fried eggs
Oeufs brouillés	Scrambled eggs
Tartine	Bread with butter

Poissons/Fruits de Mer (Fish/Seafood)

Anchois	Anchovies
Bar	Bass
Brandade de morue	Creamed salt cod
Brochet	Pike
Cabillaud/Morue	Fresh cod
Calmar	Squid
Coquilles St-Jacques	Scallops
Crevettes	Shrimp
Daurade	Sea bream
Ecrevisses	Prawns/Crayfish
Harengs	Herring
Homard	Lobster
Huîtres	Oysters
Langoustine	Prawn/Lobster
Lotte	Monkfish
Moules	Mussels
Palourdes	Clams
Saumon	Salmon
Thon	Tuna
Truite	Trout

Viande (Meat)

Agneau	Lamb
Boeuf	Beef
Boudin	Sausage
Boulettes de viande	Meatballs
Brochettes	Kabobs
Cassoulet	Casserole of white beans, meat
Cervelle	Brains
Chateaubriand	Double fillet steak
Choucroute garnie	Sausages with sauerkraut
Côtelettes	Chops
Côte/Côte de boeuf	Rib/T-bone steak
Cuisses de grenouilles	Frogs' legs
Entrecôte	Rib or rib-eye steak
Épaule	Shoulder
Escalope	Cutlet
Foie	Liver
Gigot	Leg
Porc	Pork
Ris de veau	Veal sweetbreads
Rognons	Kidneys
Saucisses	Sausages
Selle	Saddle
Tournedos	Tenderloin of T-bone steak
Veau	Veal

Methods of Preparation

A point	Medium
A l'étouffée	Stewed
Au four	Baked
Ballotine	Boned, stuffed, and rolled
Bien cuit	Well-done
Bleu	Very rare
Frit	Fried
Grillé	Grilled
Rôti	Roast
Saignant	Rare

Volailles/Gibier (Poultry/Game)

Blanc de volaille	Chicken breast
Canard/Caneton	Duck/Duckling
Cerf/Chevreuil	Venison (red/roe)
Coq au vin	Chicken stewed in red wine
Dinde/Dindonneau	Turkey/Young turkey
Faisan	Pheasant
Lapin/Lièvre	Rabbit/Wild hare
Oie	Goose
Pintade/Pintadeau	Guinea fowl/Young guinea fowl
Poulet/Poussin	Chicken/Spring chicken

Légumes (Vegetables)

Artichaut	Artichoke
Asperge	Asparagus
Aubergine	Eggplant
Carottes	Carrots
Champignons	Mushrooms
Chou-fleur	Cauliflower
Chou (rouge)	Cabbage (red)
Laitue	Lettuce
Oignons	Onions
Petits pois	Peas
Pomme de terre	Potato
Tomates	Tomatoes

Fruits/Noix (Fruits/Nuts)

Abricot	Apricot
Amandes	Almonds
Ananas	Pineapple
Cassis	Blackcurrants
Cerises	Cherries
Citron/Citron vert	Lemon/Lime
Fraises	Strawberries

Framboises	Raspberries
Pamplemousse	Grapefruit
Pêche	Peach
Poire	Pear
Pomme	Apple
Prunes/Pruneaux	Plums/Prunes
Raisins/Raisins secs	Grapes/Raisins

Desserts

Coupe (glacée)	Sundae
Crème Chantilly	Whipped cream
Gâteau au chocolat	Chocolate cake
Glace	Ice cream
Tarte tatin	Caramelized apple tart
Tourte	Layer cake

Drinks

A l'eau	With water
Avec des glaçons	On the rocks
Bière	Beer
Blonde/brune	Light/dark
Café noir/crème	Black coffee/with steamed milk
Chocolat chaud	Hot chocolate
Eau-de-vie	Brandy
Eau minérale	Mineral water
gazeuse/non gazeuse	*carbonated/still*
Jus de . . .	. . . juice
Lait	Milk
Sec	Straight or dry
Thé	Tea
au lait/au citron	*with milk/lemon*
Vin	Wine
blanc	*white*
doux	*sweet*
léger	*light*
brut	*very dry*
rouge	*red*

France Essentials

PLANNING TOOLS, EXPERT INSIGHT, GREAT CONTACTS

There are planners and there are those who, excuse the pun, fly by the seat of their pants. We happily place ourselves among the planners. Our writers and editors try to anticipate all the issues you may face before and during any journey, and then they do their research. This section is the product of their efforts. Use it to get excited about your trip to France, to inform your travel planning, or to guide you on the road should the seat of your pants start to feel threadbare.

GETTING STARTED

We're really proud of our Web site: Fodors.com is a great place to begin any journey. Scan Travel Wire for suggested itineraries, travel deals, restaurant and hotel openings, and other up-to-the-minute info. Check out Booking to research prices and book plane tickets, hotel rooms, rental cars, and vacation packages. Head to Talk for on-the-ground pointers from travelers who frequent our message boards. You can also link to loads of other travel-related resources.

> ## WORD OF MOUTH
>
> After your trip, be sure to rate the places you visited and share your experiences and travel tips with us and other Fodorites in Travel Ratings and Talk on www.fodors.com.

■ RESOURCES

ONLINE TRAVEL TOOLS

All About France The **Centre des Monuments Nationaux** (⊕ www.monum.fr, runs 200 monuments—from the Arc de Triomphe to Chambord—is chock-full of information. If you're château hopping, **Chateaux and Country** (⊕ www.chateauxandcountry.com) has a brief overview of hundreds of châteaux all over France. **Eurail** (⊕ www.eurail.com) has all the info about the many railway passes available for travel through France and the rest of Europe. **Eurostar** (⊕ www.eurostar.com) is the main contact for the Chunnel train that connects Paris and London. The **French Embassy** (⊕ www.france.diplomatie.fr) is helpful for information on the French government. The **French Ministry of Culture** (⊕ www.culture.fr) provides a portal to all the cultural happenings and institutions throughout France. **French National Museums** (⊕ www.rmn.fr) is the main site for the Réunion des musées nationaux, which administers the country's biggest museums. **Rail Europe** (⊕ www.raileurope.com) gives you the scoop on many different discount rail passes through France and Europe. **SNCF** (⊕ www.sncf.fr/index. htm) is the main clearinghouse for the French national railway network, invaluable for schedules and prices. **Weather Reports** (⊕ www.meteo.fr) helps you track the highly variable weather in France.

Currency Conversion Google (⊕ www.google.com) does currency conversion. Just type in the amount you want to convert and an explanation of how you want it converted (e.g., "14 Swiss francs in dollars"), and then voilà. **Oanda.com** (⊕ www.oanda.com) also allows you to print out a handy table with the current day's conversion rates. **XE.com** (⊕ www.xe.com) is a good currency conversion Web site.

Safety Transportation Security Administration (TSA; ⊕ www.tsa.gov)

Time Zones Timeanddate.com (⊕ www.timeanddate.com/worldclock) can help you figure out the correct time anywhere in the world.

Weather Accuweather.com (⊕ www.accuweather.com) is an independent weather-forecasting service with especially good coverage of hurricanes. **Weather.com** (⊕ www.weather.com) is the Web site for the Weather Channel.

Other Resources CIA World Factbook (⊕ www.odci.gov/cia/publications/factbook/index.html) has profiles of every country in the world. It's a good source if you need some quick facts and figures.

VISITOR INFORMATION

France Tourism Information Maison de la France (☎ 514/288–1904 ⊕ www.franceguide.com) is the national site for French tourism.

LOCAL TOURIST OFFICES

See the Essentials sections in individual chapters for local tourist office telephone numbers and addresses.

Tourism Web Sites Tourism in France (⊕ www.tourisme.fr) has links to 3,500 tourist offices. **Bordeaux Tourist Office** (⊕ www.bor-

Trip Insurance Resources

INSURANCE COMPARISON SITES		
Insure My Trip.com	800/487–4722	www.insuremytrip.com
Square Mouth.com	800/240–0369	www.squaremouth.com
COMPREHENSIVE TRAVEL INSURERS		
Access America	866/807–3982	www.accessamerica.com
CSA Travel Protection	800/873–9855	www.csatravelprotection.com
HTH Worldwide	888/243–2358 or 610/254–8700	www.hthworldwide.com
Travelex Insurance	888/457–4602	www.travelex-insurance.com
Travel Guard International	800/826–4919 or 715/345–0505	www.travelguard.com
Travel Insured International	800/243–3174	www.travelinsured.com
MEDICAL-ONLY INSURERS		
International Medical Group	800/628–4664	www.imglobal.com
International SOS	215/942–8000 or 713/521–7611	www.internationalsos.com
Wallach & Company	800/237–6615 or 504/687–3166	www.wallach.com

deaux-tourisme.com) is the main site for this southwest France region. **Lyon Tourist Office** (⊕ www.lyon-france.com) is a helpful portal to this important hub of the country. **Monaco Tourist Office** (⊕ www.visitmonaco.com) welcomes you to this glitzy resort in the south of France. **Normandy Tourist Board** (⊕ www. normandy-tourism.org) is a great site for the region. The **Office du Tourisme et Congresses de Paris** (⊕ www.parisinfo.com) is the main site for the Paris tourist office. **Provence Tourist Office** (⊕ www.visitprovence.com) is a helpful site to all things Provençal. **Riviera Tourist Office** (⊕ www.guideriviera.com) is one of the helpful overview sites devoted to the Côte d'Azur. **Strasbourg Tourism Office** (⊕ www.strasbourg.com) is devoted to one of the hubs of the Alsace-Lorraine region.

■ THINGS TO CONSIDER

General Information & Warnings U.S. Department of State (⊕ www.travel.state.gov).

GEAR

SHIPPING LUGGAGE AHEAD

Imagine globetrotting with only a carry-on in tow. Shipping your luggage in advance via an air-freight service is a great way to cut down on backaches, hassles, and stress—especially if your packing list includes strollers, car seats, etc. There are some things to be aware of, though. First, research carry-on restrictions; if you absolutely need something that's isn't practical to ship and isn't allowed in carry-ons, this strategy isn't for you. Second, plan to send your bags several days in advance to U.S. destinations and as much as two weeks in advance to some international destinations. Third, plan to spend some money: it will cost least $100 to send a small piece of luggage, a golf bag, or a pair of skis to a domestic destination, much more to places overseas. Some people use Federal Express to ship their bags, but this can cost even more than air-freight services. All these services insure your bag (for most, the limit is $1,000, but you should verify that amount); you can, however, purchase additional insurance for about $1 per $100 of value.

Contacts Luggage Concierge (☎800/288–9818 ⊕www.luggageconcierge.com). **Luggage Express** (☎866/744–7224 ⊕www.usxpluggageexpress.com). **Luggage Free** (☎800/361–6871 ⊕www.luggagefree.com). **Sports Express** (☎800/357–4174 ⊕www.sportsexpress.com) specializes in shipping golf clubs and other sports equipment. **Virtual Bellhop** (☎877/235–5467 ⊕www.virtualbellhop.com).

PASSPORTS

All U.S. citizens, even infants, need only a valid passport to enter France for stays of up to 90 days.

We're always surprised at how few Americans have passports—only 25% at this writing. This number is expected to grow in coming years, when it becomes impossible to reenter the United States from trips to neighboring Canada or Mexico without one. Remember this: a passport verifies both your identity and nationality—a great reason to have one.

U.S. passports are valid for 10 years. You must apply in person if you're getting a passport for the first time; if your previous passport was lost, stolen, or damaged; or if your previous passport has expired and was issued more than 15 years ago or when you were under 16. All children under 18 must appear in person to apply for or renew a passport. Both parents must accompany any child under 14 (or send a notarized statement with their permission) and provide proof of their relationship to the child.

There are 13 regional passport offices, as well as 7,000 passport acceptance facilities in post offices, public libraries, and other governmental offices. If you're renewing a passport, you can do so by mail. Forms are available at passport acceptance facilities and online.

The cost to apply for a new passport is $97 for adults, $82 for children under 16; renewals are $67. Allow six weeks for processing, both for first-time passports and renewals. For an expediting fee of $60 you can reduce this time to about two weeks. If your trip is less than two weeks away, you can get a passport even more rapidly by going to a passport office with the necessary documentation. Private expediters can get things done in as little as 48 hours, but charge hefty fees for their services.

■TIP➔Before your trip, make two copies of your passport's data page (one for someone at home and another for you to carry separately). Or scan the page and e-mail it to someone at home and/or yourself.

U.S. Passport Information U.S. Department of State (☎877/487–2778 ⊕travel.state.gov/passport).

U.S. PASSPORT EXPEDITERS

A. Briggs Passport & Visa Expediters (☎800/806–0581 or 202/464–3000 ⊕www.abriggs.com).

American Passport Express (☎800/455–5166 or 603/559–9888 ⊕www.americanpassport.com).

Passport Express (☎800/362–8196 or 401/272–4612 ⊕www.passportexpress.com).

Travel Document Systems (☎800/874–5100 or 202/638–3800 ⊕www.traveldocs.com).

Travel the World Visas (☎866/886–8472 or 301/495–7700 ⊕www.world-visa.com).

TRIP INSURANCE

What kind of coverage do you honestly need? Do you even need trip insurance at all? Take a deep breath and read on.

We believe that comprehensive trip insurance is especially valuable if you're booking an expensive or complicated trip (particularly to an isolated region) or if you're booking far in advance. Who knows what could happen six months down the road? But whether you get insurance has more to do with how comfortable you are assuming all that risk yourself.

Comprehensive travel policies typically cover trip-cancellation and interruption, letting you cancel or cut your trip short because of a personal emergency, illness, or, in some cases, acts of terrorism in your destination. Such policies also cover evacuation and medical care. Some also cover you for trip delays because of weather or mechanical problems as well as for lost baggage. Another type of coverage to look for is financial default—that is, when your trip is disrupted because a tour operator, airline, or cruise line goes out of business. Generally you must buy this when you book your trip or shortly thereafter, and it's only available to you if your operator isn't on a list of excluded companies.

If you're going abroad, consider buying medical-only coverage. Neither Medicare nor some private insurers cover medical expenses anywhere outside the United States besides Mexico and Canada (including time aboard a cruise ship, even if it leaves from a U.S. port). Medical-only policies typically reimburse you for medical care (excluding that related to preexisting conditions) and hospitalization abroad, and provide for evacuation. You still have to pay the bills and await reimbursement from the insurer.

Expect comprehensive travel insurance policies to cost about 4% to 7% of the total price of your trip (it's more like 12% if you're over age 70). A medical-only policy may or may not be cheaper than a comprehensive policy. Always read the fine print of your policy to make sure that you are covered for the risks that concern to you. Compare several policies to make sure you're getting the best price and coverage available.

BOOKING YOUR TRIP

Unless your cousin is a travel agent, you're probably among the millions of people who make most of their travel arrangements online. But have you ever wondered just what the differences are between an online travel agent (a Web site through which you make reservations instead of going directly to the airline, hotel, or car-rental company), a discounter (a firm that does a high volume of business with a hotel chain or airline and accordingly gets good prices), a wholesaler (one that makes cheap reservations in bulk and then resells them to people like you), and an aggregator (one that compares all the offerings so you don't have to)? Is it truly better to book directly on an airline or hotel Web site? And when does a real live travel agent come in handy?

ONLINE

You really have to shop around. A travel wholesaler such as Hotels.com or Hotel-Club.net can be a source of good rates, as can discounters such as Hotwire or Priceline, particularly if you can bid for your hotel room or airfare. Indeed, such sites sometimes have deals that are unavailable elsewhere. They do, however, tend to work only with hotel chains (which makes them just plain useless for getting hotel reservations outside major cities) or big airlines (so that often leaves out upstarts like jetBlue and some foreign carriers like Air India). Also, with discounters and wholesalers you must generally prepay, and everything is nonrefundable. Before you fork over the dough, be sure to check the terms and conditions, so you know what a given company will do for you if there's a problem and what you'll have to deal with on your own.

■TIP➔To be absolutely sure everything was processed correctly, confirm reservations made through online travel agents, discounters, and wholesalers directly with your hotel before leaving home.

Booking engines like Expedia, Travelocity, and Orbitz are actually travel agents, albeit high-volume, online ones. And airline travel packagers like American Airlines Vacations and Virgin Vacations—well, they're travel agents, too. But they may still not work with all the world's hotels.

An aggregator site will search many sites and pull the best prices for airfares, hotels, and rental cars from them. Most aggregators compare the major travel-booking sites such as Expedia, Travelocity, and Orbitz; some also look at airline Web sites, though rarely the sites of smaller budget airlines. Some aggregators also compare other travel products, including complex packages—a good thing, as you can sometimes get the best overall deal by booking an air-and-hotel package.

WITH A TRAVEL AGENT

If you use an agent—brick-and-mortar or virtual—you'll pay a fee for the service. And know that the service you get from some online agents isn't comprehensive. For example Expedia and Travelocity don't search for prices on budget airlines like jetBlue, Southwest, or small foreign carriers. That said, some agents (online or not) *do* have access to fares that are difficult to find otherwise, and the savings can more than make up for any surcharge.

A knowledgeable brick-and-mortar travel agent can be a godsend if you're booking a cruise, a package trip that's not available to you directly, an air pass, or a complicated itinerary including several overseas flights. What's more, travel agents that specialize in a destination may have exclusive access to certain deals and insider information on things such as charter flights. Agents who specialize in types of travelers (senior citizens, gays and lesbians, naturists) or types of trips (cruises, luxury travel, safaris) can also be invaluable.

A top-notch agent planning your trip to Russia will make sure you get the correct visa application and complete it on time; the one booking your cruise may get you a cabin upgrade or arrange to have a bottle of champagne chilling in your cabin when you embark. And complain about the surcharges all you like, but when things don't work out the way you'd hoped, it's nice to have an agent to put things right.

■**TIP➜**Remember that Expedia, Travelocity, and Orbitz are travel agents, not just booking engines. To resolve any problems with a reservation made through these companies, contact them first.

Agent Resources American Society of Travel Agents (☎703/739–2782⊕www. travelsense.org).

France Travel Agents Nouvelles Frontières (☎08–25–00–08–25⊕www.nouvelles-frontieres.fr). **Soltours** (☎01–42–71–24–34).

■ ACCOMMODATIONS

The following is the price chart used throughout this book to determine price categories for most hotels in this book. Paris remains the pricey exception: for that city, the highest category is €225 and the lowest is €75. Prices are for a standard double room in high season, including tax (19.6%) and service charge; rates for any board plans will be higher.

CAT-EGORY	ALL REGIONS EXCEPT PARIS	BASQUE COUNTRY
$$$$	over €190	over €180
$$$	€120–€190	€120–€180
$$	€80–€120	€80–€120
$	€50–€80	€50–€80
¢	under €50	under €50

Most hotels and other lodgings require you to give your credit-card details before they will confirm your reservation. If you don't feel comfortable e-mailing this information, ask if you can fax it (some places even prefer faxes). However you book, get confirmation in writing and have a copy of it handy when you check in.

Be sure you understand the hotel's cancellation policy. Some places allow you to cancel without any kind of penalty—even if you prepaid to secure a discounted rate—if you cancel at least 24 hours in advance. Others require you to cancel a week in advance or penalize you the cost of one night. Small inns and B&Bs are most likely to require you to cancel far in advance. Most hotels allow children under a certain age to stay in their parents' room at no extra charge, but others charge for them as extra adults; find out the cutoff age for discounts.

APARTMENT & HOUSE RENTALS

If you want a home base that's roomy enough for a family and comes with cooking facilities, consider a furnished rental. These can save you money, especially if you're traveling with a group. Renting a *gîte rural*—furnished house in the country—for a week or month can also save you money. Gîtes are nearly always maintained by on-site owners, who greet you on your arrival and provide information on groceries, doctors, and nearby attractions. The national rental network, the Fédération Nationale des Gîtes de France, rents all types of accommodations rated by ears of corn (from 1 to 4) based on stringent criteria of comfort and quality. You can find listings for fabulous renovated farmhouses with swimming pools or simple cottages in the heart of wine country. Besides country houses, Gîtes de France has listings for B&Bs, lodges, hostels, and campsites where you can pitch your tent in the middle of farmland with not a soul in sight. If you know the region you want to visit, contact the departmental branch directly and order a photo catalog that lists every property. If you specify which dates you plan to visit, the office will narrow down the choice to rentals avail-

Online Booking Resources

AGGREGATORS

Kayak	www.kayak.com;	looks at cruises and vacation packages.
Mobissimo	www.mobissimo.com	examines airfare, hotels, cars, and tons of activities.
Qixo	www.qixo.com	compares cruises, vacation packages, and even travel insurance.
Sidestep	www.sidestep.com	compares vacation packages and lists travel deals.
Travelgrove	www.travelgrove.com	also compares cruises and packages.

BOOKING ENGINES

Cheap Tickets	www.cheaptickets.com	a discounter.
Expedia	www.expedia.com	a large online agency that charges a booking fee for airline tickets.
Hotwire	www.hotwire.com	a discounter.
lastminute.com	www.lastminute.com	specializes in last-minute travel the main site is for the U.K., but it has a link to a U.S. site.
Luxury Link	www.luxurylink.com	has auctions (surprisingly good deals) as well as offers on the high-end side of travel.
Onetravel.com	www.onetravel.com	a discounter for hotels, car rentals, airfares, and packages.
Orbitz	www.orbitz.com	charges a booking fee for airline tickets, but gives a clear breakdown of fees and taxes before you book.
Priceline.com	www.priceline.com	a discounter that also allows bidding.
Travel.com	www.travel.com	allows you to compare its rates with those of other booking engines.
Travelocity	www.travelocity.com	charges a booking fee for airline tickets, but promises good problem resolution.

ONLINE ACCOMMODATIONS

Hotelbook.com	www.hotelbook.com	focuses on independent hotels worldwide.
Hotel Club	www.hotelclub.net	good for major cities worldwide.
Hotels.com	www.hotels.com	a big Expedia-owned wholesaler that offers rooms in hotels all over the world.
Quikbook	www.quikbook.com	offers "pay when you stay" reservations that let you settle your bill at checkout, not when you book.

OTHER RESOURCES

Bidding For Travel	www.biddingfortravel. com	a good place to figure out what you can get and for how much before you start bidding on, say, Priceline.

able for those days. Be sure to plan early: renting gîtes has become one of the most popular ways to discover France.

Individual tourist offices often publish lists of *locations meublés* (furnished rentals); these are often inspected by the tourist office and rated by comfort standards. Usually they're booked directly through the individual owner, which generally requires some knowledge of French. Rentals that are not classified or rated by the tourist office should be undertaken with trepidation, as they can fall well below your minimum standard of comfort.

Vacation rentals in France always book from Saturday to Saturday (with some offering weekend rates off-season). Most do not include bed linens and towels, but make them available for an additional fee. Always check on policies on pets and children and specify if you need an enclosed garden for toddlers, a washing machine, a fireplace, etc. If you plan to have overnight guests during your stay, let the owner know; there may be additional charges. Insurance restrictions prohibit loading in guests beyond the specified capacity.

Contacts At Home Abroad (☎212/421–9165 ⊕www.athomeabroadinc.com). **Barclay International Group** (☎ 800/845–6636 or 516/364–0064 ⊕www.barclayweb.com). **Drawbridge to Europe** (☎ 888/268–1148 or 541/482–7778 ⊕www.drawbridgetoeurope. com). **Fédération Nationale des Gîtes de France** (☎01–49–70–75–75 ⊕www.gitesdefrance.fr). **French Government Tourist Office** (⇨ *Visitor Information*, above). **Homes Away** (☎ 800/374–6637 or 416/920–1873 ⊕www.homesaway.com). **Hometours International** (☎865/690–8484 ⊕thor.he.net/~hometour). **Interhome** (☎ 800/882–6864 or 954/791–8282 ⊕www.interhome.us). **Suzanne B. Cohen & Associates** (☎207/622–0743 ⊕www.villaeurope.com). **Vacation Home Rentals Worldwide** (☎ 800/633–3284 or 201/767–9393 ⊕www.vhrww.com). **Villanet** (☎ 800/964–1891 or 206/417–3444 ⊕www.rentavilla.com). **Villas & Apartments Abroad**

(☎ 800/433–3020 or 212/213–6435 ⊕www.vaanyc.com). **Villas International** (☎ 800/221–2260 or 415/499–9490 ⊕www.villasintl.com). **Villas of Distinction** (☎ 800/289–0900 or 707/778–1800 ⊕www.villasofdistinction.com). **Wimco** (☎800/449–1553 ⊕www.wimco.com).

BED-AND-BREAKFASTS

Chambres d'hôtes (bed-and-breakfasts) can mean simple lodging, usually in the hosts' home and including a simple breakfast, but can also mean a beautiful room in an 18th-century château with gourmet food and a harpsichord in the living room. Chambres d'hôtes are most common in rural France, though they are becoming more popular in Paris and other major cities. Check with local tourist offices or private reservation agencies like Hôtes Qualité Paris. Another possibility is Gîtes de France, a national organization that lists B&Bs all over the country. Often table d'hôte dinners (meals cooked by and eaten with the owners) can be arranged for a nominal fee. Note that your hosts at B&Bs, unlike those at hotels, are more likely to speak only French.

Reservation Services Bed & Breakfast.com (☎800/462–2632 or 512/322–2710 ⊕www.bedandbreakfast.com) also sends out an online newsletter. **Bed & Breakfast Inns Online** (☎800/215–7365 or 615/868–1946 ⊕www.bbonline.com). **BnB Finder.com** (☎888/547–8226 or 212/432–7693 ⊕www.bnbfinder.com). **Fédération Nationale des Gîtes de France** (☎01–49–70–75–75 ⊕www.gitesdefrance.fr). **Hôtes Qualité Paris** (☎08–92–68–30–00 ⊕www.parisinfo.com).

HOME EXCHANGES

With a direct home exchange you stay in someone else's home while they stay in yours. Some outfits also deal with vacation homes, so you're not actually staying in someone's full-time residence, just their vacant weekend place.

Exchange Clubs Home Exchange.com (☎800/877–8723 ⊕www.homeexchange.com); $59.95 for a 1-year online listing. **HomeLink**

International (☎800/638–3841 ⊕ www.
homelink.org); $80 yearly for Web-only mem-
bership; $125 includes Web access and 2 cata-
logs. **Intervac U.S.** (☎800/756–4663 ⊕ www.
intervacus.com); $78.88 for Web-only member-
ship; $126 includes Web access and a catalog.

HOSTELS

Hostels offer bare-bones lodging at low,
low prices—often in shared dorm rooms
with shared baths—to people of all ages,
though the primary market is young
travelers, especially students. Most hostels serve breakfast; dinner and/or shared
cooking facilities may also be available.
In some hostels you aren't allowed to be
in your room during the day, and there
may be a curfew at night. Nevertheless,
hostels provide a sense of community,
with public rooms where travelers often
gather to share stories. Many hostels are
affiliated with Hostelling International
(HI), an umbrella group of hostel associa-
tions with some 4,500 member properties
in more than 70 countries. Other hostels
are completely independent and may be
nothing more than a really cheap hotel.

Membership in any HI association, open
to travelers of all ages, allows you to stay
in HI-affiliated hostels at member rates.
One-year membership is about $28 for
adults; hostels charge about $10–$30 per
night. Members have priority if the hostel
is full; they're also eligible for discounts
around the world, even on rail and bus
travel in some countries.

Paris's major public hostels are run by the
Féderation Unie des Auberges de Jeunesse
(FUAJ). For about €20 you get a shower,
breakfast, and a bed (usually three to four
to a room). Maisons Internationales des
Jeunes Etudiants (MIJE) have the plushest
hostels, sometimes in historic mansions.
Private hostels have accommodations
that run from pleasant, if spartan, double
rooms to dormlike arrangements.

Information FUAJ (☎01–44–89–87–
27 ⊕ www.fuaj.org). **Hostelling International—
USA** (☎301/495–1240 ⊕ www.hiusa.org). **MIJE**
(☎01–42–74–23–45 ⊕ www.mije.com).

WORD OF MOUTH

Did the resort look as good in real life as
it did in the photos? Did you sleep like a
baby, or were the walls paper thin? Did
you get your money's worth? Rate hotels
and write your own reviews in Travel
Ratings or start a discussion about your
favorite places in Travel Talk on www.
fodors.com. Your comments might even
appear in our books. Yes, you, too, can be a
correspondent!

HOTELS

Rates are always by room, not per person.
Often a hotel in a certain price category
will have a few less-expensive rooms; it's
worth asking about. In the off-season—
usually November to Easter (except for
southern France)—tariffs can be lower. It
helps to inquire about promotional specials and weekend deals. Rates must be
posted in all rooms (usually on the back
of the door), with all extra charges clearly
shown. You might try negotiating rates
if you're planning on staying for a week
or longer.

Assume all hotel rooms have air-conditioning, telephones, television, and private bath unless otherwise noted. You
should always check what bathroom
facilities the price includes. When making
your reservation, state your preference
for shower (*douche*) or tub (*baignoire*)—
the latter always costs more. Also when
booking, ask for a *grand lit* if you want
a double bed.

If you're counting on air-conditioning you
should make sure, in advance, that your
hotel room is *climatisé* (air-conditioned).
If you throw open the windows, don't
expect (*moustiquaires* (screens). Nowhere
in Europe are they standard equipment.

The quality of accommodations, particularly in older properties and even in luxury hotels, can vary greatly from room to
room; if you don't like the room you're
given, ask to see another.

Hotels operate on the European Plan (EP, with no meal provided) unless we note that they offer a Breakfast Plan (BP), Modified American Plan (MAP, with breakfast and dinner daily, known as *demi-pension*), or Full American Plan (FAP, or *pension complète,* with three meals a day). Meal plans, which are usually an option offered in addition to the basic room plan, are generally only available with a minimum two- or three-night stay and are, of course, more expensive than the basic room rate. Inquire about meal plans when making reservations; details and prices are often stated on hotel Web sites.

It's always a good idea to make hotel reservations in Paris and other major tourist destinations as far in advance as possible, especially in late spring, summer, or fall. E-mail is the easiest way to contact the hotel (the staff is probably more likely to read English than to understand it spoken over the phone long-distance), though calling also works. But whether by fax, phone, or e-mail, you should specify the exact dates you want to stay (don't forget to notify your hotel of a possible late check-in to prevent your room from being given away); the size of the room you want and how many people will be sleeping there; the type of accommodations you want (two twins, double, etc.); and what kind of bathroom (private with shower, tub, or both). You might also ask if a deposit (or your credit-card number) is required, and if so, what happens if you cancel later. Request that the hotel fax you back so you have a written confirmation of your reservation.

If you arrive without a reservation, the tourist offices in major train stations and most towns can probably help you find a room.

Many hotels in France are small, and many are family-run establishments. Some are affiliated with hotel groups, such as Logis de France, which can be relied on for comfort, character, and regional cuisine (look for its distinctive yellow-and-green sign). A Logis de France paperback guide is widely available in bookshops. Two prestigious international groups with numerous converted châteaux and manor houses among its members are Relais & Châteaux and Small Luxury Hotels of the World; booklets listing members are available from these organizations. France also has some hotel chains. Examples in the upper price bracket are Frantel, Novotel, and Sofitel as well as InterContinental, Marriott, Hilton, Hyatt, Westin, and Sheraton. The Best Western, Campanile, Climat de France, Ibis, and Timhotel chains are more moderate. Typically, chains offer a consistently acceptable standard of modern features (modern bathrooms, TVs, etc.) but tend to lack atmosphere, with some exceptions (Best Western, for instance, tries to maintain the local character of the hotels it takes over).

Here is a sample letter you can use when making a written reservation.

Cher (Dear) *Madame, Monsieur:*

Nous voudrions réserver une chambre pour (We wish to reserve a room for) _____ (number of) *nuit(s)* (nights), *du* (from) _____ (arrival date) *au* _____ (departure date), *à deux lits* (with twin beds), or *à lit-double* (with a double bed), or *une chambre pour une seule personne* (a room for a single person), *avec salle de bains et toilette privées* (with a bathroom and private toilet). *Si possible, nous voudrions une salle de bains avec une baignoire et aussi une douche.* (If possible, we would prefer a bathroom with a tub as well as a shower.) *Veuillez confirmer la réservation en nous communicant le prix de la chambre, et le dépôt forfaitaire que vous exigez. Dans l'attente de votre lettre, nous vous prions d'agréer, Madame, Monsieur, l'expression de nos sentiments amicales.* (Can you please inform us about availabilities, the rate of room, and if any deposit is needed? With our friendliest greetings, we will wait your confirmation.)

■ AIRLINE TICKETS

Most domestic airline tickets are electronic; international tickets may be either electronic or paper. With an e-ticket the only thing you receive is an e-mailed receipt citing your itinerary and reservation and ticket numbers. The greatest advantage of an e-ticket is that if you lose your receipt, you can simply print out another copy or ask the airline to do it for you at check-in. You usually pay a surcharge (up to $50) to get a paper ticket, if you can get one at all. The sole advantage of a paper ticket is that it may be easier to endorse over to another airline if your flight is canceled and the airline with which you booked can't accommodate you on another flight.

■TIP→Discount air passes that let you travel economically in a country or region must often be purchased before you leave home. In some cases you can only get them through a travel agent.

The Sky Team Europe Pass allows discounted travel throughout Europe on any of the 10 participating airlines, including Air France, Delta, Continental, and Northwest. Prices are based on how many miles you travel.

Air Pass Info Sky Team (☎800/237–2747 from U.S. ⊕ www.skyteam.com).

■ RENTAL CARS

When you reserve a car, ask about cancellation penalties, taxes, drop-off charges (if you're planning to pick up the car in one city and leave it in another), and surcharges (for being under or over a certain age, for additional drivers, or for driving across state or country borders or beyond a specific distance from your point of rental). All these things can add substantially to your costs. Request car seats and extras such as GPS when you book.

Rates are sometimes—but not always—better if you book in advance or reserve through a rental agency's Web site. There are other reasons to book ahead, though: for popular destinations, during busy times of the year, or to ensure that you get certain types of cars (vans, SUVs, exotic sports cars).

■TIP→Make sure that a confirmed reservation guarantees you a car. Agencies sometimes overbook, particularly for busy weekends and holiday periods.

Though renting a car in France is expensive—about twice as much as in the United States—it can pay off if you're traveling with two or more people. In addition, renting a car gives you the freedom that trains cannot. Rates in Paris begin at about €35 a day and €200 per week for an economy car with air-conditioning, manual transmission, and unlimited mileage. The price doesn't usually take into account the 19.6% V.A.T. tax or, if you pick it up from the airport, the airport tax. You won't need a car in the capital, so wait to pick up your rental until the day you leave Paris.

Renting a car through local French agencies can be expensive, as they simply cannot compete with the larger international companies. These giants combine bilingual service, the security of name recognition, extensive services (such as 24-hour hotlines), and automatic vehicles. However, Rent-a-Car Prestige can be useful if you're interested in luxury cars (convertible BMWs) or large family vans (Renault Espace, for example). Note that the big international agencies like Hertz and Avis offer better prices to those clients who make reservations in their home countries; if you need to rent a car while in France, it even pays to call home and have a friend take care of it for you from there. So, to get the best deal, reserve a car before you leave home.

CAR-RENTAL INSURANCE

Everyone who rents a car wonders whether the insurance that the rental companies offer is worth the expense. No one—including us—has a simple answer.

Car Rental Resources

AUTOMOBILE ASSOCIATIONS		
American Automobile Association	315/797–5000	www.aaa.com;
		most contact with the organization is through state and regional members.
National Automobile Club	650/294–7000	www.thenac.com; membership open to CA residents only.
MAJOR AGENCIES		
Alamo	800/462–5266	www.alamo.com
Avis	800/230–4898	www.avis.com
Budget	00/527–0700	www.budget.com
Hertz	800/654–3131, 0870/844–8844 in U.K.	www.hertz.com
National Car Rental	800/227–7368	www.nationalcar.com
LOCAL AGENCIES		
Autorent	01–45–54–22–45	www.autorent.fr
Easycar		www.easycar.net
Europcar	08–25–35–83–58	www.europcar.co.uk
Locabest	01–44–72–08–05	www.locabest.fr
Rent-a-Car	01–43–45–98–99	www.rentacar.fr
Ucar	08–92–88–10–10	www.ucar-location.com
WHOLESALERS		
Auto Europe	888/223–5555	www.autoeurope.com
Europe by Car	800/223–1516, 212/581–3040 in New York	www.europebycar.com
Eurovacations	877/471–3876	www.eurovacations.com
Kemwel	877/820–0668	www.kemwel.com

It all depends on how much regular insurance you have, how comfortable you are with risk, and whether or not money is an issue.

If you own a car, your personal auto insurance may cover a rental to some degree, though not all policies protect you abroad; always read your policy's fine print. If you don't have auto insurance, then seriously consider buying the collision- or loss-damage waiver (CDW or LDW) from the car-rental company, which eliminates your liability for damage to the car. Some credit cards offer CDW coverage, but it's usually supplemental to your own insurance and rarely covers SUVs, minivans, luxury models, and the like. If your coverage is secondary, you may still be liable for loss-of-use costs from the car-rental company. But no credit-card insurance is valid unless you use that card for *all* transactions, from reserving to paying the final bill.

All companies exclude car rental in some countries, so be sure to find out about the destination to which you are traveling.

■TIP➜Diners Club offers primary CDW coverage on all rentals reserved and paid for with the card. This means that Diners Club's company—not your own car insurance—pays in case of an accident. It *doesn't* mean your car-insurance company won't raise your rates once it discovers you had an accident.

Some countries require you to purchase CDW coverage or require car-rental companies to include it in quoted rates. Ask your rental company about issues like these in your destination. In most cases it's cheaper to add a supplemental CDW plan to your comprehensive travel-insurance policy (⇨ *Trip Insurance under Things to Consider in Getting Started, above)* than to purchase it from a rental company. That said, you don't want to pay for a supplement if you're not required to buy insurance from the rental company.

An unlimited third-party liability insurance policy is compulsory for all automobiles driven in France and will be issued to you automatically as part of your rental agreement.

■TIP➜You can decline the insurance from the rental company and purchase it through a third-party provider such as Travel Guard (www.travelguard.com)—$9 per day for $35,000 of coverage. That's sometimes just under half the price of the CDW offered by some car-rental companies.

■ VACATION PACKAGES

Packages *are not* guided excursions. Packages combine airfare, accommodations, and perhaps a rental car or other extras (theater tickets, guided excursions, boat trips, reserved entry to popular museums, transit passes), but they let you do your own thing. During busy periods packages may be your only option, as flights and rooms may be sold out otherwise. Packages will definitely save you time. They can also save you money, particularly in peak seasons, but—and this is a really big "but"—you should price each part of the package separately to be sure. And be aware that prices advertised on Web sites and in newspapers rarely include service charges or taxes, which can up your costs by hundreds of dollars.

■TIP➜Some packages and cruises are sold only through travel agents. Don't always assume that you can get the best deal by booking everything yourself.

Each year consumers are stranded or lose their money when packagers—even large ones with excellent reputations—go out of business. How can you protect yourself? First, always pay with a credit card; if you have a problem, your credit-card company may help you resolve it. Second, buy trip insurance that covers default. Third, choose a company that belongs to the United States Tour Operators Association, whose members must set aside funds to cover defaults. Finally, choose a company that also participates in the Tour Operator Program of the American Society of Travel Agents (ASTA), which will act as mediator in any disputes. You can also check on the tour operator's reputation among travelers by posting an inquiry on one of the Fodors.com forums.

Organizations American Society of Travel Agents (ASTA; ☎800/965–2782 or 703/739–2782 ⊕www.astanet.com). **United States Tour Operators Association** (USTOA; ☎212/599–6599 ⊕www.ustoa.com).

■TIP➜Local tourism boards can provide information about lesser-known and small-niche operators that sell packages to only a few destinations.

■ GUIDED TOURS

Sometimes the best way to optimize your time and money when traveling is to let an experienced tour outfitter organize all of the details. In France there's no short-age of tours available, from all-inclusive bus excursions to self-guided cycling trips or guided hiking trips. Maupintour and Abercrombie & Kent are two of the best-known luxury tour operators, while Cosmos caters to smaller budgets and a more independent spirit. Smaller companies such as France Off the Beaten Path and Brendan Vacations have fewer tours but more personalized service, with special-ized tour packages available in regions throughout France.

Recommended Companies Abercrombie & Kent (☎800/554–7016 or 630/954–2944 ⊕ www.abercrombiekent.com) offers high-end trips throughout France and the rest of the world. **Brendan Vacations** (☎800/421–8446 ⊕ www.brendanvacations.com) is a fam-ily-owned company that offers packages like the nine-day Treasures of France tour. **Cosmos Tours** (☎800/276–1241 ⊕ www.cosmos.com) offers budget tour packages that combine the benefits of group travel with the freedom of independent itineraries. Nine- to 15-day tours are less than $100 a day. **France Off the Beaten Path** (☎877/846–2831 ⊕ www.traveloffthebeatenpath.com) has a selection of walking, wine, and cultural tours in the Loire Valley, Burgundy, and Provence. **Maupintour** (☎800/255–4266 ⊕ www.maupintour.com) sells deluxe escorted and independent tours, such as a 16-day Grand France tour or 6-day Paris packages that include cooking classes and river cruises. **Tour Vacations To Go** (☎800/680–2858 ⊕ www.tourvacationstogo.com) is a useful site that compares prices on France travel packages from all of the major outfitters.

SPECIAL-INTEREST TOURS
The following tour companies specialize in trips to France. The French Govern-ment Tourist Office *(⇨ Visitor Infor-mation, above)* publishes brochures on theme trips including "In the Footsteps of the Painters of Light in Provence" and "France for the Jewish Traveler."

ART & ANTIQUES
Contacts EuroPanache (☎01–53–45–66–77 ⊕ www.europanache.com) offers upscale tours that include seminars with leading art and antiques experts. **French Paintbox** (☎408/358–5875 ⊕ www.frenchpaintbox.com) has tours that include painting workshops in the South of France and the Midi-Pyré-nées region. **International Art Club** (☎No phone ⊕ www.sketching.com) organizes sketch-ing holidays in the South of France.

BIKING
Contacts Backroads (☎800/462–2848 ⊕ www.backroads.com) has a large catalog of walking and cycling tours for travelers of all ages and abilities, including a Tour de France package. **DuVine Adventures** (☎888/396–5383 or 617/776–4441 ⊕ www.duvine.com) has cycling trips through the Alps, Burgundy, the Loire Valley, and Provence. **Trek** (☎866/464–8735 ⊕ www.trektravel.com) is one of the leading bike tour operators in France, offering biking trips for both leisurely sightseeing and hard-core road cyclists.

BALLOONING
Contacts France Montgolfières (☎02–54–32–20–48 ⊕ www.france-balloons.com) operates balloon flight and hotel packages throughout France, including the Loire Valley, Burgundy, Provence, Dordogne, Auvergne, and Champagne. **French Adventures** (☎01–64–21–02–68 ⊕ www.frenchadventures.com) spe-cializes in adventure tours from two to seven days throughout France, including F1 racing, helicopter and balloon rides, and barge cruises.

FOOD & WINE
Contacts Classic Journeys (☎800/200–3887 or 858/454–5004 ⊕ www.classicjour-neys.com) has a seven-day culinary tour of Provence that includes market visits and cooking classes. **Cooking with Friends in France** (☎800/236–9067 ⊕ www.cooking-withfriends.com) offers a weeklong program of cooking classes, cultural excursions, and accommodation in a farmhouse once owned by television chef Julia Child. **Le Cordon Bleu** (☎01–53–68–22–50 ⊕ www.cordonbleu.net), the world-famous cooking academy,

offers short culinary vacations in the Loire Valley, including classes and accommodation in the 18th-century Chateau des Briottières. **Enchanted France** (☎323/931–1759 ⊕ www.enchanted-france.com) specializes in hands-on cooking tours in Arles and Provence; wine-tasting tours in Bordeaux, Champagne, and the Loire Valley; as well as golf and spa packages on the Riviera and the Dordogne. **La Varenne** (☎800/537–6486 ⊕ www.lavarenne.com) is a well-regarded cooking school run by chef Anne Willan since 1975. Guests stay at the historic Château du Feÿ and participate in the five-day Country Cooking of France program or a three-day Taste of Burgundy program. **Wine Tours, Inc.** (☎510/888–9625 ⊕ www.winetoursinc.com) specialize in wine tours to Champagne, Bordeaux, Cognac, the Loire Valley, the Rhone Valley, and Beaujolais.

GOLF

Contact ITC Golf Tours (☎800/257–4981 or 562/595–6905 ⊕ www.itcgolf-africatours.com) has packages combining golf, wine, and châteaux visits in the Loire Valley.

HIKING

Contacts Van Gogh Tours (☎800/435–6192 or 802/767–3457 ⊕ www.vangoghtours.com) offers walking-tour packages such as the Best of Provence, the Gardens and Castles of the Loire, and the Emerald Coast from St-Malo to Mont St-Michel. **The Wayfarers** (☎800/249–4620 ⊕ www.thewayfarers.com) has specialized in walking tours since 1984. Today it offers leisurely countryside walking tours of the Dordogne, Provence, Burgundy, and the Loire. It also organizes some women-only tours

HISTORY

Contacts Stephen Ambrose Tours (☎888/903–3329 or 504/821–9283 ⊕ www.stephenambrosetours.com), named in honor of

the late founder, organizes military history trips throughout Europe, including D-Day and Battle of the Bulge tours in France. **Valor Tours** (☎800/842–4504 ⊕ www.valortours.com) specializes in trips to historic battlefields such as Normandy, Chateau Thierry, and Rheims.

HORSEBACK RIDING

Contact Equitours (☎800/545–0019 ⊕ www.ridingtours.com) offers guided horseback riding adventures throughout France for visitors of all skill levels.

LANGUAGE PROGRAMS

Contact French-American Exchange (☎800/995–5087 ⊕ www.frenchamericanexchange.com) has six vacation centers around France open to all ages and language levels, even absolute beginners.

MUSIC

Contacts Dailey-Thorp Travel (☎800/998–4677 or 307/673–1555 ⊕ www.daileythorp.com) organizes luxurious excursions focusing on classical music and opera festivals throughout Europe. There's usually a Paris tour on the annual schedule. **Music and Markets** (☎877/260–6383 ⊕ www.musicetc.us) runs specialized tours in Provence and Bordeaux of open markets and music festivals.

SKIING

Contact Value Holidays (☎800/558–6850 or 262/241–6373 ⊕ www.valhol.com) has all-inclusive ski packages to Chamonix, Courcheval, Val d'Isere, and Val Thorens.

VOLUNTEER PROGRAMS

Contact Volunteers for Peace (☎802/259–2759 ⊕ www.vfp.org) sponsors social, environmental, or cultural volunteer projects.

.

TRANSPORTATION

■TIP➔Ask the local tourist board about hotel and local transportation packages that include tickets to major museum exhibits or other special events.

■ BY AIR

Flying time to Paris is 7½ hours from New York, 9 hours from Chicago, 11 hours from Los Angeles, and 1 hour from London. Flying time between Paris and Nice is 1¼ hours.

Airlines & Airports Airline and Airport Links.com (⊕www.airlineandairportlinks. com) has links to many of the world's airlines and airports.

Airline Security Issues Transportation Security Administration (⊕www.tsa.gov) has answers for almost every question that might come up.

AIRPORTS

There are two major gateway airports to France, both just outside the capital: Orly, 16 km (10 mi) south of Paris, and Charles de Gaulle, 26 km (16 mi) northeast of the city. At Charles de Gaulle, also known as Roissy, there's a TGV station at Terminal 2 where you can connect to trains going all over the country. Many airlines have less frequent flights to Lyon, Nice, Marseille, Bordeaux, and Toulouse. Or you can fly to Paris and get a connecting flight to other destinations in France.

Airport Information Charles de Gaulle/ Roissy (☎01–48–62–22–80 ⊕www.adp.fr). **Orly** (☎01–49–75–15–15 ⊕www.adp.fr).

AIRPORT TRANSFERS

Charles de Gaulle/Roissy: From Charles de Gaulle, the least expensive way to get into Paris is on the RER-B line, the suburban express train, which runs daily from 5 AM to 11:30 PM. Each terminal has an exit where the free RER shuttle bus (a white-and-yellow bus with the letters ADP in gray) will pass every 7 to 15 minutes to take you on the short ride to the nearby RER station: Terminal 2A and Terminal 2C (Exit 8), Terminal 2B and Terminal 2D (Exit 6), Terminal 2E (Exit 2.06), Terminal 2F (Exit 2.08). Trains to central Paris (Les Halles, St-Michel, Luxembourg) depart every 15 minutes. The fare (including métro connection) is €8.10, and journey time is about 30 minutes.

The Air France shuttle is a comfortable option to get to and from the city—you don't need to have flown the carrier to use this service. Line 2 goes from the airport to Paris's Charles de Gaulle Étoile and Porte Maillot from 5:45 AM to 11 PM. It leaves every 15 minutes and costs €12, which you can pay on board. Passengers arriving in Terminal 1 need to take Exit 34; Terminals 2B and 2D, Exit 6; Terminals 2E and 2F, Exit 3. Line 4 goes to Montparnasse and the Gare de Lyon from 7 AM to 9 PM. Buses run every 30 minutes and cost €13. Passengers arriving in Terminal 1 need to look for Exit 34, Terminals 2A and 2C need to take Exit C2, Terminals 2B and 2D Exit B1, and Terminals 2E and 2F Exit 3.

Another option is to take Roissybus, operated by the Paris Transit Authority, which runs between Charles de Gaulle and the Opéra every 20 minutes from 6 AM to 11 PM; the cost is €8.50. The trip takes about 45 minutes in regular traffic, about 90 minutes in rush-hour traffic.

Taxis are your least desirable mode of transportation into the city. If you're traveling at peak tourist times, you may have to stand in a very long line with a lot of other disgruntled European travelers (most of whom smoke). Journey times, and as a consequence, prices, are unpredictable. At best, the journey takes 30 minutes but it can take as long as one hour.

Airport Connection is the name of just one of a number of van services that serve both Charles de Gaulle and Orly

Travel Times from Paris

To	By Air	By Car or Bus	By Train
Nice	1¼ hours	7–8 hours	5 hours
Lyon	45 minutes	4½ hours	2 hours
Montpellier	1 hour	7 hours	3½ hours
Marseille	1 hour	7 hours	3 hours
Bordeaux	1 hour	6 hours	3 hours
Lille	30 minutes	2½ hours	1 hour

airports. Prices are set, so it costs the same no matter how long the journey takes. To make a reservation, call or fax your flight details at least one week in advance to the shuttle company and an air-conditioned van with a bilingual chauffeur will be waiting for you upon your arrival. Note these shuttle vans pick up and drop off other passengers.

Orly: From Orly, the most economical way to get into Paris is to take the RER-C or Orlyrail line. Catch the free shuttle bus from the terminal to the train station. Trains to Paris leave every 15 minutes. Passengers arriving in either the South or West Terminal need to use Exit G. The fare is €5.75, and journey time is about 35 minutes. Another option is to take the monorail service, Orlyval, which runs between the Antony RER-B station and Orly Airport daily every four to eight minutes from 6 AM to 11 PM. Passengers arriving in the South Terminal should look for Exit K, those arriving in the West terminal, Exit W. The fare to downtown Paris is €9.10.

You can also take an Air France bus from Orly to Les Invalides on the Left Bank and Montparnasse; these run every 15 minutes from 6 AM to 11 PM. (You need not have flown on Air France to use this service). The fare is €9, and the trip takes between 30 and 45 minutes, depending on traffic. Those arriving in Orly South need to look for Exit L; those arriving in Orly West, Exit D. The Paris Transit Authority's Orlybus is yet another option; buses leave every 15 minutes for the Den-fert-Rochereau métro station; the cost is €5.80. You can economize using RATP Bus 285, which shuttles you from the airport to Line 7, métro Villejuif Louis Arragan station, for the price of a city bus ticket. It operates daily from 6:45 AM (from 5:15 AM weekdays) to 12:45 AM at the Orly Sud terminal.

Contacts Air France Bus (☎08-92-35-08-20 recorded information in English ⊕www.cars-airfrance.com). **Airport Connection** (☎01-43-65-55-55 🖷01-43-65-55-57 ⊕www.airport-connection.com). **Paris Airports Service** (☎01-55-98-10-80 🖷01-55-98-10-89 ⊕www.parisairportservice.com). **RATP (including Roissybus, Orlybus, Orlyval)** (☎08-92-68-77-14, €0.35 per min ⊕www.ratp.com).

FLIGHTS

As one of the world's most popular destinations, Paris is serviced by many international carriers. Air France, the French flag carrier, offers numerous flights between Paris's Charles de Gaulle Airport and New York City's JFK Airport; Newark, New Jersey; and Washington's Dulles Airport; as well as Boston, Atlanta, Miami, Chicago, Houston, San Francisco, Los Angeles, Toronto, Montréal, and Mexico City. Most other North American cities are served through Air France partnerships with Delta and Continental. American-based carriers are usually less expensive, but offer fewer nonstop flights. Delta Airlines has flights to Paris from Atlanta, Cincinnati, and New York City's JFK. Continental Airlines has nonstop flights to Paris from Newark and

Houston. Another popular carrier is United, with nonstop flights to Paris from Chicago, Denver, Los Angeles, Miami, Philadelphia, Washington, and San Francisco. American Airlines offers daily nonstop flights to Paris's Charles de Gaulle Airport from numerous cities, including New York City's JFK, Miami, Chicago, and Dallas/Fort Worth. Northwest offers a daily departure to Paris from its hub in Detroit.

Airline Contacts Air Canada (☎888/247–2262 in U.S. and Canada, 00–800–8712–7786 in France ⊕www.aircanada.com). **Air France** (☎800/237–2747 in U.S., 08–25–86–48–64 in France [€0.15 per min] ⊕www.airfrance. com). **American Airlines** (☎800/433–7300, 08–10–87–28–72 in France ⊕www.aa.com). **British Airways** (☎800/247–9297 in U.S., 08–25–82–50–40 in France ⊕www. britishairways.com). **Continental Airlines** (☎800/523–3273 for U.S. reservations, 800/231–0856 for international reservations, 01–71–23–03–35 in France ⊕www.continental. com). **Delta Airlines** (☎800/221–1212 for U.S. reservations, 800/241–4141 for international reservations, 08–00–30–13–01 in France ⊕www.delta.com). **Northwest Airlines** (☎800/225–2525, 08–90–71–07–10 in France ⊕www.nwa.com). **United Airlines** (☎800/864–8331 for U.S. reservations, 800/538–2929 for international reservations, 08–10–72–72–72 in France ⊕www.united. com). **USAirways** (☎800/428–4322 for U.S. and Canada reservations, 800/622–1015 for international reservations, 08–10–63–22–22 in France ⊕www.usairways.com). **Zoom Air** (☎866/359–9666 in U.S. and Canada, 0800–213–266 in France ⊕www.flyzoom.com).

Within Europe BMI Baby (☎0871–224–0224 in U.K., 08–90–71–00–81 in France ⊕www.bmibaby.com). **British Airways** (☎0870/8509–850 in U.K., 08–25–82–54–00 in France ⊕www.britishairways.com). **British Midland** (☎0870/6070–222 in U.K., 01–55–69–83–06 in France ⊕www.flybmi. com). **EasyJet** (☎0990/292–929 in U.K., 08–26–10–26–11 in France ⊕www.easyjet. com). **Ryanair** (☎0871–246–0000 in U.K., 08–

92–23–23–75 in France ⊕www.ryanair.com). **Virgin Express** (☎08–21–23–02–02 ⊕www. virginexpress.com).

∎ BY BARGE & YACHT

Canal and river trips are popular in France, particularly along the picturesque waterways in Brittany, Burgundy, and the Midi. For further information, ask for a "Tourisme Fluvial" brochure at any French tourist office. It's also possible to rent a barge or crewed sailboat to travel around the coast of France, particularly along the Côte d'Azur.

Barge Companies Abercrombie & Kent (☎800/554–7016 or 630/954–2944 ⊕www. abercrombiekent.com). **En-Bateau** (☎04–67–13–19–62 ⊕en-bateau.com). **European Waterways** (☎800/217–4447 or 212/688–9489 ⊕www.gobarging.com). **French Country Waterways** (☎800/222–1236 or 781/934–2454 ⊕www.fcwl.com). **Maine Anjou Rivières** (☎08–05–80–10–83 ⊕www.maine-anjou-rivieres.com). **Viking River Cruises** (☎877/668–4546 or 818/227–1234 ⊕www. rivercruises.com).

∎ BY BOAT

A number of ferry and hovercraft routes link the United Kingdom and France. Prices depend on the length of the journey and the number of people traveling. Driving distances from the French ports to Paris are as follows: from Calais, 290 km (180 mi); from Cherbourg, 358 km (222 mi); from Caen, 233 km (145 mi); from St-Malo, 404 km (250 mi).

Dover–Calais P&O European Ferries (☎0870/598–0333 ⊕www.poferries.com) has up to three sailings a day; the crossing takes about 75 minutes. **Seafrance** (☎0870/443–1653 ⊕www.seafrance.fr) operates up to 15 sailings a day; the crossing takes about 90 minutes.

Portsmouth & Poole–Cherbourg, Caen & St-Malo Brittany Ferries (☎0870/907–6103 ⊕www.brittanyferries.co.uk) has four sailing per day between Caen and Portsmouth, one crossing daily between St-Malo and Portsmouth, and from two to five crossings daily between Poole and Cherbourg.

∎ BY BUS

If you're traveling to or from another country, train service can be just as economical as bus travel, if not more so. The largest international operator is Eurolines France, whose main terminal is in the Parisian suburb of Bagnolet (a half-hour métro ride from central Paris, at the end of métro Line 3). Eurolines runs many international routes to more than 37 European destinations, including a route from London to Paris, usually departing at 8:30 AM, arriving at 5:30 PM; noon, arriving at 9 PM; and 9:30 PM, arriving at 7:30 AM. Fares are €71 round-trip (under-25 youth pass €65). Other Eurolines routes include: Amsterdam (7 hrs, €73); Barcelona (15 hrs, €155); and Berlin (10 hrs, €137). There are economical passes to be had—15-day passes run €169–€329, a 30-day pass will cost €229–€439. These passes offer unlimited coach travel to all Eurolines European destinations.

France's excellent train service means that long-distance buses are rare; regional buses are found mainly where train service is spotty. In rural areas the service can be unreliable, and schedules can be incomprehensible for those who don't speak French. Your best bet is to contact local tourism offices.

Bus Information Eurolines France (📞08–92–89–90–91 in France, 0870/580–8080 in U.K. ⊕www.eurolines.fr).

∎ BY CAR

An International Driver's Permit, valid for trips of fewer than 90 days, is not required but can prove useful in emergencies such as traffic violations or auto accidents, particularly when a foreign language is involved. Drivers in France

must be over 18 years old to drive, but there is no top age limit (if your faculties are intact).

If you're driving from the United Kingdom to the Continent, you have a choice of either the Channel Tunnel or ferry services. Reservations are always a good idea, but are essential at peak times.

GASOLINE

Gas is expensive, especially on expressways and in rural areas. When possible, buy gas before you get on the expressway and keep an eye on pump prices as you go. These vary enormously—anything from €0.90 to €1.25 per liter. The cheapest gas can be found at *hypermarchés* (large supermarkets). Credit cards are accepted everywhere. In rural areas it's possible to go for miles without passing a gas station, so don't let your tank get too low.

PARKING

Parking is a nightmare in Paris and many other metropolitan areas. "Pay and display" metered parking is usually limited to two hours in city centers. Parking is free on Sunday and national holidays. Parking meters showing a dense yellow circle indicate a free parking zone during the month of August. In smaller towns, parking may be permitted on one side of the street only—alternating every two weeks—so pay attention to signs. In France, illegally parked cars are likely to be impounded, especially those blocking entrances or fire exits. Parking tickets are €11 for the first, €33 for the second, and there's no shortage of the blue-uniformed parking police. Parking lots, indicated by a blue sign with a white P, are usually underground and are generally expensive.

ROAD CONDITIONS

France has 8,000 km (5,000 mi) of expressway and 808,000 km (502,000 mi) of main roads. For the fastest route between two points, look for roads marked A for *autoroute*. A *péage* (toll) must be paid on most expressways: the rate varies but can be steep. The N (*route nationale*) roads—which are sometimes divided highways—and D (*route départementale*) roads are usually also wide and fast.

There are excellent links between Paris and most French cities, but poor ones between the provinces (the principal exceptions are A26 from Calais to Reims, A62 between Bordeaux and Toulouse, and A9/A8 the length of the Mediterranean coast).

Though routes are numbered, the French generally guide themselves from city to city and town to town by destination name. When reading a map, keep one eye on the next big city toward your destination as well as the next small town; most snap decisions will have to be based on town names, not road numbers.

ROADSIDE EMERGENCIES

If you have car trouble on an expressway, go to a roadside emergency telephone. If you have a breakdown anywhere else, find the nearest garage or contact the police. There are also 24-hour assistance hotlines valid throughout France (available through rental agencies and supplied to you when you rent the car), but do not hesitate to call the police in case of any roadside emergency, for they are quick and reliable, and the phone call is free. There are special phones just for this purpose on all highways; you can see them every few kilometers—just pick up the bright orange phone and dial 17. The French equivalent of the AAA is the Club Automobile de l'Ile de France, but it only takes care of its members and is of little use to international travelers.

Emergency Services Police (☎17).

RULES OF THE ROAD

Drive on the right and yield to drivers coming from streets to the right. However, this rule does not necessarily apply at traffic circles, where you should watch out for just about everyone. You must wear a seat belt, and children under 12 may not travel in the front seat. Speed limits are 130 kph (80 mph) on expressways (*autoroutes*), 110 kph (70 mph) on divided highways (*routes nationales*), 90 kph (55 mph) on other roads (*routes*), 50 kph (30 mph) in cities and towns (*villes* and *villages*). French drivers break these limits all the time, and police dish out hefty on-the-spot fines with equal abandon. Do not expect to find traffic lights in the center of the road, as French lights are usually on the right- and left-hand sides.

If you're driving through France during the traditional holiday months (Christmas, Easter, July–September) you might be asked to pull over by the Police National at busy intersections. You will have to show your papers (*papiers*)— including car insurance—and submit to an "alcotest" (you guessed it, a Breathalyzer test). The rules in France have become stringent because of the high incidence of accidents on the roads; anything above 0.5 grams of alcohol in the blood—which, according to your size, could simply mean two to three glasses of wine—and you are over the limit. This does not necessarily mean a night in the clinker, but your driving privileges in France will be revoked on the spot and you will pay a hefty fine. Don't drink and drive, even if you're just crossing town to the sleepy little inn on the river. Local police are notorious for their vigilance.

Some important traffic terms and signs to note: SORTIE (exit); SENS UNIQUE (one-way); STATIONNEMENT INTERDITE (no parking); and IMPASSE (dead end). Blue rectangular signs indicate a highway; green rectangular signs indicate a major direction; triangles carry illustrations of a particular traffic hazard; speed limits are indicated in a circle with the maximum limit circled in red.

■ BY TRAIN

The SNCF, France's national rail service, is fast, punctual, comfortable, and comprehensive. Traveling across France, you have various options: local trains, overnight trains with sleeping accommodations, and the high-speed TGV (Trains à Grande Vitesse).

TGVs average 255 kph (160 mph) on the Lyon–southeast line and 300 kph (190 mph) on the Lille and Bordeaux–southwest lines and are the best and the fastest domestic trains. They operate between Paris and Lille/Calais, Paris and Brussels, Paris and Amsterdam, Paris and Lyon–Switzerland–Provence, Paris and Angers–Nantes, and Paris and Tours–Poitiers–Bordeaux. As with other main-line trains, a small supplement may be assessed at peak hours.

It's possible to get from one end of France to the other without traveling overnight, especially on TGVs. Otherwise, you have a choice between high-price *wagons-lit* (sleeping cars) and affordable *couchettes* (bunks, six to a compartment in second class, four to a compartment in first, with sheets and pillow provided, priced at around €15).

Get to the station a half hour before departure to ensure you'll have a good seat. Before boarding, you must punch your ticket (but not Eurailpass) in one of the orange machines at the entrance to the platforms, or else the ticket collector will fine you €15 on the spot. Smoking has been forbidden in TGVs for several years, and now the ban applies to all public transportation in France. Even lighting up in the bathrooms or connecting compartments will land you an on-the-spot fine starting at €65.

In Paris there are six international rail stations: Gare du Nord (northern France, northern Europe, and England via Calais or Boulogne); Gare St-Lazare (Normandy and England via Dieppe); Gare de l'Est (Strasbourg, Luxembourg, Basel, and central Europe); Gare de Lyon (Lyon, Marseille, Provence, Geneva, and Italy); and Gare d'Austerlitz (Loire Valley, southwest France, and Spain). Note that Gare Montparnasse has taken over as the main terminus for trains bound for southwest France.

There are two classes of train service in France; first (*première*) or second (*deuxième*). First-class seats offer more legroom, plusher upholstery, private reading lamps, and computer plugs on the TGV, not to mention the hush-hush environment for those of you who want to sleep. The price is also nearly double.

There are two kinds of rail passes: those you must purchase at home before you leave for France, including the France Rail Pass, the Eurail Selectpass, and those available in France from SNCF. The SNCF passes are available at any train station in France. Your rail pass does not guarantee you a seat on the train you wish to ride, however. You need to book ahead even if you're using a rail pass.

If you plan to travel outside Paris, consider purchasing a France Rail Pass, which allows three days of unlimited train travel in a one-month period. If you travel solo, first class will run you $261, second class is $222: you can add up to six days on this pass for $38 a day. For two people traveling together on a Saver Pass, the cost in first class is $223, second class is $191; each additional day costs $33. Another option is the France Rail 'n Drive Pass (combining rail and rental car).

France is one of 18 countries in which you can use EurailPasses, which provide unlimited first-class rail travel in all of the participating countries for the duration of the pass. If you plan to rack up the miles, get a standard pass.

These are available for 15 days ($635), 21 days ($829), one month ($1,025), two months ($1,449), and three months ($1,789). If your plans call for only limited train travel between France and another country, consider a two-country pass, which costs less than a EurailPass. With the two-country pass you can get four flexible travel days between France and Italy, France, Spain, or Switzerland for $329. In addition to standard EurailPasses, ask about special plans. Among these are the Eurail Selectpass Youth (for those under age 26) and the Eurail Selectpass Saver (which gives a discount for two or more people traveling together). Whichever of the above passes you choose, remember that you must purchase your Eurail passes before leaving for France.

You can get a reduced fare if you're a senior citizen (over 60). There are two options: for the Prix Découverte Senior, all you have to do is show a valid ID with your age and you're entitled to up to a 25% reduction in fares in first and second class. The second, the Carte Senior, is better if you're planning on spending a lot of time traveling; it costs €49, is valid for one year, and entitles you to up to a 50% reduction on most trains with a guaranteed minimum reduction of 25%. It also entitles you to a 30% discount on trips outside France.

With the Carte Enfant Plus, for €65 children under 12 and up to four accompanying adults can get up to 50% off most trains for an unlimited number of trips. This card, valid for a year, is perfect if you're planning to spend a lot of time traveling in France with your children. You can also opt for the Prix Découverte Enfant Plus: when you buy your ticket, simply show a valid ID with your child's age and you can get a significant discount for your child and a 25% reduction for up to four accompanying adults.

If you purchase an individual ticket from SNCF in France and you're under 26, you automatically get a 25% reduction when you flash a valid ID. If you're under 26 and plan to ride the train quite a bit, consider buying the Carte 12–25 (€49), which offers unlimited 50% reductions for one year.

If you don't benefit from any of these reductions and if you plan on traveling at least 200 km (132 mi) round-trip and don't mind staying over a Saturday night, look into the Prix Découverte Séjour. This ticket gives you a 25% reduction.

With an advance arrangement, SNCF will pick up and deliver your luggage at a given time. For instance, if you're planning on spending a weekend in Nice, SNCF will pick up your luggage at your hotel in Paris in the morning before checkout and deliver it to your hotel in Nice, where it will be awaiting your arrival. The cost is €25 for the first bag, and €11 for two additional bags, with a maximum of three bags per person.

Short of flying, taking the Channel Tunnel is the fastest way to cross the English Channel: 35 minutes from Folkestone to Calais, 60 minutes from motorway to motorway, or 2 hours and 40 minutes from London's Waterloo Station to Paris's Gare du Nord. The Belgian border is just a short drive northeast of Calais. High-speed Eurostar trains use the same tunnels to connect London's Waterloo Station directly with Midi Station in Brussels in around 2½ hours.

British Rail also has four daily departures from London's Victoria Station, all linking with the Dover–Calais–Boulogne ferry services through to Paris. There's also an overnight service on the Newhaven–Dieppe ferry. Journey time is about eight hours. Credit-card bookings are accepted by phone or in person at a British Rail travel center.

There's a vast range of prices for Eurostar—round-trip tickets range from €520 for first class to €105 for second class depending on when and where you travel.

Channel Tunnel Car Transport Eurotunnel (☎0870/535-3535 in U.K., 070/223210 in Belgium, 03-21-00-61-00 in France ⊕ www.eurotunnel.com). **French Motorail/Rail Europe** (☎0870/241-5415 ⊕ www.raileurope.co.uk/frenchmotorail).

Channel Tunnel Passenger Service Eurostar (☎0870/518-6186, in U.K. ⊕ www.eurostar.co.uk). **Rail Europe** (☎888/382-7245 in U.S., 0870/584-8848 in U.K.; inquiries and credit-card bookings ⊕ www.raileurope.com).

Information BritRail Travel (☎866/274-8724 in U.S. ⊕ www.britrail.com). **Eurail** (⊕ www.eurail.com). **SNCF** (☎08-36-35-35-35 ⊕ www.sncf.fr/indexe.htm). **SNCF Luggage Delivery Service** (☎36-35 from any landline in France, then dial 41 ⊕ www.sncf.fr).

ON THE GROUND

■ BUSINESS SERVICES & FACILITIES

France has no 24-hour copy shops like Kinkos, but larger cities have chains that provide similar printing services. Look for an *imprimeur* (printer) or *services graphiques* (graphics services), usually found around university or business districts.

■ COMMUNICATIONS

INTERNET

If you use a major Internet provider, getting online in France shouldn't be difficult. Most hotels have in-room broadband connections or wireless access. If you need to spend a lot of time online, make sure to ask when you book a room if there's a charge for the service. Remember to bring an adapter for the European-style plugs.

If you're not at your hotel, there are still many place to get online. Wi-Fi hot spots can be found at many of the cafés and public libraries in Paris and other metropolitan areas. In smaller towns ask at the local tourism office where you can get connected.

Access Numbers in Paris AOL (☎01–70–27–01–23). **Compuserve** (☎08–60–00–73–10).

Contacts Cybercafes (⊕www.cybercafes.com) lists more than 4,000 Internet cafés worldwide.

PHONES

The good news is that you can now make a direct-dial telephone call from virtually any point on Earth. The bad news? You can't always do so cheaply. Calling from a hotel is almost always the most expensive option; hotels usually add huge surcharges to all calls, particularly international ones. In some countries you can phone from call centers or even the post office. Calling cards usually keep costs to a minimum, but only if you purchase them locally. And then there are mobile

phones (⇨ *below*), which are sometimes more prevalent—particularly in the developing world—than landlines; as expensive as mobile phone calls can be, they are still usually a much cheaper option than calling from your hotel.

The country code for France is 33. The first two digits of French numbers are a prefix determined by zone: Paris and Ile-de-France, 01; the northwest, 02; the northeast, 03; the southeast, 04; and the southwest, 05. Numbers that begin with 06 are for mobile phones (and are notoriously expensive). Pay close attention to the numbers beginning with 08; 08 followed by 00 is a toll-free number but 08–36 numbers are very costly, at least €0.35 per minute.

Note that when dialing France from abroad, drop the initial 0 from the number. For instance, to call a telephone number in Paris from the United States, dial 011–33 plus the phone number minus the initial 0 (phone numbers in this book are listed with the full 10 digits, which you use to make local calls).

CALLING WITHIN FRANCE

The French are very fond of their mobile phones (*portables*), meaning that telephone booths are more scarce than ever. Look for public phones in airports, post offices, train stations, on the street, and subway stations. You can use your own credit card or an international calling card, available for sale at newsstands or post offices. Insert your card and follow directions on the screen (it should give you the option to read in English). Keep in mind that credit cards work on a €20 minimum—you'll have exactly 30 days after the first call you put on your card to use up the credit. If you're using a phone card, simply dial the toll-free number on the back of the card, enter the identification number from the back of the card, and follow the instructions in English.

At this writing, prices were falling, and a local call made between 8 AM and 7 PM cost €0.04 per minute. Low rates of €0.02 per minute apply weekdays between 7 PM and 8 AM, all day on weekends, and all national holidays.

CALLING OUTSIDE FRANCE
To make a direct international call out of France, dial 00, then the country code (1 for the United States), the area code, and number.

Telephone rates have decreased recently in France because the French Telecom monopoly finally has some competition. As in most countries, the highest rates fall between 8 AM and 7 PM; you can expect to pay €0.25 per minute for a call to the United States, Canada, or some of the closer European countries such as Great Britain, Belgium, Italy, and Germany. Rates are slashed in half when you make that same call between 7 PM and 8 AM, at just €0.12 per minute. To call home with the help of international directory assistance costs a hefty €6 per call; if this doesn't dissuade you, dial 00–33 plus the code of the country you'd like to call and a bilingual operator will come on the line. Try not to make calls directly from your hotel unless you're using a phone card; they charge heavily for local calls and slap a service charge on for international calls. Your best bet is to buy a French phone card, a *télécarte,* which can be used from any phone and will end up saving you a bundle.

Access Codes AT&T Direct (☎800/222–0300 for information , 08-00-99-00-11, 08-00-99-01-11). **MCI WorldPhone** (☎800/444-4444 for information , 08-00-99-00-19). **Sprint International Access** (☎800/793-1153 for information , 08-00-99-00-87).

CALLING CARDS
The rare French person who doesn't have a mobile phone uses *télécartes* (phone cards), which you can buy just about anywhere, from post offices to magazine kiosks to métro stations. Their rates are the best you can find. There are two télécartes available; *une pétite* that costs €9 for 50 units or *une grande* that costs €16.25 for 120 units. Scratch the card to uncover your personal PIN, dial the toll-free number and the number you wish to reach (be it local or international) and the operator will tell you the exact amount of time you have to chat.

MOBILE PHONES
If you have a multiband phone (some countries use different frequencies from what's used in the United States) and your service provider uses the world-standard GSM network (as do T-Mobile, Cingular, and Verizon), you can probably use your phone abroad. Roaming fees can be steep, however: 99¢ a minute is considered reasonable. And overseas you normally pay the toll charges for incoming calls. It's almost always cheaper to send a text message than to make a call, since text messages have a low set fee (often less than 5¢).

If you just want to make local calls, consider buying a new SIM card (note that your provider may have to unlock your phone for you to use a different SIM card) and a prepaid service plan in the destination. You can then have a local number and can make local calls at local rates. If your trip is extensive, you could also simply buy a new cell phone in your destination, as the initial cost will be offset over time.

■**TIP→If you travel internationally frequently, save one of your old mobile phones or buy a cheap one on the Internet; ask your cell phone company to unlock it for you, and take it with you as a travel phone, buying a new SIM card with pay-as-you-go service in each destination.**

Contacts Cellular Abroad (☎800/287-5072 ⊕www.cellularabroad.com) rents and sells GMS phones and sells SIM cards that work in many countries. **Mobal** (☎888/888-9162 ⊕www.mobalrental.com) rents mobiles and sells GSM phones (starting at $49) that will operate in 140 countries. Per-call rates vary throughout the world. **Planet Fone** (☎888/988–4777 ⊕www.planetfone.com) rents cell phones, but the per-minute rates are expensive.

■ CUSTOMS & DUTIES

There are two levels of duty-free allowance for travelers entering France: one for goods bought in another European Union country and the other for goods obtained anywhere else. In the first category, you may import duty-free: 300 cigarettes or 150 cigarillos or 75 cigars or 400 grams of tobacco; 5 liters of table wine and (1) 1½ liters of alcohol over 22% volume (most spirits), (2) 3 liters of alcohol under 22% by volume (fortified or sparkling wine), or (3) 3 more liters of table wine, 90 milliliters of perfume, 375 milliliters of toilet water, and other goods to the value of €365 (€95 for those under 15).

In the second category, you may import duty-free: 200 cigarettes or 100 cigarillos or 50 cigars or 250 grams of tobacco (these allowances are doubled if you live outside Europe); 2 liters of wine and (1) 1 liter of alcohol over 22% volume (most spirits), (2) 2 liters of alcohol under 22% volume (fortified or sparkling wine), or (3) 2 more liters of table wine, 60 milliliters of perfume, 250 milliliters of toilet water, and other goods to the value of €45 (€25 for those under 15).

Information in France Direction des Douanes (☎01–40–40–39–00 ⊕www. douane.gouv.fr).

U.S. Information U.S. Customs and Border Protection (⊕www.cbp.gov).

■ EATING OUT

All establishments must post their menus outside, so study them carefully before deciding to enter. Most restaurants have two basic types of menu: à la carte and fixed-price (prix-fixe or *un menu*). The prix-fixe menu is usually the best value, though choices are more limited. Most menus begin with a first course (*une entrée*), often subdivided into cold and hot starters, followed by fish and poultry, then meat; it's rare today that anyone orders something from all three.

A few pointers on French dining etiquette: diners in France don't negotiate their orders much, so don't expect serene smiles when you ask for sauce on the side. Order your coffee after dessert, not with it. When you're ready for the check, ask for it: no professional waiter would dare put a bill on your table while you're still enjoying the last sip of coffee. And don't ask for a doggy bag; it's just not done. The French usually drink wine or mineral water—not soda or coffee—with their food. You may ask for a carafe of tap water if you don't want to order wine or pay for bottled water.

MEALS & MEALTIMES

What's the difference between a bistro and a brasserie? Can you order food at a café? Can you go to a restaurant just for a snack? The following definitions should help.

A restaurant traditionally serves a three-course meal (first, main, and dessert) at both lunch and dinner. Although this category includes the most formal, three-star establishments, it also applies to humble neighborhood spots. Don't expect to grab a quick snack. In general, restaurants are what you choose when you want a complete meal and when you have the time to linger over it.

Many say that bistros served the world's first fast food. After the fall of Napoléon, the Russian soldiers who occupied Paris were known to bang on zinc-top café bars, crying "*bistro*"—"quickly" in Russian. In the past, bistros were simple places with minimal decor and service. Although nowadays many are quite upscale, with beautiful interiors and chic clientele, most remain cozy establishments serving straightforward, frequently gutsy cooking.

Brasseries—ideal places for quick, one-dish meals—originated when Alsatians fleeing German occupiers after the Franco-Prussian War came to Paris and opened restaurants serving specialties from home. Pork-based dishes, *choucroute* (sauerkraut), and beer (*brasserie* also means brewery) were—and still are—mainstays here. The typical brasserie is convivial and keeps late hours. Some are open 24 hours a day—a good thing to know since many restaurants stop serving at 10:30 PM.

Like bistros and brasseries, cafés come in a confusing variety. Often informal neighborhood hangouts, cafés may also be veritable showplaces attracting chic, well-heeled crowds. At most cafés the regulars congregate at the bar, where coffee and drinks are cheaper than at tables. At lunch tables are set, and a limited menu is served. Sandwiches, usually with *jambon* (ham), *fromage* (cheese, often Gruyère or Camembert), or *mixte* (ham and cheese), are served throughout the day. *Casse croûtes* (snacks) are also offered. Cafés are for lingering, for people-watching, and for daydreaming. If none of these options fit the bill, head to the nearest *traiteur* (deli) for picnic fixings.

Breakfast is usually served from 7:30 AM to 10 PM, lunch from noon to 2 PM, and dinner from 7:30 PM to 10 PM. Restaurants in Paris usually serve dinner until 10:30 PM.

Unless otherwise noted, the restaurants listed in this guide are open daily for lunch and dinner.

PAYING

By French law, prices must include tax and tip (*service compris* or *prix nets*), but pocket change left on the table in basic places, or an additional 5% in better restaurants, is always appreciated. Beware of bills stamped SERVICE NOT INCLUDED in English.

Credit cards, or *cartes bancaires* are widely accepted (although American Express is usually only accepted in more upscale shops, restaurants, and hotels). A few tiny boutiques and bistros may have signs posted that say they do not accept cards. It's best to ask beforehand if you're not sure. Always have cash in smaller towns or in case the "machine isn't working," which happens frequently.

The following is the price chart used throughout this book to determine price categories for all restaurants. Prices are per person for a main course at dinner, including tax (19.6%) and service; note that if a restaurant offers only prix-fixe (set-price) meals, it's given a price category that reflects the full prix-fixe price.

For guidelines on tipping see Tipping below.

CATEGORY	ALL REGIONS EXCEPT	BASQUE COUNTRY
$$$$	over €30	over €25
$$$	€23–€30	€17–€25
$$	€17–€22	€12–€17
$	€11–€16	€8–€12
¢	under €11	under €8

RESERVATIONS & DRESS

Regardless of where you are, it's a good idea to make a reservation if you can. In some places, it's expected. We only mention them specifically when reservations are essential (there's no other way you'll ever get a table) or when they are not accepted. For popular restaurants, book as far ahead as you can (often 30 days), and reconfirm as soon as you arrive. (Large parties should always call ahead to check the reservations policy.) We mention dress only when men are required to wear a jacket or a jacket and tie.

■ ELECTRICITY

The electrical current in France is 220 volts, 50 cycles alternating current (AC); wall outlets take Continental-type plugs, with two round prongs.

Consider making a small investment in a universal adapter, which has several types of plugs in one lightweight, compact unit. Most laptops and mobile phone chargers are dual voltage (i.e., they operate equally well on 110 and 220 volts), so require only an adapter. These days the same is true of small appliances such as hair dryers. Always check labels and manufacturer instructions to be sure. Don't use 110-volt outlets marked FOR SHAVERS ONLY for high-wattage appliances such as hair dryers.

Contacts Steve Kropla's Help for World Traveler's (⊕ www.kropla.com) has information on electrical and telephone plugs around the world. Walkabout Travel Gear (⊕ www. walkabouttravelgear.com) has good coverage of electricity under "adapters."

■ EMERGENCIES

The National Medical System in France is excellent and was recently ranked number one by the World Health Organization, but there are certain things you must understand to get optimum care. For minor emergencies—the flu, food poisoning, a bad respiratory infection—you should contact a generalist who will actually visit you in your home or hotel, medical bag in hand, at any hour of the day or night, whether you're in the city or on the outskirts of a tiny town. At the moment, hospital emergency rooms are undergoing a crisis and are to be used only for emergencies. They operate on a strict priority system, which could leave you with your high temperature or sprained ankle waiting for hours.

France's emergency services are conveniently streamlined and universal and quite simple to use, so no matter where you are in the country you can dial the same phone numbers. Every town and village has a *médecin de garde* (on-duty doctor) for flus, sprains, tetanus shots, and similar problems. Larger cities have a remarkable service called "SOS Doctor" (or "SOS Dentist" for dental emergencies); just dial information (12) and they will put you through. To find out who's on call on any given evening, call any *généraliste* (general practitioner), and a recording will refer you to the available doctors and specialists. If you need an X-ray or emergency treatment, call an ambulance, and you'll be whisked to the hospital of your choice—or the nearest one. Note that outside Paris it's very difficult to find English-speaking doctors.

Pharmacies have an important role in French culture; they can be helpful with minor health problems and come equipped with blood pressure machines and first-aid kits. They also can be consulted for a list of practicing doctors in the area, nearby hospitals, private clinics, or health centers. Hotels are required to post emergency exit maps with multilingual instructions to be followed in case of fire on the inside door of every room. On the street the French phrases that may be needed in an emergency are: *Au secours!* (Help!), *urgence* (emergency), *samu* (ambulance), *pompiers* (firemen), *poste de station* (police station), *médecin* (doctor), and *hôpital* (hospital).

If you need assistance in an emergency, you can go to your country's embassy. Proof of identity and citizenship are generally required to enter. If your passport has been stolen, get a police report, then contact your embassy for assistance.

■ HOURS OF OPERATION

Banks are generally open weekdays from 9 AM to 5 PM, and some are also open on Saturday. Except for those in Paris, most close for a lunch break. In general, government offices and businesses are open 9–5.

Gas stations in cities and towns are generally open 8 AM to 8 PM every day except Sunday. Those located at the entryways into each city or along the highways are open daily 24 hours a day.

The usual opening times for museums and other sights are from 9:30 AM to 5 PM or 6 PM. Many outside Paris close for lunch. Most are closed one day a week (generally Monday or Tuesday) and on national holidays. National museums are free to the public the first Sunday of every month.

Pharmacies are generally open 8:30 AM to 8 PM every day except Sunday; on the door of every pharmacy is a list of those closest that are open Sunday or 24 hours.

Large stores in big towns are open from 9 AM or 9:30 AM until 7 PM or 8 PM. Smaller shops often open earlier (8 AM) and close later (8 PM) but take a lengthy lunch break (1–4), particularly in the south of France. Corner groceries frequently stay open until around 10 PM. Some Paris stores are beginning to stay open on Sunday, although it's still uncommon.

HOLIDAYS
With 11 national *jours feriés* (holidays) and five weeks of paid vacation, the French have their share of repose. In May there's a holiday nearly every week, so be prepared for stores, banks, and museums to shut their doors for days at a time. Be sure to call museums, restaurants, and hotels in advance to make sure they'll be open.

Note that these dates are for the calendar year 2008: January 1 (New Year's Day); March 23 and 24 (Easter Sunday and Monday); May 1 (Labor Day); May 8 (V.E. Day); May 1 (Ascension); May 11 and 12 (Pentecost Sunday and Monday); July 14 (Bastille Day); August 15 (Assumption); November 1 (All Saints); November 11 (Armistice); December 25 (Christmas).

∎ MAIL

Post offices, or PTT, are found in every town and are recognizable by a yellow LA POSTE sign. They're usually open weekdays 8 AM to 7 PM, Saturday 8–noon. The **main Paris post office** (⊠*52 rue du Louvre, 1er*) is open 24 hours, seven days a week.

SHIPPING PACKAGES
Letters and postcards to the United States and Canada cost €0.90 for 20 grams. Letters and postcards within France cost €0.53. Stamps can be bought in post offices and in cafés displaying a red TABAC sign outside. It takes, on the average, three days for letters to arrive in Europe, and five days to reach the United States.

If you're uncertain where you'll be staying, have mail sent to the local post office, addressed as "poste restante," or to American Express, but remember that during peak seasons American Express may refuse to accept mail. The French postal service has a €0.45 per item service charge.

Sending overnight mail from major cities in France is relatively easy. Besides DHL, Federal Express, and UPS, the French post office has overnight mail service, called Chronopost, which is much cheaper for small packages. Keep in mind that certain things cannot be shipped from France to the United States, such as perfume and any meat products.

Express Services DHL (⊠8 rue St-Foy, Opéra/Grands Boulevards, 2e, Paris ☏01–53-00-75-00 ⊠59 av. Iéna, Trocadéro, 16e, Paris ☏01-45-01-91-00 ⊕www.dhl.com). **Federal Express** (⊠63 bd. Haussmann, Champs-Élysées, 8e, Paris ☏01-40-06-90-16 ⊕www.fedex.com). **UPS** (⊠34 bd. Malesherbes, Champs-Élysées, 8e, Paris ⊠107 rue Réaumur, Beaubourg-Les Halles, 2e, Paris ☏08-00-87-78-77 for information all over France ⊕www.ups.com).

■ MONEY

The following prices are for Paris; other areas are often cheaper (with the notable exception of the Côte d'Azur). Keep in mind that it's less expensive to eat or drink standing at a café or bar counter than to sit at a table. Two prices are listed, *au comptoir* (at the counter) and *à salle* (at a table). Sometimes orders cost even more if you're seated at a terrace table. Coffee in a bar: €1–€1.50 (standing), €1.50–€5 (seated); beer in a bar: €2 (standing), €3–€6 (seated); Coca-Cola: €2–€3 a can; ham sandwich: €3–€5; 2-km (1-mi) taxi ride: €6; movie-theater seat: €9 (the first show of the morning is always cheaper); foreign newspaper: €1–€4.

Prices throughout this guide are given for adults. Substantially reduced fees are almost always available for children, students, and senior citizens.

ATMS & BANKS

Your own bank will probably charge a fee for using ATMs abroad; the foreign bank you use may also charge a fee. Nevertheless, you can usually get a better rate of exchange at an ATM than you will at a currency-exchange office or even when changing money in a bank. And extracting funds as you need them is a safer option than carrying around a large amount of cash.

■TIP➔PIN numbers with more than four digits are not recognized at ATMs in many countries. If yours has five or more, remember to change it before you leave.

Fairly common in Paris and other cities, most towns, and even some villages (as well as in airports and train stations), ATMs are one of the easiest ways to get euros. Don't, however, expect to find ATMs in rural areas.

To get cash at ATMs in France, your PIN must be four digits long. Note that the machine will give you two chances to enter your correct PIN number; if you make a mistake on the third try, your card will be held, and you'll have to return to the bank the next morning to retrieve it. You may have better luck with ATMs with a credit or debit card that is also a Visa or MasterCard, rather than just your bank card.

CREDIT CARDS

France is a credit-card society. Credit cards are used for just about everything, from the automatic gas pumps (now starting to pop up all over the country), to the tolls on highways, payment machines in underground parking lots, stamps at the post office, and even the most minor purchases in the larger department stores. A restaurant or shop would either have to be extremely small or remote not to have some credit-card or debit-card capability. However, some of the smaller restaurants and stores do have a credit-card minimum, usually around €15, which normally should be clearly indicated; to be safe, ask before you order. Do not forget to take your credit-card receipt, as fraudulent use of credit-card numbers taken from receipts is on the rise. Note that while MasterCard and Visa are usually welcomed, American Express isn't always accepted.

It's a good idea to inform your credit-card company before you travel, especially if you're going abroad and don't travel internationally very often. Otherwise, the credit-card company might put a hold on your card because of unusual activity—not a good thing halfway through your trip. Record all your credit-card numbers—as well as the phone numbers to call if your cards are lost or stolen—in a safe place, so you're prepared should something go wrong. MasterCard and Visa have general numbers you can call (collect if you're abroad) if your card is lost, but you're better off calling the number of your issuing bank, since Master-Card and Visa usually just transfer you to your bank; your bank's number is usually printed on your card.

If you plan to use your credit card for cash advances, you'll need to apply for a PIN at least two weeks before your trip. Although it's usually cheaper (and safer) to use a credit card abroad for large purchases (so you can cancel payments or be reimbursed if there's a problem), note that some credit-card companies *and* the banks that issue them add substantial percentages to all foreign transactions, whether they're in a foreign currency or not. Check on these fees before leaving home, so there won't be any surprises when you get the bill.

■**TIP➔**Before you charge something, ask the merchant whether he or she plans to do a dynamic currency conversion (DCC). In such a transaction the credit-card *processor* (shop, restaurant, or hotel, not Visa or MasterCard) converts the currency and charges you in dollars. In most cases you'll pay the merchant a 3% fee for this service in addition to any credit-card company and issuing-bank foreign-transaction surcharges.

Dynamic currency conversion programs are becoming increasingly widespread. Merchants who participate in them are supposed to ask whether you want to be charged in dollars or the local currency, but they don't always do so. And even if they do offer you a choice, they may well avoid mentioning the additional surcharges. The good news is that you *do* have a choice. And if this practice really gets your goat, you can avoid it entirely thanks to American Express; with its cards, DCC simply isn't an option.

In this guide, the following abbreviations are used: **AE**, American Express; **D**, Discover; **DC**, Diners Club; **MC**, MasterCard; and **V**, Visa.

Reporting Lost Cards American Express (☎800/992-3404 in U.S., 336/393-1111 collect from abroad ⊕www.americanexpress. com). **Diners Club** (☎800/234-6377 in U.S., 303/799-1504 collect from abroad ⊕www. dinersclub.com). **Discover** (☎800/347-2683 in U.S., 801/902-3100 collect from abroad ⊕www.discovercard.com). **MasterCard** (☎800/622-7747 in U.S., 636/722-7111 collect from abroad ⊕www.mastercard.com). **Visa** (☎800/847-2911 in U.S., 410/581-9994 collect from abroad ⊕www.visa.com).

CURRENCY & EXCHANGE

The advent of the euro makes any whirlwind grand European tour all the easier. From France, you can glide across the borders of Austria, Germany, Italy, Spain, Holland, Ireland, Greece, Belgium, Finland, Luxembourg, and Portugal with no pressing need to run to the local exchange booth to change to yet another currency before you even had the time to become familiar with the last. You'll be able to do what drives many tourists crazy—to assess the value of a purchase (for example, to realize that eating a three-course meal in a small restaurant in Lisbon is cheaper than that ham sandwich you bought on the Champs Élysées). Initially, the euro had another benefit because it was created as a direct competitor with the U.S. dollar and was envisioned to be, therefore, of nearly equal value. Unfortunately, exchange rates have seen the euro soar and the dollar take a hit. At this writing, one euro equals U.S. $1.38.

These days, the easiest way to get euros is through ATMs; you can find them in airports, train stations, and throughout the city. ATM rates are excellent because they're based on wholesale rates offered only by major banks. It's a good idea, however, to bring some euros with you from home and always to have some cash on hand as backup.

TRAVELER'S CHECKS & CARDS

Some consider this the currency of the caveman, and it's true that fewer establishments accept traveler's checks these days. Nevertheless, they're a cheap and secure way to carry extra money, particularly on trips to urban areas. Both Citibank (under the Visa brand) and American Express issue traveler's checks in the United States, but Amex is better known and more widely accepted; you can also avoid hefty surcharges by cashing Amex checks at Amex offices. Whatever you do, keep track of all the serial numbers in case the checks are lost or stolen.

American Express now offers a stored-value card called a Travelers Cheque Card, which you can use wherever American Express credit cards are accepted, including ATMs. The card can carry a minimum of $300 and a maximum of $2,700, and it's a very safe way to carry your funds. Although you can get replacement funds in 24 hours if your card is lost or stolen, it doesn't really strike us as a very good deal. In addition to a high initial cost ($14.95 to set up the card, plus $5 each time you "reload"), you still have to pay a 2% fee for each purchase in a foreign currency (similar to that of any credit card). Further, each time you use the card in an ATM you pay a transaction fee of $2.50 on top of the 2% transaction fee for the conversion—add it all up and it can be considerably more than you would pay when simply using your own ATM card. Regular traveler's checks are just as secure and cost less.

Contacts American Express (☎ 888/412–6945 in U.S., 801/945–9450 collect outside U.S. to add value or speak to customer service ⊕ www.americanexpress.com).

▌ RESTROOMS

You can find pay-per-use toilet units on Parisian streets costing 50¢. Small children should not use these alone, as the cleaning system has weight sensors that might not sense their presence. Bathrooms in the larger métro stations and in all train stations cost 50¢. In other cities, your best bets may be fast-food chains, large department stores, and hotel lobbies. Do not be alarmed if you don't see any light switches—once the bathroom door is shut and locked, the lights will go on.

Highway rest stops also have bathrooms, which are equipped with changing tables

for babies and even showers during summer months. Many public restrooms are not the cleanest places in the world, especially for children, so it's in your best interest to be prepared and always carry a small box of tissues with you.

Find a Loo The Bathroom Diaries (⊕ www. thebathroomdiaries.com) is flush with unsanitized info on restrooms the world over—each one located, reviewed, and rated.

▌ SAFETY

Beware of petty theft—purse snatching, pickpocketing, and the like—throughout France, particularly in Paris and along the Côte d'Azur. Use common sense: avoid pulling out a lot of money in public; wear a handbag with long straps that you can sling across your body, bandolier style, with a zippered compartment for your money and passport. Men should keep their wallets up front. When withdrawing money from cash machines, be especially aware of your surroundings and anyone standing too close. If you feel uneasy, press the cancel button (*annuler*) and walk to an area where you feel more comfortable. Incidents of credit-card fraud are on the rise in France, especially in urban areas; be sure to collect your receipts, as these have recently been used by thieves to make purchases over the Internet. Car break-ins, especially in isolated parking lots where hikers set off for the day, are on the rise. It makes sense to take valuables with you or leave your luggage at your hotel.

Note one cultural difference: a friendly smile or steady eye contact is often seen as an invitation to further contact; so, unfortunately, you should avoid being overly friendly with strangers—unless you feel perfectly safe.

▌**TIP➔Distribute your cash, credit cards, IDs, and other valuables between a deep front pocket, an inside jacket or vest pocket, and a hidden money pouch. Don't reach for the money pouch once you're in public.**

▌TAXES

All taxes must be included in posted prices in France. The initials TTC (*toutes taxes comprises*—taxes included) sometimes appear on price lists but, strictly speaking, they're superfluous. By law, restaurant and hotel prices must include 19.6% taxes and a service charge. If they show up as extra charges, complain.

A number of shops offer V.A.T. refunds to foreign shoppers. You're entitled to an export refund of the 19.6% tax, depending on the item purchased, but it's often applicable only if your purchases in the same store reach a minimum of €430 (for EU residents) or €175 (for others, including U.S. and Canadian residents). In most instances, you need to fill out a form, which must then be tendered to a customs official at your last port of departure.

Global Refund is a Europe-wide service with 225,000 affiliated stores and more than 700 refund counters at major airports and border crossings. Its refund form, called a Tax Free Check, is the most common across the European continent. The service issues refunds in the form of cash, check, or credit-card adjustment.

V.A.T. Refunds Global Refund (☎ 800/566–9828 ⊕ www.globalrefund.com).

▌TIME

The time difference between New York and Paris is 6 hours (so when it's 1 PM in New York, it's 7 PM in Paris). The time difference between London and Paris is 1 hour; between Sydney and Paris, 8–9 hours; and between Auckland and Paris, 12 hours. France, like the rest of Europe, uses the 24-hour clock, which means that after noon you continue counting forward: 13h00 is 1 PM, 22h30 is 10:30 PM. The European format for abbreviating dates is day/month/year, so 7/5/05 means May 7, not July 5.

▌TIPPING

The French have a clear idea of when they should be tipped. Bills in bars and restaurants include a service charge, but it's customary to round out your bill with some small change unless you're dissatisfied. The amount varies: anywhere from €0.50, if you've merely bought a beer, to €1–€2 (or more) after a meal. Tip taxi drivers and hair stylists about 10%. In some theaters and hotels, coat-check attendants may expect nothing (if there's a sign saying POURBOIRE INTERDIT—tips forbidden); otherwise give them €0.50–€1. Washroom attendants usually get €0.50, though the sum is often posted.

If you stay in a hotel for more than two or three days, it's customary to leave something for the chambermaid—about €1.50 per day. In expensive hotels you may well call on the services of a baggage porter (bellhop) and hotel porter and possibly the telephone receptionist. All expect a tip: plan on about €1.50 per item for the baggage porter, but the other tips will depend on how much you've used their services—common sense must guide you here. In hotels that provide room service, give €1 to the waiter (this does not apply to breakfast served in your room). If the chambermaid does some pressing, give her €1 on top of the charge made. If the concierge has been helpful, it's customary to leave a tip of €10–€20.

Gas-station attendants get nothing for gas or oil but €0.75 or €1.50 for checking tires. Train and airport porters get a fixed €1–€1.50 per bag, but you're better off getting your own baggage cart if you can (a €1 coin—refundable—is necessary in train stations only). Museum guides should get €1–€1.50 after a guided tour.

INDEX

PHOTO CREDITS

Frontmatter: 4, *Danilo Donadoni/age fotostock.* 8 (top), *Joe Viesti/viestiphoto.com.* 8 (bottom), *Doug Scott/age fotostock.* 9, *Doug Pearson/Agency Jon Arnold Images.* 10 (top), *D. Guilloux/viestiphoto.com.* 10 (bottom), *S. Cozzi/ viestiphoto.com.* 11 (top), *SGM/age fotostock.* 11 (bottom), *Ken Ross/viestiphoto. com.* 12 (top), *T. Gilou/viestiphoto.com.* 12 (bottom), *SuperStock/age fotostock.* 13, *Walter Bibikow/ viestiphoto.com.* 14, *Doug Scott/age fotostock.* 15 (left), *K. Degendre/viestiphoto.com.* 15 (right), *Ken Ross/viestiphoto.com.* 16, *Joe Viesti/viestiphoto.com.* 17 (both), *Robert Fisher.* 22, *Juan Carlos Muñoz/ age fotostock.*
Chapter 1: Paris: 23, *Art Kowalsky/Alamy.* 24, *Kader Meguedad/Alamy.* 25, *Alessandro Villa/age fotostock.* 27, *ImageGap/Alamy.* 33, *Directphoto.org/Alamy.* 34 (top left), *Photodisc.* 34 (bottom left), *TAOLMOR/Shutterstock.* 34 (top right), *Renaud Visage/age fotostock.* 34 (bottom right), *Robert Harding Picture Library Ltd/Alamy.* 35 (left), *Stock Connection Blue/Alamy.* 35 (top right), *Peter Barritt/age fotostock.* 35 (bottom right), *Dennis Cox/Alamy.* 36 (left), *Frank Peterschroeder/Bilderberg/Aurora Photos.* 36 (right), *Glenn Zumwalt/Alamy.* 46, *Directphoto.org/Alamy.* 47 (top left), *The Print Collector/Alamy.* 47 (bottom left), *Directphoto.org/Alamy.* 47 (top right), *Scott Warren/Aurora Photos.* 47 (bottom right), *Gabrielle Chan/Shutterstock.* 61 (top), *Paul Hahn/Laif/Aurora Photos.* 61 (bottom), *SuperStock/age fotostock.* 62 (top), *Ivan Vdovin/age fotostock.* 62 (bottom), *Renaud Visage/age fotostock.* 63 (top left), *Sylvain Grandadam/age fotostock.* 63 (top right), *Robert Haines/Alamy.* 63 (bottom), *Paul Hahn/Laif/ Aurora Photos.* 64 (top), *Carsten Madsen/iStockphoto.* 64 (bottom), *Renaud Visage/age fotostock.* 65 (top left), *Kalpana Kartik/Aurora Photos.* 65 (top right), *Mehdi Chebil/Alamy.* 65 (bottom), *Corbis.* 66, *Sylvain Grandadam/age fotostock.* **Chapter 2: Ile-de-France:** 139, *Malcolm Freeman/Alamy.* 140, *Alberto Paredes/age fotostock.* 141, *Jason Cosburn/Shutterstock.* 143, *Robert Taylor/iStockphoto.* 150-51, *AM Corporation/Alamy.* 152 (top), *Elias H. Debbas II/Shutterstock.* 152 (second from top), *Jason Cosburn/Shutterstock.* 152 (fourth from top and bottom), *Michael Booth/Alamy.* 153 (center), *Jens Preshaw/ age fotostock.* 153 (bottom), *The Print Collector/Alamy.* 154 (top), *Michel Mory/iStockphoto.* 154 (center), *Mike Booth/Alamy.* 154 (bottom), *Tommaso di Girolamo/age fotostock.* 155, *Hemis/Alamy.* 156 (second from top), *Jason Cosburn/Shutterstock.* 156 (third from top), *Guy Thouvenin/age fotostock.* 156 (bottom), *Visual Arts Library (London)/Alamy.* 157 (top), *Guy Thouvenin/age fotostock.* 158, *Jim Tardio/iStockphoto.* **Chapter 3: The Loire Valley:** 197, *Kevin Galvin/age fotostock.* 198, *P. Narayan/ age fotostock.* 199 (top), *Scott Hortop/Alamy.* 199, *P. Narayan/age fotostock.* 200, *PCL/Alamy.* 210-11, *SuperStock/age fotostock.* 210 (bottom), *David Lyons/Alamy.* 211 (inset), *Renaud Visage/Alamy.* 212 (top left and top right), *P. Narayan/age fotostock.* 213 (top left), *Duncan Gilbert/iStockphoto.* 213 (top right), *S. Greg Panosian/iStockphoto.* 213 (bottom right), *Visual Arts Library (London)/Alamy.* 214 (top), *Sylvain Grandadam/age fotostock.* 214 (bottom left), *Images Etc Ltd/Alamy.* 214 (bottom right), *Vittorio Sciosia/Alamy.* **Chapter 4: Normandy:** 251, *San Rostro/age fotostock.* 252, *Paolo Siccardi/age fotostock.* 253, *Anger O./age fotostock.* 255, *SuperStock/age fotostock.* 284-285, *Wojtek Buss/age fotostock.* 286, *Impact Productions/Alamy.* 287 (top left), *Sylvain Grandadam/age fotostock.* 287 (top right), *Wojtek Buss/age fotostock.* 287 (bottom left), *Martin Florin Emmanuel/Alamy.* 287 (bottom right), *Visual Arts Library (London)/Alamy.* 288, *Danilo Donadoni/age fotostock.* 289, *Renaud Visage/age fotostock.* 290, *Bruno Morandi/age fotostock.* **Chapter 5: Brittany:** 295, *Danilo Donadoni/age fotostock.* 296,

iStockphoto. 297, *SuperStock/age fotostock.* 298, *Cro Magnon/Alamy.* 324, *Renault Philippe/age foto-stock.* **Chapter 6: Champagne Country:** 337, *Doug Pearson/age fotostock.* 338, *SuperStock/age fotostock.* 339 (top), *SuperStock/age fotostock.* 339 (bottom), *Images-of-France/Alamy.* 341, *Fulvio Zanettini/ Laif/Aurora Photos.* 349, *Cephas Picture Library/Alamy.* 350 (left), *Cephas Picture Library/Alamy.* 350 (top right), *Eric Baccega/age fotostock.* 351, (center left and right), *Cephas Picture Library/Alamy.* 351 (bottom right), *Ray Roberts/Alamy.* 352-53, *Clay McLachlan/Aurora Photos.* **Chapter 7: Alsace-Lorraine:** 365, *SGM/age fotostock.* 366 (top), *Doug Pearson/age fotostock.* 366 (bottom), *Eric Baccega/ age fotostock.* 367, *Robert Harding Picture Library Ltd/Alamy.* 368, *Nadejda Ivanova/Shutterstock.* 374, *Picture Contact/Alamy.* **Chapter 8: Burgundy:** 409, *Sylvain Grandadam/age fotostock.* 410 (top), *Michael Wojcik/Alamy.* 410 (bottom), *Tristan Deschamps/age fotostock.* 411, *R. Matina/age fotostock.* 413, *Doug Pearson/age fotostock.* 429, *Clay McLachlan/IPN/Aurora Photos.* 430 (both), *Alain Doire/ CRT Bourgogne.* 432 (bottom), *LOOK Die Bildagentur der Fotografen GmbH/Alamy.* **Chapter 9: Lyon & the Alps:** 459, *Mattes/age fotostock.* 460, *Boyer/age fotostock.* 461, *Art Kowalsky/Alamy.* 475 (left), *Art Kowalsky/Alamy.* 475 (top), *Jean-François Tripelon/Maison de la France.* 475 (bottom), *Andre Jenny/Alamy.* 476 (top), *panduh/flickr.com.* 476 (second from top), *Homer W. Sykes/Alamy.* 476 (third from top), *clipoyecuisine.canalblog.com.* 476 (fourth from top), *JTB Photo Communications, Inc./Alamy.* 476 (bottom), *Lourens Smak/Alamy.* 478, *Hemis/Alamy.* 479 (both), *Andre Jenny/Alamy.* 480 (both), *bocuse.com.* 481 (top), *Sylvain Grandadam/age fotostock.* 481 (bottom), *Jean-Marc Charles/age foto-stock.* **Chapter 10: Provence:** 521, *Doug Scott/age fotostock.* 522, *Chederros/age fotostock.* 523, *Carson Ganci/age fotostock.* 525, *Aaron Black/Aurora Photos.* 559 (top), *Chad Ehlers/age fotostock.* 559 (bottom), *Renaud Visage/age fotostock.* 560 (top), *David Barnes/age fotostock.* 560 (bottom left), *David Buffington/age fotostock.* 560 (bottom right), *Craig Lovell/viestiphoto.com.* 561 (left), *Doug Scott/age fotostock.* 561 (right), *Bruno Morandi/age fotostock.* 562 (top), *Susan Jones/age fotostock.* 562 (bottom), *Plus Pix/age fotostock.* 563 (top), *Sergio Cozzi/viestiphoto.com.* 563 (bottom), *Plus Pix/age foto-stock.* 564, *Sergio Cozzi/viestiphoto.com.* 565 (top), *P. Cherfils/viestiphoto.com.* 565 (center), *SGM/age fotostock.* 565 (bottom), *Doug Scott/age fotostock.* 566, *L'Occitane en Provence.* **Chapter 11: The French Riviera:** 601, *Michael Amme/Laif/Aurora Photos.* 602 (left), *Ian Dagnall/Alamy.* 602 (right), *Walter Bibikow/ age fotostock.* 603, *Barry Mason/Alamy.* 605, *Eric Alexandre/Sunset/Aurora Photos.* 636, *Owen Franken.* 637 (top left), *Enrico Bartolucci/viestiphoto.com.* 637 (top right), *Owen Franken.* 637 (bottom), *George Haling/age fotostock.* 638-39, *Owen Franken.* 640 (top), *Alain Llora/Le Moulin de Mougins.* 641 (top), *Owen Franken.* 641 (bottom), *M. Cristofori/viestiphoto.com.* **Chapter 12: The Midi-Pyrénées & Langue-doc-Roussillon:** 681, *Javier Larrea/age fotostock.* 682, *Agence Images/Alamy.* 683, *Alan Copson/age fo-tostock.* 685 (top), *Paul Shawcross/Alamy.* 685 (bottom), Fanelie Rosier/iStockphoto. 714, *Agence Images/Alamy.* **Chapter 13: The Basque Country, Gascony & Hautes-Pyrénées:** 729, *Agence Images/ Alamy.* 731 (both), *Agence Images/Alamy.* 733, *Juan Carlos Muñoz/age fotostock.* 739, *BERNAGER E./age fotostock.* 740 (top left and top right), *Javier Larrea/age fotostock.* 740 (bottom), *Profimedia In-ternational s.r.o./Alamy.* 741 (top right), *Robert Fried/Alamy.* 741 (center left), *Le Naviose/age fotostock.* 741 (center right and bottom), *Mark Baynes/Alamy.* 742, *Mark Baynes/Alamy.* **Chapter 14: Bordeaux & the Wine Country:** 765, *Peter Horree/Alamy.* 766, *Chad Ehlers/Alamy.* 767, *J.D. Dallet/age fotostock.* 768, *Chris Cheadle/Alamy.* 769, *Neil Sutherland/Alamy.* **Chapter 15: The Dordogne:** 789, *P. Narayan/ age fotostock.* 790, *Lagui/Shutterstock.* 791 (bottom), *S. Greg Panosian/iStockphoto.* 793, *Iain Frazer/ Shutterstock.* **Color Section:** Latin Quarter: *P. Narayan/age fotostock.* Centre Beaubourg: *Photodisc.* Notre Dame: *Danilo Donadoni/age fotostock.* Louvre: *P. Narayan/age fotostock.* Sleeping Beauty's Château de Ussé: *SuperStock/age fotostock.* Versailles: *Wojtek Buss/age fotostock.* Beaune: *SuperStock/age foto-stock.* Giverny: *SuperStock/age fotostock.* Mont-St-Michel: *Sylvain Grandadam/age fotostock.* Lyon's famous *bouchon* taverns: *Hemis/Alamy.* Roussillon: *Peter Adams/age fotostock.* Alsace's famous Wine Road: *Rieger Bertrand/age fotostock.* Sarlat-la-Caneda: *Wilmar Photography/Alamy.* Provence's Laven-dar Route: *SGM/age fotostock.* St-Tropez: *JLImages/Alamy.*

NOTES

ABOUT OUR WRITERS

Author of *Fodor's Escape to Provence, Escape to the Riviera,* and *Provence and the Côte d'Azur,* **Nancy Coons** has become adept at describing the golden light of Arles from under the iron-gray clouds back home in Lorraine at her 300-year-old farmhouse.

Paris shopping updater **Jennifer Ditsler-Ladonne** has long made Paris's inexhaustible array of boutiques her specialty. If you're looking for rare medieval arcana or Paris's wild edible mushrooms, she's the person to call, as we did for our Paris shopping update.

John Fanning is a writer of novels, short stories, and plays. He is also a co-director of La Muse writers' and artists' retreat (*www.lamuseinn.com*) in southern France. John updated the Bordeaux, Dordogne, and Midi-Pyrénées/Languedoc-Roussillon chapters of this guide.

Sarah Fraser spent several years growing up in Central America but re-entry to her native Canadian cold prompted frequent escapes to anywhere hot. So she packed her bags and went in search of the perfect tapenade in the South of France. For this edition, she updated our Provence and Côte d'Azur chapters and wrote our special feature on the Lavender Route.

Simon Hewitt headed to Paris straight from studying French and art history at Oxford. It was a return to base; his grandmother was French, as is his daughter Anais. He is a Paris correspondent for *Art & Auction.* His main hobby is cricket and is now national coach. For this edition, he updated our chapters on the Ile-de-France, the Loire Valley, Brittany, Normandy, and Champagne Country, and wrote our special feature on all things bubbly.

Paris food critic **Rosa Jackson**'s love affair with French pastries began at age four, when she spent her first year in Paris. Further experiments with éclairs and croissants led her to enroll in the Paris Cordon Bleu. Now splitting her time between Nice and Paris, Rosa has eaten in hundreds of French restaurants—and always has room for dessert. She wrote our Paris dining section and special feature on foods of the Riviera.

Christopher Mooney originally came to Paris to study French philosophy, smoke Gîtanes cigarettes, and hang out in cafés. Fourteen years later he's still there, now happily ensconced as co-editor of *Paris Ritz* magazine and *Paris-Athénée* magazine; his articles have appeared in *Elle* and *Condé Nast Traveler.* Chris updated our chapters on Alsace-Lorraine and Burgundy and wrote our special feature on Burgundy wines.

As a travel writer, Paris Exploring updater **Lisa Pasold** writes for the *Chicago Tribune* and the *Globe and Mail.*

George Semler lives over the border in Spain, but he has skied, hiked, and explored every side of the Pyrénées. For this edition, he updated our chapters on Lyon and the Alps and the one on Basque Country, plus writing our special features on Lyonnais cuisine and Basque culture. He contributes to *Saveur.*

Heather Stimmler-Hall came to Paris as a university student in 1995 and has since made a career out of reading between the lines of glossy hotel brochures. She writes for the London *Times, Elle,* and her own monthly e-newsletter, *www.secretsofparis.com,* and has updated our Smart Travel Tips chapter and Paris lodging section for this edition.